Henry Barclay Swete

The Psalms of Solomon

With the Greek fragments of the Book of Enoch

Henry Barclay Swete

The Psalms of Solomon
With the Greek fragments of the Book of Enoch

ISBN/EAN: 9783337037802

Printed in Europe, USA, Canada, Australia, Japan

Cover: Foto ©Lupo / pixelio.de

More available books at **www.hansebooks.com**

THE GREEK VERSIONS
OF THE TESTAMENTS
OF THE TWELVE PATRIARCHS

Edited from nine MSS together with

THE VARIANTS
OF THE ARMENIAN
AND SLAVONIC VERSIONS
AND SOME HEBREW FRAGMENTS

by

ROBERT HENRY CHARLES

OXFORD UNIVERSITY PRESS

GEORG OLMS VERLAGSBUCHHANDLUNG · HILDESHEIM

2., unveränderte Auflage 1960
Printed in Germany
Druck: Wolf, Heppenheim (Bergstr.)
Einband: Dingeldein, Darmstadt-Arheilgen

TO

R. SINKER, D.D.
F. C. CONYBEARE, M.A.
WILHELM BOUSSET, D.D.
W. R. MORFILL, M.A.

WHO HAVE RENDERED YEOMAN SERVICE
TOWARDS THE RECOVERY AND ELUCIDATION OF
THIS ANCIENT TEXT

PREFACE

A NEW text of the Testaments of the Twelve Patriarchs has long
been needed. It is now nearly forty years since Dr. Sinker published
a reproduction of the Cambridge MS. with the variants of the Oxford
MS. Ten years later he edited collations of the Vatican and Patmos
MSS. Dr. Sinker's own work was very accurate so far as it went,
but he made no attempt to deal with the relations of the MSS. to
each other and to the archetypes from which they were derived.
The MSS. evidence was, indeed, hardly adequate for such a task,
and, moreover, the presuppositions under which he worked—as also
all other students of the Testaments till within the last few years,
i.e. that the Testaments were written originally in Greek and by
a Christian author—precluded the possibility of ever attaining to
a satisfactory text.

For deliverance from the latter misleading presupposition, that
the Testaments were of Christian authorship, scholars are indebted
in the main to the meritorious articles of F. C. Conybeare. By
means of the Armenian Version this scholar established the high
probability that all the Christian allusions in the Testaments are
the interpolations of Christian scribes in an originally Jewish work,
and therein confirmed the earlier hypothesis of Grabe and Schnapp.
My own study of the Armenian Version has more than convinced
me of the validity of Conybeare's contention. In the prosecution
of this study I have spared no pains. I have used the collations
of the three Armenian MSS. which Mr. Conybeare has cited in his
articles, and which he most kindly placed at my service, and likewise
six other MSS., two of which I have collated for the first time.

For deliverance from the other false presupposition, that the
Testaments were written originally in Greek, the first steps were
taken by Grabe and Kohler when they put forward the suggestion
of a Hebrew original, but neither scholar advanced any evidence in
support of his hypothesis. The first positive evidence was furnished
by Gaster, but since this evidence was so very exiguous in quantity—in all amounting to the explanation of one, or at most two,
corrupt passages in the Greek by retranslation into Hebrew—and since
even the weight of this slight evidence was handicapped through

its connexion with extravagant claims on behalf of a comparatively late Hebrew Testament of Naphtali, the hypothesis of a Hebrew original was still looked upon as highly questionable, or even as undeserving of serious consideration, when the present editor undertook a close study of the Testaments. The firstfruits of that study appeared in the *Encyclopaedia Biblica*, I. 237–241, and the grounds there advanced for a Hebrew original were accepted in the following year by Bousset, who at the same time contributed valuable articles on the Jewish authorship of the Testaments. The sustained study of the intervening years has transformed a good working hypothesis of ten years ago into an indispensable postulate. Nearly every page of the Greek text exhibits passages which can neither be explained nor translated unless by retroversion into Hebrew.

Some of the Sections in the following Introduction have already appeared in the Introduction to my Commentary.

My obligations to friends and scholars are deep and manifold. First of all, to the Trustees of the Hibbert Trust for a subvention towards the cost of publication of the Text: to Dr. Sinker, who, when I informed him of my intention of editing the text, most generously lent me the collation of *h*, the first Mt. Sinai MS., which had been made for him by Mrs. Gibson: to Mrs. Gibson and Mrs. Lewis for the endless pains they took in securing for me a photographic reproduction of *i*, the second Sinai MS.: to the Directors of the Paris and Vatican Libraries for permission to photograph their MSS. of the Testaments: to Professor Lake for photographing the Mt. Athos MS.: to Mr. Cowley for his ever ready help in regard to the Aramaic fragments: and to Dr. James, the Provost of King's, for a collation of portions of Dr. Sinker's text with the Cambridge MS. My warm thanks are specially due to Professor Morfill, who retranslated into Greek for this edition the two recensions of the Slavonic Version: and, finally, I am indebted for the Greek Index to the kindness of Miss Poole.

The Editor will be grateful for corrections. In dealing with such a vast mass of manuscript evidence in several languages he cannot hope to escape errors of various kinds. Some of these will be found in the list of Corrigenda on pp. lviii–lix. I cannot conclude without recording my thanks to the readers and compositors for their skilled services in this most difficult Text.

R. H. CHARLES.

CONTENTS

CONTENTS

INTRODUCTION

§ 1. Short Account of the Book.

The Testaments were originally written in Hebrew by a Pharisaic upholder of the Maccabean priest-kings in the closing years of the second century B. C.   In the course of the next century the Hebrew text was interpolated with additions emanating from bitter opponents of the Maccabean dynasty.   In the early decades of the Christian era the text was current in two forms, which are denoted by H^a and H^β in this edition.   The former of these was translated not later than A. D. 50 into Greek, and this translation was used by the scholar who rendered the second Hebrew recension into Greek. The first Greek translation was used by our Lord, by St. Paul, and other New Testament writers.   In the second and following centuries it was interpolated by Christian scribes, and finally condemned indiscriminatingly along with other apocryphs.   For several centuries it was wholly lost sight of, and it was not till the thirteenth century that it was rediscovered through the agency of Robert Grosseteste, bishop of Lincoln, who translated it into Latin, under the misconception that it was a genuine work of the twelve sons of Jacob, and that the Christian interpolations were a genuine product of Jewish prophecy.   The advent of the Reformation brought in critical methods, and the book was unjustly disparaged as a mere Christian forgery for nearly four centuries.   The time has at last arrived for this book, so noble in its ethical side, to come into its own, and the text with all the documentary authorities is now laid before the student.

§ 2. The Greek MSS.

a. Bodley MS. Baroccio 133.   Quarto.   This paper MS. contains several treatises by different hands of the latter part of the fourteenth century. The Testaments occupy ff. 179^a–205^b. Their title and those of Judah and Gad are written in red. There are two copies of this MS. on paper, one in the Bodley MS. Smith 117 belonging to the close of the seventeenth century, and the second in Emmanuel College, Cambridge. This MS. is remarkable for a large number of omissions, at times of entire chapters. A collation of it is given in Dr. Sinker's edition, but it is wanting in accuracy. It is cited by him as O.

b. University Library, Cambridge, Ff. 1. 24. Quarto. This parchment MS. contains four works, of which the Testaments are the fourth, written on ff. 203^a–262^b. It is written in double columns, twenty lines in a column. It belongs to the tenth century. The initials and titles are in red except the first, which is in gold. It was from this MS. that Grosseteste's Latin Version was made. His handwriting, according to Dr. James, is found on the margin. Grabe professes to have given a transcript of this MS. as his text.

Of this MS. there are three copies. The first two are in the University Library and in the Library of Trinity College, Cambridge, respectively, and the third in the Library of Queen's College, Oxford.

This MS. forms the text of Dr. Sinker's edition. Dr. James has tested its accuracy for me, and found it to be above all praise. I have therefore used Dr. Sinker's transcript of the MS. in the present edition. It is cited by him as C.

c. Vatican Library, Cod. Graec. 731. This is a small octavo MS. written on paper with twenty-two or twenty-three lines on each page. Besides the Testaments it contains extracts from the Fathers. The Testaments are given on ff. 97^a–167^b. The script of the latter belongs probably to the thirteenth century. This is the most important of all the MSS. A fairly accurate collation of this MS. by Guidi is given by Sinker in his separately published Appendix to his edition of the Testaments and cited by him as R. I procured photographs of this MS. for the present edition.

d. Vatican Library, Gk. 1238. This is a vellum MS. in three volumes of the LXX, belonging to the thirteenth century. On the close of the LXX follows the Testament of Job, ff. 340^a–349^b, and on 350–380 our present text. There are from thirty-three to thirty-nine lines on each page. Strangely enough, above the general title of the Testaments—Διαθῆκαι τῶν ιβ πατριαρχῶν υἱῶν Ἰακώβ—appear the words Λεπτῆς Γενέσεως, which is one of the titles of the Book of Jubilees. That there was a close relation between these books we know independently. A collation of this MS. was published by Conybeare in the *J. Q. R.*, Oct., 1900, and Jan., 1901, but I thought it advisable to have the MS. photographed for this edition.

e. Mount Athos MS. This MS. is written in two columns of forty lines each, in a good hand of the tenth century. The Testaments are given on ff. 197^b–229^a. This MS. is of great interest as it contains three large additions to the text, the first before καὶ ἐπὶ πύργους in T. Lev. ii. 3 consisting of a prayer of Jacob, the second after the word ἡμερῶν in T. Lev. xviii. 2, and the third after τῆς γῆς in T. Ash. vii. 2. The third consists of two and two-third columns of certain Christian disquisitions on love and the Trinity. The second is the remarkable Greek Fragment, which we print in Appendix III, and which we show elsewhere to be a translation from a Hebrew work, which was probably an original source of the Testaments. Professor Lake photographed this MS. for me on Mount Athos.

f. Paris MS. 938. This is a beautifully written MS. of the tenth century. The Testaments are given on the first seventy-two folios. Each page contains twenty-three lines. On fol. 1^a there is a list of Old Testament names, including those of the twelve patriarchs, with their meanings. The Testaments proper begin on 1^b. It is characteristic of this MS. that after the title of each Testament it adds the meaning of the proper name, and also that at the conclusion of each Testament it adds the number of years that the patriarch lived. In the latter feature it is followed by the first Slavonic recension (S^1). After the Testaments follow the Testament of Job and other writings. This MS. was photographed for me with a view to the present edition. Dr. Sinker collated this MS. as far back as 1887, but never published the collation.

g. MS. 411 in the Library of the Monastery of St. John the Evangelist in Patmos. It is a quarto MS. written on parchment and assigned by H. O. Coxe to the sixteenth century. This very inaccurate MS. was collated for Dr. Sinker's Appendix, by whom it is cited as P.

h. Mount Sinai MS., No. 547, in the Library of St. Catherine. See Gardthausen, *Cat. Codd. Graec. Sinaiticorum*, p. 132. This MS., 14·5 by 10·35 cm., was written in the seventeenth century. It contains seventeen lines on each page. It is incomplete and comes to an end with T. Jos. xv. 7. This MS. has the following peculiar introduction: Ἰωάννου τοῦ ποτὲ ἑβραίου εἴδησις τῶν διαθηκῶν τῶν ιβ υἱῶν τοῦ πατριάρχου Ἰακὼβ μεταφρασθεῖσα ἀπὸ Ἰουδαικοῦ διαλέκτου εἰς Ἑλληνικήν. The statement is true, but where the scribe got it we cannot determine. This MS. was copied for Dr. Sinker by Mrs. Gibson in Feb., 1892. This copy, together with photographs of the T. Jos. i–xii. 3ᵃ, xv. 1–7, Dr. Sinker most kindly placed at my disposal.

i. Mount Sinai MS. This MS. was discovered accidentally in the Convent Library in the spring of 1906 by Mrs. Gibson. She was searching for *h* with a view to a more correct collation on my behalf. Notwithstanding every effort she, like as the Archbishop of Sinai who had previously sought for it, failed to find it. Just before leaving Mount Sinai, however, she came across this second MS., and photographed the greater part of it for me, i. e. down to T. Ash. vii. 6, when her camera broke down. Unfortunately the negatives of T. Naph. viii. 2ᵇ–ix. 2ᵇ; T. Gad i. 9–iv. 1, v. 3ᵇ–vi. 2ᵇ; T. Ash. i. 7ᵇ–ii. 7, iv. 5–vi. 3ᵈ were either lost or proved to be failures. When the photographs of this MS. reached me the first ninety-six pages of my text had already passed through the press. Accordingly I add in Appendix VI a collation of the Testaments of Reuben, Simeon, Levi, and Jud. i–xx, where it differs from *h*, with which it is closely connected. This MS. was written not earlier than the seventeenth century It contains twenty-one to twenty-three lines in each page. It has the same peculiar introduction as *h*. See preceding MS.

§ 3. The Armenian MSS.

There are many MSS. of this version. The first five are designated by the symbols attached to them in the Venetian edition of the text by the Mechitarist fathers. The rest owe their designation to the present editor. When cited they appear as Aᵃ, Aᵇ, &c.

Aᵃ. Mechitarist Library of St. Lazzaro, Venice, No. 345. This MS., 5 × 7 inches, was written in the year 1220 on paper. This MS. contains also the history of the Prophet Jeremiah. It belongs to the first recension of the text.

Aᵇ*. Mechitarist Library of St. Lazzaro, No. 280. This MS., 7½ × 11 inches, was written in two columns of forty-two lines each, on paper, in the year 1418. This MS. is the worst representative of the second recension of the Armenian Version. It contains also the history of Asenath.

Aᵇ. Mechitarist Library of St. Lazzaro, No. 679. This MS., 6 × 10 inches, was written towards the close of the fifteenth century,

in double columns of twenty-six lines each.   It consists of 679 folios.
This MS. belongs to the first recension.   Its collation in the Armenian
Text is not infrequently incorrect and defective, as I have discovered
through Father Carékin's copy of six of the Testaments in this MS.,
which he made for Mr. Conybeare, and which the latter most kindly
placed at my disposal.   I have introduced the needful corrections
into the Text on the basis of Carékin's collation.

A^c. Mechitarist Library of St. Lazzaro, No. 229.   This MS. Bible.
8 × 10 inches, was written on vellum in double columns of fifty lines
each in the year 1655.

A^d. Mechitarist Library of St. Lazzaro, No. 1366.   This MS. Bible
was written in the sixteenth century on paper in double columns of
forty-three lines each.

A^e. This MS. Bible was written in the sixteenth century, and
belongs to the London Bible Society.   It is designated as B by
Conybeare, whose collation I have used.

A^f. This MS. Bible, which belongs to the Catholicos of the
Armenian Church at Edschmiadzin, in Armenia, was there photographed by Conybeare in 1891.   The MS. is written in two columns
of fifty lines each in a beautiful hand.   Unfortunately the negatives
reproduced the pages of the Edschimiadzin MS. on so minute a scale
that it was impossible to print them.   Moreover, a few of the
columns were out of focus.   Notwithstanding, the present editor
has been able to decipher five-sixths of the text by holding the
negatives between himself and the sunlight and studying the
negatives letter by letter and word by word.   This MS. is closely
related to A^{cdef}, and has been of great service where the collations
of these MSS. were slightly inaccurate or defective.

A^g. This MS. Bible, which was written in the seventeenth
century, belongs to Lord Zouche.   I owe all my citations of its
text to Conybeare's collation.

A^h. Bodleian Library, Oxford, No. e. 30.   Only five Testaments
are found in this MS., and in the following order: Simeon (fol. 168^a),
Levi (173^a), Joseph (183^b), Benjamin (195^b), Judah (202^a).   The MS.
is written in two or more hands, and there are two types of text.
Fortunately the four first mentioned Testaments and T. Judah
i-xiv. 8^{abc} (i. e. ἕαν . . . . αἰσχρομομφορείν) belongs to the first recension,
and only T. Jud. xiv. 8^{cde}-xxvi to the second.   This MS. thus attests
the same type of text as A^{ab}, but it is more closely related to A^a
than to A^b.

All the preceding MSS. have been used by the present editor.
There are three others of two of which he has no knowledge.

A^i. A Vatican MS. of the Bible, cited once by Conybeare. See *J. Q. R.*, viii. (1896), p. 260. It belongs to the seventeenth century.

A^k. Mechitarist Library in Vienna, No. 126 (Dashian's *Catalog der Armenischen Handschriften der Mechitaristen-Bibliothek zu Wien*, 1895, p. 71, 411 sqq.). This MS. was written in the year 1388. On the first 105ᵃ folios it contains the history of Joseph and Asenath. Then follow the Testaments. Of these the Testaments of Reuben, Dan, and Naphtali are missing. The order of the remaining nine is peculiar, agreeing in the first five with that of A^h. Thus we have: Simeon, Levi, Joseph, Benjamin, Judah, Issachar, Zebulun, Gad, Asher. A study of the titles of these Testaments given in Sinker's Appendix, p. 25, and the German translation of the T. Jud. xxiv–xxvi and T. Benj. x. 8ᵇ–xii by Dr. Paul Hunanian, makes it at once clear that A^k belongs to the first Armenian recension, and furthermore that A^k is more nearly related to A^{ah} than to A^b and to A^h than to A^a.[1]

A^l. The Hofbibliothek, Vienna, No. 11 (Dashian's *Katalog der Armenischen HSS.*, p. 19, 1891).

§ 4. THE ARMENIAN VERSION FOUND IN TWO RECENSIONS: THEIR RELATIONS: THEIR AFFINITIES WITH THE GREEK MSS.: ITS VALUE.

The two recensions. As we have already observed in the preceding section, there are two recensions of the text, which are represented in this edition as A^a and A^β. A^a, which is found in non-Biblical MSS., includes four MSS., A^{abhk}, of which the last, A^k, is known to the editor only through the translation of Dr. Paul Hunanian in Sinker's Appendix, p. 25. The relations of these four MSS. to each other can be represented as follows :—

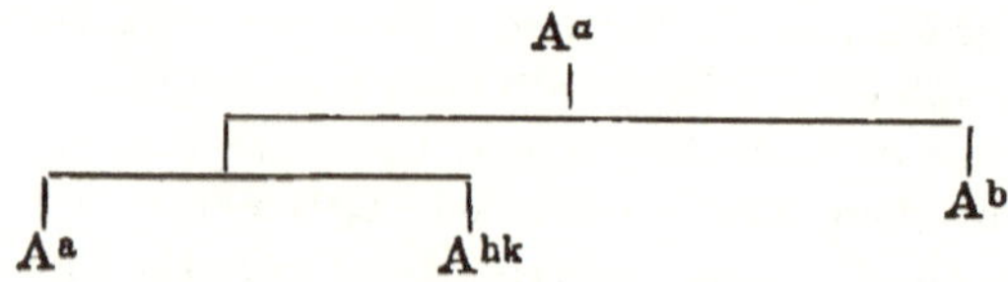

---

[1] Thus the titles of the Testaments of Simeon, Levi, Joseph, and Benjamin in A^k agree with those in A^{abh}, but that of Judah in A^k agrees only with that in A^b. A^k, like A^{ah}, rejects the additions of A^b in T. Jud. xxiv. 2, 5, 6; xxv. 3. It agrees with A^h in T. Jud. xxiv. 5, xxvi. 1 against A^{ab}, but with A^{ab} against $A^{h\beta}$ in xxv. 4.

A[b] is a good MS. in many respects and occasionally alone preserves the true text, but it is disfigured by many small additions of words and phrases.

A[β], which is found always (?) in Biblical MSS., includes in this edition A[b*cdefg]. Of these A[b*] stands aloof from the rest. Its idiosyncrasies are innumerable, but in a few rare cases, where it differs from A[cdefg], it has the support of the best Greek MSS. Cf. T. Benj. xii. 1. Unfortunately it was adopted by the Mechitarist editor of the Armenian text as his chief authority. The relations of these six MSS. might be represented as follows:—

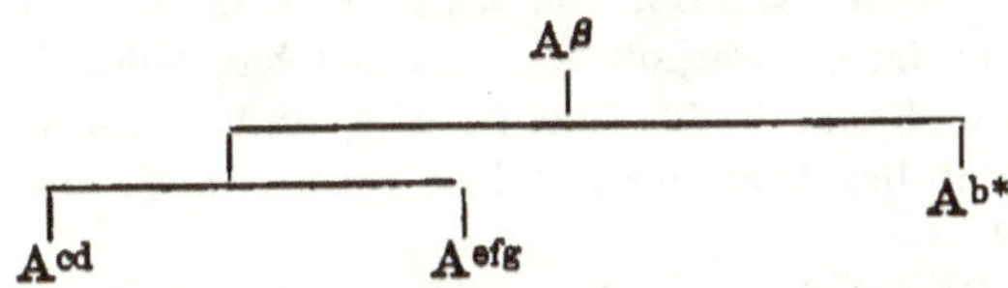

Relations of the two recensions. The variations between A[a] and A[β] are very great, but the bulk of them appear to have arisen within the Version. Very many of them are simply due to the confusion of like words with each other. Instances of this nature are pointed out on nearly every page of my text. Other differences apparently arose from an attempt of the scribe of A[a] to abbreviate the text as it is found in A[β].[1] But over and above these there are certain important sections, where the differences between the two recensions goes back to the Greek, such as in T. Lev. ii. 7–10, xiv. 1, 3–5, where A[a] agrees with *a* against *β*, and one notable section, T. Lev. iii. 1–5, where A[a] is less corrupt than *a* and gives the nearest reproduction of the original Hebrew archetype.

Affinities of A with the Greek MSS. Exclusive of such passages as the above, A, taken as a whole, agrees with *β* S against *a*. This agreement holds in an innumerable number of passages and frequently on a large scale, as in T. Lev. v. 1[b]; T. Jud. v. 6, 7, vii. 2–3, 9, x. 5, xviii. 1, xx. 2–4, xxvi. 3; T. Iss. i. 11, vii. 9; T. Zeb. iv. 1–6, ix. 7; T. Dan i. 9; T. Naph. i. 12; T. Gad ii. 3–5, vi. 3; T. Asher ii. 3, vi. 6; T. Jos. viii. 5, xvi. 2–3; T. Benj. vii. 4, viii. 2, xii. In one considerable passage, owing to hmt., i.e. in T. Benj. iv. 5, A agrees with *a* against *β*, and likewise in a number of unimportant phrases, where the agreement may be accidental.[2]

---

[1] Thus in the T. Judah the text of A[a] is less by a third than that of A[β], but this is an extreme case.

[2] Cf. T. Jos. iv. 5 (n. 35).

But within β there are two types of text to which *aef* and *bdg* belong respectively, and A agrees all but universally with *bdg*, when *bdg* differ from *aef*. In one passage, T. Zeb. viii. 6, A agrees with *aef* (ὕπαρξιν) against a (πρόσωπον). Here *bg* differ from all the MSS. and Versions and *d* gives a text conflated from *bg* and *aef*.

Value of A. The value of A will be best understood when we come to deal with the Christian interpolations in the text. These are by no means absent from A, but they are present in a much less degree in A than in a and β. This is specially the case in the last two Testaments. But not only is A notable for its comparative freedom from interpolation, but A^a has alone transmitted the purest form of text in T. Lev. iii. 1–5, and A alone preserved the text where it has been wholly lost by $a\beta$ in T. Jos. xix. 3–7 ; T. Benj. ii. 6–8.

But A is guilty of the sin of omission, and that almost on every page. These omissions are brought before the reader in my text by the use of the brackets ⌐ ⌐. All words thus enclosed are omitted by A.

Furthermore, the text of A is often corrupt. At times the meaning can only be guessed at. In my retranslations of A into Greek I have reproduced the irregularities of this Version.

§ 5. EDITION OF THE ARMENIAN TEXT.

Only one edition of the text has as yet appeared. This is given on pp. 27–151 of the TREASURY OF OLD AND NEW FATHERS: *Non-canonical Writings of the Old Testament*, Venice, 1896, by H. Sargis Josepheanz (Թանգարան Հին և Նոր Նախնեաց. Ա. Անկանոն գիրք Հին կտակարանաց).

This edition consists of a reproduction of A^{b*} with variants in the notes from A^{abcd}. The editor could not unfortunately have chosen a worse MS. for his text. Fortunately, however, in the case of the Testaments of Simeon and Levi, where A^a and A$^\beta$ differ very greatly, he has given, by the advice of Mr. Conybeare, A^{ab} on the left hand pages and A^{b*cd} on the pages facing them.

My study of this text has led me to form a low opinion of its accuracy. The editor is frequently careless as to the order of the text, and thus represents a divergence between A and $a\beta$ where there is none in the MSS. He is indefinite in his statements on the notes. Thus not unfrequently he says 'one line is missing', and gives the reader no help in determining its length. Happily, by the aid of

A^{bbefg}, I have been able to ascertain his meaning. The title of the T. Joseph is wrongly given for A^{ab}. Again A^b is not infrequently wrongly cited, as the copy of this MS. by Father Carékin shows. I cannot help drawing the same inference with regard to A^{cd} from my study of A^{efg}, which are closely related to A^{cd}, and with regard to A^a from my study of A^h, these two MSS. being made from the same archetype.

Notwithstanding, this scholar has rendered a great service to the students of the Testaments, and materially lightened the labours of his successors. But it is to be hoped that either he or some other Armenian scholar will undertake a critical edition of this much needed work, in which A^{b*} will be banished from the text and not always cited in the notes. In the meantime the students of this literature must content themselves with the knowledge of A that is given in my notes. I have in my notes either silently or expressly corrected Josepheanz's text when needful, and so far as I am aware I have not omitted a single important variant in either A^α or A^β.

§ 6. TRANSLATIONS OF THE ARMENIAN VERSION.

Paul Hunanian. A German translation has been made by this scholar of the T. Jud. xxiv–xxvi and of T. Benj. x. 8–xii from the Armenian MS. A^k and is given in Sinker's *Appendix*, pp. 26–27.

Conybeare. The chief help towards our knowledge of the Armenian Version has been rendered by this scholar in his contributions to the *J. Q. R.*, 'A collation of Sinker's Texts of the Testaments of Reuben and Simeon with the old Armenian Version,' 1896, vol. viii. 260–268: 'A collation of Armenian Texts of the Testaments of Judah, Dan, Joseph, Benjamin' (viii. 471–485). In these articles Conybeare has retranslated into Greek or Latin the chief variants in the three MSS. A^{beg}.

Preuschen: 'Die armenische Uebersetzung der Testamente der Zwölf Patriarchen' in the *Zeitschrift für NTliche Wissenschaft*, 1900, i. 106–140. This article gives almost a complete list of the Armenian MSS. and a translation into German of the T. Levi. The translator makes many good suggestions and attempts in some of the corrupt passages a reconstruction of the text. He has rightly shown that the editor of the Armenian text was wrong in making A^{b*} the basis of his text.

Issaverdens, *The Uncanonical Writings of the Old Testament*, pp. 349–

479, Venice, 1901. Dr. Issaverdens has here attempted to translate the Testaments into English, but the task was wholly beyond him. It is not that his English was defective, but that his entire training was not apparently fitted to prepare him for such an undertaking. He ought to have followed closely the printed Armenian text, and, where this text exhibited two very different recensions, have rendered each independently. As it is, he ostensibly follows the longer recension, but frequently adopts a reading from the shorter without informing his reader. No hint is given that at times ten, twenty, or thirty words or even a whole page is wanting in the shorter recension. Sometimes he gives, as a rendering of the Armenian text, the rendering of the Greek text of Sinker, where the Armenian is at variance with the Greek. Occasionally he adds a clause from the Greek which is missing in the Armenian without even a hint to that effect. Finally, his renderings are frequently inaccurate. In short, this translation, while of interest to the general reader, is absolutely worthless to the scholar.

§ 7. THE SLAVONIC VERSION.

This version is late. It is based on the type of text represented by *aef*, and of these three it attaches most closely to *f*; for S¹ always and occasionally S² agree in making the addition at the close of each Testament that is to be found in *f* alone of the Greek MSS. But S has affinities also with other MSS. than *aef*; thus in T. Lev. ix. 1 it agrees with *a* in reading τὸν προπάτορα ἡμῶν which β, A omit: in T. Gad i. 4 *a*, S¹ read ὑπάρχων νέος, where β, A have τρυφερὸς ὤν, and in T. Lev. xii. 1 ἐξ αὐτῆς where β, A read αὐτῷ: in T. Benj. iv. 3 *c*, S read θεοῦ where β has ἀγαθοῦ, and in T. Lev. ix. 11 *a*, *d*, Aᵃ, S¹ agree in omitting six words through hmt. Such instances, though they are not numerous, are sufficient to prove that the Greek MS. from which S was translated had sporadically come under the influence of *a*.

§ 8. THE TWO SLAVONIC RECENSIONS.

The two Slavonic Recensions of the Testaments of the Twelve Patriarchs are primarily taken from the so-called Palea (Greek παλαιά), which contain short accounts of events mentioned in the Old Testament with the addition of traditional stories and comments of the Fathers of the Church. These Palea sometimes appear in separate collections and are sometimes prefixed to the translations of Byzantine chronicles. Their origin is certainly Byzantine. Of the two recensions the short one has undergone many changes from the Greek original. The editor of the Palea has shortened the 'Testaments' as they already existed in a complete Slavonic translation, and following a polemical course against the Jews, he has here and there introduced references to them. Besides the alterations mentioned the editor of the Palea has changed the order of the 'Testaments', having placed the Testament of Joseph before all the others, and having connected it with the death of Jacob. Tichonravov, the Russian editor, has not followed this peculiarity, and some variations have been introduced from a Palea on vellum of 1406, written at Kolemna. The shorter redaction of the Testaments is contained in a vellum MS. of the fourteenth century. preserved in the Monastery of St. Alexander Nevski.

The Complete Recension is from a Palea of the year of 1477, preserved in the Synodal Library at Moscow, No. 210, pp. 146–189.

Some variations from the complete redaction of the Testaments have been introduced from an uncial MS. in a Miscellany of fifteenth to sixteenth centuries, belonging to the Chief Archives of the Ministry of Foreign Affairs at Moscow, and including among other things a part of the chronography of John Malalas.

It will be seen that with the exceptions indicated the two redactions agree.

Tichonravov's work is entitled : Pamiatniki Otrechennoi Russkoi, Literaturi Sobrani i izdani Nikolaem Tikhonravovim [1]. 2 vols. St. Petersburg, 1863.

W. R. MORFILL.

§ 9. THE GREEK VERSION FOUND IN TWO FORMS, α AND β. THEIR RELATIONS AND THE CHARACTERISTICS OF THEIR REPRESENTATIVES.

The Greek Version is found in two forms which are denoted by α and β in this edition. I do not call them recensions, for I hope later to prove that these forms go back to the Hebrew.

α and its characteristics. α is represented by three MSS. *chi.* The relations of *chi* to each other may be represented as follows:

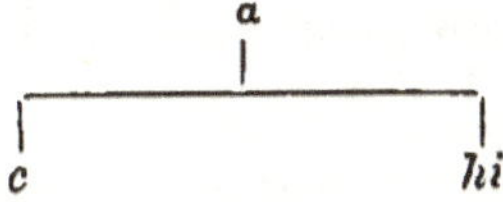

---

[1] Памятники отреченной литературы собраны и изданы Николаемъ Тихонра-вовымъ. St. Petersburg, 1863.

hi are derived from one and the same parent [1], but are late MSS. and show some signs of a mixed ancestry. In T. Zeb. i. 7[b]–ii. 1[a] they supply the text of *a* which *c* omits through hmt. These MSS. diverge occasionally from *c* : thus they support β, A$^\beta$, S[1] against *c* in T. Lev. iii. 8 (n. 49) ; β, S[1] against *c*, A in T. Sim. i. 10 (n. 68) ; β, (A), S[1] against *c* in T. Sim. vii. 1 (n. 2) ; β, A, S[1] in T. Lev. vi. 3 (n. 8) against *c* ; β, S in T. Zeb. ix. 5 (n. 27) against *c*, A.

a is rather disfigured by omissions such as T. Reub. ii. 3[b]–4[a] ; T. Lev. ix. 2[b] (n. 8), 11[b] (through hmt. n. 49) 14[b] ; xii. 5–7 (n. 27) ; xiii. 2 ; T. Jud. iii. 4 (through hmt.) ; vi. 1–2 ; xii. 6–10 ; xxi. 7[d] (n. 54) ; T. Naph. viii. 4[b], 6[c].

Though freer than β from Christian interpolations, yet *a*, too, shows many signs of the Christian scribe's activity in this direction [2]. But we shall return to this subject in a later Section.

One notable depravation of the text occurs in T. Jud. xii. 6–10, where *a* has omitted the text of the Testament and substituted in its stead an abbreviated form of the LXX of Gen. xxxviii. 20, 24–30.

β and its characteristics. β is represented by six MSS., *abdefy*. These MSS. are not so closely related to each other as *hi*, but represent two diverging types of text. Of these *aef* show many affinities with *a*, and *bdg* with A. As we have shown elsewhere (see § 7), S is derived from *aef*. It is noteworthy that *acf* exhibit one uniform type of text agreeing on the whole very closely with each other, whereas *bdg*, though undoubtedly exhibiting a certain type of text, differ very largely from each other. Thus *g* is remarkable for its large omissions, *d* for its large additions and conflations, and *b* for its frequent small changes of the text. Furthermore, *bdg* are remarkable also for large additions to the text in T. Zeb. Thus vi. 4–6, vii–viii. 3, ix. 8[cd] are found alone in *bdg*. These, if not from the original Testament, are from a Semitic source.

We shall begin with *b*. In some cases its variants are due to emendation. Thus in T. Lev. xvii. 2 the priesthood of an ancient

---

[1] *h* is not derived from *i* nor *vice versa* ; for *i* omits where *h* does not, and *h* omits where *i* does not. Besides, there is a large number of variations between them. See Appendix VI.

[2] In the following passages *c* adds περὶ χ̄ῡ (= περὶ χριστοῦ) in the margin (unless otherwise noted). T. Sim. vi. 5 (in text) ; T. Lev. iv. 1, x. 2, xvi. 3, T. xviii. 2 ; T. Iss. vii. 7 ; T. Naph. viii. 2 (on top of page) ; T. Ash. vii. 3 ; T. Jos. xix. 3 ; T. Benj. iii. 8, ix. 2. Of the above *hi* omit the first three additions in the T. Lev. ; *h* omits the address in the T. Sim., and *i* the addition in the T. Naph. Otherwise *hi* agree with *c*, except that they go a step further and in all cases embody the additions in the text.

worthy is said to have been πλήρης μετὰ Κυρίου, i.e. " עַם שָׁלֵם, 'perfect with the Lord.' But the scribe of *b*, failing naturally to understand this Semitic Greek, wrote πλήρης μετὰ φόβου Κυρίου. Likewise as an emendation we should explain the addition of ζήσεσθε in T. Jud. xvi. 2 against all other authorities, and the change of συντρέχει into συνεργεῖ in T. Benj. iv. 5, of συγγένῃ into συμπεισθῆς in T. Jos. vii. 3 as also in iv. 3, of διαβουλίου into διαβόλου in T. Ash. i. 9, of πατράσιν into πέρασιν in T. Dan v. 10, of δώσει into βοῶν in T. Dan v. 9, of ἀπέθνησκε into ἀπέθανεν in T. Lev. xi. 7 (n. 34), and of πρόσεχε into μὴ πρόσεχε in T. Lev. ix. 9, in nearly every case with disastrous results. Again, without a shadow of authority, it adds καὶ ἐθαύμαζον at the close of T. Jos. xvii. 5. Finally, in T. Zeb. viii. 6, it gives a most unlikely text along with *g*. On the other hand, in T. Jud. v. 2, the words καὶ νότου, which it inserts·after δυσμῶν, though not found in any other Greek MS., nor in A or S, are found in the Hebrew Midrash which contains fragments of the Testament: see Appendix I (p. 237, line 4 ראובן . . . מן הדרום). In some cases it agrees with A against *a*, β–*b* (T. Naph. ii. 8 (n. 62)). Thus, on the whole, it is clear that, though in many respects *b* is a good representative of the type *bdg*, it would form an insecure foundation on which to construct a text.

d. This is a most interesting MS. It exhibits peculiar readings on almost every page. First of all *d* is a conflate text. This is manifest in the titles of the Testaments, where it combines the readings of *a* and *β*. Such conflations are common in *d*. See T. Jud. vi. 3 (n. 17); T. Zeb. viii. 6 (n. 22); T. Jos. iv. 7 (n. 44); xvi. 5 (n. 23). In other cases *d* shows affinities with *a*. Thus in T. Lev. xiii. 8ᵃ *d* supports *a* against β–*d*, A, S; *a*, A in reading σοφία, where β–*d* read αὐτή in T. Lev. xiii. 8; and by reading ὑμῶν, which β–*d* om., in xiv. 7; and *a*, Aᵃ, S¹ in omitting a clause in ix. 11. Again, *d* agrees at times with *aef* against *bg*. Cf. T. Gad v. 9 (n. 59), viii. 1 (n. 4); T. Ash. iv. 2 (n. 10). In one passage, T. Jud. ix. 5, I have adopted παραθήσας into the text on the testimony of *d*, A. In another passage, T. Benj. vi. 4 (n. 26), it seems alone to have preserved the original text.

Thus *d*, which is naturally related to *b*, A, shows many traces of the influence of *a* and *aef*.

g. This is a very corrupt MS. and is chiefly remarkable for its omissions. It is very closely related to A, and *g*, A occasionally agree against all the other authorities. T. Naph. viii. 4ᵍ, *g*, A along with *e* are right against *a*, *abdf*.

We shall now attempt to represent, on a genealogical table, the affinities between the various MSS. and Versions:—

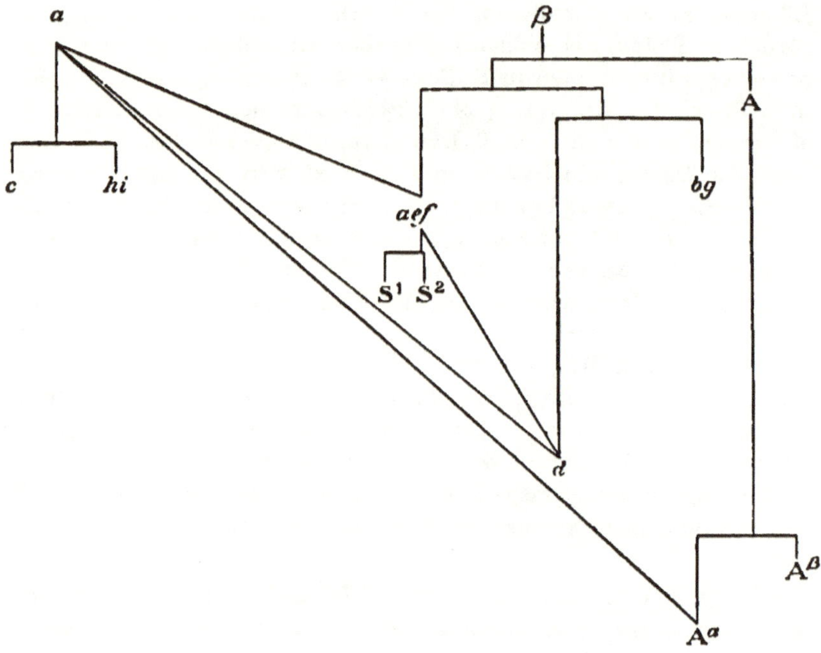

In this table the main connexions are represented. It fails, however, to exhibit the occasional influence of various descendants of β on *hi*.

§ 10. EDITIONS OF THE GREEK VERSION.

Grabe, *Spicilegium Patrum*, I, Oxon., 1698: 2nd ed., 1714. The text of the Testaments in this edition is given according to *b*, but inaccurately, and a few of the variations of *a* appended. With this was printed Grosseteste's Latin translation, for which two Bodley MSS. were used.[1]

Fabricius, *Codex pseudepigraphus Vet. Testamenti*, I. Hamburg, 1713. This is simply a reprint of Grabe's text.

Gallandi, *Bibliotheca Veterum Patrum*, I. Venetiis, 1788. This also is a reprint of Grabe's text.

---

[1] The actual 'copy' that Grabe sent to the press is preserved in Queen's College, Oxford (No. 214). See Sinker, p. ix.

Sinker, *Testamenta XII Patriarcharum, ad fidem codicis Cantabri-giensis edita : accedunt lectiones cod. Oxoniensis.* Cambridge, 1869. We have here a most accurate reproduction of *b*, but we cannot speak so well of the collation of *a*, which is given in the footnotes. This contains many serious errors.

Testamenta XII Patriarcharum : Appendix containing a Collation of the Roman and Patmos MSS. and bibliographical Notes. Cambridge, 1879. These are the MSS. denoted by *c, g* in the present edition. The collation of *c* was made for Dr. Sinker by Guidi, and is on the whole accurately done. I have discovered four errors through the photographic reproduction which I had executed for me in the Vatican. On p. 4 Dr. Sinker has expressed the conviction that 'in any future critical revision of the text the Cambridge MS. must form the basis'. *b* is undoubtedly a valuable MS., but it can never again enjoy this distinction.

§ 11. The Greek Version—a Translation from the Hebrew.

Apart from Grabe, no notable scholar has advocated a Hebrew original till within the last decade and a half. Even Grabe, though he declared for a Hebrew original, advanced no linguistic arguments in support of his contention. It is remarkable that such an eminent critic as Dillmann could write (Herzog, *Real-Encyc.*[2], xii. 362): 'Since the publication of Nitzsch's study all are agreed that the book is not a translation, but was originally written in Greek.' The judgement of Dr. Sinker is still more pronounced (*Test. XII Patr.*, p. 31): 'The Testaments in their present form were no doubt written in the Hellenistic Greek, in which we now possess them, presenting as they do none of the peculiar marks which characterize a version. Whether there were a Hebrew work, on which the present was modelled, a supposition by no means improbable in itself, we cannot tell, nor is it a matter of much importance.'

To two Jewish scholars, Kohler[1] and Gaster, within the last fourteen years, belongs the honour of re-opening the question of the Hebrew origin of the Testaments. Only Gaster[2], however, has offered any linguistic evidence. But his article on the question, though it contains a few excellent points, failed to establish his thesis. Shortly after the above articles were written the present editor began his study of the Testaments, in the course of which he early came to the conclusion—which he set forth later in the

---

[1] *J. Q. R.*, 1893, v. 400–406.

[2] 'The Hebrew text of one of the Testaments of the XII Patriarchs' (*Proceedings of the Society of Bibl. Archaeology*, Dec. 1893, Jan. 1894).

Encyclopaedia Biblica (I, 241, 1899)—that the bulk of this work was written before 100 B.C., therein confirming an earlier speculation of Kohler. Since that date a close examination of the Greek text has brought to light a number of facts that puts its derivation from a Hebrew original beyond the possibility of question. The results of this examination will now be placed before the reader.[1] Before entering on this subject it is worth observing that both the Greek MSS. *h* and *i* state at the outset that the Greek is a translation from the Hebrew. See p. xi *ad fin.*

I. *Hebrew constructions and expressions are to be found on every page. Though the vocabulary is Greek, the idiom is frequently Hebraic and foreign to the genius of the Greek language.*

T. Reub. iii. 8 συνίων ἐν τῷ νόμῳ = בן בתורה ; iv. 6 οὐκ ἐν καιρῷ αὐτῶν = בלא עתם ; vi. 11 ἐν αὐτῷ ἐξελέξατο = בו בחר. T. Sim. iv. 4 ἠγάπησά με σὺν τοῖς ἀδελφοῖς μου (α) = אהבני עם־אחי 'loved me as (he did) my brothers'. So β, A, S¹ ὡς τοὺς ἄλλους ἀδελφούς. v. 4 ἐν Λευὶ ἀδικήσουσι = יָרֵעוּ בלוי ; v. 5 οὐ δυνήσονται πρὸς Λευί (β, S¹) = לא יכלו ללוי 'they shall not overcome Levi'. The same Hebraism recurs in T. Iss. iv. 4 ; T. Dan v. 4. vi. 6 δοθήσονται . . . εἰς καταπάτησιν (β) = ... ינתנו ... למרמס 'they shall be trodden under foot'. This idiomatic use of נתן is common. Cf. use of שים in Is. x. 6. T. Lev. viii. 14 ἐπικληθήσεται αὐτῷ ὄνομα καινόν = יקרא לו שם חדש ; xviii. 10 Ἀδάμ = אדם, and should here be rendered by ἀνθρώπους. T. Jud. vii. 1 (*hi*, β) ὄχλος βαρύς = חיל כבד 'a numerous army'; ix. 8 βεθ = בת, κόρους = כורים, νφης = איפה ; xii. 8 ἕως τῆς ζωῆς μου is clearer in the Hebrew than in the Greek, it = בחיי 'so long as I lived'; xx. 4 ἐν στήθει ὀστέων αὐτοῦ, which is absolutely unintelligible, is full of significance in the Hebrew = בלב עצמו 'on his very heart'. In xxi. 5 ἐσθίειν τὴν τράπεζαν αὐτοῦ = אכל שלחנו. Most probably the peculiar Greek προκόψουσιν ἐπὶ κακῷ ἐν πλεονεξίᾳ in xxi. 8 is to be explained by retroversion into the Hebrew יוסיפו להרע בבצע 'they will grow worse in covetousness'; xxv. 1 ἔξαρχοι σκήπτρων = 'chiefs of tribes' (שבטים) ; xxv. 2 ἡ τρυφὴ τὸν Νεφθαλείμ = 'Eden (blessed) Naphtali', for τρυφή = ערן. In T. Iss. v. 7 ἐκλήρωσεν ἐν αὐτοῖς (β) = הנחיל להם. T. Gad ii. 2 προσεθέμην αὐτῷ μῖσος = הוספתי שנא אתו 'I hated him still more'. T. Ash. i. 5 ἐν οἷς τὰ δύο διαβούλια . . διακρίνοντα αὐτά. Here ἐν οἷς . . . διακρίνοντα αὐτά appears to be a poor rendering of אשר . . . בחרים בם. T. Ash. iii. 1 ὁ θεὸς ἀναπαύεται εἰς αὐτήν = אלהים ישכן בה 'God hath His

---

[1] The present editor has already published some of the following results in the *Encycl. Bibl.*, i. 239-240; Hastings, *Bibl. Dict.*, iv. 724; *Hibbert Journal*, April, 1905, pp. 562 sqq.

habitation therein'. T. Jos. ii. 3 ἔδωκέ με ὁ Κύριος εἰς οἰκτιρμοὺς ἐνώπιον=נתן אתי לרחמים לפני (cf. Dan. i. 9) 'granted me to find mercy in the sight of'; xii. 2 κλοπῇ ἔκλεψαν=גנב גנבו; xii. 3 ποίησον μετ' αὐτοῦ κρίσιν = עשה משפט עמו. T. Benj. x. 11 κατοικήσετε ἐπ' ἐλπίδι ἐν ἐμοί = תשבו לבטח בי 'Ye shall dwell securely with me'. The same misrendering is found in the LXX of Ezek. xxviii. 26; xxxiv. 28, and elsewhere.

The above instances are sufficient in themselves to prove the derivation of our text from a Hebrew original. The bulk of the above expressions could hardly, on any hypothesis, have been written for the first time in Greek. But the evidence can be multiplied fourfold, both in quantity and in conclusiveness, as we shall see as we proceed.

II. *Dittographic renderings of the same Hebrew phrase, and expressions in the Greek implying dittographs in the Hebrew MS. before the translator.*

In T. Sim. iv. 8 κλόνον παρέχει τῇ ψυχῇ καὶ τρόμον τῷ σώματι= ירגיז הנפש וירעיד הגוף, and is thus a dittographic rendering of the first two lines, ἀγριοῖ . . τὴν ψυχὴν καὶ φθείρει τὸ σῶμα, though φθείρει supposes יאבד instead of ירעיד. In T. Naph. iii. 5 ἀπὸ κατοικησίας . . . τάξας τὴν γῆν ἀοίκητον is a clear instance of dittography. The original here may have been מבלי יושב, which has been rendered first as ἀπὸ κατοικησίας, and a second time as ἀοίκητον.

In vi. 2 (β, A, S') the impossible μεστὸν ταρίχων ἐκτὸς ναυτῶν has arisen from a dittograph in the Hebrew; for μεστὸν ταρίχων = מלא מלוחים, a corrupt dittography of בלא מלחים = ἐκτὸς ναυτῶν.[1]

Again, in T. Gad vi. 6 μετανοεῖ τοῦ πλημμελῆσαι εἰς σὲ καὶ τιμήσει σε καὶ φοβηθήσεται καὶ εἰρηνεύσει (β–af, A, S'). Here the idea of fear is quite alien to the context, which deals with the case of a man repenting of the wrong he had done to a good man: φοβηθήσεται= יֶחֱרַד, a dittograph of יְהַדֵּר=τιμήσει.

We should possibly explain T. Iss. iv. 4 in this way. Thus in εἶδεν ἐπιλέξασθαι κάλλος θηλείας we might take ἐπιλέξασθαι κάλλος= בָּחֹר בְּחֵן and regard the first word as a dittograph of the second. Then the text would run 'he looketh not on the beauty of women'. Otherwise for εἶδεν (which c, ab read) we should read οἶδεν with def (A). Then οἶδεν ἐπιλέξασθαι=ידע לבחר, or, if ἐπιδέξασθαι (a, β–fg) is original, we should have ידע לרצות='cannot have pleasure in'.

On the same principle we should explain T. Jud. iii. 3 τὸν Ἀχὼρ βασιλέα=המלך האחר, i. e. τὸν ἕτερον βασιλέα, a phrase which occurs in

---

[1] This fact was first pointed out by Gaster (P. S. B. A., Dec., 1893).

the previous verse and has been wrongly repeated in this verse. See
notes *in loc.*

Again, the impossible text in T. Lev. viii. 14 ποιήσει ἱερατείαν νέαν
κατὰ τὸν τύπον τῶν ἐθνῶν εἰς πάντα τὰ ἔθνη is very probably to be
explained in the same way. The words κατὰ τὸν τύπον ... ἔθνη =
לצלם הגוים לכל הגוים. Here I take צלם as corrupt for מליץ = μεσίτης.
Then either we omit הגוים or לכל־הגוים as a dittograph. Thus we
arrive at: 'He will establish a new priesthood to be a mediator for
the Gentiles.' The clause occurs in the description of John Hyrcanus,
whom the author regarded as the Messiah. Moreover, throughout
the entire Testaments the salvation of the Gentiles is confidently
expected. But the most notable dittograph occurs in T. Naph. viii.
4, 6 :—

Ἐὰν οὖν καὶ ὑμεῖς ἐργάσησθε τὸ καλόν,
εὐλογήσουσιν ὑμᾶς οἱ ἄνθρωποι καὶ οἱ ἄγγελοι,
καὶ ὁ Θεὸς δοξασθήσεται ἐν τοῖς ἔθνεσιν δι' ὑμῶν,
καὶ ὁ διάβολος φεύξεται ἀφ' ὑμῶν,
καὶ τὰ θηρία φοβηθήσονται ὑμᾶς,
καὶ ὁ Κύριος ἀγαπήσει ὑμᾶς,
[καὶ οἱ ἄγγελοι ἀνθέξονται ὑμῶν].

Τὸν δὲ μὴ ποιοῦντα τὸ καλόν,
καταράσονται αὐτὸν καὶ οἱ ἄγγελοι καὶ οἱ ἄνθρωποι,
καὶ ὁ Θεὸς ἀδοξήσει ἐν τοῖς ἔθνεσιν δι' αὐτοῦ,
καὶ ὁ διάβολος οἰκειοῦται αὐτὸν ὡς ἴδιον σκεῦος,
καὶ πᾶν θηρίον κατακυριεύσει αὐτῷ
καὶ ὁ Κύριος μισήσει αὐτόν.

Here, if we compare ver. 6 with ver. 4, we see that the six lines in
ver. 6 correspond line for line with the first six in ver. 4. The
seventh line in 4 is thus against the structure of the stanza. It is
also against the parallelism. On retranslation into Hebrew we find
that it = ומלאכים יאחזוכם, which is a dittograph of ואלהים יאהבכם.[1]

III. *Paronomasiae which are lost in Greek can be restored by
retranslation into Hebrew.*

We can recover a dozen or more paronomasiae by retranslation,
the most of these having to do with the names of the patriarchs.
T. Sim. ii. 2 ἡ μήτηρ μου ἐκάλεσέ με Συμεῶνα ὅτι ἤκουσε Κύριος τῆς
δεήσεως αὐτῆς = אמי קראה את שמי שמעון כי שמע יי תפלתה.

T. Lev. vi. 1 ἀσπίδα . . . διὸ καὶ τὸ ὄνομα τοῦ ὄρους Ἀσπίς = שריון . . . על כן שם ההר שריון. Here the play is on different meanings of the same word.[1] T. Lev. xi. 2 ἐκάλεσε τὸ ὄνομα αὐτοῦ Γηρσάμ, ὅτι ἐν τῇ γῇ ἡμῶν πάροικοι ἦμεν (β, Aβ, S¹)= גרים . . . גרשם; xi. 5, 6 μέσος . . . ἵστατο πάσης τῆς συναγωγῆς· διὰ τοῦτο ἐκάλεσα τὸ ὄνομα αὐτοῦ Καάθ (β, Aβ)= קהת . . . קהל. See Appendix III, 66-7, where we have the same play on the name implied in the Aramaic and Greek Fragments ; xi. 7 ἐκάλεσα αὐτὸν Μεραρεῖ ὅ ἐστι πικρία μου (β)= מררי . . . ; מררי; xi. 8 Ἰωχαβὲδ ἐγεννήθη . . . ἔνδοξος γὰρ ἤμην (β)= כי . . . יכבד נולדה; נכבד אני.

T. Jud. i. 3 ἐπωνόμασέν με Ἰούδαν, λέγουσα· ἀνθομολογοῦμαι τῷ Κυρίῳ = אודה . . . יהודה.

T. Iss. i. 15 διὰ τοῦτον τὸν μισθὸν ἐκλήθην Ἰσαχάρ = בשכר נקראתי ישׁשכר; v. 8 τῷ δὲ Γὰδ ἐδόθη ἀπολέσαι τὰ ἐπερχόμενα πειρατήρια τῷ Ἰσραήλ גדודים . . . לגד. This last verse has by some accident been inserted in Issachar, whereas it ought, of course, to have appeared in the T. Gad.

T. Zeb. i. 3 Ζαβυλὼν δόσις ἀγαθή = זבד טוב . . . זבלון; iii. 3 καταπατήσομεν αὐτήν, ἀνθ' ὧν εἶπεν ὅτι βασιλεύσει ἐπί = ירדה ב . . . נרדה (Late Hebrew).

T. Naph. i. 6 ἐν πανουργίᾳ ἐποίησε Ῥαχὴλ . . . διὰ τοῦτο ἐκλήθην Νεφθαλείμ (β-g) = לכן נקראתי נפתלי . . . נפתלה רחל; i. 12 ἔτεκε τὴν Βάλλαν λέγων· καινόσπουδός μου ἡ θυγάτηρ· εὐθὺς γὰρ τεχθεῖσα ἔσπευδε θηλάζειν = בהלה לינק . . . בהלה בתולתי כי . . . ילד את־בלהה לאמר.

T. Ash. i. 2 ἀκούσατε, τέκνα Ἀσήρ . . . καὶ πᾶν τὸ εὐθὲς . . . ὑποδείξω ὑμῖν = אורה אתכם . . . שמעו בני אשר וכל הישר; i. 9 θησαυρὸς τοῦ διαβουλίου = אוצר היצר.

T. Benj. i. 6 Βενιαμίν, ὅ ἐστιν υἱὸς ἡμερῶν = בן־ימין . . . בנימין; x. 8 οἱ μὲν εἰς δόξαν οἱ δὲ εἰς ἀτιμίαν= אלה לכבד ואלה לקלון.

IV. *Many passages which are obscure or wholly unintelligible in the Greek become clear on retranslation into Hebrew.*

Many phrases and clauses given under No. I could be brought under this head, such as those in T. Jud. xx. 4 ; T. Jos. ii. 3 ; T. Benj. x. 11, &c. But there are many more such.

---

[1] ἀσπίς is a bad rendering, as שריון means here body armour or coat of mail as in Sam. xvii. 5; 2 Chron. xxvi. 14. θώραξ is given in T. Jud. iii. 5 as another rendering (see Midr. in Appendix I, p. 236, line 4), and is on the whole satisfactory, for in later times θώραξ appears to mean defensive armour generally.

T. Reub. iii. 5 πνεῦμα ψεύδους †ἐν ἀπωλείᾳ καὶ ζήλῳ† τοῦ πλάττειν λόγους καὶ κρύπτειν λόγους αὐτοῦ ἀπὸ γένους καὶ οἰκείων. The context requires a parallel to ἀπὸ γένους καὶ οἰκείων, which underlies, no doubt, the obelized words. These = לשואה וקנאה, which I take to be a corruption of לשנא ומקנא. Thus we get: 'The spirit of lying which aims at practising deceits on an enemy or rival and concealments from kindred and friends.'

In T. Lev. ii. 7 we have the peculiar expression εἶδον ἐκεῖ ὕδωρ πολὺ κρεμάμενον (α, Aᵃ). Here κρεμάμενον is surely impossible. In β, Aᵝ (i. e. Hᵝ) where the text has been expanded into an account of the seven heavens, the explanatory gloss is added: ἀνάμεσον τούτου κἀκείνου. Here κρεμάμενον = כוקיע which seems corrupt for ברקיע, or rather ורקיע = ἐν τῷ στερεώματι or rather καὶ τὸ στερέωμα. The firmament or raqia is actually the name of the second heaven in the Talmudic account of the Seven Heavens (Chag. 12ᵇ). In this earlier account the firmament is simply mentioned as being in the first (α) or second heaven (β).

In T. Lev. ii. 8 (α, β, Aᵝ) the second heaven is said to be brighter and more brilliant than the first, ἦν γὰρ καὶ ὕψος (καὶ γὰρ ὕψος ἦν, β, Aᵝ) ἐν αὐτῷ ἄπειρον. Clearly there is something wrong here. The greater brightness of the second heaven cannot be due to its greater loftiness. The error, therefore, lies in the ὕψος. This word = גֹּבַהּ, which is corrupt for נֹגַהּ = φῶς or φέγγος. Thus the brightness of the second heaven was due to a boundless light (φῶς ἄπειρον) that was therein. This light may have been physical, if we may adopt the Talmudic view which represents the sun, moon, and stars as being in the second heaven (Chag. 12ᵇ). The angel, ii. 9, bids Levi not to be surprised at this heaven, for he will presently see a far brighter one.

In T. Lev. xviii. 9 καταπαύσουσιν εἰς κακά is a most peculiar expression but becomes at once clear on retranslation. Thus it = יחדלו להרע 'shall cease to do evil'.

T. Jud. iv. 3 †ἐλευθερώσαμεν τὴν † Χεβρών. Here, from the parallel accounts in the Midrash (Appendix I), Chron. Jerach. xxxvi. 6 and the Book of Jashar (*Dict. des Apocr.* ii. 1176), we must regard Χεβρών = חברון as a corruption of חצור, i. e. Hazor. In the next place, since our text as well as the three authorities mentioned above have to do with the capture and not the deliverance of Hazor, ἐλευθερώσαμεν must be corrupt. This word = חפשנו, corrupt for תפשנו or כבשנו = ἐλάβομεν or ἐκυριεύσαμεν.

T. Jud. v. 3 οἱ ἐπὶ τοῦ τείχους ... †ἐφελκύσθησαν πρὸς ἡμᾶς 'Those on the wall ... †were drawn down† against us'. This gives no satisfactory sense. We require some such statement as 'they attacked us' or 'drew themselves up against us'; for the sons of Jacob were scaling the wall to attack the city. Here then ἐφελκύσθησαν = ארכו (cf. LXX in Num. ix. 19; Josh. xxiv. 31) which appears to be corrupt for ערכו=παρετάξαντο 'drew themselves up in array against us'.

T. Jud. viii. 2 †παρακαλέσας δέδωκέ μοι. Here παρακαλέσας can hardly mean 'invited', since it is already said that the king had talked with Judah and Ieram and had made a feast for them. Hence I take παρακαλέσας δέδωκε = נחם ונתן, corrupt for בְּחֻמְּי נתן 'when I was heated with wine he gave me his daughter to wife'. Judah's drunkenness explains his marrying a Canaanite. For another possible explanation see note in loc.

T. Jud. ix. 3 καὶ ἤρθη †νεκρὸς ἐν ὄρει Σιείρ, καὶ πορευόμενος ἐν Ἀνονιρὰμ ἀπέθανεν (β, S¹). The words καὶ πορευόμενος ... ἀπέθανεν are omitted by a as unintelligible, and A changes it into ἐν ᾧ ἐπορεύοντο ἐτάφη ἐν Ἀναν. But a comparison of the Midrash Wajjis. and the Chron. Jerach. (see note 20, p. 79) shows that this clause belongs to the original text and in the form in which it appears in β, S¹. Moreover, these authorities help us to discover how the corruption in νεκρός arose. νεκρός = נבלה, whereas these have נחלה = τετραυματισμένος. Thus Esau was wounded on Mount Seir and died as he was passing over Anoniram.

T. Jud. xi. 2 (β, S¹) συνέπεσα πρὸς αὐτήν. Similar phrases occur in xiii. 3 (β–d, A, S¹), and in T. Jos. ix. 5 (a, β–d, S¹). The sense required is obvious: συνέπεσα πρὸς αὐτήν = נפלתי לה, corrupt for בעלתי לה = συνεγενόμην αὐτῇ. This sense suits all the passages.

T. Jud. xiii. 3 ἐν κάλλει γυναικῶν (β) seems quite unsuitable here, and is omitted by a, Aᵇ. Perhaps there was a corruption of חדר= 'apartment' into הרר = κάλλει. Then we should render 'in the women's apartment'.

T. Jud. xxi. 6 οἱ μὲν †κινδυνεύουσιν αἰχμαλωτιζόμενοι, οἱ δὲ πλουτοῦσιν ἁρπάζοντες τὰ ἀλλότρια. Here, instead of κινδυνεύουσι, we require a verb forming an antithesis to πλουτοῦσιν. κινδυνεύουσιν = יִסְכְּנוּ (late Hebrew). In earlier Hebrew it = πτωχεύουσι.

T. Dan i. 7 συνήργει μοι λέγον (a om.). συνήργει is here impossible. It=יעזור, which I take to be corrupt for יעיר = ἤγειρε 'stirred me up saying'.

T. Dan i. 8 (beg) ἵνα ὥσπερ πάρδαλις †ἐκμύζουσα ἔριφον, οὕτως ἐκμυζήσω τὸν Ἰωσήφ. Here ἐκμυζᾶν 'to suck'=מצץ, corrupt for רצץ 'to crush'. Hence 'to crush Joseph as a leopard, &c.'

T. Dan iv. 4 †τέρπει τὴν ἀκοήν, καὶ οὕτως ὀξύνει τὸν νοῦν. Here it is manifestly some hearsay that gives provocation 'and makes the mind keen to perceive'. Now τέρπει τὴν ἀκοήν = הרנין השמועה where

הרנין is corrupt for הרגין. Hence the clause = 'the thing said giveth provocation'.

T. Dan v. 3 ἀγαπήσατε τὸν κύριον ἐν πάσῃ τῇ † ζωῇ (c, β–d, A, S') ὑμῶν καὶ ἀλλήλους ἐν ἀληθινῇ καρδίᾳ. Here the parallelism shows ζωῇ to be corrupt. h d read ψυχῇ, but this looks like a scribe's emendation, though it gives the right idea. Perhaps בכל חייכם or בכל ימיכם is corrupt for בכל מאדכם = 'with all your strength'.

T. Dan v. 6 †ὑπακούσονται τοῦ παρεδρεύειν τοῖς υἱοῖς Λευί. Here 'will obey with a view to attending constantly on' cannot be original. ὑπακούσονται = יַקְשִׁיבוּ, corrupt for יַקְשְׁרוּ = 'will conspire'. The latter verb occurs in the late Heb., T. Naph. ix. 2 (p. 243).

T. Dan v. 10 (a, beg) τὴν ἐκδίκησιν τοῦ νίκους δώσει τοῖς πατράσιν ἡμῶν. Since the promise refers to the future πατράσιν can hardly be right. I conjecture that אבותינו is corrupt for אויבינו and that accordingly we must render here 'will execute an everlasting vengeance on our enemies'.

T. Gad iii. 3 τὸ μῖσος ἐτύφλωσε τὴν ψυχὴν αὐτοῦ, ὡς κἀγὼ † ἔβλεπον ἐν τῷ Ἰωσήφ (β, A, S'). Here κἀγὼ ἔβλεπον ἐν = גם אני אראה ב, which may be corrupt for גם אתי עִוְּרָה ב. Thus we have: 'hate blinded his soul as it blinded me also in regard to Joseph.'

T. Gad vii. 6 ὁ γὰρ πένης ... ὑπὲρ πάντας †πλουτεῖ ὅτι οὐκ ἔχει τὸν περισπασμὸν τῶν ματαίων ἀνθρώπων. According to the text the poor man is rich because he is free from the sore travail of men seeking to be rich. But what we require here is a statement that he is happy—not that he is rich—because he is free from disquieting cares. Here πλουτεῖ = יְעֻשַׁר, corrupt for יְאֻשַׁר = μακαριστός ἐστι. The LXX of Prov. xxxi. 28 implies the converse corruption.

T. Gad vii. 7 ἐξάρατε οὖν τὸ †μῖσος ἀπὸ τῶν ψυχῶν ὑμῶν καὶ ἀγαπήσατε ἀλλήλους ἐν εὐθύτητι καρδίας. This chapter of Gad deals with envy or jealousy on the part of the poor man towards his wealthier or more prosperous neighbour. Ver. 7 closes the chapter with a general admonition bearing on the subject of the chapter. This admonition should refer, therefore, to ζῆλος or φθόνος, not to μῖσος. The corruption arose in the Hebrew קִנְאָה (= ζῆλος) being corrupted into שִׂנְאָה.

T. Ash. ii. 1 ψυχὴ ἐν λόγοις† ἀφιστῶσα τὸ καλὸν ὑπὲρ τοῦ κακοῦ. So a reads. The text of β–g, A λέγουσα, φησί seems to be a corruption of λόγοις ἀφιεῖσα: ἀφιστῶσα = מסירה, which I take to be corrupt for סמכה = ἀντιλαμβανομένη. Thus we have 'a person may support the good with words on behalf of an evil design'.

T. Ash. v. 2 διὸ καὶ τὸν θάνατον ἡ αἰώνιος ζωὴ †ἀναμένει. The interpolations being omitted, this verse runs: 'Death succeedeth to life, night to day, and darkness to light: wherefore also eternal life †awaiteth death.' h, β read ἀναμένει, c (A ?) διαμένει. For τόν before θάνατον g reads μετά. This is a mere scribal guess, but it is in the right direction. Now διαμένει with its notion of 'continuance', even of 'continuance after death', is not the idea that the preceding words suggest. It is that of succession, that we expect. διαμένει may be an emendation of the impossible ἀναμένει. I propose that the original ran as follows: אחר המות חיי־־העולם יקומו = μετὰ τὸν θάνατον ἡ αἰώνιος ζωὴ ἀκολουθεῖ, but that this was corrupted into את המות חיי העולם יקֻמו = β. It appears that it was the loss or corruption of אחר in H, or μετά in a, β that led to the subsequent depravation of the text. If we could assume its loss in a, β then ἀναμένει could be a corruption of ἀνατελεῖ.

T. Ash. vi. 4 τὰ τέλη τῶν ἀνθρώπων δεικνύουσι τὴν δικαιοσύνην αὐτῶν †καὶ γνωρίζονται† τοῖς ἀγγέλοις Κυρίου καὶ τοῦ Βελίαρ. β–dg read γνωρίζοντες instead of καὶ γνωρίζονται which a attests, and dg γνωριζόντων. The construction in a cannot be right, nor yet its sense. β is better in both respects. It is the soul's recognizing the angels of the Lord or of Beliar that makes it joyful or troubled at the hour of death, not its recognition by these angels. The participial construction of β is near what is required and may point to ב with the infin. in Hebrew. In the notes on my text I have conjectured that we have here a confusion of יִוָּדְעוּ = γνωρίζονται and יִוָּעֲדוּ = συναντῶσι, the same confusion as the LXX implies in Amos iii. 3. Perhaps this is not necessary, but I think it gives better sense, and, what is more, it explains the impossible text of a. The Hebrew may have been בהועדם למלאכים or בעוד יועדו למלאכים.

T. Jos. viii. 5 ὅτι διὰ προφάσεως ἀπηλλάγην τῆς Αἰγυπτίας. Here διὰ προφάσεως, if it can stand, must either be rendered 'by (this) means', or 'by a false charge'. But the latter rendering is questionable and the former would require the demonstrative pronoun. Hence I suggest that διὰ προφάσεως = מִתַּאֲנָת, corrupt for מִתַּאֲוֹת (the LXX and Vulg. imply the same corruption in Prov. xviii. 1). Thus we have 'praising God that I was delivered from the lustful desire of the Egyptian woman'. Cf. iii. 10.

T. Jos. xi. 7 καὶ ἐπλήθυνεν αὐτὸν ἐν χρυσίῳ καὶ ἀργυρίῳ καὶ †ἔργῳ (a). β, A, S omit καὶ ἔργῳ, probably as unintelligible. But by retranslation the source of the corruption springs to light. ἔργῳ = עבדה, which the translator read as עֲבֹדָה (= ἔργῳ); but which he should have read as עֲבֻדָּה = 'household servants'. The entire clause will be found in the Hebrew, T. Naph. i. 3 (p. 239), where Naphtali speaks of 'silver and gold and household servants'.

T. Benj. iv. 2 ὁ γὰρ ἀγαθὸς ἄνθρωπος †οὐκ ἔχει σκοτεινὸν ὀφθαλμόν†, ἐλεεῖ γὰρ πάντας. So far as I am aware the expression σκοτεινὸν ὀφθαλμόν is unexampled, and seems to spring from a corruption in the Hebrew. οὐκ ἔχει σκοτεινὸν ὀφθαλμόν = אין לו עין חשך. Here אין is to be rejected as a dittograph of עין, and חשך to be taken as a corruption of חשה. Thus we have האיש הטוב לו עין חשה כי חמל על־כל, 'The good man hath a pitiful eye, for he hath compassion on all'. Cf. Ezek. xvi. 5 לא־חסה עליך עין . . . , לחמלה עליך.

T. Benj. iv. 5 τῷ ἀγαπῶντι τὸν θεὸν †συντρέχει. Here συντρέχει = ירון, corrupt for ירצה 'approveth'.

T. Benj. viii. 3 ὥσπερ γὰρ ὁ ἥλιος οὐ μιαίνεται †προσέχων ἐπὶ κόπρον . . . οὕτω καὶ ὁ καθαρὸς νοῦς ἐν τοῖς μιασμοῖς τῆς γῆς συνεχόμενος μᾶλλον †οἰκοδομεῖ, αὐτὸς δὲ οὐ μιαίνεται. Here προσέχων (c, β–f) = בְּהִזָּהֵר (cf. Sir. xiii. 13), but the word should have been punctuated בְּהַזְהִיר = λάμπων. Strangely enough f has λάμπων here, which is probably only a lucky hit of its scribe. Or προσέχων = בהופיע על (cf. LXX on Job x. 3), which should here have been rendered λάμπων. Next, οἰκοδομεῖ = יבנה which I take to be corrupt for יָזֻבֶּה. Thus the simile in the text becomes perfect.

T. Benj. ix. 1 †ἀνανεωθήσεσθε. Perhaps we have here a corruption of תחרשו (= 'ye will desire' or 'perpetrate') not תחדשו.

In all the above cases we have dealt only with corruptions in the text, where there was no divergence among the MSS. or Versions. Yet the bulk of the restorations is so obvious that we might take as proven our contention without further evidence. And yet the strongest evidence is still to come. In the next Section we shall discuss only those passages in the text where the MSS. and Versions attest different readings, α generally standing in opposition to β, A, S. By means of the evidence thus forthcoming we hope to advance a stage further than we have yet reached, and to prove not only that our book is derived from a Hebrew original, but also that the Hebrew existed in two recensions, Hα and Hβ, and that α and β did not originate in the Greek but are derived respectively from Hα and Hβ.

§ 12. α AND β ARE DERIVED RESPECTIVELY FROM THE TWO LOST HEBREW RECENSIONS Hα AND Hβ. TABLE OF AFFINITY OF ALL THE TEXTUAL AUTHORITIES.

α and β are not, strictly speaking, Greek recensions, for their chief points of divergence[1] did not originate in the Greek, but go

[1] There are of course some omissions in α due to hmt. and others possibly to

back to two diverse forms of text already existing in the Hebrew, which we denote as Hᵃ and Hᵝ.

Of these two recensions, Hᵃ and Hᵝ, sometimes one gives the correct text, sometimes the other. Whilst, therefore, it is best to print a and add the main variations from β in the margin,[1] the translator will follow a different course, and follow in one case a, in another β.

I shall begin this list of variations between Hᵃ and Hᵝ with a few of the most remarkable taken from different Testaments and then proceed in order through the Testaments. The variants will be underlined.

a   β, A, S¹

T. Benj. xii. 2 ἐκοιμήθη ὕπνῳ καλῷ   ἀπέθανε ... ἐν γήρει καλῷ
Here β, A, S are undoubtedly right, מת בשֵׂיבָה טובה. In Hᵃ, on the other hand, שׂיבה has been corrupted into שֵׁינה. The same corruption was present in both Hᵃ and Hᵝ in T. Dan vii. 1 ; T. Ash. viii. 1 ; T. Jos. xx. 4, and both Hebrew recensions are right in T. Iss. vii. 9. In the late Hebrew T. Naph. i. 1, the correct Hebrew phrase is found. See App. II. p. 239.

a   β, A, S¹

T. Ash. vi. 6 εἰσφέρει αὐτὸν εἰς ζωὴν αἰώνιον   παραμυθεῖται αὐτὸν ἐν ζωῇ
Here it is Hᵃ that is right and not Hᵝ. The angel of peace conducts the good soul into eternal life. Here εἰσφέρει=ינחה, which in Hᵝ was corrupted into ינחם=παραμυθεῖται. On T. Benj. vi. 1 we have confirmation of the text of Hᵃ, which reads ὁ γὰρ ἄγγελος τῆς εἰρήνης ὁδηγεῖ τὴν ψυχὴν αὐτοῦ.

a   β, A, S¹

T. Ash. vi. 5 ὅτε γὰρ πονηρὰ ἡ ψυχὴ   ὅτε γὰρ τεταραγμένη ἡ ψ.
       ἀπέρχεται   ἀπέρχεται
Here Hᵝ is right. The troubled or peaceful condition of the soul at death shows its character. Here רעוישה=τεταραγμένη was corrupted in Hᵃ into רשׁעה=πονηρά.

a (aef)   bdg, A

T. Jos. iv. 7 ἀντεφιλονείκει   ἐσιώπησε.
Here Hᵃ read התחרתה and Hᵝ התחרשׁה.

a   β

T. Reub. iv. 1 μοχθοῦντες ἐν ἔργοις καλοῖς   μοχθοῦντες ἐν ἔργοις καὶ ἀπο-
       καὶ ἐν γράμμασιν   πλανώμενοι ἐν γράμμασιν

accident. These I do not include in the above, though some of them may have originated in the Hebrew.

[1] All the variants of a and β are given in the notes.

Here a, which is in part supported by A, is clearly right and β corrupt. ἐν ἔργοις καλοῖς = במעשים ישרים, of which ישרים was corrupted in H[β] into וישרים = καὶ ἀποπλανώμενοι.[1]

T. Reub. iv. 7 φέρει . . . πρόσκομμα τῷ Βελίαρ (a). Here β–af, A, S[1] are right; ποιεῖ . . . γέλωτα παρὰ τῷ Βελίαρ. γέλωτα = משחק (or שחוק), which in H[a] was corrupted into מוקש.

	a	β, A
T. Gad i. 4	ὑπάρχων νέος	τρυφερὸς ὤν

Here H[a] was נער and H[β] עלג. It is doubtful which is original.

	a	β, A, S[1]
T. Gad v. 4	ὁ φόβος τοῦ θεοῦ οἰκεῖ ἐν αὐτῷ	ὁ φ. τ. θ. νικᾷ τὸ μῖσος

Here the context is in favour of β, A, S[1], since it is dealing with the question of hatred. H[a] = תדור בנפשו, corrupt for תוכל לשנאה (= νικᾷ τὸ μῖσος) which stood in H[β].

	a (A)	β, S[1]
T. Benj. x. 4	καταλειμπάνω	διδάσκω

Here H[a] was מניה and was no doubt right. It is found in late Hebrew, T. Naph. i. 3 אני מניח. In H[β] this word was corrupted into מניד or מורה.

The above instances are sufficient to establish the existence of two distinct types in the Hebrew, H[a] and H[β]. We shall now proceed systematically through the Testaments, adducing similar phenomena in support of this view.

	a	β–d, A–a, S[1]
T. Reub. iv. 10	πονηροῦ	ὁρατοῦ

The reading of H[β] ראוי is perhaps best here. 'The God of our fathers delivered him from manifest and hidden death.' This was corrupted in H[a] into רע or רשע = πονηροῦ.

	a	β, A, S[1]
T. Reub. v. 2	διὰ τοῦ σχήματος	δυνάμεως

Here H[a], i. e. הור or הן = σχήματος, is undoubtedly right, as the context proves; for it has just been stated that 'since they have no . . . strength (δύναμιν) over man, they use wiles by outward attractions (σχήμασιν), that they may draw him to themselves. And whom they cannot bewitch with outward attractions, him they overcome by craft'. הן in H[a] was corrupted into און.

	a	β, A
T. Lev. iii. 2	ἡμέραν κρίσεως	ἡμέραν προστάγματος

Here προστάγματος may = דת, corrupt for דין = H[a].

---

[1] Or we might take καλοῖς to be = מובים, which was corrupted into ומבים = καὶ ἀποπλανώμενοι.

In T. Lev. viii. 15 a has παρουσία αὐτοῦ <u>ἀγαπητή</u>, while β–af, A, S have παρ. αὐτοῦ <u>ἄφραστος</u>. The former=ידיד which was corrupted into סוד=ἄφραστος. In 'An Original Source of the Testaments' (App. III. 83) Levi is called אל ידיד. We might also compare the Messianic phrase μονογενοῦς προφήτου in T. Benj. ix. 2. There μονογενοῦς=יחיד. Is this corrupt for ידיד?

In T. Lev. xiii. 5 a reads ὑγιασμένοι ἦτε=תרפאו, and β, A^β, S εὕρητε=תמצאו, both of which appear corrupt for תאצרו=θησαυρίσητε. Thus we have

> 'Work righteousness upon the earth
> That ye may have it as a treasure in heaven'.

	a	β, A^β
T. Lev. xiv. 3	ἥλιος	οὐρανός

Here H^β had שמים, which in H^a was corrupted into שמש.

	a, aef, S	bdg, A^β
T. Lev. xv. 3	οἱ <u>μισοῦντες</u>	οἱ <u>θεωροῦντες</u>

Here a has captured some of the MSS. belonging to β, and =השונאים, which was corrupted into הרואים.

	a	β, A^β
T. Lev. xv. 3	<u>χαρήσονται</u> ἐπὶ τῇ ἀπωλείᾳ ὑμῶν	<u>φεύξονται</u> ἀφ' ὑμῶν

Here H^a was יחדו and H^β ידרו.

	a	β, A, S^1
T. Jud. xxvi. 1	<u>κατέχουσι</u>	<u>κατευθύνουσιν</u>

This variation may have arisen within the Greek, but if not, it may be explained as follows. H^a=שׁוֹמְרִים and H^β מְיַשְּׁרִים.

	a, β–bg, S^1	bg, A
T. Zeb. i. 5	<u>ἐβεβαίωσα</u>	<u>ἐσκέπασα</u> ἐπί

Here a has influenced aef and d. H^β = כסיתי ל, which may be corrupt for כָּרַתִּי ל (or קִימְתִּי) of H^a, 'I made a covenant with my brothers not to tell my father.' But the original Hebrew word is doubtful here.

	a	β, S^1
T. Zeb. ii. 4	<u>μὴ φέρων</u> ἐγὼ τῶν οἰμωγῶν	<u>εἰς οἶκτον ἦλθον</u> ἐγώ

A is vague here, but favours β, S^1. Here H^a seems original, and may have read לא נשאתי נהי which could have been corrupted into באתי אל נהי. It is true that נשא נהי in Jer. ix. 9, 17 means 'to take up a wailing'.

	c, β–d	d, A
T. Zeb. ii. 5	<u>ἐβόμβει</u> ἡ καρδία	<u>ἐθαμβήθη</u> ἡ καρδία

Here c, β–d are original, being derived from Jer. iv. 19 הומה לי לבי.

ἐθαμβήθη=תמה, which could be an easy corruption of המה, but the corruption may have arisen within the Greek; for the agreement of *bg* with *c* is difficult, though possibly H$^\beta$ may have had both readings.

	a	*aef*, A
T. Zeb. viii. 6	τὸ πρόσωπον ἀφανίζει	τὴν ὕπαρξιν ἀφανίζει

Here H^a=פנים and H$^\beta$=אונים. The context is probably in favour of the former. *bg* give here a text of their own.

	a	*β*, A, S¹
T. Dan i. 4	ἐθέμην περὶ τοῦ θανάτου	ἡδόμην περὶ τοῦ θανάτου

Here the variation may have arisen in the Greek, but it might go back to the Hebrew. See note *in loc.*

	a	*β*, A, S¹
T. Dan iii. 1	αὐτὴν τὴν ψυχὴν ἐκταράσσει	αὐτῇ τῇ ψυχῇ αὐτὸς γίνεται ψυχή

Here both H^a and H$^\beta$ give good sense but the latter is more striking. The variation might be accounted for within the Hebrew. H$^\beta$=היה רופש לנפש and H^a=היה רופש. Cf. Ezek. xxxiv. 18, 19.

	a, aef, S¹	*bd*, A
T. Naph. i. 8	εὐλογίας Ῥαχιήλ	εὐχὰς Ῥαχιήλ

Here H^a read תהלת corrupted into תפלה.

	a	*β*, A, S¹
T. Naph. iii. 2	οἱ ἀστέρες οὐ καλύψουσι τὴν τάξιν αὐτῶν	οἱ ἀστ. οὐκ ἀλλοιοῦσι τ. τάξιν αὐτῶν

Here H$^\beta$ has preserved the original text, יְשַׁנּוּ corrupted in H^a into יְכַסּוּ=καλύψουσι.

T. Naph. iv. 2. See note *in loc.*

	a	*β*, A, S¹
T. Gad iv. 3	σπουδάζει	θέλει

Here H$^\beta$ read יחפץ corrupted (?) into יחפז in H^a.

	a	*β*, (A), S¹
T. Gad vi. 6	ἡσύχασον μὴ ἐλέγξῃς	ἡσύχασον μὴ ἐξάξῃς

H^a = חדל מהוכח, H$^\beta$ = חדל מהכעס, where the latter is probably a corruption of the former.

T. Gad vii. 3   ἐξέτασον κρίματα κυρίου

	a	*β*	A
	καὶ καταλάμψει	καὶ οὐ (*bf* om.) καταλείψει	καὶ οὐκ ἐγκαταλείψεις[1]

καὶ ἡσυχάσει τὸ διαβούλιόν σου.

Here all the authorities are alike at fault. The context suggests that in the corrupt verb we should have some synonym of ἡσυχάσει, and the moment we retranslate we discover what is lacking. Thus

---

[1] So by a change of one letter.

καταλείψει = יָנִיח, which is corrupt for יָנוּח = ἀναπαύσεται. Thus ἀναπαύσεται καὶ ἡσυχάσει = ינוח ושקט, which two verbs are conjoined in Job iii. 26. The corruption of ינוח into יניח led to the insertion of the negative in the β, A. On the other hand καταλάμψει (a) presupposes יָנִיהַ, which is thus another corruption of the original ינוח.

T. Gad vii. 5

	a, β	A
	εἰ ἀφαιρεῖται αὐτὰ ἐν κακοῖς	εἰ ἀφαιρεῖται τὸν πλοῦτον ἐν κακοῖς

This is a difficult passage. If A has preserved the original text, then we have the very unusual instance of a, β agreeing against A. In that case we must suppose all the existing MSS. of β to have been corrupted since the Armenian Version was made. Since this is wholly unlikely I assume that A has simply restored the original text by conjecture. For that it is the original seems manifest. Thus in ver. 4 our author speaks of a man growing rich by evil means (ἐκ κακῶν τις πλουτήσει). Hence ἐν κακοῖς naturally means 'got by evil means', and the phrase πλοῦτον ἐν κακοῖς = חֹן מֵעָוֶל, which goes back to Prov. xiv. 11 הון מהבל. Now this text lay behind the corrupt ἀφαιρεῖται αὐτά, which = יסירהו corrupt for יסיר הון = ἀφαιρεῖται πλοῦτον.

T. Ash. i. 8. Here Hª read תדבק (= προσκολλᾶται (h)) corrupted into תקבל = προσλαμβάνει (β, A, S¹). For προσκολλᾶται c reads καὶ προσκολλώμενος.

	a	β, A, S¹
T. Jos. v. 1	ἀνελῶ τὸν ἄνδρα μου φαρμάκῳ	ἀνελῶ τὸν Αἰγύπτιον καὶ
	καὶ λήψομαί σε	οὕτως νομίμως λήψομαί σε

Here Hª seems to be original. It = בחמה which in Hβ was corrupted into בחקה and transposed into the next clause.

	a	β, A, S¹
T. Jos. iv. 3	τῆς δολιότητος αὐτῆς	τῆς Αἰγυπτίας

Hª = תרמיתה and Hβ המצרית.

	a, β–bg	bg, A
T. Jos. iv. 7	ἀντεφιλονείκει	ἐσιώπησε

Hª = התחרתה (so Symmachus renders (φιλονεικεῖν) in Ps. xxxvi. 1) which may be a corruption of Hβ התחרישה = ἐσιώπησε.

	a	β, A, S¹
T. Jos. v. 2	γίνωσκε ὅτι ἐγὼ ἐξαγγελῶ	ἐγὼ ἐξαγγελῶ τὴν ἐπίνοιαν
	πᾶσιν τὴν ἐπίνοιάν σου ταύτην	τῆς ἀσεβείας σου πᾶσιν

Here, as in the last instance, there is a transposition of a word from its right clause to the adjoining one. Hª = ירע (i. e. γίνωσκε), while H^β read רע (i.e. τῆς ἀσεβείας) and placed it after מומת (ἐπίνοιαν).

	a	*β*, A, S[1]
T. Jos. vii. 2	ἐθεράπευσεν αὐτὴν <u>ἐν λόγοις</u>	ἐθεράπευσεν αὐτὴν <u>μὴ ἀσθενοῦσαν</u>

Here H^a read במלות and H^β לא חולה or the former במילול (late Hebrew) and the latter לא אמללה.

	a	*β–d*, A, S[1]
T. Jos. viii. 5	<u>συνείχετο ἀπὸ τῆς λύπης</u>	<u>ἠσθένει ἀπὸ τ. λ.</u>

Here H^a may have read נכלאה and H^β נלאתה.

	c	*β*, A, S[1]
T. Jos. x. 6	<u>οὐκ ἐπήρθην ἐν κακῷ</u>	<u>ἐμέτρουν ἐμαυτόν</u>

Here H^a read לא רוממתי נפשי (that is, taking ἐν κακῷ as a corruption of ἐμαυτῷ, i. e. ἐμαυτόν as in β, A, S¹). Or רוממתי is a corruption of דוממתי.[1] Thus we have the phrase in Ps. cxxxi. 2 'I kept myself quiet'. From this we could explain the reading of β, A, S¹; for ἐμέτρουν=מרותי, an easy corruption of דוממתי or indeed of רוממתי.

	a	*β–d*, (A), S[1]
T. Jos. xvi. 5	δοὺς αὐτοῖς ὀγδοήκοντα χρυσοὺς <u>ἀνελάβετό με</u>	δοὺς αὐτοῖς ὀγδ. χ. <u>ἀντ' ἐμοῦ</u>

H^a = לקחני. Was there such a form as חלפי in H^β = ἀντ' ἐμοῦ.

	c	*β–a*, A
T. Jos. xvii. 5	ἤθελον	ἐκέλευσεν

Here H^β = צוא, corrupt for H^a אוה = ἤθελον.

From the above evidence, which could be enlarged, we must conclude that there existed two recensions of the original Hebrew, which we have already designated as H^a and H^β. Since in the main these recensions, as they appear in *a* and *β*, differed from each other chiefly in words and phrases, most of which are explicable through simple internal corruptions, the Greek translation of H^a must have been used as a guide by the translator of H^β or vice versa.[2] In a few passages, however, the divergence is on a larger scale. The reader will find such an one in the T. Lev. ii. 7–iii, where the description of the Three Heavens belonged to the original Hebrew archetype and is more or less faithfully preserved in *a*, A^a, the latter being here influenced by *a*. After H^a and H^β originated, the description of the Three Heavens was changed in H^β into one of the seven heavens.

---

[1] The LXX and Vulg. read conversely דוממתי as רוממתי in Ps. cxxxi. 2.

[2] In the Book of Daniel we have a good parallel. The variations between the versions of Theodotion and the LXX in i–iii, vii–xii of that book go back to the Semitic.

As this was done clumsily, naturally it has been detected. In many cases it is impossible to get back to Hᵃ owing to the defective text of α.   Cf. T. Gad ii. 3–4 ; T. Naph. i. 12.

There are many omissions in Hᵃ or α through hmt, and some where no such explanation is possible (cf. T. Gad vi. 3, i. e. the clause ἐξορίσας τὸν ἰὸν τοῦ μίσους).   In some passages Hᵃ, in others Hᵝ (or possibly only α or β) omitted passages owing to the inconsistencies or unintelligibleness of the transmitted text.   Thus Hᵃ omits a clause in T. Jud. ix. 3 because it conflicts with the preceding corrupt clause, but here Hᵝ, supported by the Midrash Wajjis. and Chron. Jer., happily retains it, while in T. Ash. vi. 2 Hᵝ (or only β) omits on the same ground a clause which happily Hᵃ retains notwithstanding its inconsistency.   Again, in T. Jos. xi. 7 בעבדה was omitted in Hᵝ through some scribe misunderstanding it, or the wrong rendering ἐν ἔργῳ was omitted in β because of its unintelligibleness.

We are now in a position to represent by a diagram the relations of the lost and existing documents of the Testaments :—

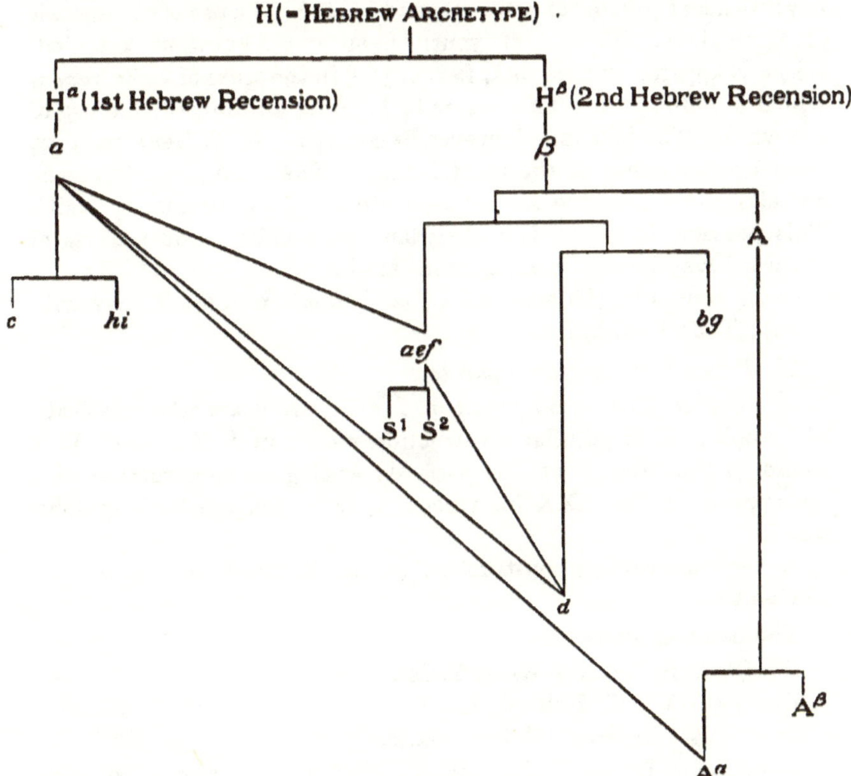

§ 13. Linguistic Character of the Greek Version.

I do not propose to discuss this question exhaustively, but only to bring forward the chief characteristics of this Version. These I shall treat under the following heads :—

    I. Peculiar use of certain nouns, &c.

    II. Peculiar use of certain phrases.

    III. Prepositions and particles.

    IV. Hebraisms.

I. *Peculiar use of nouns and other words.*

The translator's use of certain words is in some instances rare, in others unexampled. Thus he uses τόξα as = δόρατα in T. Jud. iii. 3, ix. 3 : ὀλιγοψυχία (T. Gad iv. 7) in the sense of 'hastiness of spirit'—a use however which is established in the LXX : πλάσμα (T. Naph. ii. 5) in the sense of inclination (יצר) : σκῆπτρον (T. Jud. xxv. 1) in the sense of 'tribe', but this is simply a Hebraism (being a rendering of שׁבט) : φιληδονία seems to be used merely as a synonym of ἡδονή—have we here a parallel of φιλοσοφία and σοφία ? The use of νεωτερισμός (T. Reub. ii. 2) in the sense of 'youth' is, so far as I know, unexampled. ἔνδυμα is apparently used in T. Lev. x. 3 (β) in the sense of καταπέτασμα, which is found in a. This seems to be quite an unjustifiable use of the word. The text may however be corrupt. In T. Benj. ix. 4 we have a peculiar use of the word ἅπλωμα. The word properly means an 'altar cloth', but the context seems to require the meaning 'veil'. This passage, however, is a Christian interpolation, and the use of the word may be due to an ignorant scribe.

ἕτερος is used in the sense of ἄλλος T. Reub. ii. 3 (a), T. Lev. viii. 12 (a) ; T. Jud. ix. 6, &c.

II. *Peculiar use of certain phrases.*

μετὰ ἔτη δύο τῆς τελευτῆς (T. Reub. i. 2) = 'two years after the death of Joseph'. This peculiar construction recurs in T. Zeb. i. 1. It is found in Plut. *Coriol.* 11. A perfectly analogous construction with πρό appears in the LXX in Amos i. 1, iv. 7, and the N. T. in John xii. 1.

A very interesting construction of ἔχω is found in four of the Testaments.

The passages are—

εἶχε (β, A, S¹ ἔμελλε a) τεκεῖν, T. Iss. ii. 2.

εἶχόν με ἀνελεῖν, T. Jud. vii. 7.

ἄτεκνος εἶχον ἀποθανεῖν, T. Jud. xix. 2.

εὐλογῆσαί σε ἔχει (a), T. Jos. xii. 3. Here β A, S¹ have εὐλογήσει σε.

ἀπολῦσαι ἡμᾶς ἔχει (a), T. Jos. xv. 7. Here *aef*, S¹ have ἀπολύσει (*bdg* ἀπέλυσεν) ἡμᾶς.

We have here strange uses of ἔχω. In the first three cases we should have had ἄν inserted in Classical Greek, but in N. T. times this omission is not infrequent: cf. John ix. 33, xv. 22, xix. 11; Gal. iv. 15, &c. We have now to touch briefly on this peculiar use of ἔχω with an infinitive.

Such phrases as we have cited above from the Testaments in connexion with ἔχω and an infinitive[1] are rather frequent in sixth century Greek writers, from whom Stephanus in his *Thesaurus* gives many quotations. But this usage was well established about 200 A.D. both in Greek and Latin. In Latin we find it in the third century in Cyprian, *De dom. Orat.* 34 'manifestari habebat', 'was to be manifested'; *De Haeret. baptiz.* 73 'unum habet esse et baptisma', 'there must be also one baptism'; Ep. lii. 3 'eici de ecclesia et excludi habebat', and many others. Earlier it is found in Tertullian, writing between 197–220, *Resurr. Carnis* 27 'habemus allegorizare'; *De Pudic.* 13 'erudiri haberent'; *De Virg. veland.* 1 'nasci non habebat', &c. I am not aware of any earlier instances of this use in Latin; but there are in Greek. Thus it is extremely frequent in Clement of Alexandria (ed. Dind.) i. 4 εἰ μήτι γε τοῦ νῦν με λυποῦντος ἐκεῖ χεῖρον παθεῖν ἔχω (quoted from Jannaris' *Historical Greek Grammar* 553 sq. where some dozen of other instances from the same author will be found). Thus the usage existed in Greek towards the close of the second century. But we can establish its currency about the middle and beginning of this century; for in Hermas, *Sim.* ix. 10. 5 we find μικρὸν ἔχω ἀκαιρεθῆναι, καὶ πάντα σοι ἐπιλύσω—'I shall be busy for a little and then I will explain everything to you': and in Ignatius, *Rom.* 2 οὔτε γὰρ ἐγώ ποτε ἕξω καιρὸν τοιοῦτον θεοῦ ἐπιτυχεῖν· οὔτε ὑμεῖς, ἐὰν σιωπήσητε, κρείττονι ἔργῳ ἔχετε ἐπιγραφῆναι—'for neither shall I myself ever have an opportunity such as this ... nor will ye, if ye be silent, win the credit of any nobler work '.

Thus we have traced this usage back to about 100 A. D., and now by means of the Greek Version (a) of the Testaments we are able to prove that it was in vogue full half a century earlier. The examples we have given from Hermas and Ignatius enable us to understand how εὐλογῆσαί σε ἔχει in a = 'will bless thee', as indeed we find εὐλογήσει σε in β. Perhaps an element of necessity may lurk in the phrase.

---

[1] Of course the use of ἔχω with an infinitive in the sense of *possum* is Classical as well as Hellenistic.

ἤθελε . . . ἀνελεῖν, T. Reub. i. 7 = 'would have killed'. Here ἄν is omitted as in the passages just discussed. ἐθέλω is here merely used as an auxiliary, and is Classical. Cf. Aesch. *Eum.* 429 οὐ δοῦναι θέλει = οὐκ ἄν δοίη: also Aristophanes, *Vespae* 536. Μέλλω is used in the same way in T. Iss. ii. 2 (a).

In the first three passages where the constructions εἶχε τεκεῖν, εἶχον . . . ἀνελεῖν, and εἶχον ἀποθανεῖν occur, we have simply the use of the same idiom in the past tense. To the omission of ἄν in these constructions we have already referred.

III. *Prepositions and particles.*

ἄν is used with the pres. ind., T. Lev. xiii. 9.

ἄν = ἐάν. See Index.

ἵνα with subjunctive as a periphrasis for the imperative, T. Iss. i. 6 ἵνα σχῶ ταῦτα as in N. T. Cf. Eph. v. 33; Gal. ii. 10, &c.

ἐν. This is a very hard worked preposition : it occurs nearly 600 times. In the bulk of these its use is normal. It occasionally expresses the instrument. Two or three times it = εἰς. In a few cases its presence is superfluous, being merely a translation of the Hebrew ב, as after ἐκλέγομαι in T. Reub. vi. 11, or after ἀδικεῖν in T. Sim. v. 4, or after κληρόω in T. Iss. v. 7 (β).

μετά = עם in phrase ποίησον μετ' αὐτοῦ κρίσιν.

σύν apparently = 'like', being a translation of עם in T. Sim. iv. 4.

ὑπὲρ τούτου = περὶ τούτου in T. Gad i. 8 (hi).

IV. *Hebraisms.* Only a few are given under this heading. See § 11.

ἀπὸ προσώπου τῆς πονηρίας, T. Lev. x. 3 = מפני הרע.

πᾶς . . . οὐ, T. Jud. xv. 4 ; T. Iss. vii. 3, 7.

ἐκ τῶν πνευμάτων, T. Dan i. 7 (a) = מרוחות 'one of the spirits.'

δύο δύο, T. Ash. i. 4 (v. 1) = שנים שנים, i. e. δισσός.

ἐν κατέναντι τοῦ ἑνός, T. Ash. i. 4 = האחד נגד האחר.

ἐν πρώτοις, T. Benj. x. 8 = בראשונא.

κατὰ τὴν ψυχὴν αὐτοῦ, T. Benj. iv. 5 = כנפשו.

οἷα . . . οὕτως, T. Reub. i. 10, אשר . . . כזאת.

§ 14. The Date of the Original Hebrew.

The date of the groundwork of the Testaments is not difficult to determine. Thus Reuben (T. Reub. vi. 10–11) admonishes his sons : Πρὸς τὸν Λευὶ ἐγγίσατε ἐν ταπεινώσει καρδίας ὑμῶν ἵνα δέξησθε εὐλογίαν ἐκ τοῦ στόματος αὐτοῦ . . . ὅτι ἐν αὐτῷ ἐξελέξατο Κύριος βασιλεύειν ἐνώπιον παντὸς τοῦ λαοῦ. Here a high-priest who is also a king is referred to. Such a combination of offices naturally makes us think of the

Maccabean priest-kings of the second century B. C. The possibility of doubting this reference is excluded by the words that immediately follow: καὶ προσκυνήσατε τὸ σπέρμα αὐτοῦ ὅτι ὑπὲρ ὑμῶν ἀποθανεῖται ἐν πολέμοις ὁρατοῖς καὶ ἀοράτοις· καὶ ἐν ὑμῖν ἔσται βασιλεὺς αἰώνιος. A similar statement is made in T. Sim. v. 5. Thus the high-priest is not only a high-priest and civil ruler, but also a warrior. That the Maccabean high-priests are here designed cannot be reasonably doubted. But the identification becomes undeniable as further characteristics of this priestly dynasty come to light. It was to be a new priesthood and to be called by a new name (T. Lev. viii. 14 ἱερατείαν νέαν . . . ὄνομα καινόν). Now the Maccabean high-priests were the first to assume the title ‘priests of the Most High God’—the title anciently borne by Melchizedek. But the praises accorded in this book could not apply to all the Maccabean priest-kings of the nation. As it was written by a Pharisee, it could not have been composed after the breach arose between John Hyrcanus and the Pharisees towards the close of the second century B. C. Thus the period of composition lies between 153 when Jonathan the Maccabee assumed the high-priesthood and the year of the breach of John Hyrcanus with the Pharisees,—some time, therefore, between 153 and 109. But the date can be determined between closer limits. To one member of the Maccabean dynasty are the prophetic gifts assigned in our text (T. Lev. viii. 15) in conjunction with the functions of kingship and priesthood. Now, in all Jewish history the triple offices were ascribed to only one individual, John Hyrcanus. Hence we conclude that the Testaments were written between 137 and 107. For an attempt to define the date of composition within much closer limits see § 15 in the Introduction to my Translation and Commentary.

§ 15. Date of the Greek Version.

We can only touch on this question here. It will be dealt with in some fullness in my Commentary.

The α Version seems to have been translated first, indeed before 50 A. D.; for it is twice quoted by St. Paul. The first passage is in Rom. i. 32 οὐ μόνον αὐτὰ ποιοῦσιν ἀλλὰ καὶ συνευδοκοῦσιν τοῖς πράσσουσιν, which is taken almost verbally from T. Ash. vi. 2 ὅτι οἱ διπρόσωποι δισσῶς †κολάζονται (rd. ἁμαρτάνουσι) ὅτι καὶ πράσσουσι τὸ κακὸν καὶ συνευδοκοῦσι τοῖς πράσσουσιν. Since bg A omit the words ὅτι . . . πράσσουσιν, we conclude that, though it is now found in α, adef, S¹, it was originally wanting in β and probably also in Hᵝ. For as we have already seen (Table on p. **xxxix**) *acf* were early influenced by *a*, and *d* is conflate in character. Hence in reality the passage was preserved only by *a* originally.

The second passage is the well-known one in 1 Thess. ii. 16 ἔφθασεν δὲ ἐπ' αὐτοὺς ἡ ὀργὴ (+ τοῦ θεοῦ DEFG Itala, Vulg. Gothic) εἰς τέλος, which is borrowed from T. Lev. vi. 11 ἔφθασεν δὲ (+ ἐπ' β) αὐτοὺς ἡ ὀργὴ τοῦ θεοῦ εἰς τέλος. Here β reads Κυρίου for τοῦ θεοῦ. The ἐπί is omitted by *a* through a simple scribal error.

On the ground of the above quotations we assume, therefore, that *a* was used by St. Paul, and that H*a* was therefore translated into Greek at latest before 50 A. D.

When H*β* was translated we have no definite means of determining. It was in all likelihood done subsequently to H*a*. The translator of H*β* appears to have had the translation of H*a* before him, and to have followed it, unless where there were manifest divergencies between H*a* and H*β*.

The wide influence that the Testaments had on the New Testament writers will be treated at length in my Commentary.

§ 16. Title of the Book.

The general title was probably Διαθῆκαι τῶν Πατριαρχῶν. So they are designated in A. But it varies in the different authorities. In *a*, *bd* it appears as Διαθῆκαι τῶν δώδεκα Πατριαρχῶν τῶν (*hi*, *d* om.) υἱῶν Ἰακώβ (+ τοῦ Πατριάρχου *a*); *a* αἱ δ. τῶν ιβ′ πατρ. πρὸς τοὺς υἱοὺς αὐτῶν; *c* om., *f* δ. σὺν θεῷ τῶν ιβ′ υἱῶν τοῦ Ἰακώβ. In the Stichometry of Nicephorus, the Synopsis of Athanasius, and the anonymous list of books edited by Montfaucon, Pitra, and others, the book is simply called Πατριάρχαι.

The title of the individual Testaments is very differently given in the MSS. *a* uniformly gives :—

> διαθήκη Ῥουβὴμ τοῦ πρωτοτόκου (πρώτου *i*) υἱοῦ Ἰακὼβ (*c* om. τοῦ . . .
> Ἰακὼβ) καὶ Λείας,
> διαθήκη Συμεὼν τοῦ δευτέρου υἱοῦ Ἰακὼβ καὶ Λείας,
> διαθήκη Λευὶ τοῦ τρίτου υἱοῦ Ἰακὼβ καὶ Λείας,
> διαθήκη Ἰούδα τοῦ τετάρτου υἱοῦ Ἰακὼβ καὶ Λείας,
> διαθήκη Δὰν τοῦ ἑβδόμου υἱοῦ Ἰακὼβ καὶ Βάλλας,

and so with the necessary changes in number and name of mother. In *β*, A, the matter is more complex. *a* gives simply the name of the patriarch. A fuller form is generally found in *befg*, while the title in *d* is generally conflated from *befg* and *a*. Hence we may, I think, neglect *ad* in this matter. In *f* there are generally additions

containing the interpretation of the name. These additions may also
here be neglected. *g* takes a line of its own. Thus the title of
Reuben is δ. 'Ρ., of Issachar δ. 'Ισ. εʹ, and of Joseph ιαʹ. Only that
of Simeon agrees with *b*. In all the rest it takes a line of its own.
Hence on the whole we may ignore it at present. In *bef* then we
find the following, ignoring peculiar additions in *ef*:—

διαθήκη 'Ρουβὴμ περὶ ἐννοιῶν,

διαθήκη Συμεὼν περὶ φθόνου,

διαθήκη Λευὶ περὶ ἱερωσύνης καὶ ὑπερηφανείας,

διαθήκη 'Ιούδα περὶ ἀνδρείας καὶ φιλαργυρίας (*e* om. κ. φιλ.) καὶ πορνείας
(*f* om. κ. πορν.),

διαθήκη 'Ισαχὰρ περὶ ἁπλότητος (ἀγαθότητος *e f*),

διαθήκη Ζαβουλὼν περὶ εὐσπλαγχνίας καὶ ἐλέους,

διαθήκη Δὰν περὶ θυμοῦ καὶ ψεύδους,

διαθήκη Νεφθαλεὶμ (+ ηʹ *b*) περὶ φυσικῆς ἀγαθότητος,

διαθήκη Γὰδ (+ θʹ *b*) περὶ μίσους,

διαθήκη 'Ασὴρ (+ ιʹ + *b*) περὶ δύο προσώπων κακίας καὶ ἀρετῆς,

διαθήκη 'Ιωσὴφ (+ ιαʹ *b*) περὶ σωφροσύνης,

διαθήκη Βενιαμὴν (+ ιβʹ *b*) περὶ διανοίας (*ef* ἐννοίας) καθαρᾶς.

In A the titles are—

1. A^nefg Βίβλος τῶν παραλειπομένων, λόγοι τοῦ 'Ρ. διαθήκη (+ αʹ A^efg),
   but A^h reads δ. 'Ρ. υἱοῦ 'Ιακὼβ υἱοῦ 'Ισαὰκ υἱοῦ 'Αβραάμ.

2. A^abhk δ. Συμεὼν υἱοῦ 'Ιακὼβ υἱοῦ 'Ισαὰκ υἱοῦ 'Αβραάμ,
   A^b*cdfg δ. Συμεὼν (+ περὶ φθόνου A^fg).

3. δ. Λευὶ περὶ ἱερωσύνης (+ καὶ ὑπερηφανείας A^β).

4. δ. 'Ιούδα τοῦ τετάρτου περὶ ἀνδρείας (A^hk δικαιοσύνης) καὶ φιλαργυρίας
   καὶ πορνείας.

5. δ. 'Ισαχάρ.

6. δ. Ζαβουλὼν (+ υἱοῦ 'Ισραὴλ υἱοῦ 'Ισαάκ A^ab).

7. δ. Δὰν περὶ ὑπερηφανείας καὶ ψεύδους.

8. δ. Νεφθαλεὶμ περὶ φυσικῆς ἀγαθότητος (A^d om. περὶ . . . ἀγαθ.).

9. δ. Γὰδ περὶ μίσους.

10. δ. 'Ασὴρ περὶ διπλόης καὶ ἀρετῆς.

11. δ. 'Ιωσὴφ περὶ φθόνου (A^b*cd om. π. φθ.).

12. δ. Βενιαμήν ιβʹ.

When we compare *bef* and A, we discover that they agree in the
titles of Judah, Naphtali, Gad, Asher, and with A^β in Levi, but that
they are wholly or in part different in Reuben, Issachar, Zebulun,
ᴰan, Joseph, Benjamin, and in most MSS. in Simeon. Since, therefore, within β there is a great variety of attestation, and since further,

even where there is unity in β as in *bef*, we find that A is more often at variance with *bef* than in agreement with them, we may conclude that the part of the titles particularizing special virtues or vices are really later additions. Hence the original title in Greek of the Testament of Reuben may have had one of two forms: either simply διαθήκη Ῥουβήμ or this with the addition τοῦ πρωτοτόκου υἱοῦ Ἰακὼβ καὶ Λείας as in *a*, and similarly with regard to the rest of the Testaments. The short title in *a* which gives merely the name of the patriarch is not original, but merely due to the desire for brevity which characterizes the work of the scribe of this MS.

The Hebrew form was צוואת ראובן. Compare Hebrew Test. Naph., p. 239.

§ 17. Jewish Additions to the Text.

A large body of these additions can be classed under one head as interpolated at a certain period and written with a well-defined object. The period is about 70–40 B.C., and the object of the additions is the overthrow of the Maccabean high-priesthood, which in the first century had become guilty of all lewdness and baseness. The additions in question are:

(1) *First century* B.C. *Additions.*

    T. Lev. **x, xiv–xvi.**

    T. Jud. **xvii. 2–xviii. 1 (?), xxi. 6–xxiii, xxiv. 4–6.**

    T. Zeb. **ix.**

    T. Dan **v. 6–7, vii. 3 (?).**

    T. Naph. **iv.**

    T. Gad **viii. 2.**

    T. Ash. **vii. 4–7.**

These passages are more or less closely bound together by sharing in a common aim, i. e. the denunciation of the present evil state of things under the later Maccabees, T. Lev. **x, xiv–xvi**; T. Jud. **xxii**; T. Zeb. **ix. 4–5**; they condemn the nation as again guilty of apostasy, T. Zeb. **ix. 9**; T. Naph. **iv. 4**; T. Gad **viii. 2**; T. Ash. **vii. 5–6**; they predict a second captivity, T. Jud. **xxiii. 3**; T. Naph. **iv. 5**; an ultimate redemption either by God Himself or through the agency of a Messiah from Judah, T. Lev. **xvi. 5**; T. Jud. **xxiv. 4–6**; T. Naph. **iv. 5**; and a blessed return to their own land, T. Jud. **xxiii. 5**; T. Ash. **vii. 7**; T. Zeb. **ix. 9.**

In all the above characteristics these first century B. C. passages agree with the Psalms of Solomon. In fact, the language in T. Lev. **xiv–xvi.** and T. Jud. **xxiii.** almost verbally agrees in some instances with that of these Psalms. With them, too, the hope of a Messiah from Judah is put forward afresh, and the certainty of an ultimate redemption prophesied. All the old glories of the Maccabees are forgotten, and no doubt the expectation of a Messiah from Levi, which was so fondly cherished by the faithful in the latter half of the second century, was now regarded as no better than a delusion of the evil one.

Another characteristic of these additions is their frequent citation of the Book of Enoch, as in T. Lev. x. 5, xiv. 1, xvi. 1 ; T. Jud. xviii. 1 ; T. Dan v. 6 ; T. Naph. iv. 1. Only in two other passages is this book quoted, i. e. in T. Sim. v. 4, and T. Benj. ix. 1. In the latter case this reference is omitted by A and may safely be regarded as an interpolation, and in all probability the former is also an interpolation, although it is attested by all existing authorities. From this frequent reference to Enoch, we may reasonably conclude the existence of certain sections in that literature which have not been preserved in the 1 Enoch (the Ethiopic Enoch), but have been republished in the later 2 Enoch (the Slavonic Enoch).

(2) *Other additions of various dates.* There are a few other additions which cannot be brought under the first head. They are of various dates and spring from various sources.

T. Reub. ii. 3–iii. 2. This passage is dealt with fully in the notes in my Commentary, and is there shown to have been derived ultimately from the doctrine of Stoicism. It is manifestly at variance with its present context. It is difficult to determine when it was incorporated. The fact of its appearing both in α and β, A, S¹ is in favour of its having been interpolated in the original Hebrew; but more likely it was first added in α and then copied into β. The chief reason against accepting the former hypothesis is the difficulty of explaining πνεῦμα, which is here used repeatedly with a meaning confined to the Stoics, as that of a sense, organ, or appetite. רוח was never, so far as I can ascertain, used with this signification. Yet it is possible to assume that some Jew did violence to the usual meanings of this word and used it, in the absence of any other possible word, as a rendering of the Stoic word πνεῦμα. This is constantly done by Greek Jews when translating from Hebrew. Some such document then as T. Reub. ii. 3–iii. 2 may have existed in Hebrew and have been added to the original text of the Testaments by some Jewish scribe.

T. Lev. xvii. 1–9. An addition from a Hebrew source.

T. Reub. vi. 7 ; T. Lev. xviii. 5ᵈ; T. Iss. v. 4ᶜ, 5ᵇ. Scribal additions. The first passage relates to Levi only.

T. Zeb. vi. 4–6, vii–viii. 3. See Introduction to my Commentary, § 18.

T. Naph. v. 5. A dittograph from ver. 3.

T. Gad vi. 5. Probably originally a marginal gloss.

T. Jos. x. 5–xviii. It is not improbable that this large section either displaced part of the original Testament or was added in the Hebrew. It was written in Hebrew as the rest of the Testaments. In addition to the grounds enumerated in p. 172 of my Commentary we should observe that, whereas the duty of truthfulness is emphatically laid down throughout the Testaments, yet in x. 5–xviii Joseph lies several times to screen his brethren, xi. 2, 3, xiii. 6–9, xv. 2–3, xvi. 6. Further, the style of i–x. 4 is poetical, that of x. 5–xviii is prosaic.

§ 18. Christian Additions to the Text.

These additions are found in nearly all the Testaments and were made at different periods.

T. Sim. vi. 5 ὡς ἄνθρωπος. The passage without this addition describes simply a Theophany, references to which are frequent in the Testaments, T. Lev. ii. 11, v. 2, viii. 11 ; T. Jud. xxii. 2 ; T. Zeb. ix. 9 ; T. Naph. viii. 3 ; T. Ash. vii. 3.

vi. 7^c ὅτι ὁ θεὸς σῶμα λαβὼν καὶ συνεσθίων ἀνθρώποις ἔσωσεν ἀνθρώπους. A manifest Christian interpolation.

vii. 2^b θεὸν καὶ ἄνθρωπον.

vii. 2^c σώσει [πάντα τὰ ἔθνη καὶ] τὸ γένος τοῦ Ἰσραήλ. So a, β. The bracketed words are a Christian addition. The author can look forward to the salvation of the Gentiles, but he would not set their salvation before that of Israel. See note below on T. Jos. xix. 11. A speaks here only of the salvation of mankind. The same interpolation recurs in T. Jos. xix. 11 (c, β) σώζων [πάντα τὰ ἔθνη καὶ] τὸν Ἰσραήλ, where A has simply ἡ σωτηρία τοῦ Ἰσραήλ.

T. Lev. iv. 1^b ἐπὶ τῷ πάθει τοῦ ὑψίστου. This Christian addition transforms an account of the Judgement into a description of the events accompanying the Crucifixion. The addition moreover was made by a Patripassianist.

iv. 4^{bc} ἕως ἐπισκέψεται κύριος πάντα τὰ ἔθνη ἐν σπλάγχνοις

[υἱοῦ] αὐτοῦ ἕως αἰῶνος

[πλὴν οἱ υἱοί σου ἐπιβαλοῦσι χεῖρας ἐπ' αὐτὸν τοῦ

ἀνασκολοπίσαι αὐτόν].

The Christian interpolations here transform an account of God's coming to dwell with men (cf. v. 2 ἕως ἐλθὼν κατοικήσω ἐν μέσῳ τοῦ Ἰσραήλ) into a prediction of God's sending His Son, and of His crucifixion by the priests.

x. 2 εἰς τὸν Σωτῆρα τοῦ κόσμου χριστόν. The context deals with the wickedness of the high-priests in the first century B.C.

xiv. 1. Here a alone, by the addition of the words ἐπ' αὐτόν, transforms a purely Jewish passage into a Christian one.

2. οἵτινες ἐπιβαλοῦσι τὰς χεῖρας αὐτῶν ἐπὶ τὸν Σωτῆρα τοῦ κόσμου. An addition from the same hand as iv. 4ᶜ.

xvi. 3. This verse may refer to the murder of some Jewish worthy. See my notes *in loc.* Otherwise it is a Christian addition.

xvii. 2 καὶ ἐν ἡμέραις χαρᾶς αὐτοῦ ἐπὶ σωτηρίᾳ κόσμου αὐτὸς ἀναστήσεται. This may or may not be an interpolation. It is unintelligible in its present context.

xviii. 7 ἐν τῷ ὕδατι. This slight addition changes a description of the glorification of John Hyrcanus into a description of the baptism of Christ.

xviii. 9 ὁ δὲ Ἰσραὴλ ἐλαττωθήσεται ἐν ἀγνωσίᾳ
    καὶ σκοτισθήσεται ἐν πένθει.
An anti-Jewish Christian addition.

T. Jud. xxiv. 4. Possibly a Christian interpolation.

T. Iss. vii. 7ᶜ. According to some of the MSS. this line is Christian. See notes.

T. Zeb. ix. 8. This verse in a, aef, A, Sˡ describes a Theophany in very startling words—' Ye shall see Him (i. e. God) in Jerusalem.' But these words are found in the genuine text of Ps. lxxxiv. 7 as in the LXX ὀφθήσεται ὁ θεὸς ἐν Σιών. So also the Syriac and Vulg. This very phrase is found in T. Naph. viii. 3. In *bdg*, however, we have the Christian addition ἐν σχήματι ἀνθρώπου.

T. Dan v. 10 ἐκ τῆς φυλῆς ['Ιούδα καὶ] τοῦ Λευί. Here the interpolator is clumsy. He ought to have changed φυλῆς to φυλῶν. Besides, the order betrays the interpolator's hand. In the original Testaments, when the two tribes are mentioned together, Levi always precedes Judah. See T. Sim. vii. 1 ; T. Gad viii. 1 ; T. Jos. xix. 11.

13 Κύριος ἔσται ἐν μέσῳ αὐτῆς [τοῖς ἀνθρώποις συναναστρεφόμενος] καὶ ὁ Ἅγιος Ἰσραὴλ βασιλεύων ἐπ' αὐτῆς [ἐν ταπεινώσει καὶ πτωχείᾳ καὶ ὁ πιστεύων ἐπ' αὐτῷ βασιλεύσει ἐν τοῖς ἀνθρώποις ἐν ἀληθείᾳ]. The text describes a Theophany as it does frequently elsewhere (see note above on T. Sim. vi. 5). The Christian additions transform it into a prophecy of Christ.

vi. 7. β, Sˡ add Σωτήρ against a, A.

vi. 9 ἵνα δέξηται ὑμᾶς ὁ Σωτὴρ τῶν ἐθνῶν· ἐστι γὰρ ἀληθὴς καὶ μακρόθυμος, πρᾷος καὶ ταπεινός, καὶ ἐκδιδάσκων διὰ τῶν ἔργων τὸν νόμον Κυρίου. In its present form this is undoubtedly Christian.

T. Naph. viii. 2 διὰ γὰρ τοῦ †Ἰούδα ἀνατελεῖ ἡ σωτηρία τῷ Ἰσραήλ,
    καὶ ἐν† αὐτῷ εὐλογηθήσεται Ἰακώβ.

viii. 3 διὰ † τοῦ σκήπτρου αὐτοῦ † ὀφθήσεται ὁ θεὸς [κατοικῶν ἐν ἀνθρώποις] ἐπὶ τῆς γῆς.

In my Text and Commentary I have, with Bousset, emended τοῦ Ἰούδα into αὐτῶν, since the preceding words are ἐντείλασθε τοῖς τέκνοις ὑμῶν ἵνα ἑνοῦνται τῷ Λευὶ καὶ τῷ Ἰούδα. τοῦ Ἰούδα would thus be due to a Christian scribe who likewise changed αὐτοῖς into αὐτῷ and τῶν σκήπτρων αὐτῶν into τοῦ σκήπτρου αὐτοῦ. Perhaps, however, the singular is right throughout, and Λευί stood originally instead of Ἰούδα, but T. Jos. xix. 11 is against this.

T. Ash. vii. 3 ἕως οὗ ὁ ὕψιστος ἐπισκέψηται τὴν γῆν, καὶ αὐτὸς ἐλθὼν [ὡς ἄνθρωπος μετὰ ἀνθρώπων ἐσθίων καὶ πίνων] καὶ συντρίβων τὴν κάραν τοῦ δράκοντος ἐπὶ τοῦ ὕδατος, οὗτος σώσει τὸν Ἰσραὴλ καὶ πάντα τὰ ἔθνη [θεὸς εἰς ἄνδρα ὑποκρινόμενος].

The original text described God's coming to earth and destroying the primeval dragon in the waters (Ps. lxxiv. 13) and saving Israel and all mankind, as the chief prophets taught. The Christian additions are obvious.

T. Jos. xix. 8. For a full treatment of this passage see notes *in loc.*

xix. 11 (a, β) ἀνατελεῖ ὑμῖν [ὁ ἀμνὸς τοῦ θεοῦ, ὁ αἴρων τὴν ἁμαρτίαν τοῦ κόσμου], σώζων [πάντα τὰ ἔθνη καὶ] τὸν Ἰσραήλ.

The method of the interpolator becomes manifest if we compare the above with the text of A, i. e. ἀνατελεῖ ἡ σωτηρία τοῦ Ἰσραήλ. The order ἔθνη καὶ ... Ἰσραήλ betrays the hand of the Christian interpolator. See also next passage.

T. Benj. vii. 8 (c, β, S¹) περὶ τοῦ ἀμνοῦ τοῦ θεοῦ καὶ σωτῆρος τοῦ κόσμου. This is a Christian interpolation as well as the last words of the verse ἐν αἵματι διαθήκης ἐπὶ σωτηρίᾳ ἐθνῶν καὶ τοῦ Ἰσραὴλ καὶ καταλύσει Βελίαρ καὶ τοὺς ὑπηρέτας. Observe the order 'Gentile ... Jew'. A omits both passages.

ix. 3–5. Obviously Christian. This is the only passage where A has admitted Christian interpolations in T. Benj.

T. Benj. x. 7 (c, β) ἡμεῖς ἀναστησόμεθα ... προσκυνοῦντες τὸν βασιλέα τῶν οὐρανῶν [τὸν ἐπὶ γῆς φανέντα ἐν μορφῇ ἀνθρώπου ἐν ταπεινώσει, καὶ ὅσοι πιστεύσωσιν αὐτῷ ἐπὶ τῆς γῆς χαρίσονται σὺν αὐτῷ]. A omits the interpolation. The hand of the interpolator is obvious.

x. 8 (c, β) κρινεῖ Κύριος ἐν πρώτοις τὸν Ἰσραὴλ περὶ τῆς ἀδικίας [ὅτι παραγενόμενον θεὸν ἐν σαρκὶ οὐκ ἐπίστευσαν αὐτῷ]. A omits the interpolation.

x. 9 (c, β) καὶ τότε κρινεῖ πάντα τὰ ἔθνη [ὅσα οὐκ ἐπίστευσαν αὐτῷ ἐπὶ τῆς γῆς φανέντι]. A omits the interpolation.

xi. Here the interpolators have been hard at work. While one interpolator transformed the original, which spoke only of Benjamin,

into a prophecy of Christ (c), the other transformed it into a prophecy
of St. Paul (β). The original text is preserved in A. See notes *in loc.*

§ 19. MIDRASH WAJJISSAU CONTAINING HEBREW FRAGMENTS OF THE TESTAMENT OF JUDAH.

It is not necessary to dwell on this subject. Only the part of the
Midrash, which has preserved fragments of the Testament of Judah
is here given. The Midrash is reprinted in Appendix I from
Jellinek's *Bet ha-Midrasch* iii. 1–3. The questions naturally arise: Is
the Midrash based on the Testament of Judah? or, Are both works
so far as they relate to Judah based on a common original? A comparison of both works with Jub. xxxiv. 1–9 will, I think, make it
clear that in the middle of the second century B. C. there existed an
account of the war of the Amorite kings against Jacob and his sons.
This account both Jubilees and the Testaments laid under contribu-
tion, the latter more fully than the former. Further elements of
this early history are contained in the Midrash just mentioned; for
these help to explain the over-abbreviated descriptions in both
Jubilees and the Testaments. On the other hand, later elements
have entered on a large scale into the section of the Book of Jashar
which deals with this subject.

§ 20. LATE HEBREW TESTAMENT OF NAPHTALI.

I have printed this Testament in Appendix II. My text follows
the Oxford MS., which I designate as A. I have used Gaster's[1]
collation of P, which is a twelfth-century MS. now in Paris, and
borrowed from his edition some readings which he in turn has taken
from Wertheimer's edition (printed at Jerusalem in 1890). Furthermore, for the sake of convenience, I have adopted the division into
chapters which appears in Kautzsch's *Apokr. und Pseudep.* ii. 489–
492. For the division into verses the present editor is responsible.

Dr. Gaster, to whose text reference has just been made, is of
opinion that in the Hebrew text which is printed in our Appendix
'we have undoubtedly the original version of the Testament, free
from any interpolation'. Further, he adds: 'In comparing this (the
Hebrew Testament) with the Greek Version, we are struck by the
great disparity between the two. In the Hebrew version, whole
chapters of the Greek are missing, whilst in the Greek, the whole
of the Hebrew is condensed into four-and-a-half chapters, the contents

---

[1] Gaster, 'The Hebrew Text of one of the Testaments of the XII Patriarchs,'
Proceedings of the Society of Biblical Archaeology, Dec. 1893; Jan. 1894.

transposed and mangled almost beyond recognition. The Greek counterpart of the Hebrew makes no sense and has no meaning at all; whilst the Hebrew is rounded off and complete, and perfectly clear.' These theses of Dr. Gaster have not been accepted in the world of scholarship. Almost universally, scholars who have worked on this field of literature deny the validity of his conclusions. In the first place, the style of the Hebrew is late. In the next place, even if it were early, it could lay no claim to being the original of the Greek 'Testament'. All that could be urged is that the two texts possess an exiguous[1] amount of common material. In all other respects they diverge, and the evidence points to the conclusion that the Hebrew text is, in fact, based directly or indirectly on the primitive Hebrew text from which the Greek Testament was translated.

On the following grounds we cannot accept the present Hebrew text as the original Testament of Naphtali.

(1) The Hebrew Testament does not end as all the Testaments do in the patriarch taking leave of his children.

(2) There is throughout the Hebrew Testament a strong personal feeling of hostility to Joseph. Thus his brethren complain that they have been exiled through his being a bond servant in Egypt (i. 10). Furthermore not a single word in favour of Joseph's personal character is uttered.

On the other hand, in the Greek Testaments, wherever Joseph as an individual is mentioned, he is praised either explicitly or implicitly.[2] And this is true in the single personal reference to him in the Greek Testament of Naphtali i. 8. Where the name Joseph stands for Northern Israel, as in T. Naph. v. 7, vi. 6, &c., the matter is different, and the attitude to Joseph in this relation is the same in both the Greek and Hebrew Testaments.

(3) The account of the senses and powers of man in x. 6 of the Hebrew Testament could not be the original of ii. 8 in the Greek Testament. There are four Hebrew lists of the senses, including that in the Hebrew Testament (see notes *in loc.* in my Translation), and the last is the most remote from the Greek Testament, which can be best explained from the list in Berakoth 61[a]b.

(4) The conceptions of Michael in the two Testaments do not agree. In the Hebrew (viii. 4) he is represented as the head of the

---

[1] The text in my Appendix amounts to five pages. The verbal coincidences in these five pages with the Greek Testament amount to about one-third of a page. In one or two passages, however, it is helpful in explaining corruptions in the Greek text, as I have shown in my notes.

[2] T. Reub. iv. 8; T. Sim. iv. 4, 6; T. Lev. xiii. 9; T. Zeb. viii. 4, &c., &c.

seventy angels, who instructed the seventy families that sprang from
Noah in the seventy languages. Michael's duty is to be the bearer
of God's commands to men. But in the original Testaments Michael
plays a loftier rôle. He is not merely the angelic patron of Israel,
but the intercessor for the righteous of all nations, their protector
against Beliar, and the Mediator between God and Man.

(5) The late and conflate character of this late Hebrew *réchauffé*
is shown by the fact that it contains two phrases drawn from two
other Testaments, i. e. in i. 4 ('my silver . . . my gold . . . all my substance') from T. Jos. xi. 6, and in i. 8 ('the Lord and I are witnesses')
from T. Lev. xix. 3.

§ 21. ARAMAIC AND GREEK FRAGMENTS CONTAINING PHRASES AND CLAUSES FROM AN ORIGINAL SOURCE OF THE TESTAMENT OF LEVI AND THE BOOK OF JUBILEES.

Of the Aramaic texts which are printed in Appendix III, the
Cambridge fragments were first discovered by Mr. H. L. Pass in the
Geniza collection of the University Library, and identified by him as
a part of the Testaments of the XII Patriarchs. He subsequently
published them in the *J. Q. R.*, xii. 651 sqq. The Oxford fragment
was found some time later by Mr. Cowley among the Geniza fragments in the Bodleian Library, and briefly described in the Catalogue.
No. 2835, 27. The two fragments were written on vellum by the
same hand, and not later, in the opinion of Mr. Pass, than the eleventh
century.

Both the above fragments were recently published in the *J. Q. R.*
1907, 566–83, by Mr. Cowley and the present editor. The deciphering
and translation of the Oxford fragment were almost wholly the task
of Mr. Cowley, my part being limited to occasional suggestions or
corrections, and attempts at getting behind the Aramaic and Greek
fragments to the original presupposed by them.

The Greek fragment was found by me in a tenth century MS. of
the Testaments, which Professor Lake photographed for me on
Mount Athos, and which is denoted by the letter *e* in this edition.
This fragment is interpolated in the midst of a verse in the Testament
of Levi, i. e. xviii. 2. This fragment is unique in Greek literature,
just as the Aramaic fragments are likewise unique in Aramaic. It
is very remarkable that these Greek and Aramaic fragments agree
word for word, where they coexist. Into their mutual relations
I shall enter presently. So far as the Greek corresponds with the
Aramaic, it is printed in parallel columns with it in the article in
the *J. Q. R.* just referred to. These Aramaic and Greek fragments

are reprinted with additional notes in Appendix III of my Text, and likewise another Greek fragment, to which there is no corresponding Aramaic. The last is now printed on pp. 250–52.

There is also a small Syriac fragment of the same work, which was reprinted by Mr. Pass from Wright's *British Museum Catalogue*. This I have given on p. 254, and corrected by a fresh collation of the MS. the mistake that occurs in the Catalogue and passed from the *Catalogue* into Mr. Pass's reprint.

The fragments—a source of the Testaments. A short study of the fragments serves to show that they are not derived from the Testaments, but are part of a work which formed a common source both of the Testaments and of the Book of Jubilees.

We must now study the relations of the Greek and Aramaic fragments and, in case we discover that both are versions, determine the original language of the work.

The Aramaic and Greek fragments are versions of a common original, neither being a translation of the other.

We shall now study these fragments alike in their relation to each other and to the Testaments. First then we will show that both the Aramaic and the Greek are translations, not originals, and that neither is a translation of the other.

The Aramaic is a translation and not an original work. The first evidence in favour of the Aramaic being a translation is the appearance of a dittograph in ver. 69.

The text twice states the reason for which Levi called his son's name Merari. ' And I was greatly distressed regarding him (מר לי עלוהי להדה) because as soon as he was born he died ' (מית). This statement is nonsense ; for Merari did not die. But the true text— a duplicate one for the most part—immediately follows : ' And I was greatly distressed regarding him (הווה מריר לי עלוהי סניא) because he was like to die ' (ימות). The simplest explanation of this dittograph is that we have here two renderings, one incorrect and the other correct, of the same Hebrew original. The difference in the word used for 'greatly' (סניא and להדה) in the two cases is noteworthy. The second and correct rendering is supported by the Testament of Levi xi. 7 ἐκάλεσα αὐτὸν Μεραρεῖ, ὅ ἐστι πικρία μου ὅτι καίγε αὐτὸς ἀπέθνησκεν (*was like to die*).

Again, the peculiar style of the Aramaic fragment is against its being an original production, since it embodies Hebrew words, two of these being artificially Aramaised, two or more Syriac words, and words belonging to different types of Aramaic. To the explanation of some of these peculiarities we shall address ourselves later.

Finally, we might draw attention to the non-Aramaic use of דין in ver. 13 in the sense of 'privilege' or 'right'; for the context shows that דין כהנותא is a rendering of משפט כהנים in Deut. viii. 3.

The Aramaic is not a translation of the Greek fragment. This is at once evident if we compare the Aramaic of ver. 22 with the Greek; for where the former $=$ ἀπὸ σκώληκος καὶ τότε λαβὲ αὐτά· οὕτως γὰρ εἶδον τὸν Ἀβραὰμ τὸν πατέρα μου προσέχοντα, the Greek has merely ἀπὸ παντὸς μολυσμοῦ. In ver. 23 the Greek is again defective over against a full Aramaic text. Again, the Aramaic in verses 17, 25, 31 could not be derived from the corrupt text of the Greek. Nor could the correct Aramaic ($=$σὺ γυναῖκα) in ver. 17 be derived from the impossible Greek σὺ †πρῶτος, nor in ver. 20 the Aramaic ($=$ πᾶν τοῦτο) from the Greek ὁλοκάρπωσιν, nor in 32 where it $=$ ταύρῳ βοῶν and the Greek has ταύρῳ τῷ δευτέρῳ. The above instances, which could be multiplied, will suffice. Finally, the comparative list of the trees in ver. 24 proves in itself the impossibility of the Greek being the source of the Aramaic.

The Greek is a translation and not an original work. The possibility of the Greek being the original is precluded by the fact that it exhibits several Semitic idioms such as ὧν ἐστιν ὁ καπνὸς αὐτῶν ($=$ אשר . . . עשנם), ἐκκαίειν ἐν αὐτοῖς (בער בם), μεγάλη ἀπὸ πάσης σαρκός (גדולה מכל בשר), πρόσεχε σεαιτῷ ἀπὸ παντός (השמר לך מכל). Several of its corrupt or unintelligible passages, moreover, can be explained by retranslation into Hebrew. See notes, verses 13, 49 (i. e. κρίσιν), 17. Likewise the dittograph in ver. 17 (see note 13) points to the Greek being a translation.

The Greek fragment is not a translation of the Aramaic. For in ver. 17 where the Aramaic $=$γυναῖκα, the Greek has πρῶτος: in ver. 19 where Aramaic $=$ ἐν οἴκῳ θεοῦ, the Greek has ἐν τοῖς ἁγίοις: in 20 where Aramaic$=$πᾶν τοῦτο, the Greek has ὁλοκάρπωσιν: in 32 where Aramaic $=$ταύρῳ βοῶν, the Greek has ταύρῳ τῷ δευτέρῳ. Again, in ver. 27, where the Aramaic has an unintelligible expression, the Greek has ἐπὶ τῆς κεφαλῆς αὐτῆς. Finally, the list of trees in the Greek (ver. 24) could not be derived from that in the Aramaic.

Now that it is clear that the two versions are derived from a Semitic original we have next to determine of what language this original was. The determination of this question is complicated by the fact to which we have already drawn attention, namely, the presence in the text of Hebrew words and of Syriac words.[1] There

---

[1] Owing to the presence of the Syriac words in the text, Fraenkel (*Theol. Littera-turzeitung*, 1907, No. 17, col. 475) maintains that the Aramaic is 'undoubtedly' a translation from the Syriac. But the facts adduced above show that the evidence in favour of his contention is extremely weak in comparison with that in favour of a Hebrew original.

are two Syriac words in the Aramaic, and with these we shall at once deal. The words in question, are דפרנא and נשיפא. To the presence of these in the text we drew attention in our article in the *J. Q. R.*, where we summed up in favour of a Hebrew original. First, though דפרנא is a Syriac word, it may likewise have been used in the other Aramaic dialects. However this may be, it is found in the Book of Jubilees xxi. 12—a book universally acknowledged by scholars to have been written in Hebrew. There it appears in the form *dêfrân*[1]. Its appearance, therefore, in the present text need cause us no further trouble. In ver. 4 there is another word which can be best explained from Syriac affinities, but the word itself is not found in Syriac. Thus there remains only the one undoubted Syriac word נשיפא. If there was no counterbalancing evidence in favour of a Hebrew original, the presence of this word might form a presumption in favour of a Syriac original, but nothing more. But the evidences in favour of a Hebrew original are very strong. They are as follows :—

(1) *Five Hebrew words are found in the text.* These are פר, רחע, חדשא, מישפחה, הרת. Here רחע is simply an artificial Aramaised form of the Hebrew רחין. It is found four times in verses 20, 21, 26, 28. How can we explain the presence of this Hebrew word unless on the supposition that the translator had a Hebrew original before him ? If he had a Syriac original, its presence here is inexplicable. On that supposition he should have transliterated the Syriac word before him by סהא or אשיג. חדשא (ver. 72) is a like artificial formation from the Hebrew חדש. Why did the translator use such a word, if he did not find it in the text before him ? The translator, who, it is clear, was most careless and slovenly or ignorant, knew quite well the Aramaic word for 'month'; for ירחא is found in verses 68 and 70. Again, הרת (='conceived') which occurs twice (66, 70) is a pure Hebrew word. Even a kindred root is not found in any Aramaic language. מישפחה (='clan', ver. 17) is also a Hebrew word and not found in any Aramaic language in this sense. Finally פר (='bullock', ver. 32) is a pure Hebrew word, and could not have been found in a pure Syriac original. A good translator would have rendered it by תור in Aramaic.

---

[1] On the other hand it is to be observed that the list of trees in the Greek corresponding to Bodleian col. *c* shows several transliterations of Aramaic names of trees. But this argument is not conclusive. For it would not be unnatural to use, even in a Hebrew document in the second century B.C., the popular Aramaic names of trees, where a large number is given. Moreover, in certain cases the Hebrew name may either have been forgotten or have become so unfamiliar as to make it advisable to give the ordinary names which these trees bore even amongst the minority who knew Hebrew.

(2) *A paronomasia which was manifestly intended is discovered by retranslation into Hebrew.* In ver. 67 Levi calls his second son Kohath because that 'to him would be the gathering of all the people'. Here the Aramaic words are קהת ... כנישת. Now, if these are given in Hebrew we have an obvious paronomasia קהת ... קהלת. To prove that this is no mere imagination, it is only necessary to point to the fact that in the case of Levi's first son Gershom, and his third and fourth children Merari and Jochebed, and of Kohath's son Amram (ver. 76), the paronomasia is manifest even in the Aramaic translation. But it was impossible to render the play on Kohath in Aramaic. It is equally impossible in Syriac.

(3) *Divergencies between the two versions, difficult expressions and corrupt passages can be explained by retranslation into Hebrew.* In ver. 32 the Aramaic has פר תורין, whereas the Greek has τῷ ταύρῳ τῷ δευτέρῳ. The former = פר הישור (cf. Judges vi. 26), the latter הפר הישני. Thus this confusion could easily arise in Hebrew.

We have already drawn attention to the peculiar expression in ver. 19 κρίσιν ἱερωσύνης or דין כהנותא. Neither κρίσις nor דין can bear here legitimately the meaning the context requires. The phrase is a rendering of משפט הכהנים (Deut. xviii. 3). It cannot be explained from a Syriac background.

In ver. 17 the corruption in the Greek σὺ †πρῶτος . . . λαβὲ σεαυτῷ, where for πρῶτος the Aramaic rightly reads γυναῖκα (אנתתא) can be explained by retroversion into Hebrew, but not into Syriac. πρῶτος = ראישן, a corruption of אישה. In ver. 27 we have the converse corruption, where the Aramaic reads אישה corrupt for ראישה, i. e. רישא = κεφαλή. In the same verse we have another passage which cannot be explained except on the hypothesis of a Hebrew original, μὴ βεβηλώσῃς τὸ σπέρμα σου μετὰ †πολλῶν, a corruption of πορνῶν, as the Aramaic (זניאן) shows. But in T. Levi ix. 10 we find ἀλλοφύλων ἐθνῶν, and this is the sense required by the context, and especially by Jubilees, that the priestly line was not to be defiled by foreign marriages. The text of the Testaments presupposes זרות which must have been corrupted to זנות (or זנוי) from which the Aramaic reading is derived.

In ver. 37 the corrupt form ἀποδεδείκτω comes from ἀποδείκνυμι = הורה. Here either the 2nd or 3rd sing. fut. is required, i. e. יוֹרֶה. But this can also mean 'cast' or 'sprinkle', the meaning the context requires here.

In ver. 20 the Aramaic reads πᾶν τοῦτο, and the Greek ὁλοκάρπωσιν. Here the latter = עולות, which may have been corrupted into כל־זאת = πᾶν τοῦτο. But this is unlikely.

CORRIGENDA

PAGE 1. l. 3 of notes.   For '$\sigma\upsilon\nu\theta\hat{\omega}$' read '$\sigma\grave{\upsilon}\nu\ \theta\epsilon\hat{\omega}$'.

    l. 7 of notes.   For 'ag read δ. Ῥουβίμ (Ῥουβ (*sic*) g)' read 'a reads Ῥουβίμ, g δ. Ῥουβ.'

    l. 11 of notes.   For 'Σ' read 'Ῥ'.

  6. l. 7.   For '$\sigma\upsilon\nu\iota\grave{\omega}\nu$' read '$\sigma\upsilon\nu\iota\omega\nu$'.

  7. n. 99.   For 'Eden' read 'Eder'.

11. n. 58.   For 'S' read 'S¹'.

15. For '$\Sigma\upsilon\mu\epsilon\acute{\omega}\nu$' in title read '$\Sigma\upsilon\mu\epsilon\grave{\omega}\nu$'.

19. l. 9.   Underline $\acute{o}\gamma\kappa o\hat{\upsilon}\mu a\iota$ and add *hi*, β $\kappa a\kappa o\hat{\upsilon}\mu a\iota$ in margin.

25. l. 7 in marg.   For '$\lambda\upsilon\theta\rho\omega\theta\acute{\eta}\sigma\epsilon\sigma\theta\epsilon$' read '$\lambda\upsilon\tau\rho\omega\theta\acute{\eta}\sigma\epsilon\sigma\theta\epsilon$'.

    n. 57.   For 'a reads' read 'c. *hi* read'.

26. n. 22.   For 'Jos. xix. 7' read 'Jos. xix. 11'.

    n. 28.   For '$\ddot{o}\pi\omega\varsigma\ \kappa a\iota$' read '$o\ddot{\upsilon}\tau\omega\varsigma.\ \kappa a\iota$'.

    n. 1.   For 'S' read 'S¹'.

27. l. 20 in marg.   For 'cfg' read 'efg'.

    n. 5.   For '$d =$' read 'd adds', and add 'S¹' after 'A'.

28. n. 23.   For 'adds ... $\epsilon\pi\iota$' read 'reads $\tau o\hat{\iota}\varsigma\ \tau o\iota\chi o\iota\varsigma$ for $\tau\epsilon\iota\chi o\upsilon\varsigma$'.

32. l. 7.   In A^a add '$\sigma o\iota$' after '$\delta\epsilon\iota\chi\theta\acute{\epsilon}\nu\tau\omega\nu$'.

    n. 2.   For '$\sigma\tau\upsilon\gamma\nu\acute{o}\varsigma$' read '$\delta\epsilon\iota\nu\acute{o}\varsigma$'.

34. Delete n. 45.

37. n. 15.   For '$c, dh.\ abef$' read '$c, d.\ h, abef$'.

38. l. 9 ab imo.   Delete 'h'.

45. n. 80.   For 'c' read 'a'.

46. n. 8.   After 'A$^\beta$' add 'S¹'.

47. n. 44.   For 'af' read 'a, f'.

55. At end of n. 14 add 'a om. $\epsilon\pi\iota\ K\acute{\upsilon}\rho\iota o\nu$'.

56. l. 8.   Middle column.   Delete '†' before '$\acute{\upsilon}\pi\acute{\epsilon}\rho$'.

57. l. 19 in marg.   Delete 'a, A$^\beta$ om. $\kappa a\tau\grave{a}$ ... $\epsilon\pi a\iota\rho\acute{o}\mu\epsilon\nu o\iota$'.

61. XVIII. 2^b.   For '$\hat{\omega}\iota$' read '$\hat{\omega}$'.

81. l. 14, col. 1.   For '$\tau\grave{\eta}\nu\ \mu\eta\tau\rho\grave{o}\varsigma$' read '$\tau\hat{\eta}\varsigma\ \mu\eta\tau\rho\acute{o}\varsigma$'.

87. l. 12 in marg.   For '$\nu\upsilon\mu\phi\eta\theta\epsilon\hat{\iota}\sigma a\nu$' read '$\nu\upsilon\mu\phi\epsilon\upsilon\theta\epsilon\hat{\iota}\sigma a\nu$'.

99. l. 2.   For ⌈   ⌉ read [   ].

    n. 5.   After 'A' add 'S¹'.

105. n. 2.   For 'a.' read 'a,'.

107. n. 53.   For '$\pi\rho o\chi\omega\rho\epsilon\hat{\iota}$⌉ ($\pi\rho o\sigma\chi\omega\rho\epsilon\hat{\iota}$ af' read '$\pi\rho o\epsilon\chi\acute{\omega}\rho\epsilon\iota$⌉ ($\pi\rho o\sigma\chi\omega\rho\epsilon\hat{\iota}$ af, $\pi\rho o\chi\omega\rho\epsilon\hat{\iota}$ b'.

108. n. 5.   After '$abef$' add 'S¹'.

110. l. 4.   For '*$O\grave{\upsilon}$' read '$O\grave{\upsilon}$'.

112. l. 8.   For '$\mu\grave{\epsilon}$' read '$\mu\grave{\eta}$'.

116. In marg. after '$\beta-g$' add 'A'.

    n. 1.   For '$abef$' read 'bef'.

117. n. 27.   Add 'β' after 'A'.

120. l. 11.   For '$\delta\epsilon$' read '⌐$\delta\epsilon$⌐'.

124. l. 16.   For '⌐$*\sigma\acute{\nu}\epsilon\sigma\iota\nu$ $\kappa\alpha\grave{\iota}$' read '$*\sigma\acute{\nu}\epsilon\sigma\iota\nu$ ⌐$\kappa\alpha\grave{\iota}$'.

125. l. 4 in marg.   For 'a, af' read 'a, f', and for 'VII–VIII. 2' read 'VII–VIII. 3'.

  n. 5.   For 'bd, g reads' read '$b. d$ reads $\kappa\rho\upsilon\phi\acute{\iota}\omega\varsigma$, g'.

133. n. 27.   For 'c, e read $\epsilon\grave{\iota}\varsigma$ $\mu\acute{\iota}\sigma\upsilon\varsigma$' read '$c, e$ read $\epsilon\grave{\iota}\varsigma$ ($\grave{\epsilon}\nu$ e) $\mu\acute{\iota}\sigma\upsilon\varsigma$', and delete ('$\grave{\epsilon}\nu\mu\acute{\iota}\sigma\omega\varsigma$ e)'.

149. l. 6 in marg.   For 'β–g' read 'β–d'.

150. l. 9 ab imo in notes.   For 'G' read '$a\beta$'.

151. n. 16.   For 'Ps. lxix. 10, 23' read 'Ps. lxix. 10'.

153. l. 5 read $\dot{\alpha}\rho\mu\epsilon\nu\acute{\iota}\zeta\upsilon$ (smooth breathing with c, $def.$). b (ay ?) give the rough breathing.

156. n. 8.   For 'T. Jos. xix. 7' read 'T. Jos. xix. 11'.

  n. 32.   Emendation suggested not necessary.   Take $\ddot{\alpha}\nu$ as $\dot{\epsilon}\acute{\alpha}\nu$.

160. n. 69.   For '$\kappa\alpha\tau\grave{\alpha}$ $\pi\acute{\alpha}\nu\tau\alpha$' read '$\kappa\alpha\grave{\iota}$ $\pi\acute{\alpha}\nu\tau\alpha$', and for '$\ddot{\sigma}\theta\epsilon\nu$ $\kappa\alpha\acute{\iota}$. d, A add $\pi\acute{\alpha}\nu\tau\alpha$' read '$\ddot{\sigma}\theta\epsilon\nu$ $\kappa\alpha\grave{\iota}$ $\pi\acute{\alpha}\nu\tau\alpha$'.

162. n. 21.   For 'c' read 'c, A'.

163. n. 12.   For '$\kappa\rho\iota\theta\hat{\eta}$' read '$\kappa\rho\iota\theta\hat{\eta}$ $\kappa\alpha\acute{\iota}$'.

  n. 16.   Delete '(a $\alpha\dot{\upsilon}\tau\hat{\omega}$)'.

167. l. 8. Add in marg. 'βAS $\dot{\upsilon}\mu\hat{\omega}\nu$'.

169. n. 13.   For '$\dot{\epsilon}\nu\kappa\alpha\tau\alpha\lambda\epsilon\iota\phi\theta\acute{\eta}\sigma\eta$' read '$\dot{\epsilon}\gamma\kappa\alpha\tau\alpha\lambda\epsilon\iota\phi\theta\acute{\eta}\sigma\eta$'.

170. l. 2.   Add * before '$\dot{\epsilon}\acute{\alpha}\nu$'.

173. n. 42.   After 'c (reading $\pi\rho\sigma\sigma\kappa\sigma\lambda\lambda\acute{\sigma}\mu\epsilon\nu\sigma\varsigma$)' add '$h$ reads $\pi\rho\sigma\sigma\kappa\sigma\lambda\hat{\alpha}\tau\alpha\iota$'.

174. ver. 4 (A).   For '$\epsilon\acute{\iota}\sigma\iota\nu$' read '$\epsilon\grave{\iota}\sigma\grave{\iota}\nu$'.

  n. 1. For '$a.$' read '$a,$'.

176. l. 15 in marg.   For 'β, S^1' read 'β, A, S^1'.

177. n. 27.   For ab, S^1' read 'b, S^1'.

182. n. 1.   For '$abef$, S^1 read' read 'a read ^{2}$\iota\omega\sigma\acute{\eta}\phi$, bef S^1'.

183. ver. 5^c.   For 'Kα$\grave{\iota}$' read '$\kappa\alpha\grave{\iota}$'.

  n. 23.   For 'af' read 'aef'.

  n. 24.   For 'beg' read 'bg'.

192. l. 6.   For '$\sigma\upsilon\gamma\gamma\epsilon\nu\hat{\eta}$' read '$\sigma\upsilon\gamma\gamma\acute{\epsilon}\nu\eta$', and likewise in n. 16.

193. n. 58.   For '$\alpha\dot{\upsilon}\tau\hat{\eta}\varsigma$' read '$\alpha\dot{\upsilon}\tau\sigma\hat{\upsilon}$'.

195. n. 37.   For מֵאֶת read מֵאֶת.

208. l. 11.   Read '^{2}Hλιουπόλεως'.

211. ll. 5–7, col. 2.   For '[$\kappa\alpha\grave{\iota}$ $\sigma\grave{\iota}$ $\ddot{\epsilon}\lambda\alpha\phi\sigma\iota$] . . . $\alpha\dot{\upsilon}\tau\hat{\omega}\nu$' read '[$\kappa\alpha\grave{\iota}$ $\sigma\grave{\iota}$ $\ddot{\epsilon}\lambda\alpha\phi\sigma\iota$ . . . $\alpha\dot{\upsilon}\tau\hat{\omega}\nu$]'.

213. n. 30.   For 'T. Asher viii. 2' read 'T. Asher viii. 1'.

216. ver. 6, l. 3.   For '$\alpha\dot{\upsilon}\tau\grave{\sigma}\nu$' read '$\alpha\dot{\upsilon}\tau\grave{\sigma}\nu$'.

217. n. 14.   For מְצוּקָה read מָצוּק and for לְהָצִיקָה read לְהָצִיק.

222. l. 3.   Underline '$\pi\lambda\acute{\alpha}\nu\eta\varsigma$'.

223. n. 43.   For '$\delta\iota\pi\lambda\sigma\hat{\upsilon}\varsigma$' read '$\delta\iota\pi\lambda\hat{\alpha}$'.

224. n. 12.   Delete this note and the obeli before '$\dot{\alpha}\pi\acute{\omega}\lambda\epsilon\iota\alpha$' in the three versions in ver. 2.

  n. 16. Delete the suggestion and see the discussion of this passage in the Introduction, § 10.

BRACKETS AND ABBREVIATIONS USED IN THIS EDITION.

H denotes the lost Hebrew original, of which, however, small fragments have been preserved.

H^a denotes the first Hebrew recension.

H^β denotes the second Hebrew recension.

a denotes the Greek translation of H^a, and is represented by the Greek MSS. *chi*.

β denotes the Greek translation of H^β, and is represented by the Greek MSS. *abdefg*.

abcdefghi denote the nine Greek MSS. of the Testaments.

A denotes the Armenian Version.

A^a denotes the first recension of the Armenian Version, and is represented by the Armenian MSS. A[abh].

A^β denotes the second recension of the Armenian Version, and is represented by the Armenian MSS. A[b*cdefg].

A[abcde], &c. denote the Armenian MSS.

S^1 denotes the first Slavonic recension.

S^2 denotes the second Slavonic recension.

hmt. = homoioteleuton.

⌐ ¬ The use of these brackets in the text means that the words so enclosed are not found in A.

( ) Words so enclosed are supplied by the Editor.

† † Words so enclosed are corrupt.

[ ] Words so enclosed are interpolated.

THE TEXT. The printed Greek text represents a except in a few cases. Where words are printed in thick type the reader is to understand that the text of β differs, and that this is found in the margin. Only the chief variants are thus denoted.

ΔΙΑΘΗΚΑΙ ΤΩΝ ΔΩΔΕΚΑ ΠΑΤΡΙΑΡΧΩΝ ΤΩΝ ΤΙΩΝ ΙΑΚΩΒ ΤΟΥ ΠΑΤΡΙΑΡΧΟΥ

Διαθήκη ῾Ρουβὴμ τοῦ πρωτοτόκου υἱοῦ ᾽Ιακὼβ καὶ Λείας[1].

I. ᾽Αντίγραφον[2] διαθήκης ῾Ρουβήμ[3], ὅσα[4] ἐνετείλατο τοῖς υἱοῖς[5] αὐτοῦ, ⌈*πρὶν ἢ[6] ἀποθανεῖν αὐτόν, *ἐν ἑκατοστῷ[7] *εἰκοστῷ πέμπτῳ[8] ἔτει τῆς ζωῆς αὐτοῦ⌉. 2. *Μετὰ ἔτη δύο τῆς τελευτῆς[9] ᾽Ιωσὴφ ⌈τοῦ ἀδελφοῦ αὐτοῦ⌉[10], ἀρρωστή-   β–d,A,S[1] σαντος[11] ῾Ρουβήμ[12], συνήχθησαν[13] *ἐπισκέψασθαι αὐτὸν[14] ᾽Ιωσήφ. υἱοὶ[15] αὐτοῦ καὶ υἱοὶ[16] τῶν υἱῶν αὐτοῦ[17].

3. Καὶ[18] εἶπεν αὐτοῖς[19]· Τέκνα[20] μου, *ἰδοὺ ἐγὼ[21] ἀπο-

General Title. α, bd as in text (save that h prefixes αι, and bd om. τοῦ πατρ. and d om. τῶν [20]). a reads αι δ. τῶν ιβ΄ πατρ. πρὸς τοὺς υἱοὺς αὐτῶν, f δ. συνθῶ τῶν ιβ΄ υἱῶν τοῦ ᾽Ιακώβ, g δ. τῶν υἱῶν ᾽Ιακὼβ ἤγουν τῶν δώδεκα πατρ. e om. A = διαθῆκαι τῶν πατριαρχῶν.

[1] Title of Testament. h as in text, but with ῾Ρουβίμ. c reads δ. ῾Ρουβὴμ καὶ Λίας (sic). A comparison of the titles of two other Testaments shows that h is right. ag read δ. ῾Ρουβίμ (῾Ρουβ (sic) g), bef δ. ῾Ρουβὴμ (f ῾Ρουβὴν) περὶ ἐννοιῶν (+ ῾Ρουβὴμ υἱὸς πρωτότοκος ᾽Ιακὼβ καὶ Λίας e), d α΄ δ. ῾Ρουβὴμ α΄ υἱοῦ . . . , f adds ἑρμηνεύεται ῾Ρουβὴν πνᾶ θῡ. A^aefg = βίβλος τῶν παραλειπο-μένων, λόγοι τοῦ ῾Ρ. διαθήκη (+ α΄ A^efg), A^b = διαθήκη καὶ λόγοι ῾Ρ. ἀπὸ τῶν παραλειπομένων βίβλου, A^h διαθήκη Σ. υἱοῦ ᾽Ιακὼβ υἱοῦ ᾽Ισαὰκ υἱοῦ ᾽Αβραάμ, A^c = διαθήκη α΄ ῾Ρ.   [2] a reads ἀντίγραφα, and in other Testaments.   [3] c, bdef. h, ag read ῾Ρουβίμ.   [4] h reads ὅς. A^ab = ὡς.   [5] g reads τοὺς υἱούς. [6] α, aef. bg read πρίν, d πρὸ τοῦ.   [7] g reads ἐν τῷ ρ΄. d reads ἀρρωστή-σαντος γὰρ αὐτοῦ ἐν τῷ ἑκατοστῷ.   [8] e reads κε΄ g ι΄.   [9] This peculiar coustruction is found elsewhere first (?) in Plut. Coriol. 11, μεθ᾽ ἡμέρας ὀλίγας τῆς τοῦ πατρὸς τελευτῆς. A perfectly analogous construction with πρό appears in LXX, Amos i. 1; iv. 7; 2 Macc. xv. 36; John xii. 1; Joseph. Ant., xv. 11. 10. For ἔτη δύο τῆς τελ. g reads δὲ ἔτη τελ.   [10] α, d. β–d, A, S om.   [11] α, A. abef read ἀρρωστοῦντι. g ἀρρωστῶν. d om.   [12] ef. α, a read ῾Ρουβίμ. A αὐτοῦ. g οὗτος. bd, S^1 om.   [13] g reads συνῆξε. h συνηχθῆσαι (sic). d adds οἱ ἀδελφοὶ αὐτοῦ.   [14] g, A^a om., while A^bb*cdefg trs. after υἱῶν αὐτοῦ.   [15] c. h, abe read οἱ υἱοί. d om. with next six words. e om. next word (αὐτοῦ). g reads τοὺς υἱούς.   [16] c^1, b. c^2h, adef read οἱ υἱοί g τοὺς υἱούς.   [17] g reads αὐτῶν.   [18] d adds προσκαλεσάμενος τοὺς υἱοὺς αὐτοῦ. A^b* add οὗτος ἀναστὰς ἐκάθισεν καί. A^b add ῾Ρουβήμ.   [19] A^a om. d adds ἀναστήσατέ με ἀδελφοί μου καὶ λέξω ὑμῖν Γνωστὸν ὑμῖν ἔστω.

θνήσκω καὶ πορεύομαι ὁδὸν[22] τῶν[23] πατέρων μου[24].   4.
*Ἰδὼν δὲ[25] ⌜ἐκεῖ⌝ *Ἰούδαν καὶ Γὰδ καὶ Ἀσήρ[26], τοὺς
ἀδελφοὺς αὐτοῦ, εἶπεν αὐτοῖς· Ἀναστήσατέ[27] με[28], ὅπως
εἴπω τοῖς *ἀδελφοῖς μου καὶ τοῖς τέκνοις[29] μου, ὅσα ἔχω
ἐν τῇ καρδίᾳ μου κρυπτά[30]· *ἰδοὺ γὰρ ἐκλείπω ἀπὸ τοῦ
νῦν ἐγώ[31].   5. *Καὶ ἀναστὰς[32] κατεφίλησεν αὐτοὺς καὶ
*εἶπεν αὐτοῖς[33]. Ἀκούσατε, *ἀδελφοί μου καὶ υἱοί μου[34], ἐνω-
τίσασθε[35] Ῥουβὴμ[36] τοῦ πατρὸς ὑμῶν ὅσα ⌜ἐγὼ⌝[37] ἐντέλλομαι
ὑμῖν[38].   6. Καὶ[39] *ἰδοὺ ἐπιμαρτύρομαι ὑμῖν τὸν Θεὸν τοῦ
οὐρανοῦ σήμερον[40], *ὅπως μὴ πορευθῆτε[41] ἐν ἀγνοίᾳ νεότητος[42]
⌜καὶ πορνείᾳ⌝, *ἐν ᾗ[43] ἐξεχύθην ἐγὼ καὶ ἐμίανα[44] κοίτην[45]
τοῦ πατρός μου Ἰακώβ[46].   7. *Λέγω δὲ ὑμῖν[47] ὅτι *ἔπληξέ

Marginal notes (left margin):

β-dg, A, S¹ με, ἀδελφοί μου (f, A S¹ om.).

β-d, A, S¹ κλαύσας εἶπεν.

β-dg, A♭*deg ἀδελφοί μου.

S adds λόγον μετανοίας καί.   [20] c, bg read τεκνία.   [21] α, A. abefg, S¹
read ἐγώ, d ὅτι ἐγώ.   [22] d om. but adds τὴν ὁδόν in marg. A = μετὰ
πατέρας μου but զկնի (= μετά) is probably corrupt for զուղի = ὁδόν.
[23] abf om.   [24] g om. all ver. 4 and first seven words of ver. 5.   [25] α, af.
be, A read καὶ ἰδών. For Καὶ ἰδὼν ... τοῖς τέκνοις μου d reads ταῦτα εἰπὼν
ἀνεστέναξε καὶ εἶπεν· Ἀκούσατε ἀδελφοί μου καὶ τέκνα μου.   [26] e reads Γ. καὶ
Ἀ. καὶ Ἰ.   [27] e reads αναστησαται.   [28] β-dg, A, S¹ add as in margin.
[29] a reads υἱοῖς with ἀδελφοῖς above it.   [30] A trs. before ἐν τῇ καρδίᾳ.
[31] h, af. bde¹, A, S (save that A εἰμὶ ἐγώ) read ἐκλείπων (b ἐκλιπὼν) γὰρ ἐγώ
(d om.) εἰμι ἀπὸ τοῦ νῦν. d supports text save that it om. ἐγώ. c om.
entire clause. e² reads ἐκλείπω γὰρ ἐγὼ ἰδοὺ ἀ. τ. ν.   [32] d reads προσκλαύσας.
[33] α, d (save that h om. καί and d om. αὐτοῖς). β-d, A, S¹ read as in marg.
[34] α, Ac, S¹ (save that α om. μου¹⁰). β-dg, A♭*defg read ἀδελφοί μου, d, A♭
τέκνα (+μου d). g om.   [35] g om. d, A insert καί before ἐνω. d adds τοὺς
λόγους. f υἱοί.   [36] α, a read Ῥουβίμ.   [37] c, aef. h, bdg, A, S¹ om.
[38] g om.   [39] α, dg om.   [40] β, A♭♭cdeg, S¹ (save that A♭ om. σήμερον and
Acdeg trs. it before τὸν Θεόν). α reads τὸν Θεὸν τοῦ οὐρ. καὶ τῆς γῆς προτειθημοι
(sic) ὑμῖν (for προτ. ὑμῖν h reads σήμερον). προτίθεμαι may here = הערכתי
corrupt for העידתי = ἐπιμαρτύρομαι. β could mean 'I call to witness against
you the God of heaven' (הַעִידֹתִי בָּכֶם אֶת־אֱלֹהִים הַשׁ׳). Cf. Deut. iv. 26.
But the context requires 'I charge you by the God, &c.' Hence we should
expect (as in VI. 9 of this Testament) ὁρκῶ ὑμᾶς τὸν Θεὸν τοῦ οὐρανοῦ τοῦ
μὴ πορευθῆναι = הִשְׁבַּעְתִּיכֶם בָּאלֹהִים אֲשֶׁר לֹא תִתְהַלְּכוּ. As a corruption of
השבעתי we might explain שַׂמְתִּי = προτίθεμαι, the reading in α.   [41] α. β
reads τοῦ μὴ πορευθῆναι.   [42] For following καί d reads ἐν ὑμῶν. A♭♭*cdeg
= ἐν νεότητι. A♭ om.   [43] d om.   [44] β adds τήν.   [45] e reads κύτην.
[46] d trs. before τοῦ πατρός.   [47] α. β reads λέγω γὰρ ὑμῖν, A διὰ τοῦτο καὶ
λέγω ὑμῖν, S ἥμαρτον σὺν Βάλλᾳ τῇ δούλῃ τοῦ πατρός μου.   [48] α, dg. ef read
ἔπληξέν με. a ἐξέπληξέ με. b ἐνέπληξέ με. d adds κύριος, e ὁ θεός.   [49] α,
ag. bdef read πληγὴν μεγάλην. A♭*deg = μεγάλως, but A♭♭c support text.

με[48] *πληγῇ μεγάλῃ[49] *ἐπὶ τῆς λαγόνος[50] μου ἕως[51] μῆνας[52] ἑπτά· καὶ εἰ μὴ *ὁ πατήρ μου Ἰακὼβ[53] προσηύξατο[54] *περὶ ἐμοῦ πρὸς Κύριον[55] ἤθελε[56] Κύριος[57] ἀνελεῖν με. 8. Ἤμην γὰρ[58] ἐτῶν τριάκοντα ὅτε ἔπραξα τὸ πονηρὸν ἐνώπιον Κυρίου[59]· καὶ ἐμαλακίσθην *μῆνας ἑπτὰ[60] ἕως θανάτου.   9. Καὶ *μετὰ τοῦτο[61] ἐν προαιρέσει ψυχῆς μου *ἑπτὰ ἔτη[62] μετενόησα *ἐνώπιον Κυρίου[63].

10. Καὶ[64] οἶνον καὶ σίκερα οὐκ ἔπιον, καὶ κρέας[65] οὐκ εἰσῆλθεν *ἐν τῷ στόματί[66] μου· καὶ πᾶν[67] ἄρτον ἐπιθυμίας[68] οὐκ ἔφαγον[69] *ἀλλ' ἤμην[70] πενθῶν ἐπὶ τῇ ἁμαρτίᾳ μου[71], μεγάλη γὰρ ἦν, *οἷα οὐ γέγονεν ἐν Ἰσραὴλ οὕτως[72].

II. Καὶ νῦν[1] ἀκούσατέ μου, τέκνα μου[2], ἃ[3] εἶδον περὶ τῶν ἑπτὰ[4] πνευμάτων τῆς πλάνης ἐν τῇ μετανοίᾳ μου[5].   2. Ἑπτὰ οὖν[6] πνεύματα ἐδόθη[7] κατὰ τοῦ ἀνθρώπου[8] καὶ ταῦτά[9] εἰσιν[10] *αἱ κεφαλαὶ[11] τῶν ἔργων τοῦ νεωτερισμοῦ.

h, β, S
ἐγευ-
σάμην.
β, S[1] καὶ
οὐ μὴ
γένηται.
β, A, S
ἀνθρώπου
ἀπὸ τοῦ
Βελίαρ.
β–fg,
A[a], S
κεφαλή.

e adds ὁ Θεός.   [50] α, af. bdeg read ἐν (deg ἐπὶ) ταῖς (g τοῖς) λαγῶσι. [51] α. β reads ἐπί.   [52] A = ἐνιαυτούς, but q̇w̄δ̇u is corrupt for q̇w̄δ̇u = μῆνας.   [53] α, e. dg, A read Ἰ. ὁ πατήρ μου, abf, S[1] Ἰ. ὁ π. ἡμῶν. For the order followed in the text see also last verse.   [54] eg read ηὔξατο.   [55] ag read πρὸς Κ. περὶ ἐμοῦ. h, A[b] om. περὶ ἐμοῦ.   [56] g reads ἠθέλησεν. Before this word bef add ὅτι against α, adg. If the ὅτι is genuine here, it is as Sinker suggests a rendering of כִּי. Cf. 1 Sam. xiv. 30: also Exod. xxii. 22; Is. vii. 9.   [57] d adds ὁ Θεός.   [58] α, abef, A[abdeg], S[1]. dg, A[b*c] read δέ.   [59] α adds καὶ τοῦ πατρός μου.   [60] α, g. β–g, A, S[1] read ἑπτὰ μῆνας and β, A, S[1] trs. these words before ἐμαλακίσθην.   [61] α, A. β, S om.   [62] A[abb*deg] trs. after Κυρίου.   [63] h om. Κυρίου and next six words.   [64] c, A. β, S[1] om.   [65] α, defg read κρέα.   [66] α. β reads εἰς τὸ στόμα.   [67] α, b. adefg read πάντα. S om.   [68] S om.   [69] c, A, h, β, S read as in margin.   [70] α, d (but d reads καὶ for ἀλλ'). β–d, A, S om.   [71] g om. rest of verse.   [72] c (save that for Ἰσραὴλ it reads Ἰλη̄μ̄). c alone preserves the Hebrew idiom. Thus οἷα ... οὕτως = כָּמוֹהוּ‎ ‎נִהְיָתָה אֲשֶׁר. A = καὶ οὔποτε ἐν Ἰσραὴλ γέγονεν τοιαύτη. All the other Gr. MSS. make the sentence future. abdef, S read καὶ οὐ μὴ γένηται ἐν (+ τῷ b) Ἰσραὴλ οὕτως. h ἀνταμοιβὴ γένοιτο ἐν Ἰσραὴλ οὕτως.

II. [1] d om. g om. next four words.   [2] α, A[abb*cd]. β, A[eg] om. S reads Ρουβὴμ τοῦ πατρὸς ὑμῶν. c adds καὶ διηγήσομαι ὑμῖν. h om. next twelve words.   [3] S[1] = ὅς.   [4] g om. For περὶ τῶν ἑπτὰ πνευμάτων S reads τὰ ἑπτὰ πνεύματα.   [5] g adds ἀρκεῖ μοι εἰς διδασκαλίαν ὑμῶν and om. to III. 9 inclusive.   [6] α. β, S om. A = γάρ.   [7] de read ἐδόθησαν.   [8] α. β, A, S add as in marg.   [9] α, d. abef read αὐτά.   [10] α, ef. Other MSS. εἰσί.   [11] α, f, A[bb*cd]. abde, A[a], S κεφαλή.   [12] α. A = αὖθις. β, S om.

α om.
τοῦ εἶναι
... ὁρά-
σεως
through
hmt.

[3. Καὶ ἕτερα[12] ἑπτὰ πνεύματα ἐδόθη[13] ⌜αὐτῷ⌝[14] *ἐπὶ τῆς κτίσεως[15] τοῦ εἶναι ἐν αὐτοῖς πᾶν ἔργον ἀνθρώπου. 4. Πρῶτον πνεῦμα ζωῆς, μεθ' ἧς ἡ σύστασις[16] κτίζεται. Δεύτερον πνεῦμα ὁράσεως, μεθ' ἧς γίνεται ἐπιθυμία. 5. Τρίτον πνεῦμα ἀκοῆς μεθ' ἧς γίνεται[17] διδασκαλία. Τέταρτον πνεῦμα[18] ὀσφρήσεως, μεθ' ἧς *γίνονται γεύσεις δεδομέναι[19] *εἰς ὁλκὴν[20] ἀέρος καὶ ἀναπνοῆς[21]. 6. Πέμπτον πνεῦμα[22] λαλιᾶς, μεθ' ἧς γίνεται γνῶσις. 7. Ἕκτον πνεῦμα γεύσεως μεθ' ἧς *γίνεται βρῶσις[23] *βρωμάτων τε καὶ πομάτων[24], καὶ ἰσχὺς ἐν αὐτῷ[25] κτίζεται *ὅτι ἐν βρώμασίν ἐστιν ἡ ὑπόστασις τῆς ἰσχύος[26]. 8. Ἕβδομον πνεῦμα σπορᾶς καὶ συνουσίας[27], μεθ' ἧς συνέρχονται[28] διὰ τῆς φιληδονίας[29] ἁμαρτίαι[30]. 9. Διὰ τοῦτο *ἔσχατόν ἐστι τῆς κτίσεως[31] καὶ πρῶτον τῆς νεότητος, ὅτι *ἀγνοίας πεπλήρωται[32], καὶ

β-bg, A
νεωτε-
ρισμόν.

αὕτη τὸν νεώτερον[33] ὁδηγεῖ ὥσπερ[34] τυφλὸν ἐπὶ βόθρον καὶ ὡς κτῆνος ἐπὶ κρημνόν[35].

III. *Ἐπὶ πᾶσιν δὲ[1] τούτοις ὄγδοον[2] πνεῦμα[3] τοῦ ὕπνου

The section II. 3—III. 2 which relates to the senses is bracketed as an interpolation. [13] *d* reads ἐδόθησαν. [14] *h*, β, S. *c* trs. after κτίσεως. A om. [15] A corrupt = ἐπὶ πάντων κτισμάτων. *c* adds αὐτῷ. α om. rest of verse and first eleven words of ver. 4 through hmt. [16] *bd*, S². *aef* read ἡ κίνησις. *d* adds τοῦ ἀνθρώπου. A = πάντα τὰ κτίσματα. S¹ = τὰ θελήματα. [17] α, *ab*, S. *def* read δέδοται. A = ἀκούεται. [18] A = τό. [19] α and A, save that *h* reads γίνεται. *abef*, S read ἐστὶν (ἐστὶ *ab*) ἡ (*b* om.) γεῦσις δεδομένη. *d* εὐωδία διδομενης (*sic*). [20] α, *af*. *be* read εἰς συνολκήν. *d* συνολκεῖν. [21] α. β, A read πνοῆς. Perhaps we should read ἐκπνοήν. [22] *h* om. next seven words through hmt. [23] *h* reads γένοιτο βρώσεις. [24] α, *a*. *be¹*, S read βρωτῶν τε καὶ ποτῶν. *d* βροτῶν καὶ πόσεως. *e²f* βρωμάτων τε καὶ ποτῶν. A = βρωτῶν (cf. *d*) τε καὶ ποτόν. [25] α, *aef*. *d* reads αὐτῇ. *b* αὐτοῖς. A = αὐτῷ or αὐτῇ. [26] There appears to be a doublet or a marginal gloss here. A = ὅτι τὸ βρῶμά ἐστι ἰσχύς. [27] *d* reads συνουσιασμοῦ. [28] α. *afd*, S read συνέρχεται. *b* συνεισέρχεται. *e* γίνεται. A adds wrongly εἰς ἀλλήλους. [29] A*ab* loosely = α, β but A^b*cde¹f corrupt. A^b* wrongly adds ἐν ᾗ. [30] α. β, S read ἡ ἁμαρτία. [31] A = μετὰ πάντα ταῦτα τὰ κτίσματα—a loose rendering of our text. [32] *h* reads αγνοι πεπληρισατο. [33] α, *b*, S. *adef*, A read as in margin. [34] α. β reads ὡς. [35] *c,d* read κρυμνον, *e* κρεμνον.

III. [1] α. *aef*, A read καὶ ἐπὶ πᾶσι. *bd*, S ἐπὶ πᾶσι. [2] *abf*, A, S. *e* reads ἤ, *h* ἕβδομον. *c, d* om. [3] *h, d* add τό. [4] *h* om. [5] *c* reads ὧν. [6] *a* reads ἐσκοτίσθη. [7] *c* prefixes ἡ. A = στάσις, ὑπόστασις or στερέωμα. For φύσεως A*ab read by internal corruption οἰκήσεως and om. next four

ἐστί[4], μεθ᾽ οὗ[5] ἐκτίσθη[6] ἔκστασις[7] φύσεως καὶ εἰκὼν τοῦ θανάτου.

2. *Τούτοις τοῖς[8] πνεύμασι συμμίγνυται[9] *τὰ πνεύματα[10] *τῆς πλάνης[11].]

3. Πρῶτον[12] *τὸ τῆς πορνείας πνεῦμα[13] ἐν τῇ φύσει[14] καὶ[15] *ταῖς αἰσθήσεσιν[16] ἔγκειται[17]. *Δεύτερον πνεῦμα[18] ἀπληστείας[19] γαστρός[20]. 4. Τρίτον πνεῦμα[21] μάχης ἐν τῷ ἥπατι καὶ ἐν[22] τῇ χόλῃ. Τέταρτον[23] πνεῦμα ἀρεσκείας[24] καὶ μαγγανείας[25], ἵνα διὰ[26] περιεργείας[27] ὡραῖος[28] ὀφθῇ[29]. 5. Πέμπτον πνεῦμα ὑπερηφανείας[30] ἵνα καυχᾶται[31] καὶ μεγαλοφρονῇ[32]. *Ἕκτον πνεῦμα[33] ψεύδους[34] †ἐν ἀπωλείᾳ καὶ ζήλῳ†[35] τοῦ *πλάττειν λόγους καὶ κρύπτειν λόγους[36] ⌈αὐτοῦ⌉[37] *ἀπὸ γένους[38] καὶ οἰκείων[39]. 6. Ἕβδομον πνεῦμα *ἀδικίας, μεθ᾽ ἧς[40]

words.   [8] A = τούτοις τοῖς οὖν ἑπτά.   [9] h, a read συμμίγνυνται.   [10] α, aef. bd, A, S read τὸ πνεῦμα.   [11] h reads τοῖς πλάνοις.   [12] h reads καὶ πρῶτον.   [13] α, ae, A. b, S read τὸ τῆς πορ. d τὸ πν. τῆς πονηρείας. f τὸ τῆς πονηρίας πν.   [14] A[abe] = οἰκήσει.   [15] ad, A read καὶ ἐν.   [16] A = τοῖς (A[ab] om.) αἰσθητοῖς.   [17] c reads ἔγγηται. e ἔγκιται. h ἔγκυται. A ἐστί.   [18] c reads δύο πνεύματα.   [19] bd. h, af read ἀπληστίας, e ἀπλιστείας, c ἀπληστεία.   [20] α. af read ἐν γαστρί. bde, A, S read ἐν τῇ γαστρί.   [21] α om.   [22] α, d, A. β–d om.   [23] h reads τρίτον.   [24] α reads ἀρεσκίας. d αὐταραισκίας.   [25] c, b read μαγγανίας. h illegible. A = ἐν μαγγανείαις and om. ἵνα διὰ περιεργείας, but ꜰ seems to be a corrupt compression of ꜰ = καὶ μαγγανείας ἵνα διὰ περιεργείας.   [26] d reads δή.   [27] c, bf. ae read περιεργίας. d περιεργασις. h περιεργεία. On A see note 25.   [28] h om.   [29] h, a[2]. Other MSS. ὀφθῇ.   [30] b. af read ὑπερηφανίας. c, de ὑπεριφανείας. h ὑπερηφανεία.   [31] b reads κινῆται. For καυχᾶται καί A reads καυχώμενος.   [32] a[1]be. α, df read μεγαλοφρονεῖ. a[2] μεγαλαυχεῖ.   [33] c om.   [34] de read ψεῦδος. A (corrupt) = σκληρολογίας. Read ꜰ.   [35] This phrase is corrupt. The context requires a parallel to ἀπὸ γένους καὶ οἰκείων. ἐν ἀπωλ. καὶ ζήλῳ = בשנאה וקנאה which I take to be corrupt for לשנא ולקנא = ἐχθρῷ καὶ ἀντιζήλῳ, ‘to an enemy and rival.’ For ἀπωλείᾳ c[1], def give the form ἀπολείᾳ, h reads ἀπειλίας. For ζήλῳ A[ab*cd] read ἐν ζήλῳ.   [36] h, af, A[abcd] (save that h adds μαγγανίας after λόγους[10] and A[abcd] imply ἔργα for λόγους[20]). So also e (save that λόγους καὶ κρύπτειν is a marginal addition by the original hand). A[b*], S[2] support text but A[b*] om. λόγους[10] and S[2] om. λογ.[20] c, b, S[1] om. καὶ κρύπτειν λόγους. d reads κρύπτειν λόγους καὶ πράττειν αὐτούς.   [37] d, A, S[2] om. d adds ὡς. c om. next four words.   [38] h reads ἀπὸ συγγενῶν αὐτοῦ. S = διὰ τὸν οἶκτον.   [39] d, S prefix τῶν. A adds αὐτοῦ.   [40] c reads ἀδικία καί. e καὶ κλοπαί.   [41] α, ae (over erasure) f. b, A, S read κλοπή. d κλοπῆς.

β–g, A,
S ποιήσῃ.

β, S¹ ὕπνου, τὸ ὄγδοον πνεῦμα.

α, ae, πλάνη καὶ φαντασία.

be, A ὑμᾶς· διδάσκω ὑμᾶς.

α ὄψιν.

κλοπαὶ[41] καὶ γρηπίσματα[42], ἵνα ἐμπλήσει[43] φιληδονίαν καρδίας αὐτοῦ. Ἡ γὰρ ἀδικία συνεργεῖ[44] *τοῖς λοιποῖς[45] πνεύμασιν διὰ τῆς δοσοληψίας[46].　　[7. Ἐπὶ[47] πᾶσι δὲ[48] τούτοις *τὸ πνεῦμα[49] τοῦ ὕπνου[50] συνάπτεται[51] *ὅ ἐστι[52] *πλάνης καὶ φαντασίας[53].]　　8. Καὶ οὕτως ἀπόλλυται πᾶς νεώτερος[54], σκοτίζων[55] τὸν νοῦν ⌐αὐτοῦ⌐[56] ἀπὸ τῆς ἀληθείας, καὶ μὴ *συνιὼν ἐν[57] τῷ νόμῳ τοῦ θεοῦ[58], μήτε[59] ἀκούων[60] νουθεσίας[61] πατέρων αὐτοῦ[62] ὡς[63] κἀγὼ ἔπαθον[64] ἐν τῷ νεωτερισμῷ μου.　　9. Καὶ νῦν, τέκνα μου[65], τὴν ἀλήθειαν ἀγαπᾶτε[66] καὶ αὕτη[67] *φυλάξει ὑμᾶς[68]. Ἀκούσατε ⌐λόγους⌐[69] Ῥουβὴμ τοῦ πατρὸς ὑμῶν[70].

10. Μὴ[71] προσέχετε[72] ὄψει[73] γυναικείᾳ[74] μήτε[75] συνδιάζετε[76] μετὰ *θηλείας ὑπάνδρου[77] μήτε[78] περιεργάζεσθε[79] πρᾶξιν[80] γυναικῶν.

[42] e (over erasure) f. ab, S² read γρυπίσματα. α γρηπιάσματα. d ἁρπαγῆς. A = γρήπισμα, S¹ = συκοφαντεία.　　[43] α (h reading -σῇ) = שׁבעי. β–g, A, S read ποιήσῃ (ποιήσει f) = עשׂה.　　[44] a reads συνεργεῖται. d αὐτοῦ συνεργεῖ.　　[45] A = πᾶσι τοῖς.　　[46] α, af, A. d reads δωροληψείας ἢ προσωποληψίας. e δωροληψίας. b, S¹ δολολειψίας.　　[47] d reads ἐν. Ver. 7. This verse may be the model on which III. 1, 2 were composed, or it may be due to the same hand.　　[48] α, A. β om. S¹ reads καί before ἐπί.　　[49] d reads τῷ πνεύματι.　　[50] β, S¹ add as in margin against α. For τὸ πνεῦμα τοῦ ὕπνου τὸ ὄγδ. πν. A gives τῷ ὀγδόῳ πνεύματι ἄλλο πνεῦμα.　　[51] e reads συνέπεται.　　[52] c, af, A. h, e ᾧ ἐστι. bd, S om.　　[53] A^{ab*cdeg}. α, ae read πλάνη καὶ φαντασία. b, S πλάνη καὶ φαντασίᾳ. d τῆς πλάνης καὶ τῆς φαντασίας. f πνεῦμα καὶ φαντασία. A^b πλάνη τῶν ἀφανῶν.　　[54] A = νεότης. S¹ om.　　[55] c reads σκορπίζων.　　[56] α. β, A, S¹ om.　　[57] = ב בן. c om. preceding μή.　　[58] A^c = κυρίου.　　[59] d reads μηδέ.　　[60] α. abef, S read ὑπακούων. d εἰσακούων. For ἀκούων . . . πατέρων A^{cdeg} read νουθετούμενος ὑπὸ πατέρων.　　[61] c reads νουθεσίαν.　　[62] e om.　　[63] c, af. bde read ὥσπερ. h om.　　[64] A = ἐπατήθην (?). Cf. IV. 1 note 13.　　[65] α, de, A. abf, S om.　　[66] α. abdef, A, S read ἀγαπήσατε.　　[67] S = οὕτως.　　[68] h reads φυλάξατε. be (but obelized in e) A^{ab} add (+ ἐγὼ A^b) διδάσκω ὑμᾶς. A^{bcd} = καὶ διδάσκω ὑμᾶς. A^{b*} = καὶ οὖν διδ. ὑ. Perhaps this clause was omitted by α, adfy through hmt. S¹ om. rest of verse.　　[69] α, aef. bd, A om.　　[70] d adds καὶ ἐνωτίσασθε ἃ διδάσκω ὑμᾶς.　　[71] h, A read καὶ μή.　　[72] c, abd, S². h reads προσέχητε. e προσέχεται. f πρόσχετε. S¹ = ὁρᾶτε.　　[73] c. h reads ὄψιν. adefg εἰς ὄψιν. b ἐν ὄψει.　　[74] c though in the form γυναικία. h, A read γυναικῶν. af γυναικείαν. bdeg, S γυναικός.　　[75] α, adf. beg read μηδέ.　　[76] α. The usual form would be συνδυάζετε. β–dg, S¹ read ἰδιάζετε. d ἰδιάζεσθε. g πλησιάζεται. A = 'do not be advisers of' or 'do not confer with'—a rendering which supports α. h om. next five words.　　[77] d reads θηλύας ὑπάρδρου.

11. Εἰ μὴ γὰρ εἶδον ἐγὼ[81] Βάλλαν λουομένην[82] ἐν σκεπινῷ[83] τόπῳ, οὐκ *ἂν ἔπιπτον[84] εἰς τὴν ἀνομίαν[85] τὴν μεγάλην. 12. Συλλαβοῦσα γὰρ ἡ διάνοιά μου τὴν γυναικείαν[86] γύμνωσιν[87] οὐκ εἴασέ[88] με ⸢ὑπνῶσαι⸣[89], ἕως οὗ[90] ἔπραξα τὸ βδέλυγμα[91]. 13. Ἀπιόντος[92] γὰρ Ἰακὼβ[93] τοῦ[94] πατρός μου[95] πρὸς Ἰσαὰκ τὸν πατέρα αὐτοῦ, ὄντων ἡμῶν ἐν Γαδὲρ[96] πλησίον[97] Ἐφραθὰ[98] *ἐν Βηθλεέμ[99], *ἦν ἡ Βάλλα μεθυσθεῖσα καὶ ἦν κοιμωμένη ἀκάλυπτος[100] ἐν τῷ κοιτῶνι ⸢αὐτῆς⸣[101]. 14. *Εἰσελθὼν οὖν ἐγὼ καὶ θεασάμενος[102] τὴν γύμνωσιν αὐτῆς ἔπραξα τὴν ἀσέβειαν, ⸢μὴ αἰσθανθείσ(ης) αὐτῆς⸣[103], καί, καταλιπὼν αὐτὴν κοιμωμένην, ἐξῆλθον. 15. *Καὶ εὐθέως[104] ἄγγελος *τοῦ θεοῦ[105] ἀπεκάλυψεν τῷ πατρί μου[106] περὶ τῆς ἀσεβείας μου· καὶ ἐλθὼν[107] ἐπένθησεν[108] *ἐπ᾽ ἐμοὶ[109], μηκέτι *αὐτῆς ἁψάμενος[110].

Marginal readings: β, S¹ ἀπόντος. | β, S ἡμῶν. | β–g, S¹ B. ἦν μεθύουσα καὶ. | β–g, S¹ κἀγὼ εἰσελθὼν καὶ ἰδών. | β, A, S¹ ἀσέβειαν. | β, A, S¹ μου Ἰακώβ. | β, A, S¹ ἐπένθει.

A = θηλειῶν ὑπάνδρων. For θηλείας c, e read θηλίας. [78] c, dg. a¹be, S¹ read μηδέ. a²f μή. [79] a²e read περιεργάζεσθαι. [80] abf. de, Aᵇᶜᵈᵉᵍ read πράξεις. α ὄψιν. g ποτε πρόσωπον. Aᵇ* κάλλος καὶ πράξεις. Text doubtful. [81] a om. [82] g om. next three words. [83] b. a reads σκιπινῷ, c, f σκηπινῷ. d σκεπενῷ. e σκεπεινῷ. h σκοτεινῷ. Cf. Jub. xxxiii. 2 in loco occulto. [84] α, df. abg, S¹ read ἐνέπιπτον. e ἔπιπτον. [85] d adds ἐκείνην. e ταύτην. [86] a reads τῆς γυναικός. [87] h reads γυμνίαν (sic). [88] c, e read ἔασεν. [89] A om. [90] h, fg om. [91] h, abfg. c, e read βδέλλυγμα. d βδέλλυμα· d adds ἐνώπιον κυρίου. [92] c, A and Jub. xxxiii. 1 Et abiit ad patrem suum Isaac. β, S¹ read ἀπόντος. g compresses this verse and first ten words of the next as follows: τοῦ πατρὸς γὰρ Ἰ. ἐν τῷ οἴκῳ μὴ παρόντως, εὗρον Β. μεθύονταν κ. κοιμωμένην, εἰσελθὼν ἔπρ. τὴν ἀ. μετ᾽ αὐτῆς. [93] α prefixes τοῦ. A trs. after πατρός μου. [94] h reads καί. [95] α, A. β, S¹ read ἡμῶν. [96] d reads Γάδ. See Gen. xxxv. 21. [97] e reads πλησίων. [98] c, be, Aᵇᵇ*ᶜᵈᵉᵍ. af read Εὐφρανθά. d Εὐφραθά. h Ὑφραθά. Aᵃ Ἀφραταί, S¹ Ἐφφρατά. [99] α, af, S¹ b reads οἴκου Βηθ. de καὶ Βηθλεέμ. Cf. Jub. xxxiii. 1, 'The tower of Eden of Ephrath,' and xxxii. 34, 'Ephrath that is Bethlehem.' Cf. Gen. xxxv. 19. A = ἐν Βενιαμείν. [100] α (h prefixing καί), A. abef, S¹ read B. ἦν μεθύουσα καὶ κοιμ. (+ καὶ f) ἀκάλυπτος (-ως ae, ἀκάλυφος b) κατέκειτο. d Βαλλὰν ἦν μεθύ. καὶ κοιμ. ἀκάληπτα κατέκοιτο. [101] α. β, A, S¹ om. [102] α. abdef, A, S¹ as in margin. [103] c. h reads μὴ αἰσθείσης αὐτῆς. β, A, S om. [104] a reads καὶ εὐθύς. d εὐθέως δὲ ἅμα τὸ πρᾶξαί με τὴν ἀνομίαν ταύτην. [105] adg, A read κυρίου. [106] d om. β, A, S¹ add Ἰακώβ which A trs. before τῷ πατρί. A adds ἣν ἔπραξα. [107] A adds Ἰακώβ. [108] α. abg, A, S¹ read as in margin. def ἐπένθη (sic). [109] bdeg, A(?). af read ἐμέ. h με. c om. [110] α. β–g, S¹ read ἀψά. αὐτῆς. g ἀψά. αὐτήν. A = ἀψά. Βάλλαν.

β-d,A,S[1]
προσέ-
χετε.

β, S[1] καὶ
ἀποπλα-
νώμενοι.

IV. Μὴ οὖν προσέχετε, ⌐τέκνα μου⌐[1], κάλλος[2] γυναικῶν[3], μηδὲ ἐννοεῖσθε[4] τὰς πράξεις αὐτῶν· ἀλλὰ πορεύεσθε ἐν[5] ἁπλότητι καρδίας, ἐν φόβῳ κυρίου[6], καὶ μοχθοῦντες[7] ἐν ἔργοις *καλοῖς, καὶ[8] *ἐν γράμμασι, καὶ ἐν τοῖς ποιμνίοις[9] ὑμῶν, ἕως οὗ[10] *ὁ κύριος δώῃ ὑμῖν[11] *σύζυγον, ἣν αὐτὸς θέλει[12], ἵνα μὴ πάθητε[13], ὡς κἀγώ[14]. 2. Ὅτι[15] ἄχρι[16] τελευτῆς

β-de, S[1]
Ἰακώβ.

τοῦ πατρός μου[17] οὐκ εἶχον[18] παρρησίαν ἀτενίσαι[19] εἰς *τὸ πρόσωπον αὐτοῦ[20], ἢ λαλῆσαί *τινι τῶν ἀδελφῶν[21] μου[22], διὰ[23]

β, S[1]
ἁμαρτίας.

τοὺς ὀνειδισμούς[24]. 3. *Καὶ ἕως[25] νῦν ἡ συνείδησίς[26] μου[27] συνέχει[28] με περὶ τῆς ἀσεβείας[29] μου. 4. Καίγε

β-dg, A,
S[1] ὅτι.

πολλὰ[30] *παρεκάλεσέν[31] με[32] ὁ πατήρ μου[33], καὶ[34] ηὔξατο περὶ ἐμοῦ *πρὸς κύριον[35], ἵνα παρέλθῃ[36] *ἀπ' ἐμοῦ[37] ἡ ὀργὴ κυρίου[38], καθὼς καὶ[39] ἔδειξέ[40] μοι[41] κύριος. Ἀπὸ δὲ[42] τότε

IV. [1] α, d (save that c om. μου). β–d, A, S om. [2] adef read κάλλει. [3] g reads γυναικός. d om. next five words. [4] c adds εἰς. [5] af om. [6] α, β–ag, A, S. ag read θεοῦ. [7] b reads μοχθῶντες. A = μοχθεῖτε. [8] c. But A = δικαιοσύνης καὶ ζητεῖτε and so, though conflate and loose, supports it. h reads καί. β, S καὶ (+ μὴ S[1]) ἀποπλανώμενοι. c om. next three words through hmt. (?) Here c καλοῖς καί = וְשָׂרִים which was corrupted into וְשָׂרִים = καὶ ἀποπλανώμενοι. [9] A = διδασκαλίαν καὶ τὸ ποιμενικὸν ἔργον. For γράμμασι S[1] reads μέθη. [10] α, dg. abef om. [11] h, β, A, S save that d om. ὁ before κύριος and de read δωει for δώῃ. c reads δοη ὑμῖν κύριος. For the nine words that follow c reads εἰς τὸ ἐπισκέψασθαι ἡμᾶς. [12] d reads συζύγους εἰς γυναῖκας ἃς αὐτὸς θελήσει. [13] c, β–e, A. e reads ἀπατηθηται. h απωθνητε. [14] A adds ἔπαθον. [15] α, β–bd, A. b, S[1] om. d reads λέγω γὰρ ὑμῖν ὅτι. [16] α, g add τῆς. [17] α, de[1]g, A. abe[2]f, S[1] read ἡμῶν. d adds Ἰακώβ. [18] g reads εἶχα. [19] d reads τοῦ ατενηναι. e ατενεισαι [20] α, d. abfg, S[1] read πρόσωπον Ἰακώβ. e τὸ πρόσ. τοῦ πατρὸς Ιρκ. A = τὸ πρόσ. Ιακ. τοῦ πατρός μου. [21] A = παρρησίᾳ τοῖς ἀδελφοῖς. [22] α, de, A. abf, S[1] om. [23] g reads περί. [24] h adds αὐτοῦ. A ἐμοῦ. [25] α, bfg, S[1]. d reads ἀλλὰ καὶ ἕως τοῦ. a καὶ ἕως τοῦ. A ὅτι ἕως. e om. together with next four words. [26] d reads σύνησις. [27] h om. [28] e reads συνέχειν. h om. [29] α. β, S[1] read as in margin. A may = either. [30] α. A = πολλάκις. β, S[1] om. [31] α, β–g. g reads ἠλέησεν. [32] β, A, S. α om. [33] A adds καὶ εἶπεν. g adds βλέπων με συνπεπτωκοτα. [34] α, dg. abef, A, S[1] read ὅτι. [35] α, β, A[b*d], S[1]. A[abceg] om. α om. next seven words through hmt. [36] g reads ἀπέλθῃ. [37] A = ἀπό σου but b psʦ is corrupt for jfʦʦ = ἀπ' ἐμοῦ. [38] eg read τοῦ θεοῦ, but g trs. it before ἡ ὀργή. [39] c, A[b*]. h, β, A[abcdeg], S[1] om. [40] e reads ἔδειξεν. d ἐμαλάκισε. [41] d reads με. c adds ὁ, g αὐτὸς ὁ. [42] α, A. β, S om. g adds καί before ἀπό. [43] α. This is at all events an ancient reading. But there are two other varieties.

*ἕως νῦν[43] παρεφυλαξάμην[44], καὶ οὐχ ἥμαρτον.   5. Διὰ τοῦτο[45] *τέκνα μου[46], *⌜λέγω ὑμῖν⌝[47], φυλάξατε[48] ⌜πάντα⌝[49] ὅσα ἐντέλλομαι[50] ὑμῖν, καὶ οὐ μὴ ἁμάρτητε[51].   6. *Βόθρος γάρ ἐστι ψυχῆς ἡ ἁμαρτία τῆς πορνείας[52], χωρίζουσα ἀπὸ[53] θεοῦ καὶ προσεγγίζουσα *τοῖς εἰδώλοις[54], ὅτι αὕτη *ἐστὶν ἡ[55] πλανῶσα τὸν νοῦν *καὶ τὴν διάνοιαν[56], καὶ κατάγει[57] νεανίσκους εἰς ᾅδην, οὐκ ἐν καιρῷ αὐτῶν.

7. Καὶ γὰρ πολλοὺς ἀπώλεσεν ἡ πορνεία· ὅτι κἂν *γέρων ᾖ τις[58], κἂν[59] εὐγενής, ⌜κἂν πλούσιος, κἂν πένης⌝[60], *ὀνειδισμὸν ἑαυτῷ φέρει παρὰ τοὺς υἱοὺς τῶν ἀνθρώπων καὶ †πρόσκομμα τῷ Βελίαρ[61].   8. *Ἠκούσατε γὰρ περὶ Ἰωσὴφ πῶς ἐφύλαξεν ἑαυτὸν ἀπὸ[62] γυναικός, καὶ τὰς ἐννοίας ἐκαθάρισεν[63] ἀπὸ πάσης[64] πορνείας, ⌜καὶ⌝[65] εὗρεν χάριν ἐνώπιον θεοῦ[66] καὶ ἀνθρώπων.   9. *Καὶ γὰρ[67] πολλὰ ἐποίησεν αὐτῷ ἡ Αἰγυπτία, καὶ μάγους προσεκάλεσέν[68] καὶ *φάρμακα αὐτῷ προσήνεγκε[69].

dg, A
μετα-
νοῶν.
β–g, A,
S¹ μου.
β, A, S¹
ὄλεθρος.
bdg, A, S¹
πορνεία.
de, A, S¹
ὄνειδος
ἑαυτὸν
ποιεῖ καὶ
γέλωτα
παρὰ τῷ
(τοῦ de)
B. καὶ
τοῖς υἱοῖς
τῶν ἀν-
θρώπων.
β, A, S¹

ἐπειδὴ γὰρ ἐφύλαξεν ἑαυτὸν Ἰωσὴφ ἀπὸ πάσης.   β, A, S¹ κυρίου.

aef ἕως ἐννοιῶν.   b νῦν.   dg, A μετανοῶν (A = ἐν μετανοίᾳ).   S¹ = οὖν. [44] c reads ἐφυλαξάμην.   A[abcdes] = καὶ ἐφυλαξάμην or καὶ παρεφυλ.   A[b*] = ἔζων καὶ ἐφυλ. or παρεφυλ.   [45] α adds οὖν.   [46] d trs. after ἐντέλλομαι ὑμῖν. g reads τεκνία μου.   [47] α. g reads παρακαλῶ ὑμᾶς.   β–g, A, S om.   [48] b reads φυλάξασθε.   [49] d trs. after ὅσα.   e, A om.   [50] e reads ἐνετειλάμην. [51] α, afg.   b, S¹ read ἁμαρτήσητε.   de αμαρτειτε (-ειται e).   [52] α. So also af (save that af read ἡ διὰ τῆς πορνείας for τῆς πορνείας).   bde¹g, S¹ read ὄλεθρος γὰρ ψυχῆς (d om.) ἐστιν (g ἐστὶ ψυχῆς) ἡ πορνεία.   A = ὄλεθρος (A[ab] τελευτὴ) γὰρ φθάσει ἐπὶ ψυχήν, καὶ ἡ πορνεία.   e² reads ὄλεθρος γὰρ ψυχῆς ἐστιν ἡ ἁμαρτία ἡ διὰ τῆς πορνείας and is thus a conflate text.   It is possible that βόθρος and ὄλεθρος may be different renderings of שחת.   [53] α, dg.   abef om.   [54] d reads τῷ Βελίαρ.   g εἰδώλοις.   [55] α, β–bg, A.   bg read ἐστί.   [56] g reads τῆς διανοίας.   [57] d reads κατάγουσα.   [58] α, d.   β–dg, S¹ read κἂν ᾖ τις γέρων. g εἴτις γέρων ὤν.   [59] α, d.   β–d read ἤ.   g adds εἴη after εὐγενής.   [60] α. β, A, S¹ om.   [61] α. af read ὀνειδισμὸν ἑαυτῷ ποιεῖ παρὰ τῷ (τὸν f) B. καὶ τοῖς υἱοῖς τῶν ἀνθ.   bg ὄνειδος αὐτὸν (αὐτῶν g) ποιεῖ καὶ γέλωτα παρὰ τῷ B. καὶ τοῖς υἱοῖς τῶν ἀνθ.   de, A, S read as in margin save that A[b*cdes] om. ἑαυτόν. πρόσκομμα = מוקש a corruption (?) of שחוק (or משחק) = γέλωτα.   [62] α (save that h adds τοῦ after περί).   β, A, S¹ read as in margin (save that for ἐπειδὴ γάρ A reads τοίνυν γάρ).   [63] af. c reads ἐκαθάρησεν.   b (g?) ἐκαθαίρισεν. de ἐκαθέρισεν.   h om.   [64] A[ab] om.   [65] α. β, A, S om.   [66] α. β, A, S¹ read as in margin.   [67] A[b*cdes] om.   [68] c. h, β read παρεκάλεσεν.   e adds καὶ φαρμακούς.   A[b] ἡ Αἰγυπτία περὶ Ἰωσήφ.   [69] α, β–de (save that h reads αὐτοῦ for αὐτῷ).   d reads αὐτῷ διάφορα επινεγκε πῦρ φίλτρον αὐτῆς διεγεῖραι τοῦτον βουλομένης.   e αὐτῷ φιλημάτων προσήνεγκεν.   g, A προσήνεγκεν αὐτῷ.

καὶ[70] οὐκ ἐδέξατο[71] τὸ διαβούλιον τῆς ψυχῆς αὐτοῦ[72] ἐπιθυμίαν
πονηράν.

β-d,
Αβ, S[1]
ὁρατοῦ
καί.

10. Διὰ τοῦτο[73] ὁ θεὸς τῶν πατέρων ὑμῶν[74] ἐρρύσατο
αὐτὸν ἀπὸ παντὸς πονηροῦ[75] κεκρυμμένου θανάτου.

β, Α, S[1]
κατισχύ-
σει.

11. Ἐὰν γὰρ μὴ κατισχύσει[76] ἡ πορνεία[77] *τὴν ἔννοιαν[78]
ὑμῶν[79], οὐδὲ ὁ[80] Βελίαρ *δύναται κατισχῦσαι[81] ὑμῶν[82].

β, S[1] ὅτι
μὴ ἔχου-
σαι.

V. Πονηραὶ ⌜γάρ⌝[1] εἰσιν αἱ γυναῖκες, τέκνα[2] μου, *καὶ ἐν

β, Α, S[1]
δυνάμεως
... κατα-
γωνίσα-
σθαι.

τῷ μὴ ἔχειν αὐτὰς[3] ἐξουσίαν *ἢ δύναμιν[4] ἐπὶ *τὸν ἄνδρα[5],
δολιεύονται[6] ἐν σχήμασιν[7] ὅπως[8] αὐτὸν[9] *πρὸς ἑαυτὰς[10]
ἐπισπάσονται[11].   2. Καὶ[12] ὃν[13] διὰ *τοῦ σχήματος[14] οὐκ
ἰσχύουσιν[15] καταγοητεύσασθαι[16], τοῦτον[17] δι᾿[18] ἀπάτης καταγωνίζονται[19].   3. ⌜Ὅτι⌝ καίγε[20] *περὶ αὐτῶν[21] εἶπέν[22]

---

[70] Α = ἀλλά. α adds αὐτός.   [71] h reads κατεδέξατο.   [72] h trs. before τῆς
ψυχῆς. α adds ἥ.   [73] α adds οὖν.   [74] c, h, Α, S[1] read ἡμῶν. β μου.   [75] α =
רע or רעי. This apparently was corrupted into רָאִי. Hence β, Α[b*cdeg],
S[1] which read ὁρατοῦ καί (g om.). d ἀοράτου. Α[a] = ἀνδρὸς ἀοράτου καί. Α[b]
ἀνδρὸς ἀπὸ ἐκείνου ὁρατοῦ καί. S[1] adds πονηροῦ and om. κεκρυμμένου.   [76] c,
defg. h, ab read κατισχύσῃ.   [77] Α = ἡ πονηρία.   [78] α, bef. a reads τῆς
ἐννοίας. d ἐν ταῖς ψυχαῖς. g, Α[b*ceg] τῆς καρδίας. Α[abd] = τὰς ἐννοίας.   [79] h,
β-ab. ab, S[1] om. c, Α[ab*d] read ἡμῶν. d ἡμῶν καὶ ἐν τῇ διανοίᾳ. Α[b] = τῶν
ἀνθρώπων.   [80] bg om.   [81] α. β, Α, S read κατισχύσει.   [82] Α = ἡμῶν.

V. [1] α. β, Α, S[1] om.   [2] g reads τεκνία.   [3] α, Α (save that for αὐτάς
c read αὐτούς and h αὐταῖς). β, S[1] read as in margin.   [4] Α[b*cdeg] om.
For ἐξουσίαν ... ἐπί g reads δυν. κ. ἐξουσίαν πρός.   [5] α. Α = ἄνδρας.
abefg, S[1] read τὸν ἄνθρωπον, d τῶν ἀνθρώπων.   [6] d reads δειλιεύονται.   [7] d
adds πάντα τρόπον ἐπινοούμεναι.   [8] α, d. β-d, S[1] read πῶς.   [9] α, β-d.
d, Α read αὐτούς.   [10] c, df. h, beg read πρὸς αὐτάς. a ἐπ᾿ αὐτάς.   [11] α,
β-fg. f reads ἐπισπάσωνται. g περισπάσονται. Α = ἰσχύσουσιν ἐπισπάσασθαι.
[12] h om.   [13] d reads ὧν τινων.   [14] α. β, Α, S[1] read δυνάμεως. α alone
gives the right sense. σχῆμα means 'anything that appeals to the senses'
in the text. Hence α may = הוד corrupted into הן or אן = β, Α, S[1].
[15] e Α[bb*cdeg]. c reads ἴσχνον. abfg, S[1] ἰσχύει. h, Α[a] ἰσχύσονται. d κατισχύ-
σωσι.   [16] c. h reads γοητεύσασθαι. β, Α καταγωνίσασθαι. It is noteworthy
that though Α = β here it uses a different word for the καταγων. following.
Possibly καταγοητεύασθαι = לנבל which may have been corrupted into
לכלה = καταγωνίσασθαι. But καταγοητεύσασθαι may be simply a corruption of καταγωνίσασθαι.   [17] d reads τούτων.   [18] d adds τῆς ματαίας καὶ
κενῆς.   [19] c, df, Α. abg, S[1] read καταγωνίζεται. h ἀγωνίσονται. e ἡττῶσιν.
[20] α. β-dg, S[1]. d reads καί. g γάρ. Α καί, which with next two words
it trs. after μοι.   [21] Α = περὶ τούτου.   [22] Α adds καὶ περὶ τούτου.
[23] d adds οὕτως εἰπών. g ἀκούσατε.   [24] g om. c adds καίγε.   [25] h om,

μοι ὁ ἄγγελος τοῦ Θεοῦ, καὶ ἐδίδαξέ με[23], ὅτι[24] αἱ[25] γυναῖκες
ἡττῶνται[26] *τῷ πνεύματι τῆς πορνείας[27] *ὑπὲρ τὸν ἄνδρα[28],
καὶ *ἐν καρδίᾳ[29] μηχανῶνται[30] *κατὰ τῶν ἀνθρώπων[31], καὶ[32]
*διὰ τῆς κοσμήσεως[33] πλανῶσιν ⸤αὐτῶν⸥[34] τὰς δια-   β, A, S¹
νοίας[35], *καὶ διὰ[36] τοῦ βλέμματος *τὸν ἰὸν[37] ἐνσπείρουσιν[38],   πρῶτον
καὶ τότε *τῷ ἔργῳ[39] αἰχμαλωτίζουσιν[40].   4. Οὐ γὰρ   τάς.
δύναται γυνὴ *ἄνδρα βιάσαι εἰς πρόσωπον ἀλλ' ἐν σχήμασι   β, A, S¹
πορνικοῖς τοῦτον πανουργεύεται[41].   5. *Λοιπὸν φεύγετε   ἄνθρω-
τέκνα μου τὴν πορνείαν[42], *καὶ προστάσσετε[43] ταῖς γυναιξὶν   πον βιά-
ὑμῶν[44]. καὶ ταῖς θυγατράσιν ⸤ὑμῶν⸥[45], ἵνα μὴ κοσμῶσι[46]   σασθαι.
τὰς[47] κεφαλὰς αὐτῶν[48] καὶ τὰς ὄψεις[49] *πρὸς ἀπάτην
διανοίας[50], ὅτι πᾶσα γυνὴ[51] δολιευομένη ἐν τούτοις εἰς κόλασιν[52]
αἰώνιον[53] τετήρηται[54].   6. Οὕτως γὰρ[55] ἔθελξαν τοὺς
Ἐγρηγόρους[56] ⸤τοὺς⸥[57] πρὸ τοῦ κατακλυσμοῦ· *ἐκεῖνοι γὰρ[58]   β, A, S¹
συνεχῶς[59] ὁρῶντες ⸤αὐτὰς⸥[60] ἐγένοντο[61] ⸤καὶ⸥[62] ἐν[63] ἐπιθυμίᾳ   κἀκεῖνοι.

[26] g reads πλέον ἡττ. A^b = πλέον. A^a om. S¹ = ἐμπίπτονται.   [27] α, abd,
A. e reads τῷ πάθει τῆς πορ. f τὸ πνεῦμα τῆς πονηρίας. g ἐν τῷ περὶ τῆς
πορνείας. S¹ = εἰς τὴν πορνείαν.   [28] α. abe²f, S¹ read ὑπὲρ τὸν ἄνθρωπον.
e¹ ὑπὲρ τῶν ἀνθρώπων. d, A ὑπὲρ τοὺς ἄνδρας. g reads as abef but puts
immediately after ἡττῶνται.   [29] g reads διὰ τοῦτο.   [30] e reads μηχανοῦνται.
h μηχανίζονται. S¹ = ἐγείρονται.   [31] α, bdef. a reads κ. τῶν ἀνθρώπων
πνευμάτων both in same hand with ἀνθ. above πν. g κ. τοῦ ἀνθρώπου.
A = κατὰ τῶν ἀνδρῶν. S¹ ἐπὶ τὸν ἄνδρα.   [32] c om.   [33] d reads διὰ
μὲν τ. κοσμ. A reads ꝗɯɾɼʒ ꝗɳꝑ (= πῶς τινας) which is corrupt for
ꝗɯɾɼɳɪʃɾ = διὰ τῆς κοσμήσεως.   [34] a reads αὐτόν. A om. β, A, S¹ add
πρῶτον which g trs. before αὐτῶν.   [35] a adds αἰχμαλωτίζουσαι.   [36] d
reads διὰ δέ. A = (+ καί, A^os) πρῶτον γὰρ διά.   [37] h reads τοῦ ἰοῦ.   [38] c²h,
beg, A, S. c¹(?), af read ἐνσπείρουσαι. d ἐπισπείρουσιν and omits rest of
verse.   [39] c, be, A, S¹. afg read τὸ ἔργον. h ἔργον.   [40] a om. e adds
αὐτούς.   [41] α (save that c reads πορνικῆς for πορνικοῖς). β, A, S¹ read as
in margin.   [42] α (save that h trs. φεύγ. after μου). β–g, A, S¹ read
φεύγ. οὖν τὴν πορ. τ. μου. So also g, save that it om. μου and trs. τέκνα
before τὴν πορ.   [43] d reads καὶ ἐντέλλεσθε. g προστάττετε δὲ καί.   [44] h
om. fg om. next four words.   [45] c, de. h, ab, A, S om.   [46] c. h reads
κοσμήσονται. β–e κοσμῶνται. e κοσμήσωσιν.   [47] h om.   [48] α, A. β, S¹
om.   [49] β, S¹ add αὐτῶν.   [50] α, β–b (save that d adds τῆς before διαν.),
A, S. b om.   [51] h adds μή.   [52] A^b add κακίστην.   [53] α. d reads
αἰωνίαν. β–d τοῦ αἰῶνος.   [54] h reads τηρίζονται.   [55] g om.   [56] b reads
Ἐγγρ.   [57] β, A, S om.   [58] α, d. β–d, A, S read κἀκεῖνοι.   [59] c trs.
after ὁρῶντες.   [60] h, β, S. c reads τὰς γυναῖκας. A om.   [61] α, β–e. e reads
ἐπεγίνετο. A = ἐγείροντο.   [62] α. β, A, S¹ om.   [63] eg om.   [64] A^bb*cdeg.

<table>
<tr><td>

α, β–g, S¹
ἀλλήλων.

β, A, S¹
ἀνθρώ-
πους.

β, A, S¹
εἰ θέλετε
καθαρεύ-
ειν τῇ
διανοίᾳ,
φυλά-
ξασθε.

h, β, S¹
πάσης
θηλείας.

β, S¹
ὄνειδος
τοῦ
Βελίαρ αἰώνιον.

</td><td>

αὐτῶν[64], καὶ συνέλαβον[65] τῇ διανοίᾳ *τὴν πρᾶξιν[66]· *μετε-σχηματίζοντο γὰρ[67] εἰς ἄνδρα[68] καὶ ἐν τῇ συνουσίᾳ τῶν ἀνδρῶν *αὐτῶν συνεφαίνοντο αὐταῖς[69].   7. *Κἀκεῖναι ⌐δὲ⌐[70] ἐπιθυμοῦσαι *τῇ διανοίᾳ τῆς φαντασίας[71] αὐτῶν ἔτεκον[72] γίγαντας. Ἐφαίνοντο γὰρ αὐταῖς[73] *οἱ Ἐγρήγοροι[74] *ἕως τοῦ οὐρανοῦ φθάνοντες[75].

    VI. Φυλάξατε[1] οὖν[2] ἀπὸ τῆς[3] πορνείας, καὶ *ἔστε καθα-ρεύοντες[4] τῇ διανοίᾳ· *φυλάξατε καὶ[5] *τὰς αἰσθήσεις ὑμῶν[6] ἀπὸ γυναικῶν[7].   2. Κἀκείνας[8] δὲ[9] ἐντέλλεσθε[10] μὴ συνδιάζειν[11] ἀνδράσιν[12], ἵνα καὶ αὐταὶ καθαρεύωσι[13] τῇ διανοίᾳ[14].   3. *Αἱ γὰρ συνεχεῖς συντυχίαι[15], κἂν μὴ πραχθῇ[16] τὸ ἀσέβημα, αὐταῖς[17] μέν ἐστι νόσος ἀνίατος[18], ἡμῖν[19] δὲ *εἰς ὄλεθρον Βελίαρ καὶ ὄνειδος αἰώνιον[20].   4. Ὅτι ἡ[21] πορνεία *οὔτε

</td></tr>
</table>

---

[64] g reads μετ᾽ αὐτῶν. α, β–g, S¹ ἀλλήλων (ἀλλήλοις e). Aᵃ om.   [65] d reads συλλαβόντες.   [66] g reads τῇ πράξει   [67] c.. h reads κατεσχηματίζοντο. β, A, S¹ καὶ (d om.) μετεσχηματίζοντο.   [68] α. β, A, S¹ read ἀνθρώπους.   [69] d reads τῶν συναφραινάντων αὐτοῖς.   [70] α. β–b, A, S¹ read κἀκεῖναι. b κἀκεῖνοι.   [71] c, af, A. be, S¹ τῇ δ. τὰς φαν. d τὰς φαν. g τὰς διανοίας καὶ φαν. h τῇ δ. καὶ φαντασίᾳ.   [72] e reads ἔτικτον.   [73] f reads αὐτοῖς. g om.   [74] b reads Ἐγγρήγορες. g adds ἐκεῖνοι.   [75] c, β–d, S¹. A = ὡς φθάνοντες εἰς οὐρανόν. For φθάν. d reads φαίνοντες. h φθάσοντας.

VI. [1] α. β–bg read φυλάξασθε. bg, S¹ φυλάσσεσθε.   [2] g, S¹ add τέκνα. h adds ἑαυτούς.   [3] g om.   [4] α (save that I have emended ἔσται into ἔστε). β–e, S¹ read εἰ θέλετε καθαρεύειν. e ἐὰν θέλεται καθαροὶ εἶναι. a adds ἐν.   [5] α. aef read φυλάξασθε. bd, S¹ φυλάσσετε. g φυλάσσεσθε.   [6] c, adf, Aᵇ*ᶜᵈᵉᵍ. h, beg, S¹ read τὰς αἰσθήσεις. Aᵃᵇ τὰς ψυχὰς ὑμῶν καὶ τὰς αἰσθ.   [7] c. A = πασῶν γυναικῶν. h, β, S¹ read πάσης (h om.) θηλείας (g φιλίας).   [8] α, f. β–f read κἀκείναις.   [9] d om.   [10] α, g. β–eg, S¹ read ἐντείλασθε. e παραγγέλλεται.   [11] α, de. a reads συνδοιάζειν. bfg συνδυάζειν. Aᵃᵇ read [Armenian]. Aᵇ*ᶜᵈ [Armenian] = γυμνοῦσθαι which are corrupt possibly for [Armenian] = συνδυάζειν. Aᵉⁱᵍ read [Armenian] = ἐνδοιάζειν. S¹ reads μετὰ ἀνθρώπων for μὴ ... ἀνδράσιν.   [12] α. A = ἀνδράσιν αὐτῶν. β reads ἀνθρώποις.   [13] c, abg. d reads καθαρεύουσαι. e καθαραί εἰσιν. h, f καθαρεύουσιν.   [14] d adds εἰρήνην ἔχουσιν.   [15] α, β–de. So d but om. συνεχεῖς. e reads ἐν γὰρ ταῖς συνεχεῖς (sic) συντυχίαις.   [16] h, β–g, A, S¹. c reads δεχθῇ. g προελθει.   [17] g reads αὐτοῖς.   [18] Aᵇ* = μυσαρά. Other Armenian MSS. = μεγάλη.   [19] c, bdf, Aᵃᵇ, S¹. h, aeg, Aᵇ*ᶜᵈᵉfᵍ read ὑμῖν.   [20] α (save that c reads ὄλεθρος τῷ). β, S¹ read as in margin, save that d adds παρά before τοῦ. A = ὄνειδος μέγα.   [21] c reads πᾶσα.   [22] A reads [Armenian] (= καὶ οὐδέν) which is corrupt for [Armenian] = οὔτε σύνεσιν

σύνεσιν οὔτε[22] †εὐσέβειαν[23] ἔχει ἐν ἑαυτῇ ˙καὶ[24] πᾶς[25] ζῆλος κατοικεῖ[26] ἐν τῇ ἐπιθυμίᾳ αὐτῆς[27].

5. Διὰ τοῦτο ⌜οὖν λέγω ὑμῖν⌝[28] ζηλώσετε[29] ⌜τοὺς υἱοὺς τοῦ[30] Λευί⌝ καὶ ζητήσετε[31] ὑψωθῆναι ὑπὲρ αὐτούς[32], ἀλλ᾽[33] οὐ ἰσχύσετε[34].   6. Ὁ γὰρ Θεὸς[35] ποιήσει[36] τὴν ἐκδίκησιν[37] αὐτῶν ⌜*ὑμεῖς δὲ ἀποθανεῖτε[38] θανάτῳ πονηρῷ⌝.   7. Τῷ γὰρ[39] Λευὶ ἔδωκεν *ὁ Θεὸς[40] τὴν ἀρχὴν[41] [καὶ τῷ Ἰούδα *μετ᾽ αὐτοῦ[42], *ἐμοὶ δὲ[43] καὶ *τῷ Δὰν[44] καὶ τῷ[45] Ἰωσήφ[46], *τοῦ εἶναι εἰς[47] ἄρχοντας].   8. Διὰ τοῦτο[48] ἐντέλλομαι ὑμῖν ἀκούειν τοῦ[49] Λευί, *ὅτι αὐτὸς γνώσεται[50] νόμον θεοῦ[51], καὶ *διαστελεῖ εἰς[52] κρίσιν καὶ θυσιάσει[53] ὑπὲρ τοῦ[54] Ἰσραὴλ μέχρι τελειώσεως χρόνων[55] *ἀρχιερεὺς χριστός[56], ὃν[57] εἶπεν[58] ὁ[59] Κύριος.

Marginal readings (right column): β–d, A, S¹ · διὰ τοῦτο. · β δυνήσεσθε. · β, A, S κυρίου. · h, A διατελεῖ. · β, A, S παντός.

οὔτε.   [23] = מסירות which may be corrupt for חבמה, or εὐσέβειαν is corrupt for εὐλάβειαν as in Mic. vii. 2; Sir. xi. 17.   [24] h reads ἀλλά. [25] c reads πρός.   [26] f reads οἰκεῖ.   [27] α, β, Aᵇ*, S¹. Aᵃᵇᶜᵈᵉᵍ = αὐτῶν. [28] α (but h reads δέ for οὖν). d reads οἶδα ὅτι. A καὶ ὑμεῖς. β–d, A, S¹ om.   [29] a, S¹. α, bg, A read ζηλώσατε. d ζηλοῦτε. ef ζηλώσητε.   [30] α. β om. [31] afg, S¹. h, be, A read ζητήσατε. c, d ζητεῖτε.   [32] β, A. α reads αὐτῶν. [33] A adds κἂν ζητήσητε.   [34] Em. from c ἰσχύσητε. h ἰσχύσατε. adeg read δυνήσεσθε. b δυνήσασθε. f δυνήσησθε. A adds ὑπὲρ αὐτούς.   [35] g reads κύριος.   [36] β. α reads ποιεῖ. A = ἐποίησε.   [37] A = ἐκλογὴν ἐξ.   [38] α. β, S¹ read καὶ ἀποθανεῖσθε (+ ὑμεῖς g). A om. together with next two words.   [39] A = δέ.   [40] α, ae. bg, S¹ read κύριος. f ὁ κύριος. d κύριος ὁ θεός.   [41] d reads χάριν. The rest of the verse is spurious.   [42] α, ef. ag, A read μετ᾽ αὐτόν (which A trs. before τῷ Ἰ.). b μετ᾽ αὐτῶν. d μετ᾽ αὐτῷ. S¹ om.   [43] α, d. β–d read κἀμοί. d om. next three words.   [44] h. c reads τῷ Γάδ. β–d Δάν.   [45] c, d. h, β–d om.   [46] d adds καὶ τῷ Δάν.   [47] α, β–b. b reads τοῦ εἶναι ἐπί. Aᵃᵇᵇ*ᶜᵈ = μετ᾽ αὐτούς. So also Aᵉˢ save that they prefix καί.   [48] c adds οὖν.   [49] d reads τῷ.   [50] h reads ὅταν διαγνώσατε. For γνώσεται A reads γνωρίσει. S² συνίησι.   [51] α. β, A, S as in margin.   [52] c, β–bg (save that d om. εἰς), S. Here διαστελεῖ (= יזהיר) εἰς = 'he will admonish in respect of judgement.' h, g, A read διατελεῖ εἰς 'will fulfil in respect of.' b διαστέλλει εἰς. All these readings appear unsatisfactory. Perhaps δια(σ)τελεῖ εἰς is corrupt for διατελέσει. Hence διατελέσει κρίσιν = יעשה משפט. In other words the civil authority of Levi (i.e. of the Maccabees) would be referred to here. Possibly διαστελεῖ may be used (uniquely?) as διατελεῖται 'he will issue ordinances.' A adds καὶ εἰς δίκας.   [53] α (c θυσιαση), e, A, S². af reads θυμιάσει. b, S¹ θυσίας. d θυσίαν. g θύσει.   [54] α. β, A, S read as in margin.   [55] d reads χρόνον.   [56] Emended from h which reads ἀρχιερεὺς χριστοῦ. c, β, S read ἀρχιερέως χριστοῦ (d κυρίου). Aᵇᵇ*ᶜᵈᵉˢ = τοῦ εἶναι ἱερέα τῆς διαθήκης χριστοῦ (Aˢ κήρυκος). Aˢ = τοῦ εἶναι *c* λαλεῖν. 9. Ὁρκῶ ὑμᾶς τὸν Θεὸν τοῦ οὐρανοῦ[60] τοῦ[61] ποιεῖν[62] ἀλήθειαν *ἕκαστος πρὸς τὸν πλησίον αὐτοῦ[63] *καὶ ἀγάπην ἔχειν ἕκαστος πρὸς τὸν ἀδελφὸν αὐτοῦ[64].   10. Καὶ πρὸς τὸν[65] Λευὶ ἐγγίσατε[66] ἐν ταπεινώσει καρδίας ⌜ὑμῶν⌝[67], ἵνα *δέξησθε εὐλογίαν[68] ἐκ τοῦ[69] στόματος αὐτοῦ.   11. Αὐτὸς γὰρ[70] εὐλογήσει τὸν Ἰσραὴλ καὶ τὸν Ἰούδαν· *ὅτι ἐν αὐτῷ[71]

β-f, S[1] πάντων τῶν λαῶν.

ἐξελέξατο Κύριος[72] βασιλεύειν[73] ἐνώπιον[74] *παντὸς τοῦ λαοῦ[75].   12. Καὶ προσκυνήσατε[76] *τὸ σπέρμα[77] αὐτοῦ, ὅτι[78] ὑπὲρ ὑμῶν[79] ἀποθανεῖται[80] ἐν πολέμοις ὁρατοῖς καὶ[81] ἀοράτοις. καὶ *ἐν ὑμῖν ἔσται[82] *βασιλεὺς αἰώνιος[83].

VII. *Καὶ ἀπέθανε Ῥουβίμ, ἐντειλάμενος τοῖς υἱοῖς αὐτοῦ ταῦτα[1].   2. *Καὶ ἔθεντο[2] αὐτὸν ἐν σορῷ, *ἕως

ἱερέα τῆς διαθήκης. I take it that the original text referred to Ps. cx. 4 or to the thought therein implied which was current at the time. [57] *ef* read ὦν. [58] A[a] add ἐκείνῳ. [59] α, *f*, A[bb*cdeg]. β-f, A[a], S om. [60] *c* adds καὶ τῆς γῆς. [61] α. β om. [62] *h*. β, S read ποιῆσαι. *c* λαλεῖν, a reading possibly due to Zech. viii. 16 (cf. Eph. iv. 25). A = περιπατῆσαι ἀληθείᾳ. [63] α, *bdef* (save that *e* reads μετὰ τοῦ πλ.), A, S[1]. *ag* read ἕκαστον πλησίον αὐτοῦ. [64] α, *aef* (save that *aef* om. ἔχειν, *af* read ἕκαστον and *e* μετὰ τοῦ ἀδελφοῦ). *dg* read ἀγάπην ἐχέτω (+ ὁμοίως ἕκαστος πρὸς τ. ἀδ. αὐτοῦ *g*). *b*, S[1] om. entire clause. A = ἀγάπην ἔχετε πρὸς τοὺς ἀδελφοὺς ὑμῶν. [65] A[b] reads τοὺς υἱούς. [66] *d* trs. to beginning of clause and for καί reads δὲ καί. [67] α, *g*. *d* reads ἡμῶν. β-dg, A, S om. [68] *h* reads δείξητε ἐν λόγῳ (?) [69] *aef* om. [70] *d* om. [71] *d* reads διότι αὐτόν. [72] *h* prefixes ὁ. [73] α, *aef*. *bdg*, S[1] read βασιλεῦσαι. [74] *c*. *h* reads ἐπί. β, S[1] om. [75] α (save that *h* om. τοῦ), A. β-f, S[1] read πάντων (+ τῶν *bg*, S) λαῶν. *f* πάντα τὸν λαόν. [76] *h*, *b*, S. *aef* read προσκυνήσετε. *c* προσκυνήσειται. *d* προσκυνῆσαι. *g* προσκυνήσητε. A = text or *aef*. [77] *c*, β-bd. *h*, *bd* read τῷ σπέρματι. [78] *d* om. next three words. [79] *h*, *ef*, A[ab*cdeg], S[1]. *c*, *abg*, A[b] read ἡμῶν. *d* om. [80] α, β-d, A[b], S[1]. A[ab*cdeg] read ἀποθανοῦνται. *d* om. [81] *d* reads τε καί. [82] α. β, S[1] read ἔσται ἐν ὑμῖν (ἡμῖν *d*). A = ἔσονται ἐν ὑμῖν. [83] α, *d*. β-d, S[1] read β. αἰώνων. A = βασιλεῖς αἰώνιοι. Here S makes a large Christian addition. See Appendices.

VII. [1] α, *af*, A. So also *be* save that they omit ταῦτα. *dg* read ταῦτα (καὶ *g*) ἐντειλάμενος Ῥουβὶμ τοῖς υἱοῖς αὐτοῦ ἐτελεύτησε (ἀπέθανε *g*), and add πρεσβύτης καὶ πληρις (sic) ἡμερῶν, ὑπάρχων ἐτῶν ρκε. S[1] = καὶ οὕτως εἰπὼν ἀπέθανε Ῥ. ὁ πρῶτος τοῦ Ἰ. υἱός, καὶ ἔζησε ἔτη ρκε΄. S[2] ταῦτα λέξας ἀπέθανε ὁ Ῥ. ὁ πρωτόγονος τοῦ Ἰ. ἔζη δὲ 125 ἔτη καὶ ἀπέθανε. [2] *d* reads κατέθετο δέ [3] *h*, *bef*, A, S. *c* reads καί. *ad* ἕως ὅτου (*d* οὗ). *g* ἕως. [4] *c* reads ἐξενέγκοντες. *g* ἐξενέγκαντες. [5] α, *d*, A. β-d, S[1] om. [6] *e* reads ἐν σορῷ Χ. καί. A om. [7] *g* om. [8] β-e, A, S[1] add τῷ διπλῷ, *e* τὸ διπλοῦν. [9] *h*.

ὅτε[3] ἀνενέγκαντες[4] αὐτὸν ἐξ Αἰγύπτου ἔθαψαν αὐτὸν[5] ⌜ἐν
Χεβρών⌝[6], ἐν τῷ[7] σπηλαίῳ[8] *ὅπου ὁ πατὴρ αὐτοῦ[9].

Διαθήκη Συμεὼν τοῦ δευτέρου υἱοῦ Ἰακὼβ καὶ Λίας [1].

I. *Ἀντίγραφον λόγων[2] Συμεών, ἃ[3] ἐλάλησε τοῖς υἱοῖς
αὐτοῦ[4], *πρὸ τοῦ ἀποθανεῖν[5] αὐτὸν[6] *ἐν ἑκατοστῷ εἰκοστῷ
ἔτει[7] τῆς ζωῆς αὐτοῦ[8] *ἐν ᾧ χρόνῳ[9] ἀπέθανεν Ἰωσὴφ ⌜ὁ ἀδελφὸς
αὐτοῦ⌝[10]. 2. *Ἀρρωστοῦντος τοῦ Συμεὼν ἦλθον ἐπισκέψασθαι αὐτὸν οἱ υἱοὶ αὐτοῦ[11] καὶ[12] ἐνισχύσας ἐκάθισε[13], καὶ
κατεφίλησεν[14] αὐτοὺς καὶ εἶπεν[15].

II. Ἀκούσατε[1], *τέκνα μου[2], Συμεὼν τοῦ πατρὸς ὑμῶν
⌜καὶ ἀναγγελῶ ὑμῖν⌝[3] ὅσα ἔχω *ἐν τῇ καρδίᾳ μου[4].

af. So practically c μετὰ τοῦ πατρὸς αὐτοῦ. be read ὅπου οἱ πατέρες αὐτοῦ.
g, A ὅπου οἱ πατέρες αὐτῶν. d ὅπου καὶ οἱ πατ. αὐτοῦ κατετέθησαν. S¹ = τοῦ
πατρὸς αὐτοῦ. f adds Ῥουβὴν υἱὸς Ἰακὼβ α΄ υἱὸς Λίας α΄ ἔζησεν ἔτη ρκε. See
note 1 for like addition in S.

I. [1] α (save that h adds τοῦ before Ἰακώβ). a reads Συμεών. bfg, A¹ᵍ,
S¹ read διαθ. Συμ. β (f om.) περὶ φθόνου (φθόνον f) d is conflate διαθ.
Συμ. υἱοῦ Ἰακὼβ καὶ Λίας δευτέρ. περὶ φθόνου: also e διαθ. Συμ. περὶ φθόνον·
Συμεὼν υἱὸς Ἰακὼβ καὶ Λίας β΄. Aᵇᵇʰ = διαθ. Συμ. υἱοῦ Ἰακώβ, υἱοῦ Ἰσαάκ, υἱοῦ
Ἀβραάμ. Aᵇ*ᶜᵈ διαθ. Συμ. [2] h, abfg, S¹. c reads διαθήκη. de, Aᵃᵇ ἀντίγραφον διαθήκης. Aᵇ*ᶜᵈᵉᵍ ἀντίγ. λόγων διαθήκης. [3] α, bfg. a reads ὧν. de ὅσα.
[4] α, d om. next ten words through hmt. [5] β–bd, Aᵇ*ᶜᵈᵉᶠᵍ. b reads πρὸ
τοῦ θανεῖν. Aᵇᵇʰ = ὅτε ἔμελλε ἀποθανεῖν. [6] af om. [7] abef (save that be
om. ἐν), Aᵇ*ᶜᵈ. g, Aᵃᵇᵉᶠᵍ, S¹ read ἐν τῷ ἑκατοστῷ ἔτει καὶ κε΄ (Aᵉᵍ κζ΄). [8] Aᵃᵇ
add καὶ δευτέρῳ ἔτει. [9] α. abdf, A, S¹ read ἐν ᾧ ἔτει. e ἐν ἔτη (sic) ὅ.
g om. together with next verse. [10] α, d. β–d, A, S¹ om. [11] α, af,
save that h, af om. τοῦ and f reads ἀρρωστοῦντι. be, S¹ read ἦλθον γὰρ
ἐπισκέψασθαι αὐτὸν ἀρρωστοῦντα οἱ υἱοὶ αὐτοῦ (b om. οἱ . . . αὐτοῦ). Aᵇᵇʰ =
ἦλθον οἱ υἱοὶ αὐτοῦ ἐπισκ. αὐτὸν ἀρρωσ. and so also Aᶜᵈᵉᶠᵍ save that they om.
οἱ υἱ. αὐτοῦ. Aᵇ* = καὶ ἐλθόντες συνήχθησαν οἱ υἱ. αὐτοῦ ἐπισκ. αὐτόν. d and
g give a third form of text. d reads ἀρρωστήσας προσκαλεσάμενος τοὺς υἱοὺς
αὐτοῦ. g ἀρωστήσας (sic) ἐκάλεσεν αὐτούς. Cf. S² ἐκάλεσεν υἱούς. S¹ = οἱ
γὰρ υἱοὶ ἦλθον ἐπισκέψασθαι αὐτόν. [12] A adds Συμεών. g om. the next six
words. [13] α, ef read ἐκάθησε. [14] h reads καταφιλήσας and om. following
καί. [15] g reads φησί. b, Aᵇ*, S¹ add αὐτοῖς.

II. [1] c, β–d, Aᵉᶠᵍ. d om. h, Aᵇᵇ*ᶜᵈ add μου. [2] α, d, A. g reads τεκνία
μου. β–dg, S¹ read τέκνα. √β–e, A⁻ᵇ, S¹ add ἀκούσατε. [3] α. β, S¹ om.
For Aᵃᵇ see next note. [4] e reads ἐπὶ καρδίας μου. d adds κρυπτά. Aᵃᵇ

2. Ἐγὼ ἐγεννήθην ἐξ Ἰακὼβ *υἱὸς δεύτερος τῷ πατρί
μου[5],
*καὶ Λία[6] ἡ μήτηρ μου ἐκάλεσέ με[7] Συμεῶνα[8],
ὅτι[9] ἤκουσε Κύριος τῆς δεήσεως αὐτῆς[10].

3. *Δυνατὸς γὰρ ἐγενόμην[11] σφόδρα
οὐκ ἐδειλίασα[12] πρᾶξιν[13]
οὐδὲ ἐφοβήθην *ἀπὸ παντὸς πράγματος[14].

4. Ἡ γὰρ καρδία μου ἦν σκληρά,
καὶ *τὰ ἥπατά[15] μου ἀκίνητα
καὶ τὰ σπλάγχνα μου ἀσυμπαθῆ[16].

5. *Ἐπειδὴ καὶ[17] ἡ ἀνδρεία[18] ἀπὸ[19] ὑψίστου δίδοται[20]
τοῖς[21] ἀνθρώποις, ἐν ψυχαῖς καὶ[22] σώμασιν. 6. *Ἐν γὰρ
τῷ καιρῷ τῆς νεότητός μου πολλὰ[23] ἐζήλωσα[24] τὸν[25] Ἰωσήφ,
ὅτι[26] *ἠγάπα αὐτὸν ὁ πατήρ μου[27] ⌈παρὰ πάντας⌉[28]. 7.
καὶ[29] ἐστήριξα[30] ἐπ᾽[31] αὐτὸν τὰ ἥπατά μου ὥστε[32] ἀνελεῖν
αὐτόν, *ὅτι ὁ ἄρχων[33] τῆς πλάνης καὶ[34] τὸ πνεῦμα τοῦ ζήλου[35]
ἐτύφλωσέ μου τὸν νοῦν, *μὴ προσέχειν[36] *αὐτῷ ὡς ἀδελφῷ[37],
μηδὲ[38] φείσασθαι *τῷ πατρί μου Ἰακώβ[39]. 8. Ἀλλ᾽ ὁ

bdg, A,
S[1] καὶ ἐν
τῷ καιρῷ
ἐκείνῳ.

β-a, S[1]
ἡμῶν.

β, A, S
ἀποστεί-
λας.

add ἀναγγέλλειν ὑμῖν. A[b*] λέγειν ὑμῖν. A[cdefg] om. See preceding note.
[5] c. h reads δεύτ. υἱὸς τοῦ πατρός μου. β, A, S[1] read τοῦ πατρός μου υἱὸς δεύτ.
(δεύτ. υἱός e, A[b*cd]). [6] ag read καί. d Λία τοίνυν. [7] A[abb*] τὸ ὄνομά μου.
[8] h, ag read Συμεών. [9] A[ab] = καί. [10] A[ab] = τῆς μητρός μου. [11] α. β,
A[b*cdefg], S[1] read δυν. ἐγενόμην. A[ab] = καὶ ἐγενόμην δυν. [12] d adds πᾶσαν.
[13] e reads πρᾶξαι. [14] S[1] = στάσιν. [15] A[ab] = ἡ κοιλία. [16] e reads
ἀσυμπάθητα. [17] α. β reads ὅτι καί. A = καὶ ὅτι. [18] h adds μου.
[19] d reads παρά. g ἕως. [20] α, β-abg (c, d giving the form διδωται). abg,
A, S read δέδοται. [21] e reads τοῖς υἱοῖς τῶν. A = πᾶσιν. [22] β, S add ἐν.
[23] α. aef read ἐν τῷ καιρῷ οὖν ἐκείνῳ τῆς νεότητος ἐν ᾧ. bdg, A, S[1] καὶ (+ ἐγὼ A)
ἐν τῷ καιρῷ ἐκείνῳ. [24] h reads ἐζημίωσα? [25] h om. bd read τῷ. [26] d
reads ἐν φθόνῳ διότι. [27] α, A. β-a, S[1] read ἠγάπα αὐτ. ὁ πατὴρ ἡμῶν.
a ἠγαπᾶτο αὐτὸς τῷ πατρί. [28] α. β, A, S[1] om. [29] A[abefg] om. [30] α, af.
be read ἐστήρισα. d ἐσκλήρυνα. g ἔστησα. [31] c om. [32] α. β reads τοῦ.
[33] d reads ὁ γὰρ ἄρχων. For ἄρχων A[b*cdefg] read ἄγγελος. [34] α. g om.
β-dg, S read ἀποστείλας. d Σατὰν ἀποστείλας. A[ab] = ἀπεστάλη ἐπὶ ἐμὲ καί.
A[b] ἐκίνησέ με εἰς ζῆλον καί. A[rdefg] ἀπέστειλε τὸ πνεῦμα τοῦ ζήλου καί. [35] ef
read ζήλους. [36] d reads τοῦ μὴ προσ. A[abbcdef] = μὴ ἀφείς (+ με A[cd]) προσ.
A[b*] = καὶ μὴ ἀφιέναι προσ. A[b] καὶ οὐκ ἠφίει προσ. [37] g reads αὐτὸν ὡς
ἀδελφόν and om. rest of verse. [38] α, d. β-d A, S[1] read καὶ μή. [39] α,
A[ab]. abef, A[hb*cdes], S[1] read Ἰακ. τοῦ π. μου. d Ἰακ. τοῦ π. ἡμῶν. A[abb] add
γηράσκοντος. [40] dg om. next four words through hmt. For next word
A[b*cdefg] read αὐτῶν. [41] A[abh] om. [42] S[2] reads τοῦ πατρός. [43] α. abefg,

θεὸς[40] αὐτοῦ καὶ[41] ὁ θεὸς *τῶν πατέρων[42] ἡμῶν[43] *ἀπέστειλε τὸν ἄγγελον αὐτοῦ καὶ[44] ἐρρύσατο[45] αὐτὸν ἐκ τῶν χειρῶν μου[46]. 9. Ὡς γὰρ[47] ἐγὼ ἐπορεύθην[48] *ἐν Σικίμοις[49] ἐνέγκαι[50] ἄλειμμα[51] τοῖς ποιμνίοις[52] καὶ 'Ρουβὶμ[53] εἰς[54] Δοθαείμ[55], ὅπου[56] τὰ ἐγχρῄζοντα[57] ἡμῖν[58] καὶ πᾶσα[59] ἡ ἀπόθεσις ἦν[60], Ἰούδας[61] ὁ ἀδελφός μου[62] ἐπώλησεν αὐτὸν[63] τοῖς Ἰσμαηλίταις. 10. Καὶ *ὁ 'Ρουβὶμ ἀκούσας ταῦτα[64] ἐλυπήθη[65]. ἤθελε[66] γὰρ αὐτὸν[67] ἀπαγαγεῖν[68] πρὸς τὸν πατέρα[69]. 11. Ἐγὼ δὲ[70] *ταῦτα ἀκούσας[71] ὠργίσθην ἐπὶ[72] τὸν[73] Ἰούδαν[74] ⌈σφόδρα⌉[75], ὅτι[76] ζῶντα αὐτὸν ἀπέλυσεν· καὶ *ἐποίησα μῆνας πέντε ὀργιζόμενος ἐπ' αὐτόν[77]. 12. Καίγε συνεπόδισέ με *ὁ Κύριος[78] καὶ ἐκώλυσεν δρᾶσιν[79] χειρῶν ⌈ἀπ' ἐμοῦ⌉[80]. *ὅτι ἡ χείρ μου ἡ δεξιὰ ἡμίξηρος γέγονεν ἐπὶ ἡμέρας ἑπτά[81].

Marginal notes:
β-d, A[abh], S[1] αὐτοῦ.
β, A, S[1] ἡμῶν.
β, A, S[1] ἐλθὼν 'Ρουβήμ.
β-af, S[1] διασῶσαι.
β, A[b*cdefg], S[1] ὠργίσθην.

A[abh], S[1] read αὐτοῦ. A[b*cdefg] αὐτῶν. d, S[2] μου. A[abh] add Ἰακώβ, Ἰσαὰκ καὶ Ἀβραάμ (Ἀ., Ἰ. καὶ Ἰακ. A[b]). [44] α, A. abefg, S[1] read ἀποστειλας τ. ἀγγ. αὐτοῦ. d, S[2] om. [45] a om. [46] a adds ἐξείλατο. [47] h reads καί. A = οὖν. [48] e reads ἀπῆλθον. [49] be. h, adf read ἐν Σικήμοις. g εἰς Σίκημον. c om. [50] β (save that g reads ἐνεγκεῖν), A. c reads ενεγκε. h ἤνεγκα. [51] d reads ἀλήμματα. A[abh] = φάρμακον but A[b*cdef] agree with text. [52] A[abh] = τοῖς προβάτοις ποιμνίων ἡμῶν. [53] α, d. β-d reads 'Ρουβήμ. Slightly corrupt in A[ah]. [54] c reads καί. h om. [55] ab, A[b]. c reads Δωδαείμ. d Δοδαιν. eg Δοθεμ. f Δοθαημ. h om. A[b*cdefg] = αὐλὴν ἡμῶν, but A[abh] agrees with text. [56] c reads ἤνεγκε. de, A add ἦν. [57] β-d. d read χρεωδη. α reads χρήζοντα. g adds ἦν. [58] d reads ἡμῶν, [59] e om. [60] α. A[b*cdefg] read ἡμῶν. β om. [61] c, f, A[b*cd] add δέ. [62] α. β, A, S[1] read ἡμῶν. [63] A[ab] = Ἰωσήφ. [64] c. h is conflate ἐλθὼν 'Ρουβὶμ καὶ ἀκούσας ταῦτα. β, A[b*cd], S[1] ἐλθὼν 'Ρουβήμ (Ρουβίμ d). A[ab] = ἦλθε 'Ρ. ὁ ἀδελφὸς ἡμῶν καί. d adds καὶ μὴ εὑρὼν αὐτόν. [65] dg add σφόδρα. [66] e reads ἦλθεν. [67] h om. [68] c, A[b*cdef]. h, af read διασωθῆναι. bdeg, S[1] διασῶσαι. A[ab] conflate = διασῶσαι καὶ ἀπαγαγεῖν. [69] d, A[b*cdefg] add αὐτοῦ, [70] g reads γάρ. [71] α. A[abh] = ἐλθών. β, A[b*cdefg] om. [72] be read πρός. [73] def om. [74] A[ab] read αὐτόν. A[b*cdeg] Δάν. [75] α. β, A, S[1] om. [76] d reads διότι. [77] α, β (save that for ἐπ' αὐτόν abdef read αὐτῷ, g αὐτόν). A[ab] = οὕτως ὠργίσθην ἐπ' αὐτὸν μῆν. πέντε. A[b*cdeg] καὶ ἦν ἐπ' αὐτὸν ὀργιζόμενος (A[fg] om.) μ. π. e, A[b*cdef] add ἐπὶ τῷ λόγῳ τούτῳ, g ἐπὶ τοῦτο. d περὶ τούτου διότι ἐβουλόμην ἐγὼ ἀποκτεῖναι αὐτόν. [78] α. adef, A read κύριος. bg, S ὁ θεός. [79] A[b] = 'efficacy.' A[ah] κακίαν. A[b*cdefg] = 'robbery' (as if from δράσσομαι). [80] β trs. before δρᾶσιν against a. A om. d adds λέγω γὰρ ὑμῖν before ὅτι. [81] α. bdg support text, save that bg read ἦν and d ἐγένετο for γέγονεν. aef, A[b*cdefg], S[1] also support text, save that they read ἦν for γέγ. (which e trs. before ἡμίξ.) and ξ' (ἑξήκοντα f) for ζ', while A[b*cdefg], S[1] read ξηρά,

13. Καὶ ἔγνων, τέκνα[82], ὅτι *περὶ Ἰωσὴφ[83] *τοῦτό μοι συνέβη[84]. καὶ[85] μετανοήσας ἔκλαυσα[86] καὶ[87] ηὐξάμην *Κυρίῳ τῷ Θεῷ[88] ἵνα[89] *ἀποκατασταθῇ ἡ χείρ μου[90] καὶ[91] ἀποσχῶ[92] ἀπὸ *παντὸς μολυσμοῦ καὶ φθόνου[93] ⌜καὶ ἀπὸ πάσης ἀφροσύνης⌝.   14. Ἔγνων[94] γὰρ ὅτι πονηρὸν πρᾶγμα ἐνεθυμήθην ἐνώπιον κυρίου[95] καὶ[96] *Ἰακὼβ τοῦ πατρός μου[97] *διὰ Ἰωσὴφ[98] *τὸν ἀδελφόν μου, φθονήσας αὐτῷ[99].

III. Καὶ νῦν, τέκνα[1] μου[2] ⌜ἀκούσατέ μου καὶ⌝[3] φυλάξασθε[4] ἀπὸ *τοῦ πνεύματος[5] τῆς πλάνης καὶ τοῦ φθόνου.   2. Καὶ γὰρ ὁ φθόνος κυριεύει *πάσης τῆς διανοίας τοῦ ἀνθρώπου[6] καὶ οὐκ ἀφίησιν[7] αὐτὸν ⌜οὔτε φαγεῖν, οὔτε πιεῖν, οὔτε⌝ ποιῆσαί τι[8] ἀγαθόν.   3. Ἀλλὰ[9] *πάντοτε ὑποβάλλει[10] ἀνελεῖν[11] τὸν φθονούμενον· *καὶ ὁ μὲν φθονούμενος πάντοτε ἀνθεῖ, ὁ δὲ φθονῶν μαραίνεται[12].   4. Δύο ⌜οὖν⌝[13] ἔτη[14] *ἐν φόβῳ

β–bd κυρίῳ ἵνα ἀποκατασταθῶ.

β, A, S omit.
β, S[1] τῶν πνευμάτων.

A[abh] = καὶ ἐξηράνθη ἐπὶ τριάκοντα ἡμέρας.   [82] *de*, A add μου.   [83] *d* reads διὰ Ἰ. τὸν ἀδελφόν μου.   [84] α, β–*e*. *e* reads μοι τοῦτο συνέβη. A[b*cdeg] συνέβη μοι τοῦτο. A[abh] = τοῦτο (A[b] om.) συνέβη μοι.   [85] A[a] om.   [86] A[b*cdefg] add ἐδάκρυσα.   [87] A[abh] add δάκρυσι.   [88] α, *d*. β–*d*, A[b*cdeg], S[1] read κυρίῳ. A[abh] = τῷ θεῷ.   [89] A[b*cdefg] = καί. *d* adds ἐάν.   [90] α, *d*, A[abh]. *aefg* read ἀποκατασταθῶ. *b*, S[1] ἀποκατάσταση τὴν χεῖρά μου. *d* adds ὡς τὸ πρότερον ὑγιῆ. A[b*cdefg] = ἀποκατεστάθην.   [91] *d* om.   [92] α. *beg* ἀπόσχομαι. *ab* (in margin) *df*, S[1] ἀπόσχωμαι. A = ἀπεσχόμην.   [93] A[abh] = ἀπὸ ζήλου καὶ παντὸς μολ. A[b*cdefg] = ἀπὸ παν. ζήλου καὶ μολ.   [94] *d* reads ἔγνω.   [95] A[abh] = θεοῦ.   [96] *g* om.   [97] *abefg* (save that *bg* om. μου), A[abhh*cdefg] (save that A[b] reads ἡμῶν and A[abh] trs. Ἰακ. after μου), S[1]. *d* reads ἐνώπιον οἴκου τοῦ πατρός μου. α ἐν Ἰακ. τῷ πατρί μου.   [98] *g* reads περὶ Ἰωσ. A[abh] om.   [99] α, *bdg* (save that *g* reads τοῦ ἀδ. μου, *h*, *dg* αὐτόν and *d* adds ἀδίκως). *aef*, S[1] read τὸν ἀδ. ἡμῶν, φθονήσας αὐτῷ. A[abh] = φθονήσας τῷ ἀδ. μου (ἡμῶν A[b]) Ἰωσήφ (A[b] om.). A[b*cdefg] = φθον. τοῖς ἀδελφοῖς μου.

III. [1] *g* reads τεκνία.   [2] *h*, β–*b*, A. *c*, *b*, S om.   [3] α. β, A, S om.   [4] A[abh*] add τὰς ψυχὰς ὑμῶν.   [5] α, A, S[2]. β, S[1] read τῶν πνευμάτων.   [6] *c* β–*g*, S[1]. *h*, *g*, A[c*cdefg] read πάσας τὰς διανοίας τοῦ ἀνθρώπου. A[abh] παντὸς ἀνθρώπου.   [7] *e* reads ἀφίουσιν.   [8] *af* read τό. A[abh] om.   [9] *bg*, S om.   [10] α, β–*dg*, S. *d* reads πάντοτε ὑποβ. τῷ φθονοῦντι ἄνω. *g* πάντοτε ὑποβάλλων πρὸς τὸν φθ. A[abh] = ὑποβάλλει ἀνθρώπῳ πάντοτε. A[b*cdefg] πάντοτε ὑποβάλλει αὐτῷ. Thus *bg*, A point to the currency of some such reading as that of *d*.   [11] A[abh] add πάντα.   [12] α, β (save that *e* reads φθόνον for φθονῶν). A[b*cdefg] = καὶ ᾧ μὲν φθονοῦσι, οὗτος πάντοτε ἀνθεῖ· ὁ δὲ φθονῶν φθίνων (a dittography) μαραίνεται. A[abh] καὶ ὁ μὲν μακάριος πάντοτε ὁμοῖος ἄνθει, ἐγὼ δὲ φθόνῳ φθίνων ἐμαραινόμην.   [13] α. β, A, S[1] om.   [14] *h*, β, S[1] add ἡμερῶν. *g* trs. ἡμερῶν after κυρίῳ.   [15] *c* om.   [16] α, *f*, A. β–*f*, S[1] read ἐν ν. τὴν ψ. μου.

κυρίου[15] ἐκάκωσα *τὴν ψυχήν μου ἐν νηστείᾳ[16]· καὶ ἔγνων
ὅτι ἡ[17] λύσις τοῦ φθόνου διὰ φόβου[18] θεοῦ[19] γίνεται[20].
5. Ἐὰν γάρ[21] τις ἐπὶ Κύριον καταφύγῃ, *ἀποτρέχει τὸ
πονηρὸν πνεῦμα ἀπ' αὐτοῦ[22], καὶ γίνεται ἡ διάνοια[23] κούφη.
6. Καὶ λοιπὸν συμπαθεῖ[24] τῷ φθονουμένῳ[25], καὶ[26] συγγινώσκει[27]
*τοῖς ἀγαπῶσιν[28] αὐτόν[29], καὶ οὕτως[30] παύεται τοῦ φθόνου.

(margin: bdg, A οὐ καταγινώσκει.)

IV. *Ἦν δὲ ὁ πατήρ μου ἐρωτῶν[1] ⸢περὶ ἐμοῦ⸣[2] *ὅτι
ἑώρακέ με σκυθρωπόν[3], καὶ[4] ἔλεγον αὐτῷ[5] *ὅτι τὰ ἥπατά μου
ὀγκοῦμαι[6].   2. Ἐπένθουν γὰρ *παρὰ πάντας[7] ὅτι ἐγὼ
ἤμην[8] αἴτιος *τῆς πράσεως[9] Ἰωσήφ.   3. *Καὶ ὅτε[10]
κατέβημεν εἰς Αἴγυπτον, καὶ[11] ἔδησέ[12] με[13] ὡς κατάσκοπον[14],
ἔγνων ὅτι δικαίως πάσχω[15] καὶ οὐκ ἐλυπούμην[16].   4. Ἰωσήφ
δὲ[17] ἦν *ἀγαθὸς ἀνήρ[18], καὶ[19] ἔχων[20] πνεῦμα θεοῦ *ἐν αὐτῷ[21],

[17] af om.   [18] h, bdef, A, S¹. c, ag read φόβον.   [19] α, β–d, S¹. d reads κυρίου θεοῦ. A = κυρίου.   [20] g reads ἐγγίνεται.   [21] b om.   [22] d reads τὸ πον. πνεῦμα φεύγει ἀπ' αὐτοῦ. A[abhb*] support text, but A[cdeg] = φεύγει αὐτὸς ἀπὸ τοῦ πον. πνεύματος. A[abh] om. next fifteen words καὶ γίνεται . . . αὐτόν. But A[b*cdeg] attest them.   [23] g adds τοῦ ἀνθρώπου, A[b*cdlg] αὐτοῦ.   [24] c reads συμπαθῶν. f συμπαθῇ.   [25] A[cde] = ὁ φθονῶν. A[b*] τῷ φθονοῦντι.   [26] af om.   [27] α, aef, S¹. bg, A[b*cde] = οὐ καταγινώσκει, but this gives almost the same sense as the text. Neither seems right. συγγινώσκει = יסלח which may be corrupt for ישמח = 'rejoices' or ישבח 'commends.' d = οὐκέτι καταγινώσκει.   [28] α, aef. bdg = τῶν ἀγαπώντων.   [29] d reads αὐτῶν.   [30] A[b*cd] = οὕτως τότε. A[ab] om. A[g] om. last five words.

IV. [1] α. abdef read καὶ ἦν (+ οὖν e) ἐρωτῶν ὁ πατήρ. For g see note 3. A[ab] = ἠρώτησέ με ὁ πατήρ μου. A[b*cdeg] τότε ἦν ἐρωτῶν ὁ π. μου.   [2] S¹ reads ἐμέ. A om.   [3] α, df (c reading ἑόρακεν and d omitting με). So also abe, save that they read ἑώρα (and e adds ὄντα after σκυθ.). g gives the verse so far as follows: βλέπων δὲ ὁ πατήρ μου τότε ἐμὲ σκυθρωπὸν ἠρώτα περὶ ἐμοῦ. A[b] adds διὰ τί εἶ σκυθρωπὸς σφόδρα; A[b*cdeg] add καὶ ἀπεκρίθην αὐτῷ.   [4] d, A[ab] add ἐγώ.   [5] c, d, A[b*cdeg]. h reads ἐγώ. abcfg, A[abh], S¹ om. A[abh] add προφάσει.   [6] c. h, d read ὅτι τ. ἥ. μου κακοῦμαι. abefg τ. ἥ. μου κακοῦμαι ἐγώ. A = τὰ ἄλγη τῶν ἡπάτων μου. d adds καὶ διὰ τοῦτό εἰμι σκυθρωπός. S¹ reads μόλις.   [7] a reads παρὰ πάντα. d πάντοτε. A[abh] add τοὺς ἀδελφούς μου. The verse is thus given in g ἐγὼ γὰρ ἀεὶ ἐπένθουν ὡς ὢν αἴτιος τοῦ κακοῦ.   [8] f adds ὁ.   [9] h, af add τοῦ. d reads παρὰ πάντας εἰς τόν.   [10] A[abh] = ὅτε γάρ. A[efg] ὅτε. g reads καί ὡς and om. next word.   [11] A[b] adds Ἰωσήφ.   [12] h, abde, A, S¹. c reads ἴδεν. f ἔδεισεν. g ἠδήλωσεν and om. preceding καί.   [13] h reads μοι. A[abh] add μόνον.   [14] e, A[abh] add καί. A[cdefg] add διότι.   [15] A[b*cdefg] add τοῦτο.   [16] g reads ἐλυπήθην.   [17] d adds ἐπειδή.   [18] α. bdeg, A, S read ἀν. ἀγ. af ἀγαθός.   [19] g om.

β, Δα, S¹
ὡς τοὺς
ἄλλους
ἀδελ-
φούς.
β, Α, S¹
ψυχῆς
*καὶ ἐν
ἀγαθῇ
καρδίᾳ³²,
ἐννοοῦν-
τες *'Ιω-
σὴφ τὸν
πατρά-
δελφον
ὑμῶν³³.
β, S¹ ἐν
αὐτῷ.

εὔσπλαγχνος καὶ ἐλεήμων ὑπάρχων²² οὐκ²³ ἐμνησικάκησέν με²⁴, ἀλλὰ²⁵ ἠγάπησέ με *σὺν τοῖς ἀδελφοῖς μου²⁶.   5. Φυλάξασθε οὖν ὑμεῖς²⁷, τέκνα²⁸ μου, ἀπὸ²⁹ παντὸς ζήλου καὶ φθόνου³⁰ καὶ πορεύεσθε ἐν *ἁπλότητι καρδίας³¹, ἵνα δῷ³⁴ ⌈καὶ ὑμῖν⌉³⁵ ὁ Θεὸς χάριν καὶ δόξαν καὶ εὐλογίαν *ἐπὶ τὰς κεφαλὰς ὑμῶν³⁶, καθὼς³⁷ ἴδετε³⁸ *ἐν 'Ιωσήφ³⁹.   6. Πάσας⁴⁰ τὰς ἡμέρας⁴¹ οὐκ⁴² ὠνείδισεν ἡμᾶς⁴³ *περὶ τοῦ πράγματος τούτου⁴⁴, ἀλλ'⁴⁵ ἠγάπησεν ἡμᾶς ὡς τὴν *ψυχὴν αὐτοῦ⁴⁶ καὶ ὑπὲρ τοὺς υἱοὺς αὐτοῦ⁴⁷ ἐδόξασεν⁴⁸ ἡμᾶς, καὶ⁴⁹ *πλοῦτον καὶ κτήνη καὶ καρπὸν⁵⁰ *ἐχαρίσατο ἡμῖν⁵¹.   7. *Καὶ ὑμεῖς⁵², τέκνα μου⁵³, ἀγαπήσατε⁵⁴ ἕκαστος τὸν ἀδελφὸν⁵⁵ αὐτοῦ⁵⁶ ἐν ἀγαθῇ καρδίᾳ, καὶ *ἀποστήσεται ἀφ' ὑμῶν τὸ

β, Α, S¹ πᾶσιν ἡμῖν.

²⁰ e trs. after θεοῦ.   ²¹ α, df. abeg, A^{b*cdefg} read ἐν ἑαυτῷ. d adds καί.   ²² α. a, A read καί. bdefg, S¹ om.   ²³ g reads οὐ γάρ.   ²⁴ bde read μοι. g adds ποτέ.   ²⁵ α, ef, A. abd, S¹ read ἀλλὰ καί. g ἀλλὰ μᾶλλον.   ²⁶ α. β, A^{abh}, S¹ read ὡς τοὺς ἄλλους ἀδελφούς (+ αὐτοῦ ef + μου A^{abh}). A^{b*} = ὡς πάντας τοὺς ἀδ. αὐτοῦ. A^{cdefg} ὡς π. τοὺς ἄλλους ἀδ. αὐτοῦ.   ²⁷ c. dg read καὶ ὑμεῖς and trs. after τέκνα μου. h, abef, S¹ om. g trs. ver. 5 after ver. 6.   ²⁸ A^{b*cdefg} = ἀδελφοὶ καὶ τέκνα.   ²⁹ d reads ἐπί.   ³⁰ d adds καθὼς καὶ αὐτὸς 'Ιωσὴφ ὁ πατράδελφος ἡμῶν ἐφύλαξεν ἑαυτόν.   ³¹ α. bdeg, S¹ read ἁπλότ. ψυχῆς. af, A^{ab*cdefg} ἁπλότητι.   ³² A^{ah} = καθαρᾷ καρδίᾳ. A^b = καρδίᾳ. A^{b*cdefg} = καὶ καθαρᾷ καρδίᾳ. a om. next six words.   ³³ fg, A^{abh}, S¹ (save that A^{abh} read ἀδελφὸν ἡμῶν). A^{b*cdefg} read τὸν ἀδελφὸν ἡμῶν 'Ιωσήφ. be τὸν πατράδελφον ὑμῶν (+ 'Ιωσήφ e). d τὸ ἀμνησίκακον αὐτοῦ καὶ καθὼς οἴδατε ἐν αὐτῷ, οὕτω καὶ ὑμεῖς ποιεῖτε πάσας τὰς ἡμέρας τῆς ζωῆς ὑμῶν.   ³⁴ h, afg. c reads δωει. bd δῴη. e δώσει.   ³⁵ A om. d adds κύριος.   ³⁶ g om. For ὑμῶν d reads ἡμῶν.   ³⁷ f reads καθό.   ³⁸ α, ef. abg, S¹ read εἴδετε. d δέδωκε.   ³⁹ α. A^{abh} = ἐν 'Ιωσ. πραχθέν. β, S¹ read ἐν αὐτῷ. A^{b*cdefg} = αὐτόν. d adds τεκνία μου.   ⁴⁰ c, bdg, A^{abh}. h, aef, S¹ read καὶ πάσας. A^{b*cde} = πάσας γάρ.   ⁴¹ d, A add τῆς ζωῆς αὐτοῦ.   ⁴² c reads ἀλλ' οὐκ. It is possible that ver. 6 should begin with οὐκ ὠνείδ. and that πάσας τ. ἡμέρας belongs to ver. 5.   ⁴³ A^{abh} add οὐδὲ ἐποίησεν ἡμῖν.   ⁴⁴ α. β reads περὶ τ. λόγου τούτου. So A^{b*cdefg}, but in gen. plur. A^{abh} = κατὰ τοὺς λόγους τούτους, or possibly = α. g om. next seven words.   ⁴⁵ d adds μᾶλλον.   ⁴⁶ c reads ἑαυτοῦ ψ.   ⁴⁷ b, A^{b*cdefg} add καί.   ⁴⁸ h reads ἐδίδαξεν (?)   ⁴⁹ A^{b*cd} om.   ⁵⁰ α, β, S¹ (save that c reads κτηνοι (sic) and β, S¹ καρπούς). A^{abh} = πλοῦτον (+ καὶ A^h) κτηνῶν καὶ καρπῶν. A^{b*cdeg} = πλούτῳ κτηνῶν καὶ καρπῶν.   ⁵¹ c (h?). af read ἐχ. πᾶσιν ἡ. be, S¹ πᾶσιν ἡ. ἐχ. d ἡ. ἐχ. g πάντα ἡ. ἐχ. Ά = ἐχ. ἡ. πᾶσιν which A^{abh} trs. before πλοῦτον.   ⁵² bd, S¹ add οὖν. g om. together with next two words.   ⁵³ h om. b adds ἀγαπητά. A^{abh} om. next nine words.

πνεῦμα τοῦ φθόνου[57].   8. Ὅτι[58] ἀγριοῖ τοῦτο[59] τὴν ψυχήν[60],
καὶ φθείρει *τὸ σῶμα[61], *ὀργὴν καὶ πόλεμον παρέχει τῷ διαβουλίῳ[62], καὶ εἰς[63] αἵματα[64] παροξύνει, καὶ εἰς ἔκστασιν ἄγει[65]
*τὴν διάνοιαν[66], καὶ κλόνον[69] παρέχει τῇ ψυχῇ[70] καὶ τρόμον
τῷ σώματι.   9. *Ὅτι καὶ[71] ἐν ὕπνῳ *τις ζῆλος[72] κακίας
αὐτὸν[73] φαντάζουσα[74] κατεσθίει[75] καὶ[76] πνεύμασι πονηροῖς[77]
διαταράσσει[78] τὴν ψυχὴν αὐτοῦ, καὶ ἐκθροεῖσθαι τὸ σῶμα ποιεῖ,
καὶ ἐν ταραχῇ διυπνίζει[79] τὸν νοῦν, καὶ ὡς[80] πνεῦμα πονηρὸν
*καὶ ἰοβόλον[81], *οὕτως φαίνεται[82] τοῖς ἀνθρώποις[83].

V. Διὰ τοῦτο Ἰωσὴφ ἦν[1] ὡραῖος *τῷ εἴδει[2], καὶ καλὸς
*τῇ ὄψει, ὅτι[3] οὐκ ἐνοίκησεν[4] *ἐν αὐτῷ[5] οὐδὲν[6] πονηρόν· ἐκ

Right margin: β, ΑΒ, S¹ διάνοιαν ⌐καὶ οὐκ ἐᾷ τὴν σύνεσιν ἐν ἀνθρώποις ἐνεργεῖν⌐[67]. *ἀλλὰ καὶ τὸν ὕπνον ἀφαιρεῖ[68]. β, ΑΒ, S ἰοβόλον ἔχων.

[54] g reads ἀγαπᾶτε.   [55] d reads πλησίον.   [56] af read ὑμῶν.   [57] α, g, A^{b*cdefg}. abdf, S¹ read ἀποστήσατε κτλ. e ἀποστησαται ὑμῶν τὸ πν. τοῦ ζήλου. A^{abb} = ἀπόστητε ἀπὸ πονηροῦ φθόνου.   [58] g om.   [59] α, abdg, A^{cdeg}, S¹. e reads τούτῳ. f τούτων. A^{abb*} = φθόνος which A^{ab} trs. before ἀγριοῖ.   [60] A^{b*cdefg} = τὸ σῶμα. A^{ab} = τὸν ἄνθρωπον, but text is corrupt. d om. next five words.   [61] A = τὴν ψυχήν. g adds καί. A^{abb} om. next ten words.   [62] α, β (save that α reads τῷ διαβόλῳ and bdg τὸ διαβούλιον). A^{b*cdefg} = ὅτι ὀργὴ καὶ πόλεμός εἰσι τὰ διαβούλια αὐτοῦ. S¹ supports text save that it om. ὀργήν.   [63] A^{b*cdeg} om.   [64] d reads αἷμα. A^{b*cdefg} = θυμόν.   [65] d trs. after διάνοιαν.   [66] A reads զմարդն = τὸν ἄνθρωπον corrupt for զմիտն = τ. διάνοιαν. A^{abb} om. rest of chap. and v. 1, 2.   [67] A^{b*cdefg} om. For σύνεσιν g reads συνείδησιν. b om. ἐν and for ἐνεργεῖν g reads εἰρηνεύειν.   [68] be, A^{b*cdefg}. g reads ἀλλὰ τὸν ὕπνον ἀφαιρεῖται. af om. d reads ἀλλὰ πάντα ἀβούλως καὶ ἀσκόπως πράττει· ἀφαιρεῖται δέ.   [69] d reads κλοιόν. e κλωνον.   [70] d reads τὴν ψυχὴν καὶ τὸν ὕπνον.   [71] c, A^{b*cdeg}. h, af read ὅτι γε. bde, S¹ ὅτι καί γε. g ὅτι.   [72] c reads ζῆλον. d ζῆλός τις.   [73] c, befg, A^{b*cdes}. ad read αὐτῶν. h om. For κακίας αὐτὸν φαντ. d reads φαντάζων αὐτῶν κακίαν σφοδρῶς.   [74] h, β-dg. c reads φαντάζεται. d (see preceding note) g φαντάζων. A^{b*cdefg} = φαντάζεται καί or φαντάζων.   [75] c om. A^{b*cdefg} add αὐτόν.   [76] β adds ἐν.   [77] g reads πονηρίας.   [78] A^{b*cdefg} = παραπέμπει, but յուղարկէ may be corrupt for յուզէ = διαταράσσει.   [79] c. h, β, S read διυπνίζεσθαι. A^{bdeg} = ἐκθροεῖσθαι ποιεῖ but զարհուրեցուցանէ may be corrupt for զարթուցանէ = διυπνίζει.   [80] α, beg, A^{b*cdefg}, S¹. af read ἐν. d ὥσπερ.   [81] g reads εἰσβολήν. β, S¹ add ἔχων. A^{b*cdefg} ἔχων ἐν ἑαυτῷ.   [82] a reads οὗτος φαίν. ἔχων.   [83] d adds ὁ τῷ τὸν φθόνον ἁλισκόμενος πνι ὡς ἄνος.

V. [1] d trs. before Ἰωσ.   [2] A^{b*cd} trs. according to Armenian text after ὅτι οὐκ, but not so A^{cte}. g om. together with next two words.   [3] d reads τῷ προσώπῳ διότι.   [4] h(?), abf, A^{b*cdes}. eg read ἐνοικεῖ. c, d ἐνίκησεν.   [5] bdeg, A^{b*cdes}. α reads εἰς αὐτόν. af αὐτῷ.   [6] g trs. after πονηρόν. d om.

γὰρ [7] τῆς ταραχῆς τοῦ πνεύματος τὸ πρόσωπον δηλοῖ [8].   2. Καὶ νῦν, τέκνα μου [9],

> Ἀγαθύνατε τὰς καρδίας ὑμῶν [10] ἐνώπιον Κυρίου [11],
> καὶ [12] εὐθύνατε τὰς ὁδοὺς ὑμῶν ἐνώπιον τῶν [13] ἀνθρώπων [14]
> καὶ ἔσεσθε εὑρίσκοντες χάριν *ἐνώπιον Κυρίου καὶ ἀνθρώπων [15].

β, A, S¹
πάντων
τῶν.

3. *Φυλάξασθε οὖν [16] *ἀπὸ τῆς πορνείας [17],
> ὅτι *ἡ πορνεία [18] μήτηρ [19] ἐστὶ [20] τῶν κακῶν,
> χωρίζουσα [21] *ἀπὸ τοῦ [22] θεοῦ καὶ προσεγγίζουσα [23] τῷ Βελίαρ [24].

β, A, S
ἐν Λευί.

β, S
Λευί.

β, Aᵃᵇ
μου
Ἰακώβ.

4. Ἑώρακα γὰρ ἐγὼ [25] ἐν χαρακτῆρι γραφῆς [26] Ἐνώχ, ὅτι οἱ [27] υἱοὶ ὑμῶν [28] *ἐν πορνείᾳ [29] φθαρήσονται, καὶ *τοῖς υἱοῖς Λευὶ [30] *ἀδικήσουσιν ἐν ῥομφαίᾳ [31].   5. Ἀλλ' οὐ δυνήσονται πρὸς Λευὶ ἀντιστῆναι [32], ὅτι *πόλεμον Κυρίου πολεμήσει [33] καὶ νικήσει ⌈πᾶσαν⌉ [34] παρεμβολὴν [35] ὑμῶν.   6. Καὶ ἔσονται ὀλιγοστοὶ [36] ἐπιμεριζόμενοι [37] *ἐν τῷ [38] Λευὶ καὶ *ἐν τῷ [39] Ἰούδᾳ [40] καὶ οὐκ [41] ἔσται ἐξ ὑμῶν *τις εἰς ἡγεμονίαν [42] καθὼς καὶ ὁ πατὴρ ἡμῶν [43] προεφήτευσεν [44] *ἐν ταῖς [45] εὐλογίαις [46].

---

[7] α. β–d read ἐκ γ. ταραχῆς. d ἐν γ. ταραχῇ.   [8] d reads δηλεῖ.   [9] a, S¹ om.   [10] d reads ἡμῶν.   [11] α, β. Aᵇ*ᶜᵈᵉᶠᵍ = θεοῦ.   [12] c om. next five words.   [13] h reads θεοῦ καί.   [14] dg, Aᵇ*ᶜᵈᵉᶠᵍ om. next eight words through hmt.   [15] α. abf, S¹ read θεοῦ καὶ ἀνθρώπων. e παρὰ θεῷ καὶ ἀν̅ο̅ι̅ς̅.   [16] α. β–e, S¹ read καὶ φυλάσσεσθε. e καὶ φυλάξασθαι. A = (+ καὶ Aʰ) φυλάξασθε.   [17] c, A. β read τοῦ μὴ πορνεύειν. h τοῦ πρὸ τῆς πορνείας (?).   [18] Aᵃᵇ = αὐτή.   [19] g reads μεῖζον.   [20] β, A, S¹ add πάντων.   [21] e reads ἀποστερίζουσα.   [22] c, d. h reads ἀπό. abefy om.   [23] d reads ἐγγίζουσα.   [24] h, β (save that e reads τοῦ for τῷ), A. c reads τῷ διαβόλῳ.   [25] α, Aᵃᵇʰ. β, Aᵇ*ᶜᵈ om.   [26] β–g. α, g read γραφίδι. Is γραφίδι a dittographic rendering and γραφῆς an emendation?   [27] ab om.   [28] d reads ἡμῶν. g om. afg add μεθ᾽ ὑμᾶς. b, S μεθ᾽ ὑμῶν. d μεθ᾽ ἧς against α, e, A.   [29] d reads ἡ πορνεία.   [30] α. β–g, A, S read as in margin. g reads ἐλέει.   [31] Aᵃᵇʰ = πορεύσονται ἐν ῥομφαίᾳ (for *npnιℓ* is corrupt for *υρηιℓ*).   [32] α, A. β, S om.   [33] h reads πολεμοῦνται πολέμοις (?). Aᵃᵇʰ = πολ. κ. ἐπολέμουν. Aᵇ*ᶜᵈᵉᶠᵍ, S² πολ. κ. πολεμοῖ.   [34] a, A om.   [35] c reads προσβολήν. Aᵇ*ᶜᵈᵉᶠᵍ internally corrupt but Aᵃᵇʰ right.   [36] d reads ολιγοροι. Aᵃᵇʰ = ἔνδοξοι ὑμεῖς δὲ ὀλιγοστοί.   [37] a reads μεριζόμενοι. Aᵃᵇ om.   [38] f reads ἐπί.   [39] α, af. bdeg om.   [40] α, af. bde, Aᵃᵇʰ read Λευὶ καὶ Ἰούδᾳ. g Λ. καὶ τῷ Ἰ. Aᵇ*ᶜᵈᵉᶠᵍ = Ἰούδᾳ καὶ Λευί.   [41] b om.   [42] c. β, S¹ read εἰς ἡγ. h τις ἡγεμονεῖ. A = ἡγεμών.   [43] α, A. abd read μου. efg, S¹ om. β, Aᵃᵇʰᵉᶠᵍ add Ἰακώβ. Aᵇ*ᶜᵈ trs. it before ὁ πατήρ.   [44] e trs. after εὐλογίαις.   [45] α. abefg, S read ἐν. d om.   [46] d adds περὶ Λευὶ καὶ Ἰούδα. A adds αὐτοῦ.

VI. Ἰδοὺ εἴρηκα[1] ὑμῖν πάντα[2], *ὅπως δικαιωθῶ ἀπὸ τῆς
ἁμαρτίας ὑμῶν[3].   2. Ἐὰν δὲ[4] ἀφέλητε[5] ἀφ' ὑμῶν τὸν
φθόνον καὶ πᾶσαν σκληροκαρδίαν[6],

> Ὡς[7] ῥόδον ἀνθήσει[8] τὰ ὀστᾶ μου[9] ἐν Ἰσραήλ,
> καὶ[10] ὡς κρίνον *ἡ σάρξ μου[10] ἐν Ἰακώβ,
> καὶ ἔσται[11] *ἡ ὀσμή μου ὡς[12] ὀσμὴ Λιβάνου[13]
> καὶ πληθυνθήσονται[14] ἅγιοι[15] *ἐξ ἐμοῦ[16] *ἕως αἰῶνας
>   αἰώνων[17]
> καὶ *οἱ κλάδοι[18] αὐτῶν[19] εἰς μακρὰν ἔσονται.

3. Τότε ἀπολεῖται[20] τὸ[21] σπέρμα Χαναάν
> *καὶ ἐγκατάλειμμα[22] οὐκ ἔσται ἐν[23] τῷ Ἀμαλήκ,
> ⌜καὶ ἀπολοῦνται πάντες οἱ Καππαδόκαι⌝[24]
> *καὶ πάντες οἱ Χετταῖοι ἐξολοθρευθήσονται[25].

4. Τότε[26] ἐκλείψει[27] *ἡ γῆ[28] Χάμ,
> καὶ πᾶς ὁ[29] λαὸς ἀπολεῖται.
> Τότε καταπαύσει *πᾶσα ἡ γῆ[30] ἀπὸ ταραχῆς,
> *καὶ πᾶσα ἡ[31] ὑπ' οὐρανῶν[32] ἀπὸ πολέμου.

α	β, S
5. Τότε[33] †σημεῖον[34] ἐνδοξασθήσεται[35] *μέγα τῷ Ἰσραήλ[36],	5. Τότε[37] †σημεῖον (Σήμ b d) ἐνδοξασθήσεται

Margin: β, S¹ προείρηκα. — β-e, S ἁμαρτίας τῶν ψυχῶν. — β, ΑΒ, S¹ σκληροτραχηλίαν. — β, Α, S ὡς κέδροι ἅγιοι. — A^ab omit ver. 4.

VI. [1] α, A, S². β, S¹ read προείρηκα. [2] h reads τοῦτο. S¹ om. [3] α, e¹, A^b*cdeg (save that e reads πάσης for τῆς and A^b*cdefg add ἐγώ after δικαιωθῶ). β-e, S support text but add τῶν ψυχῶν after ἁμαρτίας, and d reads ἐπί for ἀπό and ἡμῶν for ὑμῶν. e² ἀπὸ πάσης ἁμ. τῶν ψ. ὑμῶν. A^abh = τὰ σκάνδαλα τῶν υἱῶν ὑμῶν. [4] A^ab om. A^h = καί. A^b*cdefg = γάρ. [5] abg, S¹. α reads ἀφελέσθαι. d ἀφελειται. e ἀφεληται. f ἀφελετε. A^abh add τοῦτο. [6] α. β, A^b*cdefg read as in margin. A^abh om. with four preceding words. [7] d reads Τότε ὡς. [8] A^abh = ἀνθήσουσιν οἱ υἱοὶ ὑμῶν καί. [9] h om. [10] A^abh om. [11] A^b* = ὀζήσει. [12] beg, A (save that A^ab om. μου), S¹. h, df om. c, a read ὡς. [13] d adds ἡ εὐωδία μου. [14] α, adfg, A^b*cdeg. h, b read πληθυνθήσεται. e πληθυνθήσεσθαι. A^abh = τιμηθήσεται. [15] α. β, A, S, read as in margin. [16] d, A^abh om. [17] α. β, A, S¹ read ἕως αἰῶνος. [18] h reads αἱ κοιλάδες. [19] c, β-d, S. h, A^b*cdeg read αὐτοῦ. d αὐτόν. A^ab = Ἰούδα. β-d add ἕως. [20] c reads απολυται. [21] bg, A^ab om. [22] h om. [23] α. β om. [24] Α' om. For Καππαδόκαι bdef read Καππάδοκες. [25] A^abh = καὶ πᾶσιν τοῖς ἔθνεσιν. [26] h om. A^b*cdefg = καί. [27] c reads ἐκλειψη. def ἐκλήψει. A^b*cdefg = ἐξολοθρευθήσεται. [28] h reads ψυχή. [29] α, defg. ab om. [30] α, def, A^b*cd. ab read ἡ γῆ πᾶσα. g πᾶσα γῆ. [31] A^b* = ἤ. [32] c, e. But text may be a corruption of abdfg, S¹ οὐρανόν. h reads οὐρανούς. [33] καὶ τότε in A^b*cd, S¹ and καὶ ὅτε of g are secondary. [34] α, aef, S¹.

ὅτι Κύριος ὁ Θεὸς φαι-
νόμενος ἐπὶ τῆς γῆς
ἥξει[38] [ὡς ἄνθρωπος][39]
καὶ σώζων[40] * ἐν αὐτῷ[41] τὸν
'Αδάμ.

Ab*cdeg

5. καὶ τότε Σὴμ ἐνδοξασθήσεται
ὅτι Κύριος ὁ Θεός, μέγας τοῦ
'Ισραήλ, [ἐνδοξασθήσε-
ται][42] ἐπὶ γῆς [καὶ] φανήσεται [ὡς ἄνθρωπος].

ὅτι Κύριος ὁ Θεός, μέ-
γας[43] τοῦ 'Ισραήλ, φαι-
νόμενος[44] ἐπὶ[45] γῆς [ὡς
ἄνθρωπος]
καὶ σώζων ἐν αὐτῷ[46] τὸν
'Αδάμ.

Aabh

5. τότε † Σὴθ ἐνδοξασθήσεται
ὅτι Κύριος ὁ Θεὸς ἡμῶν
φανήσεται ἐπὶ γῆς [ὡς
ἄνθρωπος]
καὶ σώζει[47] † αὐτὸς πάλιν †..

g om. bd, Ab*cdefg read Σήμ. Aabh Σήθ. S2 σημεῖα. It is impossible to
determine with any certainty what stood in the original. Σήθ is simply
corrupt for Σήμ. Hence the choice lies between σημεῖον and Σήμ. If the
latter (which is clear in meaning but less strongly attested) were original,
it would be difficult to account for its change into the obscure σημεῖον.
On the other hand, while the emendation of σημεῖον into Σήμ is easy, it is
hard to see why a Christian scribe should give a more Jewish character
to the text. If σημεῖον is original in α, β, σημεῖον ἐνδοξ. may be a rendering
of יְכַבֵּד צִיּוֹן which should have been read as יְכַבֵּד צִיּוֹן = δοξάσει Σιών.
The subject of the verb would then be μέγας τοῦ 'Ισραήλ. Thus we have:
'The Mighty One of Israel will glorify Zion.' Even if Shem is original,
the above change of ἐνδοξασθ. into δοξάσει seems necessary. In favour
of Σήμ might be cited Jub. vii. 12, 'God shall dwell in the dwelling of
Shem,' and the Onkelos Targum on Gen. ix. 27, 'May He cause His
Shekinah to rest in the dwellings of Shem.' [35] Read δοξάσει. See
preceding note. [36] α. The text is corrupt for μέγας τοῦ 'Ισρ. which is
rightly preserved in β, Ab*cdefg, S1 though trs. into the next clause. Aabh
om. this clause. [37] g reads καὶ ὅτε and for σημ. ἐνδοξ. reads δοξασθήσεται.
[38] α only. Probably interpolated. [39] Christian interpolation, though
found in α, β–a, S. a om. [40] h reads σώσει. [41] α, be1fg. d reads ἐν
αὐτῇ. a, S1 ἐν ἑαυτῷ. Aabh = αὐτός. The phrase seems in some form to
be original. But ἐν αὐτῷ τὸν 'Αδάμ = בו האדם, where I take בו to be
corrupt for לו, which should then be rendered ἑαυτῷ or omitted. See
T. Lev. ii. 11, note. Τὸν 'Αδάμ is here used of the human race—a use
intelligible in a translation from Hebrew but not in a piece of original
Greek. The Greek equivalent of the phrase occurs in T. Lev. ii. 11 in the
same connexion. [42] A dittography from the preceding line. [43] g om.
[44] g reads φθονούμενος. [45] g adds τῆς. [46] af read ἑαυτῷ. [47] Possibly

6. Τότε δοθήσεται[48] πάντα τὰ πνεύματα τῆς πλάνης[49] εἰς
   καταπάτησιν[50]
  καὶ οἱ⌜[51] ἄνθρωποι[52] βασιλεύσουσιν[53] τῶν[54] πονηρῶν πνευμάτων[55].

7. Τότε ἀναστησόμαι[56] κἀγὼ[57] ἐν[58] εὐφροσύνῃ
  καὶ εὐλογήσω[59] τὸν ὕψιστον ἐπὶ[60] τοῖς θαυμασίοις αὐτοῦ
  [ὅτι ὁ[61] Θεὸς σῶμα λαβών, καὶ[62] συνεσθίων ἀνθρώποις
   *ἔσωσεν ἀνθρώπους[63]].

VII. Καὶ νῦν, τέκνα[1] μου, ἐπακούσατε[2] τοῦ[3] Λευὶ καὶ τοῦ[4]
   'Ιούδα[5]
  καὶ[7] μὴ ἐπαίρεσθε[8] ἐπὶ τὰς δύο γενεὰς[9] ταύτας,
  ὅτι ἐξ αὐτῶν[10] ἀνατελεῖ ἡμῖν[11] τὸ σωτήριον ⌜τοῦ Θεοῦ⌝[12].
2. *'Αναστήσει γὰρ[13] Κύριος[14] ἐκ[15] τοῦ Λευὶ ὡς[16] ἀρχιερέα
  *καὶ ἐκ[17] τοῦ 'Ιούδα[18] ὡς[15] βασιλέα[19] [Θεὸν καὶ ἄνθρω-
   πον][20].

Marginal: h, β (A), S¹ ὑπακούετε τοῦ Λευὶ καὶ ἐν 'Ιούδα λυθρωθήσεσθε[6]. β φυλάς.

[Armenian] is corrupt for *[Armenian]* = σώσει. As a result of the above criticism I propose to restore ver. 5 as follows:

> Τότε Σὴμ (or Σιὼν) δοξάσει μέγας τοῦ 'Ισραήλ
> ὅτι Κύριος ὁ Θεὸς φανήσεται ἐπὶ τῆς γῆς
> καὶ σώσει τοὺς υἱοὺς τοῦ 'Αδάμ.

But μέγας τοῦ 'I. may be an interpolation. It is omitted by A^abb. In that case read the first line as follows:

> Τότε Σὴμ (or Σιὼν) δοξασθήσεται.

[48] α. β reads δοθήσονται.   [49] A^abb add τοῦ Βελίαρ.   [50] h reads κατάπαυσιν. g ἕως. A^abb *[Armenian]* = ὄλεθρον corrupt for *[Armenian]* (so A^b*cdefg) = text.   [51] ab om.   [52] A^ab read *[Armenian]* (A^a om.) *[Armenian]* = νῦν μή corrupt for *[Armenian]* = ἄνθρωποι.   [53] g reads βασιλεύουσι. d adds ἐπί.   [54] A^b*cdefg read πάντων τῶν.   [55] e om.   [56] A = ἀναστησόμεθα.   [57] α reads ἐγώ. β, A, S¹ om.   [58] d om.   [59] A = εὐλογήσομεν.   [60] b reads ἐν. A^a om. with next three words, A^b with next two.   [61] bdfg om. g om. next word.   [62] A^b*cd add περιπατῶν καί.   [63] befg, A^b*cdefg, S¹. α reads ἔσ. αὐτόν. a ἔσ. αὐτούς. d σώσει ἀνθρώπους. A^abb om.

VII. [1] b reads τεκνία.   [2] c. h, f read ὑπακούσατε. abde, S¹ ὑπακούετε. g ὑπακούσετε. A^b* add μοι ὅτι. A^cd καὶ ὅτι. S² om.   [3] α, ef. a reads τόν. dg, A^befg, S¹ τῷ. b om. A^ab*cd, S² = ἐν.   [4] c. h, β, A, S read ἐν.   [5] S¹ = 'Ιωσήφ.   [6] h, β, A^abb, S². c alone om. A^b*cdefg = λυτρωθησόμεθα. A^b add ὅτι ἐκ γένους αὐτοῦ γεννηθήσεται κύριος ὁ θεός. S¹ = ἔσται λύτρωσις.   [7] A^ab om.   [8] c, e read επερεσθε, h ἐπαιρεσθαι.   [9] α. β, S read φυλάς. A = ἀδελφούς.   [10] e reads αὐτοῦ.   [11] c, df, A. h, abeg, S read ὑμῖν.   [12] A om.   [13] α, befg A, S. a reads ἀναστήσει. d καὶ ἀναστ.   [14] c om.   [15] d reads ἐκ μέν. A^ab read τὸν Λευί.   [16] dg om.   [17] d reads ἐκ δέ.

οὗτος²¹ σώσει *[πάντα τὰ ἔθνη καὶ] τὸ γένος τοῦ Ἰσραήλ²².

3. Διὰ τοῦτο ταῦτα²³ ἐντέλλομαι ὑμῖν²⁴ ἵνα²⁵ καὶ ὑμεῖς ἐντέλλεσθε²⁶ τοῖς τέκνοις ὑμῶν²⁷, ὅπως²⁸ φυλάξωσιν αὐτὰ²⁹ εἰς τὰς³⁰ γενεὰς αὐτῶν³¹.

VIII. *Καὶ ὡς¹ συνετέλεσεν² Συμεὼν ἐντελλόμενος³ τοῖς υἱοῖς⁴ αὐτοῦ⁵, ἐκοιμήθη⁶ *μετὰ τῶν πατέρων αὐτοῦ⁷ *ὢν ἐτῶν ἑκατὸν εἴκοσι⁸. 2. Καὶ ἔθηκαν αὐτὸν ἐν *θήκῃ ξυλίνῃ⁹, *τοῦ ἀναγαγεῖν τὰ ὀστᾶ αὐτοῦ¹⁰ ἐν Χεβρών. Καὶ ἀνήγαγον¹¹ *αὐτὰ ἐν πολέμῳ Αἰγυπτίων κρυφῇ¹². 3. *Τὰ γὰρ ὀστᾶ τοῦ Ἰωσὴφ ἐφύλαττον¹³ *οἱ Αἰγύπτιοι¹⁴ ἐν τοῖς μνήμασι¹⁵ τῶν

Left marginal notes:

β καί.
β, A, S¹
καὶ ἐκοιμήθη.
dg, A
ρκε'.
β, Aᵃᵇᵇʰ,
S ξυλων
ἀσήπτων.
α, d, Aᵃᵇ
εἰς τὸ

ἀναγαγεῖν αὐτόν.   α αὐτὸν ἐν κρυφῇ τὰ ὀστᾶ.   β, A, S¹ ταμιείοις.

---

¹⁸ c reads θεοῦ.   ¹⁹ g reads βασιλεύειν. h adds καί.   ²⁰ α, β (save that h prefixes καί), Aᵃᵇᵇʰᵉᶠᵍ (save that Aʰ prefixes καί), S¹. Aᵇ* = καί ἐστι οὗτος θεός. Aᶜᵈ = καὶ θεόν. S² = καὶ ἄνθρωπον. Bracketed as a Christian interpolation.   ²¹ α, β–b. b, S reads οὕτως. Aᵃᵇ = καί. Aᵇ*ᶜᵈᵉᶠᵍ = καὶ οὗτος.   ²² α, β, S. A = πάντα ἄνθρωπον (γένη Aᵇ*ᶜᵈᵉᶠᵍ) καὶ ἔθνη ἀνθρώπων. I have bracketed πάντα τὰ ἔθνη καί as an interpolation. Cf. T. Jos. xix. 7. Our author can look forward to the salvation of the Gentiles, but he would not set their salvation before that of Israel. d adds γνωστὸν οὖν ἔστω ὅτι.   ²³ c, aef, S². b reads πάντα. A by internal corruption = ἐγώ. h, dg, S¹ om.   ²⁴ d adds πάντα ταῦτα.   ²⁵ Aᵇ*ᶜᵈᵉᵍ om. d reads ὅπως.   ²⁶ α, g. a reads ἐντελεῖσθε. b ἐντείληθε. df ἐντείλεσθε. e ἐντείλασθε.   ²⁷ Aᵇ add ἵνα καὶ αὐτοὶ ἐντείλωνται τοῖς τέκνοις αὐτῶν. So also Aᵃ according to Text, but this is probably wrong as Aʰ om.   ²⁸ d reads ἵνα. h ὅπως καί.   ²⁹ f reads ταῦτα. A = ταύτας (Aᵇ*ᶜᵈᵉᶠᵍ om.) τὰς ἐντολάς.   ³⁰ e om.   ³¹ Here S¹ makes a Christian addition and at its close gives a duplicate edition of chap. VII. after recension β. See Appendix.

VIII. ¹ c, g, Aᵇ. h, β–dg, Aᵃᵇ*ᶜᵈᵉᶠᵍ, S read καί. d ὡς δέ.   ² S¹ = ταῦτα εἰπὼν ἀπέθανεν.   ³ Aᵃᵇᵇʰ = τὰς ἐντολὰς ταύτας. Aᵇ*ᶜᵈᵉᶠᵍ = τὰς (Aᵇ* om.) ἐντολάς.   ⁴ h, afg read τέκνοις.   ⁵ See note 1. d adds ἐξάρας τοὺς πόδας αὐτοῦ.   ⁶ c, d. h, β–d, A, S¹ read καὶ ἐκοιμήθη. d adds καὶ προσετέθη.   ⁷ S¹ = ἐν τῷ αἰωνίῳ ὕπνῳ.   ⁸ c. h reads ἐτῶν δὲ ρ̄κ̄. ab, S² ἑκατὸν εἴκοσι ἐτῶν. dg χρόνων (d om.) ὑπάρχων ρ̄κ̄ε̄. ef, S¹ ἐτῶν ρ̄κ̄. Aᵃᵇʰᶜᵈᵉᶠᵍ = ρκέ (ρκζ g) ἔτει τῆς ζωῆς αὐτοῦ. Aᵇ* = ρκέ ἐτῶν. Here A is wrong throughout.   ⁹ α. d reads ξυλίνη θήκη. abef θήκῃ ξύλων. g θήκῃ and omits the rest of the Testament, substituting in its stead ἕως ἀνήγαγον αὐτὸν θάψαντες ἐν Χεβρὼν μετὰ τῶν πατέρων αὐτοῦ. β–dg, Aᵃᵇʰ, S add ἀσήπτων, d ἀσήπτῳ against α, Aᵇ*ᶜᵈᵉᶠᵍ.   ¹⁰ abef, Aᵇ*ᶜᵈᵉᵍ, S. α, d, Aᵃᵇ read εἰς τὸ (ἕως τοῦ d) ἀναγ. αὐτόν.   ¹¹ α, ef. abd read ἀνήνεγκαν.   ¹² β–d, S. So also A which = αὐτὸν ἐν κρυφῇ ἐν πολ. Αἰγυπτίων. α has here an ungrammatical text αὐτὸν ἐν κρυφῇ τὰ βασιλέων[16].   4. Ἔλεγον γὰρ ⌜αὐτοῖς⌝[17] οἱ ἐπαοιδοί[18], ὅτι ἐν ἐξόδῳ τῶν[19] ὀστῶν Ἰωσὴφ[20] ἔσται ἐν πάσῃ * τῇ γῇ[21] σκότος καὶ γνόφος καὶ πληγὴ[22] μεγάλη[23] τοῖς Αἰγυπτίοις, ὥστε μετὰ λύχνου[24] μὴ[25] ἐπιγινώσκειν ἕκαστος[26] * τὸν ἀδελφὸν[27] αὐτοῦ.

IX. * Καὶ ἔκλαυσαν[1] οἱ[2] * υἱοὶ Συμεὼν[3] τὸν πατέρα αὐτῶν[4].   Καὶ ἦσαν * εἰς Αἴγυπτον[5] ἕως ἡμέρας ἐξόδου αὐτῶν[6] * ἐν χειρὶ Μωϋσῆ[7].

β, S¹ Αἰγύπτῳ. β, S¹ αὐτῶν κατὰ τὸν νόμον τοῦ πένθους. β, S¹ αὐτῶν ἐξ Αἰγύπτου. β–ab, Α, S αὐτοῦ πρὸ τοῦ ἀποθανεῖν αὐτόν (τῆς τελευτῆς αὐτοῦ cfg, S¹). β–d, S¹ ὤφθη.

Διαθήκη Λευὶ τοῦ τρίτου υἱοῦ Ἰακὼβ καὶ Λίας[1].

I. Ἀντίγραφον λόγων[2] Λευί[3], ὅσα διέθετο[4] τοῖς υἱοῖς αὐτοῦ[5] κατὰ πάντα ἃ[6] ποιήσουσιν[7], καὶ ὅσα συναντήσει αὐτοῖς * ἕως ἡμέρας κρίσεως[8].   2. Ὑγιαίνων[9] γὰρ[10] ἦν ὅτε ἐκάλεσεν αὐτοὺς πρὸς ἑαυτόν· * ἀπεκαλύφθη δὲ[11] αὐτῷ ὅτι

ὀστᾶ which *d* emends into τὰ ὀστᾶ αὐτοῦ ἐν πολ. Αἰγ. ἐν κρυφῇ. *d* adds καὶ ἔθαψαν αὐτὸν ἐν τῷ σπηλαίῳ τῷ διπλῷ ὅπου καὶ οἱ πατέρες αὐτοῦ ἐτέθησαν. Cf. *g* in note 9.   [13] *d* reads ἐφύλαττον δὲ αὐτοῦ.   [14] A^b*cdefg om. *d* adds τὰ ὀστᾶ Ἰωσήφ.   [15] α. *a* reads ταμιείοις. *bf* ταμείοις. *de* ταμίοις. A^b*cdefg supports β.   A^ab = οἰκήμασι.   [16] *bg*, A^ab(?) read βασιλείων.   [17] *d* reads αὐτῶν. *h*, A om.   [18] *d* reads αὐτῶν. A^abb = οἱ Αἰγύπτιοι καὶ οἱ ἐπαοιδοὶ αὐτῶν. A^cdefg οἱ ἐπαοιδοὶ καὶ οἱ μάγοι.   [19] α, Α. β om.   [20] A adds ἐξ Αἰγύπτου.   [21] α, A^abbcdefg. *b*, A^b*, S¹ read τῇ Αἰγύπτῳ. The rest of β gives conflate readings. *af* τῇ γῇ Αἰγύπτου. *de* γῇ Αἰγύπτου (Αἰγύπτῳ *d*).   [22] A^ab trs. before καὶ γνόφος and om. next three words.   [23] β adds σφόδρα. A^b*cdefg add σφόδρα πᾶσιν.   [24] *f* reads λύχνων.   [25] *d*, A^b*cdefg add δύνασθαι.   [26] *af* read ἕκαστον. A^ab = τις.   [27] *f* reads τῶν ἀδελφῶν.

IX. [1] *d* reads ἔκλαυσαν τοίνυν.   [2] *b* om.   [3] A^b*cdefg = ἀδελφοὶ Συμεὼν καὶ οἱ υἱοί.   [4] β, S¹ add as in margin. After πένθους *d* further adds μ' ἡμέρας. καὶ ἐπέστρεψαν εἰς Αἴγυπτον.   [5] *d* reads ἐκεῖ.   [6] β–d, S add ἐξ (ἀπ' *b*) Αἰγύπτου.   [7] *d* reads τῷ δὲ θεῷ ἡμῶν δόξα εἰς αἰῶνας. *f*, S add Συμεὼν υἱὸς Ἰακὼβ β' υἱὸς Λίας (+ β'. ἔζησεν ἔτη ρκ *f*).

I. [1] α. Attestation of β, A divided. A^abb read διαθήκη Λευὶ περὶ ἱερωσύνης. *bf*, A^cdefg, S¹ δ. Λ. περὶ ἱερωσύνης καὶ ὑπερηφανείας (+ Λευὶ ἑρμηνεύεται ὑπὲρ ἐμοῦ μισθός *f*). *a* Λευί. *de* present conflate texts. *de*, A^b* δ. Λ. υἱὸς (υἱοῦ *e*, A^b*) τρίτος (*e*, A^b* om.) Ἰακὼβ περὶ ἱερ. καὶ ὑπερη.   [2] *d* reads διαθήκης. A = ἀποκρίσεων λόγων which seems to be merely a dittographic rendering of λόγων.   [3] *h* adds τοῦ τρίτου υἱοῦ Ἰακ. καὶ Λείας, and om. next seven words. A^b* om. next five words.   [4] A = ἔδωκε.   [5] *d* = πρὸ τοῦ ἀποθανεῖν αὐτόν. *efg*, A πρὸ τῆς τελευτῆς αὐτοῦ.   [6] *g* reads ὅσα.   [7] *a* adds αὐτοί.   [8] *h* reads ἐν ἡμέρᾳ κ. A^abb om.   [9] Ver. 2 is very confused in A^abb and

Margin: β, Αβ συνελήφθην καὶ ἐτέχθην ἐκεῖ(ἐν Χαρρὰν Αβ) καὶ μετὰ ταῦτα. β, Α, S ὅτε. β, S μετὰ Σ. τὴν ἐκδίκησιν.

μέλλει ἀποθνήσκειν[12]. *Καὶ ὅτε[13] συνήχθησαν[14], *εἶπεν πρὸς αὐτούς[15].

II. Ἐγὼ Λευὶ[1] ἐν Χαρρὰν[2] ἐγεννήθην[3] καὶ[4] ἦλθον[5] σὺν τῷ πατρί μου[6] εἰς[7] Σίκημα[8]. 2. Ἤμην[9] δὲ[10] νεώτερος[11], ὡς[12] ἐτῶν εἴκοσι, *καὶ τότε[13] ἐποίησα[14] *τὴν ἐκδίκησιν μετὰ Συμεὼν[15] *τῆς ἀδελφῆς ἡμῶν Δείνας[16] *ἀπὸ Ἐμμώρ[17]. 3. Ὡς δὲ ἐποίμαινον[18] ἐν Ἀβελμαούλ[19], πνεῦμα συνέσεως Κυρίου ἦλθεν ἐπ' ἐμέ[20], καὶ *ἐθεώρουν πάντας ἀνθρώπους[21] *ἀφανίσαντας τὴν ὁδὸν αὐτῶν[22], καὶ *ἐπὶ τείχους οἰκοδομεῖτο ἡ ἁμαρτία καὶ ἐπὶ πύργους ἡ ἀδικία ἐκάθητο[23]. 4. Καὶ

β, Α[cdeg], S[1] ὅτι τείχη (adf τεῖχος) ᾠκοδόμησεν ἑαυτῇ ἡ ἀδικία καὶ ἐπὶ πύργους ἡ ἀνομία κάθηται.

defective in A[b*]. A[abh] = καὶ (A[ab] om.) ὅτε ἦν αὐτός (then space in A[b] in which [Armenian] (= ὑγιαίνων) probably stood originally) ὤφθη (or ἀπεκαλύφθη) αὐτῷ ὅρασις ὅτι μέλλω (μέλλεις A[b]). ἐκάλεσε πρὸς ἑαυτὸν τοὺς υἱοὺς αὐτοῦ. καὶ ὅτε συνήχθησαν πρὸς αὐτόν, εἶπεν π. αὐτούς. A[b*] om. ὑγιαίνων and the next seven words with the exception of γάρ. [10] α, A[b*def]. β, S[1] om. [11] α, A[cdef]. d reads ἀπεκ. γάρ. af ὤφθη δέ. beg, S[1] ὠ. γάρ. [12] A[b*] add διὰ τοῦτο εἶπεν συνάγειν τοὺς ἀδελφοὺς καὶ υἱοὺς αὐτοῦ. [13] f reads ὅτε δέ. A[b*cdef] = καὶ ἐγένετο ὅτε. [14] A[abh], S[1] add πρὸς αὐτόν. [15] S[1] reads περὶ τῆς ὄψεως ἐν τῇ ἱερωσύνῃ καὶ περὶ προφητείας ἔλεξεν πρὶν ἀποθανεῖν.

II. [1] de read Λευίς. d adds ὁ πατὴρ ἡμῶν. [2] ab. c, df read Χαρρά. h, eg Χαρά. A, S read this Χαρά as χαρᾷ and A adds ἐν Χαρράν also after ἐγεννήθην. [3] α, A[abh]. β reads συνελήφθην καὶ ἐτέχθην ἐκεῖ (ἐκεῖ ἐτέχ. f, ἐτέχ. only g). A[b*cdef] = συνελήφθην καὶ ἐτέχ. ἐν Χαρράν. S ἠρξάμην καὶ ἐγεννήθην. S[1] adds καὶ ἦν αὐξανόμενος ἐν τῷ οἴκῳ τοῦ πατρός μου. [4] α. g om. β–d, A[cdef], S[2] read καὶ μετὰ ταῦτα. S[1] καὶ ἐπεί. A[b*] add μετὰ ὀκτὼ ἔτη. [5] c reads ηλθων. e ἐλθών. g οἰκῶν. [6] α, d, A. abefg, S om. [7] de read ἐν. [8] h, eg. c reads Σύκημα. ab Σίκιμα. d Σικίμοις. f Σήκημα. A[b*] adds καὶ ὅτε ἦμεν ἐν Σικίμοις. [9] c reads εἴμην. [10] S[1] om. [11] g om. [12] α, def, A[b*cdef]. b reads ὡσεί. ag om. [13] α. β, A, S read ὅτε. [14] α, β, S. A = ἐποιήσαμεν. [15] α. β reads μετὰ Σ. τὴν ἐκδίκησιν. A = τὴν ἐκδίκ. ἐγὼ καὶ Συμεὼν ὁ ἀδελφός μου. [16] α, β (save that abef read Δίνας), A[abhef], S. A[b*cd] = Δ. τῆς ἀδ. ἡμῶν. [17] α, e. adfg read ἀπὸ τοῦ (f om.) Ἐμώρ. b ἀπὸ τ. Ἐμμώρ. A = ἀπὸ τῶν Ἀμορραίων, which it trs. before τῆς ἀδελφῆς. [18] b reads ἐποιμαίνομεν. A[abh] = ἦν ἐν τῷ ποιμνίῳ ἡμῶν, and om. next eight words. A[b] om. v. 3, 4. [19] abg, S. α, e[2]f read Ἐβαλμαούλ. de[1](?), A[b*cdef] Ἀβελμαούμ. [20] c reads ἐμοί. [21] h, A. c reads ἐθεώρουν ἀνθ. β–d, S πάντας ἑώρουν ἀνθ. d πάντας ἀνθ. ἐθεώρουν. [22] α, β–d, S. d reads ὄντας ἀφανεῖς τῇ ὁδῷ αὐτῶν. A = ἀφανισθέντας (or ὅτι ἠφανίσθησαν) ταῖς ὁδοῖς αὐτῶν. A[abh] om. rest of verse and first nine words of ver. 4. [23] α (save that h adds

* ἤμην λυπούμενος[24] * ὑπὲρ γένους τῶν υἱῶν τῶν[25] ἀνθρώπων
καὶ[26] ηὐξάμην *τῷ Κυρίῳ[27] ὅπως σωθῶ[28].   5. Τότε
ἐπέπεσέ[29] με[30] ὕπνος, καὶ ἐθεασάμην ὄρος[31] ὑψηλὸν *καὶ
ἤμην ἐν αὐτῷ[32].

6. Καὶ ἰδοὺ ἀνεῴχθησαν[33] οἱ οὐρανοί *, καὶ ἄγγελος Κυρίου[34]
εἶπε *πρός με[35]· *Λευί, ⌐Λευί⌐[36], εἴσελθε.

β, Aᵇ*ᵍ,
S τοῦτο
ὄρος ἀσ-
πίδος ἐν
'Αβελ-
μαούλ.
β, A, S
Λευί.

τούς after the first ἐπί). β, Aᶜᵈᵉᵍ, S¹ read as in margin save that e om. ὅτι,
for ἑαυτῇ, which af om., d reads ἐν αὐτῇ τῇ ὁδῷ, e ἑαυτῆς, g ἐν ἑαυτῇ; for ἀδικία
e reads κακία, g εὐδοκία; for ἐπὶ πύργους Aᶜᵈᵉᵍ read ὡς πύργος, Aᵇ* ὡς ἐπὶ
πύργον; for ἀνομία Aᵇ*ᶜᵈᵉᵍ read ἀδικία, Aᵇ* ἐπὶ ἀδικίαν; for κάθηται e reads
ἐκάθητο. g om. ἡ before ἀνομία. Before καὶ ἐπὶ πύργους e makes the
following long addition. Τότε ἐγὼ ἔπλυνα τὰ ἱμάτιά μου, καὶ καθαρίσας αὐτὰ
ἐν ὕδατι καθαρῷ. καὶ ὅλος ἐλουσάμην ἐν ὕδατι ζῶντι. καὶ πάσας τὰς ὁδούς μου
ἐποίησα εὐθείας· τότε τοὺς ὀφθαλμούς μου καὶ τὸ πρόσωπόν μου ἦρα πρὸς τὸν
οὐρανόν. καὶ τὸ στόμα μου ἤνοιξα καὶ ἐλάλησα· καὶ τοὺς δακτύλους τῶν χειρῶν
μου καὶ τὰς χεῖράς μου ἀνεπέτασα εἰς ἀλήθειαν κατέναντι τῶν ἁγίων· καὶ ηὐξάμην
καὶ εἶπα· Κύριε γινώσκεις πάσας τὰς καρδίας καὶ πάντας τοὺς διαλογισμοὺς ἐννυῶν
(sic)· σὺ μόνος ἐπίστασαι· καὶ νῦν τέκνα μου μετ' ἐμοῦ. καὶ δός μοι πάσας
ὁδοὺς ἀληθείας· μάκρυνον ἀπ' ἐμοῦ Κύριε τὸ πνεῦμα τὸ ἄδικον καὶ διαλογισμῶν τῶν
πονηρῶν καὶ πορνείαν. καὶ ὕβριν ἀπόστρεψον ἀπ' ἐμοῦ. Δειχθήτω μοι Δέσποτα
τὸ πνεῦμα τὸ ἅγιον· καὶ βουλὴν καὶ σοφίαν καὶ γνῶσιν καὶ ἰσχὺν δός μοι ποιῆσαι
τὸ (sic) ἀρέσκοντά σοι καὶ εὑρεῖν χάριν ἐνώπιόν σου· καὶ αἰνεῖν τοὺς λόγους σου
μετ' ἐμοῦ Κύριε. καὶ μὴ κατισχυσάτω με πᾶς σατανᾶς πλανῆσαί με ἀπὸ τῆς ὁδοῦ
σου· καὶ ἐλέησόν με καὶ προσάγαγέ με εἶναί σου δοῦλος καὶ λατρεῦσαί σοι καλῶς·
τεῖχος εἰρήνης σοι γενέσθαι κύκλῳ μου. καὶ σκέπη σου τῆς δυναστείας σκεπασάτω
ἀπὸ παντὸς κακοῦ. παραδως διὸ δὴ καὶ τὴν ἀνομίαν ἐξάλειψον ὑπὸ κάτοθεν τοῦ
οὐρανοῦ· καὶ συντελέσαι τὴν ἀνομίαν ἀπὸ προσώπου τῆς γῆς· καθάρισον τὴν καρδίαν
μου Δέσποτα ἀπὸ πάσης καθαρσίας· καὶ πρὸς ἀροῦμαι πρός σε αὐτός· καὶ μὴ ἀπο-
στρέψεις τὸ πρόσωπόν σου ἀπὸ τοῦ υἱοῦ παιδός σου 'Ιακώβ. σὺ Κύριε εὐλόγησας
τὸν 'Αβραὰμ πατέρα μου καὶ Σαρρὰν μητέρα μου. καὶ εἶπας δοῦναι αὐτοῖς σπέρμα
δίκαιον εὐλογημένον εἰς τοὺς αἰῶνας· εἰσάκουσον δὲ καὶ τῆς φωνῆς τοῦ παιδός σου
Λευὶ γενέσθαι σοι ἐγγύς, καὶ μέτοχον ποίησαν τοῖς λόγοις σου ποιεῖν κρίσιν ἀληθινὴν εἰς πάντα τὸν αἰῶνα, ἐμὲ καὶ τοὺς υἱούς μου εἰς πάσας τὰς γενεὰς τῶν αἰώνων,
καὶ μὴ ἀποστήσῃς τὸν υἱὸν τοῦ παιδός σου ἀπὸ τοῦ προσώπου σου πάσας τὰς ἡμέρας
τοῦ αἰῶνος· καὶ ἐσιώπησα ἔτι δεόμενος. a om. next two verses.   [24] α (save
that c reads εἴμην for ἤμην), Aᶜᵈᵉᵍ. β, Aᵇ*ᶠ, S read ἐλυπούμην.   [25] α (save
that c om. second τῶν), dfg (save that they add τοῦ before γένους, and f
reads περὶ for ὑπέρ). be, S read περὶ τοῦ γ. τῶν ἀνθ. Aᵇ*ᶜᵈᵉᵍ = ὑπὲρ τῶν
υἱῶν τῶν ἀνθ.   [26] d adds ταῦτα θεωρῶν.   [27] α. β–d read κυρίῳ. d πρὸς
κύριον. Aᵃᵇᵇ τῷ θεῷ and add καὶ ᾐτησάμην παρ' αὐτοῦ.   [28] α, β, Aᵃᵇᵇ. Aᵇ*ᶜᵈᵉᵍ
= σώσῃ αὐτούς (Aᵃˡᵍ om.). S = σωθῶσιν.   [29] eg read ἔπεσεν.   [30] c. h
reads μοι, β ἐπ' ἐμέ.   [31] A adds τι.   [32] α. α is supported by Aᵃᵇᵇ

α	Aᵃ	β, Aᵝ, S¹
7. *Καὶ εἰσῆλθον τὸν πρῶτον οὐρανὸν καὶ εἶδον ἐκεῖ ὕδωρ πολὺ κρεμάμενον[37]. 8. Καὶ ἔτι εἶδον δεύτερον οὐρανὸν πολὺ φωτεινότερον καὶ φαιδρότερον· *ἦν γὰρ καὶ †ὕψος ἐν αὐτῷ[38] ἄπειρον. 9. Καὶ εἶπον τῷ ἀγγέλῳ· Τί ἐστι ταῦτα οὕτως; καὶ εἶπέ μοι ὁ ἄγγελος· *Μὴ θαυμάζε περὶ τούτου, ἄλλον γὰρ οὐρανὸν ὄψει φαιδρότερον καὶ ἀσύγ-	7. Καὶ εἰσελθὼν[39] ἐγὼ εἰς τὸν πρῶτον οὐρανὸν 8. †Καὶ παρέπεμψε ἤνεγκέ με†[40] πρὸς τὸν δεύτερον. 7. Καὶ εἶδον ἐκεῖ ὕδωρ πολὺ κρεμάμενον. 9. Καὶ εἶπον αὐτῷ· Τί ἐστι τοῦτο, Κύριε;	7. Καὶ εἰσῆλθον[41] ἐκ τοῦ πρώτου οὐρανοῦ εἰς τὸν δεύτερον[42] καὶ εἶδον[43] ἐκεῖ ὕδωρ κρεμάμενον ἀνάμεσον τούτου κἀκείνου. 8. Καὶ ἔτι[44] εἶδον τρίτον[45] οὐρανὸν πολὺ[46] φωτεινότερον *καὶ φαιδρότερον[47] παρὰ τοὺς δύο· καὶ *γὰρ †ὕψος ἦν ἐν αὐτῷ ἄπειρον[48]. 9. Καὶ εἶπον τῷ ἀγγέλῳ· Διατί οὕτως[49]; καὶ εἶπεν ὁ ἄγγελος *πρός με[50]. Μὴ

which = καὶ ἤμην ἐν τῷ ὄρει. β, Aᵇ*ᶠ, S read τοῦτο (οὗ τὸ f + τὸ g) ὄρος ἀσπίδος (ἀσπίδων g, Aᵇ*ᶠᵍ) (+ ὅ ἐστι Aᵇ*ᶠᵍ, ὀνόματι S¹) ἐν Ἀβελμαούλ (e²f "Εβελ", Aᵇ*ᶠᵍ "μαουμ, S¹ corrupt). Aᶜᵈᵉ = τοῦτο ὄρος ὅ ἐστι ἐν Ἀβελμαούμ.   [33] α, f. Other MSS. ἠνεῴχ. Aᵃᵇʰ add μοι.   [34] Aᵃᵇʰ = ἦλθεν πρός με ἄγγελος θεοῦ καί. For Κυρίου d reads τοῦ θεοῦ.   [35] Aᵇ om. d om. rest of verses, vers. 7, 8 and first twelve words of ver. 9 through hmt.   [36] α. β, A, S read Λευί. Aᵃᵇʰ add ἴθι.   [37] It will be observed that α and Aᵃ agree almost word for word. The latter text has been dislocated by the insertion of a portion of ver. 8 in the midst of ver 7. For πολὺ κρεμ. c reads πολλὺ κρεμμάμενον. [38] c adds τό. Sense is quite unsatisfactory; why should this heaven be brighter because of its loftiness? Hence the error appears to lie in ὕψος. This = נֹגַהּ corrupt for נֹגַהּ = φέγγος or φῶς. This is fitting as the holy ones live therein.   [39] Probably the substantive verb was lost after the participle մտեալ (= εἰσελθών). Then the text would = εἰσῆλθον. [40] This corrupt clause together with next three words are a fragmentary survival of ver. 8, but may have been wrongly transposed here owing to the influence of Aᵝ.   [41] Aᵝ = εἰσελθών.   [42] Aᵝ add οὐρανόν.   [43] f reads ἴδον. [44] b, S² om.   [45] In Aᵝ երիր (= τρίτον) could easily fall out before երկին (= οὐρανόν). f om. next word.   [46] Aᵝ om.   [47] ab, Aᵉ, S² om. S¹ reads καὶ καθαρώτερον and trs. after δύο.   [48] g reads ὕψος πνευμάτων τῶν ἀπείρων.   [49] Aᵝ = δή ἐστι τοῦτο οὕτως.   [50] eg om.   [51] This clause is lost by Aᵃ, which also wrongly omits the initial καί of the next verse.

α	Aᵃ	β, Aᵝ, S¹
κριτου⁵¹. 10. Καὶ⁵² ἐν τῷ ἀνελθεῖν σε ἐκεῖ, στήσῃ⁵³ ἐγγὺς τοῦ Κυρίου καὶ λειτουργὸς αὐτῷ⁵⁴ ἔσῃ καὶ μυστήρια αὐτοῦ ἐξαγγελεῖς τοῖς ἀνθρώποις καὶ περὶ †τοῦ μέλλοντος λυτροῦσθαι τὸν†⁵⁵ Ἰσραὴλ κηρύξεις.	καὶ εἶπέν μοι· 10. ᾽Εν τῷ ἀνελθεῖν σε ἐκεῖ †ζήσῃ†⁵⁶ ἐνώπιον τοῦ Κυρίου καὶ ἔσῃ λειτουργὸς αὐτοῦ καὶ τὰ μέλλοντα μυστήρια αὐτοῦ ἐξαγγελεῖς τοῖς ἀνθρώποις.	θαύμαζε⁵⁷ ἐπὶ τούτοις, ἄλλους γὰρ *τέσσαρας οὐρανοὺς ὄψει⁵⁸ φαιδροτέρους⁵⁹ *καὶ ἀσυγκρίτους⁶⁰, 10. ῞Οτε⁶¹ ἀνέλθῃς ἐκεῖ· ⌐ὅτι⌐⁶² σὺ ἐγγὺς Κυρίου στήσῃ, καὶ λειτουργὸς αὐτοῦ⁶³ ἔσῃ καὶ μυστήρια αὐτοῦ ἐξαγγελεῖς τοῖς ἀνθρώποις⁶⁴ καὶ περὶ *λυτρώσεως τοῦ⁶⁵ Ἰρσαὴλ κηρύξεις.

β, S τοῦ μέλλοντος λυτροῦσθαι τόν.
β, A, S =ἐν.

11. Καὶ διὰ σοῦ καὶ τοῦ⁶⁶ Ἰούδα ὀφθήσεται Κύριος τοῖς⁶⁷ ἀνθρώποις⁶⁸.

⌐Σώζων· †ἐν ἑαυτῷ† πᾶν γένος ἀνθρώπων⌐⁶⁹.

Vers. 10–12. These verses seem out of place here. Both as respects substance and form they would read well after IV. 2. Moreover, as III. 1 implies that Levi has already seen the heavens, we should expect a description of the third heaven here. But these inconsistencies are due to the writer, not to subsequent transpositions of the text; for according to V. 1 Levi is not admitted into the third heaven till he has heard the long disquisition in II. 10—IV. ⁵²α. Lost in Aᵃ. ⁵³Em. from h ἵστασαι. c reads ἔσωσε. Right reading preserved in β, Aᵝ, and originally in Aᵃ. See note 55. With the statement in this line compare Jub. xxxi. 13, 'Cause thee to approach Him to serve in His sanctuary.' ⁵⁴h reads αὐτοῦ. ⁵⁵Text altered by a Christian scribe. β has suffered similarly. As Aᵃ omits, Aᵝ alone preserves the original = λυτρώσεως. ⁵⁶This corrupt reading is due to an internal corruption of [Armenian] (or [Armenian]) = στήσῃ into [Armenian] = ζήσῃ. ⁵⁷d reads θαυμάζεις. f erases. ⁵⁸d reads οὐρανοὺς ὑπὲρ ἄνω ὄψεις. S reads οὐρανοὺς ὄψει, οἵ εἰσι πλανῆται καὶ ὀνομάζονται ζῶναι. ⁵⁹Aᵝ add τούτων. ⁶⁰d reads καὶ ἀσυγκριτωτέρους. g ἀσυγκρίτως. S¹ κ. θαυμαστοτέρους αὐτῶν. d adds λέγω γάρ σοι and om. next three words. ⁶¹Aᵝ adds γάρ. ⁶²The insertion of ὅτι here gives a different turn to the context. ⁶³Aᶜᵈᵉᶠ om. Aᵇˣ reads κυρίου. ⁶⁴d reads υἱοῖς τῶν ἀνθρώπων. ⁶⁵So Aᵝ. β, S read corruptly as in margin. ⁶⁶α. β om. ⁶⁷α. β–d, A, S read ἐν. d om. ⁶⁸Aᵃ om. rest of chap. and Aᵝ om. next line. ⁶⁹This clause = ויישע בו כל־האדם, where I take

A^a omit
ver. 12.

12. *Καὶ ἐκ μερίδος Κυρίου ἡ ζωή σου[70],
καὶ αὐτὸς ἔσται σοι[71] ἀγρὸς[72] *καὶ ἀμπελὼν[73]
καὶ[74] καρπός[75] *χρυσίον καὶ ἀργύριον[76].

α	A^a	β, A^β, S¹
III. Ἄκουσον οὖν[1] περὶ τῶν δειχθέντων σοι οὐρανῶν· ὁ κατώτερος *διὰ τοῦτό σοί ἐστι στυγνός, ἐπειδὴ[2] ὁρᾷ πάσας[3] τὰς ἀδικίας τῶν ἀνθρώπων. 2. Καὶ ἔχει πῦρ χιόνα καὶ[4] κρύσταλλον ἡτοιμασμένον[5] εἰς	III. Ἄκουσον οὖν περὶ τῶν δειχθέντων †ὁράσεων[6]· ὁ πρῶτος[7] οὐρανὸς διὰ τοῦτο †ὃν κατενόησας[8] σοι ἐπειδὴ † ἑώρας[9] ἀδικίας †τὰ ἔργα†[10] ἀνθρώπων. 2. Ὁ δὲ δεύτερος ἔχει πῦρ καὶ χιόνα καὶ κρύ-	III. Ἄκουσον οὖν[11] περὶ ἑπτὰ οὐρανῶν. *Ὁ κατώτερος[12] διὰ τοῦτο[13] στυγνότερός[14] ἐστιν, ἐπειδὴ ὁρᾷ[15] ⌐πάσας⌐[16] τὰς[17] ἀδικίας[18] τῶν[17] ἀνθρώπων. 2. Ὁ[19] δεύτερος ἔχει πῦρ χιόνα[20] κρύσταλλον

ꞇ to be corrupt for ꞁ, which may = 'for Himself,' or may be an instance
of the redundant expression of the pronoun before the noun (an Aramaism,
but found in Hebrew. Cf. Gen. ii. 19; Exod. ii. 6; Jos. i. 2, &c.)
Hence read ἑαυτῷ or simply om. Cf. Sim. vi. 5. A om. entire line.
For ἐν ἑαυτῷ of c, h (e?), S² read ἐν αὐτῷ, afg, S¹ ἑαυτῷ, b ἐν αὐτοῖς, d om.
For ἀνθρώπων h reads ἀνθρώπου. [70] Cf. Isaac's blessing of Levi, Jub.
xxxi. 16, 'Let His table be thine.' For μερίδος S¹ reads τιμῆς. [71] α, dfg.
abe read σου. [72] β–α, A^β. α corruptly reads καρπός. a, A^β ἀγροί.
[73] α, adefg. b, S¹ read ἀμπελών. A = ἀμπελώνων. [74] α, e¹g, A^β. β–eg, e², S¹
om. [75] c. h, β, S¹ read καρποί. A^β καρπίμων. [76] c, ag. h reads χρυσίων
καὶ ἀργυρίων. bef, S¹ χρυσίον ἀργύριον. d, A^β read καὶ (+ θησαυρὸς A^b*)
χρυσίον καὶ ἀργυρίου.

III. [1] h reads δή. [2] h reads διατί ἐστι στυγνός, ἐπεί. [3] A, d om. [4] h om.
[5] h reads ἡτοιμασμένα. [6] Corrupt for οὐρανῶν. [7] This word is only found
elsewhere in d. [8] So A^a ꞇꞇ which may be corrupt for
ꞇꞇ = στυγνός ἐστι, or ꞇꞇ = ὁ κατώτερος. In the
latter case A^a would be akin to d (see note 15) but the ὁ κατώτερος is in
this case trs. from its place before οὐρανός. A^a therefore = ὁ πρῶτος οὐρανὸς
διὰ τοῦτο στυγνός ἐστι or ὁ πρῶτος ὁ κατώτερος διὰ τοῦτο, being in this latter
case defective. [9] This corruption, as the last, is native to A. [10] An
intrusion owing to which we have the genitives τῆς ἀδικ. and τῶν ἀνθ.
The word ꞇꞇ may be a corruption of the missing word for στυγνός.
See note 8. [11] d om. [12] d reads ὁ πρῶτος οὗτος κατώτερος. See note 8.
[13] d adds καί. [14] A^β, S¹ read στυγνός. [15] g reads συνορᾷ. b οὗτος παρά.
[16] d, A om. [17] bg, A om. [18] S¹ = μυστήρια, though S² supports text.
[19] A^β add δέ. [20] e reads χάλαζα χιών. A^β inserts καί before and after χιόνα.

α	Aᵃ	β, Aᵝ, S¹
ἡμέραν κρίσεως ἐν τῇ δικαιοκρισίᾳ τοῦ Θεοῦ· ἐν αὐτῷ γάρ εἰσι πάντα τὰ πνεύματα τῶν ἐπαγωγῶν εἰς ἐκδίκησιν τῶν ἀνθρώπων. 3. Ἐν δὲ τῷ δευτέρῳ εἰσὶν αἱ δυνάμεις τῶν παρεμβολῶν οἱ ταχθέντες εἰς ἡμέραν κρίσεως ποιῆσαι ἐκδίκησιν τοῖς πνεύμασι τῆς πλάνης καὶ τοῦ Βελίαρ· καὶ ἐπ᾽ αὐτούς εἰσιν οἱ ἅγιοι. 4. Ἐν τῷ ἀνωτέρῳ δὲ πάντων καταλύματι²¹ ἤ²² μεγάλη δόξα ὑπεράνω²³ πάσης ἁγιότητος.	στάλλον εἰς ἡμέραν τῶν προσταγμάτων²⁴ ἡτοιμασμένον. 　 4. *Ὁ δὲ ἅγιος²⁵ τῶν ἁγίων ἐστὶ ὑπεράνω πάσης ἁγιότητος.	ἕτοιμα²⁶ *εἰς ἡμέραν²⁷ προστάγματος Κυρίου ἐν τῇ δικαιοκρισίᾳ τοῦ θεοῦ· ἐν αὐτῷ²⁸ εἰσι πάντα τὰ πνεύματα *τῶν ἐπαγωγῶν²⁹ εἰς ἐκδίκησιν τῶν ἀνόμων³⁰. 3. Ἐν³¹ τῷ τρίτῳ³² εἰσὶν αἱ δυνάμεις *τῶν παρεμβολῶν³³, *οἱ ταχθέντες εἰς ἡμέραν κρίσεως³⁴ ποιῆσαι ἐκδίκησιν³⁵ *τοῖς πνεύμασι τῆς πλάνης³⁶ καὶ³⁷ τοῦ Βελίαρ. *Οἱ δὲ³⁸ εἰς τὸν τέταρτον οἱ³⁹ ἐπάνω τούτων ἅγιοι⁴⁰ εἰσιν. 4. Ὅτι ἐν τῷ ἀνωτέρῳ πάντων καταλύει ἤ⁴¹ μεγάλη δόξα⁴⁰ ἐν ἁγίῳ ἁγίων ὑπεράνω πάσης ἁγιότητος.

²¹ c. *h* reads καταλύει δὲ ἤ. 　 ²² *h*. c om. 　 ²³ *h*. c om., but β, A, S¹ support *h*. 　 ²⁴ The plural has probably originated in Aᵃ. Here Aᵃ agree with β, Aᵝ, which have προστάγματος, whereas α has κρίσεως. Both words are independent renderings of מִשְׁפָּט. 　 ²⁵ Corrupt for ἐν ἁγίῳ. ²⁶ e reads ἑτοιμασμένα. 　 ²⁷ d reads εἰσὶν ἐν ἡμέρᾳ. 　 ²⁸ d, Aᵝ add δέ. ²⁹ Aᵇ = εἰς δρόμους (?). g om. τῶν. 　 ³⁰ β–a, Aᵝ, S°. ef, S¹ ανωμ. a ἀνθρώπων. 　 ³¹ g, Aᵝ prefix καί. 　 ³² g adds οὐρανῷ. 　 ³³ Aᵇ has ժամանակաց (= τῶν χρόνων) which may be corrupt for բանակաց = τῶν παρεμβολῶν. ³⁴ Aᵝ = καὶ τεταγμέναι εἰσὶν εἰς δικαιοκρισίαν, but the Armenian for δικαιοκρισίαν is internally corrupt for ἡμέραν κρίσεως. dg read αἱ ταχθησαι (-εῖσαι g) for οἱ ταχθ. 　 ³⁵ bdg add ἐν. 　 ³⁶ Aᵝ = τῶν δικαίων πλάνης (corrupt). 　 ³⁷ Aᵇ*ᶜᵈ = ἀπό. Aᵉᶠᵍ om. 　 ³⁸ d om. A = καί. 　 ³⁹ aef, Aᵝ. bg om. d reads δὲ οὐρανόν and dg om. ἐπ. τούτων. For οἱ ... τούτων Aᵝ = οἵ εἰσιν ἐν σκηνώμασι αὐτοῦ where ի վրանս նորա is corrupt for ի վեր նոցա = ἐπάνω τούτων.

α	Aᵃ	β, Aᵝ, S¹

α

5. Ἐν τῷ μετ᾽ †αὐτῶν⁴² εἰσιν ἀρχάγγελοι οἱ λειτουργοῦντες καὶ ἐξιλασκόμενοι πρὸς Κύριον ἐπὶ πάσαις ταῖς ἀγνοίαις τῶν δικαίων, 6. Προσφέροντες τῷ Κυρίῳ ὀσμὴν εὐωδίας⁴³ λογικὴν⁴⁴ καὶ ἀναίμακτον θυσίαν. 7. Ἐν δὲ τῷ ὑποκάτω εἰσὶν⁴⁵ ἄγγελοι οἱ φέροντες ἀποκρίσεις τοῖς ἀγγέλοις τοῦ προσώπου κυρίου. 8. Ἐν δὲ τῷ⁴⁶ μετ᾽ †αὐτῶν⁴⁷ εἰσιν θρόνοι καὶ⁴⁸ ἐξουσίαι, ἐν ᾧ *ἀεὶ ὕμνον τῷ θεῷ προσφέροντες⁴⁹.

Aᵃ

5. *Αἱ δὲ δυνάμεις⁵⁰ τῶν ἀγγέλων εἰσὶ λειτουργοῦντες.

8. Καὶ ὑμνοῦντες τὸν Κύριον, 7. Οἱ καὶ *πρεσβεῖς εἰσι τῆς θεότητος⁵¹.

β, Aᵝ, S¹

5. *Ἐν τῷ⁵² μετ᾽ αὐτὸν⁵³ οἱ⁵⁴ ἄγγελοί εἰσι *τοῦ προσώπου⁵⁵ Κυρίου⁵⁶ οἱ λειτουργοῦντες *καὶ ἐξιλασκόμενοι⁵⁷ πρὸς Κυρίον ἐπὶ πάσαις⁵⁸ ταῖς *ἀγνοίαις τῶν δικαίων⁵⁹. 6. Προσφέρουσι δὲ Κυρίῳ⁶⁰ ὀσμὴν εὐωδίας⁶¹ *λογικὴν καὶ ἀναίμακτον προσφοράν. 7. Ἐν δὲ τῷ ὑποκάτω εἰσὶν οἱ⁶² ἄγγελοι οἱ φέροντες τὰς ἀποκρίσεις *τοῖς ἀγγέλοις⁶³ τοῦ προσώπου Κυρίου. 8. *Ἐν δὲ τῷ μετ᾽ αὐτόν⁶⁴ εἰσι *θρόνοι καὶ ἐξουσίαι⁶⁵, ἐν ᾧ *ἀεὶ ὕμνοι⁶⁶ τῷ θεῷ προσφέρου-

⁴⁰ Aᵝ add τοῦ θεοῦ.   ⁴¹ d om.   ⁴² α, d. β–dg, Aᵝ read αὐτόν. Here and in ver. 8 αὐτῶν seems corrupt.   ⁴³ c adds τήν.   ⁴⁴ c. h reads λογικῆς.   ⁴⁵ h adds οἱ.   ⁴⁶ h. c reads τό.   ⁴⁷ c, e. h, g read αὐτῷ. α–eg αὐτόν.   ⁴⁸ h om.   ⁴⁹ c. h, in dependence on β, reads ὕμνοι τῷ θ. προσφέρονται.   ⁵⁰ This phrase seems to be drawn from ver. 3.   ⁵¹ Apparently a free rendering of ver. 7.   ⁵² Aᵝ καί.   ⁵³ β–dg, S¹. d reads αὐτῶν. g αὐτῷ.   ⁵⁴ d, Aᵝ om.   ⁵⁵ d = τοῦ.   ⁵⁶ Aᵝ = αὐτοῦ. d om. next two words.   ⁵⁷ S¹ om. but not S². Aᵝ om. the καί.   ⁵⁸ f reads πᾶσιν. Aᵇ* om.   ⁵⁹ d reads αἰτήσεσι τῶν ἐν ἀγνοίᾳ ἐσφαλμένων τοῖς δικαίοις. In A by adding ܠܐ before ܓܦܘܢܬ݂ܘܢ (= γνώσει) we obtain ἀγνοίᾳ.   ⁶⁰ Aᵝ trs. after εὐωδίας.   ⁶¹ d reads εὐωδίαν.   ⁶² d om.   ⁶³ g reads τῶν ἀγγέλων.   ⁶⁴ abf, S¹. deg read ἐν δὲ τῷ μετὰ τούτων (e αὐτῶν, g αὐτῷ). Aᵝ = καὶ μετ᾽ αὐτούς.   ⁶⁵ a, Aᵝ. bdef, S¹ read θρόνοι ἐξουσ. g οἱ θρ. αἱ ἐξουσ.   ⁶⁶ aefg, Aᵝ. b reads ὕμνοι ἀεί. d ἀεὶ ὑμνοῦσι.   ⁶⁷ h adds ὁ.   ⁶⁸ h. c reads τρέμωμεν.   ⁶⁹ c. h reads ἄβυσσοι.   ⁷⁰ d om. Aᵝ, S = προσφέρουσι.   ⁷¹ de

<table>
<tr><td>

α

9. Ὅταν οὖν ἐπιβλέψει[67] Κύριος ἐφ᾽ ἡμᾶς οἱ πάντες τρέμομεν[68] καὶ ὁ οὐρανὸς καὶ ἡ γῆ καὶ *ἡ ἄβυσσος[69] ἀπὸ προσώπου τῆς μεγαλωσύνης αὐτοῦ σαλεύονται.

</td><td>

Aα

9. Ὅταν οὖν ἐπιβλέψῃ Κύριος ἐπὶ πᾶσαν κτίσιν, ἐσαλεύθησαν οἱ οὐρανοὶ καὶ ἡ γῆ καὶ αἱ ἄβυσσοι.

</td><td>

β, Aβ, S[1]

ται[70]. 9. Ὅταν οὖν ἐπιβλέψῃ[71] Κύριος[72] ἐφ᾽ ἡμᾶς πάντες ἡμεῖς σαλενόμεθα[73], καὶ[74] οἱ οὐρανοὶ καὶ ἡ γῆ καὶ αἱ[75] ἄβυσσοι ἀπὸ[76] προσώπου[77] τῆς μεγαλωσύνης *αὐτοῦ σαλεύονται[78].

</td></tr>
</table>

10. Οἱ δὲ υἱοὶ τῶν ἀνθρώπων ἐν[79] τούτοις[80] ἀναισθητοῦντες[81] ἁμαρτάνουσι *καὶ παροργίζουσι τὸν ὕψιστον[82].

IV. Νῦν οὖν γίνωσκε[1] ὅτι ποιήσει Κύριος κρίσιν ἐπὶ τοὺς υἱοὺς τῶν ἀνθρώπων.

  β–g, A, S γινώσκετε.

Ὅτι[2] πετρῶν[3] σχιζομένων,
καὶ τοῦ ἡλίου σβεννυμένου[4]
καὶ ὑδάτων[5] ξηραινομένων
καὶ τοῦ[6] πυρὸς καταπτήσσοντος[7]
καὶ πάσης ⌜τῆς⌝[8] κτίσεως κλονουμένης[9]
καὶ τῶν ἀοράτων πνευμάτων[10] τηκομένων[11]
καὶ[12] τοῦ ᾅδου σκυλευομένου[13] [ἐπὶ τῷ πάθει τοῦ ὑψίστου][14]
* οἱ ἄνθρωποι ἀπειθοῦντες ἐπιμενοῦσι ταῖς ἀδικίαις[15].

  h, A σκοτιζομένου.

  β–d, Aβ ἀπιστοῦντες.

read ἐπιβλέψει. [72] d adds ὁ θεός. [73] d adds καὶ οὐ μόνον ἡμεῖς ἀλλά. [74] Aβ om. [75] adf. b reads οἱ. eg om. [76] d reads μὴ φέροντες τοῦ. [77] d adds αὐτοῦ καί. [78] beg. af read αὐ. σαλευθήσονται. d τῆς ὑπερβαλλούσης δόξης. Aβ αὐτοῦ. [79] af. bdeg, S read ἐπί. [80] Aβ add πᾶσιν. [81] A reads ἀναισθητοῦσι and Aα om. rest of verse. Aβ add διὰ τοῦτο. [82] All MSS. of A om. but Ab*.

IV. [1] α, g. β–g, A read γινώσκετε. [2] c reads καὶ ὅτι. The following clauses in the genitive absolute are rendered in A by clauses with verbs in the future indicative. [3] c. h, β. S prefix τῶν. [4] h, A read σκοτιζομένου. [5] α, A. β prefixes τῶν. [6] Aβ om. [7] Aα has *[Armenian]* = ἀπειληθήσεται. Aβ has *[Armenian]* = λευκὸν ἔσται. [8] α, f. β–f, A om. [9] Aα has *[Armenian]* = ἀπολοῦνται being corrupt for *[Armenian]* = κλονήσονται which appears in Aβ. [10] h reads κτισμάτων. [11] A[abbcdefg] have *[Armenian]* = διωχθήσονται corrupt for *[Armenian]* (so Ab*) = τήξονται. [12] b om. This line is transposed before the preceding one by Aβ. [13] a reads σκυλλομένου. [14] Bracketed as a Christian interpolation. For τῷ πάθει g reads τὸ πάθος, and for ὑψίστου d reads χριστοῦ and for ἐπί reads ἐν. [15] For this and the following line Aα reads καὶ διὰ τοῦτο ἐν ⌜τῇ⌝[16] κολάσει κριθήσονται.

2. Εἰσήκουσεν[17] ⌜οὖν⌝[18] ὁ ὕψιστος τῆς προσευχῆς[19] σου *τοῦ διελεῖν[20] σε ἀπὸ[21] ἀδικίας[22] καὶ γενέσθαι αὐτῷ[23] *υἱὸν καὶ θεράποντα[24] καὶ λειτουργὸν[25] τοῦ προσώπου αὐτοῦ.

β, A, S
γνώσεως
φωτεινόν.

3. Φῶς[26] γνώσεως[27] φωτιεῖς[28] *ἐν τῷ Ἰακώβ[29], καὶ[30] ὡς[31] ἥλιος *ἔσῃ[32] παντὶ[33] σπέρματι[34] Ἰσραήλ.

α, β, A^β, S	A^a
4. Καὶ δοθήσεταί σοι εὐλογία· *καὶ παντὶ τῷ σπέρματί σου[35]	4. Καὶ γενήσεται ἐν ταῖς ἐσχάταις ἡμέραις πέμψει ὁ Θεὸς
ἕως[36] ἐπισκέψεται[37] Κύριος πάντα τὰ ἔθνη[38] ἐν σπλάγχνοις [υἱοῦ][39] αὐτοῦ* ἕως αἰῶνος[40].	[τὸν υἱὸν αὐτοῦ] τοῦ σώζειν τὰ κτίσματα
[Πλὴν[41] οἱ υἱοί σου ἐπιβαλοῦσι χεῖρας *ἐπ' αὐτὸν[42] *τοῦ ἀνασκολοπίσαι[43] αὐτόν]	[καὶ υἱοί σου ἐπιβαλοῦσι χεῖρας καὶ ἀνασκολοπίσουσι αὐτόν]

εἰπὼν τοῦτο αὖθις εἰπέν μοι. I have read ἀπειθοῦντες with α, d. β–d, A^β, S read ἀπιστοῦντες. Before ταῖς abd, A^β, S add ἐν, and for ταῖς A^β read ταῖς αὐταῖς. A^β read οἱ δὲ ἀνθ. for οἱ ἀνθ. [16] α. β, A om. [17] Before εἰσήκ. A adds ἰδού, d σοῦ δέ. [18] d, A om. g reads γοῦν. [19] c reads εὐχῆς. [20] A = καὶ διεῖλε. [21] β adds τῆς. [22] A^β = ἀνομίας. [23] abef, A, S. d reads αὐτοῦ. c σεαυτῷ. h σοι αὐτῷ. g om. [24] α, β, A^cfg, S. A^a = θεράποντα. A^b*cd εἰς θεράποντα καὶ υἱόν. [25] A^a add πιστόν. [26] d prefixes ὅτι. A^b*cd prefix καί. [27] abefg, S add φωτεινόν, d, A^cfg αὐτοῦ φωτινόν, A^b*cd αὐτοῦ, A^a κυρίου. [28] beg, S. α, af, A^β read φωτιεῖ, d φωτίσεις. A^a φωτίζει σε. With ver. 3 we might compare Jub. xxxi. 15 where Isaac blesses Levi—

    'And they will declare thy ways to Jacob
    And thy paths to Israel.'

[29] α. β, A^cefg, S read ἐν Ἰακ. A^b*d = φωτεινὸν τῷ Ἰακώβ. A^a om. [30] A^a om. [31] α, e. β–eg, A, S read ὡς ὁ. g ὡσεί. [32] β. α reads ἐν. A = ἐπιλάμψεις. [33] c reads φωτί. ae, A add τῷ. [34] α reads σπέρμα. [35] c, def, A^β, S. a reads καὶ τῷ σπ. σου. bg καὶ παντὶ σπ. σου. h ἐπὶ τῷ σπ. σου. [36] dg read ἕως οὗ. [37] h, ag. c, d read ἐπισκέψειται. bf ἐπισκέψηται. e ἐπί. [38] This might be a Christian modification of πᾶν τὸ ἔθνος, the latter meaning Israel. The genuineness of ἕως ἐπισκέψεται κ.τ.λ. is supported by v. 2, where God is represented as saying ἕως ἐλθὼν κατοικήσω κτλ. [39] b reads υἱοί. dg τοῦ υἱοῦ. Bracketed as a Christian interpolation. The text deals with an O. T. theophany. Cf. v. 2.

5. ⌜Καὶ⌝[44] διὰ τοῦτο δέδωταί[45] σοι[46] βουλὴ καὶ σύνεσις
τοῦ συνετίσαι τοὺς υἱούς σου[47] *περὶ τούτου[48].

6. Ὅτι *οἱ εὐλογοῦντες[49] †αὐτὸν[50] εὐλογημένοι[51] ἔσονται[52]
*καὶ οἱ[53] καταρώμενοι †αὐτὸν[50] ἀπολοῦνται[54].

β, ΑΒ, S ὁ εὐλογῶν ..εὐλογημένος.

V. Καὶ †ἐν τούτῳ[1] ἤνοιξέ μοι[2] *ὁ ἄγγελος[3] τὰς πύλας
τοῦ οὐρανοῦ· καὶ εἶδον τὸν *ἅγιον ὕψιστον ἐπὶ θρόνου καθήμενον[4].   2. Καὶ εἶπέ μοι[5]· Λευί, σοὶ[6] ἔδωκα[7] *τὰς
εὐλογίας τῆς ἱερατείας[8] ἕως[9] ἐλθὼν[10] κατοικήσω[11] *ἐν
μέσῳ[12] τοῦ Ἰσραήλ.   3. Τότε[13] ὁ ἄγγελος[14] κατήγαγέν[15]
με ἐπὶ τὴν γῆν, καὶ ἔδωκέ[16] μοι *ὅπλον καὶ ῥομφαίαν[17], καὶ
εἶπέ μοι[18]· Ποίησον ἐκδίκησιν ἐν Συχὲμ[19] ὑπὲρ Δείνας[20]

β, Α, S ναὸν τὸν ἅγιον καὶ ἐπὶ θρόνου δόξης τὸν ὕψιστον.

[40] α, bg. aef, S read εἰς αἰῶνα. d Aβ εἰς αἰῶνα αἰῶνος.   [41] h adds οὖν. This line is a manifest Christian interpolation. It is in conflict with both the form and matter of the text.   [42] d om. a adds γε.   [43] b reads τοῦ ἀποσκολοπίσαι. Aβ = καὶ ἀνασκολοπίσουσι.   [44] A om.   [45] c, bd. h (?), a read δέδοται. ef δίδοται. g δίδεται.   [46] d trs. before δέδωται.   [47] Ab* om.   [48] α, aef, S. bdg, Aβ read π. αὐτοῦ. Aa = μὴ ἁμαρτάνειν ἐπ' αὐτόν.   [49] α, Aa. β, Aβ, S read ὁ εὐλογῶν.   [50] Apparently a corruption for σε (Schnapp).   [51] α, Aa. β, Aβ, S read εὐλογημένος.   [52] Aa. β–g, Aβ, S read ἔσται. α om. For εὐλογ. ἔσται g reads εὐλογηθήσεται. With this verse compare Isaac's blessing of Levi, Jub. xxxi. 17:

'And blessed be he that blesses thee,
And cursed be every nation that curses thee.'

[53] α, β–bd, A. bd read οἱ δέ.   [54] S1 adds καὶ ἔτι ὁ Λευὶ προσετίθει τῷ λόγῳ τοῖς υἱοῖς αὐτοῦ.

V. [1] α. Aa = εἰπὼν τοῦτο. β, Aβ om.   [2] e om.   [3] Aa trs. before ἤνοιξε.   [4] α (save that h reads καὶ for ὕψιστον). β, Ae?s, S read ναὸν τὸν ἅγιον (g om. τ. ἅγ.) καὶ ἐπὶ θρόνου δόξης τὸν ὕψιστον. Aa,b*cd = ναὸν τὸν ἅγιον καὶ τὸν ὕψιστον ἐπὶ θρόνου δόξης.   [5] d reads πρός με.   [6] c, e read σύ. Here e adds: δοθήσεται καὶ τῷ σπέρματί σου τοῦ λειτουργεῖν τῷ ὑψίστῳ ἐν μέσῳ τῆς γῆς· καὶ ἐξιλάσκεσθαι σὺ ἐπὶ ταῖς ἀγνοίαις τῆς γῆς· τότε.   [7] α, e, Aa. abfg, S read δέδωκα. d δίδωμι. Aβ = δέδοται, but by emending ⳑ into ⳑⳑ, Aβ is brought into agreement with abfg.   [8] h, β–e, Aa, S1. c reads τὰς ἱερατείας. Aβ = δύναμιν ἱερατείας, but ϙορπι.βρμ (=δύναμις) is corrupt for ϙορϛνπι.βρμ = εὐλογίαν.   [9] bd add οὐ.   [10] Aa = ἐλεύσομαι καί.   [11] α, aefg. bd read παροικήσω. Aβ may render either. Aa = ἀποκαλυφθήσομαι.   [12] α, def. β–def read ἐμμέσῳ.   [13] d reads καὶ τότε. Aa = καὶ μετὰ ταῦτα. c adds ἐλθών.   [14] d adds ὁ συμπαρών μοι. Aa add τοῦ κυρίου and trs. after ἤγαγέ με.   [15] c, dh. abef, A, S read ἤγαγε.   [16] a reads δέδωκε.   [17] Aa = ῥομ. καὶ ὅπλον.   [18] α, dg, A. β–dg, S om. Aa add ἐλθὲ καί.   [19] Aa = Αἰγυπτίοις. Aβ = Σικιμίταις.   [20] α, d. e rea Δήνας.

Aᵃ = συντελέσω. β, Aβ, S¹ οὐρανῶν. β–a, A, S¹ εἰπέ μοι. α παρεπόμενος τοῦ γένους, d προιστάμενος τοῦ γένους. A, S¹ παταχθῆναι. β–d, Aβ, S¹ πατάξαι αὐτοὺς εἰς τέλος, ὅτι πᾶν πνεῦμα πονηρὸν εἰς αὐτὸν προσβάλλει.

*τῆς ἀδελφῆς σου[21], κἀγὼ[22] ἔσομαι μετά σου[23], ὅτι Κύριος
*ἀπέστειλέν †με[24]. 4. καὶ συνετέλεσα†[25] τῷ καιρῷ ἐκείνῳ
*τοὺς υἱοὺς[26] Ἐμμώρ[27], καθὼς γέγραπται ἐν πλαξὶ[28] τῶν
πατέρων[29]. 5. Εἶπον δὲ αὐτῷ[30]· Δέομαί σου[31], Κύριε[32],
*δίδαξόν με[33] τὸ ὄνομά σου ἵνα[34] ἐπικαλέσομαί[35] σε[36] ἐν ἡμέρᾳ
θλίψεως[37]. 6. Καὶ εἶπεν[38]· Ἐγώ εἰμι ὁ ἄγγελος ὁ *παραιτούμενος τὸ γένος[39] Ἰσραήλ, τοῦ μὴ πατάξαι[40] αὐτούς[41].

---

abf, Aβ Δίνας, g τῆς Δίνας. Aᵃ om. [21] α, d, A. β–d, S om. [22] h reads ἐγώ. [23] Aᵃ om. next four words. [24] α, adf. beg read ἀπέσταλκέ (+ν e) με. For με we should expect σε. If με is right we should expect καὶ συντελέσω to follow as in Aᵃ and not κ. συνετέλεσα as in β. See next note. S¹ trs. next three verses after τὸν ὕψιστον, v. 7. [25] See preceding note. Aβ = συντελεσθήσῃ, but կատարեսցիս is corrupt for կատարեցից = συντελέσω or կատարեցի = συνετέλεσα. Aᵃ om. next twelve words. [26] Aβ = ἐν μέσῳ τῶν υἱῶν. [27] beg. α, adf read Ἐμώρ. [28] α, bd. ae¹f read πλάξεσι. g πράξεσι. β–g prefix ταῖς. [29] α. β, Aβ, S¹ read as in margin. [30] d reads αὐτοῦ. [31] α, d, A. abefg om. [32] d adds μου. [33] α. β–a, A, S¹ read εἰπέ μοι. a εἰπέ τί. [34] g, Aβ read καί. [35] c, deg. h, ab read ἐπικαλέσωμαι. f ἐπικαλοῦμαι. [36] g reads σοι. c om. [37] e, A add μου. [38] ae read εἰπέ μοι. [39] β–d = פונע לעם.* The text is uncertain. d reads προιστάμενος τοῦ γένους which = נגן על־העם (or עומד. Cf. Dan. xii. 1). Is d original and β–d a corruption of it, or is β–d original and d an emendation due to Dan. xii. 1? Next α reads παρεπόμενος τοῦ γένους, which might be another rendering of עומד על־העם in the sense 'attending on the nation'; cf. 1 Kings xxii. 19. The LXX renders עמד על by βοηθῶν in Esther viii. 11, ix. 16. But παρεπόμενος may be either a bad rendering or a corruption of παραιτούμενος. See parallel text in Test. Dan. vi. 2. Finally A = φύλαξ (or προιστάμενος?) τοῦ γένους and S¹ σώζων τ. γ., which are nearer to d than to β–d. In fact d, A imply the same original; for պահապան (= φύλαξ) is corrupt for պաշտպան = ὑπερασπιστής. On the other hand, A supports h, β–d in the parallel passage in Test. Dan. vi. 2. After γένος adg add τοῦ. [40] Can hardly be right unless we take it in the sense 'that *one* may not smite.' A, which = παταχθῆναι, and S (= διαφθείρεσθαι) are right at least in sense, and are supported by the parallel passage Test. Dan. vi. 5, ὁ ἄγγελος (i.e. Μιχαήλ) ἐνισχύσει τὸν Ἰσραήλ, μὴ ἐμπεσεῖν αὐτὸν εἰς τέλος κακῶν. [41] h reads αὐτόν. β–d, Aβ, S¹ add εἰς τέλος, ὅτι πᾶν (a, Aᵇ* om.) πνεῦμα πονηρὸν εἰς αὐτὸν (αὐτοὺς a) προσβάλλει (προβάλλει g). Aᵃ add εἰς τέλος only. d om. τοῦ μὴ . . . προσβάλλει. [42] dg om. [43] d adds δέ. bef, S¹ add

7. Καὶ⁴² μετὰ ταῦτα⁴³ ἔξυπνος γενόμενος εὐλόγησα τὸν ὕψιστον⁴⁴.

VI. Καὶ¹ ὡς ἠρχόμην πρὸς τὸν πατέρα μου εὗρον ἀσπίδα χαλκῆν *διὸ καὶ τὸ ὄνομα τοῦ ὄρους Ἀσπις² *ὅ ἐστιν³ ἐγγὺς Γεβάλ, ἐκ δεξιῶν Ἀβιμά⁴. 2. Καὶ συνετήρουν τοὺς λόγους τούτους ἐν τῇ καρδίᾳ μου. 3. *Μετὰ δὲ τοῦτο συνεβούλευσα⁵ * τῷ πατρί μου καὶ⁶ τῷ⁷ Ῥουβὴμ ⁸ἵνα εἴπῃ⁹ *τοῖς υἱοῖς¹⁰ Ἐμμώρ¹¹ τοῦ¹² μὴ¹³ *περιτμηθῆναι αὐτούς¹⁴, ὅτι¹⁵ ἐζήλωσα *διὰ τὸ βδέλυγμα¹⁶, *ὃ ἐποίησαν¹⁷ *ἐπὶ τῇ ἀδελφῇ μου¹⁸. 4. Κἀγὼ¹⁹ ἀνεῖλον τὸν Συχὲμ ἐν πρώτοις *καὶ Συμεὼν²⁰ τὸν Ἐμμώρ²¹.

Marginal text (α): τὸν ὕψιστον καὶ τὸν ἄγγελον τὸν παραιτούμενον (προασπίζοντα d, ΑΒ) τὸ γένος τοῦ Ἰσραὴλ καὶ πάντων τῶν δικαίων. α ἐν ᾧ καὶ τὸ

ὄνομα τοῦ ὄρους λέγεται Ἀσπις ὅ ἐστιν †ἐγὼ Γεβάλ. β, S¹ ἐγὼ συνεβού- λευσα. h, β, A, S¹ Ῥουβὴμ τῷ ἀδελφῷ μου. β, ΑΒ, S¹ ἐν Ἰσραήλ.

ὥσπερ. ⁴⁴β, ΑΒ, S¹ add καὶ (+ εὐλόγησα S¹) τὸν ἄγγελον (+αὐτοῦ Ab*cd but not A's) τὸν παραιτούμενον (d προασπίζοντα, A φύλακα, but A is here corrupt as in note 39 for ὑπερασπιστήν or προασπίζοντα, S¹ σώζοντα) τὸ γένος (τοῦ γένους b) Ἰσραὴλ (τοῦ Ἰσ. dg) καὶ (S¹ om.) πάντων (πάντα e, ἐν πᾶσιν S¹) τῶν (+ταγμάτων τῶν ΑΒ) δικαίων (af, S¹ om. τ. δικ., for which e reads δίκαιον).

VI. ¹d adds ἐγένετο. ²β save that g om. καί and that d adds ἐκαλεῖτο. The text of α is given in the margin where ἐγώ is corrupt for ἐγγύς. Aᵃ = διὰ τοῦτο ἐκάλεσα τὸ ὄνομα τοῦ ὄρους ἐκείνου Ἀσπις. Aᵝ = διὸ καὶ τοῦ ὄρους Ἀσπις τὸ ὄνομα ἐκάλει. With both Aᵃ, Aᵝ, compare d (note 2). ³b reads ὅτι. ⁴aef, Aᵝ. b, S¹ read Ἀβιλά, d Ἀμηβά (in which μ and β are trs.). g Αὐιμά (where ν may be due to a mistake of the collator). Aᵃᵇ = Ἀβινά. α om. ἐκ δ. A. ⁵α (save that c reads τούτῳ for τοῦτο). β, Aᵃ read καὶ (β om.) ἐγὼ συνεβούλευσα. Aᵉˢ om. Aᵇ*ᶜᵈ = καὶ εἶπον. Aᵝ om. next three words. ⁶Aᵇ*ᶜᵈ om. ⁷α. β om. ⁸All authorities but c add as in margin. ⁹α, β–ag, Aᵝ. a, Aᵃ read εἴπωσι. g ἐπί. ¹⁰g reads τοὺς υἱούς. ¹¹α. c, abeg. h, df read Ἐμώρ. A = Ἀμορραίους. ¹²Aᵝ = καί. ¹³The negative seems right though it is found in c only. Simeon advised against the circumcision of the Shechemites as he intended to avenge the outrage done to his sister. Jub. xxx. 1–4 and Jos. Ant. I. xxi. 1 omit all reference to the circumcision of the Shechemites. ¹⁴A = περιτεμεῖν τὰ σώματα αὐτῶν (αὐτούς Aᵝ). ¹⁵Aᵝ = καὶ ὅτι. ¹⁶Aᵝ = ζῆλον, i.e. ⟨Armenian⟩ corrupt for ⟨Armenian⟩ = βδέλυγμα. We must further supply ⟨Armenian⟩ = διά before this word. ¹⁷Aᵃ om. ¹⁸α. This is supported by Aᵃ which = τῆς ἀδελφῆς μου. β–g, Aᵝ, S¹ read ἐν Ἰσραήλ. The latter may be due to Gen. xxxiv. 7. g om. ¹⁹d reads καὶ εἰσελθὼν ἐγώ. ²⁰d, Aᵇ read ὁ δὲ Σ. ἀνεῖλε. ²¹g adds εἶθ᾽ οὕτως. ²²Aᵃʰ = ἦλθον … καί. ²³α, d. A = ἡμῶν. β–d, S¹ om. ²⁴α. d reads πᾶσαν. β–d, A om. ²⁵b reads ῥομφαίας. ²⁶Aᵃ = ἀκούσας. ²⁷α. β–d, S¹ om.

β–d, S¹ omit.
β–d, A, S¹ omit.
β–d omit.
β, A καὶ μετὰ ταῦτα.
β, A, S¹ †ἄλλως ἐποίησεν.
h, β–b, A, S¹ ἐμαλακίσθην.
β, A, S¹ κακὰ εἰς Σίκιμα.
β, A, S¹ Σαρρά(ν).

5. Καὶ μετὰ ταῦτα ἐλθόντες²² οἱ ἀδελφοί μου²³ ἐπάταξαν τὴν πόλιν ⌐ἐκείνην¬²⁴ ἐν στόματι μαχαίρας²⁵.

6. Καὶ ἤκουσεν²⁶ ὁ πατήρ *μου ⌐ταῦτα¬ ²⁷ *καὶ ὀργισθεὶς²⁸ ἐλυπήθη²⁹ ὅτι κατεδέξαντο³⁰ τὴν περιτομὴν καὶ³¹ ἀπέθανον³², *καὶ ἐν ταῖς εὐλογίαις³³ †παρεῖδεν ἡμῖν³⁴.

7. *Διότι ἡμάρτομεν ἐπειδὴ³⁵ παρὰ γνώμην αὐτοῦ τοῦτο πεποιήκαμεν³⁶. καίγε ἐμαλακίσθη³⁷ ἐν τῇ ἡμέρᾳ ἐκείνῃ. 8. *Ἀλλ' ἐγὼ εἶδον ὅτι ἀπόφασις θεοῦ ἦν εἰς κακὰ³⁸ διότι ἤθελον *καὶ τὴν Σαρρὰ³⁹ ⌐καὶ τὴν Ῥεβέκκα¬⁴⁰ ποιῆσαι ⌐ὃν τρόπον ἐποίησαν *τὴν Δείναν⁴¹ *τὴν ἀδελφὴν ἡμῶν⁴². καὶ ὁ⁴³ Κύριος ἐκώλυσεν αὐτούς. 9. Καὶ⁴⁴ ἐδίωξαν Ἀβραὰμ τὸν πατέρα ἡμῶν¬ ξένον ὄντα⁴⁵ καὶ κατεπόνησαν⁴⁶ τὰ ποίμνια⁴⁷ ὀγκούμενα⁴⁸ ὄντα⁴⁹, καὶ Ἐβλαὴν⁵⁰ τὸν οἰκογενῆ⁵¹ αὐτοῦ⁵² σφόδρα⁵³ ᾐκίσαντο⁵⁴.

---

d, A, S² = ἡμῶν.   ²⁸ α. β, Aβ, S¹ read καὶ ὡργίσθη καί. Aα om.   ²⁹ Aβ has *⟨Armenian⟩* (= ἐχαλέπηνε) which is corrupt for *⟨Armenian⟩* = ἐλυπήθη. Aβ add σφόδρα.   ³⁰ A adds ἐν πρώτοις.   ³¹ β, A, S¹ add μετὰ ταῦτα (τοῦτο bdg).   ³² g reads ἀπέθανε.   ³³ d om. Aα = διὸ καὶ ἐν ταῖς εὐλ. ἡμῶν. Aβ = διὰ τοῦτο καὶ τὴν εὐλ. αὐτοῦ.   ³⁴ α. β–dg, A, S¹ read ἄλλως ἐποίησεν (Aα om.). g ἄλλους ἐποίησεν. d om.   ³⁵ α (save that they read ἡμάρτωμεν). β, S¹ read ἡμάρτομεν (ἡμάρτωμεν df) γὰρ ὅτι. Aab = καὶ ἡμεῖς ἐγενήθημεν δίκαιοι καὶ ὅτι. Ah καὶ ἡμεῖς ἀδελφοὶ δίκαιοι καὶ ὅτι. Aβ = ἡμάρτομεν ἀληθῶς ὅτι. Aα is an internal corruption of the text in Aβ.   ³⁶ a reads πεποίηκε.   ³⁷ c, b. h, β–b, A, S¹ read ἐμαλακίσθην.   ³⁸ α, β (save that e reads κυρίου for θεοῦ, and g οἶδα for εἶδον and ἐστίν for ἦν, and d inserts αὕτη before ἦν). Aα = καὶ εἶδον τὴν ἀπόφασιν τῆς ὀργῆς τοῦ θεοῦ. Ab*g = ἀλλ' ἐμοῦ ἰδόντος ὅτι ἀπόφασις κακὴ ἦν περὶ αὐτῶν ἐκ θεοῦ. Acde = ἀλλ' ἐμοῦ ἰδόντος ἀπόφασιν, κακὴ ἦν περὶ αὐτῶν ἐκ θεοῦ. Here περὶ αὐτῶν is an intrusion. After κακά β, S¹ add as in margin, A ἐπὶ Σικιμίτας.   ³⁹ α. ag τὴν Σαρράν (Σαρρά g). b, S¹ εἰς τὴν Σαρράν. df καὶ τὴν Σαρράν. e καὶ τῇ Σαρρᾷ. A adds ὡσαύτως.   ⁴⁰ α. β, A, S¹ om.   ⁴¹ c. h read Δείνην. abdf Δίναν. e Δήνᾳ. g om. A om. ὃν τρόπον to πατέρα ἡμῶν inclusive.   ⁴² c, β–e. h reads τὴν ἀδ. μου. e τῇ ἀδελφῇ ἡμῶν.   ⁴³ α, e. β–e om.   ⁴⁴ bd add οὕτως.   ⁴⁵ g, Aα om. next six words.   ⁴⁶ b, S¹ read κατεπάτησαν.   ⁴⁷ d adds αὐτοῦ.   ⁴⁸ α. ade read ὀγκώμενα. bfg ὀγκόμενα.   ⁴⁹ β adds ἐπ' αὐτόν.   ⁵⁰ c. a reads Ἰεκβλαί. b Ἰεκβλαέ. d Γεβλαέν. e Ἡεβλαήν. f Ἰεβλαήν. g ἡ Ἐβάλ. (h doubtful). Aα = Ϝεμβολά. Aβ Ἀμβλαήμ. g adds καί. S¹ σὺν αὐτοῖς.   ⁵¹ abd. c, ef read οἰκογενην. g οἰκογενον. h ἀγενην.   ⁵² d om.   ⁵³ Aα om.   ⁵⁴ g. α read ἐκείσαντο. ab αἰκίσαντο. d αἰκήσ. e ἐκίσ. f ᾐκίσ.   ⁵⁵ h reads οὕτως. A = οὕτως γάρ.   ⁵⁶ bd read πάντας τοὺς ξένους.   ⁵⁷ A (+ καὶ ἐν

10. *Καίγε οὕτως[55] ἐποίουν *πᾶσι τοῖς ξένοις[56], *ἐν δυναστείᾳ ἁρπάζοντες[57] ‥*τὰς ξένας[58] καὶ †ἐξενηλάτουν[59] αὐτάς[60].   11. *Ἔφθασε δὲ αὐτοὺς ἡ ὀργὴ τοῦ θεοῦ εἰς τέλος[61].

VII. Καὶ εἶπον[1] ⌜ἐγὼ⌝[2] τῷ πατρί μου[3], Ἰακώβ[4], ὅτι ἐν σοὶ ἐξουδενώσει[5] Κύριος[6] τοὺς Χαναναίους[7] καὶ δώσει[8] τὴν γῆν αὐτῶν σοὶ καὶ τῷ σπέρματί σου μετά σε.   2. Ἔσται γὰρ ἀπὸ τῆς[9] σήμερον *ἡ Σύκημα[10] λεγομένη πόλις ἀσυνέτων[11]. ὅτι[12] ὡσεὶ[13] τις *χλευάσει μωρὸν[14] οὕτως ἐχλευάσαμεν αὐτούς[15],

[Right margin:] β–af, A, S¹ τ. γυναῖκας αὐτῶν. β–b, A, S¹ μὴ ὀργί-ζου (+μοι Αα), κύριε (+μου de, A–b, +πάτερ S¹) Ἰακώβ.

δυν. Αβ) ἥρπαζον.   [58] α, af. bdeg, A, S¹ read τὰς γυναῖκας αὐτῶν (eg om.). Αα om. rest of chap. d om. next three words.   [59] h, Αβ. c reads ἐξελάτουν. befg ξενηλατοῦντες. a ξενηλατοιῶντες. The verb here with its suffix = ידיחון which means both to banish and to seduce to idolatrous worship. (Cf. Deut. iv. 19, xiii. 14, xxx. 17, &c.). The Greek translator wrongly followed the former. We might perhaps render ἀπεπλάνων αὐτάς. In Jub. xxx. 7-17 the penalty of death is ordained for intermarriage with the heathen in connexion with *the destruction of Shechem*. Cohabitation with a Gentile was regarded as equivalent to worship of the Gentile idols. See my commentary on Jub. xxx. 10, note.   [60] α. b, S¹ read αὐτούς and adefg om. Αβ could = αὐτάς or αὐτούς.   [61] α (save that h om. αὐτούς), aef (save that they read κυρίου for τοῦ θεοῦ). b, S¹ read ἔφθασε δὲ ἡ ὀ. κ. ἐπ᾽ αὐτοὺς εἰς τ. dg διὰ τοῦτο (g om. δ. τ.) ἔφθασε (+δέ g) ἐπ᾽ αὐτοὺς ἡ ὀ. κ. εἰς τ. Αα om. and Αβ is defective and = ἔφθασε δὲ ἐπ᾽ αὐτοὺς εἰς τέλος. This verse, as Grabe (*Spicileg. Patrum*, 1698, i. 138) saw, was adopted by St. Paul in 1 Thess. ii. 16, ἔφθασεν δὲ ἐπ᾽ αὐτοὺς ἡ ὀργὴ τοῦ θεοῦ (DEFG it., Vulgate, g, o but most other authorities om. τοῦ θεοῦ). Our text appears to be based on Gen. xxxv. 5 and presupposes, as Rönsch (*Buch der Jubiläen*, pp. 390, 391), וַיַּעַן חֶמָס instead of וַיְהִי חִתַּת. The LXX follows the Hebrew: καὶ ἐγένετο φόβος θεοῦ ἐπὶ τὰς πόλεις τὰς κύκλῳ αὐτῶν and so also Jub. xxx. 26.

VII. [1]d reads εἶπαν.   [2]α. β, A om.   [3]b, Αβ om.   [4]α. β–b, A, S¹ read as in margin (save that d trs. Ἰακώβ before μή). b μὴ ὀργ. κύριε.   [5]This word must here be taken to mean ‘destroy,’ but A has followed its usual meaning ‘to despise.’ It may be a rendering of יבוז or יבז, or of the latter word as in Prov. xxvii. 7 which may mean ‘to tread under foot’ or ‘to despise.’   [6]d adds ὁ θεός.   [7]Αα (by an internal corruption) = τὰς πόλεις and om. the rest of the verse.   [8]Αβ add κύριος.   [9]α. β om.   [10]c. h reads ἡ Σήκημα. β–b Σίκημα. b Σίκιμ.   [11]d reads συνετῶν. Cf. Sir. l. 26, ὁ λαὸς μωρὸς ὁ κατοικῶν ἐν Σικίμοις.   [12]Αα om. ὡσεὶ …ὅτι through hmt.   [13]d reads ὥσπερ.   [14]h reads χλευας, d χλευάζει.   [15]h reads αὐτόν.   [16]g reads γὰρ καί. A om.   [17]α, β–b. b, S¹ reads *beg καὶ λαβόντες ἐκεῖθεν Δίναν τὴν ἀδελφὴν ἡμῶν ἀπάραντες (ἐπάραντες e).*

3. Ὅτι ⌜καίγε⌝[16] ἀφροσύνην ἔπραξαν ἐν Ἰσραὴλ μιάναντες[17] τὴν ἀδελφήν μου[18]. 4. ˙*Ἀπάραντες δὲ[19] *ἤλθομεν εἰς[20] Βεθήλ[21].

VIII. Κἀκεῖ πάλιν εἶδον[1] *ὅραμα ὡς[2] τὸ πρότερον μετὰ *τὸ ποιῆσαι ἡμᾶς ἐκεῖ[3] ἡμέρας ἑβδομήκοντα[4].

2. Καὶ εἶδον[5] ἑπτὰ ἄνδρας[6] ἐν ἐσθῆτι[7] λευκῇ[8] *λέγοντάς μοι[9]. Ἀναστὰς ἔνδυσαι τὴν στολὴν τῆς ἱερατείας, καὶ[10] τὸν στέφανον τῆς δικαιοσύνης[11], *καὶ τὸ λόγιον[12] τῆς συνέσεως

ΑΒ omit καὶ τὸ λόγιον. . προφη- τείας.

καὶ τὸν ποδήρη[13] τῆς ἀληθείας καὶ τὸ πέταλον[14] τῆς πίστεως καὶ τὴν μίτραν[15] †τῆς κεφαλῆς†[16] καὶ τὸ ἐφοὺδ τῆς προ- φητείας. 3. Καὶ[17] εἷς[18] ἕκαστος αὐτῶν[19] βαστάζοντες *ἦσαν καὶ[20] ἐπέθηκάν μοι[21] καὶ εἶπόν[22] μοι[23]. Ἀπὸ τοῦ

μιᾶναι. Α𝛽 = καὶ ἐμίαναν. adf, S¹ add Δίναν. Αᵃ om. together with next three words. [18] α, Α𝛽. β, S¹ read ἡμῶν. [19] α. adf read ἐπάραντες (ἀπάραντες d) οὖν (δέ a). Αᵃ = ἀπάραντες δὲ ἐκεῖθεν. Α𝛽 = ἕτοιμοι δέ. beg read as in margin (save that bg om. Δίναν and g om. ἐκεῖθεν and ἀπάραντες). For ἀπάραντες ... Βεθήλ S¹ reads καὶ διὰ τοῦτο ἡ ὀργὴ τοῦ κυρίου ἐξῆλθε κατ' αὐτῶν καὶ ὁ ἄγγελος τοῦ ἰσχυροῦ ἐβοήθησεν ἐμοί. [20] d om. [21] ag read Βαιθήλ. S¹ makes here a Christian addition. See Appendix.

VIII. [1] def read ἴδον. [2] b reads πρᾶγμα ὥσπερ. For ὅραμα ... πρότε- ρον S¹ reads δεινήν τινα ὄψιν. [3] h, aefg, A. So also c (save that it om. ἡμᾶς). b, S¹ reads τὸ ποιῆσαι. d om. [4] Α𝛽 = ἑξήκοντα. [5] A adds ἐκεῖ. [6] c, g, A. h, β–g read ἀνθρώπους. e trs. before ἑπτά. [7] f reads ἐσθήσεσι. [8] α, abg, A. de read λαμπρᾷ. f λευκαῖς. [9] c trs. before ἐν ἐσθ. e reads φέροντές μοι and om. next seven words. [10] Αᵇ*ᵈ = καὶ ἐπίθες. Αᶜ om. [11] Αᵃ add ἐπίθες ἐπὶ τὴν κεφαλήν σου. [12] e reads καὶ τὸν λόγον. Αᵃ = καὶ τὴν ἐντολήν. Αʰ om. next five words. Α𝛽 om. together with rest of verse. [13] abf. c reads ποδήρει. h, deg ποδηρι. Αᵃ = λόγον. It is possible that Αᵃ has transposed the words occurring before τῆς συνέσεως and τῆς ἀλη- θείας. In other words ܦܘ݁ܠ = λόγον should be read before the former and ܞܘܡܢܬ̈ܦܘܠ = ἐντολήν which is corrupt (?) for ܞܘܡܢ̈ܕܬ̈ܐܘܠ = ποδήρη. [14] g reads πηδάλιον. [15] β–ad. α, ad read μήτραν. Αᵃ = κόσμον. [16] α. bedg, Αᵃ read τοῦ σημείου. af, S¹ τοῦ στηθίου. Αᵃ adds ἐπὶ τοῖς ὤμοις σου. Here στηθίου looks like a corruption or emendation of σημείου, and may be neglected. But κεφαλῆς and σημείου have to be accounted for, and I know of no explanation. κεφαλῆς, of course, cannot be right, since, as the parallel phrases show, we require here an abstract noun. Only for σημείου we might regard ראשׁ (= κεφαλῆς) as a corruption of ישׁר or מישׁור = εὐθύτητος. Perhaps מופת (= σημείου 'miracle') might be a corruption of מישׁור. [17] d reads ταῦτα εἰπόντες καὶ προσελθόντες. [18] h. om. [19] d om. β–d adds ἕκαστον. [20] α. β, A om. d adds τὰς στολάς. [21] d adds

νῦν γενοῦ[24] εἰς ἱερέα[25], σὺ[26] καὶ *πᾶν τὸ σπέρμα[27] σου[28].
4. Καὶ[29] ὁ πρῶτος ἤλειψέ[30] με[31] ἐλαίῳ ἁγίῳ, καὶ ἔδωκέ μοι ῥάβδον[32].   5. *Καὶ ὁ[33] δεύτερος ἔλουσέ[34] με[35] ὕδατι καθαρῷ[36], καὶ ἐψώμισέν[37] με[38] *ἄρτον καὶ οἶνον[39] ἅγιον[40] καὶ περιέθηκέ[41] μοι στολὴν ἁγίαν[42] καὶ ἔνδοξον.   6. Ὁ δὲ[43] τρίτος βυσσίνην[44] *μοι περιέθηκεν[45], ὁμοίαν[46] ἐφούδ.   7. Ὁ δὲ[47] τέταρτος ζώνην *μοι περιέβαλεν[48], ὁμοίαν πορφύρας[49].
8. Ὁ[50] πέμπτος *κλάδον μοι ἐλαίας ἔδωκεν πιότητος[51].

α, β, S	Aa	Ab*	Acdefg
9. Ὁ ἕκτος στέφανόν μοι[52] *τῇ κεφαλῇ[53] περιέθηκεν[54]. 10. Ὁ[55] ἕβδομος *διάδημά μοι ἱερατείας περιέθηκεν καὶ[56] ἐ-	9–10. Καὶ ὁ ἕκτος ἐπλήρωσε τὰς χεῖράς μου θυμιάματος ὥστε	9–10. Καὶ ὁ ἕκτος διάδημα ἱερατείας περιέθηκε τῇ κεφαλῇ μου καὶ ὁ ἕβδομος ἐπλήρωσε τὰς χεῖράς μου θυ-	9–10. Καὶ ὁ ἕκτος καὶ ὁ ἕβδομος διάδημα ἱερατείας ἔδωκέ μοι καὶ πάλιν ἐπλήρωσαν τὰς χεῖρας

Right margin: β, A, S ἱερέα κυρίου σὺ καὶ τὸ σπέρμα σου ἕως αἰῶνος. — bdg, A, S¹ ῥάβδον κρίσεως. — c, β, S ἅγια ἁγίων.

[21] αὐτά. h om. next three words.   [22] abe read εἶπαν.   [23] c, Aa. h, β, Aβ om. c adds καί. Aa om. next three words.   [24] α, e. abf read γίνου. d ἔσει.   [25] α. β, Aβ add κυρίου. Aa add θεοῦ. Cp. ix. 3.   [26] f reads σοί. g καὶ σύ.   [27] α. β–df, A read τὸ σπέρμα. df τῷ σπέρματι.   [28] β–d, A add as in margin. d reads ἕως τοῦ αἰῶνος.   [29] ae read καὶ ἔτι. d τότε. Aa om.   [30] h, abdg. c reads εἴληψε. e ἤληψεν. f om.   [31] h reads μοι. f om. e adds ἐν.   [32] α. bdg, A, S¹ add κρίσεως, aef χρίσεως.   [33] α. β, Aa read ὁ. Aβ = ὁ δέ.   [34] ef read ἔλουσεν.   [35] h reads μοι. eg add ἐν.   [36] Aa = ἁγίῳ.   [37] d reads ὕψωσεν.   [38] c, aefg, A. h reads μοι. bd om.   [39] c reads in dative.   [40] h, A. c, β, S read as in margin.   [41] g reads παρέθηκεν.   [42] A = καλόν.   [43] α, Aβ. β, Aa, S¹ om.   [44] d reads βυσσίνη.   [45] α, af. bdeg read με περιέβαλεν. Aa om. with next word.   [46] h reads ὅμοιος.   [47] α, A. β om.   [48] α. a reads περιέβαλεν. bdefg μοι (με e; f om.) περιέθηκεν. S adds οὐκ ἐπὶ τὸ μέσον ἀλλὰ τὸ κατώτερον μέρος τοῦ σώματος καὶ ἡ ζώνη ἦν.   [49] α, adef. b reads πορφύρᾳ. g πορφυρίδι. g adds from ver. 10 καὶ ἐπλ. . . . κυρίῳ.   [50] Aa, b* = ὁ δέ. Acdefg καὶ ὁ.   [51] Aa = κλ. ἐλαίας πιότητος ἔδωκέ μοι. Aβ ἐν ὁμοιώματι ἐλαίας πιότητος ἔδ. μοι καὶ ἐπλήρωσαν τὰς χεῖράς μου θυμιάματος. For πιότ. c, bd read ποιότητος. S om. ἐλαίας.   [52] d reads μου. e om.   [53] d reads τὴν κεφαλήν.   [54] d adds ἱερατείας. Cf. Ab*.   [55] h reads καὶ ὁ.   [56] α, aefg (save that h om. μοι). b, S read διάδημά μοι τῇ κεφαλῇ περιέθ. ἱερατ. (save that S¹ reads τιμῆς for ἱερατείας). With this reading compare Ab*. d om.   [57] α, adfg, S. be read ἐπλήρωσαν. With this reading compare

α, β, S	Aᵃ	Ab*	Acdefg
πλήρωσε[57] τὰς χεῖράς μου θυμιάματος[58], ὥστε ἱερατεύειν με[59] Κυρίῳ, *τῷ θεῷ[60].	ἱερατεύειν με ἐνώπιον Κυρίου. (+ καὶ ὁ ἕβδομος Ab)	μιάματος ὥστε ἱερατεύειν με ἐνώπ. Κυρίου.	μου θυμίαματος ὥστε ἱερατεύειν ἐνώπ. Κυρίου.

11. *Καὶ λέγουσι[61] πρός με· Λευί[62], εἰς τρεῖς ἀρχὰς διαιρεθήσεται[63] τὸ σπέρμα σου[64], εἰς[65] σημεῖον[66] *δόξης Κυρίου ἐπερχομένου[67].

α	β, S	Aᵃ	Aβ
12. Καὶ[68] ὁ πρῶτος κλῆρος ἔσται μέγας· καὶ ὑπὲρ αὐτὸν οὐ γενήσεται ἕτερος.	12. *Καὶ ὁ [πιστεύσας] πρῶτος κλῆρος ἔσται μέγας· ὑπὲρ αὐτὸν οὐ γενήσεται[69].	12. Καὶ οἱ πιστεύσουσιν ἐν πρώτοις, αὐτοῖς ἔσται κλῆρος μέγας.	12. Καὶ[70] †Κύριος[71] (read ὃς) ἐπίστευσε ἐν πρώτοις *κλῆρος αὐτῶν ἔσται μέγας καὶ ὑπὲρ αὐτὸν οὐδεὶς ἔσται[72].

13. Ὁ δὲ[73] δεύτερος ἔσται *ἐν ἱερωσύνη[74].   14. *Ὁ δὲ[75]

Acdefg.   [58] h reads θυμιαμάτων.   [59] af om.   [60] α. β, A, S om.   [61] α, dg. aef read λέγουσι δέ. b, S εἶπαν (εἶπε S) δέ. A = καὶ λέγει.   [62] g reads Λευί, Λευί.   [63] Aᵃ = διαιρήσω.   [64] Ab* add καὶ ἔση.   [65] Aᵃ = καί.   [66] c reads συμειον.   [67] Aᵃ = δόξης παρουσίας κυρίου. Aβ = παρουσίας δοξ. κύριου. For ἐπερχομένου g reads ἐπερχομένης.   [68] c om.   [69] eg. So also b save that it trs. κλῆρος ἔσται, and S² save that it reads καὶ μείζων for μέγας. I have bracketed πιστεύσας as an intrusion. It is found also in A. With its omission our text = α. d is conflated from the above text and α. It is: καὶ ὁ πιστεύσας πρ. οὗτος ἔσται κλῆρος μέγας καὶ ὑπὲρ αὐτὸν ἕτερος οὐ γενήσεται. af carry further the corruption in our text: καὶ ἐπίστευσα· πρ. κλῆρ. ἔσται (ἔσται κλῆρ. a) καὶ μέγας ὑπὲρ αὐτὸν (αὐτῶν a) οὐ γενήσεται. S¹ καὶ ὁ πρῶτος πιστεύσας ἔσται μέγας.   [70] Ab* = ὅτι.   [71] Aβ read ϰπ (= κύριος) corrupt for πϱ = ὅς. Thus A is brought into agreement with β.   [72] Acd. Ab* = κλῆρον αὐτοῦ σοι καὶ ὑπέρ σε οὐδεὶς ἔσται μείζων. Aefg = καὶ κλῆρος αὐτῶν ἔσται μέγας (μείζων Afg and om. rest) καὶ ὑπὲρ αὐτοὺς οὐδεὶς ἔσται μείζων.   [73] h, Aβ. c, β, Aᵃ, S² om. S¹ om. entire verse.   [74] de read εἰς ἱερωσύνην. Aᵃ = ἱερεὺς μέγας. Aβ = ἱερωσύνη.   [75] c. h, Aβ, S¹ read καὶ ὁ. β, Aᵃ, S² read ὁ.   [76] Aᵃ = ἐπικληθήσεται ὄνομα αὐτοῦ but ϩπϱω = αὐτοῦ is corrupt for ϩπϱ = καινόν. Aβ = ἔσται ὄνομα αὐτοῦ, where the same corruption exists as in Aᵃ.   [77] Though all MSS. agree in this text we should read ἐν τῷ (A = ἐκ τοῦ or ἐν τῷ) if βασιλεὺς . . . ἀναστήσεται

τρίτος *ἐπικληθήσεται αὐτῷ ὄνομα καινόν[78], ὅτι βασιλεὺς †ἐκ
τοῦ†[77] Ἰούδα ἀναστήσεται καὶ ποιήσει *ἱερατείαν νέαν, κατὰ   *β-af, A
τὸν τύπον τῶν ἐθνῶν εἰς πάντα τὰ ἔθνη[78].   15. Ἡ δὲ   *ἄφρα-
παρουσία[79] αὐτοῦ ἀγαπητή[80] ἐστιν[81] ὡς προφήτης[82] ὑψίστου[83]   *στος.
ἐκ σπέρματος Ἀβραὰμ τοῦ[84] πατρὸς ἡμῶν[85].   *β-af, A,*
   S ἀρχι-
   ερεῖς.

16. *Πᾶν οὖν ἐπιθυμητὸν[86] ἐν Ἰσραὴλ[87] σοὶ[88] ἔσται καὶ τῷ   *β-af, ΑΒ*
   σπέρματί σου[89].   *φυλα-*
   χθήσεται.

καὶ ἔδεσθε[90] πᾶν ὡραῖον ἐν[91] ὁράσει,   *β, A, S*
καὶ τὴν τράπεζαν Κυρίου διανεμεῖται[92] τὸ σπέρμα σου[93].   *καὶ ἐξυ-*

17. Καὶ ἐξ αὐτῶν[94] ἔσονται ἱερεῖς[95] καὶ[96] κριταὶ καὶ[96] γραμ-   *πνισθείς.*
   ματεῖς·   *β, S¹*
   ἐκείνου
καὶ[97] ἐπὶ στόματος αὐτῶν †ληφθήσεται[98] τὸ ἅγιον[99].   *ἐστί.*

18. *Ἐξυπνισθεὶς οὖν[100] συνῆκα[101], ὅτι *τοῦτο ὅμοιόν ἐστι τοῦ   For an
   Aramaic

fragment based on VIII. 18, 19; IX. 1, 6, 9, 10 see Appendix.

is genuine. The corruption may have arisen accidentally or may be due
to a Christian scribe, who wished to bring the text into line with O. T.
prophecy.   [78] α, β-d, Αβ, S (save that A^cde read ἱηρω (= αὐτοῦ) corrupt
for ἱηρ (so A^b*ef) = νέαν and S¹ πάντων τῶν χθονῶν for εἰς πάντα τὰ ἔθνη).
d reads ἱερατείαν νέαν εἰς πάντα τὰ ἔθνη. A^a = ἔλεος (but գբևբիև is corrupt for բւՇաևայբիբիև = ἱερατείαν) εἰς πάντα τὰ ἔθνη τῶν λαῶν.   [79] h,
β-e, A. c, e read παρρησία.   [80] c, af, S². bdeg, A read ἄφραστος = חבּרא (late
Hebrew) corrupt for אהוּב = ἀγαπητός. S¹ corrupt.   [81] α, A. β-d om.
d reads ἔσται.   [82] α, aef, Αβ, S¹. bdg, S³ read προφήτου. A^a om.   [83] α,
β-b, A, S¹. b, S³ read ὑψηλοῦ. d, A^a om. rest of verse.   [84] α. β om.
[85] c, β-ef, Αβ. h, ef read ὑμῶν.   [86] α. β-g, Αβ, S² read πᾶν ἐπιθυμητόν.
A^a = καὶ πάντα ἐπιθυμητά. g om. S¹ corrupt.   [87] g reads Ἱερουσαλήμ.
[88] Αβ om.   [89] A^a om. next six words. d adds ἕως τοῦ αἰῶνος.   [90] abg.
α, ef read ἔδεσθαι. d φάγεσθαι. S¹ ἔσεσθε.   [91] bdef om. For ἐν ὁράσει
Αβ reads εὐπρεπείας.   [92] α. β reads διανεμήσεται.   [93] S¹ adds τοῦτό ἐστι
οἱ ἀπόστολοι.   [94] ἐξ αὐτῶν = מהם.   [95] α, af. β-af, A, S read ἀρχιερεῖς.
d, A^a om. next four words. e adds οἱ before ἀρχιερεῖς and κριταί.   [96] α,
β-af, A^ef, af, A^b*cd om.   [97] α, A^a, S³. β-e, Αβ, S¹ read ὅτι. e ὥστε.
[98] af. The same text is implied in c λυφθήσεται and h λειφθήσεται. β-af,
Αβ read φυλαχθήσεται. S¹ τελεῖται. A^a = ἀναστήσεται φυλακή. None of
these readings is satisfactory. It is possible that the text originally
referred to the blessing pronounced by Levi (cf. Reub. vi. 10; Jub. xxxi.
15): 'The blessing of the Lord will be given in their mouths.' Sir. l. 20.
[99] A^a add τοῦ κυρίου.   [100] h. c om. together with next word. β, A, S
read καὶ ἐξυπνισθείς.   [101] A^ab (internally corrupt) = ἐμεμψάμην. A^b =
ἐκεῖ συνῆκα. Αβ զարբևագայ (= ἐθαύμασα) corrupt for բևագայ = συνῆκα.
[102] α. So almost A which = ἦν τοῦτο τὸ ὅραμα ὅμοιον τοῦ πρώτου (+ ὁράμα-

46 ΔΙΑΘΗΚΗ ΛΕΥΙ [VIII. 18]

β, S[1]
παντί.
β-d,
A[cdefg]
πρῶτου ὀνείρου[102].   19. *Καὶ ἔκρυψα καίγε τοῦτο[103] ἐν τῇ καρδίᾳ μου, καὶ οὐκ ἀνήγγειλα *αὐτό τινι ἀνθρώπῳ[104] *ἐπὶ τῆς γῆς[105].

πρὸς
'Ισαὰκ
μετὰ τοῦ
πατρὸς
ἡμῶν.
β, Aa, S
πάντας
τοὺς
λόγους
τῶν
ὁράσεών
μου.
α omit
καὶ οὐκ ..
Βεθήλ.
β, A, S[1]

IX. *Καὶ μεθ' ἡμέρας[1] δύο ἀνέβην[2] ἐγὼ καὶ 'Ιούδας *μετὰ τοῦ πατρὸς ἡμῶν 'Ιακὼβ πρὸς 'Ισαὰκ[3] ⌐τὸν προπάτορα ἡμῶν⌐[4].   2. Καὶ εὐλόγησέν με *ὁ πατὴρ τοῦ πατρός μου[5] κατὰ[6] *τῶν ὁραμάτων ὧν[7] εἶδον· *καὶ οὐκ ἠθέλησε πορευθῆναι μεθ' ἡμῶν εἰς Βεθήλ[8].   3. ⌐'Ως δὲ ἤλθομεν εἰς Βεθήλ⌐[9], εἶδεν[10] ὁ πατήρ μου 'Ιακὼβ[11] ὅραμα[12] περὶ ἐμοῦ, ὅτι ἔσομαι αὐτοῖς εἰς ἱερέα[13].   4. Καὶ ἀναστὰς[14] *τῷ πρωὶ[15] *ἀπεδεκάτωσε πάντα[16] δι' ἐμοῦ ⌐τῷ Κυρίῳ⌐[17].   5. Καὶ ⌐οὕτως⌐[18] ἤλθομεν εἰς Χεβρὼν τοῦ καταμεῖναι[19] ἐκεῖ[20].   6. Καὶ ὁ[21] 'Ισαὰκ ἐκάλει με συνεχῶς *τοῦ ὑπομνῆσαί[22] *με νόμου[23] Κυρίου[24], καθὼς *ἔδειξέ μοι[25] ὁ ἄγγελος[26].   7. Καὶ ἐδίδασκέ

ἱερέα πρὸς τὸν θεόν.   af, Aa ἄγγ. κυρίου.

τος Aa).   abef read τοῦτο ὅμοιον ἐκείνου (ἐκείνῳ a) ἐστί.   So also d (save that for ἐκ. ἐστί it reads ἐστὶν ἐκείνου.   g τοῦτο τὸ σημεῖον ἐκείνου ἐστὶν ὁμ.   [103] befg, S.   So h (save that it reads κἀγώ for καίγε) and c (save that it reads τοῦτο καίγε).   ad read καίγε ἔκρ. (+ καὶ d) τοῦτο.   Aa = καὶ ἔκρ. τοῦτο.   Aβ κἀγὼ ἔκρυψα.   [104] α (save that c reads αὐτῷ).   β, S[1] read αὐτὸ (αὐτῷ e) παντὶ ἀνθρώπῳ.   Aa = τινί.   Aβ, Aram. = παντὶ ἀνθρώπῳ.   [105] Aa = ἕως τοῦ νῦν.   Aram. om.

IX. [1] d reads μετὰ δὲ ἡμέρας.   [2] α, dfg. ab, A, S read ἀνέβημεν.   e ἀνέβενον (sic).   [3] α, d, S (save that S om. 'Ιακώβ).   β-d, A[cdefg] read πρὸς 'Ισαὰκ μετὰ τοῦ πατρὸς (τὸν πατέρα b) ἡμῶν.   A[b*] = πρὸς 'Ισ. τὸν πατέρα ἡμῶν.   Aa = πρὸς 'Ισ. τὸν πατέρα τοῦ πατρὸς ἡμῶν.   [4] α (save that h reads πατέρα for προπάτορα), S.   All other authorities om.   [5] Aa om.   [6] d reads καί.   [7] α.   β, Aa, S read πάντας τοὺς λόγους τῶν ὁράσεών (τῆς ὁράσεώς g, Aa, S[2]) μου (dg om.) ὧν (ὡς g).   Aβ = πάντας τοὺς λόγους μου ὧν.   [8] β, Aβ.   Aa = καὶ οὐκ ἠθέλ. πορευθῆναι αὐτός.   α om.   [9] α, beg. adf A om. through hmt.   For ἤλθομεν e reads ἦλθον, and for ὡς δέ g reads ὡς καί.   [10] d reads τότε ἴδε καί.   A = καὶ εἶδεν.   [11] f trs. before ὁ πατήρ.   g, Aa om.   [12] α, af.   β-af, A read ἐν ὁράματι.   [13] α.   bdeg, S[1] add πρὸς τὸν θεόν.   af τῷ θεῷ.   A ἐνώπιον τοῦ κυρίου.   [14] A = ἀνέστη καί.   [15] c, deg.   af read ἀπὸ π.   b τὸ π.   h τῇ πρωίᾳ.   [16] A = προσήνεγκε τὰς δεκάτας.   [17] A om.   [18] α.   β, A om.   [19] b reads καταλῦσαι.   S[1] = κατὰ δύναμιν.   [20] α, A.   β, S[1] om.   [21] α.   β om.   [22] af read τοῦ ὑπομνηματίσαι.   A = καὶ ὑπέμνησε.   [23] de read με (d om.) λόγον.   [24] Aβ om. next five (cf. text of af, Aa) words through hmt.   [25] α, bg.   adef, A(?) read ἐδίδαξέ με (μοι d).   [26] beg, S[1] add τοῦ θεοῦ.   af, Aa add κυρίου.   [27] d reads μοι.   [28] A = ἱερατικόν.   [29] g, A trs.   A[a, 28] = ὁλοκ. καὶ θυσ.   [30] α (save that h reads ἑκουσίων).   β-g, S[1]

*με²⁷ νόμον ἱερωσύνης²⁸, *θυσιῶν, ὁλοκαυτωμάτων²⁹, *ἀπαρ-
χῶν ἐκουσίου, σωτηρίου³⁰. 8. *Καὶ ἦν καθ' ἑκάστην ἡμέραν
συνετίζων με³¹, *καὶ ἀσχολούμενος εἰς ἐμὲ³² *ἔλεγέ μοι³³.
9. Πρόσεχε³⁴ σεαυτῷ³⁵ ἀπὸ τοῦ πνεύματος τῆς πορνείας.
τοῦτο γὰρ³⁶ †ἐνδελεχῆ ἐστιν†³⁷ *καὶ μέλλει μιαίνειν³⁸ διὰ³⁹
τοῦ σπέρματός σου⁴⁰ *τὰ ἅγια⁴¹. 10. *Λαβὲ οὖν σεαυτῷ⁴²
*γυναῖκα, ἔτι⁴³ νέος ὤν, *μὴ ἔχουσαν μῶμον μήτε βεβηλω-
μένην, μήτε ἀπὸ γένους⁴⁴ ἀλλοφύλων⁴⁵ ἐθνῶν. 11. Καὶ
πρὸ⁴⁶ τοῦ εἰσελθεῖν σε⁴⁷ εἰς τὰ ἅγια, λούου· καὶ ἐν τῷ θύειν
σε⁴⁸, νίπτου⁴⁹· καὶ ἀπαρτίζων πάλιν⁵⁰ τὴν θυσίαν, νίπτου.
12. *Δώδεκα οὖν δένδρων ἐχόντων φύλλα⁵¹ ἀνάγαγε⁵² τῷ⁵³

β–g, S¹
ἐκουσίων
σωτη-
ρίων.
β, Aefg,
S¹ εἰς ἐμὲ
ἦν ἀσχο-
λούμενος
ἐνώπιον
κυρίου
καί.
α, d, Aa,
S¹ omit
καὶ ἀπαρ.
... νί-

πτου. β–g δένδρων ἀεί.

read ἀπαρχῶν ἑκουσίων, σωτηρίων. g ἀπαρχῶν. Aβ = καὶ ἀπαρχῶν ἑκουσίων
καὶ σωτηρίου. Aa om. together with all but two last words of next verse.
S adds ὥστε ἱερατεύειν τῇ καθαρότητι ἐννοίας τῷ ὑψίστῳ θεῷ. ³¹ α, β–dg, S.
Aβ = καὶ (Acdfg om.) συνεχῶς οὕτως ἦν συνετίζων καὶ ἐδίδασκε. dg read καὶ ἦν
καθ' ἑκάστην συνετίζον με καὶ εἰς ἐμὲ ἀσχολ. (εἰς ἐμὲ ἀσχολ. καὶ συνετίζον με g)
ἦν (g om.) ἐνώπιον κυρίου (+τοῦ θεοῦ d). ³² α. β–dg, Aefg, S¹ read καὶ εἰς
ἐμὲ ἀσχολ. ἦν (e om.) ἐνώπιον κυρίου. For text of dg see preceding note.
Acd = καὶ μοι παρήγγελλε ἐνώπιον κ. but ⲓⲙⲱⲡⲛⲉⲃⲣⲕⲣ = παρήγγ. is corrupt
for ⲓⲙⲱⲣⲱⲓⲙⲕⲣ (A°. A^fg corrupt forms of it) = ἀσχολούμενος ἦν. ³³ α.
ad, Aβ, S read καὶ (+ἐν τοῖς νουθετήμασιν S) ἔλεγέ μοι. be read καὶ ἔλεγε,
f κατέλεγέν μοι. g λέγων. ³⁴ b adds μή before πρόσεχε. f reads προσχές.
³⁵ α, af, S¹. bdg, Aβ read τέκνον. e, Aram. Frag. 16 τέκνον σεαυτῷ. f adds
καί. Aa reads τέκνον but trs. before πρόσεχε. ³⁶ e om. ³⁷ α (for ἐνδε-
λεχές). adefg read ἐνδελεχεῖ. b, S¹ ἐνδελεχιεῖ. A = ἀπατᾷ σε. I have
bracketed the text as corrupt. ³⁸ b trs. after σου. ³⁹ c reads ἀπό.
⁴⁰ c reads μου. ⁴¹ Aa = τὸν νόμον σου. Aβ = τὴν παραθήκην σου (Afg om.),
where ⲋⲱⲓⲱⳝⲏ ⲣⲛ may be corrupt for ⲋⲱⲓⲱⳡⲱⲓ ⲣⲛ = διὰ τοῦ σπέρματός
σου. ⁴² e reads λαβέ σου οὖν. Aa = λαβὲ σύ σοι. ⁴³ g reads εἰς γυναῖκα
ὅτι. ⁴⁴ A = ἵνα μὴ ἔχῃς μῶμον ἐν σοὶ καὶ (+μηδεμίαν Aa) βεβήλωσιν καὶ μὴ
ᾖ (+γυνὴ A^s) ἀπὸ γένους. For μήτε ... μήτε of af, μηδὲ ... μηδέ are found
in ab and μηδὲ ... μήτε in de. g om. μήτε βεβηλωμένην. ⁴⁵ α, e¹. β–e, Aβ,
S¹ add ἤ, Aa. μηδέ or μήτε. ⁴⁶ g om. ⁴⁷ α, de. abfg om. ⁴⁸ α. β om.
⁴⁹ α, e give the form νήπτου, g as νιπται (bis). a reads εἰς αὐτά. A = ἁγίασον
σεαυτόν. α, d, Aa, S¹, om. next six words through hmt., and Aa om. the
rest of the chapter. ⁵⁰ e trs. after θυσίαν. ⁵¹ α. β–g read δώδεκα
δένδ. ἀεὶ ἐχ. So nearly Aβ = ἐκ τῶν δώδεκα [+καὶ A^b×cd] ἀεὶ ἐχόντων.
g δώδεκα δένδ. ἀπεχόντων. ⁵² α, adefg. b reads ἄναγε. Aβ = ἀνάξεις.
⁵³ bd om. ⁵⁴ a adds καὶ πᾶσαν θυσίαν ἅλατι ἁλιεῖς. ⁵⁵ e reads καὶ ἐμέ.
⁵⁶ α. β om. ⁵⁷ df, Aβ om. next three words through hmt. h om. next

β, S[1]
πετεινοῦ
καθαροῦ.
α omit
καὶ ...
ἁλιεῖς.
β, A, S
πάσης.
β, A, S[1]
ἀσεβοῦν-
τες, πλα-
νῶντες
(πλα-
νᾶσθε A).
β, A, S
σύν.

Κυρίῳ[54] *ὡς κἀμὲ[55] Ἀβραὰμ ἐδίδαξε.   13. Καὶ ἐκ[56] παντὸς ζώου καθαροῦ[57] ⌈καὶ πετεινοῦ⌉[58] πρόσφερε θυσίαν *τῷ Κυρίῳ[59]. 14. Καὶ *παντὸς πρωτογεννήματός σου[60] καὶ οἴνου[61] πρόσφερε *ἀπαρχὰς εἰς θυσίαν Κυρίῳ[62] ⌈τῷ θεῷ⌉[63]. *Καὶ πᾶσαν θυσίαν ἅλατι ἁλιεῖς[64].

X. *Καὶ τανῦν[1] φυλάξατε[2] *ὅσα ἐγὼ ἐντέλλομαι ὑμῖν, τέκνα, ἐπειδὴ ὅσα ἐγὼ ἤκουσα παρὰ τῶν πατέρων μου ⌈ἀνήγγειλα ὑμῖν⌉[3].   2. ⌈Καὶ ἰδοὺ⌉[4] ἀθῷός εἰμι[5] τῆς[6] ἀσεβείας[7] ὑμῶν[8] *καὶ παραβάσεως[9] ἣν ποιήσετε ἐπὶ *τῇ συντελείᾳ[10] *τῶν αἰώνων[11] [εἰς τὸν σωτῆρα τοῦ κόσμου χριστόν][12] *πλανῶντες τὸν Ἰσραήλ[13], καὶ ἐπεγείροντες[14] *ἐπ' αὐτὸν[15] κακὰ μεγάλα[16] *παρὰ Κυρίου[17].   3. Καὶ ἀνομήσετε[18] *ἐν τῷ[19] Ἰσραήλ[20], ὥστε μὴ βαστάζειν[21] τὴν[22] Ἱερουσαλὴμ[23] ἀπὸ προσ-

---

five words.   [58] β, S[1] read as in margin.   [59] adef, A[b*cde], S[1]. ab κυρίῳ. g τῷ θεῷ. c αὐτῷ. A[g] om. to τῷ θεῷ.   [60] α, a (save that h, a om. σου). bf read π. πρωτογενήματος. deg πρώτου γενήματος (γενν. g). A[β] = πάντων κτηνῶν καὶ ἀπὸ καρπῶν, but ⲙⲣ︤ϣⲙⲛⲅ ⲉⲧ ϫⲱⲣⲥ︤ⲛⲃⲱⲅ appears to be corrupt for ⲙⲡⲱⲣ︤ϩ︤ⲓⲛⲅ ⲱⲣ︤ⲥⲛⲃⲱⲅ = πρωτογεννημάτων.   [61] a reads οἴνων. [62] α (save that c reads ἀρχάς). af read ἀπ. θυσίαν τῷ (f om.) κυρίῳ. b ἀπαρχάς. d κυρίῳ ἀπαρχάς. eg, A[β] ἀπαρχὰς τῷ κυρίῳ.   [63] α. β, A[β], S[1] om. β-bdf read τῷ κ. b om.   [64] β-d (save that e reads ἁλίσεις), A[β]. d reads καὶ πᾶσαν δὲ θ. ἅ. ἁλατιεῖς. Gk. Frag. 29 (see Appendix) supports text.

X. [1] c. h reads καὶ οὖν. β, A νῦν οὖν.   [2] b reads φυλάξασθε.   [3] α (save that h adds μου after τέκνα). β-d agrees with text (save that beg om. ἐγώ after ὅσα[10] and β-d om. ἐγώ after ὅσα[20], and for ἐπειδή read ὅτι). d, A agree in omitting ἀνήγγειλα ὑμῖν. d, A[β] read τέκνα μου ὅτι (A[β] om.) ὅσα ἤκουσα παρὰ τῶν πατέρων μου ἐντέλλομαι ὑμῖν. A[α] = ὅσα νῦν ἐντέλλομαι ὑμῖν ὅσα ἤκουσα παρὰ τῶν πατέρων μου. A[α] contains τέκνα also but has trs. it before φυλάξατε.   [4] α. β, A. om.   [5] g reads ὑμῖν. A adds ἀπ' ἐκείνου.   [6] α β, A, S read πάσης.   [7] d reads ἀδικίας.   [8] g trs. after παραβ.   [9] c, β. h reads καὶ ὡς ἀσέβειαν. A[β] = καὶ παραβάσεων. A[a] om. but not A[b] as Text represents.   [10] c. h, e read τῆς (e om.) συντελείας: β συντελείᾳ.   [11] e reads τοῦ αἰῶνος.   [12] Bracketed as a Christian interpolation. The last word is found only in c.   [13] α. β, S[1] read ἀσεβοῦντες (ἀθετοῦντες a, S[1]) πλανῶντες (eg om.) τὸν Ἰσρ. (e om. τ. Ἰ.). A = ἀσεβοῦντες πλανᾶτε τὸν Ἰσρ. h om. next thirteen words through hmt.   [14] A = ἐπεγείρετε.   [15] c. abfg, S[2] read αὐτῷ. d αὐτόν. e ἑαυτοῖς. A = ὑμῖν. S[1] om.   [16] A = σφόδρα μεγάλα. d adds ἐπερχόμενα αὐτῷ.   [17] bdfg, A. c, a read παρὰ κυρίῳ. e om.   [18] β-d. c reads ανομεισητε. d ἀνομήσει. A = ἀνομεῖτε.   [19] c. β, A, S[1] read σύν. ἀνομεῖν ἐν = ‎בְּ‎ ‎מָשַׁע‎.   [20] c om. next ten words. h resumes with ὥστε after its lacuna.   [21] h. afy read βαστάσαι. be βαστάξαι. d, A δύνασθαι

ώπου τῆς²⁴ πονηρίας ὑμῶν, ἀλλὰ σχισθήσεται²⁵ τὸ καταπέτασμα²⁶ τοῦ ναοῦ, ὥστε μὴ καλύψαι²⁷ τὴν²⁸ ἀσχημοσύνην ὑμῶν.   4. Καὶ²⁹ διασπαρήσεσθε³⁰ αἰχμάλωτοι³¹ ἐν³² τοῖς ἔθνεσιν, καὶ ἔσεσθε *εἰς ὄνειδος καὶ εἰς κατάραν ἐκεῖ³³.   5. Ὁ γὰρ οἶκος, ὃν ἂν³⁴ ἐκλέξεται³⁵ Κύριος³⁶, *Ἰερουσαλὴμ κληθήσεται³⁷, καθὼς *περιέχει ἡ βίβλος³⁸ Ἐνὼχ τοῦ δικαίου.

XI¹. Ὅτε οὖν *ἔλαβον γυναῖκα, ἐγὼ εἴκοσι καὶ ὀκτὼ ἐτῶν ὑπῆρχον², *ἦν δὲ αὐτῇ ὄνομα Μελχά³.   2. Καὶ συλλαβοῦσα ἔτεκεν υἱόν⁴, καὶ ἐκάλεσα⁵ τὸ ὄνομα αὐτοῦ⁶ Γηρσάμ⁷, ὅτι *ἐν γῇ παροικίας ἦμεν⁸.   3. *Καὶ εἶδον⁹ περὶ αὐτόν¹⁰,

Marginal readings:
β–d, S σχίσαι τὸ ἔνδυμα.
β, A, S² ἐκεῖ εἰς ὀνειδισμὸν καὶ εἰς κατάραν καὶ εἰς καταπάτημα.
For Aramaic and Greek

Fragments based on XI. 1, 5, 6, 7, 8; XII. 1–7; XIII. 1, 3, 4, 7, 8, 9 see Appendix.   β–e S¹ ᾗ ὄνομα Μελχά.   β, (Aβ) S¹ τῇ γῇ ἡμῶν πάροικοι. After ἦμεν bde, A, S¹ add Γηρσὰμ γὰρ παροικία γράφεται.

βαστάσαι.   ²²f om.   ²³Aᶜᵈ read Ἰσραήλ. Aᵃ add πόλιν.   ²⁴h. β om. ²⁵c, d, A. h reads σχισθήσονται. ab, S σχίσαι. e σχισε. f σχίσει. g σχήσετε.   ²⁶c. h reads καταπετάσματα. β, A, S¹ ἔνδυμα. Since ἔνδυμα is never used as a translation of פָּרֹכֶת, the veil which divided the holy place from the holy of holies, nor of מָסָךְ, it is possible that τοῦ ναοῦ is an interpolation and that the text spoke merely of the rending of the garments whereby their shame should be exposed. Cf. Isa. xxii. 8.   But if καταπέτασμα is original then τοῦ ναοῦ is so also.   Aᵃ add κόσμου before τοῦ ναοῦ in the sense of 'ornament.'   ²⁷α. β–b read καλύπτειν. b κατακαλύπτειν.   ²⁸α. β om.   ²⁹d reads καὶ οὐ μόνον ταῦτα γενήσεται οὕτως ἀλλὰ καὶ ὑμεῖς.   ³⁰c, abg. h reads διασπαρεῖσθαι and om. next six words. def read διασπαρί (εἰ d, ἤ e) σεσθαι.   ³¹d, Aβ om. S¹(?) reads ὁμόφυλοι. ³²A adds πᾶσιν.   ³³α. β, Aβ, S² read ἐκεῖ (b om.) εἰς ὀνειδισμὸν καὶ εἰς κατάραν (g om. καὶ εἰς κατ.) καὶ εἰς καταπάτημα. Aᵃ reads εἰς κατάραν καὶ εἰς ὀνειδ. καὶ εἰς καταπάτημα ἀλλοτρίων. S¹ εἰς ὀνειδ. καὶ εἰς καταπάτημα.   ³⁴d om. ³⁵h, f. c reads ἐκλέξεται. adg ἐκλέξηται. b ἐξελεξηται. e ἐξελέξεται. A ἐξελέξατο. Aᵃ add ἑαυτῷ.   ³⁶e om.   ³⁷d reads Ἰηλ ἅγιον ἔσται. f om. ³⁸α, deg. abf read περιέχει βίβλος. A = γέγραπται (Aʰ om.) ἐν βίβλοις.

XI. ¹g om. XI.–XII. 3 S¹ om. XI.–XIII. here but adds them after XIX.   ²α (save that c reads χρόνων for ἐτῶν). β, Aβ, S¹ read ἐλ. γυναῖκα, ἤμην ἐτῶν εἴκοσι ὀκτώ (κη΄ ἐτῶν ἤμην ade, εἴκοσι καὶ ὀκτὼ ἐτῶν ἤμην f). Aᵃ = ἤμην ἐγὼ ἐτῶν εἴκοσι καὶ ὀκτὼ ἔλαβον ἐγώ μοι γυναῖκα.   ³α (save that c reads Μελχέ). e which is dependent on α reads ἦν δὲ ὄνομα αὐτῆς Μελχώ. A is an expansion of α. It = καὶ ἦν τὸ ὄνομα τῆς γυναικός μου Μελχά. β–e, S¹ read ᾗ ὄνομα Μελχά.   ⁴α, d, Aᵇ*, Gk. Frag. 63. a reads παροικηλόν. bef, Aᶜᵈᵉᶠ, S¹ om. Ver. 2 is very corrupt in Aᵃ. It = καὶ ὅτε ἦμεν ἐν Γεσέμ, ὅτι πάροικοι ἦμεν ἐν τῇ γῇ ἐν ᾗ ἦμεν· Γεσέμ γὰρ παροικία μεταγράφεται.   ⁵h, d, S¹, Gk. Frag. 63. c, abef, Aβ read ἐκάλεσε.   ⁶ adds παροικία.

β (Αβ), S¹ εἶδον δὲ ἐν ὁρά-ματι ὅτι μέσος ἐν ὑψηλοῖς ἵστατο πάσης τῆς συνα-γωγῆς.
β, Α τρίτον.

ὅτι οὐκ ἔστιν¹¹ ἐν τῇ¹² πρώτῃ τάξει.   4. Καὶ¹³ ὁ Καὰθ¹⁴ ἐγεννήθη *ἐν τῷ¹⁵ τριακόστῳ πέμπτῳ¹⁶ ἔτει¹⁷ ⌜τῆς ζωῆς μου⌝¹⁸ *πρὸς ἀνατολὰς ἡλίου¹⁹.   5. *Καὶ εἶδον ἐν ὁράματι· ἐν ὑψηλοῖς ἵστατο μεσῶν τῆς συναγωγῆς²⁰.   6. *Διὰ τοῦτο ἐκάλεσα τὸ ὄνομα αὐτοῦ Καάθ²¹, [ὅ ἐστιν ἀρχὴ μεγαλείου καὶ συμβιβασμός]²².   7. Καὶ *τρίτον υἱὸν²³ ἔτεκέν μοι τὸν Μεραρεῖ²⁴ τῷ²⁵ τεσσαρακοστῷ²⁶ ἔτει²⁷ *τῆς ζωῆς μου²⁸, καὶ

---

⁷Aᵃ = Γεσέμ.   ⁸α (save that h reads ὑμῶν (?) for ἡμεν). β, A, S read ἐν τῇ γῇ ἡμῶν (αὐτοῦ f. ἐν ᾗ ἡμεν A. e om.) πάροικοι ἡμεν (πάροικος ἤμην e). bde, A, S¹ add Γηρσὰμ (Γεσέμ Aᵃ) γὰρ παροικία γράφεται (μεταγράφεται A) against α, aef.   ⁹α, Αβ. bef read εἶδον δέ. af ἰδών. d ἰδον γάρ. Aᵃ om. together with rest of verse.   ¹⁰β reads αὐτοῦ.   ¹¹b reads ἔσται.   ¹²α, d, Αβ. β–d om.   ¹³d gives ver. 4 as follows: καὶ ἐν τῷ λ̅ε̅ ἔτει πάλιν συλλαβοῦσα ἔτεκέ μοι υἱὸν δεύτερον κατὰ ἀνατολὰς ἡλίου.   ¹⁴a reads Κάθ here and elsewhere. Aᵇ adds υἱός μου.   ¹⁵α. β om.   ¹⁶Aᵃ om. Aram. Frag. = τετάρτῳ. Gr. Frag. 68 reads ἐνιαυτῷ corrupt(?) for τετάρτῳ.   ¹⁷Aᵇ* om.   ¹⁸α. β, A, S¹ om.   ¹⁹Aᵃ om.   ²⁰α (save that c om. ἐν before ὁράματι). β reads εἶδον δὲ ἐν ὁράματι, ὅτι μέσος (μέσον adf, μεσῶν e) ἐν ὑψ. (+δρυσὶ S¹) ἵστ. πάσης τῆς συναγωγῆς. A = καὶ εἶδον ἐν ὁράματι ὅτι ἐν μέσῳ πολλῶν (here [Armenian] (= πολλῶν) is a corrupt dittography of [Armenian] = ὑψηλός) ἵστατο ὑψηλὸς ὑπὲρ πᾶσαν τὴν συναγωγήν (ἐν μέσῳ τοῦ ὕψους ἵστατο ὑπὲρ πᾶσαν τ. συναγωγήν Αβ). It thus appears that A supports β. With our text we should compare the Gr. Frag. Ἑώρακα ὅτι ἐπ' αὐτῷ ἔσται ἡ συναγωγὴ παντὸς τοῦ λαοῦ. There may be a paronomasia in קהת and קהל = συναγωγή.   ²¹Aᵃ read Καάθ only. For ἐκάλεσα a reads ἐκάλεσε and for Καάθ S¹ reads Κυιάφα and d Κάθ.   ²²I have bracketed this clause as a gloss. Though it is found in both α, β and A, it cannot be given as an explanation of the name. It may, however, be a corrupt survival of the text which may be more truly handed down in the Gr. Frag. καὶ ὅτι αὐτὸς ἔσται ἡ ἀρχιερωσύνη ἡ μεγάλη· αὐτὸς καὶ τὸ σπέρμα αὐτοῦ ἔσονται ἀρχὴ βασιλέων ἱεράτευμα τῷ Ἰσραήλ. The MSS. evidence is as follows: α, S¹ support text (save that h, S¹ read συμβιβασμοῦ). Similarly β (save that d om. ἀρχὴ μεγ. and e reads ἑρμηνεία for ἀρχή). A = ὅ ἐστιν ἡ ἀρχὴ μεγαλείου (χρίσεως Αβ by an easy internal corruption) καὶ κρίσεως (but [Armenian] may be corrupt for [Armenian] = συμβιβασμοῦ).   ²³c. h reads τὸν υἱὸν τὸν τρίτον. β–bd, A read τρίτον. b, S¹ τρεῖς. For the first seven words d reads καὶ προσθῆσα (sic) ἔτεκέ μοι υἱόν.   ²⁴α. ae read Μεραρήν. bf Μεραρί. a om. next fifteen words through hmt.   ²⁵α, d. bef om.   ²⁶d read μ.   ²⁷Aˣ om.   ²⁸c, d. h, bef, Aᵃ read ζωῆς μου. Αβ om.   ²⁹e reads ἐπεί.   ³⁰c, e, Aᵃᵇ. So also Aram. and Gr. Frag. 69. h, bdf, Aᵇβ, S¹ read ἐκάλεσε.

ἐπειδὴ[29] ἐδυστόκησεν ἡ μήτηρ αὐτοῦ ἐκάλεσα[30] αὐτὸν[31]
Μεραρεῖ[32] ὅ ἐστι[33] *πικριασμός[34].   8. Ἡ δὲ Ἰωχαβὲδ[35]
*ἐγεννήθη ἐν Αἰγύπτῳ τῷ ἑξηκοστῷ τετάρτῳ μου ἔτει[36]. *ἔνδοξος
γὰρ ἦν τότε ἐν μέσῳ τῶν ἀδελφῶν μου[37].

XII. Καὶ ἔλαβεν ὁ[1] Γερσὰμ[2] γυναῖκα[3] καὶ ἔτεκεν[4]
*ἐξ αὐτῆς[5] τὸν Λομνὴ[6] καὶ Σεμεῆ[7].   2. *Οἱ δὲ[8] υἱοὶ
Καὰθ[9] Ἀβραάμ[10], Ἰσαχάρ[11], Χεβρὼν[12] καὶ[13] Ὀζηήλ[14].
3. ⌜Καὶ οἱ[15] υἱοὶ Μεραρεῖ Μοολὶ[16] καὶ Μωυσής[17]⌝.   4. Καὶ
τετάρτῳ ἔτει ἐτέχθη ἐν Αἰγ.   β, Α αὐτῷ.

(right margin): h, bdf, Ab, S1 ἐκάλεσε. β, S1 πικρία μου ὅτι καίγε αὐτὸς ἀπέθνησκεν. β, S1 ἑξηκοστῷ

---

[31] e reads αὐτῶν.   Aᵃ, Aram. and Gr. Frag. 69 = τὸ ὄνομα αὐτοῦ.   [32] α. b reads Μεραρί.   d Μεραρή.   ef Μεραρήν (-ιν f).   [33] Α = ἑρμηνεύεται.   [34] c. β–e, Α read πικρία μου.   h κρασμος.   e πικρασμοῦ.   β adds ὅτι καίγε (καὶ d) αὐτὸς ἀπέθνησκεν (ἀπέθανεν b).   [35] α, bg.   β–bg read Ἰωχαβίθ (Ἰυχ. af)   Aᵃ = Γεναβάδ.   Aᵇ* Ναχαβίθ.   Aᶜᵈˡˢ Ἰοχαβίθ.   [36] α (save that c reads ἐγεννήθην).   Aᵃ = ἐγεννήθη (or ἐτέχθη) μοι ἑξήκοντα τετάρτῳ ἔτει ζωῆς μου, ἐν ᾧ ἦν ἐν Αἰγ.   β–d, S1 read ἑξηκοστῷ (ἑξήκοντα f, ξ e) τετάρτῳ ἔτει (τεσσάρων ἐτῶν f) ἐτέχθη ἐν Αἰγ.   Aᵝ = ὅτε ἦν ἑξήκ. τεσσάρων ἐτῶν ἐτέχθη μοι (Aᵇ* om.) ἐν Αἰγ.   d stands alone and gives ver. 8 thus: καὶ ἐν τῷ ξ τετάρτῳ ἔτει τῆς ζωῆς μου ἐν Αἰγ. συλλαβοῦσα ἔτεκέ μοι θυγατέρα τὴν Ἰωχαβίθ.   This slightly agrees with Aram. Frag. 71.   [37] h.   So c (save that it reads ει τωτε ἐν μέσῳ).   β reads ἤμην τότε (e om.) ἐμμέσῳ (ἐν μέσῳ def) τ. ἀδ. μου.   Aᵃ = καὶ τότε ἦν ἐνδ. ἐν μέσῳ ἀδελφῶν πολλῶν.   Aᵝ = καὶ ἦν τότε ἐνδ. ἐν μ. τῶν ἀδ. μου.

XII. [1] b om.   [2] Aᵇ = Γεθσών.   Aᵃ add ἑαυτῷ.   [3] Aᵇ*ᶜᵈ add συνέλαβεν.   Aᵉˢ καὶ συνέλαβεν.   [4] S1 = ἐγεννήθη.   [5] α, S1.   β, Α read αὐτῷ.   Aᵃ add υἱόν.   [6] c, f.   h reads Λομνεί and om. next nine words.   a reads Λομήν.   b Λομνί.   d Λομνήν.   e Λωμνήν.   Aᵃ, deg Λουμί.   Aᵇ* Λουνμί.   Aᶜ Λομί.   Exod. vi. 17 לִבְנִי and so Aram. Frag.   [7] c.   b reads τὸν Σεμεί.   adf Σεμεί.   e τὸν Σενεήν.   Aᵃ = Σεμί.   Aᵇ Συμί.   Aᵇ*ᶜᵈ Σεμηί.   Aᵉˢ Σεμνεί.   Exod. vi. 17 שִׁמְעִי.   [8] c.   ef, Aᵃ read καὶ οἱ.   ab καί.   For the first four words of ver. 2 d reads ἔλαβε καὶ Κἀθ γυναῖκα καὶ ἔτεκεν αὐτῷ.   [9] c adds εἰσίν.   [10] c, d.   b reads Ἀμβράμ.   Cf. LXX. Exod. vi. 18.   aef Ἀβράμ.   Α = Ἀμράμ.   So Exod. vi. 18 עַמְרָם, and also Aram. Frag.   d adds καί.   [11] c, adef, Aᵃ.   b reads Ἰσαάρ.   Aᶜᵈ = Ἰσαχαρά.   Aᵇ* Ισαχαρ και Ισαχαρα.   d adds καί.   Exod. vii. 18 and Aram. Frag. 75 יִצְהָר.   [12] b reads Χεβρώ.   [13] α, d, A.   Other MSS. om.   [14] c.   h reads Ὀζωήλ.   adf, Aᵝ Ὀζιήλ.   b Ὀζήλ.   e Οὐζηήλ.   Aᵃ = Οὐζίλ.   Aᵇ Οὐζιήλ.   [15] c, ef.   h, ab om.   For the first four words d reads ὁμοίως δὲ καὶ ὁ Μεθαρὴ ἔλαβεν αὐτῷ γυναῖκα καὶ ἔτεκεν.   A om. ver. 3.   [16] b, S1.   c reads Μοθλί.   h Μεθχί.   af Μοθλή.   d τὸν Μααλή.   e Μωλή.   Exod. vi. 19 and Aram. Frag. 75 מַחְלִי.   [17] α.   d reads Μωνσὴ καὶ Ἀαρών.   Cf. Exod. vi. 19 מוּשִׁי.   af read Ὀμουσή.   b, S1 Ὀμουσί where the Ο may represent the vav in the Hebrew.   On the other hand, the LXX has

⌜ἐν[18] τῷ[19] *ἐνενηκοστῷ τετάρτῳ μου ἔτει⌝[20] ἔλαβεν ὁ[21]
Ἀβραὰμ[22] τὴν Ἰωχαβὲδ[23] τὴν[24] θυγατέρα μου ἑαυτῷ[25] εἰς
γυναῖκα ὅτι ἐν μιᾷ ἡμέρᾳ[26] ἐγεννήθησαν[27] αὐτὸς καὶ ἡ θυγάτηρ
μου.   5. Ὀκτὼ[28] ἐτῶν ἤμην ὅτε εἰσῆλθον[29] εἰς γῆν[30]
Χαναάν[31]· καὶ *δέκα καὶ ὀκτὼ[32] ἐτῶν[33] ὅτε[34] ἀπέκτεινα
*τὸν Συχέμ[35]· καὶ *δέκα καὶ ἐννέα[36] ἐτῶν[37] ἱεράτευσα[38]
καὶ *εἴκοσι καὶ ὀκτὼ[39] ἐτῶν[40] ἔλαβον[41] γυναῖκα· καὶ τεσσαράκοντα[42] (καὶ ὀκτὼ)[43] ἐτῶν[44] εἰσῆλθον εἰς Αἴγυπτον·
6. *Καὶ ἰδού ἐστε, τέκνα μου, τρίτη γενεά[45].   7. Ἰωσὴφ[46]
ἑκατοστῷ *ὀγδόῳ καὶ δεκάτῳ μου ἔτει[47] ἀπέθανεν.

XIII. Καὶ *νῦν, τέκνα μου[1], ἐντέλλομαι ὑμῖν,
φοβεῖσθε[2] *Κύριον τὸν Θεὸν ὑμῶν[3] ⌜ἐξ ὅλης τῆς καρδίας
ὑμῶν⌝[4],

Ὁμουσεί also.   e reads βουσήν.   [18] c, d. Other MSS. om.   A om. to ἔτει
inclusive.   [19] be om.   [20] c. So also h, b (save that h om. μου and b trs.
it after ἔτει).   e reads ϛ̅δ̅ ἔτει Μωυσή.   af ἐνενηκ. ἔτει μου σὺν τῷ τετάρτῳ
(καὶ τετάρτῳ f).   d ἐνενηκ. ἔτει τῆς ζωῆς μου.   S[1] corrupt.   [21] c, bf. Other
MSS. om.   [22] α, de. af read Ἀβράμ.   b Ἀμβράμ.   A = Ἀμράμ.   d adds
ὁ υἱὸς Κάθ.   [23] a. c reads Ἠοχαβέλ.   h Ἰωχαβέλ.   d, A[a,cdeg] Ἰωχαβέθ.   e
Ἰωχαβέ. af Ἰοχαβέθ.   A[b] = Ὀχαβεθ.   [24] c, d. Other MSS. om.   [25] c, adf,
A[a,eg]. b reads αὐτῷ.   e αὐτήν.   h, A[b*cd] om.   [26] A[β] = ἔτει.   [27] α om.
rest of chap.   [28] e reads η′. Aram. Frag. 78 ὀκτωκαίδεκα.   [29] g reads
ἦλθον.   [30] ag om.   [31] A[β] = Χαναανιτῶν. d om. next nine words.   [32] afg.
b, A read ὀκτωκαίδεκα.   e Ι̅Η̅.   [33] f om.   [34] A[a] = ἤμην ὅτε. A[b*] om.
g om. next nine words.   [35] A = τοὺς Σικιμίτας.   [36] af. de read Θ̅.
b, A ἐννεακαίδεκα.   [37] bde. af read ἔτη. A[a] add ἤμην ὅτε.   [38] af, A[a]
add τῷ κυρίῳ.   [39] f, A. a read κ′ καὶ η′. de Κ̅Η̅. bg εἰκοσιοκτώ. S[1] εἴκοσι.
[40] A[a,eg] add ἤμην ὅτε.   [41] A[a] add μοι.   [42] de read μ̅.   [43] Added in
accordance with Aram. Frag. 79.   [44] A[a,cdeg] add ἤμην ὅτε.   [45] aef (save
that af om. ἐστέ and e reads ἔσται). So also A[β] (save that A[b*cd] add ὑμεῖς
after ἐστέ). b, S[1] read καὶ ἰδού, τέκνα μού ἐστε, τέκνα μου, τρίτη γενεά. d καὶ
ἰδού ἐστε ἀρτίως τρίτη γενεά, ὑμεῖς τέκνα μου. A[a] = καὶ νῦν ἰδού ἐστε τέκνα μου
†τρεῖς†. g reads καὶ ἰδοὺ ἔσται τέκνα τρεῖς γενεαί.   [46] d reads Ἰωσὴφ γὰρ
ὁ ἀδελφός μου. A[β] = καὶ Ἰωσ. g, A[a] om. this verse.   [47] adf, S[1] (save
that a and S[1] om.). b reads ὀκτωκαιδεκάτῳ ἔτει. d ι′ ἐτῶν. A[β] καὶ δεκάτῳ
ἔτει αὐτοῦ ὅτε, thus agreeing with d.

XIII. [1] g om. S[1] om. next two words.   [2] α, f, S[1]. a reads φοβεῖσθαι.
beg, A ἵνα φοβεῖσθε (φοβεῖσθαι e). d ἵνα φοβῆσθε.   [3] α, adfg, A, S[2] (save
that c, adfg read ἡμῶν). e reads τὸν θεὸν ὑμῶν. b τὸν κ. S[1] τὸν κύριον ἡμῶν.
[4] c. af read ἐξ ὅλης τῆς καρδίας. beg ἐξ ὅλης καρδ. d ἐξ ὅλης καρδ. ἡμῶν.
h, A om.   [5] ag add καρδίας (+ ὑμῶν g). d κυρίου. e ψυχῆς. A[a] = εὐθύ-

καὶ πορεύεσθε ἐν ἁπλότητι⁵ *κατὰ πάντα τὸν νόμον
αὐτοῦ⁶.

2. *Διδάξατε δὲ καὶ ὑμεῖς⁷ τὰ τέκνα ὑμῶν γράμματα⁸   α om.
ἵνα ἔχωσι⁹ σύνεσιν ἐν *πάσῃ τῇ ζωῇ αὐτῶν¹⁰,   ver. 2.
ἀναγινώσκοντες¹¹ ἀδιαλείπτως¹² τὸν νόμον τοῦ Θεοῦ¹³.

3. Ὅτι¹⁴ πᾶς, *ὃς γνώσεται¹⁵ *νόμον Κυρίου¹⁶, τιμηθήσεται,
καὶ οὐκ ἔσται¹⁷ ξένος, ὅπου ὑπάγει¹⁸.

4. Καίγε πολλοὺς φίλους ὑπὲρ γονεῖς κτήσεται¹⁹
καὶ ἐπιθυμήσουσι πολλοὶ τῶν ἀνθρώπων δουλεῦσαι αὐτῷ²⁰
καὶ ἀκοῦσαι νόμον²¹ ἐκ τοῦ²² στόματος αὐτοῦ²³.

5. Ποιήσατε ⌜οὖν⌝²⁴ δικαιοσύνην²⁵, τέκνα μου, ἐπὶ τῆς γῆς,
ἵνα †εὕρητε²⁶ ἐν τοῖς οὐρανοῖς.   α ὑγια-
                                        σμένοι
                                        ἦτε.
6. Καὶ σπείρατε²⁷ ἐν *ταῖς ψυχαῖς²⁸ ὑμῶν²⁹ ἀγαθὰ
*καὶ εὑρήσετε³⁰ αὐτὰ³¹ *ἐν τῇ ζωῇ ὑμῶν³².
*Ἐὰν δὲ σπείρητε πονηρὰ³³
*πᾶσαν ταραχὴν καὶ θλῖψιν θερίσετε³⁴.

τητι, Αᵝ ἁπλότητι.   ⁶Aᵃ = κατὰ πάσας τὰς ἐντολὰς αὐτοῦ.   Aᵝ τῶν νόμων
αὐτοῦ. d om. τόν, and b reads αὐτῶν for αὐτοῦ.   ⁷e reads διδάξατε καὶ ὑμεῖς.
Aᵃ = καὶ διδάξατε.   ⁸g trs. before τὸ τέκνα.   ⁹f reads ἔχουσιν. S¹
ἔχητε.   ¹⁰de read πάσῃ ζ. αὐτῶν.   ¹¹abfg, Aᵝ, S¹. d reads καὶ ἵνα γινώσκοντες καὶ ἐπιγινώσκοντες. e ἵνα γινώσκουσιν. Aᵃ = ἀναγινώσκειν.   ¹²d
reads ἀδιαλείπτως ὦσιν and trs. after θεοῦ.   ¹³A = κυρίου.   ¹⁴c reads
διότι. Aᵉᵍ om. Aᵝ om. next five words.   ¹⁵g reads ὁ εἰδώς.   ¹⁶α, d,
Aᵃ. abfg read ν. θεοῦ. e τὸν νόμον τοῦ θεοῦ. e adds καί.   ¹⁷c reads ἐστίν.
¹⁸β. c reads ἂν εἰσέρχεται. h ἂν ἀπέρχεται.   ¹⁹h (?), ag. c, df read κτίσε-
ται. b κτήσηται. e γε ζητεῖν. S¹ adds ὧν φιλομαθής. Aᵃ om. ver. 4 and
compresses vers. 5, 6 as follows:
    Σπείρατε δικαιοσύνην (or ἐλεημοσύνην) ἐπὶ τῆς γῆς
    ἵνα θερίσητε ἀταραξίαν.
²⁰g reads αὐτόν. Aᵇ*ᶜᵈ = ὑμῖν. Aᵉᵍ om.   ²¹c, β–d. h reads νόμους. d
λόγον.   ²²aeᶦ om.   ²³Aᵇ*ᶜᵈ = ὑμῶν.   ²⁴α. β, A, S¹ om.   ²⁵c trs.
after τέκνα μου.   ²⁶β, Aᵝ, S. d adds αὐτήν and for preceding ἵνα reads
ὅπως. c reads ὑγιασμένοι εἶται (i.e. ἦτε). h ἡλιασμένοι. All readings corrupt.
εὕρητε = תמצאו and ὑγιασμένοι ἦτε = תרמאו, both of which are corrupt for
תאצרו = θησαυρίσητε. Cf. Matt. vi. 19, 20.   ²⁷α, af. bdeg read σπείρετε.
²⁸f reads τῇ ψυχῇ.   ²⁹d reads ἡμῶν.   ³⁰α (though c reads εὑρήσειται
and h εὑρήσητε). β, A read ἵνα εὕρητε. S¹ καὶ θερίσετε καὶ εὑρήσετε.   ³¹g,
S¹ om.   ³²α om. S¹ reads αἰωνίῳ for ὑμῶν.   ³³α (save that c reads
σπείρετε). abef, S¹ read ἐὰν γὰρ σπείρητε (σπείρετε ef) κακά. dg ἐὰν γὰρ
σπείρητε.   ³⁴α, β–dg (save that c reads θερησεται (sic), h, bf θερίσητε, e
θερίσεται), Aᵝ. dg read ταραχήν, πᾶσαν (d om.) θλῖψιν θερίσητε (θερησετε g).
³⁵ab, Aᵝ. c, df read κτίσασθε. h, e κτήσασθαι. g, Aᵃ κτήσεσθε.   ³⁶Aᵃ =

β, Αβ, S
θεοῦ
μετὰ
σπουδῆς.
α ἵνα.

7. Σοφίαν κτήσασθε[35] *ἐν φόβῳ[36] Θεοῦ[37]
 ὅτι[38] ἐὰν *γένηται αἰχμαλωσία,
 καὶ ὀλοθρευθῶσι πόλεις καὶ χῶραι[39]
 *καὶ χρυσὸς καὶ ἄργυρος καὶ πᾶσα[40] κτῆσις[41] ἀπολεῖται[42]
 *τοῦ σοφοῦ τὴν σοφίαν[43] †οὐδεὶς[44] δύναται[45] ἀφελέσθαι[46]
 εἰ μὴ τύφλωσις[47] ἀσεβείας[48] καὶ πώρωσις[49] ἁμαρτίας[50].

β–d, A, S
om.

8. ⌐Ἐὰν γάρ τις φυλάξῃ αὐτὸν ἐκ τῶν πονηρῶν τούτων ἔργων⌐[61]
 τότε[52] γενήσεται[53] αὐτῷ σοφία[54] καὶ *παρὰ τοῖς πολεμίοις
   λαμπρὰ[55]
 καὶ ἐπὶ[56] γῆς ἀλλοτρίας[57] πατρίς,
 καὶ ἐν μέσῳ[58] ἐχθρῶν εὑρηθήσεται[59] φίλος.

β, A
ταῦτα.
abf, A,
S¹ ἡμῶν.

9. *Πᾶς ὃς ἂν διδάσκει καλὰ καὶ πράττει[60]
 σύνθρονος ἔσται[61] βασιλέων[62],
 ὥσπερ[63] καὶ Ἰωσὴφ ὁ ἀδελφός[64] μου[65].

καὶ φόβον. [37] α, β, S¹. Aᵃ = κυρίου θεοῦ. Αβ, S² κυρίου. β, Αβ, S add μετὰ σπουδῆς. [38] α read ἵνα. [39] α. β, S¹ read γένηται αἰχ. καὶ πόλεις ἐξολοθρευθῶσι (ὀλοθρευθῶσι bf) καὶ χῶραι (S¹ om. κ. χῶραι). Aᵃ = ὅτι ὅτε γενήσονται ἐν ταραχῇ χῶραι καὶ ὀλοθρευθῶσι. Αβ = ὅτι ἐὰν γένωνται χῶραι καὶ πόλεις ὀλοθρευθῶσι. d adds καὶ ἄρουραι. [40] Aᵃ om. [41] abeg. α, df read κτίσις. [42] beg. c reads ἀπωλλεῖται. h ἀπολυται. d ἀπόλλυται. af ἀπώληται. [43] α, β–df. df read τοῦ δὲ σοφοῦ τὴν σ. Aᵃ = τὴν δὲ σοφίαν τῶν σοφῶν. Αβ τὴν δε σοφίαν. [44] e reads οὐ. [45] Aᵃ = δυνήσεται. [46] Aᵃ add ἀπ' αὐτῶν. Aᵇ ἀπ' αὐτοῦ. [47] For τύφλ ... ἁμαρτίας S¹ reads σκοτία ἁμαρτίας τύφλωσις ῥήματος ἀπὸ τῆς εὐγενείας. [48] Aᵃ om. next three words. [49] Em. from πόρρωσις of α, e. adf read πόρωσις. b πήρωσις. g πείρωσις. Αβ = πλήρωσις, a corruption of our text. [50] g reads καρδίας. [51] α (save that c reads φυλάξει, and h ἑαυτόν, and πράξεων for ἔργων). d reads ἐὰν δὲ φυλάξῃ ταῦτα. β–d, A, S om. But the τότε (α, aef) which begins the next line points to some such clause as the above. [52] α, aef, S¹. bg, A read ὅτι. d om. [53] c adds ἐν. [54] α, d (but d prefixes ἡ), A. β–d read αὐτή. Aᵃ add αὐτοῦ ὡς πόλις ἰσχυρά. S¹ reads πόλεμος and for next five words καὶ ἀπὸ τοῦ πολεμίου. [55] h, β. c reads περὶ τοὺς πολεμίους λαμπρός. A = παρὰ τῷ πολέμῳ (τοῖς πολέμοις Αβ) λαμπρότης. [56] g adds τῆς. Aᵃ om. this line and the next. [57] Αβ = ἀλλοτρίων. [58] α, ef. Other MSS. read ἐμμέσῳ. [59] c reads γενήσεται. For εὑρ. φίλος S¹ reads ἀναστρέψεται. [60] α (save that h reads διδάσκῃ). ae read ὃς ἐὰν διδάσκῃ ταῦτα καὶ πράττῃ (πράσσει e). bdg ἐὰν (+ γὰρ g) διδάσκῃ (διδάσκει d) ταῦτα καὶ πράττῃ (πράττει d). f ὃ ἐὰν διδάσκει ταῦτα καὶ πράσσει. A = ὅτι ἐὰν ὁ διδάσκεις καὶ τοῦτο πράττῃς. S¹ ἐὰν δέ τις γλίχηται τῆς διδασκαλίας καὶ σοφίας. [61] A = ἔσῃ. [62] α, β–ab, A, S². ab, S¹ read βασιλέως. [63] α. β read ὡς. [64] g reads πατράδελφος. S¹ prefixes ἁγνός. [65] α, d. abf, A, S¹ read ἡμῶν. eg ὑμῶν.

α, Aᵃ	β, Aᵝ, S¹
XIV. Ἐγὼ[1] οὖν, τέκνα μου[2], ἔγνων[3] ὅτι ἐπὶ τὰ τέλη τῶν αἰώνων ἀσεβήσετε[4] *ἐπὶ Κυρίον, χεῖρας ἐπιβάλλοντες[5] ἐν[6] κακίᾳ [ἐπ' αὐτὸν][7] καὶ ἐν[8] πᾶσι τοῖς ἔθνεσιν γενήσεσθε[9] χλευασμός.	XIV. Καὶ νῦν, τέκνα μου[10], ἔγνων ἀπὸ[11] γραφῆς[12] Ἐνώχ, ὅτι ἐπὶ τέλει[13] ἀσεβήσετε[14] ἐπὶ Κύριον, *χεῖρας ἐπιβάλλοντες ἐν πάσῃ κακίᾳ[15] καὶ αἰσχυνθήσονται *ἐφ' ὑμῖν[16] οἱ ἀδελφοὶ ὑμῶν, καὶ πᾶσι τοῖς ἔθνεσι γενήσεσθε[17] χλευασμός.

2. Καὶ γὰρ ὁ πατὴρ ἡμῶν Ἰσραὴλ καθαρός ἐστιν[18] ἀπὸ τῆς[19] ἀσεβείας[20] τῶν ἀρχιερέων [οἵτινες ἐπιβαλοῦσι[21] τὰς χεῖρας αὐτῶν ἐπὶ τὸν σωτῆρα τοῦ κόσμου][22].

α	β (S¹).	Aᵝ
3. Ὡς[23] γάρ ἐστιν ὁ †ἥλιος[24] καθαρὸς ἐνώπιον κυρίου †ἐπὶ τὴν γῆν[25], οὕτω καὶ	3. *Καθαρὸς ὁ οὐρανὸς ὑπὲρ τὴν γῆν[26] καὶ ὑμεῖς οἱ φωστῆρες τοῦ Ἰσραήλ[27],	3. Τέκνα μου, καθαροὶ γίνεσθε καθὼς οἱ οὐρανοὶ ὑπὲρ τὴν γῆν· καὶ ὑμεῖς οἱ οἱ

Aᵃ om. vers. 2, 3, 4 (to ἀνελεῖν inclusive).

XIV. [1] Aᵃ = καὶ. [2] Aᵃ add ἀναγγέλλω ὑμῖν ὅ. [3] Aᵃ add ἀπὸ γραφῆς (τῶν ἔργων Aᵇ) Ἐνώχ. [4] h. c reads ἀσεβήσουσιν. [5] α (save that c reads ἐπιβαλοῦσι). Aᵃ = καὶ χεῖρας ὑμῶν ἐπιβαλεῖτε ἐπὶ κ. ὑμῶν. [6] Aᵃ add πάσῃ (rightly). [7] α. Bracketed as a Christian addition. A, β, S¹ om. Observe addition made here by β, Aᵝ. [8] c. h om. [9] c reads γενήσεσθαι (corrupt for γενήσεσθε as in af, A). h γενήσεται. [10] e, Aᵝ. β–e, S¹ om. [11] e adds τῆς. [12] S¹ reads γενεᾶς. [13] abd, S¹. e reads τὸ τέλος. f συντελείᾳ. g τέλος. Aᵝ = ἐπὶ τὰ τέλη τῶν αἰώνων. [14] f. ahdg read ἀσεβήσητε. e ἀσεβήσεται. S¹ ἀσεβέσουσι. Aᵝ add καθὼς ποιήσουσιν πάντα τὰ ἔθνη. [15] β (save that de read ἐπιβαλόντες), S¹. Aᵝ = καὶ χεῖρας ὑμῶν ἐπιβαλεῖτε ἐπὶ κύριον. Unless we can render χεῖρας ἐπιβ. ἐν πάσῃ κακίᾳ as 'stretching out the hands to all wickedness,' we must reject either the whole clause or χεῖρας ἐπιβ. at all events. [16] bg. d om. af read ἐφ' ὑμᾶς and e ἐφ' ὑμῶν. [17] af, A. bg read γενήσεται. d γενήσετε. e γενήσεσθαι. [18] α, adefg. b, S¹ read ἔσται. Aᵝ = ἦν. [19] α, abd, Aᵇᶜᵈᵉᵍ, S¹. efg, Aᵇ* read πάσης. [20] c adds ὑμῶν καί. [21] Aᵝ = ἐπιβάλλουσι. [22] c adds χν. The clause is bracketed as a Christian interpolation. [23] h. c reads οὐ. [24] = שֶׁמֶשׁ which, since β, Aᵝ read οὐρανός, is corrupt for שמים. [25] = בארץ corrupt for מארץ or מהארץ = ὑπέρ or παρὰ τὴν γῆν. Hence read ὑπέρ or παρά, as in β, Aᵝ. [26] β–d (save that for οὐρανός, which f om., a reads ἥλιος). d om. S¹ om. ver. 3 and ver. 4 to ἀσεβείᾳ. [27] aefg. b reads οὐρανοῦ. For καὶ ὑμεῖς . . . Ἰσραήλ d reads καὶ γὰρ αὐτῷ ὡς φωστῆρές εἰσιν. [28] Aᵝ give the imperative here. [29] c reads σκοτισθεῖτε. [30] Em. from

ὑμεῖς ἐστε[28], οἱ φωστῆρες τοῦ Ἰσραήλ, παρὰ πάντα τὰ ἔθνη. 4. Καὶ ἐὰν ὑμεῖς σκοτισθῆτε[29] ἐν ἀσεβείᾳ, τί λοιπὸν τὰ ἔθνη ποιήσουσι[30] ἐν τυφλώσει διάγοντες[31]; καὶ ἐπάξετε κατάραν ἐπὶ τὸ γένος ἡμῶν[32], †ὑπὲρ οὖν†[33] τὸ φῶς τοῦνόμουτὸδοθὲνεἰς φωτισμὸν *παντὸς ἀνθρώπου[34], †τοῦτον θέλ(ήσ)ετε[35] ἀνελεῖν, ἐναντίας ἐντολὰς διδάσκοντες[36] τοῖς τοῦ θεοῦδικαιώμασιν.	†ὡς ὁ .ἥλιος καὶ ἡ σελήνη. 4. *Τί ποιήσουσιν πάντα τὰ ἔθνη, ἐὰν ὑμεῖς σκοτισθῆτε ἐν ἀσεβείᾳ; καὶ ἐπάξετε κατάραν[37] ἐπὶ[38] τὸ γένος ἡμῶν[39], †ὑπὲρ ὧν[40] τὸ φῶς τοῦ νόμου[41] τὸ δοθὲν[42] ὑμῖν[43] εἰς φωτισμὸν παντὸς ἀνθρώπου, †τοῦτον[44] θελήσετε[45] ἀνελεῖν, ἐναντίας ἐντολὰς διδάσκοντες *τοῖς τοῦ θεοῦ δικαιώμασι[46].	φωστῆρές ἐστε τοῦ Ἰσραήλ, ὡς ὁ ἥλιος καὶ ἡ σελήνη, ἔσεσθε. 4. Τί[47] ποιήσουσιν πάντα τὰ ἔθνη, ἐὰν [γὰρ][48] σκοτισθήσεσθε ἐν ἀσεβείᾳ; καὶ ἐλεύσονται κατάραι ἐπὶ τὸ γένος ὑμῶν, καὶ τὸ φῶς τὸ δοθὲν διὰ τοῦ νόμου ὑμῖν εἰς φωτισμὸν *καὶ παντὶ ἀνθρώπῳ[49], τοῦτο θελήσετε ἀνελεῖν καὶ [ἐναντίον τούτου][50] διδάξετε[51] τὰς ἐντολὰς[52] κατὰ τοῦ δικαιώματος θεοῦ.

Aa om. ver. 5 and ver. 6 to βεβηλώσετε καί inclusive.

5. Τὰς προσφορὰς[53] Κυρίου ληστεύσετε[54], καὶ *ἀπὸ τῶν

ποιήσωσιν of c. _h_ reads ποιήσειε. [31] _h_ adds ὑπὲρ οὖν. [32] _c. h_, S¹ read ὑμῶν. [33] α. This unintelligible phrase is no doubt corrupt for ὑπὲρ ὧν as in β = אשר על. Cf. Ps. civ. 14 (LXX) for ὑπέρ with genitive in this sense as a rendering of על. Aβ give καί. S¹ γάρ. [34] _d_ om. [35] _c_ reads θέλεται. _h_ θέλετε. [36] _c. h_ reads διδάξοντες. [37] β–d (save that aef read σκοτισθήσεσθε and g ὑμῖν σκοτισθήσεται, e ἐπαξηται, f ἐπαταξετε, S¹ ἐπάξουσιν). _d_ reads (almost as in α) καὶ ἐὰν ὑμεῖς σκοτισθῆτε, τί ποιήσουσι πάντα τὰ ἔθνη; ἐν γὰρ τῇ ἀσεβίᾳ ὑμῶν ἐπάξετε. [38] _g_ om. [39] _d_, S¹ read ὑμῶν. [40] _af_ read ὑπὲρ οὖ. [41] _b_, S² read κόσμου. _d_ κόσμου καὶ τοῦ νόμου. For ὑπὲρ ὧν τὸ φῶς ... δοθέν S¹ reads οἱ ἅγιοι νόμοι ἐδόθησαν. [42] abe¹f add ἐν against α, de²g, Aβ, S¹. [43] _b_ adds ἐν. _d_ adds καὶ παντὶ ἀνθρώπῳ and om. παντὸς ἀνθρώπου in next line. So also Aβ. [44] Read τοῦτο with _a_. [45] _dg_ (though the former gives the form θελήσειτε and the latter θελήσεται). abef, S¹ read θέλοντες. [46] _e_ reads τῆς τοῦ θ. δικαιοσύνης. S¹ om. rest of chap. [47] A^{cg} i.e. [Armenian]. A^{b*cd} prefix [Armenian], text then = καὶ μὴ ὅ(?) or καὶ οὐδέν. [48] Bracketed as an interpolation. [49] So also _d_. See note 43. [50] Bracketed as a dittography of the last four words of the verse. Aª om. ver. 4 save the following words, ὅτι ὑμεῖς ἐναντίον τῷ κυρίῳ διδάσκετε τὰς ἐντολὰς ὑμῶν. [51] A^{cg}. A^{b*cd} = διδάσκειν. [52] A^{g} om. next six words. [53] Aβ read [Armenian] (= τῆς ἐντολῆς) corrupt for

μερίδων⁸⁵ αὐτοῦ⁵⁶ κλέψετε⁵⁷ ἐκλεκτά, ἐσθίοντες⁵⁸ *ἐν κατα-
φρονήσει⁵⁹ μετὰ⁶⁰ πορνῶν.   6. Καὶ⁶¹ ἐν πλεονεξίᾳ τὰς
ἐντολὰς⁶² κυρίου⁶³ διδάξετε⁶⁴, *τὰς μὲν⁶³ ὑπάνδρους βεβηλώ-
σετε⁶⁶ καὶ πόρναις⁶⁷ καὶ μοιχαλίσιν⁶⁸ συναφθήσεσθε⁶⁹, *θυγατέρας δὲ⁷⁰ ἐθνῶν λήψεσθε⁷¹ εἰς γυναῖκας⁷², καὶ γενήσεται⁷⁴
*ἡ μῖξις ὑμῶν⁷⁵ ὡς⁷⁶ *Σόδομα καὶ Γόμορρα⁷⁷.   7. Καὶ⁷⁸
φυσιωθήσεσθε⁷⁹ ἐπὶ τῇ ἱερωσύνῃ ὑμῶν⁸⁰ *κατὰ τῶν ἀνθρώπων
ἐπαιρόμενοι⁸¹, οὐ μόνον δὲ τοῦτο⁸² ἀλλὰ καὶ κατὰ τῶν ἐντολῶν
τοῦ Θεοῦ⁸³.   8. *Καταφρονήσετε γὰρ τὰ ἅγια χλευάζοντες καὶ
γελοιάζοντες⁸⁴.

XV. Διὰ¹ τοῦτο² *ὁ ναός³, ὃν⁴ ἐκλέξεται⁵ κύριος⁶,
*ἔρημος ἔσται⁷ *ἐν τῇ ἀκαθαρσίᾳ ὑμῶν⁸, καὶ ὑμεῖς αἰχμά-

Marginal column (right):

> bdeg,
> AB καὶ
> πρὸ τοῦ
> θυσιάσαι
> κυρίῳ
> λήψεσθε
> τὰ ἐκ-
> λεκτά.
> β βεβη-
> λώσητε
> καὶ παρ-
> θένους
> Ἰσραὴλ
> (bg'Ιερου-
> σαλήμ)
> μια-
> νεῖτε.

β (A) γυναῖκας *καθαρίζοντες αὐτὰς καθαρισμῷ παρανόμῳ⁷³. β Γόμορρα
ἐν ἀσεβείᾳ. a, AB om. κατὰ . . . ἐπαιρόμενοι. β *φυσιούμενοι κατα-
φρονήσετε⁸⁵ τὰ ἅγια⁸⁶ ἐν καταφρονήσει⁸⁷ γελοιάζοντες⁸⁸.

ψμωπωρωζ‘υ = τῆς προσφορᾶς. [54] a. c reads ληστεύσειτε. bdfy ληστεύσητε. e ληστεύσηται. h corrupt. [55] AB read _qρωσωζΚ_ (= τὴν φιάλην)
corrupt for _qρωσβΚΚ_ = τὴν μερίδα. [56] a reads αὐτῶν. AB = κυρίου.
[57] a. α, d read κλέψειτε. bfy κλέψητε. e κλέψηται. bdeg, AB add καὶ πρὸ
τοῦ θυσιάσαι κυρίῳ (θεῷ AB) λήψεσθε (d λήψετε) τά. [58] AB = καὶ ἔδεσθε.
[59] h, β, AB, but β trs. before ἐσθίοντες and AB after πορνῶν. c reads ἐν
καταφροσύνῃ before μετά. [60] e adds τῶν. [61] b om. [62] h, b add τοῦ.
[63] e om. [64] a. h, bdf read διδάξητε. c διδαξειτε. e διδάξηται. g διαδέξηται.
[65] α. β–e, AB read τάς. e καὶ τάς. [66] α. β reads βεβηλώσητε. β adds καὶ
παρθένους Ἰσραὴλ (bg Ἰερουσαλήμ, d om.) μιανεῖτε (ef μιάνητε) against α, AB.
[67] af read πονηραῖς. [68] e reads μυχαλλίδαις. [69] Aα = ἔσται συναγωγὴ
ὑμῶν, AB ἔσονται συναγωγαὶ ὑμῶν through internal corruption. [70] α. e,
A read καὶ θυγατέρας. β–e θυγατέρας. [71] d reads λήψετε. A adds ὑμῖν.
[72] Aα = γάμον. [73] β (save that d reads καθαρίζεσθε ἑαυτὰς κ. π. and e reads
κ. α. καθαρισμὸν πυράνομον). Aα = ἐν νῷ ἔχειν καθαρίζειν αὐτὰς καθαρισμῷ
παρανομίης ὑμῶν. AB ἐν νῷ ἔχειν καθαρίζειν αὐτὰς παρανομίᾳ ὑμῶν. [74] α, β–
af. af read γίνεται. A = γενήσονται. [75] A = αἱ μίξεις ὑμῶν ἐν ἀσεβείᾳ.
[76] beg om. [77] α, β. · A = Σοδομιτῶν καὶ Γομορραίων. β adds ἐν ἀσεβείᾳ.
[78] Aα om. [79] Ab* = φυσιοῦσθε. [80] α, d, A. β–d om. [81] α, β (save
that adf om. τῶν), Aα. AB om. [82] α. d, A read ταῦτα ποιήσετε. β–d
om. [83] Aα adds ἐναντίοι ἔσεσθε. [84] α. For γελοιάζ. c reads γελιάζοντες.
Aα om. [85] aef. bdg read φυσιούμενοι καταπαίξετε. AB = ἀσεβήσετε (i. e.
ωσρωρζωκωπωΚερζρρ corrupt for _ωσρωρπωωωκωπωΚερζρρ_ = φυσιωθήσεσθε) καὶ
διαταράξετε. [86] a reads τῶν ἁγίων. g τὸ ἅγιον. [87] AB = καταφρονοῦντες
καί. [88] d reads γελιάζοντες as in c.

XV. [1] h, S¹ read καὶ διά. [2] α, adf. beg read ταῦτα. [3] e reads οὗτος.
Aα add ὑμῶν. [4] α, deg. abf read ὃν ἄν. [5] α, efg. ab read ἐκλέξηται.

Aa om.
vers. 2, 3.
b (d) g
Aβ θεω-
ροῦντες.
β, Aβ
φεύξον-
ται ἀφ'.
β–d, A, S
τοὺς
πατέρας
ἡμῶν.
c[1] Aa
ἡμῶν.
β, Aβ, S

λωτοι ἔσεσθε εἰς πάντα τὰ ἔθνη.   2. Καὶ * ἔσεσθε βδέλυγμα[9] αὐτοῖς[10], καὶ λήψεσθε[11] ὄνειδος[12] καὶ αἰσχύνην αἰώνιον παρὰ * τῆς δικαιοκρισίας[13] τοῦ Θεοῦ.   3. Καὶ πάντες οἱ μισοῦντες[14] ὑμᾶς * χαρήσονται ἐπὶ τῇ ἀπωλείᾳ[15] ὑμῶν[16].   4. Καὶ[17] εἰ μὴ[18] δι' Ἀβραὰμ καὶ Ἰσαὰκ καὶ Ἰακὼβ * τῶν πατέρων ἡμῶν ἔλεος λήψεσθε[19], εἷς[20] ἐκ τοῦ σπέρματος[21] ὑμῶν[22] * οὐ μὴ[23] καταλειφθῇ[24] ἐπὶ τῆς γῆς.

XVI. Καὶ νῦν * ἐγὼ ἔγνωκα[1] ὅτι ἑβδομήκοντα ἑβδομάδας[2] πλανηθήσεσθε[3], καὶ τὴν ἱερωσύνην βεβηλώσετε[4] καὶ * τὰ θυσιαστήρια[5] μιανεῖτε[6].   2. Καὶ τὸν νόμον ἀθετήσετε[7] καὶ λόγους προφητῶν ἐξουδενώσετε[8] * ἐν διαστροφῇ κακῇ[9]. * δι-

έγνων ἐν βίβλῳ Ἐνώχ.   β, Aβ, S τὰς θυσίας.

dg ἐξελέξηται (-εται g).   [6] e adds τόπον. Aa εἶναι τόπον τοῦ ὀνόματος αὐτοῦ. [7] g reads ἐρημωθήσεται.   [8] α, S. β–e, Aβ read ἐν ἀκαθαρσίᾳ (+ καὶ ἁρπαγῇ Aβ). e ἐπὶ ἀκαθαρσίας. Aa καὶ ἐν ἀκαθαρσίᾳ διαφθορᾶς.   [9] β–deg, S[2]. c reads βδέλυγμα. h βδελύσεσθε. deg, Aβ ἔσεσθε εἰς βδέλυγμα. For ver. 2 Aa reads καὶ αἶσχος ἔσεσθε πᾶσι τοῖς ἔθνεσι and om. ver. 3. S[1] ἔσονται βδέλυγμα. [10] α, Aβ. β–e read ἐν αὐτοῖς.   e ἐπ' αὐτούς.   [11] S[1] reads λήψονται. [12] b reads ὀνειδισμόν.   e om. following καί.   [13] Aβ = τοῦ δικαίου κριτοῦ. [14] α, aef, S. by, Aβ read θεωροῦντες. d ὁρῶντες. Do these variants point back to השונאים and הרואים.   [15] α (save that h adds εὐτελείᾳ καί before ἀπωλείᾳ). β, Aβ read φεύξονται ἀφ'. A confusion (?) of ישירו and יסורו. S om.   [16] S om. d adds μισούμενοι ὑμᾶς.   [17] h om.   [18] Aa add ἐστίν. [19] α (save that c reads ηλεος for ἐλ.). β–d, A, S[1] read τοὺς πατέρας ἡμῶν (ὑμῶν A[b*cd]). d τοῦ πατρὸς ἡμῶν, ἐπεὶ οὐδέ.   [20] A = τὸ ἐκτημόριον.   [21] Aa = γένους.   [22] h, c[2], d, Aβ. c[1], Aa read ἡμῶν. β–d, S μου.   [23] β–d, A. c reads οὐκ. h οὐ. d om.   [24] abg, S[2]. c reads εκατελυφθη. h, f καταλήφθη. d καταλιμπάνετο. e καταλίφθη. S[1] κατέλειψα.

XVI. [1] α. abefg, Aβ, S read ἔγνων. d ἀνέγνων. Aa om. first seven words of this verse. β, Aβ, S add ἐν (+ τῇ d) βίβλῳ (βιβλίῳ be) Ἐνώχ.   [2] Aβ read Ьι Ьоβ'Ь Ьрϧϥμ (= καὶ ἑπτὰ ἑσπέρας) corrupt for Ьоβ'ЬЬрϧωϥμ (= ἑβδομάδας). For ἑβδομήκ. ἑβδ. S reads ἑβδομάδα.   [3] Aa = πλανᾶσθε and om. rest of verse.   [4] c, A[es]. h, β read βεβηλώσητε. e βεβηλωσειτε. A[cd] = βεβηλώσει. A[b*] give the clause as follows: τὴν βεβήλωσιν ἐν ἱερωσύνῃ ὑμῶν ἐπιμίξετε. S[1] om. next four words.   [5] α. β, Aβ, S[2] read τὰς θυσίας. [6] α, ab. def read μιάνητε. g om.   [7] α (c ἀθετησειτε, h -ητε). befg, Aβ read ἀφανίσητε. a, S ἀφανίσετε. d om. together with the three preceding words. Aβ = ἀφανῆ ποιήσετε. The entire verse is very corrupt and defective in Aa which = καὶ ἀπολοῦνται ἐξ ὑμῶν οἱ νόμοι καὶ οἱ προφῆται· καὶ (A[ab] om.) διώξετε ἐξ ὑμῶν δικαίους.   [8] α, a. df read ἐξουδενώσητε. bg ἐξουθενώσητε. e ἐξουθενήσεται. Aβ renders ἐξουδ. in the sense of 'despise.'   [9] α. β, S[2] read

ὤξετε δὲ[10] ἄνδρας[11] δικαίους, καὶ εὐσεβεῖς μισήσετε[12], ἀληθινῶν[13]
λόγους βδελύξεσθε[14].   [3. Καὶ ἄνδρα καινοποιοῦντα[15] *β, S ὡς νομίζετε (or -σετε)*
νόμον *ἐν δυνάμει ὑψίστου[16] πλάνον[17] προσαγορεύσετε, καὶ
τέλος †ὁρμήσετε τοῦ ἀποκτεῖναι[18] αὐτόν, οὐκ εἰδότες[19] αὐτοῦ τὸ *ἀποκτε-νεῖτε.*
ἀνάστημα†[20], τὸ[21] ἀθῷον αἷμα[22] *ἐν κακίᾳ[23] ἐπὶ τῆς[24] κεφαλῆς[25]
ὑμῶν ἀναδεχόμενοι[26].]   4. *Λέγω δὲ ὑμῖν ὅτι[27] δι' αὐτὸν[28] *β–b, A, S καί.*
ἔσονται[29] τὰ ἅγια ὑμῶν ἔρημα[30] ἕως ἐδάφους[31].   5. Καὶ *β, Aβ, S ἐδάφους μεμιαμμένα.*
*τόπος ὑμῖν καθαρὸς οὐκ ἔσται[32], ἀλλ' ἔσεσθε[33] ἐν τοῖς
ἔθνεσιν εἰς κατάραν καὶ* εἰς διασκορπισμόν[34], ἕως[35] *αὐτὸς

ἐν διαστροφῇ. Aβ om. S¹ = ἐν ἀναστροφῇ.   [10]α. dg, Aβ read καὶ διώξετε
(-ητε d).   abef, S¹ read διώξετε (f -ητε).   [11]Aβ om.   [12]af, Aβ. h, beg
read μισήσητε (-ειται e).   c μισοῦντες.   d om.   [13]α, β–deg, S. deg, Aβ
read ἀληθινούς which Aβ trs. after λόγους.   [14]a. α, bfg read βδελύξησθε
(βδελλ- c).   d βδελλύξητε.   e βδελυξεισθαι.   [15]α (καὶ νόμονουντα (sic) c).
β,A read ἀνακαινοποιοῦντα.   adf, A add τόν.   In Aβ the clause καὶ ἄνδρα . . .
προσαγορεύσετε is trs. before ver. 2.   [16]α, β, S¹. Aα om. Aβ = τοῦ ὑψίστου.
A adds αὐτόν.   [17]Aα add καὶ ἀκάθαρτον.   [18]α (c reading ὁρμήσειτε,
h -ητε).   β, S read ὡς νομίζετε (a νομίσετε, f -σητε) ἀποκτενεῖτε (d ἀποκτεῖναι).
Aβ = ὡς νομίζω ἀποκτενεῖτε.   Aα ἀποκτενεῖτε.   The original text seems to be
irrecoverable.   The text of α recalls slightly Acts vii. 57, 58, ὥρμησαν
ὁμοθυμαδὸν ἐπ' αὐτόν, καὶ . . . ἐλιθοβόλουν.   Possibly the entire verse is a
Christian interpolation, but this is not probable.   We might conjecture
the origin of the three distinct readings above.   Aα = ἀποκτενεῖτε = תִּרְמוּ.
This latter word if written twice by a scribal error might have led to
the text of α and been written תִּרְאוּ לרמה = ὁρμήσετε τοῦ ἀποκτεῖναι, or
else have been written as תִּרְמוּ לרמה = νομίσετε (af) ἀποκτεῖναι which
approximates to the text of β.   The ὡς would then have to be explained
as a later addition.   [19]A = ὡς (Aᵇ = καί, Aβ om.) οὐ δυνάμενοι εἰδέναι.
[20]α, β = 'dignity.'   Aᵇˣᶜᵈᵉ read [Armenian] = ἀνάστασιν, which seems
to rest on a misinterpretation of ἀνάστημα.   Aα offers [Armenian]
= δικαιοσύνην which is obviously a corruption of Aᵇˣᶜᵈᵉ.   Aˢ reads
[Armenian] (another corruption of Aᵇˣᶜᵈᵉ) = νίκην.   [21]e om. g,
Aα prefix καί.   [22]d, A add αὐτοῦ.   [23]α, β. A = ἐν κακίᾳ ὑμῶν which
Aα trs. before τὸ ἀθῷον.   [24]α. β om.   [25]b reads κεφαλάς.   [26]g reads
δεχόμενοι.   Aα add καὶ ἐπὶ κεφαλῆς τέκνων ὑμῶν.   A = ἀναδέξεσθε.   [27]α.
β–b, A read καί.   b, S om.   [28]h reads αὐτῶν.   eg τοῦτο.   [29]c, af. h,
bdeg read ἔσται.   [30]S¹ om.   d, Aβ add καί.   [31]β, Aβ, S add μεμιαμμένα
(e μεμησημένα, g μεμιασμένα).   [32]α. β, S read οὐκ ἔσται τόπος ὑμῶν (g ὑμῖν)
καθαρός.   A = οὐκ (Aα οὐκέτι) ἔσται ὑμῶν τόπος καθαρός.   [33]β, Aβ trs. after
ἔθνεσιν.   For ἔσεσθε . . . διασκορπισμόν Aα gives ἐν τοῖς ἔθνεσιν διασκορπισθήσεσθε.   [34]e reads διεσκορπισμένοι.   g διασκορπισμόν.   [35]e adds ἄν.   [36]d
reads αὐτός.   Aα = πάλιν ὁ κύριος.   d om. next four words.   [37]h, bef.

πάλιν³⁶ ἐπισκέψηται³⁷ καὶ *οἰκτειρήσῃ καὶ³⁸ προσδέξεται³⁹
α, β, Αβ, ὑμᾶς.
S ὑμᾶς
[ἐνπίστει καὶ ὕδατι]⁴⁰.

XVII. *Καὶ ὅτι ἠκούσατε¹ περὶ τῶν ἑβδομήκοντα² ἑβδο-
μάδων³, ἀκούσατε καὶ⁴ περὶ τῆς ἱερωσύνης⁵.   2. Καθ' ἕκαστον
γὰρ ἰωβηλαῖον⁶ ἔσται ἱερωσύνη⁷. Καὶ⁸ ἐν τῷ⁹ πρώτῳ ἰωβηλαίῳ
ὁ *χριόμενος πρῶτος¹⁰ εἰς ἱερωσύνην *ἔσται μέγας¹¹, καὶ
α λαλεῖ. λαλήσει¹² Θεῷ ὡς πατρί· καὶ ἡ ἱερωσύνη αὐτοῦ πλήρης μετὰ¹³
κυρίου· [καὶ ἐν ἡμέραις¹⁴ χαρᾶς αὐτοῦ¹⁵ *ἐπὶ σωτηρίᾳ¹⁶ κόσμου
*αὐτὸς ἀναστήσεται]¹⁷.   3. Ἐν¹⁸ τῷ δευτέρῳ ἰωβηλαίῳ
β-d, Αβ, ὁ¹⁹ χριόμενος ἐν πένθει ἀγαπητοῦ²⁰ συλληφθήσεται²¹ *καὶ
S = ἀγα- ἔσται²² ἡ ἱερωσύνη αὐτοῦ τιμία²³, καὶ παρὰ πάντων²⁴ δοξα-
πητῶν. σθήσεται.   4. Ὁ δὲ τρίτος ἱερεὺς²⁵ λύπῃ παραληφθήσεται²⁶.
5. Καὶ²⁷ ὁ τέταρτος ἐν ὀδύναις²⁸ ἔσται· ὅτι²⁹ προσθήσει³⁰
*ἐπ' αὐτῷ³¹ *ἡ ἀδικία³² *εἰς πλῆθος³³. καὶ πᾶς Ἰσραὴλ

c reads ἐπισκέψειται. ag ἐπισκέψεται. A adds ὑμᾶς.   ³⁸ c. h reads οἰκτη-
ρῆσαι. abfy οἰκτειρήσας (-ισας f). e οἰκτείρας. Αβ reads ꞯѡрⱥƀѡɭ (= πάλιν)
corrupt for ꞯƀѡɠƀѡɭ as in Aᵃ = οἰκτειρήσας.   ³⁹ adg read προσδέξεται.
c -ειται.   ⁴⁰ α, β-e¹, Αβ, S.   e¹, Aᵃ om.

XVII. ¹ d reads καθὼς ἠκούσατε περί and om. next seven words. Αβ =
ὡς οὖν ἀκούετε. Aᵃ om. XVII, XVIII. S om. first seven words.   ² a
reads ὁ'.   ³ Aᵇ*ᶜᵈ = καὶ ἑπτὰ ἑσπερῶν but a very slight change restores the
text. See note 2, chap. xvi.   ⁴ a om. S reads τέκνα μου.   ⁵ c reads
ἱεροσύνης, and so generally gives this word.   ⁶ c reads ἰοβηλαῖον and so
generally. e ἰωβήλεον and so generally. g ιυυβιλαῖον. For καθ' . . . Ἰωβ. S¹
reads καὶ ἐν τῷ γένει.   ⁷ d reads ἱερωσύνης and d, S om. next five words.
⁸ b om.   ⁹ g om.   ¹⁰ α, g, Αβ. β-g read πρῶτος χριόμενος. α gives the
form χειρόμενος and f χειρώμενος. S¹ adds καὶ ὃς ἂν χρισθῇ and om. rest of
verse.   ¹¹ α, deg. abf, Αβ read μέγας ἔσται.   ¹² β, Αβ. α reads λαλεῖ. d
adds τῷ.   ¹³ b adds φόβου. πλήρης μετά = עַם עֹלָם.   ¹⁴ α. β, Αβ read
ἡμέρᾳ.   ¹⁵ e adds καί.   ¹⁶ e reads σωτηρίας. Aᵇ*ᶜᵈᵉ σωτηρία, but Aᵍ agrees
with text.   ¹⁷ α, β. Aᵇ* = γενήσεται. Aᶜᵈᵉᵍ ἀναστήσεται.   ¹⁸ α, be¹g.
ade²f read ἐν δέ. Αβ = καὶ ἐν.   ¹⁹ g reads ὡς. ae¹ om.   ²⁰ α, g. β-dg,
Αβ, S read ἀγαπητῶν. d ἀγαπητόν. e² ἀγαπητῷ.   ²¹ h reads ληφθήσεται.
²² eg om., but e adds ἔσται in margin.   ²³ S om. rest of verse.   ²⁴ α.
β reads πᾶσιν.   ²⁵ β-f add ἐν.   ²⁶ d reads παραλειφθήσεται. Αβ = περιλη-
φθήσεται. c om. next two verses, and d om. next six words through hmt.
²⁷ g om.   ²⁸ h, a, Αβ. β-a read ὀδύνῃ.   ²⁹ β, S. Αβ reads καί. h ᾧ.   ³⁰ β.
h reads προσθείη. Here προσθήσει = יֹסִיף corrupt for יֵאָסֵף = συναχθήσεται
or יֵסֵף = προστεθήσεται.   ³¹ adf. bg read ἐπ' αὐτόν. e ἀπ' αὐτοῦ. h ἐν αὐτῷ.
³² h trs. before ἐπ' αὐτῷ.   ³³ Αβ = πολλή.   ³⁴ β, Αβ. h reads μισήσει.
³⁵ h trs. after αὐτοῦ, g before μισήσουσιν.   ³⁶ g reads τῷ.   ³⁷ g reads

μισήσουσιν³⁴ ἕκαστος³⁵ τὸν³⁶ πλησίον αὐτοῦ.   6. Ὁ πέμπτος
ἐν σκότει³⁷ παραληφθήσεται³⁸.   7. Ὡσαύτως³⁹ καὶ ὁ ἕκτος
καὶ ὁ ἕβδομος⁴⁰.   8. *Ἐν δὲ τῷ ἑβδόμῳ²⁷ ἔσται μιασμός⁴¹,
ὃν οὐ δύναμαι⁴² εἰπεῖν ἐνώπιον⁴³ ἀνθρώπων· ὅτι αὐτοὶ γνώσονται οἱ ποιοῦντες αὐτά.   9. Διὰ τοῦτο ἐν αἰχμαλωσίᾳ
καὶ ἐν προνομῇ ἔσονται· καὶ ἡ γῆ αὐτῶν⁴⁴ καὶ *ἡ ὕπαρξις⁴⁵
ἀφανισθήσεται⁴⁶.

10. *Καὶ ἐν τῇ πέμπτῃ⁴⁷ ἑβδομάδι⁴⁸ ἐπιστρέψουσιν εἰς
γῆν ἐρημώσεως αὐτῶν, καὶ⁴⁹ ἀνακαινοποιήσουσιν οἶκον κυρίου⁵⁰.
11. Ἐν δὲ τῷ †ἑβδομηκοστῷ ἑβδόμῳ†⁵¹ ἥξουσιν ἱερεῖς⁵², β, ΑΒ, S
εἰδωλολατροῦντες, μοιχοί⁵³, φιλάργυροι⁵⁴ ὑπερήφανοι, ἄνομοι, ἑβδόμῳ ἑβδομα-
ἀσελγεῖς⁵⁵, παιδοφθόροι⁵⁶, κτηνοφθόροι⁵⁷.   τικῷ.

XVIII. Καὶ¹ μετὰ τὸ γενέσθαι τὴν ἐκδίκησιν αὐτῶν παρὰ β, ΑΒ, S¹
      κυρίου, *ἐκλείψει ἡ ἱερωσύνη². μάχιμοι.

2. Καὶ³ τότε ἐγερεῖ⁴ κύριος ἱερέα καινόν⁵,
    ᾧ⁶ πάντες οἱ λόγοι κυρίου⁷ ἀποκαλυφθήσονται⁸,
    καὶ αὐτὸς ποιήσει κρίσιν⁹ ἀληθείας¹⁰ ἐπὶ τῆς γῆς¹¹ *ἐν
        πλήθει¹² ἡμερῶν.

3. Καὶ ἀνατελεῖ¹³ ἄστρον αὐτοῦ¹⁴ ἐν οὐρανῷ ὡς βασιλέως¹⁵
    φωτίζων¹⁶ φῶς γνώσεως †ἐν ἡλίῳ ἡμέρα†¹⁷,

σκοτείᾳ.   ³⁸ d reads παραλειφθήσεται.   ³⁹ h reads ὡς αὐτός.   ⁴⁰ ΑΒ om.
⁴¹ h reads σπασμός.   ⁴² h reads δαμείς.   ⁴³ b, S¹ adds κυρίου καί.   ⁴⁴ α,
adefg, ΑΒ. b, S om. a om. next four words.   ⁴⁵ eg reads ἡ (αἱ g) ὑπάρ-
ξεις. ΑΒ = ἡ ἐπαρχία. bdef, S add αὐτῶν.   ⁴⁶ c, g read ἀφανισθήσονται.
⁴⁷ c. h om. together with next two words. adf read καὶ ἐν πέμπτῃ. b κ.
ἐμπέμπτῃ. eg κ. ἐν πέμπτῳ.   ⁴⁸ g reads ἑβδοματικῷ.   ⁴⁹ h om.   ⁵⁰ a
reads κυρίῳ.   ⁵¹ α. β, ΑΒ, S read ἑβδόμῳ ἑβδοματικῷ.   ⁵² beg prefix οἱ.
⁵³ α. β, ΑΒ, S¹ read μάχιμοι.   ⁵⁴ c, ad give the form φυλάργυροι.   ⁵⁵ e
reads ἀσεβεῖς.   ⁵⁶ b, ΑΒ add καί.   ⁵⁷ α trs. before ἄνομοι. eg om. abdf,
ΑΒ, S¹ support order of text.

XVIII. ¹ g om. καὶ ... ἱερωσύνη.   ² α, adef, ΑΒ, S¹ (save that c, ef
read ἐκλήψει, and d reads ἐκλείψῃ and om. ἡ, and e reads ἱερατεία, and ΑΒ
prefix καί). b reads τῇ ἱερατείᾳ.   ³ α. β, ΑΒ om.   ⁴ α, β, S¹. ΑΒ read
ἐγείρει.   ⁵ ΑΒ om.   ⁶ α, bdf, ΑΒ. ag read ὡς. e ὅ.   ⁷ d¹ reads αὐτοῦ.
d² κυρίου, as all other MSS.   ⁸ f reads ἀποκαλυφθήσωνται.   ⁹ e¹ reads τὴν
ἐκδίκησιν. e² κρίσιν, as all other MSS.   ¹⁰ α, β–dg. g, ΑΒ read ἀληθινήν.
d is conflate and reads ἀληθινὴν ἀληθείας.   ¹¹ e om.   ¹² e reads ἐμπλήθει.
¹³ d adds αὐτῷ.   ¹⁴ h reads αὐτῷ.   ¹⁵ h, dfg, ΑΒ. c, abe, S read βασιλεύς.
¹⁶ h, a¹ read φωτίζον.   ¹⁷ h, abf. c, eg, S read ὡς ἐν ἡλίῳ ἡμέρα (ἡμέρας e, S).
d ἐν ἡλίῳ ὡς ἡμέρας. ΑΒ = ὡς ἐν μεσημβρίᾳ ἐνώπιον τοῦ ἡλίου. The text =
בַיּוֹם שֶׁמֶשׁ which may be corrupt for שֶׁמֶשׁ לְיוֹם = ὡς ὁ ἥλιος (φωτίζει) τὴν

<table>
<tr><td>β, Αβ, S¹
οἰκουμένη
[ἕως
ἀναλή-
ψεως
αὐτοῦ].

Αβ =
ἐκείναις.

adg καὶ
τοῦ.

h, abg
πατρός
(+καὶ h).</td><td>

καὶ μεγαλυνθήσεται ἐν τῇ οἰκουμένῃ¹⁸.

4. Οὗτος¹⁹ ἀναλάμψει²⁰ *ὡς ὁ²¹ ἥλιος ἐν τῇ γῇ²²,
καὶ ἐξαρεῖ πᾶν σκότος *ἐκ τῆς ὑπ' οὐρανὸν²³
καὶ ἔσται εἰρήνη ἐν πάσῃ τῇ γῇ.

5. Οἱ οὐρανοὶ ἀγαλλιάσονται²⁴ ἐν ταῖς ἡμέραις αὐτοῦ²⁵,
καὶ ἡ γῆ χαρήσεται²⁶,
καὶ αἱ²⁷ †νεφέλαι²⁸ εὐφρανθήσονται²⁹.
[καὶ ἡ γνῶσις κυρίου³⁰ ἐκχυθήσεται³¹ ἐπὶ τῆς γῆς ὡς³²
ὕδωρ θαλασσῶν³³]
*καὶ οἱ ἄγγελοι τῆς δόξης τοῦ προσώπου κυρίου εὐφρανθή-
σονται ἐν αὐτῷ³⁴.

6. Οἱ οὐρανοὶ³⁵ ἀνοιγήσονται³⁶,
καὶ³⁷ ἐκ τοῦ ναοῦ τῆς δόξης³⁸ ἥξει³⁹ ἐπ'⁴⁰ αὐτὸν ἁγίασμα
μετὰ φωνῆς πατρικῆς ὡς ἀπὸ *Ἀβραὰμ πρὸς Ἰσαάκ⁴¹.

</td></tr>
</table>

ἡμέραν. The text of c, eg can thus be explained as a conflation of the above two. ¹⁸β, Αβ, S¹ add ἕως ἀναλήψεως αὐτοῦ. ¹⁹c, β–deg. h, de read οὕτως. g, Αβ καὶ οὕτως. ²⁰f reads ἀναλάμπει. Αβ ἀναβήσεται. S om. next three words. ²¹cg read ὡς, h ὁ. ²²α om. the next two lines through hmt. ²³abfg, Αβ. d reads ἐν τῇ ὑπ' οὐρανόν. e ἐν τοῖς ὑπὸ οὐρανόν. ²⁴f reads ἀγαλλιάσωνται. ²⁵α, β, S¹. Αβ = ἐκείναις. ²⁶adg. c reads χαρίσονται. h, bef χαρίσεται. Possibly we should om. χαρήσεται or εὐφρανθήσονται and combine this line with the next. See notes 28, 34. ²⁷dg, Αβ om. ²⁸This expression is strange. αἱ νεφέλαι = הענבות, which may have been corrupt for בענבורו = δι' αὐτόν. Cf. d, note 35. ²⁹f reads εὐφρανθήσωνται. The next line is an interpolation, it destroys the parallelism and is not in touch with the context. ³⁰g reads χριστοῦ. ³¹α, adf (save that c reads ἐκχηθήσεται). beg read χυθήσεται. ³²c reads ὡσεί. ³³d reads θαλάσσιον. g θαλάσσης. ³⁴This line would form the third of the tristich, when we omit the fourth (see note 29) and combine the second and third in one. The second line would (see notes 26, 28) be: καὶ ἡ γῆ χαρήσεται δι' αὐτόν. While afg add καὶ after δόξης e om. the next fifteen words through hmt. For κυρίου Αβ read αὐτοῦ. S¹ om. προσώπου. For εὐφρανθήσονται of c we find in h, bef χαρίσονται, and χαρήσονται in adg. c adds καὶ χαρήσονται after αὐτῷ. ³⁵d adds δι' αὐτόν. ³⁶f reads ἀνοιγήσωνται. ³⁷Αβ om. ³⁸Αβ add αὐτοῦ (+καὶ Αᵇ*ᶜᵈ ?). ³⁹h, d read ἥξῃ. e ἥξουσιν. ⁴⁰g reads ἀπ'. ⁴¹Αβ. This seems the best text. c, adf read Ἀβραὰμ π̅ρ̅ς καὶ (adf om.) Ἰσαάκ. h Ἀβ. πατρὸς καὶ Ἰσ. abg Ἀβ. πατρὸς Ἰσ. e π̅ρ̅ς Ἀβ. καὶ Ἰσ. καὶ Ἰακώβ. Here π̅ρ̅ς is a contraction of πρός not of πατρός. S om. ὡς ... Ἰσαάκ. ⁴²α, β–de. d reads δόξα ἐπ' αὐτὸν ἀνθήσεται. e ἡ δόξα κυρίου ἐπ' αὐτῷ μηθ. Αβ = τὴν δόξαν αὐτοῦ ἐπ' αὐτὸν ἐροῦσιν. ⁴³Αβ = γνώσεως. For καὶ ἁγ. S¹ reads ἅγιον. c adds καί.

7. Καὶ *δόξα ὑψίστου ἐπ' αὐτὸν ῥηθήσεται[42],
    καὶ πνεῦμα συνέσεως καὶ ἁγιασμοῦ[43] καταπαύσει *ἐπ'
        αὐτόν[44] [ἐν τῷ ὕδατι].
8. *Αὐτὸς γὰρ[45] δώσει τὴν μεγαλωσύνην[46] κυρίου[47] τοῖς
        υἱοῖς αὐτοῦ[48] ἐν ἀληθείᾳ εἰς τὸν αἰῶνα,
    καὶ οὐκ ἔσται διαδοχὴ[49] αὐτοῦ[50] εἰς γενεὰς *καὶ γενεὰς[51]
        ἕως τοῦ αἰῶνος.
9. Καὶ ἐπὶ *τῆς ἱερωσύνης[52] αὐτοῦ[53] *τὰ ἔθνη[54] πληθυνθή-
        σονται[55] ἐν γνώσει ἐπὶ τῆς γῆς,
    καὶ φωτισθήσονται διὰ χάριτος κυρίου.
    [ὁ δὲ Ἰσραὴλ ἐλαττωθήσεται ἐν ἀγνωσίᾳ
    καὶ σκοτισθήσεται ἐν πένθει][56]·
    ἐπὶ τῆς ἱερωσύνης αὐτοῦ ἐκλείψει[57] ἡ[58] ἁμαρτία
    καὶ οἱ ἄνομοι *καταπαύσουσιν εἰς κακά[59],
    [οἱ δὲ δίκαιοι καταπαύσουσιν ἐν αὐτῷ][60].
10. Καίγε[61] αὐτὸς[62] ἀνοίξει τὰς θύρας[63] τοῦ παραδείσου,
    *καὶ ἀποστήσει[64] τὴν ἀπειλοῦσαν ῥομφαίαν[65] κατὰ τοῦ[66]
        Ἀδάμ.

                                       β, S
                                       πᾶσα.

[42] d reads αὐτόν. α, β–e, Αβ add ἐν τῷ ὕδατι.   [45] α. β–e, Αᵒⁱˢ, S¹ read αὐτός. e οὗτος. Αᵇ*ᶜᵈ = αὐτὸς καί.   [46] Αβ read ⟦Armenian⟧ (= ἀλήθειαν) corrupt for ⟦Armenian⟧ = μεγαλωσύνην.   [47] h reads αὐτοῦ. d om.   [48] g reads τῶν ἀνθρώπων. e om. For τοῖς … ἀληθείᾳ Αβ read πᾶσι (Αᵇ*ᶜᵈ om.) οἱ ἐν ἀληθείᾳ περιπατήσουσιν.   [49] e reads πλήν.   [50] b reads αὐτῷ.   [51] h, Αβ read γενεῶν. g om.   [52] c reads τῇ ἱερωσύνῃ.   [53] b om. τὰ ἔθνη … ἱερωσύνης αὐτοῦ through hmt.   [54] h reads τὰ ἔτη. d om. S¹ reads τόποι.   [55] h om. next seven words. S¹ reads μεγαλύνονται.   [56] These words are found in all MSS. (but be) and in A, S. With the exception of ἐν ἀγνωσίᾳ which it omits they are found in the margin of e. If they are in their original form they are undoubtedly of Christian origin. I have on this ground bracketed them. The favourable references to the Gentiles in the two preceding lines are quite in keeping with the universalism of the writer. For διὰ χάριτος … ἱερωσύνης αὐτοῦ S¹ reads τῇ εὐλογίᾳ τοῦ θεοῦ Ἰσρ. ἀσθενίζεται.   [57] h, ab. Other MSS. ἐκλήψει. S¹ om.   [58] α, Αβ. β, S¹ read πᾶσα.   [59] The construction is peculiar. It seems to be a rendering of יחרלו להרע. After καταπαύσουσιν d om. next six words through hmt. For καταπαύσουσιν e reads καταπέσουσιν.   [60] Om. with e as an intrusion. So also Schnapp and Bousset. The parallelism is against it. Moreover, as Schnapp remarks, the use of καταπαύω in two dissimilar meanings in two successive lines would be strange.   [61] Αβ = ὅτι καί.   [62] c reads αὐτούς.   [63] c reads πύλας.   [64] α, dg, Αβ. be read καὶ στήσει. af ἀποστήσει.   [65] h adds τήν.   [66] g reads τόν.   [67] g reads

11. Καὶ δώσει τοῖς ἁγίοις φαγεῖν ἐκ τοῦ ξύλου τῆς ζωῆς,
   καὶ *πνεῦμα ἁγιωσύνης ἔσται[67] ἐπ' αὐτοῖς[68].

12. Καὶ ὁ Βελίαρ δεθήσεται ὑπ' αὐτοῦ,
   καὶ δώσει ἐξουσίαν τοῖς τέκνοις αὐτοῦ[69] πατεῖν ἐπὶ τὰ
   πονηρὰ πνεύματα.

13. Καὶ εὐφρανθήσεται κύριος ἐπὶ τοῖς τέκνοις αὐτοῦ[70],
   καὶ εὐδοκήσει[71] ἐπὶ *τοῖς ἀγαπητοῖς[72] αὐτοῦ *ἕως αἰῶνος[73].

14. Τοτέ ἀγαλλιάσεται Ἀβραὰμ καὶ Ἰσαὰκ καὶ Ἰακὼβ,
   κἀγὼ χαρήσομαι[74], καὶ πάντες οἱ ἅγιοι ἐνδύσονται[75]
   δικαιοσύνην[76].

XIX. Καὶ νῦν, τέκνα μου[1], πάντα ἠκούσατε[2]. Ἐκλέξασθε[3]
ἑαυτοῖς *ἢ τὸ φῶς ἢ τὸ σκότος[4], ἢ τὸν[5] νόμον[6] κυρίου, ἢ *τὰ
ἔργα τοῦ Βελίαρ[7].   2. Καὶ *ἀπεκρίθησαν αὐτῷ οἱ υἱοὶ αὐτοῦ
λέγοντες[8]. Ἐνώπιον κυρίου πορευσόμεθα[9] ⌐καὶ⌐[10] κατὰ τὸν
νόμον αὐτοῦ.   3. Καὶ εἶπεν *αὐτοῖς ὁ πατὴρ αὐτῶν[11].
Μάρτυς ἐστι[12] κύριος, καὶ μάρτυρες οἱ[13] ἄγγελοι αὐτοῦ, *καὶ
μάρτυρες ὑμεῖς καὶ μάρτυς ἐγὼ[14] *περὶ τοῦ λόγου τοῦ στόματος
ὑμῶν[15].   Καὶ *εἶπον αὐτῷ οἱ υἱοὶ αὐτοῦ[16]. Μάρτυρες[17].   4.

beg, Αβ εὐφροσύνην β-de, A ἐλέσθε οὖν. β-dg (Αα, β) ἀπεκρίθημεν ἡμεῖς τῷ πατρὶ λέγοντες. β-d, Αᵇˡⁱ, β εἴπομεν.

πνεύματι ἁγίῳ συνησείται.   [68] c, β-de. h reads πάντας. de αὐτούς. Αβ αὐτῷ.
[69] h om. b adds τοῦ.   [70] S om. next six words.   [71] b adds κύριος.
[72] a reads τοὺς ἀγαπητούς.   [73] α. abefg read ἕως τῶν αἰώνων. d εἰς τὸν αἰῶνα
τοῦ αἰῶνος. e ἕως τοῦ αἰῶνος τῶν αἰώνων.   [74] c. h, abeg read χαρίσομαι. df
χαρίσωμαι.   [75] d reads εὐφρανθήσονται.   [76] α, af, S¹. d reads ἐν δικαιοσύνῃ. beg, Αβ εὐφροσύνην. The latter seems preferable.

XIX. [1] Αᵇ*ᶜᵈ om.   [2] α, β-ag. ag, A read ἀκούσατε. e adds καὶ οἴδατε.
Αᵃ adds ἀπ' ἐμοῦ.   [3] α, d. β-dg read ἐλέσθε. g συνελέσθε. β-e, Αᵃ,ᵇᶜᵈᵉᵍ
add οὖν. Αᵇ* = ἰδού.   [4] α, de, Αᵃ (save that d om. the first ἤ). abfg,
S read ἢ τὸ σκότος ἢ τὸ φῶς. Αβ = ἢ τὸ σκότος.   [5] be om.   [6] Αᵃ read
զզոηրδա (= τὰ ἔργα) corrupt for զորէ‛ա = τὸν νόμον.   [7] α, df, Αᵃ. ab
read ἔργα Β. e (g?) ἔργα τοῦ Β. Αβ = τοῦ Β. S¹ adds πᾶν ὃ ἐννόησα εἶπον
ὑμῖν and then inserts XI.-XIII. between XIX. 1 and XIX. 2.   [8] α (save
that c adds αὐτῷ after λέγοντες). dg, S¹ follow more or less closely. d, S¹
reads ἀπεκρ. οἱ υἱοὶ αὐτοῦ (+ Λευί S¹) τῷ πατρὶ αὐτῶν λέγοντες. g ἀπεκρ.
ἐκεῖνοι καὶ εἶπον. abef ἀπεκρίθημεν ἡμεῖς τῷ πατρὶ λέγοντες. Αᵃ,β = ἀποκριθέντες τῷ πατρὶ ἡμῶν εἴπομεν. Αᵇ ἀποκριθέντες τῷ π. αὐτῶν εἶπον.   [9] h, ae.
c, bdfg read πορευσώμεθα.   [10] α. β, Α, S¹ om.   [11] α. dg read ὁ πατήρ
(+ αὐτῶν Λευὶς πρὸς αὐτούς d). abef, Αβ ἡμῖν (abef om.) ὁ πατὴρ ἡμῶν. Αᵃ
= Λευὶ ὁ πατὴρ ἡμῶν (αὐτῶν Αᵇ).   [12] α. Α = ἐστί μοι (+ σήμερον Αᵃ).
β om. S¹ adds ἡ ἡμέρα ἐμοὶ ἐπαγγελεῖται.   [13] g reads οἱ ἅγιοι.   [14] c. h, β
read καὶ μάρτυς ἐγὼ καὶ μάρτυρες ὑμεῖς. Αβ = καὶ (Αᵇ*ᶜᵈ om.) μάρτυς ἐγὼ καὶ
ὑμεῖς. Αᵃ om. S¹ καὶ μάρτυρες ἡμεῖς.   [15] α, β-dg. d reads περὶ τὸν λόγον

Καὶ οὕτως[18] ἐπαύσατο[19] Λευὶ ἐντελλόμενος τοῖς υἱοῖς αὐτοῦ,
*καὶ ἐξέτεινε τοὺς πόδας αὐτοῦ[20] ⌜ἐπὶ τῆς κλίνης⌝[21] καὶ
προσετέθη πρὸς τοὺς πατέρας αὐτοῦ, ζήσας *ἔτη ἑκατὸν
τριάκοντα ἑπτά[22].   5. Καὶ ἔθηκαν αὐτὸν ἐν[23] σορῷ, καὶ[24]
*μετὰ τοῦτο[25] *ἔθαψαν αὐτὸν ἐν Χεβρὼν[26] μετὰ[27] *Ἀβραὰμ
καὶ Ἰσαὰκ καὶ Ἰακώβ[28].

Διαθήκη Ἰούδα τοῦ τετάρτου υἱοῦ Ἰακὼβ καὶ Λείας[1].

I. Ἀντίγραφον[2] λόγων[3] Ἰούδα, ἃ[4] ἐλάλησε τοῖς υἱοῖς
αὐτοῦ πρὸ τοῦ ἀποθανεῖν αὐτόν.   2. *Συναχθέντες οὖν[5]
ἦλθον *πρὸς αὐτὸν[6] καὶ[7] εἶπεν αὐτοῖς·   3. ⌜Ἀκούσατε,   β–d, A
τέκνα μου, Ἰούδα τοῦ πατρὸς ὑμῶν· ἐγὼ⌝[8] τέταρτος υἱὸς ἐγε-   τέταρτος.

τοῦ στ. ὑμ.   g περὶ τοῦ λ. τοῦ στ. μου καὶ ὑμῶν.   A^a = περὶ τῶν λόγων τοῦ στ.
μου.   A^β περὶ αὐτοῦ καὶ περὶ τοῦ στ. αὐτοῦ.   S¹ περὶ τ. λόγων ὑμῶν.   [16] α, d,
A^b (save that d, A^b om. αὐτῷ).   ae, A^β read εἴπαμεν (+ ἡμεῖς A^β).   b εἴπωμεν.   f εἴπομεν.   g εἶπον ἐκεῖνοι.   A^{ah} = ἡμεῖς εἴπομεν.   [17] α, β–a.   a reads
μάρτυς.   A^a = ἔσται, ἔσται.   A^β μάρτυς ἔσται.   [18] A^a om.   h om. next
seven words.   [19] g reads ἀνεπαύσατο.   [20] A^a om.   [21] α, S¹.   β–d, A om.
d reads καὶ ἐκοιμήθη ἐν εἰρήνῃ.   S adds αὐτοῦ (S¹ om.) καὶ ἐκοιμήθη.   [22] α
(save that h adds καί before ἑπτά).   β–b, S read ἔτη (a om.) ρ̅λ̅ζ̅.   b ἑκατὸν
τριάκοντα ἑπτὰ ἔτη.   A^a = ἔτη ρ̅λ̅ε̅.   A^β ρ̅λ̅η̅ ἔτη.   [23] g om.   A^β add ἐν
Αἰγύπτῳ.   [24] g, A^a om.   [25] α (save that c reads τούτῳ).   β reads ὕστερον.
[26] α, β–g, S.   g reads θάψαντες ἐν Χευρών.   A^a = ἤνεγκαν αὐτὸν καὶ ἔθαψαν ἐν Χ.
A^{b*} ἤνεγκαν αὐτὸν ἐν Χ. καὶ ἔθηκαν.   A^{cdeg} ἐν Χ.   [27] α, g.   a reads ἀνὰ χεῖρας
= על־יד (cf. 2 Sam. xv. 2).   bf ἀνὰ χεῖρα.   d ἀνὰ μετά (a conflation).   e, A
ἀνὰ μέσον.   [28] g reads τῶν πατέρων αὐτοῦ.   d adds τῷ δὲ θεῷ ἡμῶν ἡ δόξα εἰς
αἰῶνας.   f, S¹ add Λευὶ υἱὸς Ἰακὼβ Γ̅ (+ καὶ S¹) υἱὸς Λίας Γ̅ ἔζησεν ἔτη ρ̅λ̅ζ̅ (for
Γ̅ ... ρ̅λ̅ζ̅, S¹ reads γυναικὸς τοῦ Ἰακώβ).

[1] Title.   α in text.   bef read δ. Ἰ. περὶ ἀνδρείας καὶ φιλαργυρίας (e, S¹ om.
κ. φιλ.) καὶ πορνείας (f, S¹ om. κ. πορ.).   To this f adds Ἰούδας ἑρμηνεύεται
ἐξομολόγησις.   a simply Ἰούδα.   d and A are conflate.   d, A^{abcdefg} read δ. Ἰ.
τοῦ τετάρτου υἱοῦ Ἰακὼβ (A^{abcdefg} om. υἱ. Ἰ.) περὶ ἀνδρείας (A^b δικαιοσύνης) καὶ
φιλ. καὶ πορνείας.   A^b = δ. Ἰ. τοῦ τετάρτου περὶ φιλ. καὶ πορν. ἀλλὰ καὶ δικαιοσύνης.   g stands alone : δ. Ἰ. περὶ ἀνδρείας καὶ περὶ τοῦ μὴ μεθύσκεσθαι οἴνῳ.
[2] d, A add διαθήκης.   [3] h om.   [4] α.   β–d read ὅσα.   d om. together
with next four words.   [5] α.   aefg read καὶ συναχθ.   b, A, S¹ συναχθ.   d καὶ
γὰρ συναχθ. οἱ υἱοὶ αὐτοῦ.   g om. next word.   [6] c om.   d reads ἐπισκέψασθαι αὐτόν.   [7] g om.   A^{b*} adds ἀναστὰς ἐκάθισε καί.   [8] α.   d reads
οἴδατε, τέκνα μου, ὅτι.   β–d, A om.   S¹ reads τέκνα μου, ἰδού, λέξω ὑμῖν πρίν με

β, A
ἤμην καὶ
σπου-
δαῖος.

β, A, S
μου
Ἰακώβ.

β-b, A(?)
ἐπηύ-
ξατο.

β-g, S¹
πιάσας
αὐτὴν
ἐποίησα
βρῶμα
τῷ πατρί
μου.

β, A, S¹
τὰς δὲ δορκάδας.

νόμην⁹ τῷ πατρί μου Ἰακώβ¹⁰, καὶ Λεία¹¹ *ἡ μήτηρ μου¹²
ἐπωνόμασέν¹³ με¹⁴ Ἰούδαν¹⁵, λέγουσα· Ἀνθομολογοῦμαι¹⁶
τῷ¹⁷ Κυρίῳ, ὅτι ἔδωκέν¹⁸ μοι¹⁹ ⌜καὶ⌝²⁰ τέταρτον υἱόν.   4.
*Ἐγὼ ὀξὺς ἤμην²¹ ἐν²² νεότητί μου²³, καὶ ὑπήκουον²⁴ τῷ
πατρί μου κατὰ πάντα λόγον²⁵.   5. Καὶ ἐτίμων²⁶ τὴν μητέρα
μου²⁷ καὶ τὴν ἀδελφὴν *τῆς μητρός μου²⁸.   6. Καὶ ἐγένετο
ὡς ἡδρύνθην²⁹ καὶ³⁰ ὁ πατήρ μου³¹ *ηὔξατό μοι³², λέγων·
Βασιλεὺς ἔσῃ³³ κατευοδούμενος³⁴ ἐν³⁵ πᾶσιν.

II. Καὶ ἔδωκέ μοι Κύριος¹ χάριν ἐν πᾶσι τοῖς ἔργοις μου,
ἔν τε² ἀγρῷ καὶ ἐν τῷ οἴκῳ.   2. Οἶδα³ ὅτι συνέδραμον
ἐλάφῳ⁴ καὶ *ἐπίασα αὐτὴν καὶ ἐποίησα αὐτὴν βρῶμα τῷ πατρί
μου καὶ ἔφαγεν⁵.   3. *Τὴν δὲ δορκάδα⁶ *διὰ τοῦ δρόμου⁷

ἀποθανεῖν τὰ πράγματά μου.   ⁹afg, A add ἐγώ.   ¹⁰α, Aᵇ*. β, Aᵃ·ᵇᵈᵉᶠᵍ
S¹ om.   ¹¹α, ag. def, A read Λία. b, S¹ om.   ¹²f reads τῇ μητρί μου
καί. g om.   ¹³α (save that they read ἐπονόμασεν). β reads ὠνόμασεν.
¹⁴Aᶜᵈᵉᶠᵍ om.   ¹⁵c, aef. h, bdg read Ἰούδα.   ¹⁶A = ἀνθομολογήσομαι.
¹⁷afg om.   ¹⁸c, bdeg. h, af read δέδωκε.   ¹⁹Aᵃᵇʰᶜᵈᵉᶠ add κύριος.   ²⁰c,
bdf, S¹. a reads καίγε. h, eg, A om.   ²¹c. h reads ἐγὼ οὖν ὀξ. ἤμην.
d ἐγώ, τέκνα μου, ὀξ. ἤμ. β-d ὀξ. ἤμ. Aᵝ = ὀξ. ἤμ. ἐγώ. Aᵃ = καθαρὸς ἤμ.
ἐγώ. S¹ ἤν. β-e, A add καὶ σπουδαῖος. e καὶ γενναίως. S¹ σπουδαῖος. Possibly
σπουδαῖος is an alternative rendering with ὀξύς of מהיר.   ²²d adds τῇ.
²³S¹ adds ὅτι ἡ ἀνδρεία ἦν ἐν τοῖς στήθεσιν καὶ ἦν ἐν ποσὶν ταχύς, καὶ κρατερὸς
ἐν τῷ σώματι καὶ πολλοὶ τῶν ἀγωνιζομένων οὐκ ἠδυνήθησαν ἀνέχεσθαι ἐπὶ τοὺς
βραχίονας καὶ ἐνίκησα τὴν βεβαιότητα τοῦ πολίτου οὐχ ὑπείκοντός μοι, καὶ εἶδεν
ὁ πατήρ μου ὅτι ὁ ἄγγελος τοῦ κρατεροῦ συνεμάχετό μοι.   ²⁴c, deg. h, S¹ read
καὶ ὑπήκουσα. abf καὶ ὑπακούων. Aᵝ om. together with next three words.
²⁵e reads τρόπον.   ²⁶α, d read ἐτίμουν. b εὐλόγουν.   ²⁷h, f om.   ²⁸g
reads αὐτῆς.   ²⁹c, ag. A corrupt form of this appears in h, f ἠνδρύνθην.
Other verbs of kindred meaning are given in b, A ἠνδρώθην. d ἠνδρειώθην.
e ἀνδριώθην.   ³⁰g om.   ³¹β, A, S¹ add Ἰακώβ.   ³²c, b. h reads ηὔξατο.
adefg, A ἐπηύξατό μοι (a om.) or Aᵝ = ηὔξατο περὶ ἐμοῦ. S¹ εὐλόγησέν με.
³³d reads ἔσει.   ³⁴α, β-b, A. b reads καὶ εὐοδούμενος. A 𐔰𐔱𐔼𐕒 (= πρωτεύων)
corrupt for 𐔿𐕒𐔼𐔸𐕔 = κατευοδούμενος.   ³⁵f reads ἐπί.

II.   ¹e¹, Aᵇ* om.   ²g reads τῷ. adef, A add τῷ.   ³b, S¹ read ὡς
εἶδον.   ⁴c, h, β read τῇ ἐλ.   ⁵α (save that h om. the second αὐτὴν and
trs. βρῶμα after μου). β-g read πιάσας αὐτὴν ἐποίησα βρῶμα (βρώματα d) τῷ
πατρί μου. g reads as β-g but trs. βρῶμα to the end. A = πιάσας (Aᵃᵇʰᶜᵈᵉᶠᵍ
om.) ἔδωκα αὐτὴν βρῶμα τῷ π. μου.   ⁶c. h reads τὰς δὲ δορκάδας. β, S¹ τὰς
δορκ. A = καὶ τὰς δορκ.   ⁷β, A trs. this phrase after ἐκράτουν against α.
A adds μου.   ⁸e reads τῷ. d om.   ⁹e reads πεδίῳ. f σπουδαίοις.

ἐκράτουν, καὶ πᾶν ὃ ἦν ἐν τοῖς[8] πεδίοις[9] κατελάμβανον.   4.
*Τὸν λέοντα[11] ἀπέκτεινα[12] καὶ ἀφειλόμην[13] ἔριφον ἐκ τοῦ
στόματος αὐτοῦ[14]. τὴν[15] ἄρκον λαβὼν ἀπὸ τοῦ ποδὸς ἀπέλυσα[16] εἰς *τὸν κρημνόν[17], *καὶ συνετρίβη[18].   5. *Τῷ
ἀγρίῳ χοίρῳ[20] κατέδραμον[21], καὶ προέλαβον[22] ⌜ἐν τῷ τρέχειν
με⌝ καὶ[23] κατεσπάραξα αὐτόν.

β–e, S[1]
κατελάμ-
βανον.
*φοράδα
ἀγρίαν
κατέ-
λαβον
καὶ
πιάσας

ἡμέρωσα[10].   4. Καὶ λέοντα.   β, A, S[1] *καὶ πᾶν θηρίον, ὃ ἐπέστρεφε ἐπ᾽
ἐμέ, διέσπων αὐτὸ ὡς κύνα[19].

[10] β–ae (save that for κατέλαβον d reads καταλαβών and g κατέδραμον), S[1]. α
reads καὶ κρατήσας ἡμέρωσα. e, A represent a third type of text. e φορ.
αγ. καταλαβως (sic) ἡμέρωσα πιάσας δορκάδα ἐκύνηγον ἐν τῇ χειρί μου. A (with
which e is related) = φοράδας ἀγ. πιάσας ἡμέρωσα αὐτάς· ζῶα ἄγρια ἐθήρευσα
ἐν χερσί μου.   [11] α. β–def, S[1] read καὶ λέοντα. ef λέοντα. A = καίγε τὸν
λέοντα (λέοντας A[β]) πολλάκις. Vers. 4–7 appear in an expanded form in
d as follows: ἄλλοτε πάλιν ποιμαίνοντός μου τὰ πρόβατα τοῦ πατρός, λέων ἐκ
τῆς ἐρήμου ἐπελθὼν ἥρπασεν ἔριφον ἐκ τῆς ἀγέλης καὶ ἐπορεύετο. καὶ ἰδὼν αὐτὸν
ἔδραμον ἐπ᾽ αὐτὸν καὶ πιάσας πυραχρῆμα ἀπέκτεινα καὶ ἀφελόμην τὸν ἔριφον ἐκ τοῦ
στόματος αὐτοῦ. ἄλλοτε πάλιν ἄρκος (sic) ἐπελθούσης τῇ ποίμνῃ λαβὼν αὐτὸν ἀπὺ
τοῦ ποδὸς ἀπεκύλησα εἰς τὸ κρημνὸν καὶ παρ᾽ αὐτὰ διερράγη. καὶ πᾶν δὲ θηρίον
ἐπεστρεφὲν (sic) ἐπ᾽ ἐμὲ διεσπάρασσον αὐτὸ ὥσπερ κύνα. 5. Καὶ παντελεῖ ἀφα-
νισμῷ παρεδίδουν. ἄλλοτε θεασάμενος κύνα ἄγριον τρέχοντος συνέδραμον αὐτό·
καὶ παραλαβὼν αὐτὸν ἐν τῷ τρέχειν με κατεσπάραξα αὐτόν. 6. Ἄλλοτε πάρδαλιν
(sic) ἐν Χεβρὼν προσεπίδησεν ἐπὶ τὸν κύνα μου τὸν παρακολουθοῦντά μοι· καὶ πιάσας
αὐτὴν ἀπὸ τῆς οὐρᾶς ἀπεκόντισα αὐτὸν ἐν τῇ γῇ καὶ εὐθέως ἐρράγη. 7. Ἄλλοτε
πάλιν διερχομένου μου ἐν τοῖς ὁρίοις Γάζης, θεασάμενος βοῶν ἀγρίων ἀγέλην νεμω-
μένην ἐπί τινα χώραν ἔκλινα τῆς ὁδοῦ καὶ πρὸς αὐτοὺς γενόμενος κρατήσας τὸν
μείζονα αὐτῶν ἀπὸ τῶν κεράτων, καὶ ἐν κύκλῳ συσσείσας καὶ σκοτίσας ῥήξας αὐτὸν
ἀνεῖλον.   [12] A = ἀποκτείνας (A[b] ἀπέκτεινον).   [13] h. c, bg read ἀφελόμην.
af ἀφειλάμην. e, A ἀφηρόμην.   [14] A[β] = αὐτῶν.   [15] α. β om. A = καὶ
τόν.   [16] α, a. g, A read ἀπηκόντισα, of which I take bdef ἀπεκύλησα to
be a corruption. Then ἀπηκόντισα and ἀπέλυσα would be independent
renderings of שלחתי.   [17] h, afg. c reads τὸν κρυμνόν. b κρημνόν. e δένδρον.
[18] α. See also d in note 11, καὶ παρ᾽ αὐτὰ διερράγη. β, A, S[1] read καὶ πᾶν
θηρίον ὃ (ab, S[1] εἰ, dg om.) ὑπέστρεφεν (b ἐπέστρεφε, df ἐπεστρεφὲν, e ἐπέ-
τρεχεν, g ἐπιστρέφων) ἐπ᾽ (b πρὸς, g εἰς) ἐμέ, διέσπων (bg διήσπουν, d διεσπάρασσον, e διησπον, f διέσπουν, A = ἀπέκτεινον) αὐτὸ ὡς (αὐτὰ A[b*e]) κύνα (a om.
ὡς κ.) By referring to the text of d, given above, it will be observed
that here again d is conflate, or is it alone not defective?   [19] See
preceding note.   [20] h, af (but a om. τῷ). befg read τῷ χ. τῷ ἀγ. c τὸν
αγριο χοιρα.   [21] α, a. β–a read συνέδραμον.   [22] h. c reads προελαβα.
abef πρόκα (bef om.) προλαβών. d παραλαβών. g προσλαβὼν ἐκ τοῦ ποδός.
In A the text = καὶ καταδραμόντος μου χοῖρον ἄγριον κατέλαβον αὐτὸν καὶ πατάξας

β, (A), S¹
αὐτὴν καὶ
ἐρράγη
ἐν τοῖς
ὁρίοις
Γάζης.
β–d, A,
S¹ ἐν
χώρᾳ
νεμόμε-
νον ἐκρά-
τησα.
β, A, S¹
καὶ ὅτε.

6. *Πάρδαλις ἐν Χεβρὼν προσεπήδησεν ἐπὶ τὸν κύνα²⁴, καὶ πιάσας²⁵ αὐτὸν²⁶ ἀπὸ τῆς κέρκου²⁷ ἀπηκόντισα²⁸ *αὐτὸν ἐπὶ τὴν πέτραν καὶ ἐρράγη εἰς δύο²⁹.

7. *Βοῦν ἄγριον εὗρον τὴν χώραν νεμόμενον, καὶ κρατήσας³⁰ τῶν κεράτων³¹ καὶ³² κύκλῳ *συσσείσας³³ *καὶ σκοτίσας³⁴ ῥίψας³⁵ ἀνεῖλον³⁶ αὐτόν³⁷.

III. *Ὅτε δὲ¹ *ἦλθον οἱ δύο βασιλεῖς τῶν Χαναναίων τεθωρακισμένοι² ἐπὶ τὰ *ποίμνια ἡμῶν καὶ λαὸς πολὺς³ *μετ' αὐτῶν⁴ *κἀγὼ μόνος⁵ δραμὼν ἐπὶ τὸν βασιλέα *τὸν ἕνα⁶ *καὶ

____

β, S¹ καὶ πολὺς λαός.

κατεσπάραξα τὰ ὀστᾶ αὐτοῦ. ²³α. β om. ²⁴α, β–d (save that *e* reads πρός for ἐπί and *g* prefixes καί). Aα = πάρδαλις ἄλλοτε ἐν Χ. προσπηδάσας ἐπὶ τὸν κ. Aβ ἄλλοτε πάρδ. ἐλθὼν ἐν Χ. καὶ προσπηδήσας ἐπὶ τ. κ. Observe that *d* agrees with Aα. See note 11. ²⁵*ag* read κρατήσας. ²⁶α. β reads αὐτήν. A om. ²⁷α, *af.* β–*af* read οὐρᾶς. ²⁸*af.* α read ἀπηκόντησα. *bdeg* ἀπεκόντισα. ²⁹α. β–d, S¹ read αὐτὴν καὶ ἐρράγη (*e* διερράγη) ἐν τοῖς ὁρίοις (*e* ἄρεσιν) Γάζης. For *d* see note 11. A = καὶ εὑρέθη (+ ἡ πάρδαλις Aᵇᵍ) ῥαγεῖσα ἐν ὁρίοις Γάζης. The εὑρέθη here is borrowed from ver. 7 where it should be restored and read as εὗρον (*q.m.h*). The phrase ἐν ὁρίοις Γάζης seems to be wrongly connected with ver. 6. *d* connects it with ver. 7. ³⁰α. β–d, A read βοῦν ἄγρ. ἐν (*f* ἐπί, *bg* om.) χώρᾳ (*fg* χώραν, A ὄρει) νεμόμενον ἐκράτησα (A κρατήσας). *be* add ἐκ. ³¹A adds αὐτοῦ. ³²*c* om. β adds ἐν. ³³*h*, β–*e*, A. *c* reads συστήσας. *e* συνσησας. Aα,ᵉᶠᵍ add αὐτόν. ³⁴α, *bf.* β–*bfg*, A⁻ᵇ* read καὶ σκοτώσας. *g* σκοτώσας. Aᵇ* = καὶ ἐσκότωσα. Aᵇ add δηλονότι ἐκμαίνας. ³⁵Aᵃᵇʰ read καὶ ἔρριψα (+ ἐν τῇ γῇ Aᵇ). Aᶜ om. Aᵇ* read καὶ ῥίψας ἐν τῇ γῇ. ³⁶Aᵃᵇʰ om. ³⁷*f* reads αὐτήν. *h* om.

III. ¹α. β–d, A, S¹ read καὶ ὅτε. *d* καὶ ἐν μιᾷ τῶν ἡμερῶν. ²A = ἦλθεν ὁ βασιλεὺς τ. Χ. τεθωρακισμένος. ³α. *abefg*, S¹ read ποίμνια (*e* πρόβατα) καὶ π. λαός (*g* πολλοὶ λαοί). *d* ποίμνια ἡμῶν τοῦ ἁρπάσαι αὐτὰ καὶ πολὺς λαός. A ποίμνια πολλῷ λαῷ (Aᵇ καὶ πολὺς λαός). ⁴Aᵇ = ἦν αὐτῷ. Aᵃᵇ*ᶜᵈᵍ om. ⁵*d* reads ἐγὼ μόνος. *g* καί. A = κἀγὼ μόνος ἦν καί. ⁶α = האחד, 'the one.' The other authorities read הצור which is well reproduced by *ae*, S¹ as Ἀσούρ, less well by *bfg* Σούρ. *d* Ἀσσυρίων. (Cf. my note on Jub. xxxiv. 4). A = Ζούρ. The omission of Ἀσούρ by α is due to its wrong (?) text in iv. 2. See note 14, p. 72. ⁷α. β, S¹ read συνέσχον (*a* συνεῖχον, *e* συνηχον) αὐτὸν καὶ ἐπὶ (*e* om.) τ. κνημῖδας (*d* ἀντικνημῖδας) κρούσας. A = συνέσχον αὐτὸν καὶ κρούσας ἐπὶ τὰς κνήμας αὐτοῦ. ⁸A = κατασπάσας. ⁹α. β–d, A, S¹ read καὶ τόν. *d* ὁμοίως καὶ τόν. ¹⁰α. β–*eg*, S¹ read Ταφουέ. *e* Γαφούς. *g* Ταφουσέ. A = τῶν Ταφίων. ¹¹*d* reads ἵππου ἄφνω. *g* τὸν ἵππον. Aᵃᵇ add αὐτοῦ. Aᵇ* add κρούσας. ¹²β, Aᵇʰᵇ*ᶜᵈᵉᶠᵍ add αὐτόν. S¹

κρούσας αὐτὸν ἐπὶ τὰς κνημῖδας[7] *κατέσπασα, καὶ οὕτως[8] ἀνεῖλον
αὐτόν. 2. *Τὸν δὲ[9] ἕτερον βασιλέα *τὸν Ταφουὲ[10]
καθήμενον ἐπὶ *τοῦ ἵππου[11] [ἀνεῖλον[12] καὶ οὕτως πάντα τὸν
λαὸν αὐτοῦ[13] διεσκόρπισα.

β, A, S[1] 'Ασοὺρ συνέσχον αὐτὸν καὶ ἐπὶ τ. κνημῖδας κρούσας.

α	β, S[1]	A
3. Καὶ[14] τὸν †'Αχὼρ βασιλέα[15]] ἄνδρα γίγαντα εὗρον[16]	3. *Τὸν 'Αχὼρ βασιλέα[17]] ἄνδρα γίγαντα[18] βάλλοντα	3. Καὶ *τὸν βασιλέα Χωρὰ] ἄνδρα[19] γίγαντα †ἔχοντα

om. rest of verse. The words ἀνεῖλον καὶ οὕτως . . . βασιλέα must be rejected
as a corrupt and in part dittographic addition. For since according to
III. 1 and IV. 1 (β, A, S[1]) Judah kills five kings and according to III. 7
Jacob kills one, there can only be one other king slain, as there are only
seven in all. This is the King of Tappuah whom Judah slays, according
to our present text in III. 2. Thus the original text cannot have dealt
with an eighth king as the present Greek text does in III. 3–5. And
yet these verses with the exception of the phrase τὸν 'Αχὼρ βασιλέα are
original; for they are found in the Midr. Wajjis and the Book of Jashar
—only in these latter with reference to the King of Tappuah. Hence
we rightly infer that verses 2–5 originally related to the King of Tappuah
only. We can, moreover, account for the origin of the added name 'Αχώρ.
For 'Αχώρ = אחור a corruption of אַחֵר = ἕτερος. Thus τὸν 'Αχὼρ βασιλέα
is merely a corrupt dittography of the opening words of ver. 2. The
earlier part of the addition arose subsequently either in the Hebrew or
in the Greek translation. To this addition there is nothing corresponding
in the other Hebrew authorities. [13] h, de, A^abhb*. c, afg, A^cdefg read
αὐτῶν. b, S[1] om. [14] α, A. d reads καὶ πάλιν ἄλλοτε. β–d om. [15] α,
β (save that g reads 'Εχὼρ β.). A^abh attempts an emendation and gives
βασιλέα Χωρά (cf. A, ver. 4). A^b*cdes give 'Οχοσορά for Χωρά. Before
discovering the corruption of the text, I took Χωρά to be corrupt for
Χωρον = חורן, i.e. בת־חורן. See Jub. xxxiv. 2–8 note. [16] It will be
observed that α gives at once the most intelligible text and the most
grammatical. On the other hand, α is defective, for the phrase ἔμπροσθεν
καὶ ὄπισθεν ἐφ' ἵππου is found also in Jashar and Chron. Jerach. [17] An
addition. See note 12. There is no verb to govern this accusative; for
ἀνελόμενος must be construed with λίθον. For d see note 14. [18] b reads
γιγάντων. d adds τῇ ἰσχύι. [19] See note 15. Observe that this order
recurs in ver. 4. [20] c. h reads ἀνειλάμην. [21] h. c reads λυτρῶν.
[22] Undoubtedly corrupt. Possibly הביתי (i.e. הִפֵּיתִי = ἐπάταξα, so A, S[1])
stood originally in the Hebrew which was corrupted into נתתי (i.e. נָתַתִּי).
δέδωκα might be corrupt for κέκρουκα; but bde read ἔδωκα. See note 27.
[23] Though in α, d it is an addition to the text. The verse originally ended

βάλλοντα τόξα καὶ ἀνηλάμενος[20] λίθον ἐξήκοντα λιτρῶν[21] καὶ ἀκοντίσας †δέδωκα[22] τῷ ἵππῳ καὶ ἀπέκτεινα αὐτὸν [σὺν τῷ ἵππῳ][23]. 4. (Wanting.)	τόξα ἔμπροσθεν καὶ ὄπισθεν ἐφ' ἵππου[24] ἀνελόμενος[25] λίθον *ἐξήκοντα λιτρῶν[26] ἀκοντίσας †ἔδωκα[27] *τῷ ἵππῳ[28] καὶ ἀπέκτεινα[29] αὐτόν[30]. 4. Καὶ *πολεμήσας τὸν †'Αχὼρ[31] ἐπὶ *ὥρας δύο[32] *ἀπέκτεινα αὐτόν[33], καὶ εἰς[34] δύο μέρη[35] ποιήσας τὴν ἀσπίδα αὐτοῦ συνέκοψα τοὺς πόδας αὐτοῦ.	περὶ τὴν ὀσφὺν†[36] ὄπισθεν καὶ ἔμπροσθεν τόξον καὶ[37] καθήμενον ἐφ' ἵππου ἀνελόμενος λίθον λιτρῶν ξ' καὶ ἀκοντίσας ἐπάταξα[38] τὸν ἵππον καὶ ἀπέκτεινα αὐτόν. 4. Καὶ πολεμήσας τὸν βασιλέα †Ναχὼρ ὡς ἐπὶ ὥρας δύο καὶ εἰς μέρη ποιήσας τὴν ἀσπίδα συνέκοψα τοὺς πόδας αὐτοῦ, καὶ οὕτως ἀπέκτεινα αὐτόν.

β, S¹ οὖν ... ἐν τῇ χειρί.
β, S¹ λίθοις σφενδονήσας αὐτούς.

5. *'Εν δὲ[39] τῷ ἐκδύειν[40] με[41] τὸν θώρακα αὐτοῦ[42], ἰδού, *ἄνδρες †ὀκτώ[43], ἑταῖροι[44] αὐτοῦ[45], ἤρξαντο πολεμεῖν με[46].

6. 'Ενειλήσας[47] *δὲ ἐγὼ[48] τὴν στολήν μου *ἐπὶ τὴν χεῖρά[49] μου ⌜καὶ⌝[50] *σφενδονήσας αὐτοῖς λίθους[51] *τέσσαρας ἐξ αὐτῶν

with ἀπέκτεινεν αὐτόν, and thus ver. 4 was lost through hmt. [24] d reads ἵππον. [25] d reads ανελωμενος. f ἀνηλάμενος. [26] def. abg, S¹ read λιτρῶν ξ. d adds ἐγὼ καί. [27] bde. afg read δέδωκα. S¹ ἐπάταξα. [28] β-e. e reads τοῦ ἵππου. d adds αὐτοῦ. [29] a adds καί. [30] d om. ag om. next nine words. [31] β-de, S¹. d reads πεζεύσας 'Αχὼρ ἐπολέμησε μετ' ἐμοῦ. e ἐπυλέμησα τ. 'Α. 'Αχώρ here also represents a corruption of אַחֵר = ἕτερον. See note 15. [32] β-ef, S¹. ef read δύο ὥρας. de add διὸ (e om.) καί. [33] This clause, which has καί prefixed in de, should be transferred to the close of the verse as in A. See note 32. [34] e reads ἐπί. [35] b reads μερίδας. [36] So A corruptly np (A^he om.) ու՛նէր զսիրանիւ իւրով. [37] A^befg om. [38] A^b reads πατάξας and om. following καί. [39] e reads καὶ ἐν. [40] A = ἐνδύεσθαι. [41] e om. aef add αὐτόν. bg αὐτοῦ. [42] α, d, A. β-d om. af add καί. [43] α, ad. bef read ὀκτὼ ἄνδρες. g πεντήκοντα ἄνδρες. A = ἐφάνησαν ἄνδρες ἑπτά (A^els ἐννέα). ἐννέα is supported by Midr. Wajjis, Chron. Jerach. and Book of Jashar, הישׁר. [44] ab, A^bb*cdef, S¹. In the other MSS. this word is written ἕτεροι. [45] c reads ἑαυτοῦ. A^a αὐτῶν. [46] α. β-e, A read πρός με. e μετ' ἐμοῦ. [47] α, adg. bf read ἐνειλίσας. e ἐνηλήσας. g, A prefix καί. [48] α. β, S¹ read οὖν. A = ἐγώ. [49] α. β, S¹ reads ἐν τῇ χειρί. For the words τὴν στολήν ... μου A reads τὴν χεῖρά (A^cd τὰς χεῖράς) μου τῇ στολῇ μου. [50] α, A. β om. [51] c (save that with h I have

β, A, S¹
καὶ
ʼΙακὼβ ὁ
πατὴρ
ἡμῶν.
β, Aᵃᵇ, S¹
ἀμέριμνος
ἦν ὁ π.
μου.
h, Aᵃᵇᵉᶠᵍ
ὅτι.

β, A, S¹ ἀνεῖλον⁵². *οἱ δὲ λοιποὶ⁵³ ἔφυγον.　7· *ʼΟ δὲ πατήρ μου ʼΙακὼβ⁵⁴ ἀνεῖλε τὸν †Βελισάθ⁵⁵, βασιλέα⁵⁶ πάντων⁵⁷ τῶν⁵⁸ βασιλέων, ⌜ἄνδρα⌝⁵⁹ γίγαντα τῇ ἰσχύι πηχῶν δώδεκα⁶⁰. 8. Καὶ ἐπέπεσεν⁶¹ ἐπ᾽ αὐτοὺς τρόμος⁶², καὶ ἐπαύσαντο πολεμοῦντες⁶³ ἡμᾶς⁶⁴.　9. *Διὰ τοῦτο ὁ πατήρ μου ἀμέριμνος ἦν ἐν τοῖς πολέμοις⁶⁵, ὅτε⁶⁶ ἐγὼ *σὺν τοῖς ἀδελφοῖς μου ἤμην⁶⁷. 10. *Εἶδε γὰρ⁶⁸ *ἐν ὁράματι⁶⁹ ⌜περὶ ἐμοῦ⌝⁷⁰ ὅτι ἄγγελος δυνάμεως⁷¹ *συνέπεταί μοι⁷² ἐν πᾶσι, τοῦ μὴ *ἅψασθαί μοι⁷³.

β-e, A, S¹
ἡττᾶσθαί
με.
β-dg, A,
S¹ καὶ

IV. *Καὶ μετὰ τοῦτο γέγονεν ἡμῖν κατὰ νότον¹ πόλεμος² μείζων³ *τοῦ ἐν Σικίμοις⁴· καὶ παραταξάμενος *σὺν τοῖς ἀδελφοῖς⁵ μου ἐδιώξαμεν⁶ χιλίους⁷ καὶ ἀπεκτείναμεν⁸ ἐξ

————————

κατὰ νότον γέγονεν ἡμῖν. β, A-ᵇ*, S¹ ἐδίωξα. β, A-ᵇ*, S¹ ἀπέκτεινα ... διακοσίους ἄνδρας καὶ τέσσαρας βασιλεῖς.

placed λίθους for λίθοις). h reads σφενδονίσας αὐτοῖς λίθους. abdg, S¹ λίθοις σφενδονίσας (bg σφενδων. d σφενδονήσας) αὐτούς (g εἰς αὐτούς). ef λίθους σφενδονήσας αὐτοῖς. A = σφενδονήσας.　⁵²g reads τοὺς δ´ ἀνεῖλον. A = ἀνεῖλον ἐξ αὐτ. ἄνδρας (Aᵃᶜᵈ om.) τέσσαρας.　⁵³α. g reads καὶ οἱ λοιποί. β-g οἱ δὲ ἄλλοι.　⁵⁴α. d reads τῷ καιρῷ ἐκείνῳ ὁ π. μου ʼΙ. β-d, A, S¹ καὶ ʼΙ. ὁ π. ἡμῶν (e, Aᵇ*ᶜᵈᵉᶠᵍ μου).　⁵⁵α, af. b reads Βεελισά. d Βελιατ. e Βεελησάθ. g Βεελισάδ. Aᵃ = Βελιασά. Aᵇʰᵇ*ᶜᵈᵉᵍ Βελιασάθ. S¹ ʼΕλισάφ. These seem to be corruptions of בעל־שילה = ʻ Lord of Shilo.ʼ　⁵⁶e trs. before Βελ.　⁵⁷d reads ἄπαντα.　⁵⁸e om.　⁵⁹α. β, A, S¹ om.　⁶⁰c,f. h, e read δέκα δύο. abdg ιβ´.　⁶¹c, abf. h, deg read ἔπεσεν.　⁶²d trs. before ἐπ᾽. A = τρόμος (+ ἡμῶν Aᵇ*ᵈ) καὶ φόβος.　⁶³e trs. to end of verse.　⁶⁴α, d. abeg read ἀφ᾽ ἡμῶν. f ἐφ᾽ ἡμᾶς.　⁶⁵α. β-g, Aᵃᵇʰ, S¹ read καὶ (β-g om.) δ. τοῦτο ἀμ. ἦν ὁ π. μου ... πολέμοις. Aᵇ*ᶜᵈᵉᵍ = καί. g om. the entire verse, but adds the first half of it, prefixing καί and om. ὁ πατήρ μου after ver. 10. d om. rest of verse.　⁶⁶c, β-dg, Aᵇ*ᶜᵈ, S¹. h. Aᵃᵇʰᵉᶠᵍ read as in margin.　⁶⁷α (save that I have corrected ειμην of c and συνήμην of h into ἤμην). β-dg read ἤμην σὺν (b ἐν) τοῖς ἀδ. μου.　⁶⁸α, β-d, Aᵃᵇʰ, S¹. d reads ὅτι εἶδεν. g εἶδεν ὁ πατήρ μου. Aᶜᵈ = εἶδεν. Aᵉᶠᵍ ἐγὼ γάρ by internal corruption.　⁶⁹e reads ὅραμα. Aᵇ*ᶜᵈ add νυκτός.　⁷⁰A om.　⁷¹d reads κυρίου. Aᵇ = κυρίου δυνάμεω.　⁷²α, afg. bd read ἔπεταί μοι. e ἦν μετ᾽ ἐμοῦ. S¹ βοηθεῖ μοι.　⁷³α ἅψασθε μαι (h μοι) for ἅψασθαί μοι. d, A read ἡττᾶσθαί με. β-de, S¹ ἡττᾶσθαι. e ἡττιθῆναί με. These appear to be independent renderings of two different moods of נגע.

IV. ¹α (save that they read νῶτον corruptly for νότον). abf, A, S¹ read καὶ κατὰ νότον γέγονεν ἡμῖν (for ἡμῖν Aᵇ*ᵈᵉ´ᵍ read μέγας). d πάλιν οὖν γέγ. ἡμῖν. e καὶ κ. τὸν νότον ἡμῖν γέγ. g ἡμῖν γέγ.　²g adds κατὰ τοῦ νώτου.　³e reads μεῖζον. d om.　⁴abg. ef read τοῦ ἐν Σικήμοις. α τοῖς ἐν Σηκήμοις. d om.　⁵α. β reads μετὰ τῶν ἀδελφῶν.　⁶α, Aᵇ* (but this reading

β, S¹ †ἄλλους δύο βασι-λεῖς† ἀνεῖλον. A ἀνεῖλον ἄλλους ἔτι βασιλεῖς τέσσα-ρας. β-de,

αὐτῶν διακοσίους⁹.   2. Καὶ ἀνῆλθον¹⁰ ἐγὼ¹¹ ἐπὶ *τοῦ τείχους¹², καὶ¹³ *ἀνεῖλον †τὸν βασιλέα αὐτῶν†¹⁴.   3. Καὶ οὕτως †ἠλευθερώσαμεν¹⁵ τὴν¹⁶ †Χεβρών¹⁷, καὶ ἐλάβομεν πᾶσαν τὴν αἰχμαλωσίαν¹⁸.

V. Καὶ¹ τῇ ἐξῆς ἀπήλθομεν² εἰς Ἀρετάν³, πόλιν κραταιὰν⁴ καὶ ἰσχυράν⁵, *ἀπειλοῦσαν ἡμῖν θάνατον⁶.   2. *Ἐγὼ δὲ καὶ ὁ Γὰδ⁷ προσήξαμεν⁸ *ἀπὸ ἀνατολῶν τῆς πόλεως⁹. Ῥουβὴμ δὲ¹⁰ καὶ ὁ¹¹ Λευὶ¹² ἀπὸ δυσμῶν¹³.   3. Καὶ

A, S¹ αἰχ. τῶν βασιλέων. β-dg, A, S¹ τειχήρη καὶ ἀπροσέγγιστον.

seems corrupt). β, A^{abhcde's}, S¹ read ἐδίωξα. A adds ἐξ αὐτῶν ἄνδρας. ⁷bde, S¹ add ἄνδρας. g ἄνδρας καὶ τέσσαρας βασιλεῖς. ⁸α, A^{b*} (seems corrupt). β, A^{abhcdefg} read ἀπέκτεινα. ⁹α. d, A read ἄνδρας διακοσίους. β-g, S¹ add ἄνδρας (d om.) καὶ τέσσαρας (b τέσσαρες, ef τεσσαρεις) βασιλεῖς. g ἄνδρας. A καὶ βασιλεῖς τέσσαρας. d om. ver. 2 through hmt. ¹⁰g reads ἀνελθών. ¹¹α, A. β om. b, S¹ add ἐπ' αὐτούς. ¹²A reads τῶν τειχέων αὐτῶν. ¹³g om. ¹⁴α, i.e. the King of Hazor, who, however, was already slain by Judah (iii. 1). β-e, S¹ read ἄλλους δύο βασιλεῖς ἀνεῖλον. e ἀνεῖλον δύο βασιλεῖς. A = ἀνεῖλον ἄλλους ἔτι βασιλεῖς τέσσαρας, where βασιλεῖς is corrupt, but τέσσαρας is right according to Midr. Wajjis. For βασιλεῖς we should read ἰσχυρούς = נבורים, as in Midr. Wajjis and Chron. Jerach. הרג לאותם ד׳ נבורים. ¹⁵α, ag. bdef read ἐλευθερώσαμεν. Text = חפשנו corrupt for תפשנו = συνελάβομεν, or for כבשנו (verb used in Midr. Wajjis here) = κατεκυριεύσαμεν. Corruption due to corruption of Ἀσούρ into Χεβρών. See note 17. ¹⁶d reads τόν. ¹⁷Corrupt for Ἀσούρ = חצור. The whole chapter relates to Hazor as in Midr. Wajjis, Chron. Jerach. xxxvi. 6, Book of Jashar (*Dict. des Apocr.*, ii. 1176). ¹⁸e reads εὐπορίαν. β-d, A, S¹ add τῶν βασιλέων. d αὐτῶν.

V. ¹b, S¹ om. Instead of καὶ τῇ . . . ἰσχυράν d reads πάλιν οὖν ἄλλῃ πόλει κραταιᾷ καὶ ἀπροσέγγιστος Ἀρετὰ ὀνομαζομένη. ²efg read ἀπήλθαμεν. ³be. d reads Ἀρετά. g Ἀβετά. α, ae²(over erasure)f, S¹ ἑτέραν. A^{abhcdefg} = Αριτα. The original word was סרטן (see Book of Jashar, ii. 1176; Chron. Jerach. xxxvi. 7). ⁴g reads κραταιᾷ and om. καί following. A^{b*} = ἀνάλωτον κραταιάν. ⁵α. β-dg, A, S¹ read τειχείρη (ef τειχηρὰν) καὶ ἀπροσέγγιστον (a προσέγγιστον ἡμῖν). g τῇ χειρὶ καὶ ὡς προσηγγίσαμεν. For text of d see note 1. ⁶a reads θαν. ἀπ. g ἀπ. ἡμῖν θανάτῳ. A = καὶ ἠπείλουν ἡμῖν θάνατον. d adds ὀργισθέντες οὖν ἡμεῖς ἐπ' αὐτὴν ἐπορεύθημεν εἰς αὐτήν. ⁷α. β, S¹ read Ἐγὼ οὖν καὶ Γάδ. A = καὶ τότε (A^{o'} ἰδοὺ) ἐγὼ καὶ Γ. ⁸d reads προσηύξαμεν. ⁹A = εἰς τὸ τεῖχος τῆς πόλεως ἀπὸ ἀνατολῶν. ¹⁰c om. ¹¹α. β om. ¹²d reads Λευίς. ¹³b adds καὶ νότου. ¹⁴A = οὕτως ἐνόμιζον and trs. after τείχους. ¹⁵d om. ¹⁶α, abf. beg, A read ἐπί. For τ. τείχους A^β read τῶν τειχέων. ¹⁷A adds καί. ¹⁸ἐφέλκειν is used

νομίσαντες[14] οἱ[15] ἀπὸ[16] τοῦ τείχους, ὅτι ἡμεῖς μόνοι ἐσμέν[17],
† ἐφελκύσθησαν[18] πρὸς[19] ἡμᾶς.

α	β, S¹	A
4. Καὶ οὕτως λάθρα οἱ ἀδελφοί μου ἐξ ἑκατέρων τῶν μερῶν τοῦ τείχους εἰσήλθομεν εἰς τὴν πόλιν.	4. Καὶ οὕτως λάθρα[20] οἱ ἀδελφοί μου[21] ἐξ ἑκατέρων * τῶν μερῶν[21] πασσάλοις * ἐπανέβησαν τῷ τείχει[22] καὶ εἰσῆλθον[23] εἰς τὴν πόλιν ἀγνοούντων αὐτῶν[24].	4. Ἀλλὰ[25] πάντες ἀδελφοὶ ἡμῶν ἐξ ἑκατέρων τῶν μερῶν πασσάλους ἐμπήξαντες[26] εἰσῆλθομεν[27] εἰς τὴν πόλιν ἀγνοούντων αὐτῶν.

α, β, S¹	A	
5. *Καὶ κατελάβομεν[28] αὐτὴν ἐν στόματι μαχαίρας, *καὶ τοὺς[29] ἐν *τῷ πύργῳ[30] καταφυγόντας *ἐν πυρὶ ἐνεπρήσαμεν καὶ οὕτως πάντας ἐλάβομεν καὶ πάντα τὰ αὐτῶν[31].	5. Καὶ ἐλάβομεν αὐτοὺς ἐν στόματι μαχαίρας, καὶ οἱ ἐν τῷ τείχει[32] κατέφυγον [καὶ εἰσῆλθον εἰς τοὺς πύργους][33] καὶ *τότε ἡμεῖς ἐμπρήσαντες τοὺς πύργους σὺν αὐτοῖς ἐλάβομεν[34].	β ἐμπρήσαντες τὸν πύργον σὺν αὐτοῖς ἐλάβομεν.

as a rendering of the hiphil of אֱרךְ in Num. ix. 19 and Jos. xxiv. 31, in
the sense of 'to prolong' in the latter passage.   A = ἐφείλκυσαν τὸν
πόλεμον. This suggests the idea that as ἐφελκύσθησαν = ארכו, the latter
may be corrupt for ערכו, which with or without מלחמה = 'set themselves
in array'—a phrase which occurs several times in the Midr. Wajjis but
not exactly in this place.   [19] α, af. bdeg read ἐφ'.   [20] b reads λαθραῖοι.
[21] b om. For ἑκατέρων S¹ reads πάντων.   [22] d reads ἀνέβησαν τὸ τεῖχος.
S¹ om. τῷ τείχει.   [23] α reads ἦλθον.   [24] g trs. before ἀγν. a om.   [25] So
A^abcdefg. A^b = καὶ οἱ ἄλλοι (ԵՒ այլ). A^b* = δέ.   [26] A^b adds ἐν τῷ τείχει.
[27] A^abb. Cf. α. A^b*cdefg = εἰσῆλθον.   [28] h. c reads κατελάβομεν. β καὶ
ἐλάβομεν.   [29] d reads τοὺς δέ.   [30] β. α reads τοῖς πύργοις. S¹ om.
[31] α. β reads ἐμπρήσαντες (bdf ἐμπρίσαντες) τὸν πύργον σὺν αὐτοῖς ἐλάβομεν
(+ πάντας f). S¹ reads ἐνεπρήσαμεν only.   [32] An error for πύργῳ.   [33] A
dittographic rendering.   [34] So A^bbefg, save that A^bb add καί before ἐλάβομεν. The Armenian text (note 4, p. 80) wrongly omits ԵՒ առար (= καὶ
ἐλάβομεν) after ՇՆբող in giving text of A^b. The ԵՒ is here an intrusion.
The same mistake is made with regard to A^acd in the same note. A^b* is
corrupt.   [35] Better form preserved in β.   [36] α, e.   [37] h reads εἰδότες.
[38] e. b reads Θαφφού. adf Θαφονέ. g Θαμβού. A^abcdes Θεωκίων. A^b* Θωκίων.
[39] bg. a om. df, A read ἐπέβαλον ἐπὶ (εἰς f) τὴν αἰχ. (+ τοῦ ἀφελέσθαι αὐτὴν
ἐξ d) ἡμῶν. e = α.   [40] A adds ἡμεῖς. Aβ om. next five words.   [41] b reads

<table>
<tr><td>

α

6. Ἐν δὲ τῷ ἀπιέναι ἡμᾶς, ἄνδρες †Βαθουὲ[35] ἐπελάβοντο[36] τὴν αἰχμαλωσίαν ἡμῶν καὶ ἰδόντες[37] ἡμεῖς συνήψαμεν πόλεμον μετ' αὐτῶν. 7. Καὶ ἀπεκτείναμεν πάντας καὶ πάλιν ἐλάβομεν τὴν αἰχμαλωσίαν ἡμῶν.

</td><td>

β, Α, S[1]

6. Καὶ ἐν τῷ ἀπιέναι ἡμᾶς, ἄνδρες Θαφφουὲ[38] *ἐπέβαλον τῇ αἰχμαλωσίᾳ ἡμῶν[39] καὶ[40] παραδόντες[41] αὐτὴν[42] τοῖς υἱοῖς ἡμῶν συνήψαμεν *πρὸς αὐτοὺς[43] ἕως[44] Θαφφουέ[45]. 7. *Κἀκείνους ἀπεκτείναμεν[46] καὶ τὴν πόλιν[47] ἐνεπρήσαμεν[48], καὶ[49] πάντα τὰ *ἐν αὐτῇ[50] ἐσκυλεύσαμεν[51].

</td></tr>
</table>

α om. vers. 1-2.   VI. Καὶ ὡς ἤμην ἐν τοῖς ὕδασι Χωζηβά[1], οἱ ἀπὸ †Ἰωβὴλ[2] ΑΒ om. ver. 1. ἦλθον ἐφ'[3] ἡμᾶς εἰς πόλεμον.   2. Καὶ *συνάψαντες ἐτρέψαμεν[4] αὐτοὺς[5] ⌐καὶ τοὺς ἀπὸ Σιλὼμ συμμάχους αὐτῶν ἀπεκτείναμεν⌐[6] καὶ οὐκ ἐδώκαμεν ⌐αὐτοῖς⌐[7] διέξοδον[8] *τοῦ

παραλαβόντες.   [42]Α = τὴν αἰχμαλωσίαν. b adds σύν.   [43]e reads πρὸς ἑαυτούς and trs. before συνήψαμεν.   [44]beg, A, S[1]. af read ἐν τῷ. d ἐν. [45]eg. b reads Θαφφού. adf Θαφονέ. Α = Θαφού.   [46]Α[bheg]. Α[acd] = ἀπεκτ. ἐκείνους, but not A[b] as Armenian text represents. d adds πάντας.   [47]d, A[b*] add αὐτῶν.   [48]a reads ἐμπρήσαντες.   [49]f, A. β-f om.   [50]β. Α[b*] = αὐτῶν.   [51]aef. bdg, S[1] read σκυλεύσαντες. Α = εἰς αἰχμαλωσίαν ἀπηγάγομεν.

VI. [1]e. a reads Χωζιβά. bd, S[1] Χουζηβά. f Χοζιβά. g Χοζηβά. Α[ah] = Χουζιφά. Α[b] Χουζιβά. This town is probably the מֹכֵבָא mentioned in 1 Chron. iv. 22 as belonging to the descendants of Shelah, son of Judah, and named כְזִיב in Gen. xxxviii. 5. Chron. Jerach. xxxvi. 8 speaks of the 'waters of יֶשׁוֹב, north of Tappuah.' The name here is corrupt but the position assigned to it, 'north of Tappuah,' is right if we may identify it with 'Ain el Kezbeh' (Encyc. Bib., i. 37, 38).   [2]b corrupt possibly for Ἀρβήλ or Ἀρβαήλ. The inhabitants of this town were destroyed by the sons of Jacob at this time according to the Book of Jashar (op. cit., ii. 1178). af, S[1] read Ἰώ. dg Ἰωήλ. e Ἰβήν. Α[a] gives Ἰωιλαταί as equivalent of οἱ ἀπὸ Ἰ.   [3]bdeg. af read πρός.   [4]b reads συνήψαμεν. Α = συνάψαντες πρὸς αὐτοὺς ἐτρέψαμεν.   [5]af add κἀκείνους ἀπεκτείναμεν.   [6]β-f (save that a reads Σολών, b Σηλώμ, e Σιλών, instead of Σιλώμ, and d reads αὐτούς instead of αὐτῶν). f, A om. entire clause. This reference, however, to the people of Shilo is found also in Chron. Jerach., xxxvi. 8. See also III. 7 above.   [7]g reads αὐτῶν. A om. [8]g reads διεξόδοις.   [9]e reads πρὸς ἡμᾶς ἐλθεῖν.   [10]α. adefg, ΑΒ read καὶ οἱ. b καί. The words οἱ δὲ ... ἡμέρᾳ appear in d as follows: τῇ δὲ ε΄ ἡμέρᾳ ἐπῆλθον ἡμῖν καὶ οἱ ἀπὸ Μεχὴρ βουλόμενοι.   [11]g reads ἐπί.   [12]c,

εἰσελθεῖν πρὸς ἡμᾶς[9].　　　3. *Οἱ δὲ πάλιν[10] ἀπὸ[11] Μαχὴρ[12]
ἐπῆλθον[13] ἡμῖν τῇ πέμπτῃ ἡμέρᾳ[14], καὶ[15] προσάξαντες πρὸς
αὐτοὺς[16] *ἐν κραταιᾷ μαχαίρᾳ[17] περιεγενόμεθα αὐτῶν[18] καὶ
ἀπεκτείναμεν *καὶ αὐτοὺς[19] πρὸ τοῦ ἀναβῆναι τὴν ἀνάβασιν[20].
4. Ὡς δὲ ἤκομεν[21] ἐν[22] τῇ πόλει[23], αἱ γυναῖκες αὐτῶν ἐκύλιον
*λίθους ἐφ' ἡμᾶς[24] ἀπὸ τῆς κορυφῆς τοῦ ὄρους ἐν ᾧ[25] *ἦν
ἡ πόλις[26].　　　5. Καὶ ὑποκρύψας[27] ἐγώ τε καὶ Συμεὼν
ἐξόπισθεν[28] ἐπελαβόμεθα[29] τῶν ὑψηλῶν, καὶ *ἐξολοθρεύσαμεν
καὶ ταύτην τὴν πολιν[30].

VII. Καὶ τῇ ἐξῆς ἐρρέθη πρὸς ἡμᾶς ὅτι *Γαὰς πόλεως ὁ
βασιλεὺς ἐν λαῷ πολλῷ[1] ἔρχεται[2] πρὸς ἡμᾶς.

Margin: β–b, Αβ καὶ οἱ. β, Α, S¹ ἡμέρᾳ λαβεῖν τὴν αἰχμαλωσίαν. β–df, Α, S¹ καρτερᾷ μάχῃ περιεγ. ὅτι ἦσαν πλῆθος δυναστῶν

ἐν αὐτοῖς.　β, Α, S¹ ὅλην τ. πόλιν ὠλοθρεύσαμεν.

dg. ab read Μεχίρ (Μαχίρ b). h, ef read Μεχείρ. In Jub. xxxvi. 2, 4
I have taken this word to be a compression of Μαχανιπακιρ, which is
actually found in Jub. xxxiv. 2. This latter form is an inversion of
Σακιρμαχανι, in other words, Shakir of Machanaim, as in Chron. Jerach.,
xxxvi. 8 ; Book of Jashar, ii. 1174.　　　[13] c reads ἀπῆλθων.　　　[14] α. β, S¹
add as in margin (save that g reads ἐχεβρών for αἰχμαλωσίαν).　d, Α = λ.
τὴν αἰχ. ἡμῶν (d om.) ἀφ' ἡμῶν.　　　[15] a om. next six words.　　　[16] α. bef
read αὐτοῖς.　dg αὐτούς.　　　[17] α, f. bg, S¹ read ἐν καρτερᾷ (g κρατερᾷ) μάχη.
d ἐν κραταιᾷ χειρὶ καὶ δυνάμει μετὰ μαχαίρας. e, Α καρτερὰν μάχην. d adds μετὰ
μαχαίρας.　　　[18] α, f, Αᵇ*. a reads καὶ αὐτῶν. β–af, Αᵃᵇᶜᵈ om.　β, Α, S¹
add ὅτι ἦσαν πλῆθος δυναστῶν (b, S¹ δυνατοὶ, d δυναστὸν, g δυνατὸν) ἐν αὐτοῖς.
[19] α. β, S¹ read αὐτούς.　Α = πολλὰ πλήθη.　　　[20] Α = ἡμᾶς τὰ ὑψηλά.　d
adds τοῦ ἡλίου.　　　[21] α, ag. ef read ἤκαμεν. bd ἤλθομεν.　　　[22] b om.　　　[23] α.
β, Α, S¹ read πόλει αὐτῶν.　　　[24] h, def. c reads λίθον ἐφ' ἡμᾶς. abg, Α, S¹
ἐφ' ἡμᾶς λίθους.　　　[25] α, e. β–e read ᾗ.　　　[26] g adds αὐτῶν. d reads ἡ πόλις
αὐτῶν.　　　[27] c, af. h reads ἀποκρύψας. bdg ὑποκρυβέντες. e ἀποκρυβέντες.
[28] Α adds τῆς πόλεως.　　　[29] be read ἐπιλαβόμεθα.　Α = ἀνήλθομεν.　　　[30] α
(save that h reads ὀλοθρεύσαμεν).　β, Α, S¹ read καὶ ὅλην τὴν πόλιν ὠλοθρεύσαμεν (bef ὀλοθρ. dg ἐξολοθρ.).

VII.　[1] α (save that h reads βαρεῖ for πολλῷ). aej read Γαὰς (+ ἡ e)
πόλις βασιλέων ἐν ὄχλῳ βαρεῖ. d agrees in substance with α and reads
ὁ βασιλεὺς τῆς πόλεως Γᾶς ἐν ὄχλῳ βαρύ (sic). b, S¹ αἱ πόλεις τῶν δύο βασιλέων
ἐν ὄ. β. g Ῥαγαὰς πόλεως βασιλέως ἐν ὄ. β.　Α = Γᾶς πόλις σὺν βασιλεῖ
δυνατῷ.　　　[2] b reads ἔρχονται.　　　[3] β–e, Α, S¹ (save that g reads γοῦν for οὖν).
α reads δὲ καὶ ὁ Γάδ (h Δάν). e is conflate, οὖν καὶ Γάδ.　　　[4] β–d (save
that e reads συμμάχην and g συμμάχους). d reads προσποιησάμενοι ἑαυτοὺς
Ἀμορραίους ὑπάρχειν καὶ ἕνεκεν τοῦ συμμαχῆσαι αὐτούς· ἡμᾶς. Α = προσποιησάμεθα ὡς Ἀμορρ. (Αᵇ προσποιησάμενοι ὡς Ἀ.　Αᵃ προφάσει) (+ καὶ ἐσχηματισάμεθα σύμμαχοι εἶναι αὐτῶν Αᵇ*).　　　[5] dg. e reads εἰσήλθαμεν. abf ἤλθομεν.

α

2. Ἐγὼ δὲ καὶ ὁ Γὰδ πορευ-
θέντες πρὸς Ἀμορραίους καὶ
προσποιησάμενοι αὐτοῖς συμμάχους εἰσήλθομεν εἰς τὴν
πόλιν αὐτῶν.

3. *Νυκτὸς δὲ βαθείας[7] ἦλθον
δὲ[8] καὶ πάντες οἱ ἀδελφοί μου,
καὶ ἀνοίξαντες τὰς πύλας αὐτοῖς, πάντας αὐτοὺς ἐξολοθρεύσαμεν[9] καὶ ἐπροενομεύ-
σαμεν[10].

β, A, S¹

2. Ἐγὼ *οὖν καὶ Δὰν[3] *προσποιησάμενοι Ἀμορραίους ὡς
σύμμαχοι[4] εἰσήλθομεν[5] εἰς τὴν
πόλιν αὐτῶν[6].

3. Νυκτὶ δὲ βαθείᾳ *ἐλθόντων τῶν ἀδελφῶν ἡμῶν[11]
ἠνοίξαμεν τὰς πύλας[12] αὐτοῖς[13] καὶ πάντας αὐτοὺς *καὶ
τὰ αὐτῶν[14] ὀλοθρεύσαμεν[15]
καὶ *πάντα τὰ[16] αὐτῶν προ-
νομεύσαντες[17] τὰ[18] τρία τείχη
αὐτῶν καθείλαμεν[19].

β, A, S¹
καὶ ἐν τῇ
Θάμνᾳ
προσεγ-
γίσαμεν.
β–d, A
τῶν πολε-
μίων βα-
σιλέων.

4. *Καὶ ἐπροσεγγίσαμεν τῇ Θάμνᾳ[20], *ἐν ᾧ[21] ἦν πᾶσα ἡ
ἀποσκευὴ[22] αὐτῶν[23]. 5. *Τότε οὖν ὑβριζόμενος παρ'
αὐτῶν ὠργίσθην[24], *καὶ ὥρμησα[25] *ἐπ' αὐτοὺς ἐπὶ τὴν
†κορυφήν[26]. κἀκεῖνοι *ἐσφενδόνιζόν με ἐν λίθοις[27] *καὶ
τόξοις[28]. 6. Καὶ εἰ μὴ Δὰν ὁ ἀδελφός μου συνεμάχησέν

d adds σὺν τῷ λαῷ αὐτῶν.   [6]A om.   [7]c. *h* reads νυκτὶ βαθείᾳ.   [8]h om.
[9]*h* reads καὶ τὰ αὐτῶν ὀλοθρεύσαμεν.   [10]*h* reads ἐπρονομεύσαμεν.   [11]*adef.*
bg read ἐλθοῦσι τοῖς ἀδελφοῖς. For ἐλθόντων . . . πύλας αὐτοῖς A gives
ἀναστάντες ἠνοίξαμεν τοῖς ἡμετέροις ἀδελφοῖς τὰς πύλας.   [12]*d* reads πόρτας.
g om. next eight words.   [13]*ae²f. bde²g* om.   [14]*d* om. *e* om. next five
words through hmt.   [15]*a* reads ὠλοθρεύσαμεν.   [16]*d*, A read τὰ ὑπάρ-
χοντα. *e* τά.   [17]*abdf. e*, A read ἐπρονομεύσομεν. *g* παρανομήσαντες. *e*, A
add καί.   [18]*deg* om.   [19]*aefg. b* reads καθείλομεν. *d* καθείλωμεν.   [20]α
(save that for ἐπροσεγγ. *h* reads προσεγγ.). β–d, A, S¹ read καὶ ἐν τῇ Θάμνᾳ
προσεγγίσιμεν (*ab* προσηγγ.). *d* διερχόμενοι δὲ διὰ τῆς Θάμμα προσηγγίσαμεν.
[21]α. β–g read οὗ. *g* ὅπου. A ἥ.   [22]*bg* read ἀποφυγή. A = ἄρξ.   [23]α.
β, A read τῶν πολεμίων βασιλέων (*d* om.). S¹ εἰς πόλεμον.   [24]α, *de* (save that
c reads ὀργίσθην and *de* om. οὖν and read ἐθυμώθην for ὠργ.). *abfg*, S¹ read
τότε ὑβριζόμενος ὠργίσθην (*bg* ἐθυμώθην. *f* ὀργίσθην). A^abcdeg = καὶ ὑβριζόμενοι
τότε παρ' αὐτῶν καὶ θυμούμενοι.   [25]*c, ef* read καὶ ὥρμησα. A = ὡρμήσαμεν.
[26]*c, β–f. f* reads πρὸς αὐτοὺς ἐπὶ τ. κορυφήν. *h* ἐπὶ τ. κ. πρὸς αὐτούς. A ἐπ'
αὐτοὺς ἕως ἦλθον ἐπὶ τ. κορυφήν. *g*, A add τοῦ ὄρους. Since the Midr.
Wajjis has ועלה ראשׁון לחומה · · · קפץ, it is possible that as our text =
קפצתי עליהם לראשׁ, the two last words are corrupt for על חומה ראשׁון and
that we should read therefore ὥρμησα (or ἀνεπήδησα) πρῶτος ἐπὶ τὸ τεῖχος.
[27]α, *af* (save that *af* om. με). *b* reads ἐσφενδόνουν ἐπ' ἐμὲ λίθοις. *deg* σφεν-
δονοῦντες (*e* σφενδονήσαντες) ἦσαν (*g* om.) ἐπ' ἐμὲ λίθοις (*e* λίθους).   [28]*e* om.

μ∈[29], *εἶχόν με ἀνελεῖν[30].   7. *Ἀπήλθομεν οὖν[31] *ἐπ' αὐτοὺς μετὰ θυμοῦ[32] καὶ *πάντες ἔφυγον[33], καὶ *ἀπελθόντες δι' ἄλλης ὁδοῦ πρὸς τὸν πατέρα ἡμῶν ἐδεήθησαν αὐτῷ[34] καὶ ἐποίησαν[35] εἰρήνην μετ' αὐτοῦ[36].   8. Καὶ οὐκ ἐποιήσαμεν[37] αὐτοῖς οὐδὲν[38] κακόν, ἀλλ'[39] *εἴχομεν αὐτοὺς ὑποφόρους[40], *καὶ ἀπεδώκαμεν[41] αὐτοῖς[42] τὴν αἰχμαλωσίαν[43] αὐτῶν[44].

α	β, A, S¹
9. Οἰκοδομήσαμεν δὲ καὶ τὴν πόλιν αὐτῶν.	9. *Καὶ οἰκοδόμησα ἐγὼ τὴν Θάμναν καὶ ὁ πατήρ μου τὴν †Ῥαβαήλ[45].

10. *Ἤμην δὲ ἐγὼ χρόνων εἴκοσι[46], ὅτε ἐγένετο[47] ὁ πόλεμος οὗτος[48].   11. Καὶ ἦσαν οἱ Χαναναῖοι φοβούμενοι *καὶ ἐμὲ[49] καὶ *τοὺς ἀδελφούς[50] μου[51].

VIII. *Ἦσαν δέ μοι[1] κτήνη πολλά, καὶ *εἶχον ἀρχιποί-μενα[2] Ἰερὰμ[3] τὸν Ὀδολομήτην[4].   2. *Πρὸς ὃν ἐλθὼν εἶδον[5] Βαρσαβὰ[6] τὸν[7] βασιλέα[8] Ὀδολάμ[9]· ⌐καὶ ἐλάλησεν ὑμῖν⌐[10].

Marginal column (β, A, S¹): β–d, A, S¹ διελθόντες δ. ά. ὁδοῦ ἐδεήθησαν τοῦ πατρός μου. β–af, S¹ ἐποίησεν. β–a, A, S¹ αὐτῶν. β, A, S¹ ἐποιήσαμεν αὐτοὺς ὑποσπόνδους. α δὲ ἐλθὼν πρός.

A = καὶ τόξα ἐτόξευον ἐπ' ἐμέ.   [29] α. β reads μοι.   [30] α, β–e. e reads ἔμελλόν με ἀνελεῖν. A = ἔχειν (A^{b*} ἐκεῖνοι λαβόντες) ἀνεῖλόν με. These words are found in Chron. Jerach., xxxvi. 11 היו הורגין את יהודה.   [31] c, g. β–dfg, A read ἐπήλθομεν οὖν. h ἐπῆλθ. δέ. d ἀνέβημεν. f, S¹ ἐπῆλθον οὖν.   [32] a reads ἐπ' αὐτούς. d πρὸς αὐτ. μ. θυμοῦ. g μ. θυμοῦ ἐπ' αὐτούς.   [33] A = ἐφυγαδεύσαμεν αὐτούς.   [34] α. β–d, A, S¹ read διελθόντες δι' ἄλλης ὁδοῦ (a δι' ἄλλης ὁ. ἐλθόντες. e διελθόντες) ἐδεήθησαν τοῦ πατρός μου (b om. A = ἡμῶν). d διελ. δι' ἄλλης ὁδοῦ ἀπῆλθον πρὸς Ἰακὼβ τὸν πατέρα ἡμῶν δεόμενοι.   [35] α, af. bdeg, S¹ read ἐποίησεν. A = ἐποιήσαμεν.   [36] α, a. β–a, A, S¹ read αὐτῶν.   [37] A = ἐγένετο.   [38] beg read οὐθέν.   [39] d adds μᾶλλον.   [40] α. Cf. Midr. Wajjis נתנו להם מס. β–d, S¹ give a different text, ἐποιήσαμεν αὐτοὺς ὑποσπόνδους (e ἐπισπόνδους). d ὑποσπόνδους αὐ. ἐποιήσαμεν. A = σπονδὰς ἐποιήσαμεν πρὸς αὐτούς. With the latter text cf. Book of Jashar (1689, fol. 79[b]) ויכרתו להם ברית שלום. and וישימום בני יעקב ברית שלום.   [41] g reads δόντες.   [42] β, S¹ add πᾶσαν against α, A.   [43] g reads ἐχεβρών. A = αἰχμαλώτους.   [44] α, d, A. β–d, S¹ om.   [45] β–d, S¹ (save that for Θάμναν of aefg, b reads Θάμνα, and for Ῥαβαήλ of aef, S¹, b reads Ῥαμβαήλ and g Ῥοβαήλ). d, A read Τότε (A = καὶ μετὰ τοῦτο) οἰκοδόμησα (A^{ab} ἐμνημόνευσα by internal corruption) ἐγὼ τ. (+πόλιν d) Θάμνας (A Θάμνα) καὶ ὁ. π. μου τὴν Ῥαβήλ (A Ῥαφαήλ).   [46] α, β–d, A read εἴκοσι ἐτῶν ἤμην. d ἤμην δὲ τότε κ' ἐτῶν.   [47] dg read γέγονεν.   [48] d reads καὶ εἰρηνεύσαμεν.   [49] c. h reads καὶ ἐμοί. β με.   [50] h reads in dat.   [51] d adds σφόδρα.

VIII. [1] α. β, A, S¹ read ἦν δέ (A om.) μοι (+καί abf, A^b, S¹).   [2] A = ἦν ὄνομα τοῦ ἀρχιποίμενος μου.   [3] α, aef. b reads Ἰράν. dg Ἡράν. A^{abhc} = Ἰράς. A^{b*dee} Ἰράμ.   [4] α, abg. d reads Ὀδωλλαμίτην. ef Ὀδολαμήτην.

β-bd
Βισσουέ.
β, A, S¹
ἔζησεν
καὶ τὰ
τέκνα
αὐτοῦ
ὑμεῖς
ἐστέ.
β, A, S¹
ἐτῶν ἐν
τῷ τεσ-
σαρα-
κοστῷ
ἔτει ζωῆς
μου.

καὶ[11] ἐποίησεν ἡμῖν πότον[12]· καὶ †παρακαλέσας[13] δέδωκέ[14] μοι τὴν θυγατέρα αὐτοῦ[15] *ὀνόματι Σαβά[16] εἰς γυναῖκα. 3. Αὐτὴ[17] ἔτεκέν μοι τὸν Ἠρ[18] καὶ τὸν[19] Αὐνὰν καὶ τὸν[20] Σηλώμ[21]. *Καὶ τοὺς μὲν δύο[22] ἀνεῖλεν[23] Κύριος· ὁ γὰρ Σηλὼμ[24] ἔζησεν[25].

IX. *Δέκα καὶ ὀκτὼ[1] *ἔτη ἐποίησεν δὲ[2] εἰρήνην[3] ὁ[4] πατήρ μου[5] μετὰ τοῦ ἀδελφοῦ αὐτοῦ Ἡσαῦ[6], καὶ οἱ[7] υἱοὶ αὐτοῦ μεθ' ἡμῶν μετὰ[8] τὸ ἐλθεῖν ἡμᾶς ἀπὸ[9] *Μεσοποταμίας ἀπὸ Λαβάν[10]. 2. Καὶ πληρωθέντων τῶν[11] δεκαοκτὼ ἐτῶν[12] ἐπανῆλθεν[13] ἡμῖν Ἡσαῦ ὁ ἀδελφὸς τοῦ πατρός μου[14] ἐν λαῷ βαρεῖ[15] καὶ ἰσχυρῷ. 3. Καὶ *ἔπαισεν ἐν τόξῳ Ἰακὼβ τὸν Ἡσαῦ[16], καὶ[17] ἤρθη[18]

β-adf, A, S¹ ἔπεσεν ἐν τόξῳ Ἰακώβ.

---

[5] β-dg, A, S¹. dg read πρὸς ὃν ἐλθὼν (g om. καὶ) ἰδών με (g om.). α reads as in margin. [6] α, aef. bd read Βαρσάν. g, A Βαρσά. [7] α. β om. [8] dy read βασιλεύς. [9] d reads Ὀδολλάμ. A = Ὀδυλομάτων. [10] c. h reads ἐλάλησεν αὐτόν. β, A om. Perhaps we should read καὶ ἐκάλεσεν ἡμᾶς. [11] d om. [12] g reads τόπον. h adds ὁ βασιλεύς. [13] A adds με. παρακαλέσας has no intelligible meaning here. It = מכחם corrupt (?) for בחמי, 'when I was heated,' i. e. by wine, or ביחמי, 'when I was hot with desire.' Cf. XI. 2, XIII. 5-7. For the same corruption cf. LXX on Is. lvii. 5. [14] α, g. β-e, S¹ read δίδωσι(ν). e δίδουσιν. A = ἐδίδου. [15] a om. [16] α. af read Βισσουέ. b Βησσούς. d Βοσεέ (which it trs. before τὴν θυγ.). e τὴν Βησουέ. g Βισουέ. A = Βερσουέ. These are all corruptions of בת-שוע. See my note on Jub. xxxiv. 20. [17] d reads καὶ συλλαβοῦσα. A = καὶ αὐτή. [18] β-a, A. α, a read Εἴρ. [19] bd om. [20] abefg om. [21] c, ag, Aᵇ*. h, β-ag read Σιλώμ. Aᵃᵇ Συλαμών. [22] α, A. abdfg read ὧν τοὺς δύο (+Ἠρ καὶ Αὐνάν d). e υἱς τοὺς δύο. bde, A, S¹ add ἀτέκνους. [23] h, g add ὁ. [24] c, a, A. h, β-a read Σιλώμ. [25] β, A, S¹ add καὶ τὰ τέκνα αὐτοῦ (a om.) ὑμεῖς ἐστέ (d om. ὑ. ἐ.).

IX. [1] α. β reads δεκαοκτώ. [2] α, af, A, S¹ (save that af, A, S¹ om. δέ). bg read ἔτη ἐποιήσαμεν. d ἐποιήσαμεν ἔτη. e ἔτη ἐποιήσατο. [3] d reads μετὰ τὸ ἐλθεῖν ἡμᾶς ἀπὸ Λαβὰν ἐκ τῆς Μεσοποταμίας ἐν εἰρήνῃ διάγοντες. [4] d adds τε. S¹ om. with next two words. [5] α. d. β-d, A read ἡμῶν. bd add καὶ ἡμεῖς. [6] c reads Ἰσαύ. [7] a om. [8] c adds δέ. [9] c, eg. h, abf read ἐκ. d om. together with next seven words. e adds τῆς. [10] A = Λαβὰν ἐκ Μεσοποταμίας τῶν Συρίων. [11] bg om. [12] β, A, S¹ add ἐγὼ (β-e, A om.) ἐν τῷ (be om.) τεσσαρακοστῷ (+ πέμπτῳ d) ἔτει (+ τῆς ad) ζωῆς μου. [13] α. β-f read ἐπῆλθεν. f ἀνῆλθεν. [14] A = ἡμῶν. [15] c, d read βαρύ. [16] a. So also α, f (save that α inserts ὁ before Ἰακώβ and reads ἐπέπεσεν, and f ἔπεσεν for ἔπαισεν). d also (see below) substantially supports our text. Either ἔπεσεν is simply a corruption of ἔπαισεν or the latter may have

† νεκρὸς [19] ἐν ὄρει Σιείρ [20].   4. * Καὶ ἡμεῖς κατεδιώξαμεν [22] β, S¹
τοὺς υἱοὺς Ἡσαῦ [23], ἦν δὲ * καὶ τούτοις πόλις ὀχυρά [24], καὶ οὐκ Σιείρ, καὶ
ἠδυνήθημεν εἰσελθεῖν ⌐ἐν αὐτῇ⌐ [25]. * περικαθίσαντες δὲ [26] ἐπο- *πορενό-
λιορκοῦμεν αὐτήν [27].   5. Καὶ ὡς οὐκ ἤνοιγον * ἡμῖν μετὰ μενος ἐν
ἡμέρας εἴκοσι [28] ⌐ὁρώντων αὐτῶν⌐ [29] προσάγω [30] κλίμακα [31] καὶ Ἀνονιρὰμ
παραθήσας [32] * τὴν ἀσπίδα ἐπὶ τῆς κεφαλῆς μου [33] καὶ [34] ἀπέθα-
ἀνῆλθον [35] * ἀποδεχόμενος τοὺς λίθους [36] καὶ [37] ἀνεῖλον * τέσσαρας νεν [21].

β, A, S¹ πόλις καὶ τεῖχος

σιδηροῦν καὶ πύλαι χαλκαῖ. α, β-d, S¹ τὴν ἀσπίδα. β, A λίθους ἕως ταλάντων τριῶν καὶ ἀνελθών (A om.).

been only a happy emendation in the Greek, and ἔπεσεν or ἐπέπεσεν may
have been a rendering of הכה which the translator took to be הָכָּה,
whereas he should have read it as הֻכָּה. The Midr. Wajjis and Chron.
Jerach. have here הכה לעשו = 'smote Esau.' Similarly Jub. xxxviii. 2.
Of the other authorities bg, A, S¹ read ἔπεσεν ἐν τόξῳ Ἰακώβ. d ἔπεσε τῷ
Ἡσαῦ ἐν τόξῳ ὁ πατήρ μου Ἰακώβ. e ἔπεσεν τὸ ξύλον. h om. next twelve
words through hmt.   [17] d adds εὐθέως.   [18] e reads ἦλθεν. d adds ὡς.
Aᵇ = ἦραν αὐτόν.   [19] g reads Ἡσαῦ. A^cdeg trs. before ἤρθη. Aᵇ om.
νεκρός = נְבֵלָה which is corrupt for נָחְלָה = τετραυματισμένος. Owing to this
corruption c om. the following clause and A, while preserving it, wrongly
alters it.   In the Midr. Wajjis and Chron. Jerach. ver. 3 appears as:
והכה לעשו . . . . ואו נחלה מן החץ נשאוהו בניו . . . . והלך ומת שם בארודיך
[20] c, bg. a reads Σικάρ. df Σιήρ. e Σιρήχ.   [21] β-bd, S¹ (save that eg read
Ἀνονηράμ). bd read καὶ πορευόμενος ἐπάνω Εἱρραμνά (Ἡράν d) ἀπέθανεν. A =
καὶ πορευομένων αὐτῶν ἐτάφη ἐν Ἀνανιράμ. Cf. Jub. xxxviii. 9. This clause
was omitted by c owing to the corruption pointed out in note 19, and
altered as above in A for the same reason.   [22] c. af read ἡμεῖς δὲ διώξαντες
ἐπί. beg, A ἡμεῖς δὲ ἐδιώξαμεν ἐπί (e ἐπεδιώξαμεν). d ἡμεῖς κατεδ. ἐπί. For τ.
υἱούς following e reads ὀπίσω τῶν υἱῶν.   [23] d reads αὐτοῦ καὶ κατέφυγον εἰς τὴν
πόλιν αὐτῶν.   [24] h. c reads καὶ ἡ τούτων πόλις ἰσχυρά. β-d, A τούτοις πόλις
(A πόλεις (+ ὀχυραὶ Aᵇ*)) καὶ τεῖχος σιδηροῦν (τείχη (+ αὐτῶν Aᵇ*) σιδηρᾶ A)
καὶ πύλαι (+ αὐτῶν A^bheg) χαλκαῖ. d ταύτης τεῖχος ὀχυρὸς καὶ πύλαι χαλκαῖ.
S¹ αὐτοῖς πόλις σιδηρᾶ καὶ πύλαι χαλκαῖ.   [25] α, bd. ef read εἰς αὐτήν. g ἐν
αὐγῇ. a, A om.   [26] af. c, e read περικαθίσαντες δέ. h περικλεισθήσαντες δέ.
b καὶ περικαθίσαντες. dg παρακαθήσαντες τοίνυν (δέ g).   [27] c, A. h, abdf, S¹
read αὐτούς. e ἐπ᾽ αὐτήν. g αὐτῇ.   [28] h. β reads μετὰ ἡμέρας εἴκοσι (εἴκ.
ἡμέρας f). c ἡμῖν ἕως ἡμ. εἴκ. A = ἡμῖν τὰς πύλας μετὰ ἡμ. εἴκ. c, d add
καί.   [29] A om.   [30] d reads προσάγων. A = προσηγάγομεν.   [31] A^bheg
πρὸς τὰ τείχη αὐτῶν. A^ab*cd insert these words before κλίμακα according
to Armenian text.   [32] d, A^abcdeg. Aᵇ* = παραθήσαντες. This participle
is necessary though α, β-d, S¹ om. it.   [33] α, β-dg. d reads ἀσπίδα ἐν τῇ
κεφαλῇ μου. g τ. ἀσπίδα ἐπὶ τ. κεφαλήν μου. A^bheg(scd?) = ἀσπίδα ἐπὶ τῶν
κεφαλῶν ἡμῶν. So also Aᵇ* but that it trs. ἀσπίδα after ἡμῶν.   [34] α,

β, (A), S¹ τῶν δυναστῶν αὐτῶν[38].   6. *Καὶ ὁ[39] Ῥουβὶμ καὶ ὁ[40] Γὰδ
καὶ τῇ
ἑξῆς ἐμ-   ἀνεῖλον ἑτέρους ἔξ[41].   7. Τότε ⌜οὖν⌝[42] αἰτοῦσιν[43] ἡμῖν[44]
βάντες.   τὰ πρὸς εἰρήνην καὶ *γενομένης βουλῆς μετὰ[45] τοῦ πατρὸς
β, A, S¹   ἡμῶν ἐδεξάμεθα αὐτούς[46].   8. Καὶ ἦσαν διδόντες[47] ἡμῖν
αὐτοὺς
ὑποφό-   πυροῦ[48] κόρους[49] πεντακοσίους[50], καὶ[51] ἐλαίου †υφης[52]
ρους.   πεντακοσίους[53], καὶ[54] οἴνου *μέτρα πεντακόσια ⌜ἕως τοῦ λιμοῦ⌝
bde, A   ὅτε[55] κατήλθομεν[56] εἰς Αἴγυπτον.
διακο-
σίους.   β–af, A βέθ.   β, A χίλια πεντακόσια ἕως ὅτε.

β–d, A^bcd. d, A^b*ᵉ om.   [35] A^b* read ἀνήλθομεν ἐπὶ τὸ τεῖχος.   [36] α.
Here the text seems to mean 'sustaining the assault of the stones.' In
this sense we should expect ὑποδεχόμενος, but Polybius (iii. 43. 3, v. 51. 1)
uses ἀποδεχόμενοι in this sense. β, A, S¹ read ἀποδεχόμενος (ὑποδεχόμενος e)
λίθους (+ ἐπὶ τῆς κεφαλῆς μου e; + μεγάλους A^(ᵃ?)b*cdeg, but A^bb om.) ἕως ταλάντων
τριῶν (ὡς τάλαντα τρία e).   [37] β–g, S¹ add ἀνελθών. g εἰσελθών.   [38] c. h reads
τέσ. τοὺς δυνατοὺς αὐτῶν. β τέσ. τοὺς (d om.) δυνατοὺς ἐξ αὐτῶν (e δυνάστας αὐτῶν).
A = αὐτῶν ἄνδρας τέσσαρας δυνατούς.   [39] α (save that h om. ὁ). afg read
καὶ ἑξῆς. bde καὶ τῇ ἑξῆς. A = καὶ μετ᾽ ἐμέ. β–adf, A, S¹ add ἐμβάντες.
d ἐλθόντες. af ἀναβάντες.   [40] α. β om.   [41] b reads ἑξήκοντα.   [42] α. d
reads οἱ λοιποί. β–d, A, S¹ om.   [43] e reads αἰτήσαντες.   [44] c. h reads ἡμῶν.
β ἡμᾶς.   [45] α. β–de read γενόμενοι βουλῆς (cf. 1 Chron. xii. 19). d γενομένου
βουλῆς μετά. e γενομένη βουλή. A^b reads [ɯɫɥɾɫɯɫ ɿɾɯɫ] = αἰτήσαντες
ἱλαροί, where however ɿɾɯɫ is corrupt for ɿɾɯɯ = βουλήν. So I have
just found A^h reads. Thus A^b = αἰτήσαντες βουλήν, a good rendering of G.
The text of A^(ᵃ?)b is not recorded in the Armenian text, but only that
of A^b*cdeg. In these MSS. ɿɾɯɫ is corrected into ɿɯɫ = πρῶτον.
Hence their text = αἰτήσαντες πρῶτον.   [46] α. β–e, A, S¹ add ὑποφόρους.
e ἐπιφόρους.   [47] A adds ἀεί.   [48] d reads σίτου which b adds in margin,
g πυρούς.   [49] h, β–e = כֹּר. c reads κόκκους. e φόρους.   [50] α, f. a reads φ'.
bde, A διακοσίους. g om.   [51] α, A. β–g, S¹ om. g reads σύν.   [52] c.
h reads υφεις, af φεύς. These seem to be corruptions of אֵיפָה, which is
transliterated in the LXX as οἰφί and οἰφεί. But the use of this word
as a measure of liquids is without parallel. We might, however, defend
its use here by appealing to a similar use of סְאָה, which though all but
universally a measure for grain is used in a few instances as a measure
for liquids. See Jer. Targ. on Exod. xxix. 4; Lev. xi. 15, 27 &c. (Levy,
Chaldäisches Wörterbuch, p. 136). It is possible, therefore, to regard βέθ
which is the text of bdeg as a correction. A^abb*cdeg = μέτρον βέθ (sic).
[53] α, ef. abd read φ', g φε'. e om. rest of verse but e² adds ἕως ὅτε κατήλθ.
εἰς Αἰγ. at foot. A^abhcdeg om. next seven words.   [54] α, A^b*. β, S¹ om.
[55] α. abfg, A^b*, S¹ read μέτρα (afg, A^b* om.) χίλια (S¹ om.) πεντακόσια (φ' ag)
ἕως ὅτε (ὅτου a). d reads μέτρα α̅φ̅ καὶ ταῦτα ἐλαμβάνομεν ἐξ αὐτῶν ἕως ὅτου.
[56] g reads ἤλθομεν.

X. *Μετὰ δὲ ταῦτα[1] Ἦρ[2] ὁ υἱός μου ἄγεται τὴν Θαμὰρ ἐκ Μεσοποταμίας θυγατέρα Ἀράμ[3] †ἑαυτῷ εἰς γυναῖκα[4].

β, A, S¹
Ἀράμ.

α

2. Ἦν δὲ ὁ Εἶρ πονηρός, καὶ ἐθανάτωσεν αὐτὸν ἄγγελος Κυρίου. 4. Καὶ ἔδωκα αὐτὴν Αὐνὰν τῷ δευτέρῳ μου υἱῷ, καὶ ἰδοὺ[5] αὐτὸν ἀνεῖλεν ὁ Κύριος. 3. Καὶ αὐτὸς οὐκ ἔγνω αὐτὴν κατὰ πανουργίαν τὴν μητρὸς αὐτοῦ[6].

β, S¹

2. *Ἦν δὲ Ἦρ[7] πονηρός, καὶ †ἠπόρει[8] περὶ τῆς[9] Θαμάρ, ὅτι οὐκ *ἦν ἐκ γῆς[10] Χανάαν· καὶ[11] *ἄγγελος Κυρίου[12] ἀνεῖλεν αὐτὸν τῇ τρίτῃ[13] νυκτί. 3. Καὶ[14] αὐτὸς οὐκ ἔγνω αὐτήν, κατὰ πανουργίαν τῆς μητρὸς αὐτοῦ[15], οὐ γὰρ ἤθελεν *ἔχειν τέκνα[16] ἀπ᾽[17] αὐτῆς. 4. *Ἐν ταῖς ἡμέραις τοῦ θαλάμου[18] *ἐπεγάμβρευσα αὐτῇ τὸν[19] Αὐνάν[20]. Καίγε οὗτος[21] ἐν πονηρίᾳ[22] οὐκ ἔγνω αὐτήν[23], ποιήσας σὺν αὐτῇ ἐνιαυτόν.

A

2. †Ὅς ἦν[24] πονηρός, καὶ ἠπόρει[25] περὶ τῆς Θαμάρ, ὅτι οὐκ ἦν ἐκ Χαναναίων. Καὶ[26] ἄγγελος Κυρίου ἀνεῖλεν αὐτὸν[27] τῇ δευτέρᾳ[28] ἡμέρᾳ[29] 4. τοῦ θαλάμου αὐτοῦ *[καὶ] ἤθελον[30] ἐπιγαμβρεῦσαι αὐτὴν τῷ Αὐνάν· καίγε οὗτος ἐν πονηρίᾳ οὐκ ἔγνω[31] *ποιήσας σὺν αὐτῇ ἐνιαυτόν[32].

X. [1] α, a. bef read μετὰ ταῦτα. dg, A καὶ μετὰ ταῦτα.   [2] c reads Εἶρ.   [3] d reads Ἀρύν, g Ἀράβ.   [4] α. β, A om.   [5] h adds καί.   [6] α om. rest of vers. 3, and 4, 5.   [7] d reads ἦν τε ὁ υἱός μου Ἦρ.   [8] b reads ἠπορεῖτο. Text may be a mistranslation of יצר לתמר, which should have been rendered ἔθλιβε τὴν Θ. or ἤχθραινε τῇ Θ. Cf. Jub. xli. 2 (Er) 'hated and would not lie with her . . . because he wished to take him a wife of the kinsfolk of his mother.'   [9] g reads τήν.   [10] e reads ἔνεγγυς.   [11] d reads διὰ τοῦτο καί.   [12] d reads ὁ ἄγγ. Κυρίου and trs. after αὐτόν.   [13] b adds ἡμέρᾳ τῇ.   [14] S¹ om.   [15] a om. οὐ γὰρ . . . μητρὸς αὐτοῦ (ver. 5) through hmt.   [16] e reads τέκνα ἔχειν.   [17] de read ἐξ.   [18] d reads ἐν ταῖς ἡμ. ἐκείναις τοῦ θαλάμου αὐτῆς επικει . . ου. g om.   [19] d reads ἐπεγ. αὐτὴν τῷ. g ἐπιγαμβρεύσας δὲ καὶ αὐτήν.   [20] S add τὸν δεύτερον υἱόν μου. See reading of α.   [21] g reads καὶ αὐτός.   [22] e reads πανουργίᾳ. d adds ὑπάρχων.   [23] g om. next eight words.   [24] Here Եր (i.e. Ἦρ) has fallen out before Եր (= ἦν).   [25] A[abhb*cd] read [Armenian] (= ἠ'λαβεῖτο) which may be corrupt for [Armenian] = ἠπόρει. A[o*g] [Armenian] = ἐθάρρει.   [26] A[ab*cd] add ὁ.   [27] A[b]

β, A, S¹
γυνή μου
Βησσουέ.
β, A, S¹
οἰνοχοοῦ-
σαν (A,
S¹ om.)
ἐν μέθῃ
οἴνου.
β, S¹
†συνέ-
πεσα
πρὸς
αὐτήν.
A †συν-
έπεσα
πρὸς
βουλὰς
αὐτῆς.

β, A, S¹

5. Καὶ ὅτε³³ ἠπείλησα αὐτῷ³⁴, συνῆλθε μὲν³⁵ αὐτῇ, *διέφθειρε δὲ τὸ σπέρμα³⁶ ἐπὶ³⁷ τὴν γῆν³⁸, κατὰ τὴν ἐντολὴν τῆς μητρὸς αὐτοῦ³⁹· καίγε οὗτος⁴⁰ ἀπέθανεν⁴¹ ἐν πονηρίᾳ⁴².

6. Ἤθελον δὲ *καὶ τὸν Σηλὼμ δοῦναι αὐτῇ⁴³, ἀλλ' ἡ *μήτηρ αὐτοῦ⁴⁴ οὐκ ἀφῆκεν⁴⁵. ⸢ἐπονηρεύσατο γάρ⸣⁴⁶, ὅτι⁴⁷ οὐκ ἦν⁴⁸ ἐκ *τῶν θυγατέρων τῶν Χαναναίων⁴⁹ *ὡς καὶ αὐτή⁵⁰.

XI. Κἀγὼ ᾔδειν¹ ὅτι πονηρὸν² γένος ἦν³ *τῶν Χαναναίων⁴, ἀλλὰ τὸ διαβούλιον⁵ τῆς νεότητος⁶ ἐτύφλωσε *τὴν διάνοιάν μου⁷.   2. Καὶ ἰδὼν⁸ αὐτὴν οἰνοχοοῦσαν⁹ ἠπατήθην, καὶ *†ἔλαβον αὐτὴν μὴ βουλευσαμένου τοῦ πατρός μου¹⁰.   3.

τὸν υἱόν μου Ἤρ.   ²⁸ Here ⲃⲣⳑⲣⲟⲣⲧⲁⲛⲟⳑⲋ = δευτέρα is corrupt for ⲃⲣⲣⲁⲣⲧⲁⲛⲟⳑⲋ = τρίτη.   ²⁹ Cf. b (see note 13) which points to existence of ἡμέρᾳ here. After ἡμέρᾳ A om. ver. 3 and first three words of ver. 4 through hmt.   ³⁰ Aᵇᵉᶠᵍ = ἤθελεν.   ³¹ Aᵇ* = ἤθελεν. Aᵇ add Θαμάρ. ³² So Aᵃʰᶜᵈᵉᶠᵍ (save that these MSS. read ποιῆσαι instead of ποιήσας). Aᵇ = καὶ οὐκ εἰσῆλθεν εἰς αὐτήν.   ³³ d reads γνοὺς ἐγώ.   ³⁴ For ἠπείλησα ... αὐτῇ S¹ reads ἀπηγόρευσα αὐτὸν μὴ συνεῖναι αὐτῇ. d adds τότε.   ³⁵ f om. ³⁶ d reads καὶ διέφθειρεν· τὸ δὲ σπέρμα· g adds αὐτοῦ.   ³⁷ f reads εἰς. ³⁸ d adds ἔρριψεν.   ³⁹ Aᵇ adds Βησσουέ.   ⁴⁰ abeg, A. d, Aᵇ read ἀλλὰ (d om.) καὶ οὗτος, f οὕτως.   ⁴¹ b trs. after πονηρίᾳ.   ⁴² Aᵃᵇ*ᶜᵈᵉᵍ add αὐτοῦ. ⁴³ d reads αὐτὴν δοῦναι καὶ τῷ Σιλὼμ εἰς γυναῖκα. For Σηλώμ of c, e, we find Σιλώμ in h, β–e, Aᵇ*, Σιλαμών in Aᵃᶜᵈ, Ζυλαμών in Aᵇ. Aᵇ, S add τὸν τρίτον υἱόν μου. For αὐτῇ Aᵇ reads Θαμάρ.   ⁴⁴ α. β, A, S read γυνή μου. β–df, S add Βησσουέ, d Βουσεέ, f Βισσουέ, A Βηρσυνέ.   ⁴⁵ de, A add με (+τοῦτο ποιῆσαι d).   ⁴⁶ c, ef. h, abdg, S¹ read ἐπονηρεύετο γάρ (+πρὸς τὴν Θαμάρ bd, S). A om. e adds ἐν Θαμάρ.   ⁴⁷ d reads διότι.   ⁴⁸ Aᵇᵇ* add Θαμάρ. ⁴⁹ α, A. β reads τῶν (abf om.) θυγατέρων Χανάαν.   ⁵⁰ α, aef. bg, Aᵃʰᵇᵇ*, S read ὡς αὐτή. d, Aᶜᵈᵉᶠᵍ om. d om. next two verses (xi. 1, 2).

XI. ¹ β–de. c reads ειδην, h ιδην, e ἴδον.   ² b, A, S¹ add τό.   ³ α, A. β om.   ⁴ α, A. β, S¹ read Χανάαν.   ⁵ a adds τῆς ψυχῆς καί.   ⁶ A, S¹ add μου.   ⁷ α, A (save that c trs. μου before τήν). abefg read τὴν καρδίαν μου (but g trs. μου before τήν).   ⁸ e reads εἰδώς.   ⁹ α. We have three distinct readings. A, S¹ = ἐν μέθῃ (+μου Aᵇ, +οἴνου S¹) = בשתי or במשתה. α reads οἰνοχοοῦσαν = משקה. But as ἠπατήθην (α ἐπατήθην) requires some such expression as ἐν μέθῃ, we might assume that משקה is a corruption of במשתה, or else adopt the reading of β, οἰνοχοοῦσαν ἐν μέθῃ οἴνου, which conjoins α and A. ˙ After ἠπατήθην S¹ adds μεθυσκόμενος. ¹⁰ α. β, S¹, and A read as in margin. How are we to explain these

*Αὐτὴ δὲ[11] *ἀπόντος ἐμοῦ[12] ἐπορεύθη καὶ *ἔλαβε τῷ[13] Σηλώμ[14] γυναῖκα[15] ἐκ *τῆς Χανάαν[16]. 4. Ἐπιγνοὺς[17] β-d γῆς. δὲ ἐγὼ[18] ὃ ἐποίησε κατηρασάμην αὐτὴν[19] ἐν ὀδύνῃ ψυχῆς μου. 5. Καίγε[20] ἀπέθανεν ἐν τῇ[21] πονηρίᾳ[22] αὐτῆς ⌜μετὰ β, A, S¹ τῶν τέκνων αὐτῆς⌝[23]. υἱῶν αὐτῆς.

strange variations? First we shall consider β, S¹ συνέπεσα πρὸς αὐτήν. This peculiar clause recurs again in xiii. 3, 7 ; Test. Jos. ix. 5. So far as I am aware, it is not only quite unexampled but quite impossible in Greek. Nor can it be explained as a corruption native to the Greek. We must therefore have recourse to the Hebrew. Yet the sense of the phrase is obvious from a comparison of the three passages. It denotes a licit or illicit sexual connexion. Now β, S¹ = (בה or) נפלתי עליה:, but this Hebrew cannot yield the needed sense. Hence I conjecture that נפלתי is corrupt for בעלתי, which in later Hebrew has exactly the senses required by the three contexts. Now turning to A, which = συνέπεσα πρὸς βουλὰς αὐτῆς, we observe that it agrees with β, S¹ in attesting the corrupt συνέπεσα, while it approximates to α in πρὸς βουλὰς αὐτοῦ. For, if we compare A and α, we see that A—πρὸς βουλὰς αὐτῆς (בעצתה) and α—μὴ βουλευσαμένου τοῦ πατρός μου point to a common original lost in β, S¹. The Greek of α = 'my father not having counselled (it).' Cp. 2 Sam. xvi. 23. But probably we should read μὴ συμβουλευσάμενος τῷ πατρί μου, as in xiii. 4, = בלא עצת אבי. For phrase, cf. 1 Chr. xii. 19. In xiii. 4, Judah says that he wished to consult his father before taking Bathshua. Since the context does not refer to the machinations of Bathshua, we conclude that α alone is right here. Our author is fond of the phrase. Cf. ix. 7 γενομένης βουλῆς μετὰ τοῦ πατρὸς ἡμῶν. See also reading of d in note 15 below, and also in note 33 on xiv. 6, where it reads ἄνευ βουλῆς τοῦ πατρός μου. Finally, ἔλαβον αὐτήν (= נשאתיה, a phrase denoting marriage) cannot be explained as being derived from or in any way connected with בעלתי, of which נפלתי (i. e. συνέπεσα) is a corruption. α as it stands represents faithfully the original α recension, as is manifest from xiii. 4, where it actually recurs : συμβουλεύσομαι τῷ πατρί μου καὶ οὕτως λήψομαι τὴν θυγατέρα σου. Thus we have here an original divergence between the two recensions. α is truly represented in our text : β (†συνέπεσα πρὸς αὐτήν) when emended = συνεγενόμην αὐτῇ, whilst A borrows partly from β and partly-from α, and from the latter in a corrupt form. [11] α, fg. abe read αὐτή, d καί. [12] α. β reads ἀπόντος μου (d om.). A^b trs. to end of sentence. [13] α, ade. b reads ἐλάβετο, fg ἔλαβεν τόν. [14] α, e. β–e Σιλώμ. [15] f reads ἄνδρα. d adds χώρις βουλή μου (sic). [16] α. β–d, S¹ read γῆς X., d, A τῶν Χαναναίων. [17] α. β reads γνούς. [18] α, deg, A. abf om. [19] α, dfg. a reads αὐτῆς,

β-d, A, S[1]
τοὺς
λόγους
τούτους.
β, A, S[1]
πύλην
β, S[1] γαμ-
οῦσαν.
β, A, S
πορνείᾳ
ἑπτὰ
ἡμέρας
παρὰ τὴν
πύλην.
β-de, A,
S[1] ἐν
ὕδασι

XII. *Μετὰ δὲ ταῦτα[1] *χηρευούσης τῆς[2] Θαμάρ[3] *μετὰ
ἔτη δύο[4] ἀκούσασα ὅτι ἀνέρχομαι[5] τοῦ[6] κεῖραι[7] τὰ πρόβατα[8],
κοσμηθεῖσα κόσμῳ νυμφικῷ, ἐκάθισεν[9] *ἐν Ἐνὰν[10] *τῇ
πόλει[11] *πρὸς τὴν πύλην[12] ⌜τοῦ πανδοχείου[13].   2. Νόμος
γὰρ *ἦν τῶν[14] Ἀμορραίων[15] τὴν †χηρεύουσαν[16] προκαθέζεσθαι[17]
ἐν[18] πορνείᾳ[19]⌝.   3. Μεθυσθεὶς οὖν ἐγὼ ἐν[20] οἴνῳ[21] οὐκ
ἐπέγνων[22] αὐτήν[23], καὶ ἠπάτησέ[24] με τὸ κάλλος αὐτῆς διὰ
τοῦ σχήματος[25] τῆς κοσμήσεως.   4. Καὶ ἐκκλίνας[26] πρὸς
αὐτὴν εἶπον[27]· Εἰσέρχομαι[28] πρός σε· καὶ[29] εἶπεν[30] ⌜Καὶ⌝[31]
τί μοι δώσεις[32]; καὶ δέδωκα[33] αὐτῇ τὴν ῥάβδον μου καὶ
†τὸ δακτύλιον[34] καὶ τὸ[35] διάδημα[36] τῆς βασιλείας μου[37]
⌜εἰς ἀρραβῶνα⌝[38].   Καὶ *ὡς συνῆλθον[39] αὐτῇ συνείληφεν[40].

(οἴνῳ f, Aᵇ) Χωζὴβ οὐκ ἐπέγνων αὐτὴν ἀπὸ τοῦ οἴνου.   β, A, S[1] εἰσέλθω.   β, A, S τὴν ζώνην.

be αὐτῇ.   [20] α. β-g, A add αὐτή.   g om. with rest of verse.   [21] α. β,
A om.   [22] β-e, A, S[1] add υἱῶν, e υἱοῦ.   [23] α. β, A, S[1] om.

XII. [1] α, d. β-d, A read μετὰ δὲ (A καὶ ἐγένετο μετὰ) τοὺς λόγους τούτους.
[2] α, β-eg, Aᵃʰᵇ*ᶜᵈᵉᶠᵍ. eg, Aᵇ read χηρεύουσα ἦν (ἡ g).   [3] e², A add καί.
[4] α (but h reads ἐπί for μετά). abfg read μ. δύο ἔτη, d ἐπὶ δύο ἔτη, e καὶ μετὰ
τρία ἔτη.   [5] h reads ἔρχομαι.   [6] α. β om.   [7] c, def read κῆραι.   [8] e adds
εν εν αν τῇ πόλει πρὸς τῇ πύλῃ νόμος γάρ. A add μου. g om. the next three
words.   [9] A prefixes καί, and for ἐν Ἐνὰν ... πανδοχείου reads πρὸς τὴν
πύλην ἐν μέσῃ τῇ πόλει. g ἐκάθησεν and trs. after πόλει.   [10] c, e. This is
Enaim (עינים) mentioned in Gen. xxxviii. 14, where the LXX has Αἰνάν.
g reads εννεα ανα, h, a ἔναντι, bd, S[1] ἀπέναντι, f εν.   [11] d reads τῆς πόλεως.
g om. h adds τῶν Ἀμορραίων.   [12] α, bd. aefg reads παρὰ (πρὸς efg) τῇ
πύλῃ.   [13] α. β, A. om. A om. next verse through hmt.   [14] α. β om.
[15] dg read Ἀμορραίοις.   [16] α. β, S[1] read as in margin and rightly.   [17] α, a.
bdg read προκαθίσαι, ef προκάθεσθαι.   [18] d adds τῇ.   [19] α. β (save that
d reads ἡμέρας ἑπτά, and aefg τῇ πύλῃ), A, S[1] read as in margin.   [20] d reads
ἐξ. h om.   [21] α. d reads οἴνου, f, Aᵇ οἴνῳ Χοζιβά (Χουζιιβ Aᵇ). β-df,
Aᵃʰᵇ*ᶜᵈᵉᶠᵍ, S[1] ὕδασι Χωζηβά (Χωζιβά a, Χωζήβ b, Χοζή g, Χουζζάβ Aᵃᵇ*ᶜᵈᵉᶠᵍ).
d om. next three words and inserts διό.   [22] c reads ἐπέγνω, f ἔγνων, A
ἐδυνήθην ἐπιγνῶναι.   [23] Aᵇ = Θαμάρ. Here β, A, S add ἀπὸ τοῦ οἴνου.
[24] h, A read ἐπάτησε.   [25] Aᵇ*ᵈ = κάλλους.   [26] ad read ἔκλινα.   [27] ad
read εἰπών.   [28] α. β, A, S[1] read εἰσέλθω.   [29] h, A read ἡ δέ.   [30] bd,
S[1] add μοι.   [31] α. β, A, S[1] om.   [32] Aᵃᵇ = θέλεις δοῦναι.   [33] α. β reads
ἔδωκα.   [34] α = חֹתָם. But β, A, S[1] read τὴν ζώνην = פָּתִיל. The latter
is right. Cf. xv. 3.   [35] g om.   [36] = בֶּגֶד or כֶּתֶר. It is unknown to
Jub. xli. 11, 18, where the same account is given as in Gen. xxxviii. 18.
[37] α, A. β om.   [38] α. β, A, S[1] om.   [39] c, adef, Aᵃʰᶜᵉᶠ, S[1]. h reads ὡς
ἦλθον, b συνελθών, g, Aᵇ*ᵇᵈ συνῆλθον.   [40] α, β-dg, Aᵇᵉᶠ. d reads παραχρῆμα

5. Ἀγνοῶν δὲ ἐγὼ⁴¹ ὃ ἐποίησα⁴², *ἤθελον ἀνελεῖν αὐτήν⁴³. ᵃἔπεμψα
*πέμψασα δὲ ἐν κρυπτῷ τοὺς ἀρραβῶνας κατῇσχυνέ με⁴⁴. τοῦ
6. *Καλέσας δὲ αὐτήν⁴⁵, ἤκουσα καὶ τοὺς ἐν μυστηρίῳ λαβεῖν
λόγους⁴⁶ *οὓς καθεύδων σὺν αὐτῇ ἐν τῇ μέθῃ μου ⌜ἐλά- τοὺς
λησα⌝⁴⁷. *Καὶ οὐκ ἠδυνήθην ἀνελεῖν αὐτήν, ὅτι παρὰ ἀρρα-
Κυρίου ἦν⁴⁸.   7. *Ἔλεγον γάρ⁴⁹· Μήποτε ἐν δολιότητι βῶνας.
ἐποίησε παρὰ ἄλλης⁵⁰ λαβοῦσα τὸν ἀρραβῶνα⁵¹.   8. α om.
*Ἀλλ' οὐδὲ⁵² ἤγγισα⁵³ αὐτῇ ἔτι⁵⁴ ἕως *τῆς ζωῆς μου⁵⁵, vers.
6-10.

συνέλαβεν. g om. Aᵇ = καὶ συνείληφεν, Aᵃᵇ*ᶜᵈ = ἣ καὶ συνειλ. : A adds ἀπ'
ἐμοῦ.   ⁴¹α. β reads ἀγν. δέ, Aᵇ = ἠγνόησα δὲ ἐγώ.   ⁴²α, dg, A. abef,
S¹ read ἐποίησεν.   ⁴³β–dg (save that a reads αὐτὴν ἀνελεῖν), A, S¹. α, dg
om.   ⁴⁴β–dg, A (save that f reads κατίσχυσεν for κατῇσχυνε, and Aᵇ
Θαμὰρ δὲ πέμψασα for πέμψ. δέ, and A τὸν ἀρραβῶνα), S¹. d reads πέμψασα
ἐν κρυπτῷ τοὺς ἀρ. κατῇσχ. με, g καὶ πέμψασα ἔκρυψεν τοὺς ἀρ. καὶ κατῇσχ. με.
Here α omits vers. 6–10, and in their stead substitutes the following
passage, which is an abbreviated form of the LXX of Gen. xxxviii. 20,
24–30, in part adapted to its new context. Ἔπεμψα τοῦ (h δέ) λαβεῖν τοὺς
ἀρραβῶνας. Καὶ οὐχ εὗρον αὐτήν, καὶ μεθ' ἡμέρας τινὰς ἠκούσθη ὅτι Θαμὰρ ἐκπε-
πόρνευκε (c ἐκπεπόρευκε) καὶ (+ἰδοὺ h) ἐν γαστρὶ ἔχει. Ἀκούσας δὲ ἐγὼ εἶπον·
Ἐξαγάγετε (ἐξαγαγέτω c) αὐτήν (αὐτὴ c) καὶ κανθήτω. Ἡ δὲ ἀπέστειλε πρός με
λέγουσα· Τοῦ ἀνθρώπου οὗτινος (εἴτινος c) ταῦτά εἰσιν, ἐγὼ ἐν γαστρὶ ἔχω·
ἐπίγνωθι οὖν τίνος ὁ δακτύλιος καὶ ἡ ῥάβδος καὶ τὸ διάδημα (τὸ δ. καὶ ἡ ρ. h).
Ἐπιγνοὺς δὲ ἐγὼ εἶπον· Δεδικαίωται Θαμὰρ ἢ ἐγώ. Καὶ οὐ προσεθέμην ἔτι τοῦ
γνῶναι αὐτήν. Ἐγένετο δὲ ἐν τῷ τίκτειν αὐτήν (h om. ἐγένετο .. αὐτήν), ἔσχε
(+ γοῦν h) δίδυμα, καὶ ὁ μὲν εἷς ἐξήνεγκε τὴν χεῖρα αὐτοῦ, καὶ λαβοῦσα ἡ μαῖα
ἔδησεν ἐπὶ τῆς χειρὸς αὐτοῦ κόκκινον λέγουσα· Οὗτος (h om.) ἐξελεύσεται πρῶτος·
ὁ δὲ ἐπισυνήγαγε τὴν χεῖρα αὐτοῦ, καὶ εὐθὺς ἐξῆλθεν ὁ ἀδελφὸς αὐτοῦ. Καὶ
ἐκάλεσεν τὸ ὄνομα αὐτοῦ Φαρές· καὶ μετὰ τοῦτο ἐξῆλθεν καὶ ὁ ἐπὶ τῆς χειρὸς αὐτοῦ
ἔχων καὶ (h om.) τὸ κόκκινον· καὶ ἐκάλεσεν τὸ ὄνομα αὐτοῦ Ζαρά.   ⁴⁵g reads
καὶ λύσας δὲ αὐτήν. Aᵇ*ᶜᵈ add πρός με καί.   ⁴⁶A adds παρ' αὐτῆς.   ⁴⁷abefg,
S¹ (save that b, S¹ trs. οὓς after μέθῃ μου). d reads οὓς ἐλάλησα καθ. πρὸς
αὐτὴν ἐν τῇ μέθῃ μου. A = ἐν ᾧ ἐν τῇ μέθῃ μου ἐκάθευδον σὺν αὐτῇ (Aᵇ*ᵈ
om. σ. αὐτῇ).   ⁴⁸This clause is trs. into ver. 7 by d. See note 51.
For ἀνελεῖν Aᵇ*ᵈ read ἰδεῖν. After ἦν A adds ἐκεῖνο.   ⁴⁹β–b. b reads
ἔλεγον δέ. Aᵃᵇʰᶜ = καὶ ἐνεθυμήθην, but ωϑξϸ is corrupt for ωυξϸ = ἔλεγον.
Hence Aᵃᵇʰᶜ = καὶ ἔλεγον ἐν τῇ καρδίᾳ. Aᵇ*ᵈᶠᵍ = καὶ νομίσας (ἐνόμιζον καὶ fg)
ἔλεγον. d adds πρὸ τοῦ ἐξειπεῖν με αὐτὴν τοὺς ἐν μυστηρίῳ λόγους μου ὅτι
ἀνελῶ αὐτήν· ὅτι.   ⁵⁰bde, S¹. afg ἄλλου. A may be either so far as form
goes.   ⁵¹d adds καὶ ἐπειδὴ εἶπέ μοι τοὺς ἐν μυστηρίῳ λόγους, οὐκ ἠδυνήθην
ἀνελεῖν αὐτήν· ὅτι παρὰ κυρίου ἦν. See note 48.   ⁵²d reads καὶ οὐκέτι, g,
Aᵃᵇᵇ*ᶜᵈᵉⁱᵍ καὶ οὐκ.   ⁵³d reads συνεγενόμην.   ⁵⁴A adds καὶ συνέσταλμαι.
d om. next five words, g next four.   ⁵⁵aef, S¹. b reads ἕως θανάτου μου,

β-dg, S   ὅτι βδέλυγμα ἐποίησα⁵⁶ ⌐τοῦτο⌐⁵⁷ ἐν ⌐παντὶ⌐⁵⁸ Ἰσραήλ⁵⁹.
ἔζησα
ἐκεῖ.   9. Καίγε οἱ ἐν τῇ πόλει ἔλεγον, μὴ *εἶναι ἐν τῇ πύλῃ
β-bd   τελισκομένην⁶⁰· ὅτι ἐξ *ἄλλου χωρίου⁶¹ ἐλθοῦσα πρὸς βραχὺ
ἀκούσατε   ἐκάθισεν ἐν τῇ⁶² πύλῃ.   10. *Καὶ ἐνόμιζον⁶³ ὅτι οὐδεὶς
τέκνα
μου.   ἔγνω ὅτι εἰσῆλθον πρὸς⁶⁴ αὐτήν.   11. Καὶ μετὰ ταῦτα
β, A, S¹   ἤλθομεν⁶⁵ εἰς Αἴγυπτον *⌐πρὸς Ἰωσήφ⌐ διὰ τὸν⁶⁶ λιμόν.
πορεύ-
εσθε.   12. *Ἤμην δὲ ἐγὼ ἐτῶν τεσσαράκοντα καὶ ἐξ⁶⁷ καὶ ἐβδομή-
β-ag,   κοντα καὶ⁶⁸ τρία ἔτη ἐποίησα⁶⁹ * εἰς Αἴγυπτον⁷⁰.
(A), S¹
μηδὲ ἐν-   XIII. *Καὶ νῦν ἐντέλλομαι ὑμῖν, τέκνα μου, ἀκούσατε
θυμήσεσι   ⌐Ἰούδα¹ τοῦ πατρὸς ὑμῶν⌐² καὶ φυλάξασθε³ τοὺς λόγους μου⁴
διαβου-   τοῦ ποιεῖν⁵ πάντα⁶ τὰ δικαιώματα Κυρίου⁷ καὶ ὑπακούειν
λίων
ὑμῶν   ἐντολὰς⁸ Θεοῦ.   2. Καὶ μὴ πονηρεύεσθε⁹ ὀπίσω τῶν ἐπι-
ἐν ὑπερη- θυμιῶν ὑμῶν¹⁰ *ἐν ὑπερηφανείᾳ καρδίας¹¹, καὶ μὴ καυχᾶσθε ἐν
φανείᾳ   *ἔργοις καὶ ἰσχύι¹² τῆς νεότητος ὑμῶν ὅτι* γε τοῦτο¹³ πονη-
καρδίας
ὑμῶν.   ρὸν ἐνώπιον¹⁴ Κυρίου¹⁵ ἐστί¹⁶.   3. Ἐπειδὴ κἀγὼ¹⁷

but Judah could not say this whilst still alive, nor yet ἡμέρας θανάτου μου,
as in A^abhcefg. A^b*d = τῆς ἡμέρας ταύτης.   ⁵⁶ g reads ἦν.   ⁵⁷ d, A om.
⁵⁸ d adds τῷ. A om.   ⁵⁹ d adds καὶ ἐτέχθησάν μοι ἐξ αὐτῆς Φαρὲς καὶ Ὀζαρά·
ἤγουν ὑμεῖς τέκνα μου, and omits ver. 9, 10.   ⁶⁰ β–d (save that for τελισκο-
μένην aef read τελωνουμένην, and for πύλῃ bg, S¹ read πόλει). A = μὴ τελεσθῆναι
τοιαῦτα ἐν τῇ πύλῃ.   ⁶¹ g reads ἄλλης χώρας.   ⁶² b om.   ⁶³ efg, A.
a reads νομίζων. A adds οὕτως. b, S¹ read ἐνόμιζεν.   ⁶⁴ a reads εἰς.
⁶⁵ d reads εἰσήλθομεν.   ⁶⁶ f reads τήν. d adds τ. ἀδελφὸν ἡμῶν after Ἰωσήφ.
⁶⁷ α (save that c reads ὀκτώ for ἔξ), S¹. bfg read σαρακοντα ἐξ ἐτῶν ἤμην,
ade μϛ' ἐτῶν ἤμην (+ τότε d).   ⁶⁸ α. β om.   ⁶⁹ α. abef, A, S¹ read ἔζησα,
d ἐζήσαμεν, g εἰμί.   ⁷⁰ α, A. β–dg, S¹ read ἐκεῖ, d μετὰ ταῦτα, g ὧδε. a
adds ἔτη.

XIII. ¹ α. aef read κ. ν. ὡς λέγω (f om. ὡς λέγω) ὑμῖν ἐντέλλομαι, ἀκούσατε
τέκνα μου Ἰ., bg, S¹ κ. ν. ὅσα ἐγὼ ὑμῖν (g om.) ἐντέλλομαι, ἀκούσατε τέκνα (+ μου
Ἰ. g + καὶ Ἰ. S¹). d νῦν οὖν τέκνα μου ἀκούσατε Ἰ. A = κ. νῦν ἀκούσατε τέκνα
μου ὅσα ἐντέλλομαι ὑμῖν.   ² A om.   ³ α. β reads φυλάξατε. β, S¹ add
πάντας.   ⁴ d adds καὶ τὰς ἐντολάς μου. A = Ἰούδα τοῦ πατρὸς ὑμῶν.   ⁵ A
reads ꞏꞏꞏ = ἔχειν, but this is corrupt for ꞏꞏꞏ (= ποιεῖν).   ⁶ b, S¹
om.   ⁷ A = ἐνώπιον Κυρίου. d om. next four words.   ⁸ α, af. b reads
ἐντολῆς, eg ἐντολαῖς. b, S¹ add Κυρίου.   ⁹ α. β, A, S¹ read πορεύεσθε.
¹⁰ α, ag. β–ag, S¹ read ὑμῶν μηδὲ ἐνθυμήσεσι (+ τῶν δὲ) διαβουλίων ὑμῶν,
A καρδιῶν ὑμῶν μηδὲ ἐνθυμήσεσι ὑμῶν.   ¹¹ α, β–a. a om. A = ἐν. ὑπερηφανείᾳ τῶν διαβουλίων ὑμῶν ἐμπίπτετε. β–f, S¹ add ὑμῶν.   ¹² α. adef read
ἰσχύι (+ καὶ d) ἔργοις, b ἔργοις ἰσχύος, g ἐν ἰσχύει ἔργον ὑμῶν. A, S¹ = ἰσχύι
ἔργων.   ¹³ c, a. h reads τό, bdef καίγε τοῦτο, g γε καὶ τοῦτο. A = τοῦτο
πᾶν. S¹ om. ὅτι . . ἐστί.   ¹⁴ α, β–bg, A^b*cdeg. bg, A^abef read ἐν ὀφθαλμοῖς.

ἐγκαυχησάμενος [18] ὅτι *ἐν πολέμοις [19] οὐκ *ἠπάτησέ με [20]
πρόσωπον *γυναικὸς εὐμόρφου [21], *καὶ ὠνείδιζον [22] 'Ρουβὶμ [23]
*τὸν ἀδελφόν [24] *μου περὶ Βάλλας [25] γυναικὸς τοῦ [26] πατρός
μου, καὶ [27] τὸ πνεῦμα *τοῦ ζήλου καὶ τῆς πορνείας [28] παρετά-
ξαντο [29] *ἐπ' ἐμέ [30], ἕως [31] †συνετέλεσα εἰς 'Ανᾶν τὴν Χανανανί-
την [32] καὶ εἰς Θαμὰρ τὴν νύμφην [33] μου. 4. *Ἔλεγον
γὰρ τῷ πενθερῷ μου ὅτι συμβουλεύσομαι τῷ πατρί μου καὶ
οὕτως λήψομαι [34] τὴν θυγατέρα σου· *ὁ δὲ οὐκ ἤθελεν, ἀλλ' [35]
ἔδειξέ [36] μοι *εἰς ὄνομα [37] τῆς θυγατρὸς αὐτοῦ *χρυσοῦ πλῆθος
ἄπειρον [38]. *βασιλεὺς γὰρ ἦν [39]. 5. *Καὶ ἐκόσμησεν
αὐτὴν [40] ἐν χρυσίῳ [41] καὶ μαργαρίταις, *καὶ ἐποίησεν αὐτὴν

α ὑπήν
τησέν
μοι πρόσ-
ωπον.
β–d, A, S
†συνέ-
πεσα εἰς
Βησουέ
τὴν Χανα-
ναίαν.
β, A, S¹
νυμφηθεῖ-
σαν τοῖς
υἱοῖς.
β–d, A,
S¹ καί.

[15] *h* reads θεοῦ. [16] α, A. β omit. [17] *efg*, A. *h* reads ἐγώ, *b*, S¹ γὰρ ἐγώ.
c, ad om. [18] *c. h* reads ἐκαύχησά μοι corrupt (?) for ἐκαυχησάμην. β–*g*, S¹
read καυχησάμενος. *g*, A καυχησάμενος ἤμην. [19] *c* trs. before ὅτι. *d* reads
καὶ πολεμιστὴς ὢν τάχα. For these and the next six words A reads οὐκέτι
ἠπατήθην ἐν πολέμοις (A[b*cdefg] om. ἐν πολ.) εὐμορφίᾳ (εὐμορφία A[h]) γυναικῶν
εὐμόρφων (A[b*d] om). [20] β–*g*. α reads ὑπήντησέν μοι—apparently a corruption of our text. *g* reads ἤττησέν με. For ἠπάτησε . . εὐμόρφου S¹
reads οὐκ ἐπέτυχόν μοι εὔμορφοι γυναῖκες. For A see preceding note.
d adds ἄνθρωπος ἐν χρυσίῳ καὶ ἀργυρίῳ οὐδέ, *g* ἄνθρωπος ἢ εἰς χρυσὸν διερρέ-
θιζον οὐδὲ εἷς. [21] α om. [22] α, *g*, A (save that α reads ὀνείδ. for ὠνείδ.).
d reads ἔτι δὲ καὶ ὀνείδιζον, *a* ὀνειδίζων, *b*, S¹ ὠνείδιζον, *ef* ὀνείδιζον. [23] α, *ad*.
β–*ad* read 'Ρουβήμ. [24] *g* reads τῷ ἀδελφῷ. [25] *dg* add τῆς. [26] α, *dg*.
abef om. [27] *b* om. *d* adds ταῦτα καυχώμενος, A τότε. [28] A = τῆς πορν.
καὶ τοῦ ζ. For ζήλου *c* reads ζήλους. [29] *b* reads παρετάξατο. [30] α. *abefg*
read ἐν (ἐπὶ *g*) ἐμοί, *d* μοι. [31] *d* adds οὐ. [32] α. β–*d* (save that *e* reads
Βησσουέ, *f* Βισσουέ for Βησουέ), A, S¹ read as in margin. *d* reads ἐνέπεσον
εἰς Βυσουέ τὴν Χ. καὶ ἔλαβον αὐτὴν γυναῖκα ὁμοίως. συνετέλεσα seems to be
a corruption native to the Greek. [33] α. β, A, S¹ (save that A, S¹ =
τῷ υἱῷ) read as in margin. [34] α (save that *c* om. τῷ πατρί μου καὶ οὕτως
λήψομαι). β–*d*, A[ab*cde], S¹ καὶ ἔλεγον τῷ π. μου Συμβουλεύσομαι (*b* συμβου-
λεύσω, *f* συμβουλεύσωμαι, A[ab*cde] συμβουλεῦσαι, but A[b] = συμβουλεύσομαι)
τῷ πατρί μου καὶ οὕτως λήψομαι. *d* reads καὶ γὰρ ὅτε ἐκάλεσέ μοι Βαρσὰν ὁ
πενθερός μου καὶ εἶπέ μοι περὶ τῆς θυγατρὸς αὐτοῦ, οὐκ εἶπον αὐτῷ· Βουλεύσομαι
περὶ τούτου τὸν πατέρα μου καὶ οὕτως λήψομαι. A[b] = καὶ ἔλεγον τ. πενθερῷ μου
Ἔρχομαι βουλεύομαι καὶ λέγω τῷ πατρί μου πρῶτον καὶ τότε λήψομαι. A adds
εἰς γυναῖκα. [35] α. *d* reads ἀλλά, β–*d*, A, S¹ καί. [36] *c* reads ἔδειξα.
[37] α. β reads ἐπ' ὀνόματι. S¹ ἀπὸ τῶν κτημάτων. [38] *d* reads χρυσοῦ πλῆθος,
f χρυσίον ἄπειρον πλῆθος, *g* χρυσίον πλ. ἄπειρον. [39] α, A[ab*cd]. β–*d*, A[befg], S¹
read ἦν γὰρ βασιλεύς. *d* om. [40] α, A–[b]. β–*d*, S¹ read καὶ αὐτὴν κοσμήσας,
d κοσμήσας δὲ καὶ αὐτήν, A[b] καὶ τὴν θυγατέρα αὐτοῦ Βηρσουέ ἐκόσμησε. [41] *c*,

Marginal notes (left column):
β, A, S¹ δείπνῳ
*ἐν κάλλει γυναι- κῶν⁴⁴.
c (A) ἐν τῇ ἡδονῇ.
β, A, S¹ πατέρων.
β-a, A, S¹ καρδίας.

οἰνοχοεῖν ἡμῖν⁴² ἐν τῷ δείπνῳ⁴³.   6. Καὶ ὁ⁴⁵ οἶνος διέστρεψέ μου *τοὺς ὀφθαλμούς⁴⁶, καὶ ἡμαύρωσέ μου τὴν καρδίαν⁴⁷ *ἢ ἡδονή⁴⁸.   7. Καὶ ἐρασθεὶς αὐτῆς *συνέπεσα εἰς αὐτήν⁴⁹, καὶ παρέβην ἐντολὴν⁵⁰ Κυρίου καὶ τὴν⁵¹ ἐντολὴν *τοῦ πατρός⁵² μου, καὶ ἔλαβον αὐτὴν⁵³ εἰς γυναῖκα.   8. Καὶ *ὁ Κύριος ἀνταπέδωκέ μοι⁵⁴ κατὰ τὸ διαβούλιον τῆς ψυχῆς⁵⁵ μου ὅτι⁵⁶ οὐκ ηὐφράνθην ἐν⁵⁷ τοῖς τέκνοις αὐτῆς⁵⁸.

XIV. Καὶ νῦν ⌜λέγω⌝¹, τέκνα μου², μὴ μεθύσκεσθε³ οἴνῳ, ὅτι⁴ ὁ⁵ οἶνος διαστρέφει⁶ τὸν νοῦν ἀπὸ τῆς ἀληθείας καὶ ἐμβάλλει ὀργὴν ἐπιθυμίας, καὶ ὁδηγεῖ εἰς πλάνην⁷ *τοὺς ὀφθαλμούς⁸.   2. Τὸ γὰρ πνεῦμα⁹ τῆς πορνείας¹⁰ τὸν οἶνον ὡς¹¹ διάκονον *ἔχει πρὸς τὴν ἡδονὴν¹² *τοῦ νοός¹³· ὅτι καίγε

---

adefg. h, b read χρυσῷ. d adds καὶ ἱματισμῷ, A^{abhb*cd} καὶ ἀργυρίῳ.   ⁴²α, d (save that c om. ἡμῖν and d om. καί), A^{bh(sc?)} (for [Armenian] (= οἰνοχοοῦσαν) is corrupt for [Armenian] = οἰνοχυεῖν), A^{elg} (save that they add ἡμῖν before οἰνοχοεῖν). abefg, S¹ read ἐποίησεν ἡμῖν οἰνοχοεῖν.   ⁴³d adds καὶ ἐθεασάμην οὕτως.   ⁴⁴β. A^{ab*cdelg} = καὶ ἦν καλὴ σφόδρα. α, A^b om. This phrase is difficult, and its difficulty probably led to its omission by α, A^b, and to the addition of a clause in d (see note 43), and the recasting of the phrase in A^{ab*cdes}. ἐν κάλλει γυναικῶν = בהדר נשים, where הָדָר is probably corrupt for חֶדֶר = 'chamber,' 'apartment.' Thus the feast was held in the women's apartment to influence Judah. Otherwise if הדר really stood in the original, we should have to insert it immediately after μαργαρίταις, where it would aptly mean: 'with the ornaments of women.'   ⁴⁵f om.   ⁴⁶h reads τὸν ὀφθαλμόν. g om. together with the next three words.   ⁴⁷c, abf, A^{abcelg}, S¹. h, de, A^{b*d} read διάνοιαν (+ καὶ τὴν καρδίαν d).   ⁴⁸h, aefg (save that g prefixes καί), S. The parallelism supports this reading. c reads ἐν τῇ ἡδονῇ. A = ἐν ὀδύνῃ where ὀδύνη is corrupt for ἡδονῇ (as Conybeare has pointed out). bd, S¹ read ἡδονή. A^{b*d} = καὶ ἔπεσε καρδία μου ἐν ὀδύνῃ (cf. d in note 47).   ⁴⁹α. β-d, S¹ read συνέπεσα, d συνέπ. αὐτῇ. A = καταπατέομαι. d reads αὐτῇ. On this phrase see note 10 on xi. 2.   ⁵⁰d om. next four words through hmt.   ⁵¹α. β, A om.   ⁵²α. β, A, S¹ read τῶν (β-g om.) πατέρων.   ⁵³A reads αὐτήν (Βηρσουέ A^b) μοι.   ⁵⁴α. β, A, S¹ read ἀνταπ. μοι Κύριος.   ⁵⁵α, a. β-a, A, S¹ read καρδίας. c om. next word.   ⁵⁶d, A^b read καί, A^{ab*cdes} διὰ τοῦτο.   ⁵⁷bd read ἐπί.   ⁵⁸c reads αὐτοῦ. A = μου (+ ἃ ἦσαν ἐκ Βηρσουέ A^b).

XIV. ¹c. h reads λέγω ὑμῖν and trans. after μου. β, A om.   ²g om.   ³h, e add ἐν.   ⁴h om.   ⁵a om.   ⁶d reads ἀποστρέφει.   ⁷dg add ἐπιθυμίας.   ⁸g om. A = τῶν ὀφθαλμῶν.   ⁹A^{b*cdes} add τῆς πλάνης καί.   ¹⁰f reads πονηρίας, g ἐπιθυμίας.   ¹¹c om.   ¹²α. β-d, A, S read πρὸς τὴν ἡδονὴν (τὰς ἡδονὰς bg) ἔχει, d ἔχει πρὸς τὰς ἡδονάς.   ¹³A = τὸν νοῦν.

*τὰ δύο ταῦτα[14] ἀφιστῶσι τὴν διάνοιαν[15] τοῦ ἀνθρώπου. β, Αβ, S δύναμιν.
3. Ἐὰν γὰρ πίῃς[16] οἶνον εἰς μέθην, *ἐν διαλογισμοῖς ῥυπαροῖς β, Α τις πίῃ.
συνταράσσει[17] *τὸν νοῦν σου[18], *καὶ ⌐εἰς πορνείαν⌐[19] ἐκθερ- β, Α, S νοῦν εἰς πορνείαν
μαίνει[20] τὸ σῶμα πρὸς *ἡδονήν, καὶ[21] πράσσει τὴν ἁμαρτίαν[22] καὶ (A om.).
καὶ οὐκ αἰσχύνεται.   4. Τοιοῦτός[23] ἐστιν ὁ πάροινος[24], β, Α, S μίξιν,
τέκνα μου, ὅτι[25] ὁ μεθύων[26] *οὐκ αἰδεῖται οὐδένα[27].   5. καὶ εἰ
*Ἰδοὺ γὰρ κἀμὲ ἐπλάνησεν μὴ αἰσχυνθῆναι τὸ πλῆθος[28] *τῆς πάρεστι
πόλεως[29]· ὅτι[30] ἐν ὀφθαλμοῖς πάντων ἐξέκλινα πρὸς τὴν τὸ τῆς
Θαμάρ, καὶ ἐποίησα *ἁμαρτίαν μεγάλην[31], καὶ *ἀνεκάλυψα ἐπιθυμίας
κάλυμμα ἀκαθαρσίας υἱῶν μου[32].   6. Πιὼν[33] τὸν[34] οἶνον[35] αἴτιον.
οὐκ αἰσχύνθην[36] τὴν[37] ἐντολὴν τοῦ[38] Θεοῦ, καὶ ἔλαβον γυναῖκα b, Α, S¹
Χαναναίαν.   7. *Συνέσεως ⌐γὰρ πολλῆς⌐[39] χρῄζει[40] ὁ πίνων[41] οἶνος.
τὸν[42] οἶνον, *τέκνα μου[43], *καὶ αὕτη ἐστὶν ἡ σύνεσις τῆς

β-bd, Α συνέσεως γάρ (g, A om.).

[14] d reads αὐτὰ τὰ δύο.   [15] α, Α^ab. β, Α^bb*cdeg, S read δύναμιν.   [16] h. c
reads πιεσε, abg, Α, S τις πίῃ, d τις πίνει τόν, ef πίει.   [17] α, β–d (save that
c reads πονηροῖς for ῥυπαροῖς and g λογισμοῖς for διαλογισμοῖς). d reads ἐν
διαλογισμοῖς πονηροῖς γίνεται· συνταράσσει γάρ. Α = διαλογισμοὶ ῥυπαίνουσιν.
[18] α. β–d, Α, S read τὸν νοῦν, d ὁ οἶνος τὸν νοῦν.   [19] α. β, Α, S read εἰς
πορνείαν καί (A om.)   [20] c reads ἐκθερμένη, d θερμαίνει.   [21] α. β, Α, S
read μίξιν, καί. β, Α, S add εἰ (d ἐὰν, aef, S¹ om.) πάρεστι (d παρῆν) τὸ τῆς
ἐπιθυμίας (d ἁμαρτίας) αἴτιον.   [22] a reads ἐπιθυμίαν.   [23] dg read ὁ τοιοῦτος
and connect with αἰσχύνεται in preceding verse, and d om. next five words,
and g next six. f reads ὅτι οὕτως.   [24] Emended from πονηρός of α, af
and πόρνος of e. b, Α, S¹ read οἶνος. Our emendation explains all these
corruptions.   [25] f adds οὕτως.   [26] Α^ab = μεθύων οἴνῳ.   [27] α. β, S
reads οὐδένα αἰδεῖται (+ οὐδὲ αἰσχύνεται ὡς ἔπαθον κἀγώ d). Α = οὐκέτι αἰδεῖται.
[28] α, β (but that β om τό). d reads ὅτι οὐκ ᾐδέσθην πλῆθος λαοῦ, οὐδὲ αἰσχύνθην
ὁλόκληρον δῆμον. For μὴ αἰσχυνθῆναι Α reads καὶ οὐδὲ ἐνόμισα.   [29] α. β–d
read ἐν τῇ πόλει, Α = τὸ ἐν τῇ πύλῃ, S ἐν ταῖς πύλαις. d om.   [30] d reads
καὶ γάρ.   [31] Α^b*d = ἀνομίαν.   [32] h, β (save that h adds τῶν before υἱῶν),
S¹. c reads ἀνεκάλυμμα ἀκαθ. υἱῶν μου. Α νῦν (Α^abb om.) ἀνεκάλυψα τοῖς
υἱοῖς μου ἔργα ἀκαθαρσίας μου. Here զηրծս = ἔργα may be corrupt for
սսրրսս = κάλυμμα.   [33] h reads πιεῖν. d gives ver. 6 as follows: Καὶ
ταῦτα πεποίηκεν ὁ οἶνος καθὼς καὶ τὸ πρότερον ἡνίκα ἔλαβον γυναῖκα Χαναναίαν ἄνευ
βουλῆς τοῦ πατρός μου· διὰ τοῦτο τοίνυν παραγγέλλω ὑμᾶς, τέκνα μου, ἵνα μὴ καὶ
ὑμεῖς τὸ αὐτὸ πάθητε.   [34] α. β om.   [35] f adds καί.   [36] h, befg. c reads
ἐσχ., a ᾐσχ.   [37] α, aef. bg om.   [38] α, fg. abef om.   [39] α. aef read
συνέσεως γάρ. bd, S¹ διὸ (διότι d) συνέσεως. g, Α = συνέσεως.   [40] In
most MSS. written χρίζει.   [41] a reads πιών.   [42] α, d. β–d om.   [43] h,
β–d. c, d om. A trs. before ὁ πίνων. Α^cefg om. next ten words.   [44] α, β

<table>
<tr><td>

β-dg
ἵνα ἕως
... πίῃ.
β-b, A
βασιλεί-
σῃ πορ-
νεύων
γυμνού-
μενος τῆς
βασι-
λείας ἐξ-
έρχεται.
β-d, A, S[1]
γυμνω-
θείς
(ἐγυμνώ-
θην g, A).
α, adf
τὴν
δόξαν.

</td><td>

οἰνοποσίας[44]. *ἕως ὅτε ἔχει αἰδῶ, πίνει[45].   8. Ἐὰν δὲ παρέλθῃ[46] τὸν ὅρον[47], ἐμβάλλει[48] εἰς[49] τὸν νοῦν αὐτοῦ[50] τὸ πνεῦμα τῆς πλάνης, καὶ ποιεῖ *τὸν μέθυσον αἰσχρορημονεῖν καὶ[51] παρανομεῖν καὶ μὴ[52] αἰσχύνεσθαι *ἀλλὰ καυχᾶσθαι[53] τῇ ἀτιμίᾳ[54] *καὶ νομίζειν εἶναι καλόν[55].

XV. Ὁ πορνεύων[1] ζημιούμενος οὐκ αἰσθάνεται[2] καὶ ἀδοξῶν[3] οὐκ αἰσχύνεται.   2. *Κἂν γάρ[4] τις *βασιλεύς ἐστι καὶ πορνεύει, γυμνοῦται τῆς βασιλείας[5], *δουλωθεὶς τῇ πορνείᾳ[6] ὡς κἀγὼ ἔπαθον[7].   3. Δέδωκα[8] τὴν ῥάβδον μου, τουτέστιν[9], τὸ στήριγμα τῆς ἐμῆς φυλῆς[10], καὶ τὴν ζώνην μου, τουτέστιν[11], τὴν δύναμιν, καὶ τὸ διάδημα[12], τουτέστιν, τὴν δόξαν τῆς βασιλείας μου[13].   4. Καίγε *μετανοήσας ἐπὶ τούτοις[14], οἶνον[15] καὶ κρέα[16] οὐκ[17] ἔφαγον[18] ἕως γήρους[19] μου[20], καὶ *πᾶσαν εὐφροσύνην[21] οὐκ εἶδον.   5. Καὶ ἔδειξέ μοι ὁ ἄγγελος τοῦ

</td></tr>
</table>

(save that *d* om. ἐστίν, and *f* om. τῆς). A[ab*d] = καὶ αὕτη ἐστὶν σύνεσις εὐφροσύνης. But *ներաժունբեան* is corrupt for *արբգունբեան* = οἰνοποσίας. A[b] = διὰ εὐφροσύνην σύνεσίς ἐστιν.   [45] α (save that *h* om. ἕως). β-dg, S[1] read ἵνα ἕως ὅτε (ὅτου *a*) ἔχει αἰδῶ, πίῃ (*b* πίνῃ, *ef* πίει), *g* ὡς ὅτε εἰδὼς ποιεῖ, *d* ἵνα μὴ σκοτισθῇ τις ἐξ αὐτοῦ. A[abb*d] = ἵνα ἕως ὅτε ἔχει οἶνον αἰδοῖ πίῃ.   [46] *d* reads παραβῇ.   [47] β-d, A, S[1] add τοῦτον.   [48] *c* reads ἐμβαλεῖ. For ἐμβάλλει ... νοῦν S[1] reads ἕρπει εἰς τὰ ὦτα.   [49] *g* om.   [50] α, *g*, A[abcefg]. A[b*d] = αὐτῶν. *b* reads καὶ ποιεῖ. *aef* om.   [51] *d* reads τῷ μεθύοντι. Here a new hand begins in A[h], and rest of this Testament belongs to A[β] not to A[a].   [52] A = ἀπὸ μηδενός.   [53] α. β-g read ἀλλὰ (+ καὶ A, *bd*) ἐγκαυχᾶσθαι. *g* om.   [54] A[b*cdefg], S[2] add αὐτοῦ. *h* reads ἀδικίᾳ, *d* ἀτομίᾳ.   [55] α. β-d, A, S[1] read νομίζοντα εἶναι καλόν (καλόν τι ποιεῖν A), *d* τὸ αποτομια ἀναισχύντως (sic).

XV. [1] For next fourteen words *b* reads καί.   [2] A = λυπεῖται, but *ուգաւյ* is corrupt for *զգաւյ* = αἰσθάνεται. For ζημιούμενος . . . ἀδοξῶν, S[1] reads καὶ γυμνούμενος οὐχ ὑποτάσσεται, ἀτάκτως. *g* om. next four words.   [3] *a* reads ἄδοξον.   [4] *d* reads καὶ γὰρ ἐάν, *g* ἐὰν γάρ.   [5] α. β, A read βασιλεύσῃ (*d* βασιλεὺς εἴη, *ef* βασιλεύσει. A = βασιλεύς τις ᾖ (πορνεύων) A[ab*cd] trs. before βασιλεύς) γυμνούμενος τῆς βασιλείας ἐξέρχεται (A[ofg] om.). *b* γυμνούμενος τῆς βασιλείας οὐκ ἐξέρχεται. S[1] βασιλεύσῃ πορνεύει γυμνούμενος καὶ ἐκ τῆς βασιλείας ἐκπίπτει.   [6] *g*, A[abb*cd] read δοῦλος (+ εἶναι A) τῆς πορνείας. A[ofg] om.   [7] α, *d*. *abef*, S[1] read γυμνωθείς, *g*, A ἐγυμνώθην.   [8] α, S[1]. β, A read ἔδωκα γάρ.   [9] A[ab] om. next ten words through hmt. but not A[h], β.   [10] *ad* read φυλακῆς.   [11] α, *adf* om. next six words through hmt.   [12] A add τῆς κεφαλῆς μου.   [13] *g* om.   [14] *d* reads πολλὰ μετὰ ταῦτα μετενόησα καί. A adds πᾶσι.   [15] *h* adds οὐκ ἔπιον. A trs. the words οἶνον and κρέα.   [16] α, *aefg*. *b* reads κρέας, *d* σίκερα.   [17] *d* reads οὐκέτι.

θεοῦ[22] ὅτι[23] *κἂν βασιλέως κἂν πτωχοῦ[24] *κατακυριεύσωσιν
αἱ γυναῖκες[25]. ⌜οὐκ ἐστὶν ἐν αὐτοῖς προκοπὴ ζωῆς⌝[26].　　6.
*Τοῦ μὲν[27] βασιλέως[28] αἴρουσιν[29] τὴν[30] δόξαν· τοῦ[31] ἀνδρείου[32]
τὴν[30] δύναμιν, *τοῦ δὲ πτωχοῦ[33] τὸ[34] *τῆς πτωχείας[35]
ἐλάχιστον στήριγμα.

XVI. Φυλάξασθε[1] οὖν[2], τέκνα μου, *τὸν ὅρον τοῦ[3] οἴνου·
*ἔστιν γὰρ[4] ἐν αὐτῷ τέσσαρα[5] πνεύματα πονηρά[6]· *ἐπιθυμίας,
πυρώσεως, ἀσωτίας καὶ αἰσχροκερδίας[7].　　2. Ἐὰν[8] πίνητε[9]
οἶνον[10] *ἐν εὐφροσύνῃ[11], *ἐστὲ αἰδούμενοι μετὰ φόβου θεοῦ[12].
*ἐὰν γὰρ ἐν εὐφροσύνῃ ἀποστῇ ὁ τοῦ Θεοῦ φόβος[13], λοιπὸν γίνεται
*μέθη, καὶ παρεισέρχεται ἡ ἀναισχυντία[14].　　3. *Εἰ δὲ
θέλετε σωφρόνως ζῆσαι, μηδ' ὅλως τοῦ οἴνου ἐφάπτεσθε[15] ἵνα μὴ

[18] α, A. β, S¹ read ἔλαβον.　　[19] abg read γήρως.　　[20] α, A⁻ᵇ. β, Aᵇ, S¹ om.
[21] c reads π. ἀφροσύνην. Aᵇ = ἄνευ πάσης εὐφροσύνης ἔζησα καί.　　[22] A =
Κυρίου.　　[23] α. β, A, S¹ add ἕως τοῦ αἰῶνος, which b, S¹ set before ὅτι.
[24] α, ag. b reads καὶ βασιλεῖ καὶ πτωχῷ, ef κἂν βασιλεῖ κἂν πτωχῷ (πτωχοῦ e).
For these words, together with the next three, d reads κἂν βασιλεὺς ᾖ κἂν
ἀνδρεῖος κἂν πτωχὸς ὁ τῷ τοιούτῳ ἁλισκόμενος πάθει γυναῖκες κατακυριεύσωσι αὐτόν,
and A⁻ᵇ γυναῖκες κατακυριεύσουσι κἂν βασιλέων κἂν πτωχῶν, Aᵇ ἐὰν βασιλέων
καὶ πτωχῶν πορνείαις γυναῖκες κατακυριεύσουσι.　　[25] α, af (save that af trs.
κατακ. after γυναῖκες). beg, S¹ read αἱ γυναῖκες κατακυριεύουσι. g adds κἂν
ἀνδρίου φανεροῦνται.　　[26] In α only. h prefixes καί.　　[27] α, β-bdg. b, S¹
read καὶ τοῦ μέν, d καὶ τοῦ. g om. A = καὶ τῶν.　　[28] g om. A = βασιλέων.
[29] α, bd, S¹. aef, A read ἀροῦσι. g om.　　[30] h om.　　[31] α. β reads τοῦ δέ.
A = τῶν.　　[32] g om. A = ἀνδρείων.　　[33] α. β-g reads καὶ τοῦ πτ., g τοῦ
δέ. A = καὶ τῶν πτωχῶν.　　[34] h, β-ag. c reads τῷ. ag, A om.　　[35] A
read an acc. by an error. g adds τό.

XVI. [1] α, β-d read φυλάσσεσθε, d φυλάσσετε.　　[2] d om.　　[3] α, β-bd, A.
bd read ὅρον.　　[4] d reads ἔχει γὰρ ὁ οἶνος.　　[5] A trs. after πονηρά.　　[6] d adds
ἅτινά ἐστι ταῦτα.　　[7] α, β (save that abef om. καί). A = ἐπιθυμία, πύρωσις
(πυρώσεως Aᵇ*ᶜᵈᵉᶠᵍ), καὶ ἀσωτία, αἰσχροκερδία (αἰσχροκερδίας Aᵇ*ᵈᵉ).　　[8] g adds
δέ.　　[9] h, abdg. c reads πίνειται, ef πίνετε.　　[10] g om.　　[11] For ἐν εὐφρ. ἐστέ
A gives καί (Aᵇ*ᶜᵈ om.) θέλετε εὐφρόσυνοι εἶναι.　　[12] α (save that h reads
τοῦ Κυρίου for θεοῦ). β-d, S¹ read μετὰ φόβου θεοῦ αἰδούμενοι (+ ζήσεσθε b).
A = μετὰ φόβου Κυρίου καὶ αἰδοῖ πίνετε. d om.　　[13] aef, A, S (save that f
reads ἀπὸ θεοῦ ὁ φοβος, ef ἀφροσύνη, a ἀπό for ἀποστῇ ὁ τοῦ, and S¹ om. γάρ
and adds καί before ἀποστῇ). b reads ἐὰν γὰρ πίνητε μὴ αἰδούμενοι καὶ ἀποστῇ
ὁ τοῦ θεοῦ φόβος. d reads καὶ απορον ὁ φόβος τοῦ θεοῦ ἀφ' ἡμῶν, g ἀποστήσεται
ὁ μισόκαλος ἀφ' ὑμῶν καί. The clause is omitted by α through hmt.,
reading only καί.　　[14] d reads μέθη ἀπὸ δὲ τῆς μέθης παρεισ. ἡ ἄναισχ. g is
utterly corrupt: ὁ τοῦ θεοῦ φόβος ἐν ταῖς καρδίαις ὑμῶν. Here c adds ὁ μὴ

ἁμαρτάνητε[16] ἐν λόγοις ὕβρεως[17] καὶ[18] μάχαις[19] καὶ[20] συκοφαντίαις[21] καὶ παραβάσεσι[22] ἐντολῶν[23] Θεοῦ[24], καὶ ἀπολεῖσθε[25]
⌈οὐκ⌉[26] ἐν καιρῷ ὑμῶν.   4. Καίγε[27] μυστήρια Θεοῦ καὶ ἀνθρώπων[28] ἀποκαλύπτει[29] ὁ οἶνος, ὡς[30] κἀγὼ *τὰς ἐντολὰς τοῦ[31]
Θεοῦ, καὶ μυστήρια Ἰακὼβ τοῦ πατρός μου ἀπεκάλυψα[32] τῇ
Χανανίτιδι[33], *ἅ μοι[34] εἶπεν *ὁ Θεὸς[35] μὴ[36] ἀποκαλύψαι[37].

XVII. *Καὶ νῦν ἐντέλλομαι[1] ὑμῖν, τέκνα μου, μὴ
ἀγαπᾶν[2] ἀργύριον[3] μηδὲ ἐπιβλέψαι[4] *εἰς κάλλος[5] γυναικῶν·
ὅτι κἀγὼ[6] διὰ χρυσίον[7] καὶ[8] εὐμορφίαν[9] ἐπλανήθην[10] εἰς
Βησουὲ[11] τὴν Χαναναίαν.   [2. *Καὶ οἶδα[12] ὅτι διὰ τὰ δύο
ταῦτα ἔσται[13] τὸ γένος μου[14] *εἰς ἀπώλειαν πορνείας[15].   3.
ὅτι καὶ[16] σοφοὺς ἄνδρας τῶν υἱῶν μου ἀλλοιώσουσιν καὶ
βασιλείαν[17] Ἰούδα *σμικρυνθῆναι ποιήσουσιν[18], ἣν ἔδωκέ

[margin:]
b–d, A, S[1]
Χαν.
Βησουέ.
β, A, S[1]
5. *Καὶ
πολέμου
καὶ
ταραχῆς
αἴτιος
γίνεται ὁ
οἶνος[38].
β, A, S[1]
ἀργύριον.
β, S[1] ἐν
πονηρίᾳ.

πίνων τὸν οἶνον μετὰ φόβου θεοῦ. Is this the lost clause in α? See note 13.
[15] α. aef read τί δὲ λέγω; μηδ' ὅλως πίνετε, bg εἰ δὲ μηδὲ ὅλως (μὴ δόλῳ g)
πίετε, d ἐγὼ δὲ λέγω ὑμῖν ἐὰν ἐστὶν ὑμῖν δυνατὸν μηδ' ὅλως πιεῖν οἶνον. A =
καὶ καλόν ἐστι ὅλως μὴ πίνειν οἶνον. S[1] λέγω δὲ εἰ ὅλως μὴ πίετε. d adds μὴ
πίετε.   [16] h. c reads ἁμαρτάνετε. β ἁμάρτητε. For the next nine words
S[1] reads ἐν μικρῷ τοιαῦτά ἐστι ὕβρις καὶ παράβασις.   [17] g om.   [18] d reads ἤ.
[19] α, g. β–g, A read μάχης.   [20] c om. d reads ἤ, and so also for the
next καί.   [21] h, g. c, β–g, A read συκοφαντίας.   [22] h. c, β, A reads
παραβάσεως.   [23] d om. g reads ἐν πόλει.   [24] d reads τοῦ θεοῦ, A[c]
κυρίου.   [25] adefy. α, b read ἀπολεῖσθαι.   [26] A om.   [27] d reads καὶ
γάρ.   [28] b, A[abb*d] add ἀλλοτρίοις.   [29] c reads ἀνακαλύπτει.   [30] d reads
καὶ γάρ.   [31] α. β reads ἐντολάς.   [32] β–abd, add Βησουέ (Βησσουέ e,
Βισσουέ f).   [33] bd, A, S[1] add Βησουέ. a Βισσουέ.   [34] α. β reads υἱς.
A = ἤ.   [35] A = Κύριος. h adds μου.   [36] d reads μηδ' ὅλως.   [37] d adds
τινι, καὶ οὐ μόνον ταῦτα πάντα τὰ σκάνδαλα ποιεῖ ὁ οἶνος.   [38] β–d (save that b
adds δέ after πολέμου), A (but reading πολέμων γὰρ καὶ ταραχῶν for first
four words), S[1]. d reads ἀλλὰ πολέμου καὶ ταραχῆς αἴτιος γίνεται. α om.

XVII. [1] α, S[2]. aefy, A[ab*cdefg] read ἐντέλλομαι, bd, S[1] ἐντέλ. οὖν. A[b] =
ἐντελλόμενος ἐντέλλομαι.   [2] g adds τό.   [3] g om. next nine words through
lmt.   [4] c. h, ef read ἐπιβλέπειν, ab ἐμβλέπειν, d βλέπειν.   [5] α, b. ae
read εἰς κάλλη, df ἐν κάλλει (d κάλλη).   [6] α. β, A read καίγε (+ ἐγώ d).
[7] α. β, A, S[1] read ἀργύριον.   [8] aef add διά.   [9] A[−b] add γυναικῶν, A[b]
γυναικός.   [10] g reads πλανηθειτε ὡς κἀγώ and om. next four words.
[11] β (save that e reads Βησσ., f Βισσουέ). α reads Αὐνᾶν. A = Βηρσουέ.
[12] α. abef, A[−b], S[1] read ὅτι οἶδα ἐγώ, g ὅτι οἶδα. A[b] = καὶ γὰρ οἶδα ἐγώ.
For these and the next five words d reads: διὰ τοῦτο εἰς ταῦτα τὰ δύο οἶδα
ἐγὼ ὅτι.   [13] α, adf, A, S[1]. beg read ἔσεσθε.   [14] A = τοῦτο.   [15] α. β,
S[1] read ἐν πονηρίᾳ. A = ἐν πορνείᾳ.   [16] α, A[abcefg]. β reads καίγε (+ καί d).

μοι Κύριος ἐν ὑπακοῇ πατρός μου¹⁹.   4. *᾿Εγὼ οὖν οὐδέ-
ποτε²⁰ *παρελύπησα ᾿Ιακὼβ τὸν πατέρα μου²¹, ὅτι²² πάντα
*ὅσα μοι ἔλεγεν²³ ἐποίουν²⁴.   5. Καὶ ᾿Αβραὰμ²⁵ ὁ
πρόπαππός²⁶ μου εὐλόγησέ με²⁷ βασιλεύειν ἐν²⁸ ᾿Ισραήλ²⁹,
*καὶ ᾿Ιακὼβ εὐλόγησέ με οὕτως³⁰.   6. Καὶ³¹ ἐγὼ οἶδα
ὅτι ἐξ ἐμοῦ στήσεται *τὸ βασίλειον³².

XVIII. *Καὶ ἔγνωκα¹ ὅσα* κακὰ ποιήσετε² ἐν³ ⌜ταῖς⌝⁴
ἐσχάταις ἡμέραις.]   2. Φυλάξασθε⁵ οὖν⁶, τέκνα μου, ἀπὸ
τῆς *πορνείας καὶ τῆς φιλαργυρίας⁷, καὶ⁸ ἀκούσατε ᾿Ιούδα
τοῦ πατρὸς ὑμῶν⁹.

3. ῞Οτι¹⁰ ταῦτα¹¹ ἀφιστᾷ¹² *τῷ νόμῳ τοῦ¹³ θεοῦ,
   καὶ τυφλοῖ¹⁴ τὸ διαβούλιον τῆς ψυχῆς,

Right margin: bdef ἐλύπησα (+ τὸν ef) λόγον ᾿Ι. τοῦ πατρός. d, A ᾿Ισαάκ. β, A, S¹ πατὴρ τοῦ πατρός. β, A, S¹ ὅτι (β-bd om.) καίγε ἀνέγνων ἐν βι-

βλοις ᾿Ενὼχ τοῦ δικαίου.

A^{b*d} om.   ¹⁷h, g read βασιλεῖς.   ¹⁸d read σμικρυνοῦσι. For the
passage ἣν ἔδωκέ μοι ... ἐποίουν, g reads πάντα ὅσα εἶπεν ὁ πατὴρ ᾿Ιακὼβ
ἐποίουν μὴ λυπήσας αὐτόν.   ¹⁹α, A^{ab*cd}. β, A^{efg}, S¹ om.   ²⁰α (save that
h reads δέ for οὖν). β-g, A, S¹ read οὐδέποτε γάρ.   ²¹α, a (save that a
reads ἐλύπητα), A^{b}. bdef, S¹ read ἐλύπησα (+ τὸν ef) λόγον ᾿Ιακὼβ (d trs.
after μου) τοῦ πατρός μου. A^{ab*cdeg} ἐλύπησα ᾿Ιακὼβ τὸν πατέρα μου λόγοις
(A^{efg} trs. λόγοις before ᾿Ιακὼβ). β undoubtedly presents the harder text.
If it goes back to the original, then ἐλύπησα τὸν λόγον = המרותי לדבר
corrupt (?) for המריתי בדבר = ἠπείθησα τῷ λόγῳ. בדבר also would explain
the text of A.   ²²d reads ἀλλά.   ²³h. c (A?) reads μοι ὅσα ἔλεγεν,
abef, A, S¹ ὅσα (+ καὶ A) εἶπεν, d προέταττέ μοι.   ²⁴f reads ἐποίησα. d adds
διὰ τοῦτο ἐκληρονόμησα τὴν εὐλογίαν ᾿Αβραάμ.   ²⁵d, A read ᾿Ισαάκ.   ²⁶Em.
from προπάππους of c. h reads προπάτορος, β, A, S¹ πατὴρ (+ πατρὸς e) τοῦ
πατρός.   ²⁷ = ברכני, which may be corrupt for בחרני = ἐξελέξατό με.
But it is better perhaps to supply λέγων after verb. See i. 6.   ²⁸c, a
om.   ²⁹g reads ᾿Ιερουσαλήμ.   ³⁰α (save that h adds αὐτός after ᾿Ιακὼβ).
aef, A^{ab*cdefg}, S¹ read κ. ᾿Ισαὰκ ὁμοίως ἐπευλόγησέ (εὐλόγ. f, S¹) με (A om.)
οὕτως (A^{b*cdefg} om.), d ὁμοίως καὶ ᾿Ιακὼβ εὐλόγησέ με, b κ. ᾿Ισαὰκ ἐπευλόγησέ με
ὁμοίως οὕτως. For last two words in b, g reads ὁ πατὴρ τοῦ πατρός μου
εὐλόγησέν με βασιλεύειν ἐν ᾿Ιερουσαλήμ.   ³¹α, b. aef, A read διότι, dg διό.
S¹ τοσοῦτον γὰρ καί.   ³²A^{b} = ἡ εὐλογία.

XVIII. ¹α. β, A, S¹ read ὅτι (β-bd om.) καίγε (ἐγὼ A) ἀνέγνων
(ἔγνων ef) ἐν βίβλοις (βίβλῳ dg) ᾿Ενὼχ τοῦ δικαίου.   ²ae read κακοποιήσετε.
³b read ἐπ'.   ⁴α. β, A om.   ⁵d reads φυλάξατε, g φυλάσσεσθε.
⁶d om.   ⁷d reads φιλαργ. καὶ τῆς πορν. g om. τῆς before φιλαργ. A^{ab} =
πορν. καὶ μέθης καὶ φιλαργ. S² φιλαργ. καὶ μέθης.   ⁸c, A. h, β, S¹ om.
f adds οὖν after ἀκούσατε. g om. with rest of verse.   ⁹d adds καὶ γινώσκετε.   ¹⁰d adds τὰ δύο πάθη.   ¹¹A^{b*d} read φιλαργυρία.   ¹²d reads

καὶ ὑπερηφάνειαν ἐκδιδάσκει[15],
καὶ οὐκ ἀφίει[16] ἄνδρα ἐλεῆσαι[17] τὸν[18] πλησίον αὐτοῦ.

4. Στερίσκει[19] τὴν ψυχὴν αὐτοῦ[20] ἀπὸ πάσης ἀγαθότητος[21],
καὶ[22] *συνέχει αὐτὸν[23] ἐν *πόνοις καὶ μόχθοις[24].
⌈Τὸν ὕπνον ἐκδιώκει ἀπ' αὐτοῦ⌉[25],
καὶ[26] καταδαπανᾷ[27] τὰς[28] σάρκας αὐτοῦ.

5. *Θυσίας Θεοῦ ἐμποδίζει[29],
⌈καὶ εὐλογίαν Θεοῦ οὐ μνημονεύει⌉[30].
*Προφήτου λαλοῦντος οὐκ ἀκούει[31],
καὶ λόγους[32] εὐσεβείας[33] προσοχθίζει[34].

6. ⌈*Δυσὶ γὰρ πάθεσιν ἐναντίοις δουλεύει[35],
*καὶ Θεῷ ὑπακοῦσαι[36] οὐ δύναται[37],
ὅτι ἐτύφλωσεν[38] τὴν ψυχὴν αὐτοῦ
καὶ ἐν ἡμέρᾳ ὡς ἐν νυκτὶ πορεύεται⌉.

XIX. Τέκνα μου, ἡ φιλαργυρία πρὸς[1] εἰδωλολατρείαν[2]

β–g, S¹ καὶ ἀφιστᾷ ὕπνον αὐτοῦ.

β, A, S¹ εἴδωλα.

ἀφιστοῦσιν.   [13] α. β–d read νόμου. d ἀπὸ νόμου θεοῦ τὸν ἄνθρωπον. A = τῶν νόμων.   [14] d reads τυφλοῦσι.   [15] d reads ἐκδιδάσκουσι.   [16] c, bfg. h reads ἀφείη, a ἀφίησι, d ἀφίουσιν, e αφει.   [17] g trs. after αὐτοῦ.   [18] A^{b*cdefg} = τούς.   [19] d reads ὑστεροῦσι γάρ. e στερεῖ καί.   [20] d om.   [21] bg read ἀγαθοσύνης.   [22] aef om.   [23] d reads συνέχουσιν αὐτὸν τὸν ἄνθρωπον.   [24] α. β–d read μόχθοις καὶ πόνοις, d πόνῳ καὶ μόχθῳ.   [25] α. abef, S¹ read καὶ ἀφιστᾷ ὕπνον (+ ἀπ' f) αὐτοῦ, d καὶ ἀφιστῶσι τὸν ὕπνον αὐτοῦ. A om. Here ἀφιστάναι and ἐκδιώκειν appear to be alternative readings of נדד. Cf. Gen. xxxi. 40. For still another rendering see Sim. iv. 8. The phrase is found in Sir. xlii. 9 ἡ μέριμνα αὐτῆς ἀφιστᾷ ὕπνον.   [26] a om.   [27] d reads ἐκδαπανῶσι.   [28] α, d. β–d om.   [29] α, β–d, S¹ (save that β–d, S¹ prefix καί and g reads Κυρίου). d reads καὶ γὰρ ἡ φιλαργυρία θυσίαν ἐμποδίζει. A = καὶ θυσίας Κυρίου χλενάζει, but [Armenian] is corrupt for [Armenian] = ἐμποδίζει.   [30] α (save that h om. καί and reads μνημονεύεται), aef, S¹ (save that a, S¹ read εὐλογίας). bdg read καὶ εὐλογίας (+ θεοῦ d, + Κυρίου g) οὐ μέμνηται. A om.   [31] α (save that c reads προφήτῃ λαλοῦντι). β, A, S¹ read καὶ προφήτῃ λαλοῦντι οὐχ ὑπακούει.   [32] α, A. β–d, S¹ read λόγῳ, d λόγον.   [33] f adds οὐ.   [34] d reads ἀποδιωχθεῖν. A = ἀνθίσταται, but [Armenian] is corrupt for [Armenian] = προσοχθίζει.   [35] α, f (save that for δουλεύει καί f reads δουλεύων). ae, S¹ read δυσὶ γὰρ πάθεσιν ἐναντίοις τῶν ἐντολῶν τοῦ θεοῦ δουλεύων, bg read δύο γὰρ πάθη ἐναντία τῶν ἐντολῶν τοῦ θεοῦ (ἐντολῆς θεοῦ ἃ ὁ g) δουλεύων, d δύο γὰρ πάθη ἀνίατα ταῦτα.   [36] α, β–b, S¹ (save that β–b, S¹ om. καί, and a reads θεοῦ): b reads θεῷ θεοῦ ὑπακούειν.   [37] d adds ὁ τοιοῦτος.   [38] α, β–bd. b reads ἐτύφλωσαν, d ἀποτυφλοῦσι.

XIX.   [1] d reads ἀπό.   [2] α (c gives the form ἠδολολατρείαν). β, A, S¹

ὁδηγεῖ[3], ὅτι[4] ἐν πλάνῃ[5] ἀργυρίου τοὺς μὴ ὄντας θεοὺς[6]
ὀνομάζουσιν, καὶ ποιεῖ *τὸν ἔχοντα[7] αὐτὴν[8] εἰς ἔκστασιν[9]
ἐμπεσεῖν.   2. Διὰ τὸ[10] ἀργύριον[11] ἐγὼ *τέκνα μου ἀπό-
λωλα[12], καὶ[13] εἰ μὴ ἡ[14] μετάνοιά μου[15] ⌈καὶ ἡ ταπείνωσίς
μου[16]⌉, καὶ αἱ[17] εὐχαὶ[18] τοῦ πατρός μου †συνέδραμον[19],
ἄτεκνος εἶχον ἀποθανεῖν.   3. Ἀλλ' ὁ Θεὸς τῶν πατέρων
μου[20] *ἠλέησέ με[21] ὅτι ἐν ἀγνωσίᾳ[22] ⌈τοῦτο⌉[23] ἐποίησα.
4. Ἐτύφλωσε[24] γάρ[25] με ὁ ἄρχων τῆς πλάνης[26], καὶ ἠγνόησα
ὡς ἄνθρωπος[27], καὶ *ὡς σάρξ[28] ἐν[29] ἁμαρτίαις φθαρείς[30].
⌈καὶ[31] ἐπέγνων[32] τὴν ἐμαυτοῦ ἀσθένειαν, νομίζων[33] ἀκαταμάχητος εἶναι⌉.

XX. Γνῶτε[1] οὖν, τέκνα μου[2], ὅτι δύο πνεύματα σχολάζουσι[3] τῷ ἀνθρώπῳ, *τὸ τῆς[4] ἀληθείας καὶ *τὸ τῆς[5]
πλάνης[6].

Right margin: β, S¹ δι' ἀργυρίου. — β–f, A, S τῆς σαρκός μου. — β, S τῆς ψυχῆς μου. — β, A, S εὐχαὶ Ἰακώβ. — β, A, S ὁ οἰκτίρμων καὶ ἐλεήμων συνέγνω. — c om. καὶ ἠγνόησα

... τῆς πλάνης (XX. 1).

read εἴδωλα.   [3] g adds τὴν ψυχήν.   [4] g om.   [5] β, S¹ add διά.   [6] A
adds θεούς.   [7] A reads τοὺς ἔχοντας.   [8] c reads αὐτόν.   [9] g reads
κοτειαν.   [10] α, A. β om.   [11] dg read ἀργυρίου. A^b adds Βηρσουὲ τῆς
γυναικός μου.   [12] α. β, A, S¹ read ἀπώλεσα τὰ τέκνα μου.   [13] A^{ab*cdes} om.,
but not A^b as in Arm. text   [14] g om. f, A^b read ἦν ἡ, and f om. next
four words.   [15] α. β–f, A, S read τῆς (b om.) σαρκός μου. A^{−b} om. next
hmt. four words. A^b om. next ten words.   [16] α. β, S read τῆς (b om.)
ψυχῆς μου.   [17] g, A om.   [18] β, A^{ab*cdefs}, S¹ add Ἰακώβ.   [19] α. β om.
A^{ab*cdefs} = ἔσωζον, A^b = οὐκ ἂν ἐσώθην καί. This passage illustrates well
the respective values of our authorities. συνέδραμον = רצו, corrupt for
נרצו = ἐδέχθησαν. Or possibly for עזרו = ἐβοήθησαν. (Cf. T. Gad, v. 9,
note). β simply omitted συνέδραμον as unintelligible, while the reading
of A may represent attempts on the part of Armenian scribes to give
sense to the text, or ἔσωζον may = עזרו, as it does a few times in the LXX.
[20] A^{ab} = ἡμῶν.   [21] α. β, A, S read ὁ (aef om.) οἰκτίρμων καὶ ἐλεήμων συνέγνω
(A ἔγνω).   [22] c. h, β read ἀγνοίᾳ.   [23] c. h reads τὸ ἄτοπον. β, A om.
[24] A = ἐσκανδάλισε.   [25] af om.   [26] c om. rest of verse together with
xx. 1 through hmt.   [27] h om. rest of verse.   [28] beg, A, S. a(?)f om.
d reads ὡς ἅπαξ.   [29] g om.   [30] d reads διαφθαρείς. A = φυρείς or
φυρθείς, a corruption of φθαρείς. A om. rest of verse.   [31] dfg om.
[32] a reads ἐπέγνω.   [33] d reads ἦν ἐνόμιζον.

XX. [1] h. befg read ἐπίγνωτε, d γινώσκετε. a om. entire chapter.
[2] ef om.   [3] h adds ἐν.   [4] A = εἰς τὴν ἀλήθειαν.   [5] g reads τῆς, A εἰς
τήν.   [6] dg om. ver. 2 and first eight words of ver. 3 through hmt.
A = πλάνην.   [7] h. c reads μέσων ἐστὶ τῆς συνηδήσεως. α defective and
corrupt in vers. 2–4.   [8] Corrupt for ἐν ᾧ?   [9] A = μέσῳ αὐτῶν (+ δυοῖν

<table>
<tr><td>

α

2. Καὶ *μέσον ἐστὶ συνειδή-
σεως[7].   3. Καὶ ἐν ἕκαστον
αὐτῶν γνωρίζει ὁ Κύριος.   4.
Καὶ οὐκ ἐστὶ καιρὸς ὃς[8] δυνή-
σεται λαθεῖν αὐτὸν τὰ ἔργα
τῶν ἀνθρώπων, ὅτι καὶ τὰ
στήθη τῶν ὀστέων αὐτῶν παρὰ
Κυρίου γέγραπται.

</td><td>

β, A, S[1]

2. Καὶ μέσον[9] ἐστὶ *τὸ τῆς
συνέσεως[10] *τοῦ νοός, οὗ ἐὰν
θέλῃ, κλῖναι[11].   3. *Καίγε
τὰ τῆς ἀληθείας καὶ τὰ τῆς
πλάνης γέγραπται ἐπὶ τὸ στῆ-
θος τοῦ ἀνθρώπου[12]. καὶ ἐν[13]
ἕκαστον αὐτῶν[14] γνωρίζει *ὁ
Κύριος[15].   4. Καὶ οὐκ ἐστὶ
καιρὸς ἐν ᾧ *δυνήσεται λαθεῖν
ἀνθρώπων ἔργα[16], ὅτι ἐν †στή-
θει ⌈ὀστέων⌉[17] αὐτοῦ† [18] ἐγγέ-
γραπται[19] ⌈ἐνώπιον Κυρίου.

</td></tr>
</table>

β, A
μαρτυρεῖ
πάντα
καὶ κατη-
γορεῖ.

β, A, S[1]
ἀγαπή-
σατε.

5. ⌈Καὶ⌉ τὸ[20] πνεῦμα τῆς ἀληθείας[21] κατηγορεῖ[22] πάντων καὶ[23] ἐμπεπύρισται ὁ ἁμαρτωλὸς[24] ⌈ἐκ τῆς ἰδίας καρδίας⌉, καὶ *ἆραι πρόσωπον ⌈πρὸς τὸν κριτὴν⌉ οὐ δύναται[25].

XXI. Καὶ νῦν, τέκνα μου[1], *παραγγέλλω ὑμῖν, ἀγαπᾶτε[2]

A[b])   [10]A = σύνεσις.   [11]A reads զոր կան եւ ունին միտք = ἦν ἐστι καὶ ἔχει νοῦς(?), corrupt for միտաց զոր կամին յեղուլ(?) = νοός, οὗ ἐὰν θέλῃ κλῖναι.   [12]b, S[1] (save that S[1] reads ἐπικλίνεται for γέγραπται). ef read καίγε (+ τὸ τῆς ἀληθείας καὶ e) τὸ τῆς πλάνης παραβάλλει ἐπὶ τὸ στ. τοῦ ἀνθρώπου. The text reflects the language of Prov. iii. 3, Jer. xxxi. 33, כתב על לב, 'to write on the heart.' στῆθος is a rendering of לב as in Ex. xxviii. 23, 26. dg om. first eight words as we have seen (see note 6) and read ταῦτα (g om.) γέγραπται (+ γὰρ g) ἐπὶ τὸ (g om.) στ. τοῦ ἀνθ. A = ὅτι ἀδικία καὶ ἀλήθεια γεγραμμέναι εἰσὶ ἐπὶ τὸ στ. τοῦ ἀνθ.   [13]d, A = ἕνα.   [14]dg read αὐτόν. A = ἀνθρώπων. S[1] hopelessly corrupt in this clause.   [15]α, g. a(?)bd, A read Κύριος, ef Κύριον.   [16]bdef, S[1] (save that f reads μαθεῖν). g reads δυνήσ. ἄνθρωπον ἔργα αὐτοῦ λαθεῖν. A[ab*cdeg] = δυνήσ. ἄνθρωπος κρύψαι, A[b] ἄνθρωπος δυνήσ. κρύψαι ἔργα αὐτοῦ. Perhaps we should read ἀνθρώπου in the text. Cf. g, A.   [17]A om., because unintelligible as it stands. But ἐν στήθει ὀστέων αὐτοῦ בלב עצמו = 'on the heart itself,' or (less likely) it is corrupt for ἐν ὀστέῳ στήθους αὐτοῦ = בעצם לבו, which has the same meaning: cf. Ex. xxiv. 10; Job xxi. 23. With the former construction, cf. Keth. 77[b] עשה בשביל כבור עצמך = 'do it on account of thy own honour.'   [18]b, S[2] read αὐτός.   [19]d reads γέγραπται.   [20]h reads τὸ δέ.   [21]A adds καί.   [22]α. β, A = μαρτυρεῖ πάντα καὶ (ef om.) κατηγορεῖ. S[1] ἀκούει ἄμφω καὶ κατηγορεῖ.   [23]A adds ὡσεί.   [24]α. β reads ἁμαρτήσας.   [25]α. β reads ἆραι π. οὐ δύν. πρὸς τ. κριτήν. A = οὐ δύν. ἆραι τὸ πρόσωπον αὐτοῦ.

XXI. [1]abg om.   [2]α. β, A, S[1] read ἀγαπήσατε.   [3]d reads Λευίν.

τὸν Λευὶ³ ἵνα⁴ διαμείνητε⁵ καὶ⁶ ⌜μὴ ἐπαίρεσθε⁷ *ἐπ' αὐτόν⁸⌝, ἵνα μὴ ἐξολοθρευθῆτε⁹. ⌜2. Ἐμοὶ γὰρ¹⁰ ἔδωκεν *ὁ θεὸς¹¹ τὴν βασιλείαν, κἀκείνῳ¹² τὴν ἱερατείαν¹³, καὶ β Κύριος ὑπέταξε¹⁴ τὴν βασιλείαν *τῇ ἱερωσύνῃ¹⁵. 3. Ἐμοὶ ἔδωκεν τὰ ἐπὶ¹⁶ γῆς, ἐκείνῳ τὰ¹⁷ ἐν οὐρανοῖς¹⁸. 4. *Οὕτως γὰρ¹⁹ *ὑπερέχει ἡ ἱερατεία τοῦ θεοῦ²⁰ τῆς ἐπιγείου²¹ βασιλείας²², ἐὰν μὴ δι' ἁμαρτίας ἐκπέσῃ²³ ἀπὸ²⁴ Κυρίου²⁵ καὶ κυριευθῇ²⁶ *ἀπὸ τῆς²⁷ ἐπιγείου βασιλείας⌝. 5. *Ὁ γὰρ ἄγγελος Κυρίου εἶπέ μοι, ὅτι αὐτὸν ὑπέρ σε ἐξελέξατο Κύριος²⁸ προσεγγίζειν²⁹ αὐτῷ³⁰, καὶ ἐσθίειν³¹ τὴν³² τράπεζαν αὐτοῦ, καὶ ⌜ἀπαρχὰς *αὐτῷ προσφέρειν³³⌝ ἐντρυφημάτων³⁴ υἱῶν Ἰσραήλ. *Σὺ δὲ ἔσῃ βασιλεὺς Ἰακώβ³⁵.

6. Καὶ ἔσῃ³⁶ ⌜ἐν αὐτοῖς³⁷ ὡς³⁸ ἡ³⁹ θάλασσα. Καθάπερ⁴⁰ γὰρ⁴¹ ἐν αὐτῇ δίκαιοι⁴² χειμάζονται⁴³, ⌜οἱ μὲν αἰχμαλωτιζόμενοι *οἱ δὲ πλουτοῦντες⁴⁴⌝, οὕτως καὶ *ἐν σοὶ πᾶν γένος⁴⁵ ἀνθρώ-

Marginal notes: β Κύριος. / β-af, S¹ ὡς ὑπερέχει ὁ οὐρανὸς τῆς γῆς, οὕτως. / β, A, S¹ καὶ γάρ. / β, S¹ ἀπαρχὰς ἐντρυφημάτων. / bdeg, A, S¹ δίκαιοι καὶ ἄδικοι.

---

⁴ d adds δι' αὐτοῦ. ⁵ hi, β, A. c reads μείνητε. A adds εἰς τὸν αἰῶνα. ⁶ hi om. ⁷ c reads ἐπέρεσθε, hi ἐπέρεσθαι, d ἐπέρετε. ⁸ α, β-af. a reads ἐπ' αὐτῷ, f εἰς αὐτόν. ⁹ A om. next three verses. ¹⁰ d reads μέν. ¹¹ ch. i, β read ὁ (β om.) Κύριος. ¹² d reads ἐκείνῳ δέ, b ἐκείνῳ. ¹³ α, abe, S¹. df read ἱερωσύνην, g εἰρήνην. g om. next six words. ¹⁴ c reads ἐπέταξε. ¹⁵ α reads ἡ ἱερωσύνη. ¹⁶ hi, df, S¹ add τῆς. ¹⁷ hi read δὲ τά, f τοῦ. ¹⁸ c reads οὐρανῷ. ¹⁹ ch. β-af, S¹ read ὡς (ὥσπερ γάρ d) ὑπερέχει ὁ (b om.) οὐρανὸς τῆς γῆς οὕτως (τοσοῦτον d), a οὕτως, f ὄντως, i οὐ γάρ. ²⁰ c. hi read υπερατεια (sic) τοῦ θεοῦ, β ὑπερέχει θεοῦ (g om.) ἱερατεία (ἱερατείας d). ²¹ β reads ἐπὶ γῆς. ²² bd om. rest of verse through hmt. ²³ c reads ἐκπέσει, g ἀποπέσει. ²⁴ α. β om. ²⁵ hi read τοῦ Κυρίου (i Θεοῦ). ²⁶ c reads κυριευθείς, g κυριευθεῖ. ²⁷ c. hi read ἐπὶ τῆς, efg read ὑπὸ τῆς, a ὑπό. ²⁸ α (save that hi add ὁ before Κύριος). β, S¹ read καὶ γὰρ αὐτὸν ὑπέρ σε (g om. ὑπ. σε) ἐξελέξατο (+ ὁ d) Κύριος. A = ἐξελέξατο γὰρ αὐτὸν Κύριος ὑπὲρ ὑμᾶς. ²⁹ α. β read ἐγγίζειν. A = ἐγγίσατε. ³⁰ d reads αὐτόν, S¹ αὐτοῖς. ³¹ A = φάγετε. ³² α. β om. ³³ α (save that hi read αὐτοῦ). β, A, S¹ om. ³⁴ b reads ἐντρυφήματα. h adds τῶν. ³⁵ α, β-bg, A, S¹ (save that d reads ἔσει and d, A add ἐν before Ἰακώβ and hi om. Ἰακ.). g reads ἐμὲ δὲ βασιλεύειν ἐν Ἰ. b om. ³⁶ d reads ἔσει, g εἶναι. ³⁷ α, efg. ab read αὐτοῖς, d ἐπ' αὐτόν. ³⁸ e reads ὡσεί. ³⁹ α, adf. g reads ἐν (θαλάσσῃ). be, A om. ⁴⁰ α. β reads ὥσπερ. ⁴¹ α, β, Aᵇ. A⁻ᵇ om. ⁴² d prefixes οἱ. bdeg, A, S¹ add καὶ (+ οἱ d) ἄδικοι. ⁴³ A read [Armenian] (= βαπτίζονται) corrupt for [Armenian] = χειμάζονται. g reads σχηματίζονται. A om. next six words. ⁴⁴ β-g. α reads οἱ δὲ πλουτοῦσιν, g πλανοῦντες δέ. d om. οὕτως καὶ ... πλουτοῦσιν by hmt. (?), and reads καί instead. ⁴⁵ β-d, A. c reads ἐσύ (sic) ὅτι τὸ γένος τῶν, hi σὺ γένος. ⁴⁶ A = Ἰσραήλ. g adds ἤγουν ἐμοί. ⁴⁷ α,

β, S¹ ἀρ-
πάζοντες.
β, A οἱ
βασιλεύ-
οντες (+
ἐν σοὶ A)
ἔσονται
ὡς κήτη.
β, S¹
θυγατέ-
ρας καὶ
υἱοὺς
ἐλευθέ-
ρους.
α om.
οἴκους...
ἁρπάσου-
σιν.

πων⁴⁶, οἱ μὲν †κινδυνεύουσιν⁴⁷ αἰχμαλωτιζόμενοι ⌐οἱ δὲ πλου-
τοῦσιν⁴⁸ ἁρπάζοντες *τὰ ἀλλότρια⁴⁹⌐.

7. Ὅτι *οἱ βασιλεῖς ὡς κήτη ἔσονται⁵⁰,
    * καταπίνοντες ἀνθρώπους⁵¹ ὡς ἰχθύας
    * υἱοὺς καὶ θυγατέρας ⌐ἐλευθέρων⌐⁵² καταδουλώσουσιν⁵³
    * οἴκους, ἀγρούς, ποίμνια, χρήματα ἁρπάσουσιν⁵⁴.

8. Καὶ πολλῶν σάρκας ⌐ἀδίκως⌐⁵⁵ κόρακας⁵⁶ *καὶ ἴβεις⁵⁷
        χορτάσουσιν⁵⁸
    ⌐καὶ προκόψουσιν⁵⁹ ἐπὶ κακῷ⁶⁰ ἐν πλεονεξίᾳ ὑψούμενοι⌐.

9. Καὶ ἔσονται ⌐ὡς⌐ καταιγίδες⁶¹ ψευδοπροφῆται⁶²,
    καὶ πάντας⁶³ δικαίους διώξουσιν⁶⁴.

XXII. Ἐπάξει¹ δὲ αὐτοῖς² Κύριος διαιρέσεις ⌐κατ᾽ ἀλλή-
       λων⌐³,
    καὶ πόλεμοι ⌐συνεχεῖς⌐ ἔσονται ἐν Ἰσραήλ⁴.

2. Καὶ ἐν ἀλλοφύλοις⁵ συντελεσθήσεται ἡ βασιλεία μου⁶,
    ἕως *τοῦ ἐλθεῖν⁷ *τὸ σωτήριον⁸ τοῦ⁹ Ἰσραήλ¹⁰,

bfg. ae read οἱ μὲν κινδυνεύσουσιν. A = κινδυνεύσει καὶ παραβήσεται and om.
rest of verse. S¹ = πεσοῦνται εἰς ἀτυχίας. Instead of κινδυνεύουσιν the text
requires some word the antithesis of πλουτοῦσιν. Now κινδυν. = יְסָּכֵן (or
יְסָּכֵן) (late Hebrew) the former of which in earlier Hebrew = πτωχεύουσι
(cf. Is. xl. 20), or text = נִסְכָּנִים corrupt for מִסְכֵּנִים = πτωχεύουσιν. The
latter is a rare word: cf. Eccles. iv. 13, v. 15, ix. 15. The former word,
though found only once in O.T., is common in later Hebrew. ⁴⁸be, S¹ read
πλουτίσουσιν, i πλουτίζωσιν. ⁴⁹α. β, S¹ om. ⁵⁰α. β, A read οἱ (a om.)
βασιλεύοντες (+ ἐν σοὶ A) ἔσονται ὡς κήτη. S¹ = ὥσπερ βασιλεύοντες ἔσονται ὡς
κήτη. ⁵¹A = καὶ καταπίονται Ἰσραὴλ ὡς ἰχ. S¹ ἐσθίοντες ἰχθύας καὶ ἀνθρώπους.
⁵²α, A (save that Aᵃᵇ read αὐτῶν and Aʰᵇ*ᶜᵈᵉˡˢ om. ἐλευθέρων). β, S¹read θυγ. καὶ
υἱοὺς ἐλευθέρους (d om.). ⁵³bg read καταδουλοῦσιν. ⁵⁴b. This line is omitted
by α but attested by β, A, S¹. Likewise the parallelism supports it.
β–b, A, S¹ read (+ καὶ A) οἴκους (χρυσίον d) καὶ ἀγροὺς καὶ (β–d om.)
ποίμνια καὶ (β, S¹ om.) χρήματα (β–b, S¹ om.) ἁρπάσουσιν (ἁρπάσωσιν f,
ἁρπάζουσιν g). ⁵⁵g prefixes καί. For πολλῶν . . . . χορτάσουσιν S¹ reads
πολλὰ σώματα τῶν ἀδίκων κόρακες καὶ καθαρματοφαγοῦσαι ὄρνιθες χορτάσουσιν.
⁵⁶a reads κόρακες. ⁵⁷β–g. c reads ἠβεῖς, hi καὶ κύνες, g ἴβεις. ⁵⁸d reads
χορτάσωσι, g χορτάζουσι. ⁵⁹c reads προσκόψουσιν. ⁶⁰α, af. bedg read τὸ
κακόν, hi κακῶν. ⁶¹c reads καταιγίδαις, g καταιγίς, S¹ ἀποστάται.
⁶²A = προφῆται. ⁶³f reads ἅπαντας, d adds τούς. ⁶⁴b reads διώξονται,
f διώξωσιν. For πάντας . . . διώξουσιν A reads πάντες οἱ δίκαιοι διωχθήσονται.
   XXII. ¹g reads ἐπανάξει. ²ci, e read αὐτούς. ³hi, A om. ⁴α om.
next two lines through hmt. d om. next line. ⁵A adds καί and thus
connects καὶ ἐν ἀλλοφ. with what precedes. ⁶A = αὐτῶν. ⁷d reads οὗ
ἔλθῃ. ⁸Aᵇ = ἡ βασιλεία. ⁹b om. ¹⁰d reads κόσμου and adds καὶ ἐν

⌜ἕως τῆς¹¹ παρουσίας¹² Θεοῦ τῆς δικαιοσύνης⌝,
*τοῦ ἡσυχάσαι τὸν Ἰακὼβ¹³ ἐν εἰρήνῃ ⌜καὶ πάντα τὰ ἔθνη⌝¹⁴.

3. Καὶ αὐτὸς φυλάξει κράτος¹⁵ βασιλείας μου ἕως¹⁶ αἰῶνος¹⁷, ὅρκῳ γὰρ ὤμοσέ μοι ὁ¹⁸ Κύριος¹⁹ μὴ ἐξαλεῖψαι²⁰ *τὸ βασίλειον ἐκ τοῦ σπέρματός μου ἕως αἰῶνος²¹.

XXIII. Πολλὴ¹ ⌜δὲ⌝ λύπη² μοί ἐστι, τέκνα μου³, διὰ τὰς ἀσελγείας⁴ καὶ γοητείας⁵ ἃς ποιήσετε ⌜εἰς τὸ βασίλειον⌝⁶, ἐγγαστριμύθοις⁷ ἐξακολουθοῦντες⁸ κληδόσι⁹ καὶ δαίμοσι¹⁰ πλάνης¹¹.
2. Τὰς θυγατέρας ὑμῶν μουσικὰς καὶ δημοσίας¹² ποιήσετε¹³, *ἐπιμιγήσεσθε δὲ¹⁴ *ἐν βδελύγμασιν¹⁵ ἐθνῶν.   3. Ἀνθ' ὧν ἐπάξει¹⁶ Κύριος *ἐφ' ὑμᾶς¹⁷ λιμὸν καὶ λοιμόν¹⁸, θάνατον καὶ ῥομφαίαν [ἐκδικοῦσαν]¹⁹, πολιορκίαν [καὶ κύνας εἰς διασπασμὸν]²⁰ ἐχθρῶν²¹ καὶ *φίλων ὀνειδισμούς²², [ἀπώλειαν²³

β–af, A, S¹ γοη-τείας καὶ εἰδωλο-λατρείας.

a, A πο-λιορκίαν ἐχθρῶν.

ἀλλοφύλοις συντελεσθήσεται ἡ βασιλεία μου.   ¹¹α. β om.   ¹²β–g add τοῦ ¹³A = καὶ τότε οἰκήσει Ἰ. (Ἰσραὴλ καινός Aᵇ).   ¹⁴Bracketed as an interpolation. It is foreign to the context and A om. c om. the τά. h om. next eight words. ¹⁵g reads τὸ κράτος τῆς. ¹⁶b adds τοῦ. ¹⁷i om. rest of verse. ¹⁸c. Other MSS. om. ¹⁹d adds τοῦ. ²⁰ch, aef. b reads ἐκλείψειν, d ἐκλεῖψαι, g, A ἔκλειψιν ποιῆσαι, S¹ λαμβάνειν. ²¹ch, A (save that c om. ἐκ τοῦ σπ. μου). β, S¹ read τὸ βασιλείόν (τὴν βασιλείαν d) μου ἐκ (καὶ bg) τοῦ σπέρματός (τῷ σπέρματί g) μου πάσας τὰς ἡμέρας (f om. π. τ. ἡμ.) ἕως (g om.) τοῦ (a om.) αἰῶνος.

XXIII. ¹c reads πολλύ. ²g trs. after ἐστι. ³aef om. ⁴c, b read ἀσελγίας, f ἀλγηδόνας. ⁵h om. β–af, A add καὶ εἰδωλολατρείας. ⁶A reads καὶ, d ἐπὶ τὸ βασιλεύειν. ⁷α reads ἐν γαστρὶ μύθους. ⁸b reads ἀκολουθοῦντες. ⁹b, A. So also g but trs. κλ. and δαιμ. πλάνης. This word is written variously in the MSS. c reads κλύδωσι, hi κλώδωσι, d κλύδοσι, e κλήδωσιν, f. κλείδοσιν. a om. ¹⁰c, e read δαίμωσιν. ¹¹β, A. c reads πλάνων, hi πάντων. ¹²S¹= ὀρχηστρίδας. ¹³hi, df read ποιήσητε. Aᵃᵇ=ποιεῖτε. ¹⁴α. β–g, Aᵃᵇᶜᵉⁱˢ read καὶ (aefom.) ἐπιμιγ., g ἐπὶ γῆς ἔσεσθε. Aʰʰ*ᵈ=ἐπιμιγήσονται. ¹⁵a reads βδελύγματι, g βδελύγματα. ¹⁶α. β–d read ἄξει, d ἤξει. ¹⁷Aᵃᵇʰʰ*ᶜᵈ om. but not Aᵉᵉ. ¹⁸Aᵃᵇ read [Armenian] (= σεισμόν) corrupt for [Armenian] = λοιμόν. Aʰʰ*ᶜᵈᵉˢ [Armenian] = φόνον. hi read λοιμοῦ and om. preceding καί. dg add καί. λοιμόν may be a corrupt dittography of λιμόν. Then λιμός, θάνατος, and ῥομφαία would be the three destroying agencies so frequently mentioned together in Jer. xiv. 12, xv. 2, &c. ¹⁹Since A om. and the word injures the parallelism I have bracketed as an interpolation. A adds καί. ²⁰Since a, A om. and the phrase seems alien to the context I have bracketed it as an intrusion. It is derived from Jer. xv. 3. By its omission ἐχθρῶν is rightly made dependent on πολιορκίαν, and this phrase is balanced by φίλων ὀνειδισμούς. a om.

β, A, S¹   καὶ *σφακελισμὸν ⌐ὀφθαλμῶν²⁴, καὶ⌐] νηπίων ⌐ἀναίρεσιν⌐²⁵
ἀναίρεσιν   *ὑπαρχόντων ἁρπαγήν²⁶, ⌐ναοῦ²⁷ θεοῦ ἐμπρησμόν²⁸, *γῆς⌐ ἐρή-
(A om.)   μωσιν²⁹, *ὑμῶν δὲ³⁰ αὐτῶν³¹ δουλείαν ἐν ἔθνεσιν.   4. Καὶ
καὶ συμ-   ἐκτεμοῦσι *τοὺς υἱοὺς³² ὑμῶν εἰς³³ εὐνούχους *ταῖς γυναιξὶν³⁴
βίων
ἀφαιρε-   αὐτῶν.   5. Ἕως³⁵ ἂν *ἐπισκέψηται κύριος ὑμῖν³⁶, *ἐν
σιν.

β, A, S¹ ἐπιστρέψητε πρὸς κύριον.

next five words.   ²¹ h reads ἐχθροῦ. With πολιορκίαν ἐχθρῶν cf. Jer.
xix. 9.   ²² α, abd, Aᵇ (Armenian text wrong here). So also Aᵇᵇ*ᵈ
with words transposed. Aᵃᶜᵉ = φίλων εἰς ὀνειδισμούς. efg read φίλων
ὀνειδισμόν.   ²³ The text is here uncertain. A comparison of the adjoining
context suggests that ἀπώλειαν καὶ σφακ. ὀφθαλμῶν is, if original, thoroughly
corrupt. Thus if ὀφθαλμῶν is original, it is unlikely that it was preceded
by two accusatives, as all the adjoining parallels are against this. But
ὀφθαλμῶν cannot be right. The preceding genitives and the following
one (two?) relate to persons. Hence ὀφθαλμῶν is either interpolated or
corrupt. (i) First if ὀφθαλμῶν is an interpolation (hi, A omit it), ἀπώλειαν
καὶ σφακελισμόν = וכלה שחת; for σφακελίζω in the only two places where
it occurs in the LXX (Lev. xxvi. 16; Deut. xxviii. 32) is a rendering of
כלה. Now this phrase could be an easy corruption of שחת כלה = ἀπώλειαν
νυμφῶν, 'the destruction of brides.' (ii) Again, if ὀφθαλμῶν is interpolated, the interpolation may extend also to the two preceding words.
The phrase καὶ σφακελισμὸν ὀφθαλμῶν would be then an addition to the
text like καὶ κύνας εἰς διασπασμόν above, and ἀπώλειαν might be taken as
a marginal gloss—explaining the rare word σφακελισμόν—which was
subsequently taken into the text. (iii) Or finally, if ὀφθαλμῶν represents
some corruption in the original, σφακελισμὸν ὀφθαλμῶν = עינים כלת, where
עינים could be corrupt for עולים = παιδίων or νηπίων. In that case σφακ.
†ὀφθαλμῶν (i. e. νηπίων) would be simply a dittography of the following
clause νηπίων ἀναίρεσιν, ἀπώλειαν having been originally as in (ii) a marginal
gloss. As I think we should adopt either (ii) or (iii), I have bracketed
the clause ἀπώλειαν ... ὀφθαλμῶν καί as an addition to the text.   ²⁴ Cf.
Lev. xxvi. 16 מכלות עינים ... שחפת, also Deut. xxviii. 32. hi, A om.
ὀφθαλμῶν and d, A the following καί. For σφακ. a reads λήμην and d
σφακελιμούς. S¹ reads καὶ πρὸ τῶν ὀφθαλμῶν.   ²⁵ α, β. A om. β, A, S¹
add καὶ συμβίων ἀφαίρεσιν (g ἀναίρεσιν, A διαίρεσιν).   ²⁶ bdg, S¹. ef read
ὑπαρχόντων ἀπαρχόντων. a om. c reads ὑπαρχόντων ἀπαρχῶν, hi ἀπαρχὴν τῶν
ἀπαρχῶν. A = καὶ (Aᵃᵇᵒᵍ om.) ἔνδειαν (but ꜰ is corrupt for
ꜰ = ἁρπαγήν) ὑπαρχόντων.   ²⁷ hi read ναῶν.   ²⁸ α, adg. For
ἐμπρησμόν of α, adg, ἐμπυρισμόν is read by β–adg.   ²⁹ a trs. before ναοῦ.
g reads εἰς ἐρήμωσιν.   ³⁰ α. β–d, S¹ read ὑμῶν, d, A καὶ ὑμῶν.   ³¹ h om.
next eight words. A adds εἰς.   ³² α. β, A, S¹ read ἐξ.   ³³ g om.   ³⁴ a

τελείᾳ καρδίᾳ³⁷ *μεταμελουμένους καὶ πορευομένους³⁸ ἐν πάσαις ταῖς ἐντολαῖς αὐτοῦ³⁹, ⌜καὶ⌝ *ἀναγάγῃ ὑμᾶς⁴⁰ ἐκ⁴¹ *τῆς αἰχμαλωσίας ⌜τῶν ἐθνῶν⌝⁴².

β, A, S¹ μεταμε-λουμένοι καὶ πορευό-μενοι.

α, β, S	A
XXIV. *Καὶ μετὰ ταῦτα¹ ἀνατελεῖ ὑμῖν² ἄστρον ἐξ Ἰακὼβ ἐν εἰρήνῃ³, καὶ ἀναστήσεται⁴ ἄνθρωπος [ἐκ τοῦ σπέρματός μου]⁵ *ὡς ἥλιος δικαιοσύνης⁶, συμπορευόμενος⁷ τοῖς ἀνθρώποις⁸ ἐν πραότητι καὶ δικαιοσύνῃ. *Καὶ πᾶσα ἁμαρτία οὐχ εὑρεθήσεται ἐν αὐτῷ⁹.	XXIV. Καὶ μετὰ ταῦτα ἀνατελεῖ τὸ ἄστρον εἰρήνης, *τοῦ ἡλίου τῆς δικαιοσύνης¹¹ καὶ συμπορεύσεται ἀνθρώποις *ἐν πραότητι καὶ δικαιοσύνῃ¹².
2. Καὶ ἀνοιγήσονται ἐπ’ αὐτῷ¹⁰ οἱ οὐρανοὶ	2. Καὶ¹³ ἀνοιγήσονται αὐτῷ οὐρανοὶ

β–b, A, S¹ ἐπισκέψηται ὑμᾶς Κύριος ἐν ἐλεεῖ καὶ ἀναγάγῃ.

reads τὰς γυναῖκας. A = εἰς δουλείαν γυναικῶν. ³⁵ α, β–bg, S¹. bg, A read καὶ ὡς. ³⁶ α, save that c gives form ἐπισκέψειται. The construction is irregular. We should expect ὑμᾶς. β, A, S¹ read ἐπιστρέψητε πρὸς Κύριον (+ καὶ A). ³⁷ α, β–bd, A. b reads εὐτελείᾳ καρδίας, d ἐν τέλει καρδίας. ³⁸ α. β, S¹ read μεταμελούμενοι καὶ πορευόμενοι (d om. καὶ πορ.). A = μεταμελήσεσθε καὶ πορεύσεσθε. ³⁹ α, A. β, S¹ read τοῦ Θεοῦ. ⁴⁰ α (but with the form ἀναγάγει). β, A, S¹ read καὶ (A om.) ἐπισκέψηται (ἐπισκέψεται a) ὑμᾶς (ἡμᾶς d) Κύριος (A^{ab*cd} om.) ἐν ἐλεεῖ καὶ ἀναγάγῃ (ἀναγάγει dg, ἐν ἀγάπῃ b). ⁴¹ α. β reads ἀπό. ⁴² hi, β–b (save that for ἐθνῶν f reads λαῶν). c reads τῶν ἐθνῶν τῆς αἰχμαλωσίας, b τῆς αἰχ. τῶν ἐχθρῶν ὑμῶν.

XXIV. ¹ c om. καί and trs. μετὰ ταῦτα after Ἰακώβ. h prefixes as title of chapter περὶ τοῦ Χριστοῦ πῶς μέλλει γεννηθῆναι. ² g om. Cf. A. ³ In T. Levi xviii. 3 we have οὐρανῷ. ⁴ e om. ⁵ Interpolated probably by the scribe who added verses 5 and 6. Verses 1–3 refer to the Messiah from Levi. ⁶ b reads ὡς ὁ ἥλιος τῆς δικαιοσύνης. A^{-b} om. The phrase is drawn from Mal. iv. 2, and ἀναστήσεται ἄνθρωπος recalls the peculiar text of the LXX of Num. xxiv. 17. ⁷ We should expect to find καὶ συμπορεύσεται as in A. ⁸ α, aef. bdg read υἱοῖς τῶν ἀνθρώπων. ⁹ There is no adequate ground for rejecting this clause as a Christian interpolation. Cf. T. Levi xvii. 9; Pss. Sol. xviii. 41, where the Messiah is to be καθαρὸς ἀπὸ ἁμαρτίας. ¹⁰ be read αὐτόν, S¹ αὐτοῖς. ¹¹ A^b. Rest om. ¹² Emended from A^{abb*dg} which = ἡσυχίᾳ καὶ δικαιοσυνῃ, for ꝫⳡⳅⲣⲡⲧⲛⲡⲉⲃⲧⲃⳅⳡⲣ is corrupt for ⲕⲛⲃⳡⳅⲡⲣⳅⲡⲧⲃⲧⲃⳅⳡⲣ = πραότητι. A^b = ἐν ἡσυχίᾳ, A^{ce} εἰρήνῃ καὶ ἡσυχίᾳ.

α, β, S

’Εκχέαι[14] πνεῦμα[15] εὐλογίαν πατρὸς ἁγίου[16],
καὶ αὐτὸς ἐκχεεῖ πνεῦμα
χάριτος ἐφ’ ὑμᾶς.

α ἐν
ἀληθείᾳ.

3. * Καὶ ἔσεσθε αὐτῷ εἰς υἱοὺς[17]
ἐν ἀληθείᾳ
* καὶ πορεύσεσθε[18] ἐν προστάγμασιν[19] αὐτοῦ πρώ-
τοις καὶ ἐσχάτοις.

4. [Οὗτος ὁ βλαστὸς Θεοῦ
ὑψίστου

β–d, S¹
εἰς ζωὴν
πάσης
σαρκός.

καὶ αὕτη ἡ πηγὴ * πᾶσι
παρέχουσα ζωήν[20]].

5. Τότε ἀναλάμψει[21] σκῆπτρον βασιλείας μου
καὶ ἀπὸ τῆς ῥίζης ὑμῶν[22]

α πηγή.

γενήσεται πυθμήν[23],

β, S¹ ἐν
αὐτῷ ἀνα-
βήσεται.

6. Καὶ * ἐξ αὐτῆς βλαστήσει[24]
ῥάβδος δικαιοσύνης[25]
τοῖς ἔθνεσιν
* κρῖναι καὶ σῶσαι[26] πάντας τοὺς[27] ἐπικαλουμέ-
νους τὸν[28] Κύριον.

A

καὶ ἐκχυθήσονται εὐλογίαι
πατρὸς ἁγίου ἐπ’ αὐτῷ[29],
καὶ αὐτὸς ἐκχεεῖ ἐφ’
† ἡμᾶς[30] πνεῦμα χάρι-
τος.

3. Καὶ ἔσεσθε αὐτῷ εἰς υἱο-
θεσίαν ἀληθείας
καὶ πορεύσεσθε ἐν τοῖς
προστάγμασιν αὐτοῦ
πρώτοις καὶ δευτέροις.

4. [Τότε ἀναβήσεται βλαστὸς
ἀπ’ ἐμοῦ]

5. Καὶ * ἀναλάμψει σκῆπ-
τρον[31] βασιλείας μου
καὶ ἀπὸ τῆς ῥίζης ὑμῶν[32]
ἀναστήσεται πυθμήν,

6. Καὶ ἀπ’ αὐτοῦ ἀναβήσε-
ται[33] ῥάβδος δικαιοσύνης
τοῖς ἔθνεσιν
κρῖναι καὶ σῶσαι πάν-
τας τοὺς ἐπικαλουμένους
Κύριον.

[13] A[beg]. A[ab*cd] om.   [14] c reads ἐκχαῖε (sic).   [15] α, β–bg. bg, S² read πνεύματος. Though A om. there seems no valid ground for marking it as an interpolation. Cf. Ps. xi. 2; Joel ii. 28 for the thought. hi, d om. next seven words through hmt.   [16] g reads αὐτοῦ, S¹ καὶ ἁγνότητα.   [17] α om.   [18] b. deg read καὶ πορεύεσθε. α, af om. a om. rest of line.   [19] hi, efg. c, bd, S read προστάγματι.   [20] α. β–d, S read εἰς ζωὴν πάσης (g om.) σαρκός, d εἰς ζωὴν αἰώνιον. a om. next two verses together with XXV. I have bracketed οὗτος . . . ζωήν as a Christian interpolation though some defence could be made.   [21] g adds δεύτερον.   [22] hi read ἡμῶν.   [23] β–ag. α reads πηγή, dg πυιμήν. How this impossible reading arose I cannot discover.   [24] c. β–ag read as in margin, hi ἐν αὐτῇ ἀναβήσεται, g ἐν αὐτῷ γενήσεται.   [25] g adds ἐν.   [26] hi, β. c reads καὶ σώσει.   [27] ef om.   [28] α. β om.   [29] A[b] adds ὅς ἐστι Χριστός.   [30] A[abc(ег?)] but ἡμᾶς is corrupt for ὑμᾶς. A[b*d] = ἀνθρώπους.   [31] A[ab]. A[hb*cde] = θαλλήσει ἀπὸ σκήπτρου.   [32] A[b] adds ἀπὸ προφητῶν.   [33] A[b] adds ὁ ἀπεσταλ-μένος.

XXV. Καὶ[1] μετὰ ταῦτα *ἀναστήσεται Ἀβραὰμ καὶ Ἰσαὰκ καὶ Ἰακὼβ εἰς ζωήν[2], *καὶ ἐγὼ[3] καὶ οἱ ἀδελφοί μου ἔξαρχοι[4] †σκήπτρων[5] ⌜ἐν Ἰσραὴλ⌝[6] ἐσόμεθα[7], *πρῶτος Λευί[8], δεύτερος ἐγώ, τρίτος Ἰωσήφ, τέταρτος Βενιαμήν[9], πέμπτος *Συμεών, ἕκτος Ἰσαχάρ[10], καὶ οὕτως *πάντες καθεξῆς[11].   2. Καὶ[12] ὁ[13] Κύριος εὐλόγησε[14] τὸν Λευί, *ὁ δ᾽[15] ἄγγελος τοῦ προσώπου[16] ἐμέ[17], *αἱ δυνάμεις[18] τῆς δόξης[19] τὸν Συμεών[20], ὁ οὐρανὸς τὸν Ῥουβίμ[21], τὸν Ἰσαχὰρ *ἡ γῆ[22], ἡ θάλασσα τὸν[23] Ζαβουλών, τὰ ὄρη τὸν Ἰωσήφ, ἡ σκηνὴ[24] *τὸν Βενιαμήν[25], οἱ φωστῆρες τὸν Δάν[26], *ἡ †τρυφὴ[27] τὸν Νεφθαλείμ[28], *ὁ ἥλιος[29] τὸν Γάδ, *ἡ σελήνη[30] τὸν Ἀσήρ.

α Ζαβου-
λών.
β–b, A
εὐλογή-
σει.

α, β, S[1]	A
3. Καὶ *ἔσεσθε εἰς λαὸν[31] Κυρίου, καὶ[32] *γλῶσσα μία[33], καὶ οὐκ ἔσται ἐκεῖ[34] *πνεῦμα πλάνης[35] τοῦ Βελίαρ, ὅτι ἐμβληθήσεται, *ἐν πυρί[36] *εἰς τὸν αἰῶνα[37].	3. Καὶ ἔσονται εἰς λαὸν Κυρίου καὶ μία γλῶσσα καὶ οὐκ ἔσται ἐν ὑμῖν πνεῦμα πλάνης ὅτι ἐμβληθήσεται μιαρὰ πνεύματα[38] εἰς κρίσιν αἰώνιον.

β ἔσται εἰς λαός.

XXV. [1] hi, g om.   [2] A = ἔσται Ἰακὼβ ζῶν καὶ Ἰσραὴλ ἀναστήσεται. c adds καί after Ἰακώβ.   [3] α reads κἀγώ, g ἐγώ.   [4] A[abc] = ἔξαρχος.   [5] α, d. bf read σκῆπτρον ἡμῶν (ὑμῶν f), eg, S[1] σκήπτρων ἡμῶν. The translator should have rendered שבטים here by φυλῶν, but A understood peculiar meaning of σκῆπτρον here and rendered by φυλῶν ἡμῶν.   [6] c reads ἐν Ἰερουσαλήμ.   [7] c, df read ἐσώμεθα.   [8] α, A. β trans. The numbers are given in e throughout this verse by the Greek letters.   [9] c, df. hi, bg read Βενιαμίν, e Βενιαμείν.   [10] β–f (save that d reads Ἡσαχάρ), A, S[1]. α reads Ζαβουλών, f Συμεών. e, S[1] add ζ Ζαβουλών.   [11] α, ef. β–ef, S[1] read καθ. πάντες. A = πάντες. S[1] adds ἐν Ἰσραήλ.   [12] d reads τότε.   [13] β om.   [14] α, b, S[1]. β–b, A read εὐλογήσει. d trs. before Κύριος.   [15] α. d reads καὶ ὁ, β–d ὁ. A = καί.   [16] d reads πατρός μου.   [17] β. α reads ἐμοί.   [18] A = καὶ ὁ ἄγγελος.   [19] A[b*] adds αὐτοῦ.   [20] d om. next four words.   [21] α. bfg read Ῥουβήμ, e Ῥουβήν.   [22] d trs. before τὸν Ἰσ.   [23] hi add Βενιαμίν.   [24] A = αἱ σκηναί.   [25] c, df. bg read τ. Βενιαμίν, e τ. Βενιαμείν. hi om.   [26] d reads Ἀδάμ.   [27] A = αἱ τρυφαί. The original was עדן ʻEden.'   [28] α, abg. def read Νεφθαλήμ.   [29] A[abceg] = δυνάμεις καὶ στηριγμοί, A[hh*d] δύναμις καὶ στηριγμός.   [30] α, β–ab. b, S[1] read ἐλαία. A = αἱ ἐλαῖαι.   [31] α, A[elg]. bdg read ἔσται εἰς λαός, ef ἔσται εἰς λαόν, A[abb*ed] ἔσονται εἰς λαόν, S[1] ἔσται ἐν τοῖς λαοῖς.   [32] g, S[1] om.   [33] f reads γλῶσσαν μίαν.   [34] α. bg, S[1] read ἔτι, e οὐκέτι, df om.   [35] d reads τῇ πλάνῃ.   [36] α, df. be read ἐν τῷ πυρί, g εἰς τὸ πῦρ.   [37] g reads τὸ αἰώνιον. dg add καὶ ἐπέκεινα.   [38] A[b] adds

<table>
<tr><td></td><td>α, β, S¹</td><td>A</td></tr>
<tr>
<td></td>
<td>

4. *Καὶ οἱ³⁹ ἐν λύπῃ τελευ-
τήσαντες ἀναστήσονται
ἐν χαρᾷ
καὶ⁴⁰ οἱ πτωχοὶ⁴¹ διὰ⁴² Κύ-
ριον⁴³ πλουτισθήσονται
καὶ οἱ *ἀποθνήσκοντες διὰ
Κύριον⁴⁶ ἐξυπνισθήσον-
ται *εἰς ζωήν⁴⁷.

5. Καὶ οἱ ἔλαφοι Ἰωσὴφ⁴⁸
δραμοῦνται ἐν ἀγαλλιά-
σει,
καὶ οἱ ἀετοὶ Ἰσραὴλ⁴⁹ πε-
τασθήσονται⁵⁰ ἐν χαρᾷ
[οἱ δὲ ἀσεβεῖς πενθήσουσιν
καὶ οἱ ἁμαρτωλοὶ κλαύ-
σονται]⁵¹
καὶ πάντες οἱ λαοὶ δοξά-
σουσι τὸν⁵² Κύριον εἰς⁵³
αἰῶνας.

</td>
<td>

4. Καὶ οἱ ἐν λύπῃ⁵⁴ τελευτή-
σαντες ἀναστήσονται
καὶ οἱ διὰ Κύριον ἀποθνή-
σκοντες ἐξυπνισθήσον-
ται.

5. Καὶ οἱ ἔλαφοι τοῦ Ἰακὼβ
δραμοῦνται⁵⁵
καὶ αἱ δαμάλεις⁵⁶ τοῦ Ἰσ-
ραὴλ πηδιάσουσιν
καὶ πάντες λαοὶ δοξάσου-
σιν⁵⁷ Κύριον εἰς αἰῶνα.

</td>
</tr>
</table>

Side-note (left of §4): After πλουτι-
σθήσον-
ται β–g,
S¹ add
*καὶ οἱ ἐν
πείνῃ
χορτα-
σθήσον-
ται⁴⁴
*καὶ οἱ ἐν
ἀσθενείᾳ
ἰσχύσου-
σιν⁴⁵.
abg, A,
S¹ Ἰακώβ.

Side-note (left of XXVI): β, A, S¹
κατευ-
θύνουσι.

XXVI. Φυλάξατε¹ οὖν τέκνα μου *πάντα τὸν² νόμον Κυρίου³, ὅτι⁴ ἐστὶν *πᾶσιν ἐλπὶς⁵ τοῖς κατέχουσιν⁶ *τὰς

τοῦ πονηροῦ. ³⁹ d reads καί, g ὡς. ⁴⁰ h om. ⁴¹ α. β, S¹ read ἐν πτωχείᾳ. ⁴² hi add τόν. ⁴³ S¹ adds ἐξυπνισθήσονται εἰς ζωὴν καί. ⁴⁴ β–g, S¹ (save that for πείνῃ ab, S¹ read πενίᾳ, d πῖνα, ef πεῖνα). ef trs. this clause after ἰσχύσου-σιν, and S¹ trs. it after ἐξυπνισθ. εἰς ζωήν. α, g, A om. An interpolation. ⁴⁵ β–d, S¹. α, d, A om. An interpolation. ⁴⁶ α (save that hi add τόν after διά). abdg read διὰ κ. ἀποθανόντες, ef διὰ κ. ἀποθνήσκοντες. ⁴⁷ α, d. β–d read ἐν ζωῇ. ⁴⁸ α, def. abg, A, S¹ read Ἰακώβ. ⁴⁹ g reads Ἰακώβ. ⁵⁰ d reads πενθήσονται. ⁵¹ I have bracketed this clause as an interpolation though found in α, β, S¹. It is omitted by A and is against the parallelism. b om. οἱ before ἁμαρτωλοί, and g reads κολασθήσονται for κλαύσονται. ⁵² α. β om. ⁵³ hi, d add τούς. ⁵⁴ Aᵃᵇ. Aʰᵇ*ᶜᵈᵉᶠᵍ = ὑπερηφανίᾳ. ⁵⁵ Aᵇ om. next line. ⁵⁶ I do not see how this reading can have arisen. ⁵⁷ Aᵇ = τοῦ Ἰσραὴλ εὐλογήσουσιν.

XXVI. ¹ hi read φυλάξασθε. ² hi, aef, Aᵃᵇ. c reads πάντοτε τόν, bg πάντα. d, Aʰᵇ*ᶜᵈᵉᶠᵍ τόν. ³ g om. ⁴ h reads ὅς. ⁵ α. β, A read ἐλπὶς πᾶσι. ⁶ α. β, S¹ read κατευθύνουσιν. A = εὐθὺ περιπατοῦσιν a free rendering of β. The genitive αὐτοῦ that follows supports α, which = שומרים of which משרים = κατευθύνουσι is a corruption. But corruption may have originated in the Greek. ⁷ α, β–b. b, S¹ read τὴν ὁδὸν αὐτοῦ.

ὁδοὺς αὐτοῦ[7].   2. *Καὶ ⌜εἶπεν αὐτοῖς ὅτι Ἰδοὺ ἐγὼ⌝[8] *ἑκατὸν *δέκα καὶ ὀκτὼ ἐτῶν[9] ἀποθνήσκω σήμερον[10].

α	β, A, S[1]
3. Μηδείς[11] με ἐνταφιάσει ἐν πολυτελεῖ ἐσθῆτι, ἀλλὰ ἀναγάγετέ[12] με ἐν Χεβρών, ἔνθα καὶ οἱ πατέρες μου.	3. Μηδείς με ἐνταφιάσῃ[13] ⌜πολυτελεῖ[14] ἐσθῆτι⌝, ἢ *τὴν κοιλίαν μου ἀναρρήξει[15], ⌜ὅτι ταῦτα μέλλουσι ποιεῖν[16] *οἱ βασιλεύοντες[17]⌝, καὶ[18] ἀναγάγετέ με εἰς[19] Χεβρὼν *μεθ’ ὑμῶν[20].

<table>
<tr><td style="text-align:center">α, β, S[1]</td><td style="text-align:center">A</td></tr>
<tr><td>4. *Καὶ ταῦτα εἰπὼν ἐκοιμήθη[21] καὶ ἐποίησαν οἱ υἱοὶ αὐτοῦ κατὰ πάντα ὅσα[22] ἐνετείλατο αὐτοῖς, *καὶ ἔθαψαν[23] αὐτὸν[24] *μετὰ τῶν πατέρων αὐτοῦ[25] *ἐν Χεβρών[26].</td><td>4. *Καὶ ἐκοιμήθη Ἰούδας μετὰ πατέρων αὐτοῦ καὶ ἐποίησαν καθάπερ ἐνετείλατο αὐτοῖς[27].</td></tr>
</table>

(margin: aef ὅτι. β, A, S[1] σήμερον ἐν ὀφθαλμοῖς ὑμῶν.   β, S[1] ἐκοιμήθη Ἰούδας.)

Διαθήκη Ἰσαχὰρ τοῦ πέμπτου υἱοῦ Ἰακὼβ καὶ Λείας[1].

I. Ἀντίγραφον λόγων Ἰσαχάρ. *Καλέσας γὰρ τοὺς υἱοὺς αὐτοῦ εἶπεν αὐτοῖς[2].

A = κατ’ αὐτόν.   [8] α. aefg read καὶ εἶπεν ὅτι (g om.), b, S[1] καὶ εἶπε πρὸς αὐτούς. d om.   [9] α. aef read ριθ (ρι΄ καὶ ἐννέα e) ἐτῶν ἐγώ. bg δεκαεννέα ἐτῶν ἐγώ, d ριθ ἐτῶν σήμερον ἐγώ. A = καὶ νῦν (A[ab] om.) ἐγὼ (A[ab*cdeg] om.) ἑκατὸν δέκα καὶ ἐννέα (A[ab*cdeg] ἐννέα καὶ δέκα). S[1] ἑκατὸν πεντήκοντα καὶ ἐννέα but the right number is given by S at end of ver. 4.   [10] d trs. before ἐγώ. See last note. β, A, S[1] add as in margin.   [11] c adds δεῖ.   [12] h reads ἀνειλασθαι (sic).   [13] b. α, adefg read ἐνταφιάσει.   [14] ade. bfg read πολυτελῆ.   [15] bdefg (save that e reads ἀναρρίξῃ and b ἀναρήξει), A. a reads ἀνιρρήξοι τὴν κ. μου.   [16] d reads ποιῆσαι.   [17] g reads βασιλεῖς.   [18] β–d. d, A read ἀλλά.   [19] β–d. d reads ἐν.   [20] bdg, A[ab*cdeg] trs. before εἰς. aef, A[b], S[1] om.   [21] α, β (save that d om. καί and β–dg, S[1] add Ἰούδας after ἐκοιμήθη, and d adds Ἰ. τοῖς υἱοῖς αὐτοῦ before it and ἐν εἰρήνῃ after it, while g adds Ἰ. before it).   [22] α, ab. efg read ἅ. For κ. π. ὅσα d reads καθά.   [23] g reads θάψαντες, d καὶ λαβόντες αὐτὸν ἔθαψαν αὐτόν.   [24] β, S[1] add ἐν Χεβρών.   [25] g om.   [26] β, S[1] om. f, S[1] add Ἰούδας υἱὸς Ἰακὼβ δ΄ υἱὸς Λίας δ΄. καὶ (f om.) ἔζησεν ἔτη ριθ.   [27] A[b]. A[ab*cdefg] read καὶ ἐποίησαν οὕτως (A[g] om. ?) καθάπερ ἐνετείλατο αὐτοῖς καὶ ἐκοιμήθη Ἰούδας μετὰ πατέρων αὐτοῦ.

I. [1] Title. α in text. bef, S read Δ. Ἰ. περὶ ἁπλότητος (ἀγαθότητος e) (+ Ἰσαχὰρ ἑρμηνεύεται μισθός f), g Δ. Ἰ. ε΄, a Ἰσαχάρ. d is conflate: Δ. Ἰ. υἱὸς Ἰακὼβ καὶ Λίας ε΄ περὶ ἁπλότητος. A[abcdef] = Δ. Ἰ. (+ υἱοῦ Ἰακὼβ A[c]).   [2] α.

ἀκούσατε[3] τέκνα[4] Ἰσαχὰρ τοῦ πατρὸς ὑμῶν[5]
ἐνωτίσασθε ῥήματα ἠγαπημένου[6] ὑπὸ Κυρίου.
2. *Ἐγὼ ἐτέχθην ⌜πέμπτος υἱὸς τῷ Ἰακὼβ⌝[7] ἐν μισθῷ τῶν
μανδραγόρων[8]. 3. Ῥουβὶμ[9] *γὰρ ⌜ὁ ἀδελφός μου⌝[10] ἤνεγκεν
μανδραγόρους[11] *ἐκ τοῦ ἀγροῦ[12], καὶ[13] προσαπαντήσασα[14]
*ἡ Ῥαχιὴλ[15] ⌜αὐτὸν⌝[16] ἔλαβεν[17] αὐτούς[18]. 4. Ἔκλαιε[19] δὲ
ὁ[20] Ῥουβίμ[21], καὶ ἐπὶ τῇ φωνῇ αὐτοῦ ἐξῆλθεν[22] Λεία ἡ
μήτηρ μου[23].

5. *Ἦσαν δὲ ταῦτα μῆλα[24] εὔοσμα[25], *ἅπερ γίνονται[26]
*ἐν τῇ γῇ Χαράν[27] ὑποκάτω φάραγγος ὑδάτων. 6. Εἶπε
δὲ Ῥαχήλ· οὐ δώσω *σοι ταῦτα[28], *ἀλλ᾽ ἵνα σχῶ ταῦτα[29]
ἀντὶ τέκνων· *παρεῖδε γάρ με ὁ Κύριος, καὶ τέκνα οὐκ ἐγέννησα
τῷ Ἰακώβ. 7. Δύο οὖν ἦσαν τὰ μῆλα[30]. Καὶ εἶπεν ἡ[31]
Λία ⌜πρὸς Ῥαχήλ⌝[32]. *Ἱκανούσθω σοι[33] ὅτι ἔλαβες τὸν

β, A, S¹ (save that β, S¹ om. γάρ and g adds οὖτος before Καλ. and om. αὐτοῖς),
and d adds πρὸ τοῦ ἀπωθανεῖν αὐτόν before εἶπεν). A^{acf} = καὶ (οὓς A^{cf}) εἶπεν,
A^b καὶ εἶπεν Ἰ. τοῖς υἱοῖς αὐτοῦ ἐν τῷ χρόνῳ τῆς τελευτῆς αὐτοῦ, A^{b*d} ὅτε ἔμελλε
τελευτᾶν τὴν ζωὴν αὐτοῦ, ἐκάλεσε τοὺς υἱοὺς αὐτοῦ καὶ εἶπεν. Probably the last
five words belong to A^b also, but the notes are uncertain. [3] A^a = ἄκουσον.
[4] d reads τεκνία. h adds μου. A^{ab*cdf} om. [5] g om. next line. [6] ci,
aef, A. h, d, S¹ read ἠγαπημένα, bg ἠγαπημένοι. [7] α, β–g. g reads πέμπτος
υἱὸς ἐτέχθην τῷ Ἰακώβ and then om. to end of Ch. II. A = ἐγὼ ἐτέχθην.
[8] c writes μανδραγούρων and so elsewhere. [9] b reads Ἰακώβ. [10] α. β–d, A,
S¹ read γάρ, d om. [11] a reads μανδραγόραν. [12] A = ἐκ τοῦ ἄκρου. [13] A
adds πρῶτον. [14] b reads προαπαντ., d ἀπαντήσασα τοῦτον. [15] α. adef read
Ῥαχήλ, b Ῥαχιήλ. [16] α. Cf. d in note 14. abef, A, S¹ om. [17] f reads
ἀπέλαβεν. [18] hi, bef, S¹. c reads τοὺς μανδραγούρους, a αὐτήν, d αὐτὰ ἐξ αὐτοῦ.
A^{ab} = ἐξ αὐτοῦ (+ τοὺς μανδραγόρους A^b. Cf. d), A^{b*d} ἐκ κόλπου αὐτοῦ, A^{cf} om.
[19] d reads ἔκλαυσε. [20] α. β om. [21] e reads Ῥουβήν, abf Ῥουβήμ. [22] A =
ἤκουσε. [23] α. β–d, S¹. d reads αὐτοῦ καὶ ἐμοῦ. A^{abcf} = αὐτοῦ. A^{b*d} om. A adds
καὶ εἶπεν τῇ Ῥαχήλ. δὸς τοὺς μανδραγόρους. d adds καὶ εἶπεν αὐτῇ· ἵνα τί ἔλαβες
τὰ μανδραγόρα τοῦ υἱοῦ μου; [24] α (save that c reads μύλα for μῆλα here
and later). a reads αὕτη δὲ ἦν μῆλα, bdef ταῦτα δὲ ἦσαν μῆλα (ὡς μᾶλα d).
A = καὶ ἦσαν οἱ μανδράγοροι μῆλα. [25] aef. α, d read εὔωσμα, b εὐώδημα.
[26] α. abd read ἃ ἐποίει, ef, S¹ ἃ ποιεῖ. A = καὶ γίνονται. [27] α (save that hi
reads Χαναάν). β, S¹ read ἡ γῆ Ἀράμ (Ἀράν d) ἐν ὕψει. A = ἐν τῇ ὕλῃ ἐν τῇ
Ἀράμ, and om. next three words. [28] c. hi, def read σοι αὐτά, ab, A αὐτά σοι.
[29] α. β, A, S¹ read ὅτι (A = ἀλλὰ) ἔσονταί μοι. [30] α (save that hi read
μοι and ἐγένη for με and ἐγέννησα). β–g, A read ἦσαν δὲ τὰ (b om.) μῆλα
(μῦλα (sic) d) δύο. A^b adds καὶ εἶπεν αὐτῇ. Σὺ υἱοὺς ἔχεις πολλούς, καὶ ἐγὼ
οὐκ ἔχω καὶ εἶπεν. [31] α. β om. [32] α (save that hi read τὴν Ῥαχιήλ).
β, A, S¹ om. [33] A = οὐκ ἔστιν ἱκανόν σοι. [34] ld, A add τῆς (b, A om.)

ἄνδρα[34] μου· μὴ καὶ ταῦτα[35] λήψῃ[36] ⌈ἀπ' ἐμοῦ⌉[37];   8.
*Εἶπε δὲ αὐτῇ 'Ραχήλ[38]. Ἔστω[39] σοι ὁ[40] 'Ιακὼβ *τῇ νυκτὶ
ταύτῃ[41] ἀντὶ τῶν μανδραγόρων ⌈*τοῦ υἱοῦ[42] σου⌉.   9. *Εἶπε
δὲ πρὸς αὐτὴν ἡ Λεία[43]. *ἐμός ἐστιν ὁ 'Ιακώβ[44], *ὅτι ἐγώ εἰμι[45]
γυνὴ[46] νεότητος αὐτοῦ.   10. *Καὶ εἶπε 'Ραχήλ[47]. *Μὴ
καυχῶ μηδὲ δόξαζε σεαυτήν[48], *ὅτι ἐμὲ πρότερόν σου ἡρμόσατο[49],
καὶ *δι' ἐμὲ[50] ἐδούλευσε *τῷ πατρὶ ἡμῶν[51] *ἔτη δεκατέσσαρα[52].

α	β, A, S¹
11. *Καὶ εἰ μὴ ὁ δόλος ἐπλήθυνεν ἐπὶ τῆς γῆς καὶ ἡ πονηρία τῶν ἀνθρώπων ἐχώρησεν, οὐκ ἂν εἰ σὺ ὁρῶσα τὸ πρόσωπον τοῦ 'Ιακώβ[53].	11. Τί σοι ποιήσω, ὅτι ἐπλήθυνεν ὁ δόλος ⌈καὶ ἡ πανουργία τῶν ἀνθρώπων καὶ ὁ δόλος προεχώρει⌉ ἐπὶ τῆς γῆς· εἰ δὲ μή, σὺ οὐκ ἂν ᾖς ὁρῶσα πρ. 'I.

12. *Οὐ γὰρ γυνὴ αὐτοῦ εἰ σύ[54], ἀλλὰ[55] δόλῳ ἀντὶ ἐμοῦ
εἰσήχθης[56].   13. *Καὶ ἐμὲ ἐπλάνησεν[57] ὁ πατήρ μου,

Marginal note (right column):
bd, A παρθενίας μου.
β, A, S¹ Λία πρὸς αὐτήν· Μὴ καυχῶ μηδὲ δόξαζε σεαυτήν· ἐμὸς γάρ ἐστιν ὁ 'I. κἀγώ.
β, S¹ ἡ δὲ 'Ραχὴλ εἶπε· Τί οὖν; ὅτι ἐμὲ προτέραν σου ἦρμοσται.

παρθενίας.   [35]A = τοὺς μανδραγόρους.   [36]hi, ab. c, def read λήψει.   [37]α.
β, A, S¹ om.   [38]α (save that hi read ἡ 'Ραχιήλ). abef, A⁻ᵇ, S¹ read ἡ δὲ
εἶπεν, d, Aᵇ εἶπε δὲ 'P.   [39]α. aef read καὶ ἔστω, bd, A, S¹ ἰδοὺ ἔστω.   [40]c.
i, β om.   [41]α. β reads τὴν νύκτα ταύτην.   [42]c reads υἱῶν.   [43]h, A. c om.
abdef read εἶπε δὲ (καὶ εἶπεν f) Λία πρὸς αὐτήν. abdef, A add μὴ καυχῶ μηδὲ
δόξαζε σεαυτόν (μηδὲ δοξάζου d, Aᵇ*ᵈ, καὶ μὴ δοξάζου b, Aᵇ).   [44]c. hi read
ἐμός ἐστιν 'I. abdef, A, S¹ read ἐμὸς γάρ ἐστιν ὁ (de om.) 'I.   [45]α. β, A, S¹
read κἀγώ.   [46]hi add ἐκ.   [47]α (save that h reads 'Ραχιήλ). abef, A read
ἡ δὲ 'P. εἶπε, d εἶπε δὲ 'P.   [48]α (save that c reads μή for μηδὲ). This phrase
has already appeared in β in the preceding verse. β, A read τί οὖν;
[49]α (for ἡρμόσατο c gives the form εἱρμώσατο and for ἐμέ hi read ἐγώ).
abef, A, S¹ read ὅτι ἐμὲ (ἐμοὶ b) προτέραν (πρῶτον b) σου (b om.) ἤρμοσται, d οὐχὶ
πρῶτον ἐμέ σου ἥρμοσε;   [50]Aᵃᵇ*ᶜᵈ trs. after ἐδούλευσε.   [51]i reads τ. π. ὑμῶν,
d, Aᵇ τῷ πατρί μου (+ Λαβαν Aᵇ). Aᵃᵇ*ᶜᵈ om.   [52]d read ἔτι ἰδεῖν corrupt for
ἔτη ιδ' (?).   [53]α (save that for τὸ πρόσωπον τοῦ h reads πρώην πρόσωπον).
β, A read τί σοι (σύ e) ποιήσω (Aᵇ*ᶜᵈ ἐποίησα), ὅτι ἐπλήθυνεν ὁ δόλος (+ σου A)
⌈καὶ ἡ πανουργία τῶν ἀνθρώπων καὶ ὁ δόλος (a om. preceding eight words
through hmt.) προχωρεῖ⌉ (προσχωρεῖ af, προχορούσιν d) ἐπὶ τῆς γῆς; Εἰ δὲ μή
(εἰ δὲ προεχώρουν d) σὺ οὐκ ἂν ᾖς ὁρῶσα (οὐκ ἂν ᾖς σὺ ὁρῶσα be, οὐ γὰρ οἶδες
σὺ τὸ d) πρόσωπον 'I. For εἰ δὲ ... 'Ιακώβ A reads εἰ ἐν ἀληθείᾳ ὢν ἦσθα, οὐκ
ἂν ἑώρας τὸ πρ. 'I. S¹ agrees with β save that for καὶ ὁ δόλος προχωρεῖ ... εἰ
δὲ μή it reads καὶ εἰ μὴ ὁ δόλος προεχώρει ἐπὶ τῆς γῆς.   [54]α, β (save that b
reads σὺ εἶ and d εἶ for εἰ σύ). A = γυνὴ γὰρ αὐτοῦ οὐκ ἦσθα.   [55]α. β read
ἀλλ' ἐν.   [56]ci, abef. h reads εἰσῆλθες, d εἰσενέχθης αὐτῷ. Aᵃᵇ*ᶜᵈ read 𝑖𝑛𝑝𝑙𝑤𝑟
= ἐδόθης (Aᵇ 𝑏𝑖𝑛𝑝𝑙𝑟 = ἔδωκας) αὐτῷ, but both these verbs may be corruptions of 𝑓𝑢𝑛𝑏𝑟 = εἰσῆλθες or εἰσήχθης.   [57]α. abef read καὶ ἐπλάνησέ με

β, S¹ με
ἰδεῖν, ὅτι
εἰ ἤμην
ἐκεῖ, οὐκ
ἐγίνετο
τοῦτο.
β–d, S¹
καὶ εἶπε
'Ρ. Λαβὲ
ἕνα μαν-
δραγόραν
καὶ ἀντὶ

*⌜καὶ μετέστησέ με τὴν νύκτα ἐκείνην⌝, καὶ[58] οὐκ εἴασε *⌜τῷ
'Ιακὼβ ἰδεῖν με, ἐπεί⌝, ἐὰν ἤμην ἐκεῖ[59], *τοῦτο αὐτῷ οὐκ ἐγένετο[60].
14. *'Αλλ' οὖν ἀντὶ τῶν μανδραγούρων ἐκμισθῶ σοι μίαν νύκτα τῷ
'Ιακώβ[61]. 15. *῎Εγνω δὲ 'Ιακὼβ τῇ Λείᾳ[62], καὶ ⌜συλλαβοῦσα⌝
*ἔτεκεν ἐμέ[63], καὶ διὰ ⌜τούτου⌝[64] τὸν μισθὸν ἐκλήθην[65] 'Ισαχάρ.
     II. Τότε ⌜οὖν⌝[1] ὤφθη τῷ[2] 'Ιακὼβ[3] ⌜ἄγγελος Κυρίου
λέγων⌝[4], *ὅτι τέκνα τέξει 'Ραχήλ[5], *ἐπειδὴ κατέπτυσεν[6] συνουσίαν[7] ἀνδρὸς καὶ ἐξελέξατο τὴν[8] ἐγκράτειαν.   2. Καὶ[9] εἰ

τοῦ ἑνὸς ἐκμισθώσω σοι μίαν νύκτα.   β ὅτι διέπτυσε.

(a om.), d, A ἐπλάνησε γάρ με.   A' om. next nineteen words.   [58] α. abdef, S¹
read καὶ μεταστήσας (καταστήσας d) με (a om.) τῇ νυκτὶ ἐκείνῃ (τὴν νύκτα ἐκείνην d).
A om.   [59] α. abef, S¹ read με ἰδεῖν ὅτι εἰ ἤμην ἐκεῖ, d με γνῶναί τοῦτο· λέγω
γάρ σοι ὅτι εἰ ἤμην ἐκεῖ. A = ἐκεῖ (+ εἰ ἤμην ἐκεῖ A[b]).   [60] α (save that h om.
αὐτῷ and i reads αὐτό). abdef, A, S¹ read οὐκ ἐγίνετο (+ σοι d) τοῦτο (+ οὕτως A).
[61] α. abef, S¹ read (corruptly) καὶ εἶπε 'Ρ. Λαβὲ ἕνα (a μίαν) μανδραγόραν (μανδράγουρον f) καὶ ἀντὶ τοῦ ἑνὸς (ἀντὶ ταύτης a) ἐκμισθώσω (ἐκμισθῶ bf, S¹) σοι
(+ αὐτόν b) μίαν νύκτα (ἐν μιᾷ νυκτί b), d καὶ ἔρρηψεν αὐτῇ τὸ ἓν μανδράγουρον
καὶ εἶπεν αὐτῇ· λαβὲ τὸ ἓν καὶ ἀντὶ τὸ ἓν ἔχε τὸν 'Ι. τὴν νύκτα ταύτην. A[ab] = Λαβὲ
εἶπεν (ἕνα A[b]) τῶν μανδραγόρων (+ καὶ τὸν ἕνα A[b]) καὶ ἀντὶ τοῦ ἕνος ἐκμισθώσω
σοι 'Ιακὼβ ἐν τῇ νυκτὶ (= ταύτῃ A[b]). A[b*cdf] = καὶ προσέθηκε 'Ραχὴλ λαλεῖν καὶ
εἶπεν. ῎Ενα τῶν μανδραγόρων λήψομαι, καὶ ἀντὶ τοῦ ἑνὸς ἐκμισθώσω σοι ἐν τῇ
νυκτί.   [62] α. β–d read ἔγνω 'Ι. τὴν Λίαν, d ἔγνω 'Ι. τῇ νυκτὶ ἐκείνῃ. A = καὶ
εἰσῆλθε 'Ι. πρὸς τὴν Λίαν (+ ἐν ἐκείνῃ τῇ νυκτί A[b]).   [63] α, df, A[ab*cd] (adding
αὐτῷ). abe read με (a om.) ἔτεκε. A[b] = ἐγέννησε 'Ι. με ἐκ Λίας.   [64] α. abdef,
A, S¹ om.   [65] c reads ἐκλήθη.

     II. [1] α. β, A, S¹ om. Before the beginning of the chapter d adds:
καὶ πάλιν ἔωθεν ἀντέστρεψε Λίαν καὶ τὸ ἕτερον μανδράγορον εἰποῦσα τῇ 'Ραχήλ.
Λαβὲ τοῦτο καὶ ἐκμισθοῦμαι αὐτὸν καὶ τῇ νυκτὶ ταύτῃ. καὶ ἔλαβε τὰ δύο μῆλα
'Ραχήλ, καὶ δέδωκεν αὐτὴ τὸν 'Ιακὼβ καὶ τῇ ἄλλῃ νυκτί.   [2] d om.   [3] hi read
πατρί μου.   [4] α, b, S¹. aef read ἄγγελος, d ἄγγελος κυρίου καὶ εἶπεν. A om.
[5] α (save that hi read 'Ραχιήλ). abef read ὅτι δύο (aef om.) τέκνα 'Ραχὴλ
τέξεται. d om. A[abb*cd] = ὅτι διὰ τοῦτο ἔτεκεν 'Ραχὴλ δύο τέκνα.   [6] α. β reads
ὅτι διέπτυσε (+ 'Ραχὴλ d). A[b] is very corrupt and for ἐπειδὴ ... ἐγκράτειαν
gives ἐπειδὴ κατέπτυσε συνουσίαν ἀνδρός, ἔδωκε αὐτῇ ἐν μισθῷ ἑνὸς μανδραγόρου
καὶ καταφρονήσει ἡρμόσατο (?) καὶ ἐξελέξατο ἐγκράτειαν. A[-b] agrees with α, β.
[7] d reads συνουσίας.   [8] α. β om.   [9] Verses 2–4 appear confusedly in d as
follows: 2. Τούτου ἕνεκε δύο τέκνα τέξεται, ὅτι ἐν τοῖς μανδραγόροις ἐπεσκέψατο
αὐτὴν ὁ Κύριος.   3. οἶδε γὰρ ὅτι διὰ τέκνα ἤθελεν συνεῖναι τῷ 'Ιακὼβ καὶ οὐ διὰ
φιληδονίαν.   2. καὶ γὰρ εἰ μὴ Λίαν ἡ μήτηρ μου ἀντὶ συνουσίας ἀπέδωτο τὰ δύο
μᾶλα, ὀκτὼ υἱοὺς εἶχε τεκεῖν. διὰ τοῦτο ἔτεκεν ἕξ, τοὺς δὲ δύο ἔτεκεν ἡ 'Ραχήλ.

μὴ Λεία[10] ἡ μήτηρ μου ἀντὶ συνουσίας ἀπέδοτο[11] τὰ δύο
μῆλα, [ἔτι][12] ὀκτὼ υἱοὺς ἔμελλε[13] τεκεῖν· διὰ τοῦτο ἓξ ἔτεκε,
*καὶ Ῥαχιὴλ τέτοκε τοὺς δύο[14] ὅτι ἐν *τοῖς μανδραγόροις[15] ἐπεσκέ-
ψατο αὐτὴν[16] ὁ[17] Κύριος.   3. Εἶδε[18] γὰρ ὅτι διὰ τέκνα
ἤθελεν συνεῖναι *τῷ Ἰακώβ[19], καὶ οὐ διὰ φιληδονίαν.
        α, β   Aab*cdf

| 4. Προσθεῖσα[20] γὰρ καὶ[21] τῇ ἐπαύριον ἀπέδωκε[22] τὸν Ἰακώβ[23]. Ἐν *τοῖς μανδραγό-ροις[15] οὖν[24] ἐπήκουσε Κύριος[25] τῇ[26] Ῥαχήλ[27]. | 4. *Καὶ τῇ ἐπαύριον προσ-θεῖσα ἀπήτησε Ἰακὼβ ἵνα λάβῃ ἔτι ἄλλον μανδραγό-ρου[28]. |

β, A, S¹ εἶχε. β-d, Aab*cdf, S¹ τοὺς δὲ δύο (+ ἡ e) Ῥαχήλ. β-dg, S¹ Ἰακώβ, ἵνα λάβῃ καὶ τὸν ἄλλον μανδρα-γόραν. β, Aab*cdf, S¹ ἱερεῖ ὑψίστου. β κπιμφ ἐκείνῳ. β-d, S¹ τῶν πατέρων μου καὶ

5. Ὅτι καί γε ποθήσασα τούτους[29] οὐκ ἔφαγεν[30], ἀλλὰ
ἀνέθηκεν[31] ταῦτα[32] ἐν οἴκῳ Κυρίου[33], προσάξασα[34] τῷ ἱερεῖ[35]
τῷ ὄντι[36] ἐν τῷ *τότε χρόνῳ[37].

  III. *Ὅτε οὖν[1] ἡδρύνθην[2] ἐγώ[3], *τέκνα μου[4], ἐπορεύθην[5]
ἐν *εὐθύτητι καρδίας[6], *καὶ ἐγενόμην[7] γεωργὸς *τῷ πατρί
μου καὶ τοῖς ἀδελφοῖς μου[8], καὶ ἔφερον καρποὺς[9] ἐξ[10] ἀγρῶν[11].

τῶν ἀδελφῶν μου.   β-af, A, S¹ ἀγρῶν κατὰ καιρὸν αὐτῶν.

---

4. ἐν τοῖς μανδραγόροις .ἐπήκουσε Κύριος τὴν Ῥαχήλ.   [10] α. β reads Λία.
[11] h, af (a trs. before ἀντί). ci, e read ἀπέδωτο, b ἀπέδω.   [12] α (save that ci
read ἔτη). β, A om.   [13] α. abef, A read εἶχε, d ἔσχε.   [14] α (save that
c reads Ῥαχηὴλ καί). abef, Aab*cd read as in margin. Ab is very corrupt:
ἡ ἔλαβεν τὰ μῆλα καὶ οὐ συνουσίας γάμον καὶ τὰ δύο τέκνα Ῥαχήλ ἔτεκεν.   [15] α
reads ταῖς μανδραγόραις.   [16] i reads ταύτην, e αὐτῇ. Ab = τὴν Ῥαχήλ.   [17] α,
aef. b om.   [18] d reads οἶδε.   [19] Aab*cdf = τῷ ἀνδρὶ αὐτῆς, Ab Ῥαχήλ τῷ Ἰακώβ.
[20] b reads προσθήσα.   [21] h om.   [22] α. abf read ἀπέδοτο, e ἀπέδωτο.
[23] abef, S¹ add as in margin, save that for τ. α. μανδραγόραν b reads τ. α.
μανδραγόρα, f τ. α. μανδράγουρον, and a τὴν ἄλλην μανδραγόραν. After μανδραγόραν b, S¹ add διὰ τοῦτο.   [24] aef. α reads καί. bd om.   [25] e reads ὁ Κ. and
trs. after Ῥ.   [26] b reads τῆς, d τήν.   [27] c reads Ῥαχηήλ, h Ῥαχιήλ.   [28] Ab is
very corrupt and reads καὶ Λία ἡ μήτηρ μου τῇ ἐπαύριον προσθεῖσα ἀπήτησε
Ἰακώβ, ἐπιπόθησις γὰρ ἦν ἐν αὐτῇ καὶ οὐ διὰ τόκον. καὶ ἔλαβεν Ῥαχήλ ἔτι ἄλλον
μανδράγορον.   [29] hi. c reads τούτοις, a αὐτάς, bdef, A αὐτούς. Ab = υἱούς.
[30] Ab adds Ῥαχήλ τὰ μῆλα.   [31] d reads ἐνέθηκεν. Ab = ἔδωκεν.   [32] α.
adef, Ab read αὐτά, b αὐτούς. Aab*cd om.   [33] Ab adds Θεοῦ. A adds καί.
[34] α. bde, S¹ read προσενέγκασα, af προσενεγκοῦσα. A = either reading.
[35] A = ἀρχιερεῖ. β, Aab*cdf, S¹ add ὑψίστου, Ab Θεοῦ ὑψίστου.   [36] Ab adds
ἀρχιερεῖ.   [37] β reads as in margin. Ab adds καὶ εὐλόγησε Ῥαχήλ ἐν δυσὶν υἱοῖς.

  III. [1] d adds ἐγώ. g reads καὶ ὅτε. A = ἀλλὰ ὅτε.   [2] hi, df read ἡνδρ.
[3] α. β, A om.   [4] g om.   [5] α, A. β reads ἐπορευόμην.   [6] Ab* =
εὐθείᾳ καρδίᾳ. d adds μου.   [7] A = γενόμενος.   [8] α, A (save that A adds

β—a, A, S¹ ἤμην. β—g,S¹ἀν-θρώπου, πορευό-μενος ἐν ἁπλότητι ὀφθαλ-μῶν· 5. διὰ τοῦτο. β, S¹ εἴ τι γὰρ ἔκαμνον πᾶσαν ὀπώραν. β, S¹ μου,

2. ⌜*Καὶ ηὐλόγει με ὁ πατήρ μου βλέπων με¹² *ὅτι ἐν ἁπλότητι πορεύομαι¹³ *ἔμπροσθεν αὐτοῦ¹⁴⌝. 3. *Καὶ οὐκ εἰμι¹⁵ περίεργος *ἐν ταῖς πράξεσίν μου¹⁶, ⌜οὐδὲ φθονερὸς¹⁷ καὶ¹⁸ βάσκανος *τῷ πλησίον μου¹⁹. 4. *Οὐ κατελάλησά τινος πώποτε²⁰, οὐδὲ²¹ ἔψεξα²² βίον ἀνθρώπου⌝²³. 5. Τριάκοντα ⌜καὶ πέντε⌝²⁴ ἐτῶν ἔλαβον²⁵ ἐμαυτῷ²⁶ γυναῖκα²⁷, ὅτι ὁ κάματος κατήσθιε τὴν ἰσχύν²⁸ μου²⁹, καὶ οὐκ ἐνενόουν³⁰ ἡδονὴν³¹ γυναικός, ⌜ἀλλὰ διὰ τοῦ κόπου³² ὁ ὕπνος μοι³³ περιεγένετο³⁴⌝. 6. Καὶ ἔχαιρε ⌜πάντοτε⌝³⁵ ἐπὶ τῇ ἁπλότητί μου *ὁ πατήρ μου³⁶ ⌜διότι³⁷ καὶ *πᾶν πρῶτον γέννημα³⁸ *διὰ τοῦ ἱερέως³⁹ τῷ⁴⁰ Κυρίῳ⁴¹ προσέφερον⁴², ἔπειτα καὶ⁴³ τῷ πατρί μου⁴⁴. 7. Καὶ ὁ⁴⁵ Κύριος ἐμυριοπλασίασε⁴⁶ τὰ ἀγαθὰ

καὶ τότε ἐγώ.   β ἐδιπλασίαζε τὰ ἀγαθά.

Ἰακώβ after πατρί μου). β—d, S¹ read as in margin, d τοῦ πατρός μου καὶ τῶν ἀδ. μου. Aᵇ om. rest of Testament. [9]A = πάντα. [10]dg read ἐκ τῶν. [11]bd, A, S¹ add αὐτῶν (b, A, S¹ om.) κατὰ καιρὸν αὐτῶν (d, A om.), eg add κατὰ τοὺς (e om.) καιροὺς αὐτῶν. A om. ver. 2. See, however, first note on ver. 6. S¹ om. ἐξ ἀγρῶν. [12]c, β (save that abd read εὐλόγησε and abdef om. με). hi read ὁ δὲ πατήρ μου βλέπων ηὐλόγησέ (i εὐλόγει) με. [13]g reads ἐν εὐθύτητι πορευόμενον. [14]α. β, S¹ om. [15]α. a reads οὐκ εἰμί, bdef, A, S¹ καὶ (ὅτι edf om.) οὐκ ἤμην, g οὐ γὰρ ἤμην. [16]g om. Aᵇ*ᵈ om. rest of verse together with ver. 4. Aᵃᶜᶠ read διὰ τοῦτο καί in their stead. [17]b reads πονηρός. [18]g reads ἤ. [19]α, adf. be read τῷ πλ. g om. [20]α. d reads ποτε. β—d om. [21]d reads οὐκ. [22]d adds ποτε. [23]β—g, S¹ add as in margin save that d adds μου after ὀφθαλμῶν. On A see note 16. [24]α, aef, S¹ (save that aef, S¹ om. καί). bdg, A om. [25]i, g read ἔλαβα. [26]hi, β—dg. c reads ἑαυτῷ. dg, A om. [27]d reads τὴν γυναῖκά μου. [28]c reads ψυχήν. [29]g om. [30]c, bd. hi, aefg read ἐνόουν. [31]d reads ἡδονῆς. For this together with next word A reads γάμον and om. next eight words. [32]g adds μου. [33]α, g. abf read μου, de με. [34]f reads περιεγίνετο. g trs. before μοι. [35]β, S¹ trs. before ἔχαιρε. A om. [36]d, A trs. before ἐπὶ τῇ ἁπλ. [37]α. bdeg, S¹ read as in margin, af εἶτα γὰρ (a om.) ἔκαμνον (ἔκαμον f) πᾶσαν ὥραν. A = εἴ τι ἔκαμνον and om. the rest of thé Chapter, reading instead καὶ οὐ διεμέρισα διὰ τοῦτο. Πάντοτε εὐλόγει ὁ πατήρ μου (Aᵃ om. ὁ π. μ.). The last five words belong to ver. 2. See last note on ver. 1. [38]c. hi read πρῶτα γέννημα, adf πᾶν πρωτογέννημα (+πρῶτον f), beg πᾶν πρωτογέννημα πρῶτον. S¹ adds καὶ τὰ πρῶτα. [39]d om. but see note 42. [40]α. β om. [41]g reads Κυρίου. [42]d adds πρῶτον διὰ τοῦ ἱερέως. [43]α. β, S¹ om. [44]e om. β adds καὶ τότε ἐγώ (+ἐξ αὐτῶν μετελάμβανον d, +ἀπήλαυον g), S¹ καὶ τότε ἐμαυτῷ. [45]α. β, S¹ om. [46]α. β, S¹ read ἐδιπλασίαζε.

αὐτοῦ[45] *ἐν ταῖς χερσί[47] μου· ᾔδει δὲ καὶ Ἰακὼβ *ὁ πατήρ
μου[45], ὅτι ὁ Θεὸς συνεργεῖ[48] τῇ ἁπλότητί μου.   8. *Πάντα
γὰρ πένησι καὶ θλιβομένοις[49] παρεῖχον *ἐκ τῶν ἀγαθῶν τῆς
γῆς[50] ἐν ἁπλότητι καρδίας μου[51]⌉.

IV. Καὶ νῦν *ἀκούσατέ μου, τέκνα[1],
    καὶ πορεύεσθε ἐν ἁπλότητι[2] ⌜καρδίας ὑμῶν⌝[3],
    ὅτι εἶδον ἐν ὑμῖν[4] ⌜πᾶσαν⌝[5] εὐαρέστησιν[6] Κυρίου[7].

2. ⌜Ὁ ἁπλοῦς χρυσίον οὐ[8] πλεονεκτεῖ
    βρωμάτων ποικίλων οὐκ ἐφίεται
    *ἐσθῆτα διάφορον οὐ θέλει[9].

3. Χρόνους πολλοὺς[10] *οὐκ †ἐπιγράφει τοῦ ζῆν†[11]
    ἀλλὰ μόνον ἐκδέχεται *τὸ θέλημα[12] τοῦ Θεοῦ⌝.

4. Καί γε *τὰ πνεύματα[13] τῆς πλάνης οὐδὲν *ἰσχύουσιν πρὸς
        αὐτόν[14],
    οὐ γὰρ[15] †εἶδεν ἐπιδέξασθαι†[16] κάλλος[17] θηλείας[18]
    ⌜ἵνα μὴ[19] ἐν[20] διαστροφῇ μιάνῃ[21] τὸν νοῦν αὐτοῦ⌝.

bdg, A
αὐτῇ.
bdeg, S¹
οὐκ ἐπι-
θυμεῖ,
τὸν πλη-
σίον οὐ
πλεονεκ-
τεῖ.
β–g, S²
ὑπογρά-
φει ζῆν.

[47] α, e. abfg read ἐν (a om.) χερσίν μου, d ἐν τῇ χειρί μου.   [48] d reads
συμπράττει, eg συνήργει.   [49] α, ef (save that hi read πᾶσι and e θλιβομένῳ).
ad read πάντα γὰρ πένητα καὶ πᾶσι θλιβομένοις (πάντα θλιβόμενον d), bg, S¹ παντὶ
γὰρ πένητι καὶ παντὶ θλιβομένῳ.   [50] α. abef, S¹ read τῆς γῆς τὰ ἀγαθά, dg τὰ
ἀγαθὰ (τὸ ἀγαθὸν g) τῆς γῆς.   [51] α, dg. abef, S¹ om.

IV. [1] d, A read τέκνα μου ἀκούσατε μοι, g ἀκ. τέκνα.   [2] A reads
նղջդինեբդուսդ = ὑγιότητα corrupt for այորղջդինեբդուսդ.   [3] c, bg
(save that b om. ὑμῶν). hi, aef read ψυχῆς ὑμῶν (i ἡμῶν). d is conflate:
καρδίας καὶ ψυχῆς ὑμῶν.   [4] α, aef, S¹. bdg, A read αὐτῇ.   [5] d, A om.   [6] A =
τὸ εὐάρεστον.   [7] Aᶜ = Θεοῦ. g om. A om. next two verses through hmt. (?).
Observe reading of Aᶜ.   [8] bdeg, S¹ read as in margin (save that g reads
πλούσιον for πλησίον).   This addition makes the construction easy, but the
reference to one's neighbour seems alien to the context.   [9] d reads
ἐσθῆτας διαφόρους οὐ βούλεται.   [10] α. β reads μακρούς.   [11] α. β–g, S² read
οὐχ (οὐκ ef) ὑπογράφει ζῆν, g οὐχὶ γράφει ζῆν, S¹ οὐ ζητεῖ ζῆν. α is undoubtedly
corrupt, and apparently also β.   The sense appears as in S¹ to be: 'he
does not long to live for long periods.'   Now ἐπιγράφει (or ὑπογράφει) τοῦ
ζῆν = מַחְקֶה לחיות which may be corrupt for לחיות (or מִחְיֶה) מְחַמֵּד =
'desires to live.'   [12] d trs. after Θεοῦ.   [13] A = τὸ πνεῦμα.   [14] β.
α reads ἰσχύσωσιν αὐτῷ (πρὸς αὐτόν h). A = ἴσχυε πρὸς αὐτόν.   [15] d om.
[16] α, β–fg (de reading οἶδεν and hi εἶ), S². fg, A read εἶδεν (οἶδεν f, ᾔδειν A)
ἐπιλέξασθαι, S¹ ἐπιβλέπει.   Possibly the original was לא ידע לרצות ב =
οὐκ οἶδεν ἐπιδέξασθαι = 'cannot have pleasure in.'   [17] d reads
κάλλους.   [18] A = γυναικῶν.   [19] i reads μή, d ἵνα μή γε.   [20] g om.
[21] h reads μιανεῖ, d μιαίνει.   [22] A = καὶ οὐ.   [23] β, A.. c reads

β ζῆλος[23]
ἐν[24] δια-
βουλίοις
*αὐτοῦ
ἐπελεύ-
σεται[25].
β, S[1], S[2]
εὐθύτητι.
β, S[1], S[2]
ἁπλό-
τητι.

5. Οὐ[22] ζηλοῖ ἐν διαβουλίοις

[οὐ βάσκανος[26] ἐκτήκει τὴν ψυχὴν αὐτοῦ][27]

*οὐδὲ ⌈περισπασμὸς⌉ ἐν ἀπληστείᾳ ἐν νοΐ[28].

6. Πορεύεται[29] δὲ[30] ἐν *ἁπλότητι ⌈ψυχῆς⌉[31]

πάντα[32] ὁρᾷ[33] ἐν *εὐθύτητι ⌈καρδίας⌉[34]

*μὴ ἐπιδεχόμενος[35] *ὀφθαλμοὺς πονηροὺς[36] ἀπὸ τῆς
  πλάνης τοῦ κόσμου

*ἵνα μὲ ἴδῃ διεστραμμένας τὰς ἐντολὰς τοῦ Κυρίου[37].

V. Φυλάξατε οὖν *τέκνα μου νόμον Θεοῦ[1],

καὶ *τὴν ἁπλότητα κτήσασθε[2],

⌈καὶ ἐν ἀκακίᾳ πορεύεσθε,

β ἐντολὰς
Κυρίου
καὶ τοῦ.

μὴ περιεργαζόμενοι τοῦ[3] πλησίον[4] τὰς πράξεις.

2. Ἀλλὰ ἀγαπήσατε[5] τὸν[6] Κύριον καὶ τὸν πλησίον[7]·
πένητα καὶ ἀσθενῆ[8] ἐλεήσατε[9]⌉.

3. Ὑποτίθετε[10] τὸν νῶτον[11] ὑμῶν εἰς τὸ γεωργεῖν

β ἔργοις
γῆς.

καὶ ἐργάζεσθε ἐν ἔργοις[12] ⌈καθ᾽ ἑκάστην γεωργίαν,
δῶρα μετ᾽ εὐχαριστείας[13] Κυρίῳ προσφέροντες[14]⌉.

ζηλεῖ, hi ζηλοῖ. [24] g adds τοῖς. [25] β, S (save that for αὐτοῦ a reads αὐτῶν, e αὐτόν). α om. A reads μου. [26] bdg, S read βασκανία. [27] Rightly omitted by A. [28] Emended from α, β, S[1] οὐδὲ (οὐ α, οὔτε g) περισπασμὸν (πορισμὸν b) ἐν ἀπληστείᾳ (ἁπλότητι c) ἐννοεῖ (ἐν νοεί i). A = καὶ οὐκ ἀπληστίαν (+ χρυσίον A[b*cdfg]) ἐνόουν. Here A[ab*cd] according to Arm. text trs. ἐνόουν before ἀπληστ. The reading of b is obviously an emendation. [29] A = ἐπορεύθην. [30] ch, ef. abdg, A, S[1] read γάρ. i om. [31] α. β, S read εὐθύτητι ψυχῆς (ζωῆς b). A = ἁπλότητι. [32] bdg, A prefix καί. [33] A = ἑώρων. [34] α. β, S as in margin. A = εὐθύτητι. [35] d reads μὴ ἀποδεχόμενος. For these words and the rest of the verse A gives μήποτε ἐπιβαλὼν τὸν ὀφθαλμὸν εἰς πλάνην. [36] α, β—bg, S[2]. bg, S[1] read ὀφθαλμοῖς (ὀφθαλμὸν g) πονηρίας. [37] α, aef, S[1] (save that f reads ὁδούς for ἐντολάς, e διεστραμμένων for διεστραμμένας, and hi Θεοῦ for Κυρίου, and aef om. τοῦ). bg read ἵνα μὴ ἴδῃ διεστραμμένως (g reads διεστραμμένα) τι (g om.) ἐντολῶν τοῦ Κυρίου (Θεοῦ g). d om. A = μὴ ἴδω διεστραμμένως καὶ βάλῃ ἐμὲ εἰς ταραχὴν αὐτῶν.

V. [1] α, adef (save that d reads Κυρίου for Θεοῦ). bg, S[1] read νόμον Θεοῦ τέκνα μου (g om.). A = νόμον Κυρίου. [2] A[—is] = κτήσασθε τ. ἁπλότητα, but A[is] agree with α, β, and A om. rest of ver. and ver. 2. [3] α. bdg, S[1] read as in margin (save that dg read μηδὲ τῶν for καὶ τοῦ and g καὶ τῶν), aef ἐντολὴν Κυρίου καὶ τοῦ. [4] dg read πλησίων. [5] α, aef. bdg read ἀγαπᾶτε. [6] α. β om. [7] d adds ὑμῶν. [8] c reads ὀρφανόν. Is this due to Ps. lxxxi. 3? [9] b reads ἐλεᾶτε. [10] hi read ἀποτίθετε, bdg ὑπόθετε. [11] g reads νοῦν. [12] β, A, S[1] add τῆς (abef om.) γῆς. A om. rest of verse. [13] hi, d add τῷ (but hi trs. τῷ K. after προσφ.). [14] g reads προσφέρετε.

4. Ὅτι[15] ἐν πρωτογεννήμασιν[16] καρπῶν[17] ⌜τῆς γῆς[18]⌝ *εὐλογήσει ὑμᾶς[19] Κύριος[20] ⌜καθὼς εὐλόγησε[21] πάντας τοὺς[22] ἁγίους[23] ἀπὸ Ἀβὲλ ἕως τοῦ νῦν⌝. 5. Οὐ γὰρ δέδοται ὑμῖν[24] ἄλλη μερὶς ⌜*εἰ μὴ[25] *τῆς πιότητος[26] τῆς γῆς *ἐν πόνοις καρπῶν[27]⌝.

(margin: bg, S¹ ἧς ἐν πόνοις οἱ καρποί.)

α, β, S¹	A
6. *Ὅτι καὶ[28] ὁ πατήρ μου[29] Ἰακὼβ[30] ἐν[31] εὐλογίαις ⌜τῆς[32] γῆς καὶ ἀπαρχῶν[33] καρπῶν[34] εὐλόγησέ με. 7. Καὶ ὁ[35] Λευὶ[36] καὶ ὁ[37] Ἰούδας ἐδοξάσθησαν[38] παρὰ Κυρίου καὶ[39] ἐν υἱοῖς Ἰακώβ. Καὶ ὁ[40] Κύριος *ἐκληροδότησεν αὐτούς[41]⌝, καὶ τῷ μὲν Λευὶ[42] ἔδωκε *τὴν ἱερατείαν[43], τῷ δὲ Ἰούδᾳ[42] τὴν βασιλείαν.	6-7. Δι᾽ ὃ καὶ ὁ πατὴρ ἡμῶν ἐν ταῖς εὐλογίαις ἡμῶν (Ab*d αὐτοῦ) ἐκληροδότησε τῷ Λευὶ τὸ πρωτεῖον καὶ Ἰούδας ἐδοξάσθη ἐν υἱοῖς Ἰακώβ.

(margin: β–d, S ἐκλήρωσεν ἐν αὐτοῖς. β–d, S¹ αὐτοῖς (+ οὖν bg) ὑπακούσατε.)

8. *Καὶ ὑμεῖς ⌜οὖν⌝ αὐτοῖς ὑπακούετε[44] καὶ[45] τῇ ἁπλότητι[46] τοῦ πατρὸς ὑμῶν περιπατεῖτε[47]· [*τῷ δὲ[48] Γὰδ ἐδόθη ἀπολέσαι τὰ *ἐπερχόμενα πειρατήρια[49] τῷ Ἰσραήλ].

(margin: β, A, S¹ ὅτι καὶ τῷ.)

---

[15] g om.   [16] α, a. β–ad read πρωτογενήμασιν. d προγεννήμασι. Aᵃ = γεννήμασιν οῖ εὐφορίᾳ. Aᵇ*ᶜᵈᶠᵍ (corrupt) = πόνοις.   [17] A adds ὑμῶν.   [18] α. β–ag read γῆς, g τῆς γῆς καί. a om. h adds εὐλογίας, i εὐλογίαν.   [19] h, dg. c reads εὐλογήσαι. b, S¹ read εὐλόγησε, aef εὐλογήσει σε. A = εὐλογηθήσεται but by a change of a single letter A becomes εὐλογήσει.   [20] A om. rest of verse.   [21] c reads εὐλογήσαι.   [22] c om.   [23] g reads δικαίους. d adds αὐτοῦ.   [24] g, A. a reads ἡμῖν, bdef, S¹ σοι. α om.   [25] α, e. abfg read ᾖ, d πλήν.   [26] d om.   [27] α, aef. bg, S¹ read as in margin. d om.   [28] α, aefg, A. b, S¹ read ὅτι, d καὶ γάρ. A = δι᾽ ὅ.   [29] α, d. β–d, A, S¹ read ἡμῶν.   [30] d trs. before ὁ πατήρ.   [31] g om.   [32] abde om.   [33] α, beg. a reads ἀπαρχῇ, d ἐν ἀπαρχαῖς, f ἀπαρχῆς.   [34] aef add γῆς.   [35] dg om.   [36] de read Λευίς.   [37] h, abe. c, dfg om.   [38] b reads ἐδοξάσθη.   [39] α. β, S¹ om.   [40] α. β read γάρ.   [41] α, d. β–d, S¹ read ἐκλήρωσεν ἐν (g om.) αὐτοῖς.   [42] c. hi, β om.   [43] hi, a read τὸ ἱερατεῖον.   [44] α. β–d, A, S¹ read αὐτοῖς (+ οὖν bg) ὑπακούσατε (ἔστε Aᵇ*ᶜ). d ἀκούσατε οὖν αὐτοῖς.   [45] a om.   [46] c adds τῆς καρδίας ὑμῶν, h μου, a τε, g τῆς ζωῆς.   [47] α. β read περιπατήσατε. A = μὴ σκανδαλισθῆτε, but there is an obvious internal corruption here. d om. rest of verse.   [48] α. β–d, A, S¹ read as in margin. The clause τῷ δὲ . . . Ἰσραήλ, which contains a play on the name Gad, is alien to the context and belonged probably to the Test. of Gad originally. It is omitted by d. Thus τῷ Γὰδ . . . τὰ

β, A, S¹
οἴδατε
(οἶδα
bdg, A).

VI. *Γινώσκετε οὖν¹, τέκνα² μου, ὅτι ἐν ἐσχάτοις καιροῖς
καταλείψουσιν³ οἱ υἱοὶ ὑμῶν τὴν ἁπλότητα
⌜καὶ κολληθήσονται τῇ ἀπληστίᾳ⌝,
⌜καὶ⌝ ἀφέντες⁴ ⌜τὴν ἀκακίαν⁵

β κακουρ-
γίᾳ.

προσπελάσουσι⁶ τῇ πανουργίᾳ⁷,
*καὶ καταλιμπάνοντες⁸ τὰς ἐντολὰς Κυρίου
*κολληθήσονται τῷ Βελίαρ⁹.

2. Καὶ ἀφέντες⌝ τὸ¹⁰ γεωργεῖν¹¹
ἐξακολουθήσουσι¹² τοῖς ⌜πονηροῖς⌝¹³ διαβουλίοις αὐτῶν
καὶ διασπαρήσονται ἐν τοῖς ἔθνεσιν
καὶ δουλεύσουσιν¹⁴ τοῖς ἐχθροῖς αὐτῶν.

3. Καὶ ὑμεῖς οὖν εἴπατε ταῦτα¹⁵ τοῖς τέκνοις ὑμῶν, ὅπως, ἐὰν
ἁμάρτωσι¹⁶, τάχιον¹⁷ ἐπιστρέψωσι¹⁸ πρὸς τὸν¹⁹ Κύριον,

4. Ὅτι ἐλεήμων ἐστὶ καὶ ἐξελεῖται²⁰ αὐτοὺς *τοῦ ἐπιστρέψαι αὐτοὺς²¹ εἰς τὴν γῆν αὐτῶν.

α	β, A, S¹
VII. *Ἰδοὺ οὖν ὡς ὁρᾶτε, ἑκατὸν εἴκοσι καὶ ἓξ ἐτῶν ὑπάρχω¹, καὶ οὐκ *ἔγνων †ἐν ἐμοὶ ἁμαρτίαν 2. γυναικὸς† πλὴν τῆς συμβίου μου².	VII. Ἑκατὸν εἰκοσιδύο ἐτῶν εἰμὶ ἐγώ, καὶ οὐκ ἔγνων ἐν ἐμοὶ ἁμαρτίαν ⌜εἰς θάνα- τον. 2. Πλὴν τῆς γυναικός μου οὐκ ἔγνων ἄλλην⌝.

Οὐκ ἐπόρνευσα³ ἐν μετεωρισμῷ ⌜ὀφθαλμῶν⌝⁴ μου⁵.

πειρατήρια = הגדודים . . . . לנגד.   ⁴⁹α. β–d read τὰ πειρ. τὰ ἐπερχόμενα.
A = τὰ πειρ. ἃ ἀποκαλυπτόμενα ἐστίν; but is corrupt for
 = ἐπερχόμενα.

VI. ¹aef, S¹ read οἴδατε, bdg, A οἶδα.   ²g reads τεκνία.   ³A = πορνεύ-
σουσι ἀπό, which may have been corrupt for πορεύσουσιν ἀπό.   ⁴A om. next
fifteen words through hmt.   ⁵hi read κακίαν.   ⁶c reads προσπελάσωσι.
⁷α. β read κακουργίᾳ.   ⁸α, ae. bf read καταλιπόντες, d καταλείποντες.   ⁹g
prefixes καί and trs. before preceding line.   ¹⁰α read τῷ.   ¹¹b reads γεωργείον.
¹²h, abde. c reads ἐξακολουθοῦσι, f ἐξακολουθήσωσιν, g ἐπακολ.   ¹³f om.
c add καί.   ¹⁴bf add ἐν.   ¹⁵f reads αὐτά. g trs. after ὑμῶν.   ¹⁶bd
read ἁμαρτήσωσι.   ¹⁷bf read τάχειον.   ¹⁸α, d. β–d read ἐπιστρέψουσι.
¹⁹c. hi, β om.   ²⁰a reads ἐξελῆται. A^{b*d} add σώσει.   ²¹α. β–g
reads τοῦ ἐπιστρέψαι. g, A read καὶ ἐπιστρέψει αὐτούς (g om.). a om.
together with next four words.

VII. ¹α (save that hi prefix καί and read ὑπάρχων for ὑπάρχω). abf, A, S¹
read as in parallel text. deg ρκβ´ (ε´ g) εἰμὶ (ἤμην e) ἐγὼ (d om.) σήμερον
(e om.).   ²α (save that hi read γυναικῶν). β, S¹ read as in parallel column
save that for ἐν ἐμοί bdg read ἐπ' ἐμέ (dg ἐμοί) and S¹ om. εἰς θάνατον. A =

3. Οἶνον⁶ εἰς ἀποπλάνησιν οὐκ ἔπιον·
  ⌜πᾶν ἐπιθύμημα τοῦ πλησίον οὐκ ἐπεθύμησα⌝⁷.
4. Δόλος⁸ οὐκ ἐγένετο⁹ *ἐν τῇ¹⁰ καρδίᾳ μου·
  ψεῦδος οὐκ ἀνῆλθε διὰ τῶν¹¹ χειλέων μου.
5. ⌜Παντὶ ἀνθρώπῳ ὀδυνομένῳ συνεστέναξα
  καὶ πτωχῷ μετέδωκα ἄρτον¹² μου⌝.
  Εὐσέβειαν ἐποίησα¹⁴ ἐν πάσαις ταῖς¹⁵ ἡμέραις μου.
  *Ἀλήθειαν ἐφύλαξα¹⁶,

α	β, S¹
6. Τὸν Κύριον ἠγάπησα¹⁷ καὶ πάντα ἄνθρωπον ἐξ ὅλης τῆς καρδίας¹⁸ μου	6. ⌜Τὸν Κύριον ἠγάπησα *ἐν πάσῃ¹⁹ ἰσχύι μου· ὁμοίως²⁰ καὶ πάντα ἄνθρωπον ἠγάπησα *ὑπὲρ τὰ²¹ τέκνα μου.

7. *Ταῦτα καὶ ὑμεῖς, τέκνα μου, ποιεῖτε²²,
  καὶ²³. πᾶν πνεῦμα τοῦ Βελίαρ φεύξεται ἀφ' ὑμῶν
  καὶ πᾶσα πρᾶξις πονηρῶν ἀνθρώπων οὐ κυριεύσει ὑμῶν²⁴
  καὶ¹¹ πᾶν ἄγριον θηρίον²⁵ καταδουλώσετε²⁶
  ἔχοντες μεθ' ὑμῶν²⁷ τὸν θεὸν τοῦ οὐρανοῦ *καὶ τῆς γῆς²⁸
  *συμπορευόμενον τοῖς ἀνθρώποις ἐν ἁπλότητι καρδίας²⁹⌝.
8. *Καὶ ταῦτα εἰπὼν ἐνετείλατο τοῖς υἱοῖς αὐτοῦ³⁰ ὅπως ἀναγά-

After ἄρτον μου β, S¹ add ⌜οὐ βέβρωκα μόνος ὅριον οὐκ ἔλυσα⌝¹³.

β–d, Aᵃᶜᶠᵍ, S¹ καὶ ἐνετείλατο αὐτοῖς.

ἔγνων ἐν ἐμοὶ ἁμαρτίαν. ³A add καί. ⁴c read ὀφθαλμῷ. ⁵ef om. ⁶A trs. after ἀποπλάνησιν. ⁷be read ἐπόθησα. ⁸The couplet δόλος ... χειλέων μου appears in A as Καὶ δόλος οὐκ ἀνῆλθε διὰ τῶν χειλέων μου καὶ οὐκ ἐψευσάμην τῷ πλησίον μου. ⁹d reads ἔγνω. ¹⁰α, df. abe read ἐν, g τῇ. ¹¹g om. ¹²α. β–ag read τὸν ἄρτον, ag τῶν ἄρτων. ¹³β save that b reads ἔφαγον for βεβρ. and d adds ποτε after βεβρ. and τινι after ἔλυσα. ¹⁴g om. next seven words. Cf. reading of adf. ¹⁵e om. ¹⁶α. adef, S¹ read ἀλ. ἐποίησα (e ἠγάπησα), b καὶ ἀλήθειαν. A καὶ ἐν ὁσιότητι ἐπορευσάμην. A om. verses 6–7. c add εὐσέβειαν ἠγάπησα. ¹⁷hi add ὁμοίως. ¹⁸c. hi read ἰσχύος. ¹⁹efg. bd read ἐν πάσῃ τῇ. a om. ²⁰d adds δέ. ²¹b reads ὡς. ²²c. hi, g read καὶ ταῦτα ποιεῖτε καὶ ὑ. τ. μου (g ποιήσατε τ. μου καὶ ὑ.). b, S¹ ταῦτα καὶ ὑ. ποιήσατε τ. μου. adef ταῦτα ποιήσατε καὶ ὑ. τ. μου. ²³c reads ταῦτα ὑμεῖς ἐὰν ποιεῖτε. ²⁴β. c reads ἀφ' ὑμῶν, hi ὑμῖν. ²⁵α, d. a reads πάντα ἄγρια θηρία, befg πάντα ἄγριον θῆρα (θηρίον f, θηρίον θῆρα e). ²⁶c. hi, f read καταδουλώσητε, ab καταδουλώσεσθε, e καταδουλώσησθε, g καταδουλώσασθε, d οὐκ ἔλθῃ πρὸς ὑμᾶς and omit next two lines. c adds in margin and hi in text περὶ τοῦ Χριστοῦ. ²⁷α. β–d read ἑαυτῶν. ²⁸α. β, S¹ om. ²⁹α, β–d, S¹ save that hi, ef read συμπορευόμενοι and α adds αὐτοῦ after καρδίας. ³⁰α. β–d, Aᵃᶜᶠᵍ, S¹ read as in margin, d, Aᵇ*ᵈ ταῦτα (+πάντα Aᵇ*ᵈ) εἰπὼν Ἰσαχὰρ τοῖς υἱοῖς αὐτοῦ ἐνετείλατο αὐτοῖς. Thus the

β–g, S¹ γωσιν αὐτὸν[31] ἐν[32] Χεβρών[33], κἀκεῖ[34] θάψωσιν αὐτὸν[35]
αὐτὸν
ἐν τῷ   ⌜μετὰ τῶν πατέρων αὐτοῦ⌝[36].
σπηλαίῳ.

α	β, S¹	A
9. Καὶ ἐκτείναςτοὺς πόδας αὐτοῦ[37] ἐκοιμήθη ἐν γήρει καλῷ ὕπνον αἰώνιον.	9. *Καὶ ἐξέτεινε τοὺς πόδας αὐτοῦ καὶ[38] ἀπέθανε[39] ἐν γήρει καλῷ, πᾶν μέλος ἔχων ὑγιές[40], καὶ ἰσχύων ὕπνωσεν ὕπνον αἰώνιον[41].	9. Καὶ ἐκτείνας τοὺς πόδας αὐτοῦ ὕπνωσεν ἐν *γῇ 'Ρακολμ[42] *ὑγιὴς ὢν[43] πάντα μέλη αὐτοῦ, καὶ ἐν ἰσχύι ὕπνωσεν ὕπνον αἰώνιον[44].

Διαθήκη Ζαβουλὼν τοῦ ἕκτου υἱοῦ 'Ιακὼβ καὶ Λείας[1].

I. *'Αντίγραφον λόγων[2] Ζαβουλών, ὧν[3] διέθετο τοῖς υἱοῖς[4] αὐτοῦ, ⌜πρὶν ἢ ἀποθανεῖν αὐτὸν⌝[5] *ἐν τῷ[6] ἑκατοστῷ *τετάρτῳ καὶ δεκάτῳ[7] ἔτει τῆς ζωῆς αὐτοῦ[8], μετὰ *οὖν δύο ἔτη[9] *τοῦ θανάτου[10] 'Ιωσήφ.   2. Εἶπεν[11] αὐτοῖς· 'Ακούσατέ μου[12],

inferior MSS. of A agree closely here with α, d.   [31] A = ὀστέα
αὐτοῦ.   [32] α, bdf. aeg read εἰς.   [33] d reads Χευρών.   [34] g reads καί.
f adds αὐτόν.   [35] β–g trs. before θάψωσιν against α. g, A om. β–g, A,
S¹ add ἐν τῷ σπηλαίῳ (+τῷ διπλῷ d, A).   [36] h, A om.   [37] hi. c om.
[38] β–d save that g reads ἐκτείνας and om. αὐτοῦ καί. d reads ὡς δὲ ἐπλήρωσεν
ἐντελλόμενος τοῖς υἱοῖς αὐτοῦ.   [39] b adds πέμπτος.   [40] d reads ὑγιῆ. g om.
rest of ver.   [41] f, S¹ add 'Ισσαχὰρ υἱὸς 'Ιακὼβ ε' (+ καὶ S¹) υἱὸς Λίας ε'
(+ καὶ S¹) ἔζησεν ἔτη ρκβ'.   [42] So A^{ab*d}, corruption of γήρᾳ καλῷ. A^{ef} are
more corrupt.   [43] A^{acfg}. A^{b*d} = ὑγιὴς ἦν.   [44] A^{b*} add εἰς δόξαν θεοῦ.

[1] Title. α in text. abef, S¹ read Δ. Ζ. περὶ εὐσπλαγχνίας καὶ ἐλέους
(+ἑρμηνεύεται Ζ. δῶρον f), d (conflate) Δ. Ζ. υἱοῦ 'Ιακὼβ καὶ Λίας ς' περὶ
εὐσπλαγχνίας καὶ ἐλεημοσύνης, g Δ. Ζ. περὶ ἐλεημοσύνης ς'. A^{ab} = Δ. Ζ. υἱοῦ
'Ισραὴλ υἱοῦ 'Ισαάκ, A^{cfg} = Δ. Ζ.   [2] α, β–abd. a reads ἀντίγραφα λόγ. b, S¹
reads ἀντίγραφα. d reads ἀντίγραφον διαθήκης. A^{abb*cd} (conflate) = ἀντίγ.
διαθήκης λόγων. A^b om. 1, 2, 3ª.   [3] ci, β–bd. h reads ᾧ, b ὅ, d ὅσα.
[4] α. β read τέκνοις.   [5] c. d reads πρὸ τοῦ ἀποθανεῖν αὐτόν. h, β–d, A, S om.
[6] β–a om.   [7] hi, d (save that h reads τεσσάρῳ). So bg, S¹ ριδ'. ef(though
corrupt) support text τέσσαρες (-ις f) καὶ δεκάτῳ, c τετάρτῳ, a τεσσαρακοστῷ
καὶ δεκάτῳ. A = εἰκοστῷ καὶ τετάρτῳ.   [8] g om. rest of verse.   [9] c. h reads
δὲ δύο ἐτῶν, i οὖν ἔτη. adef, A read δύο ἔτη, bg λβ'.   [10] d reads τῆς τελευτῆς.
[11] α. β–dg, A^{acf}, S read καὶ εἶπεν. d, A^{bb*d} καλέσας (ἐκάλεσε A^{b*d}) τοὺς υἱοὺς
αὐτοῦ (+ καὶ A^{b*d}) εἶπεν, g καλέσας αὐτοὺς εἶπεν.   [12] a add λόγων, d ol.

υἱοὶ Ζαβουλών[13], *προσέχετε ῥήμασιν[14] *τοῦ πατρὸς ὑμῶν[15].
3. Ἐγὼ[16] Ζαβουλὼν δόσις ἀγαθὴ[17] γέγονα[18] τοῖς γονεῦσί
μου· ἐν γὰρ τῷ τεχθῆναί[19] με, ηὐξήνθη[20] ὁ πατήρ μου[21]
σφόδρα καὶ τὰ πρόβατα[22] καὶ τὰ βουκόλια, ὅτε[23] *ἐν ταῖς
ποικίλαις ῥάβδοις[24] εἶχον[25] τὸν κλῆρον.   4. Οὐκ ἔγνων
⌜δὲ[26]⌝ ὅτι ἥμαρτον ἐν ταῖς ἡμέραις μου ⌜παρεκτὸς ἐννοίας⌝.   5.
Οὐ[27] μνήσκομαι[28] ὅτι παρανομίαν ἐποίησα, πλὴν τὴν ἄγνοιαν
ἣν ἐποίησα[29] ἐπὶ τοῦ[30] Ἰωσήφ, ὅτι ἐβεβαίωσα[31] τοῖς ἀδελφοῖς
μου[32] *μὴ εἰπεῖν[33] *τῷ πατρί μου[34] τὸ γενόμενον.   6. Ἀλλ'[35]
ἔκλαιον[36] ⌜ἐν κρυφῇ⌝[37] *ἡμέρας πολλὰς[38] *διὰ τὸν Ἰωσήφ[39].
*ἐφοβούμην γὰρ[40] *τοὺς ἀδελφούς μου, ⌜ὅτι[41] συνέθεντο
πάντες[42] *ὅστις ἐξείπῃ[43] τὸ μυστήριον ἀναιρεθῆναι[44] αὐτόν[45]⌝.
7. *Πλὴν ὅτε[46] ἐβούλοντο ἀνελεῖν αὐτόν[47], *ἐγὼ μετὰ δακρύων
προσεκάλουν αὐτούς[48] μὴ ποιῆσαι τὴν ἁμαρτίαν[49] ταύτην.
II. Ἦλθον[1] γὰρ ὁ[2] Συμεὼν ⌜καὶ ὁ Δὰν⌝[2] καὶ ὁ[2] Γὰδ

Margin: β–d ἕως σφόδρα. β–d, Aabcf, S εἶχεν. bg, A ἐσκέπασα ἐπί. β (A), S¹ πολλὰ διεμαρτυράμην αὐτοῖς ⌜μετὰ δακρύων⌝ τοῦ.

g om. μου.   [13] d adds τοῦ πατρὸς ὑμῶν.   [14] g reads φωνῆς. d, A read καὶ
προσέχετε (+ τοῖς d) ῥήμασιν.   [15] α, g. abef, A, S¹ read πατρὸς ὑμῶν, d μου.
[16] β, A add εἰμί. g om. ver. 3.   [17] A = ἀγαθοῖς.   [18] α. β, S¹ om.   [19] α.
β read γεννηθῆναι.   [20] α, d. β–d read ηὐξήθη.   [21] α, d, A, S². befg S¹
read ἡμῶν. a om. β–d add ἕως.   [22] α, af. bdeg read ποίμνια.   [23] d
reads ὅτι. Ab*efg = καί.   [24] α, β–b. b reads ἐν τοῖς ποικίλοις ῥάβδοις.
Abbb*cefg = ποικίλον.   [25] α, d. β–d, Aabcf, S read εἶχεν. Ab* om.
[26] α. β, A, S¹ om. b adds τέκνα μου.   [27] α. β, S¹ read οὐδέ.   [28] α, aeg.
b reads μιμνήσκομαι, df μέμνημαι. A = μέμνησθαι δύναμαι.   [29] β, A. α om.
[30] α, b. β–b om.   [31] α, β–bg, S¹ (save that aef add ἐπί). bg, A read
as in margin (though A adds τὸν λόγον after μου). Ἐσκέπασα ἐπί =
עַל כָּפִּיתִי corrupt for עַל קִיַּמְתִּי = ἐβεβαίωσα. Cf. Esther ix. 21, 31.
[32] d add τοῦ.   [33] A = καὶ οὐκ εἶπον.   [34] β, A (though A adds Ἰακώβ
and trs. after γενόμενον). α read τὸν πατέρα ἡμῶν.   [35] α, β–bdg, Ab*d.
bg, Aabcefg read καί. d om. ἀλλ'... Ἰωσήφ. Yet see note 45.   [36] b add
πολλά.   [37] α, β–afg. af read κρυφῇ. g, A om.   [38] bg om. f prefixes
ἐπί.   [39] c. hi, aefg read περὶ (+ τοῦ h) Ἰωσήφ. b om.   [40] g reads
ἀλλ' ἐφοβούμην.   [41] d reads αὐτοὺς ἐπειδὴ γάρ.   [42] β, S¹ add ὁμοῦ.   [43] α
(save that c reads ἐξείπει). bg read εἴ τις ἐξείποι, adf ὅτι (a om.) εἴ τις
ἐξείπῃ, e ἤ τις ἐξείποι.   [44] d reads ἀναιρεθήσεται.   [45] β, S¹ add μαχαίρᾳ.
After μαχαίρᾳ d adds ἔκλαιον οὖν ἐγὼ περὶ Ἰωσήφ ἡμέρας πολλὰς ἐν κρυφῇ.
[46] dg, S¹ read πλὴν ὅτι. Ab*d = καὶ ὅτε.   [47] c om. rest of verse and
ἦλθον ... τοῦ ἀνελεῖν in ii. 1 through hmt.   [48] hi. β, S read as in
margin. A = πολλάκις διεμαρτυράμην (ἐβουλόμην διαμαρτύρασθαι Aab, ὠλόλυζον
Ab*d) αὐτοῖς τοῦ.   [49] h. β, A read ἀνομίαν.

β, A, S[1]
*ἐπὶ τὸν
'Ιωσὴφ[3]
⌐τοῦ
ἀνελεῖν
αὐτόν⌐[4]
καὶ πεσὼν
ἐπὶ πρόσ-
ωπον
'Ιωσὴφ[5]
*ἔλεγεν
αὐτοῖς[6].
β, A, S[1]
ἐπαγά-
γετε ἐπ'
ἐμέ.
β, A[abc]
ἐπενέγ-
κητέ μοι.
β, S[1] εἰς

ἐπὶ τὸν 'Ιωσὴφ τοῦ ἀνελεῖν αὐτόν, καὶ ἔλεγεν αὐτοῖς μετὰ δακρύων.   2. 'Ελεήσατέ με ἀδελφοί μου[7]· οἰκτειρήσατε[8] σπλάγχνα[9] 'Ιακὼβ τοῦ πατρὸς ἡμῶν[10]. Μὴ[11] ἐπαγάγετε[12] τὰς χεῖρας ὑμῶν ⌐τοῦ[13] ἐκχέαι αἷμα ἀθῷον⌐, ὅτι οὐχ ἥμαρτον[14] εἰς ὑμᾶς.   3. Εἰ δὲ καὶ[15] ἥμαρτον, ἐν παιδείᾳ παιδεύσατέ με, ⌐ἀδελφοί μου⌐[16], *τὴν δὲ χεῖρα ὑμῶν μὴ[17] *ἐνέγκατε ἐν φόνῳ ἀδελφοῦ ὑμῶν[18] διὰ 'Ιακὼβ τὸν πατέρα ὑμῶν[19].   4. 'Ως δὲ ἔλεγεν ⌐ὀδυρόμενος⌐[20] τὰ *ῥήματα ταῦτα[21], *μὴ φέρων ἐγὼ τῶν οἰμωγῶν[22] ⌐ἠρξάμην κλαίειν⌐, καὶ τὰ ἥπατά μου ἐξεχύθησαν[23], καὶ πᾶσα[24] ἡ ὑπόστασις[25] τῶν σπλάγχνων μου ἐχαυνοῦτο[26].   5. *Ἔκλαιον δὲ σὺν τῷ 'Ιωσήφ[27] καὶ ἐβόμβει[28] ἡ καρδία μου, ⌐καὶ οἱ ἁρμοὶ τοῦ σώματός μου ἔτρεμον[29]⌐. καὶ οὐκ ἠδυνάμην στῆναι[30].   6. *'Ιδὼν δὲ 'Ιωσὴφ συνκλαίοντά με[31] αὐτῷ, κἀκείνους ἐπερχομένους[32] ἀνελεῖν αὐτόν[33], κατέφυγεν ὄπισθέν[34]

οἶκτον ἦλθον ἐγὼ καί.   β, A, S[1] ἐχαυνοῦτο ἐπὶ τὴν ψυχήν μου.   β, S[1] ἔκλαιε δὲ καὶ 'Ιωσὴφ κἀγὼ σὺν αὐτῷ.   β, S[1] ἐξέστησαν.

II. [1] *ag* read ἦλθε.   [2] *h*. β, A, S[1] om.   [3] A = ἐπ' αὐτόν. *g* om. *af* om. next eight words through hmt. *deg* S[1] add μετ' ὀργῆς.   [4] *d*, A om.   [5] *e* reads ὁ 'Ιωσήφ.   [6] A[b*d] = ἔλεγεν μετὰ δακρύων. Cf. α. A[abceig] = ἐδάκρυε καὶ ἔλεγε. *af* insert καὶ before ἔλεγεν.   [7] *d* om.   [8] *bdg*, A add τά.   [9] A read ⲩⲱⳑⳑⲃⲁⳑ (= τὸ γῆρας) which is corrupt for ⲩⲱⲏⳑⲃⲁⳑ = τὰ σπλάγχνα.   [10] *a* reads ὑμῶν.   [11] *d*, A read καὶ μή.   [12] β, S[1] add ἐπ' ἐμέ. A adds the same phrase after ὑμῶν.   [13] *g* om.   [14] *d* adds τι.   [15] *f* om.   [16] α, β–*bd*, S[1]. *bd*, A om.   [17] α (save that *c* om. δέ), β, A[abc], S[1]. A[b*deig] = καὶ μή τι (+ μοι κακά A[b*]).   [18] α. β, A[abc] read ἐπενέγκητέ μοι (*dg* ἐπ' ἐμέ, *b* om.).   [19] *c*, A. *hi*, β, S[1] read ἡμῶν.   [20] α. β, A, S[1] om.   [21] *g* reads ἐλεεινὰ ῥήματα.   [22] α. β, S[1] read as in margin save that *d* om. καί. A = οἶκτος ἔπεσεν εἰς καρδίαν μου.   [23] *dg*. *hi*, β–*dg* read ἐξελύθησαν, S[1] ἐξελύθη. *c* reads ἐξηλήθησαν. β, S[1] add ἐπ' ἐμέ. A = ἐτύπησαν ἐν ἐμοί, but ⲥⲱⲣⲱⲓⲗⲏⲓ is corrupt for ⲥⲛⲩⳃⳉⲱⲓ = ἐξεχύθη and thus supports *dg*. The text is based on Lam. ii. 11 'and my liver was poured out' (נשׁפך).   [24] *g* trs. after ὑπόστασις.   [25] A reads ⳤⲱⲣ ⳡⲟⲣⲏⳑⳏⲃⳡⲁⳑ = ὑπόστασις δυνάμεως, but the two words appear to be duplicate renderings of ὑπόστασις.   [26] β, A, S[1] add as in margin (save that *e* om. ἐπί, and *g* reads τῇ ψυχῇ for τὴν ψυχήν). ἐχαυνοῦτο is difficult—corrupt perhaps for ἐθολοῦτο. The text would then be based on Lam. i. 20, ii. 11 חמרמרו.   [27] α, A (save that A read αὐτῷ for τῷ 'Ι.). β, S[1] read as in margin save that *f* om. καί and *d* δὲ καί.   [28] *a*. *c* reads ἐβόμβοι, *hi* ἔμφοβος ἦν, *bfy* ἐβόμβη, *d*, A ἐθαμβήθη, *e* ἐβόνβει. ἐβόμβει = הָמָה, ἐθαμβήθη = תִּמָּה.   [29] *hi*. *c* reads ἔτρεχον, β ἐξέστησαν.   [30] *b* reads τοῦ στῆναι. *g* trs. before οὐκ.   [31] α. β, A, S[1] read καὶ ἰδών (εἶδεν *g*) με συνκλαίοντα.   [32] *i*, β–*g*, A, S[1]. *ch* read ἀπερχ. *g* ἀνερχ.   [33] *g*

μου, δεόμενος *τῆς πρὸς αὐτὸν βοηθείας[35].   7. *Ἐν δὲ τῷ
μεταξὺ ἀναστὰς[36] Ῥουβὴμ[37] εἶπεν[38]. *Δεῦτε ἀδελφοί μου[39], μὴ
ἀποκτείνωμεν αὐτὸν ἀλλὰ ῥίψωμεν[40] αὐτὸν εἰς ἕνα τῶν *ξηρῶν
λάκκων[41] τούτων[42], ὧν ὤρυξαν οἱ πατέρες ἡμῶν, καὶ οὐχ εὗρον
ὕδωρ[43].   8. Διὰ γὰρ τοῦτο ἐκώλυσε ὁ[44] Κύριος *τοῦ μὴ
ἀναβλῦσαι ὕδωρ[45] ἐν αὐτοῖς ἵνα *γένηται περιποίησις τῷ[46]
Ἰωσήφ.   9. *Καὶ ἐποίησαν[47] *οὕτως ἕως ὅτου[48] ἐπώλησαν[49]
αὐτὸν[50] τοῖς Ἰσμαηλίταις[51].

III.   *Εἰς γὰρ τὸ τίμημα αὐτοῦ ἐγὼ οὐκ ἐκοινώνησα,
τέκνα μου[1].   2. *Ἀλλὰ Συμεὼν[2] καὶ *ὁ Δὰν καὶ ὁ Γὰδ καὶ
τὰ τέκνα αὐτῶν[3], καὶ[4] λαβόντες *τὴν τιμὴν αὐτοῦ[5] ἐπρίαντο[6]
ὑποδήματα ἑαυτοῖς[7] *καὶ ταῖς γυναιξὶν αὐτῶν[8] ⌜καὶ τοῖς τέκνοις
αὐτῶν[9]⌝, εἰπόντες·   3. *Οὐ φαγόμεθα αὐτήν[10], ὅτι τιμή
ἐστιν *αἵματος τοῦ ἀδελφοῦ ἡμῶν[11], ἀλλὰ καταπατήσει[12]
καταπατήσωμεν[13] αὐτήν, ἀνθ᾽ ὧν εἶπεν βασιλεῦσαι[14] ἐφ᾽ αὕτη.

β, A, S¹
αὐτῶν.
β, S¹
ἀναστὰς
δέ.
β, A, S¹
ἀδελφοί.
β τοῦ
ἀναβῆναι
ὕδωρ.
β–dg, S¹
ἐποίησε
Κύριος.
β, A ab
Γὰδ καὶ
οἱ ἄλλοι
ἐξ ἀδελ-
φοὶ ἡμῶν.
β–dg,
A ab ἡμῶν
αὕτη.

adds καί.   [34] α. β read ὀπίσω.   [35] α. β–d, A, S¹ read as in margin.
d reads αὐτοῖς.   [36] α. β read as in margin. A = καὶ τότε ἀναστάς.
[37] abfg. α, d read Ῥουβίμ, e Ῥουβήν.   [38] a adds αὐτοῖς.   [39] α. β, A read
ἀδελφοί (+ μου g, A).   [40] c reads βάλλομεν.   [41] α. β, A read λάκκων
τῶν ξηρῶν.   [42] g om. rest of verse together with ver. 8.   [43] A bc add
ῥίψωμεν αὐτόν. c. om. next ten words through hmt. hi add ἐν αὐτοῖς
owing to c(?).   [44] hi. β om.   [45] hi, A. bd, S¹ read τοῦ ἀναβῆναι (εὑρεθῆναι
d) ὕδωρ, aef ὕδωρ ἀναβῆναι.   [46] c, abef, A (save that c reads γένειται and
b τοῦ). hi read γένωνται περιποιήσεις τῷ, d γένονται εἰς περιποίησιν τῷ.   [47] α,
d, A. So also g save that it prefixes ὅ. β–dg, S¹ read καὶ ἐποίησε Κύριος.
[48] α. β–g read οὕτως ἕως οὗ, g καὶ εἶθ᾽ οὕτως.   [49] α, bdeg. a reads
πέπρακαν, and trs. after Ἰσμ. f ἔπρασαν. A = ἐπωλήσαμεν.   [50] A ab =
Ἰωσήφ.   [51] c reads Ἰσραηλίταις.

III.   [1] α. β–dg, S¹ read καὶ γὰρ τὸ τίμημα (τῆς τιμῆς b, τῷ τιμήματι e) τοῦ
Ἰωσήφ, τέκνα (aef, S¹ trs. after ἐκοιν.), ἐγὼ οὐκ ἐκοινώνησα, d καὶ ἐκ τῆς τιμῆς
αὐτοῦ, τέκνα, ἐγὼ οὐκ ἐκ., g τῆς δὲ τιμῆς Ἰωσήφ μὴ γένοιτό μοι κοινωνῆσαι. A =
ἀλλὰ (A a om.) τὸ τίμημα οὐκ ἐκ. ἐγώ, τέκνα μου.   [2] g reads Σ. δέ.   [3] α. β–g,
A ab read Γὰδ καὶ οἱ ἄλλοι (ἀδελφοί ae. f om. ἄλλοι) ἐξ ἀδελφοὶ ἡμῶν (ἐξ τῶν
ἀδελφῶν μου d, ἐξ ἀδελφοί A ab), g καὶ Γάδ. A b*cdefg = Γ. καὶ οἱ ἄλλοι ἀδελφοί.
[4] bd om.   [5] α (save that c reads αὐτῶν). β, S¹ read τὴν τιμὴν τοῦ (g om.)
Ἰωσήφ. A = αὐτήν.   [6] aefg. α, b read ἐπριάσαντο, d ἠγόρασαν.   [7] d trs.
before ὑποδήματα. A b = τοῖς ποσὶν αὐτῶν.   [8] A b*d om.   [9] d om.   [10] a
reads καὶ οὐ φαγώμεθα αὐτήν and trs. after αὕτη (see margin). For αὐτήν
g, A read ἐξ αὐτῆς.   [11] α save that hi trs. ἐστιν αἵματος. β, A, S¹ read
αἵματός ἐστιν (bdg, A om.) τοῦ (efg om.) ἀδελφοῦ ἡμῶν αὕτη (dg, A ab ἐστίν,
A b*cdefg ἦν).   [12] hi, dg om.   [13] a reads καταπατήσομεν.   [14] c. hi read

ἡμᾶς[15], ⌜καὶ ἴδωμεν[16] τί ἐστι[17] *τὰ ἐνύπνια[18] αὐτοῦ⌝.   4.

β, S¹   Διὰ τοῦτο οὖν[19] ἐν ⌜γραφῇ⌝ *νόμου Μωυσέως γέγραπται[20].
'Ενώχ (A   Τὸν μὴ θέλοντα *ἀναστῆσαι σπέρμα[21] τῷ ἀδελφῷ αὐτοῦ
αὐτῶν).   ὑπολύεσθαι[22] τὸ ὑπόδημα ⌜αὐτοῦ⌝[23] καὶ ἐμπτύεσθαι εἰς τὸ
προσωπον.   5. *Καὶ οἱ ἀδελφοὶ τοῦ 'Ιωσὴφ[24] οὐκ ἠθέλησαν[25] †ζωὴν[26] ἀδελφοῦ αὐτῶν[27], καὶ ὁ[28] Κύριος ὑπέλυσεν[29]
αὐτοὺς[30] τὸ ὑπόδημα[31] *ὃ ἐφόρεσαν κατὰ ⌜'Ιωσὴφ τοῦ ἀδελφοῦ⌝
αὐτῶν[32].   6. Καὶ *γὰρ ἐλθόντες ἐν Αἰγύπτῳ[33] ⌜ὑπελύθη-
β ἔμ-   σαν[34] *ὑπὸ τῶν παίδων[35] 'Ιωσὴφ ἔξωθεν[36] τοῦ πυλῶνος, καὶ
προσθεν.   οὕτως[37] προσεκύνησαν[38] *τῷ 'Ιωσὴφ[39] κατὰ τὸν τύπον
βασιλέως[40] Φαραώ⌝[41].   7. Οὐ μόνον δὲ προσεκύνησαν
β–dg,   αὐτῷ[42] ἀλλὰ καὶ ⌜ἐνεπτύσθησαν[43] παραχρῆμα[44] πεσόν-
A, S¹   τες ἔμπροσθεν αὐτοῦ, καὶ⌝[45] ᾐσχύνθησαν[46] παρὰ[47] τῶν[48]
ἔμπρο-
σθεν.

βασιλεύσει, β–b, A ὅτι βασιλεύσει, b βασιλεύειν.   [15] A^abcefg = ὑμᾶς, A^b*d αὐτούς.
[16] hi, ade. c reads εἴδομεν, bg εἴδωμεν, f ἴδομεν.   [17] ch, f. i, β–f read ἔσται.
[18] d reads τὸ ἐνύπνιον.   [19] α. β om. A = καί.   [20] α. β, S¹ read νόμου
(d om.) 'Ενὼχ γέγραπται. A = νόμῳ αὐτῶν εἶπεν.   [21] h, β–d (save that f
reads σπ. ἀναστῆσαι), A. c, d read ἀναστῆναι τὸ (c om.) σπέρμα.   [22] α, g.
b, S¹ reads ὑπολυθήσεσθαι, a ὑποδήσεσθαι, ef ὑποδεθήσεσθαι, d ὑποληφθήσεται.
A^ab = ὑπολύειν. A^b*d om. and for the next eight words A^b*d read ἐμπτύ-
σουσι εἰς τὸ πρόσωπον τοῦ ὑποδήματος αὐτοῦ. A^cefg om. together with next
eight words.   [23] α. β–g, A om. g reads ὃ ἐφόρεσαν and om. rest of
ver. 4 and all ver. 5.   [24] α, β–d (save that β–d om. τοῦ). d reads κατὰ·
τοῦτον δὴ τὸν νόμον. A = καὶ γὰρ ἀδελφοὶ αὐτοῦ.   [25] α, β–adf. a reads
ἤθελον, d ἤθελης. f om.   [26] α, af, S¹. beg read εἰς ζωήν, d τὴν ζωὴν 'Ιωσὴφ
τοῦ. A = περὶ ζωῆς. Here I take οὐκ ἠθέλησαν ζωὴν ἀδελφοῦ αὐτῶν = אתיהם
לא חמפו בחיית where בחיית may be corrupt for לחיית. Hence text should
run οὐκ ἠθέλησαν περιποιήσασθαι ἀδελφὸν αὐτῶν.   [27] hi, d om. rest of ver.
through hmt.   [28] c. Other MSS. om.   [29] c reads ἐπέδυσεν.   [30] a
reads αὐτοῖς.   [31] A = τὰ ὑποδήματα.   [32] c, aef, S¹. b reads 'Ιωσήφ.
A = ἃ ἐφόρεσαν κατ' αὐτοῦ.   [33] g reads ἡμεῖς γὰρ ἐλθόντες εἰς Αἴγυπτον πρὸς
'Ιωσήφ. A πάντες γὰρ ἐλθ. εἰς Αἴγ.   [34] β–g, S¹. α reads ἀπελύθησαν,
g ὑπελύθημεν.   [35] c reads ἀπὸ τῶν ποδῶν. d add τοῦ.   [36] α, S¹. β read
as in margin.   [37] d adds συνελθόντες.   [38] g reads προσεκυνήσαμεν.
[39] c, β–dg. h reads τὸν 'Ι., d αὐτόν. g om.   [40] c, ad, S¹. hi read βασιλέα,
ef τοῦ βασιλέως. bg τοῦ.   [41] g om. next five words.   [42] c, be. h, af
read αὐτόν. d om.   [43] h, β–g. c read ἐνεμπτύσθησαν, g ἐνεπτύσθημεν.
g adds ἔμπροσθεν αὐτοῦ and om. this phrase at end of clause.   [44] bdf, S¹.
α, aeg read παρὰ σχῆμα.   [45] β, S¹ add οὕτως.   [46] g reads ᾐσχύνθημεν.
[47] c. h reads ὑπό, g ἐνώπιον, abef, A, S¹ ἔμπροσθεν, d πρός.   [48] af om.

Αἰγυπτίων[49].   8. * Ἤκουσαν γὰρ ὅσα ἐνεδείξαντο αὐτῷ   β-dg, S¹
κακά[50].   μετὰ
                                                                         ταῦτα
                                                                         γὰρ
           α   β, A, S¹   ἤκουσαν
   IV. Μετὰ δὲ τὸ †πραθῆ-   IV. * Μετὰ δὲ τὸ βάλλειν   οἱ Αἰγύ-
ναι[1] αὐτὸν ἐκάθησαν οἱ ἀδελ-   αὐτὸν εἰς τὸν λάκκον[13] * ἐκά-   πτιοι
φοί μου[2] ἐσθίειν καὶ πίνειν.   θησαν ἐσθίειν ⌜οἱ ἀδελφοί   πάντα τὰ
2. Ἐγὼ δὲ σπλαγχνιζόμενος   μου⌝[14].   2. Ἐγὼ γὰρ[15] δύο   κακὰ ἃ
τὸν Ἰωσὴφ * οὐκ ἔφαγον[3]·   ἡμέρας καὶ δύο νύκτας οὐκ   ἐποιήσα-
προσέχων[4] δὲ τῷ λάκκῳ, ἐπει-   ἐγευσάμην, σπλαγχνιζόμενος   μεν τῷ
δὴ[5] ἐφοβεῖτο[6] Ἰούδας μήπως   ἐπὶ Ἰωσήφ[16]. καὶ[17] Ἰούδας   Ἰωσήφ.
ἀποπηδήσαντες[7] Συμεὼν καὶ ὁ   οὐ συνέτρωγεν αὐτοῖς· * προσ-
Δὰν καὶ ὁ Γὰδ ἀνέλωσιν   εἶχε δὲ ⌜τῷ λάκκῳ⌝[18], * ὅτι
αὐτόν.   3. Ὁρῶντές με δὲ   ἐφοβεῖτο[19] μὴ[20] ἀποπηδήσαν-
μὴ[8] ἐσθίοντα ἔθεντό με[9] τη-   τες Συμεὼν[21] καὶ Γὰδ ἀνέ-
ρεῖν αὐτὸν ἕως οὗ ἀπεδόθη   λωσιν αὐτόν.   3. * Καὶ
* τοῖς Ἰσμαηλίταις[10].   5.   ὁρῶντες κἀμὲ μὴ ἐσθίοντα
Ἐλθὼν δὲ Ῥουβὶμ καὶ ἀκούσας   ἔθεντό με τηρεῖν αὐτὸν ἕως
ὅτι ἐπράθη[8] ἀπόντος * αὐτοῦ   οὗ ἐπράθη[22]. 4. Ἐποίησε δὲ[23]
περιεσχίσατο[11] τὸν χιτῶνα   ἐν τῷ λάκκῳ τρεῖς ἡμέρας καὶ
αὐτοῦ θρηνῶν ἔλεγεν[12]· Πῶς   τρεῖς νύκτας καὶ οὕτως * ἐπρά-

[49] g om. next verse.   [50] α (save that h adds καὶ πάντα after γάρ). abef, S¹
read as in margin (save that for ἐποιήσαμεν e reads ἐνεδειξάμεθα), d ἐν τῷ
ἀκοῦσαι πάντα τὰ κακὰ ἃ πεποιήκαμεν τῷ Ἰ. A = ἠκούσθη γὰρ ἐν πᾶσι τοῖς
Αἰγυπτίοις.

   IV. [1] Corrupt probably for βληθῆναι.   [2] c. hi read αὐτοῦ.   [3] hi trs.
before σπλαγχ.   [4] hi. c reads προσεσχών.   [5] hi add δέ.   [6] c reads ἐφοβήτω.
[7] hi. c reads ἀποπηδήσωσιν.   [8] c om.   [9] hi om.   [10] c. h (i ?) reads ὁ ὅσιος.
[11] h. c reads αὐτῷ περιεσχήσαντο.   [12] c. h (i ?) reads καὶ λέγων.   [13] g, A (save
that for αὐτόν A read Ἰωσήφ). d read ἀλλὰ τότε γὰρ μετὰ τὸ βληθῆναι αὐτὸν
εἰς τὸν λάκκον. abef, S¹ are defective and corrupt: καὶ (abe, S¹ om.) μετὰ
ταῦτα ἔβαλον (ef ἔβαλλον).   [14] d. Cf. α and Gen. xxxvii. 25 וַיֵּשְׁבוּ לֶאֱכָל־לֶחֶם.
g reads ἤρξαντο ἐσθίειν οἱ ἀδελφοί μου, A ἤθελον ἐσθίειν, S¹ ἐκάθησαν ἐσθίειν
ἐκεῖνοι. Here ⟨Armenian⟩ = ἤθελον seems corrupt for ⟨Armenian⟩ = ἤρξαντο.
abef read defectively ἐσθίειν ἐκεῖνοι.   [15] d reads δέ. g om.   [16] g read
αὐτόν.   [17] d reads ὁμοίως δέ.   [18] abefg. d reads ἀλλὰ τῷ λάκκῳ προσεῖχε.
A = ὅτι (A^{b*d} ἀλλὰ) προσεῖχε.   [19] β-d, S¹. d reads ἐφοβεῖτο γάρ. A = καὶ
ἐφοβεῖτο.   [20] d, A add πως. Cf. α.   [21] g om. next four words. For
Σ. καὶ Γ. A read Γ. καὶ Σ.   [22] β save that for τηρεῖν d reads εἰς τὸ
διατηρεῖν. A = καὶ ὁρῶν με μὴ ἐσθίοντα [καὶ θεωρῶν με μὴ γευόμενον καὶ]
Ἰούδας με ἔθετο τηρεῖν αὐτόν, ἕως οὗ ἔπρασαν αὐτόν (A^{b*} om. last clause). The

	α	β, A, S¹
	ὄψωμαι²⁴ τὸ πρόσωπον τοῦ πατρός μου Ἰακώβ; 6. Καὶ λαβὼν τὸ ἀργύριον κατέδραμεν ὀπίσω τοῖς ἐμπόροις· μὴ εὑρὼν δὲ αὐτοὺς ὑπέστρεψεν ὀδυρόμενος²⁵. καταλιπόντες²⁶ δὲ οἱ ἔμποροι τὴν πλατεῖαν ὁδὸν διόδευσαν²⁷ διὰ *Τρογλοδίτων ἐν συντόμῳ²⁸.	θη ἄσιτος²⁹. 5. *Καὶ ἀκούσας Ῥουβὴμ ὅτι ἐπράθη ἀπόντος αὐτοῦ, περισχισάμενος³⁰ *τὰ ἱμάτια αὐτοῦ³¹ ἐθρήνει³², λέγων· *Πῶς ὄψομαι³³ τὸ πρόσωπον Ἰακὼβ³⁴ τοῦ πατρός μου³⁵; 6. Καὶ λαβὼν τὸ ἀργύριον³⁶ κατέδραμε³⁷ *τοῖς ἐμπόροις³⁸, *καὶ οὐδένα εὗρεν³⁹. ἀφέντες γὰρ⁴⁰ τὴν ὁδὸν τὴν μεγάλην⁴¹ ἐπορεύθησαν⁴² ⌐διὰ Τρωγλοδύτων¬⁴³ ἐν τῇ συντόμῳ.

β, A, S¹
Καὶ οὐκ
ἔφαγεν
(+ Ῥου-
βήμ bg).
β, A, S¹
πένθει·
εὗρον.
β–g, A,
S¹ ἡμῶν
Ἰακώβ.
β, A, S¹
ἐμβάψω-
μεν.

7. ⌐*Ἦν δὲ ὁ Ῥουβὶμ λυπούμενος¬⁴⁴, καὶ οὐκ ἔφαγεν⁴⁵ ⌐ἄρτον¬ *ἐν ἐκείνῃ τῇ ἡμέρᾳ⁴⁶. *προσελθὼν οὖν ὁ Δὰν εἶπεν αὐτῷ⁴⁷· 8. Μὴ κλαῖε μηδὲ λυποῦ⁴⁸· εὕρομεν⁴⁹ γὰρ τί εἴπωμεν⁵⁰ τῷ πατρὶ ἡμῶν⁵¹. 9. Θύσωμεν ⌐μαχαίρᾳ¬⁵² *χίμαρρον αἰγῶν⁵³ καὶ μολύνωμεν⁵⁴ τὸν χιτῶνα Ἰωσήφ, καὶ *ἀποστείλωμεν

first clause in brackets is manifestly a duplicate rendering of what precedes.   ²³ d om.   ²⁴ c. h reads ὄψομαι.   ²⁵ c. hi read ὀδυνόμενος.   ²⁶ hi. c reads καταλείποντες.   ²⁷ c. hi read ἐπορεύθησαν.   ²⁸ c. hi read Τρογλοδύτων ἐν συντομίᾳ.   ²⁹ β–g, A^ace, S¹. g trs. ἄσιτος before καὶ οὕτως. A^b = ἔμεινε ἄσιτος ἕως ἔπρασαν αὐτόν, A^b*dg ἐπράθη Ἰωσήφ.   ³⁰ A^abce = καὶ ἀκούσας Ῥ. ὅτι ἐπράθη (A^ac om. ὅτι ἐπρ.) περιεσχίσατο. A^b*dfg περιεσχίσατο.   ³¹ d, A. β–d, S¹ om. A adds καί.   ³² g reads ἐθρήνησε.   ³³ d reads οἴμοι πῶς ὄψωμαι.   ³⁴ d trs. after μου.   ³⁵ a reads ἡμῶν.   ³⁶ d reads τίμημα.   ³⁷ bdeg. af read καὶ καταδραμών.   ³⁸ g reads ὀπίσω τῶν ἐμπόρων.   ³⁹ beg, A^abcefg. af, S¹ read καὶ (f om.) οὐδὲν εὑρών (εὗρεν f, S¹). d, A^b*d καὶ οὐχ εὗρεν αὐτούς.   ⁴⁰ a om. A adds ἦσαν.   ⁴¹ d reads βασιλικὴν ὁδόν. A adds ἣ ἦν ἐν τῇ συντόμῳ καὶ ἄλλην ὁδόν (A^b*d om. ὁδόν, A^efg om. καὶ … ὁδόν).   ⁴² A om. rest of verse.   ⁴³ af, S¹. bd read τραγλοκολπητῶν, d τρογλοκοπητῶν, e τρωγοκολπιτῶν, g στρογκαλῶν κολπῇ.   ⁴⁴ α. β, A, S¹ om.   ⁴⁵ hi, β–ae, A^abc, S¹. c, ae read ἔφαγον, A^b*d = ἀπώλετο through an obvious internal corruption. bg (on g see note 46), A^b add Ῥουβήμ, A^ab*cdefg Ἰωσήφ.   ⁴⁶ α. β–g, A read ἐν τῇ ἡμ. ἐκ., g τὴν ἡμέραν ἐκείνην Ῥουβήμ.   ⁴⁷ α, β–g, S¹ (save that β–eg, S¹ om. ὁ). g reads καὶ ἐλθὼν Δὰν λέγει. A = καὶ προσελθὼν Δ. εἶπεν τῷ Ῥ.   ⁴⁸ α. β read as in margin.   ⁴⁹ c. hi read εὕρωμεν. β, A, S¹ read εὗρον.   ⁵⁰ h, d. c, β–d read εἴπομεν.   ⁵¹ g om. β–g, A, S¹ add Ἰακώβ.   ⁵² α, β–bde, S¹. e reads μαχαίροις, bd, A om.   ⁵³ A^acel = χίμαρρον, A^bb*cd = τραγίσκον.   ⁵⁴ α. So LXX in Gen. xxxvii. 31. β, A, S¹ as in margin. (Here A^b omit to end of verse 1).

αὐτὸν τῷ Ἰακὼβ λέγοντες[55]. Ἐπίγνωθι, ὁ[56] *χιτὼν τοῦ υἱοῦ σου ἐστίν[57]; *καὶ ἐποίησαν οὕτως[58]. 10. ⌜Τὸν γὰρ χιτῶνα[59] ἐξέδυσαν τὸν[60] Ἰωσὴφ ἐν *τῷ πιπράσκειν[61] αὐτόν[62], *καὶ ἐνέδυσαν αὐτὸν ἱμάτιον δουλικόν[63]⌝. 11. *Ἔλαβε δὲ Συμεὼν τὸν χιτῶνα[64], ⌜καὶ⌝[65] οὐκ ἤθελε δοῦναι αὐτόν[66]. ⌜*ἐβούλετο γὰρ[67] τῇ ῥομφαίᾳ[68] *κατακόψαι αὐτόν[63]⌝, ὀργιζόμενος ὅτι οὐκ[70] ἀνεῖλεν αὐτόν. 12. Ἀναστάντες δὲ[71] *⌜πάντες⌝ εἴπομεν αὐτῷ[72], ὅτι[73] ἐὰν μὴ δῷς *τὸν χιτῶνα[74], εἴπωμεν[75] ⌜τῷ πατρὶ ἡμῶν⌝[76] ὅτι σὺ[73] μόνος ἐποίησας τὸ πονηρὸν *τοῦτο ἐν Ἰσραήλ[77]. 13. *Καὶ οὕτως δέδωκεν αὐτὸν αὐτοῖς[78]. Καὶ[73] ἐποίησαν καθὼς *εἶπεν ὁ Δάν[79].

V. Καὶ νῦν[1], τέκνα μου, παραγγέλλω[2] ὑμῖν *τοῦ φυλάσσειν[3] τὰς[4] ἐντολὰς *τοῦ Κυρίου[5] ⌜καὶ ποιεῖν ἔλεος ἐπὶ[6] τὸν

(margin:) β, Α, S[1] ἐροῦμεν (+ τῷ Ἰακὼβ Α). β, S[1] παλαιὸν δοῦλον. β, Α, S[1] τὸν δὲ χιτῶνα εἶχε Σ. β, S[1] θέλων. β, Α, S[1] ἔζησεν (+ Ἰωσήφ Α)

καὶ οὐκ ἀνεῖλεν.　β, S[1] κατ’ αὐτοῦ πάντες ὁμοῦ εἴπομεν.　β–g, Α, S[1] ἐροῦμεν.　β, S[1] ἀναγγελῶ.

[55] α save that c reads ἀποστείλομεν. β, Α, S[1] read as in margin. [56] α, def. abg, Α, S[1] read εἰ. [57] α, β–g (save that β–g add οὗτος). g reads χιτών ἐστιν τοῦ υἱοῦ σου οὗτος. Α = οὗτός ἐστιν χιτὼν υἱοῦ σου Ἰωσήφ. [58] b, S[1] om. [59] β–dg, S[1] add τοῦ πατρὸς ἡμῶν. g om. τὸν ... Ἰωσήφ. d presents a peculiar text of this verse : ὅταν δὲ ἠβουλήθησαν πιπρᾶσαι αὐτὸν ἐξέδυσαν τὸν χιτῶνα τὸν ποικίλον καὶ ἐνέδυσαν ἱμάτιον παλαιὸν ἐν σχήματι δούλου. [60] c reads τῷ. [61] α. abef, S[1] read τῷ μέλλειν πιπράσκεσθαι (b, S[1] πιπράσκειν), g γὰρ τῷ μέλλειν πιπράσκειν. For d see note 59. [62] α, β–ag. g reads τὸν Ἰωσήφ. a om. [63] α, β–g, S[1] save that for δουλικόν β–g, S[1] read παλαιὸν δούλου. g reads ἐκδύσαντες αὐτὸν τὸν χιτῶνα τοῦ πατρὸς ἐνέδυσαν παλαιὸν δουλικόν. [64] α (save that hi om. δέ). β, Α, S[1] read as in margin save that g add ὁ before Σ. [65] Α om. g om. together with next four words. [66] c reads αὐτῷ, Α = αὐτοῖς. [67] α. β, S[1] read θέλων (+ ἐν d). [68] β–g, S[1] add αὐτοῦ. [69] g read αὐτὸν διελεῖν ἀντὶ Ἰωσήφ, καὶ οὐκ ἐδίδου αὐτόν. [70] α. β, Α, S[1] read as in margin. [71] d reads οὖν. [72] α. β, S[1] read as in margin (save that g trs. κατ’ αὐτοῦ after ὁμοῦ). Α = ἡμεῖς κατ’ αὐτοῦ εἴπομεν. [73] g om. [74] α, Α[b]. d reads αὐτόν. β–d, Α[-b] om. [75] hi. β, Α, S[1] read ἐροῦμεν, c εἴπομεν. [76] α. g reads τῷ πατρί. β–g, Α, S[1] om. [77] α, (Α[b]?). β–a, Α[ab*cdes], S[1] read ἐν Ἰσραήλ, a ἐνώπιον Κυρίου. [78] α. abef, S[1] read καὶ οὕτω (οὕτως bf) δίδωσιν αὐτὸν (S[1] om.) αὐτοῖς (a trs. before αὐτόν, b om.), d τότε φοβηθεὶς δίδωσιν αὐτόν, g, Α καὶ (g om.) τότε δοὺς αὐτόν (Α om.). [79] α, β–d, S[1], Α[abb*d]. d read εἶπεν Δ. Α[ces] ἐνετείλατο αὐτοῖς ὁ Δάν.

V. [1] g reads ἰδού. [2] c, Α[abces]. hi read παραγγελῶ, β, S[1] ἀναγγελῶ. Α[b*d] om. [3] Α = φυλάσσετε. [4] g om. [5] hi, Α. c reads τοῦ θεοῦ, β Κυρίου. Α[b*] add καθὼς κἀγὼ ἐφύλαξα καὶ χάριν ἔλαβον ἀπὸ θεοῦ. Α om. καὶ ποιεῖν ἔλεος ... ὁ Κύριος through hmt. [6] e reads μετά.

πλησίον[7], καὶ εὐσπλαγχνίαν *ἔχειν πρὸς πάντας[8] οὐ μόνον
*ἐν ἀνθρώποις[9], ἀλλὰ *καὶ ἐν ἀλόγοις ζώοις[10].   2. Διὰ
γὰρ ταῦτα εὐλόγησέ με ὁ[11] Κύριος[7]. *καὶ πάντων[12] τῶν
ἀδελφῶν μου ἀσθενούντων ἐγὼ ἄνοσος παρῆλθον[13]. οἶδε[14]
γὰρ[15] Κύριος ἑκάστου τὴν προαίρεσιν[16].   3. *Ἔχετε οὖν[17]
ἔλεος ἐν[18] σπλάγχνοις ὑμῶν[19], ὅτι *εἴ τι ἂν[20] ποιήσῃ[21] τῷ
πλησίον αὐτοῦ, *οὕτω Κύριος[22] ποιήσει[23] *μετ᾽ αὐτοῦ[24].
4. *Καὶ γὰρ[25] υἱοὶ[26] τῶν ἀδελφῶν μου ἠσθένουν καὶ[27] ἀπέθνησκον διὰ Ἰωσήφ[28], ⌜ὅτι οὐκ ἐποίησαν ἔλεος *ἐν σπλάγχνοις
αὐτῶν[29]⌝. οἱ δὲ *ἐμοὶ υἱοί[30] ἄνοσοι διεφυλάχθησαν[31] καθὼς[32]
οἴδατε[33].   5. Καὶ ὅτε ἤμην *ἐν γῇ[34] Χαναὰν *εἰς τὴν
παραλίαν[35] ἐθήρευον θήραν[36] Ἰακὼβ[37] τῷ πατρί μου[38], καὶ
πολλῶν ἀγχομένων *ἐν τῇ θαλάσσῃ[39], ἐγὼ ἀβλαβὴς διέ-
μενον[40].

VI. Πρῶτος ⌜οὖν⌝[1] ἐγὼ ἐποίησα σκάφος[2] ἐπιπλέειν[3] ἐν
τῇ[4] θαλάσσῃ, ὅτι Κύριος ἔδωκέ μοι ⌜*σύνεσιν καὶ σοφίαν[5]
ἐν αὐτῷ⌝.   2. Καὶ καθῆκα[6] ξύλον ὄπισθεν αὐτοῦ[7], καὶ

Marginal notes (left):
β-d, A, S[1] ὑμῶν, τέκνα μου.
β-dg, S ἠσθένουν.
c μετ᾽ αὐτῶν.
deg, A, S[1] θήραν ἰχθύων.

---

[7] g adds αὐτοῦ.   [8] α, de. abf read πρὸς π. ἔχειν, g ἔχειν ἐπὶ π.   [9] α. bdg
read πρὸς ἀνθρώπους, aef εἰς ἀνθρώπους.   [10] ci. h om. β-g read καὶ εἰς (+ τὰ d)
ἄλογα (+ ὑμῶν d), g καὶ πρὸς ἄλογα.   [11] α, g. β-g om.   [12] A = ὅτι πάντων.
[13] d add τὸν βίον, A ἡμέρας μου.   [14] β, A, S. α read εἶδε.   [15] hi add ὁ.
[16] A[sb*d] add καρδίας.   [17] α, bdg, S[1]. ef, A read ἔχετε. a om.   [18] adefy add
τοῖς.   [19] h reads αὐτῶν. d om. β-d, A, S[1] add τέκνα μου. d adds τοῦτο
εἰδότες.   [20] α. a reads ἐάν, bg, A, S[1] ὡς ἄν, d ὅσα ἄν, e ὃ ἐάν, f εἴ τι ἐάν.
[21] h, β-def. c reads ποιήσεις, i ποιήσοι, def ποιήσει. h adds τις, i τοῖς. g om.
next six words through hmt.   [22] c. hi, β-g, S[1] read οὕτως (οὕτω i, df) καὶ ὁ
(a om.) Κύριος.   [23] hi read ποιεῖ.   [24] α. β-g read αὐτῷ, g αὐτόν. In A the
order of the words is οὕτως ποιήσει αὐτῷ Κύριος.   [25] A = διὰ τοῦτο.
A[b*cdeg] add τέκνα μου.   [26] c, A. hi, β read οἱ υἱοί.   [27] α, dg, A. β-dg,
S om.   [28] d reads τὴν ἐν τῷ Ἰωσὴφ γεναμένην παρὰ τῶν πατέρων αὐτῶν
παρανομίαν.   [29] So β, S[1] = בְּרַחֲמֵיהֶם. c reads μετ᾽ αὐτῶν = עִמָּהֶם which
appears to be a corruption of former. hi read εἰς αὐτόν.   [30] α, bdg. aef
read υἱοί μου. A = ἐμοί.   [31] A[-e] διεφυλάχθησαν. A[e] = διεφυλάχθητε.
[32] α. β read ὡς.   [33] h reads εἴδετε.   [34] hi, β-bg, A, S[1]. c, b read ἐν τῇ,
g εἰς γῆν.   [35] α. β-bg read εἰς τὴν (b om.) παράλιον.   [36] α, a. bf read
θήρα ἰχθύων, deg, A, S[1] θήραν ἰχθύων. A[b*] add τροφήν.   [37] g om.   [38] d
reads ἡμῶν.   [39] A[b] = ἐν σάλῳ. A[ab*cdeg] om.   [40] α, fg. β-fg read διέμεινα,
g ἔμεινα.

VI.   [1] α. β, A, S[1] om.   [2] d reads σκάφην.   [3] d reads ἐπιπλέον, g πλέειν
which it trs. before σκάφος. b trans. after θαλάσσῃ. A = καὶ ἔπλευσα.
[4] c, ag. hi, β-ag, A om.   [5] g reads σοφ. κ. σύνεσιν.   [6] β-d, S[1]. α read

ὀθόνην ἐξέτεινα ἐν *ἑτέρῳ ξύλῳ ὀρθῷ[8] *ἐν μέσῳ[9]. 3. Καὶ ἤμην[10] ⌜ἐν αὐτῷ⌝[11] διαπορευόμενος[12] *τοὺς αἰγιαλούς[13], *ἁλιεύων ἰχθύας[14] τῷ[15] *οἴκῳ τοῦ[16] πατρός μου ἕως ὅτου[17] ἤλθομεν εἰς Αἴγυπτον. [4. Καὶ[18] ἐκ τῆς θήρας μου *παντὶ ἀνθρώπῳ ξένῳ[19] σπλαγχνιζόμενος μετεδίδουν[20]. 5. *Εἰ δὲ ἦν ξένος, ἢ νοσῶν, ἢ[21] γηράσας, ἐψήσας[22] τοὺς ἰχθύας, καὶ *ποιήσας αὐτὰ ἀγαθῶς[23] κατὰ τὴν ἑκάστου χρείαν προσέφερον πᾶσι, συναλγῶν[24] καὶ συμπάσχων. 6. Διὰ τοῦτο καὶ ὁ Κύριος *πολλοὺς ἰχθύας ἐνέπλησέ με[25] ἐν τῇ ἄγρᾳ τῶν ἰχθύων[26]. Ὁ γὰρ μεταδιδοὺς τῷ πλησίον[27], λαμβάνει πολλαπλασίονα[28] παρὰ Κυρίου]. 7. *Πέντε οὖν ἔτη[29] ἡλίευσα[30], [παντὶ ἀνθρώπῳ *ὃν ἑωράκειν[31] μεταδιδούς, καὶ παντὶ τῷ οἴκῳ τοῦ πατρός μου ἐξαρκῶν]. 8. *Καὶ τὸ μὲν θέρος[32] ἡλίευον, *ἐν τῷ χειμῶνι δὲ[33] ἐποίμαινον μετὰ τῶν ἀδελφῶν μου.

VII. [Νῦν[1] ἀναγγελῶ ὑμῖν ἃ ἐποίησα. Εἶδον θλιβόμενον ἐν γυμνότητι χειμῶνος, καὶ σπλαγχνισθεὶς *ἐπ' αὐτόν[2], κλέψας[3] ἱμάτιον ἐκ τοῦ οἴκου *τοῦ πατρός[4] μου, κρυφέως[5] ἔδωκα τῷ θλιβομένῳ. 2. Καὶ ὑμεῖς οὖν, τέκνα μου, ἐξ ὧν παρέχει ὑμῖν[2] ὁ Θεός, ἀδιακρίτως πάντας[6] σπλαγχνιζόμενοι ἐλεᾶτε, καὶ παρέχετε *παντὶ ἀνθρώπῳ ἐν ἀγαθῇ καρδίᾳ.

ὀρθῷ
ξύλῳ.

α, af ἐν.
4–6 in
bdg only.

Bracket-
ed words
only in
bdg.

VII–
VIII. 2
only in
bdg.

καθῆρξα, d καθῆκαν. A = ἠσφάλισε. [7] A[b] = νεώς. [8] α. β, S[1] read as in margin. A = ἐν μέσῳ τοῦ ὀρθοῦ ξύλου καί. [9] ab read ἐμμέσῳ. hi add τοῦ αἰγιαλοῦ, d αὐτοῦ, A ἐν μέσῳ τοῦ νεώς. [10] b, S[1] om. [11] hi. β, S[1]. c, A om. [12] hi read ἐρχόμενος. g πορευόμενος. [13] hi, d om. g reads ἐν τοῖς αἰγ. [14] g. b, S[1] reads ἡλίευον ἰχθ., d, A καὶ ἤμην ἁλιεύων ἰχθ.—perhaps better than eg, e ἁλιεύων, α, f ἐν. a om. [15] β, A om. [16] d reads οἴκου, efg οἴκῳ. [17] α. β–b read οὖ. b om. [18] Verses 4–6 are found only in bdg. [19] bg. d reads πάντα ἄνθρωπον ξένον. [20] b reads ἐδίδουν. [21] b. g reads εἰ δὲ ξένος ἦν καί, d ἢ ἦν ὁ ξένος νοσῶν ἤ. [22] d reads ἔψον. [23] b. g reads ποιῶν αὐτοὺς ἀγαθούς (d αὐτοῖς εναγαθως ἐδέσματα). [24] d. bg read συνάγων. [25] d. bg read πολὺν ἰχθὺν ἐποίησέ μοι (save that g trs. ἐποίησέ μοι before πολύν). ἐνέπλησε = שָׂבַע which may have been corrupted into עָשָׂה = ἐποίησε. [26] d. bg read θηρᾶν. [27] bg. d reads πλησίῳ μετὰ πάσης προθυμίας. [28] bg. d reads ἑπταπλάσιον. [29] α. β–a, A, S[1] read πέντε ἔτη, a πέμπτῳ ἔτει. [30] c, β, A[abceg]. h, S[1] read ἡλίευον. A[b*d] om. [31] bg (save that g reads ὡς). d reads τὸ ἀρκοῦν. [32] α, a (save that a om. καί). bfg read τὸ θέρος, d, A καὶ (A[b*d] om.) τῷ μὲν θέρει, e τὸ δὲ θέρος, S[1] om. next word. [33] α (save that h om. δέ). β–d, A read καὶ ἐν χειμῶνι, d τῷ δὲ χειμῶνι.

VII. [1] d prefixes καί. This chapter only in bdg. [2] d om. [3] bd. g reads ἔκλεψα. [4] d. bg om. [5] bd. g reads κρυφαίως καί. [6] d. b

3. Εἰ δὲ μὴ ἔχετε δοῦναι τῷ χρῄζοντι, συμπάσχετε αὐτῷ⁷ ἐν σπλάγχνοις· ἐλέους.   4. Οἶδα⁸ ὅτι ἡ χείρ μου *οὐχ εὗρε⁹ ἐπιδοῦναι¹⁰ τῷ χρῄζοντι, καὶ ἐπὶ¹¹ ἑπτὰ σταδίους συμπορεύομενος αὐτῷ ἔκλαιον· καὶ τὰ σπλάγχνα μου *ἐστρέφετο ἐπ' αὐτῷ¹² εἰς συμπάθειαν.

VIII. Καὶ ὑμεῖς οὖν, τέκνα μου, ἔχετε εὐσπλαγχνίαν *κατὰ παντὸς ἀνθρώπου¹ ἐν ἐλέει, ἵνα καὶ ὁ Κύριος *εἰς ὑμᾶς σπλαγχνισθεὶς² ἐλεήσῃ ὑμᾶς.   2. Ὅτι καίγε³ ἐπ' ἐσχάτων τῶν⁴ ἡμερῶν ὁ Θεὸς ἀποστελεῖ⁵ *τὰ σπλάγχνα⁶ αὐτοῦ ἐπὶ τῆς⁷ γῆς, καὶ ὅπου εὕρῃ σπλάγχνα ἐλέους, ἐν αὐτῷ κατοικεῖ.   3. Ὅσον γὰρ⁸ ἄνθρωπος σπλαγχνίζεται εἰς *τὸν πλησίον αὐτοῦ⁹, τοσοῦτον *καὶ ὁ⁴ Κύριος εἰς αὐτόν.]   4. Ὅτε δὲ¹⁰ κατήλθομεν¹¹ *εἰς Αἴγυπτον¹², Ἰωσὴφ *οὐκ ἐμνησικάκησεν ἡμῖν¹³.   5. Εἰς¹⁴ ὃν *προσέχοντες καὶ ὑμεῖς, τέκνα μου ἀγαπᾶτε ἀλλήλους¹⁵, καὶ μὴ λογίζεσθε¹⁶ ἕκαστος *κακίαν πρὸς τὸν ἀδελφὸν¹⁷ αὐτοῦ.   6. Ὅτι τοῦτο⁷ χωρίζει ἑνότητα¹⁸, καὶ ⌐πᾶσαν συγγένειαν⌐¹⁹ διασκορπίζει²⁰, ⌐καὶ τὴν ψυχὴν ταράσσει⌐²¹ καὶ

Marginal note (left): bg εἰς ἡμᾶς, ἐμὲ δὲ ἰδὼν ἐσπλαγχνίσθη. εἰς ὃν ἐμβλέποντες καὶ ὑμεῖς ἀμνησίκακοι γίνεσθε τέκνα μου (g om. τ. μου) καί. β, S¹ τοῦ ἀδελφοῦ.

α	aef, A, S¹	bg
τὸ πρόσωπον ἀφανίζει²².	τὴν ὕπαρξιν ἀφανίζει.	ὁ γὰρ μνησίκακος σπλάγχνα ἐλέους οὐκ ἔχει.

reads πᾶσι, g πάντοτε.   ⁷d. bd (save that b adds πρὸς καιρόν after ἔχετε and om. αὐτῷ). g reads τῷ χρείαν ἔχοντι.   ⁸d reads καὶ γὰρ ἐγὼ ἐν μιᾷ τῶν ἡμερῶν οἶδα.   ⁹g trs. before ἡ χείρ. b add πρὸς τὸ παρόν.   ¹⁰bg. d reads τι δοῦναι.   ¹¹dg. b reads ἔτι.   ¹²bg. d reads ἐτρέφοντο.

VIII. ¹bd. g reads εἰς πάντα ἄνθρωπον.   ²b. g reads σπλ. ἐφ' ὑμᾶς, d σπλ.   ³g reads γε.   ⁴b om.   ⁵g. bd read ἀποστέλλει.   ⁶g. d reads σπλάγχνα, b τὸ σπλάγχνον.   ⁷d om.   ⁸g adds ὁ.   ⁹dg (save that d reads τό). b reads τὸν πλησίον.   ¹⁰α, β–bdg, A. bdg read γάρ, S¹ om.   ¹¹h reads ἀπήλθομεν.   ¹²ae read ἐν Αἰγύπτῳ.   ¹³α, aef, S¹. A = οὐκ ἐμνήσθη τὸ κακὸν ὃ ἐποίησα (Aᵇ*ᶜᵈᵉˢ ἐποίησαν) αὐτῷ, bg read οὐκ ἐμνησικάκησεν εἰς (g om.) ἡμᾶς, ἐμὲ δὲ (g γὰρ) ἰδὼν ἐσπλαγχνίσθη, d ἰδὼν ἡμᾶς σφόδρα ἐσπλαγχνίσθη ἐφ' ἡμῖν καὶ οὐδ' ὅλως ἐμνησικάκησεν.   ¹⁴c om.   ¹⁵α, aef, A (save that aef, A trs. καὶ ὑμεῖς after τέκνα μου and read ἀγαπήσατε). bg, S¹ read ἐμβλέποντες (g βλέποντες) καὶ ὑμεῖς ἀμνησίκακοι γίνεσθε τέκνα μου (g om. τ. μου) καὶ ἀγαπᾶτε ἀλλήλους, d βλέποντες καὶ ὑμεῖς, τ. μου, ἀγαπ. ἀλλ. ἀμνησίκακοι γίνεσθε.   ¹⁶a reads λογιζέσθω. d λογίζεσθε. A adds μηδὲ νομίζετε (a dittographic rendering).   ¹⁷c, A. h reads κακῆσαι τοῦ ἀδελφοῦ, β τὴν (aef om.) κακίαν τοῦ ἀδελφοῦ.   ¹⁸A reads [Armenian] = κακότητα, which may have been in the Greek copy before the translator.   ¹⁹S¹ reads τὴν λύπην τῆς καρδίας.   ²⁰S¹ = διατείνει.   ²¹d, A om.   ²²d is

IX. Προσέχετε ⌜οὖν⌝[1] ἐπὶ[2] τὰ ὕδατα, *καί, γνῶτε, ὅταν[3] *πορεύονται ἐπὶ τὸ αὐτό[4], λίθους, ξύλα, γῆν[5] *καὶ ἕτερά τινα[6] κατασύρουσιν[7].   2. Ἐὰν[8] δὲ εἰς πολλὰ διαιρεθῶσιν[9], ἡ γῆ ἀφανίζει[10] αὐτά, *καὶ γίνονται[11] εὐκαταφρόνητα[12]. 3. Καὶ ὑμεῖς ⌜οὖν⌝[13] ἐὰν διαιρεθῆτε, ἔσεσθε[14] οὕτως.   4. ⌜Μὴ οὖν[15] *χωρισθῆτε ἐν δυσὶ κεφαλαῖς⌝[16]. ὅτι πᾶν ὃ ἐποίησεν ὁ[17] Κύριος κεφαλὴν μίαν κέκτηται[18], *καὶ ὤμους δύο, χεῖρας δύο, πόδας δύο καὶ τὰ λοιπὰ μέλη ἅπαντα[19].   5. Ἔγνων *γὰρ ἐγὼ[20] ἐν γραφῇ τῶν[21] πατέρων μου, ὅτι[22]

> Διαιρεθήθεσθε ἐν Ἰσραήλ[23],
> καὶ δύο[24] βασιλείαις[25] ἐξακολουθήσετε[26],

πόδας ἀλλὰ σύμπαντα μέλη μιᾷ κεφαλῇ ὑπακούει.   bdg ὅτι ἐν ἐσχάταις ἡμέραις ἀποστήσεσθε ἀπὸ Κυρίου καί.

Right margin notes:

aeg, A
ὅτι ὅτε
(a ὅταν).
β, A, S
ἄμμον.
β, S
μὴ σχι-
σθῆτε εἰς
δύο κε-
φαλάς.
β, S¹ ἔχει.
β-d, A,
S¹ ἔδωκε
δύο ὤμ.
⌜χεῖρας⌝,

conflate and to the reading of *aef* adds that of *bg*. A reads
 զգյազգալգուβիւ ալյայա ապւէ = ὁμοουσίαν (?) ἀφανῆ ποιεῖ where
the noun is corrupt for զգյազգուβիւ = ὕπαρξιν. We have now to
decide between ὕπαρξιν and πρόσωπον. The former = אונים which seems
to be a corruption of פנים, as the context here is rather in favour of
the latter.

IX. [1]α, d. β-d, A om. A add τέκνα μου   [2]bg om.   [3]α. aeg, A
read as in margin, b ὅτι, f, S¹ ὅτε, d πῶς ὅτε.   [4]α. β, A read ἐπὶ τὸ
αὐτὸ (d μὲν τὸ αὐτῷ, A ὁμοθυμαδόν) πορεύονται (b πορεύεται).   [5]α, β-bd,
A, S². b, S¹ reads τήν, d καὶ τήν.   [6]α. β, A, S read ἄμμον. Have the two
readings arisen from a confusion of אֶרֶץ and חוֹל? A adds ὁμοῦ, a duplicate
rendering of ἐπὶ τὸ αὐτό.   [7]α. aef, A read καταφέρει, bd, S¹ κατασύρει,
g κατωρύσσει.   [8]d read ἐπάν.   [9]α. β read διαιρεθῇ (e διερρεθῇ).
[10]A reads ɖ֊ɯɕӌɛ (= καλύπτει) corrupt for ɖ֊ɯʃʋɛ = ἀφανίζει.   [11]α, df.
be, Aᵃᵇ read καὶ γίνεται, Aᵇˣᶜᵈ καὶ γενήσεται. ag om. S¹ corrupt.   [12]ag om.
A adds ὑπὸ πάντων.   [13]α. β, A om.   [14]A = γίνεσθε. d reads this verse as
follows: οὕτω καὶ ὑμεῖς ἔσεσθε ἐὰν διαρεθῆτε.   [15]α. β, S om.   [16]α. β, S
read as in margin (save that d adds οὖν before εἰς and g reads χωρισθεῖτε
for σχ.).   [17]α, b. β-b, A om.   [18]α. β, S¹ read ἔχει. A = χαρίσατο.
[19]α (save that hi trs. δύο bef. ὤμους and adds καὶ κεφαλὴν μίαν). abefg, S¹
read as in margin (save that e reads δύο ὤμους, πόδας, χεῖρας, S¹ δύο (...)
δύο χεῖρας καὶ δύο πόδας and that for ἀλλὰ σύμπαντα μέλη (a), b reads ἀλλὰ
πάντα τὰ μέλη τῇ and ef ἀλλὰ σὺν πᾶσιν μέλεσιν, g καὶ τὰ λοιπὰ τῇ). d reads
ἔδωκε μὲν γὰρ δύο ὤμ. χ. καὶ πόδ. ἀλλὰ πᾶσι τούτοις κἂν ὅτι διπλᾶ ἡμῖν δέδωκεν
ὁ θεός, ἀλλ' οὖν μιᾷ κεφαλῇ ὑπακούει—φυλάξασθε οὖν τέκνα μου τοῦ μὴ διαιρεθῆναι.
A = ὅτι ἔδωκε δύο ὤμ. δύο πόδ. καὶ τὰ λοιπὰ μέλη (+ καὶ Aᵇˣᶜᵈᵉᵍ + καὶ πάντα Aᵇ)
μιᾷ κεφ. (+ ἔδωκε Aᵇˣᶜᵈ) ὑπακούειν.   [20]α, A. d reads γάρ. β-d, S¹ om.
[21]α, A. β om.   [22]bdg add as in margin (save that g om. καί). g om.
διαιρ. ἐν Ἰ.   [23]a reads Ἰερουσαλήμ.   [24]Aᵇˣᶜᵈ om.   [25]aef(S²). α support

After
ποιήσετε
h, β, S
add
*καίγε
πᾶν
εἴδωλον
προσκυ-
νήσετε [27].
c, bd κα-
θήσεσθε.
β, A, S[1]
πάσαις

καὶ πᾶν βδέλυγμα ποιήσετε.

6. Καὶ αἰχμαλωτεύσουσιν [28] ὑμᾶς οἱ ἐχθροὶ ὑμῶν
καὶ κακωθήσεσθε [29] ἐν [30] ἔθνεσιν
*ἐν πολλαῖς [31] ἀσθενείαις *καὶ θλίψεσιν [32].

α	β, A, S[1]
7. Καὶ μετὰ ταῦτα μνησθέντες Κύριον †ἐπιστρέψετε [33] καὶ ἐλεήσει [34] ὑμᾶς, ὅτι ἐλεήμων ἐστὶ καὶ εὔ-σπλαγχνος, *καὶ οὐ λογίζεται [35] κακίαν τοῖς υἱοῖς τῶν ἀνθρώ-πων διότι σάρξ εἰσιν καὶ πλα-νῶνται ἐν ταῖς πονηραῖς αὐτῶν πράξεσιν [36].	7. Καὶ μετὰ ταῦτα μνησθή-σεσθε [37] Κυρίου καὶ [38] μετανοήσετε [39] καὶ ἐπιστρέψει ὑμᾶς, ὅτι ἐλεήμων ἐστὶ καὶ εὔ-σπλαγχνος, *καὶ μὴ λογιζόμενος [40] κα-κίαν *τοῖς υἱοῖς τῶν ἀνθρώπων [41] διότι σάρξ εἰσιν καὶ *τὰ πνεύματα [42] τῆς πλάνης πλανᾷ [43] αὐτοὺς ἐπὶ πάσαις πράξεσιν [44].
α, aef, A, S[1]	bdg
8. Καὶ μετὰ ταῦτα [45] ἀνα-τελεῖ [46] ⌐ὑμῖν⌐ *αὐτὸς ὁ [47] Κύριος, *φῶς δικαιο-σύνης [48]	8. Καὶ μετὰ ταῦτα ἀνατελεῖ [49] ὑμῖν αὐτὸς [50] Κύριος [51], φῶς δικαιοσύνης

text but read corruptly βασιλείας. b, A, S[1] read βασιλεῦσιν, dg βασιλεῖς.
[26] d reads ἐξακολουθήσεσθε. [27] hi, β, S against c, A add as in margin (save
that h reads τὰ εἴδωλα, and h, d om. γε). [28] d reads αἰχμαλωτίσουσιν. [29] hi,
β–bd, A, S[1]. c, bd read as in margin. [30] bdg add τοῖς. [31] α. β, A, S[1]
read ἐν (ef κπὶ) πάσαις. [32] A[ceg] om. g reads θλίψεσιν, bdg add καὶ ὀδύναις
ψυχῆς (d ψυχαῖς). [33] c reads ἐπιστρέψειται, hi ἐπιστρέψητε a mistranslation of
תשובו which should here be rendered μετανοήσετε. [34] hi. c reads ἐλεύσῃ.
ἐπιστρέψετε καὶ ἐλεήσει of α = תשובו ורחם, whereas μετανοήσετε καὶ ἐπιστρέψει
of β, A, S[1] = תנחמו והשיב which seems to be a transposition and corruption
of the original of α. In β, A, S[1] ἐπιστρέψει would have to be translated
'will bring you back,' i.e. to your own land. But this idea does not
occur till next verse. [35] Here A agrees with α. [36] α add περὶ
τοῦ (c om.) Χ̄ῡ̄. [37] aef, S[1] read μνησθέντες as in α. [38] bdg, A.
aef, S[1] om. [39] A[b*d] = ἐλεηθήσεσθε μετανοίᾳ. Cf. α. [40] adef. bg, S
read μὴ λογ. Here A = α. [41] A[b*d] = τοῖς ἀνθρώποις. [42] d,
A = τὸ πνεῦμα. [43] bg read ἀπατᾷ. [44] a prefixes ταῖς. bdg, A add
αὐτῶν. [45] c reads τοῦτο. [46] This verb is taken transitively by A.
[47] h om. [48] c. hi, A read τὸ φῶς τῆς (A om.) δικ. S[1] ἐν φωτὶ

α, aef, A, S	bdg

<table>
<tr><td>

καὶ ἐπιστρέψετε[52] *εἰς τὴν γῆν[53] ὑμῶν[54],

καὶ ὄψεσθε αὐτὸν[55] ἐν Ἰερουσαλὴμ ⌜διὰ τὸ ὄνομα αὐτοῦ *τὸ ἅγιον[56]⌝.

</td><td>

καὶ ἴασις *καὶ εὐσπλαγχνία[57] ἐν[58] ταῖς πτέρυξιν αὐτοῦ.

Αὐτὸς λυτρώσεται πᾶσαν αἰχμαλωσίαν υἱῶν ἀνθρώπων ἐκ τοῦ Βελίαρ

καὶ πᾶν πνεῦμα πλάνης πατηθήσεται[59].

καὶ ἐπιστρέψει *πάντα τὰ[60] ἔθνη εἰς παραζήλωσιν αὐτοῦ[61],

καὶ ὄψεσθε *θεὸν ἐν σχήματι ἀνθρώπου[62]

*ὃν ἂν ἐκλέξηται Κύριος Ἰερουσαλὴμ ὄνομα αὐτῷ[63].

</td></tr>
</table>

9. Καὶ[64] πάλιν ⌜ἐν *τῇ πανουργίᾳ[65] *τῶν ἔργων[66] ὑμῶν[67]⌝ παροργίσετε[68] αὐτόν,

καὶ ἀπορριφήσεσθε[69] ⌜ἀπ' αὐτοῦ⌝[70] ἕως καιροῦ συντελείας.

X. Καὶ νῦν τέκνα μου, μὴ λυπεῖσθε *ὅτι ἀποθνήσκω[1], μηδὲ συμπέσητε[2] ὅτι ἀπολήγω[3].   2. Ἀναστήσομαι γὰρ[4] πάλιν *ἐν μέσῳ[5] ὑμῶν, ⌜ὡς ἡγούμενος *ἐν μέσῳ[6] υἱῶν

δικαιοσύνης.   [49] b, S¹ read ἀνατέλλει.   [50] bd add ὁ.   [51] S¹ om. [52] S¹ reads ἐπιστρέφει.   [53] af read ἐκ τῆς γῆς, e ἐπὶ τῆς γῆς.   [54] S¹ reads αὐτοῦ.   [55] α. aef, A, S read Κύριον.   [56] c. hi read τὸ πανάγιον. aef, S¹ om.   [57] d reads εὐσπλαγχνίας.   [58] dg. b reads ἐπί.   [59] d adds καὶ φοβηθήσεται.   [60] d reads ὑμᾶς εἰς τὴν γῆν ὑμῶν καί.   [61] d om.   [62] d reads Κύριον ἐν Ἱερ. ἐν σχ. ἀνθ.   A Christian phrase.   [63] b. g reads ὃν ἂν ἐκλ. Κύριος, ἐν Ἱερ. διὰ τὸ ὄνομα αὐτοῦ, d καὶ κληθήσεται τὸ ὄνομα αὐτοῦ μεγάλης βουλῆς ἄγγελος.   [64] d adds μετὰ ταῦτα.   [65] c. hi, β read τῇ (β om.) πονηρίᾳ. [66] hi, adef, S¹ (save that adef om. τῶν).   c reads τ. πατέρων, b λόγων, g ἐργάσητε.   [67] c reads ἡμῶν, g ὑμῶς.   [68] e reads παρυργίσατε.   A = παροργίζετε.   [69] b reads ἀπορηφήσεσθε.   Aᵇ = κατοικήσετε αὖθις.   [70] α. β, S¹ om.   A adds ἐν τοῖς ἔθνεσι.

X.   [1] A = ἐπὶ λόγοις μου.   β, S¹ add ἐγώ.   g om. rest of sentence.   [2] α (save that c reads συπέσειτε). β reads συμπίπτετε.   If the text is right we should surely supply τῷ προσώπῳ.   Cf. Gen. vi. 5, or for a different construction Neh. vi. 16 ויפלו בעיניהם.   A = συνταράσσεσθε.   [3] α, ae. bfg read ἀπολείπω ὑμῶν (f om.), d ἐκλείπω ἐγώ.   A adds ἀπὸ ζωῆς.   [4] f om. [5] α, dfg. abe read ἐμμέσῳ.   [6] α, adefg. b reads ἐμμέσῳ.   [7] h om.

<table>
<tr><td>β, S¹
ὅσοι ἐφύ-
λαξαν.</td><td>αὑτοῦ⌉, καὶ⌐ εὐφρανθήσομαι[8] *ἐν μέσῳ[9] τῆς φυλῆς μου, *οἵτινες φυλάξουσιν[10] νόμον Κυρίου ⌐καὶ ἐντολὰς[11] Ζαβουλὼν πατρὸς αὐτῶν⌉.   3. Ἐπὶ δὲ τοὺς ἀσεβεῖς ἐπάξει[12] Κύριος πῦρ αἰώνιον, καὶ ἀπολεῖ[13] αὐτοὺς *ἕως γενεᾶς γενεῶν[14].   4. *Ἐγὼ δὲ νῦν[15] εἰς τὴν ἀνάπαυσίν μου[16] ἀποτρέχω[17], *ὡς καὶ[18] οἱ πατέρες μου.   5. Ὑμεῖς δὲ φοβεῖσθε</td></tr>
<tr><td>h, bd, S¹
ὑμῶν.</td><td>Κύριον[19] ⌐τὸν θεὸν ἡμῶν[20] ἐν πάσῃ ἰσχύι ὑμῶν[21] πάσας τὰς[22] ἡμέρας τῆς ζωῆς ὑμῶν⌉[23].   6. Καὶ ταῦτα εἰπὼν ἐκοιμήθη ⌐†ὕπνῳ[24] καλῷ⌉, καὶ ἔθηκαν αὐτὸν *οἱ υἱοὶ αὐτοῦ[25]</td></tr>
<tr><td>β-d, A,
S¹ ἐν
θήκῃ.</td><td>*εἰς θήκην ξυλίνην[26].   7. Ὕστερον δὲ *ἀναγαγόντες ἔθαψαν αὐτὸν ἐν Χεβρὼν[27] μετὰ τῶν πατέρων αὐτοῦ[28].</td></tr>
</table>

Διαθήκη Δὰν τοῦ ἑβδόμου υἱοῦ Ἰακὼβ καὶ Βάλλας[1].

I. Ἀντίγραφον λόγων Δάν[2], *ὧν εἶπεν[3] τοῖς υἱοῖς αὐτοῦ[4] ἐπ' ἐσχάτων[5] τῶν[6] ἡμερῶν αὐτοῦ[7] *ἐν τῷ ἑκατοστῷ εἰκοστῷ

[8] Aᵇ*ᶜᵈ read ηὐφράνθην according to printed Arm. text (?) but Aᵉ supports α, β.   [9] α, adefg. b reads ἐμμέσῳ.   [10] α. β reads as in margin. A = ὅσοι ἐφυλάξατε.   [11] g reads ἐντολήν.   [12] d adds ἐπ' αὐτούς.   [13] α. β-g read ἀπολέσει, g ἀπόλλυσιν.   [14] α. β reads ἕως γενεῶν. A = ἀπὸ τῶν υἱῶν Ἰσραήλ.   [15] α. a reads τέως δέ, b ἐγώ, def τέως οὖν (+ ἐγώ d), g ἐγώ τε.   [16] aef add ἐγώ.   [17] Aᵇ*ᶜᵈ om. rest of verse.   [18] α, Aᵃᵇ. β-d, S¹ read ὡς, d καί.   [19] d om.   [20] c, aefg. hi, bd, S¹ read ὑμῶν. hi om. next ten words through hmt.   [21] c. β, S¹ om.   [22] a om.   [23] d adds καὶ τὰ ἀρεστὰ ἐνώπιον αὐτοῦ ποιεῖτε. For addition in S see S² in loc.   [24] = שֵׁנָה corrupt for שֵׂיבָה = γήρει. The phrase is found correctly in T. Iss. vii. 9 ἐκοιμήθη ἐν γήρει καλῷ.   [25] g reads υἱοὶ αὐτοῦ. d om.   [26] c. hi read ἐν θήκῃ ξυλίνῃ, β, A ἐν θήκῃ (+ καινῇ ἐν ᾗ οὐδεὶς οὐδέποτέ τις ἐτέθη d).   [27] α. d, Aᵇ*ᵈ (save that d reads ἀγαγ.). abef, Aᵃᵇᶜᵉᶠᵍ, S¹ ἀναγαγ. αὐτὸν εἰς Χ. (ἐν Χ. e) ἔθαψαν (+ αὐτόν ᵃᵇᶜᵉᶠ), g ἀνήγαγον θάψαντες ἐν Χ.   [28] d adds τῷ δὲ θεῷ ἡμῶν εἴη δόξα εἰς αἰῶνας. Ἀμήν. f, S¹ adds Ζαβουλὼν υἱὸς Ἰακὼβ ͞ϛ υἱὸς Λίας ͞ϛ (ὁ τρίτος S¹). (+ καὶ S¹) ἔζησεν ἔτη ρ̄ιδ (ρ̄δ S¹), Aᵇ*ᵈ add εἰς δόξαν θεοῦ.

I. [1] Title. α in text. a reads Δάν, bef, S¹ Δ. Δ. περὶ θυμοῦ καὶ ψεύδους (f ψεύδους καὶ θυμοῦ· Δὰν ἑρμηνεύεται κρίσις), g ἀρχὴ λόγων διαθήκης Δ. περὶ θ. καὶ ψ. ζ΄. d is conflate Δ. Δ. υἱὸς ἕβδομος Ἰακώβ, υἱὸς Βάλλας πρῶτος περὶ θ. καὶ ψ. A = Δ. Δ. περὶ ὑπερηφανίας καὶ μίσους (+ καὶ ζήλου Aᵇ, but this addition is not in Conybeare's transcript). Here ատելութեան = μίσους is obviously an error for ստութեան = ψεύδους.   [2] Aᵇ*ᵈ add υἱοῦ Ἰακώβ.   [3] d reads ὅσα ἐλάλησεν, g ὃν εἶπεν.   [4] hi om. next five words through hmt. Aᵇ*ᵈ add καὶ θυγατράσι.   [5] f reads ἐσχάτου.   [6] ae om.   [7] Aᵇᵇ*ᶜᵈᵉᶠ = τούτων.

πέμπτῳ[8] ἔτει[9] τῆς[10] ζωῆς αὐτοῦ.   2.   *Καλέσας γάρ[11]
*τὴν πατρίαν αὐτοῦ[12] εἶπεν[13]· Ἀκούσατε υἱοὶ *Δὰν λόγων
μου[14], καὶ[15] προσέχετε[16] ῥήμασι ⌜τοῦ πατρὸς ὑμῶν⌝[17].   3.   β–dg, S
Ἐγὼ[18] ἐπείρασα ἐν καρδίᾳ μου[19] καὶ[20] ἐν πάσῃ[21] ζωῇ μου[22],   ῥήμασι
ὅτι καλὸν[23] *καὶ θεῷ εὐάρεστον ἡ ἀλήθεια[24] μετὰ δικαιοπρα-   στό-
γίας[25] *καὶ ⌜ὅτι⌝ πονηρὸν τὸ ψεῦδος[26] καὶ ὁ θυμὸς[27] πᾶσαν   ματος.
κακίαν *ἐκδιδάσκοντα τὸν ἄνθρωπον[28].   4.   *Ὁμολογῶ οὖν   β, S ἄν-
ὑμῖν σήμερον[29], τέκνα μου[30], ὅτι ἐν καρδίᾳ μου ἐθέμην[31] περὶ   θρωπον
τοῦ θανάτου[32] Ἰωσήφ, ⌜τοῦ ἀδελφοῦ μου⌝[33], *τοῦ ἀγαθοῦ ἀνδρὸς   διδάσκει.
καὶ ἀληθινοῦ[34].   5.   Καὶ ἔχαιρον ἐπὶ τῇ πράσει αὐτοῦ[35],   β, A, S¹
ὅτι[36] *ὑπὲρ ἡμᾶς[37] *ὁ πατὴρ αὐτὸν ἠγάπα[38].   6.   Τὸ γὰρ[39]   †ἡδόμην.
πνεῦμα τοῦ ζήλου[40] καὶ τῆς ἀλαζονείας[41] ἔλεγέ μοι· Καίγε   β, A, S¹
σὺ *αὐτὸς υἱὸς αὐτοῦ εἶ[42].   7.   Καὶ *ἐκ τῶν πνευμάτων[43]   ἔν.

ag om. rest of verse through hmt.   [8] α. bf read ἐν (b om.) ἑκατοστῷ
εἰκοστῷ πέμπτῳ, d ἐν ἔτει ρκέ, e ἐν ρκέ ἔτει.   [9] d om.   [10] ef om.   [11] α,
dg. aef, A⌜ɢ⌝ καὶ καλέσας, b, A⌜ᵇᵇ*ᶜᵈ⌝ καλέσας.   [12] α, β–dg, S¹. d, A read
τοὺς υἱοὺς αὐτοῦ, g αὐτούς.   [13] d, A add αὐτοῖς.   [14] hi, β (save that hi read
τοὺς λόγους), A⌜ᵃᵇ*ᶜᵈᵉᶠ⌝, S¹. c reads λόγων Δὰν τοῦ πατρὸς ὑμῶν.   A⌜ᵇ⌝ = Δ.
πατρὸς ὑμῶν.   [15] b, S om.   [16] A⌜ᵇ⌝ (by an internal corruption) = προσβλέψατε.
f adds τοῖς.   [17] α, dg (save that d om. τοῦ). β–dg, S read στόματος
(+ τοῦ b) πατρὸς ὑμῶν (ἡμῶν e). A = στόματός μου.   [18] α, A. β–d om.
d reads ὅσα.   [19] c om.   [20] g om. A⌜ᵇ*⌝ adds ἔγνων.   [21] β adds τῇ.   [22] d adds
καὶ ἔγνων.   [23] hi read τὸ κάλλος (i καλι).   [24] c, aed. bfg, S read θεῷ καὶ
εὐάρεστον (f ἀρεστὸν) ἡ ἀλ., hi θεῷ εὐάρ. καὶ ἡ ἀλ. A = ἐστὶν ἐνώπιον Κυρίου
καὶ εὐάρ. ἡ ἀλ. (ἡ ἀλ. καὶ εὐάρ. A⌜ᵇ*ᵈ⌝).   [25] c reads δικαιοπρασίας.   [26] c, β, A
(save that c reads πανπόνηρον and A om. ὅτι and adds ἐστί after πονηρόν).
hi read τὸ δὲ πονηρὸν ψ.   [27] b, S¹ add ὅτι, A⌜ᵇ⌝ καί. d adds δι' ὧν καί.
[28] c. hi, A read ἐκδιδάσκουσι (ἐκδιδάσκει A) τ. ἄνθ. β–d, S read ἄνθρωπον
(e ἀνθρώπων, a om.) ἐκδιδάσκει (διδάσκει f), d οἱ ἄνθρωποι ἐκδιδάσκονται.
[29] α, d (save that d om. οὖν), A⌜ᵃᵇᶜᵉᶠᵍ⌝. β–d, A⌜ᵇ*ᵈ⌝, S read ὁμολογῶ (+ οὖν A⌜ᵇ*ᵈ⌝)
σήμερον ὑμῖν. Before ὁμολογῶ d inserts τοίνυν ὡς ταῦτα πειράσας καὶ γνοὺς
ἀμφοτέρων τὸ διάφορον.   [30] c om.   [31] α, S². β, S¹ read ἡδόμην (bd ἡδώμην)
(+ πάνυ d) = שמחתי corrupt for שמתי = ἐθέμην. A = ἡδονὴ ἦν. We have
here the familiar phrase שום על לב.   [32] Aᵃ om.   [33] α. β, A, S¹ om.
[34] α, g. d reads τοῦ ἀδ. ἀνδ. καὶ ἀγ., aefg, A, S² τοῦ ἀνδ. τοῦ ἀγ. (g τοῦ ἀγ. ἀνδ.)
καὶ ἀλ., b, S¹ ἀνδ. ἀλ. καὶ ἀγ. g om. next six words.   [35] b, S¹ read Ἰωσήφ.
[36] d reads διότι.   [37] α, β, S¹. A⌜ᵇ⌝ = ὑπὲρ ἐμέ, A⌜ᵃᵇ*ᶜᵈᵉᶠᵍ⌝ πλέον.   [38] α, β–dg
(save that b read αὐτοῦ), S¹. dg, A⌜ᵃᵇᶜ⌝ read ἠγάπα αὐτὸν ὁ πατὴρ ἡμῶν (g αὐτοῦ,
A⌜ᵇᶜ⌝ μου). For ὑπὲρ … ἠγάπα A⌜ᵇ*ᵈᵉᶠᵍ⌝ read αὐτὸν πλέον (A⌜ᵃᶠᵍ⌝ πλέον αὐτόν)
ἠγ. ὁ πατήρ μου.   [39] d, A⌜ᵇ*ᵈ⌝ om.   [40] e reads ζήλους.   [41] A = τοῦ
μίσους.   [42] α (save that c om. αὐτοῦ after υἱός). β reads υἱὸς αὐτοῦ (+ εἶ d).

β, A, S¹ τοῦ Βελίαρ †συνήργει[44] μοὶ, ὅτι[45]· *Λαβὲ τὸ ξίφος καὶ ⌜ἐν
λέγον. τούτῳ⌝[46] ἄνελε τὸν Ἰωσήφ[47], καὶ ἀγαπήσει σε ὁ πατήρ[48],
β-g,A,S¹ ἀποθανόντος αὐτοῦ. 8. *Τοῦτο δὲ ἦν τὸ πνεῦμα τοῦ θυμοῦ
πατήρ
σου. τὸ πεῖθόν με[49]· ὥσπερ[50] πάρδαλις †ἐκμύζουσα[51] ἔριφον,
beg, A ἵνα οὕτως *⌜ἐμοὶ ἐνέβαλεν⌝ †ἐκμυζῆσαι[52] τὸν Ἰωσήφ.
ὥσπερ.
β-d, A
†ἐκμυζή-
σω.

α	β, A, S¹
9. Ἀλλ' ὁ Θεὸς *τῶν πατέρων[53] μου οὐκ εἴασεν αὐτὸν ἐμπεσεῖν εἰς τὰς χεῖράς μου, ἵνα κατα-μόνας εὑρὼν αὐτὸν ἀνελῶ, καὶ ποιήσω[54] λυθῆναι σκῆπτρον δεύτερον τῷ Ἰσραήλ.	9. Ἀλλ' ὁ Θεὸς Ἰακὼβ[55] *τοῦ πατρός μου[56] οὐκ ἐνέβαλεν[57] αὐτὸν εἰς τὰς χεῖράς μου *ἵνα εὕρω[58] αὐτὸν μόνον, οὐδὲ εἴασέν με[59] *τὸ ἀνόμημα τοῦτο ποιῆ-σαι[60] ἵνα μὴ[61] λυθῶσι[62] δύο σκῆπτρα ἐν Ἰσραήλ.

II. Καὶ νῦν, τέκνα μου, ἰδοὺ[1] ἐγὼ ἀποθνήσκω, καὶ ἐν ἀληθείᾳ λέγω ὑμῖν, ὅτι[2] ἐὰν[3] μὴ φυλάξητε[4] ἑαυτοὺς·ἀπὸ *τοῦ πνεύματος[5] *τοῦ ψεύδους καὶ τοῦ θυμοῦ[6], καὶ ἀγαπήσητε[7]

A = υἱὸς εἶ αὐτοῦ (A^b Ἰακώβ). [43] α. β-d, A read ἐν τῶν πν. The former, however, is a familiar Hebraism. d reads τὸ πνεῦμα. [44] a reads συνήργησε. Text = יעיר corrupt(?) for יאמר if α is right. [45] α. bdeg, S¹ read λέγων, f, A καὶ ἔλεγεν (+ μοι A), a λέγον. [46] α. β-g, A, S¹ read λαβὲ τ. ξίφος τοῦτο καὶ ἐν αὐτῷ (df, A om. ἐν αὐτῷ), g τὸ ξ. τοῦτο λαβὲ καὶ ἐν αὐτῷ. [47] d adds ἐν αὐτῷ. [48] β-g, A, S¹ add σου. [49] c, abef, S¹ (save that abef, S¹ read ἐστί for δὲ ἦν). hi agree with c but gives a different order: τοῦτο δὲ τὸ πεῖθόν με πνεῦμα ἦν τοῦ θυμοῦ, d ταῦτά μοι τὸ πνεῦμα τοῦ θυμοῦ ὑπέβαλλεν, g, A τὸ δὲ (τόδε τὸ A) πνεῦμα τοῦ θυμοῦ πάλιν (A om.) ἔπειθέν με. d om. rest of verse. [50] c. hi read ὡς γάρ, af ἦν γὰρ ὥσπερ, beg ἵνα ὥσπερ (bg ὡς). [51] ae, S². α, f give the form ἐκμίζουσα, bg, S¹ ἐκμύζᾳ. Conscious of the impossibility of the text A restored it as follows: ἵνα ἐκμυζήσω αἷμα Ἰωσήφ, ὡς ἐκμυζᾷ πάρδαλις αἷμα ἐρίφου. But we can hardly accept this restoration. The corruption lies in ἐκμύζουσα which = מצץ corrupt for רצץ = συντρί-βουσα (in late Hebrew). Similarly for ἐκμυζῆσαι in the next line we should read συντρῖψαι. [52] α (c giving form ἐκμιζῆσαι, hi ἐκμύζουσα). β-df read ἐκμυζήσω, f ἐκμιζῆσω S¹ ἐξεμύζησα. For the corruption in text and the reading of A see note 51. [53] c. hi read τοῦ πατρός. [54] c. hi read ποιῆσαι. [55] beg, A, S¹. adf om. [56] β-d, A (save that b, A read ἡμῶν), S. d reads τῶν πατέρων μου. [57] d reads ἔβαλε. [58] β, S¹. A reads καὶ οὐχ εὗρον. [59] b om. [60] bfg. ae read τοῦτο τ. ἀν. ποιῆσαι, d, A ποιῆσαι τὸ ἀν. τοῦτο. [61] bg om. [62] d reads καταλυθῶσιν.

II. [1] b, S om. [2] c reads καί. [3] aef read εἰ. [4] hi, eg. c, af read φυλάξετε, b διαφυλάξητε, d φυλάξατε. [5] a om. [6] A = τῆς πλάνης καὶ τοῦ ψεύδους. Here ֍ꜰ֍ (= πλάνης) is undoubtedly corrupt.

τὴν ἀλήθειαν καὶ τὴν μακροθυμίαν, ἀπολεῖσθε[8].   2. Τύφλωσις *γάρ ἐστιν ὁ θυμὸς καὶ οὐκ ἐᾷ ὁρᾶν πρόσωπόν τινος ἐν ἀληθείᾳ[9]. 3. ⌐Ὅτι⌐, κᾶν πατήρ, *ἢ μήτηρ[10] ἐστίν[11], ⌐ὡς πολεμίοις[12] προσ-έχει[13] αὐτοῖς[14]· *ἢ⌐ ἀδελφός ἐστιν[15] οὐκ οἶδεν[16]· ἢ[17] *προφήτης Κυρίου, παρακούει[18]· ἢ[17] δίκαιος[19], οὐ βλέπει· ⌐*ἢ φίλος[20], οὐ γνωρίζει⌐.   4. *Περιβάλλεται γὰρ ⌐αὐτὸν⌐ τὸ πνεῦμα τοῦ θυμοῦ τὸ δίκτυον τῆς πλάνης[21] καὶ τυφλοῖ τοὺς[22] ὀφθαλμοὺς αὐτοῦ, καὶ[1] διὰ τοῦ ψεύδους σκοτοῖ[23] τὴν διάνοιαν ⌐αὐτοῦ⌐[24], καὶ τὴν ἰδίαν ὅρασιν παρέχει αὐτῷ.   5. *Ἐν τίνι δὲ[25] περιβάλλει τοὺς ὀφθαλμοὺς αὐτοῦ[26] ; *ἐν μίσει καρδίας[27] κατὰ τοῦ ἀδελφοῦ αὐτοῦ[28] *εἰς φθόνον[29].

III. *Καὶ γὰρ πονηρὸς ὁ θυμός[1], τέκνα μου, *ὡς καὶ αὐτὴν τὴν ψυχὴν ἐκταράσσει[2].   2. Καὶ τὸ μὲν σῶμα *ἴδιον ποιεῖται[3] τοῦ θυμώδους[4], *τῆς δὲ ψυχῆς[5] κατακυριεύει, καὶ παρέχει *τῷ

Margin:
β, A, S¹ ἐστὶν ἐν τῷ θυμῷ, τέκνα μου, καὶ οὐκ ἔστι τις ὁρῶν πρόσωπον ἐν ἀληθείᾳ.
β-a, A, S¹ τοὺς φυσικούς.
be, A, S¹ ἐν μίσει καρδίας καὶ διδωσιν αὐτῷ καρδίαν

ἰδίαν (A πολεμίαν ἐναντίων, S¹ om.).   β-a, A, S¹ καὶ γὰρ αὐτῇ τῇ ψυχῇ αὐτὸς γίνεται ψυχή.

----

[7] a reads ἀγαπήσετε.   [8] hi, abef. c reads ἀπόλλυσθαι, d ἀπωλείᾳ ἀπολεῖσθε, g ἵνα μὴ ἀπόλλυσθε.   [9] α. β, A, S¹ read as in margin, save that af om. ἐστίν, f om. τις, g om. μου, bd add θυμώδης after τις, and A trs. ἐν ἀληθείᾳ before ὁρῶν.   [10] c, aefg, A. b reads κᾶν μήτηρ, hi ἡμῶν, d ὑμῶν.   [11] g om.   [12] f reads πολέμιον, g πυλέμιος.   [13] β. c reads προσέχειν, h προσέχων.   [14] b reads ἑαυτοῖς.   [15] α. β-f read ἐὰν (+ δὲ a) ᾖ ἀδελφός, f ἐὰν ἀδελφὸς εἰ (sic). A = ἀδελφόν.   [16] f reads ἴδεν.   [17] α. β reads ἐάν. A = καί.   [18] A = προφήτου Κυρίου οὐκ ἀκούει. g om. Κυρίου, and rest of verse after παρακούει.   [19] c reads δικαίου. A[b]i[g] = τὸν δίκαιον. A[ab*cd] τοὺς δικαίους.   [20] h. c reads ἢ φίλους, β, S¹ φίλον.   [21] α (save that c reads αὐτό). β, S¹ read περιβάλλει (περιβαλεῖ e) γὰρ αὐτὸν (αὐτῷ aefg, αὐτὸ d) τὸ πν. τοῦ θ. τὰ δίκτυα τῆς πλάνης. A = περιβάλλει γὰρ τὸ πν. τῆς πλάνης τὰ δ. τῆς ἀσελγείας.   [22] hi, a. c om. β-a, A read as in margin.   [23] α read σκοτεῖ, d σκοτιεῖ.   [24] d om. rest of verse and ἐν τίνι ... καρδίας in ver. 4.   [25] a reads ἐντείνει. A = καὶ τότε, S¹ ἐν αὐτῷ.   [26] A adds καὶ κυκλοῖ, a duplicate rendering.   [27] hi, b. c, e read εἰς μίσους καρδίας, ag ἐκ μίσους, f ἐν μίσους καρδίαν (ἐνμίσως e) ἰδίαν. be, A, S add as in margin, d καὶ δίδωσιν αὐτῷ ἰδίαν καρδίαν διεγείρων αὐτόν.   [28] b om.   [29] A[ab] = καὶ φθόνος, A[b*cdef g] καὶ φθόνερος and connect with next chapter.

III.   [1] α, β-bd. bd read πονηρὸς ὁ θυμός. A[b*cd] = πονηρές ἐστι θυμῷ, A[ab] (internally corrupt) περιβάλλει θυμόν. On A see also preceding note   [2] α. β-ag, A, S¹ read as in margin, save that d adds καὶ before αὐτῇ. a om. g reads αὐτὴ ἡ ψυχὴ αὐτοῦ γὰρ ψύχος.   [3] b reads ἰδιοποιεῖται.   [4] c reads μύσους.   [5] α, β (save that h, ag om. δέ), A[b*d]. A[abcef g] = τῶν δὲ ψυχῶν.   [6] hi read τὸ σῶμα.   [7] α, g. β-g, S¹ read as in margin, A = ἰδίαν but om.

β-g, S¹ | σώματι⁶ ⌐δύναμιν⌐, ἵνα ποιήσῃ⁸ πᾶσαν⌐ ἀνομίαν⁹.   3. *Καὶ
δύναμιν | ὅταν ταῦτα πάντα πράξῃ τὸ σῶμα, δικαιοῖ τὰ πραχθέντα καὶ ἡ
ἰδίαν. | ψυχή¹⁰, ἐπειδὴ οὐ βλέπει ὀρθῶς.   4. *Διὰ τοῦτο¹¹ ὁ θυμού-
β-d (A), | μενος¹², *ἐὰν μὲν ᾖ¹³ *δυνατὸς ⌐τῷ σώματι⌐¹⁴, *τριπλῆν ἐν
S¹πράξῃ, | τῷ θυμῷ τὴν δύναμιν κέκτηται¹⁵· μίαν¹⁶ μὲν ἀπὸ¹⁷ τῆς βοηθείας
ἡ ψυχὴ | *τῶν ὑπουργούντων¹⁸· *δεύτερον δὲ¹⁹ διὰ τοῦ πλούτου *πείθων
δικαιοῖ τὸ | καὶ νικῶν [αὐτὸν] ἀδίκως²⁰· *τρίτον τὴν²¹ φυσικὴν ἔχων
πραχθέν. | *δύναμιν δι' αὐτῆς δρᾷ²² τὸ κακόν²³.   5. Ἐὰν δὲ ἀσθενὴς
β, A, S¹ | ᾖ ὁ²⁴ θυμούμενος²⁵, *διπλοῦν τὸ τῆς ὀργῆς πάθος ἐν αὐτῷ
βλέπει. | ἀναφύει²⁶· βοηθεῖ *γὰρ αὐτῷ ὁ θυμὸς²⁷ πάντοτε ἐν παρανο-
β, S¹ τρι- | μίᾳ²⁸.   6. Τοῦτο τὸ πνεῦμα ἀεὶ μετὰ τοῦ ψεύδους²⁹ ⌐ἐκ
πλῆν ἔχει | δεξιῶν τοῦ Σατανᾶ πορεύεται, ἵνα *ἐν ὠμότητι καὶ ³⁰ψεύδει⌐
τὴν δύν. | γίνονται³¹ αἱ πράξεις αὐτοῦ³².
ἐν τῷ |
θυμῷ. | IV. Οὐκοῦν σύνετε¹ τὴν δύναμιν τοῦ θυμοῦ² ὅτι³ †ματαία
β, A, S¹ |
τοῦ |
σώματος |
καὶ δι' |
ἑαυτοῦ |
δρῶν.   β-d, A, S¹ διπλῆν ἔχει τὴν δύναμιν παρὰ τὴν (af om.) τῆς
φύσεως.

δύν. ἵνα ποιήσῃ πᾶσαν.   ⁸hi, bdg (but g trs. after ἀνομίαν).   c, ef read
ποιήσει, a ποιήσῃς.   ⁹d reads παρανομίαν, A^bcefg τὰς ἰδίας ἀνομίας A^ab*d τὴν
ἰδίαν ἀνομ.   ¹⁰α (save that c reads πράξει for πράξῃ, and τὸ πραχθὲν καὶ
ὑψοῖ for τὰ . . . ψυχή).   β-d, A^b, S¹ read καὶ ὅταν (+τι A) πράξῃ (ef πράξει.
A om. according to printed text, but A^befg attest it at any rate), ἡ (b, A^b om.)
ψυχὴ (A^b om.) δικαιοῖ τὸ πραχθέν, d τότε ἡ ψυχὴ δικαιοῖ τὸ πραχθέν.   ¹¹A^b*d
read δι' ὅ.   ¹²hi read θυμός. A^b*cdefg add ἔστι..   ¹³a reads ἐὰν μένῃ, f κᾶν
μὴ ᾖ.   ¹⁴α. β, A^b*cdefg read δυνατός. A^ab om.   ¹⁵α, A^b*cdefg. β, S¹ read as
in margin, save that f om. τήν and g reads πολλήν for τριπλῆν. A^ab = δύναμις
ἐν τῷ θυμῷ.   ¹⁶d reads καὶ μίαν.   ¹⁷b, S¹ read διὰ τῆς δυνάμεως καί.
g διά.   ¹⁸A = τῆς συνεργούσης. d adds αὐτῷ.   ¹⁹dg read δευτέραν,
e δευτέρα.   A = καὶ δεύτερον.   ²⁰α. β-a, A, S¹ read παραπείθων (a παρα-
πείθειν, +αὐτῷ d) καὶ νικῶν (a νικᾶν) ἐν ἀδίκῳ (d, A ἐν ἀδικίᾳ).   I have
bracketed the αὐτόν in the text as an interpolation.   ²¹α, g. β-adg
read τρίτην τήν (ef om.), d, A τρίτον δὲ τήν, a om.   ²²α. β, A, S¹ as in
margin (save that A reads δρᾶν).   ²³d om. next verse.   ²⁴g om.
²⁵c reads κοιμούμενος.   ²⁶α. β-d, A, S¹ read as in margin, save that
for παρὰ . . . φύσεως A reads καὶ εἰ παρὰ φύσεως (corrupt).   ²⁷α (save
that hi read αὐτόν). β-d read γὰρ αὐτοῖς ὁ θυμός, A^b*defg = αὐτῷ, S¹ αὐτοῖς.
A^abc om.   c adds αὐτῷ.   ²⁸A adds θυμοῦ.   ²⁹A reads արասասակ թեւսնp
(= θυμοῦ) corrupt for ասակ թեւսնp = ψεύδους.   α, A om. next ten words
through hmt.   ³⁰aefg. b read ἐν ὀμότητι, d ἐν ὀμώτητι, S¹ ἐπὶ τὸ πλέον
and om. following καί.   ³¹ab, A read γίνωνται.   ³²g reads αὐτῶν.
    IV. ¹d adds τέκνα μου.   ²d adds καὶ φεύγετε οὖν αὐτήν.   ³g reads

ἐστίν[4]. 2. Ἐν γὰρ λόγῳ **παροξύνεται**[5] πρῶτον· εἶτα[6] *ἐν *bdg*, A, S^1
ἔργοις[7] †δυναμοῖ[8] τὸν ὀργιζόμενον[9], καὶ[10] ἐν *ζημίαις πικραῖς παροξύνει.
διαταράσσει τὸ διαβούλιον αὐτοῦ[11], καὶ οὕτως διεγείρει ἐν θυμῷ
μεγάλῳ τὴν ψυχὴν αὐτοῦ. 3. Ὅτε[12] οὖν λαλεῖ τις *καθ' ὑμῶν[13],
⌈ὑμεῖς⌉ μὴ[14] *κινεῖσθε εἰς ὀργήν[15], καὶ ἐάν τις[16] ἐπαινέσῃ[17]
ὑμᾶς ὡς[18] **ἁγίους**[19], μὴ ἐπαίρεσθε[20]· μήτε[21] μεταβάλλεσθε[22] *bdg*, A, S^1 ἀγαθούς.
⌈μήτε⌉ εἰς τέρψιν μήτε εἰς ἀηδίαν[23]. 4. Πρῶτον γὰρ[24]
τέρπει[25] τὴν ἀκοήν, καὶ οὕτως[26] ὀξύνει τὸν νοῦν[27] *τοῦ νοῆσαι[28] β, S^1
τὸ †ἐρεθισθέν[29], καὶ[30] θυμωθεὶς νομίζει[31] δικαίως ὀργίζεσθαι[32]. καὶ τότε.
5. Ἐὰν δὲ[33] * ζημίᾳ ἢ ἀπωλείᾳ τινὶ περιπέσητε[34], τέκνα[35], β, S^1
⌈μὴ ἐκθροεῖσθε[36]⌉· ὅτι ⌈αὐτὸ⌉ τὸ πνεῦμα[37] *ποιεῖ ἐπιθυμῆσαι[38] θυμωθῇ διὰ τοῦ
τοῦ ἀπολλυμένου[39] ἵνα * **θυμῷ πέσῃ διὰ τοῦ πάθους**[40]. πάθου.

διδασκαλία παρὰ θυμοῦ. [4] *ὅτι μ. ἐστίν* = כי הבל corrupt (?) for כי יחבל = *ὅτι διαφθείρει.* [5] α, *aef. bdg*, A, S^1 read as in margin. [6] A = *καὶ εἶτα.* [7] *g* om. [8] = יגבר corrupt(?) for יְמָרֵר = *ἐξαγριοῖ* (cf. Dan. viii. 7). [9] *b* reads *ἐρεθιζόμενον.* [10] *h* om. [11] *hi*, β (save that for *πικραῖς aefg*, S^1 read *μικραῖς*, and *d μακραῖς*, and β reads *ταράσσει*). *c* reads *πικραῖς ζ. διαταράσσει τὸν ἐρεθιζόμενον.* A = *ζ. μικραῖς προπέμπει τὸ δ. αὐτοῦ*, but յուղարկէ is corrupt for յուզէ = *ταράσσει.* *a* om. rest of verse through hmt. [12] *g* reads *ὅτι.* [13] *d* reads *καθ' ἡμῶν.* A = *μεθ' ὑμῶν.* [14] *b* om. [15] α, β (save that β reads *θυμόν* for *ὀργήν*). A = *κινείσθω ἡ καρδία ὑμῶν εἰς θυμόν.* [16] *a* om. [17] *h. c* reads *ἐπαινέσει*, *abg ἐπαινῇ*, *de ἐπαινεῖ*, *f επαινα.* [18] *e* om. [19] α, *aef. bdg*, A, S^1 read *ἀγαθούς.* [20] A adds *εἰς μετεωρισμόν* (?). [21] α, *def. abg* read *μηδέ.* S^1 om. [22] *h* adds *μὴ ἐπαίρεσθε.* S^1 om. [23] *adf.* α reads *ἀϊδίαν*, *e δειδίαν*, *g αἰδείαν* which are corruptions of the form in the text. *b* emends into *εἰδέαν.* A reads *խռովութիւն* (= *ταραχάς*) which may be a loose rendering of *ἀηδίαν.* S^1 = *ἐπιθυμίαν δόξης.* *d* adds *κατακυριεύεσθε ὑπὸ τοῦ λόγου.* [24] *c* reads *μέν.* [25] *g* reads *τρέπει*, perhaps rightly. A = *τέρψις εὐφραίνει.* [26] A^{-ab} = *τότε.* A^{ab} om. together with next three words. [27] *c* adds *ἡμῶν.* [28] α. *d* reads *πρὸς τὸ νοῆσαι*, β–*d νοῆσαι.* A = *καὶ συνετίζει.* [29] α, β–*dg. dg* read *ῥηθέν.* If *dg* is not right, we should emend *ἐρεθισθέν* into *ἐρεθίσαν.* A = *διαβούλιον τοῦ ἐρεθίσαντος* (?). *d* adds *καὶ ὅταν νοήσει αὐτό.* [30] α, A. β, S^1 read *καὶ* (*d* om.) *τότε.* A adds *ὁ.* [31] *d* adds *ὅτι.* [32] *a* reads *ὀργιζόμενος*, *d ὀργίζεται.* A^{ab} om. rest of chapter. [33] *beg* om. [34] *hi*, β, $A^{b*cdefg}$ (save that *hi* give accusatives instead of datives, *b ἐάν* for *ἢ* and *περιπέσῃ* for *περιπέσητε* and *g* om. *τινί* and A^{b*cd} trans. *ζημίᾳ* and *ἀπ.*). *c* reads *ζημίαν ἢ ἀπωλείᾳ τινὶ περιπεσεῖ.* [35] *bde* add *μου.* [36] *c. h*, β--*g* read *θροεῖσθε*, *g προίεσθε.* [37] $A^{b*cdefg}$ add *πλάνης.* [38] α. *abeg*, S^1 read *ἐπιθ. ποιεῖ*, *df ἐπιθυμεῖν σε ποιεῖ*, $A^{b*cdefg}$ = *ἐπεθύμησε ποιεῖν τοῦτο* (A^g om.). [39] *g.* α read *ἀπολλομένου*, *b ἀπολωμένου*, *df ἀπολλωμένου*, *e ἀπωλουμένου*, *a*, S^1 *ἀπολωλότος.* $A^{b*cdefg}$ = *καὶ εἰς τὸ τελειοῦν* (A^{b*cd} *τελειώσας*) *τὴν ἀπώλειαν.* [40] α. β, S^1 read as in margin (save that *d* reads *θυμωθείς*). $A^{b*cdefg}$ = *λυπηθῇ*

6. Καὶ[41] ἐὰν ζημιωθῆτε ἑκουσίως *ἢ ἀκουσίως[42] *μὴ
λυπεῖσθε[43]· ἀπὸ γὰρ λύπης[44] ἐγείρεται[45] καὶ[46] θυμὸς[47] ⌐μετὰ
ψεύδους⌐.   7. *Ἔστι δὲ διπρόσωπον κακὸν ὁ θυμὸς μετὰ

β, A, S¹
τὸ δια-
βούλιον.

ψεύδους[48], καὶ συναίρονται[49] ἀλλήλοις ἵνα ταράξωσι[50] *τὴν
καρδίαν[51]· ταρασσομένης δὲ τῆς ψυχῆς συνεχῶς, ἀφίσταται
ὁ[52] Κύριος ἀπ' αὐτῆς καὶ κυριεύει αὐτῆς· ὁ Βελίαρ.

bdg, A,
S¹ τὰς
ἐντολάς.

V. Φυλάξατε[1] οὖν, *τέκνα μου[2], *τὴν ἐντολὴν[3] τοῦ[4] Κυρίου
        καὶ τὸν νόμον αὐτοῦ τηρήσατε[5]·
        ἀπόστητε[6] ἀπὸ τοῦ[7] θυμοῦ[8],
        καὶ μισήσατε[9] τὸ ψεῦδος,
        ἵνα[10] *Κύριος κατοικήσει ἐν ὑμῖν[11]
        καὶ φεύξεται[12] *ἀφ' ὑμῶν[13] ὁ Βελίαρ.
    2. Ἀλήθειαν φθέγγεσθε[14] ἕκαστος πρὸς τὸν πλησίον αὐτοῦ
        καὶ οὐ μὴ ἐμπέσητε εἰς μῆνιν[15] *καὶ ταραχάς[16],
        ἀλλ' ἔσεσθε[17] ἐν εἰρήνῃ ἔχοντες τὸν θεὸν *τῆς εἰρήνης[18]
        καὶ *οὐ μὴ κατισχύσει[19] ὑμῶν[20] πόλεμος.

(but Aᵉ over line θυμωθῇ) διὰ πόθου τοῦ ἀπολωλότος. a om. rest of chapter.
[41] c. h, β, A^b*cdefg om.   [42] b om.   [43] A^b*cdefg = καὶ ταραχθῆτε.   [44] A^b*cdefg
by easy internal corruption = θυμοῦ.   [45] α, d, A, S¹. β–ad read ἐγείρει.
[46] c. hi, β, A^b*cde'g om.   [47] α, A. β–a read θυμόν.   [48] de, A^b*cdeg (save
that d read πρόσωπον). b, S¹ read διπρόσωπον κακὸς θυμὸς (b θυμὸν) μετὰ
ψεύδους. α, fg om. through hmt.   [49] de. hi, f read συναιρῶνται, c συναινῶνται
(sic), bg συνερῶνται, which are corrupt forms of the word in the text.
συναίρονται ἀλλήλοις means 'unite with one another,' 'assist one another,'
and is so rendered by A^b*cdefg. S¹ = συμμίσγονται and accordingly supports
reading of bg, which it took to be from συνεράω. It might be possible to
regard συνερῶνται as a present middle Attic form of συνερέω, 'to support,'
'advocate,' but this is unlikely.   [50] α, b, g. de read ταράξουσιν, f πράξουσιν.
A = προπέμψωσιν. Same corruption as in ver. 1.   [51] α. β, A^b*cdefg, S¹
as in margin (save that ef read τὰ διαβούλια). d adds τῆς ψυχῆς.   [52] α,
dg. bef, A om.

    V. [1] df read φυλάσσετε.   [2] a om.   [3] α, aef, S². bdg, A, S¹ read as in
margin.   [4] dg om.   [5] α, abef. d read ἐκζητήσατε, g τηρήσετε. A = μὴ
ἐκκλίνετε.   [6] bg add δέ.   [7] α, e. β–e, A om.   [8] A read ⲙⲡⲛⲓⲡ[ⲃⲉⲗⲥ]
(= ψεύδους) corrupt for ⲩⲣⲙⲩⲇⲓⲛⲛⲓⲡ[ⲃⲉⲗⲥ] = θυμοῦ.   [9] hi read μισεῖτε.
[10] hi, g add ὁ.   [11] A^ab*cd trs. Κύριος . . . ὑμῖν and φεύξεται . . . Βελίαρ. For
κατοικήσει which c, f read, we find κατοικήσῃ in hi, β–f. a om. next line.
[12] α. bfg read φύγῃ, de φεύγει.   [13] hi om.   [14] c, β–a. hi read φθέγξετε,
a λαλεῖτε.   [15] b, S¹ reads ἡδονήν.   [16] A^b*d om.   [17] A adds πάντοτε.
[18] A = τὸν εἰρηνοποιόν. a om. rest of chapter and vi. 1–7.   [19] c reads οὐ
μὴ κατησχήσει. A = καταπαύσεται.   [20] dg, A = ἐν (d om.) ὑμῖν.   [21] bg
read καὶ (b om.) ἀγαπᾶτε.   [22] d reads θεόν.   [23] c, befg (save that g om.

3. Ἀγαπήσατε[21] τὸν Κύριον[22] ἐν πάσῃ *τῇ ζωῇ[23] ὑμῶν[24] *καὶ ἀλλήλους[25] ἐν ἀληθινῇ[26] καρδίᾳ.

4. *Ἐγὼ οἶδα[27] ὅτι ἐν ταῖς[28] ἐσχάταις ἡμέραις ἀποστήσεσθε[29] τοῦ Κυρίου,
καὶ προσοχθιεῖτε[30] τῷ[31] Λευί,
καὶ πρὸς τῷ[32] Ἰουδὰ[33] παρατάξεσθε[34],
ἀλλ' οὐ δυνήσεσθε[35] πρὸς αὐτούς[36]·
*ἄγγελος γὰρ Κυρίου ὁδηγεῖ ἑκατέρους[37],
ὅτι ἐν αὐτοῖς[38] στήσεται ὁ[39] Ἰσραήλ.

5. Καὶ *ὡς ἂν ἀποστήσεσθε[40] ἀπὸ[41] Κυρίου[42], *ἐν πάσῃ κακίᾳ[43] *πορευόμενοι ποιήσετε τὰ βδελύγματα τῶν ἐθνῶν ἐκπορνεύοντες ἐν[44] γυναιξὶν ἀνόμων[45] καὶ ἐν πάσῃ πονηρίᾳ[46] ἐνεργούντων[47] ⌐ἐν ὑμῖν⌐ *τῶν πνευμάτων[48] τῆς πονηρίας[49].

6. [Ἀνέγνων γὰρ[50] ἐν βίβλῳ Ἐνὼχ[51] τοῦ δικαίου ⌐καὶ ἔγνων⌐[52] ὅτι ὁ[53] ἄρχων ὑμῶν[54] ὁ Σατανᾶς ἐστιν[55] *καὶ ὅτι[56] τὰ πνεύματα τῆς πονηρίας[57] καὶ τῆς ὑπερηφανίας

Margin: β, S οἶδα γάρ. β ὡς ἂν ἀπο- στῆτε. defg, S^1 πορευό- μενοι καὶ (g, S^1 om.) ποι- οῦντες. β, A, S^1 πλάνης. defg, A ὅτι. bdeg, A, S^1 πάντα τά πνεύ- ματα. β, A, S^1 πορνείας.

τῇ), A, S^1. h, d read τῇ (h om.) ψυχῇ. [24] f reads ἡμῶν. [25] hi, β (save that f om. καί), A. c om. [26] A = καθαρᾷ. [27] α (save that h adds γάρ before οἶδα), A. β, S^1 read as in margin. [28] c. h, β, A om. [29] c reads ἀποστείτε ἀπό. [30] c, beg. h reads προσώχθητε, df προσωχθήσετε. A = ἐπαναστήσεσθε. [31] b reads τόν. [32] α, β om. [33] α. β reads Ἰουδάν. [34] α (save that c gives παρατάξεισθε), ef (save that f gives παρατάξησθε). bdg, A read ἀντιτάξεσθε. [35] c reads δυνήσειται, g δύνασθε. [36] α, β, A^b. $A^{ab*cdefg}$ = αὐτόν. [37] hi, A (save that eg om. γάρ and g, A read ὁδηγήσει and for ἑκατέρους A^{ab} read αὐτούς, A^{b*defg} αὐτόν, A^c ἔτι). c om. hi add αὐτούς. [38] $A^{ab*defg}$ = αὐτῷ. [39] α. β om. [40] α. β reads as in margin (save that g om. ἄν). A = ἀποστάντες. [41] c adds τοῦ. [42] A^b = αὐτοῦ. [43] A^{-i} reads [Armenian] = ἐπιθυμίᾳ corrupt(?) for [Armenian] = ἐν κακίᾳ. This phrase A trs. after next word. [44] α. β, S^1 read πορευόμενοι (πορεύεσθε b) καὶ (bg, S^1 om.) ποιοῦντες βδελύγματα (βδέλυγμα g) ἐθνῶν, ἐκπορνεύοντες (ἐκπορεύοντες b, S^1, καὶ πορεύοντες g) ἐν. $A^{(a?)b}$ = πορεύσεσθε (πορεύεσθε A^b) καὶ ποιοῦντες βδέλυγμα ἐκπορνεύοντες ἐν ἔθνεσιν ἐν. A^{b*dfg} = πορεύσεσθε καὶ ποιοῦντες βδ. ἐν ἔθν. ἐκπορνεύοντες ἐν. $A^{c(e)}$ βδελυσσόμενοι βδ. ἐν ἔθν. ἐκπορνεύοντες ἐν. [45] c, S^1 read ἀνόμοις. [46] dg read πορνείᾳ. [47] α, β–g. A^{b*defg} read [Armenian] (= ἀφρονοῦντος) corrupt(?) for [Armenian] = ἐνεργοῦντος. A^b (i.e. [Armenian]) = ἔθνει ἄλλος γίνεσθαι (?). A^s = ἐθνῶν (?) γίνεσθαι ἄλλος. [48] hi om. A = τοῦ πνεύματος. [49] α. β, A^{abefg} S^1 read as in margin. A^{b*d} = πορνείας καὶ πλάνης. [50] c om. [51] d trs. after δικαίου. [52] c. hi read καὶ εὗρον. bdefg, A, S^1 om. [53] g om. [54] d om. [55] α. β trs. before ὁ Σ. A, S^1 = ἔσται. [56] f, A^{abcefg}, S^1 read ὅτι, A^{b*d} καί. bdeg, A, S^1 add πάντα. [57] α, f. be, A, S^1 read πορνείας, dy πλάνης καὶ (d om.) τῆς πορνείας. A^s

bdg, A
τῷ Λευὶ
†ὑπακού-
σονται.   †ὑπακούσονται[58] *τοῦ παρεδρεύειν[59] τοῖς υἱοῖς Λευί, τοῦ ποιεῖν[60]
αὐτοὺς ἐξαμαρτάνειν ἐνώπιον Κυρίου.

   7. Καὶ *οἱ ἐμοὶ υἱοὶ[61] συνεγγίζοντές[62] εἰσι τοῦ[63] Λευὶ
καὶ συναμαρτάνοντες[64] αὐτοῖς[65] ἐν πᾶσιν.
*οἱ δὲ υἱοὶ τοῦ[66] Ἰούδα ἔσονται ἐν πλεονεξίᾳ
ἁρπάζοντες[67] ἀλλότρια ὡς[68] λέοντες.]

   8. ⌐Καὶ⌐[69] διὰ τοῦτο ἀπαχθήσεσθε[70] [σὺν αὐτοῖς][71] *εἰς
αἰχμαλωσίαν[72]
κἀκεῖ ἀπολήψεσθε[73] *πάσας τὰς πληγὰς Αἰγύπτου[74]
καὶ πάσας τὰς[75] πονηρίας[76] τῶν ἐθνῶν.

   9. Καὶ οὕτως[77] ἐπιστρέψαντες[78] πρὸς Κύριον ἐλεηθήσεσθε[79]
καὶ ἄξει ὑμᾶς[80] εἰς τὸ ἁγίασμα αὐτοῦ
*καὶ δώσει[81] ὑμῖν εἰρήνην[82].

   10. Καὶ ἀνατελεῖ ὑμῖν *ἐκ τῆς φυλῆς [Ἰούδα καὶ] τοῦ Λευὶ
τὸ σωτήριον Κυρίου[83]

β, S¹ καὶ
αὐτός.   *αὐτὸς γὰρ[84] ποιήσει πρὸς τὸν Βελίαρ πόλεμον[85]

om. next three words.   [58] bdg, A⁻ᵇ add τῷ Λευί before this verb. Aᵇ adds
οὐ. If the former is a later addition (α, ef, S¹ om. it), ὑπακούσονται can
hardly be right. Probably יקשיבו to which ὑπακούσονται goes back is corrupt
for יקשרו = συστρέψονται, 'will conspire.' S¹ ὑπακούεσθαι ἄρξονται.   [59] A
= καὶ παρεδρεύσουσι, S¹ καὶ ἀρέσκειν.   [60] h, d read τοῦ ποιῆσαι, A καὶ
ποιήσουσι.   [61] α. β read οἱ (b om.) υἱοί μου.   [62] α. β reads ἐγγίζοντες.
[63] α. β‑af, S¹ read τῷ, f, A τοῖς υἱοῖς.   [64] c. hi, bef read συνεξαμαρτάνοντες,
dg ἐξαμαρτάνοντες (+ εἰσί g). g, Aᵃ add εἰσί, Aᵇᵒᵉˢ ἔσονται.   [65] d trs. after
πᾶσιν. g om. For αὐτοῖς Aᵇ*ᶜᵈᶠ give ἱερεῦσιν.   [66] α. b reads καὶ υἱοί,
d ἀλλὰ καὶ οἱ υἱοί, efg, A καὶ οἱ υἱοί.   [67] befg add τά.   [68] d adds οἱ.
[69] α. β, A, S¹ om.   [70] A = ἐλεύσεσθε. g om. next six words.   [71] added
by interpolator of verses 6, 7.   [72] α, d. bef read ἐν αἰχμαλωσίᾳ.
[73] c reads ἀπαλείψεσθε.   [74] Aᵇ*ᶜᵈᶠᵍ = σὺν αὐτοῖς πληγὰς ἐν Αἰγυτίοις.   [75] b om.
[76] d reads πορνείας.   [77] A = μετὰ ταῦτα. The text requires some such
expression.   [78] hi, befg, S. c reads ἐπιστρέψασθαι, d, A ἐπιστρέψετε.
[79] A = καὶ ἐλεήσει ὑμᾶς.   [80] g adds κύριος.   [81] f, A, S¹. The same text
is implied in all the other MSS. but b. c καὶ δόει, h, e καὶ δώῃ, d καὶ δώει,
g καὶ δόσει, b βοῶν.   [82] hi add περὶ τοῦ Χριστοῦ as title before verses 10–13.
A adds εἰς τὸν αἰῶνα.   [83] Aᵇ*ᵈ = σωτήριον ἐξ οἴκου Ἰ. καὶ ἐκ φυλῆς Λευί. β om. τοῦ
before Λευί. For κυρίου g reads τοῦ θεοῦ. Here A adds καὶ δώσει εἰρήνην ἕως
τοῦ αἰῶνος (+ τῷ Ἰσραὴλ Aᵇ*)—a doublet from the preceding verse. I have
bracketed Ἰούδα καὶ as an interpolation, for if it were original we should
have φυλῶν and not φυλῆς. Cf. T. Sim. vii. 1, T. Gad viii. 1, T. Jos. xix. 6.
[84] α. β, S¹ read as in margin. A = καί.   [85] A⁻ᵇ trs. before πρὸς τόν.
Here Aᵇ*ᶜᵈ add καὶ ψυχὰς ἁγίων πρὸς ἑαυτὸν καλέσει, καὶ ἐπιστρέψει καρδίας
ἀπειθῶν πρὸς τὸν κύριον, which are drawn and expanded from ver. 11.

καὶ τὴν ἐκδίκησιν τοῦ νίκους δώσει τοῖς[86] †πατράσιν[87]
    ὑμῶν[88].

11. Καὶ τὴν αἰχμαλωσίαν λήψεται[89] ἀπὸ τοῦ Βελίαρ, [τὰς
    ψυχὰς τῶν ἁγίων][90]
*καὶ ἐπιστρέψει[91] καρδίας[92] ἀπειθεῖς[93] πρὸς Κύριον.
καὶ δώσει *τοῖς ἐπικαλουμένοις αὐτὸν[94] εἰρήνην αἰώνιον.

12. Καὶ *ἀναπαύσονται ἐν Ἐδὲμ ἅγιοι[95]
καὶ ἐπὶ *τῆς νέας[96] Ἰερουσαλὴμ εὐφρανθήσονται δίκαιοι
*ἥτις ἐστι δόξα θεοῦ αἰώνιος[97].

13. Καὶ οὐκέτι ὑπομενεῖ[98] Ἰερουσαλὴμ ἐρήμωσιν
*οὐδὲ αἰχμαλωτισθήσεται Ἰσραήλ[99],
ὅτι[100] Κύριος ἔσται[101] *ἐν μέσῳ[102] αὐτῆς[103] [τοῖς ἀνθρώ-
    ποις συναναστρεφόμενος][104]
καὶ ὁ[105] Ἅγιος Ἰσραὴλ βασιλεύων[106] ἐπ᾽ αὐτῆς[107] [ἐν
    *ταπεινώσει καὶ πτωχείᾳ[108], καὶ ὁ πιστεύων *ἐπ᾽
    αὐτῷ[109] *βασιλεύσει ἐν τοῖς ἀνθρώποις ἐν ἀληθείᾳ[110]].

Margin (on §§12–13):
β–ad, A, S¹ ἥτις ἔσται εἰς δόξασμα θεοῦ ἕως τοῦ αἰῶνος.
β–a, S¹ ἐν ἀληθείᾳ ἐν τοῖς οὐρανοῖς.

A^els om. next sixteen words.   [86] ef om.   [87] b reads πέρασιν—a bad emendation of πατράσιν found in all other MSS. and in A, S¹. But πατράσιν ὑμῶν, which is impossible, = אבותיכם which is corrupt for אויביכם = πολεμίοις ὑμῶν, and the line = 'and he will execute an everlasting vengeance on your enemies' (i.e. ויתן נקמת נצח באויביכם). For text of A see note 85.   [88] df. α, beg, S¹ read ἡμῶν. A = αὐτοῦ.   [89] dg which g trs. before τὴν αἰχ. c reads λάβε (?), hi, bef λάβῃ.   [90] α. β reads ψυχὰς ἁγίων, S¹ ψυχῶν ἁγίων. A^abels read καὶ τὰς ψ. τῶν ἁγ. See ver. 10, note 85 where A^b*cd wrongly insert 11^ab. I have bracketed τὰς ... ἁγίων as a Christian addition.   [91] f om.   [92] d reads ψυχάς.   [93] A^−b = ἀπειθῶν. [94] A trs. after αἰώνιον.   [95] So A^bels. Possibly also A^ac though printed Arm. Text represents A^abc as ἐν Ἐ. ἀναπ. ἅγ. A^b*d = πάντες ἅγ. ἐν Ἐ. ἀναπ. [96] bg, A, S¹. c reads τῆς βασιλείας, hi, ef τῆς νέας ἁγίας (ἁγίας καὶ νέας e, ἁγίας νέας, f), d τὴν ἁγίαν καὶ δικαίαν, S² τῆς ἁγίας. The reading ἁγίας may be due to קדש being written corruptly a second time as קדש.   [97] α (save that h reads Κυρίου). befg, A, S¹ read as in margin (save that ef, A, S¹ read ἐστί and g θεῷ αἰωνίῳ), d ἕως τοῦ αἰῶνος.   [98] f reads ὑπομείνῃ. For ὑπομ. Ἰ. ἐρήμωσιν A gives Ἰ. ἐρημωθήσεται.   [99] d reads οἱ δὲ αἰχμαλωτισθήσονται. For αἰχμαλωτισθήσεται b reads αἰχμαλωτίζεται. hi add ὁ before Ἰσραήλ.   [100] d reads ὁ.   [101] hi read ἐστί.   [102] bd read ἐμμέσῳ.   [103] A = αὐτῶν.   [104] A Christian(?) interpolation. In T. Jud. xxiv. 1 this is said of the Messiah. The phrase is used with reference to wisdom in Bar. iii. 37. A = καὶ τοῖς ἀνθ. συναναστρεφήσεται.   [105] b om.   [106] A = βασιλεύσει. [107] α, ef, A. d read ἐπ᾽ αὐτήν, b, S¹ ἐπ᾽ αὐτούς, g ἐν αὐτοῖς.   [108] α, β, A^abcg (save that bdg add ἐν before πτωχείᾳ). A^b*cdf = εἰρήνη.   [109] c, bef. hi read ἐπ᾽ αὐτόν, dg ἐν αὐτῷ.   [110] α. bdeg read βασ. ἐν ἀληθ. (+ καὶ g) ἐν τοῖς

VI. Καὶ νῦν *φοβήθητε τὸν Κύριον¹, τέκνα μου, καὶ προσέχετε ἑαυτοῖς² ἀπὸ τοῦ Σατανᾶ καὶ *τῶν πνευμάτων³ αὐτοῦ.   2. Ἐγγίσατε⁴ τῷ θεῷ καὶ τῷ ἀγγέλῳ *τῷ παραιτουμένῳ ὑμᾶς⁵· ὅτι οὗτός ἐστι μεσίτης θεοῦ καὶ ἀνθρώπων καὶ⁶ ἐπὶ τῆς εἰρήνης τοῦ⁷ Ἰσραὴλ κατέναντι⁸ *τῆς βασιλείας τοῦ †θεοῦ στήσεται⁹·   3. Διὰ¹⁰ τοῦτο σπουδάζει ὁ ἐχθρὸς ὑποσκελίζειν¹¹ πάντας τοὺς ἐπικαλουμένους *τὸν Κύριον¹².   4. Οἶδε γὰρ ὅτι *ἐν ᾗ ἡμέρᾳ¹³ ἐπιστρέψει¹⁴ Ἰσραήλ, συντελεσθήσεται ἡ βασιλεία τοῦ ἐχθροῦ.   5. Αὐτὸς γὰρ¹⁵ ὁ ἄγγελος *τῆς εἰρήνης¹⁶ *ἐνισχύσει τὸν Ἰσραὴλ¹⁷ μὴ ἐμπεσεῖν¹⁸

Margin: α παρεπομένῳ ὑμῖν. β–ab, A, S¹ καὶ κατέναντι. bg(A),S¹ ἐχθροῦ. β, A, S¹ πιστεύσει.

οὐρανοῖς.   f ἐν ἀληθ. βασ. ἐν τ. οὐρ.   Aᵃᵇ = βασ. ἐν ἀληθ. ἕως τῶν οὐρανῶν. Aᵇ*ᶜᵈᵉᶠˢ βασ. ἐν ἀληθ. ἕως τοῦ αἰῶνος.   The confusion of ουνοις and ανπυις could easily arise.

VI. ¹c reads φοβεῖτε τὸν θεόν.   ²c reads ἑαυτούς. A adds καὶ φυλάξασθε —a doublet of προσ. ἑαυτοῖς.   ³A = κακοῦ πνεύματος.   ⁴α, β–bd. b, S¹ read ἐγγίζετε δέ, d ἐγγίσατε δέ. A = καὶ ἐγγίσατε.   ⁵β–d. The other authorities diverge from β–d and from each other. α reads τῷ παρεπομένῳ ὑμῖν (ἡμᾶς hi). Cf. α in T. Levi v. 6: d reads αὐτοῦ τοῦ μὴ πατάξαι ὑμᾶς εἰς τέλος. For τῷ ἀγγ.... ὑμᾶς A reads ὁ ἄγγελος συγγινώσκει ὑμῖν. Here խնայէ, which = φείδεται or συγγινώσκει, may be a misrendering of παραιτεῖται, since in late Greek παραίτησις = 'forgiveness,' or խնայէ may be corrupt for խնամէ = φροντίζει, ἐπιμελεῖται, which would point to נתן עליכם as in T. Lev. v. 6, 7. S¹ = ᾧ δεδομένοι ἐστέ. In T. Levi v. 6 we have followed β–d and taken it to be a rendering of פונע לעם. The text = 'who intercedeth for you' = פֹּנֵעַ לָכֶם or סניגורכם in Mishnic and Talmudic Hebrew. See note on T. Levi v. 6. We might perhaps assume different Hebrew originals in Levi v. 6 and in Dan. vi. 2, on the ground of the divergence of d, A(?), S¹ in the two passages. But the fact that α gives παρεπόμενος and β–d παραιτούμενος in both passages implies the same Hebrew original in both. Hence the text is doubtful.   ⁶b om.   ⁷α. β om.   ⁸α, b. β–ab, A, S¹ read as in margin. Text = לפני which may mean 'in the presence of' or after עמד 'against.'   ⁹α, def (save that d trs. στήσεται before τῆς and f before τοῦ). bg, S¹ read τῆς βασ. τοῦ ἐχθροῦ στήσεται (g στήσεσθε). Is θεοῦ right? If not the false text might be explained by a corruption of איב into אל. Though ἐχθροῦ is weakly attested it gives an excellent sense. It has the support of A, though this version is here corrupt, reading ἐχθρας τῶν βασιλέων.   ¹⁰g, A read καὶ διά.   ¹¹d reads ὑποσκελλίσαι (sic).   ¹²A = τὸ ὄνομα τοῦ κυρίου. Aᵇ*ᶜᵈᵉᶠˢ om. next eight words.   ¹³c, b. h, ef read ἐν ᾗ ἂν ἡμέρᾳ (e ἡμέραν), dg ἦν (ᾗ d) ἂν ἡμέραν.   ¹⁴α (hi ἐπιστρέψῃ). bfg read πιστεύσει, de πιστεύσῃ. Aᵃᵇ read զաւրանայցէ (= δυναμωθήσεται) corrupt for հաւատայցէ = πιστεύσει.   ¹⁵bf, S¹ om.   ¹⁶g om.   ¹⁷c reads

αὐτὸν εἰς τέλος [19] κακῶν [20].   6. Ἔσται δὲ ἐν καιρῷ τῆς [21] ἀνομίας [22] *τοῦ Ἰσραὴλ [23] (οὐκ ἔσται) [21] ἀφιστάμενος [25] *ἀπ' αὐτῶν [26] *ὁ Κύριος [27], καὶ [28] *μετελεύσεται ἐπ' ἔθνει ζητοῦντι τὸ θέλημα αὐτοῦ [29], ὅτι *οὐδεὶς τῶν ἀγγέλων ἔσται ἴσος αὐτῷ [30]. 7. Τὸ δὲ ὄνομα αὐτοῦ [1] ἐν *παντὶ τόπῳ Ἰσραὴλ [32] ⌐καὶ ἐν τοῖς [33] ἔθνεσιν⌐ [34].

8. Διατηρήσατε οὖν [33] ἑαυτούς [35], τέκνα μου, ἀπὸ παντὸς *ἔργου πονηροῦ [36], καὶ ἀπορρίψατε *ἀφ' ὑμῶν τὸν θυμὸν καὶ τὸ ψεῦδος [37] ⌐καὶ ἀγαπήσατε τὴν ἀλήθειαν καὶ τὴν μακροθυμίαν⌐.

β † ἔθνη ποιοῦνται †.

β, A, S¹ ἔσται ἐν.

β, S¹ ἔθνεσιν Σωτήρ.

β-g πᾶν.

ἐπιστρέψει τὸν Ἰσραὴλ καὶ ἐνισχύσει. A adds καί according to printed Arm. Text but certainly A[befg] do not.   [18] d reads ἐκπεσεῖν.   [19] hi, befg, A. c reads χεῖρας, d βάθος.   [20] A = κακόν.   [21] α, A[be]. β, A[-be] om.   [22] d reads ἀνομαλίας.   [23] hi read αὐτοῦ ὁ Ἰσραήλ, g Ἰσραήλ.   [24] I have added these words. If we do not so the loss of one or more clauses must be assumed before καὶ μετελεύσεται, for ver. 6 deals with the restoration of Israel through the angel of peace.   [25] A = ἀποστήσεται.   [26] hi read ἀπ' αὐτοῦ. g trs. after κύριος.   [27] α, g. β-g, A, S read κύριος. We should perhaps bracket ὁ κύριος as an interpolation. This verse relates to the action of the angel of peace. See note 24. But the αὐτοῦ after θέλημα supports it.   [28] α, A. β, S om.   [29] c (save for the corruption of ἔθνη for ἔθνει). Text = יהפך לגוי בעה רצונו. בעה is of course very unusual in this sense in Hebrew. It is probably a corruption of עָבַד = ποιοῦντα, which is the reading of all the other MSS. hi, befy read μετελεύσεται ἐπὶ ἔθνη (b ὄπισθε) ποιοῦντα τὸ θ. αὐτοῦ (τὸ ἀληθὲς ἄλειμμα g), d μεταστραφήσεται ἐπὶ τὰ ἔθνη ποιοῦντα τ. θ. α. A = μετελεύσεται ἐπὶ τὰ ἔθνη καὶ τὸ θέλημα αὐτοῦ τελειώσει. S¹ ἔσται ἐν ἔθνεσιν ποιῶν τὸ θέλημα αὐτοῦ. Here c alone is right, in reading the singular ἔθνει. The other texts did not arise from a deliberate transformation of the text in the Christian interest but from the miswriting of ἔθνει as ἔθνη. We have seen above that μετελεύσεται (μεταστραφήσεται d) = יהפך, which is here to be taken transitively = ἐπιστρέψει, 'he will transform.' On the other hand, if we do not insert the negative before ἀφιστάμενος, we must assume the loss of some words before καὶ μετελεύσεται referring to Israel's repentance or conversion. If in these Israel was the subject then יהפך would be rendered 'they will become a nation.'   [30] α, β-b, A, S¹ (save that h, e read ἴσως, i ἴσῳ, d trs. ἔσται after αὐτοῦ, and A, S¹ om. ἔσται). b reads οὐδενὶ τῶν ἀγγ. ἔσται ὡς αὐτῷ.   [31] β, A, S¹ add ἔσται.   [32] α, β, S¹ (save that g om. τόπῳ, d om. Ἰσραήλ, and h adds ἐν bef. Ἰσ.). A = ἐν πάσῃ γῇ καὶ ἐν Ἰσραήλ.   [33] g om.   [34] β, S add σωτήρ (g σωτηρία). After this a resumes.   [35] aef om.   [36] α, β, A (save that c om. ἔργου and d reads πον. ἔργου).   [37] α. β, S¹ read τὸν θ. καὶ πᾶν (g τό) ψεῦδος (+ ἀφ' ὑμῶν d). A has elements of α and β and = ἀφ' ὑμῶν ψεῦδος καὶ

β, A, S¹
(+ τὸν A)
νόμον
θεοῦ.
β, S¹
δικαιο-
σύνη τοῦ
νόμου
τοῦ.
β μου.
β, A, S¹
κατε-
φιλησεν
αὐτοὺς
καί.
β, A, S¹
† ὕπνον
αἰώνιον†.
β–d, A,

9. Καὶ ἃ ἠκούσατε³⁸· παρὰ τοῦ πατρὸς ὑμῶν, μετά- δοτε³⁹ ⌈καὶ⁴⁰ ὑμεῖς⁴¹⌉ τοῖς τέκνοις ὑμῶν⁴², [ἵνα δέξηται⁴³ ὑμᾶς ὁ Σωτὴρ⁴⁴ τῶν ἐθνῶν· *ἐστὶ γὰρ ἀληθὴς καὶ μακρόθυμος, πρᾶος καὶ ταπεινός⁴⁵, καὶ⁴⁶ ἐκδιδάσκων⁴⁷ διὰ τῶν ἔργων *τὸν νόμον Κυρίου⁴⁸]. 10. Ἀπόστητε οὖν ἀπὸ πάσης ἀδικίας καὶ κολλήθητε⁴⁹ τῇ δικαιοσύνῃ τοῦ⁵⁰ Θεοῦ⁵¹, καὶ ἔσται τὸ γένος ὑμῶν⁵² εἰς σωτηρίαν *ἕως τοῦ αἰῶνος⁵³. 11. *Καὶ θάψατέ με⁵⁴ ἐγγὺς τῶν πατέρων μου.

VII. Καὶ ταῦτα εἰπὼν *καταφιλήσας αὐτοὺς¹ *ὕπνωσεν †ὕπνῳ καλῷ². 2. Καὶ³ ἔθαψαν αὐτὸν *οἱ υἱοὶ αὐτοῦ. Καὶ⁴ μετὰ *τοῦτο ἀπήνεγκαν⁵ ⌈τὰ ὀστᾶ αὐτοῦ⌉⁶ … *ἔνθα ἦν⁷ Ἀβραὰμ⁸ καὶ Ἰσαὰκ καὶ Ἰακώβ⁹. [3. Πλὴν οὖν¹⁰ προεφήτευσεν αὐτοῖς¹¹ ⌈Δὰν⌉¹² ὅτι ἐπιλά-

S¹ ταῦτα ἀνήνεγκαν ⌈τὰ ὀστᾶ αὐτοῦ⌉ (+ καὶ κατέθηκαν f (dg), A, S¹) σύνεγγυς.

πάντα θυμόν. ³⁸ g, A read ἀκούετε. ³⁹ d om. ⁴⁰ hi read δέ. ⁴¹ d adds ποιεῖτε ἀναγγείλατε δὲ αὐτὰ καί. ⁴² a adds αὐτῶν, ef αὐτά, g ἀναγγείλατε. ⁴³ hi add καί. ⁴⁴ b reads πατήρ. The clause ἵνα … ἐθνῶν in its present form is obviously Christian. The words that follow might be taken as referring to Dan. (Cf. i. 3), but it is safer to bracket them as an addition. ⁴⁵ d reads ἐστὶ γὰρ ἀλ. καὶ μ. ἐν πᾶσι, πραΰς τε καὶ ταπεινός, g ἐν πᾶσι γὰρ ἀλ. καὶ μ. ἐστι, ταπ. καὶ πρᾶος. ⁴⁶ g om. ⁴⁷ c reads διδάσκων. ⁴⁸ α. β, A, S¹ read as in margin. ⁴⁹ hi read κολληθήσεσθε. ⁵⁰ α, A. β, S¹ add νόμου τοῦ (bg om.). ⁵¹ α, β–b, Aᵇᵇ*ᵈᵉᶠˢ. b, Aᶜᵉᶠˣ, S¹ read κυρίου. Aˢ om. b om. rest of verse. ⁵² c, A. hi read ἡμῶν, β, S μου. ⁵³ g reads εἰς τοὺς αἰῶνας. ⁵⁴ α, β–dg, Aᵇ*ᵈ, S¹. d reads θ. δέ με, g θάψαντες οὖν, Aᵃᵇᶜ καὶ νῦν, τέκνα μου, θάψατέ με.

VII. ¹ α. β, A, S¹ read as in margin. ² c. β, A read ὕπνωσεν ὕπνον αἰώνιον, hi ἐκοιμήθη. d adds πρεσβύτης καὶ πλήρης ἡμερῶν ὑπάρχων. Here c = שכב בשינה טובה, where שינה is corrupt for שיבה. Cf. T. Zab. x. 6. β, A = שכב שינת עולם, which I take to be a corruption of c (emended). The addition in d confirms the emendation of c. ³ This verse appears in d as follows: καὶ ἐνέγκαντες οἱ υἱοὶ αὐτοῦ θήκην ξύλων ἀσήπτων κατεσκευασμένην κατέθεντο αὐτὸν ἐν αὐτῇ. μετὰ ταῦτα δὲ ἀνέγκαντες ἔθαψαν αὐτὸν ἐν Χευρὼν μετὰ τῶν πατέρων αὐτοῦ. Καὶ οὗτοι μέν εἰσιν οἱ λόγοι οὓς ἐνετείλατο Δὰν τοῖς υἱοῖς αὐτοῦ. ⁴ g om. ⁵ α, Aᶜ. β–d read ταῦτα ἀνήνεγκαν. ⁶ f, Aᵇᵇ*ᵈᵉᶠˢ, S¹ add καὶ κατέθηκαν (+ αὐτά f), g adds θέντες. Such an addition is found in d (see note 3), and is needed. Hence with f (dg), A⁻ᶜ, S¹ add καὶ κατέθηκαν. ⁷ α. β–d, A, S¹ read σύνεγγυς (g ἐγγύς). ⁸ g om. rest of chapter. ⁹ This forms the natural close of the Testament. Verse 3 is the addition of a later hand. It is still more severe on Dan than v. 5, 8. ¹⁰ α. adef om. b, S¹ read ὡς. ¹¹ d reads ἐπ’ αὐτούς. A = περί

θωνται¹³ τοῦ¹⁴ Θεοῦ αὐτῶν¹⁵ καὶ ἀλλοτριωθήσονται¹⁶ γῆς¹⁷ ⌐bd, A
κλήρου¹⁸ αὐτῶν, ⌐καὶ γένους Ἰσραήλ⌐, καὶ πατριᾶς ⌐† τοῦ νόμου.
σπέρματος αὐτῶν⌐¹⁹].

h, β-bg
τελευτῆς.
β, A, S¹
μηνὸς
ὑγιαίνον-
τος
αὐτοῦ.
β-dg, A,
S¹ αὐτοῖς
καὶ
κώθωνα.

Διαθήκη Νεφθαλεὶμ τοῦ ὀγδόου υἱοῦ Ἰακὼβ καὶ Βάλλας¹.

I. Ἀντίγραφον διαθήκης Νεφθαλεὶμ ἧς² διέθετο³ ἐν καιρῷ ⌐τῆς ἐξόδου⌐⁴ αὐτοῦ ἐν ἔτει *ἑκατοστῷ καὶ τριακοστῷ⁵ τῆς⁶ ζωῆς αὐτοῦ⁷.   2. Συνελθόντων⁸ τῶν υἱῶν αὐτοῦ⁹ ἐν τῷ¹⁰ ἑβδόμῳ μηνί, μιᾷ¹¹ τοῦ μηνός¹², ἐποίησε δεῖπνον αὐτοῖς¹³.   3. *Καὶ τὸ πρωὶ¹⁴ μετὰ τὸ ἐξυπνισθῆναι¹⁵ αὐτὸν εἶπεν αὐτοῖς¹⁶

αὐτῶν.   ¹²h, d, A om.   ¹³bf. α, ae read ἐπιλάθονται, d ἐπιλησθήσονται. ¹⁴α, S¹. bd, A read as in margin. aef om.   ¹⁵Aᵇ*ᵈ om. next five words through hmt.   ¹⁶α, abe. d reads ἀπηλλοτριωθήσονται, f ἀλλοτριωθήσωνται. ¹⁷h, d om.   ¹⁸d reads κλήρους. S¹ om.   ¹⁹α. adef, S¹ read as α but prefix αὐτῶν καί. b reads αὐτῶν οὕτως καὶ γέγονεν. d adds ὅπερ καὶ γέγονεν ἐπ' αὐτούς. A is here wanting. Of the above readings the hardest is that of α, adef, S¹. If this verse was added in the Hebrew, we might regard עמם which is presupposed by τοῦ σπέρματος αὐτῶν as a corruption of זרע = καὶ διασπαρήσονται or מצאם = γέγονεν ἐπ' αὐτούς as in d. But the text is quite uncertain. At the close d adds τῷ θεῷ ἡμῶν εἴη δόξα εἰς αἰῶνας. Ἀμήν, f, S¹ Δὰν υἱὸς Ἰακὼβ ϛ υἱὸς Βάλλας ᾱ ἔζησεν ἔτη ρκε΄.

I. ¹Title. α in text. a reads Νεφθαλείμ, bef, Aᵃᶜᶠ δ. N. (+η΄ b) περὶ φυσικῆς ἀγαθότητος, d (conflate from α and abef) δ. N. υἱὸς Ἰακὼβ η΄ υἱὸς Βάλλας β περὶ φυσ. ἀγαθότητος, g δ. N. περὶ πλεονεξίας η΄. Aᵇ = Aᵃᶜᶠ (¶save that for φυσ. ἀγαθότητος it reads ἀγαθῶν ἤθους), Aᵇ* = δ. N. υἱοῦ Ἰακὼβ περὶ φυσικοῦ ἀγαθοῦ, Aᵈ δ. N. f adds Νεφθαλεὶμ ἑρμηνεύεται πλατυσμός. ²b, S¹ read ὦν, g ἦν.   ³d reads ἔθετο.   ⁴c. hi, adef read τῆς (d. om.) τελευτῆς, bg, S¹ τέλους. A om.   ⁵h, aef (save that f om. καί and ae read ρλ΄), A, S¹. c, g read ἑκατοστῷ which g trs. before ἔτει. b reads ἑκατοστῷ τριακοστῷ δευτέρῳ, d ρλβ.   ⁶ef om.   ⁷c om.   ⁸d adds γάρ. Aᵇ* adds a doublet συναχθέντων, or rather it= συνῆλθον συνήχθησαν οἱ υἱοὶ αὐτοῦ. For verses 2–3 and the first three words of 4, g reads ποιήσας δεῖπνον συνῆξε τοὺς υἱοὺς αὐτοῦ καὶ ἔφη πρὸς αὐτούς.   ⁹d adds πρὸς αὐτόν.   ¹⁰α, d. abef om.   ¹¹α, aef, A, S¹. d reads ἐν ἡμέρᾳ μιᾷ, b τετάρτῃ.   ¹²β-dg, A, S¹ add as in margin.   ¹³α. β-dg, A, S¹ read as in margin (save that b reads αὐτός for αὐτοῖς and A ꝯⱳⱳⱳ (= χαρά corrupt for ꝓⱳⱳⱳ = κώθωνα), d αὐτοῖς καὶ ηὐτρέπησε κοιτῶνα καὶ ἐκοιμήθησαν.   ¹⁴α (save that c reads τῷ), b (save that it trs. τὸ π. after αὐτόν. a reads

β, A, S¹ εὐλογῶν.

β, S¹ ἐκραται-ωσεν.

β, S¹ ἀποθανεῖ-ται.

β-g, A, S¹ ἐπὶ τῶν μηρῶν Ῥαχὴλ ἔτεκέ με.

β-g, S¹ ἐκλήθην.

ὅτι[17] Ἀποθνήσκω· καὶ[18] οὐκ ἐπίστευσαν[19] αὐτῷ. 4. Καὶ[20] *δοξάζων τὸν[21] Κύριον[22] *ἐκραταιώθη καὶ εἶπεν[23], ὅτι Μετὰ τὸ δεῖπνον τὸ χθὲς *ἀπέθανεν ἡ σάρξ μου[24]. 5. *Ἤρξατο δὲ[25] λέγειν[26]. Ἀκούσατε, τέκνα *μου, υἱοὶ Νεφθαλείμ, ἀκούσατε λόγους πατρός ὑμῶν[27]. 6. Ἐγὼ ἐγεννήθην ἀπὸ Βάλλας[28], ⸢καὶ⸣[29] ὅτι[30] ἐν πανουργίᾳ ἐποίησε[31] Ῥαχιήλ[32], καὶ ἔδωκεν *ἀντ᾽ αὐτῆς[33] Βάλλαν[34] *τῷ Ἰακώβ[35], καὶ *συλλαβοῦσα ἔτεκέ με ἐπὶ τῶν γονάτων τῆς Ῥαχιήλ[36], ⸢καὶ⸣[37] διὰ τοῦτο *ἐκάλεσε τὸ ὄνομά μου[38] Νεφθαλείμ. 7. *Ἠγάπησε γάρ[39] με Ῥαχιήλ[40] πάνυ[41], ὅτι ἐπὶ *τῶν γονάτων[42] αὐτῆς ἐγεννήθην⸣, καὶ ἔτι[43] ἀπαλὸν ὄντα *με κατεφίλει[44] λέγουσα· *Δοίη μοι ἀδελφόν[45] σου ἐκ τῆς κοιλίας μου κατά σε. 8. Ὅθεν καὶ ὅμοιός μου[46] ἦν ⸢κατὰ πάντα⸣[47] Ἰωσὴφ[48] κατὰ τὰς †εὐλογίας[49] Ῥαχιήλ.

β-g μηρῶν.   β-g ἴδοιμι ἀδελφόν.   bd, A εὐχάς.

καὶ, ef καὶ πρωί, d, A τῇ δὲ (καὶ τῇ A) ἐπαύριον. [15] d reads ἐξυπνίσαι. [16] d adds τεκνία μου, γνωστὸν ὑμῖν ἔστω. [17] d adds ἐγώ, A[b*] ἰδοὺ ἐγώ. [18] d adds πορεύομαι ὁδὸν πατέρων μου· οἱ δὲ ἀκούσαντες ταῦτα. [19] α, d, A[abe]. abef, A[b*d] read ἐπίστευον. [20] d reads ὁ δέ. [21] α. β-g, A, S¹ read as in margin. [22] A = θεόν. [23] α. β, S¹ read as in margin. A = ἐκραταιώθη ἐνθυμούμενος. [24] α. -β, S¹ read as in margin. A = ἀποθνήσκω. [25] α. β-dg read ἤρξ. οὖν, d, A καὶ ἤρξατο. [26] b adds τοῖς υἱοῖς αὐτοῦ, A αὐτοῖς. [27] α, β-dg. d, A read μου (A[b*cdf] om.) N. τοῦ πατρὸς ὑμῶν (d ἡμῶν). d adds ἐνωτίσασθε ὅσα ἐγὼ ἐντέλλομαι ὑμῖν. [28] a reads Βάλας. d adds Ἰακὼβ τῷ πατρί μου, υἱὸς ὄγδοος. For Βάλλας . . . to end of chapter g reads B. τῆς παιδίσκης Ῥ. ὄγδοος υἱὸς τῷ Ἰ. τῷ πατρί μου. [29] d, A om. [30] d reads ὅτε. [31] f adds ἡμᾶς. [32] α, a. bdef read Ῥαχήλ. A' om. next two lines to Ῥαχήλ (see margin) through hmt. [33] b reads ἀνθ᾽ ἑαυτῆς. d adds τὴν παιδίσκην. b add τήν. [34] A[b] adds τὴν μητέρα μου. [35] A[ab*cd] om. d adds διό. [36] α. β-g, A, S¹ read as in margin, save that d reads τὸν μηρόν and a Ῥαχιήλ, and A ἐτέχθην for ἔτεκέ με. A om. next nineteen words through hmt(?). [37] c. hi, β, S¹ om. [38] α. β-g, S¹ read as in margin. [39] α (save that c prefixes ὅτι). β-g, S¹ read καὶ ἠγάπησε. [40] α, a. β-ag read (+ ἡ e) Ῥαχήλ. [41] α. β-g, S¹ om. [42] α. β-dg read τῶν μηρῶν, d τὸν μηρόν. [43] b reads εἴδει. [44] α, d (save that hi read ἐπεφίλει). β-dfg, A read κατεφίλει με, f κατεφίλει. [45] So I have emended β-g, ἴδοιμι ἀδελφόν (ἀδελφούς e) in accordance with A which = δοίη μοι κύριος ἀδελφόν. α is very corrupt, ἴδει (ιδη hi) μοι ὁ ἀδελφός. ιδει or ιδη might be corrupt for εἴη, but this would not explain A. Our text = מי יתן or לי יתן. [46] α, d. β-dg read μοι. A = ἐγώ and adds τῷ before Ἰωσήφ. [47] α. β-g read ἐν πᾶσιν (πάσῃ d). [48] hi, b prefix ὁ. [49] α, aef = תהלת corrupt for תפלת = εὐχάς which bd, A read

9. Ἡ δὲ[50] μήτηρ μου *Βάλλα ὑπῆρχε[51] θυγάτηρ Ῥουθαίου[52], ἀδελφοῦ Δεβόρρας[53], τῆς τροφοῦ Ῥεβέκκας[54]· ἥτις[55] ἐν μιᾷ ἡμέρᾳ ἐτέχθη[56] ἐν ᾗ καὶ Ῥαχιήλ[57].   10. Ὁ δὲ Ῥουθαῖος[58] ἐκ τοῦ γένους ἦν[59] Ἀβραάμ, Χαλδαῖος, θεοσεβής, ἐλεύθερος καὶ εὐγενής.   11. *Καὶ αἰχμαλωτισθεὶς[60] ἠγοράσθη ὑπὸ Λαβάν· καὶ ἔδωκεν αὐτῷ Εὐνάν[61] τὴν παιδίσκην αὐτοῦ[62] εἰς[63] γυναῖκα, ἥτις[64] ἔτεκε θυγατέρα, καὶ ἐκάλεσεν *τὸ ὄνομα αὐτῆς[65] Ζέλφαν[66], *ἐπ' ὀνόματι[67] τῆς πόλεως[68] ἐν ᾗ αἰχμαλωτίσθη[69].   12. *Καὶ μετὰ τοῦτο ἔτεκεν τὴν Βάλλαν[70], λέγων·

α	bef, (A), S[1]	β-ad, A, S[2] καὶ ἐπειδὴ κοῦφος ἤμην.
†Καινοποιός μου ἡ θυγάτηρ·	*Καινόσπουδός μου ἡ θυγάτηρ[71]· *εὐθὺς γὰρ τεχθεῖσα ἐπιλαβομένη τοῦ μαζοῦ ἔσπευδεν θηλάζειν[72].	β-d A, S[2] ἔταξέ με. bdg, A ἀποστολὴν καὶ ἀγγελίαν.

II. *Ἐγὼ ἤμην κοῦφος[1] ⌜τοῖς ποσὶν⌝[2] *ὡς ἡ[3] ἔλαφος ⌜καὶ⌝[4] ἔταξέ με ὁ πατήρ μου ⌜Ἰακώβ⌝[5] εἰς πᾶσαν ἀγγελίαν[6], *καίγε ὡσεὶ[7] ἔλαφόν με ηὐλόγησεν[8].   2. Καθὼς[9] γὰρ *οἶδεν ὁ

margin.   [50] c adds ἡ.   [51] α, A. β-dg read ἐστὶ B.   d ἦν and trs. after Ῥουθ.   [52] h, a. c reads Ἡροθαίου. i Ῥουθέου. b Ῥωθέου. def, A Ῥουθέου.   [53] a reads Δεββόρας.   [54] c reads Ῥεβέκας. A[b] adds γυναικὸς Ἰσαάκ.   [55] c reads ὅτι. For ἥτις ... Ῥαχιήλ A reads ἥτις καὶ ἐν μιᾷ ἑσπέρᾳ ἐτέχθησαν αὐτὴ (ἡ μήτηρ Βάλλας A[b]) καὶ Ῥ.   [56] d reads ἐγενήθη.   [57] α, a. β-ag read Ῥαχήλ. b prefixes ἡ.   [58] α, a. b reads Ῥόθεος, def Ῥούθεος.   [59] ef om.   [60] d reads ὅστις αἰχμαλωτίσθη ἀπὸ τῆς ἑαυτοῦ πόλεως.   [61] hi, f. c reads Ἐνάν, a Ἐνί, be Αἰνάν, d Ἐδνάν. A = Ζεννάν. S om.   [62] d reads αὐτῆς.   [63] af om.   [64] c reads ὅτι.   [65] hi, β-b, A. c reads τὸ ὀν. αὐτοῦ, b αὐτήν.   [66] d reads Ζεβάλ.   [67] β-g. c reads κατ' ὀνόματι, hi ἐπωνομάσθη.   [68] α, f. β-f, A, S[1] read κώμης.   [69] b reads ἠχμαλωτεύθη.   [70] α. β-d read καὶ (b om.) ἑξῆς (ἐξ ἧς b) ἔτεκεν τὴν Βάλλαν (Λαβάν a but Βάλαν in second hand), d καὶ πάλιν ἔτεκεν αὐτῷ τὴν Β. ἐξ ἧς ἐγεννήθην ἐγώ. ad om. rest of verse.   [71] bf, S[1]. e καινος σπουδος μου ἡ θ. A = καινοσπουδασμὸς(?) ἡ θ. μου. α read as in margin. There was a play upon the name in the original. Βάλλαν, λέγων· καινόσπουδός μου ἡ θ. = בִּלְהָה לאמר נבהלה בתי.   [72] bef, S[1] (save that b, S[1] om. ἐπιλ. τοῦ μ.). A slightly corrupt = εὐθὺς γὰρ ἐτέχθη (τεχθεὶς A[a]) καὶ ἐπιλαβομένη τοῦ μαζοῦ μητρὸς αὐτῆς καὶ ἔσπευδε θηλάζειν. This clause is omitted by α, adg.

II. [1] c. hi read ἐγὼ δὲ εἰμὶ κοῦφος. β-ad, A, S[2] as in margin. a ἐπεὶ δὲ κ. ἤμην. d ἐγώ, τεκνία μου, ἐγενόμην κοῦφος.   [2] b adds μου.   [3] c, d. hi read ὡσεί, β-d ὡς.   [4] α, d. β-d, A, S[2] om.   [5] g, A om.   [6] α, aef. bdg, A read as in margin.   [7] c. Other MSS. καίγε ὡς. A = ὡς γάρ.   [8] ci, afg. h, bd read εὐλ.   [9] For verses 2-8 g reads καὶ ἐποίουν τὰς ἐντολὰς αὐτοῦ κατὰ τάξιν, καὶ

Margin:
b (def?),
A κτίσις
ὑψίστου.
bd (A?)
ἄρχεται.
bd, A
πᾶν
πλάσμα.
bdef, A
ὡς.
bdef, A
αὐτοῖ;
καὶ ὡς *ὁ
νοῦς⁴¹
αὐτοῦ,
οὕτω⁴²
καὶ *ἡ

κεραμεὺς¹⁰ τὸ σκεῦος πόσον χωρεῖ, καὶ πρὸς αὐτὸ¹¹ φέρει τὸν¹²
πηλόν, οὕτω¹³ καὶ ὁ Κύριος πρὸς ὁμοίωσιν τοῦ πνεύματος¹⁴
ποιεῖ¹⁵ τὸ σῶμα, καὶ πρὸς τὴν δύναμιν τοῦ σώματος¹⁶ *τὸ
πνεῦμα ἐπιτίθησιν¹⁷. 3. Καὶ¹⁸ οὐκ *ἔστιν ἐνλεῖπον¹⁹ *ἐν
ἐκ τοῦ ἑνὸς²⁰ *τρίτον τριχός²¹· *σταθμῷ γὰρ καὶ μέτρῳ²²
καὶ κανόνι πᾶσα ⌜ἡ⌝²³ *κτίσις ἐγένετο²⁴. 4. Καὶ καθὼς²⁵
οἶδεν²⁶ ὁ κεραμεὺς ἑνὸς ἑκάστου τὴν χρῆσιν †ὡς²⁷ ἱκανή²⁸,
οὕτω²⁹ καὶ ὁ Κύριος οἶδε τὸ σῶμα, ἕως τίνος διαρκέσει ἐν *τῷ
ἀγαθῷ³⁰, καὶ πότε ἔρχεται³¹ *ἐν κακῷ³². 5. Ὅτι οὐκ ἔστι
πλάσμα³³ καὶ πᾶσα ἔννοια ἣν ⌜οὐκ⌝ ἔγνω Κύριος· *πάντα γὰρ³⁴
ἄνθρωπον³⁵ ἔκτισεν κατ' εἰκόνα ἑαυτοῦ³⁶. 6. *Ὡς γὰρ³⁷ ἡ
ἰσχὺς αὐτοῦ³⁸, οὕτω³⁹ καὶ τὸ ἔργον αὐτοῦ⁴⁰· ὡς⁴⁶ *ὁ ὀφθαλμὸς⁴⁷
αὐτοῦ, οὕτως⁴⁸ καὶ †ὁ ὕπνος αὐτοῦ· ὡς⁴⁹ ἡ ψυχὴ αὐτοῦ,

τέχνη⁴³ αὐτοῦ· ⌜καὶ ὡς ἡ προαίρεσις⁴⁴ αὐτοῦ, οὕτω⁴² καὶ ἡ πρᾶξις
αὐτοῦ· ὡς⁴⁵ ἡ καρδία αὐτοῦ, οὕτω⁴² καὶ τὸ στόμα αὐτοῦ⌝.

ἕτερα τινὰ πολλὰ φυσιόγνωμικά. ¹⁰α, A. β read ὁ κ. οἶδεν. ¹¹h, aef. c, d read αὐτῷ, b αὐτόν. The clause πρὸς αὐτῷ ... πηλόν is given corruptly and unintelligibly in A αὐτὸ μᾶλλον ἢ φέρει τὸ ἀγαθόν(?). ¹²b om. ¹³α, bd. aef read οὕτως. ¹⁴d reads σώματος. ¹⁵d adds καί. ¹⁶A = πνεύματος. ¹⁷α. β–dg read τὸ πν. ἐντίθησι, d τίθησι τὸ πνεῦμα. A = τίθησι τὸ σῶμα (A^{b*d} τὴν ὑπόστασιν or τὸν ἄνθρωπον). ¹⁸d om. ¹⁹c, e (save that c read ἐνλείπων), a read ἐ. ἐλλεῖπον, bd ἐ. λοιπόν, f ἐ. ἐλλείπων, hi(?) ποιεῖ τὸ σῶμα (repeated from ver. 2). ²⁰d reads αὐτοῦ αἰῶνος. a om. rest of verse together with verses 3–7, and substitutes διὰ τοῦτο, τέκνα μου, ἔστω πάντα τὰ ἔργα ὑμῶν ἐν τάξει εἰς ἀγαθὸν ἐν φόβῳ θεοῦ, καὶ μηδὲν ἄτακτον ποιεῖτε ἐν καταφρονήσει μηδὲ ἔξω καιροῦ αὐτοῦ which is really ver. 9 of this chapter. ²¹d reads τριστίχῳ γάρ. A = βραχὺ μέρος τριχός. ²²α, β–de. d reads σταθμῷ καὶ μέτρῳ, e σταθμοῦ γ. κ. μέτρου, A μέτρῳ γ. κ. σταθμῷ. ²³α. β, A om. ²⁴α. b, A = κ. ὑψίστου, def κ. ὑψοῦται. Possibly נכונה ('was established') stood originally in the text, subsequently corrupted into הורמה = ὑψοῦται. ²⁵α. bef read καθάπερ. d καθώσπερ. ²⁶d om. A = πρὸς ὁμοίωσιν τοῦ πνεύματος ποιεῖ (repeated from ver. 2). ²⁷= מה which should here be rendered τί. ²⁸α, ef. b read ἱκανεῖ, d ἱκανεῖν. ²⁹α, bdf. e reads οὕτως. ³⁰α. bef read ἀγαθῷ, d ἀγαθοῖς. ³¹α, ef. bd read as in margin, and apparently rightly, A = ἀρχόμενον ποιεῖ(?). ³²A = τὸ κακόν. ³³α, ef. bd, A read as in margin. ³⁴A = καὶ πάντα. ³⁵f om. ³⁶df read αὐτοῦ. ³⁷α. bdef, A read as in margin. ³⁸d reads τοῦ ἀνθρώπου. ³⁹hi, ef read οὕτως. ⁴⁰After αὐτοῦ α om. the clauses found in the margin, which apparently belong to the original. For text of S² which though slightly corrupt and defective supports bdef, A, see Appendix. ⁴¹bef, A. d reads ἡ προαίρεσις. ⁴²bd. ef read οὕτως. ⁴³def, A. b reads τὸ ἔργον. ⁴⁴bef. d reads τέχνη. ⁴⁵bef. d reads καὶ ὡς. ⁴⁶α, bef. d, A read καὶ ὡς. ⁴⁷d reads οἱ ὀφθαλμοί. ⁴⁸α, ef. bd read οὕτω.

οὕτως⁴⁸ καὶ ὁ λόγος αὐτοῦ⁵⁰, ἢ ἐν νόμῳ Κυρίου, ἢ ἐν νόμῳ⁵¹
τοῦ⁵² Βελίαρ.   7. Καὶ ὡς⁵³ κεχώρισται ἀνάμεσον *τοῦ
φωτὸς καὶ ἀνάμεσον τοῦ σκότους⁵⁴ *ὁράσεώς τε καὶ ἀκοῆς⁵⁵,
οὕτως⁵⁶ κεχώρισται ἀνάμεσον ἀνδρὸς καὶ *ἀνδρός, καὶ ἀνάμεσον
γυναικὸς καὶ⁵⁷ γυναικός⁵⁸, καὶ οὐκ ἔστιν εἰπεῖν ὅτι †*ἐν τῷ
ἑνὶ τοῖς προσώποις ἡττόμενον ἦν †⁵⁹.

Right margin:

α ἔργοις.

bdef, A, S φωτὸς καὶ σκότους.

α ἀνάμεσον.

Aᵇ οὐκ ἔστιν ὅμοιος εἰς τῷ ἑνὶ προσώποις ἢ νοΐ.

b, A καὶ τρίχας πρὸς δόξαν.

	OTHIOTH OF "R. AKIBA" (ed. Jellinek, *Bet ha-Midrasch*, III. 42-43). (The underlined phrases are found in ver. 8.)
8. *Πάντα ⌈γὰρ⌉⁶⁰ ἐν τάξει ἐποίησεν ὁ Θεὸς καλά· τὰς πέντε αἰσθήσεις ἐν τῇ κεφαλῇ *καὶ τὸν τράχηλον συνάψας τῇ κεφαλῇ⁶¹, *προσθεὶς αὐτῇ καὶ τρίχας εἰς εὐπρέπειαν καὶ δόξαν⁶²· εἶτα⁶³ καρδίαν *εἰς φρόνησιν⁶⁴, κοιλίαν εἰς †διάκρισιν⁶⁵, *στόμαχον εἰς...⁶⁶	לא ברכת ראש אלא לכבוד.... עינים אלא לראות... אזנים אלא לשמוע... וחוטם להריח לחיים לה טעים טעמי מאכל שנים לשוחקות ושט להבליע קנה למשוך ולהוציא לב להבין בינה הכליות ליעץ ריאה

⁴⁸A = καὶ ὡς.   ⁵⁰d adds καὶ πορεύεται εἰς ἕκαστος.   ⁵¹α, bdef. A
reads ἔργοις perhaps rightly. Cf. T. Levi, xix. 1.   ⁵²b om.   ⁵³β−d, A.
d reads ὥσπερ. α ὡς οὐ, hi οὐ.   ⁵⁴α. bdef, A, S read as in margin, save
that d adds ἀνάμεσον before σκότους.   ⁵⁵hi, bef (save that bef om. τε).
c reads καὶ ἀκοῆς. A = καὶ ἀκοῆς καὶ ὁράσεως. d om.   ⁵⁶α, ef. bd
read οὕτω. α adds οὐ.   ⁵⁷bdef, A, S¹. α read as in margin. S² om.
⁵⁸d adds καὶ πάντα ἐκ προαιρέσεως γίνεται ἀμφοτέρων.   ⁵⁹α (save that h read
ἡτούμενος, i ἡτούμεος). bef support text, save that for ἡττ. ἦν b read ἢ τῶν
ὁμοίων, e ἡττῶν ἡττουν ὅμοιον, f ἧττον ἤγουν ὅμοιον. d reads ἐν τῷ ἑνί(i) αὐτοῖς
προσώποις ἧττον ἐποίησεν ἢ ἔλαττον. Aᵃᵇ*ᶜᵈᵉ = τῷ ἑνὶ ἑνὶ ἢ προσώποις ἢ νοΐ ὅμοιος.
For οὐκ ἔστιν... ἦν Aᵇ reads οὐκ ἔστι ὅμοιος εἰς τῷ ἑνὶ προσώποις ἢ νοΐ. This
is defective but right apparently so far as it goes, and in Aᵃᵇ*ᶜᵈ we are
accordingly to read τῷ ἑνὶ εἰς.   ⁶⁰d reads τὰ πάντα, f πάντα.   ⁶¹abdef
(save that df add ἐν before τῇ). b, A read καὶ τὸν τράχηλον συνάπτει (A
συνῆπτε) τῇ κ. α om. through hmt. a add καί.   ⁶²α, aef (save that ef
read πρός for εἰς). d reads προσθεὶς αὐτῷ καὶ τρίχας πρὸς δόξ. καὶ εὐπρ. b, A
read as in margin, S¹ καὶ τρίχας τῆς κεφαλῆς πρὸς εὐπρ. κ. δόξαν.   ⁶³A = καί.
⁶⁴A = εἰς εὐφροσύνην, καί.   ⁶⁵Probably corrupt for διαχώρησιν. Thus
κοιλίαν εἰς διαχώρησιν would = כרם לריעה which is found in R. Akiba's
list of the senses and faculties: see Jellinek's *Bet ha-Midrasch*, III. 42.
d adds τροφῆς.   ⁶⁶d. All other MSS. and A, S¹ read στομάχου. Supply

†κάλαμον[67] πρὸς †ὑγείαν[68], ἧπαρ[69] πρὸς θυμόν, χολὴν πρὸς πικρίαν, ⌐καὶ⌐[70] *σπλῆνα πρὸς γέλωτα[71], νεφροὺς ⌐εἰς πανουρ-γίαν[72], ψύας[73]⌐ εἰς δύναμιν, *†πλευρὰν εἰς τὸ καθεύδειν†[74], ὀσφὺν[75] εἰς ἰσχύν, καὶ τὰ ἐξῆς.

לשאוב כבד לכעוס מרה לזרוק
מחול לשחוק כרס לריעה קורקבן
להטחינה קיבה לשינה

β-g, S¹ θήκην.
β-ad, S¹ ἀκοῦ-σαι, οὐ δύναται.
β-g, S¹ δυνή-σεσθε ποιεῖν.

9. Οὕτως[76] ⌐οὖν⌐ *ἔστωσαν, τέκνα μου, πάντα τὰ ἔργα ὑμῶν ἐν τάξει εἰς ἀγαθόν[77] ἐν φόβῳ Θεοῦ, καὶ μηδὲν ἄτακτον ποιήσητε[78] ἐν καταφρονήσει, μηδὲ[79] ἔξω[80] *καιροῦ αὐτοῦ[81]. 10. *Ὅτι ἐὰν εἴπῃς τῷ ὀφθαλμῷ, Ἄκουε, οὐ δυνήσεται.[82]

ἀλεσμόν. Thus στόμαχον εἰς ἀλεσμόν = להטחינה קורקבן the phrase which occurs immediately after כרס לריעה in R. Akiba's list of the senses. See note 65. [67] α, ab, S². d reads κολασμόν, e καὶ λεμόν, f καὶ λαιμόν. A = καλάμους (+ τὸν ἀνώτερον καὶ τὸν κατώτερον A[b]), S¹ = τὸ σῶμα καὶ κοιλίαν. κάλαμον = קנה which should here have been rendered λάρυγγα. [68] πρὸς ὑγείαν = לשלום corrupt for למשוך as we see from R. Akiba's list קנה למשוך. Hence we should read here πρὸς εἰσπνοήν. [69] α reads ὕπαρ. [70] df, A om. [71] c (save that it reads σπλῆναν). h, A read σπλῆνας (d σπλῆναν) εἰς γέλωτα, abef, S¹ εἰς γέλωτα σπλῆνα (e σπλῆναν, f σπλίνα). [72] = עָרְמָה 'prudence' or עֵצָה 'counsel.' [73] bdf. α reads ψύας, a ψόας, e ψοίας. Text = כסלים. [74] α. β-g, S¹ read πλευρὰν (πλευράς bd, S¹) εἰς θήκην. A = εἰς τὸ τιθέναι ὀσφῦς. Printed Arm. Text here wrongly trs. ὀσφῦς and πλευράς. Here πλευράς seems secondary to πλευράν, since the converse change is unlikely. But πλευράν gives no good sense either in the α or the β text. It is therefore probably corrupt for πλεύμονα. Accordingly α = πλεύμονα εἰς τὸ καθεύδειν = ריאה לשכוב, which, on turning to Akiba's first list, we see is corrupt for ריאה לשאוב, for that phrase is found there, and different forms of it in the Akiba's second list, Berakh. 61ᵃ and Hebrew T. Napth. εἰς τὸ τιθέναι in A points to לשום or להושיב. [75] d reads ὀσφῦς, A πλευράς. [76] Verse 8 is here omitted by a, having been trs. by that MS. before ver. 7. See note 20. [77] hi. c reads τέκνα μου, ἔστωσαν πάντα ὑμῶν ἐν τάξει εἰς ἀγαθόν. g reads τέκνα μου, καὶ ὑμεῖς πάντα τὰ ἔργα ὑμῶν ἐν τάξει ποιεῖτε τὰ ἀγαθά, adef, A (+ διὰ τοῦτο a) τέκνα μου, ἔστω πάντα τὰ ἔργα ὑμῶν ἐν τάξει εἰς ἀγαθόν (d, A ἀγαθὰ καί), b, S¹ τέκνα μου, ἐν τ. ἔστε εἰς ἀγαθά. [78] α. b-e read ποιεῖτε, e ποιῆτε. A adds καί. [79] hi read μή. [80] d adds τοῦ. [81] A = καιρῶν ὑμῶν, but ձերոց (= ὑμῶν) is corrupt for իւրոց (= αὐτοῦ). [82] α, A. β-ad, S¹ support text (save that for Ἄκουε, οὐ δυν. they read as in margin). a reads οὐ δύναται οὖν ἐὰν εἴπῃς τῷ ὀφ. ἀκοῦσαι, d ὅτι ὥσπερ εἴπῃς τῷ ὀφ. ῥήματα, ἀκοῦσαι οὐ δύναται χωρὶς τὸ οὖς. [83] A = σκότος.

οὕτως οὐδὲ *ἐν σκότει[83] *ὄντες δύνασθε ποιεῖν[84] ἔργα[85] c, ef καινοῖς. df, A^b
φωτός.
III. Μὴ οὖν σπουδάζετε[1] *ἐν πλεονεξίᾳ[2] *διαφθεῖραι τὰς σκοπῶν-τες.
πράξεις ὑμῶν[3], ἢ ἐν *λόγοις κενοῖς ἀπατᾶν[4] τὰς ψυχᾶς ὑμῶν, β–g, A^ab
ὅτι[5] σιωπῶντες[6] ἐν *καθαρότητι καρδίας[7] συνήσετε[8] τὸ θέλημα διαβόλου.
τοῦ Θεοῦ[9] κρατεῖν[10], καὶ ἀπορρίπτειν τὸ θέλημα τοῦ Βελίαρ[11]. β, S¹ ἀλ-λοιοῦσι.
2. Ὁ[12] ἥλιος καὶ ἡ[12] σελήνη καὶ οἱ[12] ἀστέρες οὐ †καλύψουσι[13] β, S¹
τὴν[14] τάξιν αὐτῶν· οὕτω[15] καὶ ὑμεῖς μὴ ἀλλοιώσητε[16] νόμον ἐπηκο-λούθη-
Θεοῦ[17] ἐν ἀταξίᾳ τῶν[18] πράξεων ὑμῶν[19].   3. Ἔθνη πλα- σαν λί-θοις καὶ
νηθέντα *καὶ ἀφέντα Κύριον[20] ἠλλοίωσαν[21] τὴν[22] τάξιν αὐτῶν, ξύλοις
καὶ *ὑπήκουσαν ξύλοις καὶ λίθοις[23], πνεύμασι[24] πλάνης.   4. ἐξακο-λουθή-
Ὑμεῖς δὲ *μὴ οὕτως[25], τέκνα μου, γινώσκοντες[26] ἐν τῷ[27] σαντες.

[84] α. β–g, S¹ read as in margin of page 148 (save that for ποιεῖν bd read ποιῆσαι), g ποιήσητε. A = δύναται ποιεῖν.   [85] d reads ἔργον.

III. [1] d reads σπεύδετε.   [2] A trs. after διαφθεῖραι.   [3] h, β (save that h reads ἡμῶν), S¹. c reads διαφθαρῆναι ὑμῶν τὰς πράξεις. A = διαφθεῖραι γῆν ἐν ταῖς πράξεσι ὑμῶν. dg om. next eight words through hmt.   [4] c, abef, A, S¹ (save that c, ef read καινοῖς for κενοῖς). hi read λόγῳ καὶ κενοῖς ἀτύποις ἀπατῶντες.   [5] d reads ἀλλά.   [6] α, abeg, S. df, A^b read σκοπῶντες, A^ab*cde ὑπήκοοι but this text is merely a corruption of A^b.   [7] g, A read καθαρᾷ καρδίᾳ.   [8] α, aeg, A. b, S¹ read δυνήσετε, d ζητήσατε.   [9] A^b = κυρίου θεοῦ.   [10] h, β–g, S. c read κρατέως, i κραταίως, g, A ποιεῖν.   [11] α, d. β–d, A^ab read διαβόλου. A^b*cde = Σατανᾶ. hi add καθώς.   [12] α. β om.   [13] So α which = ישבי (i.e. יֹבַסּו) corrupt for ישׁנּו = ἀλλοιοῦσι which is read by β, S¹. A = κωλύουσιν but խառնանեն is corrupt for փոխեն = ἀλλοιοῦσι. See note 16 where A^b*cde give rightly the latter verb.   [14] α, d. β–d om.   [15] c, d. Other MSS. οὕτως.   [16] c, b read ἀλλοιώσετε, A^ab = κωλύσητε—the same corruption as noticed in note 13. A^b*cde = ἀλλοιώσητε.   [17] A^c = κυρίου. c adds καί.   [18] α. β om.   [19] d reads ἡμῶν.   [20] d reads ἀπὸ κυρίου. A = ἀφῆκαν κύριον. b adds τὸν before κύριον.   [21] d reads ἠλλοίωσε, g ἠλλοιώθησαν.   [22] c. g reads κατὰ τήν. hi, β–g om.   [23] α (save that hi read λίθοις καὶ ξύλοις). β, A^ab*cde, S¹ read as in margin, save that d reads ἐπηκολούθησε, and for ξύλοις f reads ξύλα, and for ἐξακολουθήσαντες A^ab*cde read καὶ ἐξακολουθεῖν. A^b reads as A^ab*cde but adds λατρείας after ξύλοις. The text of β, A, S¹ is unsatisfactory. Possibly neither text is original, and we should read ὑπήκουσαν ξύλοις καὶ λίθοις ἐξακολουθήσαντες.   [24] A^bb*cde = πνεύματι, A^a προσώποις.   [25] d reads οὕτως μὴ ποιεῖτε.   [26] α. β–dg, S¹ read γνόντες, dg, A (+ ἀλλά) γνῶτε. For ἐν τῷ στερεώ-ματι . . . πάντα d reads ἐκ τῶν δημιουργημάτων ἀπὸ στερεώματος καὶ ἀπὸ γῆς καὶ θαλάσσης καὶ ἀπὸ πάντων τὸν Κύριον δημιουργήσαντα καὶ ποιήσαντα, and A στερέωμα οὐρανοῦ καὶ θαλάσσης καὶ ἐν πᾶσι τοῖς δημιουργήμασιν (A^b*cd

<table>
<tr><td>c ὅτι
ἐνήλλα-
ξαν.
c, d
αὐτῶν.</td><td>στερεώματι, ἐν γῇ καὶ[28] ἐν[29] θαλάττῃ, καὶ[28] ἐν[30] πᾶσι τοῖς δημιουργήμασι *Κύριον τὸν[31] ποιήσαντα πάντα[32], ἵνα μὴ γένησθε[33] ὡς Σόδομα, ἥτις[34] ἐνήλλαξε[35] τάξιν φύσεως αὐτῆς[36]. 5. Ὁμοίως[37] δὲ[38] καὶ[39] οἱ Ἐγρήγοροι[40] ἐνήλλαξαν τάξιν φύσεως αὐτῶν, οὓς[41] κατηράσατο[42] Κύριος ἐπὶ τοῦ κατακλυσμοῦ[43], δι' οὓς[44] *ἀπὸ κατοικησίας καὶ ἄκαρπον τάξας τὴν γῆν [ἀοίκητον][45].</td></tr>
<tr><td>bdg, A, S¹
ἀνέγνων.
β, A, S¹
κατὰ
πᾶσαν.</td><td>IV. Ταῦτα[1] λέγω ὑμῖν[2], τέκνα μου, ὅτι ἔγνων[3] ἐν τῇ[4] γραφῇ[5] Ἐνώχ, ὅτι καίγε[6] ὑμεῖς ἀποστήσεσθε ἀπὸ Κυρίου[7], πορευόμενοι κατὰ πᾶσαν ἀνομίαν[8] ἐθνῶν[9], καὶ ποιήσετε[10] πᾶσαν πονηρίαν[11] Σοδόμων[12]. 2. Καὶ ἐπάξει Κύριος ὑμῖν αἰχμα-</td></tr>
</table>

πάντα τὰ δημιουργήματα). Here երկնի (= οὐρανοῦ) is corrupt for երկրի = γῆς. Although the cases of the text are not in order, A clearly goes back to α, β. [27] α. β om. [28] g om. [29] c, β–df. hi, f om. See text of d and A under note 26. [30] c, g. Other MSS. om. [31] d reads τὸν Κύριον δημιουργήσαντα καί. A = τὸν (A^ab om.) Κύριον τόν. [32] α, g. b, A, S read ταῦτα πάντα. aef τὰ πάντα. d om. [33] abeg. c reads γήνεσθε. hi, f γίνεσθαι. d γίνεσθε. [34] hi, β–ad, A. c reads ὅτι. d οἵτινες. a om. together with next six words. [35] hi, befg. c reads as in margin. d ἤλλαξαν. [36] hi, β–d, A, S¹. c, d read as in margin. d adds οὓς καὶ ἐτέφρωσε Κύριος. [37] f reads ὅμως. [38] c, d om. [39] a adds ὡς. For the rest of the verse d reads ἐπὶ τοῦ κατακλυσμοῦ οὓς κατηράσατο ὁ Κύριος. [40] α, aefg. b read ἐγρήγορες. a om. next four words. [41] be add καί. [42] hi read κατηργήσατο. [43] a om. rest of verse. [44] α, ef. bg, A read δι' αὐτούς, S¹ ἕνεκα γὰρ αὐτῶν ζωῆς. [45] α (save for ἀποκατοικήσας of α I read ἀπὸ κατοικησίας as in bdefg. c reads δείξας for τάξας which is found in hi, bdefg). ἀπὸ κατοικησίας = מבלי־יושב. Hence ἀοίκητον (before which α adds καί) is bracketed as a dittography. bdefg read as in text, save that for ἀπὸ κατοικησίας καί g reads ἀπό τε οἰκίας ἀπό τε and bdefg read καρπῶν for ἄκαρπον). A = εἰς (A^ss om.) ἄλλην φύσιν καρπῶν τάξας καὶ τὴν ἀνόητον (A^b*cde προσποιητόν). But բնութիւն (= φύσιν) is corrupt for բնակութիւն = κατοικησίαν and առնականան (= προσποιητόν) and առնականան (= ἀνόητον) are corrupt for անբնակ = ἀοίκητον. Thus A does not imply a text different from G. S¹ = ἐκέλευσεν εἶναι κατακλυσμόν.

IV. [1] d adds δέ. [2] bg, S¹ om. [3] α, aef. bdg, A, S¹ read as in margin. [4] c, A. hi, β, S om. [5] bg, A add ἁγίᾳ. [6] α, def. b, S read καίγε καί. g γε καί. A = καί. [7] d reads Θεοῦ. S¹ = γραφῆς τοῦ νόμου τοῦ Κυρίου. [8] bd read πονηρίαν against all other MSS. and A, S. [9] hi om. rest of verse. A^b*d om. next four words. [10] β, A, S¹ add κατά. [11] bd read ἀνομίαν against all other MSS. and A, S. [12] g reads δαιμόνων, A^abc (Arm. printed Text) ἐθνῶν but A^b*de give Σοδόμων. [13] d, A, S om. [14] d reads

λωσίαν, καὶ δουλεύσετε ⌈ἐκεῖ⌉[13] *τοῖς ἐχθροῖς[14] ὑμῶν, καὶ πάσῃ κακώσει[15] καὶ θλίψει †συναναστραφήσεσθε[16], ἕως ἀναλώσει[17] Κύριος πάντας ὑμᾶς. 3. Καὶ σμικρυνθέντες[18] ἐπιστρέψετε[19] καὶ ἐπιγνώσεσθε Κύριον τὸν Θεὸν ὑμῶν[20] καὶ ἐπιστρέψει ὑμᾶς εἰς τὴν γῆν ὑμῶν κατὰ[21] τὸ πολὺ αὐτοῦ ἔλεος[22]. 4. Καὶ ἔσται ὅταν[23] *ἐξέλθωσιν εἰς τὴν γῆν τῶν[24] πατέρων αὐτῶν, πάλιν ἐπιλήσονται[25] τοῦ[26] Κυρίου καὶ ἀσεβήσουσιν[27]. 5. Καὶ διασπερεῖ[28] αὐτοὺς Κύριος[29] ἐπὶ πρόσωπον[30] πάσης τῆς γῆς, *ἄχρις οὗ ἔλθῃ[31] *τὸ σπλάγχνον Κυρίου[32], ἄνθρωπος *ποιῶν δικαιοσύνην καὶ ποιῶν ἔλεος[33] εἰς πάντας τοὺς *μακρὰν καὶ τοὺς ἐγγύς[34].

V. Ἐν γὰρ *τῷ τεσσαρακοστῷ ἔτει τῆς[1] ζωῆς μου, εἶδον[2] *⌈ὅραμα⌉ ἐν τῷ ὄρει τοῦ Ἐλαιῶνος[3] κατὰ ἀνατολὰς Ἱερουσαλήμ, ὅτι[4] ὁ ἥλιος καὶ ἡ σελήνη ἔστηκαν[5]. 2. Καὶ ἰδοὺ Ἰσαὰκ[6] ὁ πατὴρ *τοῦ πατρός[7] μου[8] ἔλεγεν[9] ἡμῖν· Προσδραμόντες

Margin:

bg, S †συγκαλυφθήσεσθε.

A συγκαμφθήσεσθε(?).

β, A, S¹ μετὰ τὸ ὀλιγωθῆναι ὑμᾶς καὶ σμικρυνθῆναι.

β–α,

A, S¹ ἥξουσιν ἐν γῇ.

β–d,

A, S¹

ἔτει τεσσαρακοστῷ.   β–dg, S¹ λέγει.

τοὺς ἐχθρούς.   [15] hi read κακίᾳ.   [16] α, adef. bg read συγκαλυφθήσεσθε. A ταπεινωθήσεσθε or συγκαμφθήσεσθε. Original doubtful. If συναναστραφήσεσθε = 'ye shall wrestle with' (cf. Gen. xxx. 8), it may = תֵּהָפְכוּ which is unlikely in itself and may be a corruption of תִּשָּׁעֵלוּ = ταπεινωθήσεσθε (A), or συγκαμφθήσεσθε. Then συγκαλυφθήσεσθε would be a corruption of συγκαμφθήσεσθε. These Greek words are confused in LXX of 2 Kings iv. 35; Ps. lxix. 10, 23. If, on the other hand, συναναστραφήσεσθε = תִּשְׁבוּ, the latter may be corrupt for תִּכָּנְעוּ = ταπεινωθήσεσθε, and συγκαλυφθήσεσθε = תִּכָּסוּ a corruption of תִּכָּנְעוּ.   [17] b reads ἂν ἀναλώσῃ. A^{b*cde} = ἀναγνώσει but A^{ab} support text.   [18] α. β, A, S¹ read as in margin (save that g om. ὀλιγωθ. ὑμᾶς καί).   [19] α, bg. ae read ἐπιστρέψεσθε. df ἐπιστρέψητε.   [20] c reads ἡμῶν and om. next seven words through hmt.   [21] hi read διά. g om.   [22] a om. rest of chapter.   [23] h reads ὅτι.   [24] α. bdefg, A, S¹ read as in margin (save that g reads ἔλθωσιν).   [25] dg, A. α, e read ἐπιλάθονται. bf ἐπιλάθωνται.   [26] α. β om.   [27] A^{b*cde} = ὑπερήφανοι ἔσονται, but the corruption is native to these MSS. A^{ab} = text.   [28] α, A. be, S¹ read διασπείρει. d διασπαρεῖ. f διασπαριεῖ.   [29] d om. hi prefix ὁ.   [30] α, g. bdef read προσώπου. For πρόσωπον πάσης A reads πᾶν τὸ πρόσωπον.   [31] b reads ἄχρι τοῦ ἐλθεῖν.   [32] A^{ab} = Κύριος. A^{b*cde} Κύριος σπλάγχνῳ.   [33] A reads ποιῶν ἐλ. καὶ δικαιοσύνην.   [34] d reads ἐγγὺς καὶ τοὺς μακράν.

V. [1] α, d. β–d, A, S¹ read as in margin.   [2] def read ἴδον. a adds ἐν ὀνείρῳ ὅτι.   [3] α, A (save that A om. ὅραμα). abeg, S¹ read ἐν ὄρεσιν ἐλαίου (ae ἐλαιῶν, g ἰλεῶν). df ἐν ὁράσει (+ μου d) ἔλεον.   [4] a om.   [5] d reads ἵσταντο ἐνώπιον ὑμῶν. g ἕστηκεν. A adds καὶ πάντες (+ ἡμεῖς A^b) προσεδράμομεν.   [6] g reads Ἰακώβ.   [7] g om.   [8] A = ἡμῶν.   [9] α, A.

β, S[1]
πάντες
ὁμοῦ ἐπε-
δράμο-
μεν.
β, A, S[1]
ἀλλή-
λοις Λευί.
β, S[1]
φθάσας
γὰρ 'I.
ἔλαβεν.
A ἐν
παρα-
δείσῳ.
β Πέρ-
σαι, 'Ελι-
μαῖοι, Γε-
λαχαῖοι
(aef Χελ-
καῖοι).

*κρατήσατε ἕκαστος[10] κατὰ δύναμιν[11], ⸢καὶ *τοῦ πιάσαντος[12] ἔσται ὁ ἥλιος καὶ ἡ σελήνη⸣. 3. Καὶ[13] *ἐδράμομεν πάντες ὁμοῦ[14] ⸢καὶ⸣[15] ὁ[16] Λευὶ[17] ἐκράτησε τὸν ἥλιον *καὶ ὁ 'Ιούδας φθάσας ἐπίασε τὴν σελήνην[18], καὶ ὑψώθησαν ἀμφότεροι σὺν αὐτοῖς[19]. 4. Καὶ ὄντος[20] τοῦ Λευὶ *ὡς ὁ ἥλιος[21], ⸢ἰδοὺ⸣[22] νέος[23] *τις ἐπιδίδωσιν[24] αὐτῷ βαΐα φοινίκων δώδεκα, καὶ 'Ιούδας *ἐγένετο λαμπρὸς[25] ὡς *ἡ σελήνη[26], καὶ *ἦσαν ὑπὸ τοὺς πόδας αὐτῶν[27] δώδεκα ἀκτῖνες[28]. [5. Καὶ προσδραμόντες *οἱ δύο ὅτε[29] Λευὶ[30] καὶ 'Ιούδας[31] ἐκράτησαν αὐτούς[32]].

6. Καὶ ἰδοὺ ταῦρος ἐπὶ τῆς γῆς, ἔχων δύο[33] κέρατα μεγάλα, καὶ πτέρυγας[34] ἀετοῦ ἐπὶ[35] νώτου αὐτοῦ· καὶ θέλοντες ἡμεῖς[36] πιάσαι[37] αὐτόν, οὐκ ἠδυνήθημεν. 7. *ἐλθὼν δὲ 'Ιωσὴφ κατέλαβεν[38] αὐτόν, καὶ συνανῆλθεν[39] αὐτῷ εἰς τὸ[40] ὕψος. 8. Καὶ εἶδον *ὅτι ἤμην παρεκεῖ[41], καὶ ἰδοὺ γραφὴ *ἁγία ὤφθη ἡμῖν[42], λέγουσα[43]. 'Ασσύριοι[44], Μῆδοι[45], Πέρσαι[46],

---

β–dg, S[1] read as in margin. dg λέγων. [10]g reads ἕκαστος κρατῆσαι. c adds τόν, h τά. [11]A adds αὐτοῦ. [12]c, β–ag, S. hi read τοῦτο ποιήσαντος. a τοῦ κρατήσαντος. g om. [13]d adds ἅμα τῷ λόγῳ. [14]α. β, S[1] read as in margin. A = ἐν τῷ ἐπιτρέχειν ἡμᾶς. [15]d adds προσδραμών. [16]a om. [17]e reads Λευίς. [18]c, β (save that adf om. ὁ, and for ἐπίασε a reads ἐκράτησε, and g om. καὶ ὁ and trs. φθ. after ἐπίασε), A[20]. hi read τὴν δὲ σελήνην ὁ 'I. φθ. ἐπίασεν. A[b] = καὶ 'I. ἔφθασε ἐπίασε, A[b*d] καὶ 'I. τὴν σελήνην. [19]S[1] reads ἡμῖν. [20]β–g, S. α reads (+ οὕτως καὶ h) ὄντως. g γεγονότος. A = ἔχοντος. εἶναι ὡς = בְּ הָיָה. [21]α, g. β–dg, S read ὡς ἡλίου. d σὺν τῷ ἡλίῳ. A = τὸν ἥλιον. [22]α. β, A, S[1] om. [23]α, aef. bd read νεανίας. g νεᾶνις. S[1] om. [24]S[1] = ἐδόθη. [25]α. β–e, A, S[1] read ἦν (e om.) λαμπρός (d λαμπρὸς ἦν). [26]c reads ὁ ἥλιος over an erasure. [27]α. β, A, S[1] read ὑπὸ τ. πόδας αὐτῶν (bd, A, S[1] αὐτοῦ) ἦσαν (A[bb*cd] om.). [28]hi, f read τινές. [29]c. hi read ὅτε. β, A, S[1] as in margin. Ver. 5 is bracketed as a dittography of ver. 3[ab]. [30]β–d prefix ὁ. de read Λευίς. [31]eg prefix ὁ. [32]hi, f. c reads αὐτάς. β–fg, A[b], S[1] ἑαυτούς. g, A[ab*cde] ἑαυτοῖς. [33]d, A[b*cde] read ιβʹ. [34]α, dg, A. abef, S read πτέρυγες. [35]β add τοῦ. [36]α, A. β, S om. [37]a reads κρατῆσαι. aef trs. after αὐτόν. [38]α (save that hi om. δέ). β, S read as in margin. A = 'I. δὲ ἔλαβεν. [39]ag read συνῆλθεν. [40]β om. [41]α. β–d, S[1] read ὅτι ἤμην (+ παρὼν aef) ἐκεῖ (+ που bg, S[1]). d, A represent a different text. d ὅτι ἤμεν ἐν κύποις (corrupt for κήποις 'gardens'). A αὐτὸν ὅτι ἦν ἐν (+ τῇ A[bb*cde]) παραδείσῳ. Possibly παρεκεῖ and παρὼν ἐκεῖ and ἐκεῖ που in α, β–d are different corruptions of ἐν παραδείσῳ. [42]S[1] = ἐπ' αὐτῷ. [43]A = καὶ ἔλεγε. [44]A (corrupt) = 'Ασιατικοί. [45]i, β, S[1]. c reads Μήδιοι. h Μηδε. A = καὶ

Χαλδαῖοι[47], Σύροι[48], κληρονομήσουσιν αἰχμαλωσίαν[49] τὰ δώδεκα σκῆπτρα τοῦ Ἰσραήλ.

VI. *Καὶ πάλιν[1] μετὰ ἡμέρας[2] ἑπτὰ εἶδον *ὅτι ὁ πατήρ μου Ἰακὼβ ἵστατο[3] ἐν τῇ θαλάσσῃ Ἀμνείας[4], καὶ ἡμεῖς[5] σὺν αὐτῷ[6].   2. Καὶ ἰδοὺ πλοῖον ἤρχετο[7] ἀρμενίζον[8] *ἐκτὸς ναυτῶν[9] καὶ κυβερνητῶν[10]· ἐπεγέγραπτο *δὲ τῷ πλοίῳ[11] *ὅτι πλοῖον[12] Ἰακώβ.   3. *Καὶ λέγει[13] ἡμῖν ὁ πατὴρ ἡμῶν[14]. *Δεῦτε ἀνέλθωμεν[15] εἰς τὸ πλοῖον ἡμῶν.   4. *Ὡς δὲ εἰσήλθομεν[16] γίνεται[17] χειμὼν σφοδρός[18], καὶ λαῖλαψ ἀνέμου[19]

Margin: β,A[ab],S[1] μῆνας. β, S[1] τὸν πατέρα ἡμῶν Ἰ. ἑστῶτα. β, A, S[1] ἡμεῖς οἱ υἱοὶ αὐτοῦ. β, A, S[1] μεστὸν ταρίχων

ἐκτὸς ναυτῶν.   β-bg, A, S[1] ἀναβῶμεν.

Πάρθοι.   [46] A[ab] om. Here β, A add against α Ἐλιμαῖοι (d, A Ἐλαμῆται. ef Ἐλ(+λ e)υίμεροι. A[b] = Λίμαψοι. S[1] Ἀλλόφυλοι. a om.), Γελαχαῖοι (aef Χελκαῖοι. g Γεθγέοι. A = Γαλάται which it trs. to end of list. S[1] = Χερουλκαι). The latter appears to be a corrupt dittography of Χαλδαῖοι.   [47] Seems lost by A unless we take Γαλάται to be a corruption of Χαλδαῖοι. See note 46. If this word is original it should be restored before Μῆδοι.   [48] c, d read Σύριοι. A = Ἀσσύριοι. The whole text in A = Ἀσιατικοί, καὶ Πάρθοι, Πέρσαι (A[ab] om.) καὶ Ἐλαμῆται (A[b] Λίμαψοι), Ἀσσύριοι καὶ Γαλάται—very corrupt.   [49] α, df. abe, A, S[1] read ἐν (ae om.) αἰχμαλωσίᾳ. g om.

VI. [1] α, bg, A[abb*cd], S[1]. aef, A[ef] read πάλιν. d ταῦτα ἴδον τότε πάλιν δέ.   [2] α. β, A[ab] S[1] read as in margin. A[b*cdef] = ἔτη. The confusion between μῆνας and ἡμέρας arose in the Greek.   [3] α, A. β, S read as in margin (save that b read ἑστηκότα for ἑστῶτα).   [4] c, g. hi read Ἀμνείᾳ. abef Ἰαμνίας. d(A?) Ἰαμνείας. S[1] Χαμνίας.   [5] α. β, A, S[1] add as in margin (save that g om. οἱ).   [6] dg read μετ' αὐτοῦ.   [7] d reads ἤρχοντο and trs. before πλοῖον. g trs. after ἀρμενίζον.   [8] c, df read ἀρμενίζων. S[1] adds σὺν ἱστίοις.   [9] α. β, A S[1] read as in margin (save that S[1] reads φορτίον for ταρίχων, and g, A ναύτου for ναυτῶν). As Gaster has pointed out μεστὸν ταρίχων = מלא מלוחים a corrupt dittography of בלא מלוחים = ἐκτὸς ναυτῶν.   [10] α, f. β-f, A, S[1] read κυβερνήτου.   [11] c, A, S[1]. h, β read δὲ τὸ πλοῖον. i τὸ δὲ πλοῖον.   [12] α. β-bd, S[1] read πλοῖον. d οὕτως, πλοῖον. b om. A = τοῦ.   [13] d reads εἶπε δέ.   [14] aef om. g om. next six words through hmt.   [15] α (save that hi read ἔλθωμεν). abef, A, S[1] read as in margin. b ἐμβῶμεν.   [16] α, β (save that hi, d[1] read ἤλθομεν for εἰσῆλθ.), S. A = καὶ ἀνήλθομεν. d adds ἐν αὐτῷ. A[b*] σὺν αὐτῷ εἰς ναῦν.   [17] d, A read καὶ (d om.) ἐγένετο.   [18] g trs. before χειμών. A[b*cdef] = σφόδρα which A[b*cd] trs. after λαῖλαψ. A[ab] om. with next four words.   [19] hi read ἄνεμος. A = ἐπὶ τῇ θαλάσσῃ but ⲣⲟ̅ⲛⲉⲫⲛⲓⲗ may be corrupt for ⲋⲏⲛⲉ̅ⲇⲏ̅ⲩ = ἀνέμου.   [20] α, aef, A[ef]. bd, S[1] read μεγάλου. g μεγάλη. According to printed Arm. Text A[abb*cd] omit but not so A[ef].   [21] α, β-bg, S[1]. b reads ἐφήπταται. g, A (+ ὡς εἰ A) ἀφίπταται. Rab. T. Napth.

bd, S μεγάλου. μέγας[20], καὶ ἀφίσταται[21] ὁ πατὴρ ἡμῶν[22] ἀφ' ἡμῶν, ὁ[23]

β, A, S¹ καὶ 'I. ἐπὶ ἀκατίου φεύγει. κρατῶν *τοὺς αὐχένας[24]. 5. Καὶ[25] ἡμεῖς[26] χειμαζόμενοι ἐπὶ τὸ πέλαγος *ἐφερόμεθα, καὶ[27] ἐπληρώθη τὸ πλοῖον ὑδάτων[28], *ἐν τρικυμίαις[29] περιρησσόμενον[30], ὥστε[31]

⌈χωριζό-μεθα δὲ καὶ ἡμεῖς ἐπὶ σανίδων δέκα⌉. *καὶ συντρίβεσθαι[32] αὐτό[33]. 6. *Ὁ δὲ Ἰωσὴφ ἐπὶ ἀκατίῳ ἐπορεύθη[34]. ἡμεῖς δὲ διεχωρίσθημεν ἐπὶ σανίδων ἐννέα[35]. Λευὶ δὲ καὶ Ἰούδας ἦσαν *ἐπὶ τὸ αὐτό[36]. 7. Καὶ[37] διεσπάρημεν[38] πάντες εἰς[39] τὰ πέρατα *τῆς γῆς[40]. 8. Ὁ δὲ Λευὶ[41] περιβαλλόμενος[42] σάκκον[43] ἐδέετο[44] *τοῦ Κυρίου[45]. 9. Ὡς

β–d, S¹ πέρατα. δὲ ἐπαύσατο ὁ χειμών, *ἔφθασε τὸ σκάφος ἐπὶ τῆς γῆς[46], ⌈ὥσπερ⌉[47] ἐν εἰρήνῃ. 10. Καὶ ἰδοὺ ἦλθεν[48] ὁ πατὴρ

β, S¹ περὶ πάντων. ἡμῶν[49] καὶ πάντες[50] ὁμοθυμαδὸν ἠγαλλιασάμεθα[51].

ἡμῶν ἐδέετο.

v. 1 reads יתעלם מעלינו. Possibly the reading of *bg*, A is a corruption of that of α, β–*bg*, S¹ which might be a rendering of מעלינו (יתעלה or) יעלה. We might then explain עלם as a corruption of עלה. [22] α, A. β, S om. [23] β, A, S. α om. *i* adds κράζων καί. [24] S¹ = τὰ ἱστία. [25] *d* reads τότε. [26] *g* adds οἱ. [27] *d* reads φερόμενοι. [28] *g* prefixes τῶν. *d* trs. before τὸ πλοῖον. [29] *b* reads τρικυμίας. [30] *beg*, A, S. α reads περιρρησόμενον. *d* περιφερόμενον. *f* περισπώμενον. *ch* φερόμενοι. *i* φερόμενον. Perhaps ἐν τρικυμίαις περιρησσόμενον = דכוה בגלי הים ' pounded by the waves of the sea.' Rab. T. Napth. v. 5 reads והיכוה גלי הים אל סלע 'and the waves of the sea smote it to the rocks,' where היכוה should be emended into הדיחוה = ' drove it ' or ' dashed it,' if אל סלע is genuine. [31] Perhaps corrupt for ἔστε = ' until ' or a mistranslation of עד אשר. [32] *d*, A read συντριβῆναι. [33] A = τὸ πλοῖον. [34] α (save that *h* reads Ἰακώβ for Ἰωσήφ). β, A, S¹ read as in margin (save that *d* reads τότε for καί). [35] *c* (save that I have corrected the vox nulla πασανιδων into σανίδων). *hi* support text (save that for σανίδων ἐννέα they read πᾶσαν ὁδὸν οἱ ἐννέα). β, S¹ read as in margin (save that *d* om. δέ and *g* reads ἐπὶ σαννίδια νέα). [36] *d* reads δὲ τὸ αὐτὸ ἐν σανῆδι. A = ἐν τῷ μέσῳ but ի Միջոցն is corrupt for ի Միասին = ἐπὶ τὸ αὐτό. [37] α, A. β, S¹ om. [38] α, *bdg*, A. *aef*, S¹ read διεσπάρησαν. β, S¹ add οὖν οἱ (*aef* om.). *def* add οὖν. [39] α, *dg*. *abef* read ἕως εἰς. [40] α, A. *d* reads πάντα. β–d, S¹ om. [41] *de* read Λευίς. [42] *b* reads περιβαλόμενος. [43] *hi*, *d* read σάκκῳ. *g* trs. σάκκον before περιβ. [44] α. β, S¹ read as in margin (save that *d* reads ὑπέρ for περί). A = ἐδέετο περὶ ἡμῶν. [45] *d* reads τῷ κυρίῳ. [46] α (save that *hi* read ἐπὶ τὴν γῆν). β, A, S¹ read τὸ σκ. ἔφθασεν ἐπὶ τ. γῆν. [47] *dg*, A om. [48] *b* adds Ἰακώβ. [49] *dg*, A add Ἰακώβ. [50] *hi*, A (though A trs. after ὁμοθυμαδόν). *c* reads πάλιν. β, S¹ om. [51] α. β reads ἠγαλλιώμεθα.

VII. Ταῦτα[1] τὰ δύο ἐνύπνια εἶπον[2] τῷ πατρί μου[3] καὶ[4] εἶπέ μοι· Δεῖ *ταῦτα πληρωθῆναι[5] κατὰ *τοὺς καιροὺς[6] αὐτῶν, *πολλὰ τοῦ Ἰσραὴλ ὑπομείναντος[7].　β–d, S¹ τά.

2. Τότε[8] λέγει μοι ὁ πατήρ μου· Πιστεύω[9] *τῷ θεῷ[10] ὅτι ζῇ[11] Ἰωσήφ[12]· ὁρῶ γὰρ ⌐πάντοτε⌐[13] ὅτι Κύριος ἀριθμεῖ[14] αὐτὸν μεθ᾽ ἡμῶν.　3. Καὶ κλαίων ἔλεγε[15]. *Οἴμοι, τέκνον μου Ἰωσήφ, ζῆς[16], καὶ *οὐ βλέπω σε[17], *καὶ σὺ οὐχ[18] ὁρᾷς Ἰακὼβ τὸν γεννήσαντά σε.　4. *Ἐποίησε οὖν καὶ ἐμὲ δακρῦσαι[19] ἐν[20] τοῖς λόγοις τούτοις[21]. *Ἐγὼ δὲ[22] *ἐκαιόμην τοῖς σπλάγχνοις[23] μου[24] ἀναγγεῖλαι[25] ὅτι πέπραται[26] ⌐Ἰωσήφ⌐[27]. *ἀλλ᾽ ἐφοβούμην[28] τοὺς ἀδελφούς μου[29].　β–d, S¹ ὅτι.　β–g, A, S¹ ζῆς Ἰ. τέκνον μου. β, A, S¹ ἡμᾶς.

VIII. Καὶ[1] ἰδού[2], τέκνα μου[3], ὑπέδειξα ὑμῖν καιροὺς ἐσχάτους †ὅτι[4] πάντα γενήσεται ἐν Ἰσραήλ.　2. Καὶ ὑμεῖς ⌐οὖν⌐[5], ἐντείλασθε τοῖς τέκνοις ὑμῶν[6] ἵνα ἐνοῦνται τῷ Λευὶ καὶ τῷ[7] Ἰούδα.　β–d, A, S¹ ἰδού.

VII. [1] α, A. β–d, S¹ om. d reads τότε.　[2] d, A = διηγησάμην.　[3] A[b] add Ἰακώβ.　[4] h om. i om. to πατήρ μου (ver. 2) inclusive.　[5] α, bg, S¹. aef read αὐτὰ πληρωθῆναι. d γὰρ πληρωθῆναι ταῦτα πάντα, τέκνα μου. A = ταῦτα πάντα πληρωθῆναι.　[6] α, d. aef read καιρούς. bg, A, S¹ τὸν (b, A, S¹ om.) καιρόν.　[7] A = καὶ πολλὰ τὸν Ἰ. ὑπομεῖναι(?).　[8] α adds οὖν.　[9] g reads πίστευσον.　[10] α, d. A = τῷ Κυρίῳ. β–d, S¹ om. d adds τέκνα μου.　[11] hi, g add ὁ. d τὸ τέκνον μου.　[12] A adds καὶ ἐγὼ οὐχ ὁρῶ αὐτόν.　[13] hi read πάντα.　[14] c, A. hi, β, S¹ read συγκαταριθμεῖ.　[15] A adds πάντοτε here, which it om. in previous verse.　[16] α. β–g, A, S¹ read as in margin (save that adef trs. Ἰ. after τέκνον μου). g reads ποῦ ἦς τέκνον μου Ἰ.　[17] d reads οὔτε σε βλέπω ἐγώ. α, A[ab] om. rest of verse and A[b*cdef] trs. it wrongly after τούτοις in ver. 4. See note 21.　[18] d reads οὔτε σὺ πάλιν. af καὶ οὐχ.　[19] α (save that hi om. οὖν). β–d, A, S¹ read (+ καί a) ἐποίησε δὲ (af, A om.) καὶ ἡμᾶς δακρῦσαι. d ταῦτα λέγων καὶ ἡμᾶς κλαῦσαι ἐποίησεν.　[20] α, af. bdeg read ἐπί.　[21] c, aefg, A. hi, d read αὐτοῦ. b, S¹ αὐτοῦ τούτοις. Heιe A[b*cdef] add καὶ πάλιν εἶπε· καὶ σὺ οὐχ ὁρᾷς Ἰ. τὸν γεννήσαντά σε. See note 17.　[22] α. β–d, A, S¹ read καί. d ἐγώ.　[23] A ἐκαίοντο τὰ σπλάγχνα.　[24] α, A. β, S¹ om. d, A add καὶ ἠβουλόμην (+ μέν d).　[25] A adds αὐτῷ.　[26] g reads πέπρακται.　[27] α. β, A, S¹ om.　[28] d reads ἐφοβ. δέ.　[29] d adds μήποτε γνόντες ἀποκτείνουσί με.

VIII. [1] α, d. β–d, A, S¹ om.　[2] d, A add οὖν.　[3] g om.　[4] Text requires πῶς. Hence, since ὅτι = כי, the latter may have been corrupt for איך.　[5] d adds τέκνα μου.　[6] A[b] add καὶ τὰ τέκνα ὑμῶν τοῖς τέκνοις αὐτῶν.　[7] d om. a om. next nine words. h adds περὶ τοῦ Χριστοῦ before following verses.　[8] Read αὐτῶν as Bousset suggests. Text due to Christian scribe. Salvation proceeds jointly from Levi and Judah: cf.

Διὰ γὰρ †τοῦ Ἰούδα†[8] ἀνατελεῖ[9] ἡ[10] σωτηρία[11] τῷ Ἰσραὴλ[12]
καὶ ἐν †αὐτῷ[13] εὐλογηθήσεται[14] Ἰακώβ.

β, Α, S[1]
διὰ γάρ.

3. Διὰ[15] †τοῦ σκήπτρου αὐτοῦ[16] ὀφθήσεται ὁ[17] Θεὸς [κατοικῶν
ἐν ἀνθρώποις[18]] ἐπὶ τῆς γῆς,
τοῦ[19] σῶσαι *τὸ γένος τοῦ[20] Ἰσραήλ,

g,
A[abb*det]
ἐπισυνά-
ξαι.

* καὶ ἐπισυνάξει[21] δικαίους ἐκ τῶν[22] ἐθνῶν.

4. *Ἐὰν ⌜οὖν καὶ ὑμεῖς⌝[23] ἐργάσησθε τὸ καλόν[24],
εὐλογήσουσιν ὑμᾶς *οἱ ἄνθρωποι καὶ οἱ ἄγγελοι[25],

β–ag, Α,
S[1] ἐάν.

καὶ ὁ[26] Θεὸς δοξασθήσεται ἐν τοῖς ἔθνεσιν *δι' ὑμῶν[27],

β, Α, S[1]
καλόν,
τέκνα
μου.

καὶ ὁ διάβολος φεύξεται ἀφ' ὑμῶν,
⌜καὶ τὰ θηρία φοβηθήσονται ὑμᾶς⌝[28],
*καὶ ὁ Κύριος ἀγαπήσει ὑμᾶς[29],
[καὶ οἱ ἄγγελοι ἀνθέξονται ὑμῶν][30].

bdg, Α, S[1]
ἀγαθήν.

5. *Ὡς ἄν τις[31] τέκνον[32] †ἐκθρέψῃ[33] καλῶς[34] μνείαν ἔχει
καλήν[35],
οὕτως[36] καὶ *ἐπὶ τοῦ καλοῦ ἔργου μνήμη παρὰ Θεοῦ ἀγαθή[37].

T. Sim. vii. 1; T. Lev. ii. 11; T. Dan. v. 4; T. Gad viii. 1; T. Jos.
xix. 7.   [9] *ef* add ὑμῖν.   [10] α. β om.   [11] *ef* read σωτήρ.   [12] *d* om.
next line and to τοῦ Ἰσραήλ in ver. 3.   [13] Read αὐτοῖς. See note 8.
[14] *g* om. next seven words. *h* adds τῷ.   [15] α. β–g, A, S read as in
margin.   [16] Read τῶν σκήπτρων αὐτῶν. See note 8.   [17] *c*. Other MSS.
om.   [18] *eg*, S read οὐρανοῖς. The clause in brackets may be an addition
of the Christian scribe who made the changes in ver. 2.   [19] α. β om.
[20] *c*. *h* reads γένος τῷ. β, S[1] τὸ γένος. A = πᾶν τὸ γ.   [21] *g*, A[abb*def] read
ἐπισυνάξαι. A[c] καὶ ἐπισυνάξας. Perhaps we should read καὶ ἐπισυνάξαι. A
adds πάντας.   [22] *g* om.   [23] α (save that *c* prefixes καί). *ag* read ἐὰν γάρ.
β–ag, A, S[1] as in margin.   [24] *g* reads ἀγαθόν. β, A, S[1] add as in margin.
[25] α, *abeg*, A, S[1] (save that *abe*, S[1] prefix καί). *df* read καὶ οἱ ἀγγ. καὶ οἱ ἀνθ.
A[ab] om. next four lines and καὶ οἱ ἄγγελοι of fifth line through hmt.
[26] *b* om.   [27] *h* reads δι' ἡμῶν. *d* ἐν ὑμῖν. *bd*, S[1] trs. δι' ὑμῶν and ἐν ὑμῖν
respectively before ἐν τοῖς.   [28] A, S[1] om.   [29] *eg*, A[b*cdef], S. A[ab]
wanting through hmt. See note 25. This line is original though
it is missing in α, *abdf*. See next note.   [30] Though om. only by *a*,
I have bracketed this line as an interpolation. The preceding line
forms the proper end of the stanza : compare last line of ver. 6. The
interpolation arose apparently from a corrupt dittography of the preceding verse. The text = ומלאכים יאחזוכם a corrupt dittography of
ואלהים יאהבכם.   [31] α, *aef*, A. *b*, S[1] read ὡς ἄν τις γάρ. *d* ὥσπερ γὰρ ἐάν τις.
g ὡς γὰρ ἄν τις (?).   [32] *dg* trs. after ἐκθρέψει. A reads τέκνα and trs. after
καλῶς. For ἐκθρέψει we must read ἐκθρέψας with A[b*cdf].   [33] *abf*. α, *deg* read
ἐκθρέψει.   [34] *c* reads καλόν, *h* καλῶν. A = ἐπιμελῶς.   [35] α, *aef*. *bdg*,

6. Τὸν δὲ μὴ *ποιοῦντα τὸ[38] καλόν,
καταράσονται αὐτὸν[39] καὶ[40] *οἱ ἄγγελοι καὶ οἱ ἄνθρωποι[41],
*καὶ ὁ Θεὸς ἀδοξήσει ἐν τοῖς ἔθνεσιν δι᾽ αὐτοῦ[42],
*καὶ ὁ[43] διάβολος οἰκειοῦται *αὐτὸν ὡς ἴδιον σκεῦος[44],
καὶ πᾶν θηρίον κατακυριεύσει αὐτῷ[45]
καὶ[46] ὁ Κύριος μισήσει αὐτόν.

7. Καὶ γὰρ[47] αἱ ἐντολαὶ τοῦ νόμου[48] διπλαῖ εἰσιν
⌜καὶ⌝[49] μετὰ τέχνης πληροῦνται[50].

8. Καιρὸς γὰρ συνουσίας[51] γυναικός[52]
καὶ καιρὸς ἐγκρατείας[53] εἰς προσευχὴν αὐτοῦ[54].

9. Καὶ *αἱ δύο τοῦ Θεοῦ εἰσι[55], καὶ εἰ μὴ ἐγένοντο[56] ἐν
τῇ[57] τάξει αὐτῶν ἁμαρτίαν *μεγίστην παρεῖχον τοῖς ἀνθρώποις·
τὸ αὐτὸ[58] καὶ *ἐπὶ τῶν λοιπῶν ἐντολῶν[59] ἐστι[60]. 10.
Γίνεσθε οὖν *σοφοὶ ἐν θεῷ, τέκνα μου[61], καὶ φρόνιμοι, ἰδόντες[62]
τάξιν ἐντολῶν[63] αὐτοῦ[64] καὶ θεσμοὺς παντὸς πράγματος[65], ὅπως
*ἀγαπήσει ὑμᾶς ὁ Κύριος[66].

β–a, A, S[1] γυναικὸς αὐτοῦ.

β, A δύο ἐντολαί (+ θεοῦ def).

β–ad, A, S[1] παρέχουσιν· οὕτως ἐστί.

β, A, S[1] σοφοὶ ἐν θεῷ.

β–g, A, S[1] εἰδότες.

A, S[1] read as in margin. g adds περὶ αὐτοῦ. d om. next line through hmt. [36] c reads οὕτω. [37] A = τὸ ἀγαθὸν ἔργον παρὰ Θεῷ ἀγαθὴν ἔχει (A[b*cd] ἕξει) μνείαν. For Θεοῦ b reads Θεῷ. [38] ef read ποιοῦντα. a ὄντα. [39] α, A. d reads τοῦτον which it trs. before καταράσ. β–d, S om. [40] α, aef. bdg, A, S[1] om. [41] α, adg, A (save that d adds Κυρίου after ἄγγελοι). bef, S[1] read οἱ ἄνθ. καὶ οἱ ἄγγ. [42] β–d, A, S[1] (save that b reads ἀδοξήσῃ and g om. ὁ before Θεός). α om. d reads καὶ ὁ θ. δοξάσειεν αὐτῷ. [43] d reads ὁ δέ. A = ὁ. [44] α, bdg (save that d reads αὐτῷ). aef read αὐτῷ ὡς ἰδίῳ σκεύει. [45] c, d. h reads αὐτόν. abeg αὐτοῦ. [46] d reads ἔτι δὲ καί. [47] A[b*cde] add πᾶσαι. [48] A = κυρίου. [49] a reads ἀλλὰ καί and trs. these three lines ending προσευχὴν αὐτοῦ after παρέχουσιν (ver. 9). [50] A read կարգի (= τάξεως) corrupt (?) for կատարին = πληροῦνται. [51] d adds ὁ καιρός. [52] α, a. β–a, A, S[1] read as in margin. [53] f reads ἐργασίας. [54] h, β, S[1] (save that g reads προσευχῆς). c reads εἰς σευχην αὐτῶν. A = καὶ τοῦ προσευχὰς ποιεῖν. [55] α. bdg, A, S[1] read δύο (+ αὗται A) ἐντολαί εἰσι (+ τοῦ Θεοῦ d). Here d is conflate. ef read αἱ δύο ἐντολαὶ Θεοῦ εἰσι. a om. together with preceding καί. [56] α. abg, A, S read γένωνται. d γένοινται. e γένονται. f γίνονται. [57] α, A. β, S[1] om. [58] α (save that h reads μεγάλην). β–ad, A, S[1] read as in margin (save that f read παρέχωσιν). a reads παρέχουσιν and om. rest of verse, d reads παρέχουσιν πᾶσι τοῖς μὴ πρεπόντως ἀλλὰ καταφρονητικῶς ταῦτα πράττουσιν οὕτως δέ ἐστι. [59] A[b*] = πᾶσαι ἐντολαί. [60] α. β, A, S[1] om. [61] α (save that c trs. σοφοί after θεῷ). β, A, S[1] read as in margin. [62] α, g. β–g, A, S[1] read as in margin. [63] A[a] = ἐντολῆς. [64] g reads Θεοῦ. [65] f trs. A = πάντων πραγμάτων. [66] α, adefg (save that d om. ὁ). b, A, S[1] read ὁ Κ. ἀγαπήσει ὑμᾶς.

IX. *Καὶ πολλὰ¹ τοιαῦτα ἐντειλάμενος² αὐτοῖς παρεκάλεσεν ἵνα μετακομίσωσι³ τὰ ὀστᾶ αὐτοῦ⁴ *ἐν Χεβρών, καὶ
θάψωσι αὐτὸν⁵ μετὰ τῶν πατέρων αὐτοῦ⁶.   2. Καὶ⁷ φαγὼν
* καὶ πιὼν⁸ ἐν ἱλαρότητι ψυχῆς⁹ συνεκάλυψε¹⁰ τὸ πρόσωπον
αὐτοῦ καὶ ἀπέθανε.   3. Καὶ ἐποίησαν *οἱ υἱοὶ αὐτοῦ¹¹
*κατὰ πάντα¹² ὅσα¹³ ἐνετείλατο αὐτοῖς¹¹ Νεφθαλεὶμ¹⁴ ὁ
πατὴρ αὐτῶν¹⁵.

Διαθήκη Γὰδ τοῦ ἐννάτου υἱοῦ Ἰακὼβ καὶ Ζέλφας¹.

I. Ἀντίγραφον διαθήκης Γάδ², ἃ³ ἐλάλησε⁴ τοῖς υἱοῖς
αὐτοῦ⁵ ἐν *τῷ ἑκατοστῷ εἰκοστῷ πέμπτῳ ἔτει τῆς ζωῆς⁶
αὐτοῦ, *λέγων αὐτοῖς⁷.   2. *⌈Ἀκούσατε, τέκνα μου⌉· ἐγὼ
ἐγενόμην ἔννατος υἱὸς⁸ τῷ Ἰακώβ⁹, καὶ¹⁰ ἤμην¹¹ ἀνδρεῖος ἐπὶ
τῶν ποιμνίων¹².   3. *Ἐγὼ οὖν¹³ ἐφύλαττον ⌈ἐν τῇ¹⁴

(margin: β, A, S / ἔννατος / υἱὸς ἐγεν-/νήθην.)

IX. ¹A = πολλὰ οὖν. For καὶ πολλὰ ... παρεκάλεσεν d reads ταῦτα ἐντειλάμενος Ν. τοῖς υἱοῖς αὐτοῦ καὶ ἄλλα πολλὰ τοιαῦτα διετάξατο αὐτοῖς.   ²Aª
= ἐνετείλατο. A^{b*d} διηγησάμενος (through an internal corruption).   ³deg
read μετακομίσουσιν. g adds αὐτοῦ.   ⁴g om.   ⁵adef (save that ae read
εἰς and de θάψουσιν). bg, A, S¹ read εἰς (g ἐν) Χ. καὶ θάψωσι (g θάψουσι).
α om. through hmt. (?).   ⁶g adds ὃ καὶ ἐποίησαν.   ⁷A^{abb*cd} according
to printed text om. but not A^{ef}.   ⁸f om. d adds καὶ πάντα. g σὺν αὐτοῖς.
⁹d adds πράξας.   ¹⁰e reads συνεκαλύψατο.   ¹¹g om.   ¹²β–g, A, S¹.
hi read πάντα. c, g om.   ¹³d reads ἅ. g adds εἶπεν καί.   ¹⁴d om.
¹⁵d adds τῷ δὲ Θεῷ ἡμῶν κ.τ.λ. f, S¹ adds Νεφθαλεὶμ υἱὸς Ἰακὼβ η´, υἱὸς
Βάλλας β´ (S¹ reads καὶ Λείας for η´ υἱ. Βάλλας)· ἔζησεν ἔτη ρλβ´. g οὕτως. Ἀμήν.

¹Title. α as in text. β–ad, S read Διαθήκη Γὰδ θ´ (bef, S om. g trs. before
Διαθήκη) περὶ μίσους (+ Γὰδ ἑρμηνεύεται πειρατήριον f). a Γάδ. d Γ. υἱὸς Ἰ. θ´ υἱὸς
Ζ. a´ περὶ μίσους πειρατήριον. A = Δ. Γ. περὶ ὁράσεως, but [Armenian] is
corrupt for [Armenian] = μίσους.   ²hi add τοῦ ἐννάτου υἱοῦ Ἰ. A^{b*}
adds υἱοῦ Ἰακώβ.   ³dg read ὅσα. α adds ἐποίησε καί. This may have arisen
through ידבר being repeated in the MS. as יעבד.   ⁴β–dg, S add αὐτός.
⁵d adds πρὸ τοῦ ἀποθανεῖν αὐτόν.   ⁶α, A (save that h om. εἰκοστῷ). bf, S
read ἔτει ἑκατοστῷ εἰκοστῷ πέμπτῳ (b ἑβδόμῳ) ζωῆς. aeg ἔτει ρκε´ (+ τῆς ag)
ζωῆς. d ρκε´ ἔτει τῆς ζωῆς.   ⁷α. A^{abcd} = καὶ εἶπεν αὐτοῖς. b reads λέγων.
dg καλέσας γὰρ εἶπεν αὐτοῖς (g αὐτοὺς εἶπεν). aef, S¹ om. A^{b*} = συνήγαγε τοὺς
υἱοὺς αὐτοῦ καὶ θυγατέρας καὶ εἶπεν αὐτοῖς. S² ἐκαλέσατο γὰρ τοὺς υἱοὺς αὐτοῦ
καὶ εἶπεν. Here S² agrees closely with dg, A^{b*}.   ⁸α. β, A, S read as
in margin (save that d prefixes ἐγώ, τέκνα μου, b reads ἕβδομος for ἔννατος,
and bg ἐγενόμην for ἐγεννήθην).   ⁹d adds ἡ δὲ μήτηρ μου Ζέλφας παιδίσκης
Λίας.   ¹⁰d reads ἐγώ.   ¹¹A^{ab*def} om.   ¹²d adds σφόδρα. A^{ab} om.
next eight words through hmt.   ¹³α. A^{b*cdef} = καὶ ἐγώ. β, S read ἐγώ.

νυκτὶ⌐ *τὸ ποίμνιον¹⁵, καὶ ὅταν¹⁶ ἤρχετο ὁ¹⁷ λέων, ⌐ἢ ὁ λύκος⌐¹⁸, *ἢ πᾶν θηρίον¹⁹ ἐπὶ *τὴν ποίμνην²⁰, κατεδίωκον²¹ αὐτό²², καὶ *φθάνων ἐκράτουν²³ *τὸν πόδα αὐτοῦ τῇ χειρί μου²⁴ καὶ *ἠκόντισα αὐτὸ ὡσεὶ λίθου βολήν, καὶ²⁵ *ἀνῄρουν αὐτό²⁶.   4. Ὁ οὖν Ἰωσὴφ ⌐ὁ ἀδελφός μου⌐²⁷ ἐποίμαινε μεθ' ἡμῶν, ἕως²⁸ ἡμέρας τριάκοντα²⁹, καὶ *ὑπάρχων νέος³⁰ ἐμαλακίσθη³¹ ὑπὸ³² τοῦ καύσωνος³³.   5. Καὶ³⁴ ὑπέστρεψεν ἐν³⁵ Χεβρὼν πρὸς τὸν πατέρα ἡμῶν³⁶· καὶ ἀνέκλινεν *αὐτὸν πλησίον αὐτοῦ³⁷, ὅτι ἠγάπα αὐτὸν πάνυ³⁸.   6. Καὶ εἶπεν Ἰωσὴφ τῷ πατρὶ ἡμῶν³⁹, ὅτι οἱ⁴⁰ υἱοὶ ⌐Ζέλφας καὶ⌐ Βάλλας⁴¹ θύουσι ⌐τὰ θρέμματα⌐⁴² τὰ καλὰ⁴³ καὶ ἐσθίουσιν⁴⁴ αὐτὰ παρὰ γνώμην *Ῥουβὶμ καὶ Ἰούδα⁴⁵.   7. *Ἦν γὰρ ἰδὼν⁴⁶ ὅτι ἄρνα⁴⁷ ἐξειλάμην⁴⁸ *ἐκ τοῦ⁴⁹ στόματος τῆς⁵⁰ ἄρκου, κἀκείνην⁵¹

Right margin:

β-df, A, S¹ ἢ πάρδαλις, ἢ ἄρκος ἢ πᾶν θηρίον.

β-a, A, S¹ πιάσας.

β-d, (A), S¹ γυρίσας ἐσκότουν καὶ ἀκοντίσας αὐτὸ ἐπὶ δύο σταδίους

(+ καὶ b, S) οὕτως (g om.).   β, A τρυφερὸς ὤν.   b, A, S¹ αὐτοῦ.
β, S¹ Ἰ. καὶ Ῥ.   β, A, S εἶδεν γάρ.

---

14 α. β om.   15 g reads τὸ πρωτοποίμνιον and trs. before ἐν τῇ νυκτί.
16 g reads ὅτε.   17 α, b. β-b om.   18 α. β-ad, S¹ read ἢ λύκος. d, A omit. For λέων ἢ λύκος a reads λύκος ἢ λέων.   19 α. β-df, A, S¹ read as in margin (save that g reads ἄρκτος). d ἢ ἄρκος ἢ ἄλλο τι θηρίον. f ἢ πανθήρ. a om. A adds τὸ ὁρμώμενον ἐπὶ τὸ ποίμνιον.   20 c reads τὸ ποίμνιον.   21 A^abc read in 3rd plural.   22 i, a read αὐτόν. A = αὐτά.   23 α (save that c reads φθανουν). β-a, A, S¹ read as in margin (save that b reads πιάζων). a reads κρατήσας.   24 α, β (save that c om. μου), S¹. A = τῇ χ. (A^b*d ταῖς χερσί) μου τὸν πόδα αὐτῶν. d adds ἢ τὴν οὐρὰν αὐτοῦ.   25 α (save that they give the form ἠκόντηζα). β-d, S¹ read as in margin (save that b, S¹ read γυρεύων and ἀκόντιζον and a αὐτόν). d γυρίσας αὐτὸν ἐσκότουν, εἶθ οὕτως ἀκοντίζων αὐτὸ ἐπὶ δύο σταδίους ἔρριπτον καὶ οὕτως. A = γυρίσας περὶ ἐμοῦ ἐσκότουν (+ ἐκμαίνας A^b + αὐτά A^b*cdef) καὶ ἠκόντιζον ὡς δύο σταδίους, οὕτως.   26 α, def. a reads ἀν. αὐτόν. bg, S¹ ἀνῄρουν. A = ἀνὴρ ἦν ἐγώ—an obvious corruption of our text.   27 α. β, A, S¹ om.   28 α. β-g read ὡς. g om.   29 d reads κ'.   30 α, S¹. β, A read as in margin (save that ef read τρυφερώτερος). Here text = ‏נַעַר‎ and β, A = ‏עֹלֶל‎.   31 a reads ἐκαυματίσθη.   32 α, af. bdeg read ἀπό.   33 b reads καύματος.   34 d om.   35 c, d. hi, β-d read εἰς.   36 α, β-b. b, A, S¹ read as in margin.   37 A = πλησίον τοῦ πατρὸς αὐτοῦ. S¹ om. rest of verse.   38 α, A (save that A trs. bef. ἠγάπα). β om. For next three words i reads Ἰ. εἶπεν.   39 α, β, S¹. a (over ἡμῶν), A read αὐτοῦ.   40 b om.   41 a reads Βάλας. For the next eight words d reads κατεσθίουσι τὸ ποίμνιον.   42 α. β, A, S¹ om.   43 A = κάλλιστα.   44 α. β read κατεσθίουσιν.   45 α, A. β, S¹ as in margin.   46 c. hi read ὃν γὰρ ἰδόντες. β, A^abcef, S read as in margin (save that dg read οἶδε and e ἴδεν for εἶδεν). A^b*d = διότι.   47 c. Other MSS. ἀρνόν. g trs. before ὅτι.   48 α, ef.

β, (A), S
καὶ
ἐνεκότουν
τῷ ʼΙ.
περὶ τοῦ
λόγου
τούτου.

β, S¹
αὐτοῦ εἰς
Αἴγυπ-
τον.

β, S οὔτε
δι᾽ ὀφθ.
οὔτε δι᾽
ἀκοῆς.

ἐθανάτωσα, *τὸν δὲ⁵² ἀρνὸν ἔθυσα· *περὶ οὗ ἐλυπούμην⁵³, ὅτι οὐκ *ἠδύνατο ζῆν⁵⁴· καὶ⁵⁵ ἐφάγομεν αὐτόν⁵⁶. 8. *Καὶ ὑπὲρ τοῦτο ἐνεκότουν τῷ ʼΙωσὴφ⁵⁷ ⌜ἕως ἡμέρας διαπράσεως αὐτοῦ⁵⁸. 9. Καὶ τὸ πνεῦμα τοῦ⌐⁹ μίσους ἦν ἐν ἐμοί⌝, καὶ⁶⁰ οὐκ ἤθελον⁶¹ *οὔτε †δι᾽ ἀκοῆς οὔτε δι᾽ ὀφθαλμῶν⁶² ἰδεῖν τὸν ʼΙωσήφ, ὅτι⁶³ κατὰ πρόσωπον⁶⁴ ἤλεγξεν ἡμᾶς ⌜λέγων⌝⁶⁵, ὅτι χωρὶς⁶⁶ ʼΙούδα⁶⁷ ἠσθίομεν *τὰ θρέμματα⁶⁸· *πάντα γὰρ⁶⁹ ὅσα ἔλεγε *τῷ πατρὶ⁷⁰ ἐπείθετο αὐτῷ.

II. Ὁμολογῶ τοίνυν¹ τὴν ἁμαρτίαν μου, τέκνα², ὅτι πλειστάκις ἤθελον³ ἀνελεῖν αὐτόν, *ἐπειδὴ ἐμίσουν αὐτὸν ἐκ ψυχῆς⁴. 2. Καίγε διὰ τὰ ἐνύπνια⁵ *προσεθέμην αὐτῷ τὸ

β, A, S¹ καὶ (Aᵇᶜ ὅτι d διότι) κατὰ πρόσωπον ἡμῶν.   β–g, A, S¹ ὅτι ἕως (ἐκ A) ψυχῆς ἐμίσουν αὐτόν (+ καὶ ὅλως οὐκ ἦν ἐν ἐμοὶ ἧπατα ἐλέους εἰς αὐτόν bg, A)   β, S¹ μῖσος.

a reads ἐξειλόμην. bg ἐξηλόμην. d ἐξελόμην.   ⁴⁹d reads ἀπό, g ἐκ.   ⁵⁰hi, abef. c reads τοῦ. dg om.   ⁵¹A = τὴν ἄρκον.   ⁵²α. β, A, S read καὶ τόν. ⁵³Aᵇ*ᵈ om. For ἐλυπούμην a reads ἐλυπήθην.   ⁵⁴A = ἔζη.   ⁵⁵g om. ⁵⁶b adds καὶ εἶπε τῷ πατρὶ ἡμῶν. d, Aᵇ* τοῦτον ἰδὼν ʼΙ. κατελάλησεν ἡμᾶς πρὸς ʼΙακώβ, καὶ ἐμνησικάκησεν (for last five words Aᵇ reads τῷ πατρὶ αὐτοῦ). ⁵⁷α (hi reading τούτου). β, S read as in margin (save that d om. καί, f reads ῥήματος for λόγου, and g τόν before ʼΙ.).   A = ἡμεῖς ἐνεκοτοῦμεν τῷ ʼΙ. περὶ τοῦ λ. τούτου.   ⁵⁸β, S¹ add as in margin.   ⁵⁹d reads μου. ⁶⁰Aᵇ* read ἕως καί.   ⁶¹A reads 𐔉 (= ἠδυνάμην) corrupt for 𐔉 = ἤθελον.   ⁶²α. β, S read as in margin (save that g reads οὐδὲ … οὐδέ). A combines the three following words (ἰδεῖν τ. ʼΙ.) with what precedes as follows: δι᾽ ὀφθ. ἰδεῖν τὸν ʼΙ. οὔτε δι᾽ ἀκοῆς ἀκούειν περὶ αὐτοῦ. We should add ἀκούειν with A after δι᾽ ἀκοῆς. The phrase would then = לשמע באזנים. Cf. Ps. xliv. 2, &c. or δι᾽ ἀκοῆς = בשמע corrupt for לשמע = ἀκούειν.   ⁶³α, Aᵇᶜ. d reads διότι. β–d, Aᵃᵇ*ᵈᵉᶠ, S¹ καί.   ⁶⁴α. β, A, S¹ read πρόσωπον ἡμῶν. ⁶⁵α. β, A, S¹ om.   ⁶⁶α. β reads ἄνευ.   ⁶⁷d adds καὶ ʼΡουβίμ.   ⁶⁸g reads αὐτά. Aᵇ*ᵈ = ἀρνόν.   ⁶⁹α. β–d, A, S¹ read κατὰ πάντα. d ὅθεν καί. d, A add πάντα.   ⁷⁰d reads τῷ πατρὶ ἡμῶν. So presumably A though text represents them as = ὁ πατὴρ ἡμῶν. Aᵇ* add ʼΙωσήφ after ἔλεγε and ʼΙακώβ after ἡμῶν. d om. ἐπείθετο αὐτῷ.

II. ¹α. β reads νῦν.   ²h, A add μου.   ³d reads ἠβουλήθην.   ⁴α (save that h reads ἐμίσησα). β–g, S¹ read as in margin (save that S¹ adds πάσης before ψυχῆς). g om. A = καὶ (Aᵉᶠ ὅτι) ἐκ ψυχῆς ἐμ. αὐτόν. The ἕως seems corrupt in β, S¹. bg, A add as in margin (save that g om. ὅλως and for ἧπατα ἐλέους reads ἔλεος).   ⁵Aᵇ* adds αὐτοῦ.   ⁶α, A (save that h, A om. αὐτῷ). Yet the pronoun seems necessary. See reading of d.

μῖσος⁶, καὶ ἤθελον αὐτὸν⁷ ἐκλεῖξαι⁸ *ἐκ γῆς⁹ ⌈ζώντων⌉¹⁰, ὃν
τρόπον¹¹ ἐκλείχει¹² ὁ μόσχος τὰ χλωρὰ *τοῦ πεδίου¹³.

β, A, S¹
ἀπὸ (efg
ἐπὶ) τῆς
γῆς.

α	β, A, S¹
3. Καὶ κρυφῆ πράσας αὐτὸν Ἰούδας τοῖς Ἰσμαιλίταις. 5. Οὕτως¹⁴ ὁ Θεὸς τῶν πατέρων ἡμῶν ἐρρύσατο αὐτὸν ἐκ τῶν χειρῶν ἡμῶν, ἵνα μὴ ποιήσωμεν ἐν τῷ Ἰσραὴλ ἀνομίαν μεγάλην.	3. Διὸ¹⁵ ἐγὼ καὶ Συμεὼν¹⁶ πεπράκαμεν αὐτὸν τοῖς Ἰσμαηλίταις [*τριάκοντα χρυσίων¹⁷, καὶ τὰ δέκα ἀποκρύψαντες τὰ εἴκοσι ἐδείξαμεν τοῖς ἀδελφοῖς ἡμῶν¹⁸]. 4. Καὶ οὕτως τῇ πλεονεξίᾳ ἐπληροφορήθημεν¹⁹ τῆς ἀναιρέσεως αὐτοῦ. 5. Καὶ ὁ Θεὸς τῶν πατέρων μου²⁰ ἐρρύσατο αὐτὸν ἐκ τῶν χειρῶν μου, ἵνα μὴ²¹ ποιήσω ἀνόμημα²² ἐν Ἰσραήλ.

The text presupposes הוֹסַפְתִּי שְׂנֹא אֹתוֹ. Cf. Gen. xxxvii. 8. I here follow
Aᵉˡ; for printed Arm. Text reads προσετεθέμεθα (?) αὐτῷ τ. μ. β, S as in
margin. d adds εἰς αὐτόν.   ⁷d, A trs. after next word.   ⁸h, b, S¹. c, e
read ἐκλίξαι, f ἐκλῆξαι which are corruptions of the text. Num. xxii. 4
which was in the mind of the writer also supports the text. Here the
LXX = ἐκλίξει ἡ συναγωγὴ αὕτη πάντας τοὺς κύκλῳ ἡμῶν, ὡς ἐκλίξει ὁ μόσχος
τὰ χλωρὰ ἐκ τοῦ πεδίου. Notwithstanding, the expression put into Gad's
mouth is very difficult. d, A, which read ἐξαλεῖψαι, offer a more attractive
text. Of this word ἐκλεῖψαι in a and ἐκθλῖψαι in g could be easy
corruptions. Moreover ἐκλεῖξαι could be explained from ἐκλείχει in the
next clause.   ⁹d reads ἐκ τῆς γῆς τῶν. Aᵇ* om.   ¹⁰c reads ζόντα.
a om. rest of verse.   ¹¹According to Armenian Text Aᵃᵇᵇ*ᶜᵈ add ἐξαλείψας,
but this may be an error of the editor as Aᵉˡ om.   ¹²d reads ἐκλῆξει.
¹³α. bd, S¹ read as in margin. efg, A τὰ (eg, A om.) ἐπὶ τῆς γῆς. With
text compare Num. xxii. 4 ירק השרה.   ¹⁴c reads οὗτος.   ¹⁵f adds καί.
g δέ. Aᵉ om.   ¹⁶β–b, A, S². b, S¹ read Ἰούδας.   ¹⁷abef (save that be
read χρυσῶν). g reads εἰς τριάκοντα χρυσᾶ. d εἰς χρυσίνους λ´. The words in
brackets, though found in β, A, S¹, are a Christian interpolation.   ¹⁸a om.
¹⁹β–bg, S¹. bg, A read ἐπληροφορήθην. deg, A add περί. The expression
is strange. It seems to be a development of that in Eccles. viii. 11
לַעֲשׂוֹת . . . . . מָלֵא לֵב. Our text = מלאנו להרגנו = ' we were bent on slaying
him.' Perhaps מלאנו is defective for מלא לבנו = 'our heart was filled'
(i.e. bent on).   ²⁰β, Aᵃ, S¹. Aᵇ om. Aᵇ*ᶜᵈᵉf read ἡμῶν as in α.   ²¹b om.
²²fg read ἀνομίαν. d adds μέγα (as in α), and so originally A; for 'ի մէջ իսր''
(= ἐν μέσῳ τοῦ Ἰσραήλ) is corrupt for մեծ յիսր'' = μέγα ἐν Ἰσρ.

b, A, S
ἀκούσατε,
τέκνα
μου.

β-fg, S¹
ὁ μισῶν
βδελύσσ-
εται.

β, S¹
δίκαια.

β, A, S¹
ἐν τῷ
Ἰωσήφ.

III. Καὶ νῦν ἀκούσατε[1] λόγον[2] ἀληθείας[3], *τοῦ ποιεῖν[4] δικαιοσύνην, καὶ πάντα[5] νόμον[6] ὑψίστου, καὶ μὴ[7] πλανᾶσθε[8] *τῷ πνεύματι[9] τοῦ μίσους[10], ὅτι κακόν ἐστιν ἐπὶ πάσαις ταῖς[11] πράξεσι τῶν[11] ἀνθρώπων. 2. *Πᾶν ὃ[12] ἐὰν[13] ποιεῖ[14] ὁ μισῶν[15], *βδελυκτόν ἐστιν[16]· ἐὰν *δέ τις[17] ποιεῖ[18] τὸν[19] νόμον Κυρίου, *τοῦτον οὐκ ἐπαινεῖ[20]· ἐάν τις[21] φοβεῖται[22] Κύριον καὶ θέλει *τὸ δίκαιον[23], *τοῦτον οὐκ ἀγαπᾷ[24]. 3. Τὴν ἀλήθειαν ψέγει[25], *τῷ κατορθοῦντι φθονεῖ[26], *καταλαλιὰν ἀσπάζεται[27], ὑπερηφανίαν ἀγαπᾷ[28], ὅτι τὸ μῖσος ἐκτυφλοῖ[29] τὴν ψυχὴν αὐτοῦ, ὡς[30] κἀγὼ[31] ⌜τότε⌝[32] ἔβλεπον[33] *τὸν Ἰωσήφ[34].

---

[1] b, A^{er}, S add τέκνα μου, but A^{abb*cd} according to printed text prefix these words. See note 3.　　[2] c, g. h, β-g, A, S read λόγους.　　[3] defy add τέκνα μου.　　[4] A reads καὶ ποιήσατε.　　[5] bd, A, S. α, aef read πᾶν. g τόν.　　[6] g adds τοῦ. A reads λόγους.　　[7] h om.　　[8] b, S read πλανᾶσθαι.　　[9] f reads τὸ πνεῦμα.　　[10] A reads *մոլորութիւն* (= πλάνης) corrupt for *ատելութիւն* = μίσους.　　[11] α. β om.　　[12] f reads παρό. A = ὅτι πᾶν.　　[13] d om.　　[14] c, def. h, abg read ποιῇ (+ καλόν h).　　[15] g reads δίκαιος.　　[16] α. β-fg, S¹ read as in margin. f βδελλοιος ἔσται. g οὐ μή σε βδελύσσεται. A^{ab} = βδέλυγμά ἐστι αὐτῷ. A^{b*cdef} βδελυκτὸν (or βδέλυγμα) δοκεῖ αὐτῷ. Here αὐτῷ is an intrusion. Hence A supports α. βδελύσσεται and βδελυκτόν may both be renderings of נִתְעַב, but if βδελύσσεται is taken actively, as it can be in β-fg, then it presupposes מְתַעֵב.　　[17] α, A. β, S om.　　[18] h, bg read ποιῇ.　　[19] α, A. β om.　　[20] a reads οὐκ ἐπ. τοῦτον. A = πάντες ἐπαινοῦσιν αὐτόν. h adds τὸ πνεῦμα τῆς πλάνης.　　[21] c. Other MSS. om.　　[22] α, ef. abdg read φοβῆται. h adds τόν.　　[23] α, A. β, S¹ read as in margin.　　[24] A = τοιοῦτον τίς ἐστιν ὃς οὐκ ἀγαπᾷ. h reads τοῦτο for τοῦτον and adds τὸ πνεῦμα after ἀγαπᾷ.　　[25] h reads ὅτι λέγει and trs. before τὴν ἀλ. A corruptly adds ὃς before τὴν ἀλ.　　[26] c om. For κατορ. d reads καταρχοῦντι. A reads *պղծէ զճանապարհս իւր նախանձի* = μιαίνει τὴν ὁδὸν αὐτοῦ φθονεῖ. But *պղծէ* is corrupt for *նախանձի*, before which if we replace the ὅς wrongly added before τὴν ἀλήθειαν (see note 23), A = τῷ κατορθοῦντι φθονεῖ. A^{b*d} adds *որ* before *նախանձի*.　　[27] A = ὅτι (A^{b*d} om.) τῇ ματαιότητι προσκυνεῖ; but *ունայնութիւն երկրպագէ* is corrupt(?) for *չարախօսութիւն ընդունի* = καταλαλιὰν ἀσπάζεται.　　[28] a om. rest of verse. h adds ὁ μακρύνων ἀπὸ προσώπου Θεοῦ. d adds καὶ ἁπλῶς εἰπεῖν πᾶν πονηρὸν ἔργον καὶ πᾶσαν ἄλλην σατανικὴν πρᾶξιν ἐπισπᾶται.　　[29] α. beg, A, S read ἐτύφλωσε. d ἀποτυφλεῖ. f ἀποτυφλοῖ.　　[30] α, f. β—a read καθώς.　　[31] h, g read ἐγώ.　　[32] α. β, A, S¹ om.　　[33] d reads ἔπαθον and trs. after Ἰωσήφ. ὡς ... ἐν τῷ Ἰ. = כי גם אני אראה בי" which may be corrupt for כי גם אתי עִוְּרָה בי" = ὡς κἀμὲ ἐτύφλωσε ἐν τῷ Ἰ.　　[34] α. β, A, S¹ read as in margin.

IV. Φυλάξασθε οὖν, τέκνα μου[1], ἀπὸ τοῦ μίσους, ὅτι ⸀καὶ[2] εἰς[3] αὐτὸν τὸν Κύριον ἀνομίαν[4] ποιεῖ.   2. Οὐ γὰρ θέλει ἀκούειν ⸀λόγων[5] ἐντολῶν[6] αὐτοῦ περὶ ἀγάπης *τοῦ πλησίον[7] *⸀καὶ⸀ εἰς Θεὸν ἁμαρτάνει[8].   3. ⸀Ἐὰν γὰρ πέσῃ ὁ ἀδελφός[9], *σπουδάζει εὐθὺς[10] ἀναγγεῖλαι τοῖς[11] πᾶσιν, καὶ σπεύδει *περὶ αὐτοῦ ἵνα κριθεὶς[12] καὶ κολασθεὶς ἀποθάνῃ.   4. Ἐὰν δὲ *δοῦλός τις ᾖ[13], συμβαλεῖ[14] αὐτὸν πρὸς τὸν κύριον αὐτοῦ, καὶ ἐν πάσῃ θλίψει[15] *ἐπιχαίρει αὐτῷ[16], εἴπως[17] θανατωθῇ[18].   5. *Τῷ γὰρ φθόνῳ συνεργεῖ τὸ μῖσος[19], καὶ[20] κατὰ τῶν εὐπραγούντων· *ἐν προκοπῇ[21] ἀκούων καὶ[22] ὁρῶν πάντοτε ἀσθενεῖ.   6. Ὥσπερ[23] ἡ ἀγάπη ⸀καὶ⸀ τοὺς νεκροὺς *θέλει ζωοποιῆσαι[24] καὶ τοὺς ἐν[25] ἀποφάσει θανάτου θέλει[26]

β, S¹ εὐθὺς θέλει.

β, A, S¹ ἵνα κριθῇ περὶ αὐτῆς.

A διαβαλεῖ.

b, A, S¹ ἐπιχειρεῖ.

β-af,A, S¹ θανατώσει αὐτόν.

β, S¹ ὥσπερ γάρ.

IV. [1] g om.   [2] α. β, A, S¹ om.   [3] af read ἐπί.   [4] α, be¹g, S¹. ade²f, A read ἀνομεῖν.   [5] c, abe, S. hi read λόγους. d νόμον. f λόγον. g adds Θεοῦ.   [6] For the next nine words g reads Θεοῦ αὐτοῦ περὶ ἀγάπης οὐ μέλλει αὐτῷ εἰς τὸν πλησίον καὶ εἰς τὸν Θεόν.   [7] f reads τῶν πλησίων.   [8] d reads διὰ τοῦτο ἁμαρτάνει καὶ εἰς Θεόν.   [9] β, S (save that b reads πταίσῃ for πέσῃ). α, A om. but wrongly. adef add αὐτοῦ.   [10] α. β, A, S¹ read as in margin (save that A trs. the words). σπουδάζει in α = יחם, a correction of יחמץ = θέλει of β, S¹.   [11] α. β om.   [12] α (save that h reads ὑπέρ and hi κριθῇ). β, A, S¹ read as in margin (save that a reads αὐτόν and dg αὐτοῦ for αὐτῆς).   [13] α (save that they read εἰ for ᾖ and hi trs. τις after εἰ). β, A, S¹ read ᾖ δοῦλος (af δοῦλος ᾖ).   [14] ci. h, β, S¹ read συμβάλλει and A^{abb*def} read as in margin. A^c corrupt. Here A may be an unjustifiable change of the text. συμβαλεῖ here = יָשִׂיחַ or יַגִּידֶנָּה. Cf. Jer. xliii. 3.   [15] d adds αὐτοῦ.   [16] α, β-b (save that d om. αὐτῷ). b, S¹ read ἐπιχειρεῖ κατ' αὐτοῦ (a αὐτῷ). A = ἐπιχειρεῖ διατελεῖν (or ἀφαιρεῖν) αὐτὸν καὶ θέλει (A^β λογίζεται). It is obvious that there is an internal dittography in A. If ἐπιχειρεῖ is right ἐν πάσῃ θλίψει is probably a mistake for πᾶσαν θλῖψιν. We should then have the familiar phrase כל־רעה יחשב עליו.   [17] hi read εἴπερ. d ὅπως.   [18] α, af. bdeg, A, S¹ read as in margin (save that de read θανατώσῃ).   [19] α. β-ab, A, S¹ read τὸ γὰρ μῖσος συνεργεῖ (bd, S¹ ἐνεργεῖ) τῷ φθόνῳ (d φόνῳ). af ὁ γὰρ φθόνος συνεργεῖ τῷ φόνῳ.   [20] d reads the next six words as follows: ἀκούων τὴν κατ' αὐτῶν εὐπραγούντων προκοπεῖν. For κατά … ἀσθενεῖ A = ἀντιστρατεύεται (i. e. զինի but A^ef rightly read զինի = ἐστί) κατὰ τῶν εὖ ποιούντων πάντοτε ὅτι προκοπὴν αὐτῶν πάντοτε ἀκούων καὶ ὁρῶν ἀσθενεῖ (A^{b*cdef} om. καὶ ὁρῶν ἀσθενεῖ and for προκοπὴν A^cef read μῖσος through an internal corruption).   [21] α. ae read τῇ προκοπῇ. bg, A, S¹ τὴν προκοπήν. f om.   [22] α, bf. ade read ἢ καί. g ἤ.   [23] α. β, S¹ read as in margin. A = καὶ ὥσπερ.   [24] g trs.   [25] c om.   [26] hi, β-b, A, S. b reads θελήσει. c om.   [27] α, df, A. β-df, S¹ om.

ἀνακαλέσασθαι, οὕτως καὶ[27] τὸ μῖσος τοὺς ζῶντας θέλει
ἀποκτεῖναι, καὶ *τοὺς ἐν ὀλίγῳ ἁμαρτήσαντας[28] οὐ θέλει ζῆν.
7. Τὸ γὰρ πνεῦμα τοῦ μίσους *διὰ τῆς[29] ὀλιγοψυχίας
συνεργεῖ τῷ Σατανᾷ ἐν πᾶσιν εἰς θάνατον τῶν ἀνθρώπων,
τὸ δὲ πνεῦμα τῆς ἀγάπης *ἐν μακροθυμίᾳ[30] συνεργεῖ *τῷ
νόμῳ[31] τοῦ Θεοῦ εἰς σωτηρίαν τῶν[32] ἀνθρώπων.

V. ⌜Κακὸν οὖν[1] ἐστι[2] τὸ μῖσος⌝, ὅτι *ἐνδελεχεῖ συνεχῶς[3]
*τῷ ψεύδει, λαλῶν[4] κατὰ τῆς[5] ἀληθείας, καὶ τὰ μικρὰ μεγάλα
ποιεῖ[6], τὸ *φῶς σκότος[7] παρέχει[8], καὶ[9] τὸ γλυκὺ πικρὸν λέγει[10],
⌜καὶ⌝ συκοφαντίαν[11] ἐκδιδάσκει *καὶ ὀργὴν[12] ⌜ἐκταράσσει⌝[13]
καὶ πόλεμον ⌜διεγείρει⌝[14], καὶ ὕβριν[15] καὶ πᾶσαν πλεονεξίαν,
κακῶν[16] καὶ[17] ἰοῦ διαβολικοῦ τὴν καρδίαν ἐκπληροῖ[18].   2.
*Ταῦτα οὖν[19] ἐκ πείρας[20] λέγω ὑμῖν, τέκνα μου, ὅπως
ἐξώσητε[21] τὸ μῖσος *τὸ διαβολικόν[22], καὶ κολληθῆτε τῇ
ἀγάπῃ τοῦ[23] Θεοῦ[24].   3. Ἡ[25] δικαιοσύνη[26] ἐκβάλλει τὸ
μῖσος[27], ἡ ταπείνωσις ἀναιρεῖ *τὸ ζῆλος[28]· ὁ γὰρ δίκαιος καὶ

β (A), S[1]
σκότος
φῶς.

β, A ὀρ-
γὴν καὶ
πόλεμον.

abe,
A^{abcdef},
S τ. μῖσος.

---

[28] d reads τοὺς ἁμαρτ. ἐν ὀλίγῳ.   A = ἕνεκα σμικρῶν ἁμαρτιῶν.   [29]A = καί.
The phrase διὰ τ. ὀλιγ. = מִקֹּצֶר רוּחַ.   Cf. Prov. xiv. 29 ; Pss. Sol. xvi. 11.
[30]A = καὶ μακροθυμίας.   [31]c reads τὸ πνεῦμα.   [32]β–dg om.

V. [1]bg, S[1] om.   [2]α. β, S om.   [3]A reads ꝏ (= συνεχῶς)
which may be corrupt for ꝏ = ἐνδελεχεῖ συνεχῶς.   [4]β, S[1]
(save that a reads λαλοῦν). c reads τὸ εὖ λαλῶν. hi τὸ ψεῦδος λαλεῖ.
A = τὸ ψεῦδος λαλῶν (A^{b*cdef} λαλεῖν). With ἐνδελεχεῖ ... ψεύδει, cf. Ecclus.
xx. 25 ὁ ἐνδελεχίζων ψεύδει.   [5]a reads τάς.   [6]A = ποιῶν.   [7]α, S[2].
β, A, S[1] read as in margin (save that d, A read σκότος ὡς φῶς).   [8]hi, ef.
c reads λαλεῖ. bd, S[1] read προσέχει. g, A βλέπει. S[2] ποιεῖ. a om. In
Is. v. 20 the phrase is שִׂמִים חֹשֶׁךְ לְאוֹר. Here παρέχει might be a rendering
of שׂום but is never found as such. g, A βλέπει = יֶשְׁעָה. προσέχει properly
= שׂום לֵב. Perhaps τὸ φῶς σκότος παρέχει = יֶשְׁעָה אוֹר לְחֹשֶׁךְ.   [9]c, A. hi, β om.
[10]h reads λαλεῖ. i καλεῖ.   [11]c, β–a. hi συκοφαντίαις. a συκοφαντίας.
c adds τις.   [12]α, β–bd, A, S[2]. d reads καὶ ἐνεργεῖ. b, S[1] om.   [13]α.
β, A, S[1] om.   [14]α. β, A, S om.   [15]a om. rest of verse.   [16]c om.
[17]hi om.   [18]α (save that c, d[2] read ἐκπληρεῖ), d[1]. β–ad read πληροῖ.
[19]α. β–b, A read ταῦτα. b, S[1] καὶ ταῦτα.   [20]A reads ꝏ
(= ἁπλότητος) corrupt for ꝏ = πείρας.   [21]β–b, A^{ab*cdef}. α
reads ἐξώσετε. b, S[1] φεύξεσθε. For ὅπως ... διαβολικόν A^b reads ὅπως μὴ
μισῆτε ἀλλήλους· μῖσος γὰρ ἔργον τοῦ διαβόλου.   [22]α. β–b, A read τοῦ
διαβόλου. b, S[1] om.   [23]g om.   [24]ci, d, A. h, β–d, S read κυρίου.
[25]d reads ὅτι ἡ μέν. hi om. clause ἡ δικ. ... μῖσος.   [26]d, A add πατέρων.
[27]d om. next five words. A adds καί.   [28]α, A^{b*}. abe, A^{abcdef}, S read τ.
μῖσος. f τ. ψεῦδος. g τὸν φθόνον.   [29]g reads ἀδικίαν.   [30]h reads ἄλλων.

ταπεινὸς αἰδεῖται ποιῆσαι ἄδικον[29], ⌜οὐχ ὑπ' ἄλλου[30] καταγινωσκόμενος[31]⌝ ἀλλ'[32] ὑπὸ τῆς ἰδίας καρδίας[33], ὅτι Κύριος
ἐπισκοπεῖ[34] *τὴν ψυχὴν[35] αὐτοῦ[36].   4. *Οὐ καταλαλεῖ[37]
*ἀνδρὸς ὁσίου[38], ἐπειδὴ ὁ φόβος τοῦ Θεοῦ[39] *οἰκεῖ ἐν αὐτῷ[40].
5. Φοβούμενος γὰρ[41] μὴ προσκροῦσαι[42] Κυρίῳ[43], οὐ θέλει τὸ
καθόλου[44] οὐδὲ[45] ἕως ἐννοίας[46] ἀδικῆσαι ἄνθρωπον.   6.
Ταῦτα *ἐγὼ ἔσχατον[47] ἔγνων μετὰ τὸ μετανοῆσαί[48] με περὶ[49]
Ἰωσήφ[50].   7. Ἡ γὰρ κατὰ Θεὸν ἀληθὴς[51] μετάνοια[52]
[ἀναιρεῖ *τὴν ἄγνοιαν[53] καὶ] φυγαδεύει τὸ σκότος, καὶ φωτίζει
τοὺς ὀφθαλμοὺς καὶ γνῶσιν παρέχει τῇ ψυχῇ, καὶ ὁδηγεῖ *τὸ
διαβούλιον[54] *πρὸς σωτηρίαν[55].   8. *Καὶ οὐκ ἔμαθεν
ἀπὸ ἀνθρώπων τοῦτο ἀλλ' οἶδε διὰ μετανοίας τοὺς ἐπιστρέφοντας
δέχεσθαι[56].   9. Ἐπήγαγε γάρ[41] μοι ὁ Θεὸς νόσον ἥπατος,
καὶ εἰ μὴ[57] *αἱ εὐχαὶ[58] τοῦ πατρός μου[59] *ἐβοήθησάν μοι[60],

β-d, A,
S¹ τὸ δια-
βούλιον.
β, A, S¹
νικᾷ τὸ
μῖσος.
β-af, A,
S ⌜καὶ⌝ ἃ
οὐκ ἔμα-
θεν ἀπὸ
ἀνθρώ-
πων οἶδε
διὰ τῆς
μετα-
νοίας.
bg, A, S
εὐχαὶ
Ἰακώβ.

β-a, S πατρός μου.

[31] h reads κατά τινος κωλούμενος. g διδασκόμενος.   [32] For נֵ לְאִ (= οὐκ εἰ)
read לְאִ נֵ = εἰ μή or ἀλλά.   [33] g reads συνειδήσεως.   [34] α, β-bd. b reads
ἐπισκέπει, d ἐπιβλέπει.   [35] α. β-d, A, S read as in margin (save that
A, S read τὰ διαβούλια). d ἐπ' αὐτόν.   [36] α, bg. β-bg, S¹ om. A = αὐτῶν.
[37] d reads καὶ διὰ τοῦτο οὐ καταλεῖ (sic). A = καὶ οὐ καταλαλεῖ.   [38] α,
β-bd. b reads ἀνδρός, d ἄνδρα ὅσιον. A = ἀνδρὸς ἀληθοῦς. c adds αὐτοῦ.
[39] c, β-be. h reads κυρίου. b, A, S¹ ὑψίστου. e Χριστοῦ.   [40] α. β, A, S¹
read as in margin. α = ירור בנפשו. β, A, S¹ יוכל לשנאת.   [41] d om.
[42] c, Aᵇ. h, bdfg read προσκρούσει. ae προσκρούσῃ.   [43] A adds αὐτοῦ καί.
[44] a reads καθόλον.   [45] β. α reads οὔτε. Aᵃᵇᵇ*ᶜᵈ καί. Aᵉˡ om.   [46] α, β-b.
b, A, S read ἐννοιῶν.   [47] α, β-d, S. d reads δ' ἐγὼ ἔσχατον. Aᵃᵇᶜᵈᵉᶠ = γὰρ
πάντα ἐγὼ ὕστερον. Aᵇ* γὰρ ἰδὼν ὕστερον. I do not see how this corruption
in A arose.   [48] Aᵇ*ᶜᵈᵉᶠ (by internal corruption) = ἀσεβῆσαι.   [49] bdefg add
τοῦ.   [50] Aᵇ*ᶜᵈᵉᶠ add ἐν τῷ μετανοῆσαί με.   [51] β. c reads ἀληθεῖς. h ἀληθινή.
[52] c reads μετάνοιαι.   [53] α, β-bd. b reads ἀπείθειαν. S¹ ἔχθραν. d om.
As A omits bracketed clause and as this clause not only spoils the balance
of the rest but is also actually expressed in substance later, I have
bracketed it as a disturbing gloss.   [54] Aᵃ om. A reads τῷ διαβουλίῳ
καὶ ὁδηγεῖ τὴν ψυχήν for τῇ ψυχῇ . . . τὸ διαβούλιον.   [55] c reads τῆς σωτηρίας.
[56] α (save that c reads ὑπό and h om. καί and τούς, adds τῆς after διά, and
reads verbs in 1st sing.). af read καὶ οὐκ ἔμαθεν ἀπὸ (ὑπὸ a) ἀνθρώπων, οἶδε
διὰ τῆς μετανοίας τοὺς ἐπιστρέφοντας δέχεσθαι. β-af, A, S¹ read as in margin
(save that A reads μετάνοια for δ. τῆς μ. d reads παρά. e ὑπό and g διὰ
τῶν for ἀπό). There is some radical corruption in all the MSS. and
Versions.   [57] d adds ἦσαν.   [58] a reads εὐχαί, g εὐχή. bg, A, S add
Ἰακώβ.   [59] adef add Ἰακώβ.   [60] α, A = עזרוני. a reads ἔφθασαν. β-a,

<table>
<tr><td>

β, A, S
διαφώνη-
σεν ἀπ'
ἐμοῦ τὸ
πνεῦμά
μου.
β, A, S
μῆνας
ἔνδεκα.
β, A, S
Ἰωσήφ,
ἕως ἵνα
πραθῇ.
bdg, A,
S¹ τὸν
ἀδελφόν.
bdg, A, S¹
ἀγαπῶν-
τες.

</td><td>

ὀλίγου δεῖν[61] *ἐξέλειπε τὸ πνεῦμα μου[62].   10. Δι' ὧν γὰρ
ὁ[63] ἄνθρωπος παρανομεῖ, δι' ἐκείνων[64] κολάζεται.   11.
Ἐπεὶ ⌜οὖν⌝ ἔκειτο[65] τὰ ἥπατα μου ἀνίλεως[66] κατὰ τοῦ Ἰωσήφ,
*τῷ ἥπατι[67] πάσχων[68] ἀνίλεως ἐκρινόμην ἐπὶ *χρόνους δέκα[69],
καθ' *ὧν χρόνων[70] ἐνεῖχον[71] τῷ Ἰωσήφ[72].

VI. *Καὶ νῦν[1], τέκνα μου, ⌜παραινῶ ὑμῖν⌝[2]· ἀγαπᾶτε[3]
ἕκαστος *τὸν πλησίον[4] αὐτοῦ[5], καὶ ἐξάρατε τὸ μῖσος ἀπὸ τῶν
καρδιῶν ὑμῶν· ἀγαπήσατε[6] ἀλλήλους[7] ἐν ἔργῳ καὶ λόγῳ καὶ
διανοίᾳ ψυχῆς.   2. *Ἐγὼ γὰρ[8] κατὰ πρόσωπον τοῦ πατρός
μου[9], εἰρηνικὰ[10] ἐλάλουν τῷ Ἰωσήφ· *ἐξερχόμενος δὲ ἐξ αὐτοῦ[11]
τὸ πνεῦμα *τοῦ μίσους ἐσκότιζέ μου τὸν νοῦν[12], καὶ ἐτάρασσέ[13]
*μου τὸν λογισμὸν[14] *πρὸς τὸ[15] ἀνελεῖν αὐτόν[16].   3. Ἀγαπή-
σατε[17] ἀλλήλους ἀπὸ καρδίας, καὶ ἐάν τις[18] *ἁμαρτήσει εἰς σέ[19],

</td></tr>
</table>

β-d, A-ᵇ, S¹ καὶ ἐξελθόντος μου.   β, A, S¹ τὴν ψυχήν μου.

S om.   If ἔφθασαν here is not a conjecture of the Greek scribe, it = נגעו
as it does generally in the LXX. Is the latter a corruption of עורו which
α, A presuppose here, or of נרצו, which we have conjectured as the original
in the parallel passage in T. Jud. xix. 2 where α reads συνέδραμον = ו רצו ?
[61] α, adg. bef om.   [62] α (save that h reads ἐξέλιπε). β, A, S read as in
margin (save that ag, Aᵃᵇ om. ἀπ' ἐμοῦ and A reads ἐχωρίσθη). g adds ἐπ' ἐμέ.
[63] α, deg. abf, A, S om.   [64] β-d, A, S add καί.   [65] α, g, A. d reads ἔκειτο.
α ἀνέκειτο. bef ἐνέκειτο.   [66] d om. next seven words through hmt. See
note 69.   [67] a om.   [68] A = ἔπασχον καί.   [69] α. β, A, S read as in
margin. d adds κατὰ τοῦ Ἰωσήφ· διὰ τοῦτο ἔπασχον αὐτὰ ἀνίλεως. g adds
καί. a om. rest of verse.   [70] α. bd read ὅσον χρόνον. efg ὃν χρόνον.
[71] g, A read εἶχον (+ κακὸν μῖσος A). d trs. after Ἰωσήφ.   [72] β, A, S add
as in margin (save that d om. ἵνα). For πραθῇ Aᵇ* read ἐπράσαμεν.

VI. [1]Aᵇ add Ὦ ἀγαπητοί, ἀληθής ἐστι ὁ λόγος οὗτος ὅτι δι' ὧν μελῶν καὶ
ἁμαρτάνει, δι' ἐκείνων καὶ κολάζεται καὶ νῦν.   [2]α (save that c reads παρανῶ).
β, A, S om.   [3]α, β-aef. b, S¹ read ἀγαπήσατε. dg ἀγαπητά.   [4]α, aef.
bdg, A, S¹ read as in margin.   [5]d adds ἀγαπησάτω καὶ τὸν πλησίον αὐτοῦ
(conflate).   [6]α (save that h reads ἀγαπᾶτε), aef, S². A, bdg, S¹ read as
in margin.   [7]d, Aˢ add καί.   [8]A = διὰ ὃ καὶ ἐγώ.   [9]α, d, A. β-dg
read ἡμῶν. g om.   [10]Aᵇ = ἐν εἰρηνικοῖς.   [11]α. d reads ἐξερχομένου δὲ
αὐτοῦ ἀπὸ προσώπου τοῦ πατρὸς ἡμῶν, Aᵇ ἐξερχομένου δέ μου ἐκ τοῦ πατρός
μου. β-d, Aᵃᵇ*ᶜᵈᵍ, S¹ read as in margin (save that g om. μου).
[12]Aᵇ*⁽ᶜᵈ?⁾ read πλάνης ἐσκότιζε τὴν ψυχήν μου εἰς μῖσος. For μου hi
read με ὑπό.   [13]A reads յուղարկէր (= προύπεμπε) corrupt for յուզէր
= ἐτάρασσε.   [14]α (save that hi om. μου). β, A, S¹ (save that a trs.
μου before τήν) as in margin.   [15]bd read τοῦ.   [16]a om. rest of
chapter and vii. 1-6.   [17]ch, ef, A. ef, A add οὖν. i, bdg, S¹ read

<table>
<tr><td>

α

εἰπὲ αὐτῷ εἰρήνην[20], καὶ ἐν
τῇ ψυχῇ σου μὴ κρατήσῃς
δόλον· καὶ ἐὰν μετανοήσας
ὁμολογήσῃ[21], ἄφες αὐτῷ[22].

</td><td>

β, A, S[1]

εἰπὲ αὐτῷ *ἐν εἰρήνῃ[23], ἐξ- A[b*cde]
ορίσας τὸν ἰὸν τοῦ μίσους, καὶ[24] εἴπετε.
ἐν τῇ[25] ψυχῇ σου μὴ κρατή- A[b] ὑμῶν.
σῃς δόλον· καὶ ἐὰν *ὁμολογή- Lk 17[3].
σας μετανοήσῃ[26] *ἄφες αὐτῷ[27].

</td></tr>
</table>

4. Ἐὰν δὲ ἀρνεῖται[28], μὴ φιλονείκει αὐτῷ, μήποτε[29] ὀμόσαντος
αὐτοῦ δισσῶς ἁμαρτάνεις[30],   5. [Μὴ[31] ἀκούσῃ[32] ἐν μάχῃ ἀλλότριος[33] τὸ[34] μυστήριόν σου[35], *ἵνα μὴ[36] μισήσας[37] *ἐχθράνῃ
σε[38], καὶ μεγάλην ἁμαρτίαν ἐργάσηται[39] ⌈ἐν σοί⌉[40]· ὅτι
πολλάκις *δολοφωνεῖ σε[41] ἢ περιεργάζεταί σε[42] ἐν κακοῖς[43]]

ἀγαπᾶτε οὖν (i om.).   [18] α, ef. bdg om.   [19] c. hi, f read ἁμαρτήσῃ εἰς σέ,
bdg, S ἁμάρτῃ εἰς σέ. e ἁμαρτει εἰς σέ.   A = ἁμαρτήσετε εἰς ἀλλήλους.
[20] c. hi read εἰρήνη σοι.   [21] c reads ὁμολογήσει.   [22] α om. next six words
through hmt.   [23] A[ab] = εἰρήνην. dg add καί.   [24] d om.   [25] bdg om.
[26] β-ad, A[a], S[1] (save that f reads μετανοήσει). d μὲν μετανοήσῃ ὁμολογήσῃ.
A[b] = ὁμολογήσαντες μετανοήσητε. A[b*cde] ὁμολογήσας μετανοήσῃς.   [27] A[b] =
ἄφετε ἀλλήλοις. g om. next six words through hmt. S[1] adds μὴ καταφρονεῖ
αὐτοῦ.   [28] α, β-ad, A[b], S[1]. d reads ἄρνηται. A[bb*cde] = ἀρνῇ.   [29] d
reads μή.   [30] α. beg read ἁμαρτήσῃς. df ἁμαρτήσεις. A[b] adds αἴτιος γὰρ τῆς
ὁμοσίας εἰ.   [31] A corruptly reads καί and so destroys the sense of what
follows. I have bracketed all ver. 5 except the final clause as an interpolation. Verses 3, 4, 6, 7 deal wholly and in a most original manner with
the subject of forgiveness, and with this subject the bracketed clauses have
no relation. This interpolation appears to be based on Prov. xxv. 8–10
with possibly a consciousness of Sir. xix. 8–9, and deals with the danger
men run, when their tempers are roused in a legal suit, of divulging secrets
to strangers, and so of exposing themselves to attack from these strangers.
The final clause λαβὼν ἀπό σου τὸν ἰόν, which according to ver. 3 (β, A, S[1])
refers to evil of personal resentment passing from the breast of the
offended man to the offender whom he passionately reproves, cannot
apply to the stranger in ver. 5, but follows naturally on the words
μὴ φιλονείκει in ver. 4: 'don't get into a passion, lest catching the poison
from thee (i.e. he too falling into a passion) he take to swearing, &c.'
[32] df read ἀκούσει. A[b] = ἀκούσουσιν.   [33] g reads ἀλλοτρίῳ. A trs. before
ἐν μάχῃ. A[b] = ἀλλότριοι.   [34] α. β om.   [35] α. β, A, S read ὑμῶν.   [36] A[a]
= καί. A[abbb*cd] om.   [37] A = μισήσῃ σε (A[b*cde] ὑμᾶς) καί.   [38] α, b, A[ab] (save
that b trs. ἐχθ. σε). efg, S[1] read ἐχθράνη. d ἐχθραίνει. S[1] om. following
καί. A[b*cde] ἐχθροὶ ἦτε.   [39] A[(-ab ?)] = ἐργάσησθε. A[ab] om. rest of verse.
[40] α. bd, S read κατά σου. efg διά σου.   [41] hi, f. c reads δολοφωνῆσαι.
b δολοφωνῆσαι. d δολοφονῆσαι. e δολοφονεῖ σε. g δολοφωνῆσε (sic). But these

β, S,
(A?)
ἐξάξῃς.
   *λαβὼν ἀπό σου⁴⁴ τὸν ἰόν.   6. Ἐὰν *δὲ ἀρνήσηται⁴⁵ καὶ *αἰδεσθῇ ἐλεγχόμενος⁴⁶, ἡσύχασον⁴⁷ μὴ †ἐλέγξῃς⁴⁸ αὐτόν·

β, S¹ τοῦ
μηκέτι
πλημμ.
   ὁ γὰρ ἀρνούμενος⁴⁹ μετανοεῖ *τοῦ πλημμελῆσαι⁵⁰ *εἰς σέ⁵¹, *καὶ [φοβηθεὶς] εἰρηνεύει⁵².   7. Ἐὰν δέ *ἐστιν ἀναιδής⁵³,

β–af, A,
S¹ ἀλλὰ
καὶ τιμή-
σει σὲ
[καὶ
φοβηθή-
σεται]καὶ
εἰρηνεύ-
σει.
β, S¹ τις.
   καὶ ἐνίσταται⁵⁴ τῇ κακίᾳ, *καὶ οὕτως⁵⁵ ἄφες αὐτῷ ἀπὸ καρδίας, καὶ δὸς⁵⁶ ⌜τῷ Θεῷ τὴν ἐκδίκησιν.

   VII. Ἐὰν *δὲ εἷς¹ ὑπὲρ ὑμᾶς εὐοδοῦται μὴ λυπεῖσθε², ἀλλ᾽³ εὔχεσθε ὑπὲρ αὐτοῦ⁴⌝ ἵνα τελειωθῇ⁵· *οὕτως γάρ ἐστιν ὑμῖν συμφέρον⁶.   2. Καὶ ἐὰν ἐπὶ πλεῖον ὑψοῦται, μὴ φθονεῖτε ⌜αὐτῷ⌝⁷, μνημονεύοντες ὅτι πᾶσα σὰρξ ἀποθανεῖται. Κυρίῳ δὲ ὕμνους⁸ προσφέρετε⁹ τῷ παρέχοντι τὰ καλὰ καὶ¹⁰

bdeg, A, S¹ τελείως εὐοδοῦται.

may imply δόλῳ φωνήσει. A⁻ᵃᵇ renders the phrase together with ἢ περιερ-γάζεται as follows: παρασκευάζεται πολλάκις δολοφονεῦσαί σε. S¹ = δολυφονήσει σε.   ¹²β, S. α om.   ⁴³α. β reads κακῷ.   ⁴⁴α, _b_, A, S. _def_ read ἀπό σου λαβών. _g_ ἀπολαβών.   ⁴⁵α (_c_ reading ἀρνήσειτε, such itacisms being frequent in this MS.). _befg_, S¹ read οὖν ἀρνεῖται. _d_ οὖν ἀρνῆτε (i.e. for ἄρνηται). A = οὖν ἀρνῆσθε. A adds τοῦτο.   ⁴⁶A = αἰδεσθῆτε (Aᵇ*ᶜᵈᵉ ἐπιλείπητε) ἐλεγχόμενοι. After αἰδεσθῇ _d_ adds ὑπό σου.   ⁴⁷α, _efg_. _b_, S¹ read καὶ (_b_ om.) ἡσυχάσθη. _d_ εἰς εὐχάς. A = ἡσυχάσατε. A adds καί.   ⁴⁸α (_c_ reading ἐλλεγξης). The text may be right, if ἡσύχ. μὴ ἐλέγξῃς = 'cease from reproving.' _bg_, S¹ read as in margin. _def_ ἐξάξεις. A = δημοσιεύητε.   ⁴⁹A adds τοιαῦτα.   ⁵⁰α. β, S¹ read as in margin. A = καὶ οὐ πλημμελεῖ.   ⁵¹A = τινί.   ⁵²α. β–af, A, S¹ read as in margin (save that _d_ om. ἀλλά and σέ and adds σοί after φοβηθ. and μετά σου after εἰρην. and A gives the three verbs in the 3rd present indicative: cf. α), _f_ καὶ φοβηθήσεται καὶ εἰρηνεύσει. φοβηθείς or its equivalent καὶ φοβηθήσεται are bracketed as interpolations. The idea of 'fear' is alien to the context. Perhaps φοβηθήσεται (= יירא) arose through a dittography of ייקר = τιμήσει.   ⁵³α. β–a, A, S¹ read ἀναιδής (_d_ ἀναίδεια) ἐστιν.   ⁵⁴_c_ (A?) reads ἀνίσταται.   ⁵⁵_f_ om. For this phrase together with rest of sentence A gives: καὶ ἐὰν οὕτως ᾖ, ἄφες αὐτῷ ἀπὸ ὅλης καρδίας σου, καὶ δὸς ταῖς χερσὶν αὐτοῦ ἵνα τελείως †ὁδηγήσει†, συμφέρει γὰρ οὕτως. Here the last six words constitute the latter half of vii. 1 where they should be restored. ᴍⁿᵃᵃⁿ (= ὁδηγήσει) is corrupt for _ʃᵃᵣⁿᵗⁱ_ = εὐοδηθήσεται. Hence A supports _bdeg_, S.   ⁵⁶A om. last four words of this verse and first twelve of next.

   VII. ¹_c_. _hi_ read δέ τις. β, S¹ τις. A om.   ²_hi_ om. next two words through hmt. (?).   ³_c, f._ _beg_, S add καί. _d_ μᾶλλον.   ⁴_c_ reads ἑαυτοῦ.   ⁵α, _f_ (save that _f_ prefix καί). _bdeg_, A, S¹ read as in margin. (See note 56, chap. VI.)   ⁶α (save that _hi_ trs. ἐστὶν ὑμῖν), A. _beg_, S¹ read ἴσως γὰρ ὑμῖν συμφέρει οὕτως. _f_ οὕτως γ. ὑμῖν συμφέρει. _d_ om.   ⁷_c_. _h_ reads αὐτοῦ.

συμφέροντα * πᾶσιν ἀνθρώποις[11]. 3. Ἐξέτασον * κρίματα Κυρίου[12] καὶ †καταλάμψει[13] καὶ ἡσυχάσει[14] τὸ διαβούλιόν σου. 4. Ἐὰν δὲ[15] ἐκ κακῶν[16] τις πλουτήσει, ὡς Ἡσαῦ ὁ πατράδελφός[17] μου, μὴ ζηλώσητε[18]· ὅρον[19] ⌈δὲ⌉[20] Κυρίου ἐκδέξασθε[21]. 5. Εἰ[22] ἀφαιρεῖται[23] †αὐτὰ[24] * ἐν κακοῖς[25], ἢ μετανοήσαντι[26],

(right margin:) befg οὐ (bf om.) †καταλείψει. β, Α εἰ γάρ. Α τὸν πλοῦτον.

bg, (A), S¹ μετανοοῖσιν.

---

i αὐτόν. β, A, S om. [8] *b* reads ὕμνον. *hi* add καὶ ᾠδάς. [9] *hi* read προσφέροντα and om. next six words. *d* adds ἀπαίστως (sic). [10] *ef* add τά. [11] *d* reads τοῖς ἀνθ. πᾶσιν. [12] *hi, befg*, A, S¹ (save that *b*, S¹ read κυρίῳ). *c* reads κρῖμα τῷ Κυρίῳ. *d* κρῖμα Κυρίου. [13] α. *b* reads οὕτως καταλείψει. *dg* οὐκ ἐγκαταλείψει (*g* καταλείψει). *ef* οὐ (*f* om.) καταλήψει. A = οὐκ ἐνκαταλειφθήσῃ but by a change of one letter it = οὐκ ἐγκαταλείψεις. S¹ = μὴ καταλείψητε. A[abb*cd] trs. after τὸ διαβούλιόν σου according to printed Arm. Text but not A[al]. First of all καταλήψει (*ef*) is a corruption of καταλείψει. There remain then καταλάμψει of α and some compound of λείψει in β, A, S¹. But καταλάμψει is impossible. It may be a corruption of καταλείψει, or it may attest a corruption already existing in the Hebrew original: that is, it = תֵעָלֵם corrupt for תֵעָזֵב = καταλείψει. Thus it appears that καταλείψει must for the present be accepted. But this word admits of no intelligible meaning in the present context. Hence if it is right, something is wrong in the context. Now according to *deg*, A, S¹, a negative should be inserted before καταλείψεις. If then καταλείψεις is to be retained, the negative must be inserted and the clause interpreted in the sense of a prohibition as in S¹: 'thou shalt not forsake,' i.e. τὰ κρίματα. But the absence of the negative in α, *bf* makes it not improbable that the negative is an intrusion in the text. In that case καταλείψει = תֵעָזֵב corrupt for יָנוּחַ = ἀναπαύσεται, which would go well with ἡσυχάσει = יִשְׁקֹט. For the conjunction of these two verbs cf. Job iii. 26. Possibly only יָנוּחַ alone stood in the text originally. Then this through a dittograph became יָנִיחַ וְיָנוּחַ. Hence the Versions. [14] A = ἡσύχασον. [15] β–*f*, A, S¹ add καί. [16] A = κακίας. [17] *hi* read ἀδελφὸς τοῦ πατρός. [18] α, *d* read ζηλώσειτε. [19] = מוֹעֵד 'the time appointed by the Lord.' [20] *h*, *defg*, S¹. *c* reads δή. *b* γάρ. A om. [21] *h* reads δέξασθαι. ἐκδέξ. in the sense of ὑπομείνατε = קַוֵּה. Cf. Ps. xxxvii. 9, 10. [22] α. *beg* read ἢ γάρ (corrupt for εἰ γάρ). *df*, A εἰ γάρ. S¹ = οὗτος γάρ. [23] A = ἀφαιρῆσθε. S¹ φέρει (corrupt). ἀφαιρεῖσθαι seems = לָקַח here. A better rendering would have been κτᾶσθαι. [24] A reads τὸν πλοῦτον. S¹ om. [25] S = τὸ κακόν (corrupt). *d* om. next three words. But ἐν κακοῖς may = בְרָשִׁעִים corrupt for מֵרָשִׁעִים 'from the wicked.' [26] Em. from μετανοήσας a mistranslation in α, *ef*. *bg*, A, S¹ read plural as in margin. For ἢ . . . ἀφίησι A reads καὶ μετανοεῖτε, ἄφεσις ἔσται ὑμῖν.

befg, S¹ ἀφίησι²⁷ ἤ²⁸ ἀμετανόητος²⁹ τηρεῖται³⁰ εἰς *αἰωνίαν κόλασιν³¹.
ἀμετα-
νοήτω
τηρεῖ (ef 6. Ὁ γὰρ πένης³², ἐὰν ἀφθόνως ἐπὶ πᾶσι Κυρίῳ εὐαρεστῇ³³,
τηρήσει). οὗτος³⁴ *ὑπὲρ πάντας³⁵ †πλουτεῖ³⁶, ὅτι οὐκ ἔχει τὸν *περι-
β-α, A, S σπασμὸν τῶν ματαίων ἀνθρώπων³⁷. 7. Ἐξάρατε οὖν³⁸ τὸ
καὶ ἄ-
φθονος †μῖσος³⁹ ἀπὸ τῶν ψυχῶν ὑμῶν, καὶ ἀγαπήσατε⁴⁰ ἀλλήλους ἐν
ἐπὶ πᾶσι εὐθύτητι καρδίας.
Κυρίῳ
VIII. Εἴπατε *⌈δὲ⌉ ταῦτα καὶ ὑμεῖς¹ τοῖς τέκνοις ὑμῶν,

εὐχαριστῶν.   β, A, S¹ πονηρὸν περισπασμὸν τῶν.

²⁷ g om.   ²⁸ d reads καί. A = δέ.   ²⁹ Em. from ἀμετανοήτως of α (an obvious corruption as ω is frequently written for o in c). This emendation is supported by τηρεῖται and by A. The text appears to be modelled on Job xxi. 30 לַיּוֹם אֵיד יֵחָשֵׂךְ רָע. befg, S¹ read as in margin. d ἀμετανοήτοις μένουσι. A = ἐὰν μὴ μετανοῆτε (= ἀμετανόητοι).   ³⁰ α. A = τηρεῖσθε which though differing in person supports α. 'The unrepentant are reserved.' The other MSS. and S make God the subject of the verb—a mistake due to their putting ἀμετανόητος in the dative. bdg read τηρεῖ (+ αὐτούς d). ef τηρήσει (f τηρήσῃ).   ³¹ d, A. α, f read εἰς αἰῶνας τὴν κόλασιν where αἰῶνας seems corrupt for αἰῶνος. beg εἰς (+ τὸν g) αἰῶνα τὴν (εἰς g) κόλασιν.   ³² S¹ = ταπεινός but S² = text.   ³³ α (save that h reads ἄφθονος and εὐάρεστον). bdefg, A, S read as in margin (save that g adds καί before ἐπί). A adds ἐστί after εὐχαριστῶν.   ³⁴ Em. from οὕτως of c. Cf. αὐτός of β-f, S. A = τοιοῦτος. h, f οὕτω.   ³⁵ α. defg read παρὰ πάντας (f παντός). A = either α or deg. bg, S read παρὰ πᾶσι.   ³⁶ g reads πλουτιεῖ. Text = עָשַׁר corrupt for אָשַׁר = μακαριστός ἐστι. (So Symmachus renders on Ps. xli. 3.) The poor man is happy (not 'rich' as the corrupt text states) because, as the next clause states, he is free from the sore travail of men (i.e. of men seeking to be rich).   ³⁷ α. β, A, S¹ read as in margin (save that g om. τῶν). πονηρὸν περισπασμόν = עִנְיַן רָע which is found in Eccles. i. 13, v. 13.   ³⁸ d om.   ³⁹ Since verses 1–6 deal with the duty of banishing envy or jealousy, ver. 7 which treats only of hatred cannot be in its right position here, if the text is uncorrupt. For the writer could not reasonably conclude a disquisition on jealousy with the exhortation 'put away therefore hatred.' But the verse rightly belongs here as the text is corrupt. μῖσος = שִׂנְאָה which is corrupt for קִנְאָה = ζῆλος. The corruption is probably to be explained by the occurrence of the phrase 'put away hatred from your hearts' in vi. 1.   ⁴⁰ α, aef. bg read ἀγαπᾶτε. d, Aᵒⁱ om. καὶ ἀγαπᾶτε together with rest of verse and first eight words of next chapter. Καὶ ἀγάπη εἰς ἀλλήλους ... καρδίας are added by a later hand at foot of page in d.

VIII. ¹ h, ef (save that hi read δή). c reads δὴ ταῦτα ὑμεῖς. abg, A, S δέ

ὅπως τιμήσωσιν †Ἰούδα[2] καὶ Λευὶ[3] †ὅτι ἐξ αὐτῶν ἀνατελεῖ
*⌜ὑμῖν⌝ Κύριος σωτηρίαν[4] *τῷ Ἰσραήλ[5].　　　2. *Ἐγὼ γὰρ
ἔγνων[6], ὅτι ἀποστήσονται[7] τὰ τέκνα ὑμῶν ἀπ' αὐτοῦ[8], καὶ[9]
πάσῃ πονηρίᾳ καὶ κακώσει καὶ διαφθορᾷ ἔσονται ἀπὸ[10] Κυρίου.
3. *Καὶ ἡσυχάσας ὀλίγον εἶπε πάλιν[11]· Τέκνα μου, ὑπακούσατε[12]
⌜τοῦ πατρὸς ὑμῶν[13]⌝, καὶ θάψατέ με ἐγγὺς[14] τῶν πατέρων
μου.　　　4. *Καὶ ἐξάρας τοὺς πόδας[15] αὐτοῦ ἐκοιμήθη ἐν
εἰρήνῃ[16].　　　5. Καὶ μετὰ *ἔτη πέντε[17] ἀνήγαγον αὐτὸν
*εἰς Χεβρών, καὶ ἔθηκαν αὐτὸν μετὰ τῶν πατέρων αὐτοῦ[18].

adef,
σωτήρ.
β, A, S
ἐπὶ τέλει
ἀποστή-
σονται.
β–g, A, S
ἐνώπιον.
β, A
καὶ ὀλ.
ἡσυχά-
σας π.
εἶπεν.

Διαθήκη Ἀσὴρ τοῦ δεκάτου υἱοῦ Ἰακὼβ καὶ Ζέλφας[1].

I. Ἀντίγραφον διαθήκης Ἀσήρ[2], ἃ[3] ἐλάλησε τοῖς υἱοῖς

(g, A om.) καὶ ὑμεῖς ταῦτα (g om). d om. together with next three words. hi
add περὶ τοῦ Χριστοῦ.　　[2] α. β–d read Ἰούδαν. d τὸν Ἰούδαν. We should read
Λευὶ καὶ Ἰούδαν as is found universally: cf. Testaments of Sim. vii. 2, Levi
ii. 11, viii. 14, Dan. v. 4, &c.　　[3] bg prefix τόν. e reads Λευίν.　　[4] α, g, A
(save that c reads ἡμῖν Κύριος σωτηρία and g, A om. ὑμῖν). b, S read Κύριος
σωτῆρα. adef ὑμῖν (d om. in repetition of clause at foot of page) Κύριος
σωτήρ.　　[5] α, ab, A^{b*}, S. def, A^{b*} read τοῦ Ἰ. g ἐν τῷ Ἰ. A^{abcdef} = παντὶ Ἰ.
[6] α. β, S read ἔγνων γάρ. A = καὶ ἔγνων.　　[7] α. β, A, S read as in margin
(save that for τέλει af read τούτου and d reads ἀναστήσονται for ἀποστ.).
[8] b, S¹ read ἀπ' αὐτῶν, but S² = text. d ἐπ' αὐτόν.　　[9] β adds ἐν.　　[10] α.
β–g, A, S read as in margin. Both seem independent renderings of
‏מִבֵּֽית‎. g reads ἐν οἴκῳ.　　[11] α. β–d, A read as in margin. S¹ = καὶ ὀλ.
ἡσυχάσας εἶπεν. b adds αὐτοῖς. S om. next seven words. For ver. 3 d reads
ταῦτα ἐντειλάμενος Γὰδ τοῖς υἱοῖς αὐτοῦ.　　[12] g reads ἐπακούσατε.　　[13] a om.
For bracketed words A reads μου.　　[14] α. β reads σύνεγγυς.　　[15] α, β
(save that d om. καί) = ‏רגליו‎ ‏אסף‎ (cf. Gen. xlix. 33). A = καὶ καταφιλήσας
τοὺς υἱούς, but ⸮ is corrupt for ⸮ = α,
β. S¹ καὶ ἐκτείνας τοὺς πόδας.　　[16] d adds καὶ ἔθηκαν αὐτὸν ἐν θήκῃ καινῇ.　　[17] α.
β, A, S¹ reads πέντε ἔτη.　　[18] α, bg, A (save that bg, A trs. εἰς Χ. after
αὐτόν, and g, A read ἔθαψαν, and g adds ἅμα). aef, S¹ read εἰς Χ. καὶ
ἔθαψαν (S¹ = ἔθηκαν) αὐτὸν ἐκεῖ. d καὶ ἔθαψαν ἐν Χ. ἐν τῷ σπηλαίῳ τῷ διπλῷ
μετὰ Ἀβραὰμ καὶ Ἰσαὰκ καὶ Ἰακώβ. d adds τῷ δὲ θεῷ ἡμῶν. f, S¹ Γὰδ υἱὸς
Ἰακὼβ θ, υἱὸς Ζέλφας α. ἔζησε (S¹ = ζήσας) ἔτη ρκε΄. g τέλος τῶν λόγων
διαθήκης Γάδ· οὗτος ἦν Ζέλφας πρῶτος υἱός· ἔζησεν ἔτη ρκε΄.

[1] Title. α as in text. a reads Ἀσσήρ. bef, S¹ δ. Ἀ ἱ (ef, S¹ om.) περὶ
δύο προσώπων κακίας καὶ ἀρετῆς (+ Ἀσσὴρ ἑρμηνεύεται πλοῦτος ἢ μακάριος f).
d δ. Ἀ. υἱοῦ Ἰακὼβ ἱ υἱοῦ Ζέλφας παιδίσκης Λίας περὶ δύο προσώπων κακίας
καὶ ἀρετῆς. g λόγος ἱ δ. Ἀ. περὶ διδασκαλίας καὶ ἀληθείας. A = δ. Ἀ. (+ υἱοῦ

αὐτοῦ *ἐν ἑκατοστῷ εἰκοστῷ πέμπτῳ ἔτει τῆς[4] *ζωῆς αὐτοῦ[5].
2. *Ὑγιαίνων ⌐γὰρ⌐[6] *εἶπε πρὸς αὐτούς[7]· Ἀκούσατε,
τέκνα[8] Ἀσήρ, τοῦ πατρὸς ὑμῶν, καὶ[9] πᾶν τὸ εὐθὲς[10] ἐνώπιον
*τοῦ Θεοῦ[11] ὑποδείξω[12] ὑμῖν[13].   3. Δύο ὁδοὺς *ἔδωκεν
ὁ Θεὸς τοῖς υἱοῖς τῶν ἀνθρώπων[14], καὶ δύο διαβούλια, ⌐καὶ
δύο πράξεις, *καὶ δύο τρόπους[15]⌐, *καὶ ⌐δύο⌐ τέλεα[16].   4.
Διὰ τοῦτο πάντα[17] δύο[18] δύο εἰσίν[19], ἐν κατέναντι τοῦ ἑνός.

β, A, S[1]
ἐν καλῷ,
πᾶσα
πρᾶξις
αὐτῆς
ἐστιν.

5. Ὁδοὶ *⌐γὰρ⌐ εἰσιν[20] δύο, καλοῦ καὶ κακοῦ· ἐν οἷς[21] εἰσι
τὰ δύο[22] διαβούλια ἐν στέρνοις[23] ἡμῶν[24] *διακρίνοντα αὐτά[25].
6. Ἐὰν οὖν[26] ἡ ψυχὴ θέλει[27] *†καλῶς πορευθῆναι†, πάσας
τὰς πράξεις αὐτῆς ποιεῖ[28] ἐν δικαιοσύνῃ, *κἂν ἁμάρτῃ[29] εὐθὺς[30]

Ἰακὼβ A[b]*) περὶ διπλόης καὶ ἀρετῆς.   [2]f reads Ἀσσήρ always.   [3]ad read
ὅσα.   [4]α, A (save that h om. εἰκοστῷ).   bf, S[1] read ἐν (b om.) ἑκατοστῷ
εἰκ. ἔκτῳ (b om.) ἔτει, und aeg ἐν (eg om.) ρ (ἑκατοστῷ g) κϛ′ ἔτει (+ τῆς a).
d ἐν τῷ ρκϛ′ ἔτει τῆς.   [5]g om.   [6]α. afg, A[abcdef] read ὑγιαίνων. bde,
S[1] ἔτι ὑγιαίνων. A[b]* = ἀσθενήσας.   [7]A[b]* = ἐκάλεσε αὐτοὺς καὶ εἶπεν.
[8]aef, A om.   [9]A = ὅτι.   [10] = יָשָׁר a paronomasia with אָשֵׁר (i.e.
Ἀσήρ).   [11]d reads κυρίου ποιήσατε καί. g adds ὑμῶν.   [12]A[bb*d] read
ὑπέδειξα.   [13]d adds αὐτό.   [14]d reads ὑπέδειξεν ὁ θ. τοῖς ἀνθρώποις.
[15]α, adef. b, S[2] read κ. δύο τόπους. g κ. δ. πόνους. S[1] om.   [16]h. ci, e read
κ. δ. τέλεια. bdg, S[1] κ. δ. τέλη. af om.   [17]def read τὰ πάντα.   [18]b om.
d reads ἐκ. A[ef] om. next ten words through hmt.   [19]A adds ὅτι.
a om. next four words.   [20]α. β, S[1] om. A = εἰσίν.   [21]hi, β–g.
c reads αἷς. g, A ᾧ. οἷς refers to καλοῦ καὶ κακοῦ, but if αἷς is right it refers
to ὁδοί, which noun might again be referred to by αὐτάς (abeg). If ἐν
αἷς and αὐτάς may be taken together, we should regard them as corruptions
of αἷς ... ἐν αὐταῖς. Thus the text would imply אשר ... בהם.   [22]d om.
[23]α reads corruptly ἑτέροις.   [24]hi, d read ὑμῶν.   [25]α, f. β–df read
δ. αὐτάς. d om. A = καὶ διάκρισις αὐτῶν. See note 21.   [26]dg om.
[27]d reads θελήσῃ εἶναι.   [28]α (save that c reads αὐτοῖς). β, A, S[1] read as
in margin (save that g om. αὐτῆς). In order to deal with the corruption
in καλῶς πορευθῆναι (α) and ἐν καλῷ (β, A, S[1]) we must observe that in
verses 3, 5 our author has spoken of two inclinations in the breast of
man, which are directed towards good and evil. In verses 6–8 the
result of man's following one or other of these two is set forth, of
following the good inclination in verses 6–7 and of following the evil in
ver. 8. The soul (ver. 6) has to decide between them. Now καλῶς
πορευθῆναι appears to be a rendering of בטוב לצאת which may be
a corruption of ביצר הטוב. If so, we should read ἐν τῷ καλῷ διαβουλίῳ.
In ver. 8 the corresponding phrase ביצר הרע is likewise corruptly given
in the Greek ἐν πονηρῷ ... τὸ διαβούλιον, where the corruption is native

μετανοεῖ.　　7. Δίκαια *γὰρ λογιζομένη[31] καὶ ἀπορρίπτουσα[32] τὴν πονηρίαν ἀνατρέπει εὐθὺς τὸ κακόν[33], καὶ[34] ἐκριζοῖ[35] τὴν ἁμαρτίαν.　・8. Ἐὰν δὲ *ἐν †πονηρῷ[36] κλίνῃ[37] †τὸ διαβούλιον†[38], *πᾶσα πρᾶξις αὐτῆς ἐστιν[39] ἐν πονηρίᾳ, καὶ[40] ἀπωθουμένη[41] τὸ ἀγαθόν, *καὶ προσκολλώμενος[42] τὸ κακόν, καὶ κυριευθεὶς[43] ὑπό[44] τοῦ Βελίαρ· κἂν[45] ἀγαθὸν[46] πράξει[47], ⌐ἐν πονηρίᾳ[48] αὐτὸ[49] μεταστρέφει[50]⌐.　　9. *Ὅτε γὰρ[51] ἄρξεται[52] *τὸ ἀγαθὸν ποιεῖν[53], τὸ τέλος τῆς πράξεως *εἰς πονηρὸν αὐτῷ ἐλαύνει[54]· ἐπειδὴ ὁ[55] θησαυρὸς[56] τοῦ διαβουλίου[57] πονηροῦ[58] πνεύματος πεπλήρωται[59].

προσλαμ-
βάνει.
β, S
ὡς ἀγ.
ποιῶν.
β–b, A, S¹
αὐτοῦ εἰς
κακο-
ποίησιν
ἐλαύνει.
β–dg ἰοῦ
πονηροῦ.

to the Greek.　[29] bde, A, S¹.　α, afg read καὶ ἡ (g κἂν) ἁμαρτία.　[30] h reads αὐτῇ, i αὐτῆς.　[31] α, g (save that c om. γάρ). abef, S¹ read γ. λογιζόμενος. d γ. λογιζόμεθα. A = γ. λογίζεται.　[32] α, g. β–g read ἀπορρίπτων. A = ἀπορρίπτει.　[33] A adds ἀπ' αὐτοῦ.　[34] c om.　[35] α, d read ἐκριζεῖ.　[36] d = ἐστὶ πονηρόν. See note 38.　[37] h, ae, Aᵇ*ᶜᵈᵉᶠ, bdfg, S read κλίνει. c ἐκκλίνει. Aᵃᵇ λογίσεται (by internal corruption).　[38] Read τῷ διαβουλίῳ or rather read the whole clause thus: ἐὰν δὲ κλίνῃ ἐν τῷ πονηρῷ διαβουλίῳ. The ψυχή is here as in ver. 6 the subject of κλίνῃ. Observe the αὐτῆς after πρᾶξις. This verse is concerned with the evil inclination (יצר הרע = τὸ πονηρὸν διαβούλιον), which naturally pursues evil, as the good inclination pursues good.　[39] g reads πᾶσαι αἱ π. αὐτῷ. d, Aᵇ*ᶜᵈᵉᶠ om. αὐτῆς in this clause.　[40] g reads ὅτι καί.　[41] g (though in the form ἀποθουμένη). α, def read ἀποθούμενος. a, S¹ ἀποθέμενος. b ἀπωθούμενος.　[42] c (reading προσκολλόμενος). The participle should be feminine as ψυχή is subject. So also κυριευθείς. β, A, S¹ read as in margin (save that d reads καὶ λαμβάνει). α = תִּדְבַּק. β, A, S¹ = תְּקַבֵּל.　[43] See note 42.　[44] h, g reads ἀπό.　[45] d reads καί.　[46] defg, S, A add τι.　[47] a reads πράξῃ.　[48] g reads πονηρίᾳ ἐστὶ κακόν and om. next two words.　[49] c, be, S¹. h reads αὐτόν. af αὐτῷ. d αὐτοῦ.　[50] α, be, S. af read μεταστραφήσεται. d καταστρέφει.　[51] α, af. β–af read ὅταν γάρ. A = καὶ ὅταν.　[52] h. c reads ἄρξειτε which in this MS. would represent ἄρξηται. β ἐνάρξηται.　[53] α. β, S read as in margin (save that g om. ὡς and dg read ποιοῦσα). A = ἀγαθῶν ἔργων. d adds τότε.　[54] α (save that h reads αὐτόν). β–b, A, S¹ read as in margin.(save that dg read αὐτῆς and g κακοποιῖαν). b, S² αὐτοῦ εἰς κακὸν ποιεῖν ἀνελαύνει. g, A add αὐτόν.　[55] g om.　[56] In θησαυρὸς τοῦ διαβουλίου there was a play upon words in the original אצר יצר. See Taylor, Sayings of the Fathers², p. 151.　[57] α, adef, S. b reads διαβόλου. g om. abef, A add ἰοῦ. This word may have arisen through a dittography of the last three letters of διαβουλίου or possibly it may have been lost through hmt. S adds κατακυριεύεται ὑπὸ τοῦ Βελίαρ ἐπεί (καί S²).　[58] α, β, S. A = πονηροῦ πονηρίας.　[59] g reads γεγένηται. a trs. before πνεύματος.

β-g, A
†λέ-
γουσα,
⌐φησί⌐†.

abg, A, S¹
ἄγει.

β, A, S¹
λειτουρ-
γοῦντα
αὐτῷ ἐν
κακῷ.

II. *῎Εστιν οὖν[1] ἡ[2] ⌐ψυχὴ *ἐν λόγοις †ἀφιστῶσα[3] τὸ καλὸν ὑπὲρ *τοῦ κακοῦ[4], καὶ *τὸ τέλος[5] *τοῦ πράγματος[6] εἰς κακίαν †ἄγων[7]. 2. ῎Εστιν[8] ἄνθρωπος ὃς[9] οὐκ οἰκτείρει[10] *λειτουργοὺς αὐτοῦ[11]· καίγε τοῦτο διπρόσωπον[12], ἀλλὰ τὸ ὅλον πονηρόν ἐστιν.

α	β, A, S¹
3. ῎Εστιν ἄνθρωπος ἀγαπῶν πονηρευόμενον †ὅ ἐστι πονηρία†[13], ὅτι καὶ ἀποθανεῖν αἱρεῖται ἐν κακῷ· καὶ περὶ τούτου φανερόν ἐστι†τὸ ὅλον†[14] διπρόσωπόν ἐστι τὸ δὲ πᾶν κακὴ πρᾶξις.	3. Καί[15] ἐστιν ἄνθρωπος ἀγαπῶν τὸν[16] πονηρευόμενον· *ὡς αὐτός ἐστιν ἐν πονηρίᾳ[17], ὅτι ⌐καὶ⌐ ἀποθανεῖν αἱρεῖται ἐν κακῷ *δι' αὐτόν[18]· καὶ περὶ τούτου φανερὸν ὅτι διπρόσωπόν[19] ἐστι· τὸ δὲ πᾶν κακὴ πρᾶξις.

α	β, S¹	A
4. †Καίγε ἀγάπη οὖσα, ἐν πονηρίᾳ ἐστὶν ὁ συγκρύπτων[20]τὸ κακὸν ὑπὲρ τὸ ὄνομα τὸ καλόν·† τὸ δὲ τέλος τῆς πράξεως ἔρχεται εἰς κακόν.	4. †Καίγε ἀγάπη οὖσα, *ἐν πονηρίᾳ[21] ἐστὶν συγκρύπτουσα†τὸ κακόν, ὅπερ[22] ἐστὶν[23] τῷ[24] ὀνόματι ὡς καλόν[25]· τὸ δὲ τέλος τῆς πράξεως ἔρχεται εἰς κακόν.	4. Εἰ καὶ ἐν ἀγάπῃ εἰσίν, ἐν πονηρίᾳ εἰσιν συγκρύπτοντες τὸ κακὸν ὃ ὀνόματι ὡς καλὸν φαίνεται· τὸ δὲ τέλος τῆς πράξεως †ἐστὶ[26] εἰς κακόν.

II. [1]α. β–dg, S¹. d reads ἔστι. g ἔστιν γάρ. A = καὶ ἔστιν. [2]α. β, A, S¹ om. [3]α. ἀφιστῶσα = מסירה corrupt (?) for מסכנה = ἀντιλαμβανομένη 'helps.' We should then read τοῦ καλοῦ for τὸ καλόν. β–g read as in margin (save that d adds δῆθεν before φησί), but their text can only be regarded as a bad emendation of α, or at all events a no less corrupt text. g reads φησὶ θέλουσα. A = λέγουσα. S¹ = ποιοῦσα, φησί—all equally unsatisfactory. [4]d reads τὸ κακόν and om. rest of verse. [5]af read τῷ τέλει. [6]A^{ab} = τῶν πραγμάτων. A^{b*cd} ἔξω. [7]α, ef. This should be ἄγουσα or ἄγον. abg, A, S¹ read ἄγει. a om. verses 2–4. [8]A^{b*cdf} read καί. A° καί ἐστιν. [9]α, d, A. S¹ read ὅστις. befg ὅτι. [10]d reads κατοικτειρεῖ (sic). S¹ ἀγαπᾷ. [11]α. β (save that d adds τόν before λειτουργ.), A, S¹ read as in margin. [12]d reads πονηρόν ἐστι καὶ διπρόσωπον and om. next five words. [13]This is either a gloss or a corruption of the text found in β, A, S. [14]Bracketed as a dittographic rendering of הכל in the next clause and thrust in here by mistake. [15]bdg, A, S. ef om. [16]bdeg, S¹. f, A om. [17]f. d, A, S¹ read ὡς καὶ αὐτὸς ὑπάρχων ἐν πονηρίᾳ. beg ὡσαύτως ἐστὶν ἐν πονηρίᾳ. Here ὡς appears to be used causally. Thus the object of this clause is to explain the preceding clause. But since the

5. Ἄλλος[27] κλέπτει, ἀδικεῖ[28], ἁρπάζει, πλεονεκτεῖ[28], καὶ ἐλεεῖ[29] πτωχούς· διπρόσωπον μὲν ⌜καὶ⌝[30] τοῦτο, *τὸ δὲ ὅλον[31] πονηρόν[32] ἐστιν.   6. *Ὁ πλεονεκτῶν[33] τὸν[34] πλησίον[28] παροργίζει τὸν Θεόν, καὶ[35] τὸν ὕψιστον[36] ἐπιορκεῖ καὶ τὸν πτωχὸν[37] ἐλεεῖ[38]· τὸν ἐντολέα[39] *τοῦ νόμου[40] Κύριον[41] ἀθετεῖ[42] καὶ παροξύνει, καὶ τὸν πένητα ἀναπαύει.   7. ⌜Τὴν⌝[43] ψυχὴν σπιλοῖ, καὶ⌝ τὸ σῶμα λαμπρύνει[44], πολλοὺς ἀναιρεῖ καὶ ὀλίγους ἐλεεῖ, καὶ τοῦτο[45] διπρόσωπόν[46] ἐστι, *τὸ δὲ ὅλον πονηρόν ἐστιν[47].   8. Ἄλλος[48] μοιχεύει *καὶ πορνεύει[49] καὶ ἀπέχεται ἐδεσμάτων[50]· καὶ[51] νηστεύων κακοποιεῖ, καὶ τῇ[35] δυναστείᾳ *τοῦ πλούτου[52] πολλοὺς κατασύρει[53], καὶ ἐκ[54] τῆς ὑπερόγκου[55] κακίας ποιεῖ[56] ⌜τὰς⌝[57] ἐντολάς[58]· καὶ

[margin: β,S¹ τοὺς πτωχούς.]
[margin: bdg, A καὶ τῷ καὶ πλούτῳ.]

real explanation is given in the ὅτι clause, we must regard the ὡς clause either as corrupt or as interpolated. d adds καὶ τοσοῦτον. [18]A = αὐτοῦ. [19]g reads διπρόσωπος. [20]α (save that c reads συγκύπτων). But ὁ συγκρύπτων is difficult. If we retain it ἀγάπη οὖσα must be taken as a concessive clause by itself, 'though love be present.' If ver. 4 refers to the same subject as ver. 3 then ὁ συγκρύπτων seems wrong. This phrase = המחביא which may be corrupt for האוהב = ὁ ἀγαπῶν. But the closing words in ver. 3 imply that the subject of that verse is fully dealt with. If this is so, then a lacuna should be marked at the beginning of ver. 4. [21]defg. b, S¹ read πονηρία. [22]defg. b, S¹ read ὥσπερ. ὑπέρ in α may be a corruption of ὅπερ, and τὸ ὄνομα a corruption of τῷ ὀνόματι. [23]e om. [24]d adds μέν. [25]bdg read καλῷ. [26]A reads ⟨Arm.⟩ (= ἐστίν) corrupt for ⟨Arm.⟩ (= ἔρχεται). [27]d adds δέ. For ἄλλος A reads ἄλλοι here and in the subsequent verses. A adds πάλιν. [28]a om. [29]β, S add τούς. [30]h, a, A om. [31]b reads ὅλον δέ. [32]e reads πονηρῶν. [33]α, β–bd. bd, S¹ read πλεονεκτῶν. A=πλεονεκτεῖ and adds καί before παροργίζει. [34]α reads τῷ. a om. [35]g om. [36]A adds Θεόν. [37]g reads Θεόν. [38]b reads ἐλεᾷ. a om. rest of verse. [39]d reads ποιητήν. Aᵃ=ἐντολήν, Aᵇ corrupt. [40]β, A, S. α om. [41]d trs. after ἀθετεῖ. [42]A reads ⟨Arm.⟩ (= ψεύδεται) corrupt for ⟨Arm.⟩ = ἀθετεῖ. [43]d reads καὶ τήν. [44]h om. A adds καί. [45]bdg add μέν. [46]A = διπλόη. [47]c, β–b (save that c, d om. ἐστιν). h, b om. A = καὶ κακὸν τὸ ὅλον. S¹ καὶ τοῦτο χεῖρον. [48]A = ἄλλοι πάλιν with following verbs in the plural. [49]b, A, S¹. adefg read πορνεύει. c πορνεία. hi om. This phrase is probably an interpolation. [50]c reads ἐκδεσμάτων. b αἰδεσμάτων. Aᵇ*ᶜᵈᵉᶠ = ἐδέσματος. [51]d om. [52]α, aef, S¹. bdg, A read as in margin. A adds αὐτῶν. [53]α. β–d read παρασύρει. d ἐπισύρει. [54]= 'immediately after' but probably מרע (= ἐκ κακίας) is corrupt for ברע = 'notwithstanding his wickedness.' [55]c reads ὑπὲρ οἴκου. [56]If the preceding ἐκ retains its ordinary meaning, this word can hardly be

τοῦτο διπρόσωπόν ἐστιν[59], *τὸ δὲ ὅλον[60] κακόν ἐστιν. 9.
Οἱ τοιοῦτοί εἰσι[61] δασύποδες, ὅτι[62] ἐξ ἡμισείας εἰσὶ καθαροί, τὸ
δ' ἀληθὲς[63] ἀκάθαρτοί εἰσι. 10. *Καὶ γὰρ[64] ὁ Θεὸς ἐν ταῖς
πλαξὶ[65]· τῶν ἐντολῶν[66] οὕτως εἶπεν.

bdg ὡς ὕες εἰσί. β, A, S¹ οὐρανῶν.

III. Ὑμεῖς[1] δέ[2], *τέκνα μου[3], μὴ γίνεσθε *κατ' αὐτοὺς[4]
διπρόσωποι, ἀγαθότητος καὶ κακίας, ἀλλὰ τῇ ἀγαθότητι μόνῃ[5]
κολλήθητε, ὅτι ⌈Κύριος⌉[6] ὁ Θεὸς *ἀναπέπαυται ἐπ'[7] αὐτήν[8], καὶ
οἱ ἄνθρωποι *αὐτὴν ποθοῦσιν[9]. 2. *Τὴν ⌈δὲ⌉ κακίαν ἀποδράσατε[10], ἀναιροῦντες *τὸ διαβούλιον[11] ἐν ταῖς ἀγαθαῖς ὑμῶν
πράξεσι, ὅτι οἱ διπρόσωποι *οὐκ εἰσὶ τοῦ Θεοῦ[12], ἀλλὰ ταῖς
ἐπιθυμίαις αὐτῶν δουλεύουσιν, ἵνα τῷ Βελίαρ ἀρέσωσιν, καὶ
τοῖς ὁμοίοις[13] αὐτῶν ἀνθρώποις.

β, A, S¹ οὖν. β, A, S¹ ἀναπαύεται εἰς. β, A, S¹ τὸν διά-βολον. β, A, S¹ οὐ Θεῷ.

IV. Οἱ γὰρ ἀγαθοὶ ἄνθρωποι[1] *⌈καὶ⌉ μονοπρόσωποι κἂν[2]
νομισθῶσι παρὰ τῶν[3] διπροσώπων[4] ἁμαρτάνειν[5], δίκαιοί εἰσι
παρὰ τῷ[6] Θεῷ. 2. Πολλοὶ ⌈δὲ⌉[7] ἀναιροῦντες τοὺς[8] πονηρούς,
δύο[9] ποιοῦσιν ἔργα *καλοῦ τε καὶ κακοῦ[10], *τὸ δὲ ὅλον[11]
καλόν, ὅτι τὸ[12] κακὸν ἐκριζώσας ἀπώλεσεν. 3. *Ἔστι
τις μισῶν[13] τὸν ἐλεήμονα καὶ ἄδικον[14], ⌈καὶ⌉[15] τὸν μοιχὸν

β, S¹ γάρ. adef καλὸν διὰ κακοῦ.

right. In that case ποιεῖ = יַעֲשֶׂה which may be corrupt for יְעַוֵּת = διαστρέφει.
[57] α. β, A, S om. [58] A = ἔλεος. [59] e, A = δοκεῖ. g om. α, S om.
next five words through hmt. [60] adef. bg read ὅλον δέ. For τὸ δὲ . . .
ἐστίν A reads καὶ κακὸν τὸ ὅλον. [61] α, S¹. aef read ὅσοι εἰσί. bdg read
as in margin (save that g gives corruptly ὡς υἵαις ει). A οὖν εἰσιν ὡς ὕες
δασεῖς. [62] S¹ om. [63] d adds εἰπεῖν. [64] A = διὸ καί. [65] g adds πράξεσι.
S = βιβλίοις. [66] α. β, A, S¹ read as in margin. hi add ῥητῶς.

III. [1] A^{abb*cd} = καὶ ὑμεῖς. [2] α. β, A, S¹ read as in margin. [3] S om.
[4] g trs. after διπρόσωποι. S om. [5] ad, A read μόνον. [6] α. β, A,
S om. efg add καί. [7] α. β, A, S read as in margin. [8] hi read αὐτῆς.
A = τοιούτους. [9] α. β, A, S read ποθοῦσιν (A ποθήσουσιν) αὐτήν. [10] α,
β-ad, A, S (save that β-ad, A, S om. δέ). a reads τὴν δὲ κακίαν φεύγετε.
d ἀποδράσατε οὖν τ. κ. [11] α. β, A, S read as in margin. [12] α, A^b. A^b
adds δοῦλοι. β, A^{ab*cdef}, S¹ read as in margin. [13] f reads ἰδίοις.

IV. [1] α, aef. bdg read ἄνδρες. A adds εἰσίν. [2] β, A, S¹. α
corruptly reads κἂν μονοπρόσωποι (hi μονοπρόσωπον). [3] hi trs. after
διπροσώπων. [4] adef add ἀνθρώπων. [5] α reads ἁμαρτωλῶν possibly
corrupt for ἁμαρτωλοί. [6] e om. [7] α. β, S¹ read as in margin. [8] ef om.
[9] α trs. before πονηρούς. [10] α. S¹ practically the same = καλὸν καὶ κακόν.
adef read as in margin. bg, A κακὸν διὰ καλοῦ. [11] α. b reads ὅλον
ἐστὶ δέ. adefg ὅλον δ' ἐστί. A^{ab} om. together with καλόν. [12] hi, g om.
d reads τόν. [13] A = καὶ εἰσιν πάλιν τινὲς μισοῦντες. S¹ adds δέ after ἐστί.
[14] b, S¹ read ἀδικῶν. hi, A read τὸν ἄδικον. [15] α, adf. beg, A, S¹ om.

καὶ[16] νηστεύοντα[17], *καὶ αὐτό ἐστι διπρόσωπον[18], ἀλλὰ ⌐τὸ   β, Α, S¹
πᾶν⌐ ἔργον ἀγαθόν[19], ὅτι μιμεῖται[20] Κύριον, μὴ[21] †προσδοκώ-   προσ-
μενος[22] τὸ δοκοῦν καλὸν †μετὰ[23] *τοῦ ἀληθινοῦ[24] καλοῦ[25].   δεχό-
4. Ἄλλος[26] οὐ θέλει *ἰδεῖν ⌐ἡμέρας⌐ ἀγαθὰς[27] μετὰ ἀσώτων,   μενος.
ἵνα μὴ αἰσχρανεῖ[28] τὸ σῶμα[29] καὶ τὴν ψυχὴν μολυνεῖ[30].   β, S¹
*καίγε τοῦτο διπρόσωπον[31], ὅλον[32] δὲ καλόν[33] ἐστιν.   5.   κακοῦ.
*Οἱ γὰρ[34] τοιοῦτοι δορκάσι[35] καὶ ἐλάφοις[36] *εἰσιν ὅμοιοι[37],
ὅτι ἐν ἤθει ἀγρίων[38] δοκοῦσιν ἀκάθαρτοι εἶναι, *τὸ δὲ πᾶν[39]   β-de, S¹
καθαροί εἰσιν[39], ὅτι ἐν ζήλῳ Κυρίου[40] ⌐πορεύονται⌐, ἀπεχό-   ἀγρίῳ.
μενοι *ὧν καὶ ὁ Θεὸς διὰ τῶν ἐντολῶν μισῶν ἀπαγορεύει[41],   β, Α, S¹
*ἀπείργων τὸ κακὸν τοῦ ἀγαθοῦ[42].   Θεοῦ.

[16] α, Α add τόν, but β rightly om.   [17] b reads ληστεύοντα. S¹ corrupt.
[18] abef, Α, S¹. α, dg read corruptly καίγε (dg καὶ) αὐτός ἐστι (c om.)
διπρόσωπος (d διπρόσωπον).   [19] β, Α, S¹ add ἐστί.   [20] h adds τόν.
[21] d reads καί.   [22] c. hi, β, A^{ab*cd}, S¹ read as in margin. A^b = προσδέχεται
Θεός. προσδοκώμενος is a corruption of προσδεχόμενος or it is a translation
of מְקַוֶּה corrupt for מְקַבֵּל = προσδεχόμενος.   [23] = בְּ corrupt for כְּ.
Thus we have 'the seeming good as the genuine good.' Yet עִם
may have stood in this sense.   [24] d reads ἀληθινοῦ. A^{b*cdef} =
τῆς ἀληθείας.   [25] α, A^{ab}. β, S¹ read as in margin. A^{b*cdef} omit.
[26] α, aef. bdg read ἕτερος.   [27] c. h, b, S¹ read ἰδεῖν ἡμέραν ἀγαθήν (save
that ab¹, S¹ trs. ἰδεῖν after ἀγαθήν). d ἰδεῖν ἡμέραν κακήν. aefg ἀγ. ἡμέραν
ἰδεῖν. c may have been influenced by LXX of Ps. xxxiv. 12. In h, β, S¹
we have the technical use of טוֹב יוֹם as meaning a time of enjoyment
or festival. Cf. Esther viii. 17.   Text of h, β, S¹ is to be preferred.
Α = ἀγαθὸν (A^{b*cd} om.) ἰδεῖν (transposing the ἰδεῖν after ἀσώτων).   [28] ef.
ad read αἰσχράνῃ. b χράνῃ. g μιανεῖ. c (h?) ἐχθραίνει. hi ἐχεράνη (sic).
The reading of α seems a corruption of that of β.   [29] b reads στόμα.
[30] β, Α, S¹ trs. before τὴν ψ. For μολυνεῖ, hi, ad read μολύνῃ.   [31] α, abefg,
S¹ (save that c adds αὐτό and S¹ πᾶν after τοῦτο). d reads καίγε
καὶ τοῦτο ὅλον. ef add ἐστί. Α = τοῦτο οὖν διπλόη ἐστί. a om. rest of
verse.   [32] α read μᾶλλον.   [33] d²g read κακόν.   [34] α. b, S¹ read
ὅτι οἱ. adefg οἱ. Α = καὶ οἱ.   [35] be read δόρκοις. g prefixes τοῖς.   [36] g
prefixes τοῖς.   [37] α. β, Α, S¹ read ὅμοιοί εἰσιν.   [38] α, ade, A^{sf(?)}. β-ade,
S¹ read ἀγρίῳ. A^{bb*cd(?)} = ἀγριότητι.   [39] A^{b*d} om.   [40] α. β, Α, S¹ read as
in margin.   [41] h, β-g, Α, S¹ (save that h om. καὶ, f τῶν, and Α reads μισεῖν).
c reads ὧν ὁ Θεὸς μισεῖ. g οὖν τὸ πονηρόν, ἐργάζεσθε τὸ καλόν, ὅτι ὁ Θεὸς διὰ
τῶν ἐντολῶν τῶν ἔργων ὧν μισεῖ ἀπαγορεύει.   [42] β-ag, S¹ (save that bd, S¹
read ἀπείργον). c, a om. h reads τὸ κακὸν ἐκ τοῦ ἀγαθοῦ. g τὸ γινόμενον
ἀγαθόν.   Α = καὶ ἀπείργειν τὸ κακὸν τοῦ ἀγαθοῦ.

V. Ὁρᾶτε[1], τέκνα[2], πῶς δύο[3] εἰσὶν ⌜ἐν πᾶσιν⌝, ἐν[4] κατέναντι τοῦ ἑνός, *καὶ ἐν ὑπὸ τοῦ ἑνὸς[5] κέκρυπται· ⌜ἐν τῇ κτήσει ἡ πλεονεξία, ἐν τῇ εὐφροσύνῃ ἡ μέθη, ἐν τῷ γέλωτι τὸ πένθος, ἐν τῷ γάμῳ ἡ ἀσωτία⌝[6].   2. Τὴν[7] ζωὴν ὁ θάνατος διαδέχεται, τὴν δόξαν ἡ ἀτιμία, τὴν ἡμέραν ἡ νύξ[8], τὸ φῶς τὸ σκότος· τὰ δὲ πάντα[9] ὑπὸ ἡμέραν εἰσίν[10], ὑπὸ ζωὴν[11] τὰ δίκαια, ⌜ὑπὸ θάνατον τὰ ἄδικα⌝[12]·   διὸ καὶ τὸν[13] θάνατον ἡ αἰώνιος ζωὴ ἀναμένει[14].   3. Καὶ οὐκ[15] ἔστιν εἰπεῖν τὴν ἀλήθειαν ψεῦδος, οὐδὲ *τὸ δίκαιον ἄδικον[16], ὅτι πᾶσα ἀλήθεια ὑπὸ *τοῦ φωτός[17] ἐστιν, ⌜καθὼς τὰ πάντα[18] ὑπὸ *τοῦ Θεοῦ⌝[19]. 4. Ταῦτα οὖν[20] πάντα ⌜ἐγὼ⌝[21] ἐδοκίμασα ἐν τῇ ζωῇ μου, καὶ οὐκ ἐπλανήθην ἀπὸ τῆς ἀληθείας Κυρίου, καὶ[22] τὰς ἐντολὰς τοῦ ὑψίστου[23] ἐξεζήτησα[24] κατὰ πᾶσαν ἰσχύν μου πορευόμενος[25].

VI. Προσέχετε οὖν *καὶ ὑμεῖς, τέκνα μου[1], *τὰς ἐντολὰς[2] Κυρίου[3] μονοπροσώπως *ἀκολουθοῦντες τῇ ἀληθείᾳ[4].   2. Ὅτι οἱ διπρόσωποι δισσῶς †κολάζονται[5], ⌜Ὅτι καὶ πράσσουσι

β, A, S[1] ὑπὸ ζωὴν τὰ δίκαια.

β, A, S[1] πορευόμενος μονοπροσώπως εἰς τὸ ἀγαθόν.

V. [1] b, A[b*cd], S[1] add οὖν.   [2] g om. A adds μου.   [3] d adds ὁδοί. [4] a om. next five words through hmt.   [5] g repeats. After κέκρυπται d adds καὶ γὰρ ἐν τῇ κρίσει ἡ προσωποληψία, μᾶλλον δὲ ἡ δωροληψία κέκρυπται. [6] α, adef, S[1] (save that all read κτίσει for κτήσει except h which reads κρίσει, a om. ἐν ... πλεονεξία, d adds δέ after ἐν 1° and 2° and instead of ἡ ἀσωτία which α read and f om., ae, S[1] read ἡ ἀκρασία, d ἡ ἀτεκνία). bg, A om. [7] d reads πρὸς τούτοις δὲ τήν.   [8] be, S[1] add καί. a om. next four words. [9] A adds ταῦτα.   [10] bd, S[1] add καί. h om. next four words.   [11] g adds ἦν. Printed Arm. Text reads τῶν δικαίων for τὰ δίκαια.   [12] α. β, A, S[1] om. [13] g reads μετά.   [14] h, β–g. c reads διαμένει. g μόνη μένει.   [15] d om. [16] g reads ἄδικον δίκαιον.   [17] α, bd. aefg read τὸ φῶς.   [18] α, bd. aefg read ὅλα.   [19] α, d. β–d read τὸν Θεόν. aef add ἐστίν. d εἰσίν.   [20] α, A. β, S[1] om.   [21] α. β, A, S[1] om.   [22] d, A read ἀλλά. d adds πάσας. [23] h reads Κυρίου.   [24] e reads ἐζήτησα.   [25] α. β, A, S[1] read as in margin.

VI. [1] α, adef. bg, S[1] read τέκνα καὶ ὑμεῖς. A = τέκνα μου.   [2] α, b. β–b read ταῖς ἐντολαῖς.   [3] c, g. h, β–g prefix τοῦ.   [4] h, β, A, S[1] (save that g reads ἀ. τὴν ἀλήθειαν and A καὶ ἀκολουθεῖτε τ. ἀ.). c reads ποιοῦντες.   [5] A = κολασθήσονται. Text = יאשמו or יחטאו which should here have been rendered ἁμαρτάνουσι. The double nature of the sin is then stated in ver. 2. There is no mention here of punishment. In 1 Enoch v. 9 one or other of these Hebrew verbs is rendered by ἁμάρτωσιν in the Gizeh Greek Version and in the Greek followed by the Ethiopic Version is rendered by κολασθήσονται, but in this passage the former is right and the latter wrong.   [6] α, adef, S[1] (save that d reads διότι for ὅτι). bg, A wrongly om.

τὸ κακόν, καὶ συνευδοκοῦσι τοῖς πράσσουσιν[7] [6], *μιμούμενοι bg, Α τὰ
τὰ πνεύματα τῆς πλάνης καὶ κατὰ τῶν ἀνθρώπων συναγωνιζόμενοι[7].
3. ⸤Ὑμεῖς οὖν, τέκνα μου⸥[8], τὸν νόμον Κυρίου[9] φυλάξατε·
καὶ[10] μὴ προσέχετε *τῷ κακῷ ὡς καλῷ[11], ἀλλὰ κατὰ[12] τὸ
ὄντως[9] καλὸν[13] ἀποβλέπετε, καὶ διατηρεῖτε αὐτὸ ἐν πάσαις
ταῖς[14] ἐντολαῖς Κυρίου, εἰς αὐτὸ[15] ἀναστρεφόμενοι, καὶ ἐν
αὐτῷ καταπαύοντες[16].   4. Ὅτι τὰ τέλη τῶν ἀνθρώπων
δεικνύουσι[17] τὴν δικαιοσύνην αὐτῶν[18], *καὶ †γνωρίζονται[19]
*τοῖς ἀγγέλοις[20] Κυρίου, καὶ τοῦ Βελίαρ[21].   5. Ὅτε[22] γὰρ
†πονηρὰ[23] ἡ ψυχὴ ἀπέρχεται[24], βασανίζεται ὑπὸ τοῦ πονηροῦ
πνεύματος, *ὃ καὶ[25] ἐδούλευεν[26] ἐν ἐπιθυμίαις[27] καὶ ἔργοις
πονηροῖς.

Right margin: πνεύματα τῆς πλάνης μισήσατε τὰ κατὰ τῶν ἀνθρώπων ἀγωνιζόμενα. β, Α, S¹ (+καὶ Α) γνωρίζοντες (Α γνωρίζουσι).

β-ef, S¹ τοὺς ἀγγέλους.   β, Α, S¹ τεταραγμένη.

---

this clause which states the two sins of which the διπρόσωποι are guilty. This clause has been taken over bodily by S. Paul into Rom. i. 32. [7] α (save that h reads ἀγωνιζόμενοι). aef, S¹ support α but differ slightly and gave a different order: τὰ πνεύματα τῆς πλάνης μιμούμενοι (+τὰ e, S¹) κατὰ τῶν ἀνθ. ἀγωνιζόμενα. bg, A owing to the loss of the preceding clause rewrote the text. d is conflate as frequently, combining both texts. bdg, A = τὰ πνεύματα τῆς πλάνης μισήσατε τὰ (d ὅτι, g καὶ τὰ) κατὰ τῶν ἀνθρώπων (b τὸν ἄνθρωπον) ἀγωνιζόμενα (d ἀγωνίζονται). [8] α, aef, S¹. bdg, A om. [9] g om. [10] c om. [11] α, ag, A, S¹. bef read τὸ κακὸν ὡς καλόν. d τῷ καλῷ ὡς κακῷ. [12] α, aef. bd reads εἰς. g om. [13] For ὄντως καλόν A^el reads δίκαιον λόγον (by internal corruption), A^abb*cd δίκαιον καὶ καλόν. [14] α, d. abefg, A om. [15] b, S¹ read αὐτόν. [16] A read ֍ֆֹֆ֍֍ (=φροντίζοντες) corrupt for ֍֍֍֍֍ = καταπαύοντες (intransitively used). [17] α (for usual form δεικνύασι). β reads δείκνυσι. [18] S om. A^ab om. rest of VI and all VII. [19] α. abef, S¹ read γνωρίζοντες. dg γνωριζόντων. A = καὶ γνωρίζειν (= καὶ γνωρίζουσι). But all are corrupt. γνωρίζονται τοῖς ἀγγέλοις = יודעו למלאכים where the verb is corrupt for יודעו = 'meet the angels.' The LXX implies the same corruption in Amos iii. 3. Read καὶ συναντῶσι. [20] α, ef. abdg, S¹ read τοὺς ἀγγέλους. A = τὸν νόμον. [21] α. β, A, S¹ = Σατανᾶ. [22] α, aef. bdg read ἐάν. [23] α. β, A, S¹ (save that e reads τεταγμένη) read as in margin. α = רֹעשׁה which may be a corruption of רעשׁה = τεταραγμένη. The text of β is preferable, since ἥσυχος defines the opposite emotion. See next verse. [24] d reads ἐξέρχεται. e ἀνέρχεται. [25] c, g (omitting καί). h reads καὶ γάρ. β-g read ᾧ καί. [26] c. h, β, S¹ read ἐδούλευσεν. [27] h reads ἐπιθυμίᾳ. [28] α, f (omitting ἐστίν). abeg, A read ἡσύχως. d ἡσύχως εἰσέρχεται καί.

α

6. Ἐὰν δέ *ἔστιν ἥσυχος[28] *ἐν χαρᾷ[29] †γνωρίζει[30] τὸν ἄγγελον τῆς εἰρήνης, *καὶ εἰσφέρει αὐτὸν εἰς ζωὴν αἰώνιον[31].

β, A, S¹

6. Ἐὰν δὲ ἡσύχως ⌜ἐν χαρᾷ⌝ †ἐγνώρισε τὸν ἄγγελον τῆς εἰρήνης, παραμυθεῖται αὐτὸν ἐν ζωῇ.

VII. Μὴ γίνεσθε[1] ὡς Σόδομα[2], ἥτις ἠγνόησε[3] *τοὺς ἀγγέλους[4] Κυρίου, καὶ ἀπώλετο ἕως[5] αἰῶνος.   2. *Ἐγὼ γὰρ οἶδα[6] ὅτι ἁμαρτήσετε[7] καὶ παραδοθήσεσθε εἰς χεῖρας ἐχθρῶν ὑμῶν, ⌜καὶ⌝[8] ἡ γῆ ὑμῶν[9] ἐρημωθήσεται[10], καὶ τὰ ἅγια ὑμῶν καταφθαρήσονται[11], καὶ ὑμεῖς[12] διασκορπισθήσεσθε[13] εἰς τὰς τέσσαρας[14] γωνίας *τῆς γῆς[15], καὶ ἔσεσθε *εἰς διασπορὰν ἐξουδενωμένοι[16] ὡς[17] ὕδωρ[18] ἄχρηστον[19],   3. Ἕως οὗ[20] ὁ ὕψιστος ἐπισκέψηται τὴν γῆν, καὶ αὐτὸς ἐλθὼν [ὡς ἄνθρωπος[21] μετὰ ἀνθρώπων *ἐσθίων καὶ πίνων[22]], καὶ[23]

(left margin note): hi, β, A, S¹ καὶ (h, f om.) ἐν ἡσυχίᾳ συντρίβων.

[29] This phrase is omitted by A, S¹. If it is original it should be taken with γνωρίσει. But it seems to be an intrusion or a corruption. We should expect ἀπέρχεται. Cf. ver. 5.   [30] α. β, A, S read ἐγνώρισεν. Verb corrupt as in ver. 5. See note 19. Read συναντήσει or συνήντησε.   [31] α (hi reading αὐτήν). β, A, S¹ read (+καὶ S¹) παραμυθεῖται (dg, A παρακαλοῦντα, b παρακαλέσει) αὐτὸν ἐν ζωῇ (save that e reads αὐτήν and A ζωὴν αὐτοῦ). d adds αἰωνίᾳ καὶ ἀτελευτήτῳ. The text of α is to be preferred. εἰσφέρει = מְבִיאָם. This corrupted as מְנַחֲם explains aef, S¹ παραμυθεῖται and bdg, A παρακαλοῦντα. The LXX implies the same corruption in 1 Sam. xxii. 4; Is. lvii. 18. Moreover in T. Benj. vi. 1 reads ὁ γὰρ ἄγγελος τῆς εἰρήνης ὁδηγεῖ τὴν ψυχὴν αὐτοῦ where ὁδηγεῖ = מנחה or ינחי—a passage that confirms the text of α. It is noteworthy that Symmachus renders נחם as if it were ינחי in Job xxxix. 25—the converse corruption of that presupposed by β, A, S¹.

VII. [1] b, S¹ add τέκνα. d prefixes οὖν.   [2] A, S¹ read Σοδομίται followed by the requisite plurals. a om. rest of verse.   [3] A^{abb*d} read ἔγνωσαν, but A^{c f g} support text.   [4] d reads ἀγγέλους. A = τὸν ἄγγελον τῆς εἰρήνης.   [5] hi add τοῦ.   [6] c. hi, A reads ἐγὼ οἶδα. β, S¹ οἶδα γάρ.   [7] β–g. α read ἁμαρτήσητε. g ἁμαρτήσεσθε.   [8] a, A om.   [9] hi om.   [10] b om. next five words.   [11] α. β–bd read καταφθαρήσεται. d διαφθαρήσονται.   [12] d adds δέ.   [13] d adds ἐν τοῖς ἔθνεσιν.   [14] A^{b*d} = πάσας.   [15] af om.   [16] α. β, S¹ read ἐν διασπορᾷ (d διαφθορᾷ) ἐξουθενωμένοι (aefg ἐξουθενωμένοι). A = διασπαρέντες καὶ ἐξουθενωμένοι.   [17] c reads ὡσεί, the ει being added above the line.   [18] d reads εἶδος.   [19] α add here περὶ τοῦ (c om.) Χριστοῦ, c in margin and hi in text after τὴν γῆν. d τοῦ Χριστοῦ.   [20] g om.   [21] A adds καί. The bracketed clause is obviously a Christian interpolation.   [22] A =

συντρίβων²⁴ τὴν κάραν²⁵ τοῦ δράκοντος *ἐπὶ τοῦ²⁶ ὕδατος, β-g, S¹
*οὗτος σώσει²⁷ τὸν Ἰσραὴλ καὶ πάντα τὰ ἔθνη [θεὸς²⁸ εἰς ἀπειθεῖν.
ἄνδρα ὑποκρινόμενος²⁹].   4. Εἴπατε οὖν, ⌜τέκνα μου καὶ β, A, S¹
ὑμεῖς⌝³⁰ ταῦτα τοῖς τέκνοις ὑμῶν³¹, μὴ ἀπειθήσωσιν³² αὐτῷ. ἀνέγνων
5. *Ἐγὼ γὰρ ἔγνων³³ ὅτι ⌜ἀπειθοῦντες⌝³⁴ *ἀπειθήσετε, καὶ γάρ (αεf,
ἀσεβοῦντες ἀσεβήσετε³⁵, μὴ προσέχοντες³⁶ *τῷ νόμῳ³⁷ θεοῦ, S¹ ἔγνων
ἀλλ' ἐντολαῖς ἀνθρώπων *κακίᾳ διαφθειρόμενοι³⁸.   6. *Καὶ γάρ) ἐν
διὰ τοῦτο³⁹ διασκορπισθήσεσθε⁴⁰ ὡς Γὰδ καὶ⁴¹ Δάν, οἱ ταῖς
ἀδελφοί μου⁴², *καὶ ἀγνοήσετε χώρας αὐτῶν⁴³ καὶ φυλὴν καὶ πλαξὶ
γλῶσσαν⁴⁴·   7. Ἀλλ' ἐπισυνάξει ὑμᾶς⁴⁵ ἐν πίστει διὰ τῶν οὐ-
τῆς⁴⁶ εὐσπλαγχνίας αὐτοῦ, καὶ⁴⁷ δι' Ἀβραὰμ καὶ Ἰσαὰκ ρανῶν.
καὶ Ἰακώβ.   β, A, οἱ
                                                                        χώρας
                                                                        αὐτῶν
                                                                        ἀγνοή-
                                                                        σουσιν

(Α ἠγνόησαν).   β-e, A, S¹ ὑμᾶς Κύριος.   β, A, S¹ ἐλπίδα.

ἔδεται καὶ πίεται.   ²³ c, f, S¹ om. hi, β-f, A, S¹ add as in margin.   ²⁴A, S¹
= συντρίψει.   ²⁵ ch. i reads καρδίαν, β κεφαλήν.   ²⁶ g, Aᶜᶠᵍ. Aᵇ*ᵈ om.
together with ὕδατος. α, β-g read διά a change which may be due to
Christian influences, but yet διά can here mean 'in.' S¹ = τῇ βουλῇ or
τῷ ὕδατι. The text goes back to Ps. lxxiv. 13 בַּמַּיִם.   ²⁷ α, befg, S.
a reads σώσῃ. d σώσει οὕτως. Aᵇ*ᶜᵈᵍ = καὶ σώσει.   ²⁸ f reads ἕως. a om.
θεὸς ... ὑποκρινόμενος. The bracketed clause which follows is obviously
Christian.   ²⁹ hi, β-ag, S. c reads ἐπικρ. g ἀποκρ. A = φαινόμενος.
³⁰α. β, A, S om.   ³¹d adds τοῦ ἐντείλασθαι αὐτοῖς.   ³²α. β-g read
ἀπειθεῖν. g ἀπιστεῖν. A = ἀπιστήσωσιν.   ³³α. αef, S¹ and bdg, Aᵇ*ᶜᵈᶠᵍ
read as in margin (save that g reads πράξεσιν τῶν ἀνθρώπων for πλ. τῶν οὐρανῶν).
³⁴g om.   ³⁵α (save that they put the verbs in the aorist subj. and
hi add αὐτῷ after the first). β-d, A, S¹ read ἀπειθήσετε (A ἀπειθήσουσι)
αὐτῷ καὶ ἀσεβοῦντες ἀσεβήσετε (ab ἀσεβήσητε, A ἀσεβήσουσι) εἰς αὐτόν (g αὐτῷ).
d ἀπειθήσειτε εἰς αὐτόν. S¹ = αὐτῷ ἀπειθήσετε.   ³⁶g reads προσέχετε οὖν.
³⁷c, β-b. hi, b read τὸν νόμον. hi, β-f add τοῦ.   ³⁸α (save that hi read
διαφερόμενοι before κακίᾳ). defg read μονοπροσώπῳ (f μονοπροσώπων) κακίᾳ
φερόμενοι (f διαφερόμενοι). ab om. A=κακίᾳ (or εἰς κακίαν) πίπτοντές ἐστε. But
ܦ܂ܢ (= πίπτοντες) may be corrupt for ܦ܂ܢ = διαφθειρόμενοι.
S¹=μόνον ἕξετε κακίαν.   ³⁹hi. c reads καί. β, S¹ διὰ τοῦτο. A ἀλλὰ διὰ τοῦτο.
⁴⁰hi, g read σκορπισθήσεσθε.   ⁴¹i reads ὡς. b adds ὡς.   ⁴²A = ἡμῶν.
⁴³α (save that c reads ἀγνωήσειτε and h ἀγνοήσητε). β, A read as in margin.
S¹ = οὐκ ὄψονται τὴν χώραν αὐτῶν. The text of β, A is preferable owing to
next verse.   ⁴⁴β, A, S¹ add αὐτῶν.   ⁴⁵α, e. β-e, A, S¹ read as in
margin (save that Aᵉ reads ὑμᾶς θεός).   ⁴⁶c. h om. β, A, S¹ read as in
margin (save that f reads ἐλπίδος).   ⁴⁷α, d. β-d, A, S¹ om.

β-d, A, S¹
αὐτοῖς
λέγων.

β-d, A, S¹
Καὶ μετὰ
ταῦτα.

bg, A
ἀναγα-
γόντες
αὐτὸν
ἔθαψαν.

VIII. Καὶ[1] εἰπὼν αὐτοῖς ταῦτα ἐνετείλατο λέγων[2]· Θάψατέ με ἐν[3] Χεβρών[4]. Καὶ ἀπέθανεν[5] †ὕπνῳ[6] καλῷ κοιμηθείς[7]. 2. Καὶ[8] ἐποίησαν οἱ υἱοὶ αὐτοῦ ὅσα[9] ἐνετείλατο αὐτοῖς, καὶ[10] *ἀνήγαγον αὐτὸν ἐν Χεβρὼν καὶ ἔθαψαν αὐτὸν[11] μετὰ τῶν πατέρων αὐτοῦ[12].

Διαθήκη Ἰωσὴφ τοῦ ἑνδεκάτου υἱοῦ Ἰακὼβ καὶ Ῥαχιήλ[1].

β, S¹
τέκνα μου
καὶ ἀδελ-
φοί.

β, Aabc
dfg, S¹
υἱοί, τοῦ
πατρὸς
ὑμῶν.

I. Ἀντίγραφον διαθήκης Ἰωσήφ[2]. Ἐν τῷ μέλλειν αὐτὸν ἀποθνήσκειν[3], καλέσας[4] τοὺς υἱοὺς αὐτοῦ καὶ τοὺς ἀδελφοὺς ⌜αὐτοῦ⌝ εἶπεν αὐτοῖς.

2. *Ἀδελφοί μου καὶ τέκνα μου[5],

Ἀκούσατε Ἰωσὴφ[8] τοῦ ἠγαπημένου ὑπὸ[7] Ἰσραήλ[8],

Ἐνωτίσασθε *ῥήματα τοῦ στόματός μου.[9]

VIII. [1] This verse d gives as follows: καὶ ταῦτα εἰπὼν αὐτοῖς ἐκοιμήθη ἐν εἰρήνῃ. [2] α. β–d, A, S¹ read as in margin. [3] α, g. abef read εἰς. [4] h, e read Χευρών. [5] h, aef add ἐν. [6] = שׁינה corrupt for שׂיבה = γήρει. See T. Iss. vii. 9; T. Benj. xii. 2. The same corruption is found in T. Zeb. x. 6. [7] A = ἐκοιμήθη. [8] α. β–d, A, S¹ read as in margin. For καὶ ... αὐτόν 2° d reads καὶ ἀγαγόντες αὐτὸν οἱ υἱοὶ αὐτοῦ ἔθαψαν αὐτὸν ἐν Χεβρὼν ἐν τῷ σπηλαίῳ διπλῷ. [9] α. β–d, A, S¹ read ὡς. [10] g om. [11] α, aef (save that aef om. ἐν X. and h, aef om. αὐτόν 2°). S¹ = ἀνήγαγον αὐτόν (rest corrupt). bg, A read as in margin (save that g reads καὶ θάψαντες for αὐτ. ἔθ.). See d in note 8. d adds ἐν X. ἐν τῷ σπηλαίῳ διπλῷ. [12] A^b adds ἐν Χεβρών. f, S¹ read Ἀσσὴρ υἱὸς Ἰακὼβ ι΄, υἱὸς Ζέλφας β΄ (S¹ Z. β΄ καὶ υἱὸς Ἰ. ι΄) καὶ (f om.) ἔζησεν ἔτη (S¹ om.) ρκϛ΄. g adds τέλος διαθήκης Ἀσήρ· οὗτος ἐκ τῆς Ζέλφας δεύτερος ἔζησε ἔτη ρκϛ΄.

[1] Title. α as text (save that h om. τοῦ before ἑνδεκάτου and adds πρώτου after Ῥαχ.). abef, S¹ read δ. Ἰωσ. ια΄ (ef, S¹ om.) περὶ σωφροσύνης (+ Ἰωσὴφ ἑρμηνεύεται ὀνείδου (sic) ἀφαίρεσις f). d δ. Ἰωσ. τοῦ πανκάλλου (sic) υἱοῦ Ἰακὼβ ια΄, υἱοῦ Ῥαχὴλ α΄ περὶ σωφροσύνης. g ια΄ only. A = διαθήκη Ἰωσήφ (+ περὶ φθόνου A^bhefg). [2] d adds ἃ διέθετο τοῖς υἱοῖς αὐτοῦ. [3] d adds ἐν γὰρ τῷ ρι΄ ἔτει τῆς ζωῆς αὐτοῦ. [4] α add γάρ. [5] α, A^abh (save that h om. κ, τέκνα μου). β, S¹ read as in margin (save that g reads τεκνία and dg add μου after ἀδ.). A^b*cdfg om. [6] S¹ om. g adds καί. [7] c, g om. d adds Κυρίου Θεοῦ. [8] A^b* add πατρὸς ὑμῶν. [9] α. β, A^abcdfg, S¹ read as in margin (save that a reads ἡμῶν, d ῥήματα for τοῦ and A^b om. υἱοί). A^b*

3. Ἐγὼ εἶδον ἐν τῇ ζωῇ μου τὸν φθόνον καὶ τὸν θάνατον
 Καὶ[10] οὐκ ἐπλανήθην ⌜ἀλλ' ἔμεινα⌝[11] ἐν τῇ ἀληθείᾳ
  Κυρίου.
4. Οἱ[12] ἀδελφοί μου οὗτοι ἐμίσησάν με, *Ὁ δὲ Κύριος[13]
  ἠγάπησέ με·
 Αὐτοὶ[14] ἠθελόν με[15] ἀνελεῖν, *Ὁ δὲ Θεὸς[16] τῶν πατέρων
  μου[17] ἐφύλαξέν με·
 Εἰς λάκκον με[18] ἐχάλασάν, Καὶ ὁ ὕψιστος ἀνήγαγέν με[18·]
5. Ἐπράθην *εἰς δουλείαν[19], *Καὶ ὁ πάντων δεσπότης[20] β, S εἰς
  ἠλευθέρωσέν με·   δοῦλον.
 Εἰς αἰχμαλωσίαν ἐλήφθην[21], Καὶ ἡ κραταιὰ αὐτοῦ χεὶρ
  ἐβοήθησέ μοι·
 Ἐν λιμῷ συνεσχέθην, Καὶ αὐτὸς ὁ Κύριος διέθρεψέ με[22·]
6. Μόνος ἤμην[23], καὶ ὁ Θεὸς[24] παρεκάλεσέ με·
 Ἐν ἀσθενείᾳ ἤμην, καὶ ὁ Κύριος[25] ἐπεσκέψατό με[26·]
 Ἐν φυλακῇ ἤμην, καὶ ὁ †σωτὴρ[27] ἐχαρίτωσέ με[28·]
 [Ἐν δεσμοῖς καὶ ἔλυσέ με.][29]

ῥήματά μου. [10] d reads ἀλλ'. [11] α, def, S¹ (save that def read ἐμενον).
a reads ἀλλ'. bg, A om. [12] g reads ἐπεὶ γοῦν οἱ. Aᵃʰʰ*ᶜᵈᶠᵍ, S¹ καὶ οἱ, but not
Aᵇ as text states. [13] α, d. β–d, Aᵃᵇʰ, S¹ read καὶ (+ ὁ aefy) Κύριος. Aᵇ*ᶜᵈᶠᵍ
om. together with next two words. [14] g reads οὗτοι. Aᵇ*, S¹ read καί.
[15] d trs. after ἀνελεῖν. [16] c, Aᵇ. a reads καὶ ὁ Κύριος. h, bdef, Aᵃᵇ*ᵉᵈᵍ καὶ
ὁ Θεός. [17] ef om. Aᵇ = ἡμῶν. [18] c om. [19] α, A. β, S read as in
margin save that g reads ὡς δοῦλος. [20] α. β–ab, Aᵇ*ᶜᵈᵍ read ὁ πάντων
Κύριος. a καὶ ὁ Θεός. b, S καὶ ὁ Κύριος (+ ἐκ πάντων S). Aᵃᵇ om. together
with ἠλευθέρωσέν ... ἐλήφθην. [21] c, d read ἀνελήφθην. Aᵇ*ᶜᵈᶠᵍ om. next
ten words. [22] c reads μοι. [23] ch om. next sixteen words through hmt.
af om. next eight words through hmt. [24] beg, A, S. d reads Κύριος.
d, Aᵇ*, S² add τοῦ πατρός μου. [25] aef. bdg, S¹ read ὕψιστος. Aᵃᵇʰᶜᵈᶠᵍ =
Θεός. Aᵇ* = φύλαξ. [26] a om. next eight words. Aᵃᵇʰ next six
words. [27] α, β. We should read Θεός μου with Aᵇ*ᶜᵈᶠᵍ or Κύριος with
S¹. g adds ἐν πᾶσιν. [28] c reads μοι. [29] d om. It is found in all
other MSS. and in A, S. Aᵃᵇ*ᶜᵈ add Κύριος, Aᵉᶠ Θεός before ἔλυσε, but not
Aᵇʰ. I have bracketed the line as an interpolation. It may be a
dittography, and have arisen from a corrupt repetition of the preceding in
the Hebrew. Thus δεσμός and φυλακή can both go back to מַסְגֵּר.
ἐχαρίτωσε = חַנַּן which might possibly be corrupted with הִתִּיר = ἔλυσε.
ἐχαρίτωσε forms a good parallel to the two preceding verbs and ἔλυσε
does not. Finally the parallelism is destroyed by this addition,
as verses 4, 5, 6, 7 form stanzas of three lines each. a om.

β, A, S¹
Αἰγυ-
πτίων.
deg, Aᵃᵇ
ἐν
φθόνοις.
συνδού-
λων.
β–b
οὕτως
(d μετὰ
ταῦτα,
ag om.)
ὁ εὐνοῦ-
χος Φ.
β, A, S¹
ἀπω-
θεῖται.
bg, Aᵃᵇʰ,
S¹τόποις.
β, S¹
παρί-
σταται.

7. Ἐν διαβολαῖς καὶ συνηγόρησέ μοι.
  Ἐν λόγοις[30] ἐνυπνίων[31] πικροῖς[32] καὶ[33] ἐρρύσατό με[34].
  Δοῦλος[35] καὶ ὕψωσέ[36] με.

II. *Καὶ οὗτος ⌜ὁ ἀρχιμάγειρος Φαραὼ⌝[1] ἐπίστευσέ μοι τὸν οἶκον αὐτοῦ. 2. Καὶ ἠγωνισάμην πρὸς γυναῖκα ἀναιδῆ ἐπείγουσάν[2] με παρανομεῖν μετ' αὐτῆς, ἀλλ' ὁ Θεὸς *τοῦ πατρός μου[3] ἐρρύσατό[4] με ἐκ[5] φλογὸς καιομένης. 3. Ἐφυλακίσθην[6], ἐτύφθην[7], ⌜ἐξεμυκτηρίσθην⌝[8], καὶ ἔδωκέ με[9] ὁ[10] Κύριος[11] εἰς οἰκτιρμοὺς ἐνώπιον τοῦ δεσμοφύλακος.

4. Οὐ γὰρ[12] ἐγκαταλείπει[13] Κύριος[14] τοὺς φοβουμένους αὐτόν,
  *Οὐκ ἐν σκότει, ἢ δεσμοῖς[15], ἢ θλίψεσιν, ἢ ἀνάγκαις.

5. Οὐ γὰρ ὡς ἄνθρωπος ἐπαισχύνεται ὁ Θεός,
  Οὔτε[16] ὡς υἱὸς ἀνθρώπου δειλιᾷ,
  Οὔτε[17] ὡς γηγενὴς [ἀσθενεῖ ἢ][18] πτοεῖται[19],

6. Ἐν[20] πᾶσι δὲ τούτοις[21] προίσταται[22]
  Καὶ ἐν διαφόροις τρόποις[23] παρακαλεῖ[24].

ἐν δεσμοῖς to end of chapter. [30]α, β, S. A read ρω̈υμυ (= φυλακαῖς) but this is probably corrupt for ρω̈υ = λόγοις. [31]α. β, A, S¹ read Αἰγυπτίων (d Αἰγυπτίοις). [32]Aᵃᵇʰ om. [33]A adds ἐκεῖθεν. [34]f, Aᵇ*ᶜᵈᵍ om. next line. [35]α (save that h reads δοῦλον). deg, Aᵃᵇ read as in margin. b ἐν φθόνοις σὺν δόλοις. S¹ = ἐν φθόνοις σὺν πόνοις. [36]S¹ = ἐξείλατο.

II. [1]α (save that h reads αὐτός). adefg read καί (a om.) (+μετὰ ταῦτα d, +οὕτως eg, +οὗτος f) ὁ εὐνοῦχος (d οἰνοχόος) Φ. b κ. οὕτως Φωτιμὰρ ὁ ἀρχιμάγειρος Φ. A = καὶ οὕτως Πεταφρής (Aᵇ*ᶜᵈᶠᵍ Φωτιφάρ). S¹ = Καὶ οὕτως ὁ ἄρχων τῶν εὐνούχων. g adds ὁ Φωτι. [2]g. α, adef read ἐπειγούσης. b ἐπειγούσῃ. [3]h, Aᵇ*ᶜᵈᶠᵍ. c reads τῶν πατέρων μου. befg, Aᵃᵇʰ, S¹ Ἰσραὴλ τοῦ πατρός μου (g, Aᵃᵇʰ τ. π. μ. Ἰσραήλ). ad τοῦ πατρός μου Ἰακώβ (a Ἰ.τ.π.). [4]b reads ἐφύλαξε. [5]c. h, β read ἀπό. [6]g prefixes καί. [7]be read ἐτυπτήθην. [8]α, ef. bdg read ἐμυκτηρίσθην. a, A om. [9]h, bf. c, adeg read μοι. The words ἔδωκέ με . . εἰς οἰκτιρμοὺς ἐνώπιον are a literal translation of the Hebrew ‏ויתן אתי לרחמים לפני‎. Cf. Dan. i. 9. [10]α. β om. [11]h reads Θεός. [12]α, d. β–d read μὴ γάρ (efg γὰρ μή). [13]α, A. aef, S read ἐγκαταλείψει. bg ἐγκαταλίπῃ (+ποτε g). d ἐγκαταλειμπάνει. [14]α, adef, A. bg, S om. d adds πώποτε. [15]A = οὐδὲ ἐνσκοτεῖ δεσμοῖς. [16]α, adef. bg read οὐδέ. [17]α, def. abg read οὐδέ. [18]Bracketed as an interpolation. Possibly it is an alternative rendering with πτοεῖται of ‏יחת‎. [19]α. Reading of β, A, S in margin appears to be a corruption of α. [20]b (h?) read ἐπί. A = ἐν γάρ. [21]α, β–bg. bg, Aᵃᵇʰ, S¹ read as in margin. Aᵇ*ᶜᵈᵍ = Κύριος (by an internal corruption of Aᵃᵇʰ). [22]α. β, S¹ read as in margin. A = ἐστί. [23]α, β–af, A. a read τύποις. f προσώποις.

Ἐν βραχεῖ²⁵ ἀφίσταται²⁶ *εἰς τὸ²⁷ δοκιμάσαι τῆς ψυχῆς β, Α
　　τὸ διαβούλιον.　　　　　　　　　　　　　　　　　　ἀφιστά-
　　　　　　　　　　　　　　　　　　　　　　　　　　μενος.
7. *Ἐν δέκα²⁸ πειρασμοῖς *δόκιμον ἀπέδειξέ με²⁹
　　Καὶ ἐν πᾶσιν αὐτοῖς³⁰ ἐμακροθύμησα³¹.
　　Ὅτι³² μέγα φάρμακόν ἐστιν *ἡ μακροθυμία³³
　　Καὶ πολλὰ³⁴ ἀγαθὰ δίδωσιν *ἡ ὑπομονή³⁵.

III. Ποσάκις ἡ Αἰγυπτία¹ ἠπείλησέ² μοι³ θάνατον ; 　β–α, Α²,
ποσάκις⁴ τιμωρίαις⁵ ⸉με⸊⁶ παραδοῦσα⁷ ἀνεκαλέσατο⁸ [καὶ 　Sⁱ μὴ
ἠπείλησέ μοι⁹] *καὶ μὴ θέλοντός μου¹⁰ συνελθεῖν αὐτῇ ἔλεγέ¹¹ 　θέλοντι.
μοι·　　2. Κυριεύσεις¹² *κἀμοὶ καὶ πάντων τῶν ἐν τῷ οἴκῳ μου¹³, 　β, Α, Sⁱ
*ἐὰν ἐπιδῷς ἑαυτὸν¹⁴ εἰς ἐμέ, καὶ ἔσῃ ὡς δεσπότης ἡμῶν¹⁵. 　ἔλεγε δέ.
3. Ἐγὼ δὲ¹⁶ ἐμνημόνευον¹⁷ *λόγους πατρός μου¹⁸, καὶ 　β, Α, Sⁱ
εἰσερχόμενος εἰς τὸ ταμιεῖον *⸉κλαίων⸊ προσηυχόμην¹⁹ 　μου καὶ
Κυρίῳ²⁰.　　4. Καὶ ἐνήστευον ἐν τοῖς ἑπτὰ ἔτεσιν²¹ ἐκείνοις, 　πάντων
καὶ ἐφαινόμην *τῷ Αἰγυπτίῳ²² ὡς ἐν τρυφῇ διάγων· ὅτι²³ 　τῶν ἐμῶν.
　　　　　　　　　　　　　　　　　　　　　　　　　　　　　dg, Α μου
　　　　　　　　　　　　　　　　　　　　　　　　　　　　　Ἰακώβ.

S = ὀδύναις.　　²⁴Α reads ⲙⲏⲱⲝϩ (= παρακαλεῖται) corrupt for ⲙⲏⲱⲝⲃ =
παρακαλεῖ.　ɑ om. next line.　　²⁵c, d read βραχύ.　　²⁶α. β, Α read as
in margin. Sⁱ = ἐπιστάμενος.　　²⁷h reads ἐν τῷ, g καὶ εἰς τό.　　²⁸β–d, A.
α read ἐν ἔνδεκα. d διὰ τοῦτο ἐν. g ἕως δέκα. Sⁱ = ἐν ἐννέα.　　²⁹α. β–d,
Α, Sⁱ read δόκιμόν με ἀνέδειξε. d ἐδοκίμασε.　　³⁰g, Α reads τούτοις.　　³¹Α =
ἐδοκιμάσθην.　　³²d reads οἶδα ὅτι.　　³³Αᵃᵇ ἡ ὑπομονή. Αᵇ = αἱ ὑπομοναί
(not sing. as in text). Αᵇ*ᶜᵈᵍ = αἱ μακροθυμίαι. S om. next line.　　³⁴Αᵇ*ᶜᵈᵍ
om.　　³⁵Αᵇ*ᶜᵈᵍ = ὑπομένουσι.
III. ¹d adds Μέμφις. g repeats ποσ. ἡ Αἰγ. Sⁱ reads οἱ Αἰγ.　　²c reads
ὑπείλησε. e ἠθέλησεν. Sⁱ = ἠπείλησαν.　　³g om.　　⁴g adds ἡ Αἰγυπτία.
⁵h reads εἰς τιμωρίας. g τιμωρίᾳ. d ἀπειλαῖς and om. next seven words.
⁶α. β, Α, Sⁱ om.　　⁷a reads παραδοῦναι. Αᶜ = παρέδωκε.　　⁸Α = πάλιν
ἀνεκαλέσατο. For ἀνεκαλέσατο ... αὐτῇ a reads ἀλλ' ὁ Θεὸς ἐρρύσατό με. befg,
Αᵃᵇᵇ*ᶜᵈ, Sⁱ add με.　　⁹g, Αᵃᵇᵇ*ᶜᵈ om. I have bracketed καὶ ἠπείλησέ μοι
as an interpolation.　　¹⁰α, Αᵃᵇ. bdef, Sⁱ read as in margin. g μὴ θελήσας.
Αᵇ*ᶜᵈᵍ = ἀλλ' ἐγὼ οὐκ ἠθέλησα. Αᵇ καὶ (text wrong here) οὐκ ἠθέλησα.
¹¹α. β, Sⁱ read as in margin (save that a reads γάρ for δέ). Α = καὶ ἔλεγε.
For following μοι g reads ὅτι.　　¹²β–f. α, f read κυριεύσῃς.　　¹³α. β, Α, Sⁱ
read as in margin.　　¹⁴d trs. ἐὰν ... ἐμέ before κυριεύσεις. Αᵃᵇᵇ = καὶ
(Αᵃᵇ om.) ἐὰν κυριεύσῃς.　　¹⁵f om. Α = μου.　　¹⁶b, Sⁱ read οὖν.　　¹⁷α.
β reads ἐμνησκόμην.　　¹⁸c. dg, Α read λόγων (+πατέρων Αᵍ) πατρός μου
(g μου πατρός) Ἰακώβ. These (excepting Αᵍ) are right. Cf. Jub. xxxix. 6.
h, aef, Sⁱ read λόγους (aef λόγων) πατέρων μου. b λόγους πατέρων πατρός μου
Ἰακώβ.　　¹⁹c. h reads κλαίων καὶ εὐχόμενος. β, Α, Sⁱ read προσηυχόμην.
c adds τῷ.　　²⁰Α = θεῷ. d adds τῷ θεῷ. ταῦτά μοι ἐποίησα ἐπὶ ἔτη ἑπτά.
²¹Α = ἡμέραις but the corruption is native to A.　　²²c reads τοῖς Αἰγυπτίοις.

οἱ νηστεύοντες *διὰ τὸν θεὸν[24] τοῦ προσώπου τὴν χάριν[25] λαμβάνουσιν[26].　5. Ἐὰν δὲ ἀπεδήμει[27] *ὁ κύριός μου[28] οἶνον[29] οὐκ ἔπινον, *καὶ τριημερίζων[30] ἐλάμβανόν[31] ⌐μου⌐ τὴν τροφήν[32], καὶ ἐδίδουν[33] αὐτὴν ⌐τοῖς⌐[34] πένησιν καὶ ⌐τοῖς⌐[34] ἀσθενοῦσιν.　6: *Ὤρθριζον δὲ[35] πρὸς Κύριον καὶ ἔκλαιον περὶ Μεμφίας[36] τῆς Αἰγυπτίας, ὅτι σφόδρα[37] ἀδιαλείπτως ἠνόχλει[38] μοι[39]. *καὶ γὰρ[40] ἐν νυκτὶ εἰσῄει[41] *πρός με[42] λόγῳ ἐπισκέψεως.　7. Καὶ[43] ὅτι[44] τέκνον ἄρρεν[45] οὐκ ἦν αὐτῇ, καὶ[46] προσεποιεῖτο ἔχειν με ⌐ὡς⌐[47] υἱόν[48].　8. Καὶ[49] ἕως[50] χρόνου ὡς υἱόν με[51] περιεπτύσσετο, *ἐγὼ δὲ[52] ἠγνόουν *κἀκείνη δὲ ὕστερον[53] εἰς πορνείαν με ἐφελκύσατο[54].

Marginal (left): β–d, A, S¹ καί. β, A, S¹ υἱόν, καὶ ηὐξάμην πρὸς Κύριον καὶ ἔτεκεν ἄρρεν.

A[ab] om. καὶ ἐφαινόμην … διάγων.　[23] d reads καὶ γάρ. c adds γάρ.　[24] α, b. β–b read διὰ θεόν. β, A, S¹ trs. before νηστεύοντες.　[25] d reads θέσιν.　[26] α, b. β–bd read προσλαμβάνουσιν. d προλάμπουσαν κέκτηνται.　[27] aef. c, g read απεδη μοι, a corruption of ἀπεδήμει. h ἐπεδήμει. b, S¹ ἐπεδίδη μοι. d ἀπέδωτύ μοι. A[abb*cd] read Երթայի = ἀπηρχόμην or ἀπεδήμουν corrupt (?) for Երթայր = ἀπεδήμει.　[28] α. A read ներքր (=ποι) corrupt (?) for տէր իմ = ὁ Κύριός μου. β, S¹ om.　[29] d reads οἶνος.　[30] a om. A = τριῶν γὰρ ἡμερῶν and om. following μου. It would have been better if the translator had rendered οὔτε τριημερίζων, regarding the negative as governing the two verbs ἔπινον and ἐλάμβανον. See Driver, *Hebrew Tenses²*, 115. But it is possible to take the text as it stands.　[31] h (?), ef read ἐλάμβανυ. g ἐλάμβανε.　[32] α. β reads δίαιταν.　[33] h reads ἐδιδόμην. g ἐδίδου.　[34] α. β, A, S¹ om.　[35] α, d (save that c, d read ὀρθ.). aefg read ὤρθριζον (save that ef read ὀρθ.). b, S¹ καὶ ὤρθριζον. The phrase = ואשׁחר. A[b] adds at beginning καὶ ὅλην τὴν νύκτα προσηυχόμην.　[36] α, b, A[g], S¹. d reads αὐτῆς and om. τῆς Αἰγ. ef Μεμφίου. g Μεμφθείαν (with following two words in acc.). a om. A[a] = Πεμθίας. A[h] Μεμφθίας. A[b*cd] Μεφίας. A[b] corrupt.　[37] a om. A adds καί.　[38] efg. c reads ἐνόχλη. h, abd ἐνόχλει.　[39] A[b] adds τοῦ πορνεῦσαι.　[40] h. c, d read καὶ γὰρ καί. β–d, A, S¹ read as in margin.　[41] bde read εἰσίει.　[42] b, S¹ trs. after ἐπισκέψεως.　[43] bd add τὰ μὲν πρῶτα (d τ. πρ. μέν). S¹ has some corruption.　[44] d reads ἐπειδή. g ὅτε.　[45] α. β–d read ἀρρενικόν (g ἀρσενικόν). d om. and trs. τέκνον after αὐτῇ.　[46] c, a. h, β–a, A, S¹ om.　[47] g, A om.　[48] (h ?), β, A, S¹ add as in margin (save that d om. καί and ef ἄρσεν). Possibly this clause was lost through hmt. as υἱόν may have stood in c as in A instead of ἄρρεν. Before this addition d inserts ὑπολαβὼν ἐγὼ ὅτι χάριν τέκνου τοῦτο ποιεῖ and om. καὶ ἕως χρόνου … ἠγνόουν.　[49] α, A. β, S¹ om.　[50] b, S¹ add οὖν.　[51] aef, A trs. after περιεπτ. g om.　[52] α. β–df, A, S¹ read κἀγώ. f om. together with next word.　[53] α. a reads ὅτι.

9. Καὶ νοήσας ἐγὼ[55] ἐλυπήθην ἕως θανάτου[56]· *ἐξελθούσης δὲ[57] αὐτῆς ἦλθον εἰς ἐμαυτόν, καὶ ἐπένθησα[58] περὶ αὐτῆς[69] ἡμέρας πολλάς, *ὅτι ἔγνων τὸν δόλον αὐτῆς καὶ τὴν πλάνην[60]. 10. Καὶ ἔλεγον *πρὸς αὐτὴν[61] ῥήματα ὑψίστου, εἰ ἄρα ἐπιστρέψει[62] ἀπὸ τῆς ἐπιθυμίας[63] τῆς πονηρᾶς[64].

IV. *Πολλάκις οὖν[1] *ὡς ἁγίῳ ἀνδρὶ ἐν λόγοις[2] ἐκολάκευέ[3] με[4] καὶ[5] μετὰ δόλου διὰ[6] ῥημάτων ἐπαίνει[7] *τὴν σωφροσύνην[8] μου ἐνώπιον τοῦ ἀνδρὸς αὐτῆς[9], βουλομένη *κατὰ μόνας[10] ὑποσκελίσαι με. 2. *Ἐδόξαζε ⌜γάρ⌝[11] με ὡς σώφρονα *φανερῶς, καὶ ἐν κρυφῇ[12] ἔλεγέ μοι· Μὴ φοβηθῇς[13] τὸν ἄνδρα μου· καὶ γὰρ πέπεισται[14] περὶ τῆς σωφροσύνης σου[15]· ὅτι κἂν *τις αὐτῷ εἴπῃ[16] περὶ ἡμῶν, *οὐ πιστεύσει[17]. 3. *Ἐν τούτοις πᾶσιν[18] ἐγὼ[19] *χαμοκοιτῶν ἐδεόμην τοῦ Θεοῦ[20] ὅπως *ῥύσεταί με[21] ἐκ *τῆς δολιότητος αὐτῆς[22]. 4. Ὡς

Margin: β–a, A, S¹ ποσάκις. β–d, A, S¹ με. bdg, A, S¹ ἐχαμοκοίτων ἐγὼ ἐν σάκκῳ καί. aef θεοῦ ἐν σάκκῳ. β–a, A, S¹ τῆς Αἰγυπτίας.

---

be, S¹ ἔσχατον.　d κἀκείνη μάλιστα ἐπετείνετο περισσοτέρως ὁ ἔρως καί. f ὕστερον.　g ἔσχατα δέ.　A = καὶ μετὰ ταῦτα.　[54] α, befg, S¹. But with ad we should read ἐφελκύετο.　A = ἠθέλησε ἐμβάλλειν (A[b*cdfg] ἐφελκύειν). [55] α, A. β–d, S¹ om. d reads τὸν δόλον ἐγώ.　[56] d om. next six words. [57] α. β–d, A, S¹ read καὶ ἐξελθ.　[58] A[ab] add καὶ ἔκλαυσα.　[59] d adds ἐπί.　[60] d reads ἐγνωκὼς τὴν πλάνην αὐτῆς. a om.　[61] α. β reads αὐτῇ.　[62] α, defg. a reads ὑπόστρέψει. b, S¹ ἀποστρέψει.　[63] β, A, S¹ add αὐτῆς.　[64] d reads πονηρίας. A[b] adds καὶ αὐτὴ φανερῶς εἰς ὀφθαλμοὺς ἀνθρώπων ἔλεγε.

IV. [1] α. β–a, A, S¹ read as in margin (save that A[abh] is corrupt). a om. ver. 1.　[2] α, β–a, S¹ (save that dg read ἅγιον ἄνδρα). A[b*cdfg] = ὡς ἁγίοις λόγοις. A[ab] ἁγίοις λόγοις σου.　[3] α, de². be¹fg read ἐκολάκευσε.　[4] g reads μοι.　[5] b, S¹ om.　[6] d adds ματαίων.　[7] α, d, A. bef, S¹ ἐπαινοῦσα. g ἐπήνεσε. A adds με καί.　[8] h reads τῆς σωφροσύνης.　[9] A adds ἐξηγεῖτο καί. d om. rest of verse.　[10] A[b] = ἐν κρυπτῷ.　[11] α. β–d, A, S¹ read ἐδόξαζε (save that g, S¹ read ἐδόξασε). d, A read καὶ φανερῶς μὲν ἐδόξαζε.　[12] d, A read ἐν κρυπτῷ δέ.　[13] c, def read φοβηθείς.　[14] c, abef, A, S¹. h, dg read πεπίστευται.　[15] d om. rest of verse.　[16] α. β–d, A, S¹ read εἴπῃ τις αὐτῷ.　[17] α. β–d read οὐ μὴ πιστεύσῃ (e πιστεύσει).　[18] d reads ἐγὼ δὲ ταῦτα ἀκούων ἐλυπούμην μεγάλως καί.　[19] α. β om.　[20] α, aef (save that aef add ἐν σάκκῳ). bd, A, S¹ read ἐχημοκοίτων ἐγὼ (d, A om.) ἐν σάκκῳ καὶ (A καὶ ἐν σάκκῳ) ἐδεόμην τοῦ θεοῦ (A Κυρίου). g χαμαικοιτῶν ἐν σάκκῳ ἐδεόμην τ. Θεοῦ.　[21] c, bdeg. h, af read ῥύσηταί με. bdg, S¹ add ὁ (dg om.) Κύριος.　[22] α. β–a, A, S¹ read as in margin. a ταύτης. α = תרמיתה or מרמתה which may be a corruption of המצרית = τῆς Αἰγυπτίας.

β, A, S¹ δὲ οὐδὲν ἴσχυσεν[23] ⌐*ἐν τούτῳ[24], πάλιν ἐπὶ[25]⌐ λόγῳ κατη-
Κυρίου. χήσεως ἤρχετο[26] πρός με τοῦ[27] μαθεῖν[28] λόγον Θεοῦ[29].   5.
β, S¹ καὶ Καὶ ἔλεγέ[30] μοι[31]·   Εἰ θέλῃς[32] ἵνα καταλείψω[33] τὰ εἴδωλα,
τὸν Αἰ-
γύπτιον συγγενοῦ[34] μοι, *κἀγὼ πείθω τὸν ἄνδρα μου[35] ἀποστῆναι ἀπὸ[36]
πείσω. τῶν εἰδώλων, *καὶ πορευσόμεθα †ἐνώπιον Κυρίου σου[37].
abef, S¹ 6. *Ἐγὼ δὲ πρὸς αὐτὴν ἔλεγον[38] *ὅτι οὐχὶ[39] ἐν ἀκαθαρσίᾳ
ἐν νόμῳ
κυρίου θέλει[40] Κύριος τοὺς σεβομένους αὐτόν, οὔτε[41] *τοῖς μοιχεύουσιν
σου εὐδοκεῖ[42], ⌐ἀλλὰ τοῖς ἐν καθαρᾷ καρδίᾳ καὶ στόμασιν ἀμιάντοις
πορευό-
μενοι. αὐτῷ προσερχομένοις⌐[43].   7. *Κἀκείνη ἀντεφιλονείκει πλη-
β, A, S¹ ρῶσαι θέλουσα τὴν ἐπιθυμίαν αὐτῆς[44].   8. *Ἐγὼ δὲ[45]
om. ἀλλὰ
... προσ- προσετίθουν *νηστείαν καὶ[46] προσευχήν, ὅπως ῥύσεταί[47] με ὁ[48]
ερχο- Κύριος ἀπ' αὐτῆς[49].
μένοις.

———————————

bg, A ἐσιώπησε.

[23] g reads ἴσχυεν.   [24] α. β–d, A, S¹ om. d reads ἀνύσαι.   [25] g reads ἐν.
[26] α, bf, S¹. aeg, A read εἰσήρχετο. d εἰσέρχεται.   [27] α. β om. A⁻ᵇ = θέλουσα.
Aᵇ καὶ ἤθελε.   [28] Aᶠᵍ = διδάσκειν. Aᵇ*ᶜᵈ om. but Aᵃᵇ read as in text.
[29] α. β, A, S¹ read Κυρίου.   [30] g reads λέγει.   [31] A⁻ᵇ om.   [32] α. β reads
θέλεις.   [33] b reads καταλίπω.   [34] b reads συνπείσθητι. Aᵇ adds καὶ χαρίζου
μοι.   [35] α, A. β, S¹ read as in margin (save that S¹ adds Πετιφράν before
πείσω).   [36] α. β om.   [37] α (save that c reads πορευσώμεθα and h ἐν ὀνόματι
for ἐνώπιον).   Here both ἐνώπιον and ἐν ὀνόματι seem corrupt for ἐν νόμῳ.
abef, S¹ read as in margin (save that a reads πορευόμενον). dg, A καὶ ἐν
ν. Κυρίου (Aᵇ om.) σου πορευσόμεθα (d πορευσώμεθα οἱ ἀμφότεροι, A πορεύεσθαι).
[38] α. aef read ἔλεγον δὲ πρὸς αὐτήν. bg, S¹ λέγω δὲ πρὸς αὐτήν. d εἶπον δὲ
αὐτῇ. A = καὶ ἐγὼ (Aᵃᵇ*ᶜᵈᵍ om.) λέγω πρὸς αὐτήν.   [39] α. β reads οὐκ.
S¹ adds Ἀμεμφρία κυρία μου.   [40] h, b read λέγει. g ἐλεεῖ.   [41] α (save
that h adds ἐν). β reads οὐδὲ ἐν.   [42] A = εὐδοκεῖ Κύριος ἐν τοῖς μοιχεύουσιν.
[43] α. β. A, S¹ om.   [44] α (save that c reads θέλων and h om. it). aef
read κἀκείνη ἐφιλονείκει ποθοῦσα τελέσαι τ. ἐπιθυμίαν αὐτῆς. bg, A κἀκείνη
ἐσιώπησε ποθοῦσα ἐκτελέσαι (g τελέσαι) τ. ἐ. αὐτῆς (Aᵃᵇ καὶ (Aᵇ om.) τελοῦσα
τ. ἐπιθυμίαν αὐτῆς (Aᵇ μου)). d is conflate as frequently and reads: ἐκείνη
δὲ ταῦτα ἀκούσασα ἐσιώπησε μὲν κατὰ πρόσωπόν μου μηδὲν ἕτερον τολμήσασα
εἰπεῖν· τῇ δὲ διανοίᾳ αὐτῆς ἐφιλονείκει ποθοῦσα τελέσαι τ. ἐπιθυμίαν αὐτῆς.
S¹ = αὐτὴ δὲ λόγους πολλοὺς προσετίθει, and points to aef. d, S¹ may here
be neglected. bdg, A and α, aef only differ really in one word. Where
the former have ἐσιώπησε the latter have ἀντεφιλονείκει or ἐφιλονείκει. The
latter = התחרתה while ἐσιώπησε = התחרשׁה.   [45] α. β, A read κἀγώ.
[46] S¹ om.   [47] a reads ῥύσηται.   [48] abd om.   [49] d reads ἐκ τῶν τοῦ
διαβόλου παγίδων, καὶ ἐκ τῶν χειρῶν αὐτῆς.

V. *Καὶ πάλιν[1] ἐν[2] *ἑτέρῳ χρόνῳ[3] λέγει μοι· Εἰ
μοιχεῦσαι οὐ θέλεις, ἐγὼ ἀνελῶ[4] τὸν *ἄνδρα μου φαρμάκῳ καὶ[5]
λήψομαί σε εἰς[6] ἄνδρα.　　2. Ἐγὼ οὖν, ὡς ἤκουσα τοῦτο,
διέρρηξα *τὰ ἱμάτιά[7] μου, καὶ εἶπον ⌜αὐτῇ⌝[8]· Γύναι, αἰδέ-
σθητι τὸν Θεόν[9], καὶ[10] μὴ ποιήσῃς τὴν *πρᾶξιν ταύτην τὴν
πονηράν[11], ἵνα μὴ[12] ἐξολοθρευθῇς· *ἐπεὶ καίγε γίνωσκε ὅτι
ἐγὼ[13] ἐξαγγελῶ[14] *πᾶσιν τὴν ἐπίνοιάν σου ταύτην[15].　　3.
Φοβηθεῖσα[16] οὖν ἐκείνη. ἠξίου με[17] ἵνα μὴ[18] ἐξαγγείλω[19] τὴν
*ἐπίνοιαν ταύτην[20].　　4. Καὶ *ἀνεχώρησεν, ἐπιθάλπουσά
με δώροις[21] καὶ *ἀπολαύσεσι πάσαις[22].

VI. ⌜Καὶ μετὰ τοῦτο⌝[1] ἀποστέλλει[2] μοι βρῶμα ἐν γοητείᾳ

β, Α, S¹
Αἰγύ-
πτιον καὶ
οὕτως
νομίμως.
β τὴν
στολήν.
β-f, Α, S¹
Κύριον.
β, Α, S¹
ὅτι καίγε
ἐγώ.

β-d, S¹ τὴν ἐπίνοιαν τῆς ἀσεβείας σου πᾶσιν.　　β-g, Α, S¹ κακίαν αὐτῆς.
β-d, Α, S¹ πέμπουσα πᾶσαν ἀπόλαυσιν υἱῶν ἀνθρώπων.

V. [1] α. aefg, A read πάλιν. b, S¹ πάλιν δέ. d διελθόντος οὖν ἐκ τότε ἐνιαυτοῦ
ὁλοκλήρου πάλιν.　　[2] g om.　　[3] d reads μιᾷ τῶν ἡμερῶν προσελθοῦσα.
[4] α reads ἀνερῶ, and other MSS. ἀναιρῶ. I have emended as above.
[5] α (save that h adds οὕτως). β, Α, S¹ read as in margin save
that for νομίμως (which ef, A read) a reads νομίσας. b, S¹ νόμῳ,
d νομίμῳ and g om. Here φαρμάκῳ = בהמה and νομίμως = בחקה.
[6] d om.　　[7] α. β reads as in margin.　　[8] α. d reads πρὸς αὐτήν.
β-d, Α, S¹ om.　　[9] α, f. β-f, Α, S¹ read as in margin.　　[10] g om.
[11] h, aefg, A. c reads πρ. τὴν πονηράν, b, S¹ πρ. τὴν πονηρὰν ταύτην. d πονηρὰν
πρ. ταύτην.　　[12] e om.　　[13] α (save that h adds οὖν after ἐπεί).
β-g, Α, S¹ read as in margin (save that d reads καὶ for καίγε).
g reads καὶ γὰρ ἐγώ. Here γίνωσκε in α = ודע. The latter word
though wanting here in β, Α, S¹ reappears in the next clause as ודע in
β, Α, S¹. See note 15.　　[14] g, Aᵇ read ἐξαγγέλλω.　　[15] α. β-d, S¹ read
as in margin (save that g reads πᾶσαν). d τῆς καρδίας σου καὶ ἀσεβείας
σου πᾶσιν ἀνθρώποις. For πᾶσιν ... ταύτην A reads πονηρὰν πρᾶξίν σου
πᾶσιν. Here ἐπίνοιαν τῆς ἀσεβείας = בחמה ודע. See note 13.　　[16] Aᵃᵇ om.
[17] α, A. d reads μοι. β-d, S¹ om.　　[18] c, d. h reads μηδέν. β-d, A μηδενί.
[19] α, β-dg (save that aef read ἀναγγείλω). d reads ἀναγγείλαί τινι. g εἴπω.
h adds τινι.　　[20] α. β-g, Α, S¹ read as in margin. g ἀσέβειαν τῆς ἐπινοίας
αὐτῆς.　　[21] α. β reads as α save in giving θάλπουσα (a θέλπουσα) for
ἐπιθ. A = ἀναχωρήσασα δώροις ἔθαλπέ με.　　[22] α (save that the MSS. read
in accusative). β-d, Α, S¹ read as in margin (save that A reads ἔπεμπέ
μοι for πέμπουσα). d ἀποστέλλουσά μοι ἀπὸ πᾶσαν ἀπόλαυσιν.

VI. [1] α. d, S¹ read καὶ δὴ ἐν μιᾷ. β-d καί.　　[2] α, β-ag. ag, S¹ read πεφυρμένον[3].   2. *Ὡς δὲ[4] ἦλθεν ὁ[5] εὐνοῦχος ὁ κομίζων αὐτό[6], *ἀνέβλεψα καὶ[7] εἶδον *φοβερὸν ἄνδρα[8] ἐπιδιδόντα μοι *μετὰ τοῦ τρυβλίου[9] μάχαιραν· καὶ συνῆκα ὅτι[10] *περιέργεια

β–g, A, S¹   ἐστὶν εἰς ἀποπλάνησίν μου[11].   3. Καὶ ⌜ἐξελθόντος αὐτοῦ[12]⌝
μήτε   ἔκλαιον[13], *μὴ γευσάμενος μήτε ἐκείνου μήτε ἄλλου τῶν
ἐκεῖνο   ἐδεσμάτων αὐτῆς[14].   4. *Μετὰ δὲ[15] μίαν ἡμέραν ἐλθοῦσα[16]
μήτε   πρός με[17] *καὶ ἐπιγνοῦσα τὸ βρῶμα[18] λέγει[19] μοι[20]· Τί
ἄλλο τι   τοῦτο ὅτι οὐκ ἔφαγες[21] *τοῦ βρώματος[22];   5. Καὶ εἶπον
τῶν   *πρὸς αὐτήν[23]. Ὅτι[24] ἐπλήρωσας αὐτὸ ⌜γοητείας⌝[25]
ἐδεσμ.
αὐτῆς   θανάτου[26]. καὶ *πῶς εἶπας[27] ὅτι Οὐ προσεγγίζω[28] τοῖς[29]
γευσά-
μενος.   εἰδώλοις[30] ἀλλὰ τῷ[31] Κυρίῳ[32] ⌜μόνῳ⌝[33];   6. Νῦν οὖν
*β, Aᵇ*ᶜᵈᵍ
ἐπέγνω τ.   γνῶθι[34] ὅτι ὁ[35] Θεὸς *τοῦ πατρός[36] μου *δι' ἀγγέλου αὐτοῦ[37]
β. καί.
β, A, S¹   ἀπεκάλυψέ[38] μοι τὴν κακίαν σου[39], καὶ *ἐν τούτῳ ἐφύλαξα[40]
ἐτήρησα.   αὐτὸ[41] εἰς ἔλεγχόν σου, *εἴπως ἄρα[42] ἰδοῦσα[43] μετανοήσεις[44].

ἀπέστειλε. *g* adds ἕν.   [3] *h, β–b. c* reads πεφαρμακευμένον. *b* πεφυραμένον.
[4] *c. h* reads ὡς. *β, A, S¹* read καὶ ὡς.   [5] *eg* om.   [6] *β. c* reads αὐτῷ.
h αὐτός. *Aᵃᵇ*ᶜᵈᵉᵍ τὴν δίαιταν. *Aᵇ* τὸ βρῶμα. *aef, A* prefix μοι. *S¹* adds καὶ
ὁ Θεὸς ἐφανέρωσέ μοι.   [7] *d, A* = ἀναβλέψας.   [8] *α, β–b. b, A, S¹* read
ἄνδρα φ.   [9] *c* om. For μετά *g* reads διά and for τρυβλίου *d* reads τριβλίου.
By an internal corruption *A* reads θήκης.   [10] *abg, A* add ἡ.   [11] *α. β–d,*
Aᵇᵇ, S¹ read (+ ἡ *b*) περιέργεια αὕτη (*b* αὐτῆς, *Aʰ* om.) εἰς ἀποπλάνησίν (+ ψυχῆς
b) ἐστιν (*Aᵃᵇᵇ* ἤρξατο). *d* περιέργεια ἦν τοῦ Σατανᾶ καὶ εἰς ἀποπλ. ψ. ἐστιν.
*Aᵇ*ᶜᵈᵍ = ἀποπλάνησις αὕτη εἰς περιέργειαν ἐστίν μοι.   [12] *b* reads αὐτῆς.
[13] *Aᵃᵇ* om. *Aᵇ*ᶜᵈᵍ = ἠρξάμην κλαίειν καί.   [14] *α. β–g, A, S¹* read as in
margin (save that *ef* om. τι and trs. γευσάμενος before τῶν and *A* reads
ἐγευσάμην).   *g* μήτε ἐκείνου μήτε ἄλλου τῶν ἐδεσμάτων τινὸς γευσάμενος.
[15] *α, af. be, S¹* read μετὰ οὖν (*e* om.). *d* καὶ δὴ μετά. *g, A* καὶ μετά.   [16] *c*
reads ἐξελθοῦσα. *d* ἀνελθοῦσα.   [17] *g* reads μοι.   [18] *α. β, Aᵇ*ᶜᵈᵍ read
as in margin. *Aᵃᵇᵇ, S¹* om.   [19] *d* reads εἶπε.   [20] *α, dg. β–dg* read
πρός με.   [21] *bdeg* add ἀπό.   [22] *a* reads τὸ βρῶμα. *d* adds τούτου
ὅπερ τῇ χθὲς ἡμέρᾳ ἀπέστειλά σοι. *a* om. next four words.   [23] *g* reads αὐτῇ.
S¹ = πρὸς τὴν κυρίαν ἐμήν.   [24] *dg* read ἐπειδή. For ὅτι ἐπλήρωσας *S¹* reads τί
ἐποίησας ἐμοί, ὥστε τὴν ζωήν μου λαμβάνειν τὰ ὄνομα ὅτι ἔπεμψας βρῶμα πληρώσασα;
[25] *α. β, A, S¹* om.   [26] *d* reads θανατικοῦ φίλτρου διὰ τοῦτο οὐκ ἔφαγον αὐτό.
[27] *d* reads ἐπειδὴ εἶπάς μοι.   [28] *α. β–g* read ἐγγίζω. *g* ἔτι ζῶ.   [29] *α, adef, A.*
bg om.   [30] *d* adds ἀπὸ τοῦ νῦν.   [31] *α, d, β–d* om. For τῷ Κ. μόνῳ
S¹ reads ἔσομαι τοῦ Κυρίου.   [32] *g* reads θεῷ.   [33] *df* read μόνον.   [34] *d*
reads γνώθητι.   [35] *e¹* om.   [36] *A* = τῶν πατέρων.   [37] *α, A. β–dg, S¹* read
δι' ἀγγέλου. *dg* om.   [38] *c* reads ἐπεκάλυψε.   [39] *d* adds διὰ τοῦτο.   [40] *α.*
β, A, S¹ read as in margin.   [41] *d* trs. after σου.   [42] *c. h, β* read

7. *Ἵνα δὲ[45] μάθῃς[46], ὅτι[47] τῶν[48] ἐν σωφροσύνῃ θεοσεβούντων[49] οὐ κατισχύσει[50] κακία[51] *τῶν ἀσεβούντων[52]. ⌈ἰδοὺ⌉[53]
λαβὼν[54] *ἐξ αὐτοῦ ἐνώπιόν σου ἐσθίω. Καὶ τοῦτο εἰπὼν ἐπευξάμενος
οὕτως[55]. Ὁ Θεὸς τῶν πατέρων μου καὶ ὁ ἄγγελος Ἀβραὰμ[56]
*ἔσται μετ᾽ ἐμοῦ[57], ⌈ἔφαγον⌉[58].   8. Ἡ δὲ ⌈ἰδοῦσα τοῦτο⌉[58]
ἔπεσεν[59] *ἐπὶ πρόσωπον αὐτῆς[60] *εἰς τοὺς πόδας μου[61]
κλαίουσα[62]. καὶ ἀναστήσας[63] αὐτὴν ἐνουθέτησα.   9. *ἡ
δὲ[64] συνέθετό μοι[65] τοῦ[66] *μηκέτι ποιῆσαι[67] τὴν ἀσέβειαν
ταύτην[68].

VII. *Ἔτι δὲ[1] ἡ καρδία αὐτῆς *ἔκειτο εἰς τὸ κακὸν καὶ
περιεβλέπετο ποίῳ τρόπῳ με παγιδεῦσαι· στενάζουσα δὲ †συντόμως
συνέπιπτε μὴ ἀσθενοῦσα[2].   2. Ἰδὼν δὲ αὐτὴν[3] ὁ *ἀνὴρ αὐτῆς[4]
λέγει[5] ⌈πρὸς αὐτήν⌉. Τί[6] συνέπεσε τὸ πρόσωπόν σου; ἡ δὲ

Right margin: β-f, A, S¹ | ἐνώπιον αὐτῆς (+ ἀπ᾽ αὐτοῦ e) ἔφαγον (+ ἀπὸ τοῦ βρώματος A), εἰπών (καὶ εἶπον αὐτῇ A). | β, A, S¹ ἡ δὲ ἔπεσεν. | β, S καὶ ἔκλαυσε. | β, A, S¹

ἐνέκειτο εἰς (+ ἐμὲ εἰς bdg, A, S¹) ἀκολασίαν καὶ στενάζουσα συνέπιπτεν.
β, Abfg, S¹ Αἰγύπτιος.

εἰ ἄρα. e adds αὐτό.   [43] β-eg, S¹ add αὐτό.   [44] d reads μετανοήσῃ σε.
[45] d reads ἵνα. A = καὶ τοῦτο.   [46] a, A = γνώσῃ.   [47] g om.   [48] h om.
[49] h, β-a, A, S. c reads εὐσεβούντων. a θεὸν σεβόντων.   [50] α, ade. β-ade,
A, S¹ read κατισχύει. For οὐ ... ἀσεβούντων f reads οὐδὲν κακὸν ἅπτεται.
[51] g reads τὰ κακά.   [52] α, g. bde read ἀσεβούντων. af om. See note 50.
[53] α. d reads θεᾶσαι. β-d, A, S¹ om.   [54] a om. df, A read καὶ λαβών.
[55] α (save that h om. οὕτως). So almost f ἐνώπιόν σου ἀπ᾽ αὐτῶν ἐσθίω, εἰπών.
β-df, A⁻ᵇ, S¹ read as in margin (save that after αὐτῆς g adds ἐξ αὐτῆς).
d reads ἀπὸ τοῦ βρ. ἐνώπιον αὐτῆς ἔφαγον οὕτως εἰπών and Aᵇ ἀπὸ τοῦ β. ἐφ.
ἐνώπιον αὐτῆς καὶ εἶπεν.   [56] d reads τοῦ Ἀ. g Ἰσραήλ. A = αὐτοῦ.
[57] A = φυλάξει με.   [58] α. β, A, S¹ om.   [59] d reads ἐπέπεσεν. A = πεσοῦσα.
[60] bd, S read ἐπὶ πρόσωπον and d trs. after μου.   [61] Aᵇ*ᶜᵈᵍ om. For εἰς
d reads ἐπί.   [62] α. β, S read as in margin. A = ἔκλαυσε.   [63] Aᵇ*ᶜᵈ
= ἐγγίσας. Aᵍ συνετίσας.   [64] α. β reads καί.   [65] c reads με. b om.
[66] α, bd. β-bd om.   [67] α. β reads μὴ ποιῆσαι ἔτι.   [68] d adds ἀλλ᾽ ἥδε τῷ
στόματι αὐτῆς ἀπειρνεῖτο τοῦ μηκέτι ἐν τοῖς αὐτοῖς εὑρεθῆναι.

VII. [1] α, β-bd, S¹. b read ὅτι δέ. d, A ἀλλ᾽ οὖν.   [2] α (save that h reads
ὁποίῳ and c reads μοι for μή). β, A, S¹ read as in margin (save that b, S¹ om.
καί and read προσέπιπτεν, d adds τῷ προσώπῳ after συνέπ. and dg read
πρός με εἰς for εἰς ἐμὲ πρός, and that for στενάζουσα συνέπιπτεν A reads
πνεύματι συμπεσοῦσα (for [Armenian] is corrupt for [Armenian]) ἐστέναξε).
I have obelized συντόμως as corrupt for συντόνως (as also in Aq.'s Version of
Prov. xix. 13).   [3] f reads ταύτην.   [4] α, A⁻ᵇᶠᵍ. Aᵇ*ᶜᵈᶠᵍ is conflate reading
ἀνὴρ αὐτῆς ὁ Αἰγύπτιος. β, Aᵇᶠᵍ, S¹ read as in margin. d adds οὕτως συμπεσοῦσα.

Margin: β, S¹ στεναγμοὶ τοῦ πνεύματός μου. β, A, S¹ μὴ ἀσθενοῦσαν. β-d, S¹ τότε εἰσεπήδησε. bg, Aᵇ*cd ἢ εἰς φρέαρ ἢ εἰς κρημνόν.

⌈πρὸς αὐτὸν⌉[7] εἶπεν, ⌈ὅτι⌉[7] *πόνον καρδίας ἐγὼ ἀλγῶ, καὶ οἱ τοῦ πνεύματος στεναγμοὶ συνέχουσί με[8]. *Ὁ δὲ[9] ἐθεράπευσεν[10] αὐτὴν *ἐν λόγοις[11].   3. *Τότε οὖν εὐκαιρίαν λαβοῦσα[12] εἰσεπήδησε πρός με, *ἔτι ἔξω ὄντος[13] τοῦ ἀνδρὸς αὐτῆς, καὶ λέγει[14] μοι· *Ἄγχομαι, ἢ εἰς κρημνὸν ῥίπτω ἐμαυτήν[15], ἐὰν μὴ *συγγενῇ μετ’ ἐμοῦ[16].   4. *Ἐγὼ δὲ[17] νοήσας ὅτι *τὸ πνεῦμα[18] τοῦ Βελίαρ *ἐνοχλεῖ αὐτήν[19], προσευξάμενος τῷ[20] Κυρίῳ, εἶπον *πρὸς αὐτήν[21].   5. Ἵνα τί, ⌈ἀθλία⌉[22], ταράσσῃ[23] καὶ θορυβῇ[24] ἐν ἁμαρτίαις τυφλώττουσα[25]; μνήσθητι[26] ὅτι ἐὰν ἀνέλῃς σεαυτήν[27], *ἢ Ἀστηθώ[28], ἡ παλλακὴ[29] τοῦ ἀνδρός σου, ἡ[30] ἀντίζηλός[31] σου[32] κονδυλίσει[33] *τὰ τέκνα σου[34], καὶ[35] ἀπολέσεις[36] τὸ μνημόσυνόν σου ἀπὸ τῆς γῆς.

[5] d reads εἶπε.   [6] d adds σοι συνέβη ὅτι.   [7] α. β, A, S¹ om.   [8] α, β (save that d adds δυνῶν (sic) after καρδίας and for τοῦ π. στεναγμοί β, S¹ read as in margin). Aᵃᵇ*ᵈ = ἄλγος ἐστὶ καὶ στεναγμοὶ τοῦ ἥπατός μου συνέχουσί με. Aᶜᵉ = ἄλγος καρδίας συνέχει με. Aᵇ καρδίας μου ἄλγος ἐστί, καὶ στεναγμοὶ καρδίας μου συνέχουσί με (differently in printed text).   [9] α, d. β-d, S¹ = καί.   [10] α, β-b. b reads ἐθεράπευεν.   [11] α. β, A, S¹ read as in margin. ἐν λόγοις may = במילול (late Hebrew) whereas μὴ ἀσθ. = אל אמללה. Or there may be a confusion of במלה and אל תהל.   [12] α. d reads καὶ ἐν μιᾷ τῶν ἡμερῶν. β-d, S¹ read τότε. Aᵃᵇ = καὶ ἐν τῷ παρελθεῖν με. Aᵇ*cdg καὶ ἐν δευτέρᾳ ἡμέρᾳ.   [13] h, aef. bg read ἔτι ὄντος ἔξω. d ἀποδημοῦντος. c om. ἔτι . . . αὐτῆς.   [14] d reads εἶπε.   [15] α, aef, S¹ (save that h adds σοι after ἄγχομαι and ae read ἑαυτήν and S¹ read τοῖχον for κρημνόν). bg, Aᵇ*cd read ἄγχ. ἢ εἰς φρέαρ ἢ εἰς κρημνὸν ἐμαυτὴν ῥίπτω (Aᵇ*cd ῥίπτω ἐμ. ἢ εἰς κρ.). d ἐμαυτὴν θέλω ἀγχόνην χρήσασθαι ἢ εἰς κρ. ἢ εἰς φρ. ἐμ. ῥίπτω. Aᵃᵇ = ἀγχ. ἢ εἰς φρέαρ ῥίπτω ἐμαυτήν.   [16] Em. from συγγενης μ. ε. of α. aef read μοι συγγενῇ (f συγγενεῖς). b μοι συμπεισθείς. d συνέλθῃς μοι. g μοι συγγενοῦ.   [17] c, A. h reads ἐγώ. β, S¹ καί.   [18] a om.   [19] α, d, A. abef, S¹ read αὐτὴν (a αὐτῇ) ἐνοχλεῖ. g ἐνοχλεῖ.   [20] α. β om.   [21] α. β reads αὐτῇ.   [22] α. β, A, S¹ om.   [23] h, β-dg. c reads ταράσσει. d συνταράσσῃ. g ταράττει.   [24] d reads θορυβῆς. g θορυβεῖ.   [25] A = ἀναγκαίαις ἀπολομένη but ⟨Armenian⟩ may be corrupt for ⟨Armenian⟩ = τυφλώττουσα.   [26] Aᵃᵇ = γινώσκω (Aᵇ ἔγνως) τοῦτο. Aᵇ*cdg μνήσθητι τοῦτο.   [27] c, g read ἑαυτήν. S¹ adds τότε φανερῶς.   [28] α. a om. b reads ἡ Σηθώ. d ἡ Σωή. ef, Aᵇ*ᵉ ἡ Ἀσιθώ. g Ἰσιθώ. Aᵃᵇcd and S¹ corrupt.   [29] h reads παλλακίς.   [30] d adds καί.   [31] A reads ⟨Armenian⟩ (= ἐναντίον υἱοῦ) corrupt for ⟨Armenian⟩ = ἀντίζηλος.   [32] d adds γενήσεται κυρία τοῦ οἴκου σου καί.   [33] aef, A. bdg read κολαφίσει. c κονδηλῆσαι ἔχει. h κοδωλῆσαι ἔχειν. S¹ = ἀποκτενεῖ.   [34] h, β. c τὰ παιδία σου. A = τὸ τέκνον σου. d trs. τὰ τ. σου bef. κολαφίσει.   [35] d adds σύ.   [36] adf. α, e read ἀπολέσῃς. bg, S¹ ἀπολέσει. A = ἀπόλλυσι.

6. * Καὶ λέγει³⁷ πρός με· * Ἰδοὺ οὖν³⁸ ἀγαπᾷς με· * τοῦτό μοι ἀρκείτω· μόνον ἀντιποιῆσαι³⁹ *τῆς ζωῆς μου⁴⁰ ⌜καὶ *τῶν τέκνων⁴¹ μου⌝, *καὶ ἔχω⁴² προσδοκίαν ἀπολαῦσαι⁴³ ⌜καὶ⌝⁴⁴ τῆς ἐπιθυμίας μου.   7. *Οὐκ ἔγνω δὲ αὐτὴ⁴⁵ ὅτι διὰ τὸν⁴⁶ Κύριόν⁴⁷ μου εἶπον οὕτως ἐγώ⁴⁸, καὶ οὐχὶ⁴⁹ δι' αὐτήν.   8. Ἐὰν γάρ τις *ὑποπέσῃ πάθει⁵⁰ ἐπιθυμίας⁵¹ καὶ *δουλωθῇ αὐτῷ⁵² ὡς κἀκείνη, κἂν ἀγαθόν⁵³ τι ἀκούσῃ⁵⁴ εἰς *ἐκεῖνο τὸ⁵⁵ πάθος⁵⁶ *ἐκλαμβάνει αὐτὸ⁵⁷ πρὸς *τὴν πονηρὰν ἐπιθυμίαν⁵⁸.

VIII. Λέγω οὖν¹, τέκνα μου², ὅτι ὥρα *ἦν ὡσεὶ³ ἕκτη ὅτε³ ἐξῆλθεν ἀπ' ἐμοῦ⁴. *Καὶ κλίνας γόνυ⁵ πρὸς Κύριον ὅλην τὴν ἡμέραν καὶ ὅλην τὴν νύκτα⁶, πρὸς⁷ ὄρθρον ἀνέστην, δακρύων⁸ καὶ αἰτῶν⁹ λύτρωσιν *ἐξ αὐτῆς¹⁰.   2. Τέλος¹¹

Margin readings:
β,A^-b,S¹ ἀρκεῖ μοι ⌜μόνον⌝ ὅτι (af om.) ἀντιποιῆσαι.
β-d,A,S¹ καὶ οὐκ ἔγνω (eg, A ἐνόει).
β, S¹ πάθει ὑποπέσῃ ἐπιθυμίας.

πονηρᾶς.   β-ag, A, S¹ πάθος ὃ (A om.) ἥττηται.   β, S¹ ἐπιθυμίαν
πονηράν.   b-d, A, S¹ νύκτα συνάψας.   β-d, A, S¹ ἀπὸ τῆς Αἰγυπτίας.

---

³⁷ α, β-dg. d reads ἡ δ' ἔφη. g καὶ εἶπεν.   ³⁸ α, A^ab*cdfg (omitting οὖν). a reads εἰ οὖν. bfg, S¹ ἴδε οὖν. d νῦν οἶδα ὅτι. e εἰ δὲ οὖν.   ³⁹ α (both MSS. reading ἀρκήτω). β, A, S¹ read as in margin (save that d adds τοῦτο καί after μοι and b, A^-b read ἀντιποιῇ, g, A^b om. ἀρκεῖ..μόνον, and A^-b read τοῦτο instead of μόνον). If the ὅτι is retained the ἀντιποιῆσαι must be changed into ἀντιποιῇ σύ or ἀντιποιήσῃ.   ⁴⁰A^abb read τοῦ θανάτου μου. α om. μου.   ⁴¹ α reads τοῖς τέκνοις.   ⁴² α. a reads εἰ ἔχω. bdef, S¹ ἔχω (+τοίνυν d). g, A ἔχω οὖν.   ⁴³ i (?) reads ὑναπολαῦσαι. d ὅτι ἀπολαύσω.   ⁴⁴ α. β, A, S¹ om.   ⁴⁵ α. β-d, A, S¹ read as in margin. In d the whole verse reads: Καὶ ἐγὼ μὲν διὰ τὸν θεὸν εἶπον αὐτά· ἐκείνη ὑπέλαβεν ὅτι ἀγαπῶν αὐτὴν εἶπον τοῦτο.   ⁴⁶ a om.   ⁴⁷ α, β-bd, S¹. bd, A read Θεόν.   ⁴⁸ α (but h trs. before οὕτως). β, A, S¹ om.   ⁴⁹ α, ef. β-ef read οὐ.   ⁵⁰ α. β, S¹ read as in the margin (save that d reads ὑποπέσοι). For ἐὰν ... κἀκείνη A gives ἐὰν γὰρ εἰς πάθη τοιαῦτα τολμῶν (but [Armenian] is corrupt for [Armenian] = ἐπιθυμιῶν) καὶ πονηρῶν τις ὑποπέσῃ (A^b ὑποπέσῃ τις), ὡς κἀκείνη, τούτῳ δουλωθήσεται.   ⁵¹ β adds πονηρᾶς.   ⁵²α (save that h reads αὐτῇ). β, S¹ read τούτῳ (de τοῦτο) δουλωθῇ. For A see note 50.   ⁵³ A^ab=πᾶν. A^b*cdg μύριον τι, but readings are corruptions of [Armenian] = ἀγαθόν.   ⁵⁴d reads ἀκούσει.   ⁵⁵ α. β, A read τό. g om.   ⁵⁶β-ag, A, S¹ add as in margin. g adds ἡττόμενος. α, a seem wrong in omitting.   ⁵⁷A = αὐτὸ ἐκλαμβάνουσα καί.   ⁵⁸α. β, S¹ read as in margin. A = πονηρὰν ἐπιθυμίαν αὐτῆς.

VIII. ¹ α, adef, A. bg, S¹ om. β, A add ὑμῖν.   ² α, ag, A. bdef, S¹ om.   ³ d om.   ⁴ d adds τότε.   ⁵ α. aefg read κ. γόνυ κλίνας. bd, A, S¹ κἀγὼ γόνυ κλίνας.   ⁶ α, d. β-d, A, S¹ read as in margin.   ⁷ α. bdg read περὶ τόν. aef πρὸς τόν.   ⁸ d adds καὶ ταῦτα ποιῶν. A adds πρὸς Κύριον.   ⁹ For αἰτῶν ... αὐτῆς d reads αἰτοῦντός μου τοῦ λυτρωθῆναι αὐτήν.   ¹⁰ α. β-d, A, S¹

β, S¹ βίᾳ ἐπελαμβάνετό[12] μου τῶν ἱματίων, μετὰ βίας ἐφελκομένη με
(aefg
om.) εἰς συνουσίαν[13]. 3. Ὡς ⌐οὖν⌐[14] εἶδον[15] ὅτι μαινομένη[16]
κρατεῖ *κρατεῖ μου τὸν χιτῶνα, καταλείψας αὐτὸν [καὶ ἐκτιναξάμενος]
τὰ ἱμάτιά ἔφυγον γυμνός[17]. 4. *Ἐκείνη δὲ[18] ⌐κρατήσασα τοῦτον⌐[19]
μου
γυμνὸς *ἐσυκοφάντησέ με· καὶ ἐλθὼν ὁ ἀνὴρ αὐτῆς ἔβαλέ με εἰς φυλακὴν
ἔφυγον. ἐν τῷ αὐτοῦ οἴκῳ[20], καὶ τῇ ἑξῆς *μαστιγώσας ἐξέπεμψέ[21] με εἰς
β–d, A, S¹
κἀκείνη *τὴν τοῦ Φαραὼ εἱρκτήν[22]. 5. *Καὶ ὡς[23] ἤμην ἐν
ἐσυκο-
φάντησέ *τοῖς δεσμοῖς[24], ἡ Αἰγυπτία συνείχετο[25] ἀπὸ τῆς λύπης.

____

με (+ πρὸς τὸν ἄνδρα αὐτῆς b, A^abb*cd) καὶ (A^b om.) ἐνέβαλέ με εἰς
φυλακὴν ἐν οἴκῳ αὐτοῦ ὁ Αἰγύπτιος. β–d, S¹ μαστίξας με ἔπεμψε.
β–d, A, S¹ ἠσθένει.

read as in margin. A^b adds Μεμφίας. [11] h adds δέ. b, S¹ οὖν. d μόνον με
εὑροῦσα ἐν τῷ κοιτῶνι. A^ab*cd μετὰ τοῦτο ἐλθοῦσα. A^bhfg μετὰ τοῦτο. [12] c.
h, β, A, S¹ ἐπιλαμβάνεται. [13] d reads συνουσιασμόν. A^b adds from next verse
καὶ ἐγὼ κατέλειψα αὐτοῦ τὰ ἱμάτια καὶ ἔφυγον ἔξω. [14] h, A om. [15] e om.
d adds αὐτήν. g ἐγώ. [16] A adds ἐστί. [17] α. β, S¹ read as in
margin (save that d adds ἀποδυσάμενος after μου and for γυμνὸς ἔφυγον
reads ἔφυγον ἀπ' αὐτῆς γυμνός). A^ab*cd = κατέλειψα τὰ ἱμάτιά μου καὶ
γυμνὸς ἔφυγον ἀπ' αὐτῆς. A^fg κρατησάσης τὰ ἱμάτιά μου γυμνὸς ἔφυγον. A^lh
om. καὶ ἐκτιναξάμενος is bracketed as an intrusion. It may be
a rendering of וגערתי, a corrupt dittography of עזבתי = καταλείψας.
ἀποδυσάμενος in d above implies the same text as α. From α and A it is
clear that β, S¹ wrongly omit καταλείψας. [18] α. β–d, A^b read κἀκείνη.
A^ab*cdfg = καὶ τότε ἐκείνη. Ver. 4 is peculiar in d: τότε ἀποκαμοῦσα ἐκείνη καὶ
ἀπογνοῦσα τὴν θέλησιν αὐτῆς, καὶ ὅτι οὐ πείθομαι τῷ σκοπῷ αὐτῆς τῷ μυσαρῷ καὶ
εὐαγεῖ ἐσυκοφάντισέ με πρὸς τὸν Αἰγύπτιον καὶ ὀργισθεὶς κατ' ἐμοῦ ἔβαλέ με εἰς
φυλακὴν τὴν οὖσαν ἐν τῷ οἴκῳ αὐτοῦ. τῇ δὲ ἑξῆς μαστιγώσας με ἀπέστειλέ με εἰς
τὴν εἱρκτὴν Φαραὼ τοῦ βασιλέως. [19] α· (save that h reads κρατοῦσα).
β, A, S¹ om. [20] α (save that h reads ἐνέβαλε). β–d, A, S¹ read as in
margin (save that A^abb*cd according to text read συκοφαντήσασά με ἐδήλωσε
for ἐσυκοφάντησέ με, but this is not true of A^bfg: A^bfg = ἐσυκοφάντησέ με).
Observe that d (see note 18) supports the addition in b, A^abb*cd. The
order in A^bhfg is εἰς φυλ. ἐνέβαλεν ἐν οἴκῳ αὐτοῦ ὁ Αἰγ., though Arm. printed
Text represents all MSS. as giving ὁ Αἰγ. ἐνέβαλέ με εἰς φυλ. ἐν οἴκῳ αὐτοῦ.
[21] α. β–d, S¹ read as in margin. d agrees rather with α. See note 18.
[22] α. β–bd, A, S¹ read τὴν εἱρκτὴν τοῦ Φαραώ. b φυλακὴν ἐν οἴκῳ αὐτοῦ ὁ Αἰγύπτιος.
For d see note 18. [23] α, A. β–d, S¹ read ὡς οὖν. For καὶ ὡς ... λύπης
d reads καὶ ὄντος μου ἐν τῇ φυλακῇ ἡ Αἰγ. ἠρρώστει ἀπὸ τῆς λύπης καί, and om.
rest of verse, which it inserts in a modified form in ix. 4. See note 25,
p. 196. [24] α. β–d read πέδαις. [25] α. β–d, A, S¹ read as in
margin. συνείχετο may = נכלאת and ἠσθένει = נחלתה, one of which may

α	β–d, A, S¹
ἐλθοῦσα δὲ ἐπηκροᾶτό μου πῶς ηὐχαρίστουν τῷ Κυρίῳ καὶ ὕμνουν ἐν οἴκῳ *τοῦ σκότους²⁶, καὶ ἔχαιρον ἐν *ἱλαρᾷ φωνῇ²⁷ δοξάζων τὸν Θεόν μου, ὅτι διὰ προφάσεως ἀπηλλάγην²⁸ τῆς Αἰγυπτίας.	καὶ²⁹ ἐπηκροᾶτό μου³⁰ πῶς ὕμνουν³¹ Κύριον³² ἐν οἴκῳ σκότους καὶ *ἐν ἱλαρᾷ φωνῇ³³ *χαίρων ἐδόξαζον³⁴ τὸν Θεὸν³⁵ μόνον³⁶ ὅτι *διὰ προφάσεως³⁷ ἀπηλλάγην²⁸ τῆς Αἰγυπτίας.

IX. *Πολλάκις δὲ¹ ἔπεμψε πρός με λέγουσα². Εὐδό-
κησον³ ⌜πληρῶσαι τὴν ἐπιθυμίαν⌝ μου, καὶ λύω⁴ σε ἐκ⁵ τῶν
δεσμῶν, ⌜καὶ ἀπαλλάξω σε ἐκ⁶ τοῦ σκότους.   2. *Ἐγὼ   *β–af, S¹*
δὲ οὐδὲ⁷ ἕως⁸ ἐννοίας⁹ ἐξέκλινα¹⁰ πρὸς αὐτήν· *ὁ γὰρ θεὸς   *νηστεύ-οντα.*
ἀγαπᾷ¹¹ μᾶλλον τὸν¹² ἐν¹³ λάκκῳ σκότους †πιστὸν¹⁴ ἐν   *β–bd, S¹*
σωφροσύνῃ¹⁵, ἢ τὸν ἐν ταμείοις †βασιλέα¹⁶ τρυφῶντα μετ'   *βασι-λέων.*
ἀκολασίας.   3. *Εἰ δὲ¹⁷ ἐν σωφροσύνῃ διάγων *θέλει   *c, b, S¹ ὁ.*

be a corruption of the other.   ²⁶c. h reads τοῖς κόποις.   ²⁷c. h reads
ἱλαρότητι φωνῆς.   ²⁸A = ἀπήλλαξε. Clause in A = ἀπήλλαξέ με ἀπὸ
προφάσεων τῆς Αἰγυπτίας.   ²⁹g adds ἐρχομένη πολλάκις.   ³⁰Aᵇᵇ*ᶜᵈᶠ om.
These MSS. add ἀδιαλείπτως, a word which Aᵇ adds after πῶς.   ³¹fg
add τόν.   ³²b, A, S¹ add ὤν.   ³³g reads ἐν ἱλαρότητι φωνῆς. A trs.
before ἐν οἴκῳ.   ³⁴Aᵇ*ᶜᵈᶠ = δοξάζων ὕμνουν.   ³⁵b adds μου.   ³⁶A trs.
after next word and for μόνον ὅτι reads ὃς μόνος.   ³⁷Here, as A (see
note 28) shows, τῆς Αἰγυπτίας is to be taken as a genitive dependent on
προφάσεως. For διά we should expect ἀπό. Hence there may have been
a corruption of מ into ב. Now διὰ προφάσεως τῆς Αἰγ. = מֵאֲנַת המצרית,
where האנת is corrupt for תַאֲוַת. The LXX and Vulgate suppose the
same corruption in Prov. xviii. 1. Hence the clause = 'was set free
from the lustful desire of the Egyptian woman.'

IX. ¹α, df. abe, S¹ read πολλάκις. g καὶ πολλάκις. A = πολλάκις γάρ.
²Aᵇʰ = καὶ λέγει. Aᶠᵉ om. Aᵃᵇ*ᶜᵈ = εἰς τὴν φυλακήν, but here ܪܘܠܝܢ
(= φυλακή) is a corruption of ܪܘܠ = λόγος.   ³dg add τοῦ.   ⁴α, ef, A
ad, S¹ read λύσω. b λυτρώσω. g λυτρωσε, corrupt for λυτρώσω σε.   ⁵α.
β om.   ⁶α. β om. d adds καὶ τῆς δουλίας ἐλευθερώσω σε after σκότους.
⁷c. h reads ἐγὼ δέ. β–d, S¹ καὶ οὐδέ. d ἐγὼ δὲ υὐδ' ὅλως οὐδέ.   ⁸e reads ὡς.
⁹b reads ἐννοιῶν ποτέ.   ¹⁰c. h, β read ἔκλινα. g adds ποτέ.   ¹¹α.
β, S¹ read ἀγ. γὰρ ὁ θεός.   ¹²h reads τῶν.   ¹³d adds τῷ.   ¹⁴c. h reads
πιστῶν. af πιστεύοντα. β–af, S¹ read νηστεύοντα. Here the latter reading
is obviously right as the contrasting epithet τρυφῶντα in the parallel
shows. The corruption is native to α, β.   ¹⁵e reads εὐφροσύνῃ. h om.
next twelve words through hmt.   ¹⁶c, d. β–bd read as in margin.
S = βασιλικοῖς. b om.   ¹⁷aef. c, b, S¹ read ὁ δέ. g ἡ δέ (i.e. a corruption

α οἶδεν.
α καὶ
παρέχει.

β, A, S¹
καὶ τὰ
στέρνα
καί.

β, S¹ πάνυ
γὰρ ἦν
ὡραία.

α οἶδεν.   καὶ[18] δόξαν καὶ[19] οἶδεν ὁ ὕψιστος ὅτι συμφέρει, παρέχει[20] αὐτῷ καὶ ταῦτα[21] ὡς κἀμοί.   4. Ποσάκις[22] καίπερ ἀσθενοῦσα κατῄει ⌜πρός με⌝ ἐν ἀωρίᾳ[23], καὶ ἤκουσε[24] τῆς φωνῆς μου προσευχομένου[25], * καὶ ἐγὼ συνίων[26] *τοὺς στεναγμοὺς[27] ἐσιώπων[28].   5. Καὶ ⌜γὰρ⌝ *ὄντος μου[29] ἐν τῷ οἴκῳ αὐτῆς ἐγύμνου[30] τοὺς βραχίονας αὐτῆς καὶ[31] τὰς κνήμας, ⌜*ἵνα †συμπέσω εἰς αὐτήν[32]. *ἦν γὰρ⌝ καὶ ὡραία πάνυ[33] ⌜μάλιστα κοσμουμένη[34]⌝ πρὸς ἀπάτην[35] μου. Καὶ ὁ Κύριος ἐφύλαξέ με ἀπὸ τῶν ἐγχειρημάτων αὐτῆς.

h, β μετ-
έλθητε.
β, S¹ τα-
πεινώσει.
β, S¹
ἠγάπησε.

    X. Ὁρᾶτε οὖν, τέκνα μου, πόσα κατεργάζεται[1] ἡ[2] ὑπομονὴ καὶ ἡ[3] προσευχὴ μετὰ νηστείας.   2. *Οὕτως καὶ ὑμεῖς[4], ⌜ἐὰν τὴν σωφροσύνην καὶ τὴν ἁγνείαν μεταδιώκητε[5] ἐν ὑπομονῇ καὶ *προσευχῇ μετὰ νηστείας ἐν ταπεινώσει[6] καρδίας, ὁ[7] Κύριος κατοικήσει[8] ἐν ὑμῖν, ὅτι ἀγαπᾷ[9] τὴν σωφροσύνην.

for εἰ δέ).   d om. ver. 3.   [18] S = λήψεται.   [19] β–bd, S. b reads καὶ εἰ. α om.   [20] β–d, S. α read as in margin.   [21] α, be, S¹. afg read ταύτην. [22] d om. next eight words.   [23] A^b adds ἐν ἑσπέρᾳ ἐν σκότει.   [24] c, afg, S¹. h, be, A read ἤκουε. d ἠκροάσω.   [25] A^{ab*cd} = καὶ ἀνεστέναξε. A^b supports text and A^{h*} om. c adds μου. Here d adds μου διότι ὕμνουν καὶ ἐδόξαζον τὸν θεὸν ἐν οἴκῳ σκότους. καὶ ἐν ἱλαρῷ φωνῇ καὶ προσώπῳ ἔχαιρον καὶ ἐδόξαζον τὸν θεόν, ὅτι διὰ προφάσεως ἀπηλλάγην τῆς Αἰγυπτίας. παρερχομένη δὲ ἀτέναζεν which it has drawn from viii. 5.   [26] α, A. β, S¹ read συνίων δὲ ἐγώ. A^b adds ἤκουον.   [27] α. β, A, S read τοὺς στεναγμοὺς (f τοῦ στεναγμοῦ) αὐτῆς. [28] α, a. Other MSS. read ἐσιώπουν.   [29] α. β reads ὅτε ἤμην.   [30] g reads ἐγύμνοσε (sic).   [31] α. β, A, S¹ read as in margin.   [32] α, β–d, S¹. d reads ἵνα συμπ. εἰς ἔρωτα αὐτῆς. A = ἵνα σκανδαλίσῃ με, but these words are more probably a rendering of πρὸς ἀπατήν μου later, and so I have supposed in the text. Here as in Test. Jud. xi. 2 (β, S¹), xiii. 3, 7 I take συμπίπτειν to represent a corruption in the Hebrew. See note in Test. Jud. xi. 2.   [33] α. β, S¹ read as in margin. A^{abh} = καὶ ὡραία πάνυ. A^{b*cdg} om.   [34] c reads καὶ κεκοσμημένη.   [35] b reads ἀπάτησιν. g ἀγάπην. On A see note 32.

    X. [1] A = ἐστί.   [2] e om.   [3] be om.   [4] α (save that c reads ἡμεῖς). β, A, S¹ read καὶ ὑμεῖς (+ οὖν bd). A = ἐὰν γένησθε τοιοῦτοι. Verses 2–4 are very defective in A which = καὶ ὑμεῖς ἐὰν γένησθε τοιοῦτοι ἀπὸ λυπῶν καὶ θλίψεων (+ καὶ πειρασμῶν A^{ab*cd}) σωθήσεσθε διὰ κυρίου· ἢ γὰρ ἐν λόγῳ ἢ ἐν διανοίᾳ παραβήσεσθε.   [5] c. h, β read as in margin.   [6] α (save that for ἐν ταπ. h reads καὶ ταπεινότητος). β, S¹ read as in margin.   [7] α. β om. [8] α, bd, S. a reads κατοικιεῖ. efg κατοικεῖ.   [9] α. β, S¹ read as in margin.

3. *Ὅπου δὲ κατοικεῖ ὁ ὕψιστος[10], κἂν *φθόνος τις περι- β, S¹ τις
πέσῃ, κἂν δουλία, κἂν συκοφαντία[11], *ὁ Κύριος κατοικῶν ἐπ' περιπέσῃ
αὐτὸν[12] διὰ τὴν σωφροσύνην οὐ μόνον⌉ ἐκ τῶν κακῶν ῥύεται[13] φθόνῳ, ἢ
αὐτόν[14], ⌈ἀλλὰ καὶ ὑψοῖ[15] καὶ δοξάζει αὐτὸν ὡς κἀμέ.   4. δουλεία
*Πάντας⌉ γὰρ ⌈ἀνθρώπους[16] ἢ ἐν ἔργῳ⌉ *ἢ ἐν λόγῳ, ἢ ἐν ἢ συκο-
διανοίᾳ[17] †συνέρχεται[18].   5. Γινώσκουσιν[19] οἱ ἀδελφοί φαντία
μου[20] πῶς ἠγάπησέ με ὁ πατήρ μου[21], καὶ οὐχὶ[22] ὑψούμην[23] (+ἢ
⌈ἐν τῇ διανοίᾳ[24] μου⌉, καίπερ νήπιος ὑπάρχων[25], ⌈εἶχον τὸν σκότει
*φόβον τοῦ θεοῦ[26] ἐν τῇ καρδίᾳ[27] μου⌉. ᾔδειν[28] γὰρ ὅτι adefg,
πάντα[29] παρελεύσεται.   6. Καὶ *†οὐκ ἐπήρθην ἐν κακῷ† S¹).
ἀλλ'[30] ἐτίμουν *τοὺς ἀδελφούς μου[31], καὶ διὰ τὸν φόβον β–dg, S¹
πάντως
β, A, S¹ †ἐμέτρουν ἐμαυτὸν καί. γὰρ ὁ ἄνθρωπος.

---

[10] S¹ om. For κατοικεῖ ae read καὶ οἰκεῖ. g om. δέ.   [11] α. β, S¹ read as
in margin (save that d trs. τις after περιπέσῃ and f reads φθορᾷ for φθόνῳ).
a om. next eight words.   [12] c. h reads ὁ Κ. ἐπ' αὐτῶν κατοικῶν. β–a Κ. ὁ ἐν
(Κ. ἐπ' ef) αὐτῷ κατοικῶν.   [13] a reads ῥύσεται.   [14] α. β, S¹ om. For ἐκ τῶν
κακῶν . . . κἀμέ A reads ἐξ ἀλγέων καὶ θλίψεων καὶ πειρασμῶν καὶ κακῶν
(Aᵇ θλίψεως καὶ κακοῦ) σωθήσεσθε ὑπὸ τοῦ κυρίου.   [15] c, d read ὑψεῖ.
[16] α. β–dg, S¹ read as in margin (save that af om. ὁ). d καὶ γὰρ ὁ ἄνθρωπος.
g πᾶς γ. ἄνθρωπος. Aᵃᵇ*ᶜᵈᵍ = γάρ. Aᵇ ἐὰν γάρ.   [17] g reads ἢ ἐννοίας.
[18] α, aef. bg, S¹ read συνέχεται. d συνεπαίρεται. Aᵃᵇ*ᶜᵈᵍ = ἁμαρτήσεσθε.
Aᵇ ἁμάρτῃ τις. d trs. the entire verse after ἐν τῇ διανοίᾳ μου in ver. 5.
If α is right in giving the acc. ἀνθρώπους, συνέρχεται must represent
a transitive verb, possibly יבוא in the sense of 'happens to.' The subject
would then be φθόνος ἢ δουλία κ.τ.λ. in ver. 3. If β is right in giving
ἄνθρωπος, then יבוא may be corrupt for יגבה = ἐπαίρεται or συνεπαίρεται as
in d.   [19] d adds γάρ. Aᵇ, S¹ = γινώσκετε.   [20] g adds οὗτοι.   [21] d adds
Ἰακώβ.   [22] β reads οὐχ.   [23] d reads ὑψώθην. g ἡττούμην.   [24] b, S¹
read καρδίᾳ. d om. next eleven words, and substitutes ver. 4 + διὰ τοῦτο
ἐφύλαξα ἐμαυτόν· καὶ ἀπὸ λόγου καὶ ἔργου καὶ διανοίας.   [25] α. β–d reads ὤν.
[26] h, abf. c reads φόβον θεοῦ. eg τοῦ θεοῦ φόβον. eg om. next four words.
[27] b, S¹ read διανοίᾳ.   [28] d reads οἶδα.   [29] α, d, A. β–d read τὰ (f om.)
πάντα (+ταῦτα f).   [30] c (save that οὐκ ἐπήρθην is written κ ἠπάρθην).
β, A, S¹ read as in margin. h is conflate: οὐκ ἐν μέτρῳ ἑαυτῷ ἀλλά.
Of these readings those of h and β, A, S¹ are thoroughly corrupt.
c might stand: 'I did not raise myself (against them) with evil intent.'
But this is unsatisfactory. First then the negative is original or it is
not. (i) If original, we may regard ἐν κακῷ in c as a corruption of
ἐμαυτόν (β, A, S¹). Cf. h ἑαυτῷ. Then ἐπήρθην = רוממתי, which the
translator should here have rendered actively as the Pilel ἐπῆρα (or ὕψωσα).
Thus text originally = לא רוממתי נפשי = 'I did not exalt myself.' The

<table>
<tr><td valign="top">

β, A, S¹
ἐσιώπουν
πιπρα-
σκόμενος
μή.
β, A, S¹
τὸ γένος
μου ὅτι.
β, A, S¹
δυνατοῦ.
β–d, S¹
ἐλθὼν δὲ
(ef οὖν)

</td><td valign="top">

αὐτῶν[32] *καὶ πιπρασκόμενος ἐσιώπουν[33] εἰπεῖν[34] *τοῖς Ἰσμαϊλίταις[35] ὅτι[36] υἱός εἰμι Ἰακὼβ[37] ἀνδρὸς μεγάλου[38] *καὶ δικαίου[39].

XI. *Καὶ ὑμεῖς οὖν[1], *τέκνα μου[2], ⌜ἔχετε ἐν πάσῃ[3] πράξει ὑμῶν *πρὸ ὀφθαλμῶν ὑμῶν[4] *τὸν τοῦ θεοῦ φόβον[5], καὶ⌝ τιμᾶτε[6] τοὺς ἀδελφοὺς ὑμῶν· πᾶς γὰρ ὁ[7] ποιῶν[8] νόμου Κυρίου ἀγαπηθήσεται ὑπ'[9] αὐτοῦ.   2. *Ἐρχόμενος δὲ[10] *μετὰ τῶν Ἰσμαϊλιτῶν[11] *ἐπηρώτων με λέγοντες Δοῦλος εἶ; Κἀγὼ εἶπον[12] ὅτι δοῦλός[13] εἰμι[14] ἐξ οἴκου[15], ἵνα μὴ αἰσχύνω

</td></tr>
</table>

εἰς Ἰνδοκολπίτας.   β, S¹ ἠρώτων με Κἀγὼ εἶπον.

---

text of β, A, S¹ can be explained from this. Either ἐμέτρουν = מדותי a corruption of רוממתי, or ἐμέτρουν is a corruption of ἐμετεώριζον (= רוממתי). The loss of the negative would be intelligible on the latter corruption. (ii) If on the other hand the negative is not original we might explain רוממתי נפשי as a corruption of דוממתי נפשי, 'I kept myself quiet,' the phrase in Ps. cxxxi. 2, where the LXX and Vulgate render דוממתי as if it were רוממתי. If imperfects instead of perfects stood in the original, the corruptions could be similarly explained. (iii) Finally, the whole clause may be a dittography of οὐχὶ ὑψούμην ἐν τῇ διανοίᾳ μου (in ver. 5), where במדה was rewritten as ברעה.   [31]A = αὐτούς.   [32]h om. d reads αὐτόν.   [33]α. β, A, S¹ read as in margin.   [34]α. β–d, S¹ read μή (g om.) εἰπεῖν. d μὴ ἐξειπὼν αὐτοῖς but trs. after Ἰσμαϊλίταις. A = καὶ οὐκ εἶπον. ἐσιώπα εἰπεῖν = חדל לאמר.   [35]A[b] om.   [36]α. β, A, S¹ (save that d adds ἢ before ὅτι) read as in margin.   [37]h, β, A[b], S¹. c, A[ab*cdg] om.   [38]f reads δικαίου.   [39]α (save that h om. καί). β, A, S¹ read as in margin.

XI. [1]α, β, S¹. A[abb*cd] = καὶ ὑμεῖς. A[fg] = ὑμεῖς οὖν.   [2]α, d, A[ab*cd]. β–d, A[bfg] om.   [3]b om.   [4]c, adefg, S¹ (save that aef, S¹ om. ὑμῶν and d trs. after φόβον). h, b om.   [5]c, abef. h reads τὸν φόβον κυρίου. dg τὸν φ. τοῦ θεοῦ.   [6]A = ἀγαπᾶτε. h, d om. καὶ τιμᾶτε ʼ. . . ὑμῶν.   [7]e om.   [8]A[ahb*cd] read ἀγαπῶν but A[bfg] support text.   [9]h reads ἀπ'.   [10]α. β–d, S¹ read as in margin (save that g reads Ἰνδοκοπήν). d ἡνίκα δὲ ἤλθομεν εἰς Ἰνδ. A = ἐλθὼν οὖν μετ' αὐτῶν εἰς Ἰνδκαποπάτας (A[b*d] Ἰνδκακοπάτας, A[ce] Ἰνδκακπράτας).   [11]A reads οἱ Ἰσμαηλῖται and trs. after ἐπηρώτων με.   [12]α. β, S¹ read as in margin (save that bdef read ἠρώτουν and g reads καί for κἀγώ). β, S¹ have thus lost a clause. This clause is preserved also in A which = ἐπηρώτων με οἱ Ἰσμ. καὶ εἶπον· Δοῦλος εἶ ἢ ἐλεύθερος; Κἀγὼ εἶπον.   [13]be, S¹ add αὐτῶν.   [14]d adds αὐτῷ. g ἐγώ.   [15]A reads բնութենէ (= φύσεως) corrupt for բնակութենէ = οἴκου. d, A add αὐτῶν (d om.) τοῦτο δὲ (A om. δέ and A[bhfg] om. τοῦτο ἔλεγον) ἔλεγον.

τοὺς ἀδελφούς μου.   3. Λέγει δέ μοι ὁ μείζων αὐτῶν[16]· *Οὐκ εἶ δοῦλος[17], ὅτι καὶ[18] ἡ ὄψις σου δηλοῖ[19]. Ἐγὼ δὲ *λέγω αὐτοῖς[20] ὅτι[18] δοῦλος ⌜αὐτῶν⌝ ὑπάρχω[21].   4. Ὡς δὲ *εἰς Αἴγυπτον ἐφθάσαμεν ἐμάχοντο περὶ ἐμοῦ τὸ[22] *τίς προδοὺς χρυσίον λάβῃ με[23].   5. Διὸ πᾶσιν ἔδοξεν *τοῦ εἶναί[24] με εἰς Αἴγυπτον πρὸς *τὸν μετάβολον τῆς ἐμπορίας[25] αὐτῶν, ἕως ὅτου[26] ἐπιστρέψουσιν[27] φέροντες[28] ἐμπορίαν[29].   6. *Ὁ δὲ Κύριος ἔδωκέ μοι[30] χάριν ἐν ὀφθαλμοῖς τοῦ μεταβόλου καὶ ἐπίστευσέ[31] μοι τὸν οἶκον αὐτοῦ.   7. Καὶ εὐλόγησεν αὐτὸν *ὁ Θεὸς[32] ἐν[33] χειρί μου, καὶ ἐπλήθυνεν *αὐτὸν ἐν χρυσίῳ καὶ ἀργυρίῳ[34] ⌜καὶ ἔργῳ⌝[35].   8. Καὶ ἤμην μετὰ αὐτοῦ[36] *μῆνας τρεῖς[37].

XII. Κατ' ἐκεῖνον δὲ[1] τὸν καιρὸν κατῄει[2] Μεμφὶς[3] ⌜ἐν λαμπήνῃ⌝[4] *ἡ γυνὴ[5] τοῦ Πεντεφρὶ[6] ⌜μετὰ δόξης πολλῆς,

Margin: β, A, ¹ / δηλοῖ περί σου καὶ / ἠπείλει μοι ⌜ἕως θάνατον⌝. / β, A, S¹ ἤλθομεν εἰς A. / περὶ ἐμοῦ ἐμάχοντο. / β-af, A, S¹ / Κύριος. / β-d, S¹ αὐτὸν ἐν

ἀργυρίῳ καὶ χρυσίῳ.   β-d, A, S¹ μ. τρεῖς καὶ (e om.) ἡμέρας πέντε.
β, A, S¹ παρῄει.

---

[16] h om. d adds ὁ πρῶτος τοῦ τόπου.   [17] β-dg, A, S¹ add σύ. For οὐκ ... δοῦλος d reads σὺ δ. οὐκ εἶ.   [18] g om.   [19] α. β, A, S¹ read as in margin (save that a reads ἠπείλησε. d θάνατον for ἕως θ. A^ab σε for περί σου, and A om. ἕως θ.).   [20] c. h reads εἶπον αὐτοῖς. β, A, S¹ ἔλεγον.   [21] α. β reads εἰμί.   [22] α. β, A, S¹ read as in margin (save that d adds πολλοί before περί).   [23] α, β, S¹ (save that g adds τίνι after τίς, b reads προσδούς and S¹ πρῶτος προσδούς for προδούς). A = καὶ ἕκαστος ἐδίδου μέρος ἐμπορίας αὐτῶν (+ ἀντὶ ἐμοῦ A^b) ἵνα με λάβῃ (+ ἀντὶ κέρδους αὐτῶν A^ab).   [24] α. β, S¹ read εἶναι. A = ἀφιέναι.   [25] α, d, A^ahb*cdg. β-d, S¹ read μετάβολον ἐμπορίας. A^b = ἀρραβῶνα μεταβόλου ἐμπορίας.   [26] α. β-ab read οὗ. ab om.   [27] h, bd read ἐπιστρέψωσι. d ὑποστρέψωσι.   [28] A = καὶ οἴσουσι. c adds εἰς. A^b adds καὶ οὕτως ἐποίησαν.   [29] d reads τὴν ἐμπορίαν αὐτῶν. f ἐμπορίας.   [30] α. β-d read καὶ ὁ κ. ἔδωκέ μοι. d καὶ ἔδωκέ μοι κ.   [31] d reads ἐνεπίστευσε.   [32] α, af. β-af, A, S¹ read as in margin.   [33] h adds τῇ.   [34] α, d. β-d, S¹ read as in margin. A = χρυσίον καὶ ἀργύριον αὐτοῦ (A^b om.).   [35] α. β, A, S¹ om. ἔργον here = עֲבֹדָה, but we may assume that the translator should have read עֲבֻדָּה = 'household servants.' d om. rest of chapter.   [36] α, bg, A, S¹. aef read αὐτῶν.   [37] α. β-d, A, S¹ read as in margin (save that g reads τινάς for πέντε and A^ab*cd read ἡμέρας ἐνενήκοντα καὶ πέντε).

XII. [1] α, adfg. be, S¹ om. For κατ' ... κατῄει A reads παρῄει οὖν κατ' ἐκεῖνο (?).   [2] α (though written as κατιει). aef παρείη. bg, A, S¹ παρίει. d παρῆν. For A see note 1.   [3] b reads ἡ Μεμφία. adefg ἡ Μεμφίς. d adds ἡ Αἰγυπτία.   [4] α, def (though written as ἐν λαμπίνη in h). Corrupt in a

β, A, S¹ ὅτι ἤκουσε περὶ ἐμοῦ παρὰ τῶν εὐνούχων αὐτῆς[7].   2. *Καὶ
καὶ
ἐπέβαλεν λέγει τῷ ἀνδρὶ αὐτῆς[8], *ὅτι ἐπλούτησεν ὁ μετάβολος[9] ἐν
ἐπ' ἐμὲ
τοὺς χερσίν[10] *τινος νέου[11] Ἑβραίου, λέγουσι[12] δὲ ὅτι ⌐καὶ⌐[13]
ὀφθαλ-
μοὺς κλοπῇ ἔκλεψαν[14] αὐτὸν[15] ἐκ γῆς[16] Χαναάν.   3. Νῦν οὖν
αὐτῆς ποίησον μετ' αὐτοῦ[17] κρίσιν, καὶ ἀφελοῦ[18] τὸν νεανίαν[19] εἰς
⌐ὅτι εἶπον *τὸν οἶκον ἡμῶν[20], καὶ *εὐλογῆσαί σε ἔχει[21] *ὁ Θεὸς τῶν
αὐτῇ οἱ
εὐνοῦχοι Ἑβραίων[22], ὅτι χάρις *ἐκ τοῦ[23] οὐρανοῦ ἐστι *πρὸς αὐτόν[24].
περὶ
ἐμοῦ⌐.
β, A, S¹ XIII. Ὁ δὲ ⌐Πεντεφρὶς⌐[1] πεισθεὶς[2] τοῖς λόγοις ⌐αὐτῆς⌐[3]
περὶ τοῦ ἐκέλευσεν[4] †ἐλθεῖν[5] τὸν μετάβολον, *καὶ λέγει αὐτῷ[6].   *Τί
τοῦτο ὃ ἀκούω ⌐περί σου⌐[7], ὅτι κλέπτεις[8] ψυχὰς[9] ἐκ γῆς[10]
Χαναάν[11], *καὶ εἰς παῖδας μεταπωλεῖς[12];   2. *Ὁ δὲ

μεταβόλου ὅτι ἐπλούτησεν. β, A, S¹ οἰκονόμον σου (aef, S¹
οἰκόν σου) καὶ εὐλογήσει σε. bdg, S¹ ἀχθῆναι.   β-ad, S¹ εἰς π.
μετεμπολῶν.

ἡ ἐλλακπίνη. bg, A, S¹ om.   [5] h, g. c reads τῇ γυνῇ. b, A, S¹ γυνή. a om.
ef ἡ. d reads μετά.   [6] c, g (omitting τοῦ). h, adf read τ. Πεντεφρή.
be read τ. Πετεφρί (-ή e).   [7] α. β, S¹ read as in margin (save that for
ἐπέβαλεν e reads ἐπέβαλλεν and d ἰδοῦσα). A reads only καὶ (A^{ab*cd} om.)
ἐπιβλέψασα εἶδέν με.   [8] d reads καὶ ἐλθόντος τοῦ ἀνδρὸς αὐτῆς λέγει αὐτῷ.
After καί A^b adds ἐπιστρέψασα.   [9] α. β, A, S¹ read as in margin.   [10] c.
Other MSS. read χειρί.   [11] c, ef. h, a read τινός. bg, A, S¹ νέου τινός.
d νεωστί τινος.   [12] A^{ab*cd} = ἔλεξαν but A^{bhs} support text.   [13] α, adefg.
b, A, S¹ om.   [14] dg read ἔκλεψεν.   [15] h reads αὐτῶν.   [16] h, g read τῆς.
[17] A^{b*} = αὐτῶν.   [18] A adds ἀπ' αὐτοῦ.   [19] d reads νεανίσκον.   [20] α. aef,
S¹ read οἰκόν σου. bdg οἰκονόμον σου. A = οἰκονομίαν σου.   [21] α (save that
h reads σοι). β, A, S¹ read as in margin (save that d reads ἡμᾶς).
[22] c, b. h reads τῶν Ἑ. ὁ Θ. β-b ὁ τῶν Ἑ. Θ.   [23] d reads αὐτοῦ.   [24] α.
ab reads ἐπ' αὐτῷ. efg ἐπ' αὐτόν. d ἐν αὐτῷ.

XIII. [1] α, dg. af read Πεντεφρής. be, S¹ Πετεφρίς (-ής e).   [2] A = ἡσθείς.
[3] d reads αὐτοῖς.   [4] A^{abb*cdfg} om. but A^b supports text.   [5] α, aef. bdg, S¹
read as in margin. A^b = ἄγειν. A^{abb*cdfg} = ἤγαγε. c adds πρός. ἐλθεῖν
is difficult. ἐκέλευσεν ἐλθεῖν = אמר לבוא. Since bdg, S¹ = להובא and A^b
= להביא, לבוא is a corruption possibly of להביא.   [6] c om. d adds Τὴν
ἀλήθειάν μοι λέξον ἐν τάχει πρὸ τοῦ σε τιμωρήσωμαι.   [7] α, A. β-bd read τί
τοῦτο ἀκούω περί σου; b, S¹ τί ταῦτα ἀκούω; d ἤκουσα γάρ.   [8] b adds τάς.
[9] d adds ἐλευθέρας.   [10] S¹ om.   [11] b reads Ἑβραίων.   [12] α. a reads εἰς
παῖδας ἀπεμπολῶν. befg, S¹ εἰς παῖδας (S¹ δουλείαν) μετεμπολῶν (b, S¹ μετεμπωλῶν).
d εἰς π. μεταβάλλων. A = εἰς παῖδάς σοι καὶ εἰς παιδίσκας. d adds νῦν οὖν
ἀπάγγειλόν μοι, εἰ ταῦτα οὕτως ἔχῃ καθὼς ἀκούω περί σου.   [13] α. β-dg, A, S¹

μετάβολος πεσὼν εἰς τοὺς πόδας αὐτοῦ[13] *ἐδέετο λέγων[14]. β–dg, A,
Δέομαί σου[15], κύριε, *οὐκ οἶδα[16] ὃ[17] λέγεις.   3. *Καὶ S¹ πεσὼν
λέγει αὐτῷ ὁ Πεντεφρής[18]. Πόθεν ⌈οὖν⌉ *ἐστιν ὁ παῖς[19] οὖν
ὁ Ἑβραῖος[20]; καὶ[21] εἶπεν[22]. Οἱ[23] Ἰσμαϊλῖται παρέθεντό[24] ἐπὶ πρόσ-
μοι αὐτόν, ἕως ὅτου[25] ἐπιστρέψωσιν[26].   4. *Ὁ δὲ οὐκ[27] ωπον
ἐπίστευσεν αὐτῷ[28], ἀλλ' ἐκέλευσεν γυμνὸν τύπτεσθαι[29]. αὐτοῦ ὁ
Ἐπιμένοντος δὲ αὐτοῦ *τούτοις τοῖς λόγοις[30], λέγει[31] *ὁ μετά-
Πεντεφρής[32]. Ἐναχθήτω[33] οὖν[34] ὁ νεανίσκος.   5. Καὶ βολος.
εἰσαχθεὶς προσεκύνησα τῷ Πεντεφρῇ[35], τρίτος[36] γὰρ ἦν bdg, A, S¹
*ἐν ἀξιώματι παρὰ τῶν[37] Φαραὼ ⌈ἀρχόντων⌉.   6. Καὶ ὁ δὲ λέγει
(b, S¹ ἔφη, d εἶπε).

h, befg, A τύπτεσθαι αὐτόν.   aef, S¹ ἀποκριθήτω.   β, S¹ ἀρχιευνούχῳ.
β ἐν ἀξίᾳ παρὰ τῷ Φ. ⌈ἄρχων πάντων τῶν εὐνούχων, ἔχων γυναῖκας καὶ
παλλακὰς καὶ τέκνα⌉.

read as in margin (save that for πεσὼν οὖν A^abcd read καὶ ἔπεσεν, A^b* τότε ἔπ.
and A^fg ἔπ.).   d reads π. οὖν ὁ μετάβολος ἤγουν ὁ πραγματευθεὶς ἐπὶ πρόσωπον
αὐτοῦ.   g π. ὁ μετάβολος εἰς τοὺς πόδας αὐτοῦ.   εἰς τοὺς πόδας αὐτοῦ =
לרגליו, but ἐπὶ πρόσωπον αὐτοῦ = לפניו.   Which is the original?   [14]A^ahb*edfg
= καὶ λέγει.   A^b = λέγει αὐτῷ.   [15]h, ef om.   [16]A^ab*ed om. but A^bfg retain
(printed Arm. Text wrong).   [17]dg, A read τί.   [18]α.   bdg, A, S¹ read
ὁ δὲ λέγει (b, S¹ ἔφη, d εἶπε).   aef ὁ δέ.   [19]α (save that h adds σοί after
ἐστίν).   bdg, A, S¹ read σοί (g om.) ὁ παῖς.   aef ὁ παῖς σου (ae σοί).   [20]f
adds οὗτος.   [21]A = ὁ δέ.   [22]d adds ὁ μετάβολος.   [23]c om.   [24]g trs.
after αὐτόν.   [25]α.   bdeg read οὗ.   af om.   a om. also ἕως.   [26]α, b. df read
ὑποστρέψωσι.   eg ἐπιστρέψουσι.   a om.   [27]α.   β–d, A, S¹ read καὶ
(+ Πεντεφρής A^b) οὐκ.   For ὁ δὲ ... αὐτῷ d reads καὶ μὴ πιστεύσας αὐτῷ
ὁ Πεντεφρίς.   [28]c, g read αὐτόν and g adds ὁ Πεντεφρί.   [29]c, ad, S¹. h, befg,
A add αὐτόν.   d reads αὐτὸν τύπτ. γυμνόν.   [30]α, ae. dg read τοῖς λόγοις
τούτοις.   f τ. τοιούτοις λόγοις.   b om.   A, S¹ support text.   [31]d reads ἔφη.
A^ab*edfg om. together with ὁ Π., but not A^b nor A^b as Arm. Text represents.
[32]c, af. h, d read Πεντεφρίς.   bg, S¹ Πετεφρίς.   e Πετεφρής.   A^ahb*edfg om.   [33]α.
bdg read ἀχθήτω.   aef, S¹ ἀποκριθήτω = עֲנֵה, a corruption of יָבֹא = ἀχθήτω or
ἐναχθήτω.   For Ἐναχθήτω ... νεανίσκος A reads ἄγετε ὧδε (+ ἔφη A^ab*ed) τὸν
νεανίσκον (+ καὶ αὐτὸς λέγει ἡμῖν ταῦτα A^b).   [34]α.   β om.   h adds καί.   d adds
ἔμπροσθέν μου after νεανίσκος.   [35]α.   β, S¹ read as in margin (save that bd
om. the ι).   A = αὐτῷ.   d adds πρὸς τὴν γῆν.   [36]A reads երկրորդ (=
δεύτερος) corrupt for երրորդ = τρίτος.   [37]α.   A^–b = παρὰ τῷ Φ. ἀξίωμα
αὐτοῦ (?).   A^b ἀξ. αὐτοῦ παρὰ τ. Φ.   At any rate A supports α against the
addition in β, S¹.   β, S¹ read as in margin (save that d reads τοῦ for τῷ and
adds καὶ before ἄρχων, and dg γυναῖκα for γυναῖκας.   g adds καὶ before ἔχων.
b reads γυναῖκα κ. τέκνα κ. παλλακάς and S¹ adds τῷ βασιλεῖ after παρά, and

Margin: b, A Τίνος εἰ δοῦλος; — β, S^1 ἀποστέλλει πρὸς τὸν ἄνδρα (+ αὐτῆς bdg). — α τιμωρῆσαι ἀδίκως. — befg, A^{b*} ἔλθωσιν, φησίν. — β, A, S^1 αὐτόν.

διαχωρίσας[38] με[39] ἀπ' αὐτοῦ[40] λέγει[41] μοι[42]· Δοῦλος εἶ ἢ ἐλεύθερος; *ἐγὼ δὲ[43] εἶπον[44]. Δοῦλος[45]. 7. *Καὶ λέγει· Τίνος; καὶ λέγω[46]. Τῶν Ἰσμαηλιτῶν. 8. *Ὁ δὲ εἶπε[47]. Πῶς αὐτῶν ἐγένου[48] δοῦλος; καὶ[49] εἶπον· Ὅτι ἐκ γῆς[50] Χαναὰν ἐπριάσαντό[51] με. 9. *Εἶπε δὲ πρός με[52]. ⌜Ὄντως⌝[53] ψεύδῃ[54]. Καὶ ⌜εὐθὺς⌝[55] *ἐκέλευσε κἀμὲ γυμνὸν[56] τύπτεσθαι.

XIV. Ἡ δὲ Μεμφὶς[1] ἑώρα[2] διὰ *τῶν θυρίδων[3] ⌜*τυπτόμενόν με[4], *πλησίον γὰρ ἦν ὁ οἶκος αὐτῆς[5], καὶ *ἀπέστειλε πρὸς αὐτόν[6], λέγουσα⌝. Ἄδικος[7] ἡ κρίσις σου[8], ὅτι[9] τὸν κλαπέντα ⌜ἐλεύθερον⌝ *τιμωρεῖς, ὡς ἀδικήσαντα[10]. 2. Ὡς δὲ ⌜ἐγὼ⌝[11] οὐκ ἤλλαξα *τὸν λόγον μου[12] ⌜τυπτόμενος⌝, ἐκέλευσε *φυλαχθῆναί με[13], ἕως οὗ ἔλθωσιν[14] οἱ κύριοι *τοῦ παιδός[15]. 3. *Ἡ δὲ γυνὴ[16] ἔλεγε[17] πρὸς *τὸν ἄνδρα αὐτῆς[18]·

reads γυναῖκας καὶ τὰ τέκνα τῶν παλλακῶν). [38] a reads ἐκχωρίσας. [39] c reads μοι. [40] A = αὐτῶν. [41] α, A^b. β, S^1 read εἶπε. [42] aefg, $A^{ab*cdfg}$ om. [43] α, A. β, S^1 read καί. [44] d adds αὐτῷ. α om. next seventeen words through hmt. [45] d, A add εἰμί. [46] β–b, S^1 (save that a om. the second καί, and dg read εἶπον for λέγω). b, A reads καί (+ αὐτὸς A^{ab*cd}) λέγει πρός με (A^{ab*cd} om. πρός με)· Τίνος εἶ δοῦλος; καὶ λέγω (A^{abb*cd} εἶπον) αὐτῷ (A om.). [47] adef. b, A^b, S^1 καί (+ πάλιν b) λέγει μοι. g, A^{ab*cd} ὁ δὲ λέγει μοι (g om.). A^{fg} καὶ λέγει. [48] bg, A, S^1. aef read γίνη. d ἐγένετο. [49] efg add ἐγώ. [50] b reads τῆς. [51] α, g. β–g read ἐπρίαντο. [52] b reads ὁ δὲ ἠπίστησε λέγων. [53] α. b reads ὅτι. defg, A, S^1 om. [54] f reads ψεύδει. [55] α. g reads εὐθέως. β–g, A om. [56] α, A^b omitting καί. abefg, A read γυμνόν με ἐκέλευσε (g, A^{-b} trs. ἐκέλ. before γυμνόν. aef trs. it before με). d ἐκέλευσε γυμνωθῆναί με καί. S^1 = γυμνώσας ἐκέλευσε.

XIV. [1] c reads Μεμφὶ ὡς. [2] A adds με. [3] c. h, β, A, S^1 read (+ τῆς A) θυρίδος. A om. rest of verse, but inserts the latter half of it ἄδικος ... ἀδικήσαντα after the first clause in ver. 3. [4] α, adg (save that a om. με). bef read τυπτομένου μου. S^1 = πῶς ἔτυψάν με. [5] α. β, A, S^1 om. [6] α. β, S^1 read as in margin (save that g reads ἀπέστειλε). [7] b, A, S^1 add ἐστί. For the position of the clause ἄδικος ... ἀδικήσαντα in A see note 3. [8] α, b, A^{bb}, S^1. β–b, $A^{ab*cdfg}$ om. [9] h (?), β, S^1 add καί. [10] β, A, S^1 (save that e reads τιμωρῆσαι and A συνέχεις). α reads as in margin. Its corruption seems to be peculiar to itself. [11] α. β, A, S^1 om. [12] c, A^{ab*cdg}. h, a, A^b read τὸν λόγον. β–af, S^1 λόγον. f λέγων. [13] α, aef, S^1 (save that ef read ἡμᾶς). b reads φυλακισθῆναί με. dg, A ἐν (d om.) φυλακῇ βληθῆναι ἡμᾶς (A με). [14] α, ad, A^{abcdfg}, S^1. befg, A^{b*}

⌜Τί¹⁹ συνέχεις²⁰ τὸν αἰχμάλωτον καὶ εὐγενῆ παῖδα *ἐν δεσμοῖς²¹⌝, *ὃν ἔδει μᾶλλον ἄνετον εἶναι²² καὶ ὑπηρετεῖσθαι²³. 4. Ἤθελε γὰρ ὁρᾶν με²⁴ ἐν πόθῳ ⌜ἁμαρτίας⌝²⁵. *ἐγὼ δὲ²⁶ ἠγνόουν ἐν²⁷ πᾶσι τούτοις²⁸. 5. *Εἶπε δὲ πρὸς αὐτήν²⁹. Οὐκ ἐστὶ *τοῦτο τοῖς³⁰ Αἰγυπτίοις πρὸ ἀποδείξεως ἀφαιρεῖσθαι τὰ ἀλλότρια. 6. Ταῦτα ⌜οὖν⌝³¹ εἶπε *περὶ τοῦ μεταβόλου³². *Ὁ δὲ παῖς³³ *ὀφείλει ἐγκατάκλειστος εἶναι³⁴.

XV. Μετὰ δὲ¹ *ἡμέρας εἰκοσιτέσσαρας² ἦλθον οἱ Ἰσμαηλῖται· *ἦσαν γὰρ³ ἀκούσαντες⁴ ὅτι Ἰακὼβ ⌜ὁ πατήρ μου πολλὰ⁵⌝ πενθεῖ περὶ ἐμοῦ⁶, *καὶ ἐλθόντες λέγουσι⁷ πρός

Marginal notes: β, A, S¹ ὑπηρετεῖν σοι. β, A, S¹ ὁ δὲ εἶπε πρὸς τὴν Μέμφιν. dg, A ἔθος παρά (d om.) τοῖς. β–bd, A καὶ ὁ παῖς

οὖν (A ὅτι). β, A, S¹ καί. β εἶπον.

read as in margin (save that *g* trs. φησίν before ἔλθωσιν). ¹⁵ α, β–dg, S¹. *d*, A^{bfg} read μου. *g*, A^{ab*cd} αὐτοῦ. ¹⁶ α, S¹. β, A read καὶ (*d* τότε) ἡ γυνὴ αὐτοῦ (*efg* om.). ¹⁷ α. β reads λέγει. ¹⁸ α. β, A, S¹ read as in margin (save that *d* reads αὐτῷ). Instead of the next clause which A om., A inserts there the latter half of ver. 1. See note 3. ¹⁹ α. β–d read διὰ τί. *d* reads ὅτι δή. ²⁰ *a* reads συνέχει. *d* om. S¹ = ὑβρίζεις. ²¹ α. β, S¹ om. ²² α. β–d, A^{abh} read ὃν ἔδει εἶναι (*e* trs. after μᾶλλον, *fg* trs. after ἄνετον) μᾶλλον (A^{ab} om.) ἄνετον. *d* (A^{ig} ?) τοῦτον (*d* om.) ἄνετον εἶναι. A^{b*cd} = δεῖ οὖν εἶναι ἀποστάτην τὸν μετάβολον καὶ τοῦτον ἄνετον εἶναι (?). S¹ = ὃν ἔδει μᾶλλον ἔχειν ἐν τοῖς οἰκήμασιν. ²³ α. β, A, S¹ read as in margin (save that *b* reads σου and *g* trs. σοι before ὑπηρετεῖν). A^b om. next seven words. ²⁴ β–g, S¹ trs. before ὁρᾶν. ²⁵ *e* reads ἁμαρτήματος. *d* adds αὐτῆς. S¹ om. ²⁶ α. β–dg, A^g, S¹ read καί. *dg*, A^{abhb*cd} καὶ ἐγώ. ²⁷ *c*, *aef*. *h*, *bdg* read ἐπί. ²⁸ *h* om. next seven words. ²⁹ *c*. β, A^{ab*cdg}, S¹ read as in margin (save that *d*, A^{ab*cdg} read λέγει and *a* αὐτήν and *d* αὐτῇ for π. τὴν Μέμφιν). A^b = καὶ ὁ ἀνὴρ λέγει πρὸς τὴν γυναῖκα. ³⁰ *c*. *aef*, S¹ read τοῖς. *b* παρά. *d* ἔθος τοῖς. *g*, A ἔθος (*g* ἔθνος) παρὰ τοῖς. ³¹ α. β, A, S¹ om. ³² α, β, S¹. A = (+ καὶ A^{bb}) ὁ μετάβολος. ³³ α. β–bd, A read as in margin (save that for ὅτι A^{b*} read αὐτοῦ and om. rest of verse). *b* καὶ περὶ ἐμοῦ ὅτι. *d* κα εἶπεν ὅτι ὁ παῖς. S¹ = ὁ παῖς. ³⁴ *b* reads ὄφειλα ἐγκατάκλειστος εἶναι. *g* ὀφείλει κατάκλειστος εἶναι. A = ὀφείλει εἶναι ἐν δεσμοῖς. S¹ = ἔστω παρὰ τοῖς δεσμίοις.

XV. ¹ *c*, *bd*, A, S¹. *h* reads γάρ but trs. after ἡμέρας. *af* read οὖν. *eg* om. ² *c*. So *d* but in figures. *h* reads ἡμ. εἴκοσι καὶ τέσσαρας. β–dg εἰκοσιτέσσαρας (*e* κδ′) ἡμ. *g* ἡμ. τέσσαρας. ³ α. β, A, S¹ καί. ⁴ *d*, A add ὄντων αὐτῶν (A om. ὄντ. αὐτ.) εἰς γῆν Χ. ⁵ α. β, A, S¹ om. ⁶ A τοῦ υἱοῦ αὐτοῦ. S¹ om. rest of verse. ⁷ α, A^b. β reads (+ καί *d*) εἶπον.

β-dg
ἔγνωμεν.

β-d,A,S¹
καὶ πάνυ
ἤθελον
(aef
θέλων)
δακρῦ-
σαι.

β, S¹
βουλεύ-
ονται.

β, A, S¹
Ἰακώβ.

β, A, S¹
ποιήσῃ
ἐν αὐτοῖς.

β-g,A,S¹
Κυρίῳ.

με. 　　2. Τί ὅτι εἶπας σεαυτὸν[8] *δοῦλον εἶναι[9]; καὶ ἰδοὺ ⌜ἡμεῖς⌝[10] ἐγνώκαμεν[11] ὅτι *υἱὸς εἶ ἀνδρὸς μεγάλου[12] ἐν γῇ[13] Χαναάν, καὶ *ὁ πατήρ σου ⌜ἔτι⌝ πενθεῖ περί σου[14] *ἐν σάκκῳ ⌜καὶ σποδῷ⌝[15]. 　　3. *Ταῦτα ἀκούσας ἐγὼ διελύθη τὰ σπλάγχνα μου, καὶ ἡ καρδία μου ἐτάκη, καὶ ἤθελον δακρῦσαι πάνυ[16], ἀλλ'[17] ἐπέσχον ἐμαυτόν[18], ἵνα μὴ αἰσχύνω[19] τοὺς ἀδελφούς μου, ⌜*καὶ εἶπον αὐτοῖς[20] Ἐγὼ οὐκ οἶδα·[21] δοῦλός εἰμι⌝. 　　4. Τότε ⌜οὖν⌝[22] ἐβουλεύσαντο[23] πωλῆσαί με, ἵνα μὴ εὑρεθῶ ἐν *ταῖς χερσὶν αὐτῶν[24]. 　　5. Ἐφόβουντο γὰρ τὸν *πατέρα μου[25], ἵνα μὴ *ἐλθὼν ἐν αὐτοῖς ποιήσει[26] ἐκδίκησιν κινδύνου[27]. ἤκουον[28] γὰρ ὅτι μέγας ἐστὶ παρὰ Θεῷ[29] καὶ[30] ἀνθρώποις. 　　6. Τότε λέγει *αὐτοῖς ὁ μετάβολος[31]. Λύσατέ με ἀπὸ τῆς κρίσεως τοῦ[32] Πεντεφρί[33]. 　　7. *Ἐκεῖνοι δὲ προσελθόντες[34] ἤτουν[35] με[36] λέγοντες· ⌜Εἰπὲ⌝[37] ὅτι ἐν ἀργυρίῳ ἠγοράσθης[38] ἡμῖν, *κἀκεῖνος ἀπολῦσαι ἡμᾶς ἔχει[39].

β-g, S¹ προσελθόντες οὖν.　　bdg, A^{b*cdg} ἀπέλυσεν ἡμᾶς.

A^{ab*cdg} = καὶ λέγουσι. 　　[8] α, aef, A^{ab}. bdg read ἑαυτόν. A^{b*cdfg} = ἡμῖν. [9] ef, A read ὅτι δοῦλός εἰμι. g δοῦλον. 　　[10] α, d. β-d, A, S¹ om. A^{b*cdfg} om. καὶ . . . ἐγνώκαμεν. 　　[11] α, dg. β-dg read as in margin. 　　[12] α, abdf (save that d adds δυνατοῦ καί after ἀνδρός). e reads ἀνδ. μ. υἱὸς εἶ. g υἱὸς ἀνδ. μ. εἶ. 　　[13] α, def. a, A read τῇ γῇ. b, S¹ τῇ. g om. 　　[14] α, A^b (save that A^b om. περί σου). β, S¹ read πενθεῖ (+ περί σου aefg) ὁ πατήρ σου. A^{ahb*cdfg} = καὶ ἰδοὺ (A^b om.) αὐτὸς πενθεῖ περί σου. 　　[15] α. β-b, A, S¹ read ἐν σάκκῳ. b ἐν λάκκῳ. d adds περί σου. A^b adds περὶ τοῦ πατρός μου. 　　[16] α (save that h reads διελυπήθη). β-d, A, S¹ read as in margin (save that b reads πάλιν for πάνυ). d καὶ ταῦτα ἀκούσας ἐγὼ παρ' αὐτῶν πάνυ ἤθ. δακρῦσαι. 　　[17] α, g. b, A, S¹ read καί. d καὶ πάλιν and om. next two words. aef om. 　　[18] g adds καὶ εἶπον. A^b περὶ τοῦ πατρός μου. 　　[19] g reads καταισχύνω. 　　[20] h, d (omitting καί). c read κ. εἶπον αὐτῷ. abef, S¹ κ. εἶπα (f εἶπον). g om. 　　[21] d adds τοῦτο ὃ λέγετε ὑμεῖς· ἓν δὲ οἶδα ὅτι. 　　[22] α. β, A, S¹ om. 　　[23] α, A. β, S¹ read as in margin. 　　[24] α. β, A^{b*cdfg}, S¹ read χερσὶν αὐτῶν. A^{ab} αὐτοῖς. 　　[25] α. β, A, S¹ read as in margin. 　　[26] α (save that h reads ποιήσῃ αὐτοῖς for ἐν ἀ. π.). β, A, S¹ read as in margin (save that df read ποιήσει). e adds τήν. 　　[27] d reads κίνδυνον. 　　[28] b reads ἠκούσθη. 　　[29] α, g. β-g, A, S¹ read as in margin. 　　[30] g adds παρά. 　　[31] α, e, A^{ab*cdfg}. β-e, A^b, S¹ read ὁ μ. αὐτοῖς (d πρὸς αὐτούς). 　　[32] β om. 　　[33] α, d. af read Πεντεφρή. beg, S¹ Πετεφρί (e -ή). A^{abh} Πεταφρή. A^{b*cdfg} Φωτιφάρ. A^{abh} add [illegible Armenian] corrupt (?) for [illegible Armenian] as in A^{b*cdfg}. A then = δευτέρου ἄρχοντος (A^{ab} om.). 　　[34] α. β-g, S¹ read as in margin. g, A καὶ προσελθόντες. d adds οἱ Ἰσμαηλῖται. A ἔμπροσθεν αὐτοῦ. 　　[35] α, β-bd, A. bd, S¹ read αἰτοῦνται. 　　[36] g om. 　　[37] α, aef, S¹. bdg, A om. 　　[38] α, g. aef, S¹

XVI. *Ἡ δὲ Μεμφὶς εἶπε τῷ ἀνδρὶ αὐτῆς[1]· *Ἀγόρασον β, S[1] ἐδή-
τὸν νεανίαν[2], ἀκούω γάρ, φησίν[3], ὅτι πωλοῦσιν αὐτόν. λωσε.

c	β, Α, S[1]	β–df, Α, S[1] πρία-
2. Εὐθέως δὲ ἀπέστειλε εὐνοῦ-χον ἐν τοῖς Ἰσμαϊλίταις, αἰ-τοῦσά με εἰς διάπρασιν. 3. Ὁ δὲ εὐνοῦχος *μὴ θελήσας ἀγορά-σαι με[4] ἀνεχώρησεν πειράσας αὐτούς, καὶ δηλοῖ τῇ δεσποίνῃ αὐτοῦ, ὅτι πολλὴν τιμὴν αἰ-τοῦσιν τοῦ παιδός.	2. Καὶ[5] ἀπέστειλεν εὐνοῦχον τοῖς Ἰσμαηλίταις[6], *αἰτοῦσά με εἰς διάπρασιν[7]. *καλέσας οὖν ὁ ἀρχιμάγειρος τοὺς Ἰσ-μαηλίτας ᾔτει με εἰς πρᾶσιν[8]. 3. ⌈Καὶ μὴ θελήσας ἀνεχώρη-σεν⌉[9]. *Ὁ εὐνοῦχος ⌈πειρα-σθεὶς αὐτῶν⌉ δηλοῖ[10] *τῇ δεσ-ποίνῃ[11] ὅτι πολλὴν αἰτοῦσι τιμὴν ⌈τοῦ παιδός⌉.	σθαί με.

read ἐπράθης. b ἠγοράσθη. d ἐπράθη. Α[ah] = ἠγόρασας τοῦτον, Α[b] ἠγοράσατε τ.,
Α[b*cdfg] ἠγοράσαμεν τ. The chief variations seem to have arisen within α, β.
[39] h. c reads κἀκεῖνος λοιπῶν λῦσαι ἡμᾶς ἔχει. Here λοιπῶν may be corrupt
for λοιπόν. aef, S[1] read κἀκεῖνος ἀπολύσει ἡμᾶς. bdg κἀκεῖνος (+ταῦτα ἀκούσας
εὐθέως d) ἀπέλυσεν ἡμᾶς. Α καὶ ὁ μετάβολος ἀπέλυσεν (+ἡμᾶς Α[abh]).

XVI. [1]c. From this point onward h is wanting. aef read ἐδήλωσε δὲ
(+ἡ Μ. f) τῷ ἀνδρὶ αὐτῆς. b, Α, S[1] ἡ δὲ Μ. ἐδήλωσε (Α ἀπέστειλε) τῷ ἀ. αὐτῆς.
d ἐδήλωσε δὲ αὐτῷ ἡ γυνὴ αὐτοῦ. g καὶ ἐδήλωσε τῷ ἀ. αὐτῆς ἡ Μ.   [2]c. β–df,
Α, S[1] read as in margin. f reads πριάσαι με. d ἐκπρίου αὐτόν. But d is
peculiar and for ἀγόρασον . . . αὐτόν reads λέγουσα· Ἐπειδὴ ἀκούω ὅτι
πωλοῦσι αὐτὸν ἐκπρίου αὐτόν.   [3]b, S[1] read ἔφη.   [4]It will be observed
that c, bg represent only the eunuch as in treaty for the purchase of
Joseph, whereas in aef, Α, S[1], and also d (see note 9) first Potiphar acts
and next the eunuch. The loss in c, bg could have arisen through hmt.,
but probably the words referring to Potiphar are an intrusion (see
note 8). The fact that this addition is implied by d is discounted
when we consider that d is frequently conflate.   [5]β–d, S[1]. d reads
καὶ εὐθέως. Α καὶ ἕτερον (Α[b] ἄνθρωπον).   [6]d adds καὶ ἤγαγεν αὐτούς.
[7]β–bd, S[1]. bd, Α read καὶ (b om.) ᾐτεῖτό με (b om.) (+ἀπ' αὐτῶν Α) εἰς
διάπρασιν (b πρᾶσιν).   [8]aef, Α, S[1] (save that Α read ἐμπόρους for Ἰσμ.
and Α[ab*cde] add ἀπ' αἰτῶν after ᾔτει). c, bdg om. and probably rightly as
this clause conflicts with the words before and after.   [9]abef, S[1] (save
that b adds ποιῆσαι μετ' αὐτῶν after θελήσας). g, Α om. d has a very
peculiar text but gives excellent sense: for αἰτοῦσά με . . . παιδός it reads
καὶ ᾐτεῖτό με εἰς διάπρασιν παρ' αὐτῶν ὁ Πεντεφρίς· εἰπόντες δὲ πολλὴν τὴν τιμὴν
μου, καὶ μὴ θελήσας ἀπέστειλεν ἡμᾶς, ὁ δὲ εὐνοῦχος πορευθεὶς ἐδήλωσε τῇ δεσποίνῃ
αὐτοῦ ταῦτα.   [10]abef, S[1] (save that b, S[1] add δέ after ὁ and e reads αὐτοῖς).

β¹, A, S
μνᾶς
χρυσίου.
β–be, A
αἰτοῦσι.
β, A, S¹
καί.
β–d, S¹
ἀντ' ἐμοῦ,
ἑκατὸν
εἶπεν
τῇ Αἰγ.
δεδόσ-
θαι. Καί.
aef, A
αἰκισθῇ.

4. ⌜*Ἡ δὲ ἀπέστειλεν¹² *εὐνοῦχον ἕτερον¹³⌝, λέγουσα¹⁴. Ἐὰν καὶ δύο¹⁵ μνᾶς¹⁶ ζητοῦσι¹⁷ ⌜παρέχετε⌝¹⁸· μὴ φείσασθε¹⁹ ⌜χρυσίου· μόνον²⁰ πριασάμενος²¹ τὸν παῖδα ἄγαγε²² *πρός με. 5. Ἐλθὼν οὖν ὁ εὐνοῦχος⌝ καὶ²³ δοὺς²⁴ αὐτοῖς²⁵ ὀγδοήκοντα²⁶ χρυσοῦς²⁷ *ἀνελάβετό με· τῇ δὲ Αἰγυπτίᾳ εἶπεν ὅτι δέδωκα ἑκατόν. 6. Ἐγὼ δὲ²⁸ εἰδὼς²⁹ ἐσιώπησα³⁰ ἵνα μὴ αἰσχυνθῇ³¹ *ὁ εὐνοῦχος³².

XVII. Ὁρᾶτε οὖν¹, τέκνα μου², πόσα ὑπέμεινα ἵνα μὴ αἰσχύνω³ τοὺς ἀδελφούς μου. 2. Καὶ ὑμεῖς ⌜οὖν⌝ ἀγαπᾶτε ἀλλήλους, ⌜καὶ ἐν μακροθυμίᾳ⁴ *συγκρύπτετε ἀλλήλων⁵ τὰ ἐλαττώματα⌝. 3. Τέρπεται γὰρ⁶ ὁ θεὸς⁷ ⌜ἐπὶ *ὁμονοίᾳ

β καταισχύνω.

---

g reads καὶ πειρασθεὶς αὐτῶν ὁ εὐν. δηλοῖ. A = καὶ ἐδήλωσε ὁ εὐν. With A compare d (see note 9). aef make ὁ εὐνοῦχος the subject of the preceding verb ἀνεχώρησεν and af accordingly add δέ after δηλοῖ. ¹¹ g reads αὐτήν. ¹² d reads καὶ ἀποστέλλει. S¹ om. together with next three words. ¹³ c. β–d read ἕτερον εὐν. d ὕστερον εὐν. ¹⁴ A = ἡ δὲ λέγει. ¹⁵ S¹ = διακοσίας. ¹⁶ c. β, A, S¹ read as in margin. ¹⁷ c, be, S¹. β–be, A read as in margin. ¹⁸ c, a. befg read πρόσεχε. d δὸς αὐτοῖς. S¹ = προσέχετε. d om. next three words. ¹⁹ c, a²g, Aᵇᵇ. abef, S¹ read φείσασθαι. Aᵇ*ᶜᵈᶠᵍ = φεῖσαι. ²⁰ d reads μόνος. ²¹ c. β reads πριάμενος. ²² β–b. c, b, S¹ read ἀγάγετε. ²³ c. d reads μοι καί. β–d, A, S¹ καί. Vers. 5, 6 appear as follows in d: Καὶ λαβὼν ὁ εὐνοῦχος τὸ χρυσίον κατεδίωξεν ἡμᾶς καὶ ὀγδοήκοντα χρυσίνους δοὺς αὐτοῖς ἀντὶ ἐμοῦ, καὶ λαβών με παρ' αὐτοῖς ἐλθόντων ἡμῶν εἰς τὸν οἶκον ἑκατὸν εἶπεν δεδωκέναι, καὶ εἰδὼς ἐγὼ ἐσιώπησα ἵνα μὴ καταισχύνω τοὺς συνδούλους μου, μήτε μὴν αἰκισθῇ ὁ εὐνοῦχος. ²⁴ c, β–be, S¹. b reads δίδει. e δίδωσι. A = ἔδωκε. ²⁵ S¹ om. A adds ἀντ' ἐμοῦ. ²⁶ c, β (aeg reading π'). A = ἑξήκοντα. S¹ = ὀκτώ. ²⁷ c, g. β–eg read χρυσίνους. e χρυσίους. g χρυσσούς (sic). Aᵇ adds τιμὴν ἀντ' ἐμοῦ ὁ εὐνοῦχος. ²⁸ c. β–d, S¹ read as in margin (save that b reads εἰπών. e adds καί before ἑκατόν, while after δεδόσθαι be add ἀντ' ἐμοῦ. S¹ ἀντ' αὐτοῦ. g ἔλαβέν με). For d see note 23. A = καὶ εἶπεν ὅτι ὀγδοήκοντα χρυσοῦς ἔδωκε ἀντ' αὐτοῦ. Καί. Perhaps לקח (i.e. ἀνελάβετο) is corrupt for חלף = ἀντί. ²⁹ b reads ἰδών. A adds ταῦτα. bef add ἐγώ. ³⁰ A adds περὶ αὐτοῦ. ³¹ c. aef, A, S¹ read as in margin. b ἐτασθῇ. dg καταισχύνω and put last two words in acc. τοὺς εὐν. ³² Aᵇ = αὐτός. Aᵃᵇᵇ*ᶜᵈᶠᵍ om.

XVII. ¹ c, A. β, S¹ om. g om. ὁρᾶτε . . . μου. ² c, f, A. β–f, S¹ om. ³ c. β reads as in margin. ⁴ c, β–b. b reads μακροθυμίαις. ⁵ d reads διάγετε κρύπτωντες (sic) ἀλλήλους. For ἀλλήλων S¹ reads τῶν νέων. ⁶ c, bdg,

ἀδελφῶν[8] ⌜καὶ⌝ ἐπὶ προαιρέσει καρδίας[9] ⌜ἀγαθῆς⌝[10] †εὐ-
δοκοῦσιν[11] εἰς ἀγαθόν[12].   4. *Ὅτε ⌜δὲ⌝[13] ἦλθον οἱ ἀδελφοί
μου εἰς Αἴγυπτον, αὐτοὶ[14] γινώσκουσιν[15] ὅτι *ἀπέστρεψα τὸ
ἀργύριον αὐτοῖς[16], καὶ οὐκ ὠνείδισα *αὐτούς, καὶ[17] παρεκάλεσα[18] ⌜αὐτούς⌝[19].   5. Καὶ[20] μετὰ θάνατον *Ἰακώβ, τοῦ
πατρός μου[21], ⌜περισσοτέρως⌝ ἠγάπησα αὐτούς, καὶ πάντα ὅσα
ἤθελον[22] ⌜ὑπερεκπερισσοῦ⌝[23] *ἐποίουν αὐτοῖς[24].   6. *Καὶ οὐκ
ἀφῆκα[25] αὐτούς[26] θλιβῆναι *ἕως μικροῦ πράγματος[27]. καίγε
πᾶν ὃ ἦν ἐν τῇ[28] χειρί μου αὐτοῖς δέδωκα[29].   7. ⌜Καὶ⌝[30]
οἱ υἱοὶ *αὐτῶν υἱοί μου[31], *καὶ οἱ υἱοί μου ὡς δοῦλοι αὐτῶν[32],
καὶ[33] ἡ ψυχὴ *αὐτῶν ψυχή μου[34], καὶ πᾶν ἄλγημα[35] αὐτῶν

β, A, S¹ ⌜ἐκ περισσοῦ⌝ ἐποίησα.   c, A μου ψυχὴ αὐτῶν.

Margin: β, S¹ εὐδοκιμούσης εἰς ἀγάπην (a ἀγαθόν). — β-d, A, S ὡς. — β-dg, A^{b f g}, S Ἰακώβ. — β-ad, A, S¹ ἐκέλευσεν (-αν A).

A, S¹. aef om.   [7] A = κύριος.   [8] β, S¹. c reads ἐλαττώματα (sic)
ἀδελφῶν καὶ ὁμονοίᾳ. Here ἐλαττώματι may = חֶסֶר corrupt for חֶסֶד
'kindness.'   [9] A^{b*cdg} = καρδιῶν.   [10] c. β, A, S¹ om. The word
may have originated in a dittography of εἰς ἀγαθόν.   [11] c. εὐδοκοῦσιν may
be corrupt for εὐδοκούσης. But A = ὅτε (A^{b*cdg} αἱ or οἱ) εὐδοκοῦσιν. β, S¹
read as in margin (save that g reads εὐδοκιμήσει).   [12] c, a, A^{hb*cdg}. β-a
read as in margin. A^b = ἀλλήλους but this is apparently due to internal
corruption. The idea required here is not expressed by ἀγαθόν which
may be a corruption of ἀγάπην, and אהבה (= ἀγάπην) may be corrupt for
אחוה = ἀδελφότητα.   [13] c. β-d, S read καὶ ὅτε. d ὅταν οὖν. A = ὅτε.
[14] c. β-d, A, S read ὡς (+ καί A). For αὐτοί and the next seven words
d reads καὶ ἐπέγνω αὐτούς.   [15] c, A^{ab*cd}. β-bd read οἴδασιν. b, A^b ἔγνωσαν.
S = ὁρᾶτε καὶ ὑμεῖς.   [16] g, A^b read ἀπέστρεψαν τὸ ἀργύριον αὐτῶν.   [17] c.
β, S¹ read ἀλλὰ καί (d om.). A = αὐτοὺς ἀλλά.   [18] d reads παρακαλέσω.
[19] β, S. c reads αὐτοῖς. A^{(a?)b} add ἰδοὺ ἀκούουσι οἱ ἀδελφοί μου ἐὰν ψευδές τι
λαλῶ ἐγώ· ἀποδιδοῦσι εἰς πρόσωπόν μου. A^{hb*cdg} add ἀκούουσι, ἰδού, καὶ (A^h
om. ἰδού, κ.) ἐροῦσι εἰ ἐγὼ ψευδές τι λαλῶ.   [20] g reads κ. πάλιν. A =
ἀλλὰ καί (A^{fg} om.).   [21] c, d. β-dg, A^{bfg}, S read Ἰακώβ. g τοῦ πατρὸς
ἡμῶν Ἰ. A^{ab*cd} = τοῦ πατρός μου.   [22] c. a reads ἠθέλησαν. β-ad, S¹
read ἐκέλευσεν. d μοι παρήγγειλεν ὁ πατήρ μου. A = ἐκέλευσαν. The
variations arose within the Greek or c, a = אוה. The rest = צוה or צוה.
[23] c. β-d, S read ἐκ περισσοῦ. d, A om.   [24] c. β, A, S¹ read as in
margin. d adds ἐπ' αὐτούς. b adds καὶ ἐθαύμαζον.   [25] c, d, A. β-d, S
read οὐκ ἀφῆκα γάρ.   [26] a reads αὐτοῖς.   [27] S¹ = οὐ πρὸς κακὴν αἰτίαν.
A adds καὶ ἔδωκα αὐτοῖς πάντα ὅσα ἐζήτησαν.   [28] c, g. β-g om.   [29] c, β-b.
b reads ἔδωκα.   [30] c. β, A, S om.   [31] β, S¹. c reads αὐτῶν. A = μου,
υἱοὶ αὐτῶν. d om. next seven words.   [32] c, β-d, S¹ (save that g om. οἱ).
A = καὶ δοῦλοί μου, δοῦλοι αὐτῶν.   [33] c, A. β, S¹ om.   [34] β, S¹. c, A
read as in margin. A adds καὶ (A^b om.) ἡ γῆ μου γῆ αὐτῶν, a phrase which

Marginal readings (left column): bdg (A) ἀσθένειά μου ἡ γῆ μου γῆ αὐτῶν (+καί g). bef, S¹ μου βουλὴ αὐτῶν. β-ae, A, S¹ Κυρίου, τέκνα μου. β-af, S¹ ὑμᾶς ἐνταῦθα καί εὐλογή-σει ὑμᾶς.

ἄλγημά μου[36], ⌐καὶ πᾶσα μαλακία αὐτῶν *ἀσθένειά μου, καὶ[37] ἡ βουλὴ⌐ *αὐτῶν βουλή μου[38].   8. Καὶ οὐχ ὕψωσα ἐμαυτὸν[39] ἐν αὐτοῖς ⌐ἐν ἀλαζονείᾳ⌐ διὰ τὴν ⌐κοσμικήν⌐ *μου δόξαν[40], ⌐ἀλλ'[41] ἤμην ἐν αὐτοῖς ὡς εἷς τῶν ἐλαχίστων[42]⌐.

XVIII. ⌐Ἐὰν⌐[1] οὖν καὶ ὑμεῖς[2] πορευθῆτε ἐν ταῖς[3] ἐντολαῖς Κυρίου[4], ὑψώσει ὑμᾶς[5] *ὁ θεὸς[6] ⌐ἐν ἀγαθοῖς⌐ εἰς αἰῶνας. 2. ⌐Καὶ *ἐάν τις θέλει⌐[7] κακοποιῆσαι ὑμᾶς, ὑμεῖς τῇ ἀγαθοεργείᾳ[8] εὔχεσθε ὑπὲρ αὐτοῦ, καὶ ἀπὸ παντὸς κακοῦ λυτρωθήσεσθε ὑπὸ[9] Κυρίου⌐. 3. Ἰδοὺ[10] ⌐γὰρ⌐[11] ὁρᾶτε ὅτι ⌐διὰ τὴν *ταπείνωσιν καὶ τὴν μακροθυμίαν μου[12]⌐ θυγατέρα *ἱερέως ἡλιουπόλεως[13] ἔλαβον ἐμαυτῷ[14] εἰς γυναῖκα[15], καὶ ἑκατὸν τάλαντα *χρυσίου δέδονταί μοι[16] *σὺν αὐτῇ[17], *καὶ ὁ[18] Κύριός μου[19] αὐτοὺς[20] κατεδούλωσεν[21]. 4. *Καίγε

β ἀγαθοποιίᾳ. (dg κυρίου) μου.   β-a, S¹ μακροθυμίαν καί. β-ae, A, S¹ ὅτι.   β-a, A, S¹ κυρίων

bdg (omitting the καί) add after ἀσθένειά μου.   [35]S¹ = νόσος.   [36]a om. rest of chapter.   [37]c, ef (save that ef om. καί). S corrupt. bdg, A read as in margin (save that A trs. before καὶ πᾶν ἄλγημα. See note 34).   [38]c, dg. bef, S¹ read as in margin. A⁻ʰ = μία ἦν ἡμῶν πάντων ἡ βουλή. Aʰ om.   [39]bdef. c reads αὐτόν. g ἑαυτόν.   [40]c. bdef read δόξαν μου. g δόξαν.   [41]d reads καί.   [42]c, b. defg read ἐλαχιστοτέρων.

XVIII. [1]A om. and for οὖν . . . κυρίου read καί (Aᵇʰ om.) ὑμεῖς οὖν τὴν αὐτὴν ὁδὸν πορευθῆτε.   [2]e, S² add τέκνα μου.   [3]ef om.   [4]β-ae, A, S¹ add τέκνα μου against c, a.   [5]c reads ἡμᾶς. bdeg, S¹ add ἐνταῦθα (S¹ om.) καὶ εὐλογήσει ὑμᾶς (bg, S¹ om.) omitted by c, af through hmt. A attests the originality of this clause. Thus for ὑψώσει . . . αἰῶνας Aᵃᵇʰ read καὶ ὁ θεὸς δοξάσει ὑμᾶς (Aᵃ = σε?) καὶ ὑψώσει ὑμᾶς (Aᵃʰ om.) ἄνω. Here Arm. Text wrongly represents Aᵇ as twice reading σε. Possibly it is wrong also as to Aᵃ. Aᵇ*ᶜᵈᶠᵍ = ὅτι καὶ (Aᶠᵍ om. ὅτι κ.) Ἰσραὴλ Σαδαι δοξάσει ὑμᾶς καὶ ὑψώσει εἰς αἰῶνας.   [6]c, Aᵃᵇʰ. For Aᵇ*ᶜᵈᶠᵍ see preceding note. β, S¹ om.   [7]c. β-g, S read ἐὰν θέλῃ (f θέλει) τις. g ὅταν θελήσει.   [8]c. β reads as in margin.   [9]c. β reads διά. For λυτρωθήσεσθε ὑπὸ κυρίου S reads λυτρώσει ὁ κ. (+ ὑμᾶς S²).   [10]a om. verses 3, 4.   [11]g, A om.   [12]c. β, S¹ read as in margin (save that d adds μου before καί).   [13]c. So Jub. xl. 10. β-a, A, S¹ read as in margin (save that g om. μου).   [14]c, A. β-a, S¹ om.   [15]S¹ add Σειφήν.   [16]c, defg (save that d reads δέδωκε and eg δέδοται). b, S¹ read μοι χρυσίου δέδοται. A = χρυσίου ἔδωκάν μοι.   [17]A places after χρυσίου. f om. rest of verse.   [18]c. β-ae, A, S¹ read ὅτι. e om.   [19]c, g. β-ag, A, S¹ read μοι.   [20]e reads αὐτοῖς.   [21]c, de. b reads ἐδούλευσε.

καὶ[22] ὡραιότητα ἔδωκέ[23] μοι ὑπὲρ ὡραίους Ἰσραήλ, ⌜καὶ⌝ β-a, A,
ἐφύλαξέ[24] με ⌜ἕως γήρους[25] ἐν δυνάμει καὶ⌝ ἐν κάλλει· S¹ ὡς
* Καὶ γὰρ ὅμοιος ἤμην[26] ἐν πᾶσι τῷ[27] Ἰακώβ. ἄνθος
ὑπέρ.

c, β, S¹	A
XIX. Ἀκούσατε δέ[1], τέκνα μου, καὶ *περὶ ὧν †οἶδα ἐνυπνίων[2]. 2. Δώδεκα[3] ἔλαφοι ἐνέμοντο[4] *ἐν τόπῳ[5] καὶ οἱ ἐννέα[6] διεσπάρησαν *εἰς πᾶσαν τὴν γῆν[7]· ὁμοίως δὲ[8] καὶ οἱ τρεῖς.	XIX. *Ἀκούσατε οὖν[9] τὸ ἐνύπνιον ὃ εἶδον[10]. 2. Δώδεκα ἐλάφους ἑώρων[11] ὅτι ἐνέμοντο καὶ[12] ἐξ αὐτῶν ἐννέα διεσπάρησαν· οἱ δὲ τρεῖς ἐσώζοντο[13], καὶ τῇ ἡμέρᾳ τῇ ἑξῆς καὶ αὐτοὶ διεσπάρησαν.

β-b ὁ εἶδον ἐνύπνιον.

A (only for verses 3–7)

3. Καὶ ἑώρων ὅτι τρεῖς[14] ἔλαφοι τρεῖς ἀμνοὶ ἐγίνοντο καὶ ἐβόησαν πρὸς Κύριον καὶ ἐξήγαγε αὐτοὺς Κύριος[15] εἰς τόπον εὐθαλῆ καὶ ἔννδρον, καὶ ἤγαγε[16] αὐτοὺς ἐκ σκότους εἰς φῶς.
4. Καὶ ἐκεῖ ἐβόησαν πρὸς Κύριον μέχρι οὗ συνήχθησαν *πρὸς αὐτοὺς[17] οἱ ἐννέα ἔλαφοι καὶ ἐγίνοντο αὐτοὶ ὡς δώδεκα πρόβατα, καὶ μετ' ὀλίγον χρόνον ηὐξάνοντο καὶ ἐγίνοντο ποίμνια πολλά.
5. Καὶ[18] μετὰ ταῦτα ἑώρων *καὶ ἰδοὺ[15] δώδεκα βόες

g ἐδούλωσε.   [22] c. β-a read καίγε. A gives a peculiar text of ver. 4: Καὶ ἦν (+Ἀσανὲθ γυνή μου A^b) ὡραῖος ὡς ἄνθος καὶ (+ἐγὼ ἦν A^b) ὡραῖος ὑπὲρ (+πάντας A^b) ἐκλεκτοὺς Ἰσραὴλ (+καὶ σώφρων καὶ ταπεινὸς A^b) ὑπὲρ Λευὶ καὶ Ἰούδα καὶ (+ὑπὲρ A^b) Νεφθαλείμ· ἐφύλαξέ με ἐν κάλλει (for ἐφ. . . . κάλλει A^b reads πλέον ὡραῖος ἦν ἢ αὐτοί), ὅτι ὅμοιος ἦν ἐγὼ ἐν πᾶσι τῷ Ἰακώβ (+τῷ πατρί μου A^b).   [23] d reads δέδωκε.   [24] c. β-a read διεφύλαξε.   [25] c, ef. bdg read γήρως.   [26] c. β-ag read ὅτι ἐγὼ (d om.) ὅμοιος. For g see next note.   [27] dg read τοῦ. For καὶ γὰρ . . . Ἰ. g reads ἐν πᾶσι ὅμοιος τοῦ Ἰ. εἰμι.

XIX. [1] c, aef. β-aef, S¹ om.   [2] c. For οἶδα read εἶδον. b reads ὧν εἶδον ἐνυπνίων, β-b as in margin save that d reads ὅπερ. S¹ = ὧν εἶδον ἐνυπνίον· τοῦτο λέξω σοι.   [3] e reads ὅτι δώδεκα.   [4] g adds καὶ δι' ἕνα ἐτηρήθησαν.   [5] c. β, S¹ om.   [6] b adds διαιρέθησαν καί.   [7] c, β-b (save that g reads ἐπί). b, S read τῇ γῇ.   [8] c, f. β-df, S¹ om. For ὁμοίως . . . τρεῖς d reads καὶ οἱ τρεῖς ὕστερον διεσπάρησαν.   [9] A^b reads ἔλθετε οὖν πάντες, ἀκούσατε. A alone preserves the full form of the text, but in some cases it is corrupt beyond recovery.   [10] A^b adds τότε.   [11] A^b trs. before δώδεκα.   [12] A^ab*cdefg. A^b reads οἵ ἐσμὲν ἡμεῖς δώδεκα ἀδελφοί, καὶ ἑώρων γε.   [13] A^ab*cdefg. A^b = ἐνέμοντο μετ' ἀλλήλων.   [14] A^h om.   [15] A^bh om. A^h adds ἐκ σκότους εἰς φῶς καὶ ἤγαγε αὐτούς and om. six words after ἔννδρον.   [16] A^b = ἐξήγαγε. A^b trs. the clause καὶ ἤγαγε . . . φῶς before καὶ ἐξήγαγε.   [17] A^bbefg. A^ab*cd om.   [18] A^b om.

θηλάζοντες[19] μίαν δάμαλιν, ἢ ἐκ[20] . . . γάλακτος θάλασσαν
ἐποίει καὶ ἔπινον ἐξ αὐτοῦ[21] αἱ δώδεκα ποίμναι καὶ ἀνηρίθμητα
ποίμνια.   6. Καὶ τοῦ τετάρτου βοὸς ἀνέβησαν τὰ κέρατα
μέχρι τοῦ οὐρανοῦ καὶ ἐγένοντο ὡς τεῖχος τῶν ποιμνῶν, καὶ ἐν
μέσῳ τῶν δύο[22] κεράτων ἐξεβλάστησε[23] ἄλλο κέρας.   7.
Καὶ ἑώρων *μόσχον ὃς δωδεκάκις περιέβαλλε αὐτούς[24], καὶ
ἐγένετο[25] τοῖς βουσὶ ὁλοκλήρως (?) εἰς βοήθειαν.

	c, β, S[1]	A
β, S[1] προῆλ- θεν.	8. *Καὶ εἶδον[26] *ὅτι [ἐκ τοῦ Ἰούδα ἐγεννήθη] †παρθένος, [ἔχουσα στολὴν βυσσίνην, καὶ ἐξ αὐτῆς] ἐγεννήθη ἀμνὸς [ἄμω-μος][27] *καὶ ἦν[28] ἐξ ἀριστερῶν	8. Καὶ εἶδον *ἐν μέσῳ τῶν κεράτων παρθένον τινά, [ἔχου-σαν στολὴν ποικίλον καὶ ἐξ αὐτῆς] προῆλθεν ἀμνός[29], καὶ ἐξ ἀριστερῶν αὐτοῦ ὥρμων

[19] A[b*cdef] by internal corruption = νεμόμενοι (or βοσκοῦντες).   [20] A adds
an adjective = κραταιοῦ, or ἰσχυροῦ or δεινοῦ.   [21] A[bh] i. e. ⴰⴼⴻⴼ.
A[ab*cdefg] read ⴰⴼⴳⴰⴼ (= αὐτῶν) corruptly.   [22] A[efg] om. perhaps rightly.
[23] A[abh]. A[b*cdefg] read ἀνέστη.   [24] A[ab(h)cefg] (save that A[b] reads ὅπου ἦν
for ὅς, A[c] om. δωδεκάκις and αὐτούς and A[efg] om. ὅς). A[b*d] = μόσχους δώδεκα
οἳ περιέβαλλον αὐτούς.   [25] A[abhefg]. A[b*d] = ἐγένοντο.   [26] d reads ἴδον δέ.
[27] This passage has been generally rejected as a Christian interpolation.
But if we excise it wholly, the unity of the context is destroyed. It
seems undeniable that the same leader is referred to in ver. 7 and subsequently in ver. 9. In the former verse as a μόσχος he goes to the aid of
the βόες: in the latter (see A) the βόες and others rejoice in his triumphant
overthrow of their enemies. In the latter half of ver. 8 this leader is
referred to as ἀμνός. If then the translator has rightly rendered his
original, the symbolic designation of this leader is changed: from being
a μόσχος he becomes an ἀμνός. A similar transformation has already been
twice mentioned in verses 3 ἔλαφοι . . . ἀμνοὶ ἐγίνοντο, 4 ἐννέα ἔλαφοι . . .
ἐγίνοντο ὡς πρόβατα. Hence this third transformation causes no difficulty.
But some record of this transformation must have appeared. Hence the
beginning of ver. 8 must have recounted this transformation of a μόσχος
into an ἀμνός, and not the birth of a virgin of the tribe of Judah and her
bearing of a blameless ἀμνός. Even the textual evidence points to this
conclusion. A comparison of c, β with A leads to the excision of ἐκ τοῦ Ἰ.
ἐγεννήθη and ἄμωμος (om. also by f) as interpolations. Further, as we have
already shown, the context requires here an account of a transformation
and not of a birth; hence παρθένος has either been substituted for μόσχος
(=עֵגֶל) or is a mere interpolation. (Indeed where human beings are every-
where designated as animals the use of παρθένος is in itself impossible.)

αὐτοῦ ὡς λέων· καὶ πάντα τὰ θηρία ὥρμων[30] *κατ' αὐτοῦ[31] καὶ ἐνίκησεν αὐτὰ ὁ ἀμνός, καὶ ἀπώλεσεν *αὐτὰ εἰς καταπάτημα[32]. 9. Καὶ ἔχαιρον ἐπ' αὐτῷ[33] οἱ *ἄγγελοι καὶ οἱ ἄνθρωποι[34] καὶ πᾶσα[35] ἡ γῆ. 10. Ταῦτα δὲ[36] γενήσεται ἐν καιρῷ αὐτῶν[37] ἐν ἐσχάταις ἡμέραις.   11. Ὑμεῖς οὖν, τέκνα μου, φυλάξατε τὰς ἐντολὰς Κυρίου, καὶ τιμᾶτε[38] τὸν *Λευὶ καὶ τὸν Ἰούδαν[39]. ὅτι *ἐκ τοῦ σπέρματος[40] αὐτῶν ἀνατελεῖ ὑμῖν[41] [ὁ ἀμνὸς τοῦ Θεοῦ, ὁ αἴρων τὴν ἁμαρτίαν τοῦ κόσμου][42], σώζων [πάντα τὰ

πάντα[43] τὰ θηρία καὶ πάντα τὰ ἑρπετά[44], καὶ ἐνίκησεν αὐτὰ ὁ ἀμνός, καὶ ἀπώλεσεν αὐτά. 9. Καὶ ἔχαιρον δι' αὐτὸν οἱ βόες *καὶ ἡ δάμαλις [καὶ οἱ ἔλαφοι][45] ἠγάλλοντο ἅμα μετ' αὐτῶν.   10. Ταῦτα δὲ[46] δεῖ γίνεσθαι ἐν καιρῷ αὐτῶν. 11. Καὶ ὑμεῖς, τέκνα μου, τιμήσατε τὸν Λευὶ καὶ τὸν Ἰούδαν ὅτι ἐξ αὐτῶν ἀνατελεῖ ἡ[47] σωτηρία τοῦ Ἰσραήλ.

β, S[1]
Ἰούδαν
καὶ τ.
Λευὶ ὅτι
ἐξ.
β, S[1]
χάριτι.

The evidence points to the former alternative.   Finally the addition ἔχουσα στολὴν βυσσίνην would naturally be made when once παρθένος appeared in the text.   The original therefore of the first half of ver. 8 would be fairly represented by καὶ εἶδον ὅτι ἐν μέσῳ τῶν κεράτων μόσχος ἐγενήθη ἀμνός. This lamb, whose victories are recounted in the close of the verse, appears to have been a Maccabean, i. e. a descendant of Levi.   On his right fights Judah (λέων).   For according to the true text Judah is subordinate to Levi.   See ver. 6.   The above reasoning as to the interpolations holds good even if verses 7, 8, and 9 refer to different leaders.   [29] c. β–d, S[1] read καί. d om.   [29] See note 27.   For κεράτων i. e. *bηδbρωgь* (so A[befg]) A[ab*cd] according to printed Arm. Text give *bηδbρηυgь* = ἐλάφων.   [30] a. c reads ὅρμουν.   β–a ὥρμουν.   [31] g reads αὐτῷ. [32] c. adg, S[2] read αὐτὰ (d ἅπαντα) εἰς καταπάτησιν.   bef, S[1] εἰς καταπάτησιν. [33] f reads αὐτόν.   [34] g reads ἄνθ. καὶ οἱ ἀγγ.   The text is obviously secondary. A is undoubtedly to be preferred.   [35] f adds δέ.   [36] d adds τέκνα μου. [37] S[1] adds χαιρήσουσι ἐπ' αὐτῷ. g trs. ἐν κ. αὐτῶν after ἡμέραις.   [38] d reads τιμήσατε.   Cf. A.   [39] c. So A. β, S[1] read as in margin.   [40] c. β, S[1] read as in margin.   [41] c reads ἡμῖν.   g trs. before ἀνατελεῖ.   [42] Christian interpolations.   For ὁ αἴρων τ. ἁμ. τ. κόσμου which c read, β, S read χάριτι. [43] A[bhefg]. A[ab*cd] om.   [44] For καὶ πάντα τὰ ἑρπετά (= *unηπιῦρ*) we should read εἰς καταπάτημα = *'ḥ ḷηḷunιᵭῦ*.   [45] A[b*cdg]. A[ab] read καὶ ἔκγονα τῶν τριῶν ἐλάφων.   A[b] δύο τῶν τριῶν ἐλάφων.   I have bracketed the καὶ οἱ ἔλαφοι as an interpolation; for the βόες already symbolize the Twelve Tribes. [46] A[ab*cd] add πάντα against A[bhefg].   [47] A[b]. A[ab*cdhefg] om.   [48] See note 42.

ἔθνη καὶ][48] τὸν Ἰσραήλ.
12. Ἡ γὰρ βασιλεία αὐτοῦ
βασιλεία *ἔσται αἰώνιος[49]
ἥτις οὐ παρελεύσεται[50]· ἡ δὲ
ἐμὴ βασιλεία[51] ἐν ὑμῖν ἐπιτελεῖται, ὡς ὀπωροφυλάκιον[52]
ὃ[53] μετὰ τὸ θέρος ἐξαφανί-
ζεται[54].

β, S¹ οὐ φανή-σεται.

12. Ἡ γὰρ ἐμὴ βασιλεία[55]
ἡ ἐν ὑμῖν ἐπιτελεσθήσεται,
ὡς ὀπωροφυλάκιον, ὃ οὐ φανήσεται *μετὰ τὸ θέρος[56].

XX. Οἶδα ⌐γὰρ⌐[1] ὅτι μετὰ *τὴν τελευτήν μου[2] οἱ
Αἰγύπτιοι θλίψουσιν[3] ὑμᾶς[4], ἀλλ' ὁ Θεὸς[5] ποιήσει τὴν
ἐκδίκησιν ὑμῶν[6] καὶ ἐπάξει[7] ὑμᾶς εἰς *τὰς ἐπαγγελίας[8] τῶν
πατέρων ὑμῶν[9].   2. *Ὑμεῖς δὲ[10] συνανοίσετε[11] τὰ ὀστᾶ
μου[12] μεθ' ὑμῶν[13], ⌐ὅτι, ἀναγομένων[14] τῶν ὀστέων ἐκεῖ[15],
Κύριος ἐν φωτὶ ἔσται μεθ' ὑμῶν[16], καὶ ὁ[17] Βελίαρ *ἐν σκότει
ἔσται[18] μετὰ τῶν Αἰγυπτίων⌐.

β, Aᵇʰᵇ cdg, S¹ ἀλλά. bd, S μου.*

c, A

3. *Ἀσυνὲθ δὲ[19] τὴν μητέρα
ὑμῶν ἀγάγετε[20] [παρὰ τὸν
Ἱππόδρομον][21] καὶ πλησίον
Ῥαχιὴλ τῆς μητέρος μου
*θάψατε αὐτήν[22].

β, S¹

3. *Καὶ †Ζελφὰν τὴν μητέρα
ὑμῶν ἀναγάγετε καὶ[23] ἐγγὺς
Βάλλας [παρὰ *τὸν Ἱππό-
δρομον[24]] πλησίον *Ῥαχήλ,
θέτε αὐτήν[25].

---

[49] c. bd, S read αἰῶνος. aefg αἰώνιος.   [50] c, β–ab. ab, S¹ read παρασαλεύσεται.
[51] g adds καί.   [52] af. c, bdg read ὀπορόφ., e ὠπορόφ.   [53] c. β, S¹ read ὅτι.
[54] c. β, S¹ read as in margin. Here S¹ makes a large Christian addition
of several hundred words.   [55] So Aᵇʰᵉˢ (save that Aᵇʰ om. ἐμή). Printed
text corrupt.   [56] Aʰᵇ*ᶜᵈˢ. Aᵃᵇ = ἐν σώματι (through an internal
corruption).

XX. [1] c. β–dg, A, S¹ om. dg read τέκνα.   [2] Aᵇʰ = ἐμέ. Aᵇ*ᶜᵈˡ τὴν
ἔξοδόν μου.   [3] b reads θλίψωσι.   [4] c reads ἡμᾶς.   [5] d adds τῶν
πατέρων μου.   [6] d reads ὑμῖν and trs. before τὴν ἐκδίκησιν. A = αὐτῶν.
a om. rest of ver. and 2–3.   [7] c. β reads εἰσάξει.   [8] c, efg. b, A, S¹
read τὴν ἐπαγγελίαν. d τὴν γῆν τῆς ἐπαγγελίας.   [9] c, b, A, S¹. efg read
ἡμῶν. d μου.   [10] c, Aᵇ. β–a, Aᵇʰᵇ*ᶜᵈˢ, S¹ read as in margin.   [11] bg.
c reads συνανήσετε. d συνανύσατε. e συναροίσατε. f συνανύσετε.   [12] d trs.
before τά.   [13] defy add ἐκεῖ.   [14] g reads ἀγαγομένων.   [15] c. bd, S¹ read
μου. efg μου (g ὑμῶν) ἐκεῖ.   [16] c reads ἡμῶν.   [17] b om.   [18] c reads
ἐσκότισται.   [19] c. See d in note 23. Aᵇ*ᶜᵈˢ = καὶ Ζελφάν. Ver. 3 in
Aᵇʰᵇ = καὶ τὸν ἀδελφὸν (Aᵃ τοὺς ἀδελφοὺς) ὑμῶν ἀναγάγετε (Aᵃʰ ἀναπαύσατε)
καὶ ἐγγὺς τῆς ἀδελφῆς (+ μου Aᵇʰ) καὶ ἐγγὺς τῆς μητέρος θέτε αὐτόν (Aᵃ αὐτούς).
Possibly զեղբայր (ἀδελφόν) is corrupt for զասանէթ մայր = Ἀσανὲθ μητέρα.
The reading of d (see note 23) favours this conjecture.   [20] c. A =

4. Καὶ[26] *ταῦτα εἰπὼν[27] ἐκτείνας[28] τοὺς πόδας αὐτοῦ[29] *ἐκοιμήθη ὕπνῳ καλῷ[30].   5. Καὶ ἐπένθησεν[31] αὐτὸν πᾶς Ἰσραὴλ καὶ πᾶσα Αἴγυπτος πένθος μέγα.

_β, S_
ὕπνον αἰώνιον.

<table>
<tr><td>c</td><td>β, S¹</td></tr>
<tr><td>6. ⌜Καὶ ἐν τῇ ἐξόδῳ τῶν υἱῶν Ἰσραὴλ ἐξ Αἰγύπτου συνήγαγον τὰ ὀστᾶ Ἰωσήφ, καὶ ἔθαψαν αὐτὸν ἐν Χεβρὼν μετὰ τῶν πατέρων αὐτοῦ· ἐγένοντο δὲ τὰ ἔτη τῆς ζωῆς αὐτοῦ ἔτη ἑκατὸν δέκα⌝.</td><td>6. ⌜Καὶ γὰρ σὺν[32] τοῖς Αἰγυπτίοις *ὡς μέλος ἔπασχε[33], *καὶ εὐεργέτει[34] ἐν[35] παντὶ ἔργῳ *καὶ βουλῇ καὶ πράγματι παριστάμενος[36]⌝.</td></tr>
</table>

Διαθήκη Βενιαμὴν τοῦ ιβʹ υἱοῦ Ἰακὼβ καὶ Ῥαχιήλ[1].

I. Ἀντίγραφον λόγων[2] Βενιαμήν[3], ὧν[4] διέθετο[5] *τοῖς υἱοῖς[6] αὐτοῦ[7], ζήσας[8] *ἔτη ἑκατὸν εἴκοσι πέντε[9].

ἀναγάγετε.   [21] Bracketed as a gloss from the LXX of Gen. xlviii. 7. A omits.   [22] _c._ A^{ab} = θέτε αὐτόν (A^{a} αὐτούς). A^{b*cdg} = θέτε and trs. before πλησίον.   [23] _bef._ S¹. _d_ reads ἀναγάγετε δὲ καὶ Ἀσινὲτ τὴν μ. ὑμῶν καὶ τεθήτω. _ag_ om. entire verse. Thus _d_ supports _c_.   [24] S¹ = τὸ πανδοχεῖον.   [25] _d_ reads Ῥαχιήλ.   [26] _d_ om.   [27] A^{b} = μετὰ ταῦτα. A^{abb*cdg} om. _d_ adds Ἰωσήφ καὶ ἐντειλάμενος τοῖς υἱοῖς αὐτοῦ.   [28] A^{abc} = ἐξέτεινε καί. A^{b} adds Ἰωσήφ which according to printed text A^{b*cd} add after αὐτοῦ.   [29] _β–d_, A^{abhb*cd}, S. _c, d,_ A^{g} om.   [30] _c._ ὕπνῳ καλῷ = בשינה טובה corrupt for בשיבה טובה = ἐν γήρει καλῷ. Cf. T. Zeb. x. 6, T. Iss. vii. 9, T. Assher viii. 2. _β,_ S¹ read ἐκοιμήθη (+ ἐν εἰρήνῃ _d_) ὕπνον αἰώνιον. A = ἀπέθανε (+ ἑκατὸν καὶ δέκα ἐτῶν A^{b*cd}). Here ὕπ‹ν›ον αἰώνιον = שינת עולם which may likewise be a corruption of the Hebrew phrase already indicated.   [31] _e_ reads ἐπένθησαν.   [32] _aef. b_ reads καί. _dg,_ S¹ om.   [33] _aef. bg_ read ὡς ἰδίοις μέλεσι (_g_ ἴδια μέλη) συνέπασχε. _d_ συνέπασχε ἐν πάσῃ τῇ ζωῇ αὐτοῦ.   [34] _β–d. d_ reads εὐεργετῶν αὐτούς.   [35] _b_ om.   [36] _β–dg,_ S¹. _d_ reads ἀγαθῷ. διὰ τοῦτο καὶ ἐπένθησαν αὐτὸν πάντες οἱ Αἰγύπτιοι ὡς προνοητὴν αὐτῶν καὶ κηδεμόνα. _g_ καὶ λόγῳ καὶ βουλῇ παριστάμενος. _d_ adds τῷ δὲ θεῷ ἡμῶν. _f,_ S¹ Ἰωσὴφ υἱὸς Ἰακὼβ ια´ υἱός (+ καὶ S¹) Ῥαχὴλ α´ (+ καὶ S¹) ἔζησε ἔτη ρί. _g_ τέλος διαθήκης Ἰωσήφ.

I. [1] Title. _c_ in text. _β–dg,_ S read δ. Βενιαμὶν (_e_ -εὶν, _f_ -ὴν) (+ ιβ´ _b_) περὶ διανοίας (_ef_ ἐννοίας) καθαρᾶς (+ Βενιαμὴν ἑρμηνεύεται τέκνον ὀδύνης _f_). _g_ δ. Β. περὶ τοῦ ἀγαπᾶν τὸν πλησίον· λόγος ιβ´. _d_ (conflate) δ. Β. υἱοῦ Ἰ. ιβ´ υἱοῦ Ῥαχὴλ β´ περὶ διανοίας καθαρᾶς. A^{abhcdg}=δ. Β. ιβ´. A^{b*} δ. Β. υἱοῦ Ἰακὼβ Ἰσραήλ.   [2] _c, β–d,_ S¹. _d,_ A = διαθήκης (+λόγων A^{b*}).   [3] _c, df. abg_ read -ὶν. _e_ -εὶν.   [4] _d_ reads περὶ ὧν. _g_ ὅς.   [5] _β,_ A^{a}, S¹. _c_ reads ἔθετο (a mere error). A^{bb} = ἐξηγήσατο (but A^{bb} _ιϳωιιλϭωϧ_ is a corruption of A^{a}). A^{b*cdefg}

β-dg, S¹   2. *Καταφιλήσας δὲ αὐτοὺς[10] εἶπεν[11]. Ὥσπερ[12] Ἰσαὰκ
καὶ φιλή- *ἐτέχθη τῷ Ἀβραὰμ ἐν γήρει αὐτοῦ[13], οὕτως κἀγὼ τῷ[14]
σας αὐ. Ἰακώβ[15].   3. *Καὶ ἐπειδὴ[16] Ῥαχιὴλ *ἡ μήτηρ μου[17]
β-d, Aᵉᶠᵍ
ἑκατοστῷ τέθνηκε[18] γεννῶσά με, *γάλα οὐκ ἔσχον· Βαλλὰν οὖν τὴν
ἔτει παιδίσκην αὐτῆς ἐθήλασα[19].   4. Ἡ γὰρ[20] ⌈Ῥαχιὴλ μετὰ
ἐτέχθη
τῷ Ἀ. τὸ τεκεῖν[21] τὸν Ἰωσὴφ⌉ δώδεκα ἔτη ἐστείρευσεν· καὶ προσ-
β, S¹ ηύξατο *πρὸς Κύριον[22] ⌈μετὰ νηστείας[23], καὶ συλλαβοῦσα
νηστείας τέτοκε[24] με⌉.   5. Σφόδρα γὰρ[25] *ἠγάπα ⌈ὁ πατήρ μου⌉[26]
δώδεκα
ἡμέρας. τὴν Ῥαχιήλ[27], ⌈καὶ ηὔχετο δύο υἱοὺς ἰδεῖν ἐξ αὐτῆς⌉[28].
β ἔτεκεν. 6. Διὰ τοῦτο ἐκλήθην[29] *Βενιαμίν, ὅ ἐστιν υἱὸς ἡμερῶν[30].

ἐλάλησε.   [6] g reads τοὺς υἱούς.   [7] d adds ἐν ἐσχάταις ἡμέραις αὐτοῦ. Α ἐν
τετάρτῳ ἔτει (Aᵇ* ἡμέρᾳ) τῆς ἀσθενείας αὐτοῦ.   [8] d om. Aᵇ = ἔζησε.   [9] c, f,
Aᵇ*ᶜᵈᵉˡᵍ. aeg read ἔτη ρκέ. b ἴ. ἑκατὸν εἴκοσι. d ἐν τῷ ρκέ ἔτει τῆς ζωῆς αὐτοῦ.
S¹ ἔτη ρκά. Aᵃᵇᵇ = ἴ. ἑκατὸν καὶ εἴκοσι καὶ ἕν.   [10] c. β–dg, S¹ read as in
margin. g καὶ καλέσας αὐτούς. Aᵃᵇᵇᵉˡᵍ = c or β–dg. Aᵇ*ᶜᵈ φιλήσας αὐτούς.
d reads καλέσας γὰρ τοὺς υἱοὺς αὐτοῦ καὶ ἀσπασάμενος. Aᵇ* = καὶ καλέσας
τοὺς υἱοὺς αὐτοῦ πρὸς ἑαυτὸν καὶ ὅτε προσήγγισαν. Thus d and Aᵇ* are related.
[11] Aᵇ*ᶜᵈ = καὶ λέγει. d adds ἀκούσατε τέκνα Β. τοῦ πατρὸς ὑμῶν ἐνωτίσασθε ὅσα
ἐγὼ ἐντέλλομαι ὑμῖν σήμερον.   [12] c, dg. β–dg read ὡς. d adds γὰρ ὁ before
Ἰσαάκ.   [13] c, d (save that d reads ἐπὶ γήρους). β–d, Aᵉˡᵍ (also Aᵃᵇᵉ but
corruptly) read as in margin. Aᵇ = μετὰ τὸ ἑκατοστὸν ἔτος τῷ Ἀ. ἐτέχθη.
Aᵇ*ᵈ πατὴρ πατρὸς ἡμῶν ἑκατοστῷ ἔτει ἐτέχθη. For ὥσπερ ... αὐτοῦ S¹ reads
corruptly as follows: Ἐγὼ Β. ἐν τῷ γήρᾳ τοῦ πατρός μου Ἰακώβ, καὶ πάντες οἱ
ἀδελφοὶ ἦσαν νεανίαι (?). Καὶ οὕτως ὁ πατὴρ πατρὸς ἡμῶν (cf. Aᵇ*ᵈ) ἐτέχθη τῷ
Ἀβ. ἑκατοστῷ ἔτει. Aᵉˡᵍ om. next four words.   [14] d adds πατρί μου.
[15] S¹ adds ὁ δὲ Ἰακὼβ ἦν ἑκατὸν ἐτῶν.   [16] c, β–bg, Aᵃᵇ*ᶜᵈ, S¹. b reads ἐπειδὴ
οὖν. g, Aᵇᵉˡᵍ ἐπειδή.   [17] c, d, Aᵇ. β–d, Aᵃᵇ*ᶜᵈᵉˡᵍ, S¹ om.   [18] g trs. after με.
[19] c, β, S¹ (save that c reads ἔσχεν and om. τήν, a reads Βαλάν and g om. οὖν).
Α = κἀγὼ τὸ γάλα (+ Βαλλᾶς Aᵇ*ᶜᵈ) παιδίσκης (+ αὐτῆς Aᵇ*ᶜᵈ + αὐτῆς Βαλλᾶς
Aᵉˡᵍ) ἐθήλασα.   [20] d, S¹ add μήτηρ μου (S¹ ἡμῶν). For ἡ γὰρ ...
ἐστείρευσεν Α reads ἣν δὲ αὐτῇ ἔτη δώδεκα ἃ ἐστείρευσε.   [21] aef add αὐτήν.
[22] c, d. β–d read Κυρίῳ. Aᵇʰᵇ*ᵉˡᵍ add πατήρ μου (Aᵇʰᵉˡᵍ om. π. μου)
καὶ ἔδωκε αὐτῇ (+ ὁ Θεὸς Aᵇ*) γάλα ἰσχυρόν (Aᵇ* πολύ). Aᵃᶜᵈ γάλα πολύ.
[23] c. β, S¹ read as in margin (save that d reads ἡμέρας β′).   [24] c. β reads
as in margin.   [25] β, Α, S¹. c om.   [26] c. β, S¹ read ὁ πατὴρ ἡμῶν (g μου)
ἠγάπα.   [27] c. β reads Ῥαχήλ as generally.   [28] c, β–d, S¹ (save that β–d
read ἀπ' αὐτῆς, a τεκεῖν, S¹ ἔχειν for ἰδεῖν, e εὔχεται, and g trs. ἰδεῖν before δύο
υἱούς). d reads ὅθεν καὶ ηὔξατο ἵνα ἴδῃ ἐξ αὐτῆς δύο υἱούς.   [29] a om. S¹ reads
γεννηθεὶς ἐκλ.   [30] c, d (save that d reads ὅπε (sic) for ὅ). β–d, Α, S¹ read
υἱὸς ἡμ. (Aᵇ* δεξιᾶς. A⁻ᵇ* om.) ὅ (e ὅς, g, Α τοῦτ') ἐστιν Βενιαμίν (e -είν, f -ήν).

II. Ὅτε *δὲ ἦλθον εἰς Αἴγυπτον †πρὸς Ἰωσήφ[1], καὶ[2] ἐγνώρισέν[3] με ὁ ἀδελφός μου†, λέγει[4] μοι· Τί[5] εἶπαν[6] τῷ πατρί μου ὅτε[7] *με ἐπώλησαν[8];   2. Καὶ εἶπον ⌈αὐτῷ⌉ ὅτι ἔφυραν[9] τὸν χιτῶνά σου αἵματι[10] καὶ *πέμψαντες αὐτὸν εἶπον[11]· Ἐπίγνωθι[12] εἰ[13] ὁ[14] χιτὼν τοῦ υἱοῦ σου ἐστὶν[15] οὗτος.

β-d,A,S[1] οὖν εἰσῆλθον εἰς Αἴγ. καὶ ἐγνώρισέ με Ἰωσήφ, ὁ ἀδελφός μου.
dg, A, S[1] εἶπον οἱ ἀδελφοί μου.

c	β, S[1]	A
3. Καὶ λέγει μοι· Ναί, ἀδελφέ[16]. καὶ ὅτε[17] ἐξέδυσάν με τὸν χιτῶνά μου δέδωκάν με τοῖς Ἰσμαιλίταις· καὶ δέδωκάν μοι περίζωμα, καὶ φραγγελλώσαντες εἰπόν μοι τρέχειν.	3. Καὶ*λέγει μοι[18]· Ναί[19], ἀδελφέ. *Καὶ γὰρ ὅτε ἔλαβόν με οἱ Ἰσμαηλῖται, εἷς ἐξ αὐτῶν ἀποδύσας με τὸν χιτῶνα ἔδωκέ μοι περίζωμα καὶ φραγελλώσας με εἶπε τρέχειν[20].	3. *Καὶ λέγει μοι Ἰωσήφ· Ναί, ἀδελφέ[21]. ἔκλεψάν με Χαναναῖοι ἔμποροι βίᾳ.

II. [1] c, d (save that d reads εἰσῆλθον). β-d, A, S[1] read as in margin (save that be read ἀνεγνώρισε). Since most probably x. 1 originally stood before ii. 1, we should perhaps emend πρὸς Ἰωσήφ, καὶ ἐγνώρισέν με ὁ ἀδελφός μου, λέγει μοι into ἐγνώρισα Ἰωσὴφ τὸν ἀδελφόν μου· καὶ λέγει μοι, and the text of β-d, A, S[1] similarly. Benjamin recognizes Joseph as he had already seen him in a vision (x. 1). Benjamin was only six when Joseph was sold by his brethren (Jub. xxxii. 33; xlii. 20). A later account in the Book of Jashar (*Dict. des Apocr.*, II. 1222) states that Benjamin was the first to recognize Joseph by means of an astrolabe.   [2] g om. [3] be read ἀνεγνώρισεν. For ἐγνώρισεν ... λέγει μοι d reads ἀναγνωρίσας με ἔκλαυσε πικρῶς καὶ καλέσας με κατ' ἰδίαν ἔφη μοι. After ἐγνώρισέν με β-d, A, S[1] add Ἰωσήφ.   [4] eg, A[bbb*cd] read καὶ λέγει.   [5] fg read ὅτι.   [6] c, ef. abdg read εἶπον. dg, A, S[1] add οἱ ἀδελφοί μου (S[1] om.) (+ περὶ ἐμοῦ A[−]) (+ τῷ Ἰακώβ A[bbh]).   [7] c, ade, A. bfg read ὅτι.   [8] c. β, S[1] read ἐπώλησάν με. A = ἀπωλόμην.   [9] c, bd. aefg read ἔφυρον.   [10] A[b*d] om.   [11] c, S[1]. β-d read πέμψαντες εἶπον. d ἀπέστειλαν αὐτὸν πρὸς Ἰακὼβ λέγοντες. A = ἀπέστειλαν πρὸς αὐτὸν (A[b*cdefg] τὸν πατέρα + ἡμῶν A[b*]) καὶ λέγουσι (A[b*cd] εἶπον).   [12] A[bbh] = ἴδε καὶ (A[b] om.) ἐπίγνωθι.   [13] f om. For εἰ ... οὗτος A[b*cde] read τὸν χιτῶνα ὅτου ἐστὶ οὗτος. A[ab] ὅτου ἐστὶ ὁ χιτὼν οὗτος.   [14] deg om.   [15] bg om.   [16] c adds μου.   [17] c adds με.   [18] d reads εἰπέ μοι Ἰωσήφ.   [19] d adds ὄντως.   [20] β-d, S[1] (save that g reads εἶπέν μοι and a φραγγ. and S[1] om. ἔδωκε ... καί). d reads κἀγὼ ἐπορεύθην μετὰ τῶν Ἰσμ. εἷς ἐξ αὐτῶν ἀποδύσας με τὸν χιτῶνα ὃν ἐφόρουν ἔδωκέ μοι περίζωμα καὶ φραγ. εἶπε τρέχειν. A = ἔκλεψάν με οἱ Χαναναῖοι ἔμποροι βίᾳ. This clause corresponds to the first in β-d, S[1].

c	β, S¹	A
4. Εἰς δὲ ἐξ αὐτῶν ῥάβδῳ μαστίζων με, ὑπήντησεν αὐτῷ λέων καὶ ἀνεῖλεν αὐτόν. 5. Καὶ οὕτως οἱ μέτοχοι αὐτοῦ φοβηθέντες ἐν †ἀνέσει με κατέσχεν†.	4. Ἐν δὲ τῷ ὑπάγειν[22] κρύψαι *τὸ ἱμάτιόν μου[23], ὑπήντησεν[24] αὐτῷ λέων[25] καὶ ἀνεῖλεν αὐτόν. 5. Καὶ οὕτως οἱ μέτοχοι[26] φοβηθέντες *διαπωλοῦσί με τοῖς †ἑτέροις αὐτῶν[27].	4. Καὶ ἐγένετο ἐν τῷ ὑπάγειν αὐτούς, (+ καὶ A[befg]) ἔκρυπτον τὸ ἱμάτιόν μου, [εἰ]ἀπήντησέ †μοι[28] θηρίον καὶ ἀνεῖλε[29]. 5. Καὶ οὕτως[30] οἱ μέτοχοι αὐτοῦ ἐπώλησάν με τοῖς Ἰσμαηλίταις.

A (only for verses 6–8).

6. Καὶ οὐκ ἐψεύσαντο αὐτοὶ ταῦτα λέγοντες· ἤθελεν γὰρ κρύπτειν ἀπ' ἐμοῦ *τὰ ἔργα τῶν ἀδελφῶν ἡμῶν[31], καὶ ἐκάλεσε πρὸς αὐτὸν τοὺς ἀδελφοὺς αὐτοῦ[32] καὶ λέγει[33]· 7. Μὴ λέγετε τῷ πατρί μου[34] ἃ ἐποιήσατέ μοι, ἀλλ' οὕτως λέξατε καθὼς ἐξηγησάμην[35] τῷ Βενιαμίν.   8. Καὶ αἱ ἔννοιαι *γένωνται ἐν ὑμῖν[36] τοιαῦται[37] καὶ μὴ ἔλθωσιν οἱ λόγοι οὗτοι εἰς καρδίαν τὸν πατρός μου.

III. *Νῦν οὖν, τέκνα μου, καὶ ὑμεῖς ⸀ἀγαπήσατε¹ Κύριον τὸν Θεὸν τοῦ οὐρανοῦ *καὶ τῆς γῆς², καὶ³ φυλάξατε⁴ ἐντολὰς αὐτοῦ⁷, *μιμούμενοι τὸν ἀγαθὸν καὶ ὅσιον ἄνδρα ⸀Ἰωσήφ⁵.

---

[21] A[b*cdefg] (save that *efg* om. Ἰωσήφ). A[ab] read ὅτε εἶπον ταῦτα ἐθρήνει Ἰωσήφ καὶ (A[a] om.) ἔλεγέ μοι.   [22] *b*, S¹ add αὐτόν.   [23] *g* reads τὰ ἱμάτια.   [24] *g* reads ἀπήντησεν.   [25] *d* om.   [26] *d* adds αὐτοῦ.   [27] ἑτέροις corrupt for ἑταίροις. A on the whole supports β, S¹. How did ἐν ἀνέσει με κατέσχεν of c originate? The ideas (in ἀνέσει and κατέσχεν) seem contradictory. κατέσχεν is probably corrupt for κατέσχον. c, then, may = לכדוני ברוחה corrupt (?) for מכרוני לרעיהם = β, S¹. The tense ἐπώλησαν in A is preferable to the present in β, S¹.   [28] For qhu = μοι read quw = αὐτῷ.   [29] A[a(?)b*cd] add με.   [30] A[bh]. A[ab*cd] = τότε οὕτως. A[efg] = τότε.   [31] A[b]. A[ahb*cdeg] om.   [32] A[ahb*cdefg]. A[b] = ἡμῶν.   [33] A[b] adds χωρίς μου.   [34] A[d] reads ἡμῶν.   [35] A[abhcdeg]. A[b*] = ἔλεξα.   [36] A[b*cdeg]. A[ab] = μὴ γένωνται.   [37] A[b] adds ἐν ὁδῷ μὴ γνώσηται Βενιαμὶν καὶ ἐξηγήσηται τῷ Ἰακώβ.

III. ¹c, β–*bdf* (save that *ae* read τί for νῦν and *eg* trs. καὶ ὑμεῖς after ἀγαπήσατε). *b*, S¹ read καὶ ὑμεῖς οὖν τέκνα μου (+ ἀγαπητά S¹) ἀγαπήσατε. *df* ἀγαπήσατε οὖν καὶ ὑμεῖς τέκνα μου (*f* τέκνα μου καὶ ὑμεῖς). A = καὶ οὖν (A[ahb*cdefg] om.) ὑμεῖς τέκνα μου.   ²c, d. β–d, S¹ om.   ³β, S. c om.   ⁴dg add τάς.   ⁵A = μιμηταὶ γίνεσθε ἀνδρὸς ἀγαθοῦ καὶ ἀληθοῦς.

<table>
<tr><td valign="top">

c, β, S

2. Καὶ ἔστω ἡ διάνοια ὑμῶν
* εἰς τὸ ἀγαθόν[6], ὡς κἀμὲ
οἴδατε[7]. Ὅτι[8] ὁ ἔχων τὴν[9]
διάνοιαν ὀρθὴν[10] πάντα βλέπει
ὀρθῶς[11].   3. Φοβεῖσθε[12]
Κύριον καὶ ἀγαπᾶτε τὸν πλη-
σίον[13]. καὶ ἐὰν τὰ πνεύματα
τοῦ Βελίαρ εἰς πᾶσαν πονη-
ρίαν θλίψεως ἐκστήσωσι[14]
ὑμᾶς, οὐ μὴ * κατακυριεύσωσιν
ὑμῶν[15], * ὡς οὔτε[16] Ἰωσὴφ
* τὸν ἀδελφόν[17] μου. 4. Πό-
σοι[18] τῶν ἀνθρώπων * ἤθελον
αὐτὸν ἀνελεῖν[19], καὶ ὁ Θεὸς ἐσκέ-
πασεν αὐτόν[20]; ὁ γὰρ φοβού-
μενος τὸν Θεὸν καὶ ἀγαπῶν
τὸν πλησίον[21] ὑπὸ * τοῦ πνεύ-
ματος[22] τοῦ Βελίαρ οὐ δύναται
πληγῆναι, σκεπαζόμενος[23] ὑπὸ
τοῦ φόβου τοῦ Θεοῦ.   5.
Καὶ ἀπὸ[24] ἐπιβουλῆς ἀνθρώπων

</td><td valign="top">

A

2–5. Ὅτι ἕως θανάτου αὐτοῦ
οὐκ ἤθελε λέγειν περὶ αὐτοῦ·
ἀλλ’ Ἰακὼβ γνοὺς ἀπὸ Κυρίου
λέγει αὐτῷ· ἀλλ’ ὅμως αὐτὸς[25]
ἀπηρνεῖτο, * καὶ τότε[26] χαλεπῶς
ὅρκοις τοῦ Ἰσραὴλ ἐπείσθη[27].

</td><td valign="top">

β, S[1]
ἐξαιτή-
σωνται.
β, S[1]
κατα-
κυριεύσει
ὑμῶν
πᾶσα
πονηρία
θλίψεως.
β, S[1]
ἠθέλησαν
ἀνελεῖν
αὐτόν.
β, S[1]
πλησίον
αὐτοῦ.
β–a τοῦ
ἀερίου
πνεύ-
ματος.

</td></tr>
</table>

[6] *d* reads ἀγαθὴ ἕως τέλους.   *a* om. next fourteen words, ὡς . . . Κύριον inclusive.   [7] *e*, S[1] read ἴδετε.   [8] *c, d.* β–*d* om.   For ὅτι . . . ὀρθῶς S read οὕτως ζῆτε καὶ ὑμεῖς.   [9] *d* adds ἑαυτοῦ.   [10] *c, ef. bg* read ἀγαθήν. *d* καθαρὰν ἀπὸ παντὸς ἔργου κακοῦ καὶ πάσης πράξεως πονηρᾶς.   [11] *g* read ὀρθά.   [12] *d* adds οὖν τόν.   [13] *d* adds ὑμῶν.   [14] *c.* Cf. 2 Chron. xv. 6. β, S[1] read as in margin (save that *de* read ἐξαιτήσονται). Here, if β, S[1] are right, ἐὰν . . . εἰς πᾶσαν πονηρίαν †θλίψεως ἐξαιτήσωνται = אם בכל נפשיכם יבקשו מצוקה רע where I take מצוקה to be corrupt for להציקה. Hence for θλίψεως read τοῦ θλίβειν.   [15] *c.* β, S[1] read as in margin (save that β–*df* read κατακυριεύσῃ and *d* reads πᾶσαν πονηρίαν).   [16] *c. aeg* read ὡς καί. *bf*, S ὡς οὐδέ. *d* ὥσπερ.   [17] *c, ade. bfg* read τοῦ ἀδελφοῦ.   [18] *d* adds γάρ.   [19] *c.* β read as in margin. *e* om. next five words.   [20] *d* adds καὶ ἐρρύσατο αὐτὸν ἐκ τῶν χειρῶν αὐτῶν.   [21] *c.* β, S[1] read as in margin.   [22] *c.* β–*a* read as in margin (save that *g* reads ἐναερίου for ἀερίου). *a* om. For ὑπὸ τοῦ πνεύματος . . . ἐπιβουλῆς ἀνθρώπων S[1] read αὐτὸς οὐ φοβήσεται οὐδέν· εἴπερ πολὺ κακίας αὐτῷ ποιοῦσιν ἔν τινι, οὐ νικήσουσι.   [23] *dg* read σκεπόμενος.   [24] *c, adef. b* reads ὑπό. *g* ἐξ.   [25] A[b]. A[ab*cdefg] = καὶ οὕτως. A[b] om.   [26] A[b]. Other MSS. om.   [27] Text reads զարմացւալ (= ἐκοίνωσε or συνευδόκησε) which may be corrupt for զանմխբալ = ἐπείσθη.

β-dg, S ὑπὸ τῆς τοῦ Κυρίου ἀγάπης. β-b, S¹ υἱῶν. β, S¹ ὅτι (bef, S¹ εἴτι) ἐνεθυμή-θησαν πονηρὸν περὶ αὐτοῦ.

ἢ θηρίων οὐ δύναται κατα-κυριευθῆναι²⁸, βοηθούμενος *†ζῆν ἀπ' αὐτῆς† ὑπὸ τῆς ἀγάπης²⁹ ἧς³⁰ ἔχει πρὸς τὸν πλησίον.

6. *Καὶ γὰρ³¹ *ὁ Ἰωσὴφ ἐδεήθη τοῦ πατρὸς ἡμῶν³², ⌐ἵνα προσεύξηται *ὑπὲρ τῶν ἀδελφῶν αὐτοῦ³³⌐ ἵνα μὴ³⁴ λογίσηται *⌐Κύριος⌐ αὐτοῖς³⁵ *ἁμαρτίαν, ⌐ὅτι ἐποίησαν πονηρὸν εἰς αὐτόν⌐³⁶.

7. Καὶ *οὕτως ἐβόα Ἰακώβ³⁷· *ὦ τέκνον χρηστόν³⁸, ἐνί-κησας³⁹ τὰ σπλάγχνα⁴⁰ Ἰακὼβ τοῦ πατρός σου· καὶ περιλαβὼν⁴¹ αὐτὸν⁴² ἐπὶ⁴³ δύο⁴⁴ ὥρας κατεφίλει, λέγων·

c, β, S¹

8. Πληρωθήσεται⁴⁵ *περὶ σοῦ⁴⁶ προφητεία οὐράνιος⁴⁷

A

8. ⌐Πληρωθήσεται ἐπὶ σὲ ἡ προφητεία οὐράνιος ἣ λέγει

Aᵃᵇ*ᶜᵈᵉᶠᵍ trs. before ὅρκοις. For Ἰσραὴλ Aᵇ reads Ἰακώβ. ²⁸ bg read κυριευθῆναι. ²⁹ c. β-dg, S read as in margin. d ὑπὸ τῆς ἀγάπης. g ὑπὸ τοῦ Κυρίου διὰ τῆς ἀγάπης. Here c is difficult or most probably corrupt. The difficulty lies in ζῆν ἀπ' αὐτῆς. Possibly ζῆν might be taken with βοηθούμενος as expressing one idea = יָשַׁע, and ἀπ' αὐτῆς = מִיָּדָהּ corrupt for בַּאדוני = ὑπὸ τοῦ Κυρίου as in g. d om. this clause, possibly because of its corruptness. g undoubtedly gives the best sense, though we should expect διὰ τὴν ἀγαπήν. ³⁰ c, β-dg. dg read ἥν. ³¹ A = πλήν. ³² c. β-b, S read ἐδεήθη τοῦ πατρὸς ἡμῶν Ἰωσήφ (S¹ Ἰακώβ). b reads ἐδεήθην τοῦ πατρὸς ἡμῶν Ἰακώβ. A ἐδεήθη (+ Ἰωσὴφ Aᵇ) τοῦ πατρός. ³³ c. β-b read ὑπὲρ (g περὶ) τῶν υἱῶν (+ αὐτοῦ d). b περὶ τῶν ἀδελφῶν ἡμῶν. For ἵνα προσευξ. . . . αὐτοῦ S¹ read λέγων, ὦ τιμητὲ πάτερ μου Ἰακώβ, πρόσευξαι περὶ τῶν υἱῶν σου τῷ θεῷ. ³⁴ g om. ³⁵ c, d. β-d, S read αὐτοῖς ὁ (aefg om.) Κύριος. ³⁶ c. β, S¹ read as in margin (save that g, S² add ἁμαρτίαν before ὅτι (as in c). fg read πονηρά, and S¹ μου). Aᵇʰᵉᶠᵍ = ταύτην τὴν κακίαν. Aᵃᵇ*ᶜᵈ = (τοῦτο) εἰς κακίαν (+ ἵνα μὴ ἀθυμῶσι οἱ ἀδελφοί Aᵇ). ³⁷ c, β-d. d reads καὶ ἔλεγεν Ἰ. οὕτως. A = τότε Ἰακὼβ κλαίων (Aᵇ*ᶜᵈᵉᶠᵍ ἀκούων. Aʰ om.) ἐβόα καὶ ἔλεγεν. S¹ = Καὶ οὕτως σφοδρᾷ φωνῇ ἐβόα Ἰ. ³⁸ c, aef. b reads ὦ τέκνον Ἰωσήφ. d γλυκύτατον, Ἰωσήφ, ὦ τέκνον χρηστόν. g ὦ τέκνον Ἰ. ὦ τέκνον χ. A = τέκνον μου, Ἰ., τέκνον μου (Aᵉᶠᵍ om. Ἰ. τ. μ.), γλυκὺς παῖς. S¹ = εὐλογητόν. Aᵇᵇ*ᶜᵈ but not Aᵉᶠᵍ add ἐνίκησας κακίαν τῶν ἀδελφῶν σου. ³⁹ d reads ἐνέκλεισας. ⁴⁰ A reads ⲙⲗⲃⲱⲅⲓ (= γῆρυς) corrupt for ⲙⲏⲃⲱⲅⲓ = σπλάγχνα. ⁴¹ d reads παραλαβών. ⁴² Aᵇ*ᵈ om. ⁴³ afg om. ⁴⁴ A = τρεῖς through an easy internal corruption. ⁴⁵ c adds in margin περὶ Χριστοῦ. The Messianic interpretation of this passage naturally led to the additions in brackets. ⁴⁶ c. bg read ἐν σοί. d ἐπὶ σέ. aef ἐπὶ σοί. S¹ =

[περὶ⁴⁸ τοῦ ἀμνοῦ τοῦ Θεοῦ καὶ σωτῆρος τοῦ κόσμου], ὅτι ἄμωμος ὑπὸ⁴⁹ ἀνόμων παραδοθήσεται καὶ ὁ⁵⁰ ἀναμάρτητος ὑπὲρ ἀσεβῶν ἀποθανεῖται [ἐν αἵματι διαθήκης ἐπὶ σωτηρίᾳ ἐθνῶν καὶ τοῦ⁵¹ Ἰσραὴλ καὶ καταλύσει⁵² *Βελίαρ καὶ τοὺς ὑπηρέτας αὐτοῦ⁵³].

ὅτι ὁ ἄμωμος ὑπὲρ ἀνόμων †μιανθήσεται⁵⁴ καὶ ὁ ἀναμάρτητος ὑπὲρ ἀσεβῶν ἀποθανεῖται.

β, Ὑπέρ.

Α ἔλεος.
β μιμή-
σασθε
οὖν
(b om.)
ἐν ἀγαθῇ
διανοίᾳ.

IV. Ἴδετε¹ οὖν², *τέκνα μου³, τοῦ ἀγαθοῦ ἀνδρὸς⁴ τὸ τέλος⁵. μιμήσασθε⁶ ⌜*ἐν ἀγαθῷ διὰ⁷ τὴν εὐσπλαγχνίαν⌝ αὐτοῦ, ἵνα ⌜καὶ ὑμεῖς⌝ στεφάνους⁸ δόξης φορέσητε⁹. 2. Ὁ γὰρ¹⁰ ἀγαθὸς ⌜ἄνθρωπος⌝ οὐκ ἔχει σκοτεινὸν ὀφθαλμόν¹¹, ἐλεεῖ¹² γὰρ πάντας, κἂν *ἁμαρτωλοὶ ὦσιν¹³. 3. ⌜Κἂν *μὴ βούλωνται περὶ αὐτοῦ εἰς καλά¹⁴, *οὗτος τὸ ἀγαθὸν ποιῶν¹⁵ νικᾷ τὸ κακόν, σκεπόμενος¹⁶ ὑπὸ τοῦ Θεοῦ¹⁷⌝. τοὺς †ἀδικοῦντας¹⁸ ἀγαπᾷ ὡς τὴν ψυχὴν αὐτοῦ. 4. Ἐάν¹⁹ τις

β, S
βουλεύ-
ωνται
περὶ
αὐτοῦ εἰς
(ag om.)
κακά.
β ἀγαθοῦ.
β, Α, Sˡ
δὲ δι-
καίους.

ἐν σοί.   ⁴⁷c. β read (+ τοῦ f) οὐρανοῦ. Sˡ = τοῖς ἀνθρώποις. ⁴⁸d reads παρά. ⁴⁹c. β, S ὑπέρ. ⁵⁰c. β, Sˡ om. ⁵¹c, d. β–d om. ⁵²b reads καταργήσει. ⁵³c, β–d (save that b reads ὑπηρετοῦντας αὐτῷ). d reads τοῦ Β. καὶ τῶν ὑπηρετῶν αὐτοῦ πᾶσαν τὴν δύναμιν. Sˡ = Β. καὶ τὸν ὑπηρετοῦντα αὐτῷ. ⁵⁴c, β, Sˡ seem right here.

IV. ¹c, d, A. β–d εἴδετε. ²c, A. β, S om. ³c, d, A. β–d, S read τέκνα. ⁴d adds ἐκείνου. S Ἰωσήφ. ⁵c, β, S. Apparently corrupt for ἔλεος as in A, but τέλος may refer to the high position attained by Joseph; thus Benjamin's sons are exhorted to imitate his mercy that they may attain crowns of glory. Aᵇ adds τὸ τοῦ Ἰωσήφ. ⁶c, b, A. β read as in margin. Sˡ = καὶ μιμήσασθε. ⁷c apparently corrupt. β read as in margin. Sˡ = τὴν ἀγαθὴν διάνοιαν καί. ⁸A = στέφανον. ⁹c, β–g, S. g reads ἐργάσητε (sic). A = λήψησθε. ¹⁰c, Aᵃᵇ*ᶜᵈ. β, Aᵇᵉⁱᵍ, S om. ¹¹For the expression cf. Ps. lxix. 23. Yet the text seems wrong. ¹²c, β–ab. b reads ἐλεᾷ. ¹³c. β, Aᵃʰᵇ*ᶜᵈᵉⁱᵍ read ὦσιν ἁμαρτωλοί. Aᵇ ἁμαρτωλός τις ὁρᾷ. ¹⁴c. β, S read as in margin (save that def read βουλεύονται and d εἰς κακίαν). ¹⁵c. bf, S read οὕτως (Sˡ om.) ὁ (f om.) ἀγαθοποιῶν. ade αὐτὸς (οὗτος a) ἀγαθοποιῶν. g om. together with next three words. ¹⁶c, β–bg (save that c reads σκεπάμενος). b reads σκεπαζόμενος. g σκεπάζεται. Sˡ adds γάρ. ¹⁷c, S. β reads as in margin. Sˡ adds ἕνεκα τῆς ἀγαθοποιίας. ¹⁸c. β, A, Sˡ read as in margin (save that Sˡ om. δέ). c must be corrupt. ¹⁹A adds δέ.

β-af, A δοξάζηται²⁰, οὐ²¹ φθονεῖ αὐτόν²²· ἐάν τις πλουτεῖ²³, οὐ ζηλοῖ²⁴·
πιστεύων *ἐάν τις ἀνδρεῖος²⁵, ἐπαινεῖ²⁶ αὐτόν²⁷· τὸν σώφρονα ἀγαπῶν²⁸·
(A om.)
ὑμνεῖ. ⌜τὸν πένητα ἐλεεῖ²⁹· *τῷ ἀσθενοῦντι³⁰ συμπάσχει³¹· τὸν
β ἀνυμ- Θεὸν φοβεῖται³²⌝.
νεῖ.

<table>
<tr><td align="center">c, A</td><td align="center">β-a, S¹</td></tr>
<tr><td>

5. Καὶ τὸν ἔχοντα χάριν *ἀγαθοῦ πνεύματος³³ ἀγαπᾷ κατὰ τὴν ψυχὴν αὐτοῦ.

</td><td>

5. *Τὸν ἔχοντα³⁴ φόβον Κυρίου³⁵ ὑπερασπίζει³⁶· *τῷ ἀγαπῶντι³⁷ τὸν Θεὸν συντρέχει³⁸· τὸν ἀθετοῦντα τὸν ὕψιστον νουθετῶν ἐπιστρέφει³⁹· καὶ τὸν ἔχοντα χάριν *ἀγαθοῦ πνεύματος⁴⁰ ἀγαπᾷ⁴¹ κατὰ τὴν⁴² ψυχὴν αὐτοῦ.

</td></tr>
</table>

V. Ἐὰν ⌜οὖν καὶ ὑμεῖς⌝¹ ἔχετε² ἀγαθὴν³ ⌜διάνοιαν⁴, καὶ⌝ οἱ πονηροὶ ἄνθρωποι⁵ *εἰρηνεύσουσιν μεθ' ὑμῶν⁶, καὶ οἱ ἄσωτοι αἰδεσθέντες⁷ ὑμᾶς⁸ ⌜ἐπιστρέψουσιν⁹ εἰς *τὸ ἀγαθόν¹⁰, καὶ

---

²⁰ def read δοξάζεται. A°ⁱˢ om. with next five words. ²¹ S¹ = μή.
²² c. β, Aᵃʰᵇ*ᶜᵈᵉᵍ, S¹ om. Aᵇ reads ἐπὶ τῇ δόξῃ αὐτοῦ. d om. next five
words. ²³ c, aef. bg read πλουτῇ. ²⁴ a om. next eight words.
S = ζηλοῦτε. ²⁵ A⁻ᵃʰ = τὸν ἀνδρεῖον. Aᵃʰ corrupt. d adds ἤ.
²⁶ S¹ = ἐπαινεῖτε. ²⁷ c. abef, A om. d reads τοῦτον and trs. before
ἐπαινεῖ. Aᵃᵇ*ᶜᵈ add καὶ but not Aᵇʰᵉⁱˢ. Aⁱ om. rest of chapter. ²⁸ c.
β-af read πιστεύων ὑμνεῖ. A = ὑμνεῖ. S¹ ἐν πίστει ἐπαινεῖτε. f om.
A comparison of the adjoining clauses leads us to expect a single word
here as in c or A. ²⁹ S = ἐλεεῖτε. a om. next three words. ³⁰ c.
β-ad read τῷ ἀσθενεῖ. d τὸν ἀσθενῆ. ³¹ c. β-a read συμπαθεῖ. S¹ =
συμπαθεῖτε and adds ἀγαπᾶτε τοὺς ἀδελφούς, μὴ ἐπιλανθάνεσθε τῶν γονέων.
³² c = יָרֵא. β reads as in margin (save that d reads ὑμνεῖ) = יוֹדֶה.
³³ c. A = ἀπὸ Κυρίου. ³⁴ bd. ef read τῷ ἔχοντι. g τοῦ ἔχοντος. a om.
entire verse. ³⁵ def. bg, S read Θεοῦ. ³⁶ beg. df read ὑπερ-
ασπίζεται. S¹ = ὑπερασπίζετε. ·b, S¹ add αὐτοῦ. S¹ adds further : τὸν μὴ εἰδότα
τὸν θεὸν κολάζετε (al. ἐπιστρέφετε, ἀποστρέφετε) εἰς τὴν δικαίαν ὁδόν. ³⁷ d reads
τὸν ἀγαπῶντα. S¹ = τοῖς ἀγαποῦσιν. ³⁸ β-ab. b reads συνεργεῖ. S¹ =
συνεργεῖτε : συντρέχει = ירוץ which may be corrupt for ירצה = 'has pleasure
in,' but συνεργεῖ = יעזור has the support of the parallelism of the
preceding clause. ³⁹ S¹ = μὴ ἀποστρέφετε. ⁴⁰ ef. bd read πνεύματος
ἀγαθοῦ. g ἁγίου. S¹ = καὶ πνεῦμα ἀγαθόν. ⁴¹ S¹ = ἀγαπᾶτε. ⁴² g om.

V. ¹ c. a reads οὖν. β-a, Aᵃᵇ*ᶜᵈ δέ, Aᵇᵉⁱˢ, S¹ om. ² c, def. ab read
ἔχητε. g σχῆτε. A = ἦτε. ³ A = ἀγαθοί. ⁴ b, S¹ add τέκνα. ⁵ g (?)
read ἄρχοντες. ⁶ β-bd, A, S¹. c, b read εἰρηνεύσωσιν ὑμῖν (c om.)

οἱ πλεονεκτοῦντες[11] οὐ μόνον ἀποστήσονται *τοῦ πάθους[12] ἀλλὰ καὶ *τὰ τῆς[13] πλεονεξίας *ἃ εἶχον[14] δώσουσιν[15] τοῖς θλιβομένοις. 2. Ἐὰν ἦτε ἀγαθοποιοῦντες καὶ *τὰ ἀκάθαρτα[16] πνεύματα φεύξονται[17] *ἀφ' ὑμῶν[18], καὶ[19] τὰ θηρία[20] *φοβηθήσονται ὑμᾶς[21]. 3. ⌐Ὅπου γὰρ ἔνι[22] *φόβος ἀγαθῶν ἔργων καὶ φῶς[23] εἰς διάνοιαν καὶ[24] τὸ σκότος ἀποδιδράσκει ἀπ'[25] αὐτοῦ.¬ 4. *Ἐὰν ⌐γὰρ¬[26] ὑβρίσει[27] *ἄνδρα ὅσιον[28] μετανοεῖ[29], ἐλεεῖ γὰρ ⌐ὁ ὅσιος¬ τὸν λοίδωρον[30] καὶ σιωπᾷ.

aef, S¹
φῶς ἀγαθῶν ἔργων.

<table>
<tr><td align="center">c</td><td align="center">β–a, S¹</td><td align="center">A</td></tr>
<tr><td>5. Κἄν[31] τις *δίκαιον προδώσει[32], *ὁ δίκαιος προσεύχεται· εἰ καὶ πρὸς[33] ὀλίγον ταπεινωθῇ, *μετ' οὐ[34] πολὺ φαιδρότερος[35] ἀναφαίνεται, οἷος γέγονεν[36] Ἰωσὴφ ὁ ἀδελφός μου.</td><td>5. Κἄν τις ψυχὴν δικαίαν προδοίη, καὶ ὁ δίκαιος προσευχόμενος πρὸς ὀλίγον ταπεινωθῇ, μετ' οὐ πολὺ φαιδρότερος ἀναφαίνεται, οἷος γέγονεν Ἰωσὴφ ὁ ἀδελφός μου.</td><td>5. Καὶ ἐάν τις ὑβρίζῃ ψυχὴν δικαίαν,†πενθεῖ[37], ὅτι εἶδε ταπεινωθεῖσαν αὐτήν[38], καὶ μετενόησε†[39], οἷος γέγονεν Ἰ. ὁ ἀδελφός μου.</td></tr>
</table>

[d] εἰρηνεύουσι μεθ' ἡμῶν. [7] c, β–g, S¹. g reads αἰδεσθῶσιν. A = αἰδέσονται. [8] A^eʳᵍ = ἡμᾶς. [9] c reads ἐπιστρέψωσιν εἰς ὑμᾶς. [10] c. β–d read ἀγαθόν, d ἀγαθά· ὁμοίως δέ. [11] c, β–bd. bd read πλεονέκται. [12] d reads τοῦ τοιούτου πάθους. S¹ = τῆς ἁρπαγῆς. [13] c, β–ad. a reads τισὶν τῆς. d τὰ ἀπό. [14] c. β–d om. d reads συλλεγέντα αὐτοῖς εἴτε χρήματα εἴτε κτήματα. [15] d reads δίδωσιν and trs. after θλιβομένοις. g reads ἀποδώσουσιν. [16] d reads αὐτὰ τά. [17] bf read φεύξεται. [18] S¹ om. [19] c. d reads ἀλλὰ μὴν καί. β–d, A^b*cd, S¹ read καὶ αὐτά. A^abheʳᵍ om. καὶ … ὑμᾶς. [20] d adds ἀνήμερα. [21] b reads φεύξεται ἀφ' ὑμῶν φοβηθέντες. [22] g om. [23] c. aef, S¹ read as in margin. b φόβος ἀγαθῶν ἔργων. d φῶς ἀγαθὸν ἔργον. g φῶς καθαρόν and ἐν for the following εἰς. [24] c. S reads ἀνθρώπου. β om. [25] b om. [26] c, β–g, S¹. g reads ἐάν. A = κἄν. dg, A^abh add τις. [27] c, df, A^h. abe read ὑβρίσῃ. g τηρήσει. A^-h = ὑβρίζῃ. S¹ ὑβρίσητε. abe add τις. [28] d reads ἄνδρα ἅγιον. A^abh = τοῦτον τὸν ἀληθῆ. A^ab*cdeg ἄνδρα ἀληθῆ. [29] S¹ = μετάνοια ἐστίν. A^abh om. rest of verse. [30] c, bef. adg read λοίδορον. [31] a om. ver. 5. d om. κἄν τις … ἀναφαίνεται. [32] c (though δικαίῳ is emended into δίκαιον). β–ad, A^b*cdeg, S¹ agree (save that A reads ὑβρίζῃ), d ψ. δικαίου προδῶ. A^abh = ψυχήν σου (A^a om.) ὑβρίζῃ. All renderings are unsatisfactory. [33] g om. [34] be read μεθ' οὐ. [35] g reads σφοδρότερον. [36] c adds ἐν. [37] A^h om. [38] A^ab*cd trs. before ταπειν. [39] A is here hopelessly corrupt.

VI. Τὸ διαβούλιον τοῦ ἀγαθοῦ ἀνδρὸς οὐκ ἔστιν ἐν χειρὶ
πλάνης[1] πνεύματος[2] Βελίαρ· ὁ γὰρ ἄγγελος τῆς εἰρήνης
ὁδηγεῖ τὴν ψυχὴν αὐτοῦ.   2. ⌈Καὶ⌉[3] οὐχ ὁρᾷ[4] ⌈ἐμπαθῶς⌉[5]
*τὰ φθαρτά[6], οὐδὲ[7] συνάγει[8] πλοῦτον ⌈εἰς φιληδονίαν⌉[9].
3. Οὐ[10] τέρπεται ἐν[11] ἡδονῇ, ⌈[οὐ λυπεῖ τὸν πλησίον]⌉, οὐκ
ἐμπίπλαται τρυφῇ[12], οὐ πλανᾶται μετεωρισμοῖς ὀφθαλμῶν⌉[13].
Κύριος γάρ ἐστι ἡ[14] μερὶς[15] αὐτοῦ.   4. Τὸ[16] ἀγαθὸν
διαβούλιον *οὐ δέχεται δόξης ⌈οὐκ ἀτιμίας⌉[17] ἀνθρώπων, *καὶ
πάντα δόλον[18] ἢ[19] ψεῦδος ἢ[20] μάχην *ἢ λοιδωρίαν[21] *οὐκ
οἶδε[22]. *Κύριος γὰρ[23] ἐν αὐτῷ κατοικεῖ[24], καὶ φωτίζει τὴν[25]
ψυχὴν αὐτοῦ, καὶ χαίρει[26] πρὸς πάντας[27] ἐν παντὶ καιρῷ.
5. Ἡ ἀγαθὴ διάνοια[28] οὐκ ἔχει δύο γλώσσας[29] εὐλογίας καὶ
κατάρας[30], ὕβρεως καὶ ⌈τιμῆς⌉[31], ἡσυχίας καὶ ταραχῆς,
ὑποκρίσεως καὶ ἀληθείας, [πενίας καὶ πλούτου][32], ἀλλὰ *μίαν
ἔχει περὶ πάντας[33] εἰλικρινῆ[34] καὶ[35] καθαρὰν ⌈διάθεσιν⌉.
6. Οὐκ ἔχει *ὅρασιν οὔτε ἀκοὴν[36] διπλῆν· *πᾶν γὰρ ὃ[37]

VI. [1] c, β–afg, S. af, A read as in margin. g om.   [2] d reads τοῦ.
[3] c. β, A, S¹ om.   [4] g reads ἐνορᾷ. For ὁρᾷ . . . φθαρτά S¹ reads ἄγει εἰς
πειρασμὸν τοὺς φθαρτούς.   [5] d reads ἔμπροσθεν.   [6] c, aef. bdg τοῖς φθαρτοῖς.
[7] c, β–eg, A, S¹. eg read οὔτε.   [8] A reads qհunk (= οἶδε) corrupt for հnւ,unk
= συνάγει.   [9] Surely a mistranslation for ἐν φιληδονίᾳ.   [10] A = οὐδέ.
[11] c. β–g om. g reads ποτέ.   [12] c, efg. ad read τρυφῆς. b, S¹ τροφῆς.
[13] The clauses here omitted by A are possibly interpolations; for Κύριος
γάρ ἐστι ἡ μερὶς αὐτοῦ would follow naturally on φιληδονίαν ·or ἡδονῇ. At
all events οὐ λυπεῖ τὸν πλησίον is foreign to the context, and is accordingly
bracketed as such.   [14] c. β om.   [15] g om.   [16] a om. τὸ . . . ψεῦδος.
[17] c. β–a, S¹ read as in margin (save that b reads δόξης καὶ ἀτιμίας and S¹
ἐπιδέξεται). οὐκ ἀτιμίας may be a marginal gloss incorporated in the text.
In β the asyndetic structure is set right. A = οὐκ οἶδε δόξαν.   [18] β–ad,
A, S¹. d reads πάντα δὲ δόλον. c om.   [19] A = καί.   [20] c, d. β–d, S¹ om.
A = καί.   [21] c. β–d, A, S¹ read καὶ λοιδωρίαν (ae λοιδορίαν). d om.
[22] β, A, S¹. c om.   [23] d reads ὅτι Κύριος.   [24] A = ἐστί.   [25] adef om.
[26] The context seems to require a transitive verb. Χαίρει = יֶחְדֶּה corrupt
for יַחְדֵּהוּ = εὐφραίνει αὐτόν. Indeed εὐφραίνει αὐτόν is added in d (as
a dittography) after διάνοια in the next verse where it is out of place.
[27] g reads πάντα.   [28] d adds εὐφραίνει αὐτόν, a dittography from preceding
sentence. See note 26.   [29] A = διαβούλια.   [30] S¹ adds μάχην καὶ ψεῦδος
καί (sic).   [31] c. β, A, S¹ add as in margin (save that in S¹ the word for
λύπης is corrupt, and that A reads κολακείας for χαρᾶς). a om. next six
words.   [32] Bracketed as an interpolation. A om.   [33] d reads πρὸς
πάντας ἔχει. For πάντας a reads πάντων.   [34] d reads εἰληκρηνήν. A =

ποιεῖ, ⌐ἢ³⁸ λαλεῖ, *ἢ ὁρᾷ³⁹, οἶδεν ὅτι³⁹ Κύριος ἐπι‑
σκέπτει⁴⁰ τὴν⁴¹ ψυχὴν αὐτοῦ.   7. Καὶ καθαίρει τὴν
διάνοιαν αὐτοῦ πρὸς⁴² τὸ μὴ καταγνωσθῆναι ὑπὸ *τῶν ἀνθρώ‑
πων, ὁμοίως καὶ⌐ ὑπὸ Θεοῦ. Ὁμοίως δὲ καὶ τοῦ Βελίαρ τὰ ἔργα
διπλᾶ ἐστιν, καὶ ἁπλότητα ἐν αὐτοῖς οὐκ ἔχουσιν⁴³.

VII. ⌐Διὰ τοῦτο⌐, τέκνα μου, ⌐λέγω ὑμῖν⌐¹, φεύγετε τὴν
κακίαν² †⌐τοῦ Βελίαρ⌐ ὅτι μάχαιραν³ δίδωσιν⁴ τοῖς πειθομένοις
αὐτοῦ⁵.

β‑a, S¹
ὑπὸ
Θεοῦ καὶ
ἀνθρώ‑
πων· καὶ
τοῦ
Βελίαρ
δὲ πᾶν
ἔργον
διπλοῦν
ἐστι, καὶ
οὐκ ἔχει
ἁπλό‑
τ,τα.

c, bg	β‑bg, S¹	A
2. Ἡ δὲ μάχαιρα⁶ ἑπτὰ κακῶν μήτηρ	2. Ἡ δὲ μάχαιρα ἑπτὰ κακῶν μήτηρ	2. Καὶ ἡ μάχαιρά ἐστι ἑπτὰ κακῶν

ἔμπεδον or ἀσφαλῆ.   ³⁵ b, S¹ om.   ³⁶ c, β, S¹ (save that β, S¹ read οὐδέ).
Aᵇᵇ*ᶜᵈ = ἀκοὴν καὶ ὅρασιν, but Aᵉᶠᵍ support c.   ³⁷ g reads πάντα ἅ. c adds ἐάν.
³⁸ d om.   ³⁹ d reads γὰρ ὅτι ὁ.   ⁴⁰ c, b. adef read ἐπισκοπεύει. g ἐπισκοπεῖ.
a om. rest of chapter.   ⁴¹ c. β‑a om.   ⁴² g reads εἰς.   ⁴³ c (save
that I have changed ἔχωσιν into ἔχουσιν). β‑a, S¹ read as in margin
(save that d reads ἀπό for ὑπό and dg om. καί before τοῦ). For πᾶν γὰρ ὁ
ποιεῖ ... ἔχουσιν A reads πᾶς γὰρ ὃς ποιεῖ ἔργα Θεοῦ καὶ Βελίαρ διπλοῦς ἐστι καὶ
οὐχ ἁπλότης.

VII. ¹ c. β, A, S¹ om.   ² c, β, S¹. Aᵇᵇ*ᶜᵈ = πορνείαν καὶ κακίαν. Aᵇᵇ κακίαν
καὶ πορνείαν. Aᵉᶠᵍ πορνείαν.   ³ β, Aᵇ*ᶜᵈᵉᵍ, S¹. c, Aᵃᵇ read μάχαιρα. d adds
δίστομον.   ⁴ Aᵃᵇʰ = ἐν χειρί ἐστι.   ⁵ c. β, S¹ read αὐτῇ.   ⁶ The text is
doubtful.   Either μάχαιραν ... μάχαιρα or συλλαμβάνει ἡ διάνοια (c, abef) is
corrupt.   For if the latter is original, that is, if the mind conceives
through Beliar and becomes the parent of seven evil conditions of the
individual and of society, then the μάχαιρα cannot be the parent of these.
Hence if συλλαμβάνει ἡ διάνοια is original in the sense 'the mind
conceiveth,' we should strike out μάχαιραν ... μάχαιρα as an interpolation.
Thus we should have: 'Flee the malice of Beliar; for it is the mother
of seven evils.'   Next let us suppose μάχαιρα to be original.   In that
case we must regard συλλαμβάνει ἡ διάνοια as corrupt, and adopt the
reading of Aᵇ*ᶜᵈᵍ 'and the sword is the mother of seven evils, and it
receives (them) through Beliar.'   For 'and it receives' Aᵇ*ᶜᵈᵍ reads 'which
it has' (զոր ունի a corruption of Ա ասնէնէ the text of Aᵃᵇ).   Further, as
the sword cannot be said to be the mother of 'envy,' for φθόνος we must
read φόνος.   We should consider the possibility that συλλαμβάνει is
a rendering of לקח here, as the text of Aᵃᵇ supposes, or rather that
λαμβάνει originally stood here and was changed to συλλαμβάνει owing to
the phrase μήτηρ κακῶν preceding.   Then the text of β‑bg, S¹, which adds
ὅτε τίκτει, would be explained as a further depravation of the text in the
same direction.   Of the above solutions I think the first is to be preferred,

ἐστί. *πρῶτον συλλαμβάνει ἡ διάνοια διὰ τοῦ Βελίαρ[7]. †*Καὶ ἔστιν πρῶτον[8] ὁ †φθόνος[9], δεύτερον[10] ἢ[11] †ἀπώλεια[12], τρίτον ἢ[11] θλίψις, τέταρτον ἢ[11] θεηλασία[13], πέμπτον ἢ[11] ἔνδεια, ἔκτον ἢ[11] ταραχή, ἔβδομον ἡ[11] ἐρήμωσις.

ἐστί· πρῶτον συλλαμβάνει ἡ διάνοια διὰ τοῦ Βελίαρ †*ἔστιν δὲ ὅτε τίκτει πρῶτον[14] †φθόνον, δεύτερον †ἀπώλειαν, τρίτον θλίψιν, τέταρτον αἰχμαλωσίαν, πέμπτον ἔνδειαν, ἔκτον ταραχήν, ἔβδομον ἐρήμωσιν.

μήτηρ, *καὶ λαμβάνει διὰ τοῦ Βελίαρ[15]. καὶ ἔστι πρῶτον †φθόνος, δεύτερον †ἀπώλεια, τρίτον θλίψις, τέταρτον αἰχμαλωσία[16], πέμπτον ἔνδεια, ἔκτον ταραχή[17], ἔβδομον ἐρήμωσις.

3. Διὰ τοῦτο καὶ[18] ὁ Κάϊν ἑπτὰ ἐκδικίαις[19] παρεδόθη[20] ὑπὸ Θεοῦ[21]. *κατὰ γὰρ[22] *ἑκατοστὸν ἔτος[23] μίαν πληγὴν ἐπήγαγεν *ἐπ' αὐτὸν[24] ⌈ὁ[25] Κύριος⌉.

β, A, S
ἑκατὸν ἔτη.

c

4. Διακοσίων ἐτῶν πάσχει καὶ ἐννακοσιοστῷ[26] ἔτει ἐρημοῦται[27]· διὰ γὰρ 'Αβὲλ τὸν

β, A

4. Διακοσίων[28] ἐτῶν[29] πάσχει[30], καὶ ἐννακοσιοστῷ ἔτει ἐρημοῦται[31] [ἐπὶ τοῦ κατα-

and that the text should be read as follows : φεύγετε τὴν κακίαν τοῦ Βελίαρ· ὅτι συλλαμβάνει ἡ διάνοια διὰ τοῦ Βελίαρ καὶ ἑπτὰ κακῶν μήτηρ γίνεται· καὶ ἔστι πρῶτον κ.τ.λ.   [7] c, β–dg, S[1] (save that c om. διά).   d reads καὶ πρῶτον μὲν συλλαμβάνει ἡ διάνοια τὸ πονηρὸν διὰ τῆς κακίας τοῦ Βελίαρ, which is merely an expansion of β–d.   g πρῶτος συλλ. διάνοιαν τοῦ B.   [8] c, A. bg read ἔστι δὲ πρῶτος.   [9] Corrupt (?) for φόνος—the first evil that ensued on Cain's submission to Beliar. See note 6. φόνος would then be a rendering of דם.   [10] fg read β' and similarly use letters throughout rest of verse. [11] c. bg, A om.   [12] ἀπώλεια = בַּלָּהָה which the translator should here have rendered by φόβος.   [13] c. aef read αἰχμαλωσίαν. bg, A[abh] αἰχμαλωσία. A[b*cdefg] = ταραχή. αἰχμαλωσία is a rendering here of גָּלוּת = φυγή or 'exile.' Cf. Pirke Aboth v. 11.   [14] ae (save that e reads ὅ for ὅτε). d ἔστι δὲ τὸ πρῶτον τίκτει τόν. f ἔστιν δὲ ὅταν τίκτει πρῶτον. S[1] = ὅτι τ. πρ.   [15] A[abh]. A[b*cdefg] read ἃ ἔχει διὰ τοῦ Βελίαρ, but this has arisen from an internal corruption of A[abh].   [16] See note 13. [17] A[b*cd] = ὀργή. A[eg] om. A[f] = κακία.   [18] g om.   [19] bg, A (A[ab] = ἐκδικίας), S[1]. c reads ἐκδικούμενα. aef ἀδικίαις. d ἐκδικήσεσιν.   [20] c, aef, A[b*cdefg], S[1]. bg read παραδίδοται. A[abh] = ἔλαβε.   [21] c. β–g, S read τοῦ Θεοῦ. g, A = Κυρίου.   [22] A[b*d] = καὶ κατά.   [23] c. β, A, S as in margin.   [24] c. β reads αὐτῷ.   [25] dg om.   [26] c reads τῷ ἐννακοστῷ.   [27] It will be observed that aef here agree with c in omitting the phrase ἐπὶ τοῦ κατακλυσμοῦ which is found in bdg, A.   [28] dg, A add γάρ. S[1] om. διακοσίων . . .

ἀδελφὸν αὐτοῦ *ἐν πᾶσι τοῖς κακοῖς ἐκρίνετο, ὁ δὲ Λαμὲχ ἐν ἑβδομηκοντάκις ἑπτά. | κλυσμοῦ][32] διὰ Ἀβὲλ τὸν δίκαιον[33] ἀδελφὸν αὐτοῦ. *Ἐν τοῖς ἑπτὰ οὖν κακοῖς[34] *ὁ Καῒν ἐκρίνετο, ὁ δὲ Λαμὲχ ἐν τοῖς ἑβδομηκοντάκις ⌐ἑπτά⌐[35].

5. Ὅτι[36] *ἕως τοῦ αἰῶνος[37] οἱ ὁμοιούμενοι *τῷ Καῒν[38] ⌐*ἐπὶ φθόνῳ καὶ μισαδελφίᾳ τοιαύτῃ⌐ κολασθήσονται ⌐κρίσει⌐[39].

β-d, S¹ τῇ αὐτῇ κολάσει κριθή-σονται. β, S καὶ ὑμεῖς οὖν.

VIII. *Ὑμεῖς δέ[1], *τέκνα μου[2], ἀπόδρατε[3] τὴν κακίαν, ⌐*τὸν φθόνον[4] καὶ τὴν[5] μισαδελφίαν⌐, καὶ προσκολλᾶσθε[6] τῇ ἀγαθότητι ⌐καὶ τῇ ἀγάπῃ⌐[7].

c	β, S¹	A
2. Ὁ γὰρ καθαρὸς νοῦς οὐκ ἔχει μιασμὸν	2.*Ὁ ἔχων διάνοιαν καθαρὰν ἐν ἀγάπῃ οὐχ ὁρᾷ γυναῖκα εἰς πορνείαν· οὐ γὰρ ἔχει μιασμὸν[8]	2. Ὁ γὰρ ἔχων αὐτὴν οὐχ ὁρᾷ[9] γυναῖκα εἰς πορνείαν οὐδὲ γιγνώσκει μιασμὸν[10]

⌐ἐν καρδίᾳ⌐, ὅτι ἀναπαύεται[11] *ἐπ' αὐτὸν[12] τὸ[13] πνεῦμα *τοῦ Θεοῦ[14]. 3. ⌐Ὥσπερ⌐ γὰρ[15] ὁ ἥλιος οὐ μιαίνεται †προσέχων[16]

κατακλυσμου.   [29]A[ab*cd] om. but not A[befg]. A adds τῆς ζωῆς αὐτοῦ but A[cefg] om. πάσχει ... ἔτει.   [30]A[ab*cd] = ἔπαθε. A[b] ἤρξατο πάσχειν. A adds τοῦτο.   [31]A reads [Armenian] = ἀπῆλθε (+ ἀπ' αὐτοῦ A[ab*cdefg]) corrupt for [Armenian] = text.   [32]bdg, A. aef rightly om. Cf. c. A adds καὶ ἔπαθε τοῦτο.   [33]A[b*cd] om.   [34]dg, A[befg] (save that g, A[befg] om. οὖν). A[ahb*cd] = καὶ ἐν τοῖς ἑπτὰ κακοῖς (A[h] om.). a reads ἐν τοῖς ἑπτά. bef, S¹ ἐν τοῖς ἑπτακοσίοις ἔτεσιν (e om.). Here b abandons its allies dg, and a its allies ef.   [35]A = ἔκρινε αὐτόν· ἐν δὲ (A[ahb*cdefg] om. αὐτὸν ... δέ) τοῖς ἑβδομηκοντάκις τὸν Λ.   [36]c reads ὅτι γάρ. a om. entire verse. A[b] adds ἐκδικίας θεοῦ Λαμὲχ ἔπραξε ἐν Καῒν ὅτι.   [37]A = εἰς τὸ τέλος τῶν αἰώνων.   [38]d reads τὸν Κ. A[-b] = αὐτοῖς.   [39]c. β-ad, S¹ read ἐν φθόνῳ εἰς τὴν μισαδελφίαν (ef trs. εἰς τ. μισαδ. before ἐν) τῇ αὐτῇ κολάσει (g κρίσει) κριθήσονται. d ἐν φθ. ἢ μισαδελφίᾳ ἢ φθ· τῇ αὐτῇ κολάσει κατακριθήσονται. For οἱ ὁμ. ... κρίσει A reads οἱ ὁμοιούμενοι αὐτοῖς (A[b] τῷ Καῒν) κολυσθήσονται.

VIII. [1]c. β, S read as in margin (save that g om. οὖν). A = τοιγαροῦν. [2]a om. [3]c, ef. a reads φύγετε. bdg ἀποδράσατε. [4]c. β-d, S¹ read φθόνον τε. d φθόνον δέ. [5]g om. [6]a reads προσκολλήθητε. [7]g, A om. S¹ = καὶ εὐκαρδίας τῇ ἀγ. [8]β (save that d adds ἀγαθὴν καί before καθαράν, τῇ before ἀγάπῃ and τοῦ θεοῦ after it). S¹ καὶ ἔχοντες διάν. καθαρὰν ἐν ἀγ. μὴ ὁρᾶτε γυναῖκα εἰς πορνείαν καὶ μὴ ἔχετε μιασμὰν ἐν ψυχῇ καί. Compare Matt. v. 28. [9]A[efg] = ἕξει. [10]A[b*cdefg] = πορνείαν μιασμοῦ. [11]ef read ἀναπέπαυται. [12]c, d. aeg read ἐπ' αὐτῷ. bf ἐν αὐτῷ. [13]f om. [14]A = ἅγιον. [15]d om. [16]f reads λάμπων. Text = [Hebrew] which may be

ἐπὶ[17] κόπρον[18] καὶ[19] βόρβορον[20], ⌐* ἀλλὰ μᾶλλον[21] ἀμφότερα
ψύγει[22] καὶ ἀπελαύνει τὴν δυσωδίαν⌐, οὕτω καὶ ὁ καθαρὸς[23]
νοῦς ἐν τοῖς μιασμοῖς[24] τῆς[17] γῆς συνεχόμενος[25] ⌐μᾶλλον †οἰκο-
δομεῖ[26], αὐτὸς δὲ οὐ μιαίνεται⌐.

c	β, S¹	A
IX. Λέγω δὲ ὑμῖν καὶ πράξεις ἀπὸ λογίων Ἐνὼχ τοῦ δικαίου, *ὅτι πορ- νεύ(σ)ετε[1] πορνείαν Σοδόμων καὶ ἀπο- λε(ῖ)σθε ἕως βραχύ. Καὶ πάλιν ἀνανεω- θήσεσθε καὶ ἡ βα- σιλεία Κυρίου οὐκ ἔσται ἐν ὑμῖν.	IX. Ὑπονοῶ[2] δὲ καὶ[3] πράξεις *οὐ καλὰς ἐν ὑμῖν[4] ἔσε- σθαι *ἀπὸ λόγων Ἐνὼχ τοῦ δικαίου[5]. *πορνεύσετε γὰρ[6] πορνείαν Σοδόμων *καὶ ἀπολεῖσθε ἕως βραχὺ[7], καὶ *ἀνα- νεώσησθε ἐν γυ- ναιξὶν στρίνους[8]· καὶ ἡ βασιλεία Κυρίου οὐκ ἔσται ἐν ὑμῖν ὅτι *εὐθὺς αὐτὸς λήψεται[9] αὐ- τήν.	IX. Πλὴν ὑπο- νοῶ πράξεις κακίας ἔσεσθαι ἐν ὑμῖν ὅτι ἠκούσαμεν[10] ἀπὸ λόγων τῶν πατέρων ἡμῶν· ὅτι πορνεύσετε ὑμεῖς πορνείαν Σοδό- μων, ἕως *καὶ παρὰ βραχὺ ἀπολεῖσθε[11] καὶ ἀνανεωθήσεσθε εἰς στρίνους[12] γυ- ναικῶν καὶ ἡ βα- σιλεία Κυρίου οὐκ ἔσται ἐν ὑμῖν ὅτι *ἀνὴρ εὐθὺς λήψεται αὐτήν[13].

corrupt for בהשקף = παρακύπτων.   [17] d om.   [18] f reads κοπρίᾳ.   [19] c, bdg, A, S. aef read ἤ.   [20] c, β—af. a reads βόθυνον. f βορβόρῳ.   [21] g reads μᾶλλον δέ. f adds τά.   [22] a reads ψύχει.   [23] g reads κακαθαρμένος. [24] c, bdg. aef read μιάσμασι.   [25] A^{bb} read ոչ պաշտպանի = οὐ συνέχεται. A^{b*cdefg} ոչ պաշտի corrupt.   [26] c corrupt as context shows. As the sun looks down on mire and is not defiled but rather dries it up and banishes its evil odour, so the pure mind though beset with the defilements of earth is not itself defiled but rather buildeth them up! Here we require a word signifying the cleansing action of the pure mind on the pollutions of the world. Hence יבנה (= οἰκοδομεῖ) may be corrupt for יזכה = καθαρίζει.

IX. [1] So also d, A. See note 6.   [2] d, A read πλήν, τέκνα μου (A om. τ. μου), ὑπονοῶ.   [3] abdef, S¹. g, A om.   [4] β—ab. ab, S¹ read ἐν ὑμῖν οὐ καλάς.   [5] β—d, S¹. d reads ἔγνων γὰρ ἀπὸ τῆς βίβλου λόγων Ἐ. τοῦ δικ. [6] β—dg. d, A read ὅτι πορνεύσετε (as c). g πορνεύεται δέ.   [7] β (save that b reads ἀπώλησθε, g ἀπόλυσθε). S¹ καὶ ἀπολ. πολύ. a om. next five words. [8] β—a (save that g reads ἀνανεωθήσεσθε). S¹ γαμήσετε γυναῖκας βδελυράς. Perhaps תחדש (i. e. ἀνανεώσεσθε) is corrupt for תחרש = ἐργάσεσθε. [9] d reads ὁ εὐθὺς λήψεται αὐτός.   [10] A^{bhefg}. A^{ab*cd} read ἤκουσα.   [11] A^{b*cd}. A^{ab} read καὶ ἕως οὐκ (?) ἀπολεῖσθε. A^{efg} ἕως καὶ παρὰ βραχὺ ἀπόλλυται. [12] A^{b*cd}. A^{abb} = διαστροφήν.   [13] A^{b*d}. A^{abb} = εὐθεῖς λήψονται αὐτήν. A^{efg} εὐθὺς ποιεῖ (ուղէ) αὐτήν.

c, β, S¹	A

2. Πλὴν ἐν μερίδι ὑμῶν γενήσεται *ναὸς Θεοῦ¹⁴, καὶ *ἔσται ὁ ἔσχατος ἔνδοξος¹⁵ *ὑπὲρ τὸν πρῶτον¹⁶, καὶ *συναχθήσονται ἐκεῖ¹⁷ αἱ¹⁸ δώδεκα φυλαί, καὶ πάντα τὰ ἔθνη ἕως οὗ ὁ ὕψιστος ἀποστείλῃ¹⁹ τὸ σωτήριον αὐτοῦ²⁰ ἐν ἐπισκοπῇ μονογενοῦς προφήτου²¹. [3. Καὶ εἰσελεύσεται εἰς τὸν πρῶτον ναόν, καὶ ἐκεῖ Κύριος ὑβρισθήσεται²² *καὶ ἐπὶ ξύλου ὑψωθήσεται²³. 4. Καὶ ἔσται τὸ ἅπλωμα τοῦ ναοῦ σχιζόμενον²⁴ καὶ μεταβήσεται²⁵ τὸ πνεῦμα τοῦ Θεοῦ ἐπὶ τὰ ἔθνη, ὥσπερ²⁶ πῦρ ἐκχυνόμενον. 5. Καὶ ἀνελθὼν ἐκ τοῦ ᾅδου²⁷ ἔσται²⁸ μεταβαίνων²⁹ ἀπὸ³⁰ τῆς³¹ γῆς πρὸς³² οὐρανόν³³. Ἔγνων³⁴ δὲ οἷος ἔσται²⁸ ταπεινὸς ἐπὶ³⁵ γῆς, καὶ οἷος ἔνδοξος *ἐν οὐρανῷ³⁶].

2. Πλὴν ἐν μερίδι ὑμῶν γενήσεται *ἡ κληρονομία αὐτοῦ³⁷, καὶ³⁸ διὰ τὸν ναὸν Κυρίου ὕψωσέ με Ἰακώβ, ἵνα δοξασθήσωμαι ἐν αὐτῷ, καὶ αἱ δώδεκα φυλαὶ ἐκεῖ συναχθήσονται καὶ πάντα ἔθνη. [3. Καὶ Κύριος ὑβρισθήσεται καὶ ἐξουθενωθήσεται³⁹. 5. Καὶ μεταβήσεται ἀπὸ τῆς γῆς πρὸς τὸν οὐρανόν, *ἔγνων γὰρ οἷός ἐστιν ἐκ γῆς ἢ οἷος εἰς οὐρανούς⁴⁰, ἢ καὶ τί μέτρον αὐτοῦ καὶ τόπος καὶ ὁδός].

Margin (right):

aef, S¹ ἔνδοξος ἔσται.

c υἱοῦ αὐτοῦ.

c om. ἔγνων δὲ ... x. I .. εἰδέα αὐτοῦ.

---

¹⁴ c, β–b. b, S¹ ὁ ν. τοῦ θ. ¹⁵ c, dg (save that dg trs. ἔνδοξος before ἔσται). aef, S read as in margin (save that S adds ἐν ὑμῖν). b ἔνδοξος ἔσται ἐν ὑμῖν. ¹⁶ b om. and inserts a dittograph from ver. 1: ὅτι αὐτὸς λήψεται αὐτόν. ¹⁷ c. β, S¹ read ἐκεῖ συναχθήσονται and trs. after φυλαί. ¹⁸ bd om. ¹⁹ c, be. a reads ἀνατείλῃ. d ἀποστελῇ. f ἀποστελεῖ. ²⁰ d om. ²¹ β–b. c reads υἱοῦ αὐτοῦ. b om. S¹ reads ὡς εἶπον οἱ προφῆται. ²² b adds καὶ ἐξουθενωθήσεται. Cf. A. ²³ d reads ἐπὶ ξύλου σταυρούμενος. ²⁴ c reads σχισθήσεται. ²⁵ c, β–bd. bd, S¹ read καταβήσεται. ²⁶ c. β reads ὡς. ²⁷ c, bdg. a reads χάου. ef, S λαοῦ. ²⁸ d reads ἐστί. ²⁹ c, aefg. b, S read ἀναβαίνων. d καταβαίνων. ³⁰ d reads ἐπί. ³¹ c, d. β–d om. ³² c, d. β–d read εἰς. ³³ d reads οὐρανούς. c om. rest of verse and x. 1. ³⁴ b reads ἔγνω. ³⁵ adg add τῆς. ³⁶ d reads ὑπάρχει ἐν οὐρανῷ. ³⁷ Aᵉᶠˢ om. ³⁸ Aᵇʰ om. ³⁹ Aᵇˣᶜᵈᵉˢ. Aᵃᵇʰ = τιμηθήσεται. ⁴⁰ Aᵃᵇʰ. Aᵇˣᶜᵈᵉˢ om. According to Armenian Text this clause is added after ὁδός but Carekin's copy of Aᵇ and Aᵇ places it as in text.

x. 1 to
be re-
stored
before
ii. 1.

X. Ὅτε[1] δὲ *ἦν Ἰωσὴφ ἐν Αἰγύπτῳ[2], ἐπεθύμουν ἰδεῖν τὴν εἰδέαν[3] αὐτοῦ ⌈καὶ τὴν μόρφωσιν[4] τῆς ὄψεως αὐτοῦ⌉· καὶ δι᾽ εὐχῶν Ἰακὼβ τοῦ πατρός μου[5] εἶδον ⌈αὐτόν, ἐν ἡμέρα γρηγορῶν, *καθ᾽ ὃ ἦν[6] πᾶσα⌉ ἡ εἰδέα[7] αὐτοῦ.

β, A, S¹
καὶ δι-
καιοσύ-
νην
⌈ἕκαστος
μετὰ τοῦ
πλησίον
αὐτοῦ⌉
καὶ κρῖμα
εἰς πιστο-
ποίησιν.
β, S¹
ταῦτα
γὰρ ἀντὶ

2. ⌈Καὶ ταῦτα εἰπὼν λέγει αὐτοῖς⌉[8]. *Γινώσκετε οὖν[9], τέκνα μου, ὅτι[10] ἀποθνήσκω.   3. *Ποιήσατε οὖν[11] ἀλήθειαν *ἕκαστος πρὸς τὸν πλησίον αὐτοῦ[12], ⌈καὶ τὸν νόμον Κυρίου, καὶ τὰς ἐντολὰς αὐτοῦ[13] φυλάξατε⌉.   4. *Ταῦτα γὰρ ὑμῖν ἀντὶ πάσης κληρονομίας καταλειμπάνω[14]· καὶ ὑμεῖς ⌈οὖν⌉ δότε αὐτὰ[15] τοῖς τέκνοις ὑμῶν *εἰς κατάσχεσιν[16] αἰώνιον· οὕτω[17] ⌈γὰρ⌉ ἐποίησεν[18] Ἀβραὰμ καὶ Ἰσαὰκ καὶ Ἰακώβ.   5. *Ταῦτα γὰρ πάντα δέδωκαν ἡμῖν εἰς κληρονομίαν[19] *εἰπόντες· Φυλάξατε τὰς ἐντολὰς τοῦ Θεοῦ[20] ἕως ὅτου[21] ἀποκαλύψει[22] Κύριος[23] τὸ σωτήριον αὐτοῦ[24] *πᾶσι τοῖς ἔθνεσιν[25].   6. ⌈Καὶ⌉[26] τότε

π. κληρονομίας ὑμᾶς διδάσκω.   β–g, A, S¹ πάντα ταῦτα ἡμᾶς κατεκληρονόμησαν.   A ἐν πάσῃ τῇ γῇ.

X. [1] aefg, A. bd, S¹ read ὅτι.   [2] de, A. bfg, S¹ read Ἰ. ἦν ἐν Αἰγ. (af ἐν Αἰγ. ἦν). A adds καί.   [3] bfg. ade read ἰδέαν.   [4] b reads μορφήν. [5] β–af, A^bb, S¹. f, A^ab*cdes read ὑμῶν. a om. and trs. τ. π. and A trs. τ. π. μου (or ὑμῶν) before Ἰακώβ.   [6] af read καθ᾽ ἥν.   [7] bfg. ade read ἰδέα. A reads εἰδέαν ζῶσαν. d adds καὶ ἡ δόξα αὐτοῦ.   [8] c. β, A, S¹ om. [9] A = καὶ νῦν. S¹ = ὁρᾶτε οὖν.   [10] d, A^bhels om. A^ab*cd read ἰδού.   [11] g reads καὶ ποιησάτω. A = καὶ ἐντέλλομαι ὑμῖν ποιεῖν.   [12] c. β, S¹ read as in margin (save that a om. καὶ κρῖμα εἰς πιστοποίησιν).   For ἀλήθειαν ... αὐτοῦ A reads δικαιοσύνην καὶ ἀλήθειαν καὶ κρῖμα εἰς πίστιν (A^abh om. καὶ κρῖμα εἰς πίστιν) Κυρίου.   Possibly εἰς πιστοποίησιν is an attempt to render אֶמֶת.   [13] g om.   [14] c. β, S¹ read as in margin (save that b, S¹ trs. ὑμᾶς before ἀντί and dg trs. it after διδάσκω).   A = ταῦτα δίδωμι ὑμῖν ἀντὶ πάσης κληρονομίας.   Καταλειμπάνω = מַנִיחַ which is the natural word for a bequest, whereas διδάσκω = מַגִּיד or מֵבִין, or מוֹרֶה is a corruption of the former.   [15] a reads ταῦτα.   [16] A εἰς κληρονομίαν and all but A^b trs. before τοῖς τέκνοις.   [17] c, d. β–d, A, S¹ read τοῦτο.   [18] c, β–b. b reads ἐποίησαν. β–de, S¹ add καί against c, de, A.   [19] c. β–g, A, S¹ read as in margin (save that adf read ταῦτα πάντα and A adds an unintelligible καὶ (A^b om.) μᾶλλον ἤ before πάντα). g ταῦτα πάντα πάλαι κατεκλ. ἐν πίστει.̓ δέδωκαν εἰς κλ. and κατεκληρονόμησαν = הוֹרִישׁוּ.   [20] A = καὶ εἶπον· Οὕτως ποιήσατε. For φυλάξατε, a reads φυλάξασθε, g φυλάξαντες.   [21] bef read ὅτε.   [22] c, aef. β–aef read ἀποκαλύψῃ.   [23] c, e, A. b reads ὁ Κύριος, dg S¹ trs. before ἀποκαλύψει. af om.   [24] A^b om.   [25] A = ἐν πάσῃ τῇ γῇ.   [26] c. β, A, S¹ om.

ὄψεσθε[27] Ἐνὼχ *καὶ Σήθ[28], καὶ[29] Ἀβραάμ, καὶ[29] Ἰσαὰκ καὶ
Ἰακώβ ἀνασταμένους[30] ἐκ δεξιῶν ⌐αὐτοῦ⌐[31] *ἐν ἀγαλλιάσει[32].

β–d, S¹ Νῶε καὶ (aefom.) Σήμ.

c, β, S¹	A
7. Τότε καὶ ἡμεῖς ἀναστή-σομεθα[33] ἕκαστος *ἐπὶ σκή-πτρον ἡμῶν[34] προσκυνοῦντες τὸν βασιλέα *τῶν οὐρανῶν[35] [τὸν ἐπὶ γῆς φανέντα[36] ἐν[37] μορφῇ ἀνθρώπου *ἐν ταπεινώ-σει[38], καὶ ὅσοι πιστεύσωσιν[39] αὐτῷ[40] ἐπὶ τῆς[41] γῆς *χαρί-σονται σὺν αὐτῷ[42]]. 8. *Καὶ οἱ[43] πάντες ἀνα-στήσονται, οἱ μὲν εἰς δόξαν, οἱ δὲ εἰς ἀτιμίαν, καὶ κρινεῖ Κύριος[44] ἐν πρώτοις τὸν Ἰσ-ραὴλ[45] περὶ τῆς *ἀδικίας αὐτῶν[46] [ὅτι παραγενόμενον[47] Θεὸν[44] ἐν σαρκί[48], οὐκ ἐπίστευσαν αὐ-τῷ[49]]. 9. Καὶ τότε κρινεῖ πάντα τὰ ἔθνη [ὅσα οὐκ ἐπί-στευσαν αὐτῷ ἐπὶ τῆς[50] γῆς	7. Τότε ἀναστησόμεθα καὶ ἡμεῖς ἕκαστος ἐπὶ σκῆπτρον αὐτοῦ καὶ προσκυνήσομεν τὸν οὐράνιον βασιλέα.

β–g, S¹ ἐπίστευ-σαν.

8. Τότε πάντες[51] †ἀλλα-γησόμεθα[52] οἱ μὲν εἰς δόξαν[53], οἱ δὲ εἰς ἀτιμίαν· κρίνει γὰρ Κύριος ἐν πρώτοις τὸν Ἰσραὴλ περὶ τῆς ἀδικίας ἣν ἔπραξαν[54].

bdg, S¹ τότε καί.

β–d, S¹ εἰς αὐτον ἀδικίας.

9. Καὶ τότε[55] οὕτως πάντα τὰ ἔθνη[56].

β σαρκὶ ἐλευθε-ρωτίν.

[27] A^b*cdefg = ὁράτε.   [28] c. β–d, S¹ read as in margin. d, A καὶ (d, A^b om.) Νῶε.   [29] d, A^b om.   [30] c reads ἀνισταμένων.   [31] c. β, A, S¹ om.   [32] g trs. before ἀνισταμένους.   [33] β–af, S¹. c, f read ἀναστησώμεθα. a ἀνιστάμεθα.   [34] β, S¹ (save that d reads σκήπτρῳ). c om.   [35] g reads τοῦ οὐρανοῦ.   [36] c, bdg, S¹. aef read φαινόμενον.   [37] b om.   [38] c. β–a, S¹ read ταπεινώσεως. a om.   [39] c, g. β–g, S¹ read as in margin.   [40] d reads εἰς αὐτόν. e trs. before ἐπίστευσαν.   [41] c, g. β–g om.   [42] c. β–d, S¹ read συγχαρίσονται (-ήσονται ag) αὐτῷ. d συγχωρίσει αὐτῶν.   [43] c. aef read ὅτε καί. bdg, S¹ as in margin.   [44] g om.   [45] aef add καί.   [46] c. β–d, S¹ read as in margin. d εἰς ἑαυτὸν γενομένης ἀδικίας (cf. A).   [47] c, adeg. bf read παραγενάμενον.   [48] c, S¹. β reads as in margin. S¹ om. next three words.   [49] c. β–d om. d reads εἰς αὐτόν. g om. next ten words.   [50] c, g. β–g om.   [51] A^abh. A^b*cdefg read καὶ ἡμεῖς.   [52] Corrupt. The verb should be in the third plural. ⟨Armenian⟩ is a rendering of ἀλλαγησόμεθα (as in 1 Cor. xv. 51, 52) corrupt for ἀναστησόμεθα or rather ἀναστήσονται.   [53] A^bh read τιμήν.   [54] A^cfg om. next ten words.   [55] A^b reads οὕτως.   [56] A^abh om. next

c om. ver. 10.

φανέντι[87]]. 10. Καὶ ἐλέγξει ἐν τοῖς ἐκλεκτοῖς *τῶν ἐθνῶν[58] τὸν Ἰσραήλ, ὥσπερ ἤλεγξεν τὸν Ἡσαῦ ἐν τοῖς *aef ἀπι-στῆσα-σιν.* Μαδιναίοις τοῖς †ἀπατήσασιν[59] *ἀδελφοὺς αὐτῶν[60] [γενέσθαι διὰ τῆς πορνείας καὶ τῆς εἰδωλολατρείας, καὶ[81] ἀπηλ-λοτριώθησαν Θεοῦ][62], *β-α οὐ.* γενό-μενοι[63] οὖν[64] τέκνα ἐν μερίδι φοβουμένων[65] Κύριον.	10. Καὶ ἐλέγξει τὸν Ἰσραὴλ ἐν τοῖς ἐκλεκτοῖς ἔθνεσι ὥσπερ ἤλεγξε τὸν Ἡσαῦ ἐν τοῖς Μαδιαναίοις τοῖς ἀγαπήσασιν τοὺς ἀδελφοὺς αὐτῶν· γίνεσθε οὖν, τέκνα μου, *ἐν μερίδι[66] τῶν φοβουμένων Κύριον.

β, S¹ κατὰ πρόσ-ωπον.

11. ⌐Ὑμεῖς οὖν, τέκνα μου⌐[67], ἐὰν[68] πορευθῆτε[69] ἐν ἁγιασμῷ ⌐*ἐν ταῖς ἐντολαῖς[70] Κυρίου⌐, πάλιν κατοικήσετε[71] ⌐ἐπ' ἐλπίδι⌐ *ἐν ἐμοί[72], καὶ συναχθήσεται[73] *πρὸς Κύριον[74] πᾶς Ἰσραήλ.

c	β, S¹	A
XI.[1] Καὶ οὐκέτι κληθήσομαι λύκος ἅρπαξ διὰ τὰς ἁρπαγὰς ὑμῶν ἀλλὰ [ἐργάτης Κυρίου διαδιδὼν τροφὴν τοῖς ἐργαζομένοις τὸ ἀγαθόν. 2. Καὶ	XI. Καὶ οὐκέτι κληθήσομαι[2] λύκος ἅρπαξ διὰ τὰς ἁρπαγὰς ὑμῶν ἀλλ' [ἐργάτης Κυρίου διαδιδοὺς[3] τροφὴν τοῖς ἐργαζομένοις τὸ ἀγαθόν. 2. Καὶ	XI. Καὶ οὐκέτι κληθήσεται[4] *λή-σταρχος καὶ[5] λύκος διὰ τὴν ἁρπαγὴν ὑμῶν,

eight words.   [87]*g* reads φανέντα.   [58]*g*, S¹ om.   [59]*bdg*, S¹ but a manifest corruption of ἀγαπήσασιν as in A. *aef* read ἀπιστήσασιν (a corruption of the reading of *d*). *d* ἀποστήσασιν.   [60]*bd*. *aef*, S¹ read ἀδελφὸν (*ef* ἀδελφοῦ) αὐτῶν. *g* αὐτὸν ἀδελφούς.   [81]*d* reads οἵτινες καί.   [62]I have bracketed these words as an interpolation added to explain the corrupt reading ἀπατήσασιν or ἀποστήσουσιν.   [63]*d* reads γινόμενοι.   [64]*a*. β-α read οὐ, which is clearly a modification of οὖν. S¹ om.   [65]*ag* add τόν.   [66]A[b*cdefg]. A[abb] = μερίς.   [67]*c*. *abg*, S¹ read ὑμεῖς δε. *def* ὑμεῖς οὖν.   [68]A adds γάρ.   [69]*c*. β-d, S¹ read πορεύησθε (-εσθε *befg*). *d* πορεύσεσθε.   [70]*c*. β, S¹ read as in margin. *c* = עַל־פִּי, while β, S¹ = עַל־פְּנִי.   [71]β-d. *c*, *d* read κατοικήσειτε (sic).   [72]*dg* read σὺν ἐμοί and trs. before ἐπ' ἐλπίδι.   [73]*c*, *bg*, A, S¹. *aef* read συναχθήσεσθε.   [74]*b*, S¹ trs. after Ἰσραήλ against *c*, β-b, A. A = πρός με.

XI. [a]The text of β, S is here largely interpolated, and made to refer to St. Paul. In *c* the interpolation is so framed as to refer to Christ.   [2]*g* reads κληθήσεται.   [3]β-bg. *b* reads διαδιδών. *g* διδούς.   [4]A[b*] reads κληθήσεσθε.   [5]Evidently an internal corruption.

ἀναστήσεται ἐν ὑστέροις] ἀγαπητὸς Κυρίου [ἐκ σπέρματος Ἰούδα καὶ Λευὶ][6] ποιῶν εὐδοκίαν *ἐν στόματι αὐτοῦ[7], [γνῶσιν καινὴν φωτίζων πάντα τὰ ἔθνη][6].	ἀναστήσεται *ἐκ τοῦ σπέρματός[8] μου ἐν ὑστέροις καιροῖς] ἀγαπητὸς Κυρίου [ἀκούων[9] τὴν[10] φωνὴν αὐτοῦ] *καὶ ποιῶν εὐδοκίαν θελήματος αὐτοῦ[11], [γνῶσιν καινὴν φωτίζων πάντα τὰ ἔθνη	2. ἀλλ' ἀγαπητὸς *Κυρίου καὶ ποιῶν εὐδοκίαν[12] στόματος[13] αὐτοῦ.

β, S[1]

*φῶς γνώσεως[14], ἐπεμβαίνων[15] *τὸν Ἰσραὴλ[16] ἐν σωτηρίᾳ, καὶ ἁρπάζων ὡς λύκος ἀπ' αὐτῶν[17], καὶ *διδοὺς τῇ συναγωγῇ τῶν ἐθνῶν[18].   3. Ἕως[19] συντελείας *τοῦ αἰῶνος[20] ἔσται ἐν συναγωγαῖς[21] ἐθνῶν καὶ ἐν τοῖς ἄρχουσιν αὐτῶν, ὡς μουσικὸν μέλος ἐν στόματι πάντων[22].   4. Καὶ ἐν βίβλοις ἁγίαις ἔσται ἀναγραφόμενος, καὶ τὸ ἔργον καὶ ὁ λόγος αὐτοῦ· καὶ ἔσται ἐκλεκτὸς Θεοῦ[23] *ἕως τοῦ[24] αἰῶνος.   5. Καὶ[25] δι' *αὐτῶν φοιτήσει ὡς[26] Ἰακὼβ[27] ὁ πατήρ μου, λέγων· Αὐτὸς ἀναπληρώσει τὰ ὑστερήματα τῆς *φυλῆς σου[28]].

[6] Christian interpolations referring the passage to Christ.   [7] c. Cf. A[bb*cdefg]. adef, A[a] read θελήματος αὐτοῦ. The latter = המצפ the former בפיהו.   [8] g reads.ἐν τῷ σπέρματι.   [9] bdg, S[1] add ἐπὶ γῆς.   [10] adef. bg om.   [11] adef, S[1]. bg om. See note 7.   [12] A[a(?)bh]. A[b*cd] = καὶ εὐδοκίας. A[efg] καὶ ποιητῇ εὐδοκίας. But all the MSS. are corrupt.   [13] A[bb*cdefg]. A[ah] read θελήματος αὐτοῦ (A[a] om. ?).   [14] d trs. before πάντα τὰ ἔθνη. S[1] = ἐν γνώσει   [15] beg. a reads λάμπων. df ἐπιβαίνων. S[1] = εἰσάγων.   [16] β–ab, S[1]. ab read τῷ Ἰσραήλ. a trs. after σωτηρίᾳ.   [17] β–ab, S[1]. ab read αὐτοῦ.   [18] S[1] = συνάγων τὰ ἔθνη. g om. next eight words through hmt.   [19] b reads καὶ ἕως. d adds τῆς.   [20] adef (save that a om. τοῦ). b, S[1] read τῶν αἰώνων.   [21] df add τῶν.   [22] S[1] adds κατὰ τὸ ὄνομα τοῦ καλουμένου.   [23] d om.   [24] g om.   [25] a om. ver. 5. d om. next nine words.   [26] ef (save that e reads αὐτόν). b reads δι' αὐτὸν συνέτισέ με. g διὰ τοῦτο ἐφυσίωσέν με. S[1] περὶ αὐτοῦ γνωρίζεσθε. The text is absolutely uncertain.   [27] ef trs.after μου.   [28] bg. def read κοιλίας μου. Here strangely enough this divergence could be explained on the supposition of a Hebrew background. bg = מעין. def מעון.

c

XII.[1] Καὶ ταῦτα εἰπὼν ἐκτείνας τοὺς πόδας αὐτοῦ 2. ἐκοιμήθη †ὕπνῳ[2] καλῷ [καὶ ἀγαθῷ][3]. 3. Οἱ δὲ υἱοὶ αὐτοῦ ἐποίησαν ὡς προσέταξεν αὐτοῖς, καὶ ἄραντες τὸ σῶμα αὐτοῦ ἔθαψαν αὐτὸ[4] ἐν Χεβρὼν μετὰ τῶν πατέρων αὐτοῦ. 2. Ὁ δὲ ἀριθμὸς τῆς ζωῆς αὐτοῦ ἔτη ἑκατὸν εἴκοσι πέντε[5].

β, A, S[1]

XII. Καὶ[6] *ὡς ἐπλήρωσε τοὺς λόγους αὐτοῦ[7] εἶπεν[8]. Ἐντέλλομαι ὑμῖν, *τέκνα μου[9], ἀνενέγκατε[10] τὰ ὀστᾶ μου ἐξ Αἰγύπτου, καὶ *θάψατέ με[11] εἰς[12] Χεβρὼν ἐγγὺς[13] τῶν πατέρων μου. 2. Καὶ[14] ἀπέθανε Βενιαμὶν[15] *ἑκατὸν εἴκοσι πέντε[16] ἐτῶν ἐν γήρει καλῷ· καὶ ἔθηκαν αὐτὸν ἐν παραθήκῃ[17]. 3. Καὶ[18] ἐνενηκοστῷ[19] πρώτῳ[20] ἔτει ⸢τῆς[21] †ἐξόδου[22] τῶν υἱῶν Ἰσραὴλ †ἐξ Αἰγύπτου[23]⸣, *αὐτοὶ καὶ οἱ ἀδελφοὶ αὐτῶν[24] ἀνήγαγον τὰ ὀστᾶ τῶν πατέρων[25] αὐτῶν ἐν κρυφῇ *ἐν τῷ πολέμῳ Χαναάν[26], καὶ ἔθαψαν αὐτοὺς[27] ἐν Χεβρὼν[28]

XII. [1]Here the two types of text run widely apart so far as words go, and in ver. 3 there is a difference as to matter. According to *c* only the burial of Benjamin by his sons is recounted, whereas in *β*, A, S[1] it is the burial of the patriarchs generally by their sons. Even A preserves some evidence in favour of *c* as it reads ἔθαψαν αὐτόν with *c*; also *df* (see note 14) recount the burial of Benjamin only. [2]It will be observed that *β*, A, S[1] have rightly γήρει here. This corruption has occurred several times before. See T. Iss. vii. 9. [3]A dittographic rendering of בטוב. [4]*c* reads αὐτῷ. [5]*c* adds καὶ ταῖς πρεσβείαις αὐτῶν ὁ Θεὸς ἐλέει καὶ σώσον ἡμᾶς· τέλος γὰρ ἔσχεν (sic) τῶν δώδεκα πατριαρχῶν αἱ διαθῆκαι ἐν Κυρίῳ. [6]*ef* om. A[b1] adds ἐγένετο. [7]*d* reads πληρώσας Βενιαμὴν τοὺς λόγους τούτους. After ἐπλήρωσε A[b*] add Βενιαμήν. [8]A = λέγει αὐτοῖς. S[1] adds ὁρᾶτε, τέκνα μου, ὅσα ἐνόησα, εἶπον ὑμῖν. Καὶ, ἰδού, δίδωμι ἐμαυτὸν τῷ τάφῳ. [9]A[abcdeg] om. but not A[b*]. [10]*abg*, A[b*efg], S[1]. *d* reads ἀνάγαγε. *ef*, A[abbcd] ἀνενέγκαι. [11]*β–d*, A[b*], S. *d*, A[abcdefg] read θάψαι. [12]*β–df*. *df* read ἐν. [13]*f* reads μετά. [14]*d* gives ver. 2 as follows: Ταῦτα ἐντειλάμενος Βενιαμὴν τοῖς υἱοῖς αὐτοῦ ἐξάρας τοὺς πόδας αὐτοῦ ἐξέλειπεν· προσετέθη μετὰ τῶν πατέρων αὐτοῦ, πρεσβύτης καὶ πλήρης ἡμερῶν γενόμενος, ζήσας ἔτη ρκε΄. τότε ἐποίησαν οἱ υἱοὶ αὐτοῦ πάντα ὅσα ἐνετείλατο Βενιαμὴν ὁ πατὴρ αὐτῶν. This text is conflate. Its last clause it holds in common with *c* and προσετέθη … αὐτοῦ is wrongly added here from ver. 3 according to the substance of *c*. *f* om. verses 2–4 and gives in their stead a text that is practically the same as ver. 3 of *c*: Καὶ

β, A, S¹

*παρὰ τοὺς πόδας[29] τῶν πατέρων αὐτῶν.   4. *Καὶ αὐτοὶ ἐπέστρεψαν[30] ἐκ γῆς[31] Χαναάν, καὶ[32] ᾤκησαν ἐν Αἰγύπτῳ ἕως ἡμέρας ἐξόδου αὐτῶν ἐκ ⌐γῆς⌐ Αἰγύπτου[33].

ἐποίησαν οὕτως καθὼς ἐνετείλατο αὐτοῖς· καὶ ἀνενεγκόντες ἔθαψαν αὐτὸν ἐν Χεβρών. S adds ταῦτα εἰπών.   [15] S¹ adds υἱὸς τοῦ Ἰακὼβ δωδέκατος.   [16] bg. ae read ρκε΄. After ἐτῶν A^abbcdefg add ζωῆς αὐτοῦ.   [17] bg. ae read παρακαταθήκη. [18] be. a reads καὶ ἐν τῷ. d ἐν γὰρ τῷ. S¹ ἐν. g abbreviates verses 3–4 as follows: Καὶ ἔκρυπτον πρὸ τῆς ἐξόδου αὐτῶν ἀναγαγόντες καὶ θάψαντες ἐν Χεβρὼν 4. ὑπέστρεψαν εἰς Αἴγυπτον.   [19] bde. a reads ϛ΄. A^abb = δεκάτῳ. A^b*cdefg read յիննեբրրրդ (= ἐννάτῳ) corrupt for յիննունբրրրդ = ἐνενηκοστῷ.   [20] bd, A, (S¹ ʔ). ae om.   [21] e om.   [22] Corrupt for εἰσόδου.   [23] Corrupt for εἰς Αἴγυπτον. d reads ἀπό.   [24] A trs. after πατέρων αὐτῶν. S¹ = καὶ οἱ ἀδ. αὐτῶν. [25] A^b* = πατρός.   [26] ade, S¹. b reads ἐν τόπῳ λεγομένῳ Χαναάν. A = ὅτε ἦσαν ἐν πολέμῳ οἱ Χαναναῖοι.   [27] A = αὐτόν. See notes 1 and 14.   [28] d adds ἐν τῷ σπηλαίῳ τῷ διπλῷ.   [29] A = ἐγγύς.   [30] abe, A, S¹. d reads αὐτοὶ δὲ πάλιν ὑποστρέψαντες.   [31] A^b*cdefg om.   [32] d om.   [33] a adds τέλος τῶν ιβ΄ διαθηκῶν τῶν υἱῶν Ἰακώβ. d ὑπὲρ δὲ τούτων ἀπάντων οἵ τε ἀναγινώσκοντες καὶ ἀκούοντες δόξαν ἀναπέμψωμεν θεῷ εἰς αἰῶνας. Ἀμήν, ἀμήν, ἀμήν. f, S¹ Βενιαμὴν υἱὸς Ἰακὼβ ιβ΄, υἱὸς Ῥαχὴλ β΄. ἔζησεν ρκε΄. g τέλος τῶν διαθηκῶν τῶν ιβ΄ πατριαρχῶν υἱῶν Ἰσραήλ.

APPENDIX I

מדרש ויסעו

(This Midrash, which is reprinted from Jellinek's *Beth-ha Midrasch* iii. 1-3, contains Hebrew Fragments of the Testament of Judah. These are underlined.)

ויסעו ויהי חתת אלהים (בראשית ל"ה ה') . אמרו אם שני
בני יעקב עשו הדבר הגדול הזה אם יאספו כולם יכולים להחריב
את העולם . ונפל פחדו של הק״בה עליהם לכך לא רדפו אחרי בני
יעקב . רבותינו אמרו אף על פי שלא רדפו אחריהם בפעם ההיא
אבל לאחר ז' שנים רדפו תתכנסו כל מלכי האמורי על בני יעקב
ובקשו להורגם בבקעת שכם . לפי שלאחר מיכן חזר יעקב ובניו לשכם
ועמדו שם וישבו שם . אמרו לא די להם שהרגו כל אנשי שכם אלא
שיורשים את ארצם . נתקבצו כולם ובאו עליהם להורגם . כין שראה
יהודה כך קפץ לתוך מערכת הרגלים הנלחמים עמהם והרג בתחלה
לישוב _מלך_ _תפוח_ שהיה מכוסה מראשו ועד רגליו בברזל ובנחשת
והיה רוכב על סוס והיה _מורה_ חניתו בשני ידיו _מעל הסוס_ לפניו
ולאחריו לא יחטיא בכל מקום שהיה מטיל כי היה _גבור_ בכוחו לירות
בשתי ידיו . כיון שראהו יהודה לא נתירא ממנו ולא מנבורתו . קפץ
ורץ לקראתו _נטל אבן_ מן הארץ _משקלה ס' סלעים_ והשליכה עליו
והוא היה רחוק ממנו שני חלקי ריס שהוא קע״ן אמות ושליש . והוא
היה בא לקראת יהודה מקושט בכלי ברזל ומורה חניתות . _והכהו_
יהודה באותה האבן על מגינו והפילו מן הסוס . כיון שרצה לקום
רץ יהודה ובקש להורגו קודם שיקום מן הארץ . והוא מהר ועמד
על רגליו לקראת יהודה _וערך מלחמה_ בנגדו מול מגינו מול מגינו ושלף

T. Jud.
iii. 2.
iii. 3.
iii. 4.

Greek equivalents of underlined words: III. 2. Βασιλέα τοῦ
Ταφουὲ . . . καθήμενον ἐφ᾽ ἵππου.   3. καὶ βάλλοντα δόρατα αὐτοῦ (for
δόρατα Greek text gives τόξα—a bad rendering) . . . ἀφ᾽ ἵππου
ἔμπροσθεν καὶ ὄπισθεν . . . γίγαντα . . . ἀνείλετο λίθον . . . ἑξήκοντα λιτρῶν (?)
καὶ ἠκόντισε . . . καὶ ἐπάταξε αὐτόν.   4. καὶ ἐπολέμησε . . . καὶ εἰς δύο μέρη
ἐποίησε τὴν ἀσπίδα . . . καὶ συνέκοψε τοὺς πόδας αὐτοῦ.

כידונו ובקש לחתוך ראש יהודה . ויהודה הרים מגינו לנגד הכידון

קבל הכאת הכידון ופסק המגן לשנים . מה עשה יהודה גזל [1] והכהו

בכידונו וקטע שתי רגליו למעלה מן הקרסולים ואז נפל לארץ וכידונו

Jud. iii. 5.   נפל מידו וקפץ וקטע ראשו ועד שהיה חולץ שריונו באו עליו תשעה

חביריו . הראשון שהגיעו נטל יהודה אבן והכהו את ראשו ומגינו נפל

מידו ולקחו יהודה ועמד לקראת השמונה . ולוי אחיו הגיע ובא ועמד

iii. 6.   אצלו וירה בחץ והרג לאילון מלך געש . ויהודה הרג כל השמונה

iii. 7 (8).   ויעקב אביו קרב והרג לזירורי מלך שילה וכולם לא קמו לקראת בני

יעקב ועור לא היה להם לב לעמוד אלא לנום . ובני יעקב רדפו אחריהם

iv. 1.   והרג מהם יהודה ביום ההוא אלף קודם שיבא השמש . ושאר בני יעקב

יצאו מתל שכם מן המקום שהיו עומדין בצידו ורדפו אחריהם בהר

iv. 1.   עד שיצאו לחצר העיר . ולפני חצר העיר היה להם מלחמה כבדה

מן אותה המלחמה שנלחמו עמם בבקעת שכם . וירה יעקב חצים

והרג לפרעתון [2] מלך חצר ופסוסי [3] מלך סרטן וללבון [4] מלך ארם

iv. 2.   לשביר [5] מלך מחנים . ויהודה היה ראשון ועלה לחומה של חצר וערבע

נבורים ערכו מלחמה עם יהודה קודם שהגיע נפתלי אצלו שהיה עולה

אחריו וטרם שעלה הרג לאותם ד' נבורים ונפתלי קפץ ועלה אחריו .

עמד יהודה לימין החומה ונפתלי לשמאל החומה והתחילו להרוג

בהם . ושאר בני יעקב דלגו ועלו אחריהם ושברו אותם ביום ההוא

iv. 3.   וכבשו לחצר . והרגו כל הגבורים ולא הניחו איש שלא הרגוהו ושבו

כל השבי .

v. 1.   ביום השני הלכו לסרטן וגם בה היה עמם מלחמה כבדה

עיר גבוהה ותלה גבוה וכתשה לכל מי שקרב אצלה ולא היה מקום

5. Ἐν δὲ τῷ ἐκδύειν τὸν θώρακα αὐτοῦ ... ἐννέα ἑταῖροι αὐτοῦ ...
6. ἀνεῖλε ... τοὺς ὀκτώ. 7. Ἰακὼβ δὲ ὁ πατὴρ αὐτοῦ .. ἀνεῖλε .. τὸν
βασιλέα τῆς Σιλώ. 8. (καὶ οὐκέτι αὐτοῖς καρδία τοῦ στῆναι ἀλλὰ τοῦ
φεύγειν). IV. 1. καὶ ἀπέκτεινε ἐξ αὐτῶν χιλίους ... ἐγένετο αὐτοῖς
πόλεμος μείζων τοῦ ... ἐν Σικίμοις. 2. καὶ Ἰούδα ... ἀνῆλθε ἐπὶ τοῦ
τείχους ... καὶ ... ἀνεῖλε τοὺς τέσσαρας ἰσχυρούς. 3. καὶ ... κατεκυρίευσαν
τὴν Ἀσοὺρ ... καὶ ἔλαβον πᾶσαν τὴν αἰχμαλωσίαν. V. 1. καὶ τῇ δευτέρᾳ
ἡμέρᾳ ἀπῆλθον εἰς Σαρτάν. πόλιν κραταιὰν ... καὶ συνέτριψε πάντα τὸν
προσεγγίζοντα αὐτῇ καὶ ἦν ἀπροσέγγιστος, ὅτι ἰσχυρὸν τὸ τεῖχος.

---

[1] Chron. Jer. reads נחן עצמו = 'ducked his head.'   [2] Chron.
Jer. xxxvi. 5 לפרעתהו.   [3] ולסוסי.   [4] בן חלדון (or חרן).
[5] ולשכור.

לקרב אצל החומה משום שחזק היה השור ונבוה מאד ולא היה מקום

Jud. v. 2. ללוכדה . ביום ההוא כבשו אותה ועלו לחומה וקדם יהודה ועלה

ראשון מן המזרח וגד עלה מן המערב . עלו שמעון ולוי מן הצפון

עלו ראובן ודן מן הדרום . קרבו נפתלי ויששכר והדליקו צירי השערים

ועל החומה היה עמם מלחמה כבדה עד שעלו סיעת החבריהם שם .

v. 5. עמדו לנגדם על המגדל קודם שכבש יהודה את המגדל . ואחר כך

עלה יהודה לראש המגדל והרג מאתים איש על גג המגדל טרם שירד

ממנו . כל בני העיר לכדו והרגו כל הגבורים ולא החיו מהם איש . מפני

שהאנשים חזקים וקשים היו למלחמה והוציאו כל השבי משם . וחזרו

v. 6. לאחוריהם והלכו לתפוח מפני שיצאו אנשי תפוח להציל מידם השבי

vi. 1. שלקחו מחצר העיר והלכו משם לארבאל והרגו לאותן אנשים שיצאו

להציל השבי .

ביום השלישי הלכו לתפוח בעת הבוקר וכאשר היו

מקבצים השבי ובני שילה באו אצלם לעשות מלחמה אז חלצו עצמם

ויצאו אחריהם והרגו כולם קודם חצות יום תכנסו אחר הנשים לתוך

שילה ולא נתנו להם יד לעמור . בו ביום לכדו העיר והוציאו כל

השבי [ל]סיעת חבריהם שהניחו בתפוח באו אצלם ועמהם שלל תפוח .

vi. 3. ביום הרביעי היו עוברים נגד מחנה שביר[1] יצאו אף הם להציל את

השבי וירדו מהם תוך הבקעה וקפצו ועלו אחריהם והרגום קודם שעלו

vi. 4. המעלה . בו ביום יצאו אנשים ממחנה שביר[1] לנגדם עליהם היו משליכים

אבנים . בו ביום לכדום והרגו כל הגבורים והצילו לכל השבי ורבקוהו

לאותו שהיה עמהם .

vii. 1. ביום החמשי הלכו לנועש משום ששמעו

שנאספו שם עם רב מן אמוריים והיו אומרים שהיו באים עליהם ועיר

---

2. Ὁ Ἰούδας ... ἀνέβη ... ἀπὸ ἀνατολῶν καὶ ὁ Γὰδ ἀνέβη ἀπὸ δυσμῶν ... καὶ ὁ Λευὶ ... Ῥουβήμ. 5. κατέλαβεν ὁ Ἰούδας τὸν πύργου ... καὶ ἀπέκτεινε τοὺς ἄνδρας τοὺς ἐπὶ (τὸ ὄροφος) τοῦ πύργου. 6. Ἄνδρες Θαφφουὲ ἐξῆλθον τοῦ ἐξαιρεῖσθαι ἀπὸ χειρὸς αὐτῶν τὴν αἰχμαλωσίαν. VI. 1, 2. Ἀρβαήλ ... ἄνδρες Σιλὼ ἦλθον ἐπ' αὐτοὺς εἰς πόλεμον ... καὶ ἀπέκτειναν ... Σιλὼ καὶ οὐκ ἔδωκαν αὐτοῖς σθένος τοῦ στῆναι. 3. Σακίρ· ἐξῆλθον καὶ αὐτοὶ ... καὶ ἀπέκτειναν αὐτοὺς πρὸ τοῦ ἀναβῆναι τὴν ἀνάβασιν. 4. ἐπ' αὐτοὺς ἐσφενδόνιζον λίθους. 5. ἐπελάβοντο αὐτούς ... VII. 1. Γαὰς ... διότι

[1] Chron. Jer. שביר.

חזקה היתה גועש אחת מן ערי מלכי האמורי הלכו לשם ועשו

מלחמה עם העיר עד חצות היום ולא יכלו ללכדה מפני ששלש

Jud. vii. 3.   חומות היו לה חומה לפנים מחומה . והתחילו מצערין להן והיו

vii. 5.   מחרפין להן . באותה שעה עלתה חמתו של יהודה ורוח קנאת גבור

נכנסה בו וקפץ בכל כחו ועלה ראשון לחומה , ושם הגיע יהודה

vii. 6.   למות אילו לא *היה יעקב אביו ושם היה נהרג שהוא משך בקשתו[1]

vii. 5.   והרג מן ימין ומן שמאל . מן ימין היו משליכין עליו אבנים ומין שמאל

ומלפניו היו עומדין למלחמה וכולן היו מבקשין לטורדו מן החומה .

vii. 6.   וכאשר עלה דן אחיו הבריחם מעט מן החומה , ונפתלי שלישי

מאחריהם ושמעון ולוי כבשו ועלו מערב ותמשתן השעו ולא נתנו

להם יד לעמוד והרגו בהם רבים הרוגים עד זמן שהיה מושך נחל

של דם מרמן . ולקדו העיר בעת נטה השמש למערב והרגו כל

הגבורים ביום ההוא והוציאו את השבי והלכו ונפשו מחוץ לעיר

משום שיגעום היו .

ביום הששי נתקבצו כל האמוריים ובאו אצלם בלא

vii. 7.   כלי מלחמה *והיו משתחוים להם ובקשו מהם שיעשו שלום ואו עשו

vii. 8.   עמהם שלום ונתנו להם תמנה ולכל ארץ חרריה . ואו עשה יעקב

עמהם שלום ושלמו לבני יעקב כל הצאן ששבו מהם שנים באחד

vii. 9.   ונתנו להם מס והחזירו להם כל השבי †ונטה יעקב לתמנה ויהודה

לארבאל[2] ומשם והלאה עמדו בשלום עם האמוריים[3]

ἤκουσαν ὅτι συνελέχθη ἐκεῖ λαὸς πολὺς τῶν Ἀμορραίων καὶ ἐρρέθη ὅτι
ἔρχονται πρὸς αὐτούς.   3. τρία τείχη.   5. ὕβριζον αὐτούς· τότε
ἀνέβη ὀργὴ τοῦ Ἰούδα ... καὶ ὥρμησε ... πρῶτος ἐπὶ τὸ τεῖχος.
6. εἰ μὴ Ἰακὼβ πατὴρ αὐτοῦ (†συνεμάχησεν αὐτῷ, εἶχον ἀνελεῖν Ἰούδαν
Chron. Jer.).   Text is dislocated.   Transpose ושם היה נהרג
before אילו.   5. ἐσφενδόνιζον ἐπ' αὐτὸν λίθους.   6. Δὰν ὁ ἀδελφὸς
αὐτοῦ.   7. ἐδεήθησαν αὐτῶν .. καὶ τότε ἐποίησαν μετ' αὐτῶν εἰρήνην ...
καὶ τότε ἐποίησεν Ἰακὼβ μετ' αὐτῶν εἰρήνην ...   8. καὶ ἐποίησαν
αὐτοὺς ὑποφόρους καὶ ἀπέδωκαν αὐτοῖς πᾶσαν τὴν αἰχμαλωσίαν.   9. καὶ
ᾠκοδόμησε Ἰακὼβ Θάμναν καὶ Ἰούδα Ἀρβαήλ.

---

[1] Chron. Jer. בא יעקב אביו לעזרו היו הורגין את יהודה היה מת יהודה כי
יעקב משך את קשתו וירה בחצים וכלם עראות בימינא וגם שלף את
עצמם לשכרם ועשו שלום ביניהם ונתנו להם[2] חרבו . ומסרו
מנחה ושלמו להם יעקב כל צאנם ששבו כפליים וחזרו להם את השבי
ובנה יעקב וגם יהודה . Hence in text for נטה read בנה with Chron.
Jer. and T. Jud.   [*] Here Chron. Jer. add ליוסף וזה שאמר יעקב
בנו הנה נתתי לך שכם אחר שאחיך אשר לקחתי בחרבי ובקשתי

APPENDIX II

LATE HEBREW TESTAMENT OF NAPHTALI

זה צוואת נפתלי בן יעקב:

(Containing Fragments of the Ancient Testament. These are underlined.)

צוואת נפתלי: נפתלי בן יעקב נפתולי אלהים. ויהי כאשר הוזקן נפתלי
ובא בשיבה טובה ובא שלם בגבורתו ועבד משפט שוח ויחל לצוואת את
בניו ויאמר להן. בני בואו וגשו וקיבלו מצות אביכם, 2 ויענו ויאמרו
לו. הננו *שומעין לקיים¹ לכל אשר תצונו. 3 ויאמר להם. אינני מצוה
לכם לא על כספי ולא על זהבי *ולא על כל העבורה² אשר אני מניח
לכם תחת השמש. ואיני מצויכם³ דבר כבר שאינכם יכולין לעמוד בו.
אבל אני אומר לכם דבר קל שאחם יכולין לקיימו. 4 וענו והשיבו
בניו שנית ואמרו דבר אבינו כי שומעין אנו. 5 אמר להם. איני מצויכם
אלא על יראת י״י אותו תעבודו ובו תדבקו. 6 אמרו לו. ומה הוא
צריך לעבודתינו. אמר להם. לא הוא צריך לכל בריה אלא כל בריות
עולמו צריכין לו. אבל לא תהו יצר לעולמו אלא כדי שיראו מלפניו
ושלא יעשה איש לרעהו מה שלא רצה לנפשו. 7 אמרו לו. אבינו.
כלום ראיתנו שפירשנו מדרכיך ומדרכי אבותינו ימין ושמאל. 8 אמר
להן. עד י״י ואני בכם שכדבריכם כן הוא אבל יראתי על העתידות לבוא'
שלא תתעו אחרי אלילי בני נכר ולא תלכו בחוקי טיי הארצות ולא

The text follows the Oxford MS. d. 11, pp. 32 sqq., already
collated by Gaster but here collated afresh. This MS., which is of
the thirteenth century, is here designated as A. The readings from
P and J are taken from Gaster's edition. P is a twelfth-century
MS. now in Paris, and J represents the text of the Testament
printed by Wertheimer, 1890, in Jerusalem.

---

¹J. A reads שומע ולקיים.   ²J. A reads הכבודה.   ³A. P J
read מצוה אתכם.   ⁴A marg. P J. A reads לברו.

תשתתפו עם בני יוסף . זולתי עם בני לוי ועם בני יהודה .   9 אמרו לו .

ומה ראית לצוֵינו על ככה .   10 אמ' להן . לפי שידעתי שעתידין בני

יוסף לסור מאחרי י"י אלי'[1] אבותם ולהחטיא את בני ישראל ולהנלותן

מעל הארץ הטובה בארץ לא לנו . כאשר נלינו על ידו[2] לשיעבוד[3] מצרים .

T. Naph.
v. 1-3. II ועוד אספרה נא לכם החזון אשר ראיתי בהיותי רועה בצאן .

2 ראיתי והנה י"ב אחי רועים עמי בשדה . והנה אבינו בא ואמר לנו .

בניי רוצו[4] ותיפסו לפניי[5] כל אחד אשר יעלה בחלקו .   3 נענה ונאמר

לו ומה נתפוס הנה אין אנו רואים אלא השמש והירח והכוכבים[6] .

4 כשמוע לוי כן ויתפוש מרדע בידו וידלנ על השמש וישב וירכב עליו .

5 וכראות יהודה ויעש גם הוא כן ותפס מרדע ויקפץ על הירח וירכב

עליו   6 וגם כל[7] השבטים . כל אחד מהם רכב על כוכבו ומזלו בשמים .

ונשאר זולתי[8] יוסף לבדו בארץ .   7 אמר לו יעקב אבינו . בני ואתה

*למה (לא)[9] עשית כאחיך . אמר לו . אבי ומה לילודי[10] אשה בשמים

וסופן על הארץ יעמודו .

v. 6. III כדבר יוסף כן הנה שור[11] אחד גבוה עומד אצלו ולו כנפים נדולים

ככנפי החסידה וקרניו נבוהין כקרני ראימים .   2 ויאמר לו יעקב . קום

יוסף בני ורכב עליו .   3 ויקם יוסף וירכב על השור . ויעקב אבינו הלך

v. 7. מאתנו .   4 בעוד ד' שעות היה יוסף מתגאה על השור שפעמים היה

הולך ורץ ופעמים היה בו מעופף עד אשר הגיע אצל יהודה . ויושט יוסף

הנס אשר בידו ויחל להכות את יהודה אחיו .   5 אמר[12] לו יהודה . אחי

למה תכני .   6 אמר לו שבידך י"ב מרדעות ולי אחת . *עתה תנם לי[13]

ויהיה שלום .   7 ומאן[14] יהודה לתתם לו . ויכהו[15] יוסף עד שנטל ממנו

הי' שלא בטובתו ולא נשאר ביד יהודה כי אם ב' מהן .   8 אמר להן

יוסף לי' אחיו מה לכם לרוץ ליהודה[16] ולוי . סרו מאחריהן ולכו אחרי .

9 וכשמעו אחיו מפי יוסף סרו מעל לוי ויהודה כאיש אחד . ללכת אחרי

יוסף . ולא נותר עם יהודה בלתי בנימין ולוי .   10 כראות לוי[17] כן ירד

[1] P J. A reads אלקי.   [2] P J. A reads רדו.   [3] P J. A reads בשעבוד.   [4] A. P J read באו but T. Naph. v. 2 reads προσδραμόντες.
[5] A. Possibly this should be emended into לפי כח, or as Mr. Cowley suggests לפי יכלת, in accordance with T. Naph. v. 2 κατὰ δύναμιν.
P J read לפני כל.   [6] P J add אמר להם ומהם.   [7] P J read תשעת.
[8] P J add שבט.   [9] So Gaster reads, adding לא. Perhaps it would be best to read merely לא with J. P reads לו only.   [10] P J. A reads לילוד.   [11] A adds יותר.   [12] A. P J ויאמר.   [13] A. P J read תן לי עשר.   [14] A. Other MSS. וימאן.   [15] A. P J read והכהו.   [16] A adds only on marg.   [17] P J om.

בעצבון רוחו[1] מעל השמש .   11 אמר לו יוסף[2] לבנימין אחיו . בנימין
אחי הלא אחי אתה . לכה גם אתה עמי . וימאן בנימין ללכת[3] עם יוסף
אחיו .   12 ויהי כהפנות היום הנה רוח גדולה ותפריד בין יוסף לאחיו[4]
ולא נותרו שנים יחד .   13 ויהי כראותי החזון הזה ואמר[5] אותו ליעקב
אבי . ואמר לי . בני חלום הוא לא יעלה ולא יוריד כי לא משנה הוא .

IV   vi. 1.   ולא חלף זמן מרובה ויראוני[6] עוד חזון אחר .   2   שהיינו כולנו
vi. 2, 3.   עומדין עם יעקב אבינו על שפתו של ים הגדול והנה אנייה הולכת בלב
ים בלא מלח ובלא איש .   3 אמר לנו אבינו . הרואים אתם מה אני
רואה . אמרנו לו . רואין אנו .   4 אמר לנו . ממני תראו וכן תעשו .
(vi. 3.)   והפשיט יעקב אבינו את בגדיו והפיל עצמו הימה . וכלנו אחריו .   5 וקדמו
לוי ויהודה תחילה וקפצו לתוכה ויעקב עמם .   6 והנה בספינה כל טוב[7]
שבעולם .   7 אמר להן יעקב אבינו . הביטו נא אל התורן מה כתוב
עליו . שאין ספינה שאין שם שם בעלה[8] כתוב על התורן .   8 ויסתכל לוי
ויהודה ויראו והנה כתוב זו[9] האנייה לבן ברבואל[10] היא וכל טוב שיש
בה .   9 וכשמוע יעקב אבינו כן שמח ונתן קידה והעלה הודייה לה׳ב׳ה .
אמר לא דיי שברכני בארץ אלא ברכני גם בים .   10 מיד אמר לנו .
בני עתה תתגברו[11] וכל אחד מה שיתפוס הוא חלקו .   11 מיד דילג לוי על
התורן הגדול שבה וישב עליו .   12 ושיני לו קפין גם יהודה על התורן
השני הסמוך לתורן של לוי וישב גם הוא עליו .   13 ונשאר אחיי
vi. 4.   החזיקו נבר במשוטו . ויעקב אבינו תפש ב׳ הקברניטין כדי לישר הספינה
בהן .   14 ונשאר יוסף לבדו . אמר לו אבינו . יוסף בני תפוס גם אתה
משוטך . ולא אבה יוסף .   15 כראות אבי כי לא אבה יוסף לתפוס
משוטו אמר לו . בני נש הנה ותפוש אחד מהקברניטין שבידי[12] ותיישר
הספינה ואחיך ישוטו במשוטות עד שהגיעכם אל היבשה .   16 ולימדנו
לכל אחד ואחד ואמר לנו . ככה תנהיגו את הספינה ואינכם מתפחדין מכל
נלי הים ומרוח סערה אם יעמוד עליכם .

V   ויהי בכלותו לצוותו לנו ויתעלם מעלינו[12] .   2 ויחתפוס יוסף כל[13]
הקברניטין אחד מימינו ואחד משמאלו ושאר אחיי משיטין . ותשט
האנייה ותצף על פני המים .   3 ולוי ויהודה יושבים על *ב׳ התורנין[14]
לראות איזה דרך תלך האנייה .   4 כל שעה שהיה דעת יוסף ויהודה שוין .

---

[1] P om.   [2] PJ om.   [3] A om.   [4] PJ ובין אחיו.   [5] A. PJ read
ואומר.   [6] Read ואראה with O.   [7] A over an erasure. PJ read
טובות.   [8] P. A reads תעלה.   [9] A marg. P add על תורן.   [10] A.
PJ read ברכאל.   [11] A marg. PJ. A תתנבא (?).   [12] A om. but
adds on marg.   [13] A. PJ read בשני.   [14] A. PJ read התורן.

שיהודה יורה ליוסף לאיזו דרך טוב לשם יטה יוסף הספינה הלכה¹ הספינה
בשלום בלא מכשול . 5 ולפי שעה נפלה מריבה בין יוסף ליהודה . ולא
פירנס יוסף הספינה כמאמר אביו וכאילוף יהודה . ותלך הספינה דרך
עקלתון והיכוה² גלי הים [אל הסלע] עד שנשתברה .

vi. 5.

VI אז ירדו לוי ויהודה מעל התורנים להימלט איש על נפשו .
וגם שאר אחי כל אחד ממנו ונמלטנו על³ נפישנו אל היבשה .
2 והנה בא יעקב אבינו ומצאנו מטורפין אחד הנה ואחד הנה . 3 אמר
לנו . מה לכם בניי . שמא לא הינהגתם האנייה כראוי לה כאשר צויתי
לכם . 4 ונאמר לו . חי נפש עבדיך כי לא סרנו⁴ מכל אשר צויתנו.
אבל יוסף פשע⁵ בדבר שלא יישר האנייה כציויך וכאשר הורהו יהודה
ולוי בקנאו להם . 5 ויאמר לנו הראו לי איה מקומה . וירא והנה ראשי
התורנים נראין והנה צפה על פני המים . 6 וישרוק אבי ונתקבצנו⁶
אליו כלנו . 7 ויפול הימה בתחילה⁷ וירפא את הספינה . 8 ויוכח ליוסף
ואמר לו . אל תוסף בני להתל לקנא באחיך כמעט שעוברין⁸ כל אחיך
על ידך .

VII וכאשר סיפרתי החזון הזה לאבי . ספק אבי כפיו ויאנח נתזלגנה עיניו
דמעות . 2 ואחל עד בוש ולא אמר לי דבר . 3 ואתפוס יד אבי
לחבקה ולנשקה ואומרה לו . אי עבד י"י למה זלגו עיניך . 4 אמר לי .
בני על הישנות לך החזון נפל ליבי *ותשתומם נוייתי⁹ על יוסף בני . שאני
אהבתיו מכולכם ועל משחת בני יוסף אתם גולים ומתפזרין לבין האומות.
5 שחזיונך ראשון והשני כולהן¹⁰ שוין חזון אחד הוא . על כן בני אני
מצוה לכם שלא תתחברו עם בני יוסף אלא עם לוי ויהודה .

VIII וגם אנידה לכם שיפול גורלי במיטב טבור הארץ ותאכלו ותשבעו
(Deut. xxxii. 15.)
ממנדי ערניה . 2 מזהירכם אני שלא תבעטו במשמניכם ולא תמרדון
ולא¹¹ תמרו את פי י"י המשביעכם מטובי אדמתו . 3 ולא תשכחו את
י"י אלהיכם אלהי אבותיכם שבו בחר אבינו אברהם כשנתפלנו הדורות
בימי פלג . 4 כי¹² אז ירד הק' משמי מרומו והוריד ע' מלאכי שרת¹³
ומיכאל בראשון . ¹⁴ 5 א'¹² וציוה לכל אחד מהן שילמדו לע' משפחות

---

¹ A² prefixes ו.   ² A. PJ read והיטוה. Best read ורכוה or הדיחוה as T. Naph. vi. 5 suggests, or omit אל הסלע.   ³ PJ. A reads אל.   ⁴ PJ. A reads סרינו.   ⁵ A. PJ read טעה.   ⁶ PJ. A reads ונקבצנו.   ⁷ Read בתחילה.   ⁸ A. Better read נאבדו with PJ.   ⁹ A. PJ read וישתומם גופי.   ¹⁰ A. PJ read שניהם.   ¹¹ A. PJ read ואל.   ¹² PJ om.   ¹³ A. PJ read השרת.   ¹⁴ Schnapp emends rightly into בראשם.

יוצאי ירך נח ע' לשון .   6 מיד[1] ירדו המלאכים ועשו[2] כציוי בראן .
ולא נשאר לשון הקודש לשון עברי כי אם בבית שם ועבר ובבית
אברהם אבינו שהוא מבני בניהן .

IX ובו ביום הוציא מיכאל פרק מלפני הק׳ב׳ה׳ ואמר לע' אומות לכל
אחת בפני עצמה .   2 אתם ידעתם את המרד אשר אתכם ואת הקשר
אשר קשרתם על אדוני השמים והארץ . ועתה בחרו לכם היום את מי
תעבודו ומי מליצכם במרום .   3 ענה נמרוד הרשע ואמר . אני אין לי
גדול מזה שלימד[5] לי ולאומתי כפי שעה לשון כוש .   4 וענתה נם[4]
פוט ומצרים ותובל ויון ומשך ותירס וכן כל אומה ואומה בחרה
במלאכה ולא הזכירה אחת מהן שמו של הק׳ב׳ה׳ .   5 אלא כיון שאמר
מיכאל לאברהם אבינו . אברם את מי אתה תברור ולמי תעבוד . ענה
אברם אני בוחר ואני בורר אלא במי שאמר והיה העולם שיצרני במעי
אמי גויה בתוך גויה ומטיל בה רוח ונשמה . לו אברור ובו אדבק. אני
וזרעי כל ימי עולם .

X אן[1] הפריד עליהן[1] והנחיל +והגדיל[7] לכל אומה ואומה לחלקה
ולגורלה .   2 ומאז היבדלו[1] כל גויי ארמה מהק' זולתי בית אברהם
לבדו נשאר עם בוראו לעבדו ואחריו[1] יצחק ויעקב .   3 לכן בני אני
משביעכם שלא תתעו ולא תעבדו לאל אחר אלא לאותו שבחרו בו
אבותיכם[10] .   4 כי ידוע תדעו שאין כמוהו ואין מי אשר יעשה כמוהו
וכמעשיו בשמים ובארץ ואין מי אשר יפליא לעשות כגבורותיו .   5 ותבינו
מקצת כוחו[11] מבריית האדם כמה פילאי פלאות יש בו .   6 בראו מראשו
*עד רגליו . מאזניו ישמע[12] ומעיניו יביט . ומוחו יבין . ומחוטמו יריח .
ומקניהו יוציא קול ומוושטו יבנים מאכל ומשתה . ומלשונו ידבר . ובפיו
ינמור . בידיו יעשה מלאכתו . ובלבו יחשוב . ובטחולו ישחק . ובכבידו
יכעום . וקיבתו טוחנת . וברגליו הולך . וריאה [בריאה] +לנפש[13] .
ומכליותיו נעוץ .   7 ואין אחד מאובריו יתחלף מאומנותו אלא כל אחד
בשלו .   8 לפיכך נאה לאדם לשום על לבו מכל אילו מי הוא שבראו
ומי הוא שיצרו מטיפה באושה במעי האשה . ומי הוא שמוציאו לאור

T. Naph
ii. 8.

---

¹ P J. Inserted above the line in A.   ² A adds כן above the
line.   ³ P J. A reads שילמד.   ⁴ P J. A inserts above line.
⁵ A marg. P J. A om.   ⁶ A. P J read עליון. A supra lin. P J
add נוים.   ⁷ Read והגריל.   ⁸ A. P J read הבדלו.   ⁹ P J
add אבותינו.   ¹⁰ P J read אבותינו.   ¹¹ P J. A reads רוחו.
¹² P J. A reads שבו ישמע מאחניו.   ¹³ Read לשאוב. Cf. Othioth
of ' R. Akiba ' on p. 148 of text.

העולם תתן לו ראיית עינים והילוך רגלים ומעמידו ומציגו [1] על בוריו ועל
מכונו ותיכן לו נמולין טובים במקום בינה . וזרק בו נשמת חיים ורוח
טהרה מאתו .   9   ואשרי אדם אשר לא יטנף את רוח אלהים [2] הקדושה
אשר שמה ונפחה בקרבו . ואשריו אם ישיבינה טהורה לבוראה כיום
אשר [3] הופקדה בו :   10   עד הנה דברי נפתלי בן ישראל אשר הוכיח
לבניו *בנופת מיתוק חיכו [4] :
סליקא צואת נפתלי בן יעקב :

[1] A P. Read ומשינו with O.   [2] Rest missing in P J.   [3] A
adds above the line.   [4] Corrupt. Read perhaps בשיח מתוק
מנופת = 'with words sweeter than honey.'

APPENDIX III

ARAMAIC AND GREEK FRAGMENTS CONTAINING PHRASES AND CLAUSES FROM AN ORIGINAL (?) SOURCE OF THE TESTAMENT OF LEVI AND THE BOOK OF JUBILEES.

CAMBRIDGE FRAGMENT

(First 14 lines are missing)

(Col. a)			(Col. b)
.. ו . . מאת	15	3	. . . . אחי בבל עדן
דברת די כלא	16		. . . . א די הוו בשכם
למעבד כדין בכ	17		. . . . אחי ואחוי דן
יעקב אבי ורא	18		. . . . בשכם ומה
ואמרן להון ב . . . . ה ד . .	19		מ . . . . . . (עב)די חמסא ואחוי
צביין אינון בברתן ונהוי כולן א(חן)	20		אינון יהודה די אנה ושמעון
ותברין 2 נזורו עורלת בשרכון	21		אחי אזלנא לה . . דֿ לראובן
והתחמיין כ(ואתן) ותהון חתימין	22		אחונן די למד . . . שֹׁר ושור
כואתן במילת . . ט ונהוי לב(ון)	23		(י)הודה קדמא (די) שבק עצנא
(Then three columns missing.)			(A section lost here.)

Where the above texts have parts in common with the Testament of Levi, these are underlined.

BODLEIAN FRAGMENT

(Col. a)

1	שלמא וכל חמדת בכורי ארעא 4
2	כולא למאכל ולמלכות חרבא פנשא
3	וקרבא ונחשירותא ᵃ ותמלא
4	ונצפתא ᵇ וקטלא וכפנא 5 זמנין תאכול
5	חמנין תכפן וזמנין תעמול וזמנין
6	תנות וזמנין תדמוך וזמנין תנוד
7	שנת עינא 6 כען חזי לך הכין רבינך
8	מן כולא והך יהבנא לך רבות שלם
9	עלמא 7 ונגדו שבעתין מן לותי
10	ואנה אתעירת מן שנתי אדין T. Lev. viii. 18.
11	אמרת חזוא הוא דן וכדן אנה
12	מתמה די יהוי לה כל חזוא וטמרת viii. 19.
13	אף דן בלבי ולכל אינש לא גליתה
14	ועלנא על אבי יצחק ואף הוא כרן 8
15	(ברכ)ני 9 אדין כדי הוה ᶜ יעקב
16	.... עשר כל מה דיהות לה כנדרה
17	(וכדי) אנה הוית קרמי בראש
18	(כהונת)ה ולי מכל בנוהי יהב קרבן
19	.... לאל * ואלבשי לבוש כהונתא
20	(ומ)לי ידי ᵈ והוית כהין לאל עלמיא (Jub. xxxii. 3.)
21	וקרבית כל קרבנוהי וברכת לאבי viii. 10.
22	בחיותי וברכת לאחי 10 אדין כולהון
23	ברכוני ואף אבא ברכני ואשלמית

ᵃ As in Syriac. ᵇ Root in Syriac = ' to hiss with rage.'
ᶜ Corrupt for חזה. ᵈ So Jub. xxxii. 3 ' His father clothed him
in the garments of the priesthood and filled his hands.'

(Col. b) (Greek Fragment)

Aramaic (Col. b)

1. להקרבה קורבנוהי בבית אל 11 ואזלנא
2. מבית אל ושרינא בבירת אברהם
3. אבונן לות יצחק אבונה 12 וחזא ᵃ
4. יצחק אבונא לכולנא וברכנא
5. וחרי 13 וכדי ידע די אנה כהין לאל
6. עליון למארי שמיא שארי
7. לפקדה יתי ולאלפא יתי דין
8. כהנותא ואמר לי 14 לוי אזדהר
9. לך ברי ברי מן כל טומאה ומן
10. כל חטא דינך רב הוא מן כל
11. בישרא 15 ובען ברי דין
12. קושטא אחזינך ולא אטמר
13. מינך כל פתגם לאלפותך דין
14. כהונתא 16 לקדמין היזדהר לך
15. ברי מן כל פחז וטמאה ומן כל
16. זנות 17 ואנת אנתתא מן משפחתי
17. סב לך ולא תחל זרעך עם זניאן
18. ארי זרע קדיש אנת וקדיש
19. זרעך היך קודשא ארו כהין
20. קדיש אנת מתקרי לכל זרע
21. אברהם 18 קריב אנת ל(אל ו)קריב
22. לכל קדישוהי כען *אזדכי
23. בבשרך ᵇ מן כל טומאת כל נבר

Reference column: T. Lev. ix. 1? — ix. 5. — ix. 7. — ix. 9. — ix. 10. — (ix. 9 ?) — ii. 10. — (Jub. xxi. 16.)

Greek Fragment

11. καὶ ἀνήλθομεν ἀπὸ Βεθὴλ καὶ κατελύσαμεν ἐν τῇ αὐλῇ Ἀβραὰμ τοῦ πατρὸς ἡμῶν παρὰ Ἰσαὰκ τὸν πατέρα ἡμῶν. 12. καὶ ἴδεν Ἰσαὰκ ὁ πατὴρ ἡμῶν πάντας ἡμᾶς καὶ ηὐλόγησεν ἡμᾶς, καὶ ηὐφράνθη. 13. καὶ ὅτε ἔγνω ὅτι ἐγὼ ἱεράτευσα τῷ Κυρίῳ[1] δεσπότῃ τοῦ οὐρανοῦ ἤρξατο διδάσκειν[2] με τὴν κρίσιν ἱεροσύνης[3] καὶ εἶπεν· 14. Τέκνον[4] Λευί, πρόσεχε σεαυτῷ ἀπὸ πάσης ἀκαθαρσίας[5]. ἡ κρίσις σου μεγάλη ἀπὸ πάσης σαρκός. 15. καὶ νῦν[6] τὴν κρίσιν τῆς ἀληθείας ἀναγγελῶ σοι καὶ οὐ μὴ κρύψω ἀπὸ σοῦ πᾶν ῥῆμα *διδάξω σε[7] 16. πρόσεχε[8] σεαυτῷ[9] ἀπὸ παντὸς συνουσιασμοῦ καὶ ἀπὸ πάσης[10] ἀκαθαρσίας καὶ ἀπὸ πάσης πορνείας. 17. σὺ πρῶτος ἀπὸ τοῦ σπέρματος[11] λαβὲ σεαυτῷ καὶ μὴ βεβηλώσῃς τὸ σπέρμα σου μετὰ †πολλῶν[12]· ἐκ σπέρματος γὰρ ἁγίου εἶ, καὶ *τὸ σπέρμα σου ἁγίασον καὶ τὸ σπέρμα τοῦ ἁγιασμοῦ σου ἐστίν. Ἱερεὺς ἅγιος κληθήσεται τῷ[13] σπέρματι Ἀβραάμ. 18. Ἐγγὺς εἶ κυρίου καὶ σὺ[10] ἐγγὺς[14] τῶν ἁγίων αὐτοῦ. Γίνου[15] καθαρὸς ἐν τῷ σώματί[16] σου ἀπὸ πάσης ἀκαθαρσίας παντὸς ἀνθρώπου

ᵃ Emended in accordance with Gk. Frag. καὶ ἴδεν and Jubilees xxxi. 9 from והוא. ᵇ So Jub. xxi. 16 'Be pure in thy body.'

[1] Aram. = θεῷ τῷ ὑψίστῳ. [2] Aram. = παραγγέλλειν με καὶ διδάσκειν. [3] So this MS. writes this word always. [4] Aram. repeats τέκνον. [5] Aram. adds καὶ ἀπὸ πάσης ἁμαρτίας. [6] Aram. adds τέκνον. [7] Aram. = ὥστε διδάσκειν σε τὴν κρίσιν τῆς ἱερωσύνης. [8] Aram. pref. πρῶτον. [9] Aram. adds τέκνον. [10] Aram. om. [11] Aram. = γένους μου. The Aram. here is really a Hebrew word. [12] Corrupt for πορνῶν. [13] Aram. = ἅγιον τὸ σπέρμα σου ὡς τὸ ἁγίασμα, ὅτι ἱερεὺς ἅγιος σὺ κληθήσῃ τῷ παντί. Here τὸ σπέρμα σου ἁγίασον and τὸ σπέρμα τοῦ ἁγιασμοῦ σου are dittographs. [14] Aram. adds πάντων. [15] Aram. = Γίνου νῦν. [16] Here γίνου . . . σώματί σου agrees with Jub. xxi. 16. See note on Aram.

line 7 דין here T. Lev. ix. 9 has νόμον, but Gk. Frag. κρίσιν. Cf. Deut. xviii. 3 for the phrase κρίσις ἱερωσύνης, i. e. משפט כהנים.

line 16 משפחתי; cp. T. Lev. ix. 10 ἀπὸ γένους, but Gk. Frag. has ἀπὸ τοῦ σπέρματος.

(Col. c)

Aramaic (right column)

1	19 וכדי תהוי קאים למיעל לבית אל
2	הוי סחי במיא [a] ובאדין תהוי לביש
3	לבוש כהנותא 20 וכדי תהוי לביש
4	הוי תאיב תוב ורחיע ידיך
5	ורגליך עד דלא תקרב למדבחא
6	כל דנה 21 וכדי תהוי נסב [b] להקרבה
7	כל די חזה להנסקה למדבחה
8	הוי עוד תאב ורחע ידיך ורגליך
9	22 ומהקריב אעין מהצלחין ובקר
10	אינון לקודמין מן תולעא
11	ובאדין הסק אינון ארי כדנה
12	חזיתי לאברהם אבי מיזדהר
13	23 מן כל תריעשר מיני אעין אמר
14	לי די חזין להסקה מינהון למדבחה
15	די ריח חנהון בשים סליק 24 ואלין
16	אינן שמהתהון ארזא ודפרנא
17	וסגרא ואמולא [c] †ושוחא [d] †וארונא [e]
18	ברותא ותאנתא ואע משחא
19	ערא והדסה ואעי †דקתא [f] 25 אלין

Side references: T. Lev. ix. 11 (lines 1–2); ix. 11 (line 6); x. 12 (line 13).

Greek (left column)

19. καὶ ὅταν εἰσπορεύει ἐν *τοῖς
ἁγίοις[1] λούου ὕδατι πρῶτον[2] καὶ τότε
ἐνδιδύσκου τὴν στολὴν τῆς ἱεροσύνης.
20. καὶ ὅταν ἐνδιδύσκει νίπτου πάλιν
τὰς χεῖράς σου
καὶ τοὺς πόδας σου πρὸ τοῦ ἐγγίσαι
πρὸς τὸν βωμὸν προσενέγκαι ὁλοκάρπωσιν
21. καὶ ὅταν μέλλεις προσφέρειν *ὡς
ἀδίαν ἐνέγκε[3] ἐπὶ τὸν βωμόν,
πάλιν νίπτου τὰς χεῖράς σου καὶ τοὺς
πόδας σου
22. καὶ ἀνάφερε τὰ ξύλα πρῶτον[2]
(ἐ)σχισμένα, ἐπισκοπῶν αὐτὰ πρῶτον
ἀπὸ *παντὸς μολυσμοῦ[4]
23. *ιβ ξύλα[5] εἴρηκέν
μοι *ἐπὶ τὸν βωμὸν πρόσφερε[6]
ὧν ἐστιν ὁ καπνὸς αὐτῶν ἡδὺς ἀναβαίνων. 24. καὶ ταῦτα τὰ ὀνόματα
αὐτῶν, κέδρον καὶ οὐεδεφῶνα[7]
    καὶ *σχίνον καὶ στρόβιλον[8] καὶ πίτυν
καὶ †ὀλδίνα[9]
καὶ βερώθα *καν θεχὰκ[10]

---

[a] With 19–21, cf. Jub. xxi. 16 'Wash thyself with water before thou approachest to offer on the altar, and wash thy hands and thy feet before thou drawest near the altar, and when thou art done sacrificing, wash again thy hands and thy feet.' [b] = προσλαμβάνεις (?). Cf. ver. 52 for another instance of this expression. [c] Corrupt for איסטרובילא = στρόβιλος (Cowley). [d] Corrupt. Gk. Fr. and Jub. give πίτυς. Read שימא. Lévi conjectures אשוחא a species of cedar. [e] Corrupt for אורנא = κέδρος. [f] What was in the original here is uncertain. Perhaps

---

[1] Aram. = οἴκῳ θεοῦ. T. Lev. ix. 11 supports Gk. Fr. [2] Aram. om. [3] Corrupt for ὅσα δεῖ ἀνενέγκαι (Wilkins). [4] Aram. = σκώληκος καὶ τότε λαβὲ αὐτά· οὕτως γὰρ εἶδον τὸν Ἀβραὰμ τὸν πατέρα μου προσέχοντα. [5] Aram. = ἐκ πάντων τῶν δώδεκα γενῶν ξύλων. [6] Aram. = ἐξ ὧν (?) καθήκει προσφέρειν ἐπὶ τὸν βωμόν. [7] Corrupt transliteration of ודפרנא. [8] Aram. and Jub. = ἀμύγδαλον καὶ στρόβιλον. [9] Corrupt transliteration of אורנא. [10] Here καν is a corruption of καί and θεχάκ a corrupt transliteration of תאנתא. Cf. similar corruption, Jub. xxi. 12 where we have τἀνἀκ. See note f.

line 4 רחע, i.e. the Hebrew רחץ. Not Aram.

20 אינן די אמר לי די חזין [g] להסקה

21 מנהן ל(תחו)ת עלתא על מדבחה

22 וכדי (הסקת) [h] מן אעי אלין על

23 מדבחה ונורא ישרא להדלקא

καὶ κυπάρισσον καὶ δάφνην [11] καὶ
ἀσφάλαθον. 25. *Ταῦτα εἴρηκεν ὅτι
ταῦτά ἐστιν ἅ σε [12] ἀναφέρειν ὑποκάτω
τῆς ὁλοκαυτώσεως ἐπὶ τοῦ θυσιαστηρίου [13]

καὶ τὸ πῦρ τότε [14] ἄρξει ἐκκαίειν

I append here in parallel columns, the three lists of these trees, as
they help to settle the question of the mutual relations of the Aramaic
and Greek. The names of the trees are given in Greek so far as
possible :—

ARAMAIC.	GREEK FRAG.	JUB. XXI. 12.
κέδρος	κέδρος	κυπάρισσος
δεφράνα	δεφράνα	δεφράν
ἀμύγδαλος	σχῖνος	ἀμύγδαλος
στρόβιλος	στρόβιλος	στρόβιλος
πίτυς	πίτυς	πίτυς
אורנא	ὀλδίνα (i. e. אורנא)	κέδρος
βερώθα	βερώθα	βῦράθι
συκῆ	συκῆ	συκῆ
ἐλαία	κυπάρισσος	ἐλαία
δάφνη	δάφνη	μυρσίνη
μυρσίνη	ἀσφάλαθος	δάφνη
ἀσφάλαθος (?)		ἀσφάλαθος

Here the first and third lists practically imply the same original.
They diverge in their order. Jub. relegates no. 1 of Aram. to the sixth
place and possibly no. 6 of Aram. to its first place. Also it transposes
the order of 10 and 11.

The second list differs from the first and third in that it omits
ἀμύγδαλος and ἐλαία and adds σχῖνος. Again it gives κυπάρισσος where
the other lists give μυρσίνη. From these facts it is clear that the Greek
Frag. cannot be the source of the Aramaic.

דולבא = 'plane tree,' see Rosh ha-Shan., 23 a, where ten different names
are applied to the cedar. Jub. xxi. 12 = φυλάσσου εἰς τὰ ξύλα προσφορᾶς
προσφέρειν ταῦτα τὰ ξύλα ἐπὶ τὸν βωμόν (so MS. A), κυπάρισσον, δεφράν,
ἀμύγδαλον, στρόβιλον, πίτυν, κέδρον, βῦράθι, τᾶνᾶκ (corrupt transliteration of
תאנתא), δένδρον ἐλαίας, μυρσίνην, δάφνην, κέδρον ὀνομαζομένην αρβατ (corrupt
for ἀσφάλαθος) (emended text).   [g] Read חין = δεῖ.   [h] Restored by
Cowley.

Here Gk. om. καὶ ἐλαίαν.   [11] Aram. trans. before κυπάρισσον against
Gk. and Jub.   [12] Corrupt, perhaps, for ταῦτά ἐστιν (ἅ εἴρηκέν μοι) ἅ δεῖ.
So Aram.   [13] Aram. adds καὶ ὅτε . . . ἐκ τούτων τῶν ξύλων ἐπὶ τὸν βωμόν.
[i] Aram. om.

(Col. d)

1 בהון והא באדין תשרא למזרק דמא

2 על כותלי מדבחה 26 ועוד רחע ידיך

3 ורגליך מן דמא ושרי להנסקה אבריה

4 מליחי. 27 ואשה‏ᵇ הוי מתנסק לקדמין

5 ועלוהי חפי תרבא ולא יתחזה לה

6 דם ‏†נסבת תוראᶜ 28 ובתרוהי צוארה

7 ובתר צוארה ידוהי ובתר ידוהי

8 ניעא עם בן דפנא ובתר ידיאᵈ

9 ירכאתא עם שדרת חרצא

10 ובתר ירכאתא רגלין רחיען עם

11 קרביא 29 וכולהון מליחין במלח כדי

12 חזה להון כמסתהון 30 ובתר דנה נישפא

13 בליל במשחא ובתר כולא חמר נסך

14 והקטיר עליהון לבונה ויהון (כל)

15 עובדיך בסרך וכל קורבניך (לרעו)א

16 לריח ניחח קודם אל עליון 31 (וכל די)

17 תהוה עביד בסרך הוי עב(יד במדה)

18 ובמתקל לא תותר צבו די לא (הזה)

19 ולא תחסר מן חושבן *חזת.. אע(ין)ᵉ

20 חזיןᶠ להקרבה לכל די סליק למדב(חא)

21 32 לתורא רבא ככר‏ᵍ אען ליא במתקל

22 ואם תרבא בלחודוהי סליק שיתה

23 מנין ואם פר תורין הוא די סליק

ἐν αὐτοῖς, τότε ἄρξει κατασπένδειν τὸ αἷμα ἐπὶ τὸν τοῖχον τοῦ θυσιαστηρίου. 26. καὶ πάλιν νίψαι σου τὰς χεῖρας καὶ τοὺς πόδας ἀπὸ τοῦ αἵματος, καὶ ἄρξει τὰ μέλη ἀναφέρειν ἠλισμένα. 27. τὴν κεφαλὴν ἀνάφερε πρῶτον καὶ κάλυπτε αὐτὴν τῷ στέατι. καὶ μὴ ὀπτανέσθω τὸ αἷμα ἐπὶ τῆς κεφαλῆς αὐτῆς. 28. καὶ μετὰ τοῦτο τὸν τράχηλον καὶ μετὰ τοῦτο τοὺς ὤμους, καὶ μετὰ ταῦτα τὸ στῆθος μετὰ τῶν πλευρῶν, καὶ μετὰ ταῦτα τὴν ὀσφὺν σὺν τῷ νώτῳ,

καὶ μετὰ ταῦτα τοὺς πόδας πεπλυμένους σὺν τοῖς ἐνδοσθείοις. 29. καὶ πάντα ἠλισμένα ἐν ἅλατι ὡς καθήκει αὐτοῖς αὐτάρκως. 30. καὶ μετὰ ταῦτα σεμίδαλιν ἀναπεποιημένον ἐν ἐλαίῳ, καὶ μετὰ ταῦτα οἶνον σπεῖσον καὶ θυμίασον ἐπάνω λίβανον †τὸ ηεσεσθαι† [1] τὸ ἔργον σου ἐν τάξει καὶ πᾶσα προσφορά σου εἰς εὐδόκησιν καὶ ὀσμὴν εὐωδίας ἔναντι Κυρίου ὑψίστου. 31. καὶ ὅσα ἂν ποιῇς, ἐν τάξει ποίει ἃ ποιῇς ἐν μέτρῳ καὶ σταθμῷ. καὶ μὴ περισσεύσῃς μηθὲν ὅσα οὐ καθήκει. καὶ †τῷ καθηκι τῶν οὕτως ξύλα† καθήκει [2] ἀναφέρεσθαι ἐπὶ τὸν βωμόν. 32. τῷ ταύρῳ τῷ τελείῳ τάλαντον

ξύλων καθήκει αὐτῷ ἐν σταθμῷ, καὶ εἰς τὸ στέαρ μόνον ἀναφέρεσθαι ἐξ μνᾶς καὶ τῷ ταύρῳ τῷ δευτέρῳ [3] πεντήκοντα μνᾶς. καὶ εἰς τὸ στέπρ αὐτοῦ μόνον πέντε μνᾶς.

(The next four columns of the Aramaic are missing.)

ᵃ Read מליחין. ᵇ Emend into ראשא with Gk. ᶜ Gk. = על ראשה.
ᵈ Read ניעא. Cowley suggests דנא. ᵉ Read חזי די אעין. ᶠ MS. reads חזיק. ᵍ MS. reads ככר.

---

[1] Corrupt (?) for τοῦ ἔσεσθαι. [2] Defective and corrupt. Perhaps we should read μὴ ἐλαττώσῃς τοῦ λογισμοῦ τοῦ καθήκοντος τῶν ξύλων τῶν καθηκόντων. This suggestion is supported by ver. 52 below, where we have λογισμὸν τῶν ξύλων. The Aram. also favours this suggestion, and the expressions that follow ככר אעין. Wilkins suggests that οὕτως is a remnant of ἐλαττώσῃς. For conjunction of the two ideas περισσεύειν and ἐλαττοῦν see Deut. iv. 2 ; Ecclus. xlii. 21 ; Eccles. iii. 14. [3] = השני (cp. vers. 38, 41) but Aram. = השור. For phrase cf. Judg. vi. 25.

33. καὶ εἰς μόσχον τέλειον μ̄ μναῖ. 34. καὶ εἰ κριὸς ἐκ προβάτων ἢ τράγος ἐξ αἰγῶν τὸ προσφερόμενον ᾖ, καὶ τούτῳ λ̄ μναῖ, καὶ τῷ στέατι τρεῖς μναῖ. 35. καὶ εἰ ἄρνα ἐκ προβάτων ἢ ἔριφον ἐξ αἰγῶν κ̄ μναῖ· καὶ τῷ στέατι β̄ μναῖ. 36. καὶ εἰ ἀμνὸς τέλειος ἐνιαύσιος ἢ ἔριφος ἐξ αἰγῶν ῑε μναῖ, καὶ τῷ στέατι μίαν ἥμισυ μνῦν. 37. καὶ ἅλας †ἀποδεδεικτω[1] τῷ ταύρῳ τῷ μεγάλῳ ἀλῆσαι τὸ κρέας αὐτοῦ, καὶ ἀνένεγκε ἐπὶ τὸν βωμόν. σάτον καθήκει τῷ ταύρῳ. καὶ ᾧ ἂν περισσεύσει τοῦ ἁλὸς ἄλησον ἐν αὐτῷ τὸ δέρμα. 38. καὶ τῷ ταύρῳ τῷ δευτέρῳ τὰ πέντε μέρη ἀπὸ τῶν ἑξ μερῶν τοῦ σάτου. καὶ τοῦ μόσχου τὸ δίμοιρον τοῦ σάτου. 39. καὶ τῷ κριῷ τὸ ἥμισυ τοῦ σάτου, καὶ τῷ τράγῳ τὸ ἴσον. 40. καὶ τῷ ἀρνίῳ κπὶ τῷ ἐρίφῳ τὸ τρίτον τοῦ σάτου. καὶ σεμίδαλις καθήκουσα αὐτοῖς· 41. τῷ ταύρῳ τῷ μεγάλῳ[2] καὶ τῷ ταύρῳ τῷ β̄ καὶ τῷ μοσχαρίῳ, σάτον σεμίδαλιν. 42. καὶ τῷ κριῷ καὶ τῷ τράγῳ τὰ δύο μέρη τοῦ σάτου καὶ τῷ ἀρνίῳ καὶ τῷ ἐρίφῳ ἐξ αἰγῶν τὸ τρίτον τοῦ σάτου καὶ τὸ ἔλαιον. 43. καὶ τὰ τέταρτον τοῦ σάτου τῷ ταύρῳ ἀναπεποιημένον ἐν τῇ σεμιδάλει ταύτη[ν]. 44. καὶ τῷ κριῷ τὸ ἕκτον τοῦ σάτου, καὶ τῷ ἀρνίῳ τὸ ὄγδοον τοῦ σάτου καὶ ἀμνοῦ καὶ οἶνον κατὰ τὸ μέτρον τοῦ ἐλαίου τῷ ταύρῳ καὶ τῷ κριῷ καὶ τῷ ἐρίφῳ κατασπεῖσαι σπονδήν. 45. Λιβανωτοῦ σίκλοι ἐξ τῷ ταύρῳ καὶ τὸ ἥμισυ αὐτοῦ τῷ κριῷ καὶ τὸ τρίτον αὐτοῦ τῷ ἐρίφῳ, καὶ πᾶσα ἡ σεμίδαλις ἀναπεποιημένη· 46. ἢ(ν) ἂν προσαγάγεις μόνον οὐκ ἐπὶ στέατος† προσωχθίσεται[3] ἐπ' αὐτὴν λιβάνου ὁλκὴ σίκλων δύο· καὶ τὸ τρίτον τοῦ σάτου τὸ τρίτον τυῦ ὑφή ἐστιν. 47. καὶ τὰ δύο μέρη τοῦ βάτου καὶ ὁλκῆς τῆς μνᾶς ῡ σίκλων ἐστίν. καὶ τοῦ σικλίου τὸ τέταρτον ὁλκὴ θερμὸν δ̄ ἐστιν· γίνεται ὁ σίκλος ὡσεὶ ῑϛ† θερμοὶ καὶ ὁλκῆς μιᾶς. 48. καὶ νῦν, τέκνον μου, ἄκουσον τοὺς λόγους μου καὶ ἐνωτίσαι τὰς ἐντολάς μου, καὶ μὴ ἀποστήτωσαν οἱ λόγοι μου οὗτοι ἀπὸ τῆς καρδίας σου ἐν πάσαις ταῖς ἡμέραις σου, ὅτι ἱερεὺς σὺ ἅγιος κυρίου. 49. καὶ ἱερεῖς ἔσονται πᾶν τὸ σπέρμα σου· καὶ τοῖς υἱοῖς σου οὕτως ἐντεῖλον ἵνα ποιήσουσιν κατὰ τὴν κρίσιν[4] ταύτην ὡς σοὶ ὑπέδειξα. 50. Οὕτως γάρ μοι ἐνετείλατο ὁ πατὴρ Ἀβραὰμ ποιεῖν καὶ ἐντέλλεσθαι τοῖς υἱοῖς μου. 51. καὶ νῦν, τέκνον, χαίρω ὅτι ἐξελέχθης εἰς ἱεροσύνην ἁγίαν καὶ προσενεγκεῖν θυσίαν κυρίῳ ὑψίστῳ, ὡς καθήκει κατὰ τὸ προστεταγμένον τούτῳ ποιεῖν. 52. ὅταν παραλαμβάνεις θυσίαν ποιεῖν ἔναντι κυρίου ἀπὸ πάσης σαρκὸς κατὰ τὸν λογισμὸν τῶν ξύλων ἐπιδέχου οὕτως, ὡς σοὶ ἐντέλλομαι, καὶ τὸ ἅλας καὶ τὴν σεμίδαλιν καὶ τὸν οἶνον καὶ τὸν λίβανον ἐπιδέχου ἐκ τῶν χειρῶν αὐτῶν ἐπὶ πάντα κτήνη. 53. καὶ[5] ἐπὶ πᾶσαν ὥραν νίπτου τὰς χεῖρας καὶ τοὺς πόδας ὅταν πορεύει πρὸς τὸ θυσιαστήριον·

(Jub. xxi.
16–18 =
53–56.)

---

[1] A corrupt form of ἀποδείκνυμι. The context shows that an imperative is needed here. Now the 2nd sing. imper. = תורה, which the Greek translator should have rendered by βάλλε. [2] Seems to be the equivalent of τελείῳ = רבא in ver. 32. [3] Corrupt for προσενεχθήσεται. [4] = משפט. [5] With 53–56 cf. Jub. xxi. 16–18 which I here retrovert into Greek. 16. καὶ ἐπὶ πᾶσαν ὥραν γίνου καθαρὸς ἐν τῷ σώματί σου καὶ πλύνε σεαυτὸν ἐν ὕδατι πρὸ τοῦ ἐλθεῖν τοῦ προσφέρειν ἐπὶ τὸν βωμόν, καὶ νίπτου τὰς χεῖρας καὶ τοὺς πόδας πρὸ τοῦ ἐγγίσαι πρὸς τὸν βωμόν, καὶ ὅτε τὴν θυσίαν ἐτέλεσας, πάλιν νίπτου τὰς χεῖρας καὶ τοὺς πόδας. 17. καὶ μὴ ὀφθήτω πᾶν αἷμα ἐπί σοι μηδὲ ἐπὶ τῇ στολῇ σου . . . . . . κάλυπτε αὐτὸ τῇ γῇ. 18. καὶ μὴ φάγε τὸ

καὶ ὅταν ἐκπορεύεις ἐκ τῶν ἁγίων, πᾶν αἷμα μὴ ἁπτέσθω τῆς στολῆς σου· οὐκ
ἀνήψῃς αὐτῷ αὐθήμερον.　54. καὶ τὰς χεῖρας καὶ τοὺς πόδας νίπτου διὰ παντὸς ἀπὸ
πάσης τῆς σαρκός.　55. καὶ μὴ ὀφθήτω ἐπὶ σοὶ πᾶν αἷμα καὶ πᾶσα ψυχή†·[1] τὸ γὰρ
αἷμα ψυχή ἐστιν ἐν τῇ σαρκί.　56. καὶ ὃ ἐὰν ἐν οἴκῳ †ουσῃς σεαυτὸν πᾶν κρέας
φαγεῖν [κε]κάλυπτε τὸ αἷμα αὐτοῦ τῇ γῇ πρῶτον πρὶν ἢ φαγεῖν σε ἀπὸ τῶν κρεῶν καὶ

(Jub. οὐκέτι ἔσῃ ἐσθίων ἐπὶ τοῦ αἵματος.　57. *οὕτως γάρ μοι ἐνετείλατο ὁ πατήρ μου
xxi. 1.) ᾿Αβραάμ[2], ὅτι οὕτως εὗρεν ἐν τῇ γραφῇ τῆς βίβλου τοῦ Νῶε περὶ τοῦ αἵματος.
58. καὶ νῦν, ὡς σοί, τέκνον ἀγαπητόν, ἐγὼ λέγω, ἠγαπημένος σὺ τῷ πατρί σου καὶ
ἅγιος κυρίου ὑψίστου· καὶ ἠγαπημένος ἔσῃ ὑπὲρ πάντας τοὺς ἀδελφούς σου.　59. τῷ
σπέρματί σου εὐλογηθήσεται ἐν τῇ γῇ καὶ τὸ σπέρμα σου ἕως πάντων τῶν αἰώνων
†ἐνεχθήσεται ἐν βιβλίῳ μνημοσύνου ζωῆς.　60. καὶ οὐκ ἐξαληφθήσεται τὸ ὄνομά
σου καὶ τὸ ὄνομα τοῦ σπέρματός σου ἕως τῶν αἰώνων.　61. καὶ νῦν, τέκνον Λευί,
εὐλογημένον ἔσται τὸ σπέρμα σου ἐπὶ τῆς γῆς εἰς πάσας τὰς γενεὰς τῶν αἰώνων.

T. Lev. 62. καὶ ὅτε ἀνεπληρώθησάν μοι ἑβδομάδες τέσσαρες ἐν τοῖς ἔτεσιν τῆς ζωῆς μου
xi. 1. ἐν ἔτεσιν ὀγδόῳ καὶ εἰκοστῷ ἔλαβον γυναῖκα ἐμαυτῷ, ἐκ τῆς συγγενείας ᾿Αβραὰμ τοῦ
πατρός μου Μελχάν, θυγατέρα Βαθουήλ, υἱοῦ Λαβά, ἀδελφοῦ μητρός μου.　63.
xi. 2. καὶ ἐν γαστρὶ λαβοῦσα ἐξ ἐμοῦ ἔτεκεν υἱὸν πρῶτον καὶ ἐκάλεσα τὸ ὄνομα αὐτοῦ
Γηρσώμ· εἶπα γὰρ ὅτι πάροικον ἔσται τὸ σπέρμα μου ἐν γῇ, ᾗ ἐγεννήθην· πάροικοί
xi. 3. ἐσμεν ὡς τούτῳ ἐν τῇ γῇ †τῇ μητέρα νομιζομένη†.　64. καὶ ἐπὶ τοῦ παιδαρίου
ἴδον ἐγὼ ἐν τῷ ὁράματί μου, ὅτι ἐκβεβλημένος ἔσται αὐτὸς καὶ τὸ σπέρμα αὐτοῦ ἀπὸ
τῆς ἀρχῆς ἱεροσύνης ἔσται [τω σπέρμα αὐτοῦ].

αἷμα, αὐτὸ γάρ ἐστιν ἡ ψυχή· οὐκέτι ἔσῃ ἐσθίων τὸ αἷμα.　　[1] †καὶ πᾶσα ψυχή†·
τὸ γὰρ αἷμα ψυχή ἐστιν. Here Jub. xxi. 18 'And do not eat any blood;
for it is the soul,' shows what should be read.　　[2] Cf. Jub. xxi. 1
where Abraham gives these commands to Isaac, and yet agrees with
Test. Lev. ix. 6 where Isaac is represented as passing them on to Levi.

(Col. c)

(Two lines missing.)

66 . . ה כזמ
(והר)ת עוד
(וקרא)תי שמה (קהת . 67 וחזיתי) די לה
(תהו)ה כנשת כל (עמא ודי) לה תהוה
(כהנ)ותא בבתא (לכל יש)ראל
68 בשנת אר(בא ותל)תין לחיי
יליד בירחא קמ(אה בח)ד ליר(חא)
עם מדנח שמש(א) . 69 ועוד
אוספת והוית עמה וילידת לי בר
תליתוי וקראתי שמה מררי ארי
מר לי עלוהי לחדה ארי כדי יליד
הוא מית *והוה מריר לי עלוהי
סגיא מן די.ימות ᵇ ובעית והתחננת
עלוהי והיה בכל מרר 70 בשנת
ארבעין לחיי ילידת ביירחה תלית(י)
71 ועוד אוספת והויתי עמה והרת
וילידת לי ברתא ושויתי שמהא
יוכבד אמ(רת) כדי ילידת לי ליקר
ילידת לי לכבוד לישראל
72 בשנת שחין וארבע לי לחיי וילידת
בחד בחודשא שביעיא מן בתר די

Marginal references (left column): T. Lev. xi. 6. / xi. 5. / xi. 4. / xi. 7. / xi. 8.

65. Λ ἐτῶν ἤμην ὅτε ἐγεννήθη ἐν τῇ ζωῇ μου, καὶ ἐν τῷ ī μηνὶ ἐγεννήθη ἐπὶ δυσμὰς ἡλίου. 66. καὶ πάλιν συλλαβοῦσα ἔτεκεν ἐξ ἐμοῦ κατὰ τὸν καιρὸν τὸν καθήκοντα τῶν γυναικῶν καὶ ἐκάλεσα τὸ ὄνομα αὐτοῦ Καάθ. 67. καὶ* ὅτε ἐγεννήθη[1] ἑώρακα ὅτι ἐπ' αὐτῷ ἔσται ἡ συναγωγὴ παντὸς τοῦ λαοῦ, καὶ ὅτι † αὐτὸς[2] ἔσται ἡ ἀρχιεροσύνη ἡ μεγάλη, *αὐτὸς καὶ τὸ σπέρμα αὐτοῦ ἔσονται ἀρχὴ βασιλέων ἱεράτευμα τῷ Ἰσραήλ.

68. Ἐν τῷ † ἐνιαυτῷ[3] καὶ λ ἔτει[4] ἐγεννήθη ἐν τῷ πρώτῳ μηνὶ μιᾷ τοῦ μηνὸς ἐπ' ἀνατολῆς ἡλίου. 69. καὶ πάλιν συνεγενόμην αὐτῇ *καὶ ἐν γαστρὶ ἔλαβεν[1], καὶ ἔτεκέν μοι υἱὸν τρίτον καὶ ἐκάλεσα τὸ ὄνομα αὐτοῦ Μεραρήν· ἐλυπήθην γὰρ περὶ αὐτοῦ.

ᵃ This is obviously a dittograph of מר לי . . . מית preceding. The two words of לחדה and שגיא are here synonymous. This dittograph points to our text being a translation.

---

[1] Aram. om.　　[2] Read αὐτῷ with Aram.; αὐτῷ καὶ τῷ σπέρματι in next line.　　[3] Corrupt for τετάρτῳ. Cf. Aram.　　[4] Add ζωῆς μου with Aram.

(Col. d)

1	ה(עלנא ל)מצרים 73 בשנת שת
2	עשרה (ה)עלינא לארע מצרים ולבני
3	. . . . בנת אחי לעדן אשויות
4	זבניהון . . . להון בנין 74 ושם בני
5	גרשון (לבני ו)שמעי ושם בני
6	ק(הת עמר)ם ויצהר וחברון ועוזיאל
7	(ושם) בני מררי מחלי ומושי
8	75 (ונסב) לה עמרם אנתא ליוכבד ברתי
9	עד די אנה חי בשנת תשעין וא(רבע)
10	לחיי 76 וקריתי שמה די עמרם כדי
11	יליד עמרם ארי אמרת כדי יליד
12	דנה (יפיק) עמא מן א(רע מצ)רים
13	כדן (א)תקרא (שמה עמא) ראמא
14	77 ביום חד י . . . . יא הוא ויוכבד
15	ברתי 78 בר שנין ת(מ)נה עשרה העלת
16	(לא)רע כנען ובר שנין (תמ)נה[a] עשרה
17	כדי קטלית אנה לש(כם) וגמרת
18	לעבדי חמסא 79 ובר שנין תשע
19	עשרה כהנית ובר שנין תמנה
20	ועסרין נסבת לי אנתה 80 ובר
21	שנין תמנה וארבעין הויתי כדי
22	העלנא לארע מצרים . ושנין
23	תמנים ותשע הויתי חי במצרים

T. Lev. xii. 1, 2. (lines 5–6)

xii. 3. (line 7)

xii. 4. (line 8)

xii. 4. (line 14)

xii. 5. (line 15)

Syriac Fragment of Original Source[1].

(Syriac text, with numbers 78, 79, 80, 81)

[a] The writing is almost obliterated, Pass and Cowley read חשעה. But the ש, if it is ש, seems to be written over an erasure.

---

[1] See Wright's *Catalogue of Syriac MSS.*, Part II, p. 997 [Add. 17,193], which I have in accordance with MS. corrected in last line. But Levi's age, when he married, is incorrectly given, and also the number of years he lived in Egypt.

(Col. e)

1	81 והוו כל יומי חיי שבע ות.(ל)י.(ת)י(ו ום)אה	T. Lev. xix. 5.
2	שנין וחזיתי לי בנין ת(ליתאין) עד	xii. 6.
3	די לא מיתת 82 וב(שנת מאה ות)מני	xii. 7.
4	עשרה לחיי היא ש(תא) די מית בה	
5	יוסף אחי קריתי לב(ני ול)בניהון	
6	ושריתי לפקדה הנון כל ד(י) הווה	
7	עם לבבי 83 עניַת ואמרת לבנ(י שמעו)	
8	למאמר לוי אבוכן והציתו לפקודי	
9	ידיד אל. 84 אנה לכון מפקד בני ואנה	xiii. 1.
10	קושטא לכון מהחוי חביבי 85 ראש	Ps. cxix. 160.
11	עובדיכון יהוי קושטא וער	
12	עלמ(א) י(הו)י קאים עמכון צדקה	
13	86 וקוש(טא) . . . . . מלבני עלון	
14	עללה בריכא ו(זר)עא 87 די זרע	xiii. 6.
15	טאב מהנעל ודי זרע	
16	ביש עלוהי תאיב זרעה	
17	88 וכען בני ספר מוסר	
18	חוכמה אפילו[1] לבניכון ותהוי	xiii. 2.
19	חוכמתא עמכון ליקר עלם	
20	89 די אליף חוכמתא ויקר היא	xiii. 3.
21	בה ודי שאיט חובמתא[2] לבשרון	
22	מתיהב 90 חזו בני ליוסף אחי	xiii. 9.
23	(ד)מאלפא ספר ומוסר חכמא	xiii. 2.

[1] Read with Pass אליפו. [2] Emend into לבושרן.

(Col. f)

(Two lines missing.)

3	תשׁב 91	
4	לב . . . גבר . .	
5	את . . . . . מוהו	
6	וסנה . . . . . . עה לכל מ(אתא)	
7	ומדינה . . . ל לה אחא	
8	הוי בה (לַא כוא)ת נכר הוא בה	xiii. 3.
9	ולא דמ(ה בה ל)נכרי ולא דמה	
10	בה לנִּיל¹ . . . . די כולהון יהבין	
11	לה בה יקר (א)רי כולה צבִין	xiii. 4.
12	למאלף מן חוכמתה 92 רחמוה(י)	
13	סניאין ושאלי שלמיה רברבין	
14	93 ועל כורסי ייקר מהותבין לה	
15	בדיל דמשמע מילי חוכמתה	
16	94 עותר רב די יקר היא חכמתה	
17	וסימא טאבא לכל קניהא הן	xiii. 7.
18	95 יאתון מלכין תקיפין ועם רב	
19	וחיל ופרשין ורתיכין סניאין	
20	עמהם וינסבון . . . . מאת	
21	ומדינה ויבוזון כל די בהון	
22	אוצרי חוכמתא לא יבוזון	
23	ולא ישכחון מטמוריה ולא	

¹ Read לדיר = παροίκῳ.

APPENDIX IV

CHRISTIAN ADDITIONS MADE BY THE SLAVONIC SCRIBE IN S¹.*

After T. Reuben vi. 12 adds:—

Ἐννόει, Ἰουδαῖε, ὡς εὖ δοκιμάζει Ῥουβὴμ Χριστὸν εἶναι ἀρχιερέα ὅστις ὑπὲρ πάντων ἐγεύσατο τοῦ θανάτου, ὢν ἀρχιερεὺς μετὰ τὸν Λευί. Ἐξ Ἰούδα εἷλεν ὁ θεὸς αὐτὸν ὥστε κρατεῖν παντὸς τοῦ λαοῦ καὶ προσκυνεῖν τῷ σπέρματι αὐτοῦ, ὅστις ὑπὲρ ὑμῶν θανεῖται ἐν πολέμοις ὁρατοῖς καὶ ἀοράτοις. Ἐννόει δὲ σύ, ἐν γὰρ ἀοράτῳ οὐδεὶς τῶν ἐπιχθονίων δύναται ὠφέλειαν ἑαυτῷ προσφέρειν· πῶς γὰρ δύναται ὠφελεῖν, μὴ ὁρῶν τὸ ἀόρατον; διάβολος γὰρ ἔτι μαχεῖται, ἀλλὰ τῇ κλήσει τοῦ θεοῦ ὑπὸ τούτου ἐκ γένους Ἰούδα γεννηθέντος νικηθήσεται ὁ διάβολος. Καὶ προσθὲς ταύτην τὴν σκέψιν, καὶ ἔτι ἔλεξεν, αὐτὸς ἔσται ὑμῖν ὁ βασιλεὺς ὁ αἰώνιος ὡς τῷ Ῥουβὴμ ἔδοξεν ὅτι ὁ βασιλεὺς ὁ αἰώνιος γενήσεται ἀπὸ τοῦ Ἰούδα.

After viii. 3 repeats and adds:—

Καὶ νῦν, τεκνία μου, ὑπακούετε Λευὶ καὶ ἐν Ἰούδᾳ λυτρωθήσεσθε· καὶ μὴ ἐπαίρεσθε ἐπὶ τὰς δύο φυλὰς ταύτας, ὅτι ἐξ αὐτῶν ἀνατελεῖ ὑμῖν τὸ σωτήριον τοῦ θεοῦ. 2. Ἀναστήσει γὰρ κύριος ἐκ τοῦ Λευὶ ὡς ἀρχιερέα, καὶ ἐκ τοῦ Ἰούδα ὡς βασιλέα καὶ ἄνθρωπον, οὕτως σώσει καὶ πάντας ἀνθρώπους. Ὁρᾶτε, οἱ ἀθυμοῦντες, ὁ Κύριος καθίστησι ἱερέα ὑμῖν ἀπὸ Λευί, ὡς ἀρχιερέα εἶπεν ὁ θεὸς ὅτι ἠμφίεσε αὐτὸν τῇ σαρκὶ καὶ ἦν ὥσπερ ἱερεὺς κατὰ Λευί· ὡς εἶπεν πᾶσι τοῖς ἔθνεσι καὶ τὸ γένος τοῦ Ἰσραὴλ τότε πολλοὶ Ἰσραηλῖται ἐσώζοντο ἀπὸ αὐτῶν. τῶν ὑψιτέρων ἀποστόλων ἦσαν δώδεκα .. καὶ ἐννέα τῶν μαθητῶν ὑμεῖς ἔσεσθε ταλαίπωροι προριμμένοι, ἐν ὕβρει καὶ ἐν αἰκείᾳ καὶ ἐν ἐλέγχει εἰς πάντα τὰ ἔθνη. 3. Διὰ τοῦτο ἐντέλλομαι ... ὑμῖν, ἵνα καὶ ὑμεῖς ἐντείλησθε τοῖς τέκνοις ὑμῶν, καὶ ἃ εἶπον ὑμῖν ὅπως φυλάξητε εἰς τὰς γενεὰς ὑμῶν.

* The text is frequently corrupt and unintelligible. Professor Morfill's rendering reproduces the text as it stands. In some passages the corruptions are obvious.

After T. Sim. viii. 3 adds :—

Ἄκουε, ὦ Ἰουδαῖε, ὅτι λέγει ὁ Συμεών, ἑώρακα γὰρ ἐν λόγοις βιβλίων Ἑνώχ, ὅτι υἱοὶ ὑμῶν μεθ' ὑμῶν ἐν πορνείᾳ φθαρήσονται. ὡς οὐκ εἰδότες τὸν υἱὸν τοῦ θεοῦ καὶ διαφθαρέντες ἐν τοῖς ἔθνεσιν ἐν Λευὶ ἀδικήσουσιν, τοῦτο ἐστί. ὁ Χριστὸς Ἰησοῦς ἀρχιερεύς ἐστι κατὰ τὸν Λευιτικόν, αὐτὸν οἱ Ἰουδαῖοι ἐκέντησαν λόγχῃ. Ἀλλ' οὐ δυνήσονται πρὸς Λευὶ ὅτι πόλεμον Κυρίου πολεμήσει. Ὁμολόγει, Ἰουδαῖε, πρόσεχε τῷ πολέμῳ Κυρίου, ὅτι τῷ Κυρίῳ ἀνθίσταντο, καὶ ἀνθιστάμενοι τῷ σταυρῷ ἐγομφώσατε πάσχοντα κατὰ βούλησιν αὐτὸν ἐν μνημείῳ σφραγίσαντες ἐθήκατε, ἀλλὰ τῆς σφραγῖδος ὅλης σωζομένης· ἀνεγέρθη ἐκ τοῦ μνημείου ἄνευ διαφθορᾶς, ἀλλ' οὐκ ἐδυνήθη (repetition) κατέχειν τὸ θεῖον τὸ μνημεῖον ἐσφραγισμένον. ἀλλ' ὥσπερ ὁ πατὴρ Ἰακὼβ προφητεύσας εὐλόγησε οὐκ ἦν αὐτοῖς εὐλογεῖν τὰ ἔθνη. καὶ προσέθηκεν ὁ Συμεὼν εἰπεῖν τοῖς υἱοῖς, τοῦτο ἐστί, ἐλευθεροῦν τὰς ψυχὰς ὑμῶν ἀπὸ τῶν ἁμαρτιῶν, καὶ ἰδοὺ ὁ Συμεὼν προφητεύει καὶ λέγει περὶ τῆς ἀφίξεως τοῦ υἱοῦ τούτῳ καθαίρει τὴν ψυχὴν αὐτοῦ ἀπὸ τῆς πονηρᾶς πράξεως τῆς γενεᾶς τῶν Ἑβραίων, εἰ ἀφαιρήσετε· καὶ ἐκώλυσεν Συμεὼν τοὺς υἱοὺς αὐτοῦ ὥστε ἀποτρέπειν ἀπὸ φθόνου καὶ ὑπερηφανίας ἀλλ' οὐκ ἠδύνατο κωλύειν, καὶ γὰρ τότε ὁ Ἰουδαῖος ἐπληρώθη φθόνου καὶ ὑπερηφανίας καὶ δήσαντες τὸν Ἰησοῦν ἤγαγον αὐτὸν πρὸς τὸν Πιλᾶτον πρὸς τὴν κρίσιν. καὶ ὁ Πιλᾶτος εἶπεν, οὐχ εὗρον ἐν αὐτῷ οὐδεμίαν αἰτίαν· ὁ δὲ Συμεὼν εἶπεν, εἴπερ ἀποτρέπεσθε ἀπὸ φθόνου καὶ ὑπερηφανίας τότε ὥσπερ ῥόδον ἐμὰ ὀστέα ἀνθήσει ἐν Ἰσραὴλ καὶ ὥσπερ κρίνον σὰρξ ἐμὴ ἐν Ἰακὼβ καὶ ὀσμή μου ἔσται θαυμασία ὀσμή, καὶ πληθυνθήσεται ὥσπερ ἁγία κέδρος. ἡ γὰρ κέδρος ἁγία ὀνομάζεται ἢ ποῦ πρόσθεν δένδρον ἁγιάζεται; ἀλλὰ τοῖς ὀφθαλμοῖς τῆς σοφίας οἱ μεγάλοι πατριάρχαι εἶδον, ὡς ὁ Ἰησοῦς Χριστὸς ἦν ὁ υἱὸς τοῦ θεοῦ, σταυρωθῆναι ἐν κυπαρίσσῳ καὶ ἐν πεύκῃ καὶ ἐν κέδρῳ. καὶ τούτου ἕνεκα ἡ κέδρος ἁγία ὀνομάζεται, καὶ πρὸς τούτοις ὁ λόγος μου εἰς τοὺς αἰῶνας. τοῦτο ἐστὶ ἡ προφητεία περὶ τοῦ Χριστοῦ ἕως τῆς τελειώσεως τῶν κλάδων αὐτῶν καὶ μακροὶ ἔσονται. τοῦτο ἐστί· τὸ ὄνομά τοῦ Χριστοῦ παρατενεῖται ἐν τοῖς ἔθνεσιν. καὶ τότε ἔσται σημεῖον, ὅταν ὁ μέγας Κύριος φαίνηται ἐπὶ τῇ γῇ ὡς ἄνθρωπος σώζων τὸν Ἀδάμ. Ὅρα, πῶς ἑαυτῷ σώσει τὸν Ἀδάμ; ὅτι Ἀδὰμ ἦν πρῶτος ἄνθρωπος, καὶ ἔπεσεν παραβαίνων τὴν ἐντολὴν τοῦ Θεοῦ. καὶ ἕνεκα τούτου ὁ Θεὸς ἄνθρωπος ἐγένετο, λαβὼν τὴν σάρκα ἀπὸ παρθένου, ἑαυτὸς σώζων τὴν φύσιν καὶ τὸν ἄνθρωπον, καὶ τὸν Ἀδὰμ ἐγείρει καὶ τότε (εἶπεν) πάντα τὰ πνεύματα τῆς πλάνης δοθήσονται αὐτῷ εἰς πάτημα καὶ ἄνθρωποι ἄρξονται κατακυριεύειν τῶν

πονηρῶν πνευμάτων. καὶ ἐπὶ τῇ ἀναλήψει τοῦ Κυρίου ἔπεμψεν τὸ
ἅγιον αὐτῷ πνεῦμα ἐπὶ τοῖς ἁγίοις ἀγγέλοις καὶ ἔδωκεν αὐτοῖς
ἐξουσίαν καὶ δύναμιν, καὶ τοῖς λόγοις τοῦ Κυρίου ἐλαύνουσι πνεύματα
τῆς πλάνης καὶ ἡμεῖς ἕως σήμερον ἔχουσα τὰ ἅγια ὀστέα ἐν ταῖς χερσὶ
ἐτητύμως ὀσμὴ ἀκαθάρτων ψυχῶν καὶ ὁ καπνὸς ἀποφθίνει. Τότε ἐγὼ
ἐγεροῦμαι ἐν χαρᾷ καὶ εὐλογήσω τὸν ὕψιστον ἀπὸ τῶν θαυμάτων
αὐτοῦ. Ὁρᾶτε τὴν φωνὴν τῆς ἰσχύος ὅτι τοῦ Κυρίου σταυρουμένου
ἡ γῆ ἐτινάσσετο καὶ τὰ μνημεῖα ἀνεῴχθη καὶ οἱ νεκροὶ ἀνίσταντο καὶ
εὐλόγησαν τὸν ὕψιστον ἀπὸ τῶν θαυμάτων αὐτοῦ πάντες. ὡς εἶπεν
ὁ Θεός, ὁ σωτὴρ τοῦ ἀνθρώπου ἔχων τὴν σάρκα καὶ ἐσθίων σὺν τοῖς
ἀνθρώποις.

After T. Lev. vii. 4 adds :—

Ἐννόει δὲ σὺ τὴν φροντίδα, ὦ Ἰουδαῖε, καὶ εἴσελθε εἰς τὴν
ὄψιν τοῦ Λευὶ ὡς τὸν ἄγγελον θαυμάτων ἀπὸ τῶν οὐρανῶν. καὶ αὐτῷ
ὁ ἄγγελος εἶπε, σὺ ἐγγὺς τοῦ Κυρίου στήσει καὶ ἔσει ὁ ὑπηρέτης
αὐτοῦ καὶ ἀποκηρύξεις τὰ μυστήρια τοῖς ἀνθρώποις. καὶ περὶ τοῦ
θέλοντος σώζειν τὸν Ἰσραήλ. Καὶ οὕτως οὐκ ἐννοεῖς, ὦ Ἰουδαῖε, τοῦ
ἀγγέλου τοῦ Θεοῦ προφητεύοντος τοῖς πατράσιν ὑμῶν περὶ τῆς
σωτηρίας Ἰσραήλ, οὐ γὰρ τὸ ῥῆμά σοι ἐφάνη, ὅτι ἀπὸ τοῦ Ἰούδα
σώσει ὁ Κύριος πᾶν τὸ γέ⟨ν⟩ος ἀνθρώπων. Ἐννόει γάρ, ὦ ταλαίπωρε,
ὅτι οὔτε ἄγγελος οὔτε ἄνθρωπος μεσιτεύεται ἀλλὰ ὁ Θεὸς αὐτὸς
σώζει ἡμᾶς, ἰδοὺ γὰρ ὡς ἐν πρώτοις εἴπομέν σοι, ὡς ἀπὸ τῆς γενεᾶς
Ἰούδα ὁ Κύριος γίγνεται ἐκ τῆς παρθένου Μαρίας καὶ Λευὶ ἦν Λευίτης,
καὶ κατὰ τὸν πρῶτον ⟨ν⟩όμον ἦν ἱερεύς, ὥστε καθαρίζειν τὰς ἁμαρτίας τοῦ
λαοῦ, καὶ διὰ τοῦτο ἦν ἱερεὺς ὅτι ὁ ἄγγελος εἶπε τῷ Λευί, ἐκ σοῦ καὶ ἐξ
Ἰούδα ὁ Κύριος φανήσεται τοῖς ἀνθρώποις σώζων καὶ φέρων πᾶν τὸ
γένος ἀνθρώπων ἄνευ αἵματος. Ἐννόει γὰρ ὡς οἱ ἄγγελοι τοῦ Θεοῦ ἐν
τῇ λατρείᾳ τῷ Θεῷ προσφέρουσιν οὔτε τὸ αἷμα τῶν μόσχων οὔτε τὸ
αἷμα τῶν τράγων ἀλλὰ χάριν τῷ Κυρίῳ πέμπουσιν· τῆς καθαρᾶς λατρείας.
καὶ οὕτως ἡμεῖς οἱ Χριστιανοὶ πέμπουσιν τῷ Κυρίῳ τὸ σῶμα καὶ τὸ
αἷμα ὡς καθαρὰν λατρείαν κατὰ τὴν τάξιν τοῦ Μελχισεδέκ. Ἐννόει
γὰρ περὶ τούτου ἄλλου καὶ πείθου ὡς ὁ Κύριος ποιεῖ κρίσιν περὶ
τούτων τῶν ἀνθρώπων. περὶ ὑμῶν δέ, ὦ ταλαίπωροι, οὐ ποιεῖ κρίσιν
ἐν τῷ πυρὶ τῷ ἀσβέστῳ καὶ τῷ σκώληκι ἀκοιμήτῳ καὶ παρασκενάζων
ὑμᾶς ὡς πέτρας διασκορπίζων. ἐπεὶ γὰρ τὸν Κύριον προσηλώσατε, καὶ
ὁ ἥλιος ἐσβέσθη τότε οὐχ ὁ ἥλιος ἐσβέσθη ; ὅτε γὰρ ὑμεῖς τὸν κύριον
ἐσταυρώσατε, ὡς τὸ εὐαγγέλιον λέγει, τότε γὰρ σκότος ἦν ἐπὶ
πᾶσαν τὴν γῆν ἀπὸ τρίτης ὥρας ἕως ἐννάτης τῶν ὑδάτων ξηραινομένων καὶ τοῦ Ἅδου αἰχμαλωτιζομένου. λέγε δέ μοι, εἰ ὁ Ἅδης

ᾐχμαλωτίσθη, εἰ πολέμιοι ὡπλισμένοι εἰς τὸν "Ἀδην εἰσῆλθον ἀλλ' ὁ θεὸς αὐτὸς ὅτε ἔκειτο ἐν τῷ μνημείῳ, τότε γὰρ εἰσῆλθεν εἰς τὸν "Ἀδην ἐλευθερῶν τὸν Ἀδὰμ τὸν πρῶτον κλητὸν ἀπὸ τοῦ δεσμωτηρίου τοῦ "Ἀδου, ἦν γὰρ ὁ Κύριος τῆς γῆς καὶ τῆς ἀβύσσου, καὶ ἔνεκα τούτου ἦλθε ὥστε αἰχμαλωτίζειν τὸν "Ἀδην. Εἰ γὰρ ἔπαθεν, ἡ θειότης αὐτοῦ ἦν ἄνευ πάθους.

Καὶ, ἰδού, εἶπεν Λευί, ὅτε ἐγερθέντες ἤλθομεν εἰς Βεθήλ.

After viii. 4 adds:—

τοῦτό ἐστι ἐλαίῳ ἀγίῳ ᾧ χρίονται Χριστιανοὶ στάντες ἐν τῇ ἀγίᾳ κολυμβήθρᾳ βαπτισμῷ. τότε ἀγιάζονται τῷ κυρίῳ καὶ δέχονται τὸν αἰώνιον βίον.

In viii. 5 after ἔλουσέ με ὕδατι καθαρῷ adds:—

τοῦτό ἐστι τῷ τριπλῷ βαπτισμῷ ἐν τῷ ὀνόματι τοῦ πατρὸς καὶ τοῦ υἱοῦ καὶ τοῦ ἀγίου πνεύματος.

and after ἄρτον καὶ οἶνον ἄγια ἀγίων adds:—

τοῦτό ἐστι τὴν ἀγίαν εὐχαριστίαν ἐν τῇ ἐκκλησίᾳ τοῦ θεοῦ.

and at close of verse:—

τοῦτό ἐστι τὸ σημεῖον τοῦ ἀγίου βαπτισμοῦ· τοῦτο γὰρ τὸ ἱμάτιον οἱ ἄγγελοι ἐπουράνιοι ἰδόντες ἠγαλλιάσαντο· ἰδόντες γὰρ τοῦτο τὸ ἱμάτιον ταύτην τὴν στολὴν ἔνδοξον νικῶσιν τὰς στρατιὰς τῶν δαιμόνων.

After viii. 6 adds:—

καὶ οὕτως ἐκ χρόνου καὶ οὐκ εἰς ἀεὶ ἐδόθη μοι ἱερατεύειν. τοῦτό ἐστι, ὅτι μόνος ἦν εἰς τοὺς αἰῶνας καὶ εἰς τοὺς αἰῶνας μένει ὁ Ἰησοῦς ὁ θεὸς ἱερατεύειν κατὰ τὴν τάξιν τοῦ Μελχισεδέκ.

After viii. 8 adds:—

τοῦτό ἐστι λόγων εὐαγγελικῶν καὶ ἀποστολικῶν· ἀκούοντες γὰρ οἱ ἄγιοι μάρτυρες ἐγέρθησαν ἐπὶ τὴν στρατιὰν τοῦ πολεμίου.

After viii. 9 adds:—

διὰ τοῦτο γὰρ οἱ μάρτυρες ἐγέρθησαν καὶ ἐστεφανώθησαν ἐν τῇ ὀρθῇ πίστει.

After viii. 12 adds:—

τὶς προσελθὼν ἀλλ' οὐ γενήσεται ὁ λεγόμενος ὑπὸ τοῦ Ἰωάννου τοῦ βαπτιστοῦ, ὅστις ἦν ἀπὸ τῆς γενεᾶς τῶν ἱερέων· ἔσται δὲ ἀπὸ ἄλλης τινὸς μαθείας, ὅτι ἡ σωτηρία τοῦ κόσμου λέγεται εἶναι ἀπὸ τοῦ Χριστοῦ Ἰησοῦ.

After viii. 19 adds:—

Ἐννόει δέ, ὦ ταλαίπωρε Ἰουδαῖε, ὡς καὶ σοὶ ἐγένετο ἡ ὄψις τοῦ Λευὶ καὶ ἡ ἐνσωμάτωσις καὶ τὸ πάθημα τοῦ υἱοῦ τοῦ Θεοῦ, ἐγὼ σοὶ λέγω.

After πλανῶντες τὸν Ἰσραήλ in x. 2 adds:—

Τί προσδοκᾷς, ὦ Ἰουδαῖε, τίνα δὲ μένεις ἐρχόμενον τοῦ Λευὶ λέγοντος ὡς οὐκ ἐπιστεύσατε ἐν τῷ σωτῆρι τοῦ κόσμου καὶ πλανῶντες αὐτόν;

After x. 5 adds:—

ὃς γὰρ οὐ προσέχει τοῖς λόγοις μου ὁ Κύριος επ . . . . ται ἐπ' ἐμὲ πῦρ αἰώνιον.

After xix. 12 T. Joseph adds:—

Ἀκούσατε γάρ, Ἰουδαῖοι, ὅτι δηλοῖ τὸ ἐνύπνιον, εἶδε γὰρ δώδεκα ἐλάφους νεμομένους. οὗτοι δὲ ἔλαφοί εἰσι δώδεκα ἀπόστολοι, ἀγγέλλοντες θαύματα ἐν τῷ κόσμῳ, καὶ ἐννέα αὐτῶν, φησί, διεσπάρησαν ἐν ὅλῃ τῇ γῇ, διδάσκοντες καὶ βαπτίζοντες ἐν τῷ ὀνόματι τοῦ πατέρος καὶ τοῦ υἱοῦ καὶ τοῦ ἁγίου πνεύματος· ὁμοίως, φησί, οἱ τρεῖς. Οἱ τρεῖς ἐκήρυσσον καὶ ἀπέθανον οὐ λείψαντες τὸ Ἱεροσόλυμα. Ὡς ἡ γραφὴ λέγει, ὡς ὑπὸ τοῦ Ἡρώδου, τοῦ ἀνόμου, Ἰακὼβ ἀδελφὸς τοῦ Ἰωάννου ἐκτάνθη τῷ ξίφει καὶ οὕτως ὁ Στέφανος καλούμενος ὁ πρῶτος τῶν μαρτύρων ὑπὸ τῶν Ἰουδαίων κατεφονεύθη πέτροις, ὅστις ἐκοιμήθη λέγων· Κύριε, μὴ στήσῃς αὐτοῖς τὴν ἁμαρτίαν ταύτην, οὐκ οἴδασι γὰρ ὅ τι ποιοῦσιν. Ὁράω, φησί, ὅτι ἐξῆλθε παρθένος ἐξ Ἰούδα, τοῦτό ἐστι ἡ ἁγία παρθένος (ἡ μήτηρ τοῦ Θεοῦ) ἐκ τοῦ γένους τοῦ Ἰούδα ἡ θυγάτηρ τοῦ Ἰωαχίμ, ἔχουσα ἐσθῆτα βυσσίνην. τοῦτο ἐστὶ οὐ μιανθεῖσα οὐδὲ ὑβρισθεῖσα (?), ἀλλὰ καθαρὰ καὶ σφόδρα καθαρὰ ἐξ ἧς ἦλθεν ὁ ἀμνὸς ἄτερ κακίας, τοῦτο ἐστὶν ὁ υἱὸς τοῦ Θεοῦ αἰδήμων, ταπεινὸς ἄνευ λοιδορίας, ἄνευ κακίας ὅλως ἄνευ ἁμαρτίας, καὶ ἐπὶ τῇ ἀριστερᾷ ὥσπερ λέων, φησί, καὶ γὰρ ὁ λόγος τῆς θεότητος αὐτοῦ μέγας καὶ δεινὸς καὶ ἰσχυρὸς καὶ εὔγνωστος, καὶ πάντα τὰ θηρία ὥρμων κατ' αὐτόν, φησί. τοῦτό ἐστι, ὑμεῖς κατάρατοι Ἰουδαῖοι, ἑωρᾶτε τὸν υἱὸν τοῦ Θεοῦ λαμβάνοντα ταπεινὸν ὄψιν, καὶ πάντα τὰ ἄγρια θηρία ὥρμων κατ' αὐτὸν λέγοντες Λαβὲ λαβὲ σταυρώσατε, τὸ αἷμα αὐτοῦ ἐφ' ἡμῖν καὶ ἐπὶ τοῖς τέκνοις ἡμῶν. ἐνίκησεν αὐτούς, φησί, ὁ ἀμνός· τοῦτο ἐστὶ, ὁ υἱὸς τοῦ Θεοῦ ἐξεγέρθη ἀπὸ τῶν νεκρῶν. ὑμεῖς δὲ [   ] τῶν κακῶς πεπραγμένων ἐμνήσθητε καὶ ἀπωλέσατε αὐτὰ εἰς καταπάτησιν· τοῦτό

ἐστι, δώσει ὑμᾶς εἰς δουλείαν εἰς τὰ ἔθνη καὶ ἔσεσθε καταπατούμενοι
ἕως τοῦ νῦν ἐν τῇ γῇ ὑμῶν. Καὶ ἔχαιρον, φησί, ἐν αὐτῷ οἱ ἄγγελοι
καὶ οἱ ἄνθρωποι, καὶ πᾶσα ἡ γῆ. ὁ Κύριος ὁ Θεὸς ἡμῶν, βασιλεὺς τῶν
οὐρανῶν καὶ τῆς γῆς, τὰ ὕψιστα καὶ τὰ νέρτερα εἰς μίαν εὐδαιμονίαν
τοῦ εὐλογισμοῦ συναγερεῖ. Ταῦτα δὲ γενήσεται ἐν καιρῷ αὐτῶν.
Ἰακὼβ γὰρ ἦν τριῶν καὶ ἑπτὰ χ' ἐτῶν καὶ υἱὸς τοῦ Θεοῦ ἐγενήθη
ἐννέα ἐτῶν καὶ ἐχαρήσαν ἐπ' αὐτῷ ἐν ἐσχάταις ἡμέραις, τοῦτό ἐστι,
ἡ ἀρχὴ καὶ τὸ τέλος. Ἐν τῷ πρώτῳ ἦλθεν ἐκ τοῦ μὴ γενέσθαι εἰς
τὸ γενέσθαι. περὶ τούτου ἔλεγον οἱ προφῆται. Καὶ ἡμεῖς χαρήσομεν
ἐπ' αὐτῷ ἕως τῶν ἐσχάτων ἡμερῶν. ἀλλ' ὑμεῖς, τέκνα μου, φυλάξατε
τὰς ἐντολὰς τοῦ Θεοῦ Κυρίου καὶ τιμᾶτε τὸν Ἰούδαν καὶ τὸν Λευί· ὅτι
ἐξ αὐτῶν ἀνατελεῖ ὑμῖν ὁ ἀμνὸς τοῦ Θεοῦ, τοῦτό ἐστι, ἀπὸ τῆς γενεᾶς
τοῦ Ἰούδα καὶ κατὰ τὴν τάξιν τοῦ Λευὶ τὰ πρωτεῖα λαμβάνων τῇ
ἐλεημοσύνῃ σώζων πάντας τοὺς λαοὺς Ἰσραήλ, καὶ ἐνθυμοῦ σὺ Ἰσραήλ,
οὐ γὰρ μόνῳ τῷ Ἰσραὴλ ἡ σωτηρία, ἀλλὰ πᾶσι τοῖς ἔθνεσιν. Καὶ γὰρ
οὐ μόνῳ τῷ Ἰσραὴλ ἐγένετο ἡ σωτηρία, ἐγένετο ἐκ τῆς ἁγιωτάτης
παρθένου, καὶ ἔτραπε πάντα τὰ ἔθνη εἰς σωτηρίαν. καὶ ἐνθυμοῦ ὡς
ὁ ἀμνὸς τὴν παρθένον κηρύσσει, καὶ ἡ βασιλεία αὐτοῦ οὐ παρασαλεύσεται εἰς ἀεὶ καὶ εἶπεν Ἰωσήφ. .

After εἰς ἀτιμίαν in x. 8 T. Benj. adds:—

οἱ μὲν θέλοντες εἶναι ἐν τῷ μέλλοντι βίῳ . . . ἀεὶ . . . βάσανον
αἰώνιον . . . ἀγαλλιῶντες ἐπὶ τῷ ποιοῦντι τὰ ἀγαθὰ πράγματα, ἢ
συνεχῶς ἀτιμάζοντες οὐ μόνον ἀλλὰ καὶ βασανίζοντες, οἳ ἦσαν ἐνθάδε
μιαροὶ θεράποντες καὶ οὐ θέλοντες μετανοεῖν πρὶν ἢ ἐνθάδε φεύγειν
καὶ ἀφικνεῖσθαι. ὁ σκώληξ γὰρ αὐτῶν οὐ λήγει, εἶπεν ὁ Χριστός—
κρῖμα δίκαιον καὶ τὸ πῦρ οὐ σβέννυται.

After xvi. adds:—

. Καὶ ἔτι σοι λέγω, Ἰουδαῖε, ἆρ' ἤκουσας Λευὶ λέγοντος τοῖς τέκνοις τῶν
τέκνων αὐτοῦ, εἰ γὰρ ἐσταύρωσας Κύριον ὅμως οἰκτείρει καὶ δέχεται
τοὺς ἐρχομένους πρὸς αὐτὸν βαπτισθέντας ὕδατι ἐν τῷ ὀνόματι τοῦ
πατρὸς καὶ τοῦ υἱοῦ καὶ τοῦ ἁγίου πνεύματος καὶ ἐννόει ὅτι οὐκ ἐστί σοι
συγγνώμη εἰ μὴ πιστεύεις ἐν αὐτῷ καὶ δέχει τὸν βαπτισμὸν ἐν τῷ
ὀνόματι αὐτοῦ. καὶ γὰρ ὁ Θεὸς ὁ Κύριος αὐτὸς εἶπε ἐν τῷ ἁγίῳ
εὐαγγελίῳ, εἰ μὴ γενήσεταί τις τῷ ὕδατι καὶ τῷ πνεύματι, οὐκ
εἰσελεύσεται εἰς τὴν βασιλείαν τῶν οὐρανῶν. Ἀλλα σύ, ὦ Ἰουδαῖε,
μὴ ἐννόει περὶ τῶν πρότερον ὅπως μὴ ἀπολλύῃς τὴν ψυχήν σου.
Ἀποδέχου τὸν ἅγιον βαπτισμὸν καὶ ἔσει ὡς νεόγονος παῖς ἄνευ
φθορᾶς κακίας [   ]. Ἄκουε, ὦ Ἰουδαῖε, τοῦ Λευὶ λέγοντος, περὶ
τῆς ἱερατείας τοῦ Κυρίου.

APPENDIX V

RETRANSLATION OF THE SECOND RECENSION (S²) OF THE SLAVONIC VERSION BY PROFESSOR MORFILL[1]

ΔΙΑΘΗΚΗ ΡΟΥΒΗΜ

I. 2. Ἐν τῷ δευτέρῳ μετὰ ταῦτα ἔτει Ῥουβὴμ ὁ πρωτόγονος τοῦ Ἰακὼβ υἱὸς ἀρρωστῶν προσεκάλεσε τοὺς ἀδελφοὺς αὐτοῦ καὶ τὰ τέκνα, 3. καὶ ἐμήκυνε αὐτοῖς λόγον μετανοίας καὶ εἶπε· 6. ἥμαρτον σὺν Βάλλᾳ, τῇ δούλῃ τοῦ πατρός μου, 7. καὶ εἰ μὴ ὁ πατὴρ προσηύξατο τῷ Κυρίῳ ὁ ἄγγελος τοῦ Κυρίου ἔκτεινεν ἄν. 10. Ἐγὼ δὲ ἑπτὰ ἔτη οὐκ ἐγευσάμην τοῦ οἴνου καὶ τοῦ σίκερα καὶ κρέας οὐκ εἰσῆλθε εἰς τὸ στόμα μου ἤδη ἑπτὰ ἔτη διὰ τὴν ἀσέλγειαν.

II. Ἀκούσατε, τέκνα μου, πατρὸς ὑμῶν Ῥουβὴμ ὅσα εἶδον· 2. Ἑπτὰ πνεύματα τῆς πλάνης ἐδόθη κατὰ τοῦ ἀνθρώπου ἀπὸ τοῦ Βελίαρ καὶ αὐτά εἰσι κεφαλὴ τῶν ἔργων τῆς πλάνης, [αὐτὰ δὲ πειράζεται ἕκαστον ἄνθρωπον ἐν παντὶ τῷ βίῳ. οὐ φύσει ἐγγίγνεται ταῦτα τὰ συστήματα]. 3. ἀλλὰ ἐδόθη αὐτῷ εἰς αὔξησιν διὰ τὸ εἶναι ἐν αὐτοῖς πᾶν ἔργον ἀνθρώπου. 4. πρῶτον πνεῦμα ζωῆς, μεθ᾽ ἧς ἡ σύστασις κτίζεται. δεύτερον πνεῦμα ὁράσεως, μεθ᾽ ἧς γίνεται ἐπιθυμία. 5. Τρίτον πνεῦμα ἀκοῆς μεθ᾽ ἧς γίνεται διδασκαλία. Τέταρτον πνεῦμα ὀσφρήσεως, μεθ᾽ ἧς ἐστι γεῦσις δεδομένη εἰς συνολκὴν ἀέρος καὶ πνοῆς. 6. Πέμπτον βούλησις, μεθ᾽ ἧς γίνεται γνῶσις. 7. Ἕκτον πνεῦμα γεύσεως μεθ᾽ ἧς γίνεται βρῶσις βρωτῶν καὶ ποτῶν καὶ ἰσχὺς ἐν αὐτοῖς κτίζεται· ὅτι ἐν βρώμασίν ἐστιν ἡ ὑπόστασις τῆς ἰσχύος. 8. Ἕβδομον πνεῦμα σπορᾶς μεθ᾽ ἧς συνεισέρχεται διὰ τῆς φιληδονίας ἡ ἁμαρτία. 9. Διὰ τοῦτο ἔσχατον ἐστὶ τῆς κτίσεως καὶ πρῶτον τῆς νεότητος, ὅτι ἀγνοίας πεπλήρωται καὶ αὐτὴ τὸν νεώτερον ὁδηγεῖ ὡς τυφλὸν ἐπὶ βόθρον καὶ ὡς κτῆνος ἐπὶ κρημνόν. III. Ἐπὶ πᾶσι τούτοις ὄγδοον πνεῦμα τοῦ

---

[1] In this retranslation the chief and indeed most of the minor additions peculiar to the Slavonic Version are enclosed in square brackets. The text is frequently corrupt and defective, and occasionally, as in the Test. Judah, exhibits a complete inversion of the proper order of the narrative.

ὕπνου ἐστί, μεθ' οὗ ἐκτίσθη ἔκστασις φύσεως καὶ εἰκὼν τοῦ θανάτου. 2. Τούτοις τοῖς πνεύμασι συμμίγνυται τὸ πνεῦμα τῆς πλάνης. 3. Πρῶτον τὸ τῆς πορνείας ἀνθάπτεται τῆς φύσεως. δεύτερον πνεῦμα ἀπληστείας ἐν τῇ γαστρί. 4. Τρίτον πνεῦμα μάχης ἐν τῇ καρδίᾳ καὶ τῇ χολῇ. τέταρτον πνεῦμα ἀρεσκείας καὶ μαγγανείας, ἵνα διὰ περιεργείας ὡραῖος ὀφθῇ [τοῖς δυσκόλως ὁρῶσι]. 5. Πέμπτον πνεῦμα ὑπερηφανείας ἐπαινοῦντος ἑαυτὸν καὶ μεγαλοφρονοῦντος. Ἕκτον πνεῦμα ψεύδους ἐν ἀπωλείᾳ καὶ ἐν φθόνῳ ὥστε πλάττειν λόγους καὶ κρύπτειν ἀπὸ τοῦ γένους καὶ ἀπὸ τῶν οἰκείων. 6. Ἕβδομον πνεῦμα ἀδικίας, μεθ' ἧς κλοπὴ καὶ γρυπίσματα ἵνα ποιήσῃ φιληδονίαν καρδίας αὐτοῦ. Ἡ γὰρ ἀδικία συνεργεῖ τοῖς λοιποῖς πνεύμασι. 7. Ἐπὶ πᾶσι τούτοις τὸ πνεῦμα τοῦ ὕπνου συνάπτεται πλάνῃ καὶ φαντασίᾳ. 8. καὶ οὕτως ἀπόλλυται πᾶς νεώτερος, σκοτίζων τὸν νοῦν αὐτοῦ ἀπὸ τῆς ἀληθείας, καὶ μὴ συνίων ἐν τῷ νόμῳ τοῦ Θεοῦ βαίνειν, μήτε ὑπακούων νουθεσίας πατέρων αὐτοῦ· ὥσπερ κἀγὼ ἔπαθον ἐν τῇ νεότητί μου. 10. καὶ νῦν, τέκνα, μὴ προσέχετε ἐν ὄψει γυναικός. 12. συλλαβοῦσα γὰρ ἡ διάνοιά μου τὴν γυμνότητα τῶν γυναικῶν οὐκ ἔδωκέ μοι εἰρήνην ἕως οὗ ἔπραξα τὸ βδέλυγμα, [καὶ κακὸν ἐνώπιον τοῦ Θεοῦ].

VI. 8. Ἀκούσατε, τέκνα μου, Λευΐ, ὡς αὐτὸς συνίησι τὸν νόμον τοῦ Κυρίου καὶ διαστελεῖ ὑμᾶς καὶ προσοίσει θυσίας, ὑπὲρ παντὸς Ἰσραήλ, μέχρι τελειώσεως χρόνων ἀρχιερέως Χριστοῦ, ὃν εἶπε Κύριος.

[Ἐννόει, Ἰουδαῖε, ὡς εὖ δοκιμάζει Ῥουβὴμ Χριστὸν εἶναι ἀρχιερέα ὅστις ὑπὲρ πάντων ἐγεύσατο τοῦ θανάτου.] 11. ἀλλὰ Λευΐ ἦν ἐξ Ἰουδαίων ὃν ἐξελέξατο ὁ Θεὸς ὥστε κρατεῖν παντὸς τοῦ λαοῦ καὶ προσκυνεῖν τῷ σπέρματι αὐτοῦ, ὅτι ὑπὲρ ὑμῶν θανεῖται ἐν πολέμοις ὁρατοῖς καὶ ἀοράτοις. [ἐννόει δὲ σύ, τί τὸ ὁ πόλεμος ὁ ἀόρατος, ἐν γὰρ ἀοράτῳ οὐδεὶς τῶν θνητῶν δύναται ὠφέλειαν ἑαυτῷ προφέρειν. πῶς γὰρ δύναται ὠφελεῖν, μὴ ὁρῶν τὸ ἀόρατον; διάβολος γὰρ ἔτι μαχεῖται τῇ κλήσει τοῦ Θεοῦ ὑπὸ τούτου ἐκ γένους Ἰούδα γεννηθέντος νικηθήσεται ὁ διάβολος. ἀκούσατε καὶ ἐννοεῖτε ὃ ἔλεξε, καὶ ὁ Κύριος ὁ αἰώνιος ἔσται σὺν ὑμῖν. Ὡς τῷ Ῥουβὴμ ἔδοξεν ὅτι γίγνεται ὁ αἰώνιος Κύριος ἐξ Ἰούδα. ὁ γὰρ θνητὸς ὢν διὰ τοὺς αἰῶνας καὶ ἕως τοῦ διαλύεσθαι τὸν κόσμον ζήσεται εἰς τοὺς αἰῶνας.] VII. 1, 2. Ταῦτα λέξας ἀπέθανεν ὁ Ῥουβήμ, πρωτόγονος τοῦ Ἰακώβ. ἔζη δὲ 125 ἔτη καὶ ἀπέθανεν.

ΔΙΑΘΗΚΗ ΣΥΜΕΩΝ

Ἦν δὲ ὁ Συμεὼν ὁ δεύτερος υἱὸς τοῦ Ἰακώβ, καὶ ἡμέρας τῆς τελευτῆς προσερχομένης ἐκάλεσε υἱοὺς καὶ ἀδελφούς. εἶτα ἐμήκυνε τὸν λόγον αὐτοῖς. II. 5. ἀπὸ ὑψίστου ἡ ἀνδρεία δέδοται τῷ ἀνθρώπῳ ἐν ψυχαῖς καὶ ἐν σώμασι. 6. ἐζήλωσα τὸν Ἰωσήφ, τὸν ἐμὸν ἀδελφόν, 7. καὶ ὁ Σατανᾶς ὁ ἄρχων τῆς πλάνης ἀπέστειλε τὸ πνεῦμα τοῦ ζήλου, ἐτύφλωσέ μου τὸν νοῦν, καὶ ἐζήτησα κτείνειν τὸν Ἰωσήφ. 8. ἀλλὰ ὁ Θεὸς αὐτοῦ καὶ ὁ Θεὸς τοῦ πατέρος ἐμοῦ ἐρρύσατο αὐτὸν ἐκ τῶν χειρῶν μου. 12. καὶ ὁ Θεὸς οὐκ εἴασέ με ταύτην τὴν ἀνομίαν ἐργάζεσθαι.

III. Καὶ νῦν, τέκνα, φυλάξασθε ἀπὸ τοῦ πνεύματος τῆς πλάνης, ὃ διεγείρει τὸν φθόνον. 2. καὶ γὰρ ὁ φθόνος, εἰσελθὼν ἀπὸ τοῦ Βελίαρ κυριεύει πάσης τῆς διανοίας τοῦ ἀνθρώπου καὶ οὐκ ἀφίησιν αὐτὸν εὐφραίνεσθαι. 3. πάντοτε ὑποβάλλει ἀνελεῖν τὸν φθονούμενον, καὶ αὐτὸς (ὁ φθονούμενος) πάντοτε ἀνθεῖ [ἐν τῷ φόβῳ τοῦ Κυρίου] ὁ δὲ φθονῶν [μένει ἄνευ ἡσυχίας, φθόνος γὰρ ψυχὴν τεταραγμένον ποιεῖ καὶ σῶμα ἐκπλήξεσιν] μαραίνεται. IV. 8. Καὶ φθόνος ὀργὴν καὶ πόλεμον γεννᾷ καὶ εἰς αἵματα ἡγεῖται καὶ ἀφαιρεῖ τὸν ὕπνον καὶ κλόνον παρέχει τῇ ψυχῇ. [ἐννόει δὲ διανοίᾳ ὡς θεῖον πρᾶγμα ὁ ἄνθρωπος, ἀλλὰ νῦν ὅταν πνεῦμα ἐχθρὸν εἰσέρχηται ἀναγκάζει κατ' αὐτὸν δρᾶν τι.] 9. καὶ ἐν πνεύματι πονηρῷ τὴν ψυχὴν αὐτοῦ βασανίζει καὶ προφέρει φόβον τῷ σώματι [καὶ στάσιν εἰσφέρει]. καὶ γὰρ πνεῦμα ἐχθρὸν ἐγχεῖ τὸν ἰὸν αὐτοῦ. [ὥστε μὴ μέμνησθαι τοῦ ἐλέους ἐγὼ δὲ ἐννόησα καὶ] III. 4. ἐκάκωσα ἐν νηστείᾳ τὴν ψυχήν μου, καὶ ἔγνων ὅτι ἡ μέμψις τοῦ φθόνου γίνεται σὺν τῷ φόβῳ τοῦ Θεοῦ.

[Ἀλλ' ἐπεὶ ὁ ἀδελφὸς Ἰωσὴφ ἦν ἐν Αἰγύπτῳ ἠδύνατο τιμωρεῖσθαι διὰ τὸ ἐμὸν πρᾶγμα ἀνόσιον] IV. 4. Ἰωσὴφ δὲ ἀδελφὸς ἡμῶν ἦν ἀνὴρ ἀγαθὸς καὶ οὐκ ἐμνησικάκησέ μοι [ὡς κατ' αὐτοῦ ἥμαρτον, ἀλλὰ ἐνοήσατο περὶ ἡμῶν, ὡς ταῦτα βουλῇ Θεοῦ πέπρακται, καὶ ἔλεγε πάντα τὰ ἄλλα κατὰ τάξιν καὶ τούτους τοὺς λόγους προσέθηκε].

V. 4. ἑώρακα γὰρ ἐν χαρακτῆρι γραφῆς Ἑνώχ, ὅτι υἱοὶ ὑμῶν μεθ' ὑμῶν ἐν πορνείᾳ φθαρήσονται, [τοῦτό ἐστι, οὐκ εἰδότες τὸν υἱὸν τοῦ Θεοῦ διαφθειρόμενοι ἐν τοῖς ἔθνεσιν], καὶ ἐν Λευὶ ἀδικήσουσιν. [τοῦτό ἐστι, Ἰησοῦν Χριστὸν ἱερέα κατὰ τὸν Λευὶ ὃν οἱ Ἰουδαῖοι] ῥομφαίᾳ [διετρύπησαν]. 5. ἀλλ' οὐ δύνανται πρὸς Λευί, ὅτι πόλεμον Κυρίου πολεμεῖ, [ἐννόει δέ, Ἰουδαῖε, ὁ πόλεμος τοῦ Θεοῦ τι σημαίνει. καὶ οὕτως ἀντικατέστης τῷ Κυρίῳ, καὶ τῷ σταυρῷ προσήλωσας. κατὰ τὸ θέλημα τοῦ φρουροῦντος σφραγίσαντες ἐν τῷ τάφῳ κατέθηκατε, ἀλλὰ καίπερ ἔχων τὴν σφραγῖδα διασεσωμένην, ἀνέστη ἐκ τοῦ τάφου ἄνευ διαφθορᾶς, ὡς εἶπε, οὐκ ἠδύναντο καὶ οὐ δύνανται δεσμεύειν τὸν Θεόν, καίπερ σφραγίσαντες τὸν τάφον, ἀλλὰ] 6. καθὼς καὶ Ἰακὼβ προφητεύων ἐν εὐλογίαις, [καὶ οὐκ εὐλόγησε τὰ ἔθνη, καὶ Συμεὼν προσέθηκε λέγειν τοῖς υἱοῖς]. VI. 1. ἰδοὺ εἴρηκα ὑμῖν πάντα, ὅπως δικαιωθῶ ἀπὸ τῆς ἁμαρτίας τῶν ψυχῶν ὑμῶν [ἰδοὺ Συμεὼν προφητεύει καὶ λέγει τὴν ἔλευσιν τοῦ Χριστοῦ, καὶ τούτῳ καθαίρει τὴν ψυχὴν ἐκ τῶν ἀνόμων πράξεων τοῦ Ἑβραϊκοῦ γένους εἴπερ ἀφαιρήσετε φθόνον καὶ μεγαλοφροσύνην καὶ ἐπολέμησε Συμεὼν τοῖς υἱοῖς αὐτοῦ ὥστε ἀποτρέπειν αὐτοὺς ἀπὸ φθόνου καὶ μεγαλοφροσύνης, ἀλλ' οὐκ ἠδύνατο τότε πολεμεῖν, καὶ γὰρ Ἰουδαῖοι τότε προσεκαίοντο φθόνῳ καὶ μεγαλοφροσύνῃ, ἀφ' ἧς δεσμεύοντες τὸν Ἰησοῦν προσέφερον αὐτὸν τῷ Πιλάτῳ εἰς τὸ βουλευτήριον. Πιλάτος δὲ οὐχ εὑρίσκει ἁμαρτίαν ἐν αὐτῷ. Καὶ Συμεὼν εἶπεν αὐτοῖς] 2. εἰ ἀποκλίνεσθε ἀπὸ φθόνου καὶ σκληροτραχηλίας, καὶ ὀστᾶ μου ὡς ῥόδον ἀνθήσει ἐν Ἰσραὴλ καὶ ὡς κρίνον ἡ σάρξ μου ἐν Ἰακώβ, καὶ ἔσται ἡ ὀσμή μου θαυμάσιος καὶ πληθυνθήσεται ὡς κέδροι ἅγιαι.

[Ποῦ γὰρ κέδρον ἁγίαν λέγει ἢ ποῦ τὸ πρότερον δένδρον ἁγιάζεται, ἀλλ' οἱ μεγάλοι πατριάρχαι εἶδον τοῖς ὀφθαλμοῖς τῆς διανοίας καθὼς ἦν τῷ Ἰησοῦ τῷ υἱῷ τοῦ Θεοῦ κυπαρίσσῳ καὶ πεύκῃ καὶ κέδρῳ σταυροῦσθαι καὶ ἕνεκα τούτου ἡ ἁγία κέδρος ἔννοιαν ἔχει ἀπ' ἐμοῦ καὶ ἔσται εἰς ἀεὶ προφητεία καὶ ἀπὸ Χριστοῦ ἕως τοῦ χρόνου πεπληρωμένου] ἀποβλαστήματα αὐτῶν [εἰς μακρὸν χρόνον φύσεται, τοῦτό ἐστι, ὄνομα Χριστοῦ ἐκταθήσεται εἰς πάντα τὰ ἔθνη]. 5. καὶ τότε σημεῖα δοξάζεται ὅταν ὁ Κύριος ὁ ὕψιστος Θεὸς φανεῖται ἐπὶ τῇ γῇ, ὥσπερ ἄνθρωπος σώζων τὸν Ἀδάμ. [Ἰδού, ὡς ὁ Ἀδὰμ σώζεται, ὥσπερ Ἀδὰμ ἦν ὁ πρῶτος ἄνθρωπος, καὶ ἔπεσε παραβαίνων τὴν ἐντολὴν τοῦ Θεοῦ, ἕνεκα τούτου, ὁ Θεὸς ἄνθρωπος ἐγένετο, λαβὼν σάρκα ἀπὸ παρθένου σώζει σὺν αὐτῷ καὶ τὴν φύσιν καὶ τοὺς ἀνθρώπους, καὶ ἐκφέρει τὸν Ἀδὰμ καὶ δίδωσι αὐτῷ πάντα τὰ πνεύματα τῆς πλάνης εἰς τὸ κολάζειν καὶ ἄνθρωποι ἄρξονται κρατεῖν τῶν πονηρῶν πνευμάτων. καὶ ἐπὶ τῇ ἀναλήψει ὁ Κύριος ἀπέπεμψε τὸ ἅγιον πνεῦμα τοῖς ἁγίοις ἀποστόλοις καὶ ἔδωκεν αὐτοῖς δύναμιν καὶ κράτος τοῖς λόγοις τοῦ Κυρίου τὰ πνεύματα τῆς πλάνης ἐξήλασαν, καὶ ἡμεῖς εἰς ταύτην τὴν ἡμέραν τὰ ὀστᾶ τῶν ἁγίων ἔχομεν τῷ ἔργῳ τοῦ ἁγίου πνεύματος]. 6. τὰ πνεύματα τὰ ἀκάθαρτα ἀφανισθήσεται, [ὡς ὁ καπνὸς] 7. καὶ τότε ἔσονται εὐλογίαι τοῦ ὑψίστου περὶ τῶν σημείων αὐτοῦ, ὡς εἶπεν ὁ Θεὸς λαβὼν τὸ σῶμα καὶ συνεσθίων ἀνθρώποις, σώζειν τὸν ἄνθρωπον.

VII. 1. Καὶ νῦν, τέκνα μου, ἐν Λευὶ καὶ ἐν Ἰούδᾳ λυτρωθήσεσθε καὶ μὴ ἐπαίρεσθε ἐπὶ τὰς δύο φυλὰς ταύτας, ὅτι ἐξ αὐτῶν ἀνατελεῖ ὑμῖν τὸ σωτήριον τοῦ Θεοῦ. 2. Ἀναστήσει γὰρ Κύριος ἐκ τοῦ Λευὶ ὡς ἀρχιερέα, καὶ ἐκ τοῦ Ἰούδα ὡς βασιλέα καὶ ἄνθρωπον, οὕτως σώσει πάντα τὰ ἔθνη καὶ τὸ γένος τοῦ Ἰσραήλ. [Καὶ τότε πολλοὶ Ἰσραηλῖται σώζονται καὶ ἄλλοι ἀφιερώθησαν ἄνευ ἀριθμοῦ πιστεύοντες τῷ Θεῷ, ἐξ αὐτῶν καὶ τῶν μεγάλων ἀποστόλων ἦσαν 12 καὶ 70 μαθηταί. Ὑμεῖς δὲ ἄθλιοι ἐστὲ πρὸς ὕβριν καὶ ὄνειδος καὶ ἐστὲ παράδειγμα πᾶσι τοῖς ἔθνεσι]. 3. Διὰ τοῦτο ταῦτα ἐντέλλομαι ὑμῖν, ἵνα καὶ ὑμεῖς ἐντείλησθε τοῖς τέκνοις ὑμῶν ὅπως φυλάξωσιν αὐτὰ εἰς τὰς γένεας αὐτῶν.

VIII. καὶ ταῦτα συνετέλεσεν Συμεὼν τοῖς υἱοῖς αὐτοῦ ζήσας ἑκατὸν εἴκοσι ἐτῶν. 2. καὶ ἔθηκαν τὰ ὀστᾶ αὐτοῦ ἐν θήκῃ ξύλων ἀσήπτων ὡς ἀναγαγεῖν τὰ ὀστᾶ αὐτοῦ ἐν Χεβρὼν ἐκέλευσε. καὶ ἀνήνεγκαν αὐτὰ ἐν πολέμῳ Αἰγυπτίων κρυφῇ.

ΔΙΑΘΗΚΗ ΛΕΥΙ

I. 1, 2. Καὶ τότε Λευὶ ὁ τρίτος υἱὸς Ἰακὼβ υἱὸς Λέας, ἐκάλεσεν αὐτοὺς πρὸς ἑαυτὸν [ὥστε διδάσκειν αὐτοὺς τὰς περὶ ἱερωσύνης ὁράσεις, καὶ περὶ τῆς προόψεως τοῦ λόγου] πρὶν ἀποθανεῖν.

II. Ἐγὼ Λευὶ ἐν ἀγαλλιάσει ἠρξάμην καὶ ἐγενόμην, [καὶ ἀνεφυσάμην ἐν δόμῳ τοῦ πατρός μου] καὶ μετὰ ταῦτα ἦλθον σὺν τῷ πατρὶ εἰς Σίκιμα. 2. Ἤμην δὲ νέος, ὡσεὶ ἐτῶν εἴκοσι, ὅτε ἐποίησα μετὰ Συμεὼν τὴν ἐκδίκησιν τῆς ἀδελφῆς ἡμῶν Δίνας. 3. Ὡς δὲ ἐποίμαινον ἐν Ἀβελμαούλ, πνεῦμα συνέσεως Κυρίου ἦλθεν ἐπ' ἐμέ, καὶ πάντας ἑώρων ἀνθρώπους ἀφανίσαντας τὴν ὁδὸν αὐτῶν καὶ ὅτι ὡς τεῖχος ᾠκοδόμησαν τὴν ἀδικίαν καὶ ἐπὶ πύργους ἡ ἀνομία κάθηται. 4. καὶ ἐλυπούμην περὶ τοῦ γένους τῶν ἀνθρώπων, καὶ ηὐξάμην Κυρίῳ, ὅπως σωθῶσιν. 5. Τότε ἐπέπεσεν ἐπ' ἐμὲ ὕπνος, καὶ ἐθεασάμην ὄρος ὑψηλόν· τοῦτο ὄρος Ἀσπιδος ἐν Ἀβελμαούλ. 6. καὶ ἰδοὺ ἠνεῴχθησαν οἱ οὐρανοὶ καὶ ἄγγελος Θεοῦ εἶπε πρός με· Λευὶ εἴσελθε. 7. καὶ εἰσῆλθον ἐκ τοῦ πρώτου οὐρανοῦ εἰς τὸν δεύτερον, καὶ εἶδον ἐκεῖ ὕδωρ κρεμάμενον ἀνάμεσον τούτου κἀκείνου. 8. καὶ εἶδον τρίτον οὐρανὸν πολὺ φωτεινότερον παρὰ τοὺς δύο, καὶ γὰρ ὕψος ἦν ἐν αὐτῷ ἄπειρον. 9. καὶ εἶπον τῷ ἀγγέλῳ, διατί οὗτος; καὶ εἶπεν ὁ ἄγγελος πρός με, Μὴ θαύμαζε ἐπὶ τούτοις, ἄλλους γὰρ οὐρανοὺς ὄψει, [οἱ εἰσὶ πλανῆται καὶ οἱ καλοῦνται ζῶναι τέσσαρες] φαιδρότεροι καὶ δεινότεροι τούτων, 10. ὅτε ἀνέλθῃς ἐκεῖ. ὅτι σύνεγγυς Κυρίου στήσῃ καὶ λειτουργὸς αὐτοῦ ἔσῃ, καὶ μυστήρια αὐτοῦ ἐξαγγελεῖς τοῖς ἀνθρώποις, καὶ περὶ τοῦ μέλλοντος λυτροῦσθαι τὸν Ἰσραὴλ κηρύξεις· 11. καὶ περὶ Ἰούδα δείξει Κύριος ἐν ἀνθρώποις σώζων ἐν αὐτῷ πᾶν γένος ἀνθρώπων.

III. Καὶ εἶπέ μοι, ἄκουσον, καὶ γὰρ τῶν ἑπτὰ οὐρανῶν ὁ κατώτερος διὰ τοῦτο στυγνότερός ἐστιν, ὅτι ὁρᾷ πάσας τὰς ἀδικίας ἀνθρώπων. 2. ὁ δεύτερος ἔχει πῦρ, χιόνα, κρύσταλλον ἕτοιμα εἰς ἡμέραν προστάγματος Κυρίου, ἐν τῇ δικαιοκρισίᾳ τοῦ Θεοῦ. ἐν αὐτῷ εἰσὶ πάντα τὰ πνεύματα πεμπόμενα εἰς ἐκδίκησιν τῶν ἀνθρώπων. 3. Ἐν τῷ τρίτῳ εἰσὶν αἱ δυνάμεις τοῦ συντάγματος τῆς προσβολῆς ὥστε ἐν ἡμέρᾳ κρίσεως ποιῆσαι ἐκδίκησιν ἐν τοῖς πνεύμασι τῆς πλάνης καὶ τοῦ Βελίαρ. οἱ δὲ εἰς τὸν τέταρτον ἐπάνω τούτων ἅγιοι εἰσίν, 4. καὶ ἐν τῷ ἀνωτέρῳ τῶν πάντων καταλύει ἡ μεγάλη δόξα ἐν ἁγίῳ ἁγίων, ὑπεράνω πάσης ἁγιότητος. 5. Ἐν τῷ ὑπ᾽ αὐτοῖς οἱ ἄγγελοί εἰσι τοῦ προσώπου Κυρίου, οἱ λειτουργοῦντες καὶ ἐξιλασκόμενοι πρὸς Κύριον ἐπὶ πάσαις ταῖς ἀγνοίαις τῶν δικαίων. 6. προσφέρουσι δὲ Κυρίῳ ὀσμὴν εὐωδίας λογικήν, καὶ ἀναίμακτον προσφοράν. 7. Ἐν δὲ τῷ ὑποκάτω εἰσὶν οἱ ἄγγελοι οἱ φέροντες τὰς ἀποκρίσεις τοῖς ἀγγέλοις τοῦ προσώπου Κυρίου. 8. Ἐν δὲ τῷ ὑπ᾽ αὐτοῖς εἰσὶ θρόνοι τῆς ἐξουσίας, ἐν ᾧ ὕμνους ἀεὶ τῷ Θεῷ προσφέρουσιν. 9. ὅταν οὖν ἐπιβλέψῃ Κύριος ἐφ᾽ ἡμᾶς πάντες ἡμεῖς σαλευόμεθα, καὶ οἱ οὐρανοὶ καὶ ἡ γῆ ἐξ ἀβύσσου τῆς μεγαλωσύνης αὐτοῦ. 10. οἱ δὲ υἱοὶ τῶν ἀνθρώπων ἐπὶ τούτοις ἀναισθητοῦντες ἁμαρτάνουσι, καὶ παροργίζουσι τὸν Ὕψιστον.

IV. Νῦν οὖν γινώσκετε, ὅτι ποιήσει Κύριος κρίσιν ἐπὶ τοὺς υἱοὺς τῶν ἀνθρώπων, ὥσπερ τῶν πετρῶν σχιζομένων καὶ τοῦ ἡλίου σβεννυμένου καὶ τῶν ὑδάτων ξηραινομένων καὶ τοῦ ᾅδου σκυλευομένου ἐπὶ τῷ πάθει τοῦ ὑψίστου, οἱ ἄνθρωποι ἀπιστοῦντες ἐπιμενοῦσιν ἐν ταῖς ἀδικίαις. διὰ τοῦτο ἐν κολάσει κριθήσονται. 2. καὶ γὰρ ὁ ὕψιστος (εἰσήκουσε) τῆς προσευχῆς σου, τοῦ διελεῖν σε ἀπὸ τῆς ἀδικίας καὶ γενέσθαι αὐτῷ υἱὸν καὶ θεράποντα καὶ λειτουργόν. 3. φῶς γνώσεως φωτεινὸν φωτιεῖς ἐν Ἰακώβ, καὶ ὡς ὁ ἥλιος ἔσῃ παντὶ σπέρματι ἐν Ἰσραήλ. 4. καὶ δοθήσεταί σοι εὐλογία καὶ παντὶ σπέρματί σου, ἕως ἐπισκέψηται Κύριος πάντα τὰ ἔθνη ἐν σπλάγχνοις υἱοῦ αὐτοῦ ἕως αἰῶνος. πλὴν οἱ υἱοί σου ἐπιβαλοῦσι χεῖρας ἐπ᾽ αὐτόν, τοῦ κακῶσαι αὐτόν, 5. καὶ διὰ τοῦτο δώσεται σοι βουλὴ καὶ συνετίσαι τοὺς υἱούς σου περὶ αὐτοῦ, 6. ὅτι ὁ εὐλογῶν αὐτὸν εὐλογημένος ἔσται, οἱ δὲ καταρώμενοι αὐτὸν ἀπυλοῦνται.

[Καὶ οὕτως Λευὶ προσέθηκε ταύτην τὴν παραίνεσιν τοῖς υἱοῖς αὐτοῦ.] V. καὶ ἤνοιξέ μοι ὁ ἄγγελος τὰς πύλας τοῦ οὐρανοῦ καὶ εἶδον τὸν ναὸν τὸν ἅγιον. καὶ ἐπὶ θρόνου δόξης τὸν Ὕψιστον, 2. καὶ εἶπέ μοι· Λευὶ σοὶ δέδωκα τὰς εὐλογίας ἀξιώματος ἕως οὗ ἐλθὼν παροικήσω ἐμμέσῳ τοῦ Ἰσραήλ. 3. Τότε ὁ ἄγγελος ἤγαγέ με ἐπὶ τὴν γῆν καὶ ἔδωκέ μοι ὅπλον καὶ ῥομφαίαν καὶ εἶπε, ποίησον ἐκδίκησιν ἐν Συχὲμ ὑπὲρ Δίνας, κἀγὼ ἔσομαι μετὰ σοῦ ὅτι Κύριος ἀπέσταλκέ με. 7. καὶ τότε ὡς ἐξ ὕπνου ἐγερθεὶς εὐλόγησα τὸν Κύριον. 4. Καὶ συνετέλεσα τῷ καιρῷ ἐκείνῳ τοὺς υἱοὺς Ἐμμώρ, VI. 3. καὶ ἔπειτα σὺν τῷ Συμεὼν ἐζήλωσα ἐν τῇ ἀνομίᾳ ἣν ἐποίησαν ἐν Ἰσραήλ, 4. καὶ ἀνεῖλον τὸν Συχὲμ καὶ Συμεὼν τὸν Ἐμμὼρ 6. καὶ ὁ πατὴρ ἡμῶν ἀκούσας ὅσα παρενόμησαν

ἐχαλέπαινε ἐν ἡμῖν VII. 1. καὶ εἶπον τῷ πατρί μου, Κύριε Ἰακὼβ
πάτερ, μὴ ὀργίζου. 3. καὶ γὰρ ἐλυμαίνοντο τὴν Δίνην ἡμῶν. [καὶ
ἕνεκα τούτου ὁ χόλος τοῦ Θεοῦ ἐξῆλθε κατ' αὐτῶν καὶ ὁ ἄγγελος
τοῦ κρατεροῦ ἐβοήθησεν ἐμοί, ἐννόει, Ἰουδαῖε, ταύτην τὴν ἔννοιαν καὶ
ἔθιζε σεαυτὸν πρὸς τὴν ὄψιν, ἣν ἐδήλωσέ σοι ὁ Λευὶ ὁ εὐλογημένος
ὡς ἐρώτησε ὁ Λευὶ ὁ εὐλογημένος τὸν ἄγγελον θαυμάσας τὰ ἐπουράνια,
ἄγγελος εἶπεν αὐτῷ πλησίον τῷ Κυρίῳ στήσει καὶ θεράπων αὐτῷ
ἔσει καὶ τοῖς ἀνθρώποις τὰ μυστήρια ἀγγελεῖς καὶ προφητεύσεις περὶ
τοῦ μέλλοντος σώζειν τὸν Ἰσραὴλ καὶ οὕτως οὐκ ἐννοεῖς, ὦ Ἰουδαῖε,
καίπερ τοῦ ἀγγέλου τοῦ Θεοῦ προφητεύοντος τοῖς προγόνοις σου
περὶ τῆς σωτηρίας τοῦ Ἰσραήλ, ὡς ἐκ σοῦ φανήσεται περὶ Ἰούδου
ὁ Κύριος τοῖς ἀνθρώποις, σώζων, ὡς εἶπε δι' ἑαυτὸν πᾶν τὸ γένος
τῶν ἀνθρώπων. Ἐννόει, ἄθλιε, ὅτι οὔτε ἄγγελος οὔτε πρέσβυς ἀλλ'
ὁ Θεὸς αὐτὸς ἔσωσεν ἡμᾶς. Τόδε γὰρ ἐν πρώτοις ἐλέξαμέν σοι ὅτι
ἐκ γενεᾶς τῶν Ἰουδαίων ἐγένετο ὁ Κύριος ἐκ Μαρίας παρθένου, ὧν
ἱερεὺς κατὰ τὸν Λευί, ὡς γὰρ κατὰ τὴν πρώτην ἐντολὴν ἦν ἱερεὺς
ἵνα καθαρίσῃ τὰς τοῦ λαοῦ ἁμαρτίας, ἕνεκα τούτου ἱερεὺς ἦν ὁ Κύριος,
περὶ οὗ ἔλεξεν ὁ ἄγγελος τῷ Λευί· εἶπον περὶ σοῦ καὶ περὶ τοῦ
Ἰούδου ὅτι Κύριος φανήσεται ἀνθρώποις, σώζων δι' ἑαυτὸν πᾶν τὸ
γένος τῶν ἀνθρώπων ἄνευ αἵματος, ἐννοοῦντες προσφορὰν ὅτι οἱ ἄγγελοι
θρησκείαν προφέρουσι τῷ Κυρίῳ οὐκ ἐξ αἵματος μόσχων ἢ αἵματος
τράγων ἀλλ' εὐχαριστίαν τῷ Κυρίῳ καὶ καθαρὰν θρησκείαν προφέρουσιν,
καὶ οὕτως ἡμεῖς Χριστιανοὶ τὸ σῶμα καὶ τὸ αἷμα καθαρὰν θρησκείαν
κατὰ τὴν τάξιν τοῦ Μελχισεδὲκ προφέρομεν. Ἐννόει δὲ νῦν περὶ
τούτου, νῦν πάρεστι ὁρᾶν ὡς ὁ Θεὸς ποιεῖ κρίσιν περὶ τῶν υἱῶν τοῦ
ἀνθρώπου, περὶ ὑμῶν, ὦ ἄθλιοι, οὐ ποιεῖ κρίσιν ὁ Θεὸς εἰς τὸ πῦρ τὸ
ἄσβεστον καὶ εἰς τὸν σκώληκα ὃς οὐ τελεύτᾳ καὶ ἑτοιμάζων ὑμῖν λίθον
τοῦ προσκόμματος ὅτε προσηλώσατε τὸν Θεὸν τῆς δόξης ἐπὶ τῷ σταυρῷ
καὶ ὁ ἥλιος ἐξέλειψε, καὶ γὰρ οὐ τότε ὁ ἥλιος ἐξέλειψε, ἡνίκα τὸν
Κύριον ἐπὶ σταυρῷ ἐσταυρώσατε; ὡς τὸ ἅγιον εὐαγγέλιον λέγει. τότε
γὰρ ἦν σκότος ἐπὶ πάσῃ τῇ γῇ ἀπὸ τῆς τρίτης ὥρας ἕως τῆς ἐννάτης
ὑδάτων ξηραινομένων καὶ τοῦ Ἅδου αἰχμαλωτιζομένου. εἶπε γάρ μοι,
εἰ ὁ Ἅδης αἰχμαλωτίσθη στρατιῶται ὡπλισμένοι εἰς τὸν Ἅδην εἰσῆλθον,
ἀλλὰ καὶ ὁ Κύριος κείμενος ἐν τῷ μνημείῳ, τότε εἰσῆλθεν εἰς τὸν
Ἅδην. λύει τὸν πρωτογεννηθέντα Ἀδὰμ ἐκ δεσμωτηρίου, ὅτι αὐτὸς
Κύριος ἐστι τῶν οὐρανῶν καὶ τῆς γῆς καὶ τῶν κάτω, καὶ διὰ τοῦτο
ἦλθεν ὥστε αἰχμαλωτίζειν τὸν Ἅδην. καὶ ἔτι ἔπαθεν, καὶ τὸ θεῖον
[μέρος] αὐτοῦ ἦν ἄνευ πάθους, καὶ γὰρ τῷ αὐτοῦ πάθει ἔδωκεν ἀπάθειαν
τῷ γένει τῶν ἀνθρώπων. Ἄνθρωποι οὐκ εἰδότες ἐν ἀδικίᾳ μενοῦσιν,

ὑμεῖς γὰρ οἱ οὐκ ἔννοιαν ἔχοντες ταλαιπώρῳ ἐν ἀδικίᾳ μένετε καὶ
ἕνεκα τούτου κατακρίνεσθε ἐν βασάνοις, καὶ ἤκουσεν ὁ ὕψιστος τὴν
εὐχήν, καὶ ἀποτρέπου ἀπὸ τῆς πονηρίας καὶ γένου ὁ υἱὸς αὐτοῦ καὶ
θεράπων, ἐννόει γὰρ ὡς τὸ πρόσθεν ὁ υἱὸς τοῦ Θεοῦ ἦν καὶ ὑπηρέτει πρὸ
προσώπου αὐτοῦ. καὶ δώσει σοι τὴν εὐλογίαν καὶ παντὶ τῷ σπέρματί
σου, ἕως ἂν ὁ Κύριος ἐπισκέψηται πάντα τὰ ἔθνη καὶ (πέμψει) τὸν υἱὸν
αὐτοῦ εἰς ἀεὶ σὺν ἐλεημοσύνῃ. ὡς ὑμεῖς, ὦ ταλαίπωροι, ἐπεβάλετε
τὰς χεῖρας καὶ ἐκακώσατε τὸν υἱὸν τοῦ Θεοῦ καὶ ἕνεκα τούτου ἔννοια
δοθήσεται ὑμῖν ὥστε γνωρίζειν τοὺς υἱοὺς περὶ τούτου, ὡς ὁ εὐλογίζων
αὐτὸν εὐλογήσεται καὶ ὁ καταρώμενος ἐξολοθρευθήσεται. καὶ οὕτως
μέμνησθε περὶ τούτου, τίς ἐστι, εὐλογῶν τὸν υἱὸν τοῦ Θεοῦ καὶ
πιστεύοντες ἐν αὐτῷ ἐν τῇ ἀληθείᾳ, ἡμεῖς γὰρ οἱ Χριστιανοὶ προεκυνή-
σαμεν αὐτῷ, ὑμεῖς δὲ ἐσταυρώσατε, καὶ οὕτως ἐν ἀληθείᾳ ἐποιήσατε
καθ' ὑμῶν αὐτῶν τὸν ὄλεθρον. καὶ ἀπόλλυσθε ὡς μικρόν τι μέρος
διασκορπισθέντες ἐν τῇ οἰκουμένῃ. καὶ τοῦτο τὸ μέρος οὐκ ὀλίγον
λαμβάνει βάρος καὶ λύπην καὶ κάκωσιν. Ἐννόει δὲ τὸ λεχθὲν τῷ
Λευὶ ἐν τοῖς οὐρανοῖς· ἔδωκά σοι τὴν εὐλογίαν τῆς καθαρότητος, ἕως
ἐλθὼν παροικῶ ἐν τῷ Ἰσραήλ, ἀλλ' ὑμεῖς, ὦ ταλαίπωροι, οὐκ ἐννοεῖτε
ὅτι ἐλεύσεται ὁ Κύριος σώζειν τὸν Ἰσραήλ, εἰ καὶ ἐβλασφημήσατε
βλασφημίᾳ τὸν Κύριον, καὶ τούτου χάριν ἡμεῖς ἄλλοτε φέροντες νῦν
ἀπεδεξάμεθα τὸν νόμον τοῦ Θεοῦ αὐτοῦ, ἀλλ' ὑμεῖς, ταλαίπωροι, ὅμοιοι
γενόμενοι τῷ παλαιῷ σατανᾷ ἕνεκα τῆς ὑπερηφανίας εἰς τὸν ὄλεθρον
ἐπέσετε].

VIII. 1. [Καὶ εἶπεν ὁ Λευὶ· ὅτε ἦλθον πορευόμενος] εἰς Βεθήλ,
εἶδον ὅραμα δεινὸν περὶ ἁγιότητος, ὡς πρότερον. εἶδον, 2. ἑπτὰ
ἀνθρώπους ἐν ἐσθῆτι λευκῇ λέγοντάς μοι, Ἀναστὰς ἔνδυσαι τὸ ἱμάτιον
τῆς πίστεως καὶ τὴν ἐπιστήθιον χλαμύδα καὶ τὸ ἐφοὺδ τῆς προφητείας.
3. Καὶ εἷς ἕκαστος αὐτῶν ἕκαστον βαστάζοντες ἐπέθηκάν μοι καὶ
εἶπον· Ἀπὸ τοῦ νῦν γίνου εἰς ἱερέα Κυρίου, σὺ καὶ υἱοί σου καὶ
σπέρμα σου πρὸς αὐτὸν ἕως αἰῶνος. 4. καὶ ὁ πρῶτος ἤλειψεν ἐλαίῳ
ἁγίῳ καὶ ἔδωκέ μοι τὴν ζωὴν τῆς ἐλαίας [τοῦτό ἐστιν τῇ ἁγίᾳ ἐλαίᾳ ᾗ
ἀλείφονται Χριστιανοὶ ἐν τοῖς ἁγίοις λουτροῖς, καὶ τότε καθιέρωσαν
ἑαυτοὺς τῷ Κυρίῳ καὶ λήψονται τὴν ζωὴν τὴν αἰώνιον]. 5. Ὁ δεύτερος
ἔλουσέ με ὕδατι καθαρῷ, [τοῦτό ἐστι τριπλῷ βυθισμῷ, ἐν ὀνόματι τοῦ
πατρὸς καὶ τοῦ υἱοῦ καὶ τοῦ ἁγίου πνεύματος,] καὶ ἐψώμισεν ἄρτον καὶ
οἶνον, εἰς ἅγια ἁγίων, [τοῦτό ἐστι εὐχαριστίαν ἐν τῇ ἐκκλησίᾳ τοῦ
Κυρίου]. καὶ περιέθηκέ μοι στολὴν ἁγίαν καὶ ἔνδοξον, [τοῦτό ἐστι
τὸ ἅγιον σημεῖον τοῦ ἐπουρανίου βασιλέως, βαπτισμός. οἱ ἄγγελοι
γὰρ ὁρῶντες τοῦτο τὸ ἔνδοξον ἔνδυμα εἰφραίνονται, καὶ τὰ στρατεύματα

τῶν δαιμόνων ὁρῶντα φεύγει]. 6. Ὁ τρίτος βυσσίνην με περιέβαλεν, ὁμοίαν ἐφούδ, [καὶ τότε ἐξῆν μοι ἱερατεύειν κατὰ καιρὸν καὶ οὐκ εἰς τοὺς αἰῶνας τοῦτο ἐστι· εἷς μόνος ἐστὶ εἰς τοὺς αἰῶνας καὶ μένων εἰς τοὺς αἰῶνας· ὁ γὰρ Ἰησοῦς ἦν ἱερεὺς κατὰ τὴν τάξιν τοῦ Μελχισεδέκ]. 7. Ὁ τέταρτος ζώνην μοι περιέθηκεν, [οὐκ ἐν τῷ μέσῳ σώματι ἀλλ' ἐν τῷ νερτέρῳ μέρει, καὶ ἡ ζώνη ἦν] ὁμοία πορφύρᾳ. 8. Ὁ πέμπτος ἔδωκέ μοι τὴν πίστιν τῆς πιότητος, [τοῦτό ἐστι εὐαγγελικῶν καὶ ἀποστολικῶν λόγων, τούτους γὰρ ἀκούοντες οἱ ἅγιοι μάρτυρες ἐγέρθησαν ἀντὶ τοῦ στρατεύματος τοῦ πονηροῦ]. 9. Ὁ ἔκτος στέφανόν μοι τῇ κεφαλῇ περιέθηκεν, [καὶ γὰρ οἱ μάρτυρες ἐγερθέντες διὰ τὴν ἀληθινὴν πίστιν ἐστεφανώθησαν]. 10. Ὁ ἕβδομος διάδημά μοι τῇ κεφαλῇ περιέθηκεν ἱερατείας, καὶ ἐπλήρωσε τὰς χεῖράς μου θυμιάματος, ὥστε ἱερατεύειν με Κυρίῳ. 11. Εἶπε δὲ πρός με, Λευΐ, εἰς τρεῖς ἀρχὰς διαιρεθήσεται τὸ σπέρμα σου, εἰς σημεῖον δόξης Κυρίου ἐπερχομένου. 12. καὶ ὁ πιστεύσας πρῶτος κληρονόμος ἔσται καὶ μείζων ὑπὲρ αὐτὸν οὐ γενήσεται [οὕτως τῷ Ἰωάννῃ τῷ βαπτίστῃ ἐσημάνθη, ὃς ἦν ἐκ τῆς φυλῆς τῶν ἱερέων]· 13. ὁ δεύτερος διδάξει [ὡς ὁ Ἰησοῦς Χριστὸς σώσει τὸν κόσμον]. 14. Ὁ τρίτος ἐπικληθήσεται αὐτῷ ὄνομα καινόν, ὅτι βασιλεὺς ἐκ τοῦ Ἰούδα ἀναστήσεται καὶ ποιήσει ἱερατείαν νέαν κατὰ τὸν τύπον τῶν ἐθνῶν εἰς πάντα τὰ ἔθνη [τῆς ἀφίξεως αὐτοῦ]. 15. ἡ δὲ (παρουσία) ἀγαπητὴ ὡς προφήτου ὑψηλοῦ ἐκ σπέρματος Ἀβραὰμ πατρὸς ἡμῶν. 16. πᾶν ἐπιθυμητὸν ἐν Ἰσραὴλ σοὶ ἔσται καὶ τῷ σπέρματί σου· καὶ ἔδεσθε πᾶν ὡραῖον ὁράσει, καὶ τὴν τράπεζαν Κυρίου διανεμήσεται τὰ τέκνα σου [τοῦτό ἐστι ἡ ἀποστολικὴ εὐχαριστία σὺν τῷ Κυρίῳ]. 17. καὶ ἐξ αὐτῶν ἔσονται ἀρχιερεῖς καὶ κριταὶ καὶ γραμματεῖς, καὶ τὰ στόματα αὐτῶν ποιηθήσεται ἅγια. 18. Καὶ ἐξυπνισθεὶς συνῆκα ὅτι οὐχ ὅμοιόν ἐστι τῷ πρώτῳ ὁράματι. 19. Καὶ ἔκρυψα καίγε τοῦτο ἐν τῇ καρδίᾳ μου.

[Ἐννόει δὲ καί συ, ὦ ταλαίπωρε Ἰουδαῖε, ὡς καὶ σοὶ τὸ ὅραμα τοῦ Λευΐ, καὶ σοὶ ἔλεξα τὴν σωμάτωσιν καὶ τὸ πάθημα τοῦ υἱοῦ τοῦ Θεοῦ.]

IX. Καὶ μεθ' ἡμέρας δύο ἀνέβημεν ἐγὼ καὶ Ἰούδας μετὰ τοῦ πατρὸς ἡμῶν πρὸς τὸν πάππον Ἰσαάκ· 2. καὶ εὐλόγησέ με ὁ πατὴρ τοῦ πατρός μου κατὰ πάντας τοὺς λόγους τῆς ὁράσεώς μου ἧς εἶδον περὶ τῆς ἱερατείας, 7. καὶ ἐδίδαξέ με ὡς ἱερατεύειν τῷ Θεῷ τῷ ὑψίστῳ καθαρᾷ ψυχῇ. 8. καὶ ἦν καθ' ἑκάστην ἡμέραν συνετίζων με καὶ ἐν τοῖς νουθετισμοῖς εἶπέ μοι. X. [Καὶ ἔλεγε] Νῦν οὖν φυλάξασθε ὅσα ἐντέλλομαι ὑμῖν, τέκνα· ὅτι ὅσα ἤκουσα, ἀνήγγειλα ὑμῖν. 2. Ἀθῷός εἰμι ἀπὸ πάσης ἀσεβείας ὑμῶν, ἣν ποιήσετε ἐπὶ συντελείᾳ τῶν αἰώνων εἰς τὸν σωτῆρα τοῦ κόσμου, οὐ πιστεύοντες. [τίνα προσδοκᾷς, ὦ

'Ιουδαῖε, καὶ τίνα μένεις ἐρχόμενον, τοῦ Λευὶ προφητεύοντος, ἐπεὶ ἐν τῷ
σωτῆρι τοῦ κόσμου οὐ πίστιν ἔχεις] πλανῶντες τὸν 'Ισραὴλ καὶ ἐγεί-
ροντες αὐτῷ κακὸν μέγα ἀπὸ τοῦ Κυρίου. 3. Καὶ ἀνομήσετε σὺν τῷ
'Ισραήλ, ὥστε μὴ βαστάξαι τὴν 'Ιερουσαλήμ, ἀπὸ προσώπου πονηρίας
ὑμῶν, ἀλλὰ σχίσαι τὸ ἔνδυμα τοῦ ναοῦ, ὥστε μὴ κατακαλύπτειν ἀσχημοσύνην ὑμῶν. 4. Καὶ διασπαρήσεσθε αἰχμάλωτοι ἐν τοῖς ἔθνεσι
καὶ ἔσεσθε εἰς ὀνειδισμὸν καὶ εἰς κατάραν καὶ εἰς καταπάτημα. 5. ὁ
γὰρ οἶκος, ὃν ἂν ἐκλέξηται Κύριος, 'Ιερουσαλὴμ κληθήσεται. καὶ
εὕρομεν ἐν τῇ βίβλῳ 'Ενὼχ τοῦ δικαίου.

['Ιδοῦ δέ, ὦ 'Ιουδαῖε, ὡς ὁ εὐλογημένος Λευὶ εἶπέ σοι τὸ ὅραμα].
XIV. καὶ νῦν, τέκνα, ἔγνων ἀπὸ γραφῆς 'Ενώχ, ὅτι ἐπὶ τέλει ἀσεβήσετε
ἐπὶ Κύριον, χεῖρας ἐπιβάλλοντες ἐν πάσῃ κακίᾳ, καὶ αἰσχυνθήσονται
ἐφ' ὑμῖν οἱ ἀδελφοὶ ὑμῶν, καὶ πᾶσι τοῖς ἔθνεσι γενήσεται χλευασμός.
2. καὶ γὰρ ὁ πατὴρ ἡμῶν 'Ισραὴλ καθαρὸς ἐστὶν ἀπὸ τῆς ἀσεβείας τῶν
ἀρχιερέων οἵτινες ἐπιβαλοῦσι τὰς χεῖρας αὐτῶν ἐπὶ τὸν σωτῆρα τοῦ
κόσμου. 4. καὶ ἐπάξετε κατάραν ἐπὶ τὸ γένος ἡμῶν, ὅτι τὸ φῶς τοῦ
κόσμου τὸ δοθὲν ἐν ὑμῖν εἰς φωτισμὸν παντὸς ἀνθρώπου, τοῦτον
θέλοντες ἀνελεῖν, ἐναντίας ἐντολὰς διδάσκοντες τοῖς τοῦ Θεοῦ δικαιώ-
μασι. 5. τὰς προσφορὰς λαμβάνετε.

XV. Καὶ ὁ ναὸς ὃν ἂν ἐκλέξηται ὁ Κύριος (ἔρημος ἔσται) ἐν
τῇ ἀκαθαρσίᾳ ὑμῶν. καὶ ὑμεῖς αἰχμάλωτοι ἔσεσθε εἰς πάντα τὰ ἔθνη.
2. καὶ ἔσεσθε βδέλυγμα καὶ λήψεσθε ὀνειδισμὸν καὶ αἰσχύνην αἰώνιον
παρὰ τῆς δικαιοκρισίας τοῦ Θεοῦ. 3. καὶ πάντες στυγήσουσιν ἡμᾶς.
4. καὶ εἰ μὴ δι' 'Αβραὰμ καὶ 'Ισαὰκ καὶ 'Ιακὼβ τοὺς πατέρας ἡμῶν,
εἷς ἐκ τοῦ σπέρματός μου οὐ μὴ καταλειφθῇ ἐπὶ τῆς γῆς.

XVI. Καὶ νῦν ἔγνων ἐν βιβλίοις 'Ενὼχ ὅτι ἑβδομάδα πλανηθήσεσθε
καὶ τὴν ἱεροσύνην βεβηλώσετε καὶ τὰς θυσίας μιανεῖτε. 2. καὶ τὸν
νόμον ἀφανίσετε καὶ λόγους προφητῶν ἐξουθενώσετε, ἐν διαστροφῇ
διώξετε ἄνδρας δικαίους καὶ εὐσεβεῖς μισήσετε, ἀληθινῶν λόγους
βδελύξεσθε. 3. καὶ ἄνδρα ἀνακαινοποιοῦντα νόμον ἐν δυνάμει ὑψίστου,
πλάνον προσαγορεύσετε, καὶ τέλος, ὡς νομίζετε, ἀποκτενεῖτε αὐτόν,
οὐκ εἰδότες αὐτοῦ τὸ ἀνάστημα, τὸ ἀθῷον αἷμα ἐν κακίᾳ ἐπὶ κεφαλὰς
ὑμῶν ἀναδεχόμενοι. 4. Δι' αὐτὸν ἔσται τὰ ἅγια ὑμῶν ἔρημα, ἕως
ἐδάφους μεμιαμμένα. 5. καὶ οὐκ ἔσται τόπος ὑμῶν καθαρός, ἀλλ' ἐν
τοῖς ἔθνεσιν ἔσεσθε εἰς κατάραν καὶ εἰς διασκορπισμόν, ἕως· αὐτὸς
πάλιν ἐπισκέψηται, καὶ οἰκτειρήσας προσδέξηται ὑμᾶς ἐν πίστει καὶ
ὕδατι. [καὶ ὅσα σοι λέγω, ὦ 'Ιουδαῖε, ἤκουσας Λευὶ λέγοντα τοῖς
τέκνοις τῶν τέκνων αὐτοῦ ὡς τὸν Κύριον ἐσταυρώσατε αὐτὸς δὲ οἰκτείρει
καὶ ἀποδέχεται ὑμᾶς ἁγιάζοντες αὐτοὺς τῷ ὕδατι ἐν τῷ ὀνόματι τοῦ

πατρὸς καὶ τοῦ υἱοῦ καὶ τοῦ ἁγίου πνεύματος, ἐννόει δὲ ὅτι οὐκ οἰκτερεῖ
σε, εἴπερ ἐν αὐτῷ οὐ πιστεύεις καὶ οὐ τὸν βαπτισμὸν ἀποδέχει ἐν τῷ
ὀνόματι αὐτοῦ, καὶ γὰρ ὁ Κύριος αὐτὸς εἶπεν ἐν τῷ ἁγίῳ εὐαγγελίῳ
ὅτι ὁ μὴ γεννηθεὶς τῷ ὕδατι καὶ τῷ πνεύματι οὐκ ἐλεύσεται εἰς τὴν
βασιλείαν τῶν οὐρανῶν. Σὺ δέ, ὦ Ἰουδαῖε, περὶ τῶν προγόνων ἐννοῶν
ὥστε μὴ ἀπολλύναι τὴν ψυχὴν σοῦ, λαβὲ τὸν ἅγιον βαπτισμόν, καὶ
γενοῦ ὡς νεόγονον βρέφος ἄνευ μιάσματος ἐν ἁγιότητι. Ἄκουε δέ, ὦ
Ἰουδαῖε, περὶ τὴν ἱερατείαν τῷ Θεῷ τοῦ Λευὶ λέγοντος].

XVII. Ἀκούετε, ὦ τέκνα μου, περὶ τῆς ἱερατείας ἐν τίνι μένει ἐστι
ἱερατεία· 2. ὁ πρῶτος χριόμενος εἰς τὴν ἱερωσύνην μέγας ἐστι. 3. Ἐν
τῷ δευτέρῳ ὁ χριόμενος ἐν πένθει ἀγαπητῶν συλληφθήσεται, καὶ ἡ
ἱερωσύνη αὐτοῦ καθαρὰ ἔσται. 4. Ὁ δὲ τρίτος ἱερεὺς ἐν λύπῃ
παραληφθήσεται. 5. καὶ ὁ τέταρτος ἐν ὀδύνῃ ἔσται· ὅτι προσθήσει
ἐπ᾽ αὐτὸν ἡ ἀδικία εἰς πλῆθος. καὶ πᾶς Ἰσραὴλ μισήσουσιν ἕκαστος
τὸν πλησίον αὐτοῦ. 6. Ὁ πέμπτος ἐν σκότει παραληφθήσεται.
7. ὡσαύτως καὶ ὁ ἕκτος καὶ ὁ ἕβδομος. 8. καὶ ἐν παντὶ ἔσται μιασμός,
ὃν οὐ δύναμαι εἰπεῖν, ἐνώπιον τῶν ἀνθρώπων· ὅτι αὐτοὶ γνώσονται οἱ
ποιοῦντες αὐτά. 9. Διὰ τοῦτο ἐν αἰχμαλωσίᾳ ληφθήσονται, καὶ ἡ
γῆ καὶ ἡ ὕπαρξις αὐτῶν ἀφανισθήσεται. 10. [καὶ ἀνακαινοποιήσουσιν
οἶκον Κυρίου] καὶ ἐν πέμπτῃ ἑβδομάδι ἐπιστρέψουσιν εἰς γῆν ἐρημώσεως
αὐτῶν καὶ ἀνακαινοποιήσουσιν οἶκον Κυρίου. 11. Ἐν δὲ τῷ ἑβδόμῳ
ἑβδοματικῷ ἥξουσιν οἱ ἱερεῖς, εἰδωλολατροῦντες, μάχιμοι, φιλάργυροι,
ὑπερήφανοι, ἄνομοι, κτηνοφθόροι, ἀσελγεῖς.

XVIII. Καὶ μετὰ τὸ γενέσθαι τὴν ἐκδίκησιν παρὰ Κυρίου, 2. τῇ
ἱερατείᾳ τότε ἐγερεῖ Κύριος ἱερέα καινόν, ᾧ πάντες οἱ λόγοι Κυρίου
ἀποκαλυφθήσονται καὶ αὐτὸς ποιήσει κρίσιν ἀληθείας ἐπὶ τῆς γῆς ἐν
πλήθει ἡμερῶν. 3. καὶ ἀνατελεῖ ἄστρον αὐτοῦ ἐν οὐρανῷ ὡς βασιλεύς,
φωτίζων φῶς γνώσεως ἐν ἡλίῳ ἡμέρας· καὶ μεγαλυνθήσεται ἐν τῇ
οἰκουμένῃ ἕως ἀναλήψεως αὐτοῦ. 4. Ἐκεῖ ἀναλάμψει ἐν τῇ γῇ καὶ
ἐξαρεῖ πᾶν σκότος ἐκ τῆς ὑπ᾽ οὐρανὸν καὶ ἔσται εἰρήνη ἐν πάσῃ τῇ γῇ.
5. οἱ οὐρανοὶ ἀγαλλιάσονται ἐν ἐκείνῃ τῇ ἡμέρᾳ καὶ ἡ γῆ χαρίσεται καὶ
λίμναι εὐφρανθήσονται καὶ ἡ γνῶσις Κυρίου χυθήσεται ἐπὶ τῆς γῆς,
ὡς ὕδωρ θαλασσῶν. καὶ οἱ ἄγγελοι τῆς δόξης τοῦ προσώπου Κυρίου
χαρίσονται ἐν αὐτῷ. 6. Οἱ οὐρανοὶ ἀνοιγήσονται καὶ ἐκ τοῦ ναοῦ
τῆς δόξης ἥξει ὁ ἅγιος μετὰ φωνῆς τοῦ πατρός. 7. Καὶ δόξα ὑψίστου
ἐπ᾽ αὐτὸν ῥηθήσεται καὶ πνεῦμα συνέσεως καὶ ἁγιασμοῦ καταπαύσει
ἐπ᾽ αὐτὸν ἐν τῷ ὕδατι. 8. Αὐτὸς δώσει τὴν μεγαλωσύνην Κυρίου τοῖς
υἱοῖς αὐτοῦ ἐν ἀληθείᾳ εἰς τὸν αἰῶνα· καὶ οὐκ ἔσται διαδοχὴ αὐτοῦ
εἰς γενεὰς καὶ γενεὰς ἕως τοῦ αἰῶνος. 9. καὶ χῶραι τῆς ὁσιότητος

αὐτοῦ αὐξήσονται ἐν συνέσει ἐπὶ τῇ γῇ καὶ τῇ χάριτι τοῦ Θεοῦ ὁ
Ἰσραὴλ ἁγιασθήσεται· [ἐκλείψει πᾶσα ἁμαρτία] καὶ ἀμαυρωθήσεται
ἐν τῇ λύπῃ τῆς ἁγιότητος αὐτοῦ καὶ πᾶσα ἁμαρτία ἐλαττώσεται καὶ
οἱ ἄνομοι καταπαύσουσιν εἰς κακά. οἱ δὲ δίκαιοι καταπαύσουσιν ἐν
αὐτῷ. 10. Καὶ γὰρ αὐτὸς ἀνοίξει τὰς θύρας τοῦ παραδείσου καὶ
στήσει τὴν ἀπειλοῦσαν ῥομφαίαν κατὰ τοῦ Ἀδάμ. 11. καὶ δώσει τοῖς
ἁγίοις φαγεῖν ἐκ τοῦ ξύλου τῆς ζωῆς, καὶ πνεῦμα ἁγιωσύνης ἔσται
ἐπ᾽ αὐτοῖς. 12. Καὶ ὁ Βελίαρ δεθήσεται ὑπ᾽ αὐτοῦ, καὶ δώσει ἐξουσίαν
τοῖς τέκνοις αὐτοῦ τοῦ πατεῖν ἐπὶ τὰ πονηρὰ πνεύματα. 13. Καὶ
εὐφρανθήσεται Κύριος ἐπὶ τοῖς τέκνοις αὐτοῦ ἕως τῶν αἰώνων. 14. Τότε
ἀγαλλιάσεται Ἀβραὰμ καὶ Ἰσαὰκ καὶ Ἰακὼβ κἀγὼ χαρίσομαι καὶ
πάντες οἱ ἅγιοι ἐνδύσονται δικαιοσύνην.

XIX. Καὶ νῦν, τέκνα μου, πάντα ἠκούσατε· ἕλεσθε οὖν ἑαυτοῖς ἢ
τὸ σκότος ἢ τὸ φῶς, ἢ νόμον Κυρίου ἢ ἔργα τοῦ Βελίαρ.

XIII. 1. Πάντα ἃ ἐννόησα ἐντέλλεσθαι ὑμῖν, καὶ ἕνεκα τούτου
φοβεῖσθε τὸν Κύριον τὸν Θεὸν ὑμῶν πάσῃ τῇ καρδίᾳ ὑμῶν καὶ
πορεύεσθε ἐν τῇ ἁπλότητι τοῦ νόμου αὐτοῦ. 2. καὶ διδάσκετε τοὺς
υἱοὺς ὑμῶν τὰ βιβλία, ὅπως ἐννοῶσιν ἐν πάσῃ τῇ ζωῇ αὐτῶν
διδαξάμενοι τὸν νόμον τοῦ ἁγιωτάτου Θεοῦ. 3. καὶ πᾶς ὁ ἐννοῶν
τὸν νόμον τοῦ Κυρίου καθαρὸς ἔσται καὶ οὐ ξένος ἐστὶ ὅπου ἂν
ξενίζηται. 4. πολλοὶ γὰρ τῶν ἀνθρώπων ἐν τῷ βιβλίῳ τιθέναι τὰ
ὀνόματα αὐτῶν θέλουσι ὥστε ἐργάζεσθαι δι᾽ αὐτὸν καὶ ἀκούειν τὸν
νόμον ἀπὸ τῶν χειλέων αὐτοῦ. 5. Καὶ ἐργάζεσθε τὴν δικαιοσύνην,
τέκνα μου, ἐν τῇ γῇ καὶ εὑρήσετε αὐτὴν ἐν τοῖς οὐρανοῖς. 6. Καὶ
σπείρετε ἐν τῇ ψυχῇ καὶ εὐλογοῦντες καὶ θερίσετε ἐν τῇ ζωῇ ὑμῶν,
καὶ σπείραντες ἐν κακῷ κακὸν θερίσετε. 7. Ὑμεῖς δέ, τέκνα, τίθεσθε
τὴν σοφίαν ἐν τῷ φόβῳ τοῦ Κυρίου σὺν πόνῳ. εἰ δὲ πόλις ἁλίσκεται,
ἀποβάλλουσι τὸν χρυσὸν καὶ τὸν ἄργυρον καὶ πᾶν τὸ κέρδος ἀπόλλυται,
ἀλλ᾽ οὐδεὶς ἀπὸ τοῦ σοφοῦ ἀφαιρεῖν δύναται τὴν σοφίαν, ἀλλὰ μόνον
σκότωσις διὰ τὰς ἁμαρτίας καὶ τύφλωσις τῶν πραγμάτων· 8. ἐκ
τῆς εὐγενείας αὐτοῦ τότε ἔσται μάχη ἀπὸ τῶν πολεμίων καὶ ὥσπερ
πατρὶς ἐν γῇ ἀλλοτρίᾳ καὶ ἐν τοῖς πολεμίοις ἀποστρέψεται. 9. εἴ
τις τῆς μαθήσεως καὶ σοφίας ἀντιλαμβάνεται ἔσται αὐτὸς ἐπιτραπέζιος
τοῖς βασιλεῦσιν ὡς ὁ ἀδελφὸς ἡμῶν ὁ ἁγνὸς Ἰωσήφ. XIX. 2. καὶ
ἀπεκρίθησαν οἱ υἱοὶ τοῦ Λευὶ τῷ πατρὶ λέγοντες Ἐνώπιον Κυρίου
πορευσώμεθα κατὰ τὸν νόμον αὐτοῦ. 3. καὶ εἶπε Λευί· Μάρτυς ἔστω ὁ
Κύριος ὅσα ὑπέσχεσθε σήμερον. 4. καὶ ταῦτα εἰπὼν ἐκοιμήθη ζήσας
ἑκατὸν τριάκοντα ἑπτὰ ἔτη. 5. καὶ ἔθηκαν αὐτὸν ἐν σορῷ, καὶ ὕστερον
ἔθαψαν αὐτὸν ἐν Χεβρῶν ὅπου Ἀβραὰμ καὶ Ἰσαὰκ καὶ Ἰακώβ.

I. 1, 2, 3. Μετὰ ταῦτα Ἰούδα, τέταρτος υἱὸς Ἰακώβ, υἱὸς Λέας ἐκαλέσατο τοὺς υἱοὺς αὐτοῦ πρὸς ἑαυτὸν καὶ εἶπε, Τέκνα μου, πρὸ τοῦ ἀποθανεῖν ἐμέ, λέξω σοι τὰ ἔργα μου, ὅτε κράτος ἦν ἐν τῷ στέρνῳ 3..καὶ ταχὺς ἦν τοῖς ποσὶ καὶ κρατερὸς τῷ σώματι, [πολλοὶ τῶν πολεμίων οὐκ ἀνέσχον τοὺς ἐμοὺς βραχίονας καὶ ἐνίκησα κράτος πόλεως οὐκ εἰκούσης] III. 10. καὶ εἶδεν ὁ πατήρ μου Ἰακὼβ ὡς ὁ ἄγγελος τοῦ κρατεροῦ ἐβοήθησέ μοι περὶ τῆς ἀνδρείας καὶ προσεῖχεν αὐτοῖς τὸν νοῦν.

XVIII. 1. Εἶδον γὰρ ἐν τοῖς βιβλίοις τοῦ Ἐνώχ, ὅσα κακὰ ποιεῖται ἐν ταῖς ἐσχάταις ἡμέραις, 2. ἀλλὰ σώσατε ὑμᾶς ἑαυτούς, τέκνα μου, ἀπὸ πάσης πορνείας καὶ φιλαργυρίας, 3. ἥτις ἀποστερεῖ τοῦ νόμου τοῦ Κυρίου, καὶ ἐκτυφλοῖ τὰ ἐννοήματα τῆς ψυχῆς, καὶ οὐκ ἀφίει ἄνδρα ἐλεῆσαι τὸν πλησίον αὐτοῦ. 4. καὶ συνέχει αὐτὸν ἐν μόχθοις καὶ πόνοις. XIX. 2. Διὰ ἀργύριον ἐγὼ ἀπώλεσα τὰ τέκνα μου, καὶ εἰ μὴ ἡ μετάνοια σαρκός μου καὶ ἡ ταπείνωσις ψυχῆς μου, καὶ αἱ εὐχαὶ Ἰακὼβ τοῦ πατρός μου, ἄτεκνος εἶχον ἀποθανεῖν. 3. Ἀλλ' ὁ Θεὸς τῶν πατέρων μοῦ ὁ οἰκτίρμων καὶ ἐλεήμων, συνέγνω ὅτι ἐν ἀγνοίᾳ ἐποίησα. 4. Ἐτύφλωσε γάρ με ὁ ἄρχων τῆς πλάνης καὶ ἠγνόησα ὡς ἄνθρωπος καὶ ὡς σάρξ, ἐν ἁμαρτίαις φθαρείς, καὶ ἐπέγνων τὴν ἐμαυτοῦ ἀσθένειαν νομίζων ἀκαταμάχητος εἶναι XIII. 3. ὠνείδισα τὸν ἀδελφὸν Ῥουβὴμ περὶ Βάλλας τῆς γυναικὸς τοῦ πατρός, καὶ πολλάκις ἐκόμπαζον ἐν τοῖς ἀδελφοῖς τῷ σθένει τῶν πραγμάτων τῆς νεότητος οὐκ ἀπάντησεν ἐμοὶ πρόσωπον γυναικὸς εὐμόρφου ἀλλὰ τὸ πνεῦμα τοῦ ζήλου παρετάξατο ἐν ἐμοὶ καὶ ἐτύφλωσεν ἕως συνέπεσα εἰς Βησσουὲ τὴν Χαναναίαν. 6. οἶνος γὰρ διέστρεψε τοὺς ὀφθαλμούς μου, καὶ ἠμαύρωσέ μου τὴν καρδίαν ἐπιθυμίᾳ. 7. καὶ παραβὰς τὸν νόμον τοῦ Θεοῦ συνέπεσα. 8. καὶ ἀνταπέδωκέ μοι Κύριος ὅτι οὐκ ηὐφράνθην ἐπὶ τοῖς τέκνοις αὐτῆς.

XIV. Καὶ νῦν, τέκνα μου, μὴ μεθύσκεσθε οἴνῳ· ὅτι ὁ οἶνος διαστρέφει τὸν νοῦν ἀπὸ τῆς ἀληθείας, καὶ ἐμβάλλει νόημα ὀργῆς, καὶ ὁδηγεῖ εἰς πλάνην τοὺς ὀφθαλμούς. 2. Τὸ γὰρ πνεῦμα τῆς πορνείας τὸν οἶνον ὡς διάκονον πρὸς τὰς ἡδονὰς ἔχει· ὅτι καίγε τὰ δύο ταῦτα ἀφιστῶσι τὴν δύναμιν τοῦ ἀνθρώπου. 3. Ἐὰν γάρ τις πίῃ οἶνον εἰς μέθην ἐν διαλογισμοῖς ῥυπαροῖς συνταράσσει τὸν νοῦν εἰς πορνείαν καὶ ἐκθερμαίνει τὸ σῶμα πρὸς μίξιν, καὶ εἰ πάρεστι τὸ τῆς ἐπιθυμίας αἴτιον πράσσει τὴν ἁμαρτίαν καὶ οὐκ αἰσχύνεται 4. ὁ γὰρ μεθύων οὐδένα αἰδεῖται. 5. Ἰδοὺ γὰρ (ὁ οἶνος) κἀμὲ ἐπλάνησε μὴ αἰσχυνθῆναι πλῆθος ἐπὶ ταῖς πύλαις, ὅτι ἐν ὀφθαλμοῖς πάντων ἐξέκλινα πρὸς τὴν Θάμαρ, οὖσαν νύμφην, καὶ ἐποίησα ἁμαρτίαν 6. ἐν μέθῃ. καὶ οὐκ ἐφοβούμην τὴν ἐντολὴν τοῦ Κυρίου. 5. καὶ ἀνεκάλυψα κάλυμμα πᾶσιν ἐν ταῖς ἁμαρτίαις μου. 7. Καὶ νῦν, τέκνα, μὴ μεθύσκητε παρὰ φύσιν τὴν σύνεσιν ὑμῶν 8. εἴπερ μεταβάλλετε τὸν διαλογισμὸν τῆς συνέσεως ὑμῶν μέθῃ, τὸ πνεῦμα τῆς πορνείας εἰσπορεύεται εἰς (ἄνθρωπον) καὶ ποιεῖ τὸν μέθυσον αἰσχρορημονεῖν καὶ παρανομεῖν, καὶ μὴ αἰσχύνεσθαι, ἀλλὰ ἐγκαυχᾶσθαι τῇ ἀτιμίᾳ αὐτοῦ.

XV. Καὶ κατηγορούμενος οὐ ταπεινοῦται διὰ τὴν ἀτιμίαν μέμνησθε ὡς τὰ ἀγαθὰ λέγειν. 2. εἰ γὰρ βασιλεύς τις μένει μεθυσκόμενος καὶ πορνείᾳ παρέχει ἑαυτὸν γυμνούμενος ἐκ τῆς βασιλείας ταχέως ἐκπίπτει. 5. Καὶ ἔδειξέ μοι ὁ ἄγγελος τοῦ Κυρίου ὅτι τῶν ζώντων ἐν μέθῃ, ἢ βασιλέων ἢ πτωχῶν αἱ γυναῖκες κατακυριεύουσιν καὶ τοῦ μὲν βασιλέως αἴρουσιν τὴν δόξαν, τοῦ δὲ ἀνδρείου τὴν δύναμιν καὶ τοῦ πτωχοῦ ἐν τῇ πτωχείᾳ τέλειον στήριγμα.

XVI. Φυλάσσεσθε οὖν, τέκνα μου, τὰ χείλη ἐν μέθῃ, ἐστὶ γὰρ ἐν αὐτῇ τέσσαρα πνεύματα πονηρὰ ἐπιθυμίας, πυρώσεως ἀσωτίας, αἰσχροκερδίας, [ἀναιδείας]. 2. Εἰ μὴ πίνετε σὺν τῷ φόβῳ τοῦ Θεοῦ. Ἐὰν γὰρ ἐν τῷ εὐφραίνεσθαι ἀποστῇ ὁ τοῦ Θεοῦ φόβος, παρεισέρχεται ἡ ἀναισχυντία [καὶ ἀρχὴ τῆς ἁμαρτίας]. 3. Καὶ γίγνονται ἀντιλογίαι τὴν ὀργὴν γεννήσαντες, συκοφαντίαις μωραινόμενοι, καὶ γίγνεται παράβασις ἐντολῶν Θεοῦ καὶ ἔσται ἀπώλεια οὐκ ἐν καιρῷ ὑμῶν. 4. ὡς κἀγὼ ἐντολὰς Θεοῦ καὶ μυστήρια Ἰακὼβ τοῦ πατρός μου ἀπεκάλυψα τῇ Χανανίτιδι, οἷς εἶπεν ὁ Θεὸς μὴ ἀποκαλύψαι.

XVII. Καὶ νῦν ἐντέλλομαι ὑμῖν, τέκνα μου, [μὴ μεθύσκεσθαι οἴνῳ καὶ] μὴ ἀγαπᾶν ἀργύριον, μηδὲ ἐμβλέπειν εἰς κάλλος γυναικῶν ἐν τῇ ὄψει, ἐγὼ γὰρ ἐν μέθῃ εἶδον τὴν Χαναναίαν ὅλως ἐν λαμπρῷ χρυσῷ καὶ ἐπλανήθην δι’ αὐτὴν ὡς ἄνθρωπος ὢν ἐν μέθῃ καὶ τῇ ὄψει αἴτιος ἐγενόμην.

XVIII. 2. Καὶ νῦν, τέκνα μου, ἀκούσατε Ἰούδα τοῦ πατρὸς ὑμῶν, καὶ φυλάξασθε ἀπὸ τῆς φιλαργυρίας καὶ μέθης· 3. ὅτι ταῦτα ἀφιστᾷ (νόμου Θεοῦ) καὶ ὑπερηφανίαν ἐκδιδάσκει· 4. καὶ στερίσκει τὴν ψυχὴν αὐτοῦ ἀπὸ πάσης ἀγαθοσύνης, καὶ ἀφιστᾷ ὕπνον ἀπ’ αὐτοῦ καὶ καταδαπανᾷ σάρκας αὐτοῦ. 5. καὶ τὰς εὐχὰς Θεοῦ ἐμποδίζει καὶ εὐλογίας οὐ μέμνηται, καὶ προφήτῃ λαλοῦντι οὐχ ὑπακούει, καὶ λόγῳ εὐσεβείας προσοχθίζει. 6. καὶ ἐν ἡμέρᾳ ὡς ἐν νυκτὶ πορεύεται.

XII. 3, 4, 6. Ἐγὼ δὲ μωραινόμενος τῇ μέθῃ ἐδήλωσα τὰ μυστήρια τῆς καρδίας μου καὶ ἔδωκα τὴν ῥάβδον καὶ τὸ διάδημα τῆς βασιλείας μου τῇ Θάμαρ τῇ νύμφῃ μου, [ἠγνόησα γὰρ ὅτι Θάμαρ ἦν πόρνη, αἱ γὰρ ἀπὸ Μεσοποταμίας ἦσαν θυγατέρες Ἀβραάμ]. X. 1, 2. καὶ ἔδωκα αὐτὴν τῷ υἱῷ Ἢρ ἐς γάμον καὶ Ἢρ ἦν σκολιὸς καὶ ἠμέλησε τῆς Θάμαρ. αὐτοῖς οὐκ ἦν μοῖρα ἐκ γαίας Χαναάν, καὶ ὁ ἄγγελος τοῦ Θεοῦ ἔκτεινεν αὐτὸν ἐν τῇ τρίτῃ νυκτί. 3. καὶ οὐκ ἐγίνωσκεν αὐτὴν διὰ τῆς σκολιότητος, οὐ γὰρ ἤθελεν ἔχειν ἐξ αὐτῆς τέκνα. 4. ἐν ταῖς ἡμέραις τοῦ γάμου· 1. ἦν γὰρ ἐκ Μεσοποταμίας, θυγάτηρ Ἀράμ. καὶ ἔδωκα αὐτὴν τῷ υἱῷ μου Ἢρ εἰς γάμον. 2. Ἦν δὲ Ἢρ πονηρὸς καὶ ἠπορεῖτο περὶ τῆς Θάμαρ ὅτι οὐκ ἦν ἐκ γῆς Χαναάν. Καὶ ἄγγελος Κυρίου ἀνεῖλεν αὐτὸν τῇ τρίτῃ νυκτί. 3. καὶ αὐτὸς οὐκ ἔγνω αὐτήν, κατὰ πανουργίαν τῆς μητρὸς αὐτοῦ, οὐ γὰρ ἤθελεν ἔχειν τέκνα ἀπ' αὐτῆς. 4. Ἐν ταῖς ἡμέραις τοῦ θαλάμου ἐπεγάμβρευσα αὐτῇ τὸν Αὐνᾶν, τῷ δευτέρῳ υἱῷ μου, καί γε οὗτος ἐν πονηρίᾳ οὐκ ἔγνω αὐτὴν ποιήσας σὺν αὐτῇ ἐνιαυτόν, 5. καὶ ὅτε ἠπείλησα αὐτῷ συνελθεῖν τάσσων αὐτῇ, διέφθειρε τὸ σπέρμα ἐπὶ τὴν γῆν κατὰ τὴν ἐντολὴν τῆς μητρὸς αὐτοῦ, ἀλλὰ ταύτης τῆς πονηρίας γενομένης, 6. ἤθελον καὶ τὸν Σιλὼμ δοῦναι αὐτῇ, τὸν τρίτον υἱόν, ἀλλ' ἡ γυνή μου Βησσουὲ οὐκ ἀφῆκεν· ἐπονηρεύετο γὰρ πρὸς τὴν Θάμαρ, ὅτι οὐκ ἦν ἐκ θυγατέρων Φαραὼν ὡς αὐτή.

XII. 1. [Σπουδὴ γὰρ ἦν τῇ Θάμαρ ἔχειν τέκνα ἀπὸ τῆς γενεᾶς τοῦ Ἀβραάμ. Ἡ γὰρ γενεὰ τοῦ Ἀβραὰμ ἦν προστεταγμένη καὶ ἠναγκάσθη] ἡ Θάμαρ καθῆσθαι ἐπὶ ταῖς πύλαις, ὡς πόρνη, κοσμηθεῖσα κόσμῳ νυμφικῷ [καὶ φθάσασα τὴν ὁδόν μου], ὅτι ἀνέρχομαι ἀπὸ τῶν προβάτων. 3. Μεθυσθεὶς οὖν ἐγὼ οὐκ ἀπέγνων αὐτὴν ἀπὸ τοῦ οἴνου, καὶ ἠπάτησέ με τὸ κάλλος αὐτῆς, 4. καὶ ἔδωκα αὐτῇ τὴν ῥάβδον καὶ τὴν ζώνην, καὶ ἐπλησιάσθη ἐμοί, [καὶ εἶχεν ἐν τῇ κοιλίᾳ τοὺς διδύμους Φαρὲς καὶ Ἀζάρ, καὶ ἦν μυστήριον φαινόμενον ἐν τῷ τεκεῖν τὴν Θάμαρ, ἐπεὶ τὸ πρῶτον τέκνον ἐξετίθη τὴν χεῖρα, ἡ μαιεύτρια ἐδέσμευσε νῆμα κόκκινον ἐπὶ τῇ χειρί, τῇ ὠθημένῃ, ὥστε εἰδέναι τὸ τέκνον ὃ πρῶτον ἐγένετο. καὶ τὸ τέκνον ἐκάλυψε τὴν χεῖρα καὶ ἦν τὰ τέκνα ἀγγελία τοῖς λαοῖς παλαιῶν καὶ καινῶν, ὡς γὰρ ἦν τὰ παλαιὰ πρὸ τοῦ νόμου ὄντα ἀνώρθει κατὰ τὸν νόμον, ὡς εἰ τῷ νόμῳ συντηρούμενα. ἐννόει δὲ τὸν Ἄβελ καὶ τὸν Σὴθ καὶ Ἐνὼχ καὶ Ἐνώς, Νῶε καὶ Ἑβὲρ καὶ οὕτως τὸν Ἀβραὰμ ὃς ἔλειψε τὸν πατέρα χάριν τοῦ Θεοῦ, Ἰώβ τε καὶ Μελχισεδέκ, καὶ οὕτως οἱ ἄλλοι προφῆται, οἳ ἐλάλησαν περὶ τῆς ἐλεύσεως τοῦ Χριστοῦ. ἀλλὰ ὡς ἔκρυψε τὴν χεῖρα ἐν τῇ κοιλίᾳ, οὕτως τοῦ νόμου κρυπτομένου καὶ ἀτιμαζομένου ἐγεννήθη ὁ Φαρές. καὶ τότε ἐξῆλθεν ὁ Ζαρὰ καὶ ἐφαίνετο τὸ νῆμα τὸ κόκκινον, τὸ σημαινόμενον τῷ αἵματι τοῦ Χριστοῦ].

XX. Καὶ ἐπίγνωτε, τέκνα μου, ὅτι δύο πνεύματα σχολάζουσι τῷ ἀνθρώπῳ τὸ τῆς ἀληθείας καὶ τὸ τῆς πλάνης. 2. μέσον ἐστὶ τὸ τῆς συνέσεως τοῦ νοός, πρὸς ταύτης θέλει ἡ εἰλικρινὴς κλίνεσθαι καὶ κλίνεται πρὸς τὴν καρδίαν τοῦ ἀνθρώπου καὶ ἕκαστος γιγνώσκει τὴν φωνήν. 4. καὶ οὐκ ἐστὶ καιρὸς ἐν ᾧ δυνήσεται λαθεῖν ἄνθρωπων ἔργα. ὅτι ἐν στήθει ὀστέων αὐτὸς ἐγγέγραπται ἐνώπιον Κυρίου. 5. καὶ ὁ ἁμαρτωλὸς ἐκ τῆς καρδίας αὐτοῦ, καὶ ἆραι πρόσωπον οὐ δύναται πρὸς τὸν κριτήν. XXI. 1, 2. Καὶ νῦν, τέκνα, ἀγγέλλω ὑμῖν ὡς ὁ Θεὸς ἔδωκε τὴν ἱερατείαν τῷ Λευί, καὶ ἐμοὶ ἔδωκε τὴν βασιλείαν. XXII. 1. [Μεγάλη μὲν ἦν μοι ταραχὴ καὶ μετὰ ταῦτα ἔσται ἐν ταῖς ἐσχάταις ἡμέραις] πολλοὶ ἔσονται πόλεμοι ἐν τῷ Ἰσραὴλ καὶ κατ' ἀλλήλων, καὶ ἔσονται διαιρέσεις. XXIII. 3. καὶ ἐλεύσεται λιμὸς καὶ λοιμός. καὶ τὰ τέκνα ὑμῶν πείσεται πολιορκίαν καὶ πάντας τοὺς ὀλέθρους. 4. καὶ ἐκτεμοῦσιν ἐξ ὑμῶν εἰς εὐνούχους ταῖς γυναιξὶν αὐτῶν. 5. Καὶ ἐπισκέψεται ὑμᾶς Κύριος ἐν ἐλέει, [καὶ ἔσται σωτηρία τῷ Ἰσραήλ, ἐν τῇ παρουσίᾳ τοῦ Θεοῦ τοῦ ἀληθοῦς].

XXIV. Καὶ μετὰ ταῦτα ἀνατελεῖ ὑμῖν ἄστρον ἐξ Ἰακὼβ ἐν εἰρήνῃ, καὶ ἀναστήσεται ἄνθρωπος ἐκ τοῦ γένους μου ὡς ὁ ἥλιος τῆς δικαιοσύνης, συμπορευόμενος τοῖς ἀνθρώποις ἐν δικαιοσύνῃ καὶ πραότητι, καὶ πᾶσα ἁμαρτία οὐχ εὑρεθήσεται ἐν αὐτῷ. 2. Καὶ ἀνοιγήσονται ἐπ' αὐτὸν οἱ οὐρανοὶ ἐκχέαι πνεύματος εὐλογίαν πατρὸς ἁγίου καὶ αὐτὸς ἐκχεεῖ πνεῦμα χάριτος ἐφ' ὑμᾶς. 4. καὶ ἔσεσθε αὐτῷ εἰς υἱοὺς ἐν ἀληθείᾳ καὶ πορεύσεσθε ἐν προστάγμασι αὐτοῦ πρώτοις καὶ ἐσχάτοις. 5. οὗτος ὁ βλαστὸς Θεοῦ ὑψίστου καὶ αὕτη ἡ πηγὴ εἰς ζωὴν πάσης σαρκός. 6. Τότε ἀναλάμψει σκῆπτρον βασιλείας μου, καὶ ἀπὸ τῆς ῥίζης ὑμῶν γενήσεται πυθμήν, 7. καὶ ἐν αὐτῷ ἀναβήσεται ῥάβδος δικαιοσύνης τοῖς ἔθνεσι κρῖναι καὶ σῶσαι πάντας τοὺς ἐπικαλουμένους Κύριον.

XXVI. 4. Καὶ ταῦτα εἰπὼν ἐξέδωκε τὴν ψυχὴν Ἰούδας ὁ υἱὸς τοῦ Ἰακὼβ τέταρτος καὶ τῆς Λίας, ζήσας ἔτη ἑκατὸν καὶ ἐννέα καὶ δέκα· καὶ ἐξέφερον αὐτὸν οἱ υἱοὶ αὐτοῦ καὶ ἔθαψαν αὐτὸν ἐν Χεβρὼν μετὰ τῶν πατέρων αὐτοῦ.

ΔΙΑΘΗΚΗ ΙΣΑΧΑΡ ΠΕΡΙ ΑΠΛΟΤΗΤΟΣ

I. Μετὰ ταῦτα Ἰσαχὰρ καλέσας τοὺς υἱοὺς αὐτοῦ εἶπεν αὐτοῖς. ἀκούσατε, τέκνα Ἰσαχὰρ τοῦ πατρὸς ὑμῶν, ἐνωτίσασθε ῥήματα. 2. Ἐγὼ ἐτέχθην πέμπτος υἱὸς τῷ Ἰακὼβ ἐν μισθῷ τῶν μανδραγορῶν.

III. 1. [Καὶ πρὸς τούτοις εἶπεν· οὐκ οἴδατε], τέκνα μου, ὡς ἐπορευόμην ἐν εὐθύτητι καρδίας 5. καὶ πᾶς πόνος ἀνήλωσε τὸ κράτος μου. 7. Καὶ Κύριος ἐδιπλασίαζε τὰ ἀγαθὰ ἐν χερσί μου. πατρί μου πᾶν ἐποίησα τερπνὸν καὶ ἐν οὐδενὶ παρώργισα τὴν καρδίαν αὐτοῦ. καὶ ἐγὼ [ἔφερον] πᾶν τὸ βάρος τοῦ θελήματος αὐτοῦ. ἐγὼ ἦν ὁ φέρων ὑπὲρ μέτρον, καὶ εἶδεν ὁ πατὴρ ἐμὸς ὅτι ὁ Θεὸς συνεργεῖ τῇ ἁπλότητί μου. 3. Καὶ οὐκ ἤμην περίεργος ἐν ταῖς πράξεσί μου οὐδὲ φθονερὸς καὶ βάσκανος τῷ πλησίον, 4. οὐ κατελάλησά τινος, οὐδὲ ἔψεξα βίον ἀνθρώπου, πορευόμενος ἐν ἁπλότητι ὀφθαλμῶν.

IV. Καὶ νῦν ἀκούσατε, τέκνα Ἰσαχὰρ πατρὸς ὑμῶν, καὶ πορεύεσθε ἐν ἁπλότητι καρδίας. 2. Οἱ ἐν ἁπλότητι βαίνοντες οὐ θέλουσι τὸ μιαρόν, οὐκ ἐπιθυμοῦσι εὑρεῖν τοὺς θησαυροὺς τοὺς πολυτίμους. οὐ θέλουσι εἰς πλεονεξίαν, τοῦ πλησίον οὐ κατακρίνουσιν, καὶ οὐκ ἐπιφέρουσι τὸ ὄνειδος κατ' ἀνθρώπου, βρωμάτων ποικίλων οὐκ ἐφίεται. 3. χρόνους μακροὺς οὐχ ὑπογράφει ζῆν, ἀλλὰ μόνον ἐκδέχεται τὸ θέλημα τοῦ Θεοῦ [ἐν τῇ εὐγενείᾳ τῆς ταπεινοφροσύνης αὐτοῦ]. 4. καί γε τὰ πνεύματα τῆς πλάνης οὐδὲν ἰσχύουσι πρὸς αὐτόν, οὐ γὰρ εἶδεν ἐπιδέξασθαι κάλλος θηλείας, ἵνα μὴ ἐν διαστροφῇ μιαίνῃ τὸν νοῦν αὐτοῦ· 5. οὐ ζῆλος ἐν διαβουλίοις αὐτοῦ ἐπελεύσεται· οὐ βασκανία ἐκτήκει ψυχὴν αὐτοῦ οὐδὲ αἰσθάνεται τὰ στασιώδη. 6. πάντα ὁρᾷ ἐν ἁπλότητι, καὶ οὐ λήψεται πονηρὸν ὀφθαλμόν· οὐ πορεύεται ἐν τῷ κέρδει πορεύεται ἐν τῇ εὐθύτητι τῆς ψυχῆς V. καὶ φυλάττων τὸν νόμον τοῦ Κυρίου, καὶ ὑμεῖς, τέκνα μου, στῆτε ἐν ἁπλότητι [ἐν πάσαις διανοίαις ὑμῶν καὶ ἀγαπᾶτε αὐτὴν καὶ συμβιοῦτε συν αὐτῇ καὶ κολλήθησθε αὐτῇ] καὶ ἀκούσατε τὰς ἐντολὰς Κυρίου καὶ μὴ ὀνειδίζετε μηδαμῶς τῷ πλησίῳ 2. ἀλλὰ ἀγαπᾶτε τὸν Κύριον καὶ τὸν πλησίον, πένητα καὶ ἀσθενῆ ἐλεᾶτε. 3. Ὑπόθετε τὸν νῶτον ὑμῶν εἰς τὸ γεωργεῖν τὴν γῆν ὑμῶν, καὶ ἀπὸ τῶν ἔργων δῶρα μετ' εὐχαριστείας Κυρίῳ προσφέρετε, 4. καὶ ἀπὸ [τοῦ ἔργου] λήψεσθε εὐλογίαν, ὡς τὸ πρὶν Ἄβελ [καὶ εὐχαριστείαν φέρετε, τέκνα μου], 7. Λευὶ καὶ Ἰούδα, καὶ γὰρ οἱ δύο ἐδοξάσθησαν τῷ Κυρίῳ ἐν πᾶσιν τοῖς υἱοῖς Ἰακώβ, καὶ γὰρ Κύριος ἐκλήρωσεν ἐν αὐτοῖς, καὶ τῷ μὲν ἔδωκε τὴν ἱερατείαν, τῷ δὲ τὴν βασιλείαν.

VI. Ἀκούσατε οὖν, ὡς ὁρᾶτε, τέκνα μου, καὶ γὰρ ἐν ἐσχάτοις καιροῖς καταλείψουσιν οἱ υἱοὶ ὑμῶν τὴν ἁπλότητα καὶ κολληθήσονται τῇ ἀπληστίᾳ, καὶ ἀφέντες τὴν ἀκακίαν προσπελάσουσι τῇ κακουργίᾳ, καὶ καταλίποντες τὰς ἐντολὰς Κυρίου κολληθήσονται τῷ πονηρῷ, 2. καὶ ἀφέντες τὸ γεώργειον ἐξακολουθήσουσι τοῖς πονηροῖς διαβουλίοις αὐτῶν, καὶ διασπαρήσονται ἐν τοῖς ἔθνεσι καὶ δουλεύσουσι τοῖς ἐχθροῖς αὐτῶν. 3. καὶ ὑμεῖς οὖν εἴπατε ταῦτα τοῖς τέκνοις ὑμῶν. VII. 8, 9. καὶ ταῦτα εἰπὼν ἀφῆκε τὴν ψυχὴν αὐτοῦ, ζήσας ἑκατὸν εἴκοσι δύο ἔτη.

ΔΙΑΘΗΚΗ ΖΑΒΟΥΛΩΝ

Ἐπεκαλέσατο Ζαβουλὼν τοὺς υἱοὺς αὐτοῦ πρὸς ἑαυτὸν 2. καὶ εἶπεν αὐτοῖς. Ἀκούσατέ μου, υἱοὶ Ζαβουλών, προσέχετε ῥήμασι πατρὸς ὑμῶν. 3. Ἐγώ εἰμι Ζαβουλών, δόσις ἀγαθὴ τοῖς γονεῦσί μου. Ἐν γὰρ τῷ

γεννηθῆναί με, ηὐξήθη ὁ πατήρ μου ὅτι ἐν ταῖς ποικίλαις ῥάβδοις εἶχε
τὸν κλῆρον. 4. οὐκ ἔγνων, τέκνα μου, ὅτι ἥμαρτον, ὅτι παρανομίαν
ἐποίησα, πλὴν τῆς ἀγνοίας ἣν ἐποιήσαμεν ἐπὶ τὸν Ἰωσὴφ ἀδελφὸν
ἡμῶν, οὐ γὰρ ἦν τὸ θέλημά μου 6. καὶ ἔκλαιον πολλὰ 7. καὶ πολλὰ
διεμαρτυρησάμην αὐτοῖς μετὰ δακρύων, τοῦ μὴ ποιῆσαι τὴν ἀνομίαν
ταύτην [ἐν τῷ Ἰσραήλ.

II. Καὶ μετὰ ταῦτα οὐκ ἐπαυσάμην θέλειν πολλὰς ἡμέρας τῷ
Ἰωσήφ], ὅτε Συμεὼν καὶ Γὰδ ἐθέλησαν ἀνελεῖν αὐτὸν [καὶ ἔδωκα τὴν
ψυχήν μου πρὸ τῆς ψυχῆς αὐτοῦ καὶ νῦν ἀναίτιος εἰμὶ τῆς πράσεως τοῦ
ἀδελφοῦ ἡμετέρου Ἰωσήφ].

V. Ὑμεῖς δέ, τέκνα μου, ἀκούσατε ἐμοῦ καὶ φυλάσσετε τὰς ἐντολὰς
Κυρίου καὶ ποιήσατε ἔλεος ἐπὶ τὸν ἀδελφόν, καὶ εὐσπλαγχνίαν πρὸς
πάντας. 2. Διὰ γὰρ ταῦτα εὐλόγησέ με Κύριος, οἶδε γὰρ Κύριος
ἑκάστου τὴν προαίρεσιν, 3. ὡς ἔχει ἐν σπλάγχνοις ἔλεος, ὅτι ὡς ἄν τις
ποιήσῃ ἐπὶ τὸν πλησίον αὐτοῦ, οὕτως καὶ ὁ Κύριος ποιήσει ἐπ’ αὐτόν.
4. Καὶ γὰρ οἱ ἀδελφοί μου ἠσθένουν, καὶ οἱ υἱοὶ ἀπέθνησκον διὰ
Ἰωσήφ, ὅτι οὐκ ἐποίησαν ἔλεος ἐν σπλάγχνοις αὐτῶν. [Ὡς γὰρ οὐκ
ἐποίησαν ἔλεος ἐν σπλάγχνοις αὐτῶν ἐπὶ τὸν Ἰωσήφ]. Ὑμεῖς δέ,
τέκνα μου, ἐσώθητε ἄνοσοι ἀπὸ Κυρίου, καὶ ὑμεῖς αὐτοὶ οἴδατε.

VIII. 5. Καὶ νῦν ἀγαπᾶτε ἀλλήλους, καὶ μὴ λογίζεσθε κακὸν ἐπὶ τὸν
πλησίον ὑμῶν, 6. καὶ γὰρ ἡ ἀπέχθεια τὴν ψυχὴν ἀποχωρίζει [ἀπὸ τοῦ
σώματος καὶ ἀπελαύνει τὴν εὐλογίαν τοῦ Θεοῦ, ἡ γὰρ ἀπέχθεια εἰσφέρει
τὸ μόνον ἐν τέκνον ἔχειν. καὶ εἰσφέρει τὴν λύπην], καὶ ταράττει τὴν
ἔννοιαν καὶ ἀφανίζει τὴν ὕπαρξιν.

IX. Προσέχετε δέ, τέκνα, τὰ ὕδατα ὅτι ἐπὶ τὸ αὐτὸ πορεύεται,
λίθους ξύλα τὴν γῆν καὶ τὴν ἄμμον κατασύρει, 2. ἐὰν δὲ εἰς πολλὰ
διαιρεθῇ ἡ γῆ ἀφανίζει αὐτά. 3. καὶ ὑμεῖς, ἐὰν διαιρεθῆτε ἔσεσθε
οὕτως εὐκαταφρόνητοι. 4. Μὴ σχισθῆτε εἰς δύο κεφαλάς, ὅτι πᾶν ὃ
ἐποίησεν ὁ Κύριος κεφαλὴν μίαν ἔχει. Ἔδωκε δύο ὤμους, χεῖρας,
ἀλλὰ πάντα τῇ μιᾷ κεφαλῇ ὑπακούει. 5. Ἔγνων ἐν γραφαῖς πατέρων
μου ὅτι διαιρεθήσεσθε ἐν Ἰσραὴλ καὶ δύο βασιλεῖαι ἐξακολουθήσονται
καὶ πᾶν βδέλυγμα ποιήσετε, καὶ γε πᾶν εἴδωλον προσκυνήσετε. 6. καὶ
αἰχμαλωτεύσουσιν ὑμᾶς οἱ ἐχθροὶ ὑμῶν καὶ κακωθήσεσθε ἐν ἔθνεσι
καὶ ἐν ἀσθενείαις καὶ θλίψεσι. 7. Καὶ μετὰ ταῦτα μνησθήσεσθε
Κυρίου καὶ μετανοήσετε καὶ ἐπιστρέψει ὑμᾶς, ὅτι ἐλεήμων ἐστὶ καὶ
εὔσπλαγχνος, μὴ λογιζόμενος κακίαν τοῖς υἱοῖς τῶν ἀνθρώπων, διότι
σάρξ εἰσὶ καὶ τὰ πνεύματα τῆς πλάνης ἀπατᾷ αὐτοὺς ἐπὶ πάσαις
πράξεσιν αὐτῶν. 8. καὶ μετὰ ταῦτα ἀνατέλλει ὑμῖν αὐτὸς ὁ Κύριος
φῶς δικαιοσύνης καὶ ἐπανελεύσεσθε εἰς τὴν γῆν ὑμῶν καὶ ὄψεσθε

Κύριον ἐν Ἱερουσαλήμ.   9. καὶ πάλιν ἐν πονηρίᾳ ἔργων ὑμῶν παροργίσετε αὐτὸν καὶ ἀπορριφήσεσθε ἕως καιροῦ συντελείας.

X. Καὶ νῦν, τέκνα, 2. ὅσοι ὑμῶν ἀκούετε τὰς διαθήκας Ζαβουλῶν πατρὸς ὑμῶν 5. φοβεῖσθε Κύριον τὸν Θεὸν πάσῃ τῇ [ψυχῇ καὶ] ἰσχύϊ, [εἰ δέ τις μὴ ἐννοῇ τοὺς λόγους μου ἐπάξει ἐπ᾽ αὐτὸν Κύριος πῦρ αἰώνιον].   6. Καὶ ταῦτα εἰπὼν ἐκοιμήθη, ζήσας ἔτη ἑκατὸν καὶ τέσσερα καὶ δέκα, καὶ ἔθηκαν αὐτὸν οἱ υἱοὶ αὐτοῦ ἐν θήκῃ 7. καὶ ἔθαψαν αὐτὸν ἐν τῷ αὐτῷ σπηλαίῳ μετὰ τῶν πατέρων αὐτοῦ.

ΔΙΑΘΗΚΗ ΔΑΝ ΠΕΡΙ ΘΥΜΟΥ ΚΑΙ ΟΡΓΗΣ

I. 2. Καλέσας γὰρ Δὰν υἱοὺς αὐτοῦ πρὸς ἑαυτὸν εἶπε. Ἀκούσατε υἱοὶ Δάν, λόγων μου, προσέχετε ῥήμασι στόματος τοῦ πατρὸς ὑμῶν. 3. Ἐπείρασα ἐν καρδίᾳ μου καὶ ἐν πάσῃ τῇ ζωῇ μου, ὅτι καλὸν Θεῷ καὶ εὐάρεστον ἡ ἀλήθεια μετὰ δικαιοπραγίας· καὶ ὅτι πονηρὸν τὸ ψεῦδος καὶ ὁ θυμὸς καὶ πᾶσαν κακίαν ἀνθρώπους ἐκδιδάσκει.   4. Ὁμολογῶ σήμερον ὑμῖν, τέκνα μου, ὅτι ἐν καρδίᾳ μου ἐβουλευσάμην περὶ τοῦ θανάτου Ἰωσὴφ ἀνδρὸς ἀγαθοῦ καὶ ἀληθινοῦ.   5. καὶ ἔχαιρον ἐπὶ τῇ πράσει Ἰωσήφ, ὅτι ὑπὲρ ἡμᾶς ὁ πατὴρ ἠγάπα.   6. τὸ γὰρ πνεῦμα τοῦ ζήλου (καὶ) διαφθορᾶς εἶπέ μοι· 7. Λαβὲ τὸ ξίφος καὶ ἄνελε τὸν Ἰωσήφ, καὶ ἀγαπήσει σε ὁ πατήρ σου, τοῦ Ἰωσὴφ ἀποθανόντος. 8. τοῦτο εἶπε τὸ πνεῦμα τὸ πονηρὸν ἀνάγκαζον ἐμὲ καὶ ἦν ὥσπερ πάρδαλις ἐκμύζουσα ἔριφον.   [οὕτως καὶ ἐγὼ ἐφύλασσον τὸν Ἰωσήφ·] 9. Ἀλλ᾽ ὁ Θεὸς Ἰακὼβ τοῦ πατρός μου οὐκ ἔδωκέ μοι ταύτην τὴν ἀνομίαν ἐργάζεσθαι, οὐδὲ εὗρον τὸν Ἰωσὴφ μόνον.

II. 1. Καὶ νῦν, τέκνα μου, ἐγὼ ἀποθνήσκω καὶ ἐν ἀληθείᾳ λέγω ὑμῖν, ὅτι ἐὰν μὴ διαφυλάξητε ἑαυτοὺς ἀπὸ τοῦ πνεύματος τοῦ ψεύδους καὶ τοῦ θυμουμένου καὶ ἀγαπήσητε τὴν ἀλήθειαν καὶ τὴν μακροθυμίαν, ἀπολεῖσθε.   2. ἡ γὰρ ὀργὴ τυφλίζει τοὺς ἀνθρώπους καὶ ὅταν ἔρχηται ὁ θυμός, 3. οὐ γιγνώσκει τὴν ἀγάπην τῶν ἀδελφῶν.   οὐ φοβεῖται τὸν πατέρα, οὐδὲ τιμᾷ τὴν μητέρα, [οὐ πάσχει τὸν γέροντα.   οὐκ ἔχει αἰδῶ τῶν λαῶν οὐδὲ οἰκτιρμὸν τῶν τέκνων, ὅτι δεσμεύει αὐτά]. 4. περιβάλλει γὰρ αὐτὸν τὸ πνεῦμα τοῦ θυμοῦ τὰ δίκτυα τῆς πλάνης. καὶ τυφλοῖ τοὺς ὀφθαλμοὺς τῆς καρδίας, διὰ τοῦ ψεύδους σκοτοῖ τὴν διάνοιαν αὐτοῦ, καὶ τὴν ὅρασιν τὴν πονηρὰν παρέχει αὐτῷ.   5. καὶ περιβάλλει τοὺς ὀφθαλμοὺς αὐτοῦ [καὶ οὐ γιγνώσκει τὴν ἀλήθειαν] καὶ δίδωσιν αὐτῷ καρδίαν ἰδίαν κατὰ τοῦ ἀδελφοῦ εἰς φθόνον καὶ ἔχθραν.

III. 2. Καὶ ὁ θυμὸς τῆς ψυχῆς αὐτοῦ κατακυριεύει 3. ὅτε ποιεῖ τὴν ἀνομίαν καὶ δικαιοῖ ἑαυτὸν ἐν τῇ ἀνομίᾳ, [οὐ γὰρ οἶδε τὸν νόμον τοῦ

Θεοῦ, ἐγείρεται καὶ ἡ ὀξύτης τοῦ ξίφους, εἰσέρχεται εἰς τὴν κεφαλήν, καὶ ὅτε ἡ ψυχὴ αὐτοῦ ἀφαιρεῖται ἀπὸ τοῦ σώματος καὶ οὐκ ἐπανέρχεται καὶ τὰ πεποιημένα ἀεὶ πρὸ ὀφθαλμῶν ἔσται ὅτι ἐπείσθη τῇ πονηρᾷ ψυχῇ]. 6. ψυχὴ αὐτοῦ ἀεὶ μετὰ τοῦ ψεύδους ἐκ δεξιῶν τοῦ Σατανᾶ πορεύεται [καὶ ὅτε ὁρᾷ ἄνθρωπον ὀργιζόμενον πελάζεται αὐτῷ καὶ τυφλοῖ αὐτοῦ τὴν ψυχήν].

IV. 2. Καὶ οὕτως διεγείρει ἐν θυμῷ μεγάλῳ τὴν ψυχὴν αὐτοῦ. [Ἐννοεῖτε δέ, τέκνα, ὅτι ψυχὴ ἀπὸ τοῦ Σατανᾶ εἰσέρχεται εἰς ἄνθρωπον ὀργιζόμενον, ἐγείρει αὐτὸν μὴ μεμνῆσθαι τοῦ Κυρίου, ἀλλ' ἐργάζεσθαι τὴν ἀνομίαν πρὸ προσώπου τοῦ Θεοῦ καὶ μυρίων ἀγγέλων, ἀλλὰ ὡς λέγεται ἡμῖν οὕτως καὶ ὑμεῖς, τέκνα]. 3. μὴ κινήσθητε εἰς ταραγμοὺς ὀργῆς. 8. ταρασσομένης δὲ ψυχῆς ἀφίσταται Κύριος ἀπ' αὐτῆς καὶ κυριεύει αὐτῆς ὁ Βελίαρ.

V. 1. Φυλάξατε οὖν, τέκνα μου, τὴν ἐντολὴν τοῦ Κυρίου καὶ τὸν νόμον αὐτοῦ. ἀγαπᾶτε καὶ μισήσατε τὸ ψεῦδος, ἵνα φεύγῃ ἀφ' ὑμῶν ἡ ὀργή. 2. Ἀλήθειαν φθέγγεσθε ἕκαστος πρὸς τὸν πλησίον σου [καὶ φεύγεσθε ἀπὸ τοῦ πονηροῦ] καὶ οὐ μὴ κατισχύσῃ ὑμῶν πόλεμος. 3. καὶ ἀγαπᾶτε τὸν Κύριον ἐν πάσῃ τῇ ζωῇ ὑμῶν. 4. Οἶδα γὰρ ὅτι ἐν ἐσχάταις ἡμέραις ἀποστήσεσθε τοῦ Κυρίου ἐν κακοῖς βουλεύμασι πορευόμενοι. 6. Ἀνέγνων γὰρ ἐν βίβλῳ Ἐνὼχ τοῦ δικαίου 8. ὅτι πολλὰς κολάσεις καὶ πληγὰς λήψεσθε 9. καὶ οὕτως ἐπιστρέψαντες πρὸς Κύριον ἐλεηθήσεσθε 12. καὶ ἐπὶ τῆς ἁγίας Ἱερουσαλὴμ εὐφρανθήσεσθε [καὶ μετὰ ταῦτα τὸ πονηρὸν πνεῦμα ἀπατήσει ὑμᾶς εἰς τὴν ἀνομίαν ὡς εἰ μὴ ἐπικαλούμενοι ἐπὶ τῷ ὀνόματι τοῦ Θεοῦ, ἀκοῦσαι τῶν ἁγίων αὐτοῦ]. 13. ὅτι Κύριος ἔσται ἐμμέσῳ αὐτῆς (Ἱερουσαλὴμ) τοῖς ἀνθρώποις συναναστρεφόμενος καὶ ἅγιος Ἰσραὴλ οὐ γνωρισθήσεται ὑμῖν ἐν ταπεινώσει καὶ ἐν πτωχείᾳ καὶ ὁ πιστεύων ἐπ' αὐτῷ οὐ διαφθερεῖται [καὶ ἄρξονται λαβεῖν τὸν αἰώνιον βίον οἱ ἄγγελοι πιστεύσαντες ἐπ' αὐτῷ].

VI. 3. διὰ τοῦτο σπουδάζει ὁ ἐχθρὸς ὑποσκελίζειν πάντας τοὺς ἐπικαλουμένους τὸν Κύριον, 4. καὶ συντελεῖται ἡ βασιλεία τοῦ ἐχθροῦ. 6. Ἔσται δὲ ἐν καιρῷ ἀνομίας τοῦ Ἰσραὴλ ἀφιστάμενος ἀπ' αὐτῶν Κύριος, καὶ μνήσεται τῶν ἐθνῶν τῶν ποιούντων [ἐργαζομένων] τὸ θέλημα αὐτοῦ, ὅτι οὐδενὶ τῶν ἀγγέλων ἔσται ὡς αὐτῷ. 7. τὸ δὲ ὄνομα αὐτοῦ ἔσται ἐν πᾶσι τοῖς ἔθνεσιν Σωτὴρ 9. ὁ ἀληθὴς καὶ Ἱερουσαλὴμ πραῢς καὶ ταπεινὸς καὶ διδάσκεται ἐν παντὶ τῷ νόμῳ. V. 6. ὁ Σατανᾶς ἔσται βασιλεὺς ὑμῶν καὶ πᾶσαι αἱ ψυχαὶ ἀνόητοι ἔσονται ἐν μέσῳ ὑμῶν. VI. 9. Καὶ οὕτως ἐπεστειλάμην ὑμῖν, μετάδοτε καὶ ὑμεῖς τοῖς τέκνοις ὑμῶν εἰς ἀεὶ καὶ πειθόμενοι τῷ Θεῷ ἀκούσατε. 10. καὶ γένοιτο τὸ γένος μου εἰς σωτηρίαν εἰς ἀεί.

VII. 1. καὶ ταῦτα εἰπὼν κατεφίλησεν αὐτοὺς καὶ ἐκδίδωσι τὸ πνεῦμα αὐτοῦ. 2. Καὶ οἱ υἱοὶ αὐτοῦ μετὰ ταῦτα ἤνεγκαν αὐτὸν εἰς Χεβρὼν καὶ ἔθηκαν ἐν τῷ αὐτῷ σπηλαίῳ ἐν ᾧ Ἰσαὰκ καὶ Ἰακώβ. 3. καὶ πάντα τὰ ἔτη αὐτοῦ ἑκατὸν καὶ εἴκοσι καὶ πέντε.

ΔΙΑΘΗΚΗ ΝΕΦΘΑΛΕΙΜ Η ΠΕΡΙ ΦΥΣΙΚΗΣ ΑΓΑΘΟΤΗΤΟΣ

I. 1. Ἀντίγραφον διαθήκης Νεφθαλεὶμ υἱοῦ Ἰακώβ, τοῦ ὀγδόου υἱοῦ Βάλλης, τῆς δούλης Ῥαχήλ, περὶ φυσικῆς ἀγαθότητος. 5. Ἀκούσατε ἐμοῦ τοῦ πατρὸς ὑμῶν λέγοντος.

II. 1. Ἐπειδὴ κοῦφος ἤμην τοῖς ποσί μου ὡς ἔλαφος, ἔταξέ με ὁ πατήρ μου Ἰακὼβ εἰς πᾶσαν ἀποστολὴν καὶ ἄγειν καὶ φέρειν καὶ γε ὡς ἄγγελον εὐλόγησέ με. 2. καὶ γὰρ ὁ κεραμεὺς οἶδε τὸ σκεῦος, πόσον χωρεῖν θέλει ποιῆσαι καὶ οἴσει πηλὸν καὶ ποιεῖν αὐτὸ καθὼς θέλει οὕτω καὶ ὁ Κύριος πρὸς ὁμοίωσιν τοῦ πνεύματος ποιεῖ τὸ σῶμα τοῦ ἀνθρώπου καὶ πρὸς τὴν δύναμιν τοῦ σώματος τὸ πνεῦμα ἐντίθησι. 3. καὶ ἐν μέτρῳ καὶ ἀριθμῷ ἴσον ποιεῖ καὶ οὐκ ἐστὶ λοιπὸν ἓν καὶ τρίτον μέρος τριχὸς ἑκάστῳ ἀνθρώπῳ, οὕτω ὅμοιον ποιεῖ. 5. ὅτι οὐκ ἔστι πᾶν πλάσμα καὶ πᾶσα ἔννοια ἣν οὐκ ἔγνω Κύριος. 6. Ὡς ἡ ἰσχὺς αὐτοῦ, οὕτω καὶ τὸ ἔργον αὐτοῦ· καὶ ὡς ἡ προαίρεσις αὐτοῦ, οὕτω καὶ σύννοια αὐτοῦ καὶ ἡ πρᾶξις αὐτοῦ· ὡς ἡ καρδία αὐτοῦ, οὕτω καὶ τὸ στόμα αὐτοῦ· ὡς ὁ ὀφθαλμὸς αὐτοῦ, οὕτω καὶ ὁ ὕπνος αὐτοῦ. ὡς ἡ ψυχὴ αὐτοῦ, οὕτω καὶ ὁ λόγος αὐτοῦ ἢ ἐν νόμῳ Κυρίου ἢ ἐν νόμῳ Βελίαρ. 7. καὶ ὡς κεχώρισται ἀνάμεσον φωτὸς καὶ σκότους ὁράσεως καὶ ἀκοῆς· οὕτω κεχώρισται ἀνάμεσον ἀνδρὸς καὶ γυναικὸς καὶ οὐκ ἔστιν εἰπεῖν ὅτι ἐν τῷ ἑνὶ προσώπῳ ὅμοιόν ἐστι. 8. πάντα γὰρ ἐν τάξει ἐποίησεν ὁ Θεὸς καλά, ἐν τῇ μορφῇ τῆς κεφαλῆς συνημμέναι εἰσὶ τρίχες πρὸς δόξαν, εἶτα καρδίαν εἰς φρόνησιν, κοιλίαν εἰς διάκρισιν, στομάχου κάλαμον πρὸς ὑγίειαν, ἧπαρ πρὸς θυμόν, χολὴν πρὸς πικρίαν, ἀκοὴν εἰς γέλωτα, ψύας εἰς δύναμιν, πλευρὰς εἰς θήκην, ὀσφὺν εἰς ἰσχύν, καὶ πάντα καὶ πάσας τὰς αἰσθήσεις. [Φυλάσσετε τὴν ἀγάπην πρὸς τὸν Θεόν, καὶ εἰ φοβεῖταί τις τὸν Θεὸν ὅλῃ τῇ ψυχῇ καὶ πάσας τὰς αἰσθήσεις, ὅτι ὁ Θεός ἐστι καὶ κρατεῖ αὐτῶν· εἴ τις ἀποβάλλει τὴν ἀγάπην τοῦ Θεοῦ, τότε ἐν τῇ διαθέσει αὐτοῦ ἐργάζεσθαι ἄρξουσιν θυμός, λοιδορία, βαρυκαρδία, χόλος, μέθη, πολυφαγία, πορνεία, ζηλοτυπία, ἀπληστία, λοιδορία, φθόνος καὶ πᾶν βδέλυγμα]. 9. πάντα ποιήσαντας ἐν τάξει ἐν φόβῳ Θεοῦ, III. 1. καὶ σιωπῶντας τὰ μέρη τῆς καρδίας τὸ θέλημα τοῦ Θεοῦ κρατεῖν, καὶ ἀπορρίπτειν τὸ θέλημα τοῦ διαβόλου. 2. Ἥλιος γὰρ καὶ σελήνη καὶ ἀστέρες οὐκ ἀλλοιοῦσι τάξιν αὐτῶν, οὕτως καὶ

ὑμεῖς μὴ ἀλλοιώσητε [νόμον Θεοῦ] ἐν ἀταξίᾳ πράξεων ὑμῶν. 3. Ἔθνη
γὰρ πλανηθέντα ἔπεσε καὶ ἀφέντα τὸν Κύριον ἠλλοίωσαν τάξιν αὐτῶν
καὶ ἐπηκολούθησαν τοῖς εἰδώλοις καὶ ἐξηκολούθησαν πνεύμασι πλάνης.
[καὶ τοὺς βίους αὐτῶν ὁδηγοῦσιν ἐν ἀταξίᾳ καὶ ἡ ψυχὴ αὐτῶν γίνεται
βρῶμα τῷ Σατανᾷ]. 4. Ὁρᾶτε γάρ, τέκνα μου, γιγνώσκετε τὸ
στερέωμα τῆς γῆς καὶ θαλάσσης ἐν πᾶσι τοῖς δημιουργήμασιν, [καὶ]
Κύριον τὸν ποιήσαντα ταῦτα πάντα ἵνα μὴ γίνησθε ὡς Σόδομα καὶ
Γόμορρα, αἵτινες ἐνήλλαξαν τὰς τάξεις αὐτῶν.

IV. 1. Ταῦτα γὰρ ἐννόησα ἐν ταῖς γραφαῖς ('Ενώχ), ὅτι καὶ γε καὶ
ὑμεῖς ἀποστήσεσθε ἀπὸ τοῦ νόμου Κυρίου, καὶ ἄρξεσθε πορεύεσθαι
κατὰ πᾶσαν ἀνομίαν τῶν ἐθνῶν. 2. Καὶ ἐπάξει ὑμῖν Κύριος αἰχμαλωσίαν, καὶ δουλεύσετε ἐκεῖ τοῖς ἐχθροῖς ὑμῶν καὶ κακώσει (καὶ) θλίψει
ζήσετε ἕως ἂν κατακρίνῃ Κύριος πάντων ὑμῶν. 3. καὶ οὕτως ἐπιστρέψετε καὶ ἐπιγνώσεσθε Κύριον τὸν Θεὸν ὑμῶν καὶ ἐπιστρέψει ὑμᾶς
εἰς τὴν γῆν ὑμῶν κατὰ τὸ πολὺ αὐτοῦ ἔλεος. 4. καὶ ὅτε ἔσεσθε ἐν
τῇ γῇ ὑμῶν, πάλιν ἁμαρτήσεσθε καὶ Κυρίου ἐπιλήσεσθε. 5. Καὶ
ἡ μακροθυμία τοῦ Κυρίου ἐλεύσεται [ὡς] ἄνθρωπος ποιῶν δικαιοσύνην
ἀπὸ τῆς γενεᾶς 'Ιούδα, καὶ ποιῶν ἔλεος εἰς πάντας τοὺς μακρὰν καὶ
τοὺς ἐγγύς.

VIII. 2. Διὰ τούτου γὰρ ἀνατελεῖ σωτηρία, καὶ ἐν αὐτῷ εὐλογοῦνται
'Αβραάμ, 'Ισαάκ, 'Ιακώβ. 3. τὸ σκῆπτρον γὰρ αὐτοῦ φανεῖται, ὁ Θεὸς
τῆς ζωῆς ἐν τοῖς οὐρανοῖς καὶ ἐν τῇ γῇ σῴζει καὶ ἐκλέγει τοὺς
ἁγίους, [ἀλλ' ὑμεῖς οὐκ ἀκούσαντες αὐτοῦ διασπερεῖσθε κατὰ τὸ πρόσωπον
πάσης τῆς γῆς· ὑμῖν γὰρ ἐν τοῖς πρώτοις ἦν βασιλεία ἐπαγγελλομένη],
4. καὶ ὁ Θεὸς δοξάζεται ἐν τοῖς ἔθνεσι δι' ὑμᾶς· [ὑμεῖς γὰρ ἐννοούμενοι
ἠκούσατε τοῦτο] καὶ ὁ Κύριος ἐλεεῖ ὑμᾶς, καὶ οἱ ἄγγελοι ἐλεοῦσιν·
[ὑμεῖς εἰ δὲ μὴ ἀκούετε αὐτοῦ, κοινωνοὶ ἔσεσθε τῶν βασάνων· τοῖς δὲ
ἀκούουσι ἑτοιμάζονται οἱ θρόνοι καὶ ἡ δόξα ἐν τοῖς οὐρανοῖς].

IX. 1, 2. Καὶ ταῦτα εἰπὼν τὴν ψυχὴν ἀπέδωκεν ὁ Νεφθαλείμ, ὁ
ὄγδοος υἱὸς 'Ιακὼβ καὶ υἱὸς Βάλλης· ἔζη ἑκατὸν καὶ τριάκονα καὶ δύο
ἔτη καὶ ἐτάφη ἐν Χεβρὼν ἐν τῷ αὐτῷ σπηλαίῳ.

ΔΙΑΘΗΚΗ ΓΑΔ ΠΕΡΙ ΜΙΣΟΥΣ

I. 1. 'Αντίγραφον διαθήκης Γὰδ περὶ μίσους, ἐκαλέσατο γὰρ τοὺς
υἱοὺς αὐτοῦ καὶ εἶπε· 2. Ἔννατος υἱὸς ἐγενόμην τῷ 'Ιακώβ, καὶ ἤμην
ἀνδρεῖος ἐπὶ τῶν ποιμνίων. 3. Ἐγὼ ἐφύλαττον ἐν νυκτὶ τὸ ποίμνιον
καὶ ἐπεὶ ἤρχετο ἐν νυκτὶ λέων ἢ ἕτερον θηρίον ἔκτεινα αὐτόν, 7. καὶ
ἅπαξ ἄρνον ἐξειλόμην ἐκ τοῦ στόματος θηρίου καὶ ἐθανάτωσα καὶ
ἔφαγον. 6. καὶ ὁ ἀδελφός μου 'Ιωσὴφ ἰδὼν εἶπε τῷ πατρί, λέγων·

κτείνας πρόβατον οὐκ ἔδωκε τοῖς υἱοῖς Ζέλφας καὶ Βάλλας.   8. καὶ
ἐνεκότουν τῷ Ἰωσὴφ περὶ τοῦ λόγου τούτου, 9. καὶ τὸ πνεῦμα τοῦ θυμοῦ
ἦν ἐν ἐμοὶ καὶ οὐκ ἤθελον οὔτε δι' ὀφθαλμῶν οὔτε δι' ἀκοῆς ἰδεῖν τὸν
Ἰωσήφ.

II. 2, 3.   Καὶ ἠθέλησα ἐξελαύνειν βίον αὐτοῦ ἐκ τῆς γῆς, ὥσπερ
βοῦς χαράσσει ὄγμον ἀρούρας· καὶ ἐγὼ καὶ ὁ Συμεὼν ἐπωλήσαμεν τοῖς
Ἰσμαηλίταις.

III. 1.   Καὶ νῦν ἀκούσατε, τέκνα μου, λόγους ἀληθείας τοῦ ποιεῖν
δικαιοσύνην, καὶ πάντα νόμον ὑψίστου, καὶ μὴ πλανᾶσθαι τῷ πνεύματι
τοῦ μίσους, ὅτι κακόν ἐστιν παντὶ ἀνθρώπῳ.   2. πᾶν γὰρ ὃ ἐὰν ποιῇ
μισούμενόν ἐστι βδέλυγμα.   ἐὰν ποιῇ νόμον Κυρίου, τοῦτον οὐκ ἐπαινεῖ,
[τὸ γὰρ πνεῦμα τοῦ μίσους οὐ] θέλει τὴν δικαιοσύνην.   ἐάν τις φοβῆται
Κύριον, τότε ἀγαπᾷ 3. λοιδορεῖν τὴν ἀλήθειαν αὐτοῦ, τοῦ τὸν νόμον
δικαιοῦντος καταφρονεῖ, καταλαλιὰν ἀσπάζεται, ὑπερηφανίαν ἐπαινεῖ,
ὅτι τὸ πνεῦμα τοῦ μίσους ἐτύφλωσε τὴν ψυχὴν αὐτοῦ, [ὥστε μὴ
μεμνῆσθαι τοῦ Θεοῦ].

IV. 2.   Οὐ θέλει ἀκούειν τοὺς λόγους νουθετήσεως περὶ τῆς ἀγάπης
τῶν ἀδελφῶν.   3. ἐὰν γὰρ πταίσῃ, ὁ ἀδελφὸς εὐθὺς ἀγγέλλει πᾶσι, καὶ
κολασθεὶς ἀποθανεῖται.   6. ὁ ποιῶν τὰ ἀγαθὰ ἀεὶ σπουδάζει, ὡς ἀγαπῶν
καὶ θέλων τοὺς νεκροὺς ζωοποιῆσαι, καὶ τοὺς ἐν ἀποφάσει θανάτου
θέλει ἀνακαλέσασθαι, οὕτως τὸ μῖσος τοὺς ζῶντας θέλει ἀποκτεῖναι,
καὶ τοὺς ἐν ὀλίγῳ ἁμαρτήσαντας οὐ θέλει ζῆν.   7. Τὸ γὰρ πνεῦμα τοῦ
μίσους συνεργεῖ τῷ Σατανᾷ ἐν πᾶσιν εἰς θάνατον τῶν ἀνθρώπων, τὸ
δὲ πνεῦμα τῆς ἀγάπης συνεργεῖ τῷ νόμῳ τοῦ Θεοῦ εἰς σωτηρίαν
ἀνθρώπων.

V.   Κακὸν οὖν τὸ μῖσος, τὸ φῶς σκότος ποιεῖ καὶ συκοφαντίαν
ἐκδιδάσκει καὶ θυμὸν καὶ πᾶν κέρδος αἰσχρὸν ποιεῖ καὶ τῆς πράξεως
τοῦ διαβόλου τὴν καρδίαν πληροῖ.   [Ὁρᾶτε γάρ, τέκνα, λέγω ὑμῖν ὅτι]
2. ἡ δικαιοσύνη ἐκβάλλει τὸ μῖσος τοῦ διαβόλου καὶ κολλᾶται τῇ ἀγάπῃ
τοῦ Κυρίου· 3. ἀλήθεια γὰρ ἐξελαύνει τὸ μῖσος, καὶ ἡ ταπείνωσις
ἀναιρεῖ τὸ μῖσος.   Ὁ γὰρ δίκαιος αἰδεῖται ποιῆσαι ἄδικον οὐχ ὑπὸ
ἄλλου καταγινωσκόμενος, ἀλλ' ὑπὸ τῆς ἰδίας καρδίας.   6. ταῦτα ἐγὼ
ἔσχατον ἔγνων μετὰ τὸ μετανοῆσαί με περὶ τοῦ Ἰωσὴφ ἀδελφοῦ.
7. Ἡ γὰρ ἀληθὴς μετάνοια φωτίζει τοὺς ὀφθαλμούς, ἀποβάλλει καὶ
διαφθείρει τὴν ἁμαρτίαν, γνῶσιν παρέχουσα τῇ ψυχῇ, καὶ ὁδηγεῖ τὸ
διαβούλιον πρὸς σωτηρίαν.   9. Ἐπήγαγε γάρ μοι ὁ Θεὸς νόσον ἥπατος
καὶ εἰ μὴ αἱ εὐχαὶ Ἰακὼβ τοῦ πατρός μου, ὀλίγου οὐκ ἐξῆλθε ἐξ ἐμοῦ
τὸ πνεῦμα· 10. ὁ Θεὸς οἶδε δι' ὧν ἄνθρωπος παρανομεῖ, δι' ἐκείνων
καὶ κολάζεται.   11. Τὰ ἥπατά μου ἐνέκειτο ἀνίλεως κατὰ τοῦ Ἰωσήφ—

καὶ ἐκρινόμην ἐν νόσῳ (ἐπὶ μῆνας) ἔνδεκα· [διὰ ταῦτ' ἐννόησα ὅτι ὁ
Θεὸς οὕτως ἐποίησε κατ' ἐμοῦ, ὅτι καὶ] ἐγὼ τοσοῦτον χρόνον ἐνεῖχον
τῷ 'Ιωσήφ, ἕως ἂν πραθῇ.—VI. 1. καὶ νῦν, τέκνα μου, ἕκαστος λέγοι
τοῖς υἱοῖς αὐτοῦ καὶ ἀγαπήσατε ἀλλήλους ἐν ἔργῳ καὶ λόγῳ καὶ πάσῃ
διανοίᾳ [καὶ] ἐκ πάσης ψυχῆς. 3. Ἐάν τις ἁμάρτῃ εἰς σε, σὺ πρῶτον
ἐξόριζε ἀπὸ σεαυτοῦ τὸν ἰὸν τοῦ μίσους. [Αἱ γὰρ παρακλήσεις εἰς
εἰρήνην οὐκ ἀκούονται] 5. ἐν τῇ ἀλλοτρίᾳ ταραχῇ τῶν μυστηρίων ὑμῶν.
VII. 2. Εἰ δὲ ὁ ἐχθρὸς ὑμῶν ὑπερηφανὴς γίγνεται μὴ φθονήσητε,
ὅτι πάσῃ σαρκὶ καθανεῖν ἔστι. ὁ δὲ Θεὸς τὸν ἔπαινον φέρει τῷ διδόντι
τὰ ἀγαθὰ καὶ ἀναγκαῖα τοῖς ἀνθρώποις. 4. Ἐὰν δὲ ἐκ κακῶν τις
πλουτίσῃ μὴ ζηλώσητε αὐτόν. 6. ὁ γὰρ πένης καὶ ἄφθονος ἐπὶ πᾶσι
Κυρίῳ εὐχαριστεῖ, αὐτὸς παρὰ πᾶσι πλουτεῖ εὐλογητοῖς τρόποις.
VIII. 1. Εἴπατε δὲ καὶ ὑμεῖς ταῦτα τοῖς τέκνοις ὑμῶν, ὅπως
τιμήσωσιν 'Ιούδαν καὶ τὸν Λευί. ὅτι ἐξ αὐτῶν ἀνατελεῖ Κύριος σωτῆρα
τῷ 'Ισραήλ. 2. Ἔγνων γὰρ ὅτι ἐπὶ τέλει ἀποστήσονται τὰ τέκνα ὑμῶν
ἀπ' αὐτοῦ, ἐν πάσῃ πονηρίᾳ καὶ ἐν διαφθορᾷ ἔσονται ἐνώπιον Κυρίου.
4. Καὶ ταῦτα εἰπὼν προσέφερε τὴν ψυχὴν τῷ Κυρίῳ 5. καὶ ἔταφον
αὐτὸν ἐν τῷ αὐτῷ σπηλαίῳ. καὶ ἦν πάντα τὰ ἔτη τοῦ Γὰδ ἑκατὸν καὶ
πεντήκοντα καὶ πέντε, καὶ Γὰδ ἦν υἱὸς Ζέλφας ὁ τέταρτος.

ΔΙΑΘΗΚΗ ΑΣΗΡ ΠΕΡΙ ΚΑΚΙΑΣ ΚΑΙ ΑΡΕΤΗΣ

I. 1. 'Αντίγραφον διαθήκης 'Ασὴρ περὶ κακίας καὶ ἀρετῆς. 2. 'Ακού-
σατε, εἶπε, τέκνα 'Ασήρ, τοῦ πατρὸς ὑμῶν καὶ ὑποδείξω ὑμῖν πᾶν τὸ
εὐθὲς ἐνώπιον τοῦ Θεοῦ. 3. Δύο ὁδοὺς ἔδωκεν ὁ Θεὸς τοῖς υἱοῖς
τῶν ἀνθρώπων, καὶ δύο διαβούλια καὶ δύο πράξεις καὶ δύο τόπους.
4. Διὰ τοῦτο πάντα δύο ἐστίν, ἓν κατέναντι τοῦ ἑνός. 5. Δύο ἐστὶ
διαβούλια ἐν στέρνοις ἡμῶν διακρίνοντα ἡμᾶς. 6. Ἐὰν οὖν ἄνθρωπός
τις εἰς τὴν δικαιοσύνην ἐπιτρέπηται καὶ τὰ διαβούλια αὐτοῦ. Ἐὰν
πίπτῃ εἰς τὴν ἁμαρτίαν ὁ ἄνθρωπος ἢ δι' ἄγνοιαν ἐν τίνι (ἁμάρτῃ)
εὐθὺς μετανοεῖ, [καὶ διὰ τὴν μετάνοιαν αὐτοῦ καθαίρει τὰ ἁμαρτήματα
αὐτοῦ]. 7. Δίκαια γὰρ λογιζόμενος ἀνατρέπει τὸ κακὸν καὶ ἐκριζοῖ
τὴν ἁμαρτίαν. 8. εἴ τις ἐπιτρέπει εἰς ἄλλους τρόπους τὸν τρόπον
αὐτοῦ, πᾶσα πρᾶξις αὐτοῦ ἐν πονηρίᾳ [καὶ διὰ κακίαν ἐπαινεῖται, καὶ
διδάσκει τὰ χείλη αὐτοῦ ἀεὶ τὰ ψευδῆ λέγειν] καὶ ἀπωθούμενος τὸ
ἀγαθὸν λήψεται τὸ κακόν, εἴπερ θέλει τι ἀγαθὸν ποιεῖν, εἰς κακὸν
μεταστρέφει. 9. Ὅταν γὰρ εὖ ἄρξηται ὡς ἀγαθὸν ποιῶν, τὸ τέλος
τῆς πράξεως αὐτοῦ εἰς κακὸν ποιεῖν ἀνελαύνει, ὅτι ὁ θησαυρὸς τοῦ
διαβουλίου αὐτοῦ κατακυριεύεται ὑπὸ τοῦ Βελίαρ καὶ ἐπεπεπλήρωται
τοῦ πνεύματος τῆς πλάνης [ἄνθρωπος κατὰ βίαν ποιεῖ].

II. 5. Κλέπτων καὶ πλεονεκτῶν, ἀλλὰ καὶ ἔτι ἐλεεῖ τοὺς πτωχούς. διπρόσωπον μὲν καὶ τοῦτο. 8. Μοιχεύουσιν καὶ πορνεύουσιν, καὶ ἔτι ἀπέχονται ἐδεσμάτων καὶ ἄγαν τις νηστεύει. καὶ τοῦτο διπρόσωπόν ἐστι. ['Ορᾶτε οὖν, τέκνα ἐμοῦ, ὡς εἶπον] 7. τοιαῦτα γὰρ διαφθείρει τὴν ψυχήν, καθαρίζει τὸ σῶμα. 10. 'Εγώ, τέκνα, εὗρον ἐν βιβλίοις τοῦ δικαίου 'Ενώχ, λέγουσι III. 1. μὴ γίγνησθε διπρόσωποι τῇ δικαιοσύνῃ καὶ τῇ κακίᾳ, ἀλλὰ προσκολλήθητε τῷ ἀγαθῷ, ὡς ὁ Θεὸς ἀναπαύεται ἐν αὐτῷ καὶ ἄνθρωποι θέλουσιν ἐν αὐτῇ παρακύπτειν [καὶ κατὰ τὸ ἦθος τῆς κακίας μὴ ἰδεῖν τὴν χάριν]. 2. καὶ νῦν, τέκνα, φεύγετε τὴν κακίαν τοῦ Βελίαρ εἰσελθοῦσαν εἰς τὰς ἀγαθὰς ὑμῶν πράξεις.

V. 'Ορᾶτε οὖν, τέκνα, πῶς δύο ἐστὶν ἐν πᾶσιν, καὶ ἓν ὑπὸ τοῦ ἑνὸς κέκρυπται καὶ πένθος ἐν ἀδελφοῖς ἐν ποιήσει καὶ αἰσχροκέρδεια ἐν χαρᾷ κρύπτεται τῇ μέθῃ τὰ τολμηρὰ κρύπτεται καὶ ἡ λύπη ἐν ἀδελφοῖς καὶ τῇ τροφῇ. 2. ὁ θάνατος διαδέχεται τὴν ζωήν, καὶ τὴν τιμὴν διαδέχεται ἡ ἀτιμία, καὶ ὁ ποιῶν τὰ ἀληθῆ ἐστιν ἐν τῷ φωτί, ὁ δὲ ποιῶν τὴν ἀδικίαν ἐν τῷ σκότῳ πορεύεται. 4. ἐγὼ ἐν πάσῃ τῇ ζωῇ μου (ταῦτα) ἐδοκίμασα καὶ οὐκ ἐπλανήθην ἀπὸ τῆς ἀληθείας Κυρίου.

VI. 4. Τὸ γὰρ τέλος δείκνυσι τὴν δικαιοσύνην ἢ τὴν ἀδικίαν. 5. ἐπεὶ γὰρ τῇ ἐντολῇ (τοῦ Θεοῦ) ἡ ψυχή μου ἡρπάσθη τῇ χειρὶ τοῦ ἀγγέλου τοῦ Θεοῦ, ταχέως φαίνεται τὸ πνεῦμα τῆς πλάνης. 'Η γὰρ ψυχή, ἐλέγχουσα τὰς φροντίδας καὶ τὰς πράξεις, πάσχει σφόδρα ἀπὸ τοῦ πνεύματος τῆς πλάνης, ἐδούλευσεν γὰρ ἐν τούτῳ τῷ βίῳ αὐτῷ. 6. Εἰ δὲ ψυχὴ πορεύεται ἐν ἀληθείᾳ, τότε ἐν χαρᾷ ἐγνώρισε τὸν ἄγγελον τοῦ Θεοῦ, καὶ ὁ ἄγγελος παραμυθεῖται αὐτὴν εἰς τὸν αἰώνιον βίον.

VII. 'Υμεῖς δέ, τέκνα, μὴ γένεσθε ὡς Σόδομα, ἀγνοήσαντες τὰς ἐντολὰς Θεοῦ. 2. Εἶδον γὰρ ἐν βιβλίοις τοῦ 'Ενὼχ τοῦ δικαίου ὡς σφόδρα πλανᾶσθε καὶ πολλαὶ τιμωρίαι ἔσονται ἐφ' ὑμῖν καὶ ποιήσετε ἐν ξέναις χώραις, [ἀλλὰ τῇ ἐλεημοσύνῃ τοῦ Κυρίου ἐπιστρέψεσθε εἰς τὴν γῆν ὑμῶν, ὅπου ὑπέσχετο ὁ Κύριος τῷ πατρὶ ἡμῶν 'Αβραάμ], καὶ ἔσεσθε ἐκεῖ 3. ἕως ὁ 'Υψιστος ἐπισκέψηται τὴν γῆν [καὶ τοῖς ζῶσι ἐν αὐτῇ ἕξει εὐσπλαγχνίαν], καὶ αὐτὸς ἐλεύσεται ὡς ἄνθρωπος μετὰ ἀνθρώπων ἐσθίων καὶ πίνων καὶ ἐν ἡσυχίᾳ συντρίβων τὴν κεφαλὴν τοῦ δράκοντος δι' ὕδατος. Οὗτος σώσει πολλοὺς [ἐξ] 'Ισραὴλ καὶ πάντα τὰ ἔθνη, Θεὸς εἰς ἄνδρα ὑποκρινόμενος. 4. Εἴπατε οὖν ταῦτα τοῖς τέκνοις ὑμῶν μὴ ἀπειθεῖν αὐτῷ. 5. 'Ανέγνων γὰρ ἐν βιβλίοις 'Ενὼχ τοῦ δικαίου, ὅτι ἀπειθοῦντες ἀπειθήσετε αὐτῷ καὶ ἀσεβοῦντες ἀσεβήσετε εἰς αὐτόν, μὴ προσέχοντες τῷ νόμῳ τοῦ Θεοῦ. 6. Διὰ τοῦτο διασκορπισθήσεσθε εἰς τὸ εὖρος τῆς γῆς, καὶ ἔσεσθε ἐν διασπορᾷ, καὶ ἐξυυθενωθήσεσθε ὡς ὕδωρ ἄχρηστον. 7. [καὶ ὁμολογοῦντες τότε τὸ ὄνομα] τοῦ Κυρίου πάλιν πιστεύσετε καὶ ἐπιθήσει αὐτοῖς τὴν εὐσπλαγχνίαν αὐτοῦ, διὰ Ἀβραὰμ καὶ Ἰσαὰκ καὶ Ἰακώβ.

VIII. 1. Εἶτα δὲ εἶπεν αὐτοῖς· θάψατέ με εἰς Χεβρών. καὶ ἐκοίμηθη ὕπνῳ αἰωνίῳ. 2. καὶ ἔθαψαν αὐτὸν ὅτι υἱοὶ ὡς ὁ πατὴρ ἐνετείλατο αὐτοῖς. καὶ ἔζη πάντα τὰ ἔτη αὐτοῦ, ἑκατὸν καὶ εἴκοσι καὶ τρία, Ἀσὴρ ὁ υἱὸς Ἰακὼβ δέκατος, υἱὸς Ζέλφας.

ΔΙΑΘΗΚΗ ΙΩΣΗΦ

[Ἐπὶ τούτοις οἱ ἀδελφοὶ Ἰωσὴφ εἶπον· ὁ πατήρ σου λίσσεταί σε, λέγων, εἴπετε τῷ Ἰωσήφ· Συγγνῶθι αὐτοῖς τὴν σκολιότητα τῶν ἁμαρτιῶν αὐτῶν, ὡς κακὸν ἐποίησάν σοι καὶ νῦν ὁ Θεὸς ἀνίησι σκολιότητα τοῖς δούλοις (αὐτοῦ), τοῦ πατρός σου χάριν. Ὁ Ἰωσὴφ ταῦτα ἀκούσας ἐκλαύσατο ὅτε οἱ ἀδελφοὶ εἰς δούλους μετεβλήθησαν, καὶ Ἰωσὴφ σφόδρα στενάξας εἶπεν αὐτοῖς οὐχ ὥσπερ πατέρες καὶ ἀδελφοὶ πάντες]. I. 4. ὑμεῖς ἐμισήσατέ με, ἀδελφοί, ἀλλ’ ὁ Θεὸς ἠγάπησέ με, ὑμεῖς δὲ ἠθέλετέ με ἀνελεῖν καὶ ὁ Θεὸς τῶν πατέρων μου ἐφύλαξέ με, εἰς λάκκον με ἐβάλετε ἀλλ’ ὁ Ὕψιστος ἀνήγαγέ με. 5. ἐπωλήσατέ με εἰς δοῦλον, καὶ ὁ Θεὸς ἐκ πάντων ἐλευθέρωσέ με [καὶ πάσῃ τῇ Αἰγύπτῳ δοῦναι κρίσιν ἐποίησέ με], 5. εἰς αἰχμαλωσίαν ἐλήφθην καὶ ἡ κραταιὰ αὐτοῦ χεὶρ ἐβοήθησέ μοι· ἐν λιμῷ συνεσχέθην καὶ αὐτὸς ὁ Κύριος διέθρεψέ με. 6. μόνος ἤμην ἐν λάκκῳ, ἀλλ’ ὁ Θεὸς τοῦ πατρός μου παρεκάλεσέ με· ἐν ἀσθενείᾳ ἤμην ἀλλὰ ὁ σωτὴρ ἐχαρίτωσέ με, ὠνείδισάν με ἐν δεσμοῖς 7. καὶ ἐν (διαβολαῖς), ἀλλ’ ὁ Θεὸς ἐρρύσατό με, καὶ ἐν λόγοις πικροῖς οἱ Αἰγύπτιοι ἐκβάλλουσί με.

II. 2. Καὶ ἠγωνισάμην τῷ παθήματι ἐλθόντι ἐπ’ ἐμὲ ἀπὸ γυναικὸς ἐπειγούσης με παρανομεῖν μετ’ αὐτῆς ἀλλ’ ὁ Θεὸς Ἰσραὴλ τοῦ πατρός μου ἐφύλαξέ με ἀπὸ ταύτης φλογὸς καιομένης. 3. Ἐφυλακίσθην, ἐτύφθην, ἐμυκτηρίσθην καὶ ἔδωκέ με Κύριος εἰς οἰκτιρμοὺς ἐνώπιον πάντων τῶν δεσμοφυλάκων ἐν τῷ δεσμωτηρίῳ. 4. Οὐ γὰρ ἐγκαταλείψει τοὺς φοβουμένους αὐτὸν ἐν ἀληθείᾳ ἐν δεσμωτηρίῳ σκοτεινῷ οὔτε ἐν δεσμωτηρίῳ ἢ δεσμοῖς, ἢ θλίψεσιν ἢ ἀνάγκαις 5. οὐ γὰρ ὡς ἄνθρωπος ἐπαισχύνεται ὁ Θεός. οὐδὲ ὡς γηγενὴς ἀσθενεῖ ἢ ἀπωθεῖται. 6. ἐπὶ πᾶσι δὲ [τόποις] παρίσταται καὶ ἐν διαφόροις · λύπαις παρακαλεῖ παρών. 7. ἐν δέκα πειρασμοῖς ὁ Θεὸς ἐποίησέ με κρατερόν.

IV. 1, 5. Ποσάκις ἡ Αἰγυπτία σαίνουσά με εἶπε, εἴπερ συνέσει μοι ἀποβαλῶ εἴδωλον τοῦ Αἰγυπτίου Πεστεφρῆ. 7. Θέλω ὑμᾶς πιστεύσαι κατὰ τὸν νόμον τοῦ Κυρίου σου. 8. ἀποκρινάμενος αὐτῇ εἶπον·

'Αμεμεφρή, ἡ δέσποινά μου οὐ καθαρὰ καὶ Θεὸς ὁ Κύριος βούλεται τοὺς φοβουμένους αὐτὸν μὴ τοῖς λάγνοις χαρίζεσθαι. [Αὕτη δὲ μᾶλλον ἔθηκε τὴν ἐσθῆτα ὥστε περιπλέκειν ἐμέ].

VI. 1. Καὶ ἀποστέλλει μοι βρῶμα ἐν γοητείᾳ πεφυραμένον. 6. καὶ ὁ Θεὸς τοῦ πατρός μου ἀπεκάλυψε. 4. Μετὰ ταῦτα εἰσελθὼν εἰς τὴν κοίτην μου εἶπον αὐτῇ, ὅτι ἐνόμιζεν κτείνειν ἐμὲ ἀδίκως ὅτι ἔπεμψέ μοι τὸ βρῶμα τῷ (φαρμάκῳ) θανασίμῳ μεμιγμένον, καὶ 7. ὅτι γνοίης τῶν· ἐν σωφροσύνῃ θεοσεβούντων οὐ κατισχύει κακία ἀσεβούντων, λαβὼν ἐνώπιον αὐτῆς φαγεῖν ἠρξάμην· ὁ Θεὸς τῶν πατέρων μου ἐστὶ μετ' ἐμοῦ. 8. Ἡ δὲ ἔπεσεν ἐπὶ πρόσωπον εἰς τοὺς πόδας μου, καὶ ἔκλαυσε, καὶ συνέθετό μοι μὴ ποιῆσαι ἔτι τὴν ἀσέβειαν ταύτην, [καὶ ὅμως ἐξεγείρεται ταῖς φροντίσιν καὶ ἔσω ὁ δαίμων τῆς ἀκολασίας ἐπιφλέγει αὐτήν].

Μετὰ ταῦτα ὡς ἐγὼ ἦλθον πρὸς αὐτὴν διὰ τῶν ἀναγκαίων, λέγουσά μοι VIII. 2. καὶ αἴρουσα τῆς ἐσθῆτος ἔσυρέ με εἰς τὴν κοίτην αὐτῆς. Καὶ ἐγὼ συνέστρεψα ἀμφὶ ἐμαυτὸν τὴν ἐσθῆτα. καὶ ἔφυγον ἀπὸ τῆς Αἰγυπτίας. 3. ἡ δὲ οὐ δεξαμένη τὸ θέλημα ἐσυκοφάντισέ με πρὸς τὸν ἄνδρα αὐτῆς. Ἐγὼ δὴ ἐτύφθην καὶ ἐβλήθην εἰς τὸ δεσμωτήριον καὶ ἡ Αἰγυπτία ἀνίετο κατ' ἐμοῦ IX. 1. καὶ εἶπε πολλάκις πλήρωσον τὸ θέλημά μου, καὶ ἐξελευθερώσω σε ἐκ τῶν δεσμῶν καὶ σώσω σε ἐκ τοῦ δεσμωτηρίου. 2. Ἐγὼ δὲ καὶ ἐν φροντίδι οὐ συνεχώρησα αὐτῇ· ἀγαπᾷ γὰρ ὁ Κύριος τὸν ἐν στέγῃ σκοτεινῇ νηστεύοντα ἐν διανοίᾳ μᾶλλον ἢ ἐν τοῖς βασιλικοῖς μεγαλείοις τὸν ἄνδρα τρέφοντα ἑαυτὸν ἐν πορνείᾳ 3. ὁ πορευόμενος ἐν φροντίσιν λήψεται δόξαν, καὶ ὁ Θεὸς οἶδε οὗ ἔχει χρείαν, καὶ δώσει αὐτοῖς ὃ καὶ ἐμοὶ ἔδωκε.

[Νῦν οὖν, ἀδελφοί, μὴ φοβεῖσθε. ἐγὼ θρέψω ὑμᾶς καὶ δόμους ὑμετέρους. παραμυθήσομαι γὰρ λέγων αὐτοῖς. καὶ οὕτως ἦλθεν ὁ Ἰωσὴφ εἰς τὴν Αἴγυπτον καὶ οἱ ἀδελφοὶ αὐτοῦ. καὶ ἤρξατο ζῆν ἐν Αἰγύπτῳ καὶ ἐστήριξε πᾶσαν τὴν δύναμιν τῶν Αἰγυπτίων. Καὶ ὁ Ἰωσὴφ ἔζη ἔτη ἑκατὸν καὶ δέκα καὶ βλέψας τοὺς παῖδας τοῦ Ἐφραὶμ τρεῖς υἱοὺς τοῦ γένους Μάχερ, υἱοῦ Μανασσή. καὶ Ἰωσὴφ εἶδε τὴν ἡμέραν οὐ μακρὰν ἀπέχουσαν ἀπ' αὐτοῦ, καὶ προστίθεται τοῖς προγόνοις καὶ τῷ πατρί, καὶ ἤρξατο λέγειν τοῖς πλησίοις Ἰδοὺ πᾶσαι αἱ αἰσθήσεις ἀνέχουσαι τὸ σῶμά μου ἀδυνατοῦσι, καὶ τὸ κράτος ζωοτρόφον ἀπέστη ἀπ' ἐμοῦ, καὶ ἀπῆλθεν τὸ κράτος τῆς δυνάμεως καὶ νόσοι γίγνονται κρατερώτεραι ἐν ἐμοί, καὶ οὐκέτι ἔχω μέρος ἐν τοῖς ζῶσιν ἐπὶ τῇ γῇ, καὶ οὐκ ἔχω ἀπὸ τοῦ νῦν οἰκίαν καὶ μικρὸν χρόνον πρόσθεν τοῦ θανάτου λέξω τι ὑμῖν καὶ τοῖς υἱοῖς τῶν ἀδελφῶν μου].

XVII. 1. Ἠκούσατε γάρ, τέκνα μου, ὅσον ἐγὼ ἔπαθον [ἀπὸ τῶν

ἀδελφῶν μου, ἀλλὰ γινόμενος δοῦλος, μετεβλήθην]· ἵνα μὴ καταισχύνω
τοὺς ἀδελφούς 2. καὶ ὑμεῖς οὖν ἀγαπᾶτε ἀλλήλους, τέκνα μου, καὶ ἐν
μακροθυμίαις ζῆτε μὴ φέροντες αἰτίας ἄλλος ἄλλῳ. 3. Τέρπεται γὰρ
ὁ Θεὸς ἐπὶ ὁμονοίᾳ ἀδελφῶν, καὶ ἐπὶ προαιρέσει καρδίας εὐδοκεῖτε
πρὸς τὸ ζῆν. 4. καὶ ὅτι ἦλθον οἱ ἀδελφοί μου εἰς Αἴγυπτον, ὡς καὶ
αὐτοὶ ὁρῶσι, καὶ πάλιν ἔδωκα τὸ ἀργύριον αὐτῶν καὶ οὐκ ὠνείδισα τῇ
ὕβρει ἀλλὰ καὶ παρεκάλεσα αὐτούς 5. καὶ ἔτι μετὰ θάνατον Ἰακὼβ
περισσοτέρως ἠγάπησα αὐτούς. 6. οὐκ ἀφῆκα γὰρ αὐτοῖς θλιβῆναι, καὶ
ὃ ἦν ἐν χειρί μου, αὐτοῖς ἔδωκα. 7. οἱ υἱοὶ γὰρ αὐτῶν υἱοί μου. καὶ
τοὺς υἱούς μου ὡς δούλους αὐτῶν ἐποίησα. ἡ ψυχὴ αὐτῶν ἦν ψυχή μου,
καὶ πᾶν ἄλγημα αὐτῶν ἄλγημά μου καὶ πᾶσα μαλακία αὐτῶν ἀσθένειά
μου, τὸ φῶς αὐτῶν φῶς μου καὶ ἡ βουλή μου σὺν αὐτοῖς ἦν. 8. καὶ
οὐχ ὕψωσα ἐμαυτὸν ἐν αὐτοῖς ἐν ἀλαζονείᾳ διὰ τὴν κοσμικὴν δόξαν
μου, ἀλλ᾽ ἤμην ἐν αὐτοῖς ταπεινὸς [καὶ ὑφειμένος, ἐπαίρων αὐτοὺς
μᾶλλον ἢ ἐμαυτόν].

XVIII. 1. Ἐὰν οὖν ὑμεῖς, τέκνα μου, θέλητε πορεύεσθαι ἐν ταῖς
ἐντολαῖς Κυρίου [καὶ τὰ δῶρα τῆς γῆς ἐδεῖσθε καὶ ὁ στέφανος τῆς
βασιλείας πλεχθήσεται ὑμῖν. καὶ ἐπισκιασθήσεσθε τῇ χάριτι τοῦ Θεοῦ
καὶ ἐν τῇ εὐλογίᾳ τοῦ κτίστου αἱ ἀκτῖνες ἡλίου λάμψουσι ἐφ᾽ ὑμᾶς].
2. καὶ ἐὰν θέλῃ τις κακοποιῆσαι ὑμᾶς, ὑμεῖς [ἐξ ἰσχύος ὑμῶν] ἀγαθὰ
ποιοῦντες βοηθεῖτε αὐτῷ καὶ εὔχεσθε ὑπὲρ αὐτοῦ τῷ Κυρίῳ ἀπὸ παντὸς
κακοῦ [τῇ ἰσχύι καὶ κράτει αὐτοῦ] ὁ Θεὸς λυτρώσει ὑμᾶς. 3. Ἑωρᾶτε
γάρ ὅτι [Θεὸς ἐποίησέ μοι ταπεινωθέντι καὶ πωλουμένῳ καὶ συκο-
φαντηθέντι καὶ πάντα ἔπαθον τῇ ὑπομόνῃ, ἐπαινῶν τὸν Θεόν μου καὶ
ὡς κρατερὸς στρατὸς ὡπλισμένος τῷ σιδήρῳ ὁ λόγος τοῦ Κυρίου ἀφαιρεῖ
με ἐκ τῆς δουλείας καὶ ἐξ ἐπιβουλῆς καὶ κύριον τῆς Αἰγύπτου ἐν
πάσαις τύχαις ἐποίησέ με].

XIX. 1. Ἀκούσατε, τέκνα μου, ἐνύπνιον ὃ εἶδον λέξω ὑμῖν. 2. Ἰδοὺ
δώδεκα ἔλαφοι ἐνέμοντο καὶ οἱ ἐννέα διῃρέθησαν εἰς πᾶσαν τὴν γῆν·
ὁμοίως καὶ οἱ τρεῖς. 8. καὶ εἶδον ὅτι ἐκ τοῦ Ἰούδα ἐγεννήθη παρθένος,
ἔχουσα στολὴν βυσσίνην· καὶ ἐξ αὐτῆς προῆλθεν ἀμνὸς ἄμωμος. καὶ
πάντα τὰ θηρία ὥρμων κατ᾽ αὐτοῦ, καὶ ἐνίκησεν αὐτὰ ὁ ἀμνὸς καὶ
ἀπώλεσεν αὐτοὺς εἰς καταπάτησιν. 9. Καὶ ἔχαιρον ἐπ᾽ αὐτῷ οἱ
ἄγγελοι, καὶ οἱ ἄνθρωποι καὶ πᾶσα ἡ γῆ. 10. Ταῦτα δὲ γενήσεται ἐν
καιρῷ αὐτῶν [εὐφράνθησαν ἐν αὐτοῖς], ἐν ἐσχάταις ἡμέραις. 11. Ὑμεῖς
οὖν, τέκνα μου, φυλάξατε τὰς ἐντολὰς Κυρίου καὶ τιμᾶτε τὸν Ἰούδαν
καὶ τὸν Λευὶ ὅτι ἐξ αὐτῶν ἀνατελεῖ ὑμῖν ὁ ἀμνὸς τοῦ Θεοῦ, χάριτι
σώζων πάντα τὰ ἔθνη [καὶ τὸν] Ἰσραήλ. 12. Ἡ γὰρ βασιλεία
αὐτοῦ βασιλεία αἰῶνος. ἡ δὲ ἐμὴ βασιλεία ἐν ὑμῖν ἐπιτελεῖται ὡς
ὀπωροφυλάκιον· μετὰ τὸ θέρος οὐ φαίνεται.

['Άκουσον οὖν, ὦ 'Ιουδαῖε, τί λέγει τὸ ἐνύπνιον τοῦ 'Ιωσήφ. Ἑώρακα γὰρ δώδεκα ἐλάφους, καὶ ἔλαφοί εἰσιν οἱ δώδεκα ἀπόστολοι, εὐαγγελιζόμενοι τὰ σημεῖα ἐν τῷ κόσμῳ καὶ ἐννέα αὐτῶν, εἶπε, στρώννυνται ἐπὶ πᾶσαν τὴν γῆν διδάσκοντες καὶ βαπτίζοντες ἐν ὀνόματι τοῦ πατρὸς καὶ τοῦ υἱοῦ καὶ τοῦ ἁγίου πνεύματος. οὕτως εἶπον τρεῖς, καὶ οὗτοι οἱ τρεῖς ὁμοίως ἐκήρυξαν καὶ ἀπέθανον οὐκ ἐξιόντες ἐξ 'Ιερουσαλήμ. Ὡς ἡ γραφὴ ἔλεξε ὅτι Ἡρώδῃ τῷ ἀνόμῳ 'Ιακὼβ ὁ ἀδελφὸς 'Ιωάννου τῷ ξίφει ἐκτάνθη καὶ οὕτως ὁ Στέφανος ὁ διάκονος καλούμενος ἐλιθάσθη ὑπὸ τῶν 'Ιουδαίων, ὅστις ἔκραξε λέγων, Κύριε, μὴ στήσῃς αὐτοῖς τὴν ἁμαρτίαν ταύτην, οὐ γὰρ οἴδασι ὅτι ποιοῦσιν. καὶ εἶδον, εἶπεν, ὡς ἐκ τοῦ 'Ιούδα ἐγεννήθη παρθένος, τοῦτό ἐστ' ἡ μήτηρ τοῦ Θεοῦ ἐκ τοῦ γένους τοῦ 'Ιούδα, θυγάτηρ 'Ιωακίμ, ἔχουσα, εἶπε, στολὴν βυσσίνην. τοῦτό ἐστι καθαρὰ καὶ ἄνευ πλάνης, ἀλλὰ ἁγνὴ καὶ ὑπεραγνή. Ἐξ αὐτῆς, εἶπε, προῆλθεν ἀμνὸς ἄμωμος, τοῦτό ἐστιν ὁ υἱὸς τοῦ Θεοῦ, ἤπιος καὶ ταπεινὸς ἄνευ κακίας, καὶ ἄνευ πονηρίας. ἐξαιρεῖται οὐκ εἰδὼς τὴν ἁμαρτίαν, καὶ ἐξ ἀριστεροῦ αὐτοῦ ὡς λέων, εἶπε, Ἰδού ἐστι ὡς λόγος τοῦ Θεοῦ· μεγάλως καὶ δεινῶς καὶ φοβερῶς ἐπισημαίνεται καὶ πάντα τὰ θηρία ὥρμων (κατ' αὐτοῦ). Τοῦτό ἐστι, ὑμεῖς ταλαίπωροι 'Ιουδαῖοι εἴδετε τὸν υἱὸν τοῦ Θεοῦ λαβόντα ταπεινὴν μορφήν, καὶ ὡς ἄγρια θηρία ἐκράζετε καὶ ὡρμήσατε εἰπόντες, λάβετε, λάβετε, σταυρώσατε αὐτόν, γένοιτο τὸ αἷμα αὐτοῦ ἐφ' ἡμῖν καὶ ἐπὶ τέκνοις ἡμῶν.

'Ενίκησεν αὐτοῖς ἐκ νεκρῶν ἐγερθεὶς ὁ υἱὸς τοῦ Θεοῦ οὗ ὑμεῖς κατεφρονήσατε, κακῶς ποιοῦντες, καὶ ὤλεσεν αὐτὸς ἐν καταπατήσει, τοῦτό ἐστι, δίδοσθε εἰς δουλείαν ὑπὸ τὰ ἔθνη. καὶ καταπατεῖσθε ἕως τοῦ νῦν ἐν ταῖς χώραις ἡμῶν καὶ περὶ τούτου ἠγαλλιάσαντο οἱ ἄγγελοι καὶ ἄνθρωποι καὶ πᾶσα ἡ γῆ. Ὁ Κύριος ὁ Θεὸς ἡμῶν συνήψει τὰ ἄνω σὺν τοῖς κάτω ἅμα ἐν ἑνὶ φαιδρᾷ εὐλογίᾳ. τοῦτο γὰρ γενήσεται ἐν τῷ καιρῷ αὐτοῦ. 'Ιακὼβ γὰρ ἦν ἐν τῷ τρίτῳ καὶ ἑβδόμῳ ἔτει, καὶ ὁ υἱὸς τοῦ Θεοῦ ἐγένετο ἐν ἐννάτῳ ἔτει καὶ ἠγαλλιάσατο ἐν ταῖς ἐσχάταις ἡμέραις. Τούτου ἐστιν ἡ ἀρχὴ καὶ τὸ τέλος. ὁ γὰρ πρῶτον ἀπὸ τοῦ μὴ εἶναι εἰς τὸ εἶναι ἤγαγεν. περὶ τούτου οἱ προφῆται ἔλεξαν καὶ ἡμεῖς ἀγαλλιώμεθα περὶ αὐτοῦ, ἕως τῶν ἐσχάτων ἡμερῶν. Καὶ ὑμεῖς, τέκνα μου, φυλάξατε τὰς ἐντολὰς τοῦ Κυρίου. καὶ τιμᾶτε τὸν 'Ιούδαν καὶ τὸν Λευΐ, ὅτι ἐξ αὐτῶν ἀνατελεῖ ὑμῖν ὁ ἀμνὸς τοῦ Θεοῦ, τοῦτό ἐστι, ἐκ γένους 'Ιούδα καὶ κατὰ τὴν τάξιν τοῦ Λευΐ δέξεται ἡγεμονίαν τῇ χάριτι σώζων πάντα τὰ ἔθνη (καὶ) 'Ισραήλ. καὶ ἐννόει ὅτι οὐ μόνον 'Ισραὴλ ἦν ὁ σώζων ἀλλὰ πάντα τὰ ἔθνη. Ἕως γιγνόμενος οὐ μόνον 'Ισραὴλ ἔσωσε γιγνόμενος ἐξ ἁγνῆς παρθένου, καὶ πάντα τὰ ἔθνη εἰς σωτηρίαν ἔσυρε· καὶ βασιλεία αὐτοῦ βασιλεία αἰώνιος. Ἐννόει

δὲ ἆρ' οὐκ ἦν τούτου ἀμνοῦ ἡ παρθένος· καὶ ἡ βασιλεία αὐτοῦ οὐ
μεταλλάσσεται εἰς τοὺς αἰῶνας.

XX. 4. Καὶ ταῦτα εἰπὼν ἐξέτεινε τοὺς πόδας αὐτοῦ ἐν τῷ λέχει καὶ
ἐκοιμήθη ὕπνον αἰώνιον. 5, 6. Καὶ ἐπένθησαν αὐτὸν πᾶς Ἰσραὴλ καὶ
πᾶσα ἡ Αἴγυπτος ὅτι ὡς ἓν μέλος ἔπαθον σὺν αὐτῷ καὶ ἔζη Ἰωσὴφ
πάντα τὰ ἔτη ἑκατὸν καὶ δέκα (καὶ) ἀπέθανε.]

ΔΙΑΘΗΚΗ ΒΕΝΙΑΜΙΝ ΠΕΡΙ ΔΙΑΝΟΙΑΣ ΚΑΘΑΡΑΣ

[Συνεκάλεσε γὰρ Βενιαμὶν τοὺς υἱοὺς αὐτοῦ καὶ ἤρξατο λέγειν ἐν
τοῖς ὠσὶν αὐτῶν. Ἐγὼ Βενιαμὶν [υἱός]· τοῦ γήρως τοῦ πατρός μου
Ἰακὼβ καὶ ἦν νεώτερος πάντων τῶν ἀδελφῶν μου]. Ι. 2. ὡς Ἰσαάκ,
ὁ πάππος ἡμῶν, ἐτέχθη τῷ Ἀβραάμ, ἑκατοστῷ ἔτει, οὕτως κἀγὼ τῷ
Ἰακώβ, ἐν ἑκατοστῷ ἔτει. 4. ἡ γὰρ Ῥαχὴλ μετὰ τὸ τεκεῖν τὸν
Ἰωσὴφ δώδεκα ἔτη ἐστείρευσε. , καὶ προσηύξατο Κυρίῳ μετὰ σπουδῆς
δώδεκα ἡμέρας, καὶ συλλαβοῦσα ἔτεκέ με. 5. Διὰ τοῦτο ἐκλήθην
υἱὸς ἡμερῶν, ὅ ἐστι Βενιαμίν.

ΙΙΙ. 1. Καὶ ὑμεῖς οὖν, τέκνα μου, ἀγαπήσατε Κύριον τὸν Θεὸν τοῦ
οὐρανοῦ καὶ φυλάξατε ἐντολὰς αὐτοῦ, μιμούμενοι τὸν ἀγαθὸν καὶ ὅσιον
ἄνδρα Ἰωσήφ. 2. Καὶ ἔστω ἡ διάνοια ὑμῶν εἰς τὸ ἀγαθόν, ὡς κἀμὲ
οἴδατε. 3. [οὕτως ζῆτε καὶ ὑμεῖς] φοβεῖσθε Κύριον καὶ ἀγαπᾶτε τὸν
πλησίον· καὶ ἐὰν τὰ πνεύματα τοῦ Βελίαρ εἰς πᾶσαν πονηρίαν θλίψεως
ἐξαιτήσωνται ὑμᾶς, οὐ μὴ κατακυριεύσῃ ὑμῶν πᾶσα πονηρία θλίψεως,
ὡς οὐδὲ Ἰωσὴφ τοῦ ἀδελφοῦ μου. 4. Πόσοι τῶν ἀνθρώπων ἠθέλησαν
ἀνελεῖν αὐτὸν καὶ ὁ Θεὸς ἐσκέπασεν αὐτόν; ὁ γὰρ φοβούμενος τὸν
Θεὸν καὶ ἀγαπῶν τὸν πλησίον αὐτοῦ τούτῳ οὐκ ἀνάγκη τι φοβεῖσθαι.
5. καὶ εἴπερ πόλλην ὕβριν οἱ υἱοὶ τοῦ κόσμου ἐπιφέρουσι, οὐ προχω-
ρήσουσι καὶ ὑπὸ θηρίου οὐ δύναται κυριευθῆναι βοηθούμενος ὑπὸ τῆς
τοῦ Κυρίου ἀγάπης ἥτις πρὸς τὸν Θεὸν καὶ ἣν ἔχει πρὸς τὸν πλησίον.
6. καὶ γὰρ ἐδεήθην τοῦ πατρὸς ἡμῶν Ἰωσήφ, λέγων· Ὦ ἀγαθὲ πάτερ,
Ἰακώβ, προσεύχου περὶ τῶν υἱῶν σου τῷ Κυρίῳ, ἵνα μὴ λογίσηται
αὐτοῖς ὡς ἁμαρτίαν ὁ Κύριος, ὅτι ἐνεθυμήθησαν πονηρὸν περὶ ἐμοῦ. 7. Καὶ
οὕτως ἐβόα Ἰακὼβ μεγάλῃ φωνῇ, λέγων· Ὦ τέκνον εὐλογηθείς, νικᾷς
ἐμὲ τοῖς σπλάγχνοις. 8. πληρωθήτω ἐν σοὶ προφητεία ἀνθρώπων, ὁ
ἀμνὸς τοῦ Θεοῦ σώσει τὸν κόσμον. ὅτι ὅμωμος ὑπὲρ ἀνόμων ἀποθανεῖ
ἐν τῷ αἵματι τῆς διαθήκης, ἐπὶ σωτηρίᾳ ἐθνῶν καὶ Ἰσραήλ, καὶ καταργήσει Βελίαρ καὶ τὸν ὑπηρετοῦντα αὐτῷ.

IV. Καὶ ὁρᾶτε, τέκνα, τοῦ ἀγαθοῦ ἀνδρὸς Ἰωσὴφ τὸ τέλος· μιμήσασθε τὴν εὐσπλαγχνίαν αὐτοῦ, ἵνα καὶ ὑμεῖς στεφάνους δόξης

φορέσητε.   2. Ὁ ἀγαθὸς ἄνθρωπος οὐκ ἔχει σκοτεινὸν ὄμμα, ἐλεᾷ γὰρ πάντας, κἂν ὦσιν ἀμαρτωλοί.   3. κἂν βουλεύωνται περὶ αὐτοῦ εἰς κακά, οὕτως ὁ ἀγαθοποιῶν νικᾷ τὸ κακόν, σκεπαζόμενος ὑπὸ τοῦ Θεοῦ, τῆς ἀρετῆς αὐτοῦ χάριν.   4. Ἐάν τις δοξάζηται οὐ φθονεῖτε αὐτῷ, ἐάν τις πλουτῇ μὴ ζηλώσητε. τὸν πένητα ἐλεεῖτε, τῷ ἀσθενοῦντι συμπαθεῖτε, [τοὺς ἀδελφοὺς ἀγαπᾶτε, τῶν οἰκείων μὴ ἐπιλανθάνεσθε]· τὸν Θεὸν ἀνυμνεῖτε.   5. καὶ τῷ ἔχοντι φόβον Θεοῦ βοηθεῖτε, κολάζετε τὸν ἀθετοῦντα τὸν Θεὸν καὶ ἀποστρέφετε ἀπὸ τῆς ἀδίκης ὁδοῦ αὐτοῦ· ἀγαπᾶτε τὸν ἀγαπῶντα τὸν Θεὸν καὶ τῇ ψυχῇ ὑμῶν.

V. 2. Ἐὰν γὰρ συνδεδεσμένοι ἐστὲ τῇ ἀγάπῃ τοῦ Θεοῦ τὰ πνεύματα τῆς πλάνης φεύξει ὑμᾶς.   3. Ὅπου γάρ ἐστι ἀγαθὴ φροντὶς ἐν τῇ ψυχῇ τοῦ ἀνθρώπου, ἐκεῖ καὶ τὰ πνεύματα πλάνης φεύγει αὐτόν. 4. καὶ δίκαιον ἄνδρα μηδαμῶς ὑβρίζετε, καὶ ὁ δίκαιος ἀγαπᾷ τὸν κολάζοντα καὶ σιγᾷ.   5. ἐὰν γὰρ εἰς τὴν ψυχὴν κολάζεται, εὐχὰς ποιῶν φαίνεται λαμπρὸς τῷ Ὑψίστῳ. Οὕτως ἀδελφός μου Ἰωσήφ.

VI. 1. Ἀπέκλινε γὰρ τὴν ψυχὴν ἀπὸ τοῦ πνεύματος τῆς πλάνης, ἀλλ᾽ εἶχε τὸν ἄγγελον τῆς εἰρήνης τὸν κύριον τῆς ψυχῆς.   3. καὶ οὕτως ὑμεῖς, τέκνα μου, μὴ λυπῆτε τοὺς πλησίους σου 2. μηδὲ συλλέγεσθε τὸν πλοῦτον τοῦ ἀδίκου. μὴ τέρψησθε ταῖς ἀδικίαις, καὶ μὴ ἐπάγησθε τῷ αἰνίγματι τῶν ὀφθαλμῶν [εἰς τὴν κακίαν] ἀλλ᾽ ἀεί, τέκνα μου, (ὁ Κύριος) συλλήπτωρ ὑμῖν. [καὶ συζεύχθητε τοῖς δίκαια φρονοῦσιν καὶ φεύγετε, τέκνα μου, τὴν μάχαιραν τῆς πονηρίας, μάχαιρα γὰρ ἐγειρομένη τέμνει τὸν τράχηλον τοῦ ἀνθρώπου. καὶ πονηρία συναγειρομένη περὶ ἀνθρώπου θλίβει καὶ εἰς τὴν φάρυγγα τρέπεται εἰς ἄπληστον Ἅδην].

VII. 2. Ἡ δὲ μάχαιρα ἑπτὰ κακῶν μήτηρ ἐστί. πρῶτον συλλαμβάνει ἡ διάνοια διὰ τοῦ Βελίαρ. καὶ φυτεύει φθόνον. δεύτερον τὴν ἀπώλειαν, τρίτον θλίψιν, τέταρτον αἰχμαλωσίαν, πέμπτον ἔνδειαν, ἕκτον ταραχήν, ἕβδομον ἐρήμωσιν.   3. Διὰ τοῦτο καὶ ὁ Καῒν ἑπτὰ ἀδικίαις παρεδόθη ὑπὸ τοῦ Θεοῦ, διὰ τοῦ αἷμα τοῦ Ἀβὲλ τοῦ ἀδελφοῦ, κατὰ γὰρ ἑκατὸν ἔτη μίαν πληγὴν ἐπήγαγεν αὐτῷ ὁ Κύριος. Διακοσίων ἐτῶν ἀπὸ [τοῦ χρόνου] ὅτε Καῒν ἔκτεινε τὸν ἀδελφὸν αὐτοῦ.   5. Ἐν τοῖς ἑπτακοσίοις ἔτεσιν ὁ Καῒν ἐκρίνετο, ὁ δὲ Λαμὲχ ἐν τοῖς ἑβδομηκοντάκις ἑπτά. 6. ὅτι ἕως τοῦ αἰῶνος οἱ ὁμοιούμενοι τῷ Καῒν εἰς τὴν μισαδελφίαν τῷ αὐτῷ φόνῳ καὶ τῇ αὐτῇ κολάσει κριθήσονται.

VIII. Καὶ ὑμεῖς οὖν, τέκνα μου, ἀποδράσατε τὴν ἔχθραν καὶ κακίαν καὶ μισαδελφίαν καὶ προσκολλᾶσθε τῇ ἀγαθότητι καὶ τῇ ἀγάπῃ.   2. Καὶ μὴ ἔχητε αἰσχρὰ ἐν τῇ καρδίᾳ ὑμῶν, ὅτι ἀναπαύεται ἐπὶ τοιούτοις ὁ Θεός.   3. Ὥσπερ γὰρ ὁ ἥλιος οὐ μιαίνεται προσέχων ἐπὶ κόπρον καὶ βόρβορον, ἀλλὰ μᾶλλον ἀμφότερα ψύχει καὶ ἀπελαύνει τὴν δυσωδίαν, οὕτω καὶ δεῖ τὸν καθαρὸν εἶναι ἐν τοῖς μιασμοῖς τῆς γῆς.

IX. Ὑπενόησα δὲ περὶ τῶν λόγων τοῦ Ἐνὼχ τοῦ δικαίου, φύλαξασθε, τέκνα μου, ἀπὸ τῆς πορνείας Σοδόμων. Εἰ δὲ ὑμεῖς διαφθείρεσθε καὶ γαμεῖτε τὰς γυναῖκας τὰς ὑβριστικὰς καὶ οὐκ ἔσται ἐν ὑμῖν ἡ βασιλεία τῶν οὐρανῶν, ὅτι εὐθὺς αὐτὸς λήψεται αὐτήν. 2. καὶ ἀποστελεῖ ὁ Ὕψιστος τὴν σωτηρίαν αὐτοῦ τῇ ἐπισκέψει τοῦ μονογενοῦς, ὥσπερ προφήτου. 3. καὶ εἰσελεύσεται εἰς τὸν πρῶτον ναὸν καὶ ἐκεῖ Κύριος ὑβρισθήσεται καὶ ἐπὶ ξύλου ὑψωθήσεται. 4. Καὶ ἔσται τὸ ἅπλωμα τοῦ ναοῦ σχιζόμενον εἰς δύο καὶ καταβήσεται τὸ πνεῦμα τοῦ Θεοῦ, ὡς πῦρ ἐκχυνόμενον. 5. καὶ ἀνελθὼν ἐκ τῶν λαῶν ἔσται ἀναβαίνων ἀπὸ γῆς εἰς οὐρανόν. Ἔγνω δὲ οἷος ἔσται ταπεινὸς ἐπὶ γῆς, καὶ οἷος ἔνδοξος ἐν οὐρανῷ.

XI. 2. Ἀναστήσεται γὰρ ἐν ταῖς ἐσχάταις ἡμέραις ἐκ τοῦ γένους μου ἄνθρωπος ἀγαπητὸς Θεῷ καὶ ποιῶν τὰ ἐπιτήδεια γνῶσιν καινὴν φωτίζων πάντα τὰ ἔθνη [ὀνόματι τοῦ καλουμένου καὶ ἐγγράψεται ἐν ταῖς γραφαῖς τῶν ἁγίων. καὶ ὑμῖν, τέκνα μου, ὅσα ἐννόησα εἶπον]. XII. 1. [καὶ ἰδοὺ παραδίδομαι τῷ τάφῳ], καὶ θάπτετε ἐμὲ ἐν Χεβρὼν ἐγγὺς τῶν πατέρων μου. 2. καὶ ταῦτα εἰπὼν ἐκοιμήθη Βενιαμίν, υἱὸς Ἰακώβ, δωδέκατος υἱὸς Ῥαχήλ, καὶ πάντα τὰ ἔτη αὐτοῦ ἦν ἑκατὸν καὶ εἴκοσι. [καὶ πάντες οἱ υἱοὶ τοῦ Ἰακὼβ ἀπέθανον ἐν Αἰγύπτῳ, διδόντες. διαθήκας τοῖς υἱοῖς καὶ υἱωνοῖς, ὅσας εἶχον ἐν ταῖς καρδίαις αὐτῶν καὶ προεφήτευσαν προορῶντες κινούμενοι τῷ ἁγίῳ πνεύματι. τὰ μέλλοντα ἐν τῷ καιρῷ αὐτῶν τελεῖσθαι πάντα ἐγνώρισαν καὶ ἔλεγον αὐτοῖς· Ἔχετε ἀγαθὴν ἐλπίδα ὅτι ὁ Ὕψιστος ἐπισκέψεται τοὺς πένητας, καὶ ἐν σιγῇ θλίψει τοὺς ἀμελοῦντας αὐτὸν καὶ τοὺς υἱοὺς ὑμῶν τοὺς λελειμμένους ἐν τοῖς ἔτεσι διασκορπισθήσονται εἰς ὄλεθρον καὶ εἰς τὴν ὕβριν τῶν ἐθνῶν].

APPENDIX VI

Collation of the second Sinaitic MS. *i* where it diverges from
h for the Testaments of Reuben, Simeon, Levi, and Judah i–xx.[1]

T. REUBEN.

Page 1, line 3 πρώτον. l. 4 ὅσα. l. 5 after αὐτόν add καὶ ἐκάλεσε τοὺς
υἱοὺς αὐτοῦ. For ἐν read ἐν τῷ. l. 8 συνήχθησαν. P. 2, l. 11 add τὴν
after ἐμίανα. P. 3, ll. 7–8 does not om. as *h*. l. 11 οἷά μοι μὴ γένηται
ἐν Ἰσραὴλ οὕτως. P. 4, l. 9 γίνεται βρῶσις. l. 11 ἕκτον (so also *h* whose
reading is not given in notes). l. 13 ἔσχατα. l. 14 ἀγνοίας πεπλήρωται.
P. 5, l. 8 τέταρτον. μαγκανίας. l. 9 περιεργίας. l. 10 ὑπερηφανίας. om. ἵνα.
l. 10 ἀπειλίαν. P. 6, l. 7 νουθεσίαν. l. 10 αὐτὴν φυλάξατε. l. 12 προσέχετε ὄψει γυναικείᾳ. P. 7, l. 3 γύμνωσιν. l. 4 om. ἕως οὗ. l. 5 ἀπιόντος.
l. 7 εὐφαθά (*h* υρφαθά—so read in notes). l. 10 αἰσθανθείσης. P. 8, l. 6
ἀποθάνητε. l. 9 ὀνειδισμοὺς αὐτῶν. συνείδησίς μου. l. 10 ἐλέγχει με περί.
P. 9, l. 15 προσεκάλεσεν. P. 10, l. 1 ἐδέξατο. l. 4 for πονηροῦ read
πονηροῦ πράγματος. l. 5 om. γάρ. l. 6 om. οὐδὲ ... ὑμῶν through hmt.
l. 9 σεαυτάς. l. 10 ἴσχυον καταγοητεύσασθαι ... καταγωνίζονται. P. 11, l. 3
μηχανῶνται. l. 5 τὸν ἰόν. l. 10 κοσμῶσιν τάς. l. 13 τετήρηται. P. 12,
l. 1 καὶ τὴν πρᾶξιν. μετεσχηματίζοντο γάρ. l. 4 διανοίᾳ τῆς φαντασίας. l. 6
φθάνοντες. l. 8 αἰσθήσεις ὑμῶν. l. 9 συνδιάγειν (so also *h*). P. 13, l. 3
οὖν λέγω ὑμῖν. l. 10 ὅτι αὐτὸς γνώσεται. l. 12 ἀρχιερέα χριστοῦ. P. 14,
l. 4 δέξητε εὐλογίαν. l. 7 παντὸς λαοῦ (so also *h*).

T. SIMEON.

P. 15, l. 3 υἱοῦ Ἰακώβ. P. 16, l. 3 τῆς δεήσεως. P. 17, l. 4 Ῥουβὶμ
εἰς Δοδαήμ. P. 18, l. 3 ἀποστῶ (so also *h*). l. 10 πάσας τὰς διανοίας (so
also *h*). P. 19, l. 6 αὐτῷ, οὗτος. P. 20, l. 11 τέκνα μου. P. 21,
l. 1 ὡς (so also *h*). ll. 7–8 τῷ σώματι, ἢ καὶ ἐν (so also *h*). l. 11 ἐκήνισεν

[1] This MS. *i* was not discovered till the spring of 1906, when the above
section of my Text had already passed through the press. Since the two
Sinaitic MSS. *h* and *i* are derived from one archetype, I have given the readings
of *i* only where it diverges from *h*, except in some cases where *h* is omitted in
my Notes or was wrongly copied or read. In these cases *i* and *h* alike are
given.

(sic).   Copy of *h* very corrupt but probably *h* = *i*.   Since *c*, *d* read ἐνίκησεν it is probable that α read οὐκ ἐνίκησεν εἰς αὐτόν = לו לֹא לֹא.   P. 22, l. 7 οὖν ἀπό (so *h* should be read).   l. 14 πόλεμον κυρίου πολεμήσει. l. 17 τις εἰς ἡγεμονίαν.   P. 23, l. 1 ταῦτα (*h* τοῦτο).   δικαιῶ (*h* reads διάγω ?).   l. 4 ὀστᾶ μου.   l. 7 πληθυνθήσωνται.   l. 13 Χετταῖοι καί (so *h*). l. 14 τότε ἐκλείψει.   l. 17 πολέμων.   P. 25, l. 5 ἐγώ (so *h*).   l. 13 χάριν ὁ κύριος.   P. 26, l. 4 οὕτως.   καί (so *h*).   l. 7 ἐτῶν ὢν ρ̅κ̅.

T. Levi.

P. 27, l. 11 ἕως ἡμέρας κρίσεως.   P. 28, l. 7 Βαλμαούλ (so *h*).   l. 9 ἐπὶ ταύτας τοίχους.   P. 31, ver. 11, l. 3 γένος ἀνθρώπου (so *h*).   P. 32, ll. 8–9 διατί ἐστι δυνός.   ἐπειδή (sic—so *h* but reads δεινὸς ἐπεί).   P. 33, ll. 1–2 ἐν δικαιοκρισίᾳ.   l. 17 καὶ ἐν.   l. 19 καταλύει ἡ.   P. 34, l. 10 λογικόν.   P. 35, chap. iv, l. 3 οὐρανῶν (so also *h*).   P. 36, l. 9 καὶ ἐπί.   P. 37, l. 6 ἅγιον καὶ ὕψιστον.   l. 8 κατοικῆσαι (so also *h*).   P. 39 margin, second line from bottom, καὶ τὸ ὄνομα (so also *h*).   P. 40, l. 13 Ἡμεβλακὴν τὸν οἰγενήν (sic).   P. 41, l. 9 χλευάσει . . . αὐτούς.   P. 42, l. 9 πέταλον τῆς ἀληθείας καὶ τῆς πίστεως.   l. 12 μοι καὶ εἰπόν μοι.   P. 43, l. 2 ὁ μὲν πρῶτος (so also *h*).   l. 4 ἐψώμοισεν (sic) ἄρτον (so also *h*).   ἅγιον ἁγίων.   l. 6 ὁμοίαν.   P. 44, l. 6 τῷ κυρίῳ καὶ θεῷ.   P. 45, l. 10 κριταὶ γραμματεῖς (so also *h*).   P. 46, l. 1 ἔκρυψα κἀγὼ τοῦτο (so also *h*, omitting καί before ἔκρυψα).   l. 10 τὸ πρωί.   P. 48, l. 2 καὶ πετεινοῦ πρόσφερε θυσίαν αὐτοῦ.   l. 4 καὶ θεῷ ἡμῶν.   l. 6 καὶ νῦν (so also *h*).   l. 7 τέκνα μου (so also *h*).   l. 13 βαστάσαι.   P. 49, l. 5 ὃν ἐκλέξεται (so *h*).   l. 9 ἐκάλεσε. P. 50, l. 6 for ἔτεκέν μοι reads ἐκάλεσα Μεραρί (next nine (?) letters lost in photo) Μεραρὶ τῷ τεσσαρακοστῷ.   P. 51, l. 1 ἡ μήτηρ μου καὶ ἡ μήτηρ αὐτοῦ.   l. 2 πικρασμός (sic).   P. 52, l. 12 ἡμῶν.   P. 53, l. 6 διότι. l. 11 ὑγιασμένοι ἦτε.   P. 54, l. 12 πᾶς γὰρ ὅς.   P. 56, l. 7 ποιήσειν. l. 11 ἡμῶν.   l. 13 τοῦ κόσμου.   l. 21 ληστεύσητε.   P. 57, l. 3 τοῦ θεοῦ. l. 9 τὰ ἀγαθά.   P. 58, l. 1 βδελύσσεται.   l. 3 διακρίσεως (so also *h*). l. 7 καταλειφθῇ.   P. 59, l. 1 καὶ ἀληθινῶν (so also *h*).   l. 4 ὁρμήσητε ἀποκτεῖναι (so also *h*).   P. 60, l. 7 αὐτῶν πλήρης.   ll. 9–10 ἰωβηλαίῳ ἐν πένθει ἀγαπητοὶ ληφθήσεται (so also *h*).   l. 14 ἀδικία ἑαυτῷ.   P. 61, l. 3 μιασμὸς ὃν οὐ δύναμαι.   l. 9 αὐτῶν καί.   l. 15 περὶ τοῦ Χριστοῦ καὶ τότε (so also *h*).   l. 19 ἐν ἀῷ (i. e. ἀνθρώπῳ).   P. 62, ll. 7–8 νεφέλαι ἐπὶ τῆς γῆς ὡς ὕδωρ θαλασσῶν.   P. 63, ll. 9–10 ἐν γνώσει ἐπὶ τῆς γῆς καὶ φωτισθή-σονται.   l. 13 ἐπὶ τῆς γῆς ἱερωσύνῃ.   P. 65, ll. 1–2 καὶ οὗτος ἔτεινε τοὺς πόδας (so also *h*).

T. Judah.

P. 66, l. 4 ὑπήκουον.   P. 68, l. 2 αὐτήν . . . αὐτήν (so *h* also in second

case).   l. 5 συσσάσης (sic).   l. 7 ἦλθον δύο (so also *h*).   P. 69, l. 5
Ναχώρ (so also *h*).   P. 70, last line, λίθοις.   P. 75, ll. 10–11 πόλεως
βασιλεύς.   P. 76, l. 6 νυκτὶ δὲ βαθείᾳ (so also *h*).   ver. 5 τότε οὖν ἐγώ
(so also *h*).   P. 77, l. 5 οὐδὲν πονηρόν (*h* οὐδὲν πονηρὸν κακόν).   l. 7 om.
ver. 9.   ver. 11 φοβούμενοι ἐμοὶ καὶ τοὺς ἀδ. (*h* φοβ. ἐμοὶ καὶ τοῖς ἀδ.).
Chap. VIII, 1 Ὀδουλομακήτην (*h* Ὀδολομακίτην).   P. 78, l. 4 om. καὶ τοὺς
. . . Σηλώμ by hmt.   P. 79, l. 5 προσάγων (so also *h*).   P. 80, l. 5
om. πυροῦ.   P. 82, l. 13 βουλομένου (so also *h*).   P. 85, last line of
note 44 read αὐτόν for τὸ ὄνομα αὐτοῦ (so also *h*).   P. 86, l. 13 ἐπιθυμιῶν
ὑμῶν μηδὲ ἐν ἐπενθυμήσεσι τῶν διανοιῶν ὑμῶν ἐν ὑπερηφανείᾳ.   P. 87, l. 1
ἐκαυχησάμην.   l. 5 Ἀκνὰν (so also *h*) τὴν Χαναίτην.   P. 88, l. 9 ὅτι ὁ οἶνος.
P. 89, l. 2 πίνῃς.   l. 4 τὴν ἡδονήν (so also *h*).   P. 90, l. 1 ἕως ὅτι.   l. 2
ἐκβάλλει (so also *h*).   l. 7 καὶ γάρ (so also *h*).   P. 91, l. 3 τοῦ ἀνδρός
(so also *h*).   l. 8 πίνετε.   l. 9 φόβου θεοῦ.   l. 12 τὸν οἶνον (so also *h*).
P. 92, l. 13 βασιλείαν.   P. 93, l. 4 προπάπος (sic).   l. 5 Ἰακὼβ οὔτι.
P. 94, l. 8 εὐλογίαν αὐτοῦ (so also *h*).   l. 9 προφήτῃ λαλοῦντι.   P. 96, l. 1
ἐστὶ τὸ τῆς συνειδήσεως.   l. 6 κατὰ στήθη.   Here *i* is obviously right and
ch corrupt.

INDEX

[For the sake of brevity the Testaments are referred to in the following Index by their initial letters except in the case of the Testaments of Judah, Issachar, and Joseph which are denoted by Jud, Iss, Jos.]

'Αβέλ Iss 5^4; B 7^4.

'Αβελμαούλ ('Αβελμαούμ, 'Εβαλμαούλ) L 2^3 2^5 (β).

'Αβιμά ('Αβιλά, 'Αμηβά) L 6^1.

ἀβλαβής Z 5^5.

'Αβραάμ L 6^9 8^{15} 9^{12} 12^2 12^4 15^4 18^6 18^{14} 19^5; Jud 17^5 25^1; D 7^2; N 1^{10}; A 7^7; Jos 6^7; B 1^2 10^4 10^6.

ἄβυσσος L 3^9.

ἀγαθοεργεία Jos 18^2.

ἀγαθοποιέω B 4^3 (β-g) 5^2.

ἀγαθοποιΐα Jos 18^2 (β).

ἀγαθός S 3^2 4^4 4^5 (β) 4^7; L 13^6; Iss 3^7 3^8; Z 1^3 7^2; D 1^4 4^3 (bdg); N 2^4 2^9 8^5; A 1^8 1^9 3^2 4^1 4^3 4^4 4^5 5^4 (β); Jos 2^7 7^8 17^3 18^1; B 3^1 3^2 4^1 4^2 4^3 4^5 5^1 5^3 6^1 6^4 6^5 11^1 12^2 (c).

ἀγαθότης Jud 18^4; A 3^1; B 8^1.

ἀγαθύνω S 5^2.

ἀγαθῶς Z 6^5.

ἀγαλλίασις Jud 25^5; B 10^6.

ἀγαλλιάω L 18^5 18^{14}; N 6^{10}.

ἀγαπάω R 3^9; S 2^6 3^6 4^4 4^6 4^7; Jud 17^1 21^1; Iss 1^1 5^2 7^6; Z 8^5; D 1^5 1^7 2^1 5^3 6^8; N 1^7 8^4 8^{10}; G 1^5 3^2 3^3 6^1 6^3 7^7; A 2^3; Jos 1^2 1^4 7^6 9^2 10^2 10^5 11^1 17^2 17^5; B 1^5 3^1 3^3 3^4 4^3 4^4 4^5.

ἀγάπη R 6^9; G 4^2 4^6 4^7 5^2; A 2^4; Jos 17^3 (β-a); B 3^5 8^1 8^2 (β).

ἀγαπητός L 8^{15} 17^3 18^{13}; B 11^2.

ἀγγελία N 2^1.

ἄγγελος R 3^{15} 5^3; S 2^8; L 2^6 2^9 3^7 5^1 5^3 5^6 5^7 (β) 9^6 18^5 19^3; Jud 3^{10} 10^2 15^5 21^5 25^2; D 5^4 6^2 6^5 6^6; N 8^4 8^6; A 6^4 6^6 7^1; Jos 6^5 6^7 19^9; B 6^1.

ἀγίασμα L 18^6; D 5^9.

ἀγιασμός L 18^7; B 10^{11}.

ἅγιος S 6^2; L 3^3 5^1 8^4 8^5 8^{17} 9^9 9^{11} 14^6 16^4 18^{11} 18^{14}; Jud 24^2; Iss 5^4; Z 9^8; D 4^3 5^{11} 5^{12} 5^{13}; N 5^8; A 7^2; Jos 4^1; B 11^4.

ἁγιότης L 3^4.

ἁγιωσύνη L 18^{11}.

ἁγνεία Jos 10^2.

ἀγνοέω Jud 5^4 (β) 12^5 19^4; A 7^1 7^6; Jos 3^8 14^4.

ἄγνοια R 1^6 2^9; L 3^5; Jud 19^3 (h, β); Z 1^5; G 5^7.

ἀγνωσία L 18^9; Jud 19^5.

ἀγοράζω N 1^{11}; Jos 15^7 16^1 16^3 (c).

ἄγρα Z 6^6.

ἄγριος Jud 2^3 (β) 2^5 2^7; Iss 7^7; A 4^5.

ἀγριόω S 4^8.

ἀγρός L 2^{12}; Jud 2^1 21^7; Iss 1^3 3^1.

ἄγχω Jos 7^3.

ἄγω S 4^8; L 5^3 (β-dg); Jud 10^1 23^3 (β-d); D 5^9; A 2^1; Jos 13^1 (bdg) 16^4 19^3 (A) 20^3 (c, A).

ἀγωνίζομαι A 6^2 (h, β); Jos 2^2.

'Αδάμ S 6^5; L 18^{10}.

ἀδελφή L 2^2 5^3 6^3 6^8 7^3 7^4 (beg); Jud 1^5.

ἀδελφός R 1^2 1^4 1^5 4^2 6^9; S 1^1 2^7 2^9 2^{14} 4^4 4^7 8^4; L 6^5 (h, β) 6^5 11^8 13^9 14^1 (β); Jud 3^9 4^1 5^4 7^3 7^5 7^{11} 9^1 9^2 13^3 25^1; Iss 1^3 3^1; Z 1^5 1^6 2^2 2^3 2^7 3^2 (β) 3^3 3^4 3^5 4^1 5^2 5^4 6^8 8^5; D 1^4 2^3 2^5; N 1^7 1^9 7^4; G 1^4 2^3 (β) 4^3 6^1 (bdg); A 7^6; Jos 1^1 1^2 1^4 10^5 10^6 11^1 11^2 15^3 17^1 17^3 17^4; B 2^1 2^3 2^6 (A) 3^3 3^6 5^5 7^4 10^{10} 12^3 (β).

ᾅδης R 4^6; L 4^1; B 9^5.

ἀδιακρίτως Z 7^2.

ἀδιαλείπτως L 13^2; Jos 3^6.

ἀδικέω S 5^4; G 5^5; A 2^5; Jos 14^1; B 4^3.

ἀδικία R 3^6; L 2^3 3^1 4^1 4^2 17^5; D 6^{10}; B 10^8.

ἄδικος Jud 21^8 (β-af); D 3^4 (β-d); G 5^3; A 4^3 5^2 5^3; Jos 14^1.

ἀδίκως Jud 21^8; D 3^4; Jos 14^1 (a).

ἀδοξέω Jud 15^1; N 8^6.

ἀδρύνω Jud 1^6; Iss 3^1.

ἀέριος B 3^4 (β-ag).

ἀετός Jud 25^5; N 5^6.

ἀηδία D 4^3.

ἀήρ R 2^5.

ἀθετέω L 16^2; A 2^6; B 4^5 (β-a).

ἄθλιος Jos 7^5.

ἄθῷος L 10^2 16^3; Z 2^2.

αἰγιαλός Z 6^3.

Αἰγύπτιος R 4^9; S 8^2 8^3 8^4; Z 3^7 3^8 (β-dg); Jos 1^7 (β) 3^1 3^4 3^6 4^3 (β-a) 4^8 (β) 5^1 (β) 7^2 (β) 8^1 (β-d) 8^4 (β-d) 8^5 14^5 16^5 20^1 20^2 20^6 (β).

Αἴγυπτος R 7^2; S 4^3 8^4 (β) 9; L 11^8 12^5; Jud 9^8 12^{11} 12^{12}; Z 3^6 6^3 8^4; D 5^8; G 1^8 (β); Jos 11^4 11^5 17^4 20^5 20^6 (c); B 2^1 10^1 12^1 (β) 12^3 (β) 12^4.

αἰδέομαι Jud 14^4 16^2; G 5^3 6^6; Jos 5^2; B 5^1.

αἰδώς Jud 14^7.
αἰκίζω L 6^9; Jos 16^6 (aef).
αἷμα S 4^8; L 16^3; Z 2^2 3^3; B 2^2 3^8.
αἴξ Z 4^9.
ἀιρέω L 19^1 (β–de); A 2^3.
αἴρω Jud 9^3 15^6 20^6; Jos 19^{11}; B 12^3 (c).
αἰσθάνομαι R 3^{14}; Jud 15^1.
αἴσθησις R 3^3 16^1; N 2^8.
αἰσχραίνω A 4^4.
αἰσχροκερδία Jud 16^1.
αἰσχρορημονέω Jud 14^8.
αἰσχύνη L 15^2.
αἰσχύνω L 14^1 (β); Jud 14^3 14^5 14^6 14^8 15^1; Z 3^7; Jos 11^2 15^3 16^6 17^1.
αἰτέω Jud 9^7; Jos 8^1 15^7 16^2 16^3 16^4 (β–be).
αἴτιος S 4^9; Jud 14^3 (β).
αἰχμαλωσία L 13^7 17^9; Jud 4^3 5^8 5^7 (a) 6^3 (β) 7^8 23^5; Z 9^8 (bdg); D 5^8 5^{11}; N 4^2 5^8; Jos 1^6; B 7^2 (β–bg).
αἰχμαλωτεύω Z 9^6.
αἰχμαλωτίζω R 5^3; Jud 21^6; D 5^{13}; N 1^{11}.
αἰχμάλωτος L 10^4 15^1; Jos 14^3.
αἰών R 6^{12} (β–d); S 6^3; L 4^4 8^3 (β) 10^2 14^1 (a) 18^8 18^{13}; Jud 15^6 (β) 22^3 25^3 25^5; D 5^{12} (β–ag) 6^{10}; G 7^5 (a, β–d); A 7^1; Jos 18^1; B 7^5 11^3 11^4.
αἰώνιος R 5^5 6^3 6^{12}; L 15^2; Iss 7^9; Z 10^3; D 5^{11} 5^{12} 7^1 (β); G 7^5; A 5^2 6^6 (a); Jos 19^{12} 20^4 (β); B 10^4.
ἀκαθαρσία L 15^1; Jud 14^6; Jos 4^6.
ἀκάθαρτος A 2^9 4^8; B 5^2.
ἀκακία Iss 5^1 6^1.
ἀκάλυπτος R 3^{13}.
ἄκαρπος N 3^5.
ἀκαταμάχητος Jud 19^4.
ἀκάτιον N 6^6.
ἀκίνητος S 2^4.
ἀκοή R 2^5; D 4^4; N 2^7; G 1^9; B 6^6.
ἀκολασία Jos 7^1 (β) 9^2.
ἀκολουθέω A 6^1.
ἀκοντίζω Jud 3^3; G 1^3.
ἀκουσίως D 4^6.
ἀκούω R 1^5 2^1 3^8 3^9 4^8 6^8; S 2^1 2^2 2^{10} 2^{11} 3^1; L 3^1 6^6 10^1 13^4 17^1 19^1; Jud 1^3 12^1 12^6 13^1 18^2 18^5; Iss 1^1 4^1; Z 1^2 3^8 4^5; D 1^2 6^9; N 1^5 2^{10}; G 1^2 3^1 4^2 4^5 6^5; A 1^2; Jos 1^2 5^2 7^8 9^4 12^1 13^1 15^1 15^3 15^6 16^1 19^1; B 11^2 (β).
ἀκτίς N 5^4.
ἀλαζονεία D 1^6; Jos 17^8.
ἅλας L 9^{14}.
ἄλγημα Jos 17^7.
ἀλγῶ Jos 7^2.
ἄλειμμα S 2^9.
ἀλείφω L 8^4.
ἀλήθεια R 3^8 3^9 6^9; L 8^2 18^2 18^8; Jud 14^1 20^1 20^3 (β) 20^6 24^3; Iss 7^5; D 1^3 2^1 2^2 5^2 5^{13} 6^8; G 3^1 3^3 5^1; A 5^3 5^4 6^1; Jos 1^3; B 6^8 10^3.
ἀληθής D 6^9; G 5^7; A 2^9.

ἀληθινός L 16^2; D κ^4; A 4^3.
ἀλιεύω Z 6^3 6^7 6^8.
ἀλίζω L 9^{14}.
ἀλλά saepissime.
ἀλλάσσω Jos 14^2.
ἀλλήλων R 5^8 (a, β–g); Jud 22^1; Z 8^5; D 4^7 5^3; N 5^6 (β); G 6^1 6^3 7^7; Jos 17^2.
ἀλλοιόω Jud 17^3; N 3^2 3^3.
ἄλλος S 4^4 (β); L 2^9; Jud 3^6 (β–g) 4^2 (β) 7^7 12^7 12^9; Iss 2^4 (β–dg), 5^5 7^2 (β); Z 3^2 (β); G 5^3; A 2^5 2^4 4^4; Jos 6^3 19^6 (A).
ἀλλότριος L 13^8; Jud 21^6; D 5^7; G 6^5; Jos 14^5.
ἀλλοτριόω D 7^3.
ἀλλόφυλος L 9^{10}; Jud 22^2.
ἄλογος Z 5^1.
Ἀμαλήκ S 6^3.
ἁμαρτάνω R 4^4 4^5; L 3^{10} 6^7; Jud 16^3 20^5 (β); Iss 6^3; Z 1^4 2^2 2^3; G 4^2 4^6 6^3 6^4; A 1^6 4^1 7^2.
ἁμαρτία R 1^{10} 2^8 4^3 (β) 4^6; S 6^1; L 2^8 13^7 18^9; Jud 14^3 14^6 19^4 21^4 24^1; Iss 7^1; Z 1^7; N 8^9; G 2^1 6^5; A 1^7; Jos 7^5 14^4 19^{11}; B 3^6.
ἁμαρτωλός Jud 20^5 25^5; A 4^1 (a); B 4^2.
ἀμαυρόω Jud 13^8.
ἀμέριμνος Jud 3^9.
ἀμετανόητος G 7^5.
ἀμετανοήτως G 7^5 (a).
ἀμίαντος Jos 4^6.
ἄμμος Z 9^1 (β).
Ἀμνεία (Ἰαμνία, Ἰαμνεία) N 6^1.
ἄν = ἐάν c. pres. ind. D 2^3; N 8^5; A 1^8.
ἄν c. pres. ind. L 13^9; Iss 1^{11} (a) : c. pres. subj. in independent clause Iss 1^{11} : c. past imperf. R 3^{11}.
ἀμνός Jos 19^3 (A) 19^8 19^{11}; B 3^8.
Ἀμορραῖος Jud 7^2 12^2.
ἀμπελών L 2^{12}.
ἀμφότερος N 5^3; B 8^3.
ἄμωμος Jos 19^8; B 3^8.
ἀναβαίνω L 9^1; Jud 6^3 24^8 (β); Z 2^8 (β–dg); N 6^2 (β–bg); Jos 19^6 (A).
ἀνάβασις Jud 6^8.
ἀναβλέπω Jos 6^2.
ἀναβλύζω Z 2^8.
ἀναγγέλλω S 2^1; L 8^{19} 10^1; Z 5^1 (β) 7^1; N 7^4; G 4^3.
ἀναγιγνώσκω L 13^2; Jud 18^1 (β); D 5^6; N 4^1 (bdg); A 7^5 (bdg).
ἀνάγκη Jos 2^4.
ἀναγράφω B 11^4.
ἀνάγω S 8^2; L 9^{12}; Jud 23^5 26^3; Iss 7^8; Z 10^7; G 8^6; A 8^2; Jos 1^4 20^2 20^3 (β); B 12^3 (β).
ἀναδείκνυμι Jos 2^7 (β–d).
ἀναδέχομαι L 16^3.
ἀναιδής G 6^7; Jos 2^2.
ἀναίμακτος L 3^8.

ἁπλοῦς Iss 4².
ἅπλωμα B 9⁴.
ἀπό above 100 times.
ἀποβλέπω A 6³.
ἀποδείκνυμι Jos 2⁷.
ἀπόδειξις Jos 14⁵.
ἀποδεκατόω L 9⁴.
ἀποδέχομαι Jud 9⁵.
ἀποδημέω Jos 3⁵.
ἀποδιδράσκω B 5³.
ἀποδίδωμι Jud 7⁶ ; Iss 2² ; Z 4³ (a).
ἀποδράω A 3² ; B 8¹.
ἀποδύω B 2³ (β).
ἀπόθεσις S 2⁹.
ἀποθνήσκω R 1¹ 1³ 6⁶ 6¹² 7¹ ; S 1¹ ; L 1¹
    (β–ab) 1² 6⁶ 11⁷ (β) 12⁷ ; Jud 1¹ 9³ (β)
    10⁵ (β) 11⁵ 19² 25⁴ ; Iss 7⁹ (β) ; Z 1¹ 5⁴
    10¹ ; D 1⁷ 2¹ ; N 1³ 1⁴ 9² ; G 4³ 7² ;
    A 2³ 8¹ ; Jos 1¹ ; B 3³ 10² 12² (β).
ἀποκαθίστημι S 2¹⁰.
ἀποκαλύπτω R 3¹⁵ ; L 1² 18² ; Jud 16⁴ ;
    Jos 6⁶ ; B 10⁵.
ἀποκρίνω L 19² ; Jos 13⁴ (aef).
ἀπόκρισις L 3⁷.
ἀποκρύπτω G 2³ (β).
ἀποκτείνω L 12⁵ 16³ ; Jud 2⁴ 3³ 3⁴ 4¹ 5⁷
    6² 6³ ; Z 2⁷ ; G 4⁶.
ἀπολαμβάνω D 5⁸.
ἀπόλαυσις Jos 5⁴.
ἀπολαύω Jos 7⁶.
ἀπολείπω Z 10¹ (bfg).
ἀπολήγω Z 10¹.
ἀπόλλυμι R 3⁸ 4⁷ ; S 6³ 6⁴ ; L 4⁶ 13⁷ ; Jud
    16³ 19² ; Iss 5⁸ ; Z 10³ ; D 2¹ 4⁵ ; A
    4² 7¹ ; Jos 7⁵ 19⁸ ; B 9¹.
ἀπολύω S 2¹¹ ; Jud 2⁴ ; Z 3⁶ (a).
ἀποπηδάω Z 4².
ἀποπλανάω R 4¹ (β).
ἀποπλάνησις Iss 7³ ; Jos 6².
ἀπορέω Jud 10² (β).
ἀπορρίπτω Z 9⁹ ; D 6⁸ ; N 3¹ ; A 1⁷.
ἀποσκευή Jud 7⁴.
ἀποστέλλω S 2⁷ (β) 2⁸ ; L 5³ ; Z 4⁹ 8² ;
    Jos 6¹ 14¹ 16² 16⁴ ; B 9².
ἀποστολή N 2¹ (bdg).
ἀποστρέφω Jos 17⁴.
ἀποτρέχω S 3⁵ ; Z 10⁴.
ἀπόφασις L 6⁸ ; G 4⁶.
ἀποφέρω D 7².
ἀπροσέγγιστος Jud 5¹ (β–dg).
ἅπτω R 3¹⁵ ; Jud 3¹⁰.
ἀπωθέω Λ 1⁸ ; Jos 2⁵ (β).
ἀπώλεια (ἀπολεία) R 3⁵ ; L 15³ ; Jud 17²
    23³ ; D 4⁵ ; B 7².
Ἀράμ (Ἀράν, Ἀράβ) Jud 10¹ ; Iss 1⁵ (β).
ἀργύριον L 2¹² ; Jud 17¹ 19¹ 19² ; Z 4⁶ ;
    Jos 11⁷ 15⁷ 17⁴.
ἄργυρος L 13⁷.
ἀρέσκεια R 3⁴.
ἀρέσκω Λ 3².
Ἀρετά (Ἀθετά) Jud 5¹.
ἀριθμέω N 7² (c).

ἀριθμός B 12² (c).
ἀριστερός Jos 19⁸.
ἀρκέω Jos 7⁸.
ἄρκος Jud 2⁴ ; G 1³ (β–fg) 1⁷.
ἀρμενίζω N 6².
ἁρμόζω Iss 1¹⁰.
ἁρμός Z 2⁵.
ἀρνέομαι G 6⁴ 6⁶.
ἀρνός G 1⁷.
ἁρπαγή Jud 23³ ; B 11¹.
ἁρπάζω L 6¹⁰ ; Jud 21⁶ 21⁷ ; D 5⁷ ; A 2⁵ ;
    B 11².
ἅρπαξ B 11¹.
ἀρραβών Jud 12⁴ 12⁵ 12⁷.
ἀρρενικός Jos 3⁷ (β–d).
ἄρρην Jos 3⁷.
ἀρρωστέω R 1² ; S 1².
ἄρτος R 1¹⁰ ; L 8⁵ ; Iss 7⁵ ; Z 4⁷.
ἀρχάγγελος L 3⁵ (a).
ἀρχή R 6⁷ ; L 8¹¹ 11⁶.
ἀρχιερεύς R 6⁸ ; S 7² ; L 8¹⁶ (β–af) 14².
ἀρχιευνοῦχος Jos 13⁵ (β).
ἀρχιμάγειρος Jos 2¹ 16² (β).
ἀρχιποίμην Jud 8¹.
ἄρχω R 6⁷ ; Jud 3⁵ ; Z 2⁴ 5⁵ ; N 1⁵ 2¹
    (bd) 6² ; G 1³ ; A 1⁹ ; Jos 13⁵.
ἄρχων S 2⁷ ; Jud 19⁴ ; D 5⁶ ; B 11³.
ἀσέβεια R 3¹⁴ 3¹⁵ 4³ ; L 10² 13⁷ 14² 14⁴
    14⁶ (β) ; Jos 5² (β–d) 6⁹.
ἀσεβέω L 10² (β) 14¹ ; N 4⁴ ; A 7⁵ ;
    Jos 6⁷.
ἀσέβημα R 6³.
ἀσεβής Jud 25⁵ ; Z 10³ ; B 3⁸.
ἀσέλγεια Jud 23¹.
ἀσελγής L 17¹¹.
ἄσηπτος S 8² (β).
Ἀσήρ (Ἀσσήρ) R 1⁴ ; Jud 25² ; A 1¹ 1².
ἀσθένεια Jud 19⁴ 25⁴ (β–g) ; Z 9⁶ ; Jos 1²
    1⁶ 17⁷.
ἀσθενέω Z 5² 5⁴ ; G 4⁵ ; Jos 2⁶ 3⁵ 7¹ 7²
    (β) 8⁵ (β–d) 9⁴ ; B 4⁴.
ἀσθενής Iss 5² ; D 3⁵ ; B 4⁴ (β–a).
ἄσιτος Z 4⁴ (β).
Ἀσούρ Jud 3¹ (β).
ἀσπάζομαι G 3³.
Ἄσπις L 6¹.
ἀσπίς L 2⁵ (β) 6¹ ; Jud 3⁴ (β) 9⁵.
Ἀσσύριος N 5⁸.
ἀστήρ N 3².
Ἀστηθώ Jos 7⁵.
ἄστρον L 18³ ; Jud 24¹.
ἀσύγκριτος L 2⁹.
ἀσυμπαθής S 2⁴.
Ἀσυνέθ Jos 20³ (c, A).
ἀσύνετος L 7⁹.
ἀσχαλάω L 9⁸.
ἀσχημοσύνη L 10³.
ἀσωτία Jud 16¹ ; Λ 5¹.
ἄσωτος Λ 4⁴ ; B 5¹.
ἄτακτος N 2⁹.
ἀταξία N 3².
ἄτεκνος Jud 8³ (bde) 19².

ἀτενίζω R 4².
ἀτιμία Jud 14⁸ ; A 5² ; B 6⁴ 10⁶.
Αὐνάν Jud 10⁴ 17¹ (a).
αὐξάνω Z 1³ ; Jos 19⁴ (A).
αὐτό, ἐπὶ τὸ N 6⁶.
αὐχήν N 6⁴.
ἀφαίρεσις Jud 23³ (β-g).
ἀφαιρέω S 4⁸ (β) 6² ; L 13⁷ ; Jud 2⁴ ;
 G 7⁵ ; Jos 12³ 14⁵.
ἀφανίζω L 2³ 16² (β-d) 17⁹ ; Z 8⁶ (a,
 β-bg) 9².
ἄφθονος G 7⁶ (β-a).
ἀφθόνως G 7⁶.
ἀφίημι S 3² ; Jud 10⁶ 18³ ; Iss 6¹ 6² ;
 Z 4⁶ (β) ; N 3³ ; G 6³ 6⁷ 7⁵ ; Jos 17⁶.
ἀφίστημι S 4⁷ ; L 18¹⁰ ; Jud 14² 16² 18³
 18⁴ (β-g) ; D 4⁷ 5¹ 5⁴ 5⁵ 6⁶ 6¹⁰ ; N 4¹
 6⁴ ; G 8² ; A 2¹ ; Jos 2⁶ 4⁵ ; B 5¹.
ἄφραστος L 8¹⁵ (β-af).
ἀφροσύνη S 2¹³ ; L 7³.
ἄχρηστος A 7².
ἄχρι R 4².
ἄχρις N 4⁵.
Ἀχώρ Jud 3³ 3⁴ (β).
ἀωρία Jos 9⁴.

βαθύς Jud 7³.
βάτον N 5⁴.
Βάλλα R 3¹¹ 3¹³ ; Jud 13³ ; N 1⁶ 1⁹ 1¹² ;
 G 1⁶ ; Jos 20³ (β) ; B 1³.
βάλλω Jud 3³ ; Z 4¹ (β) ; Jos 8⁴.
Βαρσαβά (Βαρσάν, Βαρσά) Jud 8².
βαρύς Jud 7¹ (h, β) 9².
βασανίζω A 6⁵.
βασιλεία Jud 12⁴ 15² 15³ 17³ 21² 21⁴ 22²
 22³ 24⁵ ; Iss 5⁷ ; Z 9⁵ ; D 6² 6⁴ ; Jos
 19¹² ; B 9¹.
βασίλειον Jud 17⁶ 22³ 23¹.
βασιλεύς R 6¹² ; S 7² 8³ ; L 13⁹ 18³ ; Jud
 1⁶ 3¹ 3² 3³ 3⁷ 4¹ (β) 4² 4³ (β) 7¹ 7⁴ (β-d)
 8³ 13⁴ 15² 15³ 15⁶ 21⁶ 21⁷ ; Z 3⁶ ; Jos
 9² ; B 10⁷.
βασιλεύω R 6¹¹ ; S 6⁶ ; Jud 17⁵ 21⁷ (β)
 26³ (β) ; Z 3³ ; D 5¹³.
βασκανία Iss 4⁵ (bdg).
βάσκανος Iss 3³ 4⁵.
Βασσουέ (Βησσουέ, Βουσεέ, Βισσουέ) Jud 8²
 (β) 10⁶ (β) 13³ (β) 16⁴ (β) 17¹.
βαστάζω L 8³ 10³.
βδέλυγμα R 3¹² ; L 6³ 15² ; Jud 12⁸ 23² ;
 Z 9⁵ ; D 5⁵.
βδελυκτός G 3².
βδελύσσω L 16² ; G 3² (β-f).
βεβαιόω Z 1⁵.
βεβηλόω L 9¹⁰ 14⁶ 16¹.
βίθ Jud 9⁶ (β-af).
Βεθήλ or Βαιθήλ L 7⁴ 9² 9³.
Βηθλεέμ R 3¹³.
Βελιάρ R 2³ (β) 4⁷ 4¹¹ 6³ ; S 5³ ; L 3³ 18¹²
 19¹ ; Jud 25⁵ ; Iss 6¹ 7⁷ ; Z 9⁸ (bdg) ;
 D 1⁷ 4⁷ 5¹ 5¹⁰ 5¹¹ ; N 2⁶ 3¹ ; A 1³ 3²
 6⁴ ; Jos 7⁴ 20² ; B 3³ 3⁴ 3⁶ 6¹ 6⁷ 7¹ 7³.

Βελισάθ (Βεελισά, Βεελησάθ, Βεελισάδ)
 Jud 3⁷.
Βενιαμήν (Βενιαμίν, Βενιαμείν) Jud 25¹
 25² ; B 1¹ 1⁶ 2⁷ (A) 12² (β).
βία Jos 8².
βιάζω R 5⁴.
βιβλίον Jud 18¹ (β-bg).
βίβλος L 10⁵ 16¹ (β) ; D 5⁶ ; B 11⁴.
βιβρώσκω Iss 7⁵ (β-b).
βίος Iss 3⁴.
βλαστάνω Jud 24⁶.
βλαστός Jud 24⁴.
βλέμμα R 5³.
βλέπω Iss 3² ; D 2³ 3³ ; N 7³ ; G 3³ ;
 B 3².
βοάω Jos 19³ (A) 19⁴ (A) ; B 3⁷.
βοήθεια Z 2⁶ ; D 3⁴ ; Jos 19⁷ (A).
βοηθέω D 3⁵ ; G 5⁹ ; Jos 1⁵ ; B 3⁵.
βόθρος R 2⁹ 4⁶.
βολή G 1³.
βομβέω Z 2⁵.
βόρβορος B 8³.
βουκόλιον Z 1³.
βουλεύω Jud 11² ; Jos 15⁴ ; B 4³ (β).
βουλή L 4⁵ ; Jud 9⁷ ; Jos 17⁷ 20⁶ (β).
βούλομαι Z 1⁷ 4¹¹ ; Jos 4¹ ; B 4³.
βοῦς Jud 2⁷ ; Jos 19⁵ (A) 19⁶ (A) 19⁷ (A).
βραχίων Jos 9⁵.
βραχύς Jud 12⁹ ; Jos 2⁶ ; B 9¹.
βρῶμα R 2⁷ ; Jud 2² ; Iss 4² ; Jos 6¹ 6⁴.
βρῶσις R 2⁷.
βύσσινος L 8⁶ ; Jos 19⁸.

Γαάς Jud 7¹.
Γάδ R 1⁴ ; Jud 5² 7² (a) 9⁶ 25² ; Iss 5⁸ ;
 Z 2¹ 3² 4² ; G 1¹ ; A 7⁶.
Γαδέρ R 3¹³.
Γάζη Jud 2⁶ (β).
γάλα Jos 19⁵ (A) ; B 1³.
γαμέω Jud 12² (β).
γάμος A 5¹.
γάρ passim.
γαστήρ R 3³ ; Jud 23¹ (a).
Γεβάλ L 6¹.
Γελαχαῖος (Χελκαῖος) N 5⁸ (β).
γελοιάζω L 14⁸.
γέλως R 4⁷ (β-af) ; N 2⁸ ; A 5¹.
γενεά S 7¹ 7³ ; L 12⁶ 18⁸ ; Z 10³.
γεννάω S 2² ; L 2¹ (a) 11⁴ 11⁸ 12⁴ ; Iss 1⁶ ;
 Z 1³ (β) ; N 1⁶ 1⁷ 7³ ; Jos 19⁸ ; B 1³.
γέννημα (γένημα) L 9¹⁴ (deg) ; Iss 3⁶.
γένος R 3⁶ ; S 7² ; L 2⁴ 2¹¹ 5⁶ 5⁷ (β) 9¹⁰
 14⁴ ; Jud 11¹ 17² 21⁶ ; D 6¹⁰ 7³ ; N 1¹⁰
 8³ ; Jos 10⁶ (β).
γέρων R 4⁷.
γεύομαι R 1¹⁰ (h, β) ; Z 4² (β) ; Jos 6³.
γεῦσις R 2⁵ 2⁷.
γεωργέω Iss 5³ 6².
γεωργία Iss 5³.
γεωργός Iss 3¹.
γῆ R 1⁶ (a) ; S 6⁴, 6⁵, 8⁴ ; L 3⁹ 5³ 7¹ 8¹⁰
 11² 12⁵ 13⁶ 13⁸ 14³ 15⁴ 17⁹ 17¹⁰ 18² 18⁴

διάκονος Jud 14².
διακόσιοι Jud 4¹ 9⁸ (bde) ; B 7⁴.
διακρίνω A 1⁵.
διάκρισις N 2⁶.
διαλογισμός Jud 14³.
διαλύω Jos 15³.
διαμαρτύρομαι Z 1⁷ (β).
διαμένω Jud 21¹.
διανέμω L 8¹⁶.
διάνοια R 3¹² 4⁸ 5³ 5⁵ 5⁶ 5⁷ 6¹ 6² ; S 3² 3⁵ 4⁸ ; Jud 11¹ 13⁶ (h, de) 14² ; D 2⁴ ; G 6¹ ; Jos 10⁴ 10⁵ ; B 3² 4¹ (β) 5¹ 5³ 6⁵ 6⁷ 7² 8² (β).
διαπορεύομαι Z 6³.
διάπρασις G 1⁸ ; Jos 16².
διαπτύω Iss 2¹ (β).
διαπωλέω B 2⁵ (β).
διαρκέω N 2⁴.
διαρρήγνυμι Jos 5².
διασκορπίζω Jud 3² ; Z 8⁶ ; A 7² 7⁶.
διασκορπισμός L 16⁵.
διασπασμός Jud 23³.
διασπάω Jud 2⁴ (β).
διασπείρω L 10⁴ ; Iss 6² ; N 4⁵ 6⁷ ; Jos 19².
διασπορά A 7².
διαστέλλω R 6⁸.
διαστρέφω Jud 13⁶ 14¹ ; Iss 4⁶ ; Jos 1⁵.
διαστροφή L 16² ; Iss 4⁴.
διασώζω S 2¹⁰ (β-af).
διαταράσσω S 4⁹.
διατηρέω D 6⁸ ; A 6³.
διατί L 2⁹.
διατίθημι L 1¹ ; Z 1¹ ; N 1¹ ; B 1¹.
διαφθείρω Jud 10⁵ (β) ; N 3¹ ; A 7⁵.
διαφθορά G 8².
διάφορος Iss 4² ; Jos 2⁶.
διαφυλάσσω Z 5⁴ ; Jos. 18⁴ (β-a).
διαφωνέω G 5⁹ (β).
διαχωρίζω N 6⁸ ; Jos 13⁶.
διδασκαλία R 2⁵.
διδάσκω R 5³ ; L 5⁵ 9⁶ (β-bg) 9⁷ 9¹² 13² 13⁹ 14⁴ 14⁶ ; D 1³ (β) ; B 10⁴ (β).
δίδωμι R 2² 2³ 2⁵ 4¹ 6⁷ ; S 2⁵ 4⁵ 6⁶ ; L 4⁴ 4⁵ 5² 5³ 7¹ 8⁴ 8⁸ 14⁴ 18⁸ 18¹¹ 18¹² ; Jud 1³ 2¹ 3³ 6² 8² 9⁸ 10⁴ (a) 10⁶ 12⁴ 15³ 17³ 21² 21³ ; Iss 1⁶ 5⁵ 5⁸ ; Z 4¹¹ 4¹² 4¹³ 6¹ 7¹ 7³ ; D 2⁵ (bde) 5⁹ 5¹⁰ 5¹¹ ; N 1⁶ 1⁷ 1¹¹ ; G 6⁷ ; A 1³ ; Jos 2³ 2⁷ 3⁵ 11⁶ 16⁵ 17⁶ 18³ 18⁴ ; B 2³ 5¹ 7¹ 10⁴ 10⁵ 11².
διεγείρω D 4² ; G 5¹.
διέξοδος Jud 6².
διέρχομαι Jud 7⁷ (β-d).
δικαιοκρισία L 3² 15².
δικαιοπραγία D 1³.
δίκαιος L 3⁵ 5⁷ (β) 10⁵ 16² 18⁹ ; Jud 18¹ (β) 21⁶ 21⁹ ; D 2³ 5⁶ 5¹² ; N 8³ ; G 3² 5³ ; A 1⁷ 4¹ 5³ 5³ ; Jos 10⁶ ; B 4³ (β) 5⁵ 7⁴ (β) 9¹.
δικαιοσύνη L 8² 13⁵ 18¹⁴ ; Jud 22² 24¹ 24⁶ ; Z 9⁸ ; D 6¹⁰ ; N 4⁵ ; G 3¹ 5³ ; A 1⁶ 6⁴ ; B 10³ (β).

δικαιόω S 6¹ ; D 3³.
δικαίως S 4³ ; D 4⁴.
δίκτυον D 2⁴.
διό L 6¹ (β) ; G 1³ (β) ; A 5² ; Jos 11⁵.
διοδεύω Z 4⁶ (a).
διότι L 6⁷ (a.⁸ ; Z 9⁷.
διπλάζω Iss 3⁷ (β).
διπλοῦς R 4¹ ; D 3⁵ ; N 8⁷ ; B 6⁶ 6⁷.
διπρόσωπος D 4⁷ ; A 2² 2³ 2⁵ 2⁷ 2⁸ 3¹ 3² 4¹ 4³ 4⁴ 6².
δισσῶς G 6⁴ ; A 6².
διυπνίζω S 4⁹.
διώκω L 6⁹ 16² ; Jud 4¹ 21⁹.
Δοθαείμ (Δωδαείμ) S 2⁹.
δοκέω A 4³ 4⁵ ; Jos 11⁵.
δοκιμάζω A 5⁴ ; Jos 2⁶.
δόκιμος Jos 2⁷.
δολιεύομαι R 5¹ 5⁵.
δολιότης Jud 12⁷ ; Jos 4³.
δόλος Iss 1¹¹ 1¹² 7⁴ ; G 6³ ; Jos 3⁹ 4¹ ; B 6⁴.
δολοφονέω G 6⁵.
δόξα S 4⁵ ; L 3⁴ 5¹ (β) 8¹¹ 18⁵ 18⁶ 18⁷ ; Jud 15³ (a, adf) 15⁶ 25² ; D 5¹² ; N 2⁸ ; A 5² ; Jos 9³ 12¹ 17ˣ ; B 4¹ 6⁴ 10⁸.
δοξάζω S 4⁶ ; L 17³ ; Jud 25⁵ ; Iss 1⁹ (β) 1¹⁰ 5⁷ ; N 1⁴ 8⁴ ; Jos 4² 8⁵ 10³ ; B 4⁴.
δόξασμα D 5¹² (β-ad).
δορκάς Jud 2⁹ ; A 4⁵.
δόσις Z 1³.
δοσοληψία R 3⁶.
δουλεία Jud 23³ ; Jos 1⁵ 10³.
δουλεύω L 13⁴ ; Jud 18⁶ ; Iss 1¹⁰ 6² ; N 4² ; A 3² 6⁵.
δουλικός Z 4¹⁰.
δοῦλος Z 4¹⁰ (β-g) ; G 4⁴ ; Jos 1⁵ (β) 1⁷ 11² 11³ 13⁶ 13⁸ 15² 15³ 17⁷.
δουλόω Jud 15² ; Jos 7⁸.
δράκων A 7³.
δρᾶσις S 2¹².
δράω D 3⁴.
δρόμος Jud 2³.
δύναμαι R 4¹¹ 5⁴ 6⁵ (β) ; S 5⁵ ; L 13⁷ 17⁸ ; Jud 9⁴ 12⁶ 18⁶ 20⁴ 20⁵ ; Z 2⁵ ; D 4² 5⁴ ; N 2¹⁰ 5⁶ ; G 1⁷ ; B 3⁴ 3⁵.
δύναμις R 5¹ 5² (β) ; L 3⁸ 16³ ; Jud 3¹⁰ 14² (β) 15³ 15⁶ 25² ; D 3² 3⁴ 3⁵ (β-d) 4¹ ; N 2² 2⁸ 5² ; Jos 18⁴.
δυναστεία L 6¹⁰ ; A 2⁸.
δυνάστης Jud 6³ (β-bg) 9⁵.
δυνατός S 2³ ; D 3⁴ ; Jos 10⁶ (β).
δύο R 1² ; S 3⁴ 7¹ ; L 2⁸ (β) 9¹ ; Jud 2⁸ 3¹ 3⁴ (β) 4² (β) 8³ 12¹ 14² 17² 18⁶ 20¹ ; Iss 1⁷ 2¹ (β-dg) 2² ; Z 1¹ 4² (β) 9⁴ 9⁵ ; D 1⁹ (β) ; N 5⁵ 5⁶ 7¹ 8⁹ ; G 1³ (β) ; A 1³ 1⁴ 1⁶ 4² 5¹ ; Jos 16⁴ 19⁶ (A) ; B 1⁵ 3⁷ 6⁵.
δυσμαί Jud 5².
δυστοκέω L 11⁷.
δυσωδία B 8³.
δώδεκα L 9¹² ; Jud 3⁷ ; N 5⁴ 5⁹ ; Jos 19² 19⁴ (A) 19⁵ (A) ; B 1⁴ 9².

δωδεκάκις Jos 19⁷ (A).
δῶρον Iss 5³ ; Jos 5⁴.

ἐάν c. fut. R 4¹¹ : subj. R 6² ; S 3⁵ &c. : pres. ind. Jud 15² ; Jos 18² (c).
ἐάω R 3¹² ; S 4⁸ (β) ; Iss 1¹³ ; D 1⁹ 2².
ἑβδομάς L 16¹ 17¹⁰.
ἑβδοματικός L 17¹¹ (β).
ἑβδομήκοντα L 8¹ 16¹ 17¹ ; Jud 12¹².
ἑβδομηκοντάκις B 7⁴.
ἑβδομηκοστός L 17¹¹.
ἕβδομος R 2⁸ 3⁶ ; L 8¹⁰ 17⁷ 17⁸ 17¹¹ ; N 1² ; B 7².
Ἐβλαής (Ἠεβλαής Ἰεβλαής) L 6⁹.
Ἑβραῖος Jos 12² 12³ 13³.
ἐγγαστρίμυθος Jud 23¹.
ἐγγίζω R 6¹⁰ ; Jud 12⁸ 21⁵ (β) ; D 5⁷ (β) 6² ; Jos 6⁵ (β-g).
ἐγγύς D 6¹¹ ; N 4⁵ ; G 8³ ; Jos 20³ (β) ; B 12¹ (β).
ἐγείρω L 18² ; D 4⁶.
ἐγκατάκλειστος Jos 14⁶.
ἐγκατάλειμμα S 6³.
ἐγκαταλείπω Jos 2⁴.
ἐγκαυχάομαι Jud 13³.
ἔγκειμαι R 3³ ; Jos 7¹ (β).
ἐγκοτέω G 1⁸.
ἐγκράτεια Iss 2¹ ; N 8⁸.
Ἐγρήγορος (Ἐγγρήγορος) R 5⁶ 5⁷ ; N 3⁵.
ἐγχείρημα Jos 9⁵.
ἐγχρῄζω S 2⁹.
ἔδαφος L 16⁴.
Ἐδέμ D 5¹².
ἔδεσμα A 2⁸ ; Jos 6³.
ἐθέλω (θέλω) R 1⁷ 4¹ 6¹ (β) ; S 2¹⁰ ; L 6⁸ 9² 14⁴ ; Jud 10³ (β) 10⁶ 12⁵ 13⁴ 16⁵ 20² (β) ; Iss 2³ 4² ; Z 3⁴ 3⁵ 4¹¹ ; N 5⁶ ; G 1⁹ 2¹ 2² 3² 4² 4³ (β) 4⁶ 5⁵ ; A 1⁶ 4⁴ ; Jos 1⁴ 3¹ 4⁵ 4⁶ 4⁷ 5¹ 9³ 14⁴ 15³ 16³ 17⁵ 18² ; B 2⁶ (A) 3⁴.
ἔθνος S 7² ; L 4⁴ 8¹⁴ 9¹⁰ 10⁴ 14¹ 14³ (a) 14⁴ 14⁶ 15¹ 16⁵ 18⁹ ; Jud 22² 23² 23³ 23⁵ 24⁶ ; Iss 6² ; Z 9⁶ 9⁸ (b/g) ; D 5⁵ 5⁸ 6⁶ 6⁷ 6⁹ ; N 3³ 4¹ 8⁵ 8⁴ 8⁶ ; A 7³ ; Jos 19¹¹ ; B 3⁸ 9² 9⁴ 10⁶ 10⁹ 10¹⁰ 11² 11³.
εἰδέα B 10¹.
εἶδον R 1³ 1⁴ 1⁶ 2¹ 3¹¹ 3¹⁴ (β-g) ; S 4⁵ 6¹ ; L 2⁶ 2⁷ 2⁸ 5¹ 6⁸ 8¹ 8² 9² 9⁷ 10² 11³ 11⁵ 12⁶ ; Jud 3⁵ 3¹⁰ 5⁶ (a) 8² 10⁴ (a) 11² 14⁵ 15⁴ 26² ; Iss 1¹³ 2³ 4¹ 4⁴ 4⁶ 7¹ (a) ; Z 2⁶ 3³ 5² (a) 7¹ 8⁴ (b/g) ; D 2¹ ; N 1⁷ (β-g) 5¹ 5² 5⁴ 5⁶ 5⁸ 6¹ 6² 6¹⁰ 8¹ 8¹⁰ ; G 1⁷ 1⁹ ; A 4⁴ ; Jos 1³ 6² 6⁶ 6⁷ 6⁸ 7⁷ 7⁸ 8³ 15² 18³ 19¹ (β) 19⁵ (A) 19⁸ ; B 1⁵ 4¹ 10¹.
εἶδος S 5¹.
εἰδωλολατρεία Jud 19¹ 23¹ (β-af) ; B 10¹⁰.
εἰδωλολατρέω L 17¹¹.
εἴδωλον R 4⁶ ; Jud 19¹ (β) ; Z 9⁶ (h, β) ; Jos 4⁵ 6⁵.

εἴκοσι S 8¹ ; L 2² 11¹ 12⁵ ; Jud 7¹⁰ 9³ ; Iss 7¹ (a) ; G 2³ (β) ; B 1¹ 12².
εἰκοσιδύο Iss 7¹ (β).
εἰκοσιτέσσαρες Jos 15¹.
εἰκοστός R 1¹ ; S 1¹ ; D 1¹ ; G 1¹ ; A 1¹.
εἰκών R 3¹ ; N 2⁵.
εἰλικρινής B 6⁵.
εἰ μή R 1⁷ 3¹¹ ; L 13⁷ &c.
εἰμί R 1¹⁰ 2² 2⁹ 2⁵ (β-dg) 2⁹ passim.
εἶπον R 1³ 1⁴ 1⁵ 5³ 6⁸ ; S 1² 6¹ ; L 1² 2⁶ 2⁹ 5² 5³ 5⁵ 5⁶ 6³ 7¹ 8³ 17⁸ 18⁷ 19³ ; Jud 1² 7¹ 12⁴ 16⁴ 17⁴ (β-dg), 21⁵ 26² 26⁴ ; Iss 1¹ 1⁶ 1⁷ 1⁸ 1⁹ 1¹⁰ 1¹⁴ (β-d) 6³ 7⁸ ; Z 1² 1⁵ 2⁷ 3² 3³ 4⁷ 4⁸ 4⁹ (β) 4¹² 4¹³ 10⁶ ; D 1¹ 1² 7¹ ; N 1³ 1⁴ 2⁷ 2¹⁰ 7¹ ; G 1⁶ 6³ 8¹ 8³ ; A 1² 2¹⁰ 5³ 7⁴ 8¹ ; Jos 1¹ 4² 5² 6⁵ 6⁶ 6⁷ 7² 7⁴ 7⁷ 10⁶ 11² 12¹ (β) 13³ 13⁶ 13⁸ 13⁹ 14⁵ 14⁶ 15¹ (β) 15² 15³ 15⁷ 16¹ 16⁵ 20¹ ; B 1² 2¹ 2² 10² 10⁵ 12¹.
εἶπως G 4⁴ ; Jos 6⁶ (c).
εἰρηνεύω G 6⁶ ; B 5¹.
εἰρήνη L 18⁴ ; Jud 7⁷ 9¹ 9⁷ 22² 24¹ ; D 5² 5⁹ 5¹¹ 6² 6⁵ ; N 6⁹ ; G 6³ 8⁴ ; A 6⁶ ; B 6¹.
εἰρηνικός G 6².
εἰρκτή Jos 8⁴.
εἰς above 200 times.
εἷς L 8³ 12⁴ ; Jud 3¹ 20³ 25³ ; Iss 1¹⁴ ; Z 2⁷ 9⁴ ; D 3¹ ; N 1² 1⁹ 2³ 2⁴ 2⁷ ; G 7¹ ; A 1⁴ 5¹ ; Jos 6⁴ 19⁵ (A) ; B 2⁴ (c) 6⁵ 7³.
εἰσάγω Iss 1¹² ; Jos 13⁵.
εἰσακούω L 4².
εἴσειμι Jos 3⁶.
εἰσέρχομαι R 1¹⁰ 3¹⁴ ; L 2⁶ 2⁷ 9¹¹ 12⁵ ; Jud 5⁴ 6² 7² 9⁴ 12⁴ 12¹⁰ ; N 6⁴ ; Jos 3³ 4⁴ (aeg) ; B 2¹ (β-d) 9³.
εἰσπηδάω Jos 7³.
εἰσφέρω A 6⁶ (a).
εἶτα N 2⁸.
ἐκ about 40 times.
ἕκαστος R 6⁹ ; S 4⁷ 8⁴ ; L 8³ 9⁸ ; Jud 20³ ; Iss 5³ ; Z 5² 6⁵ 8⁵ ; D 5² ; N 5² ; G 6¹ ; B 10³ 10⁷.
ἑκάτερος Jud 5⁴ ; D 5⁴.
ἑκατόν S 8¹ ; L 19⁴ ; Jud 26² ; Iss 7¹ ; Jos 16⁵ 18³ 20⁶ (c) ; B 1¹ 7³ (β) 12².
ἑκατοστός R 1¹ ; S 1¹ ; L 12⁷ ; Z 1¹ ; D 1¹ ; N 1¹ ; G 1¹ ; A 1¹ ; B 1² (β-d) 7³.
ἐκβάλλω G 5³.
ἐκβλαστάνω Jos 19⁶ (A).
ἐκδέχομαι G 7⁴.
ἐκδιδάσκω Jud 18³ ; D 1³ 6⁹ ; G 5¹.
ἐκδικέω Jud 23³.
ἐκδίκησις R 6⁵ ; L 2² 3² 3³ 5³ 18¹ ; D 5¹⁰ ; G 6⁷ ; Jos 15⁵ 20¹.
ἐκδικία B 7³.
ἐκδιώκω Jud 18⁴.
ἐκδύω Jud 3⁵ ; Z 4¹⁰ ; B 2³ (c).
ἐκεῖ Jos 20² ; B 9² 9³.
ἐκζητέω A 5⁴.
ἐκθερμαίνω Jud 14³.
ἐκθροέω S 4⁹ ; D 4⁵.

ἐκκλίνω Jud 12[4] 14[5]; Jos 9[2].
ἐκλαμβάνω L 18[1] (c, ef) 18[9] (a-h, β-ab); Jos 7[8].
ἐκλέγω R 6[11]; L 10[5] 15[1] 19[1]; Jud 21[5]; Iss 2[1]; Z 9[8] (bdg).
ἐκλείπω R 1[4]; S 6[4]; L 18[1] 18[9]; G 5[9].
ἐκλείχω G 2[2].
ἐκλεκτός L 14[5]; B 10[10] 11[4].
ἐκμισθόω Iss 1[14].
ἐκμυζάω (ἐκμίζω, ἐκμύζω) D 1[8].
ἐκμυκτηρίζω Jos 2[3].
ἐκούσιος L 9[7].
ἐκουσίως D 4[6].
ἐκπέμπω Jos 8[4].
ἐκπίπτω Jud 21[4].
ἐκπληρόω G 5[1].
ἐκπορνεύω D 5[5].
ἐκριζόω A 1[7] 4[2].
ἔκστασις R 3[1]; S 4[8]; Jud 19[1].
ἐκταράσσω D 3[1]; G 5[1].
ἐκτείνω L 19[4]; Iss 7[9]; Z 6[2]; Jos 20[4]; B 12[1] (c).
ἐκτέμνω Jud 23[4].
ἐκτός N 6[2].
ἕκτος R 2[7] 3[5]; L 8[9] 17[7]; Jud 25[1]; Jos 8[1]; B 7[2].
ἐκτρέφω N 8[5].
ἐκτυφλόω G 3[3].
ἐκχέω R 1[6]; L 18[5]; Jud 24[2]; Z 2[2] 2[4].
ἐλαία L 8[8].
ἔλαιον L 8[4]; Jud 9[8].
ἔλαιος N 5[1] (abe).
Ἐλαιών N 5[1].
ἐλαττόω L 18[9].
ἐλάττωμα Jos 17[2].
ἐλαύνω A 1[9].
ἔλαφος Jud 2[2] 25[8]; N 2[1]; A 4[3]; Jos 19[2] 19[3] (A) 19[4] (A).
ἐλάχιστος Jud 15[6]; Jos 17[8].
ἔλεγχος Jos 6[6].
ἐλέγχω G 1[9] 6[6]; B 10[10].
ἐλεέω Jud 18[3] 19[3]; Iss 5[2]; Z 2[2] 7[2] 8[1] 9[7] (a); D 5[9]; A 2[5] 2[6] 2[7]; B 4[2] 4[4] 5[4].
ἐλεήμων S 4[4]; Jud 19[3] (β); Iss 6[4]; Z 9[7]; A 4[9].
ἔλεος L 15[4]; Z 5[1] 5[3] 5[4] 7[3] 8[2] 8[6] (bdg); N 4[3] 4[5].
ἐλεύθερος Jud 21[7]; N 1[10]; Jos 13[6] 14[1].
ἐλευθερόω Jud 4[9]; Jos 1[5].
ἐλευθερωτής B 10[8] (β).
Ἐλιμαῖος (Ἐλαμήτης) N 5[8] (β).
ἐλπίς Jud 26[1]; A 7[7] (β); B 10[11].
ἐμβαίνω Jud 9[6] (β).
ἐμβάλλω Jud 14[1] 14[8] 25[3]; D 1[8] 1[9] (β); Jos 8[4] (β-d).
ἐμβάπτω Z 4[9] (β).
Ἐμμώρ (Ἐμώρ) L 2[2] 5[4] 6[3] 6[4].
ἐμπαθῶς B 6[2].
ἐμπίμπλημι R 3[6]; Z 6[6]; B 6[3].
ἐμπίπρημι Jud 5[5] 5[7] (β).
ἐμπίπτω R 3[11] (abg); Jud 19[1]; D 1[9] (a) 5[2] 6[5].

ἐμποδίζω Jud 18[5].
ἐμπορία Jos 11[5].
ἔμπορος Z 4[6].
ἐμπρησμός Jud 23[3].
ἔμπροσθεν Jud 3[3] (β); Iss 3[2]; Z 3[6] (β) 3[7].
ἐμπτύω Z 3[4] 3[7].
ἐμπυρίζω Jud 20[5].
ἐμπυρισμός Jud 23[3] (bef).
ἐν nearly 600 times.
ἐνάγω Jos 13[4].
ἐναλλάσσω N 3[4] 3[5].
Ἐνᾶν Jud 12[1].
ἐναντίος L 14[4]; Jud 18[6].
ἐνάρχομαι A 1[9] (β).
ἔνδεια B 7[2].
ἐνδείκνυμι Z 3[8].
ἕνδεκα G 5[11] (β); Jos 2[7] (a).
ἐνδελεχέω G 5[1].
ἐνδελεχής L 9[9].
ἐνδέχομαι Iss 4[3].
ἐνδοξάζω S 6[5].
ἔνδοξος L 8[5] 11[8]; B 9[2] 9[5].
ἔνδυμα L 10[3] (β-d).
ἐνδύω L 8[2] 18[14]; Z 4[10].
ἐνειλέω Jud 3[6].
ἐνενηκοστός L 12[4]; B 12[3] (β).
ἐνεργέω S 4[8] (β); D 5[5].
ἐνέχω G 5[11].
ἔνθα Jud 26[3]; D 7[2] (a).
ἐνθυμέω S 2[14]; B 3[6] (β).
ἐνθύμησις Jud 13[2] (β-ag).
ἐνιαυτός Jud 10[4] (β).
ἐνίστημι G 6[7].
ἐνισχύω S 1[2]; D 6[5].
ἐνλείπω N 2[3].
ἐννακοσιοστός B 7[4].
ἔννατος G 1[2].
ἐννέα L 12[5]; N 6[6]; Jos 19[2] 19[4] (A).
ἐννοέω R 4[1] 4[4] (aef) 5[5] (β); Iss 3[5] 4[5] (a, β).
ἔννοια R 4[8] 4[11]; Z 1[4]; N 2[5]; G 5[5]; Jos 9[2]; B 2[8] (A).
ἐνοικέω S 5[1].
ἐνότης Z 8[6].
ἐνοχλέω Jos 3[6] 7[4].
ἐνόω N 8[2].
ἐνσπείρω R 5[3].
ἐνταφιάζω Jud 26[3].
ἐντέλλομαι R 1[1] 1[5] 4[5] 6[2] 6[8] 7[1]; S 7[3] 8[1]; L 10[1] 13[1] 19[4]; Jud 13[1] 17[1] 26[4]; Iss 7[8]; N 8[2] 9[1] 9[3]; A 8[1] 8[2]; B 12[1] (β).
ἐντίθημι N 2[2] (β-dg).
ἐντολεύς A 2[6].
ἐντολή L 14[4] 14[6] 14[7]; Jud 10[6] (β) 13[1] 13[7] 14[6] 16[3] 16[4] 18[6] (abeg) 23[5]; Iss 4[6] 5[1] (β) 6[1]; Z 5[1] 10[2]; D 5[1]; N 8[7] 8[9] 8[10]; G 4[2]; A 2[8] 2[10] 4[5] 5[4] 6[1] 6[3] 7[5]; Jos 18[1] 19[11]; B 3[1] 10[3] 10[5] 10[11].
ἐντρύφημα Jud 21[5].
ἔνυδρος Jos 19[3] (A)
ἐνύπνιον Z 3[3]; N 7[1]; G 2[2]; Jos 1[7] 19[1].
ἐνώπιον R 1[8] 1[9] 4[8] 6[11]; S 2[14] 5[2]; L 9[8]

(β) 14[3] (a) 17[8] 19[2] ; Jud 13[2] 20[4] (β) ; D 5[6] ; G 8[2] (β-g) ; A 1[2] ; Jos 2[3] 4[1] 4[5] 6[7].
ἐνωτίζομαι R 1[5] ; Iss 1[1] ; Jos 1[2].
Ἐνώχ S 5[4] ; L 10[5] 14[1] (β) 16[1] (β) ; Jud 18[1] (β) ; Z 3[4] (β) ; D 5[6] ; N 4[1] ; B 9[1] 10[6].
ἕξ Jud 9[6] 12[12] ; Iss 2[2] 7[1] (a).
ἐξαγγέλλω L 2[10] ; Jos 5[2] 5[3].
ἐξάγω G 6[6] (β) ; Jos 19[3] (A).
ἐξαιρέω Iss 6[4] ; G 1[7].
ἐξαίρω L 18[1] ; G 6[1] 7[7] 8[4].
ἐξαιτέω B 3[3] (β).
ἐξακολουθέω Jud 23[1] ; Iss 6[2] ; Z 9[5] ; N 3[3] (β).
ἐξαλείφω Jud 22[3].
ἐξαρκέω Z 6[7].
ἔξαρχος Jud 25[1].
ἐξαφανίζω Jos 19[12].
ἐξεῖπον Z 1[6].
ἐξελέγχω R 6[11].
ἐξέρχομαι R 3[14] ; Jud 15[2] (β) ; Iss 1[4] ; Z 2[4] (hi, β-dg) ; N 4[4] ; G 6[2] ; Jos 3[9] 6[3] 8[1].
ἐξετάζω G 7[3].
ἐξηγέομαι B 2[7] (A).
ἐξήκοντα Jud 3[3].
ἐξηκοστός L 11[8].
ἐξῆς Jud 5[1] 7[1] 9[6] (β) ; N 2[8] ; Jos 8[4].
ἐξιλάσκομαι L 3[5].
ἐξίστημι Z 2[5] (β) ; B 3[3].
ἔξοδος S 8[4] 9 ; N 1[1] ; Jos 20[6] (c) ; B 12[3] (β) 12[4].
ἐξολοθρεύω S 6[3] ; Jud 6[5] 7[3] (a) 21[1] ; Jos 5[2].
ἐξόπισθεν Jud 6[8].
ἐξορίζω G 6[3] (β).
ἐξουδενόω L 7[1] 16[2] ; A 7[2].
ἐξουσία R 5[1] ; L 3[8] 18[12].
ἐξυπνίζω L 8[18] ; Jud 25[4] ; N 1[3].
ἔξυπνος L 5[7].
ἔξω N 2[9] ; Jos 7[3].
ἔξωθεν Z 3[6].
ἐξωθέω G 5[2].
ἐπαγγελία Jos 20[1].
ἐπάγω L 14[4] ; Jud 22[1] 23[3] ; Z 2[2] 10[3] ; N 4[2] ; G 5[9] ; Jos 20[1] ; B 7[3].
ἐπαγωγός L 3[2].
ἐπαινέω D 4[3] ; G 3[2] ; Jos 4[1] ; B 4[4].
ἐπαίρω S 7[1] ; L 14[7] ; Jud 21[1] ; D 4[3] ; Jos 10[6].
ἐπαοιδός S 8[4].
ἐπαισχύνομαι Jos 2[5].
ἐπακολουθέω N 3[3] (β).
ἐπακούω S 7[1] ; Iss 2[4].
ἐπακροάομαι Jos 8[5].
ἐπαναβαίνω Jud 5[4] (β).
ἐπανέρχομαι Jud 9[2].
ἐπάνω L 3[3] (β).
ἐπαύριον Iss 2[4].
ἐπεγείρω L 10[2].
ἐπείγω Jos 2[2].
ἐπειδή S 2[5] (a) ; L 3[1] 6[7] (a) 10[1] &c.

ἐπεμβαίνω B 11[2].
ἐπέρχομαι L 8[11] ; Jud 6[3] 7[7] (h, β-dy) 9[2] (β-f) ; Iss 4[5] (β) 5[8] ; Z 2[6].
ἐπερωτάω Jos 11[2].
ἐπευλογέω Jud 17[5] (aef).
ἐπεύχομαι Jud 1[6] (β-b) ; Jos 6[7].
ἐπέχω Jos 15[3].
ἐπί c. gen. about 45 times: c. dat. about 40 times: c. acc. about 70 times.
ἐπιβάλλω L 4[4] 14[1] 14[2] ; Jud 5[8] (β) ; Jos 12[1] (β-d).
ἐπιβλέπω L 3[9] ; Jud 17[1].
ἐπιβουλή B 3[5].
ἐπιγαμβρεύω Jud 10[4] (β).
ἐπίγειος Jud 21[4].
ἐπιγιγνώσκω S 8[4] ; Jud 11[4] 12[3] 19[4] 20[1] (β-ad) ; Z 4[9] ; N 4[3] ; Jos 6[4] ; B 2[2].
ἐπιγράφω Iss 4[3] ; N 6[2].
ἐπιδέχομαι Iss 4[4] 4[6] ; B 6[4] (β-a).
ἐπιδίδωμι Z 7[4] ; N 5[4] ; Jos 3[2] 6[2].
ἐπιθάλπω Jos 5[4].
ἐπιθυμέω R 5[7] ; L 13[4] ; Iss 4[2] (β-af) 7[3] ; D 4[5] ; B 10[1].
ἐπιθύμημα Iss 7[3].
ἐπιθυμητός L 8[16].
ἐπιθυμία R 1[10] 2[4] 4[9] 5[6] 6[4] ; Jud 13[2] 14[1] 14[3] (β) 16[1] ; A 3[2] 6[5] ; Jos 3[10] 4[7] 7[6] 7[8] 9[1].
ἐπικαλέω L 5[5] 8[14] ; Jud 24[6] ; D 5[11] 6[3].
ἐπιλαμβάνω Jud 5[6] (a) 6[5] ; N 1[12] (bef) ; Jos 8[2].
ἐπιλανθάνω D 7[3] ; N 4[4].
ἐπιμαρτύρομαι R 1[6].
ἐπιμένω L 4[1] ; Jos 13[4].
ἐπιμερίζω S 5[6].
ἐπιμίγνυμι Jud 23[2].
ἐπίνοια Jos 5[2] 5[3].
ἐπιορκέω Λ 2[6].
ἐπιπίπτω L 2[8] ; Jud 3[8] 9[3] (a).
ἐπιπλέω Z 6[1].
ἐπίσκεψις Jos 3[6].
ἐπισκοπεύω B 6[6] (β-bg).
ἐπισκοπέω R 1[2] ; S 1[2] ; L 4[4] 16[5] ; Jud 23[5] ; Iss 2[2] ; G 5[3] ; A 7[3] ; Jos 1[6] ; B 6[6].
ἐπισκοπή B 9[2].
ἐπισπάω R 5[1].
ἐπιστρέφω L 17[10] ; Jud 2[4] (β) 23[5] (β) ; Iss 6[3] 6[4] ; Z 9[7] 9[8] ; D 5[9] 5[11] 6[4] ; N 4[3] ; G 5[8] ; Jos 3[10] 11[5] 13[3] ; B 4[5] (β-a) 5[1] 12[4].
ἐπισυνάγω N 8[3] ; A 7[7].
ἐπιτελέω Jos 19[12].
ἐπιτίθημι L 8[3] ; N 2[2].
ἐπιτρέχω N 5[3] (β).
ἐπιφέρω Z 2[3] (β).
ἐπιχαίρω G 4[4].
ἐπονομάζω Jud 1[3].
ἑπτά R 1[7] 1[8] 1[9] 2[1] 2[2] 2[3] ; S 2[12] ; L 3[1] (β) 8[2] 19[4] ; Jud 12[2] (β) ; Z 7[4] ; N 6[1] ; Jos 3[4] ; B 7[2] 7[3] 7[4].
ἐράω Jud 13[7].
ἐργάζομαι Iss 5[3] ; N 8[4] ; G 6[5] ; B 11[1].

ἐργάτης B 11[1].
ἔργον R 2[2] 2[3] 4[1] 5[3] ; L 13[8] 19[1] ; Jud 2[2] 13[2] 20[4] ; Iss 5[3] ; Z 9[9] ; D 4[2] 6[8] 6[9] ; N 2[6] 2[9] 2[10] 8[5] ; G 6[1] ; A 4[2] 4[3] 6[5] ; Jos 10[4] 11[7] 20[6] (β) ; B 2[6] (A) 5[3] 6[7] 11[4].
ἐρεθίζω D 4[4].
ἔρημος L 15[1] 16[4].
ἐρημόω Jud 23[3] ; A 7[2] ; B 7[4].
ἐρήμωσις L 17[10] ; D 5[13] ; B 7[2].
ἔριφος Jud 2[4] ; D 1[8].
ἔρχομαι R 3[15] ; S 1[2] 2[10] (β) ; L 2[1] 2[3] 5[2] 6[1] 6[8] 7[4] 9[3] 9[5] ; Jud 1[2] 3[1] 6[1] 7[1] 7[2] (abf) 7[3] 8[2] 9[1] 12[9] 12[11] 22[2] ; Z 2[1] 2[4] (β) 3[6] 4[5] (a) 6[3] ; N 2[4] 4[5] 5[7] 6[10] ; A 2[4] 7[3] ; Jos 3[9] 4[4] 6[2] 6[4] 8[4] 8[5] (a) 11[2] 11[4] (β) 13[1] 14[2] 15[1] 15[5] 17[4] ; B 2[1] 2[8] (A).
ἐρωτάω S 4[1] ; Jos 11[2] (β).
ἐσθής L 8[2] ; Jud 26[3] ; Iss 4[2].
ἐσθίω R 1[10] ; S 3[2] ; L 8[16] 14[5] 18[11] ; Jud 2[2] 15[4] 21[5] ; Iss 2[5] ; Z 3[3] 4[1] 4[2] (a) 4[3] 4[7] ; N 9[2] ; G 1[6] 1[7] 1[9] ; A 7[3] ; Jos 6[4] 6[7].
ἔσχατος R 2[9] ; Jud 18[1] 24[3] ; Iss 6[1] ; Z 8[2] ; D 1[1] 5[4] ; N 8[1] ; G 5[6] ; Jos 19[10] ; B 9[2].
ἑταῖρος Jud 3[5].
ἕτερος R 2[3] (a) ; L 8[12] (a) ; Jud 3[2] 3[5] (a, β-ab) 9[6] ; Z 9[1] ; A 1[5] (a) 4[4] (bdg) ; Jos 5[1] 16[4] ; B 2[5] (β).
ἔτι L 2[8] 9[10] ; Jud 12[7] &c.
ἑτοιμάζω L 3[2] (a).
ἕτοιμος L 3[2] (β).
ἔτος R 1[1] 1[2] 1[7] 1[9] ; S 1[1] 3[4] 8[1] ; L 2[2] 11[1] 11[4] 11[7] 11[8] 12[4] 12[5] 12[7] 19[4] ; Jud 7[10] (β) 9[1] 9[2] 12[1] 12[12] 26[2] ; Iss 1[10] 3[5] 7[1] ; Z 1[1] 6[7] ; D 1[1] ; N 1[1] 5[1] ; G 1[1] 8[5] ; A 1[1] ; Jos 3[4] 20[6] (c) ; B 1[1] 1[2] (β-d) 1[4] 7[3] 7[4] 12[2] 12[3] (β).
εὐαρεστέω G 7[6].
εὐαρέστησις Iss 4[1].
εὐάρεστος D 1[3].
εὐγενής R 4[7] ; N 1[10] ; Jos 14[3].
εὐδοκέω L 18[13] ; Jos 4[6] 9[1] 17[3].
εὐδοκία B 11[2].
εὐδοκιμέω Jos 17[3] (β).
εὐεργετέω Jos 20[6] (β).
εὐθαλής Jos 19[3] (A).
εὐθέως R 3[15] ; Jos 16[2] (c).
εὐθής A 1[2].
εὐθύνω S 5[2].
εὐθύς adv. N 1[12] (bef) ; G 4[3] ; A 1[6] 1[7] ; Jos 13[9] ; B 9[1] (β).
εὐθύτης Iss 3[1] 4[6] ; G 7[7].
εὐκαιρία Jos 7[3].
εὐκαταφρόνητος Z 9[2].
εὐλογέω R 6[11] ; S 6[7] ; L 4[6] 5[7] 9[2] ; Jud 17[5] 25[2] ; Iss 3[2] 5[4] 5[6] ; Z 5[2] ; N 1[4] (β) 2[1] 8[2] 8[4] ; Jos 11[7] 12[3] 18[1] (β-af).
εὐλογία R 6[10] ; S 4[5] 5[6] ; L 4[4] 5[2] 6[6] ; Jud 18[5] 24[2] ; Iss 5[6] ; N 1[8] ; B 6[5].
εὐμορφία Jud 17[1].

εὔμορφος Jud 13[3].
Εὐνά ('Ενά, Αἰνά, 'Εδνά) N 1[11].
εὐνοῦχος Jud 23[4] ; Jos 2[1] (β-bd) 6[2] 12[1] 13[5] (β) 16[2] 16[3] 16[4] 16[5] 16[6].
εὐοδόω G 7[1].
εὔοσμος (εὔωσμος) Iss 1[5].
εὐπραγέω G 4[5].
εὐπρέπεια N 2[8].
εὑρίσκω R 4[8] ; S 5[2] ; L 6[1] 13[5] 13[6] 13[8] ; Jud 2[7] 3[3] (a) 24[1] ; Z 2[7] 4[6] 4[8] 7[1] 8[2] ; D 1[9] ; Jos 15[4].
εὐσέβεια R 6[4] ; Jud 18[5] ; Iss 7[5].
εὐσεβής L 16[2].
εὐσπλαγχνία Z 5[1] 8[1] 9[8] (bdg) ; A 7[7] ; B 4[1].
εὔσπλαγχνος S 4[4] ; Z 9[7].
εὐφραίνω L 18[5] 18[13] ; Jud 13[8] ; Z 10[2] ; D 5[12].
εὐφροσύνη S 6[7] ; L 18[14] (beg) ; Jud 15[4] 16[2] ; A 5[1].
εὐχαριστεία Iss 5[3].
εὐχαριστέω G 7[6] (β-a) ; Jos 8[5] (a).
εὐχή Jud 19[2] ; N 1[8] (bd) ; G 5[9] ; B 10[1].
εὔχομαι R 4[4] ; S 2[13] ; L 2[4] ; Jud 1[6] ; G 7[1] ; Jos 3[7] (β) 18[2] ; B 1[5].
εὐωδία L 3[6].
ἐφάπτω Jud 16[3].
ἐφελκύω Jud 5[3].
ἐφέλκω Jos 3[8] 8[2].
ἐφίημι Iss 4[2].
ἐφούδ L 8[2] 8[6].
'Εφραθά (Εὐφραθά, Εὐφρανθά, Ὑφραθά) R 3[13].
ἐχθραίνω G 6[5].
ἐχθρός L 13[8] ; Jud 23[3] ; Iss 6[2] ; Z 9[6] ; D 6[3] 6[4] ; N 4[2] ; A 7[2].
ἔχω R 1[4] 4[2] 5[1] 6[4] 6[9] ; S 2[1] 4[4] 4[9] (β) ; L 3[2] 9[10] 9[12] 13[2] ; Jud 7[6] 7[8] 8[1] 10[3] (β) 14[2] 14[7] 19[1] 19[2] ; Iss 1[6] 2[2] (β) 7[7] ; Z 1[3] 4[11] (β) 5[1] 5[3] 7[3] 8[1] 8[6] (bdg) ; D 3[4] 5[2] ; N 5[6] 8[5] ; G 7[6] ; Jos 3[7] 7[6] 10[5] 11[1] 12[3] 13[5] (β) 15[7] 19[8] ; B 1[3] 3[2] 3[5] 4[2] 4[5] 5[1] 6[5] 6[6] 6[7] 8[2].
ἕψω Z 6[5].
ἕως c. gen. about 30 times: c. acc. 7 times.
ἕως νῦν R 4[3] 4[4].
ἕως οὗ 5 times.
ἕως ὅτι R 7[2].

Ζαβουλών Jud 25[1] (a) 25[2] ; Z 1[1] 1[2] 1[3] 10[2].
ζάω S 2[11] ; L 19[4] ; Jud 8[3] 12[12] (β-g) 16[3] ; Iss 4[3] ; Z 4[11] (β) ; N 7[2] 7[3] ; G 1[7] 2[4] 4[6] ; B 1[1] 3[5].
Ζέλφα (Ζεβάλ) N 1[11] ; G 1[6] ; Jos 20[3] (β).
ζῆλος R 3[6] 6[4] ; S 2[7] 4[5] 4[9] ; Jud 13[3] ; Iss 4[5] (β) ; D 1[6] ; G 5[3] ; A 4[5].
ζηλόω R 6[5] ; S 2[6] ; L 6[3] ; Iss 4[5] ; G 7[4] ; B 4[4].
ζημία D 4[2] 4[6].
ζημιόω Jud 15[1] ; D 4[6].

ζητέω R 6[5]; D 6[6]; Jos 16[4].
ζωή R 1[1] 2[4]; S 1[1]; L 2[12] 11[4] 11[7] 13[2] 13[6] 18[11]; Jud 9[2] (β) 12[8] 15[5] 24[4] 25[1] 25[4]; Z 1[1] 3[6] 10[8]; D 1[1] 1[3] 5[3]; N 1[1] 5[1]; G 1[1]; A 1[1] 5[2] 5[4] 6[6]; Jos 1[3] 7[6] 20[6] (c); B 12[2] (c).
ζώνη L 8[7]; Jud 12[4] (β) 15[3].
ζῷον L 9[13]; Z 5[1].
ζωοποιέω G 4[6].

ἤ saepissime.
ἡγεμονία S 5[6].
ἡγέομαι Z 10[2].
ἥδομαι D 1[4] (β).
ἡδονή Jud 13[6] 14[2] 14[3]; Iss 3[5]; B 6[3].
ἦθος A 4[5].
ἥκω S 6[5] (a); L 17[11] 18[6]; Jud 6[4]; N 4[4] (β-a).
ἥλιος L 4[1] 4[3] 11[4] 14[3] 18[3] 18[4]; Jud 24[1] 25[2]; N 3[2] 5[1] 5[2] 5[3] 5[4]; B 8[3].
Ἡλιούπολις Jos 18[3].
ἡμέρα S 2[12] 3[4] (h, β) 4[6] 9; L 1[1] 3[2] 3[3] 5[5] 6[7] 8[1] 9[1] 9[8] 12[4] 17[2] 18[2] 18[3] 18[5]; Jud 6[3] 9[5] 10[4] (β) 12[2] (β) 18[1] 18[6] 22[3] (β-f); Iss 7[5]; Z 1[4] 1[6] 4[2] (β) 4[4] (β) 4[7] 8[2] 10[5]; D 1[1] 5[4] 6[4]; N 1[9] 6[1]; G 1[4] 1[8]; A 4[4] 5[2]; Jos 3[9] 6[4] 8[1] 11[3] (β-d) 15[1] 19[10]; B 1[4] (β) 1[8] 10[1] 12[4].
ἡμερόω Jud 2[3] (β).
ἡμέτερος S 2[12].
ἥμισυς A 2[9].
ἧπαρ R 3[4]; S 2[4] 2[7] 4[1]; Z 2[4]; N 2[8]; G 5[9] 5[11].
Ἤρ (Εἴρ) Jud 8[3] 10[1] 10[2].
Ἠσαῦ Jud 9[1] 9[2] 9[3] 9[4]; G 7[4]; B 10[10].
ἡσυχάζω Jud 22[2]; G 6[6] 7[3] 8[3].
ἡσυχία A 7[3] (hi, β); B 6[5].
ἥσυχος A 6[8] (a).
ἡσύχως A 6[8] (β-f).
ἡττάομαι R 5[3]; Jud 3[10] (β-e); N 2[7]; Jos 7[8] (β-ag).
ἥττων N 2[7] (def).

θάλαμος Jud 10[4] (β).
θάλασσα L 18[5]; Jud 21[6] 25[2]; Z 5[5] 6[1]; N 3[4] 6[1]; Jos 19[5] (A).
θάλπω Jos 5[4] (β-a).
Θαμάρ Jud 10[1] 10[2] (β) 12[1] 13[3] 14[5].
Θάμνα Jud 7[4] 7[9] (β).
θάνατος R 1[8] 3[1] 4[10] 6[6]; Jud 5[1] 23[3]; Iss 7[1] (β); Z 1[1]; D 1[4]; G 4[6] 4[7]; A 5[2]; Jos 1[3] 3[1] 3[9] 6[5] 11[3] (β) 17[5].
θανατόω Jud 10[2] (a); G 1[7] 4[4].
θάπτω R 7[2]; L 19[5]; Jud 26[4]; Iss 7[8]; Z 10[7]; D 6[11] 7[2]; N 9[1]; G 8[3] 8[5] (β-bd); A 8[4] 8[2]; Jos 20[3] (c, A) 20[6] (c); B 12[1] (β) 12[3].
θαυμάζω L 2[9].
θαυμάσιος S 6[7].
Θαφφουέ (Θαφουέ, Βαθουέ) Jud 5[6].
θεάομαι R 3[14]; L 2[5].
θεηλασία B 7[2] (c, bg).

θέλγω R 5[6].
θέλημα Iss 4[3]; D 6[6]; N 3[1]; B 11[2] (β-bg).
θεός R 1[6] 3[8] 3[15] 4[6] 4[8] 4[10] 5[3] 6[6] 6[7] 6[8] 6[9]; S 2[8] 2[19] 3[4] 4[4] 4[5] 5[2] (β-dg) 5[3] 6[5] 6[7] 7[1] 7[2]; L 3[2] 3[8] 6[8] 6[11] 8[10] 9[3] (β) 9[6] (beg) 9[14] 13[1] 13[2] 13[3] (β-d) 13[7] 14[4] 14[7] 15[2] 17[2]; Jud 13[1] 14[6] 15[5] 16[2] 16[3] 16[4] 18[3] 18[5] 18[6] 19[1] 19[3] 21[2] 21[4] 22[2] 23[3] 23[5] (β) 24[4]; Iss 3[7] 4[3] 5[1] 7[7]; Z 7[2] 8[2] 9[8] (bdg) 10[5]; D 1[3] 1[9] 5[2] 5[12] 6[2] 6[9] (β) 6[10] 7[3]; N 2[8] 2[9] 3[1] 3[2] 4[3] 7[2] 8[3] 8[4] 8[5] 8[6] 8[9] 8[10]; G 2[5] 4[2] 4[7] 5[2] 5[4] 5[7] 5[9] 6[7]; A 1[2] 1[3] 2[6] 2[10] 3[1] 3[2] 4[1] 4[5] 5[3] 7[3] 7[5]; Jos 1[4] 1[6] 2[2] 2[5] 3[4] 4[3] 4[4] 5[2] 6[6] 6[7] 8[5] 9[2] 10[5] 11[1] 11[7] 12[3] 15[5] 17[3] 18[1] 19[11] 20[1]; B 3[1] 3[4] 3[8] 4[3] 4[4] 4[5] (β-a) 6[7] 7[3] 8[2] 9[2] 9[4] 10[5] 10[8] 10[10] 11[4].
θεοσεβέω Jos 6[7].
θεοσεβής N 1[10].
θεραπεύω Jos 7[2].
θεράπων L 4[2].
θερίζω L 13[6].
θέρος Z 6[8]; Jos 19[12].
θεσμός N 8[10].
θεωρέω L 2[3].
θήκη S 8[2]; Z 10[6]; N 2[8] (β-g).
θηλάζω N 1[12] (bef); Jos 19[5] (A); B 1[3].
θῆλυς R 3[10] 6[1] (h, β); Iss 4[4].
θήρα Z 5[5] 6[4].
θηρεύω Z 5[5].
θηρίον Jud 2[4] (β); Iss 7[7]; N 8[4] 8[6]; G 1[3]; Jos 19[8]; B 3[5] 5[2].
θησαυρός A 1[9].
θλίβω Iss 3[8]; Z 7[1]; Jos 17[6] 20[1]; B 5[1].
θλῖψις L 5[5] 13[6]; Z 9[6]; N 4[2]; G 4[4]; Jos 2[4]; B 3[9] 7[2].
θορυβέω Jos 7[5].
θρέμμα G 1[6] 1[9].
θρηνέω Z 4[5].
θρίξ N 2[3] 2[8].
θροέω D 4[5] (h, β-g).
θρόνος L 3[9] 5[1].
θυγάτηρ R 5[6]; L 12[4]; Jud 8[2] 10[1] 10[6] 13[4] 21[7] 23[2]; N 1[9] 1[11] 1[12]; Jos 18[3].
θυμέομαι D 3[4] 3[5].
θυμίαμα L 8[10].
θυμός Jud 7[7]; D 1[3] 1[8] 2[1] 2[2] 2[4] 3[1] 3[4] 3[5] 4[1] 4[2] 4[5] 4[6] 4[7] 5[1] 6[8]; N 2[8].
θυμόω D 4[4] 4[5] (β).
θυμώδης D 3[2].
θύρα L 18[10].
θυρίς Jos 14[1].
θυσία L 3[6] (a) 9[7] 9[11] 9[13] 9[14] 16[1] (β); Jud 18[5].
θυσιάζω R 6[8]; L 14[5] (β-af).
θυσιαστήριον L 16[1].
θύω L 9[11]; Z 4[9]; G 1[6] 1[7].
θωρακίζω Jud 3[1].
θώραξ Jud 3[5].

Ἰακώβ R 1[6] 1[7] 3[13] 3[15] (β) 4[2] (β-de); S 2[2] 2[7] 2[14] 5[6] (β) 6[2]; L 4[3] 7[1] 9[1] 9[3] 15[4] 18[14]

19[5] ; Jud 1[3] 1[6] (β) 3[7] 9[3] 16[4] 17[4] 17[5] 19[2] (β) 21[5] 22[2] 24[1] 25[1] 25[5] (abg); Iss 1[2] 1[6] 1[8] 1[9] 1[11] 1[13] 1[14] 1[15] 2[1] 2[3] 2[4] 3[7] 5[6] 5[7]; Z 2[2] 2[3] 4[5] 4[8] (β-g) 4[9] 5[5]; D 1[9] (β) 7[2]; N 1[6] 2[1] 6[1] 6[2] 7[3] 8[2]; G 1[2] 5[9] (β); A 7[7]; Jos 10[6] 15[1] 15[5] (β), 17[5] 18[4]; B 1[2] 3[7] 10[1] 10[4] 10[6] 11[5].

ἴασις Z 9[8] (bdg).

ἴβις Jud 21[8].

ἰδιάζω R 3[10] (β-g).

ἴδιος Jud 20[5]; D 2[4] 2[5] (β-ag) 3[2]; N 8[6]; G 5[3]; B 10[1] (ade).

ἰδού R 1[3] 1[4] 1[6]; S 6[1]; L 2[6] 10[2] 12[6] &c.

Ἰεράμ (Ἰράν, Ἡράν) Jud 8[1].

ἱερατεία L 5[2] 8[2] 8[10] 8[14]; Jud 21[2] 21[4]; Iss 5[7].

ἱερατεῖον Iss 5[7] (hi, a).

ἱερατεύω L 8[10] 12[5].

ἱερεύς L 8[3] 8[17] 9[3] 17[4] 17[11] 18[2]; Iss 2[5] 3[6]; Jos 18[3].

Ἰερουσαλήμ L 10[3] 10[5]; Z 9[8]; D 5[12] 5[13]; N 5[1].

ἱερωσύνη L 8[13] 9[7] 14[7] 16[1] 17[1] 17[2] 17[3] 18[1] 18[9]; Jud 21[2].

ἱκανός N 2[4].

ἱκανόω Iss 1[7].

ἱλαρός Jos 8[5].

ἱλαρότης N 9[2].

ἱμάτιον Z 4[5] (β) 4[10] 7[1]; Jos 5[2] 8[2] 8[3] (β); B 2[4] (β).

ἵνα of purpose R 3[4] 3[5] &c.: ecbatic R 4[1] &c.: after verbs of commanding L 6[3].

ἵνα μή R 4[1] 5[5]; Iss 4[4] 4[6].

ἵνα τί Jos 7[5].

Ἰνδοκολπίτη Jos 11[2] (β-d).

ἰοβόλος S 4[9].

ἰός R 5[3]; G 5[1] 6[3] (β) 6[5].

Ἰούδας R 1[4] 6[7] 6[11]; S 2[9] 2[11] 5[6] 7[1] 7[2]; L 2[11] 8[14] 9[1]; Jud 1[1] 1[3] 13[1] 17[3] 18[2] 26[1] (β); Iss 5[7]: Z 4[2]; D 5[4] 5[7] 5[10]; N 5[3] 5[4] 5[5] 6[6] 8[2]; G 1[6] 1[9] 2[3] (a, b) 8[1]; Jos 19[8] 19[11]; B 11[2] (c).

ἱππόδρομος Jos 20[3].

ἵππος Jud 3[2] 3[3].

Ἰσαάκ R 3[13]; L 9[1] 9[6] 15[4] 18[6] 18[14] 19[5]; Jud 17[5] (β-g) 25[1]; D 7[2]; N 5[2]; A 7[7]; B 1[2] 10[4] 10[6].

Ἰσαχάρ (Ἡσαχάρ) L 12[2]; Jud 25[1] 25[2]; Iss 1[1] 1[15].

Ἰσμαηλίτης S 2[9]; Z 2[9] 4[3] (a); G 2[3]; Jos 10[6] 11[2] 13[3] 13[7] 15[1] 16[2]; B 2[3].

ἴσος D 6[6].

Ἰσραήλ R 1[10] 6[8] 6[11]; S 6[2] 6[5] 7[2]; L 2[10] 4[3] 5[2] 5[6] 5[7] (β) 6[3] (β) 7[3] 8[16] 10[2] 10[3] 14[2] 14[3] 14[6] (β) 17[5] 18[9]; Jud 12[8] 17[5] 21[5] 22[1] 22[2] 25[1] 25[5]; Iss 5[8]; Z 4[12] 9[5]; D 1[9] 5[4] 5[13] 6[2] 6[4] 6[5] 6[6] 6[7] 7[3]; N 5[7] 7[1] 8[1] 8[2] 8[3]; G 2[5] 8[1]; A 7[3]; Jos 1[2] 2[2] (β-ad) 18[4] 19[11] 20[5] 20[6] (c); B 10[8] 10[10] 10[11] 11[2] 12[3] (β).

ἵστημι L 2[10] 11[5]; Jud 17[6]; Iss 4[5]; Z 2[5]; D 5[4] 6[2]; N 2[9] 5[1] 6[1].

ἰσχυρός Jud 5[1] 9[2].

ἰσχύς R 2[7]; Jud 3[7] 13[2]; Iss 3[5] 7[6] (β); Z 10[5]; N 2[6] 2[8]; A 5[4].

ἰσχύω R 5[2] 6[5]; Jud 25[4] (β-g); Iss 4[4] 7[9] (β); Jos 4[4].

ἰχθύς Jud 21[7]; Z 5[5] (β-a) 6[3] 6[5] 6[6].

Ἰωβήλ (Ἰώ, Ἰωήλ) Jud 6[1].

ἰωβηλαῖον L 17[2] 17[3].

Ἰωσήφ R 1[2] 4[8] 6[7]; S 1[1] 2[6] 2[13] 2[14] 4[2] 4[4] 4[5] 5[1] 8[3] 8[4]; L 12[7] 13[9]; Jud 12[11] 25[1] 25[2] 25[5]; Z 1[1] 1[5] 1[6] 2[1] 2[3] 2[6] 2[8] 3[1] (β-d) 3[2] (β) 3[5] 3[6] 4[2] 4[9] 4[10] 5[4] 8[4]; D 1[4] 1[7] 1[8]; N 1[8] 5[7] 6[6] 7[2] 7[3] 7[4]; G 1[4] 1[6] 1[8] 1[9] 3[3] 5[6] 5[11] 6[2]; Jos 1[1] 1[2] 20[6] (c); B 1[4] 2[1] 3[1] 3[3] 3[6] 5[5] 10[1].

Ἰωχαβέδ (Ἰωχαβέθ, Ἰωχαβέλ, Ἡοχαβέλ) L 11[8] 12[4].

καθαιρέω Jud 7[3] (β); B 6[7].

καθάπερ Jud 21[6] (a).

καθαρεύω R 6[1] 6[2].

καθαρίζω R 4[8]; L 14[6] (β).

καθαρισμός L 14[6] (β).

καθαρός L 8[5] 9[13] 14[2] 14[3] 16[5]; Λ 2[9] 4[5]; Jos 4[6]; B 6[5] 8[2] 8[3].

καθαρότης N 3[1].

καθεξῆς Jud 25[1].

καθεύδω Jud 12[6]; N 2[8].

κάθημαι Jud 3[2]; Z 4[1].

καθίζω S 1[2]; L 2[3] 5[1]; Jud 12[1] 12[9].

καθίημι Z 6[2] 9[6] (c, bd).

καθόλου G 5[5].

καθώς S 4[5] 5[6]; L 5[4] &c.

Κάϊν B 7[3] 7[4] (β) 7[5].

καινοποιέω L 16[3].

καινοποιός N 1[12] (a).

καινός L 8[14] 18[2]; N 3[1] (c, ef); B 11[2].

καινόσπουδος N 1[12] (bef).

καίπερ Jos 10[5].

καιρός R 4[6]; S 2[6]; L 5[4]; Jud 16[3] 20[4]; Iss 2[5] (β) 3[1] (β-af) 6[1]; Z 9[9]; D 6[6]; N 1[1] 2[9] 7[1] 8[1] 8[8]; Jos 12[1] 19[10]; B 6[4] 11[2] (β).

καίω N 7[4]; Jos 2[2].

κακία S 4[9]; L 14[1] 16[3]; Z 8[5] 9[7]; D 1[3] 5[5]; G 6[7]; A 2[1] 2[8] 3[1] 3[2] 7[5]; Jos 5[3] (β-g) 6[7]; B 7[1] 8[1].

κακοποιέω A 2[8]; Jos 18[2].

κακός S 5[3]; L 6[8] 10[2] 13[6] (β-dg) 16[2] 18[9]; Jud 7[8] 18[1] 21[8]; Z 3[8]; D 3[4] 4[7] 6[5]; N 2[4]; G 3[1] 5[1] 6[5] 7[4] 7[5]; A 1[5] 1[7] 1[8] 2[1] 2[2] (β) 2[3] 2[4] 2[8] 4[2] 4[3] (β) 4[5] 6[2] 6[3]; Jos 7[1] 10[3] 10[6] 18[2]; B 4[3] 7[2] 7[4].

κακουργία Iss 6[1] (β).

κακόω S 3[4] 4[1] (hi, β); Z 9[6].

κάκωσις N 4[2]; G 8[2].

κάλαμος N 2[6].

καλέω S 2[2]; L 1[2] 9[6] 10[5] 11[2] 11[7]; Jud 12[6]; Iss 1[1] 1[15]; D 1[2]; N 1[6] 1[11]; Jos 1[1] 16[2] (β); B 1[6] 2[6] (A) 11[1].

κάλλος R 4[1]; Jud 12[3] 13[5] (β) 17[1]; Iss 4[4]; Jos 18[4].

καλός R 4^1; S 5^1; L 13^9; Jud 14^8; Iss 7^9; Z 10^6; D 1^3 7^1; N 2^8 8^4 8^5 8^6; G 1^6 7^2; A 1^5 1^6 (β) 2^1 2^4 4^2 4^3 4^4 6^3 8^1; Jos 20^4; B 4^3 9^1 (β) 12^2.

κάλυμμα Jud 14^5.

καλύπτω L 10^3; N 3^2.

καλῶς N 8^5; A 1^6.

κάματος Iss 3^5.

κάμνω Iss 3^6 (β).

κανών N 2^5.

Καππαδόκαι (Καππάδοκες) S 6^3.

κάρα A 7^3.

καρδία R 1^4 3^6 4^1 5^3 6^{10}; S 2^1 2^4 4^1 4^7 5^2; L 6^2 8^{19} 13^1; Jud 11^1 (β-d) 13^2 13^6 13^8 (β-a) 20^5 23^5; Iss 3^1 3^8 4^1 4^6 7^4 7^6 (a) 7^7; Z 2^5 7^2; D 1^3 1^4 2^5 4^7 5^3 5^{11}; N 2^6 (β-ag) 2^8 3^1; G 5^1 5^3 6^1 6^3 6^7 7^7; Jos 4^6 7^1 7^2 10^2 10^5 15^3 17^3; B 2^8 (A) 8^2.

καρπός S 4^8; L 2^{12}; Iss 3^1 5^4 5^5 5^6; N 3^5 (β-a).

καρτερός Jud 6^3 (β-df).

κατά c. gen. 18 times: c. acc. 34.

καταβαίνω S 4^3.

καταγινώσκω S 3^6 (bdg); G 5^3; B 6^7.

καταγοητεύω R 5^2.

κατάγω R 4^6; L 5^3.

καταγωνίζομαι R 5^2.

καταδαπανάω Jud 18^1.

καταδέχομαι L 6^6.

καταδιώκω Jud 9^4; G 1^3.

καταδουλόω Jud 21^7; Iss 7^7; Jos 18^3.

καταιγίς Jud 21^9.

καταισχύνω Jud 12^6; Jos 17^1 (β).

κατάκειμαι R 13^1 (β-dg).

κατακληρονομέω B 10^8 (β).

κατακλυσμός R 5^6; N 3^5; B 7^4 (bdg).

κατακόπτω Z 4^{11}.

κατακυριεύω Jud 15^5; D 3^2; N 8^6; B 3^3 3^5.

καταλαλέω Iss 3^4; G 5^4.

καταλαλιά G 3^3.

καταλαμβάνω Jud 2^3 5^5; N 5^7.

καταλάμπω G 7^3.

καταλειμπάνω B 10^4.

καταλείπω R 3^{14}; L 15^4; Iss 6^1; Z 4^6 (a); Jos 4^5 8^3.

καταλιμπάνω Iss 6^1.

κατάλυμα L 3^4 (a).

καταλύω L 3^4 (β); B 3^8.

καταμένω L 9^5.

καταμόνας D 1^9 (a).

καταπαίζω L 14^8 (bdg).

καταπατέω Z 3^3.

καταπάτημα L 10^4 (β); Jos 19^8.

καταπάτησις S 6^8; Z 3^5; Jos 19^8 (adg).

καταπαύω S 6^4; L 18^7 18^9; A 6^3.

καταπέτασμα L 10^3.

καταπίνω Jud 21^7.

καταπονέω L 6^9.

καταπτήσσω L 4^1.

καταπτύω Iss 2^1.

κατάρα L 10^4 14^4 16^5; B 6^5.

καταράομαι L 4^6; Jud 11^4; N 3^5 8^6.

κατάρχω Z 6^2 (a).

κατάσκοπος S 4^3.

κατασπαράσσω Jud 2^5.

κατασπάω Jud 3^1.

κατασύρω Z 9^1; A 2^8.

κατάσχεσις B 10^4.

κατατρέχω Jud 2^5; Z 4^6.

καταφέρω Z 9^1 (aef).

καταφεύγω S 3^5; Jud 5^5; Z 2^6.

καταφθείρω A 7^2.

καταφιλέω R 1^5; S 1^2; D 7^1; N 1^7; B 1^2 3^7.

καταφρονέω L 14^8.

καταφρόνησις L 14^5 14^8 (β); N 2^9.

κατέναντι D 6^2; A 1^4 5^1.

κατεργάζομαι Jos 10^1.

κατέρχομαι Jud 9^8; Z 8^4; Jos 9^4 12^1.

κατεσθίω S 4^9; Iss 3^5; G 1^6 (β).

κατευθύνω Jud 26^1 (β).

κατευοδόω Jud 1^6.

κατέχω Jud 26^1; B 2^5 (c).

κατηγορέω Jud 20^5.

κατήχησις Jos 4^4.

κατισχύω R 4^{11}; D 5^2; Jos 6^7.

κατοικέω R 6^4; L 5^2; Z 8^2; D 5^1; N 8^3; Jos 10^2 10^3; B 6^4 10^{11}.

κατοικησία N 3^5.

κατορθόω G 3^3.

κάτω L 3^1.

καύσων G 1^4.

καυχάομαι R 3^8; Jud 13^2 14^8; Iss 1^9 (β) 1^{10}.

κέδρος S 6^2 (β).

κεῖμαι G 5^{11}; Jos 7^1.

κείρω (κήρω) Jud 12^1.

κελεύω Jos 13^1 13^4 13^9 14^2 17^5 (β-ad).

κενός N 3^1.

κεραμεύς N 2^2 2^4.

κέρας Jud 2^7; N 5^8; Jos 19^6 (A).

κέρκος Jud 2^6.

κεφαλή R 2^2 5^5; S 4^5; L 8^2 8^9 16^3; Jud 9^5; Z 9^4; N 2^8; A 7^3 (β).

κηρύσσω L 2^{10}.

κῆτος Jud 21^7.

κινδυνεύω Jud 21^5.

κίνδυνος Jos 15^5.

κινέω D 4^3.

κίνησις R 2^4 (aef).

κλάδος S 6^2; L 8^8.

κλαίω R 1^5 (β-d); S 2^{13} 9; Iss 1^4; Z 1^6 2^4 2^5 4^8 7^4; N 7^3; Jos 3^3 3^6 6^3 6^8.

κλέπτω L 14^5; Z 7^1; A 2^8; Jos 12^2 13^1 14^1.

κληδών Jud 23^1.

κληροδοτέω Iss 5^7.

κληρονομέω N 5^8.

κληρονομία B 10^4 10^5.

κλῆρος L 8^{12}; Z 1^3; D 7^3.

κληρόω Iss 5^7 (β-d).

κλῖμαξ Jud 9^5.

κλίνη L 19⁴.
κλίνω Jud 20² (β); A 1⁸; Jos 8¹ 9¹ (h, β).
κλονέω L 4¹.
κλόνος S 4⁸.
κλοπή R 3⁶; Jos 12².
κνήμη Jos 9⁵.
κνημίς Jud 3¹.
κοιλία. Jud 26³ (β); N 1⁷ 2⁶.
κοιμάομαι R 3¹³ 3¹⁴; S 8¹; Jud 26⁴; Iss 7⁹ (a); Z 10⁶; G 8⁴; A 8¹; Jos 20⁴; B 12² (c).
κοινωνέω Z 3¹.
κοίτη R 1⁶.
κοιτών R 3¹³.
κολάζω G 4³ 5¹⁰; A 6²; B 7⁵.
κολακεύω Jos 4¹.
κόλασις R 5⁵; L 4¹; G 7⁵; B 7⁵ (β-ag).
κολλάομαι Iss 6¹; D 6¹⁰; G 5²; A 3¹.
κομίζω Jos 6².
κονδυλίζω Jos 7⁶.
κόπος Iss 3⁵.
κόπρος B 8³.
κόραξ Jud 21⁸.
κύρος Jud 9⁸.
κορυφή Jud 6⁴ 7⁵.
κοσμέω R 5⁵; Jud 12¹ 13⁵; Jos 9⁵.
κόσμησις R 5³; Jud 12³.
κοσμικός Jos 17⁸.
κόσμος L 10² 14² 17²; Jud 12¹; Iss 4⁶; Jos 19¹¹; B 3⁸.
κοῦφος S 3⁵; N 2¹.
κραταιός Jud 5¹ 6³; Jos 1⁵.
κραταιόω N 1⁴.
κρατέω Jud 2³ 2⁷; N 3¹ 5² 5³ 5⁵ 6⁴; G 1³ 6³; Jos 8³ 8⁴.
κράτος Jud 22³.
κρέας R 1¹⁰; Jud 15⁴.
κρεμάννυμι L 2⁷.
κρημνός R 2⁹; Jud 2⁴; Jos 7³.
κρῖμα G 7³; B 10³ (β-a).
κρίνον S 6².
κρίνω L 4¹; Jud 24⁶; G 4³ 5¹¹; B 7⁴ 7⁵ (β) 10⁸ 10⁹.
κρίσις R 6⁸; L 1¹ 3² (a) 3³ 4¹ 8⁴ (bdg) 18²; Jos 12³ 14¹ 15⁶; B 7⁵.
κριτής L 8¹⁷; Jud 20⁸.
κρούω Jud 3¹.
κρυπτός R 1⁴; Jud 12⁵.
κρύπτω R 4¹⁰; L 8¹⁹; A 5¹; B 2⁴ (β) 2⁶ (A).
κρύσταλλος L 3².
κρυφέως (b. κρυφίως d) Z 7¹.
κρυφῆ S 8²; Z 1⁶; G 2³ (a); Jos 4²; B 12³ (β).
κτάομαι L 13⁴ 13⁷; Iss 5¹; Z 9⁴; D 3⁴.
κτῆνος R 2⁹; S 4⁶; Jud 8¹.
κτηνοφθόρος L 17¹¹.
κτῆσις L 13⁷; A 5¹.
κτίζω R 2⁴ 2⁷ 3¹; N 2⁵.
κτίσις R 2³ 2⁹; L 4¹ 13⁷ (a, df); N 2³.
κυβερνήτης N 6².
κύκλος Jud 2⁷.

κυλίω Jud 6⁴.
κυριεύω S 3²; Jud 21⁴; Iss 7⁷; D 4⁷; A 1⁸; Jos 3².
κύριος R 1⁷ 1⁸ 1⁹ 3¹⁵ (adg) 4¹ 4⁴ 4⁸ (β) 6⁸ 6¹¹; S 2² 2¹² 2¹³ 3⁴ 3⁵ 5² 5⁵ 6⁵ 7²; L 2³ 2⁴ 2⁶ 2¹⁰ 2¹¹ 2¹² 3² (β) 3⁵ 3⁶ 3⁷ 3⁹ 4¹ 4⁴ 5³ 5⁵ 6⁸ 7¹ 8³ (β) 8¹⁰ 8¹¹ 8¹⁶ 9⁴ 9⁶ 9⁸ (β) 9¹² 9¹³ 9¹⁴ 10² 10⁵ 13¹ 13³ 14¹ 14³ (a) 14⁵ 14⁶ 15¹ 17² 17¹⁰ 18¹ 18² 18⁵ 18⁸ 18⁹ 18¹³ 19¹ 19² 19³; Jud 1³ 2¹ 8³ 10² 10⁴ (a) 12⁶ 13¹ 13² 13⁷ 13⁸ 17³ 20³ 20⁴ 21² (β) 21⁴ 21⁵ 22¹ 22³ 23³ 23⁵ 24⁶ 25² 25³ 25⁴ 25⁵ 26¹; Iss 1¹ 1⁶ 2¹ 2⁴ 2⁵ 3⁶ 4¹ 4⁶ 5¹ (β) 5² 5³ 5⁴ 5⁷ 6¹ 6³ 7⁶; Z 2⁸ 2⁹ (β-dg) 3⁵ 5¹ 5² 5³ 6¹ 6⁵ 8¹ 8³ 9⁴ 9⁷ 9⁸ 10² 10³ 10⁵; D 2³ 4⁷ 5¹ 5³ 5⁴ 5⁵ 5⁶ 5⁹ 5¹⁰ 5¹¹ 5¹³ 6¹ 6³ 6⁶ 6⁹; N 1⁴ 2² 2⁴ 2⁵ 2⁶ 3³ 3⁴ 3⁵ 4¹ 4² 4³ 4⁴ 4⁵ 6⁸ 7² 8⁴ 8⁶ 8¹⁰; G 3² 4¹ 4⁴ 5² (h, β-d) 5³ 5⁶ 7² 7³ 7⁶ 8¹ 8²; A 2⁶ 3¹ 4³ 4⁵ 5⁴ 6¹ 6³ 6⁴ 7¹ 7⁷ (β-e); Jos 1³ 1⁴ 1⁵ 1⁶ 2³ 2⁴ 3³ 3⁵ 3⁶ 3⁷ (β) 4⁴ (β) 4⁵ 4⁶ 4⁸ 5² (β-f) 6⁵ 7⁴ 7⁷ 8¹ 8⁵ 9⁶ 10² 10³ 11¹ 11⁶ 11⁷ (β-af) 13² 14² 15⁵ (β-g) 18¹ 18² 18³ 19³ (A) 19⁴ (A) 19¹¹ 20²; B 1⁴ 3¹ 3³ 3⁵ (β-dg) 3⁶ 4⁵ (β-a) 6³ 6⁴ 6⁶ 7³ 9¹ 9³ 10³ 10⁵ 10⁸ 10¹⁰ 10¹¹ 11¹ 11³.
κύων Jud 2⁴ (β) 2⁶ 23³.
κώθων N 1² (β-dg).
κωλύω S 2¹²; L 6³; Z 2⁸.
κώμη N 1¹¹ (β-f).

Λαβάν Jud 9¹; N 1¹¹.
λαγών R 1⁷.
λάθρα Jud 5⁴.
λαῖλαψ N 6⁴.
λάκκος Z 2⁷ 4¹ (β) 4² 4⁴ (β); Jos 1⁴ 9².
λαλέω R 4²; S 1¹; L 17²; Jud 1¹ 8² 12⁶ 18⁵; D 4³; G 1¹ 5¹ 6²; A 1¹; B 6⁶.
λαλιά R 2⁶.
λαμβάνω S 6⁷; L 7⁴ (beg) 8¹⁷ 9¹⁰ 11¹ 12¹ 12⁴ 12⁵ 14⁵ (β-af) 14⁶ 15² 15⁴; Jud 2⁴ 4³ 5⁵ 5⁷ (a) 6³ (β) 11² 11³ 12⁵ (a) 12⁷ 13⁴ 13⁷ 14⁶ 15⁴ (β); Iss 1³ 1⁷ 1¹⁴ (β) 2⁴ (β-dg) 3⁵; Z 3² 4⁶ 4¹¹ 6⁶; D 1⁷ 5¹¹; G 6⁵; Jos 1⁵ 3⁴ 3⁵ 5¹ 6⁷ 7³ 11⁴ 18³; B 2³ (β) 9¹ (β).
Λαμέχ B 7⁴.
λαμπήνη Jos 12¹.
λαμπρός L 13⁸; N 5⁴.
λαμπρύνω A 2⁷.
λανθάνω Jud 20⁴.
λαός R 6¹¹; S 6⁴; Jud 3¹ 3² 7¹ 9² 25³ 25⁵.
λέγω R 1⁷ 4⁵ 6⁵; S 4¹ 8⁴; L 6¹ (a) 7² 8² 8¹¹ 9⁸ 16⁴ 19²; Jud 1³ 1⁶ 12⁷ 12⁹ 13⁴ 14¹ 16³ (aef) 17⁴; Iss 2¹; Z 2¹ 2⁴ 4⁵ 4⁹; D 1⁶ 1⁷ 2¹; N 1⁵ 1⁷ 1¹² 4¹ 5² 5⁸ 6³ 7² 7³; G 1¹ 1⁹ 5¹ 5²; A 2¹ (β-g) 8¹; Jos 3¹ 3¹⁰ 4² 4⁶ 5¹ 6⁴ 7² 7³ 7⁶ 8¹ 9¹ 11² 11³ 12² 13¹ 13² 13³ 13⁴ 13⁶ 13⁷ 14¹ 14³ 15¹ 15⁶ 15⁷ 16⁴; B 2¹ 2³ 2⁶ (A) 2⁷ (A) 3⁷ 7¹ 9¹ (c) 10² 11⁵.

λειτουργέω L 3^5; A 2^2 (β).
λειτουργός L 2^{10} 4^2; A 2^2.
Λευί R 6^5 6^7 6^8 6^{10}; S 5^4 5^5 5^6 7^1 7^2; L 1^1 2^1 2^6 5^2 8^{11} 19^4; Jud 5^2 21^1 25^1 25^2; Iss 5^7; D 5^4 5^6 5^7 5^{10}; N 5^3 5^4 5^8 6^8 8^2; G 8^1; Jos 19^{11}; B 11^2 (c).
λευκός L 8^2.
λέων Jud 2^4; D 5^7; G 1^3; Jos 19^8; B 2^4.
ληστεύω L 14^5.
Λία (Λεία) S 2^2; Jud 1^3; Iss 1^4 1^7 1^9 1^{15} 2^2.
Λίβανος S 6^2.
λίθος Jud 3^3 3^6 6^4 7^5 9^5; Z 9^1; N 3^3; G 1^3.
λιμός Jud 9^8 12^{11} 23^3; Jos 1^5.
λίτρα Jud 3^3.
λογίζομαι Z 8^5 9^7; A 1^7; B 3^6.
λογικός L 3^6.
λόγιον L 8^2; B 9^1 (c).
λογισμός G 6^2.
λόγος R 3^5 3^9; S 1^1; L 1^1 6^2 9^2 (β) 16^2 18^2 19^3; Jud 1^1 1^4 12^1 (β-d) 12^6 13^1 16^3 18^5; Iss 1^1; Z 1^1; D 1^1 1^2 4^2; N 1^5 2^6 3^1 7^4; G 1^8 (β) 3^1 4^2 6^1; A 2^1; Jos 1^7 3^3 3^6 4^1 4^4 7^2 10^4 13^1 13^4 14^2; B 1^1 2^8 (A) 9^1 (β) 11^4 12^1 (β).
λοιδωρία B 6^4.
λοίδωρος (λοίδορος) B 5^4.
λοιμός Jud 23^3.
λοιπός R 3^6 5^5; S 3^6; L 14^4 (a); Jud 3^6 16^2; Z 9^4; N 8^9.
Λομνή (Λομνί, Λωμνήν) L 12^1.
λούω R 3^{11}; L 8^5 9^{11}.
λύκος G 1^3; B 11^1 11^2.
λυπέω S 2^{10} 4^3; L 2^4 6^6; Jud 17^4 (β-g); Z 4^7 4^8 10^1; D 4^6; G 1^7 7^1; Jos 3^9; B 6^3.
λύπη L 17^4; Jud 23^1 25^4; D 4^6; Jos 8^5; B 6^4 (β).
λύσις S 3^4.
λυτρόω S 7^1 (h, β); L 2^{10} (a); Z 9^8 (bdg); Jos 18^2.
λύτρωσις L 2^{10} (β); Jos 8^1.
λύχνος S 8^4.
λύω Iss 7^5 (β); D 1^9; Jos 1^6 9^1 15^6.

μαγγανεία R 3^4.
μάγος R 4^9.
Μαδιναῖος B 10^{10}.
μαζός N 1^{12} (bef).
μαίνομαι Jos 8^5.
μακράν S 6^2.
μακροθυμέω Jos 2^7.
μακροθυμία D 2^1 6^8; G 4^7; Jos 2^7 17^2 18^3.
μακρόθυμος D 6^9.
μακρός Iss 4^3 (β); N 4^5.
μάλα Jos 14^3; B 8^9.
μαλακία Jos 17^7.
μαλακίζω R 1^h; L 6^7; G 1^4.
μανδραγόρας Iss 1^2 1^3 1^8 1^{14} 2^2 2^4.

μανθάνω G 5^8; Jos 4^4 6^7.
μαραίνω S 3^5.
μαργαρίτης Jud 13^5.
μαρτυρέω Jud 20^5 (β).
μάρτυς L 19^3.
μαστιγόω Jos 8^4.
μαστίζω Jos 8^4 (β-d); B 2^4 (c).
μάταιος D 4^1; G 7^6.
μάχαιρα L 6^5; Jud 5^5 6^3; Z 1^6 (β) 4^9; Jos 6^2; B 7^1 7^2.
μάχη R 3^4; Jud 6^3 (β-df) 16^3; G 6^5; B 6^4.
Μαχήρ (Μεχίρ, Μεχείρ) Jud 6^3.
μάχιμος L 17^{11} (β).
μάχομαι Jos 11^4.
μεγαλεῖος L 11^6.
μεγαλοφρονέω R 3^5.
μεγαλύνω L 18^3.
μεγαλωσύνη L 3^9 18^8.
μέγας R 1^7 1^{10} 3^{11}; S 6^5 8^4; L 3^4 8^{12} 10^2 17^2; Jud 4^1 14^5; Z 4^8 (β); D 4^2; N 5^6 6^4 8^9; G 2^5 (a) 5^1 6^5; Jos 2^7 10^6 11^3 15^2 15^6 20^5.
μέθη Jud 11^2 (β) 12^6 14^3 16^2; A 5^1.
μεθίστημι Iss 1^{13}.
μεθύσκω Jud 14^1.
μέθυσος Jud 14^4.
μεθύω R 3^{13}; Jud 12^3 14^4.
μέλλω L 1^2 2^{10} (a) 9^9; Jud 26^3 (β); Iss 2^2 (a); Jos 1^1.
μέλος Iss 7^9 (β); Z 9^4; Jos 20^6 (β); B 11^3.
Μελχά (Μελχέ, Μελχώ) L 11^1.
Μέμφις Jos 3^6 12^1 14^1 14^5 (β-ad) 16^1.
μένω Jos 1^3.
Μεραρεί L 11^7 12^3.
μερίς L 2^{12} 14^5; Iss 5^5; B 6^3 9^2 10^{10}.
μέρος Jud. 3^4 (β) 5^4.
μεσίτης D 6^2.
Μεσοποταμία Jud 9^1 10^1.
μέσος L 5^2 11^5 11^8 13^8; Jud 20^2; Z 6^2 10^2; D 5^{13}; Jos 19^6 (A).
μεστός N 6^2 (β).
μετά c. gen. above 70 times: c. dat. once: c. acc. about 40 times.
μεταβαίνω B 9^4 9^5.
μεταβάλλω D 4^3.
μετάβολος Jos 11^5 11^6 12^2 13^1 13^2 14^6 15^6.
μεταδίδωμι Iss 7^5; Z 6^4 6^6 6^7; D 6^9.
μεταδιώκω Jos 10^2.
μετακομίζω N 9^1.
μεταμέλομαι Jud 23^5.
μετανοέω R 1^9; S 2^{13}; Jud 15^4; Z 9^7 (β); G 5^6 6^3 6^6 7^5; A 1^6; Jos 6^6; B 5^4.
μετάνοια R 2^1; Jud 19^2; G 5^7 5^8.
μεταξύ Z 2^7.
μεταπωλέω Jos 13^1.
μεταστρέφω A 1^8.
μετασχηματίζω R 5^6.
μετεμπολάω Jos 13^1 (β-ad).
μετέρχομαι D 6^6; Jos 10^2 (h, β).
μετεωρισμός Iss 7^2; B 6^3.

μέτοχος B 2⁵.
μετρέω Jos 10⁶ (β).
μέτρον Jud 9⁸; N 2³.
μέχρι R 6⁸ Jos 19⁶.
μή c. part. R 3⁸ 3¹⁵; L 9¹⁰ &c.: c. imper. R 3¹⁰ &c.: c. inf. S 1⁷ 8⁴ &c.
μηδέ passim.
μηδείς saepe.
Μῆδος N 5⁸.
μηκέτι R 3¹⁵.
μῆλον Iss 1⁵ 1⁷ 2².
μήν R 1⁷ 1⁸; S 2¹¹; N 1² 6¹ (β); G 5¹¹ (β); Jos 11⁸.
μῆνις D 5².
μήποτε G 6⁴.
μήπως Z 4².
μηρός N 1⁶ (β-g) 1⁷ (β-g).
μήτηρ S 2² 5³; L 11⁷; Jud 1³ 1⁵ 10³ 10⁵ (β) 10⁶; Iss 1⁴ 2²; D 2³; N 1⁹; Jos 20³; B 1³ 7².
μηχανάομαι R 5³.
μιαίνω R 1⁶; L 7³ 9⁹ 14⁶ (β) 16¹ 16⁴ (β); Iss 4⁴; B 8³.
μιασμός L 17⁸; B 8² 8³.
μικρός G 5¹; Jos 17⁶.
μιμέομαι A 4³ 6²; B 3¹ 4¹.
μιμνήσκομαι Z 1⁵ 9⁷; Jos 3⁸ (β) 7⁵.
μῖξις L 14⁶; Jud 14³ (β).
μισαδελφία B 7⁵ 8¹.
μισέω L 15³ 16² 17⁵; D 5¹; N 8⁶; G 2¹ 3² 6⁵; A 4³ 4⁵ 6² (bdg); Jos 1⁴.
μισθός Iss 1² 1¹⁵.
μῖσος D 2⁵; G 1⁹ 2² 3¹ 3³ 4¹ 4⁵ 4⁶ 4⁷ 5¹ 5² 5³ 5⁴ (β) 6¹ 6² 6³ (β) 7⁷.
μίτρα L 8².
μνᾶ Jos 16⁴.
μνεία N 8⁵.
μνῆμα S 8³.
μνήμη N 8⁵.
μνημονεύω Jud 18⁶; G 7²; Jos 3³.
μνημόσυνον Jos 7⁵.
μνησικακέω S 4⁴; Z 8⁴.
μνησίκακος Z 8⁶ (bdg).
μοιχαλίς L 14⁶.
μοιχεύω A 2⁸; Jos 4⁶ 5¹.
μοιχός L 17¹¹; A 4⁸.
μολύνω Z 4⁹; A 4⁴.
μολυσμός S 2¹³.
μονογενής B 9².
μονοπρόσωπος A 4¹.
μονοπροσώπως A 5⁴ (β) 6¹.
μόνος Jud 3¹ 5³; Iss 4⁹ 7⁵ (β); Z 3⁷ 4¹² 5¹; D 1⁹ (β); Jos 1⁶ 4¹ 6⁵ 7⁶ 10³ 16⁴; B 5¹.
Μοολί (Μοθλί, Μεχθί, Μοθλή) L 12³.
μορφή B 10⁷.
μόρφωσις B 10¹.
μόσχος G 2²; Jos 19⁷ (A).
μουσική Jud 23².
μουσικός B 11³.
μοχθέω R 4¹.
μόχθος Jud 18⁴.
μῦθος Jud 23¹ (a).

μυκτηρίζω Jos 2³ (bdg).
μυριοπλασιάζω Iss 3⁷.
μυστήριον L 2¹⁰; Jud 12⁶ 16⁴; Z 1⁶; G 6⁵.
μῶμος L 9¹⁰.
μωρός L 7².
Μωϋσῆς S 9; L 12³; Z 3⁴.

ναός L 5¹ (β) 10¹ 15¹ 18⁶; Jud 23³; B 9² 9³ 9⁴.
ναύτης N 6².
νεανίας Jos 12⁹ 16¹.
νεανίσκος R 4⁶; Jos 13⁴.
νεκρός Jud 9³; G 4⁶.
νέμω Jud 2⁷; Jos 19².
νέος R 2⁹ 3⁸; L 2² 8¹⁴ 9¹⁰; D 5¹²; N 5⁴; G 1⁴; Jos 12².
νεότης R 1⁶ 2⁹; S 2⁶; Jud 1⁴ 11¹ 13²; Iss 1⁹.
νεφέλη L 18⁶.
Νεφθαλείμ (Νεφθαλήμ) Jud 25²; N 1¹ 1⁵ 1⁶ 9⁹.
νεφρός N 2⁸.
νεωτερισμός R 2² 2⁹ (β-bg) 3⁸.
νήπιος Jud 23³; Jos 10⁵.
νηστεία S 3⁴; Jos 4⁸ 10¹ 10²; B 1⁴.
νηστεύω A 2⁸ 4³; Jos 3⁴ 9² (β-af).
νικάω S 5⁵; D 3⁴; G 5⁴ (β); Jos 19⁸; B 3⁷ 4³.
νῖκος D 5¹⁰.
νίπτω L 9¹¹.
νοέω Iss 3⁵ (hi, β-bd); D 4⁴; Jos 3⁹ 7⁴.
νομίζω L 16³ (β); Jud 5³ 12¹⁰ 14⁶ 19⁴; D 4⁴; A 4¹.
νόμος R 3⁸ 6⁸; S 9 (β); L 9⁶ 9⁷ 13¹ 13² 13⁴ 14⁴ 16² 16¹ 19¹ 19²; Jud 12² 18³ 26¹; Iss 5¹; Z 3⁴ 10²; D 5¹ 6⁹ 6¹⁰ (β); N 2⁶ 3² 8⁷; G 3¹ 3² 4⁷; A 2⁶ 6³ 7⁵; Jos 4⁵ (β) 11¹; B 10³.
νοσέω Z 6⁵.
νόσος R 6³; G 5⁹.
νότος Jud 4¹.
νουθεσία R 3⁸.
νουθετέω Jos 6⁸; B 4⁵ (β-a).
νοῦς R 3⁸ 4⁶; S 2⁷ 4⁹; Jud 14¹ 14² 14³ 14⁸ 20² (β); Iss 4⁴ 4⁵; D 4⁴; N 2⁶ (bef); G 6²; B 8² (c) 8³.
νυμφεύω Jud 13³ (β).
νύμφη Jud 13³.
νυμφικός Jud 12¹.
νύξ Jud 7³ 10² (β) 18⁶; Iss 1⁸ 1¹³ 1¹⁴; Z 4² (β) 4⁴ (β); G 1³; A 5²; Jos 3⁶ 8¹.
Νῶε B 10⁶ (β-d).
νῶτον Iss 5³; N 5⁶.

ξενηλατέω L 6¹⁰.
ξένος L 6⁹ 6¹⁰ 13³; Z 6⁴.
ξηραίνω L 4¹.
ξηρός Z 2⁷.
ξίφος D 1⁷.
ξύλινος S 8²; Z 10⁶.

ξύλον S 8² (β); L 18¹¹; Z 6² 9¹; N 3³; B 9³.

ὀγδοήκοντα Jos 16⁸.
ὄγδοος R 3¹ 3⁷ (β); L 12⁷.
ὀγκόω S 4¹ (c); L 6⁹.
ὁδηγέω R 2⁹; Jud 14¹ 19¹; G 5⁷; B 6¹.
Ὀδολάμ (Ὀδολλάμ) Jud 8².
Ὀδολομήτης (Ὀδωλλαμίτης, Ὀδολαμήτης) Jud 8¹.
ὁδός R 1³; S 5²; L 2³; Jud 7⁷ 26¹; Z 4⁶; A 1³ 1⁵.
ὀδυνάω Iss 7⁵.
ὀδύνη L 17⁵; Jud 11⁴; Z 9⁶ (bdg).
ὀδύρομαι Z 2⁴ 4⁶ (a).
Ὀζιήλ (Ὀζίηλ, Ὀζωήλ) L 12².
ὅθεν N 1⁸.
ὀθόνη Z 6².
οἶδα L 16³; Jud 2² 11¹ 17² 17⁶; Iss 3⁷ 6¹ (β); Z 5² 5⁴ 7⁴; D 2³ 5⁴ 6⁴; N 2² 2⁴ 8¹⁰ (β-g); G 5⁸; A 7²; Jos 9³ 10⁵ 13² 15³ 16⁵ 17⁴ (β-bd) 19¹ 20¹; B 3² 4¹ (β-d) 6⁴ 6⁶.
οἰκεῖος R 3⁵.
οἰκειόω N 8⁶.
οἰκέω L 18³; G 5⁴; B 12⁴.
οἰκογενής L 6⁹.
οἰκοδομέω L 2³; Jud 7⁹; B 8³.
οἰκονόμος Jos 12³ (bdg).
οἶκος L 10⁵ 17¹⁰; Jud 2¹ 21⁷; Iss 2⁵; Z 6³ 6⁷ 7¹; Jos 2¹ 3² 8⁴ 8⁵ 9⁵ 11² 11⁶ 12³ 14¹.
οἰκτείρω L 16⁵; Z 2²; A 2².
οἰκτιρμός Jos 2³.
οἰκτίρμων Jud 19³ (β).
οἶκτος Z 2⁴ (β).
οἰμωγή Z 2⁴.
οἰνοποσία Jud 14⁷.
οἶνος R 1¹⁰; L 8⁵ 9¹⁴; Jud 9⁸ 11² (β) 12³ 13⁶ 14¹ 14² 14³ 14⁶ 14⁷ 15⁴ 16¹ 16² 16³ 16⁴; Iss 7³; Jos 3⁵.
οἰνοχοέω Jud 11² 13⁵.
οἶος B 5⁵ 9⁵.
ὀκτώ L 11¹ 12⁵; Jud 3⁵ 9¹ 26²; Iss 2².
ὄλεθρος R 4⁵ (β) 6³.
ὀλίγος G 4⁶ 5⁹ 8³; A 2⁷; Jos 19⁴ (A); B 5⁵.
ὀλιγοστός S 5⁶.
ὀλιγοψυχία G 4⁷.
ὀλιγόω N 4³ (β).
ὁλκή R 2⁶.
ὀλοθρεύω L 13⁷; Jud 6⁵ (β) 7³ (β).
ὁλοκαύτωμα L 9⁷.
ὁλοκλήρως Jos 19⁷ (A).
ὅλος L 13¹; Jud 6⁵ (β); Iss 7⁶ (a); A 2² 2³ (a) 2⁵ 2⁷ 2⁸ 4² 4⁴; Jos 8¹.
ὅλως Jud 16³; G 2¹ (bg).
ὄμνυμι Jud 22³; G 6⁴.
ὁμοθυμαδόν N 6¹⁰.
ὅμοιος L 8¹⁸; N 1⁸ 2⁷ (bef); A 3² 4⁵; Jos 18⁴.
ὁμοιόω N 2²; B 7⁵.

ὁμοίως N 3⁵; Jos 19²; B 6⁷ (a).
ὁμολογέω D 1⁴; G 2¹ 6³.
ὁμόνοια Jos 17³.
ὁμοῦ N 5³.
ὀνειδίζω S 4⁶; Jud 13³; Jos 17⁴.
ὀνειδισμός R 4² 4⁷; L 10⁴ (β); Jud 23³.
ὄνειδος R 4⁷ (β-af) 6³; L 10⁴ 15².
ὄνειρος L 8¹⁸.
ὄνομα L 5⁵ 6¹ 8¹⁴ 11¹ 11² 11⁶; Jud 8² 13⁴; Z 9³; D 6⁷; N 1⁶ 1¹¹; A 2⁴.
ὀνομάζω Jud 1³ (β) 19¹.
ὄντως Jos 13⁹.
ὀξύνω D 4⁴.
ὀξύς Jud 1⁴.
ὄπισθεν Jud 3³ (β); Z 2⁶ (a) 6².
ὀπίσω Z 2⁶ (β) 4⁶ (a).
ὅπλον L 5³.
ὅπου R 7² (β) &c.
ὀπώρα Iss 3⁶ (β).
ὀπωροφυλάκιον Jos 19¹².
ὅπως R 1⁴ 1⁶ 5¹ (a) &c.
ὅραμα L 8¹ 9² 9³ 11⁵; Jud 3¹⁰; N 5¹.
ὅρασις R 2⁴; L 8¹⁶ 9² (β); D 2⁴; N 2⁷; B 6⁶.
ὁρατός R 4¹⁰ (β-d) 6¹².
ὁράω R 3¹ 5⁶; S 4¹ 5⁴; L 2⁹ 2¹¹ 3¹; Jud 9⁵; Iss 1¹¹ 2¹ 4⁶ 7¹ (a); Z 4³ 4⁵ 6⁷ 9⁸; D 2²; N 5⁶ 7² 7³ 8⁵; G 4⁵; A 5¹; Jos 10¹ 14¹ 14⁴ 17¹ 18³ 19³ (A) 19⁵ (A) 19⁷ (A); B 6² 6⁶ 8² (β) 10⁸.
ὀργή R 4⁴; S 4⁸; L 6¹¹; Jud 14¹; Z 2¹ (deg); D 3⁵ 4³; G 5¹.
ὀργίζω S 2¹¹; L 6⁶ 7¹ (β-b); Jud 7⁵; Z 4¹¹; D 4² 4⁴.
ὀρθός Z 6²; B 3².
ὀρθρίζω Jos 3⁶.
ὄρθρος Jos 8¹.
ὀρθῶς D 3³; B 3².
ὅριον Jud 2⁶ (β); Iss 7⁵ (β).
ὅρκος Jud 22³.
ὁρκῶ R 6⁹.
ὁρμάω L 16³; Jud 7⁵; Jos 19⁸.
ὅρος L 2⁵ 6¹; Jud 6⁴ 9³ 25²; N 5¹.
ὄρος Jud 14⁸ 16¹; G 7⁴.
ὀρύσσω Z 2⁷.
ὅσιος G 5⁴; B 3¹ 5⁴.
ὀσμή S 6²; L 3⁶.
ὀστοῦν S 6² 8² 8³ 8⁴; Jud 20⁴; D 7²; N 9¹; Jos 20² 20⁶ (c); B 12¹ (β) 12³ (β).
ὄσφρησις R 2⁶.
ὀσφύς N 2⁸.
ὅταν c. ind. Z 9¹ (a); G 1³.
ὅτε passim.
ὅτι passim.
οὐ μή c. subj. vel fut. R 4⁵; L 15⁴; D 5².
οὐ μόνον L 14⁷; Iss 4³; Z 3⁷ 5¹.
οὐ, οὔτε, οὐδέ passim.
οὐκέτι B 11¹.
οὖν passim.
οὐρά Jud 2⁶ (β-af).
οὐράνιος B 3⁸ (c).

οὐρανός R 1^6 5^7 6^9; S 6^4; L 2^6 2^7 2^8 2^9 3^1 3^9 5^1 5^4 (β) 13^5 14^3 (β) 18^3 18^4 18^5 18^6; Jud 21^3 21^4 (β-af) 24^2 25^2; Iss 7^7; D 5^{13} (β-a); A 2^{10} (β) 7^5 (β); Jos 12^3 19^6 (A); B 3^1 3^8 (β) 9^5 10^7.
οὕτως passim.
ὀφείλω Jos 14^6.
ὀφθαλμός Jud 13^6 14^1 14^5 23^3 26^2 (β); Iss 3^4 (β-g) 4^6 7^2; D 2^4 2^5; N 2^6 2^{10}; G 1^9 5^7; Jos 11^1 11^6 12^1 (β); B 4^2 6^3.
ὄχλος Jud 7^1 (β).
ὀχυρός Jud 9^4.
ὄψις R 3^{10} 5^5; S 5^1; Jos 11^3; B 10^1.

παγιδεύω Jos 7^1.
πάθος L 4^1; Jud 18^6; D 3^5 4^5; Jos 7^8; B 5^1.
παιδεία Z 2^3.
παιδεύω Z 2^3.
παιδίσκη N 1^{11}; B 1^3.
παιδοφθόρος L 17^{11}.
παῖς Z 3^6; Jos 13^1 13^3 14^2 14^3 14^6 16^3 16^4.
παίω Jud 9^3.
παλαιός Z 4^{10} (β).
πάλιν L 8^1 9^{11}; Jud 5^7 (a) 6^3 (a); Z 9^9 10^2; N 4^4 6^1; G 8^3; Jos 4^4 5^1; B 9^1 (c) 10^{11}.
παλλακή Jos 7^5 13^5 (β).
πανδοχεῖον Jud 12^1.
πανουργεύω R 5^4.
πανουργία Jud 10^3; Iss 1^{11} (β) $6^{\cdot}$; Z 9^9; N 1^6 2^8.
πάντοτε S 3^3 (bis); N 7^2; G 4^5.
πάντως Jos 10^4 (β-dg).
πάνυ N 1^7 (a); G 1^5 (a); Jos 9^8 (β) 15^3.
παρά c. gen. 16 times: c. dat. 3 times: c. acc. 8 times.
παραβαίνω Jud 13^7.
παράβασις L 10^2; Jud 16^3.
παραγγέλλω Jud 21^1; Z 5^1.
παραγίγνομαι B 10^8.
παράδεισος L 18^{10}.
παραδίδωμι Jud 5^6 (β); A 7^2; Jos 3^1; B 3^8 7^3.
παραζήλωσις Z 9^8 (bdg).
παραθήκη B 12^2 (β).
παραινῶ G 6^1.
παραιτέομαι L 5^6 5^7 (β); D 6^2.
παρακαλέω R 4^4 4^9 (h, β); Jud 8^2; N 9^1; A 6^6 (bdg); Jos 1^6 2^8 17^4.
παρακούω D 2^3.
παραλαμβάνω L 17^4 17^6.
παραλία Z 5^5.
παράλιος Z 5^5 (β-bg).
παραλυπέω Jud 17^4.
παραμυθέομαι A 6^6 (aef).
παρανομέω Jud 14^8; G 5^{10}; Jos 2^2.
παρανομία Z 1^5; D 3^5.
παράνομος L 14^6 (β).
παραπείθω D 3^4 (β).
παρατάσσω Jud 4^1 13^3; D 5^4.

παρατίθημι Jud 9^5; Jos 13^3.
παραφυλάσσω R 4^4.
παραχρῆμα Z 3^7 (bdf).
πάρδαλις Jud 2^6; D 1^8; G 1^3 (β-df).
παρεδρεύω D 5^6.
παρεῖδον L 6^6; Iss 1^6.
πάρειμι (εἰμί) Jud 14^3 (β).
παρεισέρχομαι Jud 16^2.
παρεκεῖ N 5^8 (a).
παρεκτός Z 1^4.
παρεμβολή S 5^5; L 3^5.
παρέπομαι L 5^6 (a); D 6^2 (a).
παρέρχομαι R 4^4; Jud 14^8; Z 5^2; Jos 10^5 12^1 (β) 19^{12}.
παρέχω S 4^8; Jud 24^4; Iss 3^8; Z 7^2; D 2^4 3^2; N 8^9; G 5^1 5^7 7^2; Jos 9^3 16^4.
παρθένος L 14^6 (β); Jos 19^3.
παρίστημι Jos 2^6 (β) 20^6 (β).
παροικία L 11^2.
πάροικος L 11^2 (β).
πάροινος Jud 14^4.
παροξύνω S 4^8; D 4^2; A 2^6.
παρυργίζω L 3^{10}; Z 9^9; A 2^6.
παρουσία L 8^{15}; Jud 22^2.
παρρησία R 4^2.
πᾶς R 1^{10} 2^3 3^1 3^8 passim.
πάσσαλος Jud 5^4 (β).
πάσχω R 3^8 4^1; S 4^3; Jud 15^2; G 5^{11}; Jos 20^6 (β); B 7^4.
πατάσσω L 5^6 6^5.
πατέω L 18^{12}; Z 9^8 (bdg).
πατήρ R 1^3 1^5 1^6 1^7 1^8 (a) 3^8 3^9 3^{13} 3^{13} 4^2 4^4 4^{10} 7^2; S 2^1 2^2 2^6 2^7 2^8 2^{10} 2^{14} 4^1 5^6 8^1 9; L 2^1 5^4 6^1 6^3 6^6 6^9 7^1 8^{15} 9^1 9^2 9^3 10^1 14^2 15^4 17^2 18^6 (h, abg) 19^2 (β-g) 19^3 19^4; Jud 1^3 1^4 1^6 2^2 3^7 3^9 7^7 7^9 (β) 9^1 9^2 9^7 11^2 13^1 13^3 13^4 13^7 16^4 17^3 17^4 17^5 (β) 18^2 19^2 19^3 24^2 26^3 (a) 26^4; Iss 1^1 1^{10} 1^{13} 3^1 3^2 3^6 3^7 5^6 5^8 7^8; Z 1^2 1^3 1^5 2^2 2^3 2^7 4^5 4^8 4^{10} (β-dg) 4^{12} 5^5 6^3 6^7 7^1 9^5 10^2 10^4 10^7; D 1^2 1^5 1^7 1^9 2^3 5^{10} 6^9 6^{11}; N 1^5 2^1 4^4 5^2 6^1 6^3 6^4 6^{10} 7^1 7^2 9^1 9^3; G 1^5 1^6 1^9 2^5 5^9 6^2 8^3 8^5; A 1^2 8^2; Jos 1^2 (β) 1^4 2^2 3^3 6^6 6^7 10^5 15^1 15^2 15^5 17^5 20^1 20^6 (c); B 1^5 2^1 2^7 (A) 2^8 (A) 3^6 3^7 10^1 11^5 12^1 (β) 12^3.
πατράδελφος S 4^5 (β); G 7^4.
πατρία D 1^2 7^3.
πατρικός L 18^6.
πατρίς L 13^8.
παύω S 3^6; L 19^4; Jud 3^8; N 6^9.
πέδη Jos 8^5 (β-d).
πεδίον Jud 2^3; G 2^2.
πείθω D 1^8 3^4; G 1^9; Jos 4^2 4^5 13^1; B 7^1.
πεῖνα Jud 25^4 (β-g).
πεῖρα G 5^2.
πειρασμός Jos 2^7.
πειρατήριον Iss 5^8.
πειράω D 1^3; Jos 16^3.
πέλαγος N 6^5.
πέμπτος R 1^1 2^6 3^5; L 8^8 11^4 17^6 17^{10};

(β) 7^7 7^8 8^2 9^1 10^4 (β) 11^4 12^5 12^7 12^8 12^{12} 13^1 13^5 14^5 14^8 17^3 17^4 18^1 19^1 19^3 23^1 23^2 26^3 (β) 26^4; Iss 1^5 (β-g) 1^{11} (β) 7^5 7^7; Z 1^5 1^7 2^9 3^7 (β-eg) 4^4 (β) 4^9 4^{12} 4^{13} 5^1 5^3 5^4 6^1 6^5 7^1 9^4 9^6; D 1^9 3^2 4^5 5^5 5^6 5^{10} 6^8 (β); N 1^2 1^6 2^2 2^8 2^9 2^{10} 3^4 4^1 4^5 7^4 8^6 9^3; G 2^8 3^1 3^2 4^1 5^1 5^3; A 1^6 1^9 2^6 4^2 8^2; Jos 5^2 6^9 11^1 12^3 15^5 17^5 19^5 (A) 20^1; B 2^7 (A) 3^6 4^3 6^6 10^3 10^4 11^2 12^3 (c).

ποικίλος Iss 4^2; Z 1^3.
ποιμαίνω L 2^3; Z 6^8; G 1^4.
ποίμνη G 1^3; Jos 19^5 (A) 19^6 (A).
ποίμνιον R 4^1; S 2^9; L 6^9; Jud 3^1 21^7; Z 1^3 (β-af); G 1^2 1^3; Jos 19^4 (A) 19^5 (A).
ποιός Jos 7^1 (a).
πολεμέω S 5^5; Jud 3^4 (β) 3^5 3^8.
πολέμιος R 6^{12}; L 13^8; Jud 3^9 7^4 (β-d) 13^5; D 2^3.
πόλεμος S 4^8 5^5 6^4 8^2; Jud 4^1 5^6 (a) 6^1 7^{10} 22^1; D 5^2 5^{10}; G 5^1; B 12^3 (β).
πολιορκέω Jud 9^4.
πολιορκία Jud 23^3.
πόλις L 6^5 7^2 13^7; Jud 5^1 5^2 5^4 5^7 (β) 6^4 6^5 7^1 7^2 7^9 (a) 9^4 12^1 12^9 14^5; N 1^{11}.
πολλάκις G 6^8; Jos 4^1 (a) 9^1.
πολλαπλασίων Z 6^6 (bdg).
πολύς R 4^4 4^7 4^9; S 2^6; L 2^7 (a) 2^8 13^4; Jud 3^1 7^1 8^1 14^7 21^8 23^1; Iss 4^3; Z 1^6 1^7 (β) 5^5 6^6 9^2 9^6; N 4^3 7^1 9^1; A 2^7 2^8 4^2; Jos 3^9 12^1 15^1 16^3 19^4 (A); B 5^5.
πολυτελής Jud 26^3.
πόμα R 2^7.
πονηρεύομαι Jud 10^6 13^2; A 2^3.
πονηρία L 10^3; Jud 10^4 (β) 10^5 (β) 11^5 17^2 (β); Iss 1^{11} (a); Z 9^9 (h, β); D 5^5 5^6 5^8; N 4^1; G 8^2; A 1^7 1^8 2^3 2^4; B 3^3.
πονηρός R 1^8 4^9 4^{10} 5^1 6^5; S 2^{14} 3^5 4^9 5^1 6^6; L 5^6 (β-d) 13^6 13^8 18^{12}; Jud 10^2 11^1 12^2 14^4 (a, af) 16^1; Iss 4^6 6^2 7^7; Z 4^{12} 9^7 (a); D 1^3 3^1 6^8; G 7^6 (β); A 1^8 1^9 2^2 2^5 2^7 4^2 6^5; Jos 3^{10} 5^2 7^8; B 3^6 5^1.
πόνος Jud 18^4; Iss 5^5; Jos 7^2.
πορεύομαι R 1^3 1^4 4^1; S 2^9 4^5; L 9^2 13^1 19^2; Jud 7^2 (a) 9^3 (β) 11^3 13^2 (β) 18^6 23^5 24^3; Iss 3^1 3^2 3^4 (β-g) 4^1 4^6 5^1; Z 4^8 (β) 9^1; D 3^6 5^5; N 4^1 6^6; A 1^6 4^5 5^4; Jos 4^5 18^1; B 10^{11}.
πορνεία R 1^6 3^3 4^6 4^7 4^8 4^{11} 5^3 5^5 6^1 6^4; S 5^3 5^4; L 9^9; Jud 12^2 13^9 14^2 14^3 15^2 17^2 18^2; D 5^6 (β); Jos 3^8; B 8^2 (β) 9^1 10^{10}.
πορνεύω S 5^3 (β); Jud 15^1 15^2; Iss 7^2; A 2^6; B 9^1.
πόρνη L 14^5 14^6.
πορνικός R 5^4.
πορφύρα L 8^7.
ποσάκις Jos 3^1 4^1 (β-a) 9^4.

πόσος N 2^2; Jos 10^1 17^1; B 3^4.
πότε N 2^4.
πότος Jud 8^2.
πούς L 19^4; Jud 2^4 3^4 (β); Iss 7^9; Z 9^4; N 2^1 5^4; G 1^3 8^4; Jos 6^8 13^2 20^4; B 12^1 (c) 12^3 (β).
πρᾶγμα S 2^3 2^{14} 4^6; N 8^{10}; A 2^1; Jos 17^8 20^6 (β).
πρᾶξις R 3^{10} 4^1 5^6; S 2^3; Iss 3^3 5^1 7^7; Z 9^7; D 3^6; N 2^6 (β-ag) 3^1 3^2; G 3^1; A 1^3 1^6 1^8 1^9 2^3 2^4 3^2; Jos 5^2 11^1; B 9^1.
πρᾶος D 6^9.
πραότης Jud 24^1.
πρᾶσις S 4^2; D 1^5; Jos 16^2 (β).
πράσσω R 1^8 3^{12} 3^{14} 6^3; L 7^3 13^9; Jud 14^3; D 3^3; A 1^8 6^2.
προαίρεσις R 1^9; Z 5^2; N 2^6 (bef); Jos 17^3.
πρόβατον Jud 12^1; Z 1^3; Jos 19^4 (A).
προδίδωμι Jos 11^4; B 5^5.
προεῖπον S 6^1 (β).
προέρχομαι Jos 19^8 (β).
προΐστημι Jos 2^6.
πρό 7 times.
προκαθέζομαι Jud 12^2.
προκοπή Jud 15^5; G 4^5.
προκόπτω Jud 21^8.
προλαμβάνω Jud 2^5.
προνομεύω Jud 7^3.
προνομή L 17^9.
πρόπαππος Jud 17^5.
προπάτωρ L 9^1.
πρός c. dat. 4 times: c. acc. about 100 times.
προσαγορεύω L 16^3.
προσάγω Jud 6^3 9^5; Iss 2^5.
προσαπαντάω Iss 1^3.
προσβάλλω L 5^6 (β-dg).
προσδέχομαι L 16^5; A 4^3 (β).
προσδοκάω A 4^3.
προσδοκία Jos 7^6.
προσεγγίζω R 4^6; S 5^3; Jud 7^4 21^5; Jos 6^5.
προσέρχομαι Z 4^7; Jos 4^6 15^7.
προσευχή L 4^2; N 8^8; Jos 4^8 10^1 10^2.
προσεύχομαι R 1^7; Jos 3^3 7^4 9^4; B 1^4 3^6 5^5.
προσέχω R 3^{10} 4^1; S 2^7; L 9^9; Z 1^2 4^2 8^5 9^1; D 1^2 2^3 6^1; A 6^1 6^3 7^5; Jos 16^4 (β-ad); B 8^3.
προσήκω Jud 5^2.
προσκαλέω R 4^9; Z 1^7.
προσκολλάομαι A 1^8 (a); B 8^1.
πρόσκομμα R 4^7.
προσκρούω G 5^5.
προσκυνέω R 6^{12}; Z 3^6 3^7 9^6 (h, β); Jos 13^5; B 10^7.
προσλαμβάνω A 1^8 (β); Jos 3^4 (β-bd).
προσοχθίζω Jud 18^5; D 5^4.
προσπεδάω Jud 2^6.
προσπελάζω Iss 6^1.

προσποιέομαι Jud 7[2]; Jos 3[7].
πρόσταγμα L 3[2] (β); Jud 24[3].
προστάσσω R 5[5]; B 12[3] (c).
προστίθημι L 17[5] 19[4]; Iss 2[4]; N 2[8]; G 2[2]; Jos 4[8].
προστρέχω N 5[2] 5[5].
προσφέρω R 4[9]; L 3[6] 3[8] 9[13] 9[14]; Jud 21[5]; Iss 2[5] (β-g) 3[6] 5[3]; Z 6[5]; G 7[2].
προσφορά L 3[6] (β) 14[5].
πρόσωπον R 4[2] 5[4]; S 5[1]; L 3[5] (β) 3[7] 3[9] 4[2] 10[3] 18[5]; Jud 13[8] 20[5] 25[2]; Iss 1[11]; Z 2[1] (β) 3[4] 4[5] 8[6] (a); D 2[2]; N 2[7] 4[5] 9[2]; G 1[9] 6[2]; Jos 3[4] 6[8] 7[2] 13[2] (β-g); B 10[11] (β).
πρότερος L 8[1]; Iss 1[10].
προτίθημι R 1[6] (a).
πρόφασις Jos 8[6].
προφητεία L 8[2]; B 3[8].
προφητεύω S 5[6]; D 7[9].
προφήτης L 8[15] 16[2]; Jud 18[5]; D 2[3]; B 9[2].
προχωρέω Iss 1[11] (β).
πρωΐ L 9[4]; N 1[3].
πρωτογέννημα L 9[14]; Iss 3[6] (β) 5[4].
πρῶτος R 2[4] 2[9] 3[3] 5[3] (β); L 2[7] 6[4] 8[4] 8[12] 8[18] 9[14] (deg) 11[8] 17[2]; Jud 24[3] 25[1]; Iss 3[6]; Z 6[1]; D 4[2] 4[4]; B 7[2] 9[2] 9[3] 10[8] 12[3] (β).
πρωτότοκος R title.
πτέρυξ Z 9[8] (bdg); N 5[6].
πτοέω Jos 2[5].
πτωχεία Jud 15[6] 25[4] (β); D 5[13].
πτωχός Jud 15[5] 15[6] 25[4]; Iss 7[5]; A 2[5] 2[6].
πυθμήν Jud 24[5].
πύλη L 5[1]; Jud 7[3] 9[4] (β) 12[1] 12[2] (β) 12[9].
πυλών Z 3[6].
πῦρ L 3[2] 4[1]; Jud 5[5] 25[3]; Z 10[3].
πύργος L 2[3]; Jud 5[6].
πυρός Jud 9[8].
πύρωσις Jud 16[1].
πωλέω S 2[9]; Z 2[9]; Jos 15[4] 16[1]; B 2[1].
πώρωσις (πύρωσις) L 13[7].
πῶς R 4[8]; Z 4[5]; A 5[1]; Jos 6[5] 10[5].

Ῥαβαήλ (Ῥαμβαήλ, Ῥοβαήλ) Jud 7[9] (β).
ῥάβδος L 8[4]; Jud 12[4] 15[3] 24[6]; Z 1[3]; B 2[4] (c).
Ῥαχιήλ (Ῥαχήλ) Iss 1[3] 1[6] 1[7] 1[8] 1[10] 1[14] (β-d) 2[1] 2[2] 2[4]; N 1[6] 1[7] 1[8] 1[9]; Jos 20[3]; B 1[3] 1[4] 1[5].
Ῥεβέκκα L 6[8]; N 1[9].
ῥήγνυμι Jud 2[6].
ῥῆμα Iss 1[1]; Z 1[2] 2[4]; D 1[2]; Jos 1[2] 3[10] 4[1].
ῥίζα Jud 24[5].
ῥίπτω Jud 2[7]; Z 2[7]; Jos 7[3].
ῥόδον S 6[2].
ῥομφαία S 5[4]; L 5[3] 18[10]; Jud 23[3]; Z 4[11].
Ῥουβήμ (Ῥουβίμ) R 1[1] 1[2] 1[5] 3[9] 7[1]; S 2[9] 2[10]; L 6[3]; Jud 5[2] 9[6] 13[3] 25[2]; Iss 1[3] 1[4]; Z 2[7] 4[5] 4[7]; G 1[6].

Ῥουθαῖος (Ῥούθεος, Ῥώθεος, Ἡροθαῖος) N 1[9] 1[10].
ῥύομαι R 4[10]; S 2[8]; G 2[5]; Jos 1[7] 2[2] 4[3] 4[8] 10[3].
ῥυπαρός Jud 14[3].

Σαβά Jud 8[2].
σάκκος N 6[8]; Jos 4[3] (β) 15[2].
σαλεύομαι L 3[9].
σανίς N 6[6].
σάρξ S 6[2]; Jud 18[4] 19[2] (β-f) 19[4] 21[8] 24[4] (β-d); Z 9[7]; N 1[4]; G 7[2]; B 10[8].
Σαρρά L 6[8].
Σατανᾶς D 3[6] 5[6] 6[1]; G 4[7]; A 6[4] (β).
σβέννυμι L 4[1].
σέβομαι Jos 4[6].
σελήνη L 14[3] (β); Jud 25[2]; N 3[2] 5[1] 5[2] 5[3] 5[4].
Σεμεῆ (Σεμεί) L 12[1].
Σήθ B 10[6].
Σήμ B 10[6] (β-d).
σημεῖον S 6[5]; L 8[2] (β-af) 8[11].
σήμερον R 1[6]; L 7[2]; Jud 26[2]; D 1[4].
σίδηρος Jud 9[4] (β).
Σείρ (Σικάρ, Σιήρ, Σιρήχ) Jud 9[3].
σίκερα R 1[10].
Σίκιμα (Σήκημα, Σίκημα, Σύκημα) S 2[9]; L 2[1] 6[8] (β) 7[2]; Jud 4[1].
Σιλώμ (Σολών, Σηλώμ, Σιλών) Jud 6[2] 8[3] 10[6] 11[3].
σιωπάω N 3[1]; Jos 4[7] (bdg) 9[4] 10[6] 16[6]; B 5[4].
σκάφος Z 6[1]; N 6[9].
σκεπάζω B 3[4].
σκεπινός (σκεπεινός) R 3[11].
σκέπω B 4[3].
σκεῦος N 2[2] 8[4].
σκηνή Jud 25[2].
σκῆπτρον Jud 24[5] 25[1]; D 1[9]; N 5[8] 8[7]; B 10[7].
σκληροκαρδία S 6[2] (a).
σκληρός S 2[4].
σκληροτριχηλία S 6[2] (β).
σκοπέω N 3[1] (df).
σκορπίζω A 7[6] (hi, g).
σκοτεινός B 4[2].
σκοτίζω R 3[8]; L 14[4] 18[8]; Jud 2[7]; G 6[2].
σκότος S 8[4]; L 17[6] 18[4] 19[1]; N 2[7] 2[10]; G 5[1] 5[7]; A 5[2]; Jos 2[4] 8[5] 9[1] 9[2] 10[3] (β-b) 19[3] (A) 20[2]; B 5[3].
σκοτόω Jud 2[7] (adeg); D 2[4]; G 1[3] (β).
σκυθρωπός S 4[1].
σκυλεύω L 4[1]; Jud 5[7] (β).
σμικρύνω Jud 17[3]; N 4[3].
Σόδομα L 14[6]; N 3[4] 4[1]; A 7[1]; B 9[1].
σορός R 7[2]; L 19[5].
σοφία L 13[7] 13[8]; Z 6[1].
σοφός L 13[7]; Jud 17[3]; N 8[10].
σπείρω L 13[6].
σπέρμα R 6[12]; S 6[3]; L 4[3] 4[4] 7[1] 8[3] 8[11] 8[15] 8[16] 9[9] 15[4]; Jud 10[5] (β) 22[3] 24[1]; Z 3[4]; D 7[3]; Jos 19[11]; B 11[2].

σπεύδω N 1¹² (bef); G 4³.
σπήλαιον R 7¹; Iss 7⁸ (β-g).
σπιλόω A 2⁷.
σπλαγχνίζομαι Z 4² 6⁴ 7¹ 7² 8¹ 8³ 8⁴ (bdg).
σπλάγχνον S 2⁴; L 4⁴; Z 2² 2⁴ 5³ 5⁴ 7³ 7⁴ (bdg) 8² (bdg) 8⁶ (bdg); N 4⁵ 7⁴; Jos 15³; B 3⁷.
σπλήν N 2⁸.
σποδός Jos 15².
σπορά R 2⁸.
σπουδάζω D 6³; N 3¹; G 4³.
σπουδαῖος Jud 1⁴ (β).
σπουδή L 13⁷ (β).
στάδιος Z 7⁴; G 1³ (β).
σταθμός N 2³.
στειρεύω B 1⁴.
στεναγμός Jos 7² 9¹.
στενάζω Jos 7¹.
στερέωμα N 3⁴.
στερίσκω Jud 18⁴.
στέρνον A 1⁵; Jos 9⁵ (β).
στέφανος L 8² 8⁹; B 4¹.
στῆθος Jud 20³ (β) 20⁴.
στήριγμα Jud 15³ 15⁶.
στηρίζω S 2⁷.
στολή L 8⁵; Jud 3⁶; Jos 5² (β) 19⁸.
στόμα R 1¹⁰ 6¹⁰; L 6⁵ 8¹⁷ 13⁴ 19³; Jud 2⁴ 5⁵; D 1² (β-dg); N 2⁶ (β-ag); G 1⁷; Jos 1² 4⁶; B 11² (c) 11³.
στόμαχος N 2⁸.
στρέφω Z 7⁴.
στρῖνος B 9¹ (β).
στυγνός L 3¹.
συγγένεια Z 8⁶.
συγγίγνομαι Jos 4⁵ 7⁹.
συγγινώσκω S 3⁶; Jud 19³ (β).
συγκαλύπτω N 9².
συγκαταριθμέω N 7² (hi, β).
συγκόπτω Jud 3⁴ (β).
συγκρύπτω A 2⁴; Jos 17².
συγχαρίζομαι B 10⁷ (β-d).
σύζυγος R 4¹.
συκοφαντέω Jos 8⁴.
συκοφαντία Jud 16⁸; G 5¹; Jos 10³.
συλλαμβάνω R 3¹² 5⁶; L 2¹ (β) 11² 17³; Jud 12¹; Iss 1¹⁵; N 1⁶; B 1⁴ 7².
συμβαίνω S 2¹³.
συμβάλλω G 4⁴.
συμβιβασμός L 11⁶.
σύμβιος Jud 23³ (β); Iss 7² (a).
συμβουλεύω L 6³; Jud 13⁴.
Συμεών S 1¹ 1² 2¹ 2² 8¹ 9; L 2² 6⁴; Jud 6⁵ 25¹ 25²; Z 2¹ 3² 4² 4¹¹; G 2³ (β).
συμμαχέω Jud 7⁶.
σύμμαχος Jud 6² 7².
συμμίγνυμι R 3².
συμπάθεια Z 7⁴.
συμπαθέω S 3⁶; B 4⁴ (β-a).
συμπάσχω Z 6⁵ 7³; B 4⁴ (a).
συμπίπτω Jud 11² (β) 13³ (β-d) 13⁷; Z 10¹; Jos 7¹ 7² 9⁵.
συμπνίζω S 2¹².
συμπορεύομαι Jud 24¹; Iss 7⁷; Z 7⁴.

συμφαίνομαι R 5⁶.
συμφέρω G 7¹ 7²; Jos 9³.
σύν 12 times.
συνάγω R 1²; L 1²; Jud 1²; Jos 19⁴ (A) 20⁶ (c); B 6² 9² 10¹¹.
συναγωγή L 11⁵; B 11² 11⁷.
συναίρω D 4⁷.
συναλγέω Z 6⁵.
συναμαρτάνω D 5⁷ (c).
συναναστρέφομαι D 5¹³; N 4².
συναναφέρω Jos 20².
συνανέρχομαι N 5⁷.
συναντάω L 1¹.
συνάπτω R 3⁷; L 14⁶; Jud 5⁶ 6²; N 2⁸; Jos 8¹ (β-d).
συνδιάζω R 3¹⁰ (a) 6² (a, de).
συνδυάζω R 6² (bfg).
συνεγγίζω D 5⁷.
σύνεγγυς D 7² (β-dg); G 8³ (β).
συνείδησις R 4³; Jud 20² (a).
σύνειμι Iss 2³.
συνεξαμαρτάνω D 5⁷ (hi, bef).
συνέπομαι Jud 3¹⁰.
συνεργέω R 3⁶; Iss 3⁷; D 1⁷; G 4⁵ 4⁷.
συνέρχομαι R 2⁹ 3⁸; Jud 10⁵ (β) 12⁴; N 1²; Jos 3¹ 9⁴ 10⁴.
συνεσθίω S 6⁷.
σύνεσις R 6⁴; S 4⁸ (β); L 2³ 4⁵ 8² 13² 18⁷; Jud 14⁷ 20² (β); Z 6¹.
συνετίζω L 4⁵ 9⁸.
συνευδοκέω A 6².
συνεχής R 6³; Jud 22¹.
συνέχω R 4³; Jud 3¹ (β) 18⁴; Jos 1⁵ 7² 8⁵ 14³; B 8³.
συνεχῶς R 5⁶; L 9⁶; D 4⁷; G 5¹.
συνηγορέω Jos 1⁷.
σύνθρονος L 13⁹.
συνίημι L 8¹⁸; D 4¹; N 3¹; Jos 6².
συνκλαίω Z 2⁶.
συνουσία R 2⁸ 5⁶; Iss 2¹ 2²; N 8⁸; Jos 8².
συνταράσσω Jud 14³.
συντέλεια L 10²; Z 9⁹; B 11³.
συντελέω S 8¹; L 5⁴; Jud 13⁸ 22²; D 6⁴.
συντηρέω L 6².
συντίθεμαι Z 1⁶; Jos 6⁹.
σύντομος Z 4⁸.
συντόμως Jos 7¹.
συντρέχω Jud 2² 2⁵ (β-a) 19²; B 4⁵ (β-ab).
συντρίβω Jud 2⁴; N 6⁵; A 7³.
συντρώγω Z 4² (β).
συντυχία R 6³.
Σύρος N 5⁸.
συσσείω Jud 2⁷.
σύστασις R 2⁴.
συστενάζω Iss 7⁵.
Συχέμ L 5³ 6⁴ 12⁵.
σφακελισμός Jud 23³.
σφενδονάω Jud 3⁶.
σφενδονίζω Jud 7⁵.
σφόδρα Z 1³; Jos 3⁶; B 1⁵.
σφοδρός N 6⁴; B 1⁵.
σχῆμα R 5¹ 5² 5⁴; Jud 12⁵; Z 3⁷ (a, aeg) 9⁸ (bdg).

σχίζω L 4¹ 10³ ; Z 9⁴ (β) ; B 9⁴.
σχολάζω Jud 20¹.
σώζω S 6⁵ 6⁷ 7² ; L 2⁴ 2¹¹ ; Jud 24⁶ ; N 8³ ; A 7³ ; Jos 19¹¹.
σῶμα S 2⁵ 4⁶ 4⁹ 6⁷ ; Jud 14³ ; Z 2⁵ ; D 3² 3³ 3⁴ ; N 2² 2⁴ ; A 2⁷ 4⁴ ; B 12³ (c).
σωτήρ L 10² 14² ; D 6⁷ (β) 6⁹ ; G 8¹ (β-bg) ; Jos 1⁶ ; B 3⁸.
σωτηρία L 17² ; D 6¹⁰ ; N 8² ; G 4⁷ 5⁷ 8¹ ; B 3⁸ 11².
σωτήριος S 7¹ ; L 9⁷ ; Jud 22² ; D 5¹⁰ ; B 9² 10⁵.
σωφρόνως Jud 16³.
σωφροσύνη Jos 4¹ 4² 6⁷ 9² 9³ 10² 10³.
σώφρων Jos 4² ; B 4⁴.

τάλαντον Jud 9⁵ (β) ; Jos 18³.
ταμιεῖον S 8³ (β) ; Jos 3³ 9².
τανῦν L 10¹ (a).
τάξις L 11³ ; N 2⁸ 2⁹ 3² 3³ 3⁴ 3⁵ 8⁹ 8¹⁰.
ταπεινός D 6⁹ ; G 5³ ; B 9⁵.
ταπεινόω B 5⁵.
ταπείνωσις R 6¹⁰ ; Jud 19² ; D 5¹³ ; G 5³ ; Jos 10² 18³ ; B 10⁷.
ταράσσω Z 8⁶ ; D 4² 4⁷ ; G 6² ; A 6⁵ (β) ; Jos 7⁵.
ταραχή S 4⁹ 5¹ 6⁴ ; L 13⁶ ; D 5² ; B 6⁵ 7².
τάριχος N 6² (β).
τάσσω L 3³ ; N 2¹ 3⁵.
ταῦρος N 5⁶.
Ταφουέ (Ταφουσέ, Γαφούς) Jud 3² 5⁸.
ταχύς Iss 6³.
τειχήρης Jud 5¹ (β-dg).
τεῖχος L 2³ ; Jud 4² 5³ 5⁴ 7³ (β) 9⁴ (β) ; Jos 19⁶ (A).
τεκνίον R 1³ (c, bg).
τέκνον R 1³ 1⁴ 2¹ 3⁹ 4¹ 4⁵ 5¹ 5⁵ ; S 2¹ 2¹³ 3¹ 4⁵ 4⁷ 5² 7¹ 7⁸ 8¹ (h, afg) ; Lev 9⁹ (bdg) 10¹ 12⁶ 13¹ 13² 13⁵ 14¹ 18¹² 18¹³ 19¹ ; Jud 1³ 8³ (β) 10³ (β) 11⁵ 13¹ 13⁸ 14¹ 14⁴ 14⁷ 16¹ 17¹ 18² 19¹ 19² 20¹ 21¹ 23¹ 26¹ ; Iss 1¹ 1⁶ 2¹ 2³ 3¹ 4¹ 5¹ 6¹ 6³ 7⁶ (β) 7⁷ ; Z 1¹ (β) 3¹ 3² 5¹ 5³ (β-d) 7² 8¹ 8⁵ 10¹ ; D 1⁴ 2¹ 2² (β) 3¹ 4⁵ 5¹ 6¹ 6⁸ 6⁹ ; N 1⁵ 2⁹ 3⁴ 4¹ 7³ 8¹ 8² 8⁴ (β) 8⁵ 8¹⁰ ; G 1² 2¹ 3¹ (β-a) 4¹ 5² 6¹ 8¹ 8² 8³ ; A 1² 3¹ 5¹ 6¹ 6³ 7⁴ ; Jos 1² 3⁷ 7⁵ 7⁶ 8¹ 10¹ 11¹ 13⁵ (β) 17¹ 18¹ (β-ae) 19¹ 19¹¹ ; B 3¹ 3⁷ 4¹ 7¹ 8¹ 10² 10⁴ 10¹⁰ 10¹¹ 12¹ (β).
τέλειος Jud 23⁵ ; A 1³ (ci, e).
τελειόω G 7¹.
τελείως G 7¹ (β-af).
τελευτάω Jud 25⁴.
τελευτή R 1² 4² ; L 1¹ (efg) ; N 1¹ (hi, β-bg) ; Jos 20¹.
τελέω Jos 4⁷ (β).
τελείωσις R 6⁸.
τελίσκομαι Jud 12⁹ (bg).
τέλος L 5⁶ (β-d) 6¹¹ 14¹ 16³ ; D 6⁵ ; N 1¹ (bg) ; G 8² (β) ; A 1³ 1⁹ 2¹ 2⁴ 6⁴ ; Jos 8² ; B 4¹.
τελωνέομαι Jud 12⁹ (aef).
τέρπω D 4⁴ ; Jos 17³ ; B 6³.

τέρψις D 4³.
τεσσαράκοντα L 12⁵ ; Jud 12¹².
τεσσαρακοστός L 11⁷ ; Jud 9² (β) ; N 5¹.
τέσσαρες L 2⁹ (β) ; Jud 3⁶ 4¹ (β) 9⁵ 16¹ ; A 7².
τέταρτος R 2⁵ 3⁴ ; L 3³ (β) 8⁷ 11⁸ 12⁴ 17⁵ ; Jud 1³ 25¹ ; Z 1¹ ; Jos 19⁶ (A) ; B 7².
τέχνη N 2⁸ (def) 8⁷.
τήκω L 4¹ ; Jos 15³.
τηρέω R 5⁵ ; Z 4³ ; D 5¹ ; G 7⁵.
τίθημι R 7² ; S 8² ; L 19⁵ ; Z 4³ 10⁶ ; D 1⁴ ; G 8⁵ ; Jos 20³ (β) ; B 12² (β).
τίκτω R 5⁷ ; L 2¹ (β) 11² 11⁷ 11⁸ (β) 12¹ ; Jud 8³ ; Iss 1² 1¹⁵ 2¹ 2² ; Z 1³ ; N 1⁶ 1⁹ 1¹¹ 1¹² ; Jos 3⁷ (β) ; B 1² 1⁴ 7² (β-bg).
τιμάω L 13³ ; Jud 1⁵ ; G 6⁶ (β-af) 8¹ ; Jos 10⁶ 11¹ 19¹¹.
τιμή Z 3² 3³ ; Jos 16³ ; B 6⁵.
τίμημα Z 3¹.
τίμιος L 17³.
τιμωρέω Jos 14¹.
τιμωρία Jos 3¹.
τοιοῦτος N 9¹ ; A 2⁹ 4⁵ ; B 2⁸ (A) 7⁵.
τόξον Jud 3³ 7⁵ 9³.
τύπος R 3¹¹ ; L 16⁵ ; D 6⁷ ; Jos 2⁶ (bg) ; 19² 19³ (A).
τότε passim.
τότε οὖν peculiar to a, Jud 7⁵ 9⁷ ; Iss 2¹.
τράπεζα L 8¹⁶ ; Jud 21⁵.
τράχηλος N 2⁸.
τρεῖς L 8¹¹ ; Jud 7⁸ (β) 9⁵ (β) 12¹² ; Z 4⁴ (β) ; Jos·11⁸ 19² 19³ (A).
τρέμω L 3⁹ (a) ; Z 2⁵.
τρέπω Jud 6².
τρέχω Jud 2⁵ 3¹ 25⁵ ; N 5⁹ ; B 2³.
τριάκοντα R 1⁸ ; L 19⁴ ; Iss 3⁵ ; G 1⁴ 2³ (β).
τριακοστός L 11⁴ ; N 1¹.
τριημερίζω Jos 3⁵.
τρικυμία N 6⁵.
τριπλοῦς D 3⁴.
τρίτος R 2⁵ 3⁴ ; L 2⁸ (β) 3³ (β) 8⁶ 8¹⁴ 11⁷ 12⁸ 17⁴ ; Jud 10² (β) 25¹ ; D 3⁴ ; N 2³ ; Jos 13⁵ ; B 7².
Τρωγλοδίτης (Τρωγλοδύτης, &c.) Z 4⁶.
τρόμος S 4⁸ ; Jud 3⁸.
τρόπος L 6⁸ ; G 2² ; A 1³ ; Jos 2⁶ 7¹.
τροφή Jos 3⁵ ; B 11¹.
τροφός N 1⁹.
τρύβλιον Jos 6².
τρυφάω Jos 9².
τρυφερός G 1⁴ (β).
τρυφή Jud 25² ; Jos 3⁴ ; B 6³.
τύπος L 8¹⁴ ; Z 3⁶.
τύπτω Jos 2³ 13¹ 13⁹ 14¹ 14².
τυφλός R 2⁹.
τυφλόω S 2⁷ ; Jud 11¹ 18³ 18⁶ 19⁴ ; D 2⁴.
τύφλωσις L 13⁷ 14⁴ (a) ; D 2².
τυφλώττω Jos 7⁵.

ὑβρίζω Jud 7⁵ ; B 5⁴ 9³.
ὕβρις Jud 16³ ; G 5¹ ; B 6⁵.
ὑγεία N 2⁸.
ὑγιάζω L 13⁵ (a).

ὑγιαίνω L 1² ; N 1² (β) ; A 1².
ὑγιής Iss 7⁹ (β).
ὕδωρ L 2⁷ 4¹ 8⁵ 18⁵ 18⁷ ; Jud 6¹ 12³ (β-df) ; Iss 1⁵ ; Z 2⁷ 2⁸ 9¹ ; N 6⁵ ; A 7² 7³.
υἱός R 1¹ 1² 1⁵ 4⁷ 6⁵ 7¹ ; S 1¹ 1² 2² 4⁶ 5⁴ 8¹ 9 ; L 1¹ 2⁴ 3¹⁰ 4¹ 4² 4⁴ 4⁵ 5⁴ 6³ 11² 11⁷ 12² 12³ 18⁸ 19² 19³ 19⁴ ; Jud 1¹ 1³ 5⁶ (β) 9¹ 9⁴ 10¹ 10⁴ (a) 11⁵ (β) 13³ (β) 14⁵ 17³ 21⁵ 21⁷ 23⁴ 24¹ (bdg) 24³ 26⁴ ; Iss 1¹ 1² 1⁸ 2² 5⁷ 6¹ 7⁸ ; Z 1¹ 4⁹ 5⁴ 9⁷ 9⁸ (bdg) 10² 10⁶ ; D 1¹ 1² 1⁶ 5⁶ 5⁷ 7² ; N 1² 1⁵ 6¹ (β) 9³ ; G 1¹ 1² 1⁶ ; A 1¹ 1³ 8² ; Jos 1¹ 1² (β) 2⁵ 3⁷ 3⁸ 5⁴ (β-d) 10⁸ 15² 17⁷ 20⁶ (c) ; B 1¹ 1⁵ 1⁶ 2² 3⁶ (β-b) 9² (c) 12³.
ὕμνος L 3⁸ ; G 7².
ὑμνέω Jos 8⁵.
ὑπάγω L 13³ ; B 2⁴ (β).
ὑπακοή Jud 17³.
ὑπακούω R 3⁸ (β-dg) ; S 7¹ (h, β) ; Jud 1⁴ 13¹ 18⁵ (β) 18⁶ ; Iss 5⁸ ; Z 9⁴ (β) ; D 5⁵ ; N 3³ ; G 8³.
ὕπανδρος R 3¹⁰ ; L 14⁸.
ὑπαντάω Jud 13³ (a) ; B 2⁴.
ὕπαρ N 2⁸ (a).
ὕπαρξις L 17⁹ ; Z 8⁶ (aef).
ὑπάρχω S 4⁴ ; L 11¹ ; Jud 23³ ; Iss 7¹ (a) ; N 1⁹ ; G 1⁴ ; Jos 10⁵ 11³.
ὑπέρ c. gen. 9 times : c. acc. 15 times.
ὑπεράνω L 3⁴.
ὑπερασπίζω B 4⁵ (β-a).
ὑπερεκπερισσοῦ Jos 17⁵.
ὑπερέχω Jud 21⁴.
ὑπερηφανεία (ὑπερηφανία) R 3⁵ ; Jud 13² 18³ ; D 5⁶ ; G 3³.
ὑπερήφανος L 17¹¹.
ὑπέρογκος A 2⁸.
ὑπηρετέω Jos 14³.
ὑπηρέτης B 3⁸.
ὕπνος R 3¹ 3⁷ ; S 4⁸ (β) 4⁹ ; L 2⁵ ; Jud 18⁴ ; Iss 3⁵ 7⁹ ; Z 10⁶ ; D 7¹ ; N 2⁶ ; A 8¹ ; Jos 20⁴ ; B 12² (c).
ὑπνόω R 3¹² ; Iss 7⁹ (β) ; D 7¹.
ὑπό c. gen. about 25 times : c. acc. 5 times.
ὑποβάλλω S 3³.
ὑπογράφω Iss 4³ (β-g).
ὑποδείκνυμι N 8¹ ; A 1².
ὑπόδημα Z 3² 3⁴ 3⁵.
ὑποκάτω L 3⁷ ; Iss 1⁵.
ὑποκρίνομαι A 7³.
ὑπόκρισις B 6⁵.
ὑποκρύπτω Jud 6⁵.
ὑπολύω Z 3⁴ 3⁵ 3⁶.
ὑπομένω D 5¹³ ; N 7¹ ; Jos 17¹.
ὑπομιμνήσκω L 9⁶.
ὑπομονή Jos 2⁷ 10¹ 10².
ὑπονοῶ B 9¹ (β).
ὑποπίπτω Jos 7⁸.
ὑποσκελίζω D 6³ ; Jos 4¹.
ὑπόσπονδος Jud 7⁸ (β).
ὑπόστασις R 2⁷ ; Z 2⁴.
ὑποστρέφω Z 4⁶ (a) ; G 1⁵.
ὑποτάσσω Jud 21².
ὑποτίθημι Iss 5³.

ὑπουργέω D 3⁴.
ὑπόφορος Jud 7⁸ 9⁷ (β).
ὗς Λ 2⁹ (bdg).
ὑστέρημα B 11⁵.
ὕστερος L 19⁵ (β) ; Z 10⁷ ; Jos 3⁸ ; B 11².
υφης Jud 9⁵.
ὑψηλός L 2⁵ 11⁵ ; Jud 6⁵.
ὕψιστος S 2⁵ 6⁷ ; L 3¹⁰ 4¹ 4² 5¹ 5⁷ 8¹⁵ 16³ 18⁷ ; Jud 24⁴ ; Iss 2⁵ (β) ; N 2³ (b, A) ; G 3¹ ; A 2⁶ 5⁴ 7³ ; Jos 1⁴ 1⁶ (bdg) 3¹⁰ 9³ 10³ ; B 4⁵ (β-a) 9².
ὕψος L 2⁸ ; Iss 1⁵ (β) ; N 5⁷.
ὑψόω R 6⁵ ; Jud 21⁸ ; N 5³ ; G 7² ; Jos 1⁷ 10³ 10⁵ 17³ 18¹ ; B 9³.

φαιδρός L 2⁸ 2⁹ ; B 5⁵.
φαίνω R 5⁷ ; S 4⁹ 6⁵ ; Jos 3⁴ 19¹² (β) ; B 10⁷ 10⁹.
φανερός A 2³.
φανερῶς Jos 4².
φαντάζω S 4⁹.
φαντασία R 3⁷ 5⁷.
φάραγξ Iss 1⁵.
Φαραώ Z 3⁶ ; Jos 2¹ 8⁴ 13⁵.
φάρμακον R 4⁹ ; Jos 2⁷ 5¹.
φείδομαι S 2⁷ ; Jos 16⁴.
φέρω R 4⁷ ; S 2⁹ ; L 3⁷ ; Iss 1³ 3¹ ; Z 2³ 2⁴ ; N 2² 6⁵ ; Jos 11⁵.
φεύγω R 5⁵ ; L 15³ (β) ; Jud 3⁶ 7⁷ ; Iss 7⁷ ; D 5¹ ; N 6⁶ (β) 8⁴ ; Jos 8¹ ; B 5² 7¹.
φημί A 2¹ (β-g) ; Jos 14² (β-ad) 16¹.
φθάνω R 5⁷ ; L 6¹¹ ; N 5³ 5⁷ (β) 6⁹ ; G 1³ ; Jos 11⁴ (a).
φθαρτός B 6².
φθέγγομαι D 5².
φθείρω S 4⁸ 5⁴ ; Jud 19⁴.
φθονερός Iss 3³.
φθονέω S 2¹⁴ 3³ 3⁶ ; G 3³ 7² ; B 4⁴.
φθόνος S 2¹³ 3¹ 3² 3⁴ 3⁶ 4⁵ 4⁷ 6² ; D 2⁵ ; G 4⁵ ; Jos 1³ 1⁷ (β-af) 10³ ; B 7² 7⁵ 8¹.
φιλαργυρία Jud 18² 19¹.
φιλάργυρος (φυλάργυρος) L 17¹¹.
φιλέω B 1² (β-dg).
φιληδονία R 2⁴ 3⁶ ; Iss 2³ ; B 6².
φιλονεικέω G 6⁴ ; Jos 4⁷ (β-bg).
φίλος L 13⁴ 13⁸ ; Jud 23³ ; D 2³.
φλόξ Jos 2².
φοβερός Jos 6².
φοβέομαι S 2³ ; L 13¹ ; Jud 7¹¹ ; Z 1⁶ 4² 10⁵ ; D 6¹ ; N 7¹ 8⁴ ; G 3² 5⁵ 6⁶ ; Jos 2⁴ 4² 5³ 15⁵ ; B 2⁵ 3³ 4⁴ 5² 10¹⁰.
φόβος R 4¹ ; S 3⁴ ; L 13⁷ ; Jud 16² ; N 2⁹ ; G 5⁴ ; Jos 10⁵ 10⁶ 11¹ ; B 3⁴ 4⁵ (β-a) 5⁴.
φοῖνιξ N 5⁴.
φοιτάω B 11⁵.
φόνος Z 2³.
φοράς Jud 2³ (β).
φορέω Z 3⁵ ; B 4¹.
φραγγελόω B 2³.
φρόνησις N 2⁸.
φρόνιμος N 8¹⁰.
φυγαδεύω G 5⁷.
φυλακή Jos 1⁶ 8⁴.

φυλάσσω R 3[9] 4[5] 4[8] 6[1]; S 3[1] 4[5] 5[9] 7[3] 8[3]; L 8[17] (β-af) 10[1] 13[8]; Jud 13[1] 16[1] 18[2] 22[3] 26[1]; Iss 5[1] 7[5]; Z 5[1] 10[2]; D 2[1] 5[1]; G 1[3] 4[1]; A 6[3]; Jos 1[4] 2[3] 9[5] 14[2] 18[4] 19[11]; B 3[1] 10[3] 10[5].
φυλή S 7[1] (β); Jud 15[3]; Z 10[2]; D 5[10]; A 7[6]; B 9[2] 11[5].
φύλλον L 9[12].
φύρω Jos 6[1]; B 2[2].
φυσιόομαι L 14[7] 14[8] (β).
φυσικός D 2[4] (β-a) 3[4].
φύσις R 3[1] 3[3]; D 3[5] (β-d); N 3[4] 3[5].
φωνή L 18[6]; Iss 1[4]; Jos 8[5] 9[4]; B 11[2] (β).
φῶς L 4[3] 14[4] 18[3] 19[1]; Z 9[8]; N 2[7] 2[10]; G 5[1]; A 5[2] 5[3]; Jos 19[3] (A) 20[2]; B 5[3] 11[2].
φωστήρ L 14[3]; Jud 25[2].
φωτεινός L 2[8] 4[3] (β).
φωτίζω L 4[3] 18[3] 18[9]; G 5[7]; B 6[4] 11[2].
φωτισμός L 14[4].

χαίρω Iss 3[6]; D 1[5]; Jos 8[5] 19[9]; B 6[4].
χαλάω Jos 1[4].
Χαλδαῖος N 1[10] 5[8].
χαλκοῦς L 6[1]; Jud 9[4] (β).
Χάμ S 6[4].
χαμοκοιτέω Jos 4[3].
Χαναάν S 6[3]; L 12[5]; Jud 10[2] (β) 11[1] (β) 11[3]; Z 5[5]; Jos 12[2] 13[1] 13[8] 15[2]; B 12[3] (β) 12[4].
Χαναναῖος L 7[1]; Jud 3[1] 7[11] 10[6] 11[1] 13[3] (β) 14[6] 17[1].
Χανανίτος (Χανανίτης) Jud 13[3] 16[4].
χαρά L 17[2]; Jud 25[4] 25[5]; A 6[6]; B 6[5] (β).
χαρακτήρ S 5[4].
χαρίζομαι S 4[6]; L 15[3] 18[5] 18[14]; B 10[7] (a).
χάρις R 4[8]; S 4[5] 5[2]; L 18[3]; Jud 2[1] 24[2]; Jos 3[4] 11[6] 12[3] 19[11] (β); B 4[5].
χαριτόω Jos 1[6].
Χαρράν (Χαρά) L 2[1]; Iss 1[5].
χαυνόομαι Z 2[4].
Χεβρών R 7[2]; S 8[2]; L 9[5] 12[2] 19[5]; Jud 2[6] 4[3] 26[3] 26[4]; Iss 7[8]; Z 10[7]; N 9[1]; G 1[5] 8[5]; A 8[1] 8[2]; Jos 20[6] (c); B 12[1] (β) 12[3].
χεῖλος Iss 7[4].
χειμάζομαι Jud 21[6]; N 6[5].
χειμών Z 6[8] 7[1]; N 6[9].
χείρ S 2[8] 2[12] 2[19] 9; L 4[4] 8[10] 14[1] 14[2]; Jud 3[6]; Iss 3[7]; Z 2[2] 2[3] 7[4] 9[4]; D 1[9]; G 1[3] 2[5]; A 7[2]; Jos 1[5] 11[7] 12[2] 15[4] 17[6]; B 6[1].
Χετταῖος S 6[3].
χέω L 18[5] (beg).
χηρεύω Jud 12[1] 12[2].
χθές N 1[4].
χίλιοι Jud 4[1] 9[2] (β).
χίμαρρος Z 4[9].
χιτών Z 4[5] (a) 4[9] 4[10] 4[11] 4[12]; Jos 8[3]; B 2[2] 2[3].

χιών L 3[2].
χλευάζω L 7[2] 14[8].
χλευασμός L 14[1].
χλωρός G 2[2].
χοῖρος Jud 2[5].
χολή R 3[4]; N 2[8].
χορτάζω Jud 21[8] 25[4] (β-g).
χρεία Z 6[5].
χρῄζω Jud 14[7]; Z 7[3] 7[4].
χρῆμα Jud 21[7].
χρῆσις N 2[4].
χρηστός B 3[7].
Χριστός A 7[2] (a, d).
χριστός R 6[8]; L 10[2].
χρίω L 17[2] 17[3].
χρόνος R 6[8]; S 1[1]; Jud 7[10]; Iss 2[5] 4[3]; G 5[11]; Jos 3[8] 5[1] 19[4] (A).
χρύσινος Jos 16[5] (β-eg).
χρυσίον L 2[12]; Jud 13[5] 17[1]; Iss 4[2]; G 2[3] (β); Jos 11[4] 11[7] 16[4] 18[3].
χρυσός L 13[7]; Jud 13[4]; Jos 16[5].
Χωζηβά (Χωζιβά, Χουζηβά) Jud 6[1] 12[1] (β-d).
χώρα L 13[7]; Jud 2[7].
χωρέω Iss 1[11] (a); N 2[2].
χωρίζω R 4[6]; S 5[3]; Z 8[6] 9[4]; N 2[7] 6[6] (β).
χωρίον Jud 12[9].
χωρίς G 1[9] (a).

ψέγω Iss 3[4]; G 3[5].
ψευδοπροφήτης Jud 21[9].
ψεῦδος R 3[5]; Iss 7[4]; D 1[3] 2[1] 2[4] 3[5] 4[6] 4[7] 5[1] 6[8]; G 5[1]; A 5[3]; B 6[4].
ψεύδομαι Jos 13[9]; B 2[6] (A).
ψύα N 2[8] (bdf).
ψύγω B 8[3].
ψυχή R 1[9] 4[6] 4[9]; S 2[5] 3[4] 4[5] (β) 4[6] 4[8] 4[9] 6[1] (β); L 13[6]; Jud 11[4] 13[8] 18[7] 18[4] 18[6] 19[2] (β); Iss 4[1] (hi, β-bg) 4[5] 4[6]; Z 2[4] (β) 8[6] 9[6] (bdg); D 3[1] 3[2] 3[9] 4[2] 4[7] 5[11]; N 2[6] 3[1] 9[2]; G 2[1] 3[3] 5[3] 5[7] 6[1] 6[2] (β) 6[3] 7[7]; A 1[6] 2[1] 2[7] 4[4] 6[5]; Jos 2[6] 13[1] 17[7]; B 4[3] 4[5] 5[5] (β-a) 6[1] 6[4] 6[6].
ψώα N 2[8] (a).
ψωμίζω L 8[5].

ὦμος Z 9[4].
ὠμότης D 3[6].
ὠνέομαι Z 3[2]; Jos 13[8] 16[1] (β-df) 16[4].
ὥρα Jud 3[4] (β); Jos 8[1]; B 3[7].
ὡραῖος R 3[4]; S 5[1]; L 8[16]; Jos 9[5] 18[4].
ὡραιότης Jos 18[1].
ὡς = 'when,' passim.
 = 'as,' saepissime.
ὡσαύτως L 17[7]; A 2[3] (beg).
ὡσεί L 7[2]; N 2[1] (a); G 1[3] (a); Jos 8[1].
ὥσπερ saepe.
ὥστε saepe.

Oxford: Printed at the Clarendon Press by Horace Hart, M.A.

www.ingramcontent.com/pod-product-compliance
Lightning Source LLC
Chambersburg PA
CBHW032015120726
47902CB00013B/918